SERVICE INFORMATION

The Archbold service

Archbold: Criminal Pleading, Evidence and Practice consists of one main text volume (including the tables and index). This volume is re-issued annually, and is updated by cumulative supplements, the e-update service (see below) and *Archbold Review.* The service also includes a supplement containing the Sentencing Guidelines (see below). For the 2021 edition, an extra supplement is published containing Chapter 5A on Sentences and Orders on Conviction fully updated for the Sentencing Code 2020.

The supplement

Three cumulative supplements, containing updating material for the main volume, are published in each year as part of the service.

This is the second supplement of the 2021 edition.

New material is incorporated into this supplement using the same paragraph numbers as appear in the mainwork. All material new to this supplement is marked in the text by a **bold star** in the margin next to the paragraph number. ★

After consulting the main work on any given subject, reference should always be made to the same paragraph number in the current supplement to check that there have been no new developments since the main text volume was published. The supplement will also track material which has been removed or relocated as part of the re-issue process.

The back cover contains a list of all important developments included in this supplement for the first time and where they can be found.

All references in the text to cases, statutes and statutory instruments are contained in the tables printed at the beginning of this supplement.

Case citations

From the 2020 edition, *"R. v"* has been removed from the start of case citations in the text, to modernise the look-and-feel of Archbold and to ensure the text flows smoothly. However, it has been kept in place in the Table of Cases and in various instances in the text where removing it would cause confusion, such as *"R. (Party) v Smith"*.

Criminal Procedure Rules 2020 and Criminal Practice Directions

Appendix B in this supplement contains the full text of the Criminal Procedure Rules 2020 with the full text of the Criminal Practice Directions interleaved with the rules. Please refer to the table at the beginning of Appendix B to locate any given rule or practice direction, whether in this supplement, in the main work or (in most cases) in both. A separate bookmark, provided with the main work, includes the same information for the rules only.

Sentencing Guidelines and Related Authorities

The Sentencing Guidelines Supplement is part of the Archbold service. This includes the Sentencing Guidelines in full, as they are published by the Sentencing Council as well as including the relevant authorities and an abridged version of the Magistrates' Court sentencing guideline. The original pagination from the guidelines is retained in the paragraph numbering for easy reference.

Usually reissued once a year with the Main Work, a revised edition of the Sentencing Guidelines Supplement is published in early 2021 updated in line with the Sentencing Council's amendments following the enactment of the Sentencing Act 2020 and the coming into force of the Sentencing Code in December 2020. Subscribers receive the new edition as part of their subscription at no extra charge.

Please email *archbold@thomsonreuters.com* with comments/suggestions for any of the Archbold services.

Archbold e-update activation code

As a subscriber to Archbold 2021 you have free and unlimited access to the accompanying weekly e-update service and online archive. If you are a new user accessing the service for the first time then please visit *www.sweetandmaxwell.co.uk/archbold/eupdate.aspx* where you will be asked to complete a simple short registration process, and to enter the following activation code to start receiving updates:

AB2021

If you are an existing user of the e-update then your access will automatically be updated for the new edition and there is no need to re-register.

ARCHBOLD

2021

SECOND SUPPLEMENT TO THE 2021 EDITION

GENERAL EDITOR

HIS HONOUR JUDGE MARK LUCRAFT, QC, BA (Hons) (KENT)
Recorder of London and Chief Coroner of England and Wales

SUPPLEMENT EDITORS

LYND P)

SEB

SWEET & MAXWELL ON REUTERS

Published in 2021 by Thomson Reuters, trading as Sweet & Maxwell. Registered in England & Wales. Company number 1679046. Registered office 5 Canada Square, Canary Wharf, London E14 5AQ

Printed in Great Britain by Hobbs the Printers Ltd, Totton, Hampshire, SO40 3WX

Typeset by Sweet & Maxwell, 5 Canada Square, Canary Wharf, London E14 5AQ

For further information on our products and services, visit:

http://www.sweetandmaxwell.co.uk

No natural forests were destroyed to make this product; only farmed timber was used and replanted.

A CIP catalogue record for this book is available from the British Library

ISBN MAINWORK 9780414080805
ISBN SECOND SUPPLEMENT 9780414080751

TABLE OF CONTENTS

ABBREVIATIONS OF LEGISLATION

The following abbreviations have been adopted throughout.

AFA	Armed Forces Act
CAA	Criminal Appeal Act
CDA	Crime and Disorder Act
CDDA	Company Directors Disqualification Act
CEMA	Customs and Excise Management Act
CJA	Criminal Justice Act
CJCA	Criminal Justice and Courts Act
CJCSA	Criminal Justice and Court Services Act
CJIA	Criminal Justice and Immigration Act
CJPA	Criminal Justice and Police Act
CJPOA	Criminal Justice and Public Order Act
CLA	Criminal Law Act
CPIA	Criminal Procedure and Investigations Act
C(S)A	Crime (Sentences) Act
CYPA	Children and Young Persons Act
DTA	Drug Trafficking Act
DTOA	Drug Trafficking Offences Act
ECHR	European Convention on Human Rights
FSMA	Financial Services and Markets Act
LASPOA	Legal Aid, Sentencing and Punishment of Offenders Act
MCA	Magistrates' Courts Act
MHA	Mental Health Act
PACE	Police and Criminal Evidence
PCCA	Powers of Criminal Courts Act
PCC(S)A	Powers of Criminal Courts (Sentencing) Act
PJA	Police and Justice Act
POCA	Proceeds of Crime Act
RIPA	Regulation of Investigatory Powers Act
RSA	Road Safety Act
RSC	Rules of the Supreme Court (Revision)
RTA	Road Traffic Act
RTOA	Road Traffic Offenders Act
SCA	Serious Crime Act
SOA	Sexual Offences Act
SOCPA	Serious Organised Crime and Police Act
VCRA	Violent Crime Reduction Act
YJCEA	Youth Justice and Criminal Evidence Act

TABLE OF STATUTES

References in bold indicate where legislation is reproduced in full

TABLE OF INTERNATIONAL TREATIES AND CONVENTIONS

References in bold indicate where legislation is reproduced in full

TABLE OF EC REGULATIONS AND DIRECTIVES

DIRECTIVES

TABLE OF STATUTORY INSTRUMENTS

References in bold indicate where legislation is reproduced in full

TABLE OF CASES

TABLE OF NON-UK CASES

TABLE OF PRACTICE DIRECTIONS

References in bold indicate where practice directions are reproduced in full

CHAPTER 1

COMMENCEMENT OF PROCEEDINGS, THE INDICTMENT

VIII. PROCEEDINGS AGAINST CORPORATIONS AND OTHER BODIES

(2) Deferred prosecutions

Application of deferred prosecution agreements

The DPA between the *Serious Fraud Office v G4S Care and Justice Services (UK) Ltd* [2020] 7 303 is now reported as *SFO v G4S Care and Justice Services (UK) Ltd* [2021] Crim. L.R. 138, Crown Court at Southwark (William Davis J). **★1-394**

X. PROSECUTION AGENCIES' POWERS AND DUTIES

A. CROWN PROSECUTION SERVICE

(11) Power to set time limits for preliminary stages of proceedings

Extension of custody time limits

The court in *R. (DPP) v Crown Court at Woolwich*; *Lucima v Central Criminal Court* [2020] EWHC 3243 (Admin), DC identified the following non-exhaustive principles relevant to applications for extensions of custody time limits ("CTLs") during the coronavirus pandemic: **★1-442**

(i) Delay attributable to the pandemic, which means that it is neither practicable nor safe to hold the trial in question within the CTL, provides a good cause for an extension.

(ii) Whether it provides a sufficient cause depends on an examination of the individual facts of the case and of the defendant in question.

(iii) The normal requirements of exploring administratively whether a trial can be brought on elsewhere within the CTL should be followed; so too whether any non-custody cases listed for hearing can be vacated to enable a custody case to come into the list. The underlying purposes of the CTLs explained by Lord Bingham in *R. (McDonald) v Manchester Crown Court* [1999] 1 W.L.R. 841, DC, above remain as potent as ever.

(iv) If practical arrangements cannot be made, it does not follow that it will be appropriate to extend the CTL in every case even though the need to delay a trial will be clear. In some cases, a defendant should be released subject to exacting bail conditions. Factors which may come into play include:

(a) The likely duration of the delay before trial;

(b) Whether there has been any previous extension of the CTL;

(c) The age and antecedents of the defendant;

(d) The likely sentence in the event of conviction. A defendant should rarely be kept in custody if he had served, or come close to serving, the likely sentence were he convicted;

(e) The underlying reasons why bail was refused;

(f) Any particular vulnerabilities of the defendant which make remand in custody particularly difficult.

(v) In multi-handed trials, consideration should be given to whether delay could be reduced by separate trials.

(vi) The burden is on the prosecution to satisfy the statutory criteria for the granting of an extension. No formal evidence about the impact of the pandemic will be needed in the light of the publicly available material and this judgment. All parties can be expected to be familiar with the steps taken to date by HMCTS and the courts. The court should inform the parties of the listing position at that court, having regard to available and anticipated capacity, and of any inquiries made to see whether an earlier trial slot is available elsewhere.

(vii) Any extension of a CTL should be for a comparatively short period, generally not exceeding about three months, so that the court retains the power to review the position in the light of changing circumstances.

Chapter 2

The Criminal Jurisdiction of the Crown Court

I. THE CROWN COURT

C. CONSTITUTION

(4) Crown Court officers

Criminal Procedure Rules 2020 (SI 2020/759), r.25.18

Duty of court officer

★2-16 As to the amendment of r.25.18 of SI 2020/759 by the Criminal Procedure (Amendment) Rules 2021 (SI 2021/40), see Appendix B-430.

II. GENERAL JURISDICTION OF THE CROWN COURT

Courts Act 2003, s.86A

Requirement to give information in criminal proceedings

★2-34a With effect from 8 February 2021, rr.3.16(5) and 3.21(5) of the Criminal Procedure Rules 2020 (SI 2020/759) are amended by the Criminal Procedure (Amendment) Rules 2021 (SI 2021/40) so as to remove the requirement to obtain the defendant's nationality at pre-trial hearings (see § 4-120c below).

III. JURISDICTION IN RESPECT OF ACTS PERFORMED ABROAD AND FOREIGN NATIONALS

D. PARTICULAR OFFENCES

(7) Offences by Crown servants

Criminal Justice Act 1948, s.31(1)

★2-67 Section 31 of the 1948 Act applies to civil servants and not to the Prime Minister, he or she not being a Crown servant: *R. (Defending Arab Christians) v Guildford Magistrates' Court and Tony Blair)* [2020] EWHC 1850 (Admin).

VI. CRIMINAL PROCEDURE RULES

Criminal Procedure Rules 2020 (SI 2020/759), Pt 2

When the rules apply

★2-159 As to the amendment of r.2.1 of SI 2020/759 by the Criminal Procedure (Amendment) Rules 2021 (SI 2021/40), see Appendix B-5.

CHAPTER 3

BAIL, APPEARANCE OF ACCUSED FOR TRIAL, PRESENCE DURING TRIAL

I. BAIL

A. GENERAL

(5) Custody time limits

Prosecution of Offences (Custody Time Limits) Regulations 1987 (SI 1987/299), regs 2, 4–8

Custody time limits in the Crown Court

With effect from 28 September 2020, the Prosecution of Offences (Custody Time Limits) (Coronavirus) (Amendment) Regulations 2020 (SI 2020/953) temporarily amend reg.5 of SI 1987/299 (see the main work) so that in para.(3) "112 days" is replaced by "168 days" (thereby increasing the time limit for cases where a voluntary bill of indictment is preferred, or a fresh trial has been ordered by the Court of Appeal to 168 days) and in para.(6B) "182 days" is replaced by "238 days" (thereby increasing the time limit for cases where an accused has been sent for trial to 238 days). The temporary amendments do not apply to an accused who is in custody in relation to an offence and subject to a custody time limit before they come into force on 28 September 2020. The amendments will cease to have effect on 28th June 2021 (albeit will continue to have effect in relation to accused persons who are still in custody when they cease). **★3-82**

With effect from 19 February 2021, SI 2020/953 is amended by the Prosecution of Offences (Custody Time Limits) (Coronavirus) (Amendment) Regulations 2021 (SI 2021/91) so that the modifications made by SI 2020/953 do not apply in respect of an accused who is under 18 years of age when in custody for the first time in relation to an offence.

(11) Rules of Procedure

Criminal Procedure Rules 2020 (SI 2020/759), Pt 14

When this Part applies

As to the amendment of r.14.1 of SI 2020/759 by the Criminal Procedure (Amendment) Rules 2021 (SI 2021/40), see below, Appendix B-218. **★3-118**

General duties of court officer

As to the amendment of r.14.4 of SI 2020/759 by the Criminal Procedure (Amendment) Rules 2021 (SI 2021/40), see below, Appendix B-221. **★3-121**

Bail condition to be enforced in another European Union member State

With effect from 8 February 2021, r.14.16 of SI 2020/759 is omitted by r.8(e) of the Criminal Procedure (Amendment) Rules 2021 (SI 2021/40). **★3-132a**

Enforcement of measure imposed in another European Union member State

With effect from 8 February 2021, r.14.17 of SI 2020/759 is omitted by r.8(e) of the Criminal Procedure (Amendment) Rules 2021 (SI 2021/40). **★3-132b**

Application to extend a custody time limit

As to the re-numbering of the existing r.14.18 of SI 2020/759 as r.14.16 by the Criminal Procedure (Amendment) Rules 2021 (SI 2021/40), see below, Appendix B-235. **★3-133**

Appeal against custody time limit decision

As to the re-numbering of the existing r.14.19 of SI 2020/759 as r.14.17 by the Criminal Procedure (Amendment) Rules 2021 (SI 2021/40), see below, Appendix B-236. **★3-134**

Exercise of court's powers: extension of pre-charge bail

As to the re-numbering of the eixsting r.14.20 of SI 2020/759 as r.14.18 by the Criminal **★3-134a**

Procedure (Amendment) Rules 2021 (SI 2021/40) and subsequent amendment by SI 2021/40, see below, Appendix B-237.

Application to authorise extension of pre-charge bail

★3-134b As to the re-numbering of the existing r.14.21 of SI 2020/759 as r.14.19 by the Criminal Procedure (Amendment) Rules 2021 (SI 2021/40), see below, Appendix B-238.

Application to withhold information from the defendant

★3-134c As to the re-numbering of the existing r.14.22 of SI 2020/759 as r.14.20 by the Criminal Procedure (Amendment) Rules 2021 (SI 2021/40), see below, Appendix B-239.

B. SPECIFIC PROVISIONS

(1) The police

(a) The Police and Criminal Evidence Act 1984

Savings

3-172 With effect from 13 August 2020, the amendments to s.51 of the Police and Criminal Evidence Act 1984 effected by the Counter-Terrorism and Border Security Act 2019, s.23(1) and Sch.4, para.18(1) and (2) (see the main work) were brought into force: Counter-Terrorism and Border Security Act 2019 (Commencement No. 1) Regulations 2020 (SI 2020/792).

Chapter 4

Trial

I. PRELIMINARIES

C. PUBLICATION OF COURT PROCEEDINGS

(2) Reporting restrictions

(d) Photographs

Criminal Justice Act 1925, s.41

Prohibition on taking photographs, etc., in court.

4-40 With effect from 24 July 2020, the Competition Appeal Tribunal (Coronavirus) (Recording and Broadcasting) Order 2020 (SI 2020/801) provides that the offence under s.41 of the 1925 Act (see the main work) does not apply in relation to the recording and broadcast of proceedings in the Competition Appeal Tribunal in compliance with the conditions in the 2020 order. The 2020 Order expires on 25 March 2022.

G. LEGAL REPRESENTATION

(1) Right to representation

★4-67 Whether it would be unfair to continue a trial where defence counsel has withdrawn, will depend on the nature and complexity of the issues, the stage at which the defendant became unrepresented, the extent to which the defendant was responsible for the withdrawal, and whether and to what extent the defendant is able effectively to take part in the remaining stages of the trial. Ultimately, the question is whether the trial, taken overall, is fair and the primary focus must be on fairness to the defendant. This requires careful consideration of both whether the trial should continue and whether an opportunity should be afforded for the instruction of a new defence team. It may be appropriate for the latter question to be approached in stages, for example for new lawyers to be instructed in order to consider with the defendant whether an application should be made to discharge the jury. The judge is entitled to bear in mind such matters as fairness to prosecution witnesses, particularly in the case of vulnerable witnesses. The need to complete the trial within its original estimate is not a factor of significant weight, even bearing in mind the pressures on the criminal justice system and the needs of other litigants. A substantial delay is one thing, but an adjournment of a day or so to take stock and, if necessary, allow new representatives to be properly instructed is another: *Cadamartriea* [2019] EWCA Crim 1736; [2020] 4 W.L.R. 126.

K. POWER TO STAY PROCEEDINGS

(2) Abuse of process

(c) Stay necessary to protect integrity of criminal justice system

Situations akin to autrefois

In *Wangige* [2020] EWCA Crim 1319; [2021] R.T.R. 7 the court held that the test in *Dwyer* [2012] EWCA Crim 10; [2012] 2 *Archbold Review* 1 (which provides that when considering whether subsequent proceedings would be founded on "substantially the same facts", or "the same incident" as previous proceedings, it is the relevant state of affairs "as they existed to the knowledge of the prosecutor at the date the proceedings were concluded" that needs to be considered) should be modified so as to add an additional requirement by reference to what reasonably could have been known to the prosecutor by the time the proceedings were concluded. On the facts of the case the court held that proceedings for causing serious injury by dangerous driving were an abuse of process where the defendant had already been prosecuted for that incident of driving and the only change since was a new expert opinion as to the quality of the driving. ★4-88

N. PRE-TRIAL HEARINGS

(1) Case management

Criminal Procedure Rules 2020 (SI 2020/759), Pt 1

The overriding objective

As to the amendment of r.1.1 of SI 2020/759 by the Criminal Procedure (Amendment) Rules 2021 (SI 2021/40), see below, Appendix B-1. ★4-114

Criminal Procedure Rules 2020 (SI 2020/759), rr.3.1–3.15

The duty of the parties

As to the amendment of r.3.3 of SI 2020/759 by the Criminal Procedure (Amendment) Rules 2021 (SI 2021/40), see below, Appendix B-14. ★4-115

The court's case management powers

As to the amendment of r.3.4 of SI 2020/759 by the Criminal Procedure (Amendment) Rules 2021 (SI 2021/40), see below, Appendix B-15. ★4-116

(2) Plea and trial preparation hearings

Preparation for trial in the Crown Court

Criminal Procedure Rules 2020 (SI 2020/759), rr.3.21–3.33

Pre-trial hearings in the Crown Court: general rules

As to the amendment of r.3.21 of SI 2020/759 by the Criminal Procedure (Amendment) Rules 2021 (SI 2021/40), see below, Appendix B-24. ★4-120c

Criminal Practice Direction I (General matters) 3A: Case management, paras 3A.16-3A.22

Further case management hearing

As to the amendment of para.3A.21 of *Criminal Practice Direction I (General Matters) 3A: Case management* by *Criminal Practice Directions 2015 (Amendment No. 11)* [2020] EWCA Crim 1347, Lord Burnett CJ, see below, Appendix B-47. ★4-123a

VII. CRIMINAL PROCEDURE RULES: TRIAL AND SENTENCE

Criminal Procedure Rules 2020 (SI 2020/759), Pt 25

General powers and requirements

★4-265a As to the amendment of r.25.2 of SI 2020/759 by the Criminal Procedure (Amendment) Rules 2021 (SI 2021/40), see below, Appendix B-415.

XVIII. VERDICT

F. INCOMPLETE VERDICT

★4-522 The discretion to allow a jury to alter a verdict pronounced by a foreman should not be exercised to allow amendment if there has been a material opportunity for further discussion after the verdict in question was delivered, thereby potentially leading to a change of mind: *RN* [2020] EWCA Crim 937; [2020] Crim. L.R. 1082.

Chapter 5A

Sentences and Orders on Conviction (pre-Sentencing Code)

I. GENERAL PROVISIONS AND PRINCIPLES

D. SENTENCING GUIDELINES

(3) Guidance

(f) Departing from offence-specific guidelines

5A-40b A judge should only depart from a guideline for good reasons, which should be set out in their sentencing remarks so that the sentence passed can be understood; failing to explain the reason for such a departure was a serious omission: *Smith (Ashley)* [2020] EWCA Crim 933.

F. MITIGATION

(4) Selected mitigating factors

(g) Delay

5A-72 A sentencing judge is entitled to consider all factors and aspects of the conduct of the defendants and prosecution when considering the question of delay, and not merely whether the delay resulted from misconduct by the defendants: *Whitson-Dew*; *Richards* [2019] EWCA Crim 2131; [2020] 1 Cr. App. R.(S.) 56.

(p) Covid-19

5A-76e In *Att-Gen's Ref. (R. v Manning)* [2020] EWCA Crim 592; [2020] 4 W.L.R. 7 the Lord Chief Justice stated that the effect of the "lockdown" was a matter that sentencing courts could properly take into account when considering the seriousness of an offence as the impact of a custodial sentence was likely to be "heavier" on a prisoner during the Covid-19 emergency. In *Jones* [2020] EWCA Crim 764, the court took account of the specific conditions in the custodial institution in which the appellant was held following the imposition of his sentence as a result of the Covid-19 pandemic, namely being kept in his cell all day save for a 30-minute period each day and prohibited from having social visits, and reduced the sentence by 25%. In *Smith* [2020] EWCA Crim 1014, the court applied the so-called 'Covid-discount' notwithstanding the fact that the offender had been sentenced prior to the onset of the Covid-19 pandemic. However, in *Randhawa* [2020] EWCA Crim 1071, the court (differently constituted) held that the decision in *Manning* had no application.

The Sentencing Council has issued a guidance note on Covid-19 explaining that the impact of Covid-19 on conditions in prison can properly be accounted for when considering the type and length of the sentence to be imposed, that the practical realities of the effects of the Covid-19 emergency are to be accounted for and that courts should consider whether increased weight should be given to mitigating factors given all the circumstances. The note is available on the Sentencing Council's website.

J. GOODYEAR INDICATIONS

(5) The court

(b) Giving the indication

Where a *Goodyear* indication is given without regard to mitigation, it is not wrong in principle to impose the sentence indicated after having heard mitigation: *Almilhim* [2019] EWCA Crim 220; [2019] 2 Cr. App. R.(S.) 45. It is submitted, however, that best practice is for the court to explain, if only briefly, why the mitigation advanced would not result in a reduction in sentence below the indication previously given. **5A-123**

The authorities and *Goodyear* itself establish the following propositions:

(a) if the court gives a *Goodyear* indication, the defendant has a reasonable opportunity to consider his position in light of the indication. If they do not enter a guilty plea, within that period, the indication ceases to have effect;

(b) if the defendant did, within that period, plead guilty then the court would normally be bound to adhere to the indication;

(c) that, however, would not be the case in exceptional circumstance such as those that arose in *Newman* [2010] EWCA Crim 1566; [2011] 1 Cr. App. R.(S.) 68 (where the judge had plainly been in error as to the guideline category, and had not been in receipt of a pre-sentence report that raised serious concerns about dangerousness); and

(d) when there were to be additions to or departures from *Goodyear* indications that had been acted upon, that should only be done in a way which was fair for the defendant: *Utton* [2019] EWCA Crim 1341; [2020] 1 Cr. App. R.(S.) 7.

In *Hobbs* [2019] EWCA Crim 2137; [2020] 1 Cr. App. R.(S.) 57, the court confirmed that an informal discussion not complying with the Goodyear procedure is insufficient to found an appeal against sentence on the basis the sentencing judge had departed from the indication of sentence; the formality and precision of those requirements was important because it served to avoid the risk of misunderstanding, confusion and potential injustice.

K. REDUCTION IN SENTENCE FOR A GUILTY PLEA

(3) Guidance

(b) Extent of reduction of sentence

Relevance of prosecution's attitude to offer of plea to lesser offence

Where an offender had pleaded guilty to assault occasioning actual bodily harm after his PTPH in circumstances where he had faced alternative charges of wounding contrary to sections 18 and 20 of the Offences Against the Persons Act 1861 and had denied involvement, an argument that an earlier indication of a plea to assault occasioning actual bodily harm would not have been entertained or accepted by the prosecution, was beside the point and irrelevant; where the offender could not bring himself within one of the exceptions listed in the definitive guideline, the applicable credit for the plea was less than 25% due for pleading guilty at the PTPH: *Bannergee* [2020] EWCA Crim 909. **5A-141b**

In circumstances where an offender absconds and seeks to "evade justice altogether", there can be no complaint that any reduction in sentence for a guilty plea is only "very limited"; however, where the fact of absconding is reflected in reduced credit for pleading guilty, there should be no separate penalty for an offence contrary to the Bail Act 1976: *Williamson* [2020] EWCA Crim 1085. **5A-141c**

L. TOTALITY

(2) Relationship with other sentences

(e) Foreign sentences

5A-164a In *Bazegurore and Shuti* [2020] EWCA Crim 375 (a case concerning two conspiracies to "traffick" individuals, one having been prosecuted in the UK and the other in Belgium), the court concluded that there was no obligation on the domestic court to take account of the sentences imposed in the foreign court under the principle of totality. In any event, on the facts of the particular case, had the judge done so, the sentence imposed was not manifestly excessive.

III. SENTENCING HEARING

E. IMPOSITION OF SENTENCE

(3) Sentencing remarks

5A-321 In *Beckett* [2020] EWCA Crim 914, the court observed that although Chin-Charles emphasised that sentence remarks should be concise, there was a statutory duty upon the court state the reasons for deciding on the sentence to. Be imposed and to explain how the court had discharged its duty in relation to any applicable sentencing guidelines.

IV. PRIMARY DISPOSALS

H. DISQUALIFICATION FROM DRIVING

(1) Disqualification from driving following commission of any offence

(b) Guidance

5A-468a The primary purpose of disqualification from driving is to prevent a repetition of the danger which led to the offence. In the case of someone who has a bad driving record and commits an offence of high culpability a significant period of disqualification will be justified. Undoubtedly disqualification must to some extent reflect the result of the bad driving. However, it was not intended as a further punishment; the length of disqualification should not impede an offender's rehabilitation and that was particularly relevant where the offender was young: *Parkin* [2020] EWCA Crim 614.

L. SUSPENDED SENTENCE ORDERS

(3) Guidance

(ca) Covid-19

5A-621aa In *Att-Gen's Ref. (R. v Manning)* [2020] EWCA Crim 592; [2020] 4 W.L.R. 7 the Lord Chief Justice stated that the effect of the "lockdown" was a matter that sentencing courts could properly take into account when considering whether or a not a sentence ought to be suspended, bearing in mind that a custodial sentence was likely to be "heavier" on an individual during the current Covid-19 emergency when prisoners are confined to their cells for longer periods than normal and are unable to receive social visits.

M. DETERMINATE SENTENCES: GENERAL PRINCIPLES

(2) Guidance

(c) Time on remand

General

5A-638 In *Horne* [2020] EWCA Crim 487; [2020] 6 *Archbold Review* 2, the court rejected the suggestion that whether offences are "related offences" for the purposes of s.240ZA of the Criminal Justice Act 2003 should be determined by reference to the test for joinder.

Q. MINIMUM SENTENCES

(1) Introduction

Where the defendant is being sentenced for more than one offence to which a mandatory minimum sentence applies, each offence attracts the minimum prescribed term, however, in every case it remains a matter for the sentencing judge to consider (bearing in mind considerations of totality): (a) whether sentences imposed for multiple offences should be concurrent or consecutive, and (b) whether there are exceptional circumstances or particular circumstances that would make imposition of the minimum term unjust in all the circumstances (as the case may be): *Rooney* [2020] EWCA Crim 801. **5A-652**

(2) Third Class A drug trafficking offence

(b) Guidance

In relation to circumstances which may make it unjust to impose the minimum sentence, a basis of plea confirming social supply is, of itself, not enough and "there must be more": *McDonald* [2020] EWCA Crim 56; [2020] 2 Cr. App. R.(S.) 13. **5A-654**

(3) Firearms

(b) Guidance

"Exceptional circumstances"

General

It is not helpful to conceive of the "exceptional circumstances" test in s.51A of the Firearms Act 1968 as asking whether the circumstances are ordinary or wholly remarkable, and ultimately the test being whether the imposition of the minimum sentence would lead to a sentence that is arbitrary or disproportionate (bearing in mind its deterrent purpose): *Bartell (Robert)* [2020] EWCA Crim 625; [2020] 4 W.L.R. 79. **5A-661**

(4) Third domestic burglary

(b) Guidance

"Unjust"

Burden on defendant

The court in *Woofe* [2019] EWCA Crim 2249 summarised the legal principles applicable to a minimum sentence under s.110 of the Powers of Criminal Courts (Sentencing) Act 2000 (presumably also applicable to minimum sentences under s.111). Additionally, the court suggested that there may be threshold requirement for a defendant to give at least some indication of the kinds of circumstance capable of amounting to particular circumstances that might be disclosed or corroborated by a pre-sentence report before one must be obtained. **5A-681**

S. LIFE SENTENCES (NON-MURDER)

(2) The interaction of life sentences with other sentencing orders

(b) Offender serving a determinate sentence

Where a life sentence is being imposed concurrently to an extended sentence and the minimum term is to be increased to take account of that sentence, the increase to the minimum term should calculated by reference to the period remaining to be served under the offender is eligible for **5A-712** release, not until the expiry of the custodial term: *Mohammed (Raja)* [2019] EWCA Crim 2095; [2020] 1 Cr. App. R.(S.) 65.

V. SECONDARY DISPOSALS

C. PREVENTATIVE ORDERS

(2) Criminal behaviour order

(c) Guidance

Requirements and prohibitions

Blanket social media prohibition

5A-830a When considering whether prohibitions to form part of a CBO would "help" in preventing further activity of the kind that underpinned the conviction offence, deterrence was a legitimate consideration. On the particular circumstances of the case, a prohibition limiting the number of devices and the internet accounts that the offender could use (which were capable of facilitating offending of the type forming the basis of the conviction) enabled proportionate and effective monitoring: *Tofagsazan* [2020] EWCA Crim 982.

(4) Football banning orders

(c) Guidance

Making the order

Statutory test

5A-855 In *Jelf* [2020] EWCA Crim 631, the sentencing judge had erred in interpreting the first limb of the applicable test too broadly (asking whether the offence related to football matches rather than to a specific match) and accordingly the order had to be quashed; the proper application of the test was to ask whether the offence related to a particular football match (in this case, a match between England and Panama that had ended minutes before the violence forming the basis of the offence of conviction occurred).

G. RECOMMENDATION FOR DEPORTATION

(2) Guidance

(d) Nationals of EU member states

5A-942 *Hafeez v Secretary of State for the Home Department* [2020] EWCA Civ 406; [2020] 1 W.L.R. 1928 confirmed that periods of residence while imprisoned or detained do not count for the purpose of calculating the required 10 year period of residence for the Immigration (European Economic Area) Regulations 2016 (SI 2016/1052).

VI. CHILDREN AND YOUNG PERSONS

C. PRIMARY DISPOSALS

(6) Detention and training orders

(c) Guidance

Making the order

The period of detention and training

5A-1013a The youth court has an unfettered discretion in making orders under s.102(5) of the 2000 Act and it therefore is not inappropriate to make such an order for public protection even absent bad behaviour in custody: *R. (X) v Ealing Youth Court* [2020] EWHC 800 (Admin), DC.

(7) Detention under s.91 (determinate)

(c) Guidance

Multiple offences

Endorsing the decision in *M* [1998] 2 Cr. App. R.(S.) 128 (and the approach in *A.M.* (see the main work), the court in *Robinson* [2020] EWCA Crim 866 stated that where an offender falls to be sentenced for an offence or offences which do qualify for a sentence under s.91 (s.250 of the Sentencing Code), and another offence or offences which do not, a term of detention commensurate with the seriousness of all of the offences should be passed under s.91 (s.250 of the Sentencing Code) only on those offences which do qualify, and the court should order no separate penalty on those which do not. **5A-1025**

VII. CONSEQUENCES OF CONVICTION

E. AUTOMATIC LIABILITY TO DEPORTATION

(3) Guidance

(e) Relevance of liability to deportation on determination of length of sentence

Where the offender had been sentenced to an immediate custodial sentence of 14 months, and on appeal against sentence it was submitted on his behalf that the fact that the sentence made him a "foreign criminal" and that he was therefore liable to the automatic deportation provisions of the UK Borders Act 2007, it was held that the argument was not open to the offender as a matter of principle; what mattered in any sentencing exercise was what the appropriate term of imprisonment might be, with the judge always endeavouring to keep it as short as is appropriate: *Malik* [2020] EWCA Crim 957. **5A-1127a**

VIII. NON-RECENT OFFENCES

E. SENTENCING GUIDELINES

The term "measured reference" is not intended to prescribe a mathematical exercise, but rather to cause the court to reflect the previous maximum sentence as part of the composition of the sentence based on current guidelines. It must achieve a proper calibration and thereby some reduction to reflect the statutory maximum available at the date of offending: *DL* [2020] EWCA Crim 881. **5A-1137**

IX. MENTAL HEALTH DISPOSALS

A. INTRODUCTION

The Sentencing Council has issued a definitive sentencing guideline for the sentencing of offenders with mental health disorders, developmental disorders or neurological impairments. The new guideline applies to all offenders sentenced on or after 1 October 2020. It provides general guidance on the sentencing of such offenders, including providing guidance on the approach to mental health reports and the relevant mental health disposals. **5A-1168**

C. ON CONVICTION

(2) Summary of approach in post-conviction cases

The court in *Westwood* [2020] EWCA Crim 598 further considered the differences between an order under ss.37 and 41 of the Mental Health Act 1983 and an order under s.45A of that Act, explaining that the process for recall under ss.37 and 41 is much quicker than under s.45A with the potential for warrants for recall to hospital within minutes. **5A-1177**

Chapter 5ASC

Sentences and Orders on Conviction (Sentencing Code)

I. GENERAL PROVISIONS AND PRINCIPLES

A. INTRODUCTION AND THE COMMENCEMENT OF THE SENTENCING CODE

★5ASC-1 With effect from 1 December 2020, the Sentencing Act 2020 (Commencement No. 1) Regulations 2020 (SI 2020/1236) brought into force the Sentencing Act 2020 (Pts 2 to 13 of which make up a code called the Sentencing Code). The effect is that the Sentencing Code applies to any offence of which an offender was convicted on or after 1 December 2020, no matter when committed, and reference should be made to Chapter 5ASC (rather than Chapter 5A) accordingly. When sentencing offenders for offences convicted before that date (including when re-sentencing offenders for breach of orders imposed for convictions obtained before that date) reference should be made to the previous law as contained in Chapter 5A.

D. SENTENCING GUIDELINES

(3) Guidance

(e) Departing from offence-specific guidelines

5ASC-40a A judge should only depart from a guideline for good reasons, which should be set out in their sentencing remarks so that the sentence passed can be understood; failing to explain the reason for such a departure was a serious omission: *Smith (Ashley)* [2020] EWCA Crim 933.

E. AGGRAVATION

(2) Statutory aggravating factors

(b) Previous convictions

Sentencing Act 2020, s.65

★5ASC-44 With effect from 11.00 pm on 31 December 2020 ("IP completion day" as defined by s.39 of the European Union (Withdrawal Agreement) Act 2020), s.65(4) of the Sentencing Act 2020 is amended by the Sentencing Act 2020, s.417(9) and Sch.22, para.86 (as amended by SI 2020/1520 reg.5(2) so that:

(a) at the end of para. (a) the word "or" is inserted;
(b) para. (b) is omitted;
(c) para. (d) and the word "or" immediately before it are omitted;

After subs. (4), the following is inserted:

> "(4A) If the proceedings for the current offence were instituted before IP completion day (see section 397(5)), 'relevant previous conviction' in subsections (1) to (3) also includes—
> (a) a previous conviction of a relevant offence under the law of a member State by a court in that State, and
> (b) a finding of guilt in respect of a member State service offence (see subsection (6))."

In subsection (6), "(4)(d)" is replaced with "(4A)(b)".

F. MITIGATION

(4) Selected mitigating factors

(g) Delay

5ASC-84 A sentencing judge is entitled to consider all factors and aspects of the conduct of the defendants and prosecution when considering the question of delay, and not merely whether the delay resulted from misconduct by the defendants: *Whitson-Dew*; *Richards* [2019] EWCA Crim 2131; [2020] 1 Cr. App. R.(S.) 56.

(p) Covid-19

In *Att-Gen's Ref. (R. v Manning)* [2020] EWCA Crim 592; [2020] 4 W.L.R. 77 the Lord Chief Justice stated that the effect of the "lockdown" was a matter that sentencing courts could properly take into account when considering the seriousness of an offence as the impact of a custodial sentence was likely to be "heavier" on a prisoner during the Covid-19 emergency. In *Jones* [2020] EWCA Crim 764; [2021] 1 Cr. App. R.(S.) 6, the court took account of the specific conditions in the custodial institution in which the appellant was held following the imposition of his sentence as a result of the Covid-19 pandemic, namely being kept in his cell all day save for a 30-minute period each day and prohibited from having social visits, and reduced the sentence by 25%. In *Smith* [2020] EWCA Crim 1014, the court applied the so-called 'Covid-discount' notwithstanding the fact that the offender had been sentenced prior to the onset of the Covid-19 pandemic. However, in *Randhawa* [2020] EWCA Crim 1071, the court (differently constituted) held that the decision in *Manning* had no application. **★5ASC-92a**

The Sentencing Council has issued a guidance note on Covid-19 explaining that the impact of Covid-19 on conditions in prison can properly be accounted for when considering the type and length of the sentence to be imposed, that the practical realities of the effects of the Covid-19 emergency are to be accounted for and that courts should consider whether increased weight should be given to mitigating factors given all the circumstances. The note is available on the Sentencing Council's website.

In *Wilson* [2020] EWCA Crim 1284, an appeal against sentence where the appellant had been sentenced on 24 February 2020, before the implementation of the so-called 'lockdown' restrictions as a consequence of the Covid-19 pandemic, the court held that it was not the intention of the Lord Chief Justice in *Att-Gen's Ref (Manning)* (see the main work) for there to be a review of the sentences imposed in cases where the offender was presently in custody solely on the basis of pandemic.

In *Att-Gen's Ref (Marland)* [2020] EWCA Crim 1267, it had been submitted on the respondent's behalf that the effects of the restrictions imposed in consequence of the Covid-19 pandemic should be taken into consideration when determining whether to increase the sentence imposed upon the respondent; the court held that there was no force in that submission in circumstances where the court had formed the view that the sentence imposed was unduly lenient and further, in light of the length of sentence that the respondent would be serving in any event (a sentence of two years and six months' imprisonment, immediate) the pandemic was not a relevant consideration "...given the likelihood as to the time in which it will take our society to start to come out of the restrictions which Covid-19 has imposed."

In *Brass* [2020] EWCA Crim 1394, the court considered an appeal against the sentence imposed for an offence involving threatening social workers who had attended her property to assist her son during the height of the Covid-19 pandemic. The court commented that the applicant could not rely on the effects of the pandemic to obtain a lesser sentence in circumstances where her offence involved making threats to key workers who, at the height of the pandemic, were risking their own health in accordance with their employment.

In *Whittington* [2020] EWCA Crim 1560, a case in which the sentence was imposed many months before the pandemic and in which the applicant required a lengthy extension of time to make his application for leave, the court commented that while the Court of Appeal (Criminal Division), in accordance with well-understood principles, could reduce a sentence where there were proper grounds do so, it would be rarely - if ever - appropriate to do so in respect of a long sentence passed many months before the pandemic started; and that the decision in *Randhawa* [2020] EWCA Crim 1071, suggested that "the *Manning* principle" did not apply at all in such a case.

J. GOODYEAR INDICATIONS

(5) The court

(b) Giving the indication

5ASC-138 Where a *Goodyear* indication is given without regard to mitigation, it is not wrong in principle to impose the sentence indicated after having heard mitigation: *Almilhim* [2019] EWCA Crim 220; [2019] 2 Cr. App. R.(S.) 45. It is submitted, however, that best practice is for the court to explain, if only briefly, why the mitigation advanced would not result in a reduction in sentence below the indication previously given.

The authorities and *Goodyear* itself establish the following propositions:

(a) if the court gives a *Goodyear* indication, the defendant has a reasonable opportunity to consider his position in light of the indication. If they do not enter a guilty plea, within that period, the indication ceases to have effect;

(b) if the defendant did, within that period, plead guilty then the court would normally be bound to adhere to the indication;

(c) that, however, would not be the case in exceptional circumstance such as those that arose in *Newman* [2010] EWCA Crim 1566; [2011] 1 Cr. App. R.(S.) 68 (where the judge had plainly been in error as to the guideline category, and had not been in receipt of a pre-sentence report that raised serious concerns about dangerousness); and

(d) when there were to be additions to or departures from *Goodyear* indications that had been acted upon, that should only be done in a way which was fair for the defendant: *Utton* [2019] EWCA Crim 1341; [2020] 1 Cr. App. R.(S.) 7.

In *Hobbs* [2019] EWCA Crim 2137; [2020] 1 Cr. App. R.(S.) 57, the court confirmed that an informal discussion not complying with the *Goodyear* procedure is insufficient to found an appeal against sentence on the basis the sentencing judge had departed from the indication of sentence; the formality and precision of those requirements was important because it served to avoid the risk of misunderstanding, confusion and potential injustice.

K. REDUCTION IN SENTENCE FOR A GUILTY PLEA

(3) Guidance

(b) Extent of reduction of sentence

Relevance of prosecution's attitude to offer of plea to lesser offence

5ASC-161a Where an offender had pleaded guilty to assault occasioning actual bodily harm after his PTPH in circumstances where he had faced alternative charges of wounding contrary to sections 18 and 20 of the Offences Against the Person Act 1861 and had denied involvement, an argument that an earlier indication of a plea to assault occasioning actual bodily harm would not have been entertained or accepted by the prosecution, was beside the point and irrelevant; where the offender could not bring himself within one of the exceptions listed in the definitive guideline, the applicable credit for the plea was less than 25% due for pleading guilty at the PTPH: *Bannergee* [2020] EWCA Crim 909; [2020] 2 Cr. App. R.(S.) 55.

5ASC-161b In circumstances where an offender absconds and seeks to "evade justice altogether", there can be no complaint that any reduction in sentence for a guilty plea is only "very limited"; however, where the fact of absconding is reflected in reduced credit for pleading guilty, there should be no separate penalty for an offence contrary to the Bail Act 1976: *Williamson* [2020] EWCA Crim 1085; [2020] 8 *Archbold Review* 3.

(c) Timing of guilty plea

General

★5ASC-163 In *Hodgin* [2020] EWCA Crim 1388; [2020] 4 W.L.R. 147 the court emphasised that the maximum reduction of one-third for a guilty plea to an indictable-only offence will only be available to an offender who has given at the first stage of the proceedings an unequivocal indication of his intention to plead guilty; an indication that he is likely to plead guilty is not enough.

Indication in defence statement

Hardy [2020] EWCA Crim 398 is now reported at [2020] 2 Cr. App. R.(S.) 37. ★5ASC-168

L. TOTALITY

(1) General

In *Corrie* [2020] EWCA Crim 1162, in the context of a submission regarding the principle of totality, the court observed that "when concurrent sentences are imposed for a number of offences...detailed analysis of the categorisation of each offence and the individual sentences imposed are not as helpful as they would be in different circumstances." ★5ASC-186

In *Bailey* [2020] EWCA Crim 1719, a multi-handed case, it had been submitted on behalf of the appellants that the sentencing judge, having made brief reference to the principle of totality to the effect that this had been taken into account when determining sentence, had adopted an improper and inadequate approach and that, there was in fact a duty to "spell out how totality applied in each case". The court disagreed, stating that whether a judge had applied the principle of totality was a question of substance and not form; and that in the instant case the fact therefore that the judge made a single generalised statement towards the end of her sentencing remarks to the effect that she had considered totality was perfectly adequate.

(2) Relationship with other sentences

(e) Foreign sentences

In *Bazegurore and Shuti* [2020] EWCA Crim 375; [2020] 2 Cr. App. R.(S.) 27 (a case concerning two conspiracies to "traffick" individuals, one having been prosecuted in the UK and the other in Belgium), the court concluded that there was no obligation on the domestic court to take account of the sentences imposed in the foreign court under the principle of totality. In any event, on the facts of the particular case, had the judge done so, the sentence imposed was not manifestly excessive. 5ASC-190a

II. PRE-SENTENCE

A. DEFERMENT OF SENTENCE

(3) Procedure when deferring sentence

(c) Effect of deferment

In *Mizan* [2020] EWCA Crim 1553, an appeal under s.13 of the Administration of Justice Act 1960 following the imposition of a custodial sentence for a Bail Act 1976 offence of failing to surrender to court in circumstances where the offender had previously had the sentence imposed upon him deferred, the court clarified that as the court has no power to remand an offender in custody following the deferring of sentence, no question of releasing the offender on bail arises. The court could therefore not convict the offender of failing to surrender. ★5ASC-238

B. COMMITTAL FOR SENTENCE

(3) Guidance

(b) Sentencing in the Crown Court

Whether to have a Newton hearing

In *Belcher* [2020] EWCA Crim 1192 it was submitted that in circumstances where a *Newton* hearing is held in the magistrates' courts and following this, the magistrates' commit the case to the Crown Court for sentencing, the interests of justice require a further *Newton* hearing to be held in the Crown Court if the defendant disputes the basis for sentence and where the Crown Court fails to hold a further hearing, the defendant must be sentenced on the basis of plea as ★5ASC-269 advanced by the defendant. The court held that (1) *Gillan v DPP* (see the main work) held that the Crown Court had discretion to hold a further *Newton* hearing if it was in the interests of justice to do so, an example of the circumstances in which it might be appropriate to exercise that power was if the defendant identified some significant development such as the discovery of fresh evidence which was material to sentence; (2) there was a discretion to hold a second *Newton* hearing where the defendant disputed the basis for sentencing; there was no duty to do so; (3) the Court was not bound by *Gillan* but considered that it was correct to follow that decision.

III. SENTENCING HEARING

B. FACTUAL BASIS FOR SENTENCING

(1) Conviction following not guilty plea

(a) Introduction

★5ASC-306 In *Swift* [2020] EWCA Crim 1291, the sentencing judge had sentenced on the basis that the burglary was targeted and had a sexual motive (in that the offender had entered the property, gone to the victim's bedroom and began looking through her laundry); the court held that, in the circumstances of the case, this amounted to impermissible speculation and was not based on sound evidence.

(2) Following guilty plea

(f) Newton hearings

Hearing resolved in favour of defendant; Effect on sentencing guideline categorisation

★5ASC-349a In *Hewitt* [2020] EWCA Crim 1225, a case concerning a robbery, the judge had indicated that the appropriate guideline category was 2B of the street robbery sentencing guideline. The judge held a *Newton* hearing in relation to whether one of the defendants had spoken words which amounted to a threat to stab the victim; this was resolved in favour of the defendant. When sentencing, the judge had indicated that the appropriate guideline category remained 2B, following the outcome of the *Newton* hearing. On appeal against sentence, it was submitted that a *Newton* hearing was only to be held on an issue which would make a material difference to sentence and thus, the judge had erred in not altering the guideline category. The court determined that there was "nothing in these points"; a *Newton* hearing, capable of making a material difference in relation to sentence, was not restricted in its impact to whether or not a different guideline category was going to be selected; a *Newton* hearing could make a material difference within a "range", as a nuanced approach was taken in the light of all the facts and circumstances relating to culpability and to harm.

C. IMPACT STATEMENTS

(1) Victim Personal statements

(b) Guidance

★5ASC-356 In *Jones* [2020] EWCA Crim 1139, a case in which victim personal statements were provided to the court at sentencing, but had not been prepared and served in accordance with the guidance in the decision in *Perkins* (see the main work) or the *Criminal Practice Directions* (see the main work), the court observed that the failure to follow the correct procedure meant that the sentencing court made their assessment of psychological harm on evidence that was not up to date and did not give a full or reliable picture of psychological harm and that this was "an obvious danger" of such statements taken in the immediate aftermath of an offence which may well describe intense emotions and fears, but that such raw feelings subside with time in many cases. The court also observed that the sentencing court's task was to attempt to identify, if possible, cases in which serious psychological harm had been caused, but emphasised that evidence of harm falling below that level would still be taken into account.

E. IMPOSITION OF SENTENCE

(3) Sentencing remarks

In *Beckett* [2020] EWCA Crim 914, the court observed that although *Chin-Charles* emphasised that sentence remarks should be concise, there was a statutory duty upon the court to state the reasons for deciding on the sentence to be imposed and to explain how the court had discharged its duty in relation to any applicable sentencing guidelines. **5ASC-369**

I. SURCHARGE

(2) Guidance

(a) General

Cases to which the scheme does not apply

Abbott; *Hawker*; *Harrison* [2020] EWCA Crim 516; [2020] Cr. App. R.(S.) 39 is now reported at [2020] 1 WLR 3739. **5ASC-389**

(ba) Calculating the amount of surcharge

Abbott; *Hawker*; *Harrison* [2020] EWCA Crim 516; [2020] Cr. App. R.(S.) 39 is now reported at [2020] 1 WLR 3739. **5ASC-391**

(c) Relationship with confiscation

Bristowe [2019] EWCA Crim 2005 is now reported at [2020] 1 Cr. App. R.(S.) 58. **5ASC-393**

IV. PRIMARY DISPOSALS

E. FINES

(1) Legislation

(a) Power of Crown Court to fine

Sentencing Act 2020, ss.120–121, 124–127

General power of Crown Court to fine offender convicted on indictment

With effect from 1 December 2020, s.120(3) of the Sentencing Act 2020 (see the main work) is amended by reg.4(2) of the Sentencing Act 2020 (Commencement No. 1) Regulations 2020 (SI 2020/1236) so that "the commencement date" is replaced by "1 December 2020". **★5ASC-465**

H. DISQUALIFICATION FROM DRIVING

(1) General

(b) Guidance

The primary purpose of disqualification from driving is to prevent a repetition of the danger which led to the offence. In the case of someone who has a bad driving record and commits an offence of high culpability a significant period of disqualification will be justified. Undoubtedly disqualification must to some extent reflect the result of the bad driving. However, it was not intended as a further punishment; the length of disqualification should not impede an offender's rehabilitation and that was particularly relevant where the offender was young: *Parkin* [2020] EWCA Crim 614; [2020] 2 Cr. App. R.(S.) 44. **5ASC-539a**

(2) Disqualification from driving following commission of any offence

(b) Guidance

Extension and effect of disqualification from driving in custodial cases (ss.166, 167)

The new regime

There is no power to take into account early release on home detention curfew when calculat- **★5ASC-556** ing the length of the extension period under s.35A of the 1988 Act (see the main work) which is materially identical to s.166 of the Sentencing Code: *Parkin* [2020] EWCA Crim 614; [2020] 2 Cr. App. R.(S.) 44.

K. CUSTODIAL SENTENCES: GENERAL PRINCIPLES

(3) Maximum sentences

(b) Guidance

Most serious example of the offence

★5ASC-650 There is a different approach to maximum sentences in the context of non-recent offences, and the principles applicable to sentencing such offences are such that the maximum sentence for an individual offence may be merited whether or not a particular offence could be said to be in the most serious category of its kind, in accordance with the approach to sentencing 'recent' offences, and whether or not there were mitigating features: *Griffiths* [2020] EWCA Crim 732; [2020] 2 Cr. App. R.(S.) 54.

(5) Dangerous offenders

(c) Guidance

The dangerousness test

Risk: Present or future

5ASC-674 *Baker, Richards* [2020] EWCA Crim 176 is now reported at [2020] 2 Cr. App. R.(S.) 23.

L. SUSPENDED SENTENCE ORDERS

(3) Guidance

(c) Whether or not to impose a suspended sentence order

5ASC-713 *Montaut* [2019] EWCA Crim 2252 is now reported at [2020] 2 Cr. App. R.(S.) 7.

(ca) Covid-19

5ASC-713a In *Att-Gen's Ref. (R. v Manning)* [2020] EWCA Crim 592; [2020] 4 W.L.R. 77 the Lord Chief Justice stated that the effect of the "lockdown" was a matter that sentencing courts could properly take into account when considering whether or a not a sentence ought to be suspended, bearing in mind that a custodial sentence was likely to be "heavier" on an individual during the current Covid-19 emergency when prisoners are confined to their cells for longer periods than normal and are unable to receive social visits.

M. DETERMINATE SENTENCES: GENERAL PRINCIPLES

(2) Guidance

(c) Time on remand

General

5ASC-731 In *Horne* [2020] EWCA Crim 487; [2020] 6 *Archbold Review* 2, the court rejected the suggestion that whether offences are "related offences" for the purposes of s.240ZA of the Criminal Justice Act 2003 should be determined by reference to the test for joinder.

Q. MINIMUM SENTENCES

(1) Introduction

5ASC-751 Where the defendant is being sentenced for more than one offence to which a mandatory minimum sentence applies, each offence attracts the minimum prescribed term, however, in every case it remains a matter for the sentencing judge to consider (bearing in mind considerations of totality): (a) whether sentences imposed for multiple offences should be concurrent or consecutive, and (b) whether there are exceptional circumstances or particular circumstances that would make imposition of the minimum term unjust in all the circumstances (as the case may be): *Rooney* [2020] EWCA Crim 801; [2021] 1 Cr. App. R.(S.) 9.

(2) Firearms

(b) Guidance

Procedure

Starting point

For a case holding that for offences to which the minimum sentence under s.311 of the Sentencing Code (§ 5ASC-752 in the main work) applies the minimum sentence of five years is not a starting point to be adjusted and is simply a minimum sentence, no more, no less, see *Att.-Gen.'s Reference (Smith (Kelly Anne))* [2020] EWCA Crim 953; [2021] 1 Cr. App. R.(S.) 8. **★5ASC-755**

"Exceptional circumstances"

General

It is not helpful to conceive of the "exceptional circumstances" test in s.51A of the Firearms Act 1968 (s.311 of the Sentencing Code) as asking whether the circumstances are ordinary or wholly remarkable, and ultimately the test being whether the imposition of the minimum sentence would lead to a sentence that is arbitrary or disproportionate (bearing in mind its deterrent purpose): *Bartell (Robert)* [2020] EWCA Crim 625; [2020] 4 W.L.R. 79. **5ASC-758**

(4) Third Class A drug trafficking offence

(a) Legislation

With effect from 11.00 pm on 31 December 2020 ("IP completion day" as defined by s.39 of the European Union (Withdrawal Agreement) Act 2020), s.313(3) of the 2020 Act is amended by the 2020 Act, s.417(9) and Sch.22, para.90 (as amended by SI 2020/1520 reg.5(8)), so that: **★5ASC-773**

(a) para.(b) is omitted
(b) the word "or" is inserted at the end of para. (c);
(c) para. (e) and the word "or" immediately before it are omitted;

After subs.(3), the following subsection is inserted:

"(3A) If the proceedings for the index offence were instituted before IP completion day (see section 397(5)), for the purposes of subsection (1) 'relevant drug conviction' also includes–
(a) a conviction in a member State of an offence committed on or after 16 August 2010 which would, if committed in the United Kingdom at the time of the conviction, have constituted a class A drug trafficking offence, and
(b) a conviction of a member State service offence committed on or after 16 August 2010 which would have constituted a class A drug offence if committed in England and Wales at the time of conviction."

(b) Guidance

In relation to circumstances which may make it unjust to impose the minimum sentence, a basis of plea confirming social supply is, of itself, not enough and "there must be more": *McDonald* [2020] EWCA Crim 56; [2020] 2 Cr. App. R.(S.) 13. **5ASC-774**

(5) Third domestic burglary

(a) Legislation

With effect from 11.00 pm on 31 December 2020 ("IP completion day" as defined by s.39 of the European Union (Withdrawal Agreement) Act 2020), s.314(3) of the 2020 Act is amended by **★5ASC-775** the 2020 Act, s.417(9) and Sch.22, para.91 (as amended by SI 2020/1520 reg.5(9)), the effect of which is as follows:

(a) omit 'or another member State';
(b) the word "or" is inserted at the end of para. (c);
(c) para. (e) and the word "or" immediately before it are omitted;

After subs. (3), the following subsection is inserted:

"(3A) If the proceedings for the index offence were instituted before IP completion day (see section 397(5)), for the purposes of subsection (1) 'relevant domestic burglary conviction' also includes—
(a) a conviction in a member State of an offence committed on or after 16 August 2010 which would have constituted an offence of domestic burglary, if committed in England and Wales at the time of the conviction, and
(b) a conviction of a member State service offence committed on or after 16 August 2010 which would have constituted an offence of domestic burglary if committed in England and Wales at the time of conviction."

(b) Guidance

"Unjust"

Burden on defendant

5ASC-782 The court in *Woofe* [2019] EWCA Crim 2249; [2020] 2 Cr. App. R.(S.) 6 summarised the legal principles applicable to a minimum sentence under s.110 of the Powers of Criminal Courts (Sentencing) Act 2000 (presumably also applicable to minimum sentences under s.111) (ss.313 and 314 of the Sentencing Code). Additionally, the court suggested that there may be threshold requirement for a defendant to give at least some indication of the kinds of circumstance capable of amounting to particular circumstances that might be disclosed or corroborated by a pre-sentence report before one must be obtained.

(6) Repeat offences involving weapon or bladed article

(a) Legislation

★5ASC-789 With effect from 11.00 pm on 31 December 2020 ("IP completion day" as defined by s.39 of the European Union (Withdrawal Agreement) Act 2020) s.315(4) of the 2020 Act is amended by the 2020 Act, s.417(9) and Sch.22, para.92 (as amended by SI 2020/1520 reg.5(10)), the effect of which is as follows:

(a) omit 'or another member State';
(b) the word "or" is inserted at the end of para.(c);
(c) para. (e) and the word "or" immediately before it are omitted;

After subs.(4), the following subsection is inserted:

"(4A) If the proceedings for the index offence were instituted before IP completion day (see section 397(5)), for the purposes of this section 'relevant conviction' also includes—
(a) a conviction in a member State of a civilian offence which would have constituted a relevant offence if committed in England and Wales at the time of the conviction (whenever the offence was in fact committed), and
(b) a conviction of a member State service offence which would have constituted a relevant offence if committed in England and Wales at the time of conviction (whenever the offence was in fact committed)."

(7) Minimum sentences: supplementary provisions

★5ASC-792 With effect from 11.00 pm on 31 December 2020 ("IP completion day" as defined by s.39 of the European Union (Withdrawal Agreement) Act 2020), s.317 of the 2020 Act is amended by the 2020 Act, s.417(9) and Sch.22, para.93 (as amended by SI 2020/1520 reg.5(11)) as follows:

(1) In subs.(1):
  (a) for the words before "applies", the words "Subsection (2)" are substituted;
  (b) para. (c) is omitted (but not the word "or" at the end of it);

(c) in para. (d) the words ", or in any other member State," are omitted.

(2) After subs.(2), the following subsections are inserted:

> "(2A) Subsection (2B) applies where an offender has been convicted—
> (a) in any member State of a corresponding drug trafficking offence, or
> (b) in any member State of a corresponding domestic burglary offence.
>
> (2B) For the purposes of section 313 or 314 as it applies where the proceedings were instituted before IP completion day (see section 397(5)), a certificate given in accordance with subsection (3) of either or both of the following is evidence of the facts so certified—
> (a) that the offender was convicted of that offence on the date of the conviction;
> (b) that the offence was committed on a particular day, or over, or at some time during, a particular period."

(3) In subs.(4):
(a) in the definition of "corresponding drug trafficking offence", after "313(3)(b)" the words "or (3A)(a)" are inserted;
(b) in the definition of "corresponding domestic burglary offence", after "314(3)(b)" the words "or (3A)(a)" are inserted.

With effect from 11.00 pm on 31 December 2020 ("IP completion day" as defined by s.39 of the European Union (Withdrawal Agreement) Act 2020), s.318 of the 2020 Act is amended by the 2020 Act, s.417(9) and Sch.22, para.94 (as amended by SI 2020/1520 reg.5(12)) as follows: **★5ASC-793**
(a) In subs.(2) for the words "and (e)", the words "and (3A)(b)" are substituted;
(b) In subs. (3)(a) for the words "and (e)", the words "and (3A)(b)" are substituted.

R. EXTENDED SENTENCES

(2) Legislation

(a) Extended sentences for those aged 18 to 20

With effect from 11.00 pm on 31 December 2020 ("IP completion day" as defined by s.39 of the European Union (Withdrawal Agreement) Act 2020), s.267 of the 2020 Act is amended by the 2020 Act, s.417(9) and Sch.22, para.87A (as inserted by SI 2020/1520, reg.5(4)) as follows: **★5ASC-798**
(a) in subs.(3), after "listed in", the words "Part 1, 2 or 3 of" are inserted;
(b) after that subsection the following subsection is inserted:

> "(3A) But if the proceedings for the offence were instituted before IP completion day (see section 397(5)), the earlier offence condition is that, when the offence was committed, the offender had been convicted of an offence listed in Part 1, 2, 3 or 3A of Schedule 14."

(b) Extended sentences for those aged 21+

With effect from 11.00 pm on 31 December 2020 ("IP completion day" as defined by s.39 of the European Union (Withdrawal Agreement) Act 2020), s.280 of the 2020 Act is amended by the 2020 Act, s.417(9) and Sch.22, para.88A (as inserted by SI 2020/1520, reg.5(6)) as follows: **★5ASC-801**
(a) in subs. (3), after "listed in", the words "Part 1, 2 or 3 of" are inserted;
(b) after subs. (3), the following subsection is inserted:

> "(3A) But if the proceedings for the offence were instituted before IP completion day (see section 397(5)), the earlier offence condition is that, when the offence was committed, the offender had been convicted of an offence listed in Part 1, 2, 3 or 3A of Schedule 14."

(d) Earlier offences: offences listed in Schedule 14

With effect from 11.00 pm on 31 December 2020 ("IP completion day" as defined by s.39 of the European Union (Withdrawal Agreement) Act 2020), Sch.14 to the 2020 Act is amended by the 2020 Act, s.417(9) and Sch.22, para.95 (as amended by SI 2020/1520, reg.5(13)) to remove references to other EU member states, consequent upon the end of the transition period relating **★5ASC-810** to the United Kingdom's exit from the European Union. Paragraph 18 is amended; paragraphs 19 and 20 are omitted; the heading to Part 3 is amended and a new Part 3A (dealing with proceedings instituted before IP completion day) is inserted.

S. LIFE SENTENCES (NON-MURDER)

(2) The interaction of life sentences with other sentencing orders

(b) Offender serving a determinate sentence

5ASC-822 Where a life sentence is being imposed concurrently to an extended sentence and the minimum term is to be increased to take account of that sentence, the increase to the minimum term should calculated by reference to the period remaining to be served under the offender is eligible for release, not until the expiry of the custodial term: *Mohammed (Raja)* [2019] EWCA Crim 2095; [2020] 1 Cr. App. R.(S.) 65.

(6) Life (for second listed offence) (ss.273 and 283)

(a) Legislation

★5ASC-850 With effect from 11.00 pm on 31 December 2020 ("IP completion day" as defined by s.39 of the European Union (Withdrawal Agreement) Act 2020), s.273 of the 2020 Act is amended by the 2020 Act, s.417(9) and Sch.22, para.88 (as amended by SI 2020/1520, reg.5(5)) as follows:

(a) In subs.(12), in the definition of "extended sentence", in the words following para. (b), for the words following "Scotland" substitute "or Northern Ireland";

(b) in subs.(12), in the definition of "life sentence", in the words following para. (c), for the words following "Scotland" substitute "or Northern Ireland";

(c) a new subs.(12A) is inserted:

> "(12A) If the proceedings for the index offence were instituted before IP completion day (see section 397(5)), the references to 'an equivalent sentence' in the definitions of the following are to be read as also including an equivalent sentence imposed under the law of a member State—
> (a) "extended sentence", and
> (b) "life sentence"."

★5ASC-851 With effect from 11.00pm on 31 December 2020 ("IP completion day" as defined by s.39 of the European Union (Withdrawal Agreement) Act 2020), s.283 of the 2020 Act is amended by the 2020 Act, s.417(9) and Sch.22, para.88 (as amended by SI 2020/1520, reg.5(7)) as follows:

(a) In subs.(12), in the definition of "extended sentence", in the words following para. (b), for the words following "Scotland" substitute "or Northern Ireland";

(b) in subs.(12), in the definition of "life sentence", in the words following para. (c), for the words following "Scotland" substitute "or Northern Ireland";

(c) a new subs.(12A) is inserted:

> "(12A) If the proceedings for the index offence were instituted before IP completion day (see section 397(5)), the references to 'an equivalent sentence' in the definitions of the following are to be read as also including an equivalent sentence imposed under the law of a member State—
> (a) "extended sentence", and
> (b) "life sentence"."

★5ASC-855 From 11.00pm on 31 December 2020, that being "IP completion day" as defined by s.39 of the European Union (Withdrawal Agreement) Act 2020, Schedule 15 is amended by s.417(9) and Sch.22 para.96, as amended by SI 2020/1520 reg.5(14) to remove references to other EU member states, consequent upon the end of the transition period relating to the United Kingdom's exit from the European Union. Paragraph 20 is amended; paragraphs 21 and 23 are omitted; the heading to Part 4 is amended; and a new Part 4A (dealing with proceedings instituted before IP completion day) is inserted.

T. MANDATORY LIFE SENTENCE FOR MURDER

(5) Offences committed before 18 December 2003

(a) General

In *Att-Gen's Ref (Mohammed (Shahid))* [2020] EWCA Crim 766; [2020] 4 W.L.R. 114, a pre-CJA 2003 murder case in which the respondent had spent time in custody in Pakistan awaiting extradition, the court considered the length of the minimum term imposed; the court held that when considering the term that was likely to be set by the Secretary of State under the previous regime (and whether that period was inclusive of any reduction for time in custody awaiting extradition), the sentencing judge had been correct to approach the matter as one involving judicial discretion and that there was no reason to think that a judge sentencing at that time, or the Secretary of State considering that judge's recommendation, would have been any more willing to exercise it in the defendant's favour than was the judge in the present case, and accordingly the sentencing judge had not erred. **★5ASC-908**

V. SECONDARY DISPOSALS

C. PREVENTATIVE ORDERS

(1) Procedure in respect of civil orders and European protection orders

(b) Legislation

Criminal Procedure Rules 2020 (SI 2020/759), Pt 31

When this Part applies

Rule 31.1 of SI 2020/759 (see the main work) by the Criminal Procedure (Amendment) Rules 2021 (SI 2021/40), see below, Appendix B-508. **★5ASC-913**

Behaviour orders: general rules

Rule 31.2 of SI 2020/759 (see the main work) by the Criminal Procedure (Amendment) Rules 2021 (SI 2021/40), see below, Appendix B-509. **★5ASC-914**

Application for behaviour order and notice of terms of proposed order: special rules

Rule 31.3 of SI 2020/759 (see the main work) by the Criminal Procedure (Amendment) Rules 2021 (SI 2021/40), see below, Appendix B-510. **★5ASC-915**

European protection order to be given effect in another EU member State

Rules 31.9 and 31.10 are revoked. In consequence, r.31.11 is renumbered as 31.9 by the Criminal Procedure (Amendment) Rules 2021 (SI 2021/40), see below, Appendix B-518. **★5ASC-921**

(2) Criminal behaviour order

(c) Guidance

Requirements and prohibitions

Blanket social media prohibition

When considering whether prohibitions to form part of a CBO would "help" in preventing further activity of the kind that underpinned the conviction offence, deterrence was a legitimate consideration. On the particular circumstances of the case, a prohibition limiting the number of devices and the internet accounts that the offender could use (which were capable of facilitating offending of the type forming the basis of the conviction) enabled proportionate and effective monitoring: *Tofagsazan* [2020] EWCA Crim 982. **5ASC-953a**

(4) Football banning orders

(c) Guidance

Making the order

Statutory test

In *Jelf* [2020] EWCA Crim 631; [2020] 2 Cr. App. R.(S.) 52, the sentencing judge had erred in **5ASC-980** interpreting the first limb of the applicable test too broadly (asking whether the offence related to football matches rather than to a specific match) and accordingly the order had to be quashed; the proper application of the test was to ask whether the offence related to a particular football match (in this case, a match between England and Panama that had ended minutes before the violence forming the basis of the offence of conviction occurred).

(7) Serious crime prevention order

(b) Legislation

Serious Crime Act 2007, Sch.1

★5ASC-1023 With effect from the time and on the date when para.2(2) of Sch. 1 to the Immigration and Social Security Co-ordination (EU Withdrawal) Act 2020 is commenced (currently a day to be appointed), Sch.1 to the Serious Crime Act 2007 (see the main work) is amended by para.1(4)(a) of Sch.1 to the Immigration and Social Security Co-ordination (EU Withdrawal) Act 2020 (Consequential, Saving, Transitional and Transitory Provisions) (EU Exit) Regulations 2020 (SI 2020/1309) to omit references to offences contrary to s.25B of the Immigration Act 1971 wherever they appear.

G. RECOMMENDATION FOR DEPORTATION

(2) Guidance

(d) Nationals of EU member states

★5ASC-1066 With effect from 11.00 pm on 31 December 2020 (that being IP completion day as defined by s.39 of the European Union (Withdrawal Agreement) Act 2020), the Immigration (European Economic Area) Regulations 2016 (SI 2016/1052) (see the main work) are revoked by s.1 of, and Sch.1, para.2(2)) to, the Immigration and Social Security Co-ordination (EU Withdrawal) Act 2020. Saving provisions are made by Sch.3 to the Immigration and Social Security Co-ordination (EU Withdrawal) Act 2020 (Consequential, Saving, Transitional and Transitory Provisions) (EU Exit) Regulations 2020 (SI 2020/1309). The broad effect of the amendments will be to treat EU nationals the same as other foreign nationals for the purpose of deportation decisions made after the amendments come into force.

5ASC-1067 *Hafeez v Secretary of State for the Home Department* [2020] EWCA Civ 406; [2020] 1 W.L.R. 1928 confirmed that periods of residence while imprisoned or detained do not count for the purpose of calculating the required 10 year period of residence for the Immigration (European Economic Area) Regulations 2016 (SI 2016/1052).

VI. CHILDREN AND YOUNG PERSONS

B. PRINCIPLES

(2) Guidance

(f) Guilty plea

★5ASC-1079a Any reduction in sentence for guilty plea should be made after any reduction on the grounds of youth: *RB* [2020] EWCA Crim 643; [2021] Crim. L.R. 64.

C. PRIMARY DISPOSALS

(6) Detention and training orders

(b) Legislation

Sentencing Act 2020, s.233–248

Offender subject concurrently to detention and training order and sentence of detention in a young offender institution

★5ASC-1193 With effect from 1 December 2020, s.244(1) and (5) of the Sentencing Act 2020 (see the main work) is amended by reg.4(3) of the Sentencing Act 2020 (Commencement No. 1) Regulations 2020 (SI 2020/1236) so that "the commencement date" in each place it appears is replaced by "1 December 2020".

Offender subject concurrently to detention and training order and other sentence of detention

With effect from 1 December 2020, ss 245(1) and (4) of the Sentencing Act 2020 (see the main work) is amended by reg.4(4) of the Sentencing Act 2020 (Commencement No. 1) Regulations 2020 (SI 2020/1236) so that "the commencement date" in each place it appears is replaced by "1 December 2020". **★5ASC-1194**

(c) Guidance

Making the order

The period of detention and training

The youth court has an unfettered discretion in making orders under s.102(5) of the 2000 Act (s.241(5) of the Sentencing Code) and it therefore is not inappropriate to make such an order for public protection even absent bad behaviour in custody: *R. (X) v Ealing Youth Court* [2020] EWHC 800 (Admin), DC; [2020] 1 W.L.R. 3645. **5ASC-1200a**

(7) Detention under s.250 (determinate)

(c) Guidance

Multiple offences

Endorsing the decision in *M* [1998] 2 Cr. App. R.(S.) 128 (and the approach in A.M. (see the main work), the court in *Robinson* [2020] EWCA Crim 866; [2020] 2 Cr. App. R.(S.) 48 stated that where an offender falls to be sentenced for an offence or offences which do qualify for a sentence under s.91 (s.250 of the Sentencing Code), and another offence or offences which do not, a term of detention commensurate with the seriousness of all of the offences should be passed under s.91 (s.250 of the Sentencing Code) only on those offences which do qualify, and the court should order no separate penalty on those which do not. **5ASC-1216**

VII. CONSEQUENCES OF CONVICTION

E. AUTOMATIC LIABILITY TO DEPORTATION

(2) Legislation

UK Borders Act 2007, ss.32–39

Exceptions

With effect from 11.00 pm on 31 December 2020 (that being "IP completion day" as defined by s.39 of the European Union (Withdrawal Agreement) Act 2020), s.33 of the 2007 Act (see the main work) is amended by the Extradition (Provisional Arrest) Act 2020, s.1 and Sch., para.29 so as to insert a new (5)(ca) as follows: "(ca) is the subject of a certificate under section 74B of that Act,". **★5ASC-1322**

With effect from 11.00 pm on 31 December 2020 (that being "IP completion day" as defined by s.39 of the European Union (Withdrawal Agreement) Act 2020 and thus the day on which para.2(2) of Sch. 1 to the Immigration and Social Security Co-ordination (EU Withdrawal) Act 2020 was commenced), s.33(4) of the UK Borders Act 2007 (see the main work) is omitted by reg.17(1) and (2) of the Immigration and Social Security Co-ordination (EU Withdrawal) Act 2020 (Consequential, Saving, Transitional and Transitory Provisions) (EU Exit) Regulations 2020 (SI 2020/1309).

With effect from the same point in time, the amendments to s.33 of the 2007 Act which were to be effected by SI 2019/975 (see the main work) are revoked by reg.48(1) and (2)(i) of the Immigration and Social Security Co-ordination (EU Withdrawal) Act 2020 (Consequential, Saving, Transitional and Transitory Provisions) (EU Exit) Regulations 2020 (SI 2020/1309).

(3) Guidance

(c) Reducing/restructuring a sentence to affect automatic liability to deportation

★5ASC-1331 For a further case confirming that a sentencing court should not 'retro-fit' or 're-engineer' the appropriate sentence by reference to the potential immigration consequences of the sentence, see *Malik* [2020] EWCA Crim 957; [2021] 1 Cr. App. R.(S.) 7.

(e) Relevance of liability to deportation on determination of length of sentence

5ASC-1332a Where the offender had been sentenced to an immediate custodial sentence of 14 months, and on appeal against sentence it was submitted on his behalf that the fact that the sentence made him a "foreign criminal" and that he was therefore liable to the automatic deportation provisions of the UK Borders Act 2007, it was held that the argument was not open to the offender as a matter of principle; what mattered in any sentencing exercise was what the appropriate term of imprisonment might be, with the judge always endeavouring to keep it as short as is appropriate: *Malik* [2020] EWCA Crim 957.

VIII. NON-RECENT OFFENCES

A. INTRODUCTION

Most serious example of the offence

★5ASC-1333 There was a different approach to maximum sentences in the context of non-recent offences, and the principles applicable to sentencing such offences are such that the maximum sentence for an individual offence may be merited whether or not a particular offence could be said to be in the most serious category of its kind, in accordance with the approach to sentencing 'recent' offences, and whether or not there were mitigating features: *Griffiths* [2020] EWCA Crim 732; [2020] 2 Cr. App. R.(S.) 54.

E. SENTENCING GUIDELINES

5ASC-1342 The term "measured reference" is not intended to prescribe a mathematical exercise, but rather to cause the court to reflect the previous maximum sentence as part of the composition of the sentence based on current guidelines. It must achieve a proper calibration and thereby some reduction to reflect the statutory maximum available at the date of offending: *DL* [2020] EWCA Crim 881.

IX. MENTAL HEALTH DISPOSALS

A. INTRODUCTION

5ASC-1373 The Sentencing Council has issued a definitive sentencing guideline for the sentencing of offenders with mental health disorders, developmental disorders or neurological impairments. The new guideline applies to all offenders sentenced on or after 1 October 2020. It provides general guidance on the sentencing of such offenders, including providing guidance on the approach to mental health reports and the relevant mental health disposals.

C. ON CONVICTION

(2) Summary of approach in post-conviction cases

5ASC-1381 The court in *Westwood* [2020] EWCA Crim 598 further considered the differences between an order under ss.37 and 41 of the Mental Health Act 1983 and an order under s.45A of that Act, explaining that the process for recall under ss.37 and 41 is much quicker than under s.45A with the potential for warrants for recall to hospital within minutes.

X. POST-SENTENCE

C. RELEASE AND RECALL

(2) Determinate Sentences

(c) Release

Release on licence

Criminal Justice Act 2003, s.246A

Release on licence of prisoners serving extended sentence under section 254, 266 or 279 of the Sentencing Code, etc

With effect from 4 January 2021 (Prisoners (Disclosure of Information About Victims) Act 2020 (Commencement) Regulations (SI 2020/1537), s.246A of the 2003 Act (see the main work) is amended by s.2(1) and (3) of the Prisoners (Disclosure of Information about Victims) Act 2020 so as to insert a new subs.(6A) as follows: "(6A) Sections 246B and 246C contain provision that relates to the Board's function of giving directions under subsection (5) for the release of P". **★5ASC-1467**

With effect from 4 January 2021 (Prisoners (Disclosure of Information About Victims) Act 2020 (Commencement) Regulations (SI 2020/1537), s.2(1) and (2) of the Prisoners (Disclosure of Information about Victims) Act 2020 inserts new ss.246B and 246C into the 2003 Act. The effect of those sections is where an offender is serving an extended sentence for an offence of murder or manslaughter or for an indecent images offence the Parole Board must take into account the failure to disclose information about, respectively, how or where the victim's remains were disposed of, or the identity of the child, and the reasons in the Board's view, for that non-disclosure when determining whether the continued detention of the prisoner is necessary for the protection of the public. **★5ASC-1468**

(3) Indeterminate sentences

(b) Release

Crime (Sentences) Act 1997, ss.28, 30, 31

Duty to release certain life prisoners

With effect from 4 January 2021 (Prisoners (Disclosure of Information About Victims) Act 2020 (Commencement) Regulations (SI 2020/1537), s.28 of the 1997 Act (see the main work) is amended by s.1(2) of the Prisoners (Disclosure of Information about Victims) Act 2020 so as to insert a new subs.(6A) as follows: "(6A) Sections 28A and 28B contain provision that relates to the Board's function of giving directions under subsection (5) for the release of P". **★5ASC-1488**

With effect from 4 January 2021 (Prisoners (Disclosure of Information About Victims) Act 2020 (Commencement) Regulations (SI 2020/1537), s.1(1) of the Prisoners (Disclosure of Information about Victims) Act 2020 inserts new ss.28A and 28B into the 1997 Act. The effect of those sections is where an offender is serving a life sentence for an offence of murder or manslaughter or for an indecent images offence the Parole Board must take into account the failure to disclose information about, respectively, how or where the victim's remains were disposed of or, the identity of the child, and the reasons in the Board's view, for that non-disclosure when determining whether the continued detention of the prisoner is necessary for the protection of the public.

D. BREACH, VARIATION AND AMENDMENT OF PRIMARY DISPOSALS

(1) General: Criminal Procedure Rules

Criminal Procedure Rules 2020 (SI 2020/759), Pt 32

When this Part applies

As to the amendment of r.32.1 of SI 2020/759 (see the main work) by the Criminal Procedure (Amendment) Rules 2021 (SI 2021/40), see below, Appendix B-519. **★5ASC-1493**

Chapter 5B

Confiscation under the Proceeds of Crime Act 2002

I. INTRODUCTION

D. KEY PROVISIONS

(2) The hearing

Determination of defendant's interest in property (s.10A)

5B-16 There is no duty to proceed under s.10A of the Proceeds of Crime Act 2002 in every case that third party interests arise; the legislature's intention was for the making of a confiscation order to be straightforward and quasi-automatic, with s.55 of the 2002 Act providing for the interests of a third party to be dealt with at the enforcement stage if necessary: *Hilton* [2020] UKSC 29 (which concerned the "mirror" provisions applicable to Northern Ireland (ss.160A and 51 of the 2002 Act)).

II. LEGISLATION

A. PROCEEDS OF CRIME ACT 2002, PT 2

Proceeds of Crime Act 2002, ss.6–91

Effect of postponement

5B-42a Section 15 of the 2002 Act requires that the imposition of the statutory surcharge should be delayed until confiscation is concluded; however if the surcharge is imposed prior to the conclusion of confiscation proceedings, it will not be quashed by the Court of Appeal (Criminal Division) on an appeal unless, exceptionally, the final outcome of the case means that the circumstances and justice of the case makes this necessary: *Bristowe* [2019] EWCA Crim 2005; [2020] 1 Cr. App. R.(S.) 58.

Proceeds of Crime Act 2002, Sch. 2

People trafficking

★5B-177 With effect from 11.00 pm on 31 December 2020 (that being "IP completion day" and thus the commencement date of para.2(2) of Sch. 1 to the Immigration and Social Security Co-ordination (EU Withdrawal) Act 2020), para.4 of Sch.2 to the Proceeds of Crime Act 2002 (see the main work) is amended by para.(1)(3)(a) of Sch.1 to the Immigration and Social Security Co-ordination (EU Withdrawal) Act 2020 (Consequential, Saving, Transitional and Transitory Provisions) (EU Exit) Regulations 2020 (SI 2020/1309) so that ", 25A or 25B" is replaced by "or 25A".

B. SUBORDINATE LEGISLATION

Rules of court relating to confiscation, restraint and receivership proceedings

Criminal Procedure Rules 2020 (SI 2020/759), Pt 33

Sums in the hands of receivers

★5B-244 As to the amendment of r.33.59 of SI 2020/759 (see the main work) by the Criminal Procedure (Amendment) Rules 2021 (SI 2021/40), see below, Appendix B-619.

III. AUTHORITIES

Lack of discretion, abuse of process and proportionality

5B-299 Generally, there is a need for any postulated restoration to be lawful before it can be accepted for the purposes of arguing that confiscation is disproportionate: *Andrewes* [2020] EWCA Crim 1055. Thus, in *Andrewes*, where the appellant had made dishonest representations in applying for a job which he could lawfully hold but at which he had properly fulfilled his duties, he was to be taken as having given full value for his remuneration and to have made full restoration.

A. BENEFIT

(1) Property obtained

Regulatory offences

For a further confiscation case relating to planning enforcement in which it was held that the gross rent derived from letting out flats that had been converted without planning permission was criminal benefit, see *Roth (Boruch)* [2020] EWCA Crim 967; [2020] 4 W.L.R. 130. **★5B-313**

B. VALUATION OF BENEFIT FROM CRIMINAL CONDUCT (SS.79, 80)

In *Lowther* [2020] EWCA Crim 1387; [2020] 4 W.L.R. 152, the court considered whether the costs of the sale of a property were to be included in the consideration of the benefit figure. The court noted that the underlying policy aims of the Proceeds of Crime Act 2002 was to require that the sum to be paid in satisfaction of the order was no more than the amount of the defendant's realisable assets (where less than the benefit figure), and that the value of property at any relevant time was its market value, and where a property had to be sold in order to satisfy the order, it was only the net proceeds of sale that were available to meet the confiscation order. Accordingly, the court held that the costs of sale of any properties included in the benefit figure fell to be deducted only against the defendant's realisable assets in calculating the available amount and thus the recoverable amount for the purpose of fixing the amount of the confiscation order. The court further held that it followed that there was no requirement also to reduce the amount of the benefit figure, since at the benefit stage the market value of the property was what somebody would be prepared to pay for it on the open market, not the net proceeds of sale which the defendant would obtain from its sale. **★5B-326**

D. PROCEDURE AND EVIDENCE

A failure to draw up a written formal order does not render a confiscation order made by a judge a nullity: *Westbrook* [2020] EWCA Crim 1243; [2020] 4 W.L.R. 138. **★5B-338**

Chapter 6

Costs and Legal Aid

I. COSTS

B. DEFENCE COSTS ORDERS

(2) Circumstances where costs may be awarded

"In the proceedings"—s.16(6)

In *Mirchandani v Lord Chancellor* [2020] EWCA Civ 1260 the court held that in the context of s.17 of the Prosecution of Offences Act 1985, costs "in the proceedings" included proceedings in the civil courts to enforce a confiscation order. **★6-9**

II. LEGAL AID

D. ADVICE AND ASSISTANCE FOR CRIMINAL PROCEEDINGS

Criminal Legal Aid Regulations, Pt 4

Prescribed conditions

With effect from 13 August 2020, the amendments to para.12 of SI 2013/9 effected by the **6-114**

Counter-Terrorism and Border Security Act 2019, s.23(1) and Sch.4, para.30 (see the main work) were brought into force: Counter-Terrorism and Border Security Act 2019 (Commencement No. 1) is 2020 (SI 2020/792).

K. DETERMINATIONS BY A COURT AND CHOICE OF REPRESENTATIVE

(3) – Determinations

Criminal Legal Aid (Determinations by a Court and Choice of Representative) Regulations 2013 (SI 2013/614), regs 4–9

Determinations by the Court of Appeal

★6-172 Save exceptionally, decisions as to representation orders in the Criminal Division of the Court of Appeal are to be made well in advance of the hearing of an appeal. Such decisions are pre-eminently a matter for the Registrar of Criminal Appeals, but the issue can be put before the presiding Lord or Lady Justice, or the Vice President of the Court of Appeal (Criminal Division), in advance of the hearing if there is a substantive basis for appealing her decision: *Yaryare and others* [2020] EWCA Crim 1314; [2020] 4 W.L.R. 156.

Chapter 7

Criminal Appeal

III. THE COURT OF APPEAL

D. PRINCIPLE OF STARE DECISIS

7-36 *Barton* [2020] EWCA Crim 575 has now been reported at [2020] 2 Cr. App. R. 7, sub nom., *Barton; Booth.*

IV. APPEAL TO COURT OF APPEAL BY THE DEFENDANT

A. APPEAL AGAINST CONVICTION OF INDICTMENT

(3) Determination of appeals

Fresh evidence cases

7-50 For a further case confirming that the test in fresh evidence cases is whether the court believes the conviction is unsafe, and not whether the fresh evidence might reasonably have affected the decision of the trial jury to convict, see *Park* [2020] EWCA Crim 589; [2020] Crim. L.R. 936.

G. PROCEDURE FROM NOTICE OF APPEAL TO THE HEARING

(9) Bail pending appeal

Criminal Procedure Rules 2020 (SI 2020/759), rr.39.8, 39.9, 39.10

Application for bail, or to suspend a disqualification or order, pending appeal or retrial

★7-177 As to the amendment of r.39.8 of SI 2020/759 by the Criminal Procedure (Amendment) Rules 2021 (SI 2021/40), see below, Appendix B-689.

H. THE HEARING

(7) Attendance and role of prosecution

Criminal Procedure Rules 2020 (SI 2020/759), r.39.6

Respondent's notice

★7-203 As to the amendment of r.39.6 of SI 2020/759 by the Criminal Procedure (Amendment) Rules 2021 (SI 2021/40), see below, Appendix B-687.

V. APPEAL TO COURT OF APPEAL BY THE PROSECUTION

E. RULES OF PROCEDURE

Criminal Procedure Rules 2020 (SI 2020/759), Pt 38

Form of appeal notice

As to the amendment of r.38.4 of SI 2020/759 by the Criminal Procedure (Amendment) Rules 2021 (SI 2021/40), see below, Appendix B-674. **★7-268**

Respondent's notice

As to the amendment of r.38.7 of SI 2020/759 by the Criminal Procedure (Amendment) Rules 2021 (SI 2021/40), see below, Appendix B-677. **★7-271**

VII. INTERLOCUTORY APPEALS

C. PROCEDURE

Criminal Procedure Rules 2020 (SI 2020/759), Pt 37

Form of appeal notice

As to the amendment of r.37.3 of SI 2020/759 by the Criminal Procedure (Amendment) Rules 2021 (SI 2021/40), see below, Appendix B-665. **★7-317**

Respondent's notice

As to the amendment of r.37.5 of SI 2020/759 by the Criminal Procedure (Amendment) Rules 2021 (SI 2021/40), see below, Appendix B-667. **★7-319**

VIII. MISCELLANEOUS RIGHTS OF APPEAL

A. APPEALS AGAINST REPORTING OR PUBLIC ACCESS RESTRICTIONS

Criminal Procedure Rules 2020 (SI 2020/759), Pt 40

Form of appeal notice

As to the amendment of r.40.3 of SI 2020/759 by the Criminal Procedure (Amendment) Rules 2021 (SI 2021/40), see below, Appendix B-709. **★7-328**

Respondent's notice on appeal against reporting restriction

As to the amendment of r.40.6 of SI 2020/759 by the Criminal Procedure (Amendment) Rules 2021 (SI 2021/40), see below, Appendix B-712. **★7-331**

IX. APPEAL TO THE COURT OF APPEAL: PROCEDURE AND FORMS

A. PROCEDURE

Criminal Procedure Rules 2020 (SI 2020/759), Pt 36

Duty of Crown Court officer

As to the amendment of r.36.8 of SI 2020/759 by the Criminal Procedure (Amendment) Rules 2021 (SI 2021/40), see below, Appendix B-655. **★7-373**

Criminal Procedure Rules 2020 (SI 2020/759), Pt 39

When this Part applies

As to the amendment of r.39.1 of SI 2020/759 by the Criminal Procedure (Amendment) Rules 2021 (SI 2021/40), see below, Appendix B-682. **★7-380**

Form of appeal notice

As to the amendment of r.39.3 of SI 2020/759 by the Criminal Procedure (Amendment) Rules 2021 (SI 2021/40), see below, Appendix B-684. **★7-382**

XIII. ATTORNEY-GENERAL'S REFERENCES

C. PROCEDURE

Criminal Procedure Rules 2020 (SI 2020/759), Pt 41

Form of notice of reference and application for permission

★7-455 As to the amendment of r.41.3 of SI 2020/759 by the Criminal Procedure (Amendment) Rules 2021 (SI 2021/40), see below, Appendix B-718.

Respondent's notice

★7-456 As to the amendment of r.41.4 of SI 2020/759 by the Criminal Procedure (Amendment) Rules 2021 (SI 2021/40), see below, Appendix B-720.

Chapter 8

Witnesses

IV. RULES OF EVIDENCE AND QUESTIONING WITNESSES

A. MATTERS TO CONSIDER BEFORE A WITNESS GIVES EVIDENCE

(2) Special measures directions

Youth Justice and Criminal Evidence Act 1999, ss.28–30

Video recorded cross-examination or re-examination

★8-99 With effect from 24 August 2020, s.28 of the Youth Justice and Criminal Evidence Act 1999 (see § 8-98 in the main work) is brought into force for proceedings taking place before the Crown Court sitting at Basildon, Canterbury, the Central Criminal Court, Chelmsford, Croydon, Guildford, Harrow, the Inner London Sessions House, Isleworth, Lewes, Maidstone, Snaresbrook, Southwark, Stafford, Wood Green, or Woolwich, where the witness is eligible for assistance under s.16 of that Act (see § 8-73 in the main work): Youth Justice and Criminal Evidence Act 1999 (Commencement No. 18) Order 2020 (SI 2020/888).

With effect from 26 October 2020, s.28 of the Youth Justice and Criminal Evidence Act 1999 (see § 8-98 in the main work) was brought into force for proceedings taking place before the Crown Court sitting at Amersham Law Courts, Bolton, Burnley Combined Court Centre, Caernarfon Justice Centre, Cardiff, Doncaster Justice Centre South, Exeter Law Courts, Gloucester, Ipswich, King's Lynn, Lancaster, Manchester (Crown Square), Manchester (Minshull Street), Merthyr Tydfil Combined Court Centre, Newcastle Moot Hall, Newport (South Wales), Norwich Combined Court Centre, Plymouth Combined Court, Preston Crown Court and Family Court (Sessions House), Salisbury Law Courts, Southampton Combined Court Centre, St. Albans, Swindon Combined Court, Teesside Combined Court Centre, Warrington, Winchester Combined Court Centre, Worcester Combined Court, or York, where the witness is eligible for assistance under s.16 of that Act (see § 8-73 in the main work): Youth Justice and Criminal Evidence Act 1999 (Commencement No. 19) Order 2020 (SI 2020/1159).

With effect from 23 November 2020, s.28 of the Youth Justice and Criminal Evidence Act 1999 (see § 8-98 in the main work) was brought into force for proceedings taking place before the Crown Court sitting at Birmingham, Bournemouth Combined Court, Cambridge, Coventry Combined Court Centre, Derby Combined Court Centre, Great Grimsby Combined Court Centre, Hereford, Hove Trial Centre, Isle of Wight Combined Court, Kingston-Upon-Hull Combined Court Centre, Lincoln, Luton, Newcastle-upon-Tyne Combined Court Centre, Nottingham, Peterborough Combined Court Centre, Shrewsbury, Southend, Stoke-on-Trent Combined Court, Taunton Crown, County and Family Court, Truro Combined Court, or Warwick Combined Court, where the witness is eligible for assistance under s.16 of that Act (see § 8-73 in the main work): Youth Justice and Criminal Evidence Act 1999 (Commencement No. 20) Order 2020 (SI 2020/1331).

Criminal Procedure Rules 2020 (SI 2020/759), Pt 18

When this Part applies

As to the amendment of r.18.1 of SI 2020/759 by the Criminal Procedure (Amendment) Rules 2021 (SI 2021/40), see below, Appendix B-282. **★8-118**

Meaning of "witness"

As to the insertion of a new r.18.3 into SI 2020/759 by the Criminal Procedure (Amendment) Rules 2021 (SI 2021/40), see below, Appendix B-283a. **★8-119**

Making an application for a direction or order

As to the re-numbering of the existing r.18.3 of SI 2020/759 by the Criminal Procedure (Amendment) Rules 2021 (SI 2021/40) as r.18.4, see below, Appendix B-284. **★8-120**

Decisions and reasons

As to the re-numbering of the existing r.18.4 of SI 2020/759 by the Criminal Procedure (Amendment) Rules 2021 (SI 2021/40) as r.18.5, see below, Appendix B-285. **★8-121**

Court's power to vary requirements under this Part

As to the re-numbering of the existing r.18.5 of SI 2020/759 by the Criminal Procedure (Amendment) Rules 2021 (SI 2021/40) as r.18.6, see below, Appendix B-286. **★8-122**

Custody of documents

As to the re-numbering of the existing r.18.6 of SI 2020/759 by the Criminal Procedure (Amendment) Rules 2021 (SI 2021/40) as r.18.7, see below, Appendix B-287. **★8-123**

Declaration by intermediary

With effect from 5 April 2021, the existing r.18.7 of the Criminal Procedure Rules 2020 (SI 2020/759) is omitted by r.9(d) of the Criminal Procedure (Amendment) Rules 2021 (SI 2021/40). **★8-124**

Content of application for a live link direction

As to the amendment of r.18.24 of SI 2020/759 by the Criminal Procedure (Amendment) Rules 2021 (SI 2021/40), see below, Appendix B-305. **★8-141**

Application to discharge [vary or rescind] a live link direction, etc.

As to the amendment of r.18.25 of SI 2020/759 by the Criminal Procedure (Amendment) Rules 2021 (SI 2021/40), see below, Appendix B-306. **★8-142**

Representations in response

As to the insertion of new rr.18.27 - 18.32 into SI 2020/759 by the Criminal Procedure (Amendment) Rules 2021 (SI 2021/40), see below, Appendix B-307a to B-307f. **★8-143**

Criminal Practice Direction V Evidence 18E: Use of s.28 YJCEA 1999; Pre-recording of Cross-examination and Re-examination for Witnesses Captured by s.16 YJCEA 1999

As to the amendment of para.18E.1 of *Criminal Practice Direction V (Evidence) 18E: Use of s.28 YJCEA 1999; Pre-recording of Cross-examination and Re-examination for Witnesses Captured by s.16 YJCEA 1999 by Criminal Practice Directions 2015 (Amendment No. 11)* [2020] EWCA Crim 1347, Lord Burnett CJ, see below, Appendix B-320. **★8-159**

C. CROSS-EXAMINATION

(3) Protection of witnesses

(b) Protection of complainant in proceedings for sexual offences

Previous complaints, statements about sexual behaviour and false complaints

In *Fichardo* [2020] EWCA Crim 667; [2020] Crim. L.R. 1164 the court held that there must be a proper evidential basis for suggesting a complainant has made a previous false complaint and that the decision in *M* [2009] EWCA Crim 618; [2010] Crim. L.R. 792 does not permit speculative cross-examination in the hope that the complainant might admit a previous falsehood. The **★8-294** court further suggested, *obiter dicta*, that where the complainant denies making previous false complaints there is a need for the defendant to prove on the balance of probabilities that the allegation was made and was false.

Criminal Procedure Rules 2020 (SI 2020/759), Pt 22

Special measures, etc. for a witness

★8-308 As to the amendment of r.22.7 of SI 2020/759 (see the main work) by the Criminal Procedure (Amendment) Rules 2021 (SI 2021/40), see below, Appendix B-369.

Chapter 9

Documentary and Real Evidence

II. PUBLIC DOCUMENTS

D. CATEGORIES OF PUBLIC DOCUMENT

(8) Judicial documents

(g) Convictions and acquittals

Conviction of person other than the accused

"Where evidence of his having done so is admissible"

9-88 *Stevens* [2020] EWCA Crim 280 is now reported at [2020] 4 W.L.R. 101.

Discretion to exclude

9-90a *Horne* [2020] EWCA Crim 487 is now reported at [2020] 6 *Archbold Review* 2.
Stevens [2020] EWCA Crim 280 is now reported at [2020] 4 W.L.R. 101.

Chapter 10

Miscellaneous Sources of Evidence

VI. LETTERS OF REQUEST

Crime (International Co-operation) Act 2003, ss.9, 10

Domestic freezing orders

★10-31 With effect from 30 December 2020, reg.87(5) of the Law Enforcement and Security (Amendment) (EU Exit) Regulations 2019 (SI 2019/742) (see the main work) - which would have repealed s.10 of the 2003 Act (see the main work) - is omitted by the European Union (Future Relationship) Act 2020, s.9 and Sch.3, para.2(1) and (2)(a).

Sending domestic freezing orders

★10-32 With effect from 30 December 2020, reg.87(5) of the Law Enforcement and Security (Amendment) (EU Exit) Regulations 2019 (SI 2019/742) (see the main work) - which would have repealed s.11 of the 2003 Act (see the main work) - is omitted by the European Union (Future Relationship) Act 2020, s.9 and Sch.3, para.2(1) and (2)(a).

Variation or revocation of domestic freezing orders

★10-33 With effect from 30 December 2020, reg.87(5) of the Law Enforcement and Security (Amendment) (EU Exit) Regulations 2019 (SI 2019/742) (see the main work) - which would have repealed s.12 of the 2003 Act (see the main work) - is omitted by the European Union (Future Relationship) Act 2020, s.9 and Sch.3, para.2(1) and (2)(a).

Chapter 11

Hearsay Evidence

II. CRIMINAL JUSTICE ACT 2003

A. ADMISSIBILITY OF HEARSAY EVIDENCE

Admissibility in the interests of justice (s.114(1)(d))

Nguyen (Van Huong) [2020] EWCA Crim 140 is now reported at [2020] 1 W.L.R. 3084. **11-3d**

B. PRINCIPAL CATEGORIES OF ADMISSIBILITY OF HEARSAY

(4) Previous statements of witnesses

Other previous statements (s.120)

Rebuttal of suggestion of fabrication (s.120(2))

Statements admitted under s.120(2) of the Criminal Justice Act 2003 (see § 11-34 in the main work) are admissible not only to rebut a suggestion of fabrication but also as proof of the matters stated, and where a statement is introduced to rebut an allegation of recent fabrication (under s.120(2)) there is no need to meet the requirements of s.120(4) (which provides an alternative more stringent route to introducing previous consistent statements): *KH* [2020] EWCA Crim 1363. **★11-36**

Chapter 12

Privilege, Public Interest Immunity and Disclosure

III. DISCLOSURE

A. PRELIMINARY

Introduction

The Attorney-General has issued new guidelines on disclosure, which came into force on 31 December 2020, which replace the 2013 guidelines and the 2013 supplementary guidelines on digital material (see Appendix A-242 and following). Although drawn in large part from the 2013 guidelines, the material has been extensively restructured and there are new sections on sensitive material, pre-charge engagement and the disclosure of digital material. Annex C contains a new template of a disclosure management document. **★12-48**

With effect from 31 December 2020, the Criminal Procedure and Investigations Act 1996 (Code of Practice) Order 2020 (SI 2020/1330) brought into force a revised code of practice under section 23 of the Criminal Procedure and Investigations Act 1996, setting out the manner in which police officers are to record, retain and reveal to the prosecutor material obtained in the course of a criminal investigation and that may be relevant to the investigation and related matters (Appendix A-231 and following).

Third party disclosure

In *CB*; *Mohammed (Sultan)* [2020] EWCA Crim 790; [2020] 2 Cr. App. R. 20, the Court of Appeal gave detailed guidance on the retention, inspection, copying, disclosure and deletion of the electronic records held by prosecution witnesses, including in particular material stored on complainants' mobile telephones in relation to sexual offences. The court stressed that there is no **12-53** obligation on investigators to review a witness's digital material without good cause. A request to inspect digital material must, in every case, have a proper basis which will usually be that there are reasonable grounds to believe that it may reveal material relevant to the investigation or the likely issues at trial. Mobile telephones should not be obtained as a matter of routine by investigators from witnesses. There must be a proper identifiable foundation for the enquiry, not mere conjecture or speculation. The court went on to provide guidance in relation to the decision by an investigator as to how extensive an enquiry should be made into material held on digital devices and to the need to keep a witness informed as to how long a device is to be retained and as to decisions concerning disclosure. Where a witness is reluctant to permit access to a device, it may be advisable to warn him or her not to delete potentially relevant material as this may impede a fair investigation of the case. It is important to look carefully at the reasons for a refusal to permit access and to furnish the witness with an explanation and reassurance as to the procedure that will be followed if the device is made available to the investigator. If it is suggested that the proceedings should be stayed, the court will need to consider the adequacy of the trial process, and whether this will ensure that there is fairness to the defendant, particularly by way of cross-examination of the witness, coupled with appropriate judicial directions.

B. LEGISLATION

(1) Criminal Procedure and Investigations Act 1996, ss.3, 4

Initial duty of prosecutor to disclose

12-59a As to a case considering the extent of the prosecutor's duty to disclose electronic material held by prosecution witnesses, see *CB*; *Mohammed (Sultan)*, above.

(3) Codes of practice

Material obtained during criminal investigation

★12-124 As to the coming into force on 31 December 2020 of a revised code of practice setting out the manner in which police officers are to record, retain and reveal to the prosecutor material obtained in a criminal investigation, see 12-48 above.

Chapter 13

Evidence of Bad Character and Rehabilitation of Offenders

I. SUBSTANTIVE LAW

C. THE BAD CHARACTER OF NON-DEFENDANTS

The need for an evidential basis

★13-24 In *Fichardo* [2020] EWCA Crim 667; [2020] Crim. L.R. 1164 the court suggested, *obiter dicta*, that where the complainant denies making previous false complaints there is a need for the defendant to prove on the balance of probabilities that the allegation was made and was false.

The requirement of leave

13-29 *Boxall* [2020] EWCA Crim 688 is now reported at [2020] Crim. L.R. 944.

D. THE BAD CHARACTER OF DEFENDANTS

Propensity, or coincidence, or both? Two practical issues

★13-52 The criminal standard of proof applies to any dispute as to bad character, and where there is such a dispute it is preferable to, even shortly, include in a bad character direction a direction that the jury must be sure of the relevant circumstances: *Gabbana (Jason)* [2020] EWCA Crim 1473; [2020] 4 W.L.R. 160.

II. PROCEDURAL MATTERS

Jury directions

★13-79 The criminal standard of proof applies to any dispute as to bad character, and where there is such a dispute it is preferable to, even shortly, include in a bad character direction a direction that the jury must be sure of the relevant circumstances: *Gabbana (Jason)* [2020] EWCA Crim 1473; [2020] 4 W.L.R. 160.

III. REHABILITATION OF OFFENDERS

A. INTRODUCTION

For an appeal from *Hussain v Waltham Forest LBC* [2019] UKUT 339 (LC), see *Hussain v Waltham Forest LBC* [2020] EWCA Civ 1539. **★13-80**

D. OTHER EXCEPTIONS TO THE ROA 1974 SCHEME – AND HUMAN RIGHTS CHALLENGES

With effect from 28 November 2020, the Rehabilitation of Offenders Act 1974 (Exceptions) Order 1975 (Amendment) (England and Wales) Order 2020 (SI 2020/1373) amends the Rehabilitation of Offenders Act 1974 (Exceptions) Order 1975 (SI 1975/1023) (see the main work) in order to ensure that the Order complies with the Supreme Court decision in *Re Gallagher, R. (P) v Secretary of State for Justice and another, R. (G) v Secretary of State for the Home Department and another, R. (W) v Secretary of State for Justice and another* [2019] UKSC 3; [2020] A.C. 185 (see the main work). **★13-93**

Chapter 14

Evidence of Identification

I. VISUAL IDENTIFICATION

E. IDENTIFICATION USING VISUAL AIDS

(2) Identification evidence at trial

Recognition by witness

Where recognition evidence has been compiled from extensive viewing of CCTV by a police officer, from a practical point of view it may be unrealistic to expect an officer to record all their passing thoughts while watching footage time and again. Any conclusions are likely to emerge incrementally and the fine detail of an improving or changing recognition may be difficult to record in a log. However, the officer should record the "Red Letter" events, for instance, when they first begin to note similarities with a particular individual, along with any significant features that occur to them in the process of viewing. Officers should also note any factors that tend to indicate that the suspect does not match a particular individual who is being considered: *Yaryare* [2020] EWCA Crim 1314; [2020] 4 W.L.R. 156, CA. **★14-65**

(3) Photofits, identikits and sketches

In *Thomasson and Warmington* [2021] EWCA Crim 114, the Court of Appeal considered the admission of E-Fit evidence at trial, noting that the admissibility of such evidence is now regulated by Part 11 of the Criminal Justice Act 2003. Section 114 of the 2003 Act (see § 11-2 in the main work) sets out the various routes to admissibility of statements not made in oral evidence in proceedings. Section 115(2) (see § 11-4 in the main work) provides that, for the purposes of Part 11, "a statement is any representation of fact or opinion made by a person by whatever means; and it includes a representation made in a sketch, photofit or other pictorial form", which plainly covers an E-Fit picture. The reasoning expressed in *Cook* and *Constantinou* on this issue to the effect that E-Fits are "in a class of their own" or "akin to a camera" has therefore been superseded, given that they are now to be treated as hearsay evidence of a representation of fact or opinion by a person. Where a witness, with the assistance of a technician, had produced an E-Fit picture, it was not permissible to introduce evidence that a number of police officers had viewed it, none of **★14-70** whom had suggested that it resembled the appellant but had given the opinion that it looked like other individuals related to the case. Such a process would have involved the officers viewing the E-Fit picture, comparing it to their memory of the appearance of various other people, and expressing their opinion as to the match between (a) the perception of the artist who compiled the E-Fit picture as to the perception of the witness as to the man she had seen, and (b) a range of other people. Such a process is fraught risk that a jury is misled by undetected human error, and is markedly different from that where a police officer, who has not been present at the scene, gives identification evidence from photographs. The critical difference is that, in the latter situation, there is no hearsay involved, because the identifying witness is not reliant on the perception of another human being.

Chapter 15A

Investigatory Powers

III. ENTRY, SEARCH AND SEIZURE

B. POLICE AND CRIMINAL EVIDENCE ACT 1984, PT II (SS 8-23)

Police and Criminal Evidence Act 1984, s.8

Power of justice of the peace to authorise entry and search of premises

★15A-50 In *R. (Jordan) v Chief Constable of Merseyside* [2020] EWHC 2408 (Admin); [2020] A.C.D. 128, QBD (Chamberlain J), after reviewing the authorities, it was said that the correct approach when considering a challenge to a search warrant on the ground of non-disclosure is to begin by asking two questions:

(a) Did the applicant fail to disclose something which he or she was legally obliged to disclose?

(b) If so, was the non-disclosure material?

As to question (a), if there is a point that could properly be made against the grant of the warrant, but the applicant thinks there is an answer to it, he or she will generally be well advised, and may be legally obliged, to disclose both the point and the answer. In general, it is for the issuing authority, not the applicant, to decide whether the answer is a good one.

As to question (b), the test is: "might the information that should have been given to the magistrate reasonably have led him or her to refuse to issue the warrant?".

Police and Criminal Evidence Act 1984, Sch.1

Procedure

★15A-61 Rule 47.6 of the Criminal Procedure Rules 2020 (SI 2020/759) was amended with effect from 8 February 2021 by SI 2021/40, r.27(c): see Appendix B-774 for the amended text.

The two conditions in paras 2(b)(ii) and 14(d) of Sch.1 to the 1984 Act (see §§ 15A-55 and 15A-57) (that "other methods of obtaining the material ... have not been tried because it appeared that they were bound to fail" and "that service of notice of an application for an order ... may seriously prejudice the investigation") should be addressed separately, ideally by means of a short skeleton argument filed in advance of the hearing: *R. (Ashbolt) v Revenue and Customs Commissioners* [2020] EWHC 1588 (Admin); [2020] S.T.C. 1813, DC.

V. QUESTIONING AND TREATMENT OF PERSONS

C. RIGHT TO HAVE SOMEONE INFORMED WHEN ARRESTED

Police and Criminal Evidence Act 1984, s.56

15A-175 With effect from 13 August 2020, the amendments to s.56 of the 1984 Act effected by the Counter-Terrorism and Border Security Act 2019, s.23(1) and Sch.4, para.18(1) and (3), are brought into force: Counter-Terrorism and Border Security Act 2019 (Commencement No. 1) Regulations 2020 (SI 2020/792).

D. CHILDREN AND YOUNG PERSONS

Children and Young Persons Act 1933, s.34

With effect from 13 August 2020, the amendments to s.34 of the 1933 Act effected by the Counter-Terrorism and Border Security Act 2019, s.23(1) and Sch.4, para.17, are brought into force: Counter-Terrorism and Border Security Act 2019 (Commencement No. 1) Regulations 2020 (SI 2020/792). **15A-177**

E. ACCESS TO LEGAL ADVICE

Police and Criminal Evidence Act 1984, s.58

With effect from 13 August 2020, the amendments to s.58 of the 1984 Act effected by the Counter-Terrorism and Border Security Act 2019, s.23(1) and Sch.4, para.18(1) and (4), are brought into force: Counter-Terrorism and Border Security Act 2019 (Commencement No. 1) Regulations 2020 (SI 2020/792). **15A-179**

I. FINGERPRINTS, PHOTOGRAPHS, INTIMATE AND OTHER SAMPLES

Police and Criminal Evidence Act 1984, s.61

Fingerprinting

With effect from 13 August 2020, the amendments to s.61 of the 1984 Act effected by the Counter-Terrorism and Border Security Act 2019, s.23(1) and Sch.4, para.18(1) and (5), are brought into force: Counter-Terrorism and Border Security Act 2019 (Commencement No. 1) Regulations 2020 (SI 2020/792). **15A-192**

Police and Criminal Evidence Act 1984, s.61A

Impressions of footwear

With effect from 13 August 2020, the amendments to s.61A of the 1984 Act effected by the Counter-Terrorism and Border Security Act 2019, s.23(1) and Sch.4, para.18(1) and (6), are brought into force: Counter-Terrorism and Border Security Act 2019 (Commencement No. 1) Regulations 2020 (SI 2020/792). **15A-194**

Police and Criminal Evidence Act 1984, s.62

Intimate samples

With effect from 13 August 2020, the amendments to s.62 of the 1984 Act effected by the Counter-Terrorism and Border Security Act 2019, s.23(1) and Sch.4, para.18(1) and (7), are brought into force: Counter-Terrorism and Border Security Act 2019 (Commencement No. 1) Regulations 2020 (SI 2020/792). **15A-196**

Police and Criminal Evidence Act 1984, s.63

Other samples

With effect from 13 August 2020, the amendments to s.63 of the 1984 Act effected by the Counter-Terrorism and Border Security Act 2019, s.23(1) and Sch.4, para.18(1) and (8), are brought into force: Counter-Terrorism and Border Security Act 2019 (Commencement No. 1) Regulations 2020 (SI 2020/792). **15A-198**

Destruction, retention and use of fingerprints, DNA profiles, and footwear impressions

With effect from 1 October 2020, the Coronavirus (Retention of Fingerprints and DNA Profiles in the Interests of National Security) (No. 2) Regulations 2020 (SI 2020/973) extend by six months the deadline for the retention of fingerprints and DNA profiles under s.63F of the Police and Criminal Evidence Act 1984 where the controller of the fingerprints or DNA profiles has been notified by a constable or a member of the civilian staff of a police force that the fingerprints or DNA profiles may be relevant to the interests of national security, and the final day of the period for which that biometric data may be retained would otherwise fall within the period that starts with 1 October 2020 and ends with 24 March 2021. **15A-217**

With effect from 13 August 2020, s.19 of, and paras 1–4 of Sch.2 to, the Counter-Terrorism and Border Security Act 2019 come into force: Counter-Terrorism and Border Security Act 2019 (Commencement No. 1) Regulations 2020 (SI 2020/792).

15A-219 With effect from 13 August 2020, the amendments to s.63U of the 1984 Act effected by the Counter-Terrorism and Border Security Act 2019, s.23(1) and Sch.4, para.18(1) and (9), are brought into force: Counter-Terrorism and Border Security Act 2019 (Commencement No. 1) Regulations 2020 (SI 2020/792).

Material not subject to statutory restrictions

15A-220 With effect from 13 August 2020, the amendments to ss.18 and 18B of the Counter-Terrorism Act 2008, and the insertion of s.18BA into that Act, effected by the Counter-Terrorism and Border Security Act 2019, ss.19 and 23(1), Sch.2, paras 12–14, and Sch.4, para.26, are brought into force: Counter-Terrorism and Border Security Act 2019 (Commencement No. 1) Regulations 2020 (SI 2020/792).

With effect from 1 October 2020, the Coronavirus (Retention of Fingerprints and DNA Profiles in the Interests of National Security) (No. 2) Regulations 2020 (SI 2020/973) extend by six months the deadline for the retention of fingerprints and DNA profiles under s.18A of the Counter-Terrorism Act 2008 where the final day of the period for which that biometric data may be retained would otherwise fall within the period that starts with 1 October 2020 and ends with 24 March 2021.

J. INTERPRETATION

Police and Criminal Evidence Act 1984, s.65

Part V: supplementary

★15A-223 With effect from 11.00 pm on 31 December 2020 (IP completion day as defined by the European Union (Withdrawal Agreement) Act 2020, s.39) (Extradition (Provisional Arrest) Act 2020 (Commencement No. 1) Regulations 2020 (SI 2020/1652), s.65 of the 1984 Act was amended by the Extradition (Provisional Arrest) Act 2020, s.1 and Sch., para.7, so as to insert in the definition of "extradition arrest power":

"(e) section 74A of that Act;".

VIII. PROCEEDS OF CRIME ACT 2002

A. LEGISLATIVE FRAMEWORK

(1) Introduction

★15A-250 With effect from 11.00pm on 31 December 2020 (IP completion day as defined by the European Union (Withdrawal Agreement) Act 2020, s.39) (European Union (Future Relationship) Act 2020 (Commencement No. 1) Regulations 2020 (SI 2020/1662), the Proceeds of Crime Act 2002 (External Investigations) Order 2013 (SI 2013/2605) was further amended by the European Union (Future Relationship) Act 2020, s.9, and Sch.3, para.4.

XI. INVESTIGATORY POWERS ACT 2016

B. UNLAWFUL INTERCEPTION OF COMMUNICATIONS DATA

Investigatory Powers Act 2016, ss. 44–47

Postal services: interception for enforcement purposes

15A-324 With effect from 13 August 2020, the amendments to s.47 of the 2016 Act effected by the Counter-Terrorism and Border Security Act 2019, s.23(1) and Sch.4, para.33, are brought into force: Counter-Terrorism and Border Security Act 2019 (Commencement No. 1) Regulations 2020 (SI 2020/792).

C. UNLAWFUL OBTAINING OF COMMUNICATIONS DATA

15A-334 With effect from 22 July 2020, the repeal of Ch.2 of Pt 1 of the Regulation of Investigatory

XIV. OFFENCES RELATING TO CHILDREN AND YOUNG PERSONS

A. ILL-TREATMENT AND NEGLECT

(2) Cruelty

(b) Indictment

In *Morgan and Cole* [2020] EWCA Crim 378; [2020] 2 Cr. App. R. 9 it was held that a charge of "inflicting, or encouraging the infliction of, the bite mark and/or the fractured ribs or failing to prevent the infliction of those injuries", contrary to s.1 of the Children and Young Persons Act 1933 (see § 19-375 in the main work), was not bad for duplicity as although it alleged two injuries those injuries were alleged to have formed a course of conduct, in line with rule 10.2 of the Criminal Procedure Rules (see Appendix B-183 below). **19-376**

XVI. TORTURE, SLAVERY AND HUMAN TRAFFICKING

B. SLAVERY AND HUMAN TRAFFICKING

(4) Prevention orders

(a) Slavery and trafficking prevention orders

Modern Slavery Act 2015, ss.14, 17-20, 22

Slavery and trafficking prevention orders on sentencing

In *Wabelua, Alford and Karemera* [2020] EWCA Crim 783; [2021] 1 Cr. App. R.(S.) 3 the court gave guidance as to the circumstances in which a slavery and trafficking prevention order can be made under s.14 of the 2015 Act. The court held that the risk of the defendant committing the offence must be real, not remote, and must be sufficient to justify making an order. Further, the order must be necessary (that being a distinct condition) for the purpose of protecting people from the physical or psychological harm likely to occur if the defendant committed such an offence, not merely desirable or helpful in that regard. In determining whether any order is necessary, a court must consider whether the risk is sufficiently addressed by the nature and length of the sentence imposed, the presence of other controls on the defendant, and the ability of the police to apply for an order if it becomes necessary to do so in the future. Not only must the order itself be necessary but so must the individual terms, which must be both reasonable and proportionate to the purpose for which the order has been made. The terms of the order must be clear and a draft order must be provided to the court and to all defence advocates in good time to enable its terms to be considered before the sentencing hearing. **★19-452**

(6) Protection of victims

(b) Defences to criminal proceedings

Modern Slavery Act 2015, s.45

Defence for slavery or trafficking victims who commit an offence

In *S* [2020] EWCA Crim 765; [2020] 2 Cr. App. R. 18 the court held that the appellant's guilty plea to drug offences should have been quashed in circumstances where that plea was entered following a "conclusive grounds" decision that there were insufficient grounds to believe he was the victim of trafficking that was subsequently reversed, given that that decision was of critical importance and the appellant had not previously understood his ability to run the defence under s.45 of the 2015 Act notwithstanding the view of the competent authority. **★19-464**

Offences post-dating the MSA 2015

In *DPP v M* [2020] EWHC 3422 (Admin), DC the court held that conclusive grounds decision of the single competent authority are admissible expert evidence in relation to whether a person **★19-467** is a victim of exploitation for the purposes of the defence under s.45 of the 2015 Act (see § 19-464 in the main work), but are not conclusive evidence in that respect. Further, the court held that that when considering the defence under s.45(4) age is only one factor to consider when considering the situation and relevant characteristics of the defendant for the purposes of para.(4)(c), and the seriousness of the offence will be of less significance than it would in respect of the defence under s.45(1), as a child is more likely than an adult to behave without a proper understanding of the nature and consequences of his actions.

Chapter 20

Sexual Offences

II. OFFENCES

C. ASSAULT BY PENETRATION AND SEXUAL ASSAULT

(5) Elements

Intention

★20-52 It is not necessary for the prosecution to prove, on a charge of sexual assault contrary to s.3 of the Sexual Offences Act 2003 (see § 20-48 in the main work) that the defendant intended his touching of that person to be sexual; it is sufficient to show that the touching was intentional and "sexual": *Att.-Gen.'s Reference (No. 1 of 2020)* [2020] EWCA Crim 1665. See also, below, §20-54.

"Sexual"

★20-54 Whilst it is not necessary for the prosecution to prove, on a charge of sexual assault contrary to s.3 of the Sexual Offences Act 2003 (see § 20-48 in the main work) that the defendant intended his touching of that person to be sexual, the defendant's purpose in relation to the activity may be relevant when deciding if the touching was sexual by reference to s.78(b) of the 2003 Act (see § 20-32 in the main work) (whether a reasonable person would consider that, given the nature of the activity, it may be sexual and, because of the defendant's purpose, it was sexual): *Att.-Gen.'s Reference (No. 1 of 2020)* [2020] EWCA Crim 1665.

Q. OTHER STATUTORY SEXUAL OFFENCES

(2) Voyeurism

(e) Elements

20-209 *Richards* [2020] EWCA Crim 95 is now reported at [2020] 2 Cr. App. R. 16, sub nom., *Richards (Tony).*

III. NOTIFICATION AND ORDERS

D. SEXUAL HARM PREVENTION ORDERS

(2) Sexual harm prevention orders (Sexual Offences Act 2003, ss.103A–103K)

Variations, renewals and discharges

★20-277 Any purported variation of a sexual harm prevention order in the absence of a valid application by a person listed in s.103E(2) of the 2003 Act is invalid, but a failure to accord with the requirements of s.103E(3) or a failure to strictly comply with all applicable rules of procedure when varying a sexual harm prevention order are procedural defects capable of remedy: *Ashford* [2020] EWCA Crim 673; [2020] 2 Cr. App. R.(S.) 56.

to section 16A of the 1968 Act. The guideline has effect for offenders aged 18 and older who are sentenced on or after 1 January 2021.

(c) Use of firearms to resist arrest

Sentence

The Sentencing Council has published a definitive sentencing guideline for offences contrary to section 17 of the 1968 Act. The guideline has effect for offenders aged 18 and older who are sentenced on or after 1 January 2021. **★24-63**

Indictment and sentencing practice

For a further case holding that, where the use of a firearm in the course of another offence is alleged, it must be indicted, see *Solari* [2020] EWCA Crim 231; [2020] 2 Cr. App. R.(S.) 15. **24-64**

(d) Carrying firearm with criminal intent

Firearms Act 1968, s.18

Sentence

The Sentencing Council has published a definitive sentencing guideline for offences contrary to section 18 of the 1968 Act. The guideline has effect for offenders aged 18 and older who are sentenced on or after 1 January 2021. **★24-68**

(e) Carrying firearm in a public place

Firearms Act 1968, s.19

Sentence

The Sentencing Council has published a definitive sentencing guideline for offences contrary to section 19 of the 1968 Act. The guideline has effect for offenders aged 18 and older who are sentenced on or after 1 January 2021. **★24-73**

(g) Possession of firearms by persons previously convicted of crime

Firearms Act 1968, s.21

Sentence

The Sentencing Council has published a definitive sentencing guideline for offences contrary to section 21 of the 1968 Act. The guideline has effect for offenders aged 18 and older who are sentenced on or after 1 January 2021. **★24-82**

Chapter 25

Terrorism and Other Offences against the Crown and Government

III. TERRORISM

A. TERRORISM ACT 2000

(4) Membership of and support for proscribed organisations

Uniform

The offence under s.13 of the 2000 Act (see the main work) is a strict liability offence; although the person who is wearing, carrying or displaying the item or article in question must act **25-19** deliberately, in the sense that he must know that he is wearing, carrying or displaying that item or article, there is no requirement that the offender has any knowledge of the import of the item or article, or of its capacity to arouse the requisite suspicion and this is compatible with Art.10 of the ECHR (see § 16-157 in the main work): *Pwr and others v DPP* [2020] EWHC 798 (Admin); [2020] 2 Cr. App. R. 11, DC.

(5) Proscribed organisations

Terrorism Act 2000, Sch.2

25-19a With effect from 17 July 2020, Sch.2 to the Terrorism Act 2020 is amended by the Terrorism Act 2000 (Proscribed Organisations) (Amendment) (No. 2) Order 2020 (SI 2020/743) to add to the list of proscribed organisations in that Schedule, "Feuerkrieg Division".

(23) Port and border controls

Terrorism Act 2000, Sch.7

Power to stop, question and detain

25-124c With effect from 13 August 2020, s.16 of the Counter-Terrorism and Border Security Act 2019 inserts para.5A into Sch.7 to the 2000 Act (see the main work): Counter-Terrorism and Border Security Act 2019 (Commencement No. 1) Regulations 2020 (SI 2020/792).

25-124e With effect from 13 August 2020, para.6A(3A) is inserted into Sch.7 to the 2000 Act by s.18(3) of the Counter-Terrorism and Border Security Act 2019 (see the main work): Counter-Terrorism and Border Security Act 2019 (Commencement No. 1) Regulations 2020 (SI 2020/792).

(24) Detention of suspected terrorists: treatment, review and extension

Terrorism Act 2000, Sch.8

Rights: England, Wales and Northern Ireland

25-138 With effect from 13 August 2020, paras.6(4) and 7(4) are inserted into Sch.8 to the 2000 Act by s.17 of the Counter-Terrorism and Border Security Act 2019 (see the main work): Counter-Terrorism and Border Security Act 2019 (Commencement No. 1) Regulations 2020 (SI 2020/792).

25-140 With effect from 13 August 2020, the amendments to para.9 of Sch.8 to the 2000 Act effected by s.17(4) of the Counter-Terrorism and Border Security Act 2019 (see the main work) are brought into force: Counter-Terrorism and Border Security Act 2019 (Commencement No. 1) Regulations 2020 (SI 2020/792).

(25) Exercise of authorised and examining officers' powers

Terrorism Act 2000, Sch.14

Code of practice

25-167 With effect from 13 August 2020, the Port Examination Codes of Practice and National Security Determinations Guidance Regulations 2020 (SI 2020/795) gives effect to a revised code of practice entitled "*Examining Officers and Review Officers under Schedule 7 to the Terrorism Act 2000*", replacing the previous code issued under the Terrorism Act 2000 (Code of Practice for Examining Officers and Review Officers) Order 2015 (SI 2015/906) (see the main work). The revisions to the code take account of the amendments made to the 2000 Act by the Counter-Terrorism and Border Security Act 2019.

IV. IMMIGRATION OFFENCES

(2) Assisting illegal entry and related offences

Immigration Act 1971, ss.25–25C

Assisting unlawful immigration to member State [or the United Kingdom]

★25-286 With effect from IP completion day (11pm on 31 December 2020) (Immigration and Social Security Co-ordination (EU Withdrawal) Act 2020 (Commencement) Regulations 2020 (SI 2020/

1279)), s.25 of the Immigration Act 1971 (see the main work) is amended by reg.5(1) and (3) of the Immigration and Social Security Co-ordination (EU Withdrawal) Act 2020 (Consequential, Saving, Transitional and Transitory Provisions) (EU Exit) Regulations 2020 (SI 2020/1309) so that in subs.(1) in both places it occurs "a citizen of the European Union" is replaced by "a national of the United Kingdom" and to omit subs.(7)(b).

With effect from the same point in time, the amendments to s.25(1) of the 1971 Act (see the main work) which are to be effected by SI 2019/745 (see the main work) are revoked by reg.48(1) and (2)(b) of the Immigration and Social Security Co-ordination (EU Withdrawal) Act 2020 (Consequential, Saving, Transitional and Transitory Provisions) (EU Exit) Regulations 2020 (SI 2020/1309). The other amendments to s.25 made by SI 2019/745 are unaffected.

Assisting entry to United Kingdom in breach of deportation or exclusion order

With effect from IP completion day (11pm on 31 December 2020) (Immigration and Social Security Co-ordination (EU Withdrawal) Act 2020 (Commencement) Regulations 2020 (SI 2020/1279)), s.25B of the Immigration Act 1971 (see the main work) is repealed by reg.5(1) and (4) of the Immigration and Social Security Co-ordination (EU Withdrawal) Act 2020 (Consequential, Saving, Transitional and Transitory Provisions) (EU Exit) Regulations 2020 (SI 2020/1309). **★25-288**

Forfeiture of vehicle, ship or aircraft

With effect from IP completion day (11pm on 31 December 2020) (Immigration and Social Security Co-ordination (EU Withdrawal) Act 2020 (Commencement) Regulations 2020 (SI 2020/1279)), s.25C of the Immigration Act 1971 (see the main work) is amended by para.1(a) of Sch.1 to the Immigration and Social Security Co-ordination (EU Withdrawal) Act 2020 (Consequential, Saving, Transitional and Transitory Provisions) (EU Exit) Regulations 2020 (SI 2020/1309) so that in subss.(1) and (5)(b)", 25A or 25B" is replaced by "or 25A". **★25-289**

Immigration Act 1971, s.28

Proceedings

With effect from IP completion day (11pm on 31 December 2020) (Immigration and Social Security Co-ordination (EU Withdrawal) Act 2020 (Commencement) Regulations 2020 (SI 2020/1279)), s.28 of the Immigration Act 1971 (see the main work) is amended by para.1(a) of Sch.1 to the Immigration and Social Security Co-ordination (EU Withdrawal) Act 2020 (Consequential, Saving, Transitional and Transitory Provisions) (EU Exit) Regulations 2020 (SI 2020/1309) so that in subs.(2A) ", 25A or 25B" is replaced by "or 25A". **★25-294**

Chapter 26

Money Laundering Offences

I. PROCEEDS OF CRIME ACT 2002

D. APPROPRIATE CONSENT, PROTECTED AND AUTHORISED DISCLOSURES

(4) Extension of moratorium period

Criminal Procedure Rules 2020 (SI 2020/759), rr.47.62 – 47.65

When this Section applies

As to the re-numbering of s.10 of Pt 47 of SI 2020/759 (see the main work) as s.9, and the re-numbering of the existing r.47.62 as r.47.59, by the Criminal Procedure (Amendment) Rules 2021 (SI 2021/40), see below, Appendix B-830. **★26-42e**

Exercise of court's powers

As to the re-numbering, and amendment, of r.47.63 of SI 2020/759 (see the main work) as r.47.60 by the Criminal Procedure (Amendment) Rules 2021 (SI 2021/40), see below, Appendix B-831. **★26-42f**

Application for extension of moratorium period

★26-42g As to the re-numbering of r.47.64 of SI 2020/759 (see the main work) as r.47.61 by the Criminal Procedure (Amendment) Rules 2021 (SI 2021/40), see below, Appendix B-832.

Application containing information withheld from a respondent

★26-42h As to the re-numbering of r.47.65 of SI 2020/759 (see the main work) as r.47.62 by the Criminal Procedure (Amendment) Rules 2021 (SI 2021/40), see below, Appendix B-833.

II. MONEY LAUNDERING REGULATIONS

Introduction

26-58 With effect from various dates (principally 6 October 2020 and IP completion day), the Money Laundering, Terrorist Financing and Transfer of Funds (Information on the Payer) Regulations 2017 (SI 2017/692) (see the main work) are further amended by the Money Laundering and Terrorist Financing (Amendment) (EU Exit) Regulations 2020 (SI 2020/991) so as to further implement amendments made by European Parliament and Council Directive 2018/843 to European Parliament and Council Directive (EU) 2015/849 on the prevention of the use of the financial system for the purpose of money laundering or terrorist financing (the Fourth Anti-Money Laundering Directive), and to address failures of retained EU law to operate effectively and other deficiencies arising from the withdrawal of the UK from the EU. The regulations effect significant amendments which are discussed below at §§ 26-60 to 26-65.

Part 3, Customer due diligence (regs 27–38)

26-60 With effect from 6 October 2020, Pt 3 of the Money Laundering, Terrorist Financing and Transfer of Funds (Information on the Payer) Regulations 2017 (SI 2017/692) (see the main work) is further amended by the Money Laundering and Terrorist Financing (Amendment) (EU Exit) Regulations 2020 (SI 2020/991) principally to clarify the due diligence existing requirements and to extend certain due diligence requirements in relation to beneficiaries of life insurance policies.

With effect from 10 March 2022, a new reg.30A of SI 2017/692 is substituted by SI 2020/991. The new reg.30A principally expands the duties to report discrepancies in registers to a trust which is subject to registration under Pt 5 of SI 2017/692.

Part 5, Beneficial ownership information (regs 42–45)

26-62a With effect from 6 October 2020, Pt 5 of the Money Laundering, Terrorist Financing and Transfer of Funds (Information on the Payer) Regulations 2017 (SI 2017/692) (see the main work) is further amended by the Money Laundering and Terrorist Financing (Amendment) (EU Exit) Regulations 2020 (SI 2020/991) to provide that that Part applies also to non-UK trusts which are an express trust, is not a trust listed in new Sch.3A (excluded trusts) and whose trustees (in their capacity as such) acquire an interest in land in the United Kingdom; or enter into a business relationship with a relevant person, where at least one of those trustees is resident in the United Kingdom and the trust is not an EEA registered trust. A new reg.45ZA is also inserted providing for additional express trusts to be included on the register. Further from 10 March 2022, new reg.45ZB is inserted providing for certain information on that register to be accessible to certain persons.

With effect from IP completion day, further minor amendments are also effected to reg.42 by SI 2020/991 to the definitions of "EEA registered trust" and "third country entity" to ensure the law continues to operate properly.

Part 6, Money laundering and terrorist financing: supervision and registration (regs 46–60)

26-63 With effect from 6 October 2020, Pt 6 of the Money Laundering, Terrorist Financing and Transfer of Funds (Information on the Payer) Regulations 2017 (SI 2017/692) (see the main work) is further amended by the Money Laundering and Terrorist Financing (Amendment) (EU Exit) Regulations 2020 (SI 2020/991), principally to extend the time limit for art market participant or letting agents to apply for registration on the register to 10 June 2021 as a result of a potential application backlog caused by the coronavirus pandemic.

Part 8, Information and investigation (regs 65–74)

26-65 With effect from 6 October 2020, reg.74C of the Money Laundering, Terrorist Financing and

Transfer of Funds (Information on the Payer) Regulations 2017 (SI 2017/692) (see the main work) is amended by the Money Laundering and Terrorist Financing (Amendment) (EU Exit) Regulations 2020 (SI 2020/991) to correct a drafting defect.

Chapter 27

Harmful or Dangerous Drugs

I. CONTROLLED DRUGS

B. DRUG OFFENCES

(2) Production and supply of controlled drug

(b) Production of drugs

Allocation and sentence

The Sentencing Council has issued a revised sentencing guideline on drug offences and covering offences contrary to s.4(2) of the 1971 Act. It applies to all offenders aged 18 or over who are sentenced on or after 1 April 2021, regardless of the date of their offence: see §§ S-42.11 and following in the Sentencing Guidelines Supplement. ★27-31

(c) Supply of drugs

Allocation and sentence

As to the revised sentencing guideline issued by the Sentencing Council and covering offences contrary to s.4(3) of the 1971 Act, see above § 12-31. ★27-40

(3) Possession and possession with intent to supply drugs

(c) Allocation and sentence

As to the revised sentencing guideline issued by the Sentencing Council and covering offences contrary to s.5(3) of the 1971 Act, see above § 12-31. ★27-53

(4) Cultivation of cannabis plant

Allocation and sentence

As to the revised sentencing guidelines issued by the Sentencing Council and covering offences contrary to s.6 of the 1971 Act, see above § 12-31. ★27-80

E. MISCELLANEOUS OFFENCES AND POWERS

(2) Incitement

Misuse of Drugs Act 1971, s.19

The drafting error in section 19 of the 1971 Act which was identified in *Marlow* (see the main work) was corrected by the amendment effected by the SCA 2007. ★27-95

II. PSYCHOACTIVE SUBSTANCES

C. OFFENCES

Penalties

The Sentencing Council has issued a revised sentencing guideline on drug offences, which, for the first time covers offences contrary to the Psychoactive Substances Act 2016, namely s.4 ★27-141 (producing a psychoactive substance); s.5 (supplying, or offering to supply, a psychoactive substance; s.7 (possession of a psychoactive substance with intent to supply); and s.8 (importing or exporting a psychoactive substance). It applies to all offenders aged 18 or over who are sentenced on or after 1 April 2021. See §§ S-42.38 and following in the Sentencing Guidelines Supplement.

Chapter 28

Offences against Public Justice

VII. PRISON SECURITY OFFENCES

E. CONVEYING PROHIBITED ARTICLES, POSSESSION OF OFFENSIVE WEAPONS AND UNAUTHORISED PHOTOGRAPHY, ETC.

Prison Act 1952, ss.40A–40E

Sections 40B and 40C: classification of articles

★28-193 To determine whether an item is a List A, B or C article, the court should inquire first whether the item comes within the ambit of the more serious category, thereafter considering the lesser category if it is not within the definition of the former; and that if an object comes within the more serious category then, absent good reason, it should be placed in that category (even if it also fits in a definition of an article in a less serious category): *Salih and Hamasalih* [2020] EWCA Crim 658; [2020] 2 Cr. App. R.(S.) 42.

Chapter 30

Business, Revenue and Customs Offences

I. FRAUDULENT TRADING

A. FRAUDULENT TRADING

(5) Elements

30-7 The correct citation for *Barton and Booth* (see the main work) is [2020] 2 Cr. App. R. 7.

V. REVENUE AND CUSTOMS OFFENCES

D. VAT OFFENCES

(2) Offences and penalty

Fraudulent evasion of VAT

Value added Tax Act 1994, s.72

Offences

★30-150 With effect from 11.00 pm on 31 December 2020, the amendments to s.72 of the 1994 Act effected by the Taxation (Cross-border Trade) Act 2018, s.43, and Sch.8, para.63, were brought into force by the Finance Act 2016, Section 126 (Appointed Day), the Taxation (Cross-border Trade) Act 2018 (Appointed Day No. 8, Transition and Saving Provisions) and the Taxation (Post-transition Period) Act 2020 (Appointed Day No. 1) (EU Exit) Regulations 2020 (SI 2020/1642), reg.4.

E. CUSTOMS AND EXCISE MANAGEMENT ACT 1979

(1) Introduction

HMRC Commissioners and Officers

★30-157 With effect from 11.00 pm on 31 December 2020, the repeal of s.9 of the Commissioners for

Revenue and Customs Act 2005 by the Taxation (Cross-border Trade) Act 2018, s.29, and Sch.7, para.7, was brought into force by the Finance Act 2016, Section 126 (Appointed Day), the Taxation (Cross-border Trade) Act 2018 (Appointed Day No. 8, Transition and Saving Provisions) and the Taxation (Post-transition Period) Act 2020 (Appointed Day No. 1) (EU Exit) Regulations 2020 (SI 2020/1642), reg.4.

(2) Definitions and application

Interpretation

Customs and Excise Management Act 1979, s.1

Interpretation

With effect from 11.00 pm on 31 December 2020, the amendments to s.1 of the 1979 Act effected by the Taxation (Cross-border Trade) Act 2018, s.29, and Sch.7, para.4, were brought into force by the Finance Act 2016, Section 126 (Appointed Day), the Taxation (Cross-border Trade) Act 2018 (Appointed Day No. 8, Transition and Saving Provisions) and the Taxation (Post-transition Period) Act 2020 (Appointed Day No. 1) (EU Exit) Regulations 2020 (SI 2020/1642), reg.4. ★30-171

Time of importation and exportation

Customs and Excise Management Act 1979, s.5

Time of importation, exportation, etc.

With effect from 11.00 pm on 31 December 2020, the amendments to s.5 of the 1979 Act effected by the Taxation (Cross-border Trade) Act 2018, s.29, and Sch.7, para.6, were brought into force by the Finance Act 2016, Section 126 (Appointed Day), the Taxation (Cross-border Trade) Act 2018 (Appointed Day No. 8, Transition and Saving Provisions) and the Taxation (Post-transition Period) Act 2020 (Appointed Day No. 1) (EU Exit) Regulations 2020 (SI 2020/1642), reg.4. ★30-172

(4) Illegal importation

Customs and Excise Management Act 1979, s.50

Penalty for improper importation of goods

With effect from 11.00 pm on 31 December 2020, the amendments to s.50 of the 1979 Act effected by the Taxation (Cross-border Trade) Act 2018, s.29, and Sch.7, para.44, were brought into force by the Finance Act 2016, Section 126 (Appointed Day), the Taxation (Cross-border Trade) Act 2018 (Appointed Day No. 8, Transition and Saving Provisions) and the Taxation (Post-transition Period) Act 2020 (Appointed Day No. 1) (EU Exit) Regulations 2020 (SI 2020/1642), reg.4. ★30-175

Importation through the Channel Tunnel

Channel Tunnel (Customs and Excise) Order 1990 (SI 1990/2167), Sch., para.8

Penalty for improper importation of goods

With effect from 11.00 pm on 31 December 2020, the omission of para.8(a) of the schedule to the 1990 Order by reg.9(6) of SI 2018/1247 was brought into force by the Customs and Tariff (Appointed Day) (EU Exit) Regulations 2020 (SI 2020/1643). ★30-179

(5) Illegal exportation

Customs and Excise Management Act 1979, s.52A

Breach of applicable export provisions, etc.

With effect from 11.00 pm on 31 December 2020, the insertion of s.52A into the 1979 Act by the Taxation (Cross-border Trade) Act 2018, s.29, and Sch.7, para.44, was brought into force by the Finance Act 2016, Section 126 (Appointed Day), the Taxation (Cross-border Trade) Act 2018 ★30-181

(Appointed Day No. 8, Transition and Saving Provisions) and the Taxation (Post-transition Period) Act 2020 (Appointed Day No. 1) (EU Exit) Regulations 2020 (SI 2020/1642), reg.4.

Customs and Excise Management Act 1979, s.68

Offences in relation to exportation of prohibited or restricted goods

★30-182 With effect from 11.00 pm on 31 December 2020, the amendments to s.68 of the 1979 Act by the Taxation (Cross-border Trade) Act 2018, s.29, and Sch.7, para.70, were brought into force by the Finance Act 2016, Section 126 (Appointed Day), the Taxation (Cross-border Trade) Act 2018 (Appointed Day No. 8, Transition and Saving Provisions) and the Taxation (Post-transition Period) Act 2020 (Appointed Day No. 1) (EU Exit) Regulations 2020 (SI 2020/1642), reg.4.

(6) Control of persons entering or leaving the United Kingdom

Customs and Excise Management Act 1979, s.78

Customs and excise control of persons entering or leaving the United Kingdom

★30-186 With effect from 11.00 pm on 31 December 2020, the amendments to s.78 of the 1979 Act by the Taxation (Cross-border Trade) Act 2018, s.29, and Sch.7, para.78, were brought into force by theFinance Act 2016, Section 126 (Appointed Day), the Taxation (Cross-border Trade) Act 2018 (Appointed Day No. 8, Transition and Saving Provisions) and the Taxation (Post-transition Period) Act 2020 (Appointed Day No. 1) (EU Exit) Regulations 2020 (SI 2020/1642), reg.4.

(7) Interference with revenue vessels

Customs and Excise Management Act 1979, s.85

Penalty for interfering with revenue vessels, etc

★30-188 With effect from 11.00 pm on 31 December 2020, the amendments to s.85 of the 1979 Act by the Taxation (Cross-border Trade) Act 2018, s.29, and Sch.7, para.81, were brought into force by the Finance Act 2016, Section 126 (Appointed Day), the Taxation (Cross-border Trade) Act 2018 (Appointed Day No. 8, Transition and Saving Provisions) and the Taxation (Post-transition Period) Act 2020 (Appointed Day No. 1) (EU Exit) Regulations 2020 (SI 2020/1642), reg.4.

(10) Procedure

Proof and burden of proof

Customs and Excise Management Act 1979, s.154

Proof of certain other matters

★30-202 With effect from 11.00 pm on 31 December 2020, the amendments to s.154 of the 1979 Act by the Taxation (Cross-border Trade) Act 2018, s.29, and Sch.7, para.106, were brought into force by the Finance Act 2016, Section 126 (Appointed Day), the Taxation (Cross-border Trade) Act 2018 (Appointed Day No. 8, Transition and Saving Provisions) and the Taxation (Post-transition Period) Act 2020 (Appointed Day No. 1) (EU Exit) Regulations 2020 (SI 2020/1642), reg.4.

Power to examine and take account of goods

Customs and Excise Management Act 1979, s.159

Power to examine and take account of goods

★30-207 With effect from 11.00 pm on 31 December 2020, the amendments to s.159 of the 1979 Act by the Taxation (Cross-border Trade) Act 2018, s.29, and Sch.7, para.107, were brought into force by the Finance Act 2016, Section 126 (Appointed Day), the Taxation (Cross-border Trade) Act 2018 (Appointed Day No. 8, Transition and Saving Provisions) and the Taxation (Post-transition Period) Act 2020 (Appointed Day No. 1) (EU Exit) Regulations 2020 (SI 2020/1642), reg.4.

Power to search premises, vehicles and vessels, and articles

Customs and Excise Management Act 1979, ss.161-163A

Power to enter land for or in connection with access to pipe-lines

★30-211 With effect from 11.00 pm on 31 December 2020, the amendment to s.162 of the 1979 Act by the Taxation (Cross-border Trade) Act 2018, s.29, and Sch.7, para.110, was brought into force by theFinance Act 2016, Section 126 (Appointed Day), the Taxation (Cross-border Trade) Act 2018 (Appointed Day No. 8, Transition and Saving Provisions) and the Taxation (Post-transition Period) Act 2020 (Appointed Day No. 1) (EU Exit) Regulations 2020 (SI 2020/1642), reg.4.

Power to search vehicles or vessels

With effect from 11.00 pm on 31 December 2020, the amendment to s.163 of the 1979 Act by the Taxation (Cross-border Trade) Act 2018, s.29, and Sch.7, para.111, were brought into force by the Finance Act 2016, Section 126 (Appointed Day), the Taxation (Cross-border Trade) Act 2018 (Appointed Day No. 8, Transition and Saving Provisions) and the Taxation (Post-transition Period) Act 2020 (Appointed Day No. 1) (EU Exit) Regulations 2020 (SI 2020/1642), reg.4. **★30-212**

Powers of search: personal searches

Customs and Excise Management Act 1979, s.164

Power of search

With effect from 11.00 pm on 31 December 2020, the amendments to s.164 of the 1979 Act by the Taxation (Cross-border Trade) Act 2018, s.29, and Sch.7, para.112, were brought into force by the Finance Act 2016, Section 126 (Appointed Day), the Taxation (Cross-border Trade) Act 2018 (Appointed Day No. 8, Transition and Saving Provisions) and the Taxation (Post-transition Period) Act 2020 (Appointed Day No. 1) (EU Exit) Regulations 2020 (SI 2020/1642), reg.4. **★30-214**

(13) Fraudulent evasion offences

Fraudulent evasion

Customs and Excise Management Act 1979, s.170

Penalty for fraudulent evasion of duty, etc

With effect from 11.00 pm on 31 December 2020, the amendment to s.170 of the 1979 Act by the Taxation (Cross-border Trade) Act 2018, s.29, and Sch.7, para.114, was brought into force by the Finance Act 2016, Section 126 (Appointed Day), the Taxation (Cross-border Trade) Act 2018 (Appointed Day No. 8, Transition and Saving Provisions) and the Taxation (Post-transition Period) Act 2020 (Appointed Day No. 1) (EU Exit) Regulations 2020 (SI 2020/1642), reg.4. **★30-221**

(14) Penalty and sentence

Sentencing guidelines

A revised sentencing guideline has been published for drugs offences, including the fraudulent evasion of the prohibition on the importation or exportation of a controlled drug. The revised guideline applies to offenders aged 18 or over, sentenced on or after 1 April 2021. **★30-257**

Chapter 31

Offences Relating to Marriage, Public Nuisance and Obscene or Indecent Publications

III. OBSCENE OR INDECENT PUBLICATIONS AND DISPLAYS, ETC

B. LEGISLATION

(4) Protection of Children Act 1978

Protection of Children Act 1978, s.2

Evidence

In *T and M* [2020] EWCA Crim 1343, expert evidence was admitted concerning the age of an unknown male shown in a video being subjected to sexual assaults by one of the defendants, ad- **★31-109** duced to rebut the defence that the unknown male was a willing adult participant. The Court of Appeal held that the observation in Land (see the main work) to the effect that expert evidence as to the age of a child shown in a photograph was obiter and did not have meant that such expert evidence is always inadmissible. Jurors are used to reaching a conclusion about a person's age in real life or in a film, but not in assessing it where only the lower half of the body is visible.

Chapter 32

Motor Vehicle Offences

II. DRIVING OFFENCES

S. DRIVING WITHOUT INSURANCE

(4) Elements

Requirements in respect of insurance policies

Road Traffic Act 1988, s.145

32-177 Where an insurance policy may be avoided for non-disclosure but has not yet been avoided or cancelled, it remains a valid certificate of insurance for the purposes of the Road Traffic Act 1988: *R. (Linse) v Chief Constable of North Wales* [2020] EWHC 1288 (Admin); [2020] 6 *Archbold Review* 3, QBD (HH Judge Jarman QC).

X. DISQUALIFICATION FROM DRIVING, ENDORSEMENT AND PENALTY POINTS

(8) Extension of disqualification where custodial sentence also imposed

Road Traffic Offenders Act 1988, ss. 35A, 35B

Extension of disqualification where custodial sentence also imposed

★32-270 There is no power to take into account early release on home detention curfew when calculating the extension period under s.35A: *Parkin* [2020] EWCA Crim 614; [2020] 2 Cr. App. R.(S.) 44.

III. VEHICLE DOCUMENT OFFENCES

E. ROAD VEHICLES (APPROVAL) REGULATIONS 2009

32-322 With effect from 1 September 2020, the Road Vehicles (Approval) Regulations 2009 (SI 2009/717) are revoked by the Road Vehicles (Approval) Regulations 2020 (SI 2020/818).

APPENDIX A
Codes of Practice and Attorney-General's Guidelines

I. CODES OF PRACTICE

A. UNDER THE POLICE AND CRIMINAL EVIDENCE ACT 1984

(1) Introduction

The Police and Criminal Evidence Act 1984 makes provision for the issuing by the Secretary of State of codes of practice in connection with the tape-recording of interviews (s.60, § 15-236 in the main work), the visual recording of interviews (s.60A, § 15-239 in the main work), the exercise by police officers of statutory powers of "stop and search" (s.66(1)(a)(i) and (ii), § 15-2 in the main work), the exercise by police officers of statutory powers to arrest a person (s.66(1)(a)(iii), § 15-2 in the main work) the detention, treatment, questioning and identification of persons by police officers (s.66(1)(b), § 15-2 in the main work), and searches of premises and seizure of property (s.66(1)(c) and (d), § 15-2 in the main work). **A-1**

There are eight extant codes: Code A (stop and search); Code B (search and seizure); Code C (detention, treatment and questioning of persons), Code D (identification), Code E (audio-recording of interviews), Code F (visual recording of interviews), Code G (arrest) and Code H (detention, treatment and questioning of persons under section 41 of, and Schedule 8 to, the Terrorism Act 2000).

Code D came into force on 7 March 2011: Police and Criminal Evidence Act 1984 (Codes of Practice) (Revision of Codes A, B and D) Order 2011 (SI 2011/412). Code G came into force on 12 November 2012: Police and Criminal Evidence Act 1984 (Codes of Practice) (Revision of Codes C, G and H) Order 2012 (SI 2012/1798).

The Police and Criminal Evidence Act 1984 (Codes of Practice) (Revisions to Codes A, B, C, E, F and H) Order 2013 (SI 2013/2685) brought revised Codes A, B, C, E, F and H into force on 27 October 2013. The revisions were required in order to give effect to (i) the United Kingdom's obligations under European Parliament and Council Directive 2010/64/EU on the right to interpretation and translation in criminal proceedings, and (ii) the decision of the Divisional Court in *R. (C.) v Secretary of State for the Home Department* (as to which, see §§ 15-227, 16-141 in the main work).

The Police and Criminal Evidence Act 1984 (Codes of Practice) (Revisions to Codes C and H) Order 2014 (SI 2014/1237) brought revised Codes C and H into force on 2 June 2014. The revisions implemented obligations under European Parliament and Council Directive 2012/13/EU, in relation to the right to information in criminal proceedings. In particular, every detainee must be given a revised written notice setting out his rights and entitlements whilst in custody, which has been updated to reflect the new substantive rights conferred by the 2012 directive.

The Police and Criminal Evidence Act 1984 (Revision of Code A) Order 2015 (SI 2015/418) brought a revised Code A into force on 19 March 2015. The main changes were intended to make clear what constitutes "reasonable grounds for suspicion". The revised code also emphasises that where officers are not using their powers properly they will be subject to formal performance or disciplinary proceedings.

The Police and Criminal Evidence Act 1984 (Codes of Practice) (Revision of Code E) Order

2016 (SI 2016/35) brought a revised Code E on the audio recording of interviews with suspects into force on 2 February 2016. The revisions exempt four offences from the requirement that the interviews of individuals regarding indictable offences must be audio-recorded. The conditions that must be met before the exemption can apply are set out in a new annex to the code.

The Police and Criminal Evidence Act 1984 (Codes of Practice) Revision of Codes C, D and H) Order 2017 (SI 2017/103) brought revised Codes C, D and H into force on 23 February 2017. The principal revisions to Code C allow for interpretation services to be provided by live-link services; implement the amendments to the Police and Criminal Evidence Act 1984 made by the Criminal Justice and Courts Act 2015 to extend the protections provided to "juveniles" in detention from those aged under 17 to those aged under 18; and permit an appropriate adult to be removed from an interview if he prevents proper questioning. The revisions to Code H correspond to those in Code C so far as relevant. The principal revisions to Code D: update the eye-witness identification provisions to reflect new developments in case law and practice; and reflect amendments to the Police and Criminal Evidence Act 1984 made by the Anti-Social Behaviour, Crime and Policing Act 2014 in relation to the retention of fingerprints, footwear impressions and DNA profiles and samples.

The Police and Criminal Evidence Act 1984 (Codes of Practice) (Revision of Codes C, E, F, and H) Order 2018 (SI 2018/829) brought revised Codes C, E, F and H into force on 31 July 2018. The principal revisions to Code C introduce a new definition of "vulnerable" to describe a person for whom an appropriate adult must be called and a requirement for proactive steps to be taken to identify and record factors which indicate that a suspect may require help and support from an appropriate adult. More broadly changes are made to clarify the rights, entitlements and safeguards that apply to voluntary interviews, and to reflect amendments to the Police and Criminal Evidence Act 1984 made by the Policing and Crime Act 2017 in relation to the use of live links, and to ensure that the safeguards applicable to 14 to 16-year-olds also apply to 17 year olds. The revisions to Code H mirror those in Code C insofar as they apply to vulnerable suspects. Code E has been substantially revised, extending the type of interview for which audio recording shall ordinarily be used, and restricting the use of written records only to where an authorised recording device in working order is unavailable, or there is no suitable location to use such a device. The new Code also extends the types of device that may be used. The revisions to Code E are mirrored in Code F which provides additional provisions that must be complied with when making simultaneous video and audio recordings, stressing that the police are under no duty to make such a recording.

The Police and Criminal Evidence Act 1984 (Codes of Practice) (Revision of Codes C and H) Order 2019 (SI 2019/1157) brought revised Codes C and H into force on 21 August 2019. The principle revisions to the Codes relate to the personal needs of detainees, in particular their health, hygiene and welfare, and among other things, provide for the provision of menstrual and other health, hygiene and welfare products. Further amendments are also made to protect the dignity of detainees, including transgender detainees, in relation to toilet and washing facilities, and during searches.

For further details of the various versions of the codes and their revisions, see §§ 15-5 et seq. in the main work. For further details in relation to the codes generally, see the main work at §§ 15-2 et seq. (primary legislation), § 15-5 (commencement), § 15-6 (status of codes), § 15-7 (who is bound by the codes), § 15-9 (admissibility), and § 15-10 (breaches).

It should be noted that the original text of the codes has a series of errors. Only in the most obvious cases has any change been made to the wording, but the punctuation, use of case, use of number and paragraphing have been amended with a view to injecting consistency and intelligibility.

(2) Stop and search

A. CODE OF PRACTICE FOR THE EXERCISE BY: POLICE OFFICERS OF STATUTORY POWERS OF STOP AND SEARCH; POLICE OFFICERS AND POLICE STAFF OF REQUIREMENTS TO RECORD PUBLIC ENCOUNTERS

Commencement—transitional arrangements

This code applies to any search by a police officer and the recording of public encounters taking place after 00.00 on 19 March 2015.

A:1.0 General

A:1.01 This code of practice must be readily available at all police stations for consultation by A-2
police officers, police staff, detained persons and members of the public.

A:1.02 The notes for guidance included are not provisions of this code, but are guidance to police officers and others about its application and interpretation. Provisions in the annexes to the code are provisions of this code.

A:1.03 This code governs the exercise by police officers of statutory powers to search a person or a vehicle without first making an arrest. The main stop and search powers to which this code applies are set out in Annex A, but that list should not be regarded as definitive [see *Note 1*]. In addition, it covers requirements on police officers and police staff to record encounters not governed by statutory powers (see paras 2.11 and 4.12). This code does not apply to:

- (a) the powers of stop and search under:
  - (i) the Aviation Security Act 1982, s.27(2), and
  - (ii) the Police and Criminal Evidence Act 1984, s.6(1) (which relates specifically to powers of constables employed by statutory undertakers on the premises of the statutory undertakers);
- (b) searches carried out for the purposes of examination under Schedule 7 to the Terrorism Act 2000 and to which the code of practice issued under paragraph 6 of Schedule 14 to the Terrorism Act 2000 applies;
- (c) the powers to search persons and vehicles and to stop and search in specified locations to which the code of practice issued under section 47AB of the Terrorism Act 2000 applies.

A:1 Principles governing stop and search

A:1.1 Powers to stop and search must be used fairly, responsibly, with respect for people being A-3
searched and without unlawful discrimination. Under the Equality Act 2010, s.149, when police officers are carrying out their functions, they also have a duty to have due regard to the need to eliminate unlawful discrimination, harassment and victimisation, to advance equality of opportunity between people who share a relevant protected characteristic and people who do not share it, and to take steps to foster good relations between those persons. [See *Notes 1* and *1A*.] The Children Act 2004, s.11, also requires chief police officers and other specified persons and bodies to ensure that in the discharge of their functions they have regard to the need to safeguard and promote the welfare of all persons under the age of 18.

A:1.2 The intrusion on the liberty of the person stopped or searched must be brief and detention for the purposes of a search must take place at or near the location of the stop.

A:1.3 If these fundamental principles are not observed the use of powers to stop and search may be drawn into question. Failure to use the powers in the proper manner reduces their effectiveness. Stop and search can play an important role in the detection and prevention of crime, and using the powers fairly makes them more effective.

A:1.4 The primary purpose of stop and search powers is to enable officers to allay or confirm suspicions about individuals without exercising their power of arrest. Officers may be required to justify the use or authorisation of such powers, in relation both to individual searches and the overall pattern of their activity in this regard, to their supervisory officers or in court. Any misuse of the powers is likely to be harmful to policing and lead to mistrust of the police. Officers must also be able to explain their actions to the member of the public searched. The misuse of these powers can lead to disciplinary action (see paras 5.5 and 5.6).

A:1.5 An officer must not search a person, even with his or her consent, where no power to search is applicable. Even where a person is prepared to submit to a search voluntarily, the person must not be searched unless the necessary legal power exists, and the search must be in accordance with the relevant power and the provisions of this code. The only exception, where an officer does not require a specific power, applies to searches of persons entering sports grounds or other premises carried out with their consent given as a condition of entry.

A:1.6 Evidence obtained from a search to which this code applies may be open to challenge if the provisions of this code are not observed.

A:2 Types of stop and search powers

A:2.1 This code applies, subject to paragraph 1.03, to powers of stop and search as follows: A-4

- (a) powers which require reasonable grounds for suspicion, before they may be exercised; that articles unlawfully obtained or possessed are being carried such as section 1 of PACE for stolen and prohibited articles and section 23 of the Misuse of Drugs Act 1971 for controlled drugs;

(b) authorised under section 60 of the Criminal Justice and Public Order Act 1994, based upon a reasonable belief that incidents involving serious violence may take place or that people are carrying dangerous instruments or offensive weapons within any locality in the police area, or that it is expedient to use the powers to find such instruments or weapons that have been used in incidents of serious violence;

(c) [*not used*];

(d) the powers in Schedule 5 to the Terrorism Prevention and Investigation Measures (TPIM) Act 2011 to search an individual who has not been arrested, conferred by:

 (i) paragraph 6(2)(a) at the time of serving a TPIM notice;

 (ii) paragraph 8(2)(a) under a search warrant for compliance purposes; and

 (iii) paragraph 10 for public safety purposes;

see paragraph 2.18A;

(e) powers to search a person who has not been arrested in the exercise of a power to search premises (see Code B, para. 2.4).

(a) Stop and search powers requiring reasonable grounds for suspicion - explanation

General

A-5 A:2.2 Reasonable grounds for suspicion is the legal test which a police officer must satisfy before they can stop and detain individuals or vehicles to search them under powers such as section 1 of PACE (to find stolen or prohibited articles) and section 23 of the Misuse of Drugs Act 1971 (to find controlled drugs). This test must be applied to the particular circumstances in each case and is in two parts:

 (i) firstly, the officer must have formed a genuine suspicion in their own mind that they will find the object for which the search power being exercised allows them to search (see Annex A, second column, for examples); and

 (ii) secondly, the suspicion that the object will be found must be reasonable. This means that there must be an objective basis for that suspicion based on facts, information and/or intelligence which are relevant to the likelihood that the object in question will be found, so that a reasonable person would be entitled to reach the same conclusion based on the same facts and information and/or intelligence.

Officers must therefore be able to explain the basis for their suspicion by reference to intelligence or information about, or some specific behaviour by, the person concerned (see paras 3.8(d), 4.6 and 5.5).

A:2.2A The exercise of these stop and search powers depends on the likelihood that the person searched is in possession of an item for which they may be searched; it does not depend on the person concerned being suspected of committing an offence in relation to the object of the search. A police officer who has reasonable grounds to suspect that a person is in innocent possession of a stolen or prohibited article, controlled drug or other item for which the officer is empowered to search, may stop and search the person even though there would be no power of arrest. This would apply when a child under the age of criminal responsibility (10 years) is suspected of carrying any such item, even if they knew they had it. (See *Notes 1B* and *1BA*.)

Personal factors can never support reasonable grounds for suspicion

A-5a A:2.2B Reasonable suspicion can never be supported on the basis of personal factors. This means that unless the police have information or intelligence which provides a description of a person suspected of carrying an article for which there is a power to stop and search, the following cannot be used, alone or in combination with each other, or in combination with any other factor, as the reason for stopping and searching any individual, including any vehicle which they are driving or are being carried in:

(a) a person's physical appearance with regard, for example, to any of the "relevant protected characteristics" set out in the Equality Act 2010, s.149, which are age, disability, gender reassignment, pregnancy and maternity, race, religion or belief, sex and sexual orientation (see para. 1.1 and *Note 1A*), or the fact that the person is known to have a previous conviction; and

(b) generalisations or stereotypical images that certain groups or categories of people are more likely to be involved in criminal activity.

A:2.3 [*Not used.*]

Reasonable grounds for suspicion based on information and/or intelligence

A-5b A:2.4 Reasonable grounds for suspicion should normally be linked to accurate and current intelligence or information, relating to articles for which there is a power to stop and search, being carried by individuals or being in vehicles in any locality. This would include reports from members of the public or other officers describing:

- a person who has been seen carrying such an article or a vehicle in which such an article has been seen;
- crimes committed in relation to which such an article would constitute relevant evidence, for example, property stolen in a theft or burglary, an offensive weapon or bladed or sharply pointed article used to assault or threaten someone or an article used to cause criminal damage to property.

A:2.4A Searches based on accurate and current intelligence or information are more likely to be effective. Targeting searches in a particular area at specified crime problems not only increases their effectiveness but also minimises inconvenience to law-abiding members of the public. It also helps in justifying the use of searches both to those who are searched and to the public. This does not, however, prevent stop and search powers being exercised in other locations where such powers may be exercised and reasonable suspicion exists.

A:2.5 [*Not used.*]

Reasonable grounds for suspicion and searching groups

A:2.6 Where there is reliable information or intelligence that members of a group or gang habitually carry knives unlawfully or weapons or controlled drugs, and wear a distinctive item of clothing or other means of identification in order to identify themselves as members of that group or gang, that distinctive item of clothing or other means of identification may provide reasonable grounds to stop and search any person believed to be a member of that group or gang. [See *Note 9*.] **A-5c**

A:2.6A A similar approach would apply to particular organised protest groups where there is reliable information or intelligence:

(a) that the group in question arranges meetings and marches to which one or more members bring articles intended to be used to cause criminal damage and/or injury to others in support of the group's aims;

(b) that at one or more previous meetings or marches arranged by that group, such articles have been used and resulted in damage and/or injury; and

(c) that on the subsequent occasion in question, one or more members of the group have brought with them such articles with similar intentions.

These circumstances may provide reasonable grounds to stop and search any members of the group to find such articles (see *Note 9A*). See also paragraphs 2.12 to 2.18, "Searches authorised under section 60 of the Criminal Justice and Public Order Act 1994", when serious violence is anticipated at meetings and marches.

Reasonable grounds for suspicion based on behaviour, time and location

A:2.6B Reasonable suspicion may also exist without specific information or intelligence and on the basis of the behaviour of a person. For example, if an officer encounters someone on the street at night who is obviously trying to hide something, the officer may (depending on the other surrounding circumstances) base such suspicion on the fact that this kind of behaviour is often linked to stolen or prohibited articles being carried. An officer who forms the opinion that a person is acting suspiciously or that they appear to be nervous must be able to explain, with reference to specific aspects of the person's behaviour or conduct which they have observed, why they formed that opinion (see paras 3.8(d) and 5.5). A hunch or instinct which cannot be explained or justified to an objective observer can never amount to reasonable grounds. **A-5d**

A:2.7 [*Not used.*]

A:2.8 [*Not used.*]

Securing public confidence and promoting community relations

A:2.8A All police officers must recognise that searches are more likely to be effective, legitimate and secure public confidence when their reasonable grounds for suspicion are based on a range of objective factors. The overall use of these powers is more likely to be effective when up-to-date and accurate intelligence or information is communicated to officers and they are well-informed about local crime patterns. Local senior officers have a duty to ensure that those under their command who exercise stop and search powers have access to such information, and the officers exercising the powers have a duty to acquaint themselves with that information (see paras 5.1 to 5.6). **A-5e**

Questioning to decide whether to carry out a search

A:2.9 An officer who has reasonable grounds for suspicion may detain the person concerned in order to carry out a search. Before carrying out the search the officer may ask questions about the **A-5f** person's behaviour or presence in circumstances which gave rise to the suspicion. As a result of questioning the detained person, the reasonable grounds for suspicion necessary to detain that person may be confirmed or, because of a satisfactory explanation, be dispelled. [See *Notes 2* and *3*.] Questioning may also reveal reasonable grounds to suspect the possession of a different kind of unlawful article from that originally suspected. Reasonable grounds for suspicion however cannot be provided retrospectively by such questioning during a person's detention or by refusal to answer any questions asked.

A:2.10 If, as a result of questioning before a search, or other circumstances which come to the attention of the officer, there cease to be reasonable grounds for suspecting that an article of a kind for which there is a power to stop and search is being carried, no search may take place. [See *Note 3*.] In the absence of any other lawful power to detain, the person is free to leave at will and must be so informed.

A:2.11 There is no power to stop or detain a person in order to find grounds for a search. Police officers have many encounters with members of the public which do not involve detaining people against their will and do not require any statutory power for an officer to speak to a person (see para. 4.12 and *Note 1*). However, if reasonable grounds for suspicion emerge during such an encounter, the officer may detain the person to search them, even though no grounds existed when the encounter began. As soon as detention begins, and before searching, the officer must inform the person that they are being detained for the purpose of a search and take action in accordance with paragraphs 3.8 to 3.11 under *"Steps to be taken prior to a search"*.

(b) Searches authorised under section 60 of the Criminal Justice and Public Order Act 1994

A-5g A:2.12 Authority for a constable in uniform to stop and search under section 60 of the Criminal Justice and Public Order Act 1994 may be given if the authorising officer reasonably believes:

(a) that incidents involving serious violence may take place in any locality in the officer's police area, and it is expedient to use these powers to prevent their occurrence;

(b) that persons are carrying dangerous instruments or offensive weapons without good reason in any locality in the officer's police area; or

(c) that an incident involving serious violence has taken place in the officer's police area, a dangerous instrument or offensive weapon used in the incident is being carried by a person in any locality in that police area, and it is expedient to use these powers to find that instrument or weapon.

A:2.13 An authorisation under section 60 may only be given by an officer of the rank of inspector or above and in writing, or orally if paragraph 2.12(c) applies and it is not practicable to give the authorisation in writing. The authorisation (whether written or oral) must specify the grounds on which it was given, the locality in which the powers may be exercised and the period of time for which they are in force. The period authorised shall be no longer than appears reasonably necessary to prevent, or seek to prevent incidents of serious violence, or to deal with the problem of carrying dangerous instruments or offensive weapons or to find a dangerous instrument or offensive weapon that has been used. It may not exceed 24 hours. An oral authorisation given where paragraph 2.12(c) applies must be recorded in writing as soon as practicable. [See *Notes 10-13*.]

A:2.14 An inspector who gives an authorisation must, as soon as practicable, inform an officer of or above the rank of superintendent. This officer may direct that the authorisation shall be extended for a further 24 hours, if violence or the carrying of dangerous instruments or offensive weapons has occurred, or is suspected to have occurred, and the continued use of the powers is considered necessary to prevent or deal with further such activity or to find a dangerous instrument or offensive weapon that has been used. That direction must be given in writing unless it is not practicable to do so, in which case it must be recorded in writing as soon as practicable afterwards. [See *Note 12*.]

A:2.14A The selection of persons and vehicles under section 60 to be stopped and, if appropriate, searched should reflect an objective assessment of the nature of the incident or weapon in question and the individuals and vehicles thought likely to be associated with that incident or those weapons [see *Notes 10* and *11*]. The powers must not be used to stop and search persons and vehicles for reasons unconnected with the purpose of the authorisation. When selecting persons and vehicles to be stopped in response to a specific threat or incident, officers must take care not to discriminate unlawfully against anyone on the grounds of any of the protected characteristics set out in the Equality Act 2010 (see paragraph 1.1).

A:2.14B The driver of a vehicle which is stopped under section 60 and any person who is searched under section 60 are entitled to a written statement to that effect if they apply within twelve months from the day the vehicle was stopped or the person was searched. This statement is a record which states that the vehicle was stopped or (as the case may be) that the person was searched under section 60 and it may form part of the search record or be supplied as a separate record.

Powers to require removal of face coverings

A-6 A:2.15 Section 60AA of the Criminal Justice and Public Order Act 1994 also provides a power to demand the removal of disguises. The officer exercising the power must reasonably believe that someone is wearing an item wholly or mainly for the purpose of concealing identity. There is also a power to seize such items where the officer believes that a person intends to wear them for this purpose. There is no power to stop and search for disguises. An officer may seize any such item which is discovered when exercising a power of search for something else, or which is being carried, and which the officer reasonably believes is intended to be used for concealing anyone's identity. This power can only be used if an authorisation given under section 60, or under section 60AA, is in force. [See *Note 4.*]

A:2.16 Authority under section 60AA for a constable in uniform to require the removal of disguises and to seize them may be given if the authorising officer reasonably believes that activities may take place in any locality in the officer's police area that are likely to involve the commission of offences and it is expedient to use these powers to prevent or control these activities.

A:2.17 An authorisation under section 60AA may only be given by an officer of the rank of inspector or above, in writing, specifying the grounds on which it was given, the locality in which the powers may be exercised and the period of time for which they are in force. The period authorised shall be no longer than appears reasonably necessary to prevent, or seek to prevent the commission of offences. It may not exceed 24 hours. [See *Notes 10-13.*]

A:2.18 An inspector who gives an authorisation must, as soon as practicable, inform an officer of or above the rank of superintendent. This officer may direct that the authorisation shall be extended for a further 24 hours, if crimes have been committed, or are suspected to have been committed, and the continued use of the powers is considered necessary to prevent or deal with further such activity. This direction must also be given in writing at the time or as soon as practicable afterwards. [See *Note 12.*]

(c) [Not used]

(d) Searches under Schedule 5 to the Terrorism Prevention and Investigation Measures Act 2011

A:2.18A Paragraph 3 of Schedule 5 to the TPIM Act 2011 allows a constable to detain an individual to be searched under the following powers: **A-7**

(i) paragraph 6(2)(a) when a TPIM notice is being, or has just been, served on the individual for the purpose of ascertaining whether there is anything on the individual that contravenes measures specified in the notice;

(ii) paragraph 8(2)(a) in accordance with a warrant to search the individual issued by a justice of the peace in England and Wales, a sheriff in Scotland or a lay magistrate in Northern Ireland who is satisfied that a search is necessary for the purpose of determining whether an individual in respect of whom a TPIM notice is in force is complying with measures specified in the notice (see para. 2.20); and

(iii) paragraph 10 to ascertain whether an individual in respect of whom a TPIM notice is in force is in possession of anything that could be used to threaten or harm any person.

See paragraph 2.1(e).

A:2.19 The exercise of the powers mentioned in paragraph 2.18A does not require the constable to have reasonable grounds to suspect that the individual:

(a) has been, or is, contravening any of the measures specified in the TPIM notice; or

(b) has on them anything which:
- in the case of the power in sub-paragraph (i), contravenes measures specified in the TPIM notice;
- in the case of the power in sub-paragraph (ii) is not complying with measures specified in the TPIM notice; or
- in the case of the power in sub-paragraph (iii), could be used to threaten or harm any person.

A:2.20 A search of an individual on warrant under the power mentioned in paragraph 2.18A(ii) must carried [*sic*] out within 28 days of the issue of the warrant and:
- the individual may be searched on one occasion only within that period;
- the search must take place at a reasonable hour unless it appears that this would frustrate the purposes of the search.

A:2.21-2.25 [*Not used.*]

A:2.26 The powers under Schedule 5 allow a constable to conduct a search of an individual only for specified purposes relating to a TPIM notice as set out above. However, anything found may be seized and retained if there are reasonable grounds for believing that it is or it contains evidence of any offence for use at a trial for that offence or to prevent it being concealed, lost, damaged, altered, or destroyed. However, this would not prevent a search being carried out under other search powers if, in the course of exercising these powers, the officer formed reasonable grounds for suspicion.

(e) Powers to search persons in the exercise of a power to search premises

A-8 A:2.27 The following powers to search premises also authorise the search of a person, not under arrest, who is found on the premises during the course of the search:

(a) section 139B of the Criminal Justice Act 1988 under which a constable may enter school premises and search the premises and any person on those premises for any bladed or pointed article or offensive weapon;

(b) under a warrant issued under section 23(3) of the Misuse of Drugs Act 1971 to search premises for drugs or documents but only if the warrant specifically authorises the search of persons found on the premises; and

(c) under a search warrant or order issued under paragraph 1, 3 or 11 of Schedule 5 to the Terrorism Act 2000 to search premises and any person found there for material likely to be of substantial value to a terrorist investigation.

A:2.28 Before the power under section 139B of the Criminal Justice Act 1988 may be exercised, the constable must have reasonable grounds to suspect that an offence under section 139A or 139AA of the Criminal Justice Act 1988 (having a bladed or pointed article or offensive weapon on school premises) has been or is being committed. A warrant to search premises and persons found therein may be issued under section 23(3) of the Misuse of Drugs Act 1971 if there are reasonable grounds to suspect that controlled drugs or certain documents are in the possession of a person on the premises.

A:2.29 The powers in paragraph 2.27 do not require prior specific grounds to suspect that the person to be searched is in possession of an item for which there is an existing power to search. However, it is still necessary to ensure that the selection and treatment of those searched under these powers is based upon objective factors connected with the search of the premises, and not upon personal prejudice.

A:3 Conduct of searches

A-9 A:3.1 All stops and searches must be carried out with courtesy, consideration and respect for the person concerned. This has a significant impact on public confidence in the police. Every reasonable effort must be made to minimise the embarrassment that a person being searched may experience. [See *Note 4*.]

A:3.2 The co-operation of the person to be searched must be sought in every case, even if the person initially objects to the search. A forcible search may be made only if it has been established that the person is unwilling to co-operate or resists. Reasonable force may be used as a last resort if necessary to conduct a search or to detain a person or vehicle for the purposes of a search.

As to this paragraph, see *James v DPP* (§ 15-87 in the main work).

A:3.3 The length of time for which a person or vehicle may be detained must be reasonable and kept to a minimum. Where the exercise of the power requires reasonable suspicion, the thoroughness and extent of a search must depend on what is suspected of being carried, and by whom. If the suspicion relates to a particular article which is seen to be slipped into a person's pocket, then, in the absence of other grounds for suspicion or an opportunity for the article to be moved elsewhere, the search must be confined to that pocket. In the case of a small article which can readily be concealed, such as a drug, and which might be concealed anywhere on the person, a more extensive search may be necessary. In the case of searches mentioned in paragraph 2.1(b) and (d), which do not require reasonable grounds for suspicion, officers may make any reasonable search to look for items for which they are empowered to search. [See *Note 5*.]

A:3.4 The search must be carried out at or near the place where the person or vehicle was first detained. [See *Note 6*.]

A:3.5 There is no power to require a person to remove any clothing in public other than an outer coat, jacket or gloves, except under section 60AA of the Criminal Justice and Public Order Act 1994 (which empowers a constable to require a person to remove any item worn to conceal identity). [See *Notes 4* and *6*.] A search in public of a person's clothing which has not been removed must be restricted to superficial examination of outer garments. This does not, however, prevent an officer from placing his or her hand inside the pockets of the outer clothing, or feeling round the inside of collars, socks and shoes if this is reasonably necessary in the circumstances to look for the object of the search or to remove and examine any item reasonably suspected to be the object of the search. For the same reasons, subject to the restrictions on the removal of headgear, a person's hair may also be searched in public (see paragraphs 3.1 and 3.3).

A:3.6 Where on reasonable grounds it is considered necessary to conduct a more thorough search (e.g. by requiring a person to take off a T-shirt), this must be done out of public view, for example, in a police van unless paragraph 3.7 applies, or police station if there is one nearby. [See *Note 6*.] Any search involving the removal of more than an outer coat, jacket, gloves, headgear or footwear, or any other item concealing identity, may only be made by an officer of the same sex as the person searched and may not be made in the presence of anyone of the opposite sex unless the person being searched specifically requests it. [See Code C, Annex L and *Notes 4* and *7*.]

A:3.7 Searches involving exposure of intimate parts of the body must not be conducted as a routine extension of a less thorough search, simply because nothing is found in the course of the initial search. Searches involving exposure of intimate parts of the body may be carried out only at a nearby police station or other nearby location which is out of public view (but not a police vehicle). These searches must be conducted in accordance with paragraph 11 of Annex A to Code C except that an intimate search mentioned in paragraph 11(f) of Annex A to Code C may not be authorised or carried out under any stop and search powers. The other provisions of Code C do not apply to the conduct and recording of searches of persons detained at police stations in the exercise of stop and search powers. [See *Note 7*.]

Steps to be taken prior to a search

A:3.8 Before any search of a detained person or attended vehicle takes place the officer must take reasonable steps, if not in uniform (see para. 3.9), to show their warrant card to the person to be searched or in charge of the vehicle to be searched and, whether or not in uniform, to give that person the following information: **A-10**

(a) that they are being detained for the purposes of a search;
(b) the officer's name (except in the case of enquiries linked to the investigation of terrorism, or otherwise where the officer reasonably believes that giving their name might put them in danger, in which case a warrant or other identification number shall be given) and the name of the police station to which the officer is attached;
(c) the legal search power which is being exercised; and
(d) a clear explanation of:
  (i) the object of the search in terms of the article or articles for which there is a power to search; and
  (ii) in the case of:
    - the power under section 60 of the Criminal Justice and Public Order Act 1994 (see para. 2.1(b)), the nature of the power, the authorisation and the fact that it has been given;
    - the powers under Schedule 5 to the Terrorism Prevention and Investigation Measures Act 2011 (see paras 2.1(e) and 2.18A):
      - the fact that a TPIM notice is in force or (in the case of para. 6(2)(a)) that a TPIM notice is being served;
      - the nature of the power being exercised (for a search under para. 8 of Schedule 5, the warrant must be produced and the person provided with a copy of it);
    - all other powers requiring reasonable suspicion (see para. 2.1(a)), the grounds for that suspicion (this means explaining the basis for the suspicion by reference to information and/or intelligence about, or some specific behaviour by, the person concerned (see para. 2.2));
(e) that they are entitled to a copy of the record of the search if one is made (see section 4 below) if they ask within 3 months from the date of the search and:
  (i) if they are not arrested and taken to a police station as a result of the search and it is practicable to make the record on the spot, that immediately after the search is completed they will be given, if they request, either:
    - a copy of the record, or
    - a receipt which explains how they can obtain a copy of the full record or access to an electronic copy of the record; or
  (ii) if they are arrested and taken to a police station as a result of the search, that the record will be made at the station as part of their custody record and they will be given, if they request, a copy of their custody record which includes a record of the search as soon as practicable whilst they are at the station. [See *Note 16*.]

A:3.9 Stops and searches under the power mentioned in paragraph 2.1(b) may be undertaken only by a constable in uniform.

A:3.10 The person should also be given information about police powers to stop and search and the individual's rights in these circumstances.

A:3.11 If the person to be searched, or in charge of a vehicle to be searched, does not appear to understand what is being said, or there is any doubt about the person's ability to understand English, the officer must take reasonable steps to bring information regarding the person's rights and any relevant provisions of this code to his or her attention. If the person is deaf or cannot understand English and is accompanied by someone, then the officer must try to establish whether that person can interpret or otherwise help the officer to give the required information.

A:4 Recording requirements

(a) Searches which do not result in an arrest

A-11 A:4.1 When an officer carries out a search in the exercise of any power to which this code applies and the search does not result in the person searched or person in charge of the vehicle searched being arrested and taken to a police station, a record must be made of it, electronically or on paper, unless there are exceptional circumstances which make this wholly impracticable (e.g. in situations involving public disorder or when the recording officer's presence is urgently required elsewhere). If a record is to be made, the officer carrying out the search must make the record on the spot unless this is not practicable, in which case the officer must make the record as soon as practicable after the search is completed. [See *Note 16.*]

A:4.2 If the record is made at the time, the person who has been searched or who is in charge of the vehicle that has been searched must be asked if they want a copy and if they do, they must be given immediately, either:

- a copy of the record, or
- a receipt which explains how they can obtain a copy of the full record or access to an electronic copy of the record.

A:4.2A An officer is not required to provide a copy of the full record or a receipt at the time if they are called to an incident of higher priority. [See *Note 21.*]

(b) Searches which result in an arrest

A-11a A:4.2B If a search in the exercise of any power to which this code applies results in a person being arrested and taken to a police station, the officer carrying out the search is responsible for ensuring that a record of the search is made as part of their custody record. The custody officer must then ensure that the person is asked if they want a copy of the record and if they do, that they are given a copy as soon as practicable. [See *Note 16.*]

(c) Record of search

A-11b A:4.3 The record of a search must always include the following information:

(a) a note of the self-defined ethnicity, and if different, the ethnicity as perceived by the officer making the search, of the person searched or of the person in charge of the vehicle searched (as the case may be) [see *Note 18*];

(b) the date, time and place the person or vehicle was searched [see *Note 6*];

(c) the object of the search in terms of the article or articles for which there is a power to search;

(d) in the case of:

- the power under section 60 of the Criminal Justice and Public Order Act 1994 (see paragraph 2.1(b)), the nature of the power, the authorisation and the fact that it has been given [see *Note 17*];
- the powers under Schedule 5 to the Terrorism Prevention and Investigation Measures Act 2011 (see paras 2.1(e) and 2.18A):
  - the fact that a TPIM notice is in force or (in the case of para. 6(2)(a)) that a TPIM notice is being served;
  - the nature of the power, and
  - for a search under paragraph 8, the date the search warrant was issued, the fact that the warrant was produced and a copy of it provided and the warrant must also be endorsed by the constable executing it to state whether anything was found and whether anything was seized, and
- all other powers requiring reasonable suspicion (see para. 2.1(a)), the grounds for that suspicion;

(e) subject to paragraph 3.8(b), the identity of the officer carrying out the search. [See *Note 15.*]

A:4.3A For the purposes of completing the search record, there is no requirement to record the name, address and date of birth of the person searched or the person in charge of a vehicle which is searched. The person is under no obligation to provide this information and they should not be asked to provide it for the purpose of completing the record.

A:4.4 Nothing in paragraph 4.3 requires the names of police officers to be shown on the search record or any other record required to be made under this code in the case of enquiries linked to the investigation of terrorism or otherwise where an officer reasonably believes that recording names might endanger the officers. In such cases the record must show the officers' warrant or other identification number and duty station.

A:4.5 A record is required for each person and each vehicle searched. However, if a person is in a vehicle and both are searched, and the object and grounds of the search are the same, only one record need be completed. If more than one person in a vehicle is searched, separate records for each search of a person must be made. If only a vehicle is searched, the self-defined ethnic background of the person in charge of the vehicle must be recorded, unless the vehicle is unattended.

A:4.6 The record of the grounds for making a search must, briefly but informatively, explain the reason for suspecting the person concerned, by reference to information and/or intelligence about, or some specific behaviour by, the person concerned (see para. 2.2).

A:4.7 Where officers detain an individual with a view to performing a search, but the need to search is eliminated as a result of questioning the person detained, a search should not be carried out and a record is not required. [See paragraph 2.10, *Notes 3* and *22A*.]

A:4.8 After searching an unattended vehicle, or anything in or on it, an officer must leave a notice in it (or on it, if things on it have been searched without opening it) recording the fact that it has been searched.

A:4.9 The notice must include the name of the police station to which the officer concerned is attached and state where a copy of the record of the search may be obtained and how (if applicable) an electronic copy may be accessed and where any application for compensation should be directed.

A:4.10 The vehicle must if practicable be left secure.

Recording of encounters not governed by statutory powers

A:4.11 [*Not used.*]

A:4.12 There is no national requirement for an officer who requests a person in a public place to account for themselves, i.e. their actions, behaviour, presence in an area or possession of anything, to make any record of the encounter or to give the person a receipt. [See para. 2.11 and *Notes 22A* and *22B*.] **A-11d**

A:5 Monitoring and supervising the use of stop and search powers

General

A:5.1 Any misuse of stop and search powers is likely to be harmful to policing and lead to mistrust of the police by the local community and by the public in general. Supervising officers must monitor the use of stop and search powers and should consider in particular whether there is any evidence that they are being exercised on the basis of stereotyped images or inappropriate generalisations. Supervising officers must satisfy themselves that the practice of officers under their supervision in stopping, searching and recording is fully in accordance with this code. Supervisors must also examine whether the records reveal any trends or patterns which give cause for concern, and if so take appropriate action to address this. (See para. 2.8A.) **A-12**

A:5.2 Senior officers with area or force-wide responsibilities must also monitor the broader use of stop and search powers and, where necessary, take action at the relevant level.

A:5.3 Supervision and monitoring must be supported by the compilation of comprehensive statistical records of stops and searches at force, area and local level. Any apparently disproportionate use of the powers by particular officers or groups of officers or in relation to specific sections of the community should be identified and investigated.

A:5.4 In order to promote public confidence in the use of the powers, forces in consultation with police and crime commissioners must make arrangements for the records to be scrutinised by representatives of the community, and to explain the use of the powers at a local level. [See *Note 19*.]

Suspected misuse of powers by individual officers

A:5.5 Police supervisors must monitor the use of stop and search powers by individual officers to ensure that they are being applied appropriately and lawfully. Monitoring takes many forms, such as direct supervision of the exercise of the powers, examining stop and search records (particularly examining the officer's documented reasonable grounds for suspicion) and asking the officer to account for the way in which they conducted and recorded particular searches or through complaints about a stop and search that an officer has carried out. **A-12a**

A:5.6 Where a supervisor identifies issues with the way that an officer has used a stop and search power, the facts of the case will determine whether the standards of professional behaviour as set out in the Code of Ethics (see *http://www.college.police.uk/en/20972.htm*) have been breached and which formal action is pursued. Improper use might be a result of poor performance or a conduct matter, which will require the supervisor to take appropriate action such as performance or misconduct procedures. It is imperative that supervisors take both timely and appropriate action to deal with all such cases that come to their notice.

Notes for guidance

Officers exercising stop and search powers

A-13 *A:1 This code does not affect the ability of an officer to speak to or question a person in the ordinary course of the officer's duties without detaining the person or exercising any element of compulsion. It is not the purpose of the code to prohibit such encounters between the police and the community with the co-operation of the person concerned and neither does it affect the principle that all citizens have a duty to help police officers to prevent crime and discover offenders. This is a civic rather than a legal duty; but when a police officer is trying to discover whether, or by whom, an offence has been committed he or she may question any person from whom useful information might be obtained, subject to the restrictions imposed by Code C. A person's unwillingness to reply does not alter this entitlement, but in the absence of a power to arrest, or to detain in order to search, the person is free to leave at will and cannot be compelled to remain with the officer.*

A:1A In paragraphs 1.1 and 2.2B(a), the "relevant protected characteristics" are: age, disability, gender reassignment, pregnancy and maternity, race, religion or belief, sex and sexual orientation.

A:1B Innocent possession means that the person does have [sic] *the guilty knowledge that they are carrying an unlawful item which is required before an arrest on suspicion that the person has committed an offence in respect of the item sought (if arrest is necessary - see PACE Code G) and/or a criminal prosecution) can be considered. It is not uncommon for children under the age of criminal responsibility to be used by older children and adults to carry stolen property, drugs and weapons and, in some cases, firearms, for the criminal benefit of others, either:*

- *in the hope that police may not suspect they are being used for carrying the items; or*
- *knowing that if they are suspected of being couriers and are stopped and searched, they cannot be arrested or prosecuted for any criminal offence.*

Stop and search powers therefore allow the police to intervene effectively to break up criminal gangs and groups that use young children to further their criminal activities.

A:1BA Whenever a child under 10 is suspected of carrying unlawful items for someone else, or is found in circumstances which suggest that their welfare and safety may be at risk, the facts should be reported and actioned in accordance with established force safeguarding procedures. This will be in addition to treating them as a potentially vulnerable or intimidated witness in respect of their status as a witness to the serious criminal offence(s) committed by those using them as couriers. Safeguarding considerations will also apply to other persons aged under 18 who are stopped and searched under any of the powers to which this code applies. See paragraph 1.1 with regard to the requirement under the Children Act 2004, s.11, for chief police officers and other specified persons and bodies, to ensure that in the discharge of their functions, they have regard to the need to safeguard and promote the welfare of all persons under the age of 18.

A:2 In some circumstances preparatory questioning may be unnecessary, but in general a brief conversation or exchange will be desirable not only as a means of avoiding unsuccessful searches, but to explain the grounds for the stop/search, to gain cooperation and reduce any tension there might be surrounding the stop/ search.

A:3 Where a person is lawfully detained for the purpose of a search, but no search in the event takes place, the detention will not thereby have been rendered unlawful.

A:4 Many people customarily cover their heads or faces for religious reasons–for example, Muslim women, Sikh men, Sikh or Hindu women, or Rastafarian men or women. A police officer cannot order the removal of a head or face covering except where there is reason to believe that the item is being worn by the individual wholly or mainly for the purpose of disguising identity, not simply because it disguises identity. Where there may be religious sensitivities about ordering the removal of such an item, the officer should permit the item to be removed out of public view. Where practicable, the item should be removed in the presence of an officer of the same sex as the person and out of sight of anyone of the opposite sex (see Code C, Annex L).

A:5 A search of a person in public should be completed as soon as possible.

A:6 A person may be detained under a stop and search power at a place other than where the person was first detained, only if that place, be it a police station or elsewhere, is nearby. Such a place should be located within a reasonable travelling distance using whatever mode of travel (on foot or by car) is appropriate. This applies to all searches under stop and search powers, whether or not they involve the removal of clothing or exposure of intimate parts of the body (see paragraphs 3.6 and 3.7) or take place in or out of public view. It means, for example, that a search under the stop and search power in section 23 of the Misuse of Drugs Act 1971 which involves the compulsory removal of more than a person's outer coat, jacket or gloves cannot be carried out unless a place which is both nearby the place they were first detained and out of public view, is available. If a search involves exposure of intimate parts of the body and a police station is not nearby, particular care must be taken to ensure that the location is suitable in that it enables the search to be conducted in accordance with the requirements of paragraph 11 of Annex A to Code C.

A:7 A search in the street itself should be regarded as being in public for the purposes of paragraphs 3.6 and 3.7 above, even though it may be empty at the time a search begins. Although there is no power to require a person to do so, there is nothing to prevent an officer from asking a person voluntarily to remove more than an outer coat, jacket or gloves in public.

A:8 [Not used.]

A:9 Other means of identification might include jewellery, insignias, tattoos or other features which are known to identify members of the particular gang or group.

A:9A A decision to search individuals believed to be members of a particular group or gang must be judged on a case by case basis according to the circumstances applicable at the time of the proposed searches and in particular, having regard to:

(a) the number of items suspected of being carried;
(b) the nature of those items and the risk they pose; and
(c) the number of individuals to be searched.

A group search will only be justified if it is a necessary and proportionate approach based on the facts and having regard to the nature of the suspicion in these cases. The extent and thoroughness of the searches must not be excessive.

The size of the group and the number of individuals it is proposed to search will be a key factor and steps should be taken to identify those who are to be searched to avoid unnecessary inconvenience to unconnected members of the public who are also present.

The onus is on the police to be satisfied and to demonstrate that their approach to the decision to search is in pursuit of a legitimate aim, necessary and proportionate.

Authorising officers

A:10 The powers under section 60 are separate from and additional to the normal stop and search powers which require reasonable grounds to suspect an individual of carrying an offensive weapon (or other article). Their overall purpose is to prevent serious violence and the widespread carrying of weapons which might lead to persons being seriously injured by disarming potential offenders or finding weapons that have been used in circumstances where other powers would not be sufficient. They should not therefore be used to replace or circumvent the normal powers for dealing with routine crime problems. A particular example might be an authorisation to prevent serious violence or the carrying of offensive weapons at a sports event by rival team supporters when the expected general appearance and age range of those likely to be responsible, alone, would not be sufficiently distinctive to support reasonable suspicion (see paragraph 2.6). The purpose of the powers under section 60AA is to prevent those involved in intimidatory or violent protests using face coverings to disguise identity. **A-14**

A:11 Authorisations under section 60 require a reasonable belief on the part of the authorising officer. This must have an objective basis, for example: intelligence or relevant information such as a history of antagonism and violence between particular groups; previous incidents of violence at, or connected with, particular events or locations; a significant increase in knife-point robberies in a limited area; reports that individuals are regularly carrying weapons in a particular locality; information following an incident in which weapons were used about where the weapons might be found or in the case of section 60AA previous incidents of crimes being committed while wearing face coverings to conceal identity.

A:12 It is for the authorising officer to determine the period of time during which the powers mentioned in paragraph 2.1(b) may be exercised. The officer should set the minimum period he or she considers necessary to deal with the risk of violence, the carrying of knives or offensive weapons, or to find dangerous instruments or weapons that have been used. A direction to extend the period authorised under the powers mentioned in paragraph 2.1(b) may be given only once. Thereafter further use of the powers requires a new authorisation.

A:13 It is for the authorising officer to determine the geographical area in which the use of the powers is to be authorised. In doing so the officer may wish to take into account factors such as the nature and venue of the anticipated incident or the incident which has taken place, the number of people who may be in the immediate area of that incident, their access to surrounding areas and the anticipated or actual level of violence. The officer should not set a geographical area which is wider than that he or she believes necessary for the purpose of preventing anticipated violence, the carrying of knives or offensive weapons, or for finding a dangerous instrument or weapon that has been used or, in the case of section 60AA, the prevention of commission of offences. It is particularly important to ensure that constables exercising such powers are fully aware of the locality within which they may be used. The officer giving the authorisation should therefore specify either the streets which form the boundary of the locality or a divisional boundary if appropriate within the force area. If the power is to be used in response to a threat or incident that straddles police force areas, an officer from each of the forces concerned will need to give an authorisation.

A:14 [Not used.]

Recording

A:15 Where a stop and search is conducted by more than one officer the identity of all the officers engaged in **A-15** *the search must be recorded on the record. Nothing prevents an officer who is present but not directly involved in searching from completing the record during the course of the encounter.*

A:16 When the search results in the person searched or in charge of a vehicle which is searched being arrested, the requirement to make the record of the search as part of the person's custody record does not apply if the person is granted "street bail" after arrest (see section 30A of PACE) to attend a police station and is not taken in custody to the police station. An arrested person's entitlement to a copy of the search record which is made as part of their custody record does not affect their entitlement to a copy of their custody record or any other provisions of PACE Code C section 2 (custody records).

A:17 It is important for monitoring purposes to specify when authority is given for exercising the stop and search power under section 60 of the Criminal Justice and Public Order Act 1994.

A:18 Officers should record the self-defined ethnicity of every person stopped according to the categories used in the 2001 census question listed in Annex B. The person should be asked to select one of the five main categories representing broad ethnic groups and then a more specific cultural background from within this group. The ethnic classification should be coded for recording purposes using the coding system in Annex B. An additional "Not stated" box is available but should not be offered to respondents explicitly. Officers should be aware and explain to members of the public, especially where concerns are raised, that this information is required to obtain a true picture of stop and search activity and to help improve ethnic monitoring, tackle discriminatory practice, and promote effective use of the powers. If the person gives what appears to the officer to be an "incorrect" answer (e.g. a person who appears to be white states that they are black), the officer should record the response that has been given and then record their own perception of the person's ethnic background by using the PNC classification system. If the "Not stated" category is used the reason for this must be recorded on the form.

A:19 Arrangements for public scrutiny of records should take account of the right to confidentiality of those stopped and searched. Anonymised forms and/or statistics generated from records should be the focus of the examinations by members of the public. The groups that are consulted should always include children and young persons.

A:20 [Not used.]

A:21 In situations where it is not practicable to provide a written copy of the record or immediate access to an electronic copy of the record or a receipt of the search at the time (see paragraph 4.2A above), the officer should consider giving the person details of the station which they may attend for a copy of the record. A receipt may take the form of a simple business card which includes sufficient information to locate the record should the person ask for copy [*sic*], *for example, the date and place of the search, and a reference number or the name of the officer who carried out the search (unless paragraph 4.4 applies).*

A:22 [Not used.]

A:22A Where there are concerns which make it necessary to monitor any local disproportionality, forces have discretion to direct officers to record the self-defined ethnicity of persons they request to account for themselves in a public place or who they detain with a view to searching but do not search. Guidance should be provided locally and efforts made to minimise the bureaucracy involved. Records should be closely monitored and supervised in line with paragraphs 5.1 to 5.6, and forces can suspend or re-instate recording of these encounters as appropriate.

A:22B A person who is asked to account for themselves should, if they request, be given information about how they can report their dissatisfaction about how they have been treated.

Definition of offensive weapon

A:23 "Offensive weapon" is defined as "any article made or adapted for use by him for causing injury to the person, or intended by the person having it with him for such use or by someone else". There are three categories of offensive weapons: those made for causing injury to the person; those adapted for such a purpose; and those not so made or adapted, but carried with the intention of causing injury to the person. A firearm, as defined by section 57 of the Firearms Act 1968, would fall within the definition of offensive weapon if any of the criteria above apply.

ANNEX A

Summary of main stop and search powers to which Code A applies

A-16 This table relates to stop and search powers only. Individual statutes below may contain other police powers of entry, search and seizure.

Power	*Object of search*	*Extent of Search*	*Where Exercisable*
Unlawful articles general			
1. Public Stores Act 1875, s.6	HM Stores stolen or unlawfully obtained	Persons, vehicles and vessels	Anywhere where the constabulary powers are exercisable
2. Firearms Act 1968, s.47	Firearms	Persons and vehicles	A public place, or anywhere in the case of reasonable suspicion of offences of carrying rearms with criminal intent or trespassing with firearms
3. Misuse of Drugs Act 1971, s.23	Controlled drugs	Persons and vehicles	Anywhere
4. Customs and Excise Management Act 1979, s.163	Goods: (a) on which duty has not been paid; (b) being unlawfully removed, imported or exported; (c) otherwise liable to forfeiture to HM Revenue and Customs	Vehicles and vessels only	Anywhere
5. Aviation Security Act 1982, s.24B *Note: This power applies throughout the UK but the provisions of this code will apply only when the power is exercised at an aerodrome situated in England and Wales.*	Stolen articles or articles made, adapted or intended for use in the course of/in connection with conduct which constitutes an offence in the part of the UK where the aerodrome is situated or would do so, if it occurred there.	Persons, vehicles, aircraft Anything in or on a vehicle or aircraft	Any part of an aerodrome
6. Police and Criminal Evidence Act 1984, s.1	Stolen goods;	Persons and vehicles	Where there is public access
	Articles made, adapted or intended for use in the course of or in connection with, certain offences under the Theft Act 1968, Fraud Act and Criminal Damage Act 1971;	Persons and vehicles	Where there is public access
	Offensive weapons, bladed or sharply-pointed articles (except folding pocket knives with a blade cutting edge not exceeding 3 inches);	Persons and vehicles	Where there is public access
	Fireworks: category 4 (display grade) fireworks if possession prohibited,	Persons and vehicles	Where there is public access

Power	*Object of search*	*Extent of Search*	*Where Exercisable*
	adult fireworks in possession of a person under 18 in a public place.		
7. Sporting Events (Control of Alcohol etc.) Act 1985, s.7	Intoxicating liquor	Persons, coaches and trains	Designated sports grounds or coaches and trains travelling to or from a designated sporting event.
8. Crossbows Act 1987, s.4	Crossbows or parts of crossbows (except crossbows with a draw weight of less than 1.4 kilograms)	Persons and vehicles	Anywhere except dwellings
9. Criminal Justice Act 1988 s.139B	Offensive weapons, bladed or sharply pointed article	Persons	School premises
Evidence of game and wildlife offences			
10. Poaching Prevention Act 1862, s.2	Game or poaching equipment	Persons and vehicles	A public place
11. Deer Act 1991, s.12	Evidence of offences under the Act	Persons and vehicles	Anywhere except dwellings
12. Conservation of Seals Act 1970, s.4	Seals or hunting equipment	Vehicles only	Anywhere
13. Protection of Badgers Act 1992, s.11	Evidence offences under the Act	Persons and vehicles	Anywhere
14. Wildlife and Countryside Act 1981, s.19	Evidence of wildlife offences	Persons and vehicles	Anywhere except dwellings
Other			
15. Paragraphs 6 & 8 of Schedule 5 to the Terrorism Prevention and Investigation Measures Act 2011	Anything that contravenes measures specied in a TPIM notice.	Persons in respect of whom a TPIM notice is being served or is in force	Anywhere
16. Paragraph 10 of Schedule 5 to the Terrorism Prevention and Investigation Measures Act 2011	Anything that could be used to threaten or harm any person.	Persons in respect of whom a TPIM notice is in force.	Anywhere
17. [*Not used.*]			
18. [*Not used.*]			
19. Section 60 Criminal Justice and Public Order Act 1994	Offensive weapons or dangerous instruments to prevent incidents of serious violence or to deal with the carrying of such items or nd such items which have been used in incidents of serious violence	Persons and vehicles	Anywhere within a locality authorised under subsection (1)

ANNEX B

Self-defined ethnic classification categories A-17

	W
White	
A. White–British	W1
B. White–Irish	W2
C. Any other White background	W9
Mixed	**M**
D. White and Black Caribbean	M1
E. White and Black African	M2
F. White and Asian	M3
G. Any other Mixed background	M9
Asian/ Asian–British	**A**
H. Asian–Indian	A1
I. Asian–Pakistani	A2
J. Asian–Bangladeshi	A3
K. Any other Asian background	A9
Black / Black–British	**B**
L. Black–Caribbean	B1
M. Black African	B2
N. Any other Black background	B9
Other	**O**
O. Chinese	O1
P. Any other	O9
Not stated	**NS**

ANNEX C

Summary of powers of community support officers to search and seize

The following is a summary of the search and seizure powers that may be exercised by a community support officer (CSO) who has been designated with the relevant powers in accordance with Part 4 of the Police Reform Act 2002. A-17a

When exercising any of these powers, a CSO must have regard to any relevant provisions of this code, including section 3 governing the conduct of searches and the steps to be taken prior to a search.

1. [*Not used.*]				
2. Powers to search requiring the consent of the person and seizure A CSO may detain a person using reasonable force where necessary as set out in Part 1 of Schedule 4 to the Police Reform Act 2002. If the person has been lawfully detained, the CSO may search the person provided that person gives consent to such a search in relation to the following:				
Designation	**Powers conferred**	**Object of Search**	**Extent of Search**	**Where Exercisable**
Police Reform Act 2002, Schedule 4, paragraphs 7 and 7A	(a) Criminal Justice and Police Act 2001, s.12(2)	(a) Alcohol or a container for alcohol	(a) Persons	(a) Designated public place
	(b) Confiscation of Alcohol (Young Persons) Act 1997, s.1	(b) Alcohol	(b) Persons under 18 years old	(b) Public place
	(c) Children and Young Persons Act 1933, s.7(3)	(c) Tobacco or cigarette papers	(c) Persons under 16 years old found smoking	(c) Public place
3. Powers to search not requiring the consent of the person and seizure A CSO may detain a person using reasonable force where necessary as set out in Part 1 of Schedule 4 to the Police Reform Act 2002. If the person has been lawfully detained, the CSO may search the person without the need for that person's consent in relation to the following:				
Designation	**Power conferred**	**Object of Search**	**Extent of Search**	**Where Exercisable**
Police Reform Act 2002, Schedule 4, paragraph 2A	Police and Criminal Evidence Act 1984, s.32	(a) Objects that might be used to cause physical injury to the person or the CSO. (b) Items that might be used to assist escape.	Persons made subject to a requirement to wait.	Any place where the requirement to wait has been made.
4. Powers to seize without consent This power applies when drugs are found in the course of any search mentioned above.				
Designation	**Power conferred**	**Object of Seizure**		**Where Exercisable**
Police Reform Act 2002, Schedule 4, paragraph 7B	Police Reform Act 2002, Schedule 4, paragraph 7B	Controlled drugs in a person's possession.		Any place where the person is in possession of the drug.

Annex D—Deleted
Annex E—Deleted

ANNEX F

Establishing gender of persons for the purpose of searching

See Code C, Annex L. **A-17b**

(3) Search and seizure

The text that follows is of the version of the code that came into force on 27 October 2013: see A-1. **A-18**

For authorities in relation to Code B, see, in particular, § 15-180 in the main work.

B. CODE OF PRACTICE FOR SEARCHES OF PREMISES BY POLICE OFFICERS AND THE SEIZURE OF PROPERTY FOUND BY POLICE OFFICERS ON PERSONS OR PREMISES

Commencement—transitional arrangements

This code applies to applications for warrants made after 00.00 on 27 October 2013 and to searches and seizures taking place after 00.00 on 27 October 2013. **A-19**

B:1 Introduction

B:1.1 This code of practice deals with police powers to: **A-20**

- search premises
- seize and retain property found on premises and persons.

B:1.1A These powers may be used to find:

- property and material relating to a crime
- wanted persons
- children who abscond from local authority accommodation where they have been remanded or committed by a court.

B:1.2 A justice of the peace may issue a search warrant granting powers of entry, search and seizure, e.g. warrants to search for stolen property, drugs, firearms and evidence of serious offences. Police also have powers without a search warrant. The main ones provided by the Police and Criminal Evidence Act 1984 (PACE) include powers to search premises:

- to make an arrest
- after an arrest.

B:1.3 The right to privacy and respect for personal property are key principles of the Human Rights Act 1998. Powers of entry, search and seizure should be fully and clearly justified before use because they may significantly interfere with the occupier's privacy. Officers should consider if the necessary objectives can be met by less intrusive means.

B:1.3A Powers to search and seize must be used fairly, responsibly, with respect for people who occupy premises being searched or are in charge of property being seized and without unlawful discrimination. Under the Equality Act 2010, s.149, when police officers are carrying out their functions, they also have a duty to have due regard to the need to eliminate unlawful discrimination, harassment and victimisation, to advance equality of opportunity between people who share a relevant protected characteristic and people who do not share it, and to take steps to foster good relations between those persons. [See *Note 1A.*]

B:1.4 In all cases, police should therefore:

- exercise their powers courteously and with respect for persons and property
- only use reasonable force when this is considered necessary and proportionate to the circumstances.

B:1.5 If the provisions of PACE and this code are not observed, evidence obtained from a search may be open to question.

Notes for guidance

B:1A In paragraph 1.3A, "relevant protected characteristic" includes: age, disability, gender reassignment, pregnancy and maternity, race, religion/belief, sex and sexual orientation.

B:2 General

B:2.1 This code must be readily available at all police stations for consultation by: **A-21**

- police officers
- police staff
- detained persons
- members of the public.

B:2.2 The *Notes for guidance* included are not provisions of this code.

B:2.3 This code applies to searches of premises:

(a) by police for the purposes of an investigation into an alleged offence, with the occupier's consent, other than:
- routine scene of crime searches;
- calls to a fire or burglary made by or on behalf of an occupier or searches following the activation of fire or burglar alarms or discovery of insecure premises;
- searches when paragraph 5.4 applies;
- bomb threat calls;

(b) under powers conferred on police officers by PACE, ss.17, 18 and 32;

(c) undertaken in pursuance of search warrants issued to and executed by constables in accordance with PACE, ss.15 and 16 [see *Note 2A*];

(d) subject to paragraph 2.6, under any other power given to police to enter premises with or without a search warrant for any purpose connected with the investigation into an alleged or suspected offence. [See *Note 2B.*]

For the purposes of this code, "premises" as defined in PACE, s.23, includes any place, vehicle, vessel, aircraft, hovercraft, tent or movable structure and any offshore installation as defined in the Mineral Workings (Offshore Installations) Act 1971, s.1. [See *Note 2D.*]

B:2.4 A person who has not been arrested but is searched during a search of premises should be searched in accordance with Code A. [See *Note 2C.*]

B:2.5 This code does not apply to the exercise of a statutory power to enter premises or to inspect goods, equipment or procedures if the exercise of that power is not dependent on the existence of grounds for suspecting that an offence may have been committed and the person exercising the power has no reasonable grounds for such suspicion.

B:2.6 This code does not affect any directions or requirements of a search warrant, order or other power to search and seize lawfully exercised in England or Wales that any item or evidence seized under that warrant, order or power be handed over to a police force, court, tribunal, or other authority outside England or Wales. For example, warrants and orders issued in Scotland or Northern Ireland [see *Note 2B(f)*] and search warrants and powers provided for in sections 14 to 17 of the Crime (International Co-operation) Act 2003.

B:2.7 When this code requires the prior authority or agreement of an officer of at least inspector or superintendent rank, that authority may be given by a sergeant or chief inspector authorised to perform the functions of the higher rank under PACE, s.107.

B:2.8 Written records required under this code not made in the search record shall, unless otherwise specified, be made:
- in the recording officer's pocket book ("pocket book" includes any official report book issued to police officers), or
- on forms provided for the purpose.

B:2.9 Nothing in this code requires the identity of officers, or anyone accompanying them during a search of premises, to be recorded or disclosed:

(a) in the case of enquiries linked to the investigation of terrorism; or

(b) if officers reasonably believe recording or disclosing their names might put them in danger.

In these cases officers should use warrant or other identification numbers and the name of their police station. Police staff should use any identification number provided to them by the police force. [See *Note 2E.*]

B:2.10 The "officer in charge of the search" means the officer assigned specific duties and responsibilities under this code. Whenever there is a search of premises to which this code applies one officer must act as the officer in charge of the search. [See *Note 2F.*]

B:2.11 In this code:

(a) "designated person" means a person other than a police officer, designated under the Police Reform Act 2002, Pt 4 who has specified powers and duties of police officers conferred or imposed on them [see Note 2G];

(b) any reference to a police officer includes a designated person acting in the exercise or performance of the powers and duties conferred or imposed on them by their designation;

(c) a person authorised to accompany police officers or designated persons in the execution of a warrant has the same powers as a constable in the execution of the warrant and the search and seizure of anything related to the warrant. These powers must be exercised in the company and under the supervision of a police officer. [See *Note 3C.*]

B:2.12 If a power conferred on a designated person:

(a) allows reasonable force to be used when exercised by a police officer, a designated person exercising that power has the same entitlement to use force;
(b) includes power to use force to enter any premises, that power is not exercisable by that designated person except:
  (i) in the company and under the supervision of a police officer; or
  (ii) for the purpose of:
    - saving life or limb; or
    - preventing serious damage to property.

B:2.13 Designated persons must have regard to any relevant provisions of the codes of practice.

Notes for guidance

B:2A *PACE ss.15 and 16 apply to all search warrants issued to and executed by constables under any enactment, e.g. search warrants issued by a:* A-22
(a) *justice of the peace under the:*
  - *Theft Act 1968, s.26–stolen property;*
  - *Misuse of Drugs Act 1971, s.23–controlled drugs;*
  - *PACE, s.8–evidence of an indictable offence;*
  - *Terrorism Act 2000, Sched. 5, para. 1;*
  - *Terrorism Prevention and Investigation Measures Act 2011, Sched. 5, para. 8(2)(b)– search of premises for compliance purposes (see para. 10.1);*
(b) *circuit judge under:*
  - *PACE, Sched. 1;*
  - *Terrorism Act 2000, Sched. 5, para. 11.*

B:2B *Examples of the other powers in paragraph 2.3(d) include:*
(a) *Road Traffic Act 1988, s.6E(1) giving police power to enter premises under section 6E(1) to:*
  - *require a person to provide a specimen of breath; or*
  - *arrest a person following:*
    - *a positive breath test;*
    - *failure to provide a specimen of breath;*
(b) *Transport and Works Act 1992, s.30(4) giving police powers to enter premises mirroring the powers in (a) in relation to specified persons working on transport systems to which the Act applies;*
(c) *Criminal Justice Act 1988, s.139B giving police power to enter and search school premises for offensive weapons, bladed or pointed articles;*
(d) *Terrorism Act 2000, Sched. 5, paras 3 and 15 empowering a superintendent in urgent cases to give written authority for police to enter and search premises for the purposes of a terrorist investigation;*
(e) *Explosives Act 1875, s.73(b) empowering a superintendent to give written authority for police to enter premises, examine and search them for explosives;*
(f) *search warrants and production orders or the equivalent issued in Scotland or Northern Ireland endorsed under the Summary Jurisdiction (Process) Act 1881 or the Petty Sessions (Ireland) Act 1851 respectively for execution in England and Wales;*
(g) *Terrorism Prevention and Investigation Measures Act 2011, Sched. 5, paras 5(1), 6(2)(b) and 7(2), searches relating to TPIM notices (see para. 10.1).*

B:2C The Criminal Justice Act 1988, s.139B provides that a constable who has reasonable grounds to suspect an offence under the Criminal Justice Act 1988, s.139A or 139AA has or is being committed may enter school premises and search the premises and any persons on the premises for any bladed or pointed article or offensive weapon. Persons may be searched under a warrant issued under the Misuse of Drugs Act 1971, s.23(3) to search premises for drugs or documents only if the warrant specifically authorises the search of persons on the premises. Powers to search premises under certain terrorism provisions also authorise the search of persons on the premises, for example, under paragraphs 1, 2, 11 and 15 of Schedule 5 to the Terrorism Act 2000 and section 52 of the Anti-terrorism, Crime and Security Act 2001.

B:2D The Immigration Act 1971, Pt III and Sched. 2 gives immigration officers powers to enter and search premises, seize and retain property, with and without a search warrant. These are similar to the powers available to police under search warrants issued by a justice of the peace and without a warrant under PACE, ss.17, 18, 19 and 32 except they only apply to specified offences under the Immigration Act 1971 and immigration control powers. For certain types of investigations and enquiries these powers avoid the need for the Immigration Service to rely on police officers becoming directly involved. When exercising these powers, immigration officers are required by the Immigration and Asylum Act 1999, s.145 to have regard to this code's corresponding provisions. When immigration officers are dealing with persons or property at police stations, police officers should give appropriate assistance to help them discharge their specific duties and responsibilities.

B:2E The purpose of paragraph 2.9(b) is to protect those involved in serious organised crime investigations or arrests of particularly violent suspects when there is reliable information that those arrested or their associates may threaten or cause harm to the officers or anyone accompanying them during a search of premises. In cases of doubt, an officer of inspector rank or above should be consulted.

B:2F *For the purposes of paragraph 2.10, the officer in charge of the search should normally be the most senior officer present. Some exceptions are:*

(a) *a supervising officer who attends or assists at the scene of a premises search may appoint an officer of lower rank as officer in charge of the search if that officer is:*
- *more conversant with the facts;*
- *a more appropriate officer to be in charge of the search;*

(b) *when all officers in a premises search are the same rank. The supervising officer if available, must make sure one of them is appointed officer in charge of the search, otherwise the officers themselves must nominate one of their number as the officer in charge;*

(c) *a senior officer assisting in a specialist role. This officer need not be regarded as having a general supervisory role over the conduct of the search or be appointed or expected to act as the officer in charge of the search.*

Except in (c), nothing in this note diminishes the role and responsibilities of a supervisory officer who is present at the search or knows of a search taking place.

B:2G An officer of the rank of inspector or above may direct a designated investigating officer not to wear a uniform for the purposes of a specific operation.

B:3 Search warrants and production orders

(a) Before making an application

A-23 B:3.1 When information appears to justify an application, the officer must take reasonable steps to check the information is accurate, recent and not provided maliciously or irresponsibly. An application may not be made on the basis of information from an anonymous source if corroboration has not been sought. See *Note 3A*.

B:3.2 The officer shall ascertain as specifically as possible the nature of the articles concerned and their location.

B:3.3 The officer shall make reasonable enquiries to:

(i) establish if:
- anything is known about the likely occupier of the premises and the nature of the premises themselves;
- the premises have been searched previously and how recently;

(ii) obtain any other relevant information.

B:3.4 An application:

(a) to a justice of the peace for a search warrant or to a circuit judge for a search warrant or production order under PACE, Sched. 1 must be supported by a signed written authority from an officer of inspector rank or above; [Note: if the case is an urgent application to a justice of the peace and an inspector or above is not readily available, the next most senior officer on duty can give the written authority];

(b) to a circuit judge under the Terrorism Act 2000, Sched. 5 for:
- a production order;
- search warrant; or
- an order requiring an explanation of material seized or produced under such a warrant or production order,

must be supported by a signed written authority from an officer of superintendent rank or above.

B:3.5 Except in a case of urgency, if there is reason to believe a search might have an adverse effect on relations between the police and the community, the officer in charge shall consult the local police/community liaison officer:
- before the search; or
- in urgent cases, as soon as practicable after the search.

(b) Making an application

B:3.6 A search warrant application must be supported in writing, specifying:

(a) the enactment under which the application is made [see *Note 2A*];

(b)(i) whether the warrant is to authorise entry and search of:
- one set of premises; or
- if the application is under PACE, s.8, or Sched. 1, para. 12, more than one set of specified premises or all premises occupied or controlled by a specified person, and

(ii) the premises to be searched;

(c) the object of the search [see *Note 3B*];

(d) the grounds for the application, including, when the purpose of the proposed search is to find evidence of an alleged offence, an indication of how the evidence relates to the investigation;

(da) where the application is under PACE, s.8, or Sched. 1, para. 12 for a single warrant to enter and search:

(i) more than one set of specified premises, the officer must specify each set of premises which it is desired to enter and search;

(ii) all premises occupied or controlled by a specified person, the officer must specify:

- as many sets of premises which it is desired to enter and search as it is reasonably practicable to specify;
- the person who is in occupation or control of those premises and any others which it is desired to search;
- why it is necessary to search more premises than those which can be specified;
- why it is not reasonably practicable to specify all the premises which it is desired to enter and search;

(db) whether an application under PACE, s.8 is for a warrant authorising entry and search on more than one occasion, and if so, the officer must state the grounds for this and whether the desired number of entries authorised is unlimited or a specified maximum;

(e) that there are no reasonable grounds to believe the material to be sought, when making application to a:

(i) justice of the peace or a circuit judge consists of or includes items subject to legal privilege;

(ii) justice of the peace, consists of or includes excluded material or special procedure material;

[Note: this does not affect the additional powers of seizure in the Criminal Justice and Police Act 2001, Pt 2 covered in paragraph 7.7 [see *Note 3B*]];

(f) if applicable, a request for the warrant to authorise a person or persons to accompany the officer who executes the warrant [see *Note 3C*].

B:3.7 A search warrant application under PACE, Sched. 1, para. 12(a), shall if appropriate indicate why it is believed service of notice of an application for a production order may seriously prejudice the investigation. Applications for search warrants under the Terrorism Act 2000, Schedule 5, paragraph 11 must indicate why a production order would not be appropriate.

B:3.8 If a search warrant application is refused, a further application may not be made for those premises unless supported by additional grounds.

Notes for guidance

B:3A The identity of an informant need not be disclosed when making an application, but the officer should be prepared to answer any questions the magistrate or judge may have about: **A-24**

- *the accuracy of previous information from that source, and*
- *any other related matters.*

B:3B The information supporting a search warrant application should be as specific as possible, particularly in relation to the articles or persons being sought and where in the premises it is suspected they may be found. The meaning of "items subject to legal privilege", "excluded material" and "special procedure material" are defined by PACE, ss.10, 11 and 14 respectively.

B:3C Under PACE, s.16(2), a search warrant may authorise persons other than police officers to accompany the constable who executes the warrant. This includes, e.g. any suitably qualified or skilled person or an expert in a particular field whose presence is needed to help accurately identify the material sought or to advise where certain evidence is most likely to be found and how it should be dealt with. It does not give them any right to force entry, but it gives them the right to be on the premises during the search and to search for or seize property without the occupier's permission.

B:4 Entry without warrant—particular powers

(a) Making an arrest etc

B:4.1 The conditions under which an officer may enter and search premises without a warrant are set out in PACE, s.17. It should be noted that this section does not create or confer any powers of arrest. See other powers in *Note 2B(a)*. **A-25**

(b) Search of premises where arrest takes place or the arrested person was immediately before arrest

B:4.2 When a person has been arrested for an indictable offence, a police officer has power under PACE, s.32 to search the premises where the person was arrested or where the person was immediately before being arrested.

(c) Search of premises occupied or controlled by the arrested person

B:4.3 The specific powers to search premises which are occupied or controlled by a person arrested for an indictable offence are set out in PACE, s.18. They may not be exercised, except if section 18 (5) applies, unless an officer of inspector rank or above has given written authority. That authority should only be given when the authorising officer is satisfied that the premises are occupied or controlled by the arrested person and that the necessary grounds exist. If possible the authorising officer should record the authority on the Notice of Powers and Rights and, subject to paragraph 2.9, sign the notice. The record of the grounds for the search and the nature of the evidence sought as required by section 18(7) of the Act should be made in:

- the custody record if there is one, otherwise
- the officer's pocket book, or
- the search record.

B:5 Search with consent

A-26 B:5.1 Subject to paragraph 5.4, if it is proposed to search premises with the consent of a person entitled to grant entry the consent must, if practicable, be given in writing on the Notice of Powers and Rights before the search. The officer must make any necessary enquiries to be satisfied the person is in a position to give such consent. [See *Notes 5A* and *5B.*]

B:5.2 Before seeking consent the officer in charge of the search shall state the purpose of the proposed search and its extent. This information must be as specific as possible, particularly regarding the articles or persons being sought and the parts of the premises to be searched. The person concerned must be clearly informed they are not obliged to consent, that any consent given can be withdrawn at any time, including before the search starts or while it is under way and anything seized may be produced in evidence. If at the time the person is not suspected of an offence, the officer shall say this when stating the purpose of the search.

B:5.3 An officer cannot enter and search or continue to search premises under paragraph 5.1 if consent is given under duress or withdrawn before the search is completed.

B:5.4 It is unnecessary to seek consent under paragraphs 5.1 and 5.2 if this would cause disproportionate inconvenience to the person concerned. [See *Note 5C.*]

Notes for guidance

A-27 *B:5A In a lodging house, hostel or similar accommodation, every reasonable effort should be made to obtain the consent of the tenant, lodger or occupier. A search should not be made solely on the basis of the landlord's consent.*

B:5B If the intention is to search premises under the authority of a warrant or a power of entry and search without warrant, and the occupier of the premises co-operates in accordance with paragraph 6.4, there is no need to obtain written consent.

B:5C Paragraph 5.4 is intended to apply when it is reasonable to assume innocent occupiers would agree to, and expect, police to take the proposed action, e.g. if:

- *a suspect has fled the scene of a crime or to evade arrest and it is necessary quickly to check surrounding gardens and readily accessible places to see if the suspect is hiding, or*
- *police have arrested someone in the night after a pursuit and it is necessary to make a brief check of gardens along the pursuit route to see if stolen or incriminating articles have been discarded.*

B:6 Searching premises—general considerations

(a) Time of searches

A-28 B:6.1 Searches made under warrant must be made within three calendar months of the date the warrant is issued or within the period specified in the enactment under which the warrant is issued if this is shorter.

B:6.2 Searches must be made at a reasonable hour unless this might frustrate the purpose of the search.

B:6.3 When the extent or complexity of a search mean it is likely to take a long time, the officer in charge of the search may consider using the seize and sift powers referred to in section 7.

B:6.3A A warrant under PACE, s.8 may authorise entry to and search of premises on more than one occasion if, on the application, the justice of the peace is satisfied that it is necessary to authorise multiple entries in order to achieve the purpose for which the warrant is issued. No premises may be entered or searched on any subsequent occasions without the prior written authority of an officer of the rank of inspector who is not involved in the investigation. All other warrants authorise entry on one occasion only.

B:6.3B Where a warrant under PACE, s.8, or Sched. 1, para. 12 authorises entry to and search of all premises occupied or controlled by a specified person, no premises which are not specified in the warrant may be entered and searched without the prior written authority of an officer of the rank of inspector who is not involved in the investigation.

(b) Entry other than with consent

B:6.4 The officer in charge of the search shall first try to communicate with the occupier, or any other person entitled to grant access to the premises, explain the authority under which entry is sought and ask the occupier to allow entry, unless:
- (i) the search premises are unoccupied;
- (ii) the occupier and any other person entitled to grant access are absent;
- (iii) there are reasonable grounds for believing that alerting the occupier or any other person entitled to grant access would frustrate the object of the search or endanger officers or other people.

B:6.5 Unless sub-paragraph 6.4(iii) applies, if the premises are occupied the officer, subject to paragraph 2.9, shall, before the search begins:
- (i) identify him or herself, show their warrant card (if not in uniform) and state the purpose of, and grounds for, the search; and
- (ii) identify and introduce any person accompanying the officer on the search (such persons should carry identification for production on request) and briefly describe that person's role in the process.

B:6.6 Reasonable and proportionate force may be used if necessary to enter premises if the officer in charge of the search is satisfied the premises are those specified in any warrant, or in exercise of the powers described in paragraph 4.1 to 4.3, and if:
- (i) the occupier or any other person entitled to grant access has refused entry;
- (ii) it is impossible to communicate with the occupier or any other person entitled to grant access; or
- (iii) any of the provisions of paragraph 6.4 apply.

(c) Notice of powers and rights

B:6.7 If an officer conducts a search to which this code applies the officer shall, unless it is impracticable to do so, provide the occupier with a copy of a notice in a standard format: **A-29**
- (i) specifying if the search is made under warrant, with consent, or in the exercise of the powers described in paragraphs 4.1 to 4.3. Note: the notice format shall provide for authority or consent to be indicated (see paragraphs 4.3 and 5.1);
- (ii) summarising the extent of the powers of search and seizure conferred by PACE and other relevant legislation as appropriate;
- (iii) explaining the rights of the occupier and the owner of the property seized;
- (iv) explaining compensation may be payable in appropriate cases for damages [*sic*] caused entering and searching premises, and giving the address to send a compensation application [see *Note 6A*]; and
- (v) stating this code is available at any police station.

B:6.8 If the occupier is:
- present, copies of the notice and warrant shall, if practicable, be given to them before the search begins, unless the officer in charge of the search reasonably believes this would frustrate the object of the search or endanger officers or other people;
- not present, copies of the notice and warrant shall be left in a prominent place on the premises or appropriate part of the premises and endorsed, subject to paragraph 2.9 with the name of the officer in charge of the search, the date and time of the search.

The warrant shall be endorsed to show this has been done.

(d) Conduct of searches

B:6.9 Premises may be searched only to the extent necessary to achieve the purpose of the search, having regard to the size and nature of whatever is sought.

B:6.9A A search may not continue under:
- a warrant's authority once all the things specified in that warrant have been found;
- any other power once the object of that search has been achieved.

B:6.9B No search may continue once the officer in charge of the search is satisfied whatever is being sought is not on the premises [see *Note 6B*]. This does not prevent a further search of the same premises if additional grounds come to light supporting a further application for a search warrant or exercise or further exercise of another power. For example, when, as a result of new information, it is believed articles previously not found or additional articles are on the premises.

B:6.10 Searches must be conducted with due consideration for the property and privacy of the occupier and with no more disturbance than necessary. Reasonable force may be used only when necessary and proportionate because the co-operation of the occupier cannot be obtained or is insufficient for the purpose. [See *Note 6C.*]

B:6.11 A friend, neighbour or other person must be allowed to witness the search if the occupier wishes unless the officer in charge of the search has reasonable grounds for believing the presence of the person asked for would seriously hinder the investigation or endanger officers or other people. A search need not be unreasonably delayed for this purpose. A record of the action taken should be made on the premises search record including the grounds for refusing the occupier's request.

B:6.12 A person is not required to be cautioned prior to being asked questions that are solely necessary for the purpose of furthering the proper and effective conduct of a search, see Code C, paragraph 10.1(c). For example, questions to discover the occupier of specified premises, to find a key to open a locked drawer or cupboard or to otherwise seek co-operation during the search or to determine if a particular item is liable to be seized.

B:6.12A If questioning goes beyond what is necessary for the purpose of the exemption in Code C, the exchange is likely to constitute an interview as defined by Code C, paragraph 11.1A and would require the associated safeguards included in Code C, section 10.

(e) Leaving premises

A-30 B:6.13 If premises have been entered by force, before leaving the officer in charge of the search must make sure they are secure by:

- arranging for the occupier or their agent to be present;
- any other appropriate means.

(f) Searches under PACE, Schedule 1 or the Terrorism Act 2000, Schedule 5

B:6.14 An officer shall be appointed as the officer in charge of the search (see paragraph 2.10), in respect of any search made under a warrant issued under PACE Act 1984, Sched. 1 or the Terrorism Act 2000, Sched. 5. They are responsible for making sure the search is conducted with discretion and in a manner that causes the least possible disruption to any business or other activities carried out on the premises.

B:6.15 Once the officer in charge of the search is satisfied material may not be taken from the premises without their knowledge, they shall ask for the documents or other records concerned. The officer in charge of the search may also ask to see the index to files held on the premises, and the officers conducting the search may inspect any files which, according to the index, appear to contain the material sought. A more extensive search of the premises may be made only if:

- the person responsible for them refuses to:
  - produce the material sought, or
  - allow access to the index;
- it appears the index is:
  - inaccurate, or
  - incomplete;
- for any other reason the officer in charge of the search has reasonable grounds for believing such a search is necessary in order to find the material sought.

Notes for guidance

A-31 *B:6A Whether compensation is appropriate depends on the circumstances in each case. Compensation for damage caused when effecting entry is unlikely to be appropriate if the search was lawful, and the force used can be shown to be reasonable, proportionate and necessary to effect entry. If the wrong premises are searched by mistake everything possible should be done at the earliest opportunity to allay any sense of grievance and there should normally be a strong presumption in favour of paying compensation.*

B:6B It is important that, when possible, all those involved in a search are fully briefed about any powers to be exercised and the extent and limits within which it should be conducted.

B:6C In all cases the number of officers and other persons involved in executing the warrant should be determined by what is reasonable and necessary according to the particular circumstances.

B:7 Seizure and retention of property

(a) Seizure

B:7.1 Subject to paragraph 7.2, an officer who is searching any person or premises under any statutory power or with the consent of the occupier may seize anything: **A-32**

(a) covered by a warrant;
(b) the officer has reasonable grounds for believing is evidence of an offence or has been obtained in consequence of the commission of an offence but only if seizure is necessary to prevent the items being concealed, lost, disposed of, altered, damaged, destroyed or tampered with;
(c) covered by the powers in the Criminal Justice and Police Act 2001, Pt 2 allowing an officer to seize property from persons or premises and retain it for sifting or examination elsewhere.

See *Note 7B*.

B:7.2 No item may be seized which an officer has reasonable grounds for believing to be subject to legal privilege, as defined in PACE, s.10, other than under the Criminal Justice and Police Act 2001, Pt 2.

B:7.3 Officers must be aware of the provisions in the Criminal Justice and Police Act 2001, s.59, allowing for applications to a judicial authority for the return of property seized and the subsequent duty to secure in section 60 (see paragraph 7.12(iii)).

B:7.4 An officer may decide it is not appropriate to seize property because of an explanation from the person holding it but may nevertheless have reasonable grounds for believing it was obtained in consequence of an offence by some person. In these circumstances, the officer should identify the property to the holder, inform the holder of their suspicions and explain the holder may be liable to civil or criminal proceedings if they dispose of, alter or destroy the property.

B:7.5 An officer may arrange to photograph, image or copy, any document or other article they have the power to seize in accordance with paragraph 7.1. This is subject to specific restrictions on the examination, imaging or copying of certain property seized under the Criminal Justice and Police Act 2001, Pt 2. An officer must have regard to their statutory obligation to retain an original document or other article only when a photograph or copy is not sufficient.

B:7.6 If an officer considers information stored in any electronic form and accessible from the premises could be used in evidence, they may require the information to be produced in a form:

- which can be taken away and in which it is visible and legible; or
- from which it can readily be produced in a visible and legible form.

(b) Criminal Justice and Police Act 2001: specific procedures for seize and sift powers

B:7.7 The Criminal Justice and Police Act 2001, Pt 2 gives officers limited powers to seize property from premises or persons so they can sift or examine it elsewhere. Officers must be careful they only exercise these powers when it is essential and they do not remove any more material than necessary. The removal of large volumes of material, much of which may not ultimately be retainable, may have serious implications for the owners, particularly when they are involved in business or activities such as journalism or the provision of medical services. Officers must carefully consider if removing copies or images of relevant material or data would be a satisfactory alternative to removing originals. When originals are taken, officers must be prepared to facilitate the provision of copies or images for the owners when reasonably practicable. [See *Note 7C*.] **A-33**

B:7.8 Property seized under the Criminal Justice and Police Act 2001, s.50 or 51 must be kept securely and separately from any material seized under other powers. An examination under section 53 to determine which elements may be retained must be carried out at the earliest practicable time, having due regard to the desirability of allowing the person from whom the property was seized, or a person with an interest in the property, an opportunity of being present or represented at the examination.

B:7.8A All reasonable steps should be taken to accommodate an interested person's request to be present, provided the request is reasonable and subject to the need to prevent harm to, interference with, or unreasonable delay to the investigatory process. If an examination proceeds in the absence of an interested person who asked to attend or their representative, the officer who exercised the relevant seizure power must give that person a written notice of why the examination was carried out in those circumstances. If it is necessary for security reasons or to maintain confidentiality officers may exclude interested persons from decryption or other processes which facilitate the examination but do not form part of it. [See *Note 7D*.]

B:7.9 It is the responsibility of the officer in charge of the investigation to make sure property is returned in accordance with sections 53 to 55. Material which there is no power to retain must be:

- separated from the rest of the seized property; and

• returned as soon as reasonably practicable after examination of all the seized property.

B:7.9A Delay is only warranted if very clear and compelling reasons exist, for example:

• the unavailability of the person to whom the material is to be returned; or
• the need to agree a convenient time to return a large volume of material.

B:7.9B Legally privileged, excluded or special procedure material which cannot be retained must be returned:

• as soon as reasonably practicable; and
• without waiting for the whole examination.

B:7.9C As set out in section 58, material must be returned to the person from whom it was seized, except when it is clear some other person has a better right to it. [See *Note 7E.*]

B:7.10 When an officer involved in the investigation has reasonable grounds to believe a person with a relevant interest in property seized under section 50 or 51 intends to make an application under section 59 for the return of any legally privileged, special procedure or excluded material, the officer in charge of the investigation should be informed as soon as practicable and the material seized should be kept secure in accordance with section 61. [See *Note 7C.*]

B:7.11 The officer in charge of the investigation is responsible for making sure property is properly secured. Securing involves making sure the property is not examined, copied, imaged or put to any other use except at the request, or with the consent, of the applicant or in accordance with the directions of the appropriate judicial authority. Any request, consent or directions must be recorded in writing and signed by both the initiator and the officer in charge of the investigation. [See *Notes 7F* and *7G.*]

B:7.12 When an officer exercises a power of seizure conferred by sections 50 or 51 they shall provide the occupier of the premises or the person from whom the property is being seized with a written notice:

(i) specifying what has been seized under the powers conferred by that section;
(ii) specifying the grounds for those powers;
(iii) setting out the effect of sections 59 to 61 covering the grounds for a person with a relevant interest in seized property to apply to a judicial authority for its return and the duty of officers to secure property in certain circumstances when an application is made; and
(iv) specifying the name and address of the person to whom:
 • notice of an application to the appropriate judicial authority in respect of any of the seized property must be given;
 • an application may be made to allow attendance at the initial examination of the property.

B:7.13 If the occupier is not present but there is someone in charge of the premises, the notice shall be given to them. If no suitable person is available, so the notice will easily be found it should either be:

• left in a prominent place on the premises; or
• attached to the exterior of the premises.

(c) Retention

A-34 B:7.14 Subject to paragraph 7.15, anything seized in accordance with the above provisions may be retained only for as long as is necessary. It may be retained, among other purposes:

(i) for use as evidence at a trial for an offence;
(ii) to facilitate the use in any investigation or proceedings of anything to which it is inextricably linked [see *Note 7H*];
(iii) for forensic examination or other investigation in connection with an offence;
(iv) in order to establish its lawful owner when there are reasonable grounds for believing it has been stolen or obtained by the commission of an offence.

B:7.15 Property shall not be retained under paragraph 7.14(i), (ii) or (iii) if a copy or image would be sufficient.

(d) Rights of owners etc

B:7.16 If property is retained, the person who had custody or control of it immediately before seizure must, on request, be provided with a list or description of the property within a reasonable time.

B:7.17 That person or their representative must be allowed supervised access to the property to examine it or have it photographed or copied, or must be provided with a photograph or copy, in either case within a reasonable time of any request and at their own expense, unless the officer in charge of an investigation has reasonable grounds for believing this would:

(i) prejudice the investigation of any offence or criminal proceedings; or

(ii) lead to the commission of an offence by providing access to unlawful material such as pornography.

A record of the grounds shall be made when access is denied.

Notes for guidance

B:7A Any person claiming property seized by the police may apply to a magistrates' court under the Police (Property) Act 1897 for its possession and should, if appropriate, be advised of this procedure. A-35

B:7B The powers of seizure conferred by PACE, ss.18(2) and 19(3) extend to the seizure of the whole premises when it is physically possible to seize and retain the premises in their totality and practical considerations make seizure desirable. For example, police may remove premises such as tents, vehicles or caravans to a police station for the purpose of preserving evidence.

B:7C Officers should consider reaching agreement with owners and/or other interested parties on the procedures for examining a specific set of property, rather than awaiting the judicial authority's determination. Agreement can sometimes give a quicker and more satisfactory route for all concerned and minimise costs and legal complexities.

B:7D What constitutes a relevant interest in specific material may depend on the nature of that material and the circumstances in which it is seized. Anyone with a reasonable claim to ownership of the material and anyone entrusted with its safe keeping by the owner should be considered.

B:7E Requirements to secure and return property apply equally to all copies, images or other material created because of seizure of the original property.

B:7F The mechanics of securing property vary according to the circumstances; "bagging up", i.e. *placing material in sealed bags or containers and strict subsequent control of access is the appropriate procedure in many cases.*

B:7G When material is seized under the powers of seizure conferred by PACE, the duty to retain it under the code of practice issued under the Criminal Procedure and Investigations Act 1996 is subject to the provisions on retention of seized material in PACE, s.22.

B:7H Paragraph 7.14(ii) applies if inextricably linked material is seized under the Criminal Justice and Police Act 2001, s.50 or 51. Inextricably linked material is material it is not reasonably practicable to separate from other linked material without prejudicing the use of that other material in any investigation or proceedings. For example, it may not be possible to separate items of data held on computer disk without damaging their evidential integrity. Inextricably linked material must not be examined, imaged, copied or used for any purpose other than for proving the source and/or integrity of the linked material.

B:8 Action after searches

B:8.1 If premises are searched in circumstances where this code applies, unless the exceptions in paragraph 2.3(a) apply, on arrival at a police station the officer in charge of the search shall make or have made a record of the search, to include: A-36

(i) the address of the searched premises;
(ii) the date, time and duration of the search;
(iii) the authority used for the search:
- if the search was made in exercise of a statutory power to search premises without warrant, the power which was used for the search:
- if the search was made under a warrant or with written consent;
  - a copy of the warrant and the written authority to apply for it, see paragraph 3.4; or
  - the written consent;

shall be appended to the record or the record shall show the location of the copy warrant or consent;

(iv) subject to paragraph 2.9, the names of:
- the officer(s) in charge of the search;
- all other officers and any authorised persons who conducted the search;

(v) the names of any people on the premises if they are known;
(vi) any grounds for refusing the occupier's request to have someone present during the search, see paragraph 6.11;
(vii) a list of any articles seized or the location of a list and, if not covered by a warrant, the grounds for their seizure;
(viii) whether force was used, and the reason;
(ix) details of any damage caused during the search, and the circumstances;
(x) if applicable, the reason it was not practicable;
(a) to give the occupier a copy of the notice of powers and rights, see paragraph 6.7;
(b) before the search to give the occupier a copy of the notice, see paragraph 6.8;

(xi) when the occupier was not present, the place where copies of the notice of powers and rights and search warrant were left on the premises, see paragraph 6.8.

B:8.2 On each occasion when premises are searched under warrant, the warrant authorising the search on that occasion shall be endorsed to show:

(i) if any articles specified in the warrant were found and the address where found;
(ii) if any other articles were seized;
(iii) the date and time it was executed and if present, the name of the occupier or if the occupier is not present the name of the person in charge of the premises;
(iv) subject to paragraph 2.9, the names of the officers who executed it and any authorised persons who accompanied them; and
(v) if a copy, together with a copy of the notice of powers and rights was:
  - handed to the occupier; or
  - endorsed as required by paragraph 6.8; and left on the premises and where.

B:8.3 Any warrant shall be returned within three calendar months of its issue or sooner on completion of the search(es) authorised by that warrant, if it was issued by a:

- justice of the peace, to the designated officer for the local justice area in which the justice was acting when issuing the warrant; or
- judge, to the appropriate officer of the court concerned.

B:9 Search registers

A-37 B:9.1 A search register will be maintained at each sub-divisional or equivalent police station. All search records required under paragraph 8.1 shall be made, copied, or referred to in the register. [See *Note 9A.*]

Note for guidance

B:9A Paragraph 9.1 also applies to search records made by immigration officers. In these cases, a search register must also be maintained at an immigration office. [*See also Note 2D.*]

B:10 Searches under Schedule 5 to the Terrorism Prevention and Investigation Measures Act 2011

A-37a B:10.1 This code applies to the powers of constables under Schedule 5 to the Terrorism Prevention and Investigation Measures Act 2011 relating to TPIM notices to enter and search premises subject to the modifications in the following paragraphs.

B:10.2 In paragraph 2.3(d), the reference to the investigation into an alleged or suspected offence include [*sic*] the enforcement of terrorism prevention and investigation measures which may be imposed on an individual by a TPIM notice in accordance with the Terrorism Prevention and Investigation Measures Act 2011.

B:10.3 References to the purpose and object of the entry and search of premises, the nature of articles sought and what may be seized and retained include (as appropriate):

(a) in relation to the power to search without a search warrant in paragraph 5 (for purposes of serving TPIM notice), finding the individual on whom the notice is to be served;
(b) in relation to the power to search without a search warrant in paragraph 6 (at time of serving TPIM notice), ascertaining whether there is anything in the premises, that contravenes measures specified in the notice [see *Note 10A*];
(c) in relation to the power to search without a search warrant under paragraph 7 (suspected absconding), ascertaining whether a person has absconded or if there is anything on the premises which will assist in the pursuit or arrest of an individual in respect of whom a TPIM notice is force who is reasonably suspected of having absconded;
(d) in relation to the power to search under a search warrant issued under paragraph 8 (for compliance purposes), determining whether an individual in respect of whom a notice is in force is complying with measures specified in the notice [see *Note 10A*].

Note for guidance

B:10A Searches of individuals under Schedule 5, paras 6(2)(a) (at time of serving TPIM notice) and 8(2)(a) (for compliance purposes) must be conducted and recorded in accordance with Code A. See Code A, para. 2.18A for details.

(4) Detention, treatment and questioning of persons

A-38 The text that follows is of the version of the code that came into force on 21 August 2019: see above, A-1.

For authorities in relation to Code C, see, in particular, §§ 15-229 et seq. (right of access to solicitor), § 15-276 (general), § 15-407 et seq. (confessions), §§ 15-493 et seq. (discretionary exclusion of evidence) in the main work.

POLICE AND CRIMINAL EVIDENCE ACT 1984 (PACE) CODE C REVISED CODE OF PRACTICE FOR THE DETENTION, TREATMENT AND QUESTIONING OF PERSONS BY POLICE OFFICERS

Commencement - Transitional Arrangements

This Code applies to people in police detention after 00:00 on 21 August 2019 notwithstanding that their period of detention may have commenced before that time. **A-39**

C:1 General

C:1.0 The powers and procedures in this Code must be used fairly, responsibly, with respect for the people to whom they apply and without unlawful discrimination. Under the Equality Act 2010, section 149 (Public sector Equality Duty), police forces must, in carrying out their functions, have due regard to the need to eliminate unlawful discrimination, harassment, victimisation and any other conduct which is prohibited by that Act, to advance equality of opportunity between people who share a relevant protected characteristic and people who do not share it, and to foster good relations between those persons. The Equality Act *also* makes it unlawful for police officers to discriminate against, harass or victimise any person on the grounds of the 'protected characteristics' of age, disability, gender reassignment, race, religion or belief, sex and sexual orientation, marriage and civil partnership, pregnancy and maternity, when using their powers. See *Notes 1A* and *1AA.* **A-40**

C:1.1 All persons in custody must be dealt with expeditiously, and released as soon as the need for detention no longer applies.

C:1.1A A custody officer must perform the functions in this Code as soon as practicable. A custody officer will not be in breach of this Code if delay is justifiable and reasonable steps are taken to prevent unnecessary delay. The custody record shall show when a delay has occurred and the reason. See *Note 1H.*

C:1.2 This Code of Practice must be readily available at all police stations for consultation by:

- police officers;
- police staff;
- detained persons;
- members of the public.

C:1.3 The provisions of this Code:

- include the *Annexes*
- do not include the *Notes for Guidance which* form guidance to police officers and others about its application and interpretation.

C:1.4 If at any time an officer has any reason to suspect that a person of any age may be vulnerable (see *paragraph 1.13(d)*), in the absence of clear evidence to dispel that suspicion, that person shall be treated as such for the purposes of this Code and to establish whether any such reason may exist in relation to a person suspected of committing an offence (see *paragraph 10.1* and *Note 10A*), the custody officer in the case of a detained person, or the officer investigating the offence in the case of a person who has not been arrested or detained, shall take, or cause to be taken, (see *paragraph 3.5* and *Note 3F*) the following action:

(a) reasonable enquiries shall be made to ascertain what information is available that is relevant to any of the factors described in *paragraph 1.13(d)* as indicating that the person may be vulnerable might apply;

(b) a record shall be made describing whether any of those factors appear to apply and provide any reason to suspect that the person may be vulnerable or (as the case may be) may not be vulnerable; and

(c) the record mentioned in sub-paragraph (b) shall be made available to be taken into account by police officers, police staff and any others who, in accordance with the provisions of this or any other Code, are required or entitled to communicate with the person in question. This would include any solicitor, appropriate adult and health care professional and is particularly relevant to communication by telephone or by means of a live link (see *paragraphs 12.9A* (interviews), *13.12* (interpretation), and *15.3C, 15.11A, 15.11B, 15.11C* and *15.11D* (reviews and extension of detention)).

See *Notes 1G, 1GA, 1GB* and *1GC.*

C:1.5 Anyone who appears to be under 18, shall, in the absence of clear evidence that they are older, be treated as a juvenile for the purposes of this Code and any other Code. See *Note 1L.*

C:1.5A *Not used.*

C:1.6 If a person appears to be blind, seriously visually impaired, deaf, unable to read or speak or has difficulty orally because of a speech impediment, they shall be treated as such for the purposes of this Code in the absence of clear evidence to the contrary.

A-41 C:1.7 "The appropriate adult" means, in the case of a:

(a) juvenile:
  (i) the parent, guardian or, if the juvenile is in the care of a local authority or voluntary organisation, a person representing that authority or organisation (see *Note 1B*);
  (ii) a social worker of a local authority (see *Note 1C*);
  (iii) failing these, some other responsible adult aged 18 or over who is *not*:
    ~ a police officer;
    ~ employed by the police;
    ~ under the direction or control of the chief officer of a police force; or
    ~ a person who provides services under contractual arrangements (but without being employed by the chief officer of a police force), to assist that force in relation to the discharge of its chief officer's functions,

  whether or not they are on duty at the time.

  See *Note 1F*.

(b) person who is vulnerable (see *paragraph 1.4* and *Note 1D*):
  (i) a relative, guardian or other person responsible for their care or custody;
  (ii) someone experienced in dealing with vulnerable persons but who is *not*:
    ~ a police officer;
    ~ employed by the police;
    ~ under the direction or control of the chief officer of a police force;
    ~ a person who provides services under contractual arrangements (but without being employed by the chief officer of a police force), to assist that force in relation to the discharge of its chief officer's functions,

  whether or not they are on duty at the time;
  (iii) failing these, some other responsible adult aged 18 or over who is other than a person described in the bullet points in *sub-paragraph (b)(ii)* above.

See *Note 1F*.

C:1.7A The role of the appropriate adult is to safeguard the rights, entitlements and welfare of juveniles and vulnerable persons (see *paragraphs 1.4* and *1.5*) to whom the provisions of this and any other Code of Practice apply. For this reason, the appropriate adult is expected, amongst other things, to:

- support, advise and assist them when, in accordance with this Code or any other Code of Practice, they are given or asked to provide information or participate in any procedure;
- observe whether the police are acting properly and fairly to respect their rights and entitlements, and inform an officer of the rank of inspector or above if they consider that they are not;
- assist them to communicate with the police whilst respecting their right to say nothing unless they want to as set out in the terms of the caution (see *paragraphs 10.5* and *10.6*);
- help them to understand their rights and ensure that those rights are protected and respected (see *paragraphs 3.15, 3.17, 6.5A* and *11.17*).

A-42 C:1.8 If this Code requires a person be given certain information, they do not have to be given it if at the time they are incapable of understanding what is said, are violent or may become violent or in urgent need of medical attention, but they must be given it as soon as practicable.

C:1.9 References to a custody officer include any police officer who, for the time being, is performing the functions of a custody officer.

C:1.9A When this Code requires the prior authority or agreement of an officer of at least inspector or superintendent rank, that authority may be given by a sergeant or chief inspector authorised to perform the functions of the higher rank under the Police and Criminal Evidence Act 1984 (PACE), section 107.

C:1.10 Subject to *paragraph 1.12*, this Code applies to people in custody at police stations in England and Wales, whether or not they have been arrested, and to those removed to a police station as a place of safety under the Mental Health Act 1983, sections 135 and 136, as amended by the Policing and Crime Act 2017 (see *paragraph 3.16*). Section 15 applies solely to people in police detention, e.g. those brought to a police station under arrest or arrested at a police station for an offence after going there voluntarily.

C:1.11 No part of this Code applies to a detained person:

(a) to whom PACE Code H applies because:
  - they are detained following arrest under section 41 of the Terrorism Act 2000 (TACT) and not charged; or

- an authorisation has been given under section 22 of the Counter-Terrorism Act 2008 (CTACT) (post-charge questioning of terrorist suspects) to interview them.

(b) to whom the Code of Practice issued under paragraph 6 of Schedule 14 to TACT applies because they are detained for examination under Schedule 7 to TACT.

C:1.12 This Code does not apply to people in custody:

(i) arrested by officers under the Criminal Justice and Public Order Act 1994, section 136(2) on warrants issued in Scotland, or arrested or detained without warrant under section 137(2) by officers from a police force in Scotland. In these cases, police powers and duties and the person's rights and entitlements whilst at a police station in England or Wales are the same as those in Scotland;

(ii) arrested under the Immigration and Asylum Act 1999, section 142(3) in order to have their fingerprints taken;

(iii) whose detention has been authorised under Schedules 2 or 3 to the Immigration Act 1971 or section 62 of the Nationality, Immigration and Asylum Act 2002;

(iv) who are convicted or remanded prisoners held in police cells on behalf of the Prison Service under the Imprisonment (Temporary Provisions) Act 1980;

(v) Not used.

(vi) detained for searches under stop and search powers except as required by Code A.

The provisions on conditions of detention and treatment in sections 8 and 9 must be considered as the minimum standards of treatment for such detainees.

C:1.13 In this Code: A-43

(a) "designated person" means a person other than a police officer, who has specified powers and duties conferred or imposed on them by designation under section 38 or 39 of the Police Reform Act 2002;

(b) reference to a police officer includes a designated person acting in the exercise or performance of the powers and duties conferred or imposed on them by their designation;

(c) if there is doubt as to whether the person should be treated, or continue to be treated, as being male or female in the case of:

   (i) a search or other procedure to which this Code applies which may only be carried out or observed by a person of the *same* sex as the detainee; or

   (ii) any other procedure which requires action to be taken or information to be given that depends on whether the person is to be treated as being male or female;

then the gender of the detainee and other parties concerned should be established and recorded in line with *Annex L* of this Code.

(d) 'vulnerable' applies to any person who, because of a mental health condition or mental disorder (see *Notes 1G and 1GB*):

   (i) may have difficulty understanding or communicating effectively about the full implications for them of any procedures and processes connected with:
   - their arrest and detention; or (as the case may be)
   - their voluntary attendance at a police station or their presence elsewhere (see *paragraph 3.21*), for the purpose of a voluntary interview; and
   - the exercise of their rights and entitlements.

   (ii) does not appear to understand the significance of what they are told, of questions they are asked or of their replies:

   (iii) appears to be particularly prone to:
   - becoming confused and unclear about their position;
   - providing unreliable, misleading or incriminating information without knowing or wishing to do so;
   - accepting or acting on suggestions from others without consciously knowing or wishing to do so; or
   - readily agreeing to suggestions or proposals without any protest or question.

(e) "Live link" means:

   (i) for the purpose of *paragraph 12.9A*; an arrangement by means of which the *interviewing officer* who is not present at the police station where the detainee is held, is able to see and hear, and to be seen and heard by, the detainee concerned, the detainee's solicitor, appropriate adult and interpreter (as applicable) and the officer who has custody of that detainee (see *Note 1N*).

   (ii) for the purpose of *paragraph 15.9A*; an arrangement by means of which the *review officer* who is not present at the police station where the detainee is held, is able to see and hear, and to be seen and heard by, the detainee concerned and the detainee's solicitor, appropriate adult and interpreter (as applicable) (see *Note 1N*). The use of live link for decisions about detention under section 45A of PACE is subject to regulations made by the Secretary of State being in force.

(iii) for the purpose of *paragraph 15.11A*;an arrangement by means of which the *authorising officer* who is not present at the police station where the detainee is held, is able to see and hear, and to be seen and heard by, the detainee concerned and the detainee's solicitor, appropriate adult and interpreter (as applicable) (see *Note 1N*).

(iv) for the purpose of *paragraph 15.11C*; an arrangement by means of which the *detainee* when not present in the court where the hearing is being held, is able to see and hear, and to be seen and heard by, the court during the hearing (see *Note 1N*).

Note: Chief officers must be satisfied that live link used in their force area for the above purposes provides for accurate and secure communication between the detainee, the detainee's solicitor, appropriate adult and interpreter (as applicable). This includes ensuring that at any time during which the live link is being used: a person cannot see, hear or otherwise obtain access to any such communications unless so authorised or allowed by the custody officer or, in the case of an interview, the interviewer and that as applicable, the confidentiality of any private consultation between a suspect and their solicitor and appropriate adult is maintained.

A-44 C:1.14 Designated persons are entitled to use reasonable force as follows:

(a) when exercising a power conferred on them which allows a police officer exercising that power to use reasonable force, a designated person has the same entitlement to use force; and

(b) at other times when carrying out duties conferred or imposed on them that also entitle them to use reasonable force, for example:
- when at a police station carrying out the duty to keep detainees for whom they are responsible under control and to assist any police officer or designated person to keep any detainee under control and to prevent their escape;
- when securing, or assisting any police officer or designated person in securing, the detention of a person at a police station;
- when escorting, or assisting any police officer or designated person in escorting, a detainee within a police station;
- for the purpose of saving life or limb; or
- preventing serious damage to property.

C:1.15 Nothing in this Code prevents the custody officer, or other police officer or designated person (see *paragraph 1.13(a)*) given custody of the detainee by the custody officer, from allowing another person (see *(a)* and *(b)* below) to carry out individual procedures or tasks at the police station if the law allows. However, the officer or designated person given custody remains responsible for making sure the procedures and tasks are carried out correctly in accordance with the Codes of Practice (see *paragraph 3.5* and *Note 3F*). The other person who is allowed to carry out the procedures or tasks must be someone who *at that time*, is:

(a) under the direction and control of the chief officer of the force responsible for the police station in question; or

(b) providing services under contractual arrangements (but without being employed by the chief officer the police force), to assist a police force in relation to the discharge of its chief officer's functions.

C:1.16 Designated persons and others mentioned in *sub-paragraphs (a)* and *(b)* of *paragraph 1.15*, must have regard to any relevant provisions of the Codes of Practice.

C:1.17 In any provision of this or any other Code which allows or requires police officers or police staff to make a record in their report book, the reference to report book shall include any official report book or electronic recording device issued to them that enables the record in question to be made and dealt with in accordance with that provision. References in this and any other Code to written records, forms and signatures include electronic records and forms and electronic confirmation that identifies the person making the record or completing the form.

Chief officers must be satisfied as to the integrity and security of the devices, records and forms to which this paragraph applies and that use of those devices, records and forms satisfies relevant data protection legislation.

Notes for Guidance

A-45 *C:1A Although certain sections of this Code apply specifically to people in custody at police stations, a person who attends a police station or other location voluntarily to assist with an investigation should be treated with no less consideration, e.g. offered or allowed refreshments at appropriate times, and enjoy an absolute right to obtain legal advice or communicate with anyone outside the police station or other location (see paragraphs 3.21* and *3.22.*

C:1AA In paragraph 1.0, under the Equality Act 2010, section 149, the 'relevant protected characteristics' are age, disability, gender reassignment, pregnancy and maternity, race, religion/belief and sex and sexual orientation. For further detailed guidance and advice on the Equality Act, see: https://www.gov.uk/guidance/equality-act-2010-guidance.

C:1B A person, including a parent or guardian, should not be an appropriate adult if they:

- *are:*
  - ~ *suspected of involvement in the offence;*
  - ~ *the victim;*
  - ~ *a witness;*
  - ~ *involved in the investigation.*
- *received admissions prior to attending to act as the appropriate adult.*

Note: If a juvenile's parent is estranged from the juvenile, they should not be asked to act as the appropriate adult if the juvenile expressly and specifically objects to their presence.

C:1C If a juvenile admits an offence to, or in the presence of, a social worker or member of a youth offending team other than during the time that person is acting as the juvenile's appropriate adult, another appropriate adult should be appointed in the interest of fairness.

C:1D In the case of someone who is vulnerable, it may be more satisfactory if the appropriate adult is someone experienced or trained in their care rather than a relative lacking such qualifications. But if the person prefers a relative to a better qualified stranger or objects to a particular person their wishes should, if practicable, be respected.

C:1E A detainee should always be given an opportunity, when an appropriate adult is called to the police station, to consult privately with a solicitor in the appropriate adult's absence if they want. An appropriate adult is not subject to legal privilege.

C:1F An appropriate adult who is not a parent or guardian in the case of a juvenile, or a relative, guardian or carer in the case of a vulnerable person, must be independent of the police as their role is to safeguard the person's rights and entitlements. Additionally, a solicitor or independent custody visitor who is present at the police station and acting in that capacity, may not be the appropriate adult.

C:1G A person may be vulnerable as a result of a having a mental health condition or mental disorder. Similarly, simply because an individual does not have, or is not known to have, any such condition or disorder, does not mean that they are not vulnerable for the purposes of this Code. It is therefore important that the custody officer in the case of a detained person or the officer investigating the offence in the case of a person who has not been arrested or detained, as appropriate, considers on a case by case basis, whether any of the factors described in paragraph 1.13(d) might apply to the person in question. In doing so, the officer must take into account the particular circumstances of the individual and how the nature of the investigation might affect them and bear in mind that juveniles, by virtue of their age will always require an appropriate adult.

C:1GA For the purposes of paragraph 1.4(a), examples of relevant information that may be available include:

- *the behaviour of the adult or juvenile;*
- *the mental health and capacity of the adult or juvenile;*
- *what the adult or juvenile says about themselves;*
- *information from relatives and friends of the adult or juvenile;*
- *information from police officers and staff and from police records;*
- *information from health and social care (including liaison and diversion services) and other professionals who know, or have had previous contact with, the individual and may be able to contribute to assessing their need for help and support from an appropriate adult. This includes contacts and assessments arranged by the police or at the request of the individual or (as applicable) their appropriate adult or solicitor.*

C:1GB The Mental Health Act 1983 Code of Practice at page 26 describes the range of clinically recognised conditions which can fall with the meaning of mental disorder for the purpose of paragraph 1.13(d). The Code is published here: *https://www.gov.uk/government/publications/code-of-practice-mental-health-act-1983.*

C:1GC When a person is under the influence of drink and/or drugs, it is not intended that they are to be treated as vulnerable and requiring an appropriate adult for the purpose of paragraph 1.4 unless other information indicates that any of the factors described in *paragraph 1.13(d)* may apply to that person. When the person has recovered from the effects of drink and/or drugs, they should be re-assessed in accordance with *paragraph 1.4.* See *paragraph 15.4A* for application to live link.

C:1H Paragraph 1.1A is intended to cover delays which may occur in processing detainees e.g. if:

- *a large number of suspects are brought into the station simultaneously to be placed in custody;*
- *interview rooms are all being used;*
- *there are difficulties contacting an appropriate adult, solicitor or interpreter.*

C:1I The custody officer must remind the appropriate adult and detainee about the right to legal advice and record any reasons for waiving it in accordance with section 6.

C:1J Not used.

C:1K This Code does not affect the principle that all citizens have a duty to help police officers to prevent crime and discover offenders. This is a civic rather than a legal duty; but when police officers are trying to discover whether, or by whom, offences have been committed they are entitled to question any person from whom they think useful information can be obtained, subject to the restrictions imposed by this Code. A person's declaration that they are unwilling to reply does not alter this entitlement.

C:1L Paragraph 1.5 reflects the statutory definition of 'arrested juvenile' in section 37(15) of PACE. This section was amended by section 42 of the Criminal Justice and Courts Act 2015 with effect from 26 October 2015, and includes anyone who appears to be under the age of 18. This definition applies for the purposes of the detention and bail provisions in sections 34 to 51 of PACE. With effect from 3 April 2017, amendments made by the Policing and Crime Act 2017 require persons under the age of 18 to be treated as juveniles for the purposes of all other provisions of PACE and the Codes.

C:1M Not used.

C:1N For the purpose of the provisions of PACE that allow a live link to be used, any impairment of the detainee's eyesight or hearing is to be disregarded. This means that if a detainee's eyesight or hearing is impaired, the arrangements which would be needed to ensure effective communication if all parties were physically present in the same location, for example, using sign language, would apply to the live link arrangements.

C:2 Custody records

A-46 C:2.1A When a person:

- is brought to a police station under arrest;
- is arrested at the police station having attended there voluntarily; or
- attends a police station to answer bail.

they must be brought before the custody officer as soon as practicable after their arrival at the station or if applicable, following their arrest after attending the police station voluntarily. This applies to both designated and non-designated police stations. A person is deemed to be "at a police station" for these purposes if they are within the boundary of any building or enclosed yard which forms part of that police station.

C:2.1 A separate custody record must be opened as soon as practicable for each person brought to a police station under arrest or arrested at the station having gone there voluntarily or attending a police station in answer to street bail. All information recorded under this Code must be recorded as soon as practicable in the custody record unless otherwise specified. Any audio or video recording made in the custody area is not part of the custody record.

C:2.2 If any action requires the authority of an officer of a specified rank, subject to *paragraph 2.6A*, their name and rank must be noted in the custody record.

C:2.3 The custody officer is responsible for the custody record's accuracy and completeness and for making sure the record or copy of the record accompanies a detainee if they are transferred to another police station. The record shall show the:

- time and reason for transfer;
- time a person is released from detention.

C:2.3A If a person is arrested and taken to a police station as a result of a search in the exercise of any stop and search power to which PACE Code A (Stop and search) or the 'search powers code' issued under TACT applies, the officer carrying out the search is responsible for ensuring that the record of that stop and search is made as part of the person's custody record. The custody officer must then ensure that the person is asked if they want a copy of the search record and if they do, that they are given a copy as soon as practicable. The person's entitlement to a copy of the search record which is made as part of their custody record is in addition to, and does not affect, their entitlement to a copy of their custody record or any other provisions of section 2 (Custody records) of this Code. (See Code A *paragraph 4.2B* and the TACT search powers code *paragraph 5.3.5*).

C:2.4 The detainee's solicitor and appropriate adult must be permitted to inspect the whole of the detainee's custody record as soon as practicable after their arrival at the station and at any other time on request, whilst the person is detained. This includes the following *specific* records relating to the reasons for the detainee's arrest and detention and the offence concerned to which *paragraph 3.1(b)* refers:

(a) The information about the circumstances and reasons for the detainee's arrest as recorded in the custody record in accordance with *paragraph 4.3 of Code G*. This applies to any further offences for which the detainee is arrested whilst in custody;

(b) The record of the grounds for each authorisation to keep the person in custody. The authorisations to which this applies are the same as those described at items *(i)(a)* to *(d)* in the table in *paragraph 2* of *Annex M* of this Code.

Access to the records in *sub-paragraphs (a)* and *(b)* is *in addition* to the requirements in *paragraphs 3.4(b), 11.1A, 15.0, 15,7A(c) and 16.7A* to make certain documents and materials available and to provide information about the offence and the reasons for arrest and detention.

Access to the custody record for the purposes of this paragraph must be arranged and agreed with the custody officer and may not unreasonably interfere with the custody officer's duties. A record shall be made when access is allowed and whether it includes the records described in *sub-paragraphs (a)* and *(b)* above.

C:2.4A When a detainee leaves police detention or is taken before a court they, their legal representative or appropriate adult shall be given, on request, a copy of the custody record as soon as practicable. This entitlement lasts for 12 months after release.

C:2.5 The detainee, appropriate adult or legal representative shall be permitted to inspect the original custody record after the detainee has left police detention provided they give reasonable notice of their request. Any such inspection shall be noted in the custody record.

C:2.6 Subject to *paragraph 2.6A*, all entries in custody records must be timed and signed by the maker. Records entered on computer shall be timed and contain the operator's identification.

C:2.6A Nothing in this Code requires the identity of officers or other police staff to be recorded or disclosed:

(a) *Not used.*

(b) if the officer or police staff reasonably believe recording or disclosing their name might put them in danger.

In these cases, they shall use their warrant or other identification numbers and the name of their police station. See *Note 2A*.

C:2.7 The fact and time of any detainee's refusal to sign a custody record, when asked in accordance with this Code, must be recorded.

Note for Guidance

C:2A The purpose of paragraph 2.6A(b) is to protect those involved in serious organised crime investigations or arrests of particularly violent suspects when there is reliable information that those arrested or their associates may threaten or cause harm to those involved. In cases of doubt, an officer of inspector rank or above should be consulted. **A-47**

C:3 Initial action

(A) Detained persons - normal procedure

C:3.1 When a person is brought to a police station under arrest or arrested at the station having gone there voluntarily, the custody officer must make sure the person is told clearly about: **A-48**

(a) the following continuing rights, which may be exercised at any stage during the period in custody:

  (i) their right to consult privately with a solicitor and that free independent legal advice is available as in section 6;

  (ii) their right to have someone informed of their arrest as in section 5;

  (iii) their right to consult the Codes of Practice (see *Note 3D*); and

  (iv) if applicable, their right to interpretation and translation (see *paragraph 3.12*) and their right to communicate with their High Commission, Embassy or Consulate (see *paragraph 3.12A*).

(b) their right to be informed about the offence and (as the case may be) any further offences for which they are arrested whilst in custody and why they have been arrested and detained in accordance with *paragraphs 2.4, 3.4(a)* and *11.1A* of this Code and *paragraph 3.3* of *Code G*.

C:3.2 The detainee must also be given a written notice, which contains information:

(a) to allow them to exercise their rights by setting out:

  (i) their rights under *paragraph 3.1, paragraph 3.12* and *3.12A*;

  (ii) the arrangements for obtaining legal advice, see section 6;

  (iii) their right to a copy of the custody record as in *paragraph 2.4A*;

  (iv) their right to remain silent as set out in the caution in the terms prescribed in section 10;

  (v) their right to have access to materials and documents which are essential to effectively challenging the lawfulness of their arrest and detention for any offence and (as the case may be) any further offences for which they are arrested whilst in custody, in accordance with *paragraphs 3.4(b), 15.0, 15.7A(c)* and *16.7A* of this Code;

  (vi) the maximum period for which they may be kept in police detention without being charged, when detention must be reviewed and when release is required;

  (vii) their right to medical assistance in accordance with *section 9* of this Code;

  (viii) their right, if they are prosecuted, to have access to the evidence in the case before their trial in accordance with the Criminal Procedure and Investigations Act 1996, the Attorney General's Guidelines on Disclosure, the common law and the Criminal Procedure Rules; and

(b) briefly setting out their other entitlements while in custody, by:
(i) mentioning:
- the provisions relating to the conduct of interviews;
- the circumstances in which an appropriate adult should be available to assist the detainee and their statutory rights to make representations whenever the need for their detention is reviewed;

(ii) listing the entitlements in this Code, concerning;
- reasonable standards of physical comfort;
- adequate food and drink;
- access to toilets and washing facilities, clothing, medical attention, and exercise when practicable;
- personal needs relating to health, hygiene and welfare concerning the provision of menstrual and any other health, hygiene and welfare products needed by the detainee in question and speaking about these in private to a member of the custody staff (see *paragraphs 9.3A* and *9.3B*).

See *Note 3A*.

C:3.2A The detainee must be given an opportunity to read the notice and shall be asked to sign the custody record to acknowledge receipt of the notice. Any refusal to sign must be recorded on the custody record.

C:3.3 Not used.

C:3.3A An 'easy read' illustrated version should also be provided if available (see *Note 3A*).

A-48a C:3.4(a)The custody officer shall:
- record the offence(s) that the detainee has been arrested for and the reason(s) for the arrest on the custody record. See *paragraph 10.3 and Code G paragraphs 2.2 and 4.3*;
- note on the custody record any comment the detainee makes in relation to the arresting officer's account but shall not invite comment. If the arresting officer is not physically present when the detainee is brought to a police station, the arresting officer's account must be made available to the custody officer remotely or by a third party on the arresting officer's behalf. If the custody officer authorises a person's detention, subject to *paragraph 1.8*, that officer must record the grounds for detention in the detainee's presence and at the same time, inform them of the grounds. The detainee must be informed of the grounds for their detention before they are questioned about any offence;
- note any comment the detainee makes in respect of the decision to detain them but shall not invite comment;
- not put specific questions to the detainee regarding their involvement in any offence, nor in respect of any comments they may make in response to the arresting officer's account or the decision to place them in detention. Such an exchange is likely to constitute an interview as in *paragraph 11.1A* and require the associated safeguards in section 11.

Note: This *sub-paragraph* also applies to any further offences and grounds for detention which come to light whilst the person is detained.

See *paragraph 11.13* in respect of unsolicited comments.

(b) Documents and materials which are essential to effectively challenging the lawfulness of the detainee's arrest and detention must be made available to the detainee or their solicitor. Documents and materials will be "essential" for this purpose if they are capable of undermining the reasons and grounds which make the detainee's arrest and detention *necessary*. The decision about whether particular documents or materials must be made available for the purpose of this requirement therefore rests with the custody officer who determines whether detention is necessary, in consultation with the investigating officer who has the knowledge of the documents and materials in a particular case necessary to inform that decision. A note should be made in the detainee's custody record of the *fact* that documents or materials have been made available under this sub-paragraph and when. The investigating officer should make a separate note of what is made available and how it is made available in a particular case. This sub-paragraph also applies (with modifications) for the purposes of *sections 15 (Reviews and extensions of detention)* and *16 (Charging detained persons)*. See *Note 3ZA* and *paragraphs 15.0* and *16.7A*.

A-48b C:3.5 The custody officer or other custody staff as directed by the custody officer shall:

(a) ask the detainee whether at this time, they:
(i) would like legal advice, see *paragraph 6.5*;
(ii) want someone informed of their detention, see *section 5*;

(b) ask the detainee to sign the custody record to confirm their decisions in respect of (a);

(c) determine whether the detainee:
(i) is, or might be, in need of medical treatment or attention, see *section 9*;

(ii) is a juvenile and/or vulnerable and therefore requires an appropriate adult (see *paragraphs 1.4, 1.5*, and *3.15*);
(iia) wishes to speak in private with a member of the custody staff who may be of the same sex about any matter concerning their personal needs relating to health, hygiene and welfare (see *paragraph 9.3A*);
(iii) requires:
- help to check documentation (see *paragraph 3.20*);
- an interpreter (see *paragraph 3.12 and Note 13B*).

(ca) if the detainee is a female aged 18 or over, ask if they require or are likely to require any menstrual products whilst they are in custody (see *paragraph 9.3B*). For girls under 18, see *paragraph 3.20A*;
(d) record the decision and actions taken as applicable in respect of (*c*) and (ca).

Where any duties under this paragraph have been carried out by custody staff at the direction of the custody officer, the outcomes shall, as soon as practicable, be reported to the custody officer who retains overall responsibility for the detainee's care and treatment and ensuring that it complies with this Code. See *Note 3F*.

C:3.6 When the needs mentioned in *paragraph 3.5(c)* are being determined, the custody officer is responsible for initiating an assessment to consider whether the detainee is likely to present specific risks to custody staff, any individual who may have contact with detainee (e.g. legal advisers, medical staff) or themselves. This risk assessment must include the taking of reasonable steps to establish the detainee's identity and to obtain information about the detainee that is relevant to their safe custody, security and welfare and risks to others. Such assessments should therefore always include a check on the Police National Computer (PNC), to be carried out as soon as practicable, to identify any risks that have been highlighted in relation to the detainee. Although such assessments are primarily the custody officer's responsibility, it may be necessary for them to consult and involve others, e.g. the arresting officer or an appropriate healthcare professional, see *paragraph 9.13*. Other records held by or on behalf of the police and other UK law enforcement authorities that might provide information relevant to the detainee's safe custody, security and welfare and risk to others and to confirming their identity should also be checked. Reasons for delaying the initiation or completion of the assessment must be recorded. **A-49**

C:3.7 Chief officers should ensure that arrangements for proper and effective risk assessments required by *paragraph 3.6* are implemented in respect of all detainees at police stations in their area.

C:3.8 Risk assessments must follow a structured process which clearly defines the categories of risk to be considered and the results must be incorporated in the detainee's custody record. The custody officer is responsible for making sure those responsible for the detainee's custody are appropriately briefed about the risks. If no specific risks are identified by the assessment, that should be noted in the custody record. See *Note 3E* and *paragraph 9.14*.

C:3.8A The content of any risk assessment and any analysis of the level of risk relating to the person's detention is not required to be shown or provided to the detainee or any person acting on behalf of the detainee. But information should not be withheld from any person acting on the detainee's behalf, for example, an appropriate adult, solicitor or interpreter, if to do so might put that person at risk.

C:3.9 The custody officer is responsible for implementing the response to any specific risk assessment, e.g.:
- reducing opportunities for self harm;
- calling an appropriate healthcare professional;
- increasing levels of monitoring or observation;
- reducing the risk to those who come into contact with the detainee.

See *Note 3E*.

C:3.10 Risk assessment is an ongoing process and assessments must always be subject to review if circumstances change.

C:3.11 If video cameras are installed in the custody area, notices shall be prominently displayed showing cameras are in use. Any request to have video cameras switched off shall be refused.

(B) Detained persons - special groups

C:3.12 If the detainee appears to be someone who does not speak or understand English or who has a hearing or speech impediment, the custody officer must ensure: **A-50**

(a) that without delay, arrangements (see *paragraph 13.1ZA*) are made for the detainee to have the assistance of an interpreter in the action under *paragraphs 3.1* to *3.5*. If the person appears to have a hearing or speech impediment, the reference to 'interpreter' includes appropriate assistance necessary to comply with *paragraphs 3.1* to *3.5*. See *paragraph 13.1C* if the detainee is in Wales. See *section 13* and *Note 13B*;

(b) that in addition to the continuing rights set out in *paragraph 3.1(a)(i)* to *(iv)*, the detainee is told clearly about their right to interpretation and translation;
(c) that the written notice given to the detainee in accordance with *paragraph 3.2* is in a language the detainee understands and includes the right to interpretation and translation together with information about the provisions in *section 13* and *Annex M*, which explain how the right applies (see *Note 3A*); and
(d) that if the translation of the notice is not available, the information in the notice is given through an interpreter and a written translation provided without undue delay.

C:3.12A If the detainee is a citizen of an independent Commonwealth country or a national of a foreign country, including the Republic of Ireland, the custody officer must ensure that in addition to the continuing rights set out in *paragraph 3.1(a)(i)* to *(iv)*, they are informed as soon as practicable about their rights of communication with their High Commission, Embassy or Consulate set out in *section 7*. This right must be included in the written notice given to the detainee in accordance with *paragraph 3.2*.

C:3.13 If the detainee is a juvenile, the custody officer must, if it is practicable, ascertain the identity of a person responsible for their welfare. That person:

- may be:
  - the parent or guardian;
  - if the juvenile is in local authority or voluntary organisation care, or is otherwise being looked after under the Children Act 1989, a person appointed by that authority or organisation to have responsibility for the juvenile's welfare;
  - any other person who has, for the time being, assumed responsibility for the juvenile's welfare.
- must be informed as soon as practicable that the juvenile has been arrested, why they have been arrested and where they are detained. This right is in addition to the juvenile's right in *section 5* not to be held incommunicado. See *Note 3C*.

C:3.14 If a juvenile is known to be subject to a court order under which a person or organisation is given any degree of statutory responsibility to supervise or otherwise monitor them, reasonable steps must also be taken to notify that person or organisation (the 'responsible officer'). The responsible officer will normally be a member of a Youth Offending Team, except for a curfew order which involves electronic monitoring when the contractor providing the monitoring will normally be the responsible officer.

C:3.15 If the detainee is a juvenile or a vulnerable person, the custody officer must, as soon as practicable, ensure that:

- the detainee is informed of the decision that an appropriate adult is required and the reason for that decision (see *paragraph 3.5(c)(ii)* and;
- the detainee is advised:
  - of the duties of the appropriate adult as described in *paragraph 1.7A*; and
  - that they can consult privately with the appropriate adult at any time.
- the appropriate adult, who in the case of a juvenile may or may not be a person responsible for their welfare, as in *paragraph 3.13*, is informed of:
  - the grounds for their detention;
  - their whereabouts; and
- the attendance of the appropriate adult at the police station to see the detainee is secured.

A-51 C:3.16 It is imperative that a person detained under the Mental Health Act 1983, section 135 or 136, be assessed as soon as possible within the permitted period of detention specified in that Act. A police station may only be used as a place of safety in accordance with The Mental Health Act 1983 (Places of Safety) Regulations 2017. If that assessment is to take place at the police station, an approved mental health professional and a registered medical practitioner shall be called to the station as soon as possible to carry it out. See *Note 9D*. The appropriate adult has no role in the assessment process and their presence is not required. Once the detainee has been assessed and suitable arrangements made for their treatment or care, they can no longer be detained under section 135 or 136. A detainee must be immediately discharged from detention if a registered medical practitioner, having examined them, concludes they are not mentally disordered within the meaning of the Act.

C:3.17 If the appropriate adult is:

- already at the police station, the provisions of *paragraphs 3.1* to *3.5* must be complied with in the appropriate adult's presence;
- not at the station when these provisions are complied with, they must be complied with again in the presence of the appropriate adult when they arrive,

and a copy of the notice given to the detainee in accordance with *paragraph 3.2*, shall also be given to the appropriate adult.

C:3.17A The custody officer must ensure that at the time the copy of the notice is given to the appropriate adult, or as soon as practicable thereafter, the appropriate adult is advised of the duties of the appropriate adult as described in *paragraph 1.7A*.

C:3.18 *Not used.*

C:3.19 If the detainee, or appropriate adult on the detainee's behalf, asks for a solicitor to be called to give legal advice, the provisions of *section 6* apply (see *paragraph 6.5A* and *Note 3H*).

C:3.20 If the detainee is blind, seriously visually impaired or unable to read, the custody officer shall make sure their solicitor, relative, appropriate adult or some other person likely to take an interest in them and not involved in the investigation is available to help check any documentation. When this Code requires written consent or signing the person assisting may be asked to sign instead, if the detainee prefers. This paragraph does not require an appropriate adult to be called solely to assist in checking and signing documentation for a person who is not a juvenile, or is not vulnerable (see *paragraph 3.15* and *Note 13C*).

C:3.20A The Children and Young Persons Act 1933, section 31, requires that arrangements must be made for ensuring that a girl under the age of 18, while detained in a police station, is under the care of a woman. The custody officer must ensure that the woman under whose care the girl is, makes the enquiries and provides the information concerning personal needs relating to their health, hygiene and welfare described in *paragraph 9.3A* and menstrual products described in *paragraph 9.3B*. See *Note 3G*. The section also requires that arrangements must be made for preventing any person under 18, while being detained in a police station, from associating with an adult charged with any offence, unless that adult is a relative or the adult is jointly charged with the same offence as the person under 18.

(C) Detained persons - Documentation

C:3.20B The grounds for a person's detention shall be recorded, in the person's presence if practicable. See *paragraph 1.8*. **A-52**

C:3.20C Action taken under *paragraphs 3.12* to *3.20A* shall be recorded.

(D) Persons attending a police station or elsewhere voluntarily

C:3.21 Anybody attending a police station or other location (see *paragraph 3.22* and *Note 3I*) voluntarily to assist police with the investigation of an offence may leave at will unless arrested. See *Notes 1A* and *1K*. The person may only be prevented from leaving at will if their arrest on suspicion of committing the offence is necessary in accordance with Code G. See *Code G Note 2G*. **A-53**

Action if arrest becomes necessary

(a) If during a person's voluntary attendance at a police station or other location it is decided for any reason that their arrest is necessary, they must: **A-53a**
- be informed at once that they are under arrest and of the grounds and reasons as required by *Code G*, and
- be brought before the custody officer at the police station where they are arrested or (as the case may be) at the police station to which they are taken after being arrested elsewhere. The custody officer is then responsible for making sure that a custody record is opened and that they are notified of their rights in the same way as other detainees as required by this Code.

Information to be given when arranging a voluntary interview:

(b) If the suspect's arrest is not necessary but they are cautioned as required in *section 10*, the person who, after describing the nature and circumstances of the suspected offence, gives the caution must at the same time, inform them that they are not under arrest and that they are not obliged to remain at the station or other location (see *paragraph 3.22* and *Note 3I*). The rights, entitlements and safeguards that apply to the conduct and recording of interviews with suspects are not diminished simply because the interview is arranged on a voluntary basis. For the purpose of arranging a voluntary interview (see *Code G Note 2F*), the duty of the interviewer reflects that of the custody officer with regard to detained suspects. As a result: **A-53b**

  (i) the requirement in *paragraph 3.5(c)(ii)* to determine whether a detained suspect requires an appropriate adult, help to check documentation or an interpreter shall apply equally to a suspect who has not been arrested; and

  (ii) the suspect must not be asked to give their informed consent to be interviewed until *after* they have been informed of the rights, entitlements and safeguards that apply to voluntary interviews. These are set out in *paragraph 3.21A* and the interviewer is responsible for ensuring that the suspect is so informed and for explaining these rights, entitlements and safeguards.

C:3.21A The interviewer must inform the suspect that the purpose of the voluntary interview is to question them to obtain evidence about their involvement or suspected involvement in the of- **A-54** fence(s) described when they were cautioned and told that they were not under arrest. The interviewer shall then inform the suspect that the following matters will apply if they agree to the voluntary interview proceeding:

(a) Their right to information about the offence(s) in question by providing sufficient information to enable them to understand the nature of any such offence(s) and why they are suspected of committing it. This is in order to allow for the effective exercise of the rights of the defence as required by *paragraph 11.1A*. It applies whether or not they ask for legal advice and includes any further offences that come to light and are pointed out during the voluntary interview and for which they are cautioned.

(b) Their right to free (see *Note 3J*) legal advice by:

(i) explaining that they may obtain free and independent legal advice if they want it, and that this includes the right to speak with a solicitor on the telephone and to have the solicitor present during the interview;

(ii) asking if they want legal advice and recording their reply; and

(iii) if the person requests advice, securing its provision before the interview by contacting the Defence Solicitor Call Centre and explaining that the time and place of the interview will be arranged to enable them to obtain advice and that the interview will be delayed until they have received the advice unless, in accordance with *paragraph 6.6(c)* (Nominated solicitor not available and duty solicitor declined) or *paragraph 6.6(d)* (Change of mind), an officer of the rank of inspector or above agrees to the interview proceeding; or

(iv) if the person declines to exercise the right, asking them why and recording any reasons given (see *Note 6K*).

Note: When explaining the right to legal advice and the arrangements, the interviewer must take care not to indicate, except to answer a direct question, that the time taken to arrange and complete the voluntary interview might be reduced if:

- the suspect does not ask for legal advice or does not want a solicitor present when they are interviewed; or
- the suspect asks for legal advice or (as the case may be) asks for a solicitor to be present when they are interviewed, but changes their mind and agrees to be interviewed without waiting for a solicitor.

(c) Their right, if in accordance with *paragraph 3.5(c)(ii)* the interviewer determines:

(i) that they are a juvenile or are vulnerable; or

(ii) that they need help to check documentation (see *paragraph 3.20*),

to have the appropriate adult present or (as the case may be) to have the necessary help to check documentation; and that the interview will be delayed until the presence of the appropriate adult or the necessary help, is secured.

(d) If they are a juvenile or vulnerable and do not want legal advice, their appropriate adult has the right to ask for a solicitor to attend if this would be in their best interests and the appropriate adult must be so informed. In this case, action to secure the provision of advice if so requested by their appropriate adult will be taken without delay in the same way as if requested by the person (see *sub-paragraph (b)(iii)*). However, they cannot be forced to see the solicitor if they are adamant that they do not wish to do so (see *paragraphs 3.19* and *6.5A*).

(e) Their right to an interpreter, if in accordance with, *paragraphs 3.5(c)(ii)* and *3.12*, the interviewer determines that they require an interpreter and that if they require an interpreter, making the necessary arrangements in accordance with *paragraph 13.1ZA* and that the interview will be delayed to make the arrangements.

(f) That interview will be arranged for a time and location (see *paragraph 3.22* and *Note 3I*) that enables:

(i) the suspect's rights described above to be fully respected; and

(ii) the whole of the interview to be recorded using an authorised recording device in accordance with Code E (Code of Practice on Audio recording of interviews with suspects) or (as the case may be) Code F (Code of Practice on visual recording with sound of interviews with suspects); and

(g) That their agreement to take part in the interview also signifies their agreement for that interview to be audio-recorded or (as the case may be) visually recorded with sound.

A-55 C:3.21B The provision by the interviewer of factual information described in *paragraph 3.21A* and, if asked by the suspect, further such information, does not constitute an interview for the purpose of this Code and *when that information is provided*:

(a) the interviewer must remind the suspect about the caution as required in *section 10* but must not *invite* comment about the offence or put specific questions to the suspect regarding their involvement in any offence, nor in respect of any comments they may make when given the information. Such an exchange is itself likely to constitute an interview as in *paragraph 11.1A* and require the associated interview safeguards in *section 11*.

(b) Any comment the suspect makes when the information is given which might be relevant to the offence, must be recorded and dealt with in accordance with *paragraph 11.13*.

(c) The suspect must be given a notice summarising the matters described in *paragraph 3.21A* and which includes the arrangements for obtaining legal advice. If a specific notice is not available, the notice given to detained suspects with references to detention-specific requirements and information redacted, may be used.

(d) For juvenile and vulnerable suspects (see *paragraphs 1.4* and *1.5*):
 (i) the information must be provided or (as the case may be) provided again, together with the notice, in the presence of the appropriate adult;
 (ii) if cautioned in the absence of the appropriate adult, the caution must be repeated in the appropriate adult's presence (see *paragraph 10.12*);
 (iii) the suspect must be informed of the decision that an appropriate is required and the reason (see *paragraph 3.5(c)(ii)*;
 (iv) the suspect *and* the appropriate adult shall be advised:
  - that the duties of the appropriate adult include giving advice and assistance in accordance with *paragraphs 1.7A* and *11.17*; and
  - that they can consult privately at any time.
 (v) their informed agreement to be interviewed voluntarily must be sought and given in the *presence* of the appropriate adult and for a juvenile, the agreement of a parent or guardian of the juvenile is also required.

C:3.22 If the other location mentioned in *paragraph 3.21* is any place or premises for which the interviewer requires the informed consent of the suspect and/or occupier (if different) to remain, for example, the suspect's home (see *Note 3I*), then the references that the person is 'not obliged to remain' and that they 'may leave at will' mean that the suspect and/or occupier (if different) may also withdraw their consent and require the interviewer to leave.

Commencement of voluntary interview - general

C:3.22A Before asking the suspect any questions about their involvement in the offence they are suspected of committing, the interviewing officer must ask them to confirm that they agree to the interview proceeding. This confirmation shall be recorded in the interview record made in accordance with *section 11* of this Code (written record) or Code E or Code F. **A-56**

Documentation

C:3.22B Action taken under *paragraphs 3.21A* to *3.21B* shall be recorded. The record shall include the date time and place the action was taken, who was present and anything said to or by the suspect and to or by those present. **A-57**

C:3.23 *Not* used.

C:3.24 *Not* used.

(E) Persons answering street bail

C:3.25 When a person is answering street bail, the custody officer should link any documentation held in relation to arrest with the custody record. Any further action shall be recorded on the custody record in accordance with *paragraphs 3.20B* and *3.20C* above. **A-58**

(F) Requirements for suspects to be informed of certain rights

C:3.26 The provisions of this section identify the information which must be given to suspects who have been cautioned in accordance with *section 10* of this Code according to whether or not they have been arrested and detained. It includes information required by EU Directive 2012/13 on the right to information in criminal proceedings. If a complaint is made by or on behalf of such a suspect that the information and (as the case may be) access to records and documents has not been provided as required, the matter shall be reported to an inspector to deal with as a complaint for the purposes of *paragraph 9.2*, or *paragraph 12.9* if the challenge is made during an interview. This would include, for example: **A-59**

(a) in the case of a detained suspect:
 - not informing them of their rights (see *paragraph 3.1*);
 - not giving them a copy of the Notice (see *paragraph 3.2(a)*);
 - not providing an opportunity to read the notice (see *paragraph 3.2A*);
 - not providing the required information (see *paragraphs 3.2(a)*, *3.12(b)* and, *3.12A*;

- not allowing access to the custody record (see *paragraph 2.4*);
- not providing a translation of the Notice (see *paragraph 3.12(c)* and *(d)*); and

(b) in the case of a suspect who is not detained:
- not informing them of their rights or providing the required information (see *paragraphs 3.21(b)* to *3.21B*).

Notes for Guidance

A-60 *C:3ZA For the purposes of paragraphs 3.4(b)* and *15.0*:

(a) *Investigating officers are responsible for bringing to the attention of the officer who is responsible for authorising the suspect's detention or (as the case may be) continued detention (before or after charge), any documents and materials in their possession or control which appear to undermine the need to keep the suspect in custody. In accordance with Part IV of PACE, this officer will be either the custody officer, the officer reviewing the need for detention before or after charge (PACE, section 40), or the officer considering the need to extend detention without charge from 24 to 36 hours (PACE, section 42) who is then responsible for determining, which, if any, of those documents and materials are capable of undermining the need to detain the suspect and must therefore be made available to the suspect or their solicitor.*

(b) *the way in which documents and materials are 'made available', is a matter for the investigating officer to determine on a case by case basis and having regard to the nature and volume of the documents and materials involved. For example, they may be made available by supplying a copy or allowing supervised access to view. However, for view only access, it will be necessary to demonstrate that sufficient time is allowed for the suspect and solicitor to view and consider the documents and materials in question.*

C:3A For access to currently available notices, including 'easy-read' versions, see https://www.gov.uk/guidance/notice-of-rights-and-entitlements-a-persons-rights-in-police-detention.

C:3B Not used.

C:3C If the juvenile is in local authority or voluntary organisation care but living with their parents or other adults responsible for their welfare, although there is no legal obligation to inform them, they should normally be contacted, as well as the authority or organisation unless they are suspected of involvement in the offence concerned. Even if the juvenile is not living with their parents, consideration should be given to informing them.

C:3D The right to consult the Codes of Practice does not entitle the person concerned to delay unreasonably any necessary investigative or administrative action whilst they do so. Examples of action which need not be delayed unreasonably include:

- *procedures requiring the provision of breath, blood or urine specimens under the Road Traffic Act 1988 or the Transport and Works Act 1992;*
- *searching detainees at the police station;*
- *taking fingerprints, footwear impressions or non-intimate samples without consent for evidential purposes.*

C:3E The Detention and Custody Authorised Professional Practice (APP) produced by the College of Policing (see http://www.app.college.police.uk) provides more detailed guidance on risk assessments and identifies key risk areas which should always be considered. See Home Office *Circular 34/2007 (Safety of solicitors and probationary representatives at police stations).*

C:3F A custody officer or other officer who, in accordance with this Code, allows or directs the carrying out of any task or action relating to a detainee's care, treatment, rights and entitlements to another officer or any other person, must be satisfied that the officer or person concerned is suitable, trained and competent to carry out the task or action in question.

C:3G Guidance for police officers and police staff on the operational application of section 31 of the Children and Young Persons Act 1933 has been published by the College of Policing and is available at: https://www.app.college.police.uk/app-content/detention-and-custody-2/detainee-care/children-and-young-persons/#girls.

C:3H The purpose of the provisions at paragraphs 3.19 and *6.5A* is to protect the rights of juvenile and vulnerable persons who may not understand the significance of what is said to them. They should always be given an opportunity, when an appropriate adult is called to the police station, to consult privately with a solicitor in the absence of the appropriate adult if they want.

C:3I An interviewer who is not sure, or has any doubt, about whether a place or location elsewhere than a police station is suitable for carrying out a voluntary interview, particularly in the case of a juvenile or vulnerable person, should consult an officer of the rank of sergeant or above for advice. Detailed guidance for police officers and staff concerning the conduct and recording of voluntary interviews is being developed by the College of Policing. It follows a review of operational issues arising when voluntary interviews need to be arranged. The aim is to ensure the effective implementation of the safeguards in paragraphs 3.21 to 3.22B particularly concerning the rights of suspects, the location for the interview and supervision.

C:3J For voluntary interviews conducted by non-police investigators, the provision of legal advice is set out by the Legal Aid Agency at paragraph 9.54 of the 2017 Standard Crime Contract Specification. This is published at https://www.gov.uk/government/publications/standard-crime-contract-2017 and the rules mean that a non-police interviewer who does not have their own statutory power of arrest would have to inform the suspect that they have a right to seek legal advice if they wish, but payment would be a matter for them to arrange with the solicitor.

C:4 Detainee's property

(A) Action

C:4.1 The custody officer is responsible for: A-61

(a) ascertaining what property a detainee:

(i) has with them when they come to the police station, whether on:

- arrest or re-detention on answering to bail;
- commitment to prison custody on the order or sentence of a court;
- lodgement at the police station with a view to their production in court from prison custody;
- transfer from detention at another station or hospital;
- detention under the Mental Health Act 1983, section 135 or 136;
- remand into police custody on the authority of a court.

(ii) might have acquired for an unlawful or harmful purpose while in custody;

(b) the safekeeping of any property taken from a detainee which remains at the police station.

The custody officer may search the detainee or authorise their being searched to the extent they consider necessary, provided a search of intimate parts of the body or involving the removal of more than outer clothing is only made as in *Annex A*. A search may only be carried out by an officer of the same sex as the detainee. See *Note 4A* and *Annex L*.

C:4.2 Subject to *paragraph 4.3A*, detainees may retain clothing and personal effects at their own risk unless the custody officer considers they may use them to cause harm to themselves or others, interfere with evidence, damage property, effect an escape or they are needed as evidence. In this event the custody officer may withhold such articles as they consider necessary and must tell the detainee why.

C:4.3 Personal effects are those items a detainee may lawfully need, use or refer to while in detention but do not include cash and other items of value.

C:4.3A For the purposes of *paragraph 4.2*, the reference to clothing and personal effects shall be treated as including menstrual and any other health, hygiene and welfare products needed by the detainee in question (see *paragraphs 9.3A* and *9.3B*) and a decision to withhold any such products must be subject to a further specific risk assessment.

(B) Documentation

C:4.4 It is a matter for the custody officer to determine whether a record should be made of the property a detained person has with him or had taken from him on arrest. Any record made is not required to be kept as part of the custody record but the custody record should be noted as to where such a record exists and that record shall be treated as being part of the custody record for the purpose of this and any other Code of Practice (see *paragraphs 2.4, 2.4A and 2.5*). Whenever a record is made the detainee shall be allowed to check and sign the record of property as correct. Any refusal to sign shall be recorded. A-61a

C:4.5 If a detainee is not allowed to keep any article of clothing or personal effects, the reason must be recorded.

Notes for Guidance

C:4A PACE, Section 54(1) and paragraph 4.1 require a detainee to be searched when it is clear the custody officer will have continuing duties in relation to that detainee or when that detainee's behaviour or offence makes an inventory appropriate. They do not require every detainee to be searched, e.g. if it is clear a person will only be detained for a short period and is not to be placed in a cell, the custody officer may decide not to search them. In such a case the custody record will be endorsed 'not searched', paragraph 4.4 will not apply, and the detainee will be invited to sign the entry. If the detainee refuses, the custody officer will be obliged to ascertain what property they have in accordance with paragraph 4.1. A-61b

C:4B Paragraph 4.4 does not require the custody officer to record on the custody record property in the detainee's possession on arrest if, by virtue of its nature, quantity or size, it is not practicable to remove it to the police station.

C:4C Paragraph 4.4 does not require items of clothing worn by the person to be recorded unless withheld by the custody officer as in paragraph 4.2.

C:5 Right not to be held incommunicado

(A) Action

C:5.1 Subject to *paragraph 5.7B*, any person arrested and held in custody at a police station or A-62 other premises may, on request, have one person known to them or likely to take an interest in their welfare informed at public expense of their whereabouts as soon as practicable. If the person cannot be contacted the detainee may choose up to two alternatives. If they cannot be contacted, the person in charge of detention or the investigation has discretion to allow further attempts until the information has been conveyed. See *Notes 5C* and *5D.*

C:5.2 The exercise of the above right in respect of each person nominated may be delayed only in accordance with *Annex B.*

C:5.3 The above right may be exercised each time a detainee is taken to another police station.

C:5.4 If the detainee agrees, they may at the custody officer's discretion, receive visits from friends, family or others likely to take an interest in their welfare, or in whose welfare the detainee has an interest. See *Note 5B.*

C:5.5 If a friend, relative or person with an interest in the detainee's welfare enquires about their whereabouts, this information shall be given if the suspect agrees and *Annex B* does not apply. See *Note 5D.*

C:5.6 The detainee shall be given writing materials, on request, and allowed to telephone one person for a reasonable time, see *Notes 5A* and *5E.* Either or both of these privileges may be denied or delayed if an officer of inspector rank or above considers sending a letter or making a telephone call may result in any of the consequences in:

(a) *Annex B paragraphs 1* and *2* and the person is detained in connection with an indictable offence;
(b) *Not used.*

Nothing in this paragraph permits the restriction or denial of the rights in *paragraphs 5.1* and *6.1.*

C:5.7 Before any letter or message is sent, or telephone call made, the detainee shall be informed that what they say in any letter, call or message (other than in a communication to a solicitor) may be read or listened to and may be given in evidence. A telephone call may be terminated if it is being abused. The costs can be at public expense at the custody officer's discretion.

C:5.7A Any delay or denial of the rights in this section should be proportionate and should last no longer than necessary.

C:5.7B In the case of a person in police custody for specific purposes and periods in accordance with a direction under the Crime (Sentences) Act 1997, Schedule 1 (productions from prison etc.), the exercise of the rights in this section shall be subject to any additional conditions specified in the direction for the purpose of regulating the detainee's contact and communication with others whilst in police custody. See *Note 5F.*

(B) Documentation

A-62a C:5.8 A record must be kept of any:

(a) request made under this section and the action taken;
(b) letters, messages or telephone calls made or received or visit received;
(c) refusal by the detainee to have information about them given to an outside enquirer. The detainee must be asked to countersign the record accordingly and any refusal recorded.

Notes for Guidance

A-62b *C:5A A person may request an interpreter to interpret a telephone call or translate a letter.*

C:5B At the custody officer's discretion and subject to the detainee's consent, visits should be allowed when possible, subject to having sufficient personnel to supervise a visit and any possible hindrance to the investigation.

C:5C If the detainee does not know anyone to contact for advice or support or cannot contact a friend or relative, the custody officer should bear in mind any local voluntary bodies or other organisations who might be able to help. Paragraph 6.1 applies if legal advice is required.

C:5D In some circumstances it may not be appropriate to use the telephone to disclose information under paragraphs 5.1 and 5.5.

C:5E The telephone call at paragraph 5.6 is in addition to any communication under paragraphs 5.1 and 6.1.

C:5F Prison Service Instruction 26/2012 (Production of Prisoners at the Request of Warranted Law Enforcement Agencies) *provides detailed guidance and instructions for police officers and Governors and Directors of Prisons regarding applications for prisoners to be transferred to police custody and their safe custody and treatment while in police custody.*

C:6 Right to legal advice

(A) Action

A-63 C:6.1 Unless *Annex B* applies, all detainees must be informed that they may at any time consult and communicate privately with a solicitor, whether in person, in writing or by telephone, and that free independent legal advice is available. See *paragraph 3.1, Notes 1I, 6B and 6J.*

C:6.2 Not used.

C:6.3 A poster advertising the right to legal advice must be prominently displayed in the charging area of every police station. See *Note 6H.*

C:6.4 No police officer should, at any time, do or say anything with the intention of dissuading any person who is entitled to legal advice in accordance with this Code, whether or not they have been arrested and are detained, from obtaining legal advice. See *Note 6ZA.*

C:6.5 The exercise of the right of access to legal advice may be delayed only as in *Annex B.* Whenever legal advice is requested, and unless *Annex B* applies, the custody officer must act without delay to secure the provision of such advice. If the detainee has the right to speak to a solicitor in person but declines to exercise the right the officer should point out that the right includes the right to speak with a solicitor on the telephone. If the detainee continues to waive this right, or a detainee whose right to free legal advice is limited to telephone advice from the Criminal Defence Service (CDS) Direct (see *Note 6B*) declines to exercise that right, the officer should ask them why and any reasons should be recorded on the custody record or the interview record as appropriate. Reminders of the right to legal advice must be given as in *paragraphs 3.5, 11.2, 15.4, 16.4, 16.5, 2B of Annex A, 3 of Annex K* and *5 of Annex M* of this Code and Code D, *paragraphs 3.17(ii)* and *6.3.* Once it is clear a detainee does not want to speak to a solicitor in person or by telephone they should cease to be asked their reasons. See *N ote 6K.*

C:6.5A In the case of a person who is a juvenile or is vulnerable, an appropriate adult should consider whether legal advice from a solicitor is required. If such a detained person wants to exercise the right to legal advice, the appropriate action should be taken and should not be delayed until the appropriate adult arrives. If the person indicates that they do not want legal advice, the appropriate adult has the right to ask for a solicitor to attend if this would be in the best interests of the person and must be so informed. In this case, action to secure the provision of advice if so requested by the appropriate adult shall be taken without delay in the same way as when requested by the person. However, the person cannot be forced to see the solicitor if they are adamant that they do not wish to do so.

C:6.6 A detainee who wants legal advice may not be interviewed or continue to be interviewed until they have received such advice unless: **A-64**

(a) *Annex B* applies, when the restriction on drawing adverse inferences from silence in *Annex C* will apply because the detainee is not allowed an opportunity to consult a solicitor; or

(b) an officer of superintendent rank or above has reasonable grounds for believing that:

  (i) the consequent delay might:
  - lead to interference with, or harm to, evidence connected with an offence;
  - lead to interference with, or physical harm to, other people;
  - lead to serious loss of, or damage to, property;
  - lead to alerting other people suspected of having committed an offence but not yet arrested for it;
  - hinder the recovery of property obtained in consequence of the commission of an offence.

  See *Note 6A*

  (ii) when a solicitor, including a duty solicitor, has been contacted and has agreed to attend, awaiting their arrival would cause unreasonable delay to the process of investigation.

  Note: In these cases the restriction on drawing adverse inferences from silence in *Annex C* will apply because the detainee is not allowed an opportunity to consult a solicitor.

(c) the solicitor the detainee has nominated or selected from a list:

  (i) cannot be contacted;

  (ii) has previously indicated they do not wish to be contacted; or

  (iii) having been contacted, has declined to attend; and
  - the detainee has been advised of the Duty Solicitor Scheme but has declined to ask for the duty solicitor;
  - in these circumstances the interview may be started or continued without further delay provided an officer of inspector rank or above has agreed to the interview proceeding.

  Note: The restriction on drawing adverse inferences from silence in *Annex C* will not apply because the detainee is allowed an opportunity to consult the duty solicitor;

(d) the detainee changes their mind about wanting legal advice or (as the case may be) about wanting a solicitor present at the interview and states that they no longer wish to speak to a solicitor. In these circumstances, the interview may be started or continued without delay provided that:

(i) an officer of inspector rank or above:
- speaks to the detainee to enquire about the reasons for their change of mind (see *Note 6K*), and
- makes, or directs the making of, reasonable efforts to ascertain the solicitor's expected time of arrival and to inform the solicitor that the suspect has stated that they wish to change their mind and the reason (if given);

(ii) the detainee's reason for their change of mind (if given) and the outcome of the action in (i) are recorded in the custody record;

(iii) the detainee, after being informed of the outcome of the action in (i) above, confirms in writing that they want the interview to proceed without speaking or further speaking to a solicitor or (as the case may be) without a solicitor being present and do not wish to wait for a solicitor by signing an entry to this effect in the custody record;

(iv) an officer of inspector rank or above is satisfied that it is proper for the interview to proceed in these circumstances and:
- gives authority in writing for the interview to proceed and, if the authority is not recorded in the custody record, the officer must ensure that the custody record shows the date and time of the authority and where it is recorded, and
- takes, or directs the taking of, reasonable steps to inform the solicitor that the authority has been given and the time when the interview is expected to commence and records or causes to be recorded, the outcome of this action in the custody record.

(v) When the interview starts and the interviewer reminds the suspect of their right to legal advice (see *paragraph 11.2*, Code E *paragraph 4.5* and Code F *paragraph 4.5*), the interviewer shall then ensure that the following is recorded in the written interview record or the interview record made in accordance with Code E or F:
- confirmation that the detainee has changed their mind about wanting legal advice or (as the case may be) about wanting a solicitor present and the reasons for it if given;
- the fact that authority for the interview to proceed has been given and, subject to *paragraph 2.6A*, the name of the authorising officer;
- that if the solicitor arrives at the station before the interview is completed, the detainee will be so informed without delay and *a break will be taken* to allow them to speak to the solicitor if they wish, unless *paragraph 6.6(a)* applies, and
- that at any time during the interview, the detainee may again ask for legal advice and that if they do, a break will be taken to allow them to speak to the solicitor, unless *paragraph 6.6(a), (b), or (c)* applies.

Note: In these circumstances, the restriction on drawing adverse inferences from silence in *Annex C* will not apply because the detainee is allowed an opportunity to consult a solicitor if they wish.

A-65 C:6.7 If *paragraph 6.6(a)* applies, where the reason for authorising the delay ceases to apply, there may be no further delay in permitting the exercise of the right in the absence of a further authorisation unless *paragraph 6.6(b), (c)* or *(d)* applies. If *paragraph 6.6(b)(i)* applies, once sufficient information has been obtained to avert the risk, questioning must cease until the detainee has received legal advice unless *paragraph 6.6(a), (b)(ii), (c)* or *(d)* applies.

C:6.8 A detainee who has been permitted to consult a solicitor shall be entitled on request to have the solicitor present when they are interviewed unless one of the exceptions in *paragraph 6.6* applies.

C:6.9 The solicitor may only be required to leave the interview if their conduct is such that the interviewer is unable properly to put questions to the suspect. See *Notes 6D* and *6E.*

C:6.10 If the interviewer considers a solicitor is acting in such a way, they will stop the interview and consult an officer not below superintendent rank, if one is readily available, and otherwise an officer not below inspector rank not connected with the investigation. After speaking to the solicitor, the officer consulted will decide if the interview should continue in the presence of that solicitor. If they decide it should not, the suspect will be given the opportunity to consult another solicitor before the interview continues and that solicitor given an opportunity to be present at the interview. *See Note 6E.*

C:6.11 The removal of a solicitor from an interview is a serious step and, if it occurs, the officer of superintendent rank or above who took the decision will consider if the incident should be reported to the Solicitors Regulatory Authority. If the decision to remove the solicitor has been taken by an officer below superintendent rank, the facts must be reported to an officer of superintendent rank or above, who will similarly consider whether a report to the Solicitors Regulatory Authority would be appropriate. When the solicitor concerned is a duty solicitor, the report should be both to the Solicitors Regulatory Authority and to the Legal Aid Agency.

C:6.12 "Solicitor" in this Code means:
- a solicitor who holds a current practising certificate;
- an accredited or probationary representative included on the register of representatives maintained by the Legal Aid Agency.

C:6.12A An accredited or probationary representative sent to provide advice by, and on behalf of, a solicitor shall be admitted to the police station for this purpose unless an officer of inspector rank or above considers such a visit will hinder the investigation and directs otherwise. Hindering the investigation does not include giving proper legal advice to a detainee as in *Note 6D*. Once admitted to the police station, *paragraphs 6.6* to *6.10* apply.

C:6.13 In exercising their discretion under *paragraph 6.12A*, the officer should take into account in particular:

- whether:
  - the identity and status of an accredited or probationary representative have been satisfactorily established;
  - they are of suitable character to provide legal advice, e.g. a person with a criminal record is unlikely to be suitable unless the conviction was for a minor offence and not recent.
- any other matters in any written letter of authorisation provided by the solicitor on whose behalf the person is attending the police station. See *Note 6F*.

C:6.14 If the inspector refuses access to an accredited or probationary representative or a decision is taken that such a person should not be permitted to remain at an interview, the inspector must notify the solicitor on whose behalf the representative was acting and give them an opportunity to make alternative arrangements. The detainee must be informed and the custody record noted.

C:6.15 If a solicitor arrives at the station to see a particular person, that person must, unless *Annex B* applies, be so informed whether or not they are being interviewed and asked if they would like to see the solicitor. This applies even if the detainee has declined legal advice or, having requested it, subsequently agreed to be interviewed without receiving advice. The solicitor's attendance and the detainee's decision must be noted in the custody record.

(B) Documentation

C:6.16 Any request for legal advice and the action taken shall be recorded. **A-66**

C: 6.17 A record shall be made in the interview record if a detainee asks for legal advice and an interview is begun either in the absence of a solicitor or their representative, or they have been required to leave an interview.

Notes for Guidance

C:6ZA No police officer or police staff shall indicate to any suspect, except to answer a direct question, that the period for which they are liable to be detained, or if not detained, the time taken to complete the interview, might be reduced: **A-67**

- *if they do not ask for legal advice or do not want a solicitor present when they are interviewed; or*
- *if they have asked for legal advice or (as the case may be) asked for a solicitor to be present when they are interviewed but change their mind and agree to be interviewed without waiting for a solicitor.*

C:6A In considering if paragraph 6.6(b) applies, the officer should, if practicable, ask the solicitor for an estimate of how long it will take to come to the station and relate this to the time detention is permitted, the time of day (i.e. whether the rest period under paragraph 12.2 is imminent) and the requirements of other investigations. If the solicitor is on their way or is to set off immediately, it will not normally be appropriate to begin an interview before they arrive. If it appears necessary to begin an interview before the solicitor's arrival, they should be given an indication of how long the police would be able to wait before 6.6(b) applies so there is an opportunity to make arrangements for someone else to provide legal advice.

C:6B A detainee has a right to free legal advice and to be represented by a solicitor. This Note for Guidance explains the arrangements which enable detainees to obtain legal advice. An outline of these arrangements is also included in the Notice of Rights and Entitlements given to detainees in accordance with paragraph 3.2. The arrangements also apply, with appropriate modifications, to persons attending a police station or other location (see paragraph 3.22 and *Notes 3I* and *3J*) voluntarily who are cautioned prior to being interviewed. See *paragraph 3.21.*

When a detainee asks for free legal advice, the Defence Solicitor Call Centre (DSCC) must be informed of the request.

Free legal advice will be limited to telephone advice provided by CDS Direct if a detainee is:

- *detained for a non-imprisonable offence;*
- *arrested on a bench warrant for failing to appear and being held for production at court (except where the solicitor has clear documentary evidence available that would result in the client being released from custody);*
- *arrested for drink driving (driving/in charge with excess alcohol, failing to provide a specimen, driving/in charge whilst unfit through drink), or*
- *detained in relation to breach of police or court bail conditions*

unless one or more exceptions apply, in which case the DSCC should arrange for advice to be given by a solicitor at the police station, for example:

- *the police want to interview the detainee or carry out an eye-witness identification procedure;*
- *the detainee needs an appropriate adult;*
- *the detainee is unable to communicate over the telephone;*
- *the detainee alleges serious misconduct by the police;*
- *the investigation includes another offence not included in the list,*
- *the solicitor to be assigned is already at the police station.*

When free advice is not limited to telephone advice, a detainee can ask for free advice from a solicitor they know or if they do not know a solicitor or the solicitor they know cannot be contacted, from the duty solicitor.

To arrange free legal advice, the police should telephone the DSCC. The call centre will decide whether legal advice should be limited to telephone advice from CDS Direct, or whether a solicitor known to the detainee or the duty solicitor should speak to the detainee.

When a detainee wants to pay for legal advice themselves:

- *the DSCC will contact a solicitor of their choice on their behalf;*
- *they may, when free advice is only available by telephone from CDS Direct, still speak to a solicitor of their choice on the telephone for advice, but the solicitor would not be paid by legal aid and may ask the person to pay for the advice;*
- *they should be given an opportunity to consult a specific solicitor or another solicitor from that solicitor's firm. If this solicitor is not available, they may choose up to two alternatives. If these alternatives are not available, the custody officer has discretion to allow further attempts until a solicitor has been contacted and agreed to provide advice;*
- *they are entitled to a private consultation with their chosen solicitor on the telephone or the solicitor may decide to come to the police station;*
- *If their chosen solicitor cannot be contacted, the DSCC may still be called to arrange free legal advice.*

Apart from carrying out duties necessary to implement these arrangements, an officer must not advise the suspect about any particular firm of solicitors.

C:6B1 Not used.

C:6B2 Not used.

C:6C Not used.

A-67a *C:6D The solicitor's only role in the police station is to protect and advance the legal rights of their client. On occasions this may require the solicitor to give advice which has the effect of the client avoiding giving evidence which strengthens a prosecution case. The solicitor may intervene in order to seek clarification, challenge an improper question to their client or the manner in which it is put, advise their client not to reply to particular questions, or if they wish to give their client further legal advice. Paragraph 6.9 only applies if the solicitor's approach or conduct prevents or unreasonably obstructs proper questions being put to the suspect or the suspect's response being recorded. Examples of unacceptable conduct include answering questions on a suspect's behalf or providing written replies for the suspect to quote.*

C:6E An officer who takes the decision to exclude a solicitor must be in a position to satisfy the court the decision was properly made. In order to do this they may need to witness what is happening.

C:6F If an officer of at least inspector rank considers a particular solicitor or firm of solicitors is persistently sending probationary representatives who are unsuited to provide legal advice, they should inform an officer of at least superintendent rank, who may wish to take the matter up with the Solicitors Regulation Authority.

C:6G Subject to the constraints of Annex B, a solicitor may advise more than one client in an investigation if they wish. Any question of a conflict of interest is for the solicitor under their professional code of conduct. If, however, waiting for a solicitor to give advice to one client may lead to unreasonable delay to the interview with another, the provisions of paragraph 6.6(b) may apply.

C:6H In addition to a poster in English, a poster or posters containing translations into Welsh, the main minority ethnic languages and the principal European languages should be displayed wherever they are likely to be helpful and it is practicable to do so.

C:6I Not used.

C:6J Whenever a detainee exercises their right to legal advice by consulting or communicating with a solicitor, they must be allowed to do so in private. This right to consult or communicate in private is fundamental. If the requirement for privacy is compromised because what is said or written by the detainee or solicitor for the purpose of giving and receiving legal advice is overheard, listened to, or read by others without the informed consent of the detainee, the right will effectively have been denied. When a detainee speaks to a solicitor on the telephone, they should be allowed to do so in private unless this is impractical because of the design and layout of the custody area or the location of telephones. However, the normal expectation should be that facilities will be available, unless they are being used, at all police stations to enable detainees to speak in private to a solicitor either face to face or over the telephone.

C:6K A detainee is not obliged to give reasons for declining legal advice and should not be pressed to do so.

C:7 Citizens of independent Commonwealth countries or foreign nationals

(A) Action

A-68 C:7.1 A detainee who is a citizen of an independent Commonwealth country or a national of a foreign country, including the Republic of Ireland, has the right, upon request, to communicate at any time with the appropriate High Commission, Embassy or Consulate. That detainee must be informed as soon as practicable of this right and asked if they want to have their High Commission, Embassy or Consulate told of their whereabouts and the grounds for their detention. Such a request should be acted upon as soon as practicable. See *Note 7A*.

C:7.2 A detainee who is a citizen of a country with which a bilateral consular convention or agreement is in force requiring notification of arrest must also be informed that subject to *paragraph 7.4*, notification of their arrest will be sent to the appropriate High Commission, Embassy or Consulate as soon as practicable, whether or not they request it. A list of the countries to which this requirement currently applies and contact details for the relevant High Commissions, Embassies and Consulates can be obtained from the Consular Directorate of the Foreign and Commonwealth Office (FCO) as follows:

- from the FCO web pages:
  - *https://gov.uk/government/publications/table-of-consular-conventions-and-mandatory-notification-obligations*, and
  - *https://www.gov.uk/government/publications/foreign-embassies-in-the-uk*
- by telephone to 020 7008 3100,
- by email to *fcocorrespondence@fco.gov.uk.*
- by letter to the Foreign and Commonwealth Office, King Charles Street, London, SW1A 2AH.

C:7.3 Consular officers may, if the detainee agrees, visit one of their nationals in police detention to talk to them and, if required, to arrange for legal advice. Such visits shall take place out of the hearing of a police officer.

C:7.4 Notwithstanding the provisions of consular conventions, if the detainee claims that they are a refugee or have applied or intend to apply for asylum, the custody officer must ensure that UK Visas and Immigration (UKVI) (formerly the UK Border Agency) is informed as soon as practicable of the claim. UKVI will then determine whether compliance with relevant international obligations requires notification of the arrest to be sent and will inform the custody officer as to what action police need to take.

(B) Documentation

C:7.5 A record shall be made: **A-68a**

- when a detainee is informed of their rights under this section and of any requirement in paragraph 7.2;
- of any communications with a High Commission, Embassy or Consulate, and
- of any communications with UKVI about a detainee's claim to be a refugee or to be seeking asylum and the resulting action taken by police.

Note for Guidance

C:7A The exercise of the rights in this section may not be interfered with even though Annex B applies. **A-68b**

C:8 Conditions of detention

(A) Action

C:8.1 So far as it is practicable, not more than one detainee should be detained in each cell. See *Note 8C*. **A-69**

C:8.2 Cells in use must be adequately heated, cleaned and ventilated. They must be adequately lit, subject to such dimming as is compatible with safety and security to allow people detained overnight to sleep. No additional restraints shall be used within a locked cell unless absolutely necessary and then only restraint equipment, approved for use in that force by the chief officer, which is reasonable and necessary in the circumstances having regard to the detainee's demeanour and with a view to ensuring their safety and the safety of others. If a detainee is deaf or a vulnerable person, particular care must be taken when deciding whether to use any form of approved restraints.

C:8.3 Blankets, mattresses, pillows and other bedding supplied shall be of a reasonable standard and in a clean and sanitary condition. See *Note 8A*.

C:8.4 Access to toilet and washing facilities must be provided. This must take account of the dignity of the detainee. *See Note 8D*.

C:8.5 If it is necessary to remove a detainee's clothes for the purposes of investigation, for hygiene, health reasons or cleaning, removal shall be conducted with proper regard to the dignity, sensitivity and vulnerability of the detainee and replacement clothing of a reasonable standard of comfort and cleanliness shall be provided. A detainee may not be interviewed unless adequate clothing has been offered.

C:8.6 At least two light meals and one main meal should be offered in any 24-hour period. See *Note 8B*. Drinks should be provided at meal times and upon reasonable request between meals. Whenever necessary, advice shall be sought from the appropriate healthcare professional, see *Note 9A*, on medical and dietary matters. As far as practicable, meals provided shall offer a varied diet and meet any specific dietary needs or religious beliefs the detainee may have. The detainee may, at the custody officer's discretion, have meals supplied by their family or friends at their expense. See *Note 8A*.

C:8.7 Brief outdoor exercise shall be offered daily if practicable.

C:8.8 A juvenile shall not be placed in a police cell unless no other secure accommodation is available and the custody officer considers it is not practicable to supervise them if they are not placed in a cell or that a cell provides more comfortable accommodation than other secure accommodation in the station. A juvenile may not be placed in a cell with a detained adult.

(B) Documentation

A-69a C:8.9 A record must be kept of replacement clothing and meals offered.

C:8.10 If a juvenile is placed in a cell, the reason must be recorded.

C:8.11 The use of any restraints on a detainee whilst in a cell, the reasons for it and, if appropriate, the arrangements for enhanced supervision of the detainee whilst so restrained, shall be recorded. See *paragraph 3.9*.

Notes for Guidance

A-69b *C:8A The provisions in paragraph 8.3 and 8.6 respectively are of particular importance in the case of a person likely to be detained for an extended period. In deciding whether to allow meals to be supplied by family or friends, the custody officer is entitled to take account of the risk of items being concealed in any food or package and the officer's duties and responsibilities under food handling legislation.*

C:8B Meals should, so far as practicable, be offered at recognised meal times, or at other times that take account of when the detainee last had a meal.

C:8C The Detention and Custody Authorised Professional Practice (APP) produced by the College of Policing (see http://www.app.college.police.uk) provides more detailed guidance on matters concerning detainee healthcare and treatment and associated forensic issues which should be read in conjunction with sections 8 and 9 of this Code.

C:8D In cells subject to CCTV monitoring, privacy in the toilet area should be ensured by any appropriate means and detainees should be made aware of this when they are placed in the cell. If a detainee or appropriate adult on their behalf, expresses doubts about the effectiveness of the means used, reasonable steps should be taken to allay those doubts, for example, by explaining or demonstrating the means used.

C:9 Care and treatment of detained persons

(A) General

A-70 C:9.1 Nothing in this section prevents the police from calling an appropriate healthcare professional to examine a detainee for the purposes of obtaining evidence relating to any offence in which the detainee is suspected of being involved. See *Notes 9A and 8C*.

C:9.2 If a complaint is made by, or on behalf of, a detainee about their treatment since their arrest, or it comes to notice that a detainee may have been treated improperly, a report must be made as soon as practicable to an officer of inspector rank or above not connected with the investigation. If the matter concerns a possible assault or the possibility of the unnecessary or unreasonable use of force, an appropriate healthcare professional must also be called as soon as practicable.

C:9.3 Subject to *paragraph 9.6* in the case of a person to whom The Mental Health Act 1983 (Places of Safety) Regulations 2017 apply, detainees should be visited at least every hour. If no reasonably foreseeable risk was identified in a risk assessment, see *paragraphs 3.6* to *3.10*, there is no need to wake a sleeping detainee. Those suspected of being under the influence of drink or drugs or both or of having swallowed drugs, see *Note 9CA*, or whose level of consciousness causes concern must, subject to any clinical directions given by the appropriate healthcare professional, see *paragraph 9.13*:

- be visited and roused at least every half hour;
- have their condition assessed as in *Annex H*;
- and clinical treatment arranged if appropriate.

See *Notes 9B, 9C* and *9H*

C:9.3A As soon as practicable after arrival at the police station, each detainee must be given an opportunity to speak in private with a member of the custody staff who if they wish may be of the same sex as the detainee (see *paragraph 1.13(c)*), about any matter concerning the detainee's personal needs relating to their health, hygiene and welfare that might affect or concern them whilst in custody. If the detainee wishes to take this opportunity, the necessary arrangements shall be made as soon as practicable. In the case of a juvenile or vulnerable person, the appropriate adult must be involved in accordance with *paragraph 3.17* and in the case of a girl under 18, see *paragraph 3.20A* (see *Note 9CB*). **A-71**

C:9.3B Each female detainee aged 18 or over shall be asked in private if possible and at the earliest opportunity, if they require or are likely to require any menstrual products whilst they are in custody. They must be told that they will be provided free of charge and that replacement products are available. At the custody officer's discretion, detainees may have menstrual products supplied by their family or friends at their expense (see *Note 9CC*). For girls under 18, see *paragraph 3.20A*.

C:9.4 When arrangements are made to secure clinical attention for a detainee, the custody officer must make sure all relevant information which might assist in the treatment of the detainee's condition is made available to the responsible healthcare professional. This applies whether or not the healthcare professional asks for such information. Any officer or police staff with relevant information must inform the custody officer as soon as practicable.

(B) Clinical treatment and attention

C:9.5 The custody officer must make sure a detainee receives appropriate clinical attention as soon as reasonably practicable if the person: **A-72**

(a) appears to be suffering from physical illness; or
(b) is injured; or
(c) appears to be suffering from a mental disorder; or
(d) appears to need clinical attention.

C:9.5A This applies even if the detainee makes no request for clinical attention and whether or not they have already received clinical attention elsewhere. If the need for attention appears urgent, e.g. when indicated as in *Annex H*, the nearest available healthcare professional or an ambulance must be called immediately.

C:9.5B The custody officer must also consider the need for clinical attention as set out in *Note 9C* in relation to those suffering the effects of alcohol or drugs.

C:9.6 *Paragraph 9.5* is not meant to prevent or delay the transfer to a hospital if necessary of a person detained under the Mental Health Act 1983, sections 135 and 136, as amended by the Policing and Crime Act 2017. See *Note 9D*. When an assessment under that Act is to take place at a police station (see *paragraph 3.16*) the custody officer must also ensure that in accordance with The Mental Health Act 1983 (Places of Safety) Regulations 2017, a health professional is present and available to the person throughout the period they are detained at the police station and that at the welfare of the detainee is checked by the health professional at least once every thirty minutes and any appropriate action for the care and treatment of the detainee taken.

C:9.7 If it appears to the custody officer, or they are told, that a person brought to a station under arrest may be suffering from an infectious disease or condition, the custody officer must take reasonable steps to safeguard the health of the detainee and others at the station. In deciding what action to take, advice must be sought from an appropriate healthcare professional. See *Note 9E*. The custody officer has discretion to isolate the person and their property until clinical directions have been obtained.

C:9.8 If a detainee requests a clinical examination, an appropriate healthcare professional must be called as soon as practicable to assess the detainee's clinical needs. If a safe and appropriate care plan cannot be provided, the appropriate healthcare professional's advice must be sought. The detainee may also be examined by a medical practitioner of their choice at their expense. **A-73**

C:9.9 If a detainee is required to take or apply any medication in compliance with clinical directions prescribed before their detention, the custody officer must consult the appropriate healthcare professional before the use of the medication. Subject to the restrictions in *paragraph 9.10*, the custody officer is responsible for the safekeeping of any medication and for making sure the detainee is given the opportunity to take or apply prescribed or approved medication. Any such consultation and its outcome shall be noted in the custody record.

C:9.10 No police officer may administer or supervise the self-administration of medically prescribed controlled drugs of the types and forms listed in the Misuse of Drugs Regulations 2001, Schedule 2 or 3. A detainee may only self-administer such drugs under the personal supervision of the registered medical practitioner authorising their use or other appropriate healthcare professional. The custody officer may supervise the self-administration of, or authorise other custody staff to supervise the self-administration of, drugs listed in Schedule 4 or 5 if the officer has consulted the appropriate healthcare professional authorising their use and both are satisfied self-administration will not expose the detainee, police officers or anyone else to the risk of harm or injury.

C:9.11 When appropriate healthcare professionals administer drugs or authorise the use of other medications, supervise their self-administration or consult with the custody officer about allowing self-administration of drugs listed in Schedule 4 or 5, it must be within current medicines legislation and the scope of practice as determined by their relevant statutory regulatory body.

C:9.12 If a detainee has in their possession, or claims to need, medication relating to a heart condition, diabetes, epilepsy or a condition of comparable potential seriousness then, even though *paragraph 9.5* may not apply, the advice of the appropriate healthcare professional must be obtained.

C:9.13 Whenever the appropriate healthcare professional is called in accordance with this section to examine or treat a detainee, the custody officer shall ask for their opinion about:

- any risks or problems which police need to take into account when making decisions about the detainee's continued detention;
- when to carry out an interview if applicable; and
- the need for safeguards.

C:9.14 When clinical directions are given by the appropriate healthcare professional, whether orally or in writing, and the custody officer has any doubts or is in any way uncertain about any aspect of the directions, the custody officer shall ask for clarification. It is particularly important that directions concerning the frequency of visits are clear, precise and capable of being implemented. See *Note 9F.*

(C) Documentation

A-74 C:9.15 A record must be made in the custody record of:

(a) the arrangements made for an examination by an appropriate healthcare professional under *paragraph 9.2* and of any complaint reported under that paragraph together with any relevant remarks by the custody officer;
(b) any arrangements made in accordance with *paragraph 9.5*;
(c) any request for a clinical examination under *paragraph 9.8* and any arrangements made in response;
(d) the injury, ailment, condition or other reason which made it necessary to make the arrangements in *(a)* to *(c)*; See *Note 9G.*
(e) any clinical directions and advice, including any further clarifications, given to police by a healthcare professional concerning the care and treatment of the detainee in connection with any of the arrangements made in *(a)* to *(c)*; See *Notes 9E* and *9F.*
(f) if applicable, the responses received when attempting to rouse a person using the procedure in *Annex H.* See *Note 9H.*

C:9.16 If a healthcare professional does not record their clinical findings in the custody record, the record must show where they are recorded. See *Note 9G.* However, information which is necessary to custody staff to ensure the effective ongoing care and well being of the detainee must be recorded openly in the custody record, see *paragraph 3.8* and *Annex G, paragraph 7.*

C:9.17 Subject to the requirements of *Section 4,* the custody record shall include:

- a record of all medication a detainee has in their possession on arrival at the police station;
- a note of any such medication they claim to need but do not have with them.

Notes for Guidance

A-75 *C:9A A "healthcare professional" means a clinically qualified person working within the scope of practice as determined by their relevant statutory regulatory body. Whether a healthcare professional is 'appropriate' depends on the circumstances of the duties they carry out at the time.*

C:9B Whenever possible, detained juveniles and vulnerable persons should be visited more frequently.

C:9C A detainee who appears drunk or behaves abnormally may be suffering from illness, the effects of drugs or may have sustained injury, particularly a head injury which is not apparent. A detainee needing or dependent on certain drugs, including alcohol, may experience harmful effects within a short time of being deprived of their supply. In these circumstances, when there is any doubt, police should always act urgently to call an appropriate healthcare professional or an ambulance. Paragraph 9.5 does not apply to minor ailments or injuries which do not need attention. However, all such ailments or injuries must be recorded in the custody record and any doubt must be resolved in favour of calling the appropriate healthcare professional.

C:9CA Paragraph 9.3 would apply to a person in police custody by order of a magistrates' court under the Criminal Justice Act 1988, section 152 (as amended by the Drugs Act 2005, section 8) to facilitate the recovery of evidence after being charged with drug possession or drug trafficking and suspected of having swallowed drugs. In the case of the healthcare needs of a person who has swallowed drugs, the custody officer, subject to any clinical directions, should consider the necessity for rousing every half hour. This does not negate the need for regular visiting of the suspect in the cell.

C:9CB Matters concerning personal needs to which paragraph 9.3A applies include any requirement for menstrual products incontinence products and colostomy appliances, where these needs have not previously been identified (see *paragraph 3.5(c)*). It also enables adult women to speak in private to a female officer about their requirements for menstrual products if they decline to respond to the more direct enquiry envisaged under *paragraph 9.3B*. This contact should be facilitated at any time, where possible.

C:9CC Detailed guidance for police officers and staff concerning menstruating female detainees in police custody is included in the College of Policing Authorised Professional Practice (APP).

C:9D Except as allowed under The Mental Health Act 1983 (Places of Safety) Regulations 2017, a police station must not be used as a place of safety for persons detained under section 135 or 136 of that Act. Chapter 16 of the Mental Health Act 1983 Code of Practice (as revised), provides more detailed guidance about arranging assessments under the Mental Health Act and transferring detainees from police stations to other places of safety. Additional guidance in relation to amendments made to the Mental Health Act in 2017 are published at https://www.gov.uk/government/publications/mental-health-act-1983-implementing-changes-to-police-powers.

C:9E It is important to respect a person's right to privacy and information about their health must be kept confidential and only disclosed with their consent or in accordance with clinical advice when it is necessary to protect the detainee's health or that of others who come into contact with them.

C:9F The custody officer should always seek to clarify directions that the detainee requires constant observation or supervision and should ask the appropriate healthcare professional to explain precisely what action needs to be taken to implement such directions.

C:9G Paragraphs 9.15 and 9.16 do not require any information about the cause of any injury, ailment or condition to be recorded on the custody record if it appears capable of providing evidence of an offence.

C:9H The purpose of recording a person's responses when attempting to rouse them using the procedure in Annex H is to enable any change in the individual's consciousness level to be noted and clinical treatment arranged if appropriate.

C:10 Cautions

(A) When a caution must be given

C:10.1 A person whom there are grounds to suspect of an offence, see *Note 10A*, must be cautioned before any questions about an offence, or further questions if the answers provide the grounds for suspicion, are put to them if either the suspect's answers or silence, (i.e. failure or refusal to answer or answer satisfactorily) may be given in evidence to a court in a prosecution. A person need not be cautioned if questions are for other necessary purposes, e.g.: **A-76**

(a) solely to establish their identity or ownership of any vehicle;
(b) to obtain information in accordance with any relevant statutory requirement, see *paragraph 10.9*;
(c) in furtherance of the proper and effective conduct of a search, e.g. to determine the need to search in the exercise of powers of stop and search or to seek co-operation while carrying out a search; or
(d) to seek verification of a written record as in *paragraph 11.13*.
(e) *Not used.*

C:10.2 Whenever a person not under arrest is initially cautioned, or reminded that they are under caution, that person must at the same time be told they are not under arrest and must be informed of the provisions of *paragraphs 3.21* to *3.21B* which explain that they need to agree to be interviewed, how they may obtain legal advice according to whether they are at a police station or elsewhere and the other rights and entitlements that apply to a voluntary interview. See *Note 10C*.

C:10.3 A person who is arrested, or further arrested, must be informed at the time if practicable or, if not, as soon as it becomes practicable thereafter, that they are under arrest and of the grounds and reasons for their arrest, see *paragraph 3.4, Note 10B* and *Code G, paragraphs 2.2 and 4.3*.

C:10.4 As required by *Code G, section 3*, a person who is arrested, or further arrested, must also be cautioned unless:

(a) it is impracticable to do so by reason of their condition or behaviour at the time;
(b) they have already been cautioned immediately prior to arrest as in *paragraph 10.1*.

(B) Terms of the cautions

C:10.5 The caution which must be given on: **A-77**

(a) arrest; or
(b) all other occasions before a person is charged or informed they may be prosecuted; see *section 16*,

should, unless the restriction on drawing adverse inferences from silence applies, see *Annex C*, be in the following terms:

"You do not have to say anything. But it may harm your defence if you do not mention when questioned something which you later rely on in Court. Anything you do say may be given in evidence."

Where the use of the Welsh Language is appropriate, a constable may provide the caution directly in Welsh in the following terms:

"Does dim rhaid i chi ddweud dim byd. Ond gall niweidio eich amddiffyniad os na fyddwch chi'n sôn, wrth gael eich holi, am rywbeth y byddwch chi'n dibynnu arno nes ymlaen yn y Llys. Gall unrhyw beth yr ydych yn ei ddweud gael ei roi fel tystiolaeth."

See *Note 10G*

C:10.6 *Annex C, paragraph 2* sets out the alternative terms of the caution to be used when the restriction on drawing adverse inferences from silence applies.

C:10.7 Minor deviations from the words of any caution given in accordance with this Code do not constitute a breach of this Code, provided the sense of the relevant caution is preserved. See *Note 10D.*

C:10.8 After any break in questioning under caution, the person being questioned must be made aware they remain under caution. If there is any doubt the relevant caution should be given again in full when the interview resumes. See *Note 10E.*

C:10.9 When, despite being cautioned, a person fails to co-operate or to answer particular questions which may affect their immediate treatment, the person should be informed of any relevant consequences and that those consequences are not affected by the caution. Examples are when a person's refusal to provide:

- their name and address when charged may make them liable to detention;
- particulars and information in accordance with a statutory requirement, e.g. under the Road Traffic Act 1988, may amount to an offence or may make the person liable to a further arrest.

(C) Special warnings under the Criminal Justice and Public Order Act 1994, sections 36 and 37

A-78 C:10.10 When a suspect interviewed at a police station or authorised place of detention after arrest fails or refuses to answer certain questions, or to answer satisfactorily, after due warning, see *Note 10F*, a court or jury may draw such inferences as appear proper under the Criminal Justice and Public Order Act 1994, sections 36 and 37. Such inferences may only be drawn when:

(a) the restriction on drawing adverse inferences from silence, see *Annex C*, does not apply; and
(b) the suspect is arrested by a constable and fails or refuses to account for any objects, marks or substances, or marks on such objects found:
  - on their person;
  - in or on their clothing or footwear;
  - otherwise in their possession; or
  - in the place they were arrested;
(c) the arrested suspect was found by a constable at a place at or about the time the offence for which that officer has arrested them is alleged to have been committed, and the suspect fails or refuses to account for their presence there.

When the restriction on drawing adverse inferences from silence applies, the suspect may still be asked to account for any of the matters in (*b*) or (*c*) but the special warning described in *paragraph 10.11* will not apply and must not be given.

C:10.11 For an inference to be drawn when a suspect fails or refuses to answer a question about one of these matters or to answer it satisfactorily, the suspect must first be told in ordinary language:

(a) what offence is being investigated;
(b) what fact they are being asked to account for;
(c) this fact may be due to them taking part in the commission of the offence;
(d) a court may draw a proper inference if they fail or refuse to account for this fact; and
(e) a record is being made of the interview and it may be given in evidence if they are brought to trial.

(D) Juveniles and vulnerable persons

A-79 C:10.11A The information required in paragraph 10.11 must not be given to a suspect who is a juvenile or a vulnerable person unless the appropriate adult is present.

C:10.12 If a juvenile or a vulnerable person is cautioned in the absence of the appropriate adult, the caution must be repeated in the appropriate adult's presence.

C:10.12A *Not used.*

(E) Documentation

A-80 C:10.13 A record shall be made when a caution is given under this section, either in the interviewer's report book or in the interview record.

Notes for Guidance

A-81 *C:10A There must be some reasonable, objective grounds for the suspicion, based on known facts or information which are relevant to the likelihood the offence has been committed and the person to be questioned committed it.*

C:10B An arrested person must be given sufficient information to enable them to understand that they have been deprived of their liberty and the reason they have been arrested, e.g. when a person is arrested on suspicion of committing an offence they must be informed of the suspected offence's nature, when and where it was committed. The suspect must also be informed of the reason or reasons why the arrest is considered necessary. Vague or technical language should be avoided.

C:10C The restriction on drawing inferences from silence, see Annex C, paragraph 1, does not apply to a person who has not been detained and who therefore cannot be prevented from seeking legal advice if they want, see paragraph 3.21.

C:10D If it appears a person does not understand the caution, the person giving it should explain it in their own words.

C:10E It may be necessary to show to the court that nothing occurred during an interview break or between interviews which influenced the suspect's recorded evidence. After a break in an interview or at the beginning of a subsequent interview, the interviewer should summarise the reason for the break and confirm this with the suspect.

C:10F The Criminal Justice and Public Order Act 1994, sections 36 and 37 apply only to suspects who have been arrested by a constable or an officer of Revenue and Customs and are given the relevant warning by the police or Revenue and Customs officer who made the arrest or who is investigating the offence. They do not apply to any interviews with suspects who have not been arrested.

C:10G Nothing in this Code requires a caution to be given or repeated when informing a person not under arrest they may be prosecuted for an offence. However, a court will not be able to draw any inferences under the Criminal Justice and Public Order Act 1994, section 34, if the person was not cautioned.

C:11 Interviews - general

(A) Action

A-82 C:11.1A An interview is the questioning of a person regarding their involvement or suspected involvement in a criminal offence or offences which, under paragraph 10.1, must be carried out under caution. Before a person is interviewed, they and, if they are represented, their solicitor must be given sufficient information to enable them to understand the nature of any such offence, and why they are suspected of committing it (see *paragraphs 3.4(a)* and *10.3*), in order to allow for the effective exercise of the rights of the defence. However, whilst the information must always be sufficient for the person to understand the nature of any offence (see *Note 11ZA*), this does not require the disclosure of details at a time which might prejudice the criminal investigation. The decision about what needs to be disclosed for the purpose of this requirement therefore rests with the investigating officer who has sufficient knowledge of the case to make that decision. The officer who discloses the information shall make a record of the information disclosed and when it was disclosed. This record may be made in the interview record, in the officer's report book or other form provided for this purpose. Procedures under the Road Traffic Act 1988, section 7 or the Transport and Works Act 1992, section 31 do not constitute interviewing for the purpose of this Code.

C:11.1 Following a decision to arrest a suspect, they must not be interviewed about the relevant offence except at a police station or other authorised place of detention, unless the consequent delay would be likely to:

(a) lead to:
- interference with, or harm to, evidence connected with an offence;
- interference with, or physical harm to, other people; or
- serious loss of, or damage to, property;

(b) lead to alerting other people suspected of committing an offence but not yet arrested for it; or

(c) hinder the recovery of property obtained in consequence of the commission of an offence.

Interviewing in any of these circumstances shall cease once the relevant risk has been averted or the necessary questions have been put in order to attempt to avert that risk.

C:11.2 Immediately prior to the commencement or re-commencement of any interview at a police station or other authorised place of detention, the interviewer should remind the suspect of their entitlement to free legal advice and that the interview can be delayed for legal advice to be obtained, unless one of the exceptions in *paragraph 6.6* applies. It is the interviewer's responsibility to make sure all reminders are recorded in the interview record.

C:11.3 *Not used.*

A-82a C:11.4 At the beginning of an interview the interviewer, after cautioning the suspect, see *section 10*, shall put to them any significant statement or silence which occurred in the presence and hearing of a police officer or other police staff before the start of the interview and which have not been put to the suspect in the course of a previous interview. See *Note 11A*. The interviewer shall ask the suspect whether they confirm or deny that earlier statement or silence and if they want to add anything.

C:11.4A A significant statement is one which appears capable of being used in evidence against the suspect, in particular a direct admission of guilt. A significant silence is a failure or refusal to answer a question or answer satisfactorily when under caution, which might, allowing for the restriction on drawing adverse inferences from silence, see *Annex C*, give rise to an inference under the Criminal Justice and Public Order Act 1994, Part III.

C:11.5 No interviewer may try to obtain answers or elicit a statement by the use of oppression. Except as in *paragraph 10.9*, no interviewer shall indicate, except to answer a direct question, what action will be taken by the police if the person being questioned answers questions, makes a statement or refuses to do either. If the person asks directly what action will be taken if they answer questions, make a statement or refuse to do either, the interviewer may inform them what action the police propose to take provided that action is itself proper and warranted.

C:11.6 The interview or further interview of a person about an offence with which that person has not been charged or for which they have not been informed they may be prosecuted, must cease when:

(a) the officer in charge of the investigation is satisfied all the questions they consider relevant to obtaining accurate and reliable information about the offence have been put to the suspect, this includes allowing the suspect an opportunity to give an innocent explanation and asking questions to test if the explanation is accurate and reliable, e.g. to clear up ambiguities or clarify what the suspect said;

(b) the officer in charge of the investigation has taken account of any other available evidence; and

(c) the officer in charge of the investigation, or in the case of a detained suspect, the custody officer, see *paragraph 16.1*, reasonably believes there is sufficient evidence to provide a realistic prospect of conviction for that offence. See *Note 11B*.

This paragraph does not prevent officers in revenue cases or acting under the confiscation provisions of the Criminal Justice Act 1988 or the Drug Trafficking Act 1994 from inviting suspects to complete a formal question and answer record after the interview is concluded.

(B) Interview records

A-83 C:11.7(a)n accurate record must be made of each interview, whether or not the interview takes place at a police station.

(b) The record must state the place of interview, the time it begins and ends, any interview breaks and, subject to *paragraph 2.6A*, the names of all those present; and must be made on the forms provided for this purpose or in the interviewer's report book or in accordance with Codes of Practice E or F.

(c) Any written record must be made and completed during the interview, unless this would not be practicable or would interfere with the conduct of the interview, and must constitute either a verbatim record of what has been said or, failing this, an account of the interview which adequately and accurately summarises it.

C:11.8 If a written record is not made during the interview it must be made as soon as practicable after its completion.

C:11.9 Written interview records must be timed and signed by the maker.

C:11.10 If a written record is not completed during the interview the reason must be recorded in the interview record.

C:11.11 Unless it is impracticable, the person interviewed shall be given the opportunity to read the interview record and to sign it as correct or to indicate how they consider it inaccurate. If the person interviewed cannot read or refuses to read the record or sign it, the senior interviewer present shall read it to them and ask whether they would like to sign it as correct or make their mark or to indicate how they consider it inaccurate. The interviewer shall certify on the interview record itself what has occurred. See *Note 11E*.

C:11.12 If the appropriate adult or the person's solicitor is present during the interview, they should also be given an opportunity to read and sign the interview record or any written statement taken down during the interview.

C:11.13 A record shall be made of any comments made by a suspect, including unsolicited comments, which are outside the context of an interview but which might be relevant to the offence. Any such record must be timed and signed by the maker. When practicable the suspect shall be given the opportunity to read that record and to sign it as correct or to indicate how they consider it inaccurate. See *Note 11E*.

C:11.14 Any refusal by a person to sign an interview record when asked in accordance with this Code must itself be recorded.

(C) Juveniles and vulnerable persons

C:11.15 A juvenile or vulnerable person must not be interviewed regarding their involvement or suspected involvement in a criminal offence or offences, or asked to provide or sign a written statement under caution or record of interview, in the absence of the appropriate adult unless *paragraphs 11.1* or *11.18* to *11.20* apply. See *Note 11C*. **A-84**

C:11.16 Juveniles may only be interviewed at their place of education in exceptional circumstances and only when the principal or their nominee agrees. Every effort should be made to notify the parent(s) or other person responsible for the juvenile's welfare and the appropriate adult, if this is a different person, that the police want to interview the juvenile and reasonable time should be allowed to enable the appropriate adult to be present at the interview. If awaiting the appropriate adult would cause unreasonable delay, and unless the juvenile is suspected of an offence against the educational establishment, the principal or their nominee can act as the appropriate adult for the purposes of the interview.

C:11.17 If an appropriate adult is present at an interview, they shall be informed:

- that they are not expected to act simply as an observer; and
- that the purpose of their presence is to:
  - ˜ advise the person being interviewed;
  - ˜ observe whether the interview is being conducted properly and fairly; and
  - ˜ facilitate communication with the person being interviewed.

See *paragraph 1.7A*.

C:11.17A The appropriate adult may be required to leave the interview if their conduct is such that the interviewer is unable properly to put questions to the suspect. This will include situations where the appropriate adult's approach or conduct prevents or unreasonably obstructs proper questions being put to the suspect or the suspect's responses being recorded (see *Note 11F*). If the interviewer considers an appropriate adult is acting in such a way, they will stop the interview and consult an officer not below superintendent rank, if one is readily available, and otherwise an officer not below inspector rank not connected with the investigation. After speaking to the appropriate adult, the officer consulted must remind the adult that their role under *paragraph 11.17* does not allow them to obstruct proper questioning and give the adult an opportunity to respond. The officer consulted will then decide if the interview should continue without the attendance of that appropriate adult. If they decide it should, another appropriate adult must be obtained before the interview continues, unless the provisions of *paragraph 11.18* below apply. **A-84a**

(D) Vulnerable suspects - urgent interviews at police stations

C:11.18 The following interviews may take place only if an officer of superintendent rank or above considers delaying the interview will lead to the consequences in *paragraph 11.1(a)* to *(c)*, and is satisfied the interview would not significantly harm the person's physical or mental state (see *Annex G*): **A-85**

(a) an interview of a detained juvenile or vulnerable person without the appropriate adult being present (see *Note 11C*);

(b) an interview of anyone detained other than in (a) who appears unable to:
- appreciate the significance of questions and their answers; or
- understand what is happening because of the effects of drink, drugs or any illness, ailment or condition;

(c) an interview, without an interpreter having been arranged, of a detained person whom the custody officer has determined requires an interpreter (see *paragraphs 3.5(c)(ii)* and *3.12*) which is carried out by an interviewer speaking the suspect's own language or (as the case may be) otherwise establishing effective communication which is sufficient to enable the necessary questions to be asked and answered in order to avert the consequences. See *paragraphs 13.2* and *13.5*.

C:11.19 These interviews may not continue once sufficient information has been obtained to avert the consequences in *paragraph 11.1(a)* to *(c)*.

C:11.20 A record shall be made of the grounds for any decision to interview a person under *paragraph 11.18*.

(E) Conduct and recording of Interviews at police stations - use of live link

C:11.21 When a suspect in police detention is interviewed using a live link by a police officer who **A-86** is not at the police station where the detainee is held, the provisions of this section that govern the conduct and making a written record of that interview, shall be subject to *paragraph 12.9B* of this Code.

(F) Witnesses

A-87 C:11.22 The provisions of this Code and Codes E and F which govern the conduct and recording of interviews do not apply to interviews with, or taking statements from, witnesses.

Notes for Guidance

A-88 *C:11ZA The requirement in paragraph 11.1A for a suspect to be given sufficient information about the offence applies prior to the interview and whether or not they are legally represented. What is sufficient will depend on the circumstances of the case, but it should normally include, as a minimum, a description of the facts relating to the suspected offence that are known to the officer, including the time and place in question. This aims to avoid suspects being confused or unclear about what they are supposed to have done and to help an innocent suspect to clear the matter up more quickly.*

C:11A Paragraph 11.4 does not prevent the interviewer from putting significant statements and silences to a suspect again at a later stage or a further interview.

C:11B The Criminal Procedure and Investigations Act 1996 Code of Practice, paragraph 3.5 states 'In conducting an investigation, the investigator should pursue all reasonable lines of enquiry, whether these point towards or away from the suspect. What is reasonable will depend on the particular circumstances.' Interviewers should keep this in mind when deciding what questions to ask in an interview.

C:11C Although juveniles or vulnerable persons are often capable of providing reliable evidence, they may, without knowing or wishing to do so, be particularly prone in certain circumstances to providing information that may be unreliable, misleading or self-incriminating. Special care should always be taken when questioning such a person, and the appropriate adult should be involved if there is any doubt about a person's age, mental state or capacity. Because of the risk of unreliable evidence it is also important to obtain corroboration of any facts admitted whenever possible. Because of the risks, which the presence of the appropriate adult is intended to minimise, officers of superintendent rank or above should exercise their discretion under paragraph 11.18(a) to authorise the commencement of an interview in the appropriate adult's absence only in exceptional cases, if it is necessary to avert one or more of the specified risks in *paragraph 11.1.*

C:11D Juveniles should not be arrested at their place of education unless this is unavoidable. When a juvenile is arrested at their place of education, the principal or their nominee must be informed.

C:11E Significant statements described in paragraph 11.4 will always be relevant to the offence and must be recorded. When a suspect agrees to read records of interviews and other comments and sign them as correct, they should be asked to endorse the record with, e.g. 'I agree that this is a correct record of what was said' and add their signature. If the suspect does not agree with the record, the interviewer should record the details of any disagreement and ask the suspect to read these details and sign them to the effect that they accurately reflect their disagreement. Any refusal to sign should be recorded.

C:11F The appropriate adult may intervene if they consider it is necessary to help the suspect understand any question asked and to help the suspect to answer any question. Paragraph 11.17A only applies if the appropriate adult's approach or conduct prevents or unreasonably obstructs proper questions being put to the suspect or the suspect's response being recorded. Examples of unacceptable conduct include answering questions on a suspect's behalf or providing written replies for the suspect to quote. An officer who takes the decision to exclude an appropriate adult must be in a position to satisfy the court the decision was properly made. In order to do this they may need to witness what is happening and give the suspect's solicitor (if they have one) who witnessed what happened, an opportunity to comment.

C:12 Interviews in police stations

(A) Action

When interviewer and suspect are present at the same police station

A-89 C:12.1 If a police officer wants to interview or conduct enquiries which require the presence of a detainee, the custody officer is responsible for deciding whether to deliver the detainee into the officer's custody. An investigating officer who is given custody of a detainee takes over responsibility for the detainee's care and safe custody for the purposes of this Code until they return the detainee to the custody officer when they must report the manner in which they complied with the Code whilst having custody of the detainee.

C:12.2 Except as below, in any period of 24 hours a detainee must be allowed a continuous period of at least 8 hours for rest, free from questioning, travel or any interruption in connection with the investigation concerned. This period should normally be at night or other appropriate time which takes account of when the detainee last slept or rested. If a detainee is arrested at a police station after going there voluntarily, the period of 24 hours runs from the time of their arrest and not the time of arrival at the police station. The period may not be interrupted or delayed, except:

(a) when there are reasonable grounds for believing not delaying or interrupting the period would:
  (i) involve a risk of harm to people or serious loss of, or damage to, property;
  (ii) delay unnecessarily the person's release from custody; or
  (iii) otherwise prejudice the outcome of the investigation;
(b) at the request of the detainee, their appropriate adult or legal representative;
(c) when a delay or interruption is necessary in order to:
  (i) comply with the legal obligations and duties arising under section 15; or
  (ii) to take action required under *section 9* or in accordance with medical advice.

If the period is interrupted in accordance with (*a*), a fresh period must be allowed. Interruptions under (*b*) and (*c*) do not require a fresh period to be allowed.

C:12.3 Before a detainee is interviewed, the custody officer, in consultation with the officer in charge of the investigation and appropriate healthcare professionals as necessary, shall assess whether the detainee is fit enough to be interviewed. This means determining and considering the risks to the detainee's physical and mental state if the interview took place and determining what safeguards are needed to allow the interview to take place. *See Annex G.* The custody officer shall not allow a detainee to be interviewed if the custody officer considers it would cause significant harm to the detainee's physical or mental state. Vulnerable suspects listed at *paragraph 11.18* shall be treated as always being at some risk during an interview and these persons may not be interviewed except in accordance with *paragraphs 11.18* to *11.20.*

C:12.4 As far as practicable interviews shall take place in interview rooms which are adequately heated, lit and ventilated.

C:12.5 A suspect whose detention without charge has been authorised under PACE because the detention is necessary for an interview to obtain evidence of the offence for which they have been arrested may choose not to answer questions but police do not require the suspect's consent or agreement to interview them for this purpose. If a suspect takes steps to prevent themselves being questioned or further questioned, e.g. by refusing to leave their cell to go to a suitable interview room or by trying to leave the interview room, they shall be advised that their consent or agreement to be interviewed is not required. The suspect shall be cautioned as in *section 10,* and informed if they fail or refuse to co-operate, the interview may take place in the cell and that their failure or refusal to co-operate may be given in evidence. The suspect shall then be invited to co-operate and go into the interview room. If they refuse and the custody officer considers, on reasonable grounds, that the interview should not be delayed, the custody officer has discretion to direct that the interview be conducted in a cell. **A-89a**

C:12.6 People being questioned or making statements shall not be required to stand.

C:12.7 Before the interview commences each interviewer shall, subject to *paragraph 2.6A,* identify themselves and any other persons present to the interviewee.

C:12.8 Breaks from interviewing should be made at recognised meal times or at other times that take account of when an interviewee last had a meal. Short refreshment breaks shall be provided at approximately two hour intervals, subject to the interviewer's discretion to delay a break if there are reasonable grounds for believing it would:

(i) involve a:
  - risk of harm to people;
  - serious loss of, or damage to, property;
(ii) unnecessarily delay the detainee's release; or
(iii) otherwise prejudice the outcome of the investigation.

See Note 12B

C:12.9 If during the interview a complaint is made by or on behalf of the interviewee concerning the provisions of any of the Codes, or it comes to the interviewer's notice that the interviewee may have been treated improperly, the interviewer should:

(i) record the matter in the interview record; and
(ii) inform the custody officer, who is then responsible for dealing with it as in *section 9.*

Interviewer not present at the same station as the detainee– use of live link

C:12.9A Amendments to PACE, section 39, allow a person in police detention to be interviewed using a live link (see *paragraph 1.13(e)(i)*) by a police officer who is not at the police station where the detainee is held. Subject to *sub-paragraphs (a)* to *(f)* below, the custody officer is responsible for deciding on a case by case basis whether a detainee is fit to be interviewed (see *paragraph 12.3*) and should **A-89b** be delivered into the physical custody of an officer who is not involved in the investigation, for the purpose of enabling another officer who is investigating the offence for which the person is detained and who is not at the police station where the person is detained, to interview the detainee by means of a live link (see *Note 12ZA*).

(a) The custody officer must be satisfied that the live link to be used provides for accurate and secure communication with the suspect. The provisions of *paragraph 13.13* shall apply to communications between the interviewing officer, the suspect and anyone else whose presence at the interview or, (as the case may be) whose access to any communications between the suspect and the interviewer, has been authorised by the custody officer or the interviewing officer.

(b) Each decision must take account of the age, gender and vulnerability of the suspect, the nature and circumstances of the offence and the investigation and the impact on the suspect of carrying out the interview by means of a live link. For this reason, the custody officer must consider whether the ability of the particular suspect, to communicate confidently and effectively for the purpose of the interview is likely to be adversely affected or otherwise undermined or limited if the interviewing officer is not physically present and a live-link is used (see *Note 12ZB*). Although a suspect for whom an appropriate adult is required may be more likely to be adversely affected as described, it is important to note that a person who does not require an appropriate adult may also be adversely impacted if interviewed by means of a live link.

(c) If the custody officer is satisfied that interviewing the detainee by means of a live link *would not* adversely affect or otherwise undermine or limit the suspect's ability to communicate confidently and effectively for the purpose of the *interview*, the officer must so inform the suspect, their solicitor and (if applicable) the appropriate adult. At the same time, the operation of the live-link must be explained and demonstrated to them (see *Note 12ZC*), they must be advised of the chief officer's obligations concerning the security of live-link communications under *paragraph 13.13* and they must be asked if they wish to make representations that the live-link should not be used or if they require more information about the operation of the arrangements. They must also be told that at any time live-link is in use, they may make representations to the custody officer or the interviewer that its operation should cease and that the physical presence of the interviewer should be arranged.

When the authority of an inspector is required

A-89c (d) If:

(i) representations are made that a live-link should not be used to carry out the interview, or that at any time it is in use, its operation should cease and the physical presence of the interviewer arranged; and

(ii) the custody officer in consultation with the interviewer is unable to allay the concerns raised;

then live-link may not be used, or (as the case may be) continue to be used, unless authorised in writing by an officer of the rank of inspector or above in accordance with *sub-paragraph (e)*.

(e) Authority may be given if the officer is satisfied that interviewing the detainee by means of a live link is necessary and justified. In making this decision, the officer must have regard to:

(i) the circumstances of the suspect;

(ii) the nature and seriousness of the offence;

(iii) the requirements of the investigation, including its likely impact on both the suspect and any victim(s);

(iv) the representations made by the suspect, their solicitor and (if applicable) the appropriate adult that a live-link should not be used (see *sub-paragraph (b)*;

(v) the impact on the investigation of making arrangements for the physical presence of the interviewer (see *Note 12ZD*); and

(vi) the risk if the interviewer is not *physically* present, evidence obtained using link interpretation might be excluded in subsequent criminal proceedings; and

(vii) the likely impact on the suspect and the investigation of any consequential delay to arrange for the interviewer to be *physically* present with the suspect.

(f) The officer given custody of the detainee *and* the interviewer take over responsibility for the detainee's care, treatment and safe custody for the purposes of this Code until the detainee is returned to the custody officer. On that return, both must report the manner in which they complied with the Code during period in question.

C:12.9B When a suspect detained at a police station is interviewed using a live link in accordance with *paragraph 12.9A*, the officer given custody of the detainee at the police station *and* the interviewer who is not present at the police station, take over responsibility for ensuring compliance with the provisions of *sections 11* and *12* of this Code, or *Code E* (Audio recording) or *Code F* (Audio visual recording) that govern the conduct and recording of that interview. In these circumstances:

(a) *the interviewer who is not at the police station where the detainee is held* must direct the officer having physical custody of the suspect at the police station, to take the action required by those provisions and which the interviewer would be required to take if they were present at the police station.

(b) *the officer having physical custody of the suspect at the police station* must take the action required by those provisions and which would otherwise be required to be taken by the interviewer if they were present at the police station. This applies whether or not the officer has been so directed by the interviewer but in such a case, the officer must inform the interviewer of the action taken.

(c) *during the course of the interview*, the officers in (a) and (b) may consult each other as necessary to clarify any action to be taken and to avoid any misunderstanding. Such consultations must, if in the hearing of the suspect and any other person present with the suspect (for example, a solicitor, appropriate adult or interpreter) be recorded in the interview record.

(B) Documentation

C:12.10 A record must be made of the: A-90

- time a detainee is not in the custody of the custody officer, and why
- reason for any refusal to deliver the detainee out of that custody.

C:12.11 A record shall be made of the following:

(a) the reasons it was not practicable to use an interview room;

(b) any action taken as in *paragraph 12.5*; and

(c) the actions, decisions, authorisations, representations and outcomes arising from the requirements of *paragraphs 12.9A* and *12.9B*.

The record shall be made on the custody record or in the interview record for action taken whilst an interview record is being kept, with a brief reference to this effect in the custody record.

C:12.12 Any decision to delay a break in an interview must be recorded, with reasons, in the interview record.

C:12.13 All written statements made at police stations under caution shall be written on forms provided for the purpose.

C:12.14 All written statements made under caution shall be taken in accordance with *Annex D*. Before a person makes a written statement under caution at a police station, they shall be reminded about the right to legal advice. See *Note 12A*.

Notes for Guidance

C:12ZA "Live link" means an arrangement by means of which the interviewing officer who is not at the police station is able to see and hear, and to be seen and heard by, the detainee concerned, the detainee's solicitor, any appropriate adult present and the officer who has custody of that detainee. See paragraphs 13.12 to 13.14 and *Annex N* for application to live-link interpretation. A-91

C:12ZB In considering whether the use of the live link is appropriate in a particular case, the custody officer, in consultation with the interviewer, should make an assessment of the detainee's ability to understand and take part in the interviewing process and make a record of the outcome. If the suspect has asked for legal advice, their solicitor should be involved in the assessment and in the case of a juvenile or vulnerable person, the appropriate adult should be involved.

C:12ZC The explanation and demonstration of live-link interpretation is intended to help the suspect, solicitor and appropriate adult make an informed decision and to allay any concerns they may have.

C:12ZD Factors affecting the arrangements for the interviewer to be physically present will include the location of the police station where the interview would take place and the availability of an interviewer with sufficient knowledge of the investigation who can attend that station and carry out the interview.

C:12A It is not normally necessary to ask for a written statement if the interview was recorded in writing and the record signed in accordance with paragraph 11.11 or audibly or visually recorded in accordance with Code E or F. Statements under caution should normally be taken in these circumstances only at the person's express wish. A person may however be asked if they want to make such a statement.

C:12B Meal breaks should normally last at least 45 minutes and shorter breaks after two hours should last at least 15 minutes. If the interviewer delays a break in accordance with paragraph 12.8 and prolongs the interview, a longer break should be provided. If there is a short interview and another short interview is contemplated, the length of the break may be reduced if there are reasonable grounds to believe this is necessary to avoid any of the consequences in paragraph 12.8(i) to (iii).

C:13 Interpreters

(A) General

A-92 C:13.1 Chief officers are responsible for making arrangements (see *paragraph 13.1ZA*) to provide appropriately qualified independent persons to act as interpreters and to provide translations of essential documents for:

(a) detained suspects who, in accordance with *paragraph 3.5(c)(ii)*, the custody officer has determined require an interpreter, and

(b) suspects who are not under arrest but are cautioned as in *section 10* who, in accordance with *paragraph 3.21(b)*, the interviewer has determined require an interpreter. In these cases, the responsibilities of the custody officer are, if appropriate, assigned to the interviewer. An interviewer who has any doubts about whether and what arrangements for an interpreter must be made or about how the provisions of this section should be applied to a suspect who is not under arrest should seek advice from an officer of the rank of sergeant or above.

If the suspect has a hearing or speech impediment, references to "interpreter" and "interpretation" in this Code include arrangements for appropriate assistance necessary to establish effective communication with that person. See *paragraph 13.1C* below if the person is in Wales.

C:13.1ZA References in *paragraph 13.1* above and elsewhere in this Code (see *paragraphs 3.12(a), 13.2, 13.2A, 13.5, 13.6, 13.9, 13.10, 13.10A, 13.10D* and *13.11 below* and in any other Code, to making arrangements for an interpreter to assist a suspect, mean making arrangements for the interpreter to be *physically* present in the same location as the suspect *unless* the provisions in *paragraph 13.12* below, and Part 1 of *Annex N*, allow live-link interpretation to be used.

A-92a C:13.1A The arrangements *must* comply with the minimum requirements set out in Directive 2010/64/EU of the European Parliament and of the Council of 20 October 2010 on the right to interpretation and translation in criminal proceedings (see *Note 13A*). The provisions *of this* Code implement the requirements for those to whom this Code applies. These requirements include the following:

- That the arrangements made and the quality of interpretation and translation provided shall be sufficient to '*safeguard the fairness of the proceedings, in particular by ensuring that suspected or accused persons have knowledge of the cases against them and are able to exercise their right of defence*'. This term which is used by the Directive means that the suspect must be able to understand their position and be able to communicate effectively with police officers, interviewers, solicitors and appropriate adults as provided for by this and any other Code in the same way as a suspect who can speak and understand English and who does not have a hearing or speech impediment and who would therefore not require an interpreter. See paragraphs *13.12* to *13.14* and *Annex N* for application to live-link interpretation.
- The provision of a written translation of all documents considered essential for the person to exercise their right of defence and to '*safeguard the fairness of the proceedings*' as described above. For the purposes of this Code, this includes any decision to authorise a person to be detained and details of any offence(s) with which the person has been charged or for which they have been told they may be prosecuted, see *Annex M*.
- Procedures to help determine:
  - ~ whether a suspect can speak and understand English and needs the assistance of an interpreter, see *paragraph 13.1* and *Notes 13B* and *13C*; and
  - ~ whether another interpreter should be arranged or another translation should be provided when a suspect complains about the quality of either or both, see *paragraphs 13.10A* and *13.10C*.

C:13.1B All reasonable attempts should be made to make the suspect understand that interpretation and translation will be provided at public expense.

C:13.1C With regard to persons in Wales, nothing in this or any other Code affects the application of the Welsh Language Schemes produced by police and crime commissioners in Wales in accordance with the Welsh Language Act 1993. See *paragraphs 3.12 and 13.1.*

(B) Interviewing suspects - foreign languages

A-93 C:13.2 Unless *paragraphs 11.1 or 11.18(c)* apply, a suspect who for the purposes of this Code requires an interpreter because they do not appear to speak or understand English (see *paragraphs 3.5(c)(ii)* and *3.12*) must not be interviewed unless arrangements are made for a person capable of interpreting to assist the suspect to understand and communicate.

C:13.2A If a person who is a juvenile or a vulnerable person is interviewed and the person acting as the appropriate adult does not appear to speak or understand English, arrangements must be made for an interpreter to assist communication between the person, the appropriate adult and the interviewer, unless the interview is urgent and *paragraphs 11.1 or 11.18(c)* apply.

C:13.3 When a written record of the interview is made (see *paragraph 11.7*), the interviewer shall make sure the interpreter makes a note of the interview at the time in the person's language for use in the event of the interpreter being called to give evidence, and certifies its accuracy. The interviewer should allow sufficient time for the interpreter to note each question and answer after each is put, given and interpreted. The person should be allowed to read the record or have it read to them and sign it as correct or indicate the respects in which they consider it inaccurate. If an audio or visual record of the interview is made, the arrangements in Code E or F shall apply. See *paragraphs 13.12* to *13.14* and *Annex N* for application to live-link interpretation.

C:13.4 In the case of a person making a statement under caution (see *Annex D*) to a police officer or other police staff in a language other than English:

(a) the interpreter shall record the statement in the language it is made;
(b) the person shall be invited to sign it;
(c) an official English translation shall be made in due course. See *paragraphs 13.12* to *13.14* and *Annex N* for application to live-link interpretation.

(C) Interviewing suspects who have a hearing or speech impediment

C:13.5 Unless *paragraphs 11.1 or 11.18(c)* (urgent interviews) apply, a suspect who for the purposes of this Code requires an interpreter or other appropriate assistance to enable effective communication with them because they appear to have a hearing or speech impediment (see *paragraphs 3.5(c)(ii)* and *3.12*) must not be interviewed without arrangements having been made to provide an independent person capable of interpreting or of providing other appropriate assistance. **A-94**

C:13.6 An interpreter should also be arranged if a person who is a juvenile or a vulnerable person is interviewed and the person who is present as the appropriate adult, appears to have a hearing or speech impediment, unless the interview is urgent and *paragraphs 11.1 or 11.18(c)* apply.

C:13.7 If a written record of the interview is made, the interviewer shall make sure the interpreter is allowed to read the record and certify its accuracy in the event of the interpreter being called to give evidence. If an audio or visual recording is made, the arrangements in Code E or F apply.

See *paragraphs 13.12* to *13.14* and *Annex N* for application to live-link interpretation.

(D) Additional rules for detained persons

C:13.8 *Not used.* **A-95**

C:13.9 If *paragraph 6.1* applies and the detainee cannot communicate with the solicitor because of language, hearing or speech difficulties, arrangements must be made for an interpreter to enable communication. A police officer or any other police staff may not be used for this purpose.

C:13.10 After the custody officer has determined that a detainee requires an interpreter (see *paragraph 3.5(c)(ii)*) and following the initial action in *paragraphs 3.1 to 3.5*, arrangements must also be made for an interpreter to:

- explain the grounds and reasons for any authorisation for their *continued* detention, before or after charge and any information about the authorisation given to them by the authorising officer and which is recorded in the custody record. See *paragraphs 15.3, 15.4* and *15.16(a)* and *(b)*;
- to provide interpretation at the magistrates' court for the hearing of an application for a warrant of further detention or any extension or further extension of such warrant to explain any grounds and reasons for the application and any information about the authorisation of their further detention given to them by the court (see PACE, sections 43 and 44 and *paragraphs 15.2* and *15.16(c)*); and
- explain any offence with which the detainee is charged or for which they are informed they may be prosecuted and any other information about the offence given to them by or on behalf of the custody officer, see *paragraphs 16.1* and *16.3*.

C:13.10A If a detainee complains that they are not satisfied with the quality of interpretation, the custody officer or (as the case may be) the interviewer, is responsible for deciding whether to make arrangements for a different interpreter in accordance with the procedures set out in the arrangements made by the chief officer, *see paragraph 13.1A*.

(E) Translations of essential documents

C:13.10B Written translations, oral translations and oral summaries of essential documents in a language the detainee understands shall be provided in accordance with Annex M (Translations of documents and records). **A-96**

C:13.10C If a detainee complains that they are not satisfied with the quality of the translation, the custody officer or (as the case may be) the interviewer, is responsible for deciding whether a further translation should be provided in accordance with the procedures set out in the arrangements made by the chief officer, see *paragraph 13.1A*.

(F) Decisions not to provide interpretation and translation.

A-97 C:13.10D If a suspect challenges a decision:

- made by the custody officer or (as the case may be) by the interviewer, in accordance with this Code (see *paragraphs 3.5(c)(ii)* and *3.21(b)*) that they do not require an interpreter, or
- made in accordance with *paragraphs 13.10A, 13.10B* or *13.10C* not to make arrangements to provide a different interpreter or another translation or not to translate a requested document,

the matter shall be reported to an inspector to deal with as a complaint for the purposes of *paragraph 9.2* or *paragraph 12.9* if the challenge is made during an interview.

(G) Documentation

A-98 C:13.11 The following must be recorded in the custody record or, as applicable, the interview record:

(a) Action taken to arrange for an interpreter, including the live-link requirements in *Annex N* as applicable;
(b) Action taken when a detainee is not satisfied about the standard of interpretation or translation provided, see *paragraphs 13.10A* and *13.10C*;
(c) When an urgent interview is carried out in accordance with *paragraph 13.2* or *13.5* in the absence of an interpreter;
(d) When a detainee has been assisted by an interpreter for the purpose of providing or being given information or being interviewed;
(e) Action taken in accordance with *Annex M* when:
  - a written translation of an essential document is provided;
  - an oral translation or oral summary of an essential document is provided instead of a written translation and the authorising officer's reason(s) why this would not prejudice the fairness of the proceedings (see *Annex M, paragraph 3*);
  - a suspect waives their right to a translation of an essential document (see *Annex M, paragraph 4*);
  - when representations that a document which is not included in the table is essential and that a translation should be provided are refused and the reason for the refusal (see *Annex M, paragraph 8*).

(H) Live link interpretation

A-99 C:13.12 In this section and in *Annex N*, "live-link interpretation" means an arrangement to enable communication between the suspect and an interpreter who is not *physically* present with the suspect. The arrangement must ensure that anything said by any person in the suspect's presence and hearing can be interpreted in the same way as if the interpreter was physically present at that time. The communication must be by audio *and* visual means for the purpose of an interview, and for all other purposes it may be *either*, by audio and visual means, or by audio means *only*, as follows:

A-99a (a) **Audio and visual communication** This applies for the purposes of an interview conducted and recorded in accordance with Code E (Audio recording) or Code F (Visual recording) and during that interview, live link interpretation must *enable*:
  (i) the suspect, the interviewer, solicitor, appropriate adult and any other person *physically* present with the suspect at any time during the interview and an interpreter who is not *physically* present, to *see* and *hear* each other; and
  (ii) the interview to be conducted and recorded in accordance with the provisions of Codes C, E and F, subject to the modifications in *Part 2 of Annex N*.

A-99b (b) **Audio and visual or audio without visual communication.** This applies to communication for the purposes of any provision of this or any other Code except as described in (a), which requires or permits information to be given to, sought from, or provided by a suspect, whether orally or in writing, which would include communication between the suspect and their solicitor and/or appropriate adult, and for these cases, live link interpretation must:
  (i) *enable* the suspect, the person giving or seeking that information, any other person *physically* present with the suspect at that time and an interpreter who is not so present, to either see and *hear* each other, or to *hear without seeing* each other (for example by using a telephone); and
  (ii) enable that information to be given to, sought from, or provided by, the suspect in ac-

cordance with the provisions of this or any other Code that apply to that information, as modified for the purposes of the live-link, by *Part 2 of Annex N*.

C:13.12A The requirement in *sub-paragraphs 13.12(a)(ii)* and *(b)(ii)*, that live-link interpretation must enable compliance with the relevant provisions of the Codes C, E and F, means that the arrangements must provide for any written or electronic record of what the suspect says in their own language which is made by the interpreter, to be securely transmitted without delay so that the suspect can be invited to read, check and if appropriate, sign or otherwise confirm that the record is correct or make corrections to the record. **A-100**

C:13.13 Chief officers must be satisfied that live-link interpretation used in their force area for the purposes of *paragraphs 13.12(a)* and *(b)*, provides for accurate and secure communication with the suspect. This includes ensuring that at any time during which live link interpretation is being used: a person cannot see, hear or otherwise obtain access to any communications between the suspect and interpreter or communicate with the suspect or interpreter unless so authorised or allowed by the custody officer or, in the case of an interview, the interviewer and that as applicable, the confidentiality of any private consultation between a suspect and their solicitor and appropriate adult (see *paragraphs 13.2A, 13.6* and *13.9*) is maintained. See *Annex N paragraph 4*.

Notes for Guidance

C:13A Chief officers have discretion when determining the individuals or organisations they use to provide interpretation and translation services for their forces provided that these are compatible with the requirements of the Directive. One example which chief officers may wish to consider is the Ministry of Justice commercial agreements for interpretation and translation services. **A-101**

C:13B A procedure for determining whether a person needs an interpreter might involve a telephone interpreter service or using cue cards or similar visual aids which enable the detainee to indicate their ability to speak and understand English and their preferred language. This could be confirmed through an interpreter who could also assess the extent to which the person can speak and understand English.

C:13C There should also be a procedure for determining whether a suspect who requires an interpreter requires assistance in accordance with paragraph 3.20 to help them check and if applicable, sign any documentation.

C:14 Questioning - special restrictions

C:14.1 If a person is arrested by one police force on behalf of another and the lawful period of detention in respect of that offence has not yet commenced in accordance with PACE, section 41, no questions may be put to them about the offence while they are in transit between the forces except to clarify any voluntary statement they make. **A-102**

C:14.2 If a person is in police detention at a hospital, they may not be questioned without the agreement of a responsible doctor. See *Note 14A*.

Note for Guidance

C:14A If questioning takes place at a hospital under paragraph 14.2, or on the way to or from a hospital, the period of questioning concerned counts towards the total period of detention permitted. **A-103**

C:15 Reviews and extensions of detention

(A) Persons detained under PACE

C:15.0 The requirement in *paragraph 3.4(b)* that documents and materials essential to challenging the lawfulness of the detainee's arrest and detention must be made available to the detainee or their solicitor, applies for the purposes of this section as follows: **A-104**

(a) The officer reviewing the need for detention without charge (PACE, section 40), or (as the case may be) the officer considering the need to extend detention without charge from 24 to 36 hours (PACE, section 42), is responsible, in consultation with the investigating officer, for deciding which documents and materials are essential and must be made available.

(b) When *paragraph 15.7A* applies (application for a warrant of further detention or extension of such a warrant), the officer making the application is responsible for deciding which documents and materials are essential and must be made available *before* the hearing. See *Note 3ZA*.

C:15.1 The review officer is responsible under PACE, section 40 for periodically determining if a person's detention, before or after charge, continues to be necessary. This requirement continues throughout the detention period and, except when a telephone or a live link is used in accordance with *paragraphs 15.9* to *15.11C*, the review officer must be present at the police station holding the detainee. See *Notes 15A* and *15B*.

C:15.2 Under PACE, section 42, an officer of superintendent rank or above who is responsible for the station holding the detainee may give authority any time after the second review to extend the maximum period the person may be detained without charge by up to 12 hours. Except when a live link is used as in *paragraph 15.11A*, the superintendent must be present at the station holding the detainee. Further detention without charge may be authorised only by a magistrates' court in accordance with PACE, sections 43 and 44 and unless the court has given a live link direction as in *paragraph 15.11B*, the detainee must be brought before the court for the hearing. See *Notes 15C, 15D* and *15E*.

C:15.2A An authorisation under section 42(1) of PACE extends the maximum period of detention permitted before charge for indictable offences from 24 hours to 36 hours. Detaining a juvenile or a vulnerable person for longer than 24 hours will be dependent on the circumstances of the case and with regard to the person's:

(a) special vulnerability;
(b) the legal obligation to provide an opportunity for representations to be made prior to a decision about extending detention;
(c) the need to consult and consider the views of any appropriate adult; and
(d) any alternatives to police custody.

A-104a C:15.3 Before deciding whether to authorise continued detention the officer responsible under *paragraph 15.1* or *15.2* shall give an opportunity to make representations about the detention to:

(a) the detainee, unless in the case of a review as in *paragraph 15.1*, the detainee is asleep;
(b) the detainee's solicitor if available at the time; and
(c) the appropriate adult if available at the time.

See *Note 15CA*

C:15.3A Other people having an interest in the detainee's welfare may also make representations at the authorising officer's discretion.

C:15.3B Subject to *paragraph 15.10*, the representations may be made orally in person or by telephone or in writing. The authorising officer may, however, refuse to hear oral representations from the detainee if the officer considers them unfit to make representations because of their condition or behaviour. See *Note 15C*.

C:15.3C The decision on whether the review takes place in person or by telephone or by live link (see *paragraph 1.13(e)(ii)*) is a matter for the review officer. In determining the form the review may take, the review officer must always take full account of the needs of the person in custody. The benefits of carrying out a review in person should always be considered, based on the individual circumstances of each case with specific additional consideration if the person is:

(a) a juvenile (and the age of the juvenile); or
(b) a vulnerable person; or
(c) in need of medical attention for other than routine minor ailments; or
(d) subject to presentational or community issues around their detention.

See *paragraph 1.4(c)*

C:15.4 Before conducting a review or determining whether to extend the maximum period of detention without charge, the officer responsible must make sure the detainee is reminded of their entitlement to free legal advice, see *paragraph 6.5*, unless in the case of a review the person is asleep. When determining whether to extend the maximum period of detention without charge, it should also be pointed out that for the purposes of *paragraph 15.2*, the superintendent or (as the case may be) the court, responsible for authorising any such extension, will not be able to use a live link unless the detainee has *received* legal advice on the use of the live link (see *paragraphs 15.11A(ii)* and *15.11C(ii)*) and given consent to its use (see *paragraphs 15.11A(iii)* and *15.11C(iii)*. The detainee must also be given information about how the live link is used.

C:15.4A Following sections 45ZA and 45ZB of PACE, when the reminder and information concerning legal advice and about the use of the live link is given and the detainee's consent is sought, the presence of an appropriate adult is required if the detainee in question is a juvenile (see *paragraph 1.5*) or is a *vulnerable adult* by virtue of being a person aged 18 or over who, because of a mental disorder established in accordance *paragraphs 1.4* and *1.13(d)* or for *any other reason* (see *paragraph 15.4B*), may have difficulty understanding the purpose of:

(a) an authorisation under section 42 of PACE or anything that occurs in connection with a decision whether to give it (see *paragraphs 15.2* and *15.2A*); or
(b) a court hearing under section 43 or 44 of PACE or what occurs at the hearing it (see *paragraphs 15.2* and *15.7A*).

A1-04b C:15.4B For the purpose of using a live link in accordance with sections 45ZA and 45ZB of PACE to authorise detention without charge (see *paragraphs 15.11A* and *15.11C*), the reference to 'any other reason' would extend to difficulties in understanding the purposes mentioned in paragraph 15.4A that might arise if the person happened to be under the influence of drink or drugs at the time the live link is to be used. This does not however apply for the purposes of *paragraphs 1.4* and *1.13(d)* (see *Note 1GC*).

C:15.5 If, after considering any representations, the review officer under *paragraph 15.1* decides to keep the detainee in detention or the superintendent under *paragraph 15.2* extends the maximum period for which they may be detained without charge, then any comment made by the detainee shall be recorded. If applicable, the officer shall be informed of the comment as soon as practicable. See also *paragraphs 11.4* and *11.13*.

C:15.6 No officer shall put specific questions to the detainee:

- regarding their involvement in any offence; or
- in respect of any comments they may make:
  - when given the opportunity to make representations; or
  - in response to a decision to keep them in detention or extend the maximum period of detention.

Such an exchange could constitute an interview as in *paragraph 11.1A* and would be subject to the associated safeguards in *section 11* and, in respect of a person who has been charged, *paragraph 16.5*. See also *paragraph 11.13*.

C:15.7 A detainee who is asleep at a review, see *paragraph 15.1*, and whose continued detention is authorised must be informed about the decision and reason as soon as practicable after waking.

C:15.7A When an application is made to a magistrates' court under PACE, section 43 for a warrant of further detention to extend detention without charge of a person arrested for an *indictable offence*, or under section 44, to extend or further extend that warrant, the detainee: **A-104c**

(a) must, unless the court has given a live link direction as in *paragraph 15.11C*, be brought to court for the hearing of the application (see *Note 15D*);
(b) is entitled to be legally represented if they wish, in which case, *Annex B* cannot apply; and
(c) must be given a copy of the information which supports the application and states:
   (i) the nature of the offence for which the person to whom the application relates has been arrested;
   (ii) the general nature of the evidence on which the person was arrested;
   (iii) what inquiries about the offence have been made and what further inquiries are proposed;
   (iv) the reasons for believing continued detention is necessary for the purposes of the further inquiries;

Note: A warrant of further detention can only be issued or extended if the court has reasonable grounds for believing that the person's further detention is necessary for the purpose of obtaining evidence of an indictable offence for which the person has been arrested and that the investigation is being conducted diligently and expeditiously.

See *paragraph 15.0(b)*.

C:15.8 *Not used.*

(B) Review of detention by telephone or by using a live link (section 40A and 45A)

C:15.9 PACE, section 40A provides that the officer responsible under section 40 for reviewing the detention of a person who has not been charged, need not attend the police station holding the detainee and may carry out the review by telephone. **A-105**

C:15.9A PACE, section 45A(2) provides that the officer responsible under section 40 for reviewing the detention of a person who has not been charged, need not attend the police station holding the detainee and may carry out the review using a live link. See *paragraph 1.13(e)(ii)*.

C:15.9B A telephone review is not permitted where facilities for review using a live link exist and it is practicable to use them.

C:15.9C The review officer can decide at any stage that a telephone review or review by live link should be terminated and that the review will be conducted in person. The reasons for doing so should be noted in the custody record. See *Note 15F*.

C:15.10 When a review is carried out by telephone or by using a live link, an officer at the station holding the detainee shall be required by the review officer to fulfil that officer's obligations under PACE, section 40 and this Code by:

(a) making any record connected with the review in the detainee's custody record;
(b) if applicable, making the record in (a) in the presence of the detainee; and
(c) for a review by telephone, giving the detainee information about the review.

C:15.11 When a review is carried out by telephone or by using a live link, or the requirement in *paragraph 15.3* will be satisfied:

(a) if facilities exist for the immediate transmission of written representations to the review officer, e.g. fax or email message, by allowing those who are given the opportunity to make representations, to make their representations:
   (i) orally by telephone or (as the case may be) by means of the live link; or
   (ii) in writing using the facilities for the immediate transmission of written representations; and

(b) in all other cases, by allowing those who are given the opportunity to make representations, to make their representations orally by telephone or by means of the live link.

(C) Authorisation to extend detention using live link (sections 45ZA and 45ZB)

A-106 C:15.11A For the purpose of *paragraphs 15.2* and *15.2A*, a superintendent who is not present at the police station where the detainee is being held but who has access to the use of a live link (see *paragraph 1.13(e)(iii)*) may, using that live link, give authority to extend the maximum period of detention permitted before charge, if, and only if, the following conditions are satisfied:

(i) the custody officer considers that the use of the live link is appropriate (see *Note 15H*);

(ii) the detainee in question has requested and received legal advice on the use of the live link (see *paragraph 15.4*).

(iii) the detainee has given their consent to the live link being used (see *paragraph 15.11D*)

C:15.11B When a live link is used:

(a) the authorising superintendent shall, with regard to any record connected with the authorisation which PACE, section 42 and this Code require to be made by the authorising officer, require an officer at the station holding the detainee to make that record in the detainee's custody record;

(b) the requirement in *paragraph 15.3* (allowing opportunity to make representations) will be satisfied:

(i) if facilities exist for the immediate transmission of written representations to the authorising officer, e.g. fax or email message, by allowing those who are given the opportunity to make representations, to make their representations:

- in writing by means of those facilities or
- orally by means of the live link; or

(ii) in all other cases, by allowing those who are given the opportunity to make representations, to make their representations orally by means of the live link.

(c) The authorising officer can decide at any stage to terminate the live link and attend the police station where the detainee is held to carry out the procedure in person. The reasons for doing so should be noted in the custody record.

C:15.11C For the purpose of *paragraph 15.7A* and the hearing of an application to a magistrates' court under PACE, section 43 for a warrant of further detention to extend detention without charge of a person arrested for an *indictable offence*, or under PACE, section 44, to extend or further extend that warrant, the magistrates' court may give a direction that a live link (see *paragraph 1.13(e)(iv)*) be used for the purposes of the hearing if, and only if, the following conditions are satisfied:

(i) the custody officer considers that the use of the live link for the purpose of the hearing is appropriate (see *Note 15H*);

(ii) the detainee in question has requested and received legal advice on the use of the live link (see *paragraph 15.4*);

(iii) the detainee has given their consent to the live link being used (see *paragraph 15.11D*); and

(iv) it is not contrary to the interests of justice to give the direction.

C:15.11D References in *paragraphs 15.11A(iii)* and *15.11C(iii)* to the consent of the detainee mean:

(a) if detainee is aged 18 or over, the consent of that detainee;

(b) if the detainee is aged 14 and under 18, the consent of the detainee *and* their parent or guardian; and

(c) if the detainee is aged under 14, the consent of their parent or guardian.

C:15.11E The consent described in *paragraph 15.11D* will only be valid if:

(i) in the case of a detainee aged 18 or over *who is a vulnerable adult* as described in *paragraph 15.4A*), information about how the live link is used *and* the reminder about their right to legal advice mentioned in *paragraph 15.4 and* their consent, are given in the *presence of the appropriate adult*; and

(ii) in the case of a *juvenile:*

- if information about how the live link is used *and* the reminder about their right to legal advice mentioned in *paragraph 15.4* are given in the *presence of the appropriate adult* (who may or may not be their parent or guardian); and
- if the juvenile is *aged 14 or over*, their consent is given in the *presence of the appropriate adult* (who may or may not be their parent or guardian).

Note: If the juvenile is *aged under 14*, the consent of their parent or guardian is sufficient in its own right (see *Note 15I*).

(D) Documentation

A-107 C:15.12 It is the officer's responsibility to make sure all reminders given under *paragraph 15.4* are noted in the custody record.

C:15.13 The grounds for, and extent of, any delay in conducting a review shall be recorded.

C:15.14 When a review is carried out by telephone or video conferencing facilities, a record shall be made of:

(a) the reason the review officer did not attend the station holding the detainee;
(b) the place the review officer was;
(c) the method representations, oral or written, were made to the review officer, see *paragraph 15.11*.

C:15.15 Any written representations shall be retained.

C:15.16 A record shall be made as soon as practicable of:

(a) the outcome of each review of detention before or after charge, and if *paragraph 15.7* applies, of when the person was informed and by whom;
(b) the outcome of any determination under PACE, section 42 by a superintendent whether to extend the maximum period of detention without charge beyond 24 hours from the relevant time. If an authorisation is given, the record shall state the number of hours and minutes by which the detention period is extended or further extended.
(c) the outcome of each application under PACE, section 43, for a warrant of further detention or under section 44, for an extension or further extension of that warrant. If a warrant for further detention is granted under section 43 or extended or further extended under 44, the record shall state the detention period authorised by the warrant and the date and time it was granted or (as the case may be) the period by which the warrant is extended or further extended.

Note: Any period during which a person is released on bail does not count towards the maximum period of detention without charge allowed under PACE, sections 41 to 44.

Notes for Guidance

C:15A Review officer for the purposes of: **A-108**

- *PACE, sections 40, 40A and 45A means, in the case of a person arrested but not charged, an officer of at least inspector rank not directly involved in the investigation and, if a person has been arrested and charged, the custody officer.*

C:15B The detention of persons in police custody not subject to the statutory review requirement in paragraph 15.1 should still be reviewed periodically as a matter of good practice. Such reviews can be carried out by an officer of the rank of sergeant or above. The purpose of such reviews is to check the particular power under which a detainee is held continues to apply, any associated conditions are complied with and to make sure appropriate action is taken to deal with any changes. This includes the detainee's prompt release when the power no longer applies, or their transfer if the power requires the detainee be taken elsewhere as soon as the necessary arrangements are made. Examples include persons:

(a) arrested on warrant because they failed to answer bail to appear at court;
(b) arrested under the Bail Act 1976, section 7(3) for breaching a condition of bail granted after charge;
(c) in police custody for specific purposes and periods under the Crime (Sentences) Act 1997, Schedule 1;
(d) convicted, or remand prisoners, held in police stations on behalf of the Prison Service under the Imprisonment (Temporary Provisions) Act 1980, section 6;
(e) being detained to prevent them causing a breach of the peace;
(f) detained at police stations on behalf of Immigration Enforcement (formerly the UK Immigration Service);
(g) detained by order of a magistrates' court under the Criminal Justice Act 1988, section 152 (as amended by the Drugs Act 2005, section 8) to facilitate the recovery of evidence after being charged with drug possession or drug trafficking and suspected of having swallowed drugs.

The detention of persons remanded into police detention by order of a court under the Magistrates' Courts Act 1980, section 128 is subject to a statutory requirement to review that detention. This is to make sure the detainee is taken back to court no later than the end of the period authorised by the court or when the need for their detention by police ceases, whichever is the sooner.

C:15C In the case of a review of detention, but not an extension, the detainee need not be woken for the review. However, if the detainee is likely to be asleep, e.g. during a period of rest allowed as in paragraph 12.2, at the latest time a review or authorisation to extend detention may take place, the officer should, if the legal obligations and time constraints permit, bring forward the procedure to allow the detainee to make representations. A detainee not asleep during the review must be present when the grounds for their continued detention are recorded and must at the same time be informed of those grounds unless the review officer considers the person is incapable of understanding what is said, violent or likely to become violent or in urgent need of medical attention.

C:15CA In paragraph 15.3(b) and (c), "available" includes being contactable in time to enable them to make representations remotely by telephone or other electronic means or in person by attending the station. Reasonable efforts should therefore be made to give the solicitor and appropriate adult sufficient notice of the time the decision is expected to be made so that they can make themselves available.

C:15D An application to a Magistrates' Court under PACE, sections 43 or 44 for a warrant of further detention or its extension should be made between 10am and 9pm, and if possible during normal court hours. It will not usually be practicable to arrange for a court to sit specially outside the hours of 10am to 9pm. If it appears a special sitting may be needed outside normal court hours but between 10am and 9pm, the clerk to the justices should be given notice and informed of this possibility, while the court is sitting if possible.

C:15E In paragraph 15.2, the officer responsible for the station holding the detainee includes a superintendent or above who, in accordance with their force operational policy or police regulations, is given that responsibility on a temporary basis whilst the appointed long-term holder is off duty or otherwise unavailable.

C:15F The provisions of PACE, section 40A allowing telephone reviews do not apply to reviews of detention after charge by the custody officer. When use of a live link is not required, they allow the use of a telephone to carry out a review of detention before charge.

C:15G Not used.

C:15H In considering whether the use of the live link is appropriate in the case of a juvenile or vulnerable person, the custody officer and the superintendent should have regard to the detainee's ability to understand the purpose of the authorisation or (as the case may be) the court hearing, and be satisfied that the suspect is able to take part effectively in the process (see paragraphs 1.4(c)). The appropriate adult should always be involved.

C:15I For the purpose of paragraphs 15.11D and *15.11E,* the consent required from a parent or guardian may, for a juvenile in the care of a local authority or voluntary organisation, be given by that authority or organisation. In the case of a juvenile, nothing in *paragraphs 15.11D* and *15.11E* require the parent, guardian or representative of a local authority or voluntary organisation to be present with the juvenile to give their consent, unless they are acting as the appropriate adult. However, it is important that the parent, guardian or representative of a local authority or voluntary organisation who is not present is fully informed before being asked to consent. They must be given the same information as that given to the juvenile and the appropriate adult in accordance with *paragraph 15.11E.* They must also be allowed to speak to the juvenile and the appropriate adult if they wish. Provided the consent is fully informed and is not withdrawn, it may be obtained at any time before the live link is used.

C:16 Charging detained persons

(A) Action

A-109 C:16.1 When the officer in charge of the investigation reasonably believes there is sufficient evidence to provide a realistic prospect of conviction for the offence (see *paragraph 11.6*), they shall without delay, and subject to the following qualification, inform the custody officer who will be responsible for considering whether the detainee should be charged. See *Notes 11B* and *16A.* When a person is detained in respect of more than one offence it is permissible to delay informing the custody officer until the above conditions are satisfied in respect of all the offences, but see *paragraph 11.6.* If the detainee is a juvenile or a vulnerable person, any resulting action shall be taken in the presence of the appropriate adult if they are present at the time.

See *Notes 16B and 16C.*

C:16.1A Where guidance issued by the Director of Public Prosecutions under PACE, section 37A is in force the custody officer must comply with that Guidance in deciding how to act in dealing with the detainee. See *Notes 16AA* and *16AB.*

C:16.1B Where in compliance with the DPP's Guidance the custody officer decides that the case should be immediately referred to the CPS to make the charging decision, consultation should take place with a Crown Prosecutor as soon as is reasonably practicable. Where the Crown Prosecutor is unable to make the charging decision on the information available at that time, the detainee may be released without charge and on bail (with conditions if necessary) under section 37(7)(a). In such circumstances, the detainee should be informed that they are being released to enable the Director of Public Prosecutions to make a decision under section 37B.

C:16.2 When a detainee is charged with or informed they may be prosecuted for an offence, see *Note 16B*, they shall, unless the restriction on drawing adverse inferences from silence applies, see *Annex C*, be cautioned as follows:

> '*You do not have to say anything. But it may harm your defence if you do not mention now something which you later rely on in court. Anything you do say may be given in evidence.*'

Where the use of the Welsh Language is appropriate, a constable may provide the caution directly in Welsh in the following terms:

> '*Does dim rhaid i chi ddweud dim byd. Ond gall niweidio eich amddiffyniad os na fyddwch chi'n sôn, yn*

awr, am rywbeth y byddwch chi'n dibynnu arno nes ymlaen yn y llys. Gall unrhyw beth yr ydych yn ei ddweud gael ei roi fel tystiolaeth.'

Annex C, paragraph 2 sets out the alternative terms of the caution to be used when the restriction on drawing adverse inferences from silence applies.

C:16.3 When a detainee is charged they shall be given a written notice showing particulars of the offence and, subject to *paragraph 2.6A*, the officer's name and the case reference number. As far as possible the particulars of the charge shall be stated in simple terms, but they shall also show the precise offence in law with which the detainee is charged. The notice shall begin:

'*You are charged with the offence(s) shown below.*' Followed by the caution.

If the detainee is a juvenile, mentally disordered or otherwise mentally vulnerable, a copy of the notice should also be given to the appropriate adult.

C:16.4 If, after a detainee has been charged with or informed they may be prosecuted for an offence, an officer wants to tell them about any written statement or interview with another person relating to such an offence, the detainee shall either be handed a true copy of the written statement or the content of the interview record brought to their attention. Nothing shall be done to invite any reply or comment except to:

(a) caution the detainee, '*You do not have to say anything, but anything you do say may be given in evidence.*';

Where the use of the Welsh Language is appropriate, caution the detainee in the following terms:

'*Does dim rhaid i chi ddweud dim byd, ond gall unrhyw beth yr ydych yn ei ddweud gael ei roi fel tystiolaeth.*'

and

(b) remind the detainee about their right to legal advice.

C:16.4A If the detainee: **A-109a**

- cannot read, the document may be read to them;
- is a juvenile, mentally disordered or otherwise mentally vulnerable, the appropriate adult shall also be given a copy, or the interview record shall be brought to their attention.

C:16.5 A detainee may not be interviewed about an offence after they have been charged with, or informed they may be prosecuted for it, unless the interview is necessary:

- to prevent or minimise harm or loss to some other person, or the public
- to clear up an ambiguity in a previous answer or statement
- in the interests of justice for the detainee to have put to them, and have an opportunity to comment on, information concerning the offence which has come to light since they were charged or informed they might be prosecuted

Before any such interview, the interviewer shall:

(a) caution the detainee, '*You do not have to say anything, but anything you do say may be given in evidence.*'

Where the use of the Welsh Language is appropriate, the interviewer shall caution the detainee: '*Does dim rhaid i chi ddweud dim byd, ond gall unrhyw beth yr ydych yn ei ddweud gael ei roi fel tystiolaeth.*'

(b) remind the detainee about their right to legal advice.

See *Note 16B*

C:16.6 The provisions of *paragraphs 16.2* to *16.5* must be complied with in the appropriate adult's presence if they are already at the police station. If they are not at the police station then these provisions must be complied with again in their presence when they arrive unless the detainee has been released. See *Note 16C.*

C:16.7 When a juvenile is charged with an offence and the custody officer authorises their continued detention after charge, the custody officer must make arrangements for the juvenile to be taken into the care of a local authority to be detained pending appearance in court *unless* the custody officer certifies in accordance with PACE, section 38(6), that:

(a) for any juvenile; it is impracticable to do so and the reasons why it is impracticable must be set out in the certificate that must be produced to the court; or,

(b) in the case of a juvenile of at least 12 years old, no secure accommodation is available and other accommodation would not be adequate to protect the public from serious harm from that juvenile. See *Note 16D.*

Note: Chief officers should ensure that the operation of these provisions at police stations in their areas is subject to supervision and monitoring by an officer of the rank of inspector or above. See *Note 16E.*

C:16.7A The requirement in *paragraph 3.4(b)* that documents and materials essential to effectively challenging the lawfulness of the detainee's arrest and detention must be made available to the detainee and, if they are represented, their solicitor, applies for the purposes of this section and a person's detention after charge. This means that the custody officer making the bail decision (PACE, section 38) or reviewing the need for detention after charge (PACE, section 40), is responsible for determining what, if any, documents or materials are essential and must be made available to the detainee or their solicitor. See *Note 3ZA*.

(B) Documentation

A-109b C:16.8 A record shall be made of anything a detainee says when charged.

C:16.9 Any questions put in an interview after charge and answers given relating to the offence shall be recorded in full during the interview on forms for that purpose and the record signed by the detainee or, if they refuse, by the interviewer and any third parties present. If the questions are audibly recorded or visually recorded the arrangements in Code E or F apply.

C:16.10 If arrangements for a juvenile's transfer into local authority care as in *paragraph 16.7* are not made, the custody officer must record the reasons in a certificate which must be produced before the court with the juvenile. See *Note 16D*.

Notes for Guidance

A-109c *C:16A The custody officer must take into account alternatives to prosecution under the Crime and Disorder Act 1998 applicable to persons under 18, and in national guidance on the cautioning of offenders applicable to persons aged 18 and over.*

C:16AA When a person is arrested under the provisions of the Criminal Justice Act 2003 which allow a person to be re-tried after being acquitted of a serious offence which is a qualifying offence specified in Schedule 5 to that Act and not precluded from further prosecution by virtue of section 75(3) of that Act the detention provisions of PACE are modified and make an officer of the rank of superintendent or above who has not been directly involved in the investigation responsible for determining whether the evidence is sufficient to charge.

C:16AB Where Guidance issued by the Director of Public Prosecutions under section 37B is in force, a custody officer who determines in accordance with that Guidance that there is sufficient evidence to charge the detainee, may detain that person for no longer than is reasonably necessary to decide how that person is to be dealt with under PACE, section 37(7)(a) to (d), including, where appropriate, consultation with the Duty Prosecutor. The period is subject to the maximum period of detention before charge determined by PACE, sections 41 to 44. Where in accordance with the Guidance the case is referred to the CPS for decision, the custody officer should ensure that an officer involved in the investigation sends to the CPS such information as is specified in the Guidance.

C:16B The giving of a warning or the service of the Notice of Intended Prosecution required by the Road Traffic Offenders Act 1988, section 1 does not amount to informing a detainee they may be prosecuted for an offence and so does not preclude further questioning in relation to that offence.

C:16C There is no power under PACE to detain a person and delay action under paragraphs 16.2 to 16.5 solely to await the arrival of the appropriate adult. Reasonable efforts should therefore be made to give the appropriate adult sufficient notice of the time the decision (charge etc.) is to be implemented so that they can be present. If the appropriate adult is not, or cannot be, present at that time, the detainee should be released on bail to return for the decision to be implemented when the adult is present, unless the custody officer determines that the absence of the appropriate adult makes the detainee unsuitable for bail for this purpose. After charge, bail cannot be refused, or release on bail delayed, simply because an appropriate adult is not available, unless the absence of that adult provides the custody officer with the necessary grounds to authorise detention after charge under PACE, section 38.

C:16D Except as in paragraph 16.7, neither a juvenile's behaviour nor the nature of the offence provides grounds for the custody officer to decide it is impracticable to arrange the juvenile's transfer to local authority care. Impracticability concerns the transport and travel requirements and the lack of secure accommodation which is provided for the purposes of restricting liberty does not make it impracticable to transfer the juvenile. Rather, 'impracticable' should be taken to mean that exceptional circumstances render movement of the child impossible or that the juvenile is due at court in such a short space of time that transfer would deprive them of rest or cause them to miss a court appearance. When the reason for not transferring the juvenile is an imminent court appearance, details of the travelling and court appearance times which justify the decision should be included in the certificate. The availability of secure accommodation is only a factor in relation to a juvenile aged 12 or over when other local authority accommodation would not be adequate to protect the public from serious harm from them. The obligation to transfer a juvenile to local authority accommodation applies as much to a juvenile charged during the daytime as to a juvenile to be held overnight, subject to a requirement to bring the juvenile before a court under PACE, section 46.

C:16E The Concordat on Children in Custody published by the Home Office in 2017 provides detailed guid-

ance with the aim of preventing the detention of children in police stations following charge. It is available here: https://www.gov.uk/government/publications/concordat-on-children-in-custody.

C:17 Testing persons for the presence of specified Class A drugs

(A) Action

C:17.1 This section of Code C applies only in selected police stations in police areas where the provisions for drug testing under section 63B of PACE (as amended by section 5 of the Criminal Justice Act 2003 and section 7 of the Drugs Act 2005) are in force and in respect of which the Secretary of State has given a notification to the relevant chief officer of police that arrangements for the taking of samples have been made. Such a notification will cover either a police area as a whole or particular stations within a police area. The notification indicates whether the testing applies to those arrested or charged or under the age of 18 as the case may be and testing can only take place in respect of the persons so indicated in the notification. Testing cannot be carried out unless the relevant notification has been given and has not been withdrawn. See *Note 17F*. **A-109d**

C:17.2 A sample of urine or a non-intimate sample may be taken from a person in police detention for the purpose of ascertaining whether they have any specified Class A drug in their body only where they have been brought before the custody officer and:

(a) either the arrest condition, see *paragraph 17.3*, or the charge condition, see *paragraph 17.4* is met;
(b) the age condition see *paragraph 17.5*, is met;
(c) the notification condition is met in relation to the arrest condition, the charge condition, or the age condition, as the case may be. (Testing on charge and/or arrest must be specifically provided for in the notification for the power to apply. In addition, the fact that testing of under 18s is authorised must be expressly provided for in the notification before the power to test such persons applies.). See *paragraph 17.1*; and
(d) a police officer has requested the person concerned to give the sample (the request condition).

C:17.3 The arrest condition is met where the detainee:

(a) has been arrested for a trigger offence, see *Note 17E*, but not charged with that offence; or
(b) has been arrested for any other offence but not charged with that offence and a police officer of inspector rank or above, who has reasonable grounds for suspecting that their misuse of any specified Class A drug caused or contributed to the offence, has authorised the sample to be taken.

C:17.4 The charge condition is met where the detainee:

(a) has been charged with a trigger offence, or
(b) has been charged with any other offence and a police officer of inspector rank or above, who has reasonable grounds for suspecting that the detainee's misuse of any specified Class A drug caused or contributed to the offence, has authorised the sample to be taken.

C:17.5 The age condition is met where:

(a) in the case of a detainee who has been arrested but not charged as in *paragraph 17.3*, they are aged 18 or over;
(b) in the case of a detainee who has been charged as in *paragraph 17.4*, they are aged 14 or over.

C:17.6 Before requesting a sample from the person concerned, an officer must: **A-109e**

(a) inform them that the purpose of taking the sample is for drug testing under PACE. This is to ascertain whether they have a specified Class A drug present in their body;
(b) warn them that if, when so requested, they fail without good cause to provide a sample they may be liable to prosecution;
(c) where the taking of the sample has been authorised by an inspector or above in accordance with *paragraph 17.3(b)* or *17.4(b)* above, inform them that the authorisation has been given and the grounds for giving it;
(d) remind them of the following rights, which may be exercised at any stage during the period in custody:
    (i) the right to have someone informed of their arrest [see section 5];
    (ii) the right to consult privately with a solicitor and that free independent legal advice is available [see section 6]; and
    (iii) the right to consult these Codes of Practice [see section 3].

C:17.7 In the case of a person who has not attained the age specified in section 63B(5A) of PACE—

(a) the making of the request for a sample under *paragraph 17.2(d)* above;
(b) the giving of the warning and the information under *paragraph 17.6* above; and

(c) the taking of the sample,

may not take place except in the presence of an appropriate adult. See *Note 17G.*

C:17.8 Authorisation by an officer of the rank of inspector or above within *paragraph 17.3(b)* or *17.4(b)* may be given orally or in writing but, if it is given orally, it must be confirmed in writing as soon as practicable.

C:17.9 If a sample is taken from a detainee who has been arrested for an offence but not charged with that offence as in *paragraph 17.3*, no further sample may be taken during the same continuous period of detention. If during that same period the charge condition is also met in respect of that detainee, the sample which has been taken shall be treated as being taken by virtue of the charge condition, see *paragraph 17.4*, being met.

C:17.10 A detainee from whom a sample may be taken may be detained for up to six hours from the time of charge if the custody officer reasonably believes the detention is necessary to enable a sample to be taken. Where the arrest condition is met, a detainee whom the custody officer has decided to release on bail without charge may continue to be detained, but not beyond 24 hours from the relevant time (as defined in section 41(2) of PACE), to enable a sample to be taken.

C:17.11 A detainee in respect of whom the arrest condition is met, but not the charge condition, see *paragraphs 17.3* and *17.4*, and whose release would be required before a sample can be taken had they not continued to be detained as a result of being arrested for a further offence which does not satisfy the arrest condition, may have a sample taken at any time within 24 hours after the arrest for the offence that satisfies the arrest condition.

(B) Documentation

A-109f C:17.12 The following must be recorded in the custody record:

(a) if a sample is taken following authorisation by an officer of the rank of inspector or above, the authorisation and the grounds for suspicion;
(b) the giving of a warning of the consequences of failure to provide a sample;
(c) the time at which the sample was given; and
(d) the time of charge or, where the arrest condition is being relied upon, the time of arrest and, where applicable, the fact that a sample taken after arrest but before charge is to be treated as being taken by virtue of the charge condition, where that is met in the same period of continuous detention. See *paragraph 17.9.*

(C) General

A-109g C:17.13 A sample may only be taken by a prescribed person. See *Note 17C.*

C:17.14 Force may not be used to take any sample for the purpose of drug testing.

C:17.15 The terms "Class A drug" and "misuse" have the same meanings as in the Misuse of Drugs Act 1971."Specified" (in relation to a Class A drug) and "trigger offence" have the same meanings as in Part III of the Criminal Justice and Court Services Act 2000.

C:17.16 Any sample taken:

(a) may not be used for any purpose other than to ascertain whether the person concerned has a specified Class A drug present in his body; and
(b) can be disposed of as clinical waste unless it is to be sent for further analysis in cases where the test result is disputed at the point when the result is known, including on the basis that medication has been taken, or for quality assurance purposes.

(D) Assessment of misuse of drugs

A-109h C:17.17 Under the provisions of Part 3 of the Drugs Act 2005, where a detainee has tested positive for a specified Class A drug under section 63B of PACE a police officer may, at any time before the person's release from the police station, impose a requirement on the detainee to attend an initial assessment of their drug misuse by a suitably qualified person and to remain for its duration. Where such a requirement is imposed, the officer must, at the same time, impose a second requirement on the detainee to attend and remain for a follow-up assessment. The officer must inform the detainee that the second requirement will cease to have effect if, at the initial assessment they are informed that a follow-up assessment is not necessary These requirements may only be imposed on a person if:

(a) they have reached the age of 18
(b) notification has been given by the Secretary of State to the relevant chief officer of police that arrangements for conducting initial and follow-up assessments have been made for those from whom samples for testing have been taken at the police station where the detainee is in custody.

C:17.18 When imposing a requirement to attend an initial assessment and a follow-up assessment the police officer must:

(a) inform the person of the time and place at which the initial assessment is to take place;
(b) explain that this information will be confirmed in writing; and
(c) warn the person that they may be liable to prosecution if they fail without good cause to attend the initial assessment and remain for its duration and if they fail to attend the follow-up assessment and remain for its duration (if so required).

C:17.19 Where a police officer has imposed a requirement to attend an initial assessment and a follow-up assessment in accordance with *paragraph 17.17*, he must, before the person is released from detention, give the person notice in writing which:
(a) confirms their requirement to attend and remain for the duration of the assessments; and
(b) confirms the information and repeats the warning referred to in *paragraph 17.18*.

C:17.20 The following must be recorded in the custody record:
(a) that the requirement to attend an initial assessment and a follow-up assessment has been imposed; and
(b) the information, explanation, warning and notice given in accordance with *paragraphs 17.17* and *17.19*.

C:17.21 Where a notice is given in accordance with paragraph 17.19, a police officer can give the person a further notice in writing which informs the person of any change to the time or place at which the initial assessment is to take place and which repeats the warning referred to in *paragraph 17.18(c)*.

C:17.22 Part 3 of the Drugs Act 2005 also requires police officers to have regard to any guidance issued by the Secretary of State in respect of the assessment provisions.

Notes for Guidance

C:17A When warning a person who is asked to provide a urine or non-intimate sample in accordance with paragraph 17.6(b), the following form of words may be used: **A-109i**

> "*You do not have to provide a sample, but I must warn you that if you fail or refuse without good cause to do so, you will commit an offence for which you may be imprisoned, or fined, or both*".

Where the Welsh language is appropriate, the following form of words may be used:

> "*Does dim rhaid i chi roi sampl, ond mae'n rhaid i mi eich rhybuddio y byddwch chi'n cyflawni trosedd os byddwch chi'n methu neu yn gwrthod gwneud hynny heb reswm da, ac y gellir, oherwydd hynny, eich carcharu, eich dirwyo, neu'r ddau.*"

C:17B A sample has to be sufficient and suitable. A sufficient sample is sufficient in quantity and quality to enable drug-testing analysis to take place. A suitable sample is one which by its nature, is suitable for a particular form of drug analysis.

C:17C A prescribed person in paragraph 17.13 is one who is prescribed in regulations made by the Secretary of State under section 63B(6) of the Police and Criminal Evidence Act 1984. [The regulations are currently contained in regulation SI 2001 No. 2645, the Police and Criminal Evidence Act 1984 (Drug Testing Persons in Police Detention) (Prescribed Persons) Regulations 2001.]

C:17D Samples, and the information derived from them, may not be subsequently used in the investigation of any offence or in evidence against the persons from whom they were taken.

C:17E Trigger offences are:

1. *Offences under the following provisions of the Theft Act 1968:*
   section 1 (theft)
   section 8 (robbery)
   section 9 (burglary)
   section 10 (aggravated burglary)
   section 12 (taking a motor vehicle or other conveyance without authority)
   section 12A (aggravated vehicle-taking)
   section 22 (handling stolen goods)
   section 25 (going equipped for stealing etc.)
2. *Offences under the following provisions of the Misuse of Drugs Act 1971, if committed in respect of a specified Class A drug:-*
   section 4 (restriction on production and supply of controlled drugs)
   section 5(2) (possession of a controlled drug)
   section 5(3) (possession of a controlled drug with intent to supply)
3. *Offences under the following provisions of the Fraud Act 2006:*
   section 1 (fraud)
   section 6 (possession etc. of articles for use in frauds)

section 7 (making or supplying articles for use in frauds)

3A. An offence under section 1(1) of the Criminal Attempts Act 1981 if committed in respect of an offence under

(a) any of the following provisions of the Theft Act 1968:
section 1 (theft)
section 8 (robbery)
section 9 (burglary)
section 22 (handling stolen goods)

(b) section 1 of the Fraud Act 2006 (fraud)

4. Offences under the following provisions of the Vagrancy Act 1824:
section 3 (begging)
section 4 (persistent begging)

C:17F The power to take samples is subject to notification by the Secretary of State that appropriate arrangements for the taking of samples have been made for the police area as a whole or for the particular police station concerned for whichever of the following is specified in the notification:

(a) persons in respect of whom the arrest condition is met;
(b) persons in respect of whom the charge condition is met;
(c) persons who have not attained the age of 18.

Note: Notification is treated as having been given for the purposes of the charge condition in relation to a police area, if testing (on charge) under section 63B(2) of PACE was in force immediately before section 7 of the Drugs Act 2005 was brought into force; and for the purposes of the age condition, in relation to a police area or police station, if immediately before that day, notification that arrangements had been made for the taking of samples from persons under the age of 18 (those aged 14-17) had been given and had not been withdrawn.

C:17G Appropriate adult in paragraph 17.7 means the person's-

(a) parent or guardian or, if they are in the care of a local authority or voluntary organisation, a person representing that authority or organisation; or
(b) a social worker of a local authority; or
(c) if no person falling within (a) or (b) above is available, any responsible person aged 18 or over who is not:

~ *a police officer;*
~ *employed by the police;*
~ *under the direction or control of the chief officer of police force; or*
~ *a person who provides services under contractual arrangements (but without being employed by the chief officer of a police force), to assist that force in relation to the discharge of its chief officer's functions;*

whether or not they are on duty at the time.

ANNEX A: INTIMATE AND STRIP SEARCHES

A Intimate search

A-110 C:1. An intimate search consists of the physical examination of a person's body orifices other than the mouth. The intrusive nature of such searches means the actual and potential risks associated with intimate searches must never be underestimated.

(a) Action

A-110a C:2. Body orifices other than the mouth may be searched only:

(a) if authorised by an officer of inspector rank or above who has reasonable grounds for believing that the person may have concealed on themselves:
  (i) anything which they could and might use to cause physical injury to themselves or others at the station; or
  (ii) a Class A drug which they intended to supply to another or to export;

and the officer has reasonable grounds for believing that an intimate search is the only means of removing those items; and

(b) if the search is under *paragraph 2(a)(ii)* (a drug offence search), the detainee's appropriate consent has been given in writing.

C:2A. Before the search begins, a police officer or designated detention officer, must tell the detainee:-

(a) that the authority to carry out the search has been given;
(b) the grounds for giving the authorisation and for believing that the article cannot be removed without an intimate search.

C:2B. Before a detainee is asked to give appropriate consent to a search under *paragraph 2(a)(ii)* (a drug offence search) they must be warned that if they refuse without good cause their refusal may harm their case if it comes to trial, see *Note A6*. This warning may be given by a police officer or member of police staff. In the case of a juvenile or a vulnerable person, the seeking and giving of consent must take place in the presence of the appropriate adult. A juvenile's consent is only valid if their parent's or guardian's consent is also obtained unless the juvenile is under 14, when their parent's or guardian's consent is sufficient in its own right. A detainee who is not legally represented must be reminded of their entitlement to have free legal advice, see Code C, *paragraph 6.5*, and the reminder noted in the custody record.

C:3. An intimate search may only be carried out by a registered medical practitioner or registered nurse, unless an officer of at least inspector rank considers this is not practicable and the search is to take place under *paragraph 2(a)(i)*, in which case a police officer may carry out the search. See *Notes A1* to *A5*.

C:3A. Any proposal for a search under *paragraph 2(a)(i)* to be carried out by someone other than a registered medical practitioner or registered nurse must only be considered as a last resort and when the authorising officer is satisfied the risks associated with allowing the item to remain with the detainee outweigh the risks associated with removing it. See *Notes A1* to *A5*.

C:4. An intimate search under:

- *paragraph 2(a)(i)* may take place only at a hospital, surgery, other medical premises or police station;
- *paragraph 2(a)(ii)* may take place only at a hospital, surgery or other medical premises and must be carried out by a registered medical practitioner or a registered nurse.

C:5. An intimate search at a police station of a juvenile or vulnerable person may take place only in the presence of an appropriate adult of the same sex (see *Annex L*), unless the detainee specifically requests a particular appropriate adult of the opposite sex who is readily available. In the case of a juvenile, the search may take place in the absence of the appropriate adult only if the juvenile signifies in the presence of the appropriate adult they do not want the appropriate adult present during the search and the appropriate adult agrees. A record shall be made of the juvenile's decision and signed by the appropriate adult.

C:6. When an intimate search under *paragraph 2(a)(i)* is carried out by a police officer, the officer must be of the same sex as the detainee (see *Annex L*). A minimum of two people, other than the detainee, must be present during the search. Subject to *paragraph 5*, no person of the opposite sex who is not a medical practitioner or nurse shall be present, nor shall anyone whose presence is unnecessary. The search shall be conducted with proper regard to the dignity, sensitivity and vulnerability of the detainee including in particular, their health, hygiene and welfare needs to which *paragraphs 9.3A* and *9.3B* apply.

(b) Documentation

C:7. In the case of an intimate search, the following shall be recorded as soon as practicable in the detainee's custody record: **A-110b**

(a) for searches under paragraphs 2(a)(i) and (ii);
- the authorisation to carry out the search;
- the grounds for giving the authorisation;
- the grounds for believing the article could not be removed without an intimate search;
- which parts of the detainee's body were searched;
- who carried out the search;
- who was present;
- the result.

(b) for searches under paragraph 2(a)(ii):
- the giving of the warning required by *paragraph 2B*;
- the fact that the appropriate consent was given or (as the case may be) refused, and if refused, the reason given for the refusal (if any).

C:8. If an intimate search is carried out by a police officer, the reason why it was impracticable for a registered medical practitioner or registered nurse to conduct it must be recorded.

B Strip search

C:9. A strip search is a search involving the removal of more than outer clothing. In this Code, outer clothing includes shoes and socks. **A-110c**

(a) Action

C:10. A strip search may take place only if it is considered necessary to remove an article which a detainee would not be allowed to keep and the officer reasonably considers the detainee might have **A-110ca** concealed such an article. Strip searches shall not be routinely carried out if there is no reason to consider that articles are concealed.

The conduct of strip searches

A-110cb C:11. When strip searches are conducted:

(a) a police officer carrying out a strip search must be the same sex as the detainee (see *Annex L*);

(b) the search shall take place in an area where the detainee cannot be seen by anyone who does not need to be present, nor by a member of the opposite sex (see *Annex L*) except an appropriate adult who has been specifically requested by the detainee;

(c) except in cases of urgency, where there is risk of serious harm to the detainee or to others, whenever a strip search involves exposure of intimate body parts, there must be at least two people present other than the detainee, and if the search is of a juvenile or vulnerable person, one of the people must be the appropriate adult. Except in urgent cases as above, a search of a juvenile may take place in the absence of the appropriate adult only if the juvenile signifies in the presence of the appropriate adult that they do not want the appropriate adult to be present during the search and the appropriate adult agrees. A record shall be made of the juvenile's decision and signed by the appropriate adult. The presence of more than two people, other than an appropriate adult, shall be permitted only in the most exceptional circumstances;

(d) the search shall be conducted with proper regard to the dignity, sensitivity and vulnerability of the detainee in these circumstances, including in particular, their health, hygiene and welfare needs to which *paragraphs 9.3A* and *9.3B* apply. Every reasonable effort shall be made to secure the detainee's co-operation, maintain their dignity and minimise embarrassment. Detainees who are searched shall not normally be required to remove all their clothes at the same time, e.g. a person should be allowed to remove clothing above the waist and redress before removing further clothing;

(e) if necessary to assist the search, the detainee may be required to hold their arms in the air or to stand with their legs apart and bend forward so a visual examination may be made of the genital and anal areas provided no physical contact is made with any body orifice;

(f) if articles are found, the detainee shall be asked to hand them over. If articles are found within any body orifice other than the mouth, and the detainee refuses to hand them over, their removal would constitute an intimate search, which must be carried out as in *Part A*;

(g) a strip search shall be conducted as quickly as possible, and the detainee allowed to dress as soon as the procedure is complete.

(b) Documentation

A-110d C:12. A record shall be made on the custody record of a strip search including the reason it was considered necessary, those present and any result.

Notes for Guidance

A-110e *C:A1 Before authorising any intimate search, the authorising officer must make every reasonable effort to persuade the detainee to hand the article over without a search. If the detainee agrees, a registered medical practitioner or registered nurse should whenever possible be asked to assess the risks involved and, if necessary, attend to assist the detainee.*

C:A2 If the detainee does not agree to hand the article over without a search, the authorising officer must carefully review all the relevant factors before authorising an intimate search. In particular, the officer must consider whether the grounds for believing an article may be concealed are reasonable.

C:A3 If authority is given for a search under paragraph 2(a)(i), a registered medical practitioner or registered nurse shall be consulted whenever possible. The presumption should be that the search will be conducted by the registered medical practitioner or registered nurse and the authorising officer must make every reasonable effort to persuade the detainee to allow the medical practitioner or nurse to conduct the search.

C:A4 A constable should only be authorised to carry out a search as a last resort and when all other approaches have failed. In these circumstances, the authorising officer must be satisfied the detainee might use the article for one or more of the purposes in paragraph 2(a)(i) and the physical injury likely to be caused is sufficiently severe to justify authorising a constable to carry out the search.

C:A5 If an officer has any doubts whether to authorise an intimate search by a constable, the officer should seek advice from an officer of superintendent rank or above.

C:A6 In warning a detainee who is asked to consent to an intimate drug offence search, as in paragraph 2B, the following form of words may be used:

> "*You do not have to allow yourself to be searched, but I must warn you that if you refuse without good cause, your refusal may harm your case if it comes to trial.*"

Where the use of the Welsh Language is appropriate, the following form of words may be used:

"Nid oes rhaid i chi roi caniatâd i gael eich archwilio, ond mae'n rhaid i mi eich rhybuddio os gwrthodwch heb reswm da, y gallai eich penderfyniad i wrthod wneud niwed i'ch achos pe bai'n dod gerbron llys."

ANNEX B: DELAY IN NOTIFICATION OF ARREST AND WHEREABOUTS OR ALLOWING ACCESS TO LEGAL ADVICE

A Persons detained under PACE

C:1. The exercise of the rights in Section 5 or Section 6, or both, may be delayed if the person is in police detention, as in PACE, section 118(2), in connection with an indictable offence, has not yet been charged with an offence and an officer of superintendent rank or above, or inspector rank or above only for the rights in Section 5, has reasonable grounds for believing their exercise will: **A-110f**

(i) lead to:
- interference with, or harm to, evidence connected with an indictable offence; or
- interference with, or physical harm to, other people; or

(ii) lead to alerting other people suspected of having committed an indictable offence but not yet arrested for it; or

(iii) hinder the recovery of property obtained in consequence of the commission of such an offence.

C:2. These rights may also be delayed if the officer has reasonable grounds to believe that:

(i) the person detained for an indictable offence has benefited from their criminal conduct (decided in accordance with Part 2 of the Proceeds of Crime Act 2002); and

(ii) the recovery of the value of the property constituting that benefit will be hindered by the exercise of either right.

C:3. Authority to delay a detainee's right to consult privately with a solicitor may be given only if the authorising officer has reasonable grounds to believe the solicitor the detainee wants to consult will, inadvertently or otherwise, pass on a message from the detainee or act in some other way which will have any of the consequences specified under *paragraphs 1 or 2*. In these circumstances, the detainee must be allowed to choose another solicitor. See *Note B3*.

C:4. If the detainee wishes to see a solicitor, access to that solicitor may not be delayed on the grounds they might advise the detainee not to answer questions or the solicitor was initially asked to attend the police station by someone else. In the latter case, the detainee must be told the solicitor has come to the police station at another person's request, and must be asked to sign the custody record to signify whether they want to see the solicitor.

C:5. The fact the grounds for delaying notification of arrest may be satisfied does not automatically mean the grounds for delaying access to legal advice will also be satisfied.

C:6. These rights may be delayed only for as long as grounds exist and in no case beyond 36 hours after the relevant time as in PACE, section 41. If the grounds cease to apply within this time, the detainee must, as soon as practicable, be asked if they want to exercise either right, the custody record must be noted accordingly, and action taken in accordance with the relevant section of the Code.

C:7. A detained person must be permitted to consult a solicitor for a reasonable time before any court hearing.

Not used **A-110g**

C Documentation

C:13. The grounds for action under this Annex shall be recorded and the detainee informed of them as soon as practicable. **A-110h**

C:14. Any reply given by a detainee under *paragraphs 6* or *11* must be recorded and the detainee asked to endorse the record in relation to whether they want to receive legal advice at this point.

D Cautions and special warnings

C:15. When a suspect detained at a police station is interviewed during any period for which access to legal advice has been delayed under this Annex, the court or jury may not draw adverse inferences from their silence. **A-110i**

Notes for Guidance

C:B1 Even if Annex B applies in the case of a juvenile, or a vulnerable person, action to inform the appropriate adult and the person responsible for a juvenile's welfare, if that is a different person, must nevertheless be taken as in paragraph 3.13 and 3.15. **A110j**

C:B2 In the case of Commonwealth citizens and foreign nationals, see Note 7A.

C:B3 A decision to delay access to a specific solicitor is likely to be a rare occurrence and only when it can be shown the suspect is capable of misleading that particular solicitor and there is more than a substantial risk that the suspect will succeed in causing information to be conveyed which will lead to one or more of the specified consequences.

ANNEX C: RESTRICTION ON DRAWING ADVERSE INFERENCES FROM SILENCE AND TERMS OF THE CAUTION WHEN THE RESTRICTION APPLIES

(a) The restriction on drawing adverse inferences from silence

A-110k C:1. The Criminal Justice and Public Order Act 1994, sections 34, 36 and 37 as amended by the Youth Justice and Criminal Evidence Act 1999, section 58 describe the conditions under which adverse inferences may be drawn from a person's failure or refusal to say anything about their involvement in the offence when interviewed, after being charged or informed they may be prosecuted. These provisions are subject to an overriding restriction on the ability of a court or jury to draw adverse inferences from a person's silence. This restriction applies:

(a) to any detainee at a police station, see *Note 10C* who, before being interviewed, see section 11 or being charged or informed they may be prosecuted, see section 16, has:
  (i) asked for legal advice, see section 6, *paragraph 6.1*;
  (ii) not been allowed an opportunity to consult a solicitor, including the duty solicitor, as in this Code; and
  (iii) not changed their mind about wanting legal advice, see section 6, *paragraph 6.6(d)*.
  Note the condition in (ii) will:
  ~ apply when a detainee who has asked for legal advice is interviewed before speaking to a solicitor as in section 6, *paragraph 6.6(a)* or *(b)*;
  ~ not apply if the detained person declines to ask for the duty solicitor, see section 6, *paragraphs 6.6(c)* and *(d)*.

(b) to any person charged with, or informed they may be prosecuted for, an offence who:
  (i) has had brought to their notice a written statement made by another person or the content of an interview with another person which relates to that offence, see section 16, *paragraph 16.4*;
  (ii) is interviewed about that offence, see section 16, *paragraph 16.5*; or
  (iii) makes a written statement about that offence, see *Annex D paragraphs 4* and 9.

(b) Terms of the caution when the restriction applies

A-110ka C:2. When a requirement to caution arises at a time when the restriction on drawing adverse inferences from silence applies, the caution shall be:

'*You do not have to say anything, but anything you do say may be given in evidence.*'

Where the use of the Welsh Language is appropriate, the caution may be used directly in Welsh in the following terms:

'*Does dim rhaid i chi ddweud dim byd, ond gall unrhyw beth yr ydych chi'n ei ddweud gael ei roi fel tystiolaeth.*'

C:3. Whenever the restriction either begins to apply or ceases to apply after a caution has already been given, the person shall be re-cautioned in the appropriate terms. The changed position on drawing inferences and that the previous caution no longer applies shall also be explained to the detainee in ordinary language. See *Note C2*.

Notes for Guidance

A-110kb *C:C1 The restriction on drawing inferences from silence does not apply to a person who has not been detained and who therefore cannot be prevented from seeking legal advice if they want to, see paragraphs 10.2 and 3.21.*

C:C2 The following is suggested as a framework to help explain changes in the position on drawing adverse inferences if the restriction on drawing adverse inferences from silence:

(a) begins to apply:

'*The caution you were previously given no longer applies. This is because after that caution:*
(i) you asked to speak to a solicitor but have not yet been allowed an opportunity to speak to a solicitor. See paragraph 1(a); or

(ii) you have been charged with/informed you may be prosecuted. See paragraph 1(b).

'This means that from now on, adverse inferences cannot be drawn at court and your defence will not be harmed just because you choose to say nothing. Please listen carefully to the caution I am about to give you because it will apply from now on. You will see that it does not say anything about your defence being harmed.'

(b) ceases to apply before or at the time the person is charged or informed they may be prosecuted, see paragraph 1(a);

'The caution you were previously given no longer applies. This is because after that caution you have been allowed an opportunity to speak to a solicitor. Please listen carefully to the caution I am about to give you because it will apply from now on. It explains how your defence at court may be affected if you choose to say nothing.'

ANNEX D: WRITTEN STATEMENTS UNDER CAUTION

(a) Written by a person under caution

C:1. A person shall always be invited to write down what they want to say. **A-110l**

C:2. A person who has not been charged with, or informed they may be prosecuted for, any offence to which the statement they want to write relates, shall:

(a) unless the statement is made at a time when the restriction on drawing adverse inferences from silence applies, see Annex C, be asked to write out and sign the following before writing what they want to say:

'*I make this statement of my own free will. I understand that I do not have to say anything but that it may harm my defence if I do not mention when questioned something which I later rely on in court. This statement may be given in evidence.*';

(b) if the statement is made at a time when the restriction on drawing adverse inferences from silence applies, be asked to write out and sign the following before writing what they want to say;

'*I make this statement of my own free will. I understand that I do not have to say anything. This statement may be given in evidence.*'

C:3. When a person, on the occasion of being charged with or informed they may be prosecuted for any offence, asks to make a statement which relates to any such offence and wants to write it they shall:

(a) unless the restriction on drawing adverse inferences from silence, see *Annex C*, applied when they were so charged or informed they may be prosecuted, be asked to write out and sign the following before writing what they want to say:

'*I make this statement of my own free will. I understand that I do not have to say anything but that it may harm my defence if I do not mention when questioned something which I later rely on in court. This statement may be given in evidence.*';

(b) if the restriction on drawing adverse inferences from silence applied when they were so charged or informed they may be prosecuted, be asked to write out and sign the following before writing what they want to say:

'*I make this statement of my own free will. I understand that I do not have to say anything. This statement may be given in evidence.*'

C:4. When a person who has already been charged with or informed they may be prosecuted for any offence asks to make a statement which relates to any such offence and wants to write it, they shall be asked to write out and sign the following before writing what they want to say:

'*I make this statement of my own free will. I understand that I do not have to say anything. This statement may be given in evidence.*';

C:5. Any person writing their own statement shall be allowed to do so without any prompting except a police officer or other police staff may indicate to them which matters are material or question any ambiguity in the statement.

(b) Written by a police officer or other police staff

C:6. If a person says they would like someone to write the statement for them, a police officer, or other police staff shall write the statement. **A-110la**

C:7. If the person has not been charged with, or informed they may be prosecuted for, any offence to which the statement they want to make relates they shall, before starting, be asked to sign, or make their mark, to the following:

(a) unless the statement is made at a time when the restriction on drawing adverse inferences from silence applies, see *Annex C*:

> *'I, ..., wish to make a statement. I want someone to write down what I say. I understand that I do not have to say anything but that it may harm my defence if I do not mention when questioned something which I later rely on in court. This statement may be given in evidence.'*;

(b) if the statement is made at a time when the restriction on drawing adverse inferences from silence applies:

> *'I, ..., wish to make a statement. I want someone to write down what I say. I understand that I do not have to say anything. This statement may be given in evidence.'*

C:8. If, on the occasion of being charged with or informed they may be prosecuted for any offence, the person asks to make a statement which relates to any such offence they shall before starting be asked to sign, or make their mark to, the following:

(a) unless the restriction on drawing adverse inferences from silence applied, see *Annex C*, when they were so charged or informed they may be prosecuted:

> *'I, ..., wish to make a statement. I want someone to write down what I say. I understand that I do not have to say anything but that it may harm my defence if I do not mention when questioned something which I later rely on in court. This statement may be given in evidence.'*;

(b) if the restriction on drawing adverse inferences from silence applied when they were so charged or informed they may be prosecuted:

> *'I, ..., wish to make a statement. I want someone to write down what I say. I understand that I do not have to say anything. This statement may be given in evidence.'*

C:9. If, having already been charged with or informed they may be prosecuted for any offence, a person asks to make a statement which relates to any such offence they shall before starting, be asked to sign, or make their mark to:

> *'I, ..., wish to make a statement. I want someone to write down what I say. I understand that I do not have to say anything. This statement may be given in evidence.'*

C:10. The person writing the statement must take down the exact words spoken by the person making it and must not edit or paraphrase it. Any questions that are necessary, e.g. to make it more intelligible, and the answers given must be recorded at the same time on the statement form.

C:11. When the writing of a statement is finished the person making it shall be asked to read it and to make any corrections, alterations or additions they want. When they have finished reading they shall be asked to write and sign or make their mark on the following certificate at the end of the statement:

> *'I have read the above statement, and I have been able to correct, alter or add anything I wish. This statement is true. I have made it of my own free will.'*

C:12. If the person making the statement cannot read, or refuses to read it, or to write the above mentioned certificate at the end of it or to sign it, the person taking the statement shall read it to them and ask them if they would like to correct, alter or add anything and to put their signature or make their mark at the end. The person taking the statement shall certify on the statement itself what has occurred.

ANNEX E: SUMMARY OF PROVISIONS RELATING TO VULNERABLE PERSONS

A-110m C:1. If at any time, an officer has reason to suspect that a person of any age may be vulnerable (see *paragraph 1.13(d)*), in the absence of clear evidence to dispel that suspicion that person shall be treated as such for the purposes of this Code and to establish whether any such reason may exist in relation to a person suspected of committing an offence (see *paragraph 10.1* and *Note 10A*), the custody officer in the case of a detained person, or the officer investigating the offence in the case of a person who has not been arrested or detained, shall take, or cause to be taken, (see *paragraph 3.5* and *Note 3F*) the following action:

(a) reasonable enquiries shall be made to ascertain what information is available that is relevant to any of the factors described in *paragraph 1.13(d)* as indicating that the person may be vulnerable might apply;

(b) a record shall be made describing whether any of those factors appear to apply and provide any reason to suspect that the person may be vulnerable or (as the case may be) may not be vulnerable; and

(c) the record mentioned in sub-paragraph (b) shall be made available to be taken into account by police officers, police staff and any others who, in accordance with the provisions of this or any other Code, are entitled to communicate with the person in question. This would include any solicitor, appropriate adult and health care professional and is particularly relevant to communication by telephone or by means of a live link (see *paragraphs 12.9A* (interviews), *13.12* (interpretation), and *15.3C, 15.11A, 15.11B, 15.11C* and *15.11D* (reviews and extension of detention)).

See *Notes 1G, E5, E6* and *E7*.

C:2. In the case of a person who is vulnerable, "the appropriate adult" means:

(i) a relative, guardian or other person responsible for their care or custody;

(ii) someone experienced in dealing with vulnerable persons but who is not:

~ a police officer;

~ employed by the police;

~ under the direction or control of the chief officer of a police force;

~ a person who provides services under contractual arrangements (but without being employed by the chief officer of a police force), to assist that force in relation to the discharge of its chief officer's functions,

whether or not they are on duty at the time.

(iii) failing these, some other responsible adult aged 18 or over who is other than a person described in the bullet points in sub-paragraph (ii) above.

See *paragraph 1.7(b)* and *Notes 1D* and *1F*.

C:2A The role of the appropriate adult is to safeguard the rights, entitlements and welfare of 'vulnerable persons' (see *paragraph 1*) to whom the provisions of this and any other Code of Practice apply. For this reason, the appropriate adult is expected, amongst other things, to:

- support, advise and assist them when, in accordance with this Code or any other Code of Practice, they are given or asked to provide information or participate in any procedure;
- observe whether the police are acting properly and fairly to respect their rights and entitlements, and inform an officer of the rank of inspector or above if they consider that they are not;
- assist them to communicate with the police whilst respecting their right to say nothing unless they want to as set out in the terms of the caution (see *paragraphs 10.5* and *10.6*);and
- help them understand their rights and ensure that those rights are protected and respected (see *paragraphs 3.15, 3.17, 6.5A* and *11.17*).

See *paragraph 1.7A*.

C:3. If the custody officer authorises the detention of a vulnerable person, the custody officer must as soon as practicable inform the appropriate adult of the grounds for detention and the person's whereabouts, and secure the attendance of the appropriate adult at the police station to see the detainee. If the appropriate adult:

- is already at the station when information is given as in *paragraphs 3.1* to *3.5* the information must be given in their presence;
- is not at the station when the provisions of paragraph 3.1 to 3.5 are complied with these provisions must be complied with again in their presence once they arrive.

See *paragraphs 3.15* to *3.17*

C:4. If the appropriate adult, having been informed of the right to legal advice, considers legal advice should be taken, the provisions of *section 6* apply as if the vulnerable person had requested access to legal advice. See *paragraphs 3.19, 6.5A* and *Note E1*. **A-110n**

C:5. The custody officer must make sure a person receives appropriate clinical attention as soon as reasonably practicable if the person appears to be suffering from a mental disorder or in urgent cases immediately call the nearest appropriate healthcare professional or an ambulance. See Code C *paragraphs 3.16, 9.5* and *9.6* which apply when a person is detained under the Mental Health Act 1983, sections 135 and 136, as amended by the Policing and Crime Act 2017.

C:6. *Not used.*

C:7. If a vulnerable person is cautioned in the absence of the appropriate adult, the caution must be repeated in the appropriate adult's presence. See *paragraph 10.12*.

C:8. A vulnerable person must not be interviewed or asked to provide or sign a written statement in the absence of the appropriate adult unless the provisions of *paragraphs 11.1* or *11.18* to *11.20* apply. Questioning in these circumstances may not continue in the absence of the appropriate adult once sufficient information to avert the risk has been obtained. A record shall be made of the grounds for any decision to begin an interview in these circumstances. See *paragraphs 11.1, 11.15* and *11.18* to *11.20.*

C:9. If the appropriate adult is present at an interview, they shall be informed they are not expected to act simply as an observer and the purposes of their presence are to:

- advise the interviewee;
- observe whether or not the interview is being conducted properly and fairly;
- facilitate communication with the interviewee.

See *paragraph 11.17*

C:10. If the detention of a vulnerable person is reviewed by a review officer or a superintendent, the appropriate adult must, if available at the time, be given an opportunity to make representations to the officer about the need for continuing detention. See *paragraph 15.3.*

C:11. If the custody officer charges a vulnerable person with an offence or takes such other action as is appropriate when there is sufficient evidence for a prosecution this must be carried out in the presence of the appropriate adult if they are at the police station. A copy of the written notice embodying any charge must also be given to the appropriate adult. See *paragraphs 16.1* to *16.4A*

C:12. An intimate or strip search of a vulnerable person may take place only in the presence of the appropriate adult of the same sex, unless the detainee specifically requests the presence of a particular adult of the opposite sex. A strip search may take place in the absence of an appropriate adult only in cases of urgency when there is a risk of serious harm to the detainee or others. See *Annex A, paragraphs 5* and *11(c).*

C:13. Particular care must be taken when deciding whether to use any form of approved restraints on a vulnerable person in a locked cell. See *paragraph 8.2.*

Notes for Guidance

A-110o *C:E1 The purpose of the provisions at paragraphs 3.19* and *6.5A* is to protect the rights of a vulnerable person who does not understand the significance of what is said to them. A vulnerable person should always be given an opportunity, when an appropriate adult is called to the police station, to consult privately with a solicitor in the absence of the appropriate adult if they want.

C:E2 Although vulnerable persons are often capable of providing reliable evidence, they may, without knowing or wanting to do so, be particularly prone in certain circumstances to provide information that may be unreliable, misleading or self-incriminating. Special care should always be taken when questioning such a person, and the appropriate adult should be involved if there is any doubt about a person's mental state or capacity. Because of the risk of unreliable evidence, it is important to obtain corroboration of any facts admitted whenever possible.

C:E3 Because of the risks referred to in Note E2, which the presence of the appropriate adult is intended to minimise, officers of superintendent rank or above should exercise their discretion to authorise the commencement of an interview in the appropriate adult's absence only in exceptional cases, if it is necessary to avert one or more of the specified risks in paragraph 11.1. See paragraphs 11.1 and *11.18 to 11.20.*

C:E4 When a person is detained under section 136 of the Mental Health Act 1983 for assessment, the appropriate adult has no role in the assessment process and their presence is not required.

C:E5 For the purposes of Annex E paragraph 1, examples of relevant information that may be available include:

- *the behaviour of the adult or juvenile;*
- *the mental health and capacity of the adult or juvenile;*
- *what the adult or juvenile says about themselves;*
- *information from relatives and friends of the adult or juvenile;*
- *information from police officers and staff and from police records;*
- *information from health and social care (including liaison and diversion services) and other professionals who know, or have had previous contact with, the individual and may be able to contribute to assessing their need for help and support from an appropriate adult. This includes contacts and assessments arranged by the police or at the request of the individual or (as applicable) their appropriate adult or solicitor.*

C:E6 The Mental Health Act 1983 Code of Practice at page 26 describes the range of clinically recognised conditions which can fall with the meaning of mental disorder for the purpose of paragraph 1.13(d). The Code is published here: *https://www.gov.uk/government/publications/code-of-practice-mental-health-act-1983.*

C:E7 When a person is under the influence of drink and/or drugs, it is not intended that they are to be treated as vulnerable and requiring an appropriate adult for the purpose of Annex E paragraph 1 unless other information indicates that any of the factors described in paragraph 1.13(d) may apply to that person. When the person has recovered from the effects of drink and/or drugs, they should be re-assessed in accordance with Annex E paragraph 1. See paragraph 15.4A for application to live link.

ANNEX F

A-110p *Not used*

ANNEX G: FITNESS TO BE INTERVIEWED

C:1. This Annex contains general guidance to help police officers and healthcare professionals assess whether a detainee might be at risk in an interview. **A-110q**

C:2. A detainee may be at risk in an interview if it is considered that:

(a) conducting the interview could significantly harm the detainee's physical or mental state;

(b) anything the detainee says in the interview about their involvement or suspected involvement in the offence about which they are being interviewed *might* be considered unreliable in subsequent court proceedings because of their physical or mental state.

C:3. In assessing whether the detainee should be interviewed, the following must be considered:

(a) how the detainee's physical or mental state might affect their ability to understand the nature and purpose of the interview, to comprehend what is being asked and to appreciate the significance of any answers given and make rational decisions about whether they want to say anything;

(b) the extent to which the detainee's replies may be affected by their physical or mental condition rather than representing a rational and accurate explanation of their involvement in the offence;

(c) how the nature of the interview, which could include particularly probing questions, might affect the detainee.

C:4. It is essential healthcare professionals who are consulted consider the functional ability of the detainee rather than simply relying on a medical diagnosis, e.g. it is possible for a person with severe mental illness to be fit for interview.

C:5. Healthcare professionals should advise on the need for an appropriate adult to be present, whether reassessment of the person's fitness for interview may be necessary if the interview lasts beyond a specified time, and whether a further specialist opinion may be required.

C:6. When healthcare professionals identify risks they should be asked to quantify the risks. They should inform the custody officer:

- whether the person's condition:
  - ˜ is likely to improve;
  - ˜ will require or be amenable to treatment; and
- indicate how long it may take for such improvement to take effect.

C:7. The role of the healthcare professional is to consider the risks and advise the custody officer of the outcome of that consideration. The healthcare professional's determination and any advice or recommendations should be made in writing and form part of the custody record.

C:8. Once the healthcare professional has provided that information, it is a matter for the custody officer to decide whether or not to allow the interview to go ahead and if the interview is to proceed, to determine what safeguards are needed. Nothing prevents safeguards being provided in addition to those required under the Code. An example might be to have an appropriate healthcare professional present during the interview, in addition to an appropriate adult, in order constantly to monitor the person's condition and how it is being affected by the interview.

ANNEX H: DETAINED PERSON: OBSERVATION LIST

C:1. If any detainee fails to meet any of the following criteria, an appropriate healthcare professional or an ambulance must be called. **A-110r**

C:2. When assessing the level of rousability, consider:

Rousability - can they be woken?

- go into the cell
- call their name
- shake gently

Response to questions - can they give appropriate answers to questions such as:

- What's your name?
- Where do you live?
- Where do you think you are?

Response to commands - can they respond appropriately to commands such as:

- Open your eyes!
- Lift one arm, now the other arm!

C:3. Remember to take into account the possibility or presence of other illnesses, injury, or mental condition; a person who is drowsy and smells of alcohol may also have the following:

- Diabetes
- Epilepsy
- Head injury
- Drug intoxication or overdose

- Stroke

ANNEX I

A-110s *Not used*

ANNEX J

A-110t *Not used*

ANNEX K: X-RAYS AND ULTRASOUND SCANS

(a) Action

A-110u C:1. PACE, section 55A allows a person who has been arrested and is in police detention to have an X-ray taken of them or an ultrasound scan to be carried out on them (or both) if:

(a) authorised by an officer of inspector rank or above who has reasonable grounds for believing that the detainee:
  (i) may have swallowed a Class A drug; and
  (ii) was in possession of that Class A drug with the intention of supplying it to another or to export; and
(b) the detainee's appropriate consent has been given in writing.

C:2. Before an x-ray is taken or an ultrasound scan carried out, a police officer or designated detention officer must tell the detainee:-

(a) that the authority has been given; and
(b) the grounds for giving the authorisation.

C:3. Before a detainee is asked to give appropriate consent to an x-ray or an ultrasound scan, they must be warned that if they refuse without good cause their refusal may harm their case if it comes to trial, see *Notes K1* and *K2*. This warning may be given by a police officer or member of police staff. In the case of juveniles and vulnerable persons, the seeking and giving of consent must take place in the presence of the appropriate adult. A juvenile's consent is only valid if their parent's or guardian's consent is also obtained unless the juvenile is under 14, when their parent's or guardian's consent is sufficient in its own right. A detainee who is not legally represented must be reminded of their entitlement to have free legal advice, see Code C, *paragraph 6.5*, and the reminder noted in the custody record.

C:4. An x-ray may be taken, or an ultrasound scan may be carried out, only by a registered medical practitioner or registered nurse, and only at a hospital, surgery or other medical premises.

(b) Documentation

A-110ua C:5. The following shall be recorded as soon as practicable in the detainee's custody record:

(a) the authorisation to take the x-ray or carry out the ultrasound scan (or both);
(b) the grounds for giving the authorisation;
(c) the giving of the warning required by *paragraph 3*; and
(d) the fact that the appropriate consent was given or (as the case may be) refused, and if refused, the reason given for the refusal (if any); and
(e) if an x-ray is taken or an ultrasound scan carried out:
  - where it was taken or carried out;
  - who took it or carried it out;
  - who was present;
  - the result.

C:6 Not used.

Notes for Guidance

A-110ub *C:K1 If authority is given for an x-ray to be taken or an ultrasound scan to be carried out (or both), consideration should be given to asking a registered medical practitioner or registered nurse to explain to the detainee what is involved and to allay any concerns the detainee might have about the effect which taking an x-ray or carrying out an ultrasound scan might have on them. If appropriate consent is not given, evidence of the explanation may, if the case comes to trial, be relevant to determining whether the detainee had a good cause for refusing.*

C:K2 In warning a detainee who is asked to consent to an X-ray being taken or an ultrasound scan being carried out (or both), as in paragraph 3, the following form of words may be used:

> "*You do not have to allow an x-ray of you to be taken or an ultrasound scan to be carried out on you, but I must warn you that if you refuse without good cause, your refusal may harm your case if it comes to trial.*"

Where the use of the Welsh Language is appropriate, the following form of words may be provided in Welsh:

"Does dim rhaid i chi ganiatáu cymryd sgan uwchsain neu belydr-x (neu'r ddau) arnoch, ond mae'n rhaid i mi eich rhybuddio os byddwch chi'n gwrthod gwneud hynny heb reswm da, fe allai hynny niweidio eich achos pe bai'n dod gerbron llys."

ANNEX L: ESTABLISHING GENDER OF PERSONS FOR THE PURPOSE OF SEARCHING AND CERTAIN OTHER PROCEDURES

C:1. Certain provisions of this and other PACE Codes explicitly state that searches and other procedures may only be carried out by, or in the presence of, persons of the same sex as the person subject to the search or other procedure or require action to be taken or information to be given which depends on whether the detainee is treated as being male or female. See *Note L1*. **A-110v**

C:2. All such searches, procedures and requirements must be carried out with courtesy, consideration and respect for the person concerned. Police officers should show particular sensitivity when dealing with transgender individuals (including transsexual persons) and transvestite persons (see *Notes L2, L3* and *L4*).

(a) Consideration

C:3. In law, the gender (and accordingly the sex) of an individual is their gender as registered at birth unless they have been issued with a Gender Recognition Certificate (GRC) under the Gender Recognition Act 2004 (GRA), in which case the person's gender is their acquired gender. This means that if the acquired gender is the male gender, the person's sex becomes that of a man and, if it is the female gender, the person's sex becomes that of a woman and they must be treated as their acquired gender. **A-110va**

C:4. When establishing whether the person concerned should be treated as being male or female for the purposes of these searches, procedures and requirements, the following approach which is designed to maintain their dignity, minimise embarrassment and secure their co-operation should be followed:

(a) The person must not be asked whether they have a GRC (see paragraph 8);

(b) If there is no doubt as to as to whether the person concerned should be treated as being male or female, they should be dealt with as being of that sex.

(c) If at any time (including during the search or carrying out the procedure) there is doubt as to whether the person should be treated, or continue to be treated, as being male or female:

(i) the person should be asked what gender they consider themselves to be. If they express a preference to be dealt with as a particular gender, they should be asked to indicate and confirm their preference by signing the custody record or, if a custody record has not been opened, the search record or the officer's notebook. Subject to (ii) below, the person should be treated according to their preference except with regard to the requirements to provide *that* person with information concerning menstrual products and their personal needs relating to health, hygiene and welfare described in *paragraph 3.20A* (if aged under 18) and *paragraphs 9.3A* and *9.3B* (if aged 18 or over). In these cases, a person whose confirmed preference is to be dealt with as being male should be asked in private whether they wish to speak in private with a member of the custody staff of a gender of their choosing about the provision of menstrual products and their personal needs, notwithstanding their confirmed preference (see *Note L3A*);

(ii) if there are grounds to doubt that the preference in (i) accurately reflects the person's predominant lifestyle, for example, if they ask to be treated as a woman but documents and other information make it clear that they live predominantly as a man, or vice versa, they should be treated according to what appears to be their predominant lifestyle and not their stated preference;

(iii) If the person is unwilling to express a preference as in (i) above, efforts should be made to determine their predominant lifestyle and they should be treated as such. For example, if they appear to live predominantly as a woman, they should be treated as being female; except with regard to the requirements to provide that person with information concerning menstrual products and their personal needs relating to health, hygiene and welfare described in *paragraph 3.20A* (if aged under 18) and *paragraphs 9.3A* and *9.3B* (if aged 18 or over). In these cases, a person whose predominant lifestyle has been determined to be male should be asked in private whether they wish to speak in private with a member of the custody staff of a gender of their choosing about the provision of menstrual products and their personal needs, notwithstanding their determined predominant lifestyle (see *Note L3A*); or

(iv) if none of the above apply, the person should be dealt with according to what reasonably appears to have been their sex as registered at birth.

C:5. Once a decision has been made about which gender an individual is to be treated as, each officer responsible for the search, procedure or requirement should where possible be advised before the search or procedure starts of any doubts as to the person's gender and the person informed that the doubts have been disclosed. This is important so as to maintain the dignity of the person and any officers concerned.

(b) Documentation

A-110vb C:6. The person's gender as established under *paragraph 4(c)(i)* to *(iv)* above must be recorded in the person's custody record or, if a custody record has not been opened, on the search record or in the officer's notebook.

C:7. Where the person elects which gender they consider themselves to be under *paragraph 4(b)(i)* but, *following 4(b)(ii)* is not treated in accordance with their preference, the reason must be recorded in the search record, in the officer's notebook or, if applicable, in the person's custody record.

(c) Disclosure of information

A-110vc C:8. Section 22 of the GRA defines any information relating to a person's application for a GRC or to a successful applicant's gender before it became their acquired gender as 'protected information'. Nothing in this Annex is to be read as authorising or permitting any police officer or any police staff who has acquired such information when acting in their official capacity to disclose that information to any other person in contravention of the GRA. Disclosure includes making a record of 'protected information' which is read by others.

Notes for Guidance

A-110vd *C:L1 Provisions to which paragraph 1 applies include:*

- *In Code C; paragraphs 3.20A, 4.1 and Annex A paragraphs 5, 6, and 11 (searches, strip and intimate searches of detainees under sections 54 and 55 of PACE) and 9.3B;*
- *In Code A; paragraphs 2.8 and 3.6 and Note 4;*
- *In Code D; paragraph 5.5 and Note 5F (searches, examinations and photographing of detainees under section 54A of PACE) and paragraph 6.9 (taking samples);*
- *In Code H; paragraphs 3.21A, 4.1 and Annex A paragraphs 6, 7 and 12 (searches, strip and intimate searches under sections 54 and 55 of PACE of persons arrested under section 41 of the Terrorism Act 2000).*

C:L2 While there is no agreed definition of transgender (or trans), it is generally used as an umbrella term to describe people whose gender identity (self-identification as being a woman, man, neither or both) differs from the sex they were registered as at birth. The term includes, but is not limited to, transsexual people.

C:L3 Transsexual means a person who is proposing to undergo, is undergoing or has undergone a process (or part of a process) for the purpose of gender reassignment, which is a protected characteristic under the Equality Act 2010 (see paragraph 1.0), by changing physiological or other attributes of their sex. This includes aspects of gender such as dress and title. It would apply to a woman making the transition to being a man and a man making the transition to being a woman, as well as to a person who has only just started out on the process of gender reassignment and to a person who has completed the process. Both would share the characteristic of gender reassignment with each having the characteristics of one sex, but with certain characteristics of the other sex.

C:L3A The reason for the exception is to modify the same sex/gender approach for searching to acknowledge the possible needs of transgender individuals in respect of menstrual products and other personal needs relating to health, hygiene and welfare and ensure that they are not overlooked.

C:L4 Transvestite means a person of one gender who dresses in the clothes of a person of the opposite gender. However, a transvestite does not live permanently in the gender opposite to their birth sex.

C:L5 Chief officers are responsible for providing corresponding operational guidance and instructions for the deployment of transgender officers and staff under their direction and control to duties which involve carrying out, or being present at, any of the searches and procedures described in paragraph 1. The guidance and instructions must comply with the Equality Act 2010 and should therefore complement the approach in this Annex.

ANNEX MDOCUMENTS AND RECORDS TO BE TRANSLATED

A-110w C:1. For the purposes of Directive 2010/64/EU of the European Parliament and of the Council of 20 October 2010 and this Code, essential documents comprise records required to be made in accordance with this Code which are relevant to decisions to deprive a person of their liberty, to any charge and to any record considered necessary to enable a detainee to defend themselves in criminal proceedings and to safeguard the fairness of the proceedings. Passages of essential documents which are not relevant need not be translated. See *Note M1*

C:2. The table below lists the documents considered essential for the purposes of this Code and when (subject to paragraphs 3 to 7) written translations must be created and provided. See *paragraphs 13.12* to *13.14* and *Annex N* for application to live-link interpretation.

Table of essential documents:

	ESSENTIAL DOCUMENTS FOR THE PURPOSES OF THIS CODE	*WHEN TRANSLATION TO BE CREATED*	*WHEN TRANSLATION TO BE PROVIDED.*
(i)	The grounds for each of the following authorisations to keep the person in custody as they are described and referred to in the custody record: (a) Authorisation for detention before and after charge given by the custody officer and by the review officer, see Code C paragraphs 3.4 and 15.16(a). (b) Authorisation to extend detention without charge beyond 24 hours given by a superintendent, see Code C paragraph 15.16(b). (c) A warrant of further detention issued by a magistrates' court and any extension(s) of the warrant, see Code C paragraph 15.16(c). (d) An authority to detain in accordance with the directions in a warrant of arrest issued in connection with criminal proceedings including the court issuing the warrant.	As soon as practicable after each authorisation has been recorded in the custody record.	As soon as practicable after the translation has been created, whilst the person is detained or after they have been released (see Note M3).
(ii)	Written notice showing particulars of the offence charged required by Code C paragraph 16.3 or the offence for which the suspect has been told they may be prosecuted.	As soon as practicable after the person has been charged or reported.	
(iii)	Written interview records: Code C11.11, 13.3, 13.4 & Code E4.7 Written statement under caution: Code C Annex D.	To be created contemporaneously by the interpreter for the person to check and sign.	As soon as practicable after the person has been charged or told they may be prosecuted.

C:3. The custody officer may authorise an oral translation or oral summary of documents (i) to (ii) in the table (but not (iii)) to be provided (through an interpreter) instead of a written translation. Such an oral translation or summary may only be provided if it would not prejudice the fairness of the proceedings by in any way adversely affecting or otherwise undermining or limiting the ability of the suspect in question to understand their position and to communicate effectively with police officers, interviewers, solicitors and appropriate adults with regard to their detention and the investigation of the offence in question and to defend themselves in the event of criminal proceedings. The quantity and complexity of the information in the document should always be considered and specific additional consideration given if the suspect is vulnerable or is a juvenile (see Code C paragraph 1.5). The reason for the decision must be recorded (see *paragraph 13.11(e)*)

C:4. Subject to paragraphs 5 to 7 below, a suspect may waive their right to a written translation of **A-110wa**
the essential documents described in the table but only if they do so voluntarily after receiving legal

advice or having full knowledge of the consequences and give their unconditional and fully informed consent in writing (see *paragraph 9*).

C:5. The suspect may be asked if they wish to waive their right to a written translation and before giving their consent, they must be reminded of their right to legal advice and asked whether they wish to speak to a solicitor.

C:6. No police officer or police staff should do or say anything with the intention of persuading a suspect who is entitled to a written translation of an essential document to waive that right. See *Notes M2 and M3*.

C:7. For the purpose of the waiver:

(a) the consent of a vulnerable person is only valid if the information about the circumstances under which they can waive the right and the reminder about their right to legal advice mentioned in *paragraphs 3* to *5* and their consent is given in the presence of the appropriate adult.

(b) the consent of a juvenile is only valid if their parent's or guardian's consent is also obtained unless the juvenile is under 14, when their parent's or guardian's consent is sufficient in its own right and the information and reminder mentioned in *sub-paragraph (a)* above and their consent is also given in the presence of the appropriate adult (who may or may not be a parent or guardian).

C:8. The detainee, their solicitor or appropriate adult may make representations to the custody officer that a document which is not included in the table is essential and that a translation should be provided. The request may be refused if the officer is satisfied that the translation requested is not essential for the purposes described in *paragraph 1* above.

C:9. If the custody officer has any doubts about

- providing an oral translation or summary of an essential document instead of a written translation (see paragraph 3);
- whether the suspect fully understands the consequences of waiving their right to a written translation of an essential document (see *paragraph 4*), or
- about refusing to provide a translation of a requested document (see *paragraph 7*),

the officer should seek advice from an inspector or above.

Documentation

A-110wb C:10. Action taken in accordance with this Annex shall be recorded in the detainee's custody record or interview record as appropriate (see *Code C paragraph 13.11(e)*).

Notes for Guidance

A-110wc *C:M1 It is not necessary to disclose information in any translation which is capable of undermining or otherwise adversely affecting any investigative processes, for example, by enabling the suspect to fabricate an innocent explanation or to conceal lies from the interviewer.*

C:M2 No police officer or police staff shall indicate to any suspect, except to answer a direct question, whether the period for which they are liable to be detained or if not detained, the time taken to complete the interview, might be reduced:

- *if they do not ask for legal advice before deciding whether they wish to waive their right to a written translation of an essential document; or*
- *if they decide to waive their right to a written translation of an essential document.*

C:M3 There is no power under PACE to detain a person or to delay their release solely to create and provide a written translation of any essential document.

ANNEX N: LIVE-LINK INTERPRETATION (PARA. 13.12)

Part 1: When the physical presence of the interpreter is not required.

A-110x C:1. EU Directive 2010/64 (see *paragraph 13.1*), Article 2(6) provides "Where appropriate, communication technology such as videoconferencing, telephone or the Internet may be used, unless the physical presence of the interpreter is required in order to safeguard the fairness of the proceedings." This Article permits, but does not require the use of a live-link, and the following provisions of this Annex determine whether the use of a live-link is appropriate in any particular case.

C:2. Decisions in accordance with this Annex that the physical presence of the interpreter is not required and to permit live-link interpretation, must be made on a case by case basis. Each decision must take account of the age, gender and vulnerability of the suspect, the nature and circumstances of the offence and the investigation and the impact on the suspect according to the particular purpose(s) for which the suspect requires the assistance of an interpreter and the time(s) when that assistance is required (see *Note N1*). For this reason, the custody officer in the case of a detained suspect, or in the case of a suspect who has not been arrested, the interviewer (subject to *paragraph 13.1(b)*), must consider whether the ability of the particular suspect, to communicate confidently and effectively for the purpose in question (see *paragraph 3*) is likely to be adversely affected or otherwise undermined or limited if the interpreter is not physically present and live-link interpretation is used. Although a suspect for whom an appropriate adult is required may be more likely to be adversely affected as described, it is important to note that a person who does not require an appropriate adult may also be adversely impacted by the use of live-link interpretation.

C:3. Examples of purposes referred to in *paragraph 2* include:

(a) understanding and appreciating their position having regard to any information given to them, or sought from them, in accordance with this or any other Code of Practice which, in particular, include:
- the caution (see *paragraphs C10.1* and *10.12*).
- the special warning (see *paragraphs 10.10* to *10.12*).
- information about the offence (see *paragraphs 10.3, 11.1A* and *Note 11ZA*).
- the grounds and reasons for detention (see *paragraphs 13.10* and *13.10A*).
- the translation of essential documents (see *paragraph 13.10B* and *Annex M*).
- their rights and entitlements (see *paragraph 3.12* and *C3.21(b)*).
- intimate and non-intimate searches of detained persons at police stations.
- provisions and procedures to which Code D (Identification) applies concerning, for example, eye-witness identification, taking fingerprints, samples and photographs.

(b) understanding and seeking clarification from the interviewer of questions asked during an interview conducted and recorded in accordance with Code E or Code F and of anything else that is said by the interviewer and answering the questions.

(c) consulting privately with their solicitor and (if applicable) the appropriate adult (see *paragraphs 3.18, 13.2A, 13.6* and *13.9*):
  (i) to help decide whether to answer questions put to them during interview; and
  (ii) about any other matter concerning their detention and treatment whilst in custody.

(d) communicating with practitioners and others who have some formal responsibility for, or an interest in, the health and welfare of the suspect. Particular examples include appropriate healthcare professionals (see section 9 of this Code), Independent Custody Visitors and drug arrest referral workers.

C:4. If the custody officer or the interviewer (subject to *paragraph 13.1(b)*) is satisfied that for a particular purpose as described in *paragraphs 2* and *3 above*, the live-link interpretation *would not* adversely affect or otherwise undermine or limit the suspect's ability to communicate confidently and effectively for *that* purpose, they must so inform the suspect, their solicitor and (if applicable) the appropriate adult. At the same time, the operation of live-link interpretation must be explained and demonstrated to them, they must be advised of the chief officer's obligations concerning the security of live-link communications under *paragraph 13.13* (see *Note N2*) and they must be asked if they wish to make representations that live-link interpretation should not be used or if they require more information about the operation of the arrangements. They must also be told that at any time live-link interpretation is in use, they may make representations to the custody officer or the interviewer that its operation should cease and that the physical presence of an interpreter should be arranged. **A-110xa**

When the authority of an inspector is required

C:5. If: **A-110xb**

(i) representations are made that live-link interpretation should not be used, or that at any time live-link interpretation is in use, its operation should cease and the physical presence of an interpreter arranged; and

(ii) the custody officer or interviewer (subject to *paragraph 13.1(b)*) is unable to allay the concerns raised;

then live-link interpretation may not be used, or (as the case may be) continue to be used, unless authorised in writing by an officer of the rank of inspector or above, in accordance with *paragraph 6*.

C:6. Authority may be given if the officer is satisfied that for the purpose(s) in question at the time an interpreter is required, live-link interpretation is necessary and justified. In making this decision, the officer must have regard to:

(a) the circumstances of the suspect;
(b) the nature and seriousness of the offence;
(c) the requirements of the investigation, including its likely impact on both the suspect and any victim(s);
(d) the representations made by the suspect, their solicitor and (if applicable) the appropriate adult that live-link interpretation should not be used (see *paragraph 5*);

(e) the availability of a suitable interpreter to be *physically* present compared with the availability of a suitable interpreter for live-link interpretation (see *Note N3*); and
(f) the risk if the interpreter is not *physically* present, evidence obtained using link interpretation might be excluded in subsequent criminal proceedings; and
(g) the likely impact on the suspect and the investigation of any consequential delay to arrange for the interpreter to be *physically* present with the suspect.

C:7. For the purposes of Code E and live-link interpretation, there is no requirement to make a visual recording which shows the interpreter as viewed by the suspect and others present at the interview. The audio recording required by that Code is sufficient. However, the authorising officer, in consultation with the officer in charge of the investigation, may direct that the interview is conducted and recorded in accordance with Code F. This will require the visual record to show the live-link interpretation arrangements and the interpreter as seen and experienced by the suspect during the interview. This should be considered if it appears that the admissibility of interview evidence might be challenged because the interpreter was not *physically* present or if the suspect, solicitor or appropriate adult make representations that Code F should be applied.

Documentation

A-110xc C:8. A record must be made of the actions, decisions, authorisations and outcomes arising from the requirements of this Annex. This includes representations made in accordance with *paragraphs 4* and *7*.

Part 2: Modifications for live-link interpretation

A-110xd C:9. The following modification shall apply for the purposes of live-link interpretation:
(a) **Code C paragraph 13.3:** For the third sentence, *substitute:* "A clear legible copy of the complete record shall be sent without delay via the live-link to the interviewer. The interviewer, after confirming with the suspect that the copy is legible and complete, shall allow the suspect to read the record, or have the record read to them by the interpreter and to sign the copy as correct or indicate the respects in which they consider it inaccurate. The interviewer is responsible for ensuring that that the signed copy and the original record made by the interpreter are retained with the case papers for use in evidence if required and must advise the interpreter of their obligation to keep the original record securely for that purpose.";
(b) **Code C paragraph 13.4:** For sub-paragraph (b), *substitute:* "A clear legible copy of the complete statement shall be sent without delay via the live-link to the interviewer. The interviewer, after confirming with the suspect that the copy is legible and complete, shall invite the suspect to sign it. The interviewer is responsible for ensuring that that the signed copy and the original record made by the interpreter are retained with the case papers for use in evidence if required and must advise the interpreter of their obligation to keep the original record securely for that purpose.";
(c) **Code C paragraph 13.7:** After the first sentence, *insert:* "A clear legible copy of the certified record must be sent without delay via the live-link to the interviewer. The interviewer is responsible for ensuring that the original certified record and the copy are retained with the case papers for use as evidence if required and must advise the interpreter of their obligation to keep the original record securely for that purpose."
(d) **Code C paragraph 11.2, Code E paragraphs 3.4 and 4.3 and Code F paragraph 2.5.- interviews** At the beginning of each paragraph, *insert:* "Before the interview commences, the operation of live-link interpretation shall be explained and demonstrated to the suspect, their solicitor and appropriate adult, unless it has been previously explained and demonstrated (see Code C Annex N *paragraph 4*)."
(e) **Code E, paragraph 3.20 (signing master recording label)** After the *third sentence,* insert, "If live-link interpretation has been used, the interviewer should ask the interpreter to observe the removal and sealing of the master recording and to confirm in writing that they have seen it sealed and signed by the interviewer. A clear legible copy of the confirmation signed by the interpreter must be sent via the live-link to the interviewer. The interviewer is responsible for ensuring that the original confirmation and the copy are retained with the case papers for use in evidence if required and must advise the interpreter of their obligation to keep the original confirmation securely for that purpose."

Note: By virtue of *paragraphs 2.1* and *2.3 of Code F,* this applies when a visually recording to which Code F applies is made.

Notes for Guidance

A-110xe *C:N1 For purposes other than an interview, audio-only live-link interpretation, for example by telephone (see*

Code C paragraph 13.12(b)) may provide an appropriate option until an interpreter is physically present or audio-visual live-link interpretation becomes available. A particular example would be the initial action required when a detained suspect arrives at a police station to inform them of, and to explain, the reasons for their arrest and detention and their various rights and entitlements. Another example would be to inform the suspect by telephone, that an interpreter they will be able to see and hear is being arranged. In these circumstances, telephone live-link interpretation may help to allay the suspect's concerns and contribute to the completion of the risk assessment (see Code C paragraph 3.6).

C:N2 The explanation and demonstration of live-link interpretation is intended to help the suspect, solicitor and appropriate adult make an informed decision and to allay any concerns they may have.

C:N3 Factors affecting availability of a suitable interpreter will include the location of the police station and the language and type of interpretation (oral or sign language) required.

(5) Identification

The text that follows is of the version of the code that came into force on 23 February 2017: see A-1. **A-112**

In connection with Code D, see also §§ 14-39 et seq. (application of code), §§ 14-45 et seq. (identification procedures), § 14-54 (group identification, confrontation and video identification), §§ 14-57 et seq. (effect of breaches), §§ 14-60 et seq. (photographs), § 14-62 (video recordings), and § 15-270 (photographs) of the main work.

D. CODE OF PRACTICE FOR THE IDENTIFICATION OF PERSONS BY POLICE OFFICERS

Commencement—transitional arrangements

This code has effect in relation to any identification procedure carried out after midnight on 23 February 2017. **A-113**

D:1 Introduction

D:1.1 This code of practice concerns the principal methods used by police to identify people in connection with the investigation of offences and the keeping of accurate and reliable criminal records. The powers and procedures in this code must be used fairly, responsibly, with respect for the people to whom they apply and without unlawful discrimination. Under the Equality Act 2010, s.149 (public sector equality duty), police forces must, in carrying out their functions, have due regard to the need to eliminate unlawful discrimination, harassment, victimisation and any other conduct which is prohibited by that Act, to advance equality of opportunity between people who share a relevant "protected characteristic" and people who do not share it, and to foster good relations between those persons. The Equality Act also makes it unlawful for police officers to discriminate against, harass or victimise any person on the grounds of the 'protected characteristics' of age, disability, gender reassignment, race, religion or belief, sex and sexual orientation, marriage and civil partnership, pregnancy and maternity when using their powers. See *Note 1A*. **A-114**

D:1.2 In this code, identification by an eye-witness arises when a witness who has seen the offender committing the crime and is given an opportunity to identify a person suspected of involvement in the offence in a video identification, identification parade or similar procedure. These eye-witness identification procedures which are in Part A of section 3 below, are designed to:

- test the eye-witness' ability to identify the suspect as the person they saw on a previous occasion
- provide safeguards against mistaken identification.

While this code concentrates on visual identification procedures, it does not prevent the police making use of aural identification procedures such as a "voice identification parade", where they judge that appropriate. See *Note 1B*.

D:1.2A In this code, separate provisions in Part B of section 3 below, apply when any person, including a police officer, is asked if they recognise anyone they see in an image as being someone who is known to them and to test their claim that they recognise that person. These separate provisions are not subject to the eye-witnesses identification procedures described in paragraph 1.2.

D:1.2B Part C applies when a film, photograph or image relating to the offence or any description of the suspect is broadcast or published in any national or local media or on any social networking site or on any local or national police communication systems.

D:1.3 Identification by fingerprints applies when a person's fingerprints are taken to:

- compare with fingerprints found at the scene of a crime
- check and prove convictions

• help to ascertain a person's identity.

D:1.3A Identification using footwear impressions applies when a person's footwear impressions are taken to compare with impressions found at the scene of a crime.

D:1.4 Identification by body samples and impressions includes taking samples such as a cheek swab, hair or blood to generate a DNA profile for comparison with material obtained from the scene of a crime, or a victim.

D:1.5 Taking photographs of arrested people applies to recording and checking identity and locating and tracing persons who:

- are wanted for offences
- fail to answer their bail.

D:1.6 Another method of identification involves searching and examining detained suspects to find, e.g., marks such as tattoos or scars which may help establish their identity or whether they have been involved in committing an offence.

D:1.7 The provisions of the Police and Criminal Evidence Act 1984 (PACE) and this ode are designed to make sure fingerprints, samples, impressions and photographs are taken, used and retained, and identification procedures carried out, only when justified and necessary for preventing, detecting or investigating crime. If these provisions are not observed, the application of the relevant procedures in particular cases may be open to question.

D:1.8 The provisions of this code do not authorise, or otherwise permit, fingerprints or samples to be taken from a person detained solely for the purposes of assessment under section 136 of the Mental Health Act 1983.

Note for guidance

D:1A In paragraph 1.1, under the Equality Act 1949, s.149, the "relevant protected characteristics" are: age, disability, gender reassignment, pregnancy and maternity, race, religion/belief, sex and sexual orientation. For further detailed guidance and advice on the Equality Act, see: https://www.gov.uk/guidance/equality-act-2010-guidance.

D:1B See Home Office Circular 57/2003 "Advice on the use of voice identification parades".

D:2 General

A-115 D:2.1 This code must be readily available at all police stations for consultation by:

- police officers and police staff
- detained persons
- members of the public

D:2.2 The provisions of this code:

- include the Annexes
- do not include the *Notes for guidance.*

D:2.3 Code C, para. 1.4 and the *Notes for guidance* applicable to those provisions apply to this code with regard to a suspected person who may be mentally disordered or otherwise mentally vulnerable.

D:2.4 Code C, paras 1.5 and 1.5A and the *Notes for guidance* applicable to those provisions apply to this Code with regard to a suspected person who appears to be under the age of 18.

D:2.5 Code C, para. 1.6 applies to this code with regard to a suspected person who appears to be blind, seriously visually impaired, deaf, unable to read or speak or has difficulty communicating orally because of a speech impediment.

A-116 D:2.6 In this code:

- "appropriate adult" means the same as in Code C, para. 1.7
- "solicitor" means the same as in Code C, para. 6.12

  and the *Notes for guidance* applicable to those provisions apply to this code.
- where a search or other procedure under this code may only be carried out or observed by a person of the same sex as the person to whom the search or procedure applies, the gender of the detainee and other persons present should be established and recorded in line with Annex L of Code C.

D:2.7 References to a custody officer include any police officer who, for the time being, is performing the functions of a custody officer, see paragraph 1.9 of Code C.

D:2.8 When a record of any action requiring the authority of an officer of a specified rank is made under this code, subject to paragraph 2.18, the officer's name and rank must be recorded.

D:2.9 When this code requires the prior authority or agreement of an officer of at least inspector or superintendent rank, that authority may be given by a sergeant or chief inspector who has been authorised to perform the functions of the higher rank under PACE, s.107.

D:2.10 Subject to paragraph 2.18, all records must be timed and signed by the maker.

A-117 D:2.11 Records must be made in the custody record, unless otherwise specified. In any provision of this code which allows or requires police officers or police staff to make a record in their report book, the reference to "report book" shall include any official report book or electronic recording device issued to them that enables the record in question to be made and dealt with in accordance with that provision. References in this code to written records, forms and signatures include electronic records and forms and electronic confirmation that identifies the person completing the record or form.

Chief officers must be satisfied as to the integrity and security of the devices, records and forms to which this paragraph applies and that use of those devices, records and forms satisfies relevant data protection legislation.

D:2.12 If any procedure in this Code requires a person's consent, the consent of a:

- mentally disordered or otherwise mentally vulnerable person is only valid if given in the presence of the appropriate adult
- juvenile is only valid if their parent's or guardian's consent is also obtained unless the juvenile is under 14, when their parent's or guardian's consent is sufficient in its own right. If the only obstacle to an identification procedure in section 3 is that a juvenile's parent or guardian refuses consent or reasonable efforts to obtain it have failed, the identification officer may apply the provisions of paragraph 3.21 (suspect known but not available). See *Note 2A.*

D:2.13 If a person is blind, seriously visually impaired or unable to read, the custody officer or identification officer shall make sure their solicitor, relative, appropriate adult or some other person likely to take an interest in them and not involved in the investigation is available to help check any documentation. When this code requires written consent or signing, the person assisting may be asked to sign instead, if the detainee prefers. This paragraph does not require an appropriate adult to be called solely to assist in checking and signing documentation for a person who is not a juvenile, or mentally disordered or otherwise mentally vulnerable (see *Note 2B* and Code C, para. 3.15).

D:2.14 If any procedure in this code requires information to be given to or sought from a suspect, it must be given or sought in the appropriate adult's presence if the suspect is mentally disordered, otherwise mentally vulnerable or a juvenile. If the appropriate adult is not present when the information is first given or sought, the procedure must be repeated in the presence of the appropriate adult when they arrive. If the suspect appears deaf or there is doubt about their hearing or speaking ability or ability to understand English, the custody officer or identification officer must ensure that the necessary arrangements in accordance with Code C are made for an interpreter to assist the suspect.

D:2.15 Any procedure in this code involving the participation of a suspect who is mentally disordered, otherwise mentally vulnerable or a juvenile must take place in the presence of the appropriate adult. See Code C, para. 1.4.

D:2.15A Any procedure in this code involving the participation of a witness who is or appears to be mentally disordered, otherwise mentally vulnerable or a juvenile should take place in the presence of a pre-trial support person unless the witness states that they do not want a support person to be present. A support person must not be allowed to prompt any identification of a suspect by a witness. See *Note 2AB.*

D:2.16 References to:

- "taking a photograph", include the use of any process to produce a single, still or moving, visual image
- "photographing a person", should be construed accordingly
- "photographs", "films", "negatives" and "copies" include relevant visual images recorded, stored, or reproduced through any medium
- "destruction" includes the deletion of computer data relating to such images or making access to that data impossible

D:2.17 This code does not affect or apply to, the powers and procedures:

(i) for requiring and taking samples of breath, blood and urine in relation to driving offences, etc, when under the influence of drink, drugs or excess alcohol under the:
  - Road Traffic Act 1988, ss.4 to 11
  - Road Traffic Offenders Act 1988, ss.15 and 16
  - Transport and Works Act 1992, ss.26 to 38;

(ii) under the Immigration Act 1971, Sched. 2, para.18, for taking photographs, measuring and identifying and taking biometric information (not including DNA) from persons detained or liable to be detained under that Act, Sched. 2, para. 16 (administrative provisions as to control on entry etc.); or for taking fingerprints in accordance with the Immigration and Asylum Act 1999, ss.141 and 142(4), or other methods for collecting information about a person's external physical characteristics provided for by regulations made under that Act, s.144;

(iii) under the Terrorism Act 2000, Sched. 8, for taking photographs, fingerprints, skin impressions, body samples or impressions from people:

- arrested under that Act, s.41,
- detained for the purposes of examination under that Act, Sched. 7, and to whom the code of practice issued under that Act, Sched.14, para. 6, applies ("the terrorism provisions")

(iv) for taking photographs, fingerprints, skin impressions, body samples or impressions from people who have been:

- arrested on warrants issued in Scotland, by officers exercising powers mentioned in Part X of the Criminal Justice and Public Order Act 1994;
- arrested or detained without warrant by officers from a police force in Scotland exercising their powers of arrest or detention mentioned in Part X of the Criminal Justice and Public Order Act 1994.

Note: In these cases, police powers and duties and the person's rights and entitlements whilst at a police station in England and Wales are the same as if the person had been arrested in Scotland by a Scottish police officer.

D:2.18 Nothing in this code requires the identity of officers or police staff to be recorded or disclosed:

(a) in the case of enquiries linked to the investigation of terrorism;

(b) if the officers or police staff reasonably believe recording or disclosing their names might put them in danger.

In these cases, they shall use their warrant or other identification numbers and the name of their police station. See *Note 2D.*

A-118 D:2.19 In this code:

(a) "designated person" means a person other than a police officer, who has specified powers and duties conferred or imposed on them by designation under section 38 or 39 of the Police Reform Act 2002;

(b) any reference to a police officer includes a designated person acting in the exercise or performance of the powers and duties conferred or imposed on them by their designation.

D:2.20 If a power conferred on a designated person:

(a) allows reasonable force to be used when exercised by a police officer, a designated person exercising that power has the same entitlement to use force;

(b) includes power to use force to enter any premises, that power is not exercisable by that designated person except:

(i) in the company, and under the supervision, of a police officer; or

(ii) for the purpose of:

- saving life or limb; or
- preventing serious damage to property.

D:2.21 In the case of a detained person, nothing in this code prevents the custody officer, or other police officer or designated person given custody of the detainee by the custody officer for the purposes of the investigation of an offence for which the person is detained, from allowing another person (see (a) and (b) below) to carry out individual procedures or tasks at the police station if the law allows. However, the officer or designated person given custody remains responsible for making sure the procedures and tasks are carried out correctly in accordance with the Codes of Practice. The other person who is allowed to carry out the procedures or tasks must be *someone who at that time* is:

(a) under the direction and control of the chief officer of the force responsible for the police station in question; or;

(b) providing services under contractual arrangements (but without being employed by the chief officer the police force), to assist a police force in relation to the discharge of its chief officer's functions.

D:2.22 Designated persons and others mentioned in sub-paragraphs (a) and (b) of paragraph 2.21 must have regard to any relevant provisions of the codes of practice.

Notes for guidance

A-119 *D:2A For the purposes of paragraph 2.12, the consent required from a parent or guardian may, for a juvenile in the care of a local authority or voluntary organisation, be given by that authority or organisation. In the case of a juvenile, nothing in paragraph 2.12 requires the parent, guardian or representative of a local authority or voluntary organisation to be present to give their consent, unless they are acting as the appropriate adult under paragraphs 2.14 or 2.15. However, it is important that a parent or guardian not present is fully informed before being asked to consent. They must be given the same information about the procedure and the juvenile's suspected involvement in the offence as the juvenile and appropriate adult. The parent or guardian must also be allowed to speak to the juvenile and the appropriate adult if they wish. Provided the consent is fully informed and is not withdrawn, it may be obtained at any time before the procedure takes place.*

D:2AB The Youth Justice and Criminal Evidence Act 1999 guidance "Achieving Best Evidence in Criminal

Proceedings" indicates that a pre-trial support person should accompany a vulnerable witness during any identification procedure unless the witness states that they do not want a support person to be present. It states that this support person should not be (or not be likely to be) a witness in the investigation.

D:2B People who are seriously visually impaired or unable to read may be unwilling to sign police documents. The alternative, i.e. their representative signing on their behalf, seeks to protect the interests of both police and suspects.

D:2C [Not used.]

D:2D The purpose of paragraph 2.18(b) is to protect those involved in serious organised crime investigations or arrests of particularly violent suspects when there is reliable information that those arrested or their associates may threaten or cause harm to the officers. In cases of doubt, an officer of inspector rank or above should be consulted.

D:3 Identification and recognition of suspects

Part (a) Identification of a suspect by an eye-witness

D:3.0 This part applies when an eye-witness has seen a person committing a crime or in any other circumstances which tend to prove or disprove the involvement of the person they saw in a crime, for example, close to the scene of the crime, immediately before or immediately after it was committed. It sets out the procedures to be used to test the ability of that eye-witness to identify a person suspected of involvement in the offence ("the suspect") as the person they saw on the previous occasion. This part does not apply to the procedure described in Part B (see *Note 3AA*) which is used to test the ability of someone who is not an eye-witness, to recognise anyone whose image they see. A-120

D:3.1 A record shall be made of the description of the suspect as first given by the eye-witness . This record must:

(a) be made and kept in a form which enables details of that description to be accurately produced from it, in a visible and legible form, which can be given to the suspect or the suspect's solicitor in accordance with this Code; and

(b) unless otherwise specified, be made before the eye-witness takes part in any identification procedures under paragraphs 3.5 to 3.10, 3.21, 3.23 or Annex E (showing photographs to eye-witnesses).

A copy of the record shall where practicable, be given to the suspect or their solicitor before any procedures under paragraphs 3.5 to 3.10, 3.21 or 3.23 are carried out. See *Note 3E.*

D:3.1A References in this Part:

(a) to the identity of the suspect being "known" mean that there is sufficient information known to the police to establish, in accordance with Code G (arrest), that there are reasonable grounds to suspect a particular person of involvement in the offence;

(b) to the suspect being "available" mean that the suspect is immediately available, or will be available within a reasonably short time, in order that they can be invited to take part in at least one of the eye-witness identification procedures under paragraphs 3.5 to 3.10 and it is practicable to arrange an effective procedure under paragraphs 3.5 to 3.10; and

(c) to the eye-witness identification procedures under paragraphs 3.5 to 3.10 mean:
- video identification (paragraphs 3.5 and 3.6);
- identification parade (paragraphs 3.7 and 3.8); and
- group identification (paragraphs 3.9 and 3.10).

(a) Cases when the suspect's identity is not known

D:3.2 In cases when the suspect's identity is not known, an eye-witness may be taken to a particular neighbourhood or place to see whether they can identify the person they saw on a previous occasion. Although the number, age, sex, race, general description and style of clothing of other people present at the location and the way in which any identification is made cannot be controlled, the principles applicable to the formal procedures under paragraphs 3.5 to 3.10 shall be followed as far as practicable. For example:

(a) where it is practicable to do so, a record should be made of the eye-witness' description of the person they saw on the previous occasion, as in paragraph 3.1(a), before asking the eye-witness to make an identification;

(b) care must be taken not provide the eye-witness with any information concerning the description of the suspect (if such information is available) and not to direct the eyewitness' attention to any individual unless, taking into account all the circumstances, this cannot be avoided. However, this does not prevent an eye-witness being asked to look carefully at the people around at the time or to look towards a group or in a particular direction, if this appears necessary to make sure that the witness does not overlook a possible suspect simply because the eye-witness is looking in the opposite direction and also to enable the eye-witness to make comparisons between any suspect and others who are in the area;

(c) where there is more than one eye-witness, every effort should be made to keep them separate and eye-witnesses should be taken to see whether they can identify a person independently;
(d) once there is sufficient information to establish, in accordance with paragraph 3.1A(a), that the suspect is "known", e.g. after the eye-witness makes an identification, the provisions set out from paragraph 3.4 onwards shall apply for that and any other eyewitnesses in relation to that individual;
(e) the officer or police staff accompanying the eye-witness must record, in their report book, the action taken as soon as practicable and in as much detail, as possible. The record should include:
  (i) the date, time and place of the relevant occasion when the eye-witness claims to have previously seen the person committing the offence in question or in any other circumstances which tend to prove or disprove the involvement of the person they saw in a crime (see paragraph 3.0); and
  (ii) where any identification was made:
  - how it was made and the conditions at the time (e.g., the distance the eyewitness was from the suspect, the weather and light);
  - if the eye-witness's attention was drawn to the suspect; the reason for this; and
  - anything said by the eye-witness or the suspect about the identification or the conduct of the procedure.

  See *Note 3F*

D:3.3 An eye-witness must not be shown photographs, computerised or artist's composite likenesses or similar likenesses or pictures (including "E-fit" images) if in accordance with paragraph 3.1A, the identity of the suspect is known and they are available to take part in one of the procedures under paragraphs 3.5 to 3.10. If the suspect's identity is not known, the showing of any such images to an eye-witness to see if they can identify a person whose image they are shown as the person they saw on a previous occasion must be done in accordance with Annex E.

(b) Cases when the suspect is known and available

A-121 D:3.4 If the suspect's identity is known to the police (see paragraph 3.1A(a)) and they are available (see paragraph 3.1A(b)), the identification procedures that may be used are set out in paragraphs 3.5 to 3.10 below as follows:
  (i) video identification;
  (ii) identification parade; or
  (iii) group identification.

(i) Video identification

D:3.5 A "video identification" is when the eye-witness is shown images of a known suspect, together with similar images of others who resemble the suspect. *Moving* images must be used unless the conditions in sub-paragraph (a) or (b) below apply:
(a) this sub-paragraph applies if:
  (i) the identification officer, in consultation with the officer in charge of the investigation, is satisfied that because of aging, or other physical changes or differences, the appearance of the suspect has significantly changed since the previous occasion when the eye-witness claims to have seen the suspect (see paragraph 3.0 and *Note 3ZA*);
  (ii) an image (moving or still) is available which the identification officer and the officer in charge of the investigation reasonably believe shows the appearance of the suspect as it was at the time the suspect was seen by the eye-witness; and
  (iii) having regard to the extent of change and the purpose of eye-witness identification procedures (see paragraph 3.0), the identification officer believes that that such an image should be shown to the eye-witness.

  In such a case, the identification officer may arrange a video identification procedure using the image described in (ii). In accordance with the "Notice to suspect" (see paragraph 3.17(vi)), the suspect must first be given an opportunity to provide their own image(s) for use in the procedure but it is for the identification officer and officer in charge of the investigation to decide whether, following (ii) and (iii), any image(s) provided by the suspect should be used.

  A video identification using an image described above may, at the discretion of the identification officer be arranged in addition to, or as an alternative to, a video identification using *moving* images taken after the suspect has been given the information and notice described in paragraphs 3.17 and 3.18.

  See paragraph 3.21 and *Note 3D* in any case where the suspect deliberately takes steps to frustrate the eye-witness identification arrangements and procedures.

(b) this sub-paragraph applies if, in accordance with paragraph 2A of Annex A of this code, the identification officer does not consider that replication of a physical feature or concealment of the location of the feature can be achieved using a moving image. In these cases, still images may be used.

D:3.6 Video identifications must be carried out in accordance with Annex A.

(ii) Identification parade

D:3.7 An "identification parade" is when the eye-witness sees the suspect in a line of others who resemble the suspect.

D:3.8 Identification parades must be carried out in accordance with Annex B.

(iii) Group identification

D:3.9 A "group identification" is when the eye-witness sees the suspect in an informal group of people.

D:3.10 Group identifications must be carried out in accordance with Annex C.

Arranging eye-witness identification procedures–duties of identification officer

D:3.11 Except as provided for in paragraph 3.19, the arrangements for, and conduct of, the eyewitness identification procedures in paragraphs 3.5 to 3.10 and circumstances in which any such identification procedure must be held shall be the responsibility of an officer not below inspector rank who is not involved with the investigation ("the identification officer"). The identification officer may direct another officer or police staff, see paragraph 2.21, to make arrangements for, and to conduct, any of these identification procedures and except as provided for in paragraph 7 of Annex A, any reference in this section to the identification officer includes the officer or police staff to whom the arrangements for, and/or conduct of, any of these procedure has been delegated. In delegating these arrangements and procedures, the identification officer must be able to supervise effectively and either intervene or be contacted for advice. Where any action referred to in this paragraph is taken by another officer or police staff at the direction of the identification officer, the outcome shall, as soon as practicable, be reported to the identification officer. For the purpose of these procedures, the identification officer retains overall responsibility for ensuring that the procedure complies with this code and in addition, in the case of detained suspect, their care and treatment until returned to the custody officer. Except as permitted by this code, no officer or any other person involved with the investigation of the case against the suspect may take any part in these procedures or act as the identification officer.

This paragraph does not prevent the identification officer from consulting the officer in charge of the investigation to determine which procedure to use. When an identification procedure is required, in the interest of fairness to suspects and eye-witnesses, it must be held as soon as practicable.

Circumstances in which an eye-witness identification procedure must be held

D:3.12 If, before any identification procedure set out in paragraphs 3.5 to 3.10 has been held **A-122**

(a) an eye-witness has identified a suspect or purported to have identified them; or
(b) there is an eye-witness available who expresses an ability to identify the suspect; or
(c) there is a reasonable chance of an eye-witness being able to identify the suspect,

and the eye-witness in (a) to (c) has not been given an opportunity to identify the suspect in any of the procedures set out in paragraphs 3.5 to 3.10, then an identification procedure shall be held if the suspect disputes being the person the eye-witness claims to have seen on a previous occasion (see paragraph 3.0), unless:

(i) it is not practicable to hold any such procedure; or
(ii) any such procedure would serve no useful purpose in proving or disproving whether the suspect was involved in committing the offence, for example
- where the suspect admits being at the scene of the crime and gives an account of what took place and the eye-witness does not see anything which contradicts that; or
- when it is not disputed that the suspect is already known to the eye-witness who claims to have recognised them when seeing them commit the crime.

D:3.13 An eye-witness identification procedure may also be held if the officer in charge of the investigation, after consultation with the identification officer, considers it would be useful.

Selecting an eye-witness identification procedure

D:3.14 If, because of paragraph 3.12, an identification procedure is to be held, the suspect shall initially be invited to take part in a video identification unless:

(a) a video identification is not practicable; or

(b) an identification parade is both practicable and more suitable than a video identification; or
(c) paragraph 3.16 applies.

The identification officer and the officer in charge of the investigation shall consult each other to determine which option is to be offered. An identification parade may not be practicable because of factors relating to the witnesses, such as their number, state of health, availability and travelling requirements. A video identification would normally be more suitable if it could be arranged and completed sooner than an identification parade. Before an option is offered the suspect must also be reminded of their entitlement to have free legal advice, see Code C, para. 6.5.

D:3.15 A suspect who refuses the identification procedure in which the suspect is first invited to take part shall be asked to state their reason for refusing and may get advice from their solicitor and/or if present, their appropriate adult. The suspect, solicitor and/or appropriate adult shall be allowed to make representations about why another procedure should be used. A record should be made of the reasons for refusal and any representations made. After considering any reasons given, and representations made, the identification officer shall, if appropriate, arrange for the suspect to be invited to take part in an alternative which the officer considers suitable and practicable. If the officer decides it is not suitable and practicable to invite the suspect to take part in an alternative identification procedure, the reasons for that decision shall be recorded.

D:3.16 A suspect may initially be invited to take part in a group identification if the officer in charge of the investigation considers it is more suitable than a video identification or an identification parade and the identification officer considers it practicable to arrange.

Notice to suspect

A-123 D:3.17 Unless paragraph 3.20 applies, before any eye-witness identification procedure set out in paragraphs 3.5 to 3.10 is arranged, the following shall be explained to the suspect:

(i) the purpose of the procedure (see paragraph 3.0);
(ii) their entitlement to free legal advice; see Code C, para. 6.5;
(iii) the procedures for holding it, including their right, subject to Annex A para. 9, to have a solicitor or friend present;
(iv) that they do not have to consent to or co-operate in the procedure;
(v) that if they do not consent to, and co-operate in, a procedure, their refusal may be given in evidence in any subsequent trial and police may proceed covertly without their consent or make other arrangements to test whether an eye-witness can identify them, see paragraph 3.21;
(vi) whether, for the purposes of a video identification procedure, images of them have previously been obtained either:
  - in accordance with paragraph 3.20, and if so, that they may co-operate in providing further, suitable images to be used instead; or
  - in accordance with paragraph 3.5(a), and if so, that they may provide their own images for the identification officer to consider using.
(vii) if appropriate, the special arrangements for juveniles;
(viii) if appropriate, the special arrangements for mentally disordered or otherwise mentally vulnerable people;
(ix) that if they significantly alter their appearance between being offered an identification procedure and any attempt to hold an identification procedure, this may be given in evidence if the case comes to trial, and the identification officer may then consider other forms of identification, see paragraph 3.21 and *Note 3C*;
(x) that a moving image or photograph may be taken of them when they attend for any identification procedure;
(xi) whether, before their identity became known, the eye-witness was shown photographs, a computerised or artist' s composite likeness or similar likeness or image by the police, see *Note 3B*;
(xii) that if they change their appearance before an identification parade, it may not be practicable to arrange one on the day or subsequently and, because of the appearance change, the identification officer may consider alternative methods of identification, see *Note 3C*;
(xiii) that they or their solicitor will be provided with details of the description of the suspect as first given by any eye-witnesses who are to attend the procedure or confrontation, see paragraph 3.1.

D:3.18 This information must also be recorded in a written notice handed to the suspect. The suspect must be given a reasonable opportunity to read the notice, after which, they should be asked to sign a copy of the notice to indicate if they are willing to co-operate with the making of a video or take part in the identification parade or group identification. The signed copy shall be retained by the identification officer.

D:3.19 In the case of a detained suspect, the duties under paragraphs 3.17 and 3.18 may be performed by the custody officer or by another officer or police staff not involved in the investigation as directed by the custody officer, if:

(a) it is proposed to release the suspect in order that an identification procedure can be arranged and carried out and an inspector is not available to act as the identification officer, see paragraph 3.11, before the suspect leaves the station; or

(b) it is proposed to keep the suspect in police detention whilst the procedure is arranged and carried out and waiting for an inspector to act as the identification officer, see paragraph 3.11, would cause unreasonable delay to the investigation.

The officer concerned shall inform the identification officer of the action taken and give them the signed copy of the notice. See *Note 3C.*

D:3.20 If the identification officer and officer in charge of the investigation suspect, on reasonable grounds that if the suspect was given the information and notice as in paragraphs 3.17 and 3.18, they would then take steps to avoid being seen by a witness in any identification procedure, the identification officer may arrange for images of the suspect suitable for use in a video identification procedure to be obtained before giving the information and notice. If suspect's [*sic*] images are obtained in these circumstances, the suspect may, for the purposes of a video identification procedure, co-operate in providing new images which if suitable, would be used instead, see paragraph 3.17(vi).

(c) Cases when the suspect is known but not available

D:3.21 When a known suspect is not available or has ceased to be available, see paragraph 3.1A, the identification officer may make arrangements for a video identification (see paragraph 3.5 and Annex A). If necessary, the identification officer may follow the video identification procedures using any suitable moving or still images and these may be obtained covertly if necessary. Alternatively, the identification officer may make arrangements for a group identification without the suspect's consent (see Annex C, para. 34). See *Note 3D.* These provisions may also be applied to juveniles where the consent of their parent or guardian is either refused or reasonable efforts to obtain that consent have failed (see paragraph 2.12). **A-124**

D:3.22 Any covert activity should be strictly limited to that necessary to test the ability of the eyewitness to identify the suspect as the person they saw on the relevant previous occasion.

D:3.23 The identification officer may arrange for the suspect to be confronted by the eye-witness if none of the options referred to in paragraphs 3.5 to 3.10 or 3.21 are practicable. A "confrontation" is when the suspect is directly confronted by the eye-witness. A confrontation does not require the suspect's consent. Confrontations must be carried out in accordance with Annex D.

D:3.24 Requirements for information to be given to, or sought from, a suspect or for the suspect to be given an opportunity to view images before they are shown to an eye-witness, do not apply if the suspect's lack of co-operation prevents the necessary action.

(d) Documentation

D:3.25 A record shall be made of the video identification, identification parade, group identification or confrontation on forms provided for the purpose. **A-125**

D:3.26 If the identification officer considers it is not practicable to hold a video identification or identification parade requested by the suspect, the reasons shall be recorded and explained to the suspect.

D:3.27 A record shall be made of a person's failure or refusal to co-operate in a video identification, identification parade or group identification and, if applicable, of the grounds for obtaining images in accordance with paragraph 3.20.

(e) Not used

D:3.28 [*Not used.*] **A-126**

D:3.29 [*Not used.*]

(f) Destruction and retention of photographs taken or used in eye-witness identification procedures

D:3.30 PACE, s.64A, see paragraph 5.12, provides powers to take photographs of suspects and allows these photographs to be used or disclosed only for purposes related to the prevention or detection of crime, the investigation of offences or the conduct of prosecutions by, or on behalf of, police or other law enforcement and prosecuting authorities inside and outside the United Kingdom or the enforcement of a sentence. After being so used or disclosed, they may be retained but can only be used or disclosed for the same purposes.

D:3.31 Subject to paragraph 3.33, the photographs (and all negatives and copies), of suspects *not* taken in accordance with the provisions in paragraph 5.12 which are taken for the purposes of, or in connection with, the identification procedures in paragraphs 3.5 to 3.10, 3.21 or 3.23 must be destroyed unless the suspect:

(a) is charged with, or informed they may be prosecuted for, a recordable offence;
(b) is prosecuted for a recordable offence;
(c) is cautioned for a recordable offence or given a warning or reprimand in accordance with the Crime and Disorder Act 1998 for a recordable offence; or
(d) gives informed consent, in writing, for the photograph or images to be retained for purposes described in paragraph 3.30.

D:3.32 When paragraph 3.31 requires the destruction of any photograph, the person must be given an opportunity to witness the destruction or to have a certificate confirming the destruction if they request one within five days of being informed that the destruction is required.

D:3.33 Nothing in paragraph 3.31 affects any separate requirement under the Criminal Procedure and Investigations Act 1996 to retain material in connection with criminal investigations.

Part (b) Recognition by controlled showing of films, photographs and images

A-126a D:3.34 This Part of this section applies when, for the purposes of obtaining evidence of recognition, arrangements are made for a person, including a police officer, who is *not* an eye-witness (see *Note 3AA*):

(a) to view a film, photograph or any other visual medium; and
(b) on the occasion of the viewing, to be asked whether they recognise anyone whose image is shown in the material as someone who is known to them.

The arrangements for such viewings may be made by the officer in charge of the relevant investigation. Although there is no requirement for the identification officer to make the arrangements or to be consulted about the arrangements, nothing prevents this. See *Notes 3AA* and *3G*.

D:3.35 To provide safeguards against mistaken recognition and to avoid any possibility of collusion, on the occasion of the viewing, the arrangements should ensure:

(a) that the films, photographs and other images are shown on an individual basis;
(b) that any person who views the material;
    (i) is unable to communicate with any other individual to whom the material has been, or is to be, shown;
    (ii) is not reminded of any photograph or description of any individual whose image is shown or given any other indication as to the identity of any such individual;
    (iii) is not be told whether a previous witness has recognised any one;
(c) that immediately before a person views the material, they are told that:
    (i) an individual who is known to them may, or may not, appear in the material they are shown and that if they do not recognise anyone, they should say so;
    (ii) at any point, they may ask to see a particular part of the material frozen for them to study and there is no limit on how many times they can view the whole or any part or parts of the material; and
(d) that the person who views the material is not asked to make any decision as to whether they recognise anyone whose image they have seen as someone known to them until they have seen the whole of the material at least twice, unless the officer in charge of the viewing decides that because of the number of images the person has been invited to view, it would not be reasonable to ask them to view the whole of the material for a second time. A record of this decision must be included in the record that is made in accordance with paragraph 3.36.

(see *Note 3G*).

D:3.36 A record of the circumstances and conditions under which the person is given an opportunity to recognise an individual must be made and the record must include:

(a) whether the person knew or was given information concerning the name or identity of any suspect;
(b) what the person has been told *before* the viewing about the offence, the person(s) depicted in the images or the offender and by whom;
(c) how and by whom the witness was asked to view the image or look at the individual;
(d) whether the viewing was alone or with others and if with others, the reason for it;
(e) the arrangements under which the person viewed the film or saw the individual and by whom those arrangements were made;
(f) subject to paragraph 2.18, the name and rank of the officer responsible for deciding that the viewing arrangements should be made in accordance with this Part;
(g) the date time and place images were viewed or further viewed or the individual was seen;
(h) the times between which the images were viewed or the individual was seen;
(i) how the viewing of images or sighting of the individual was controlled and by whom;

(j) whether the person was familiar with the location shown in any images or the place where they saw the individual and if so, why;
(k) whether or not, on this occasion, the person claims to recognise any image shown, or any individual seen, as being someone known to them, and if they do:
(i) the reason;
(ii) the words of recognition;
(iii) any expressions of doubt; and
(iv) what features of the image or the individual triggered the recognition.

D:3.37 The record required under paragraph 3.36 may be made by the person who views the image or sees the individual and makes the recognition; and if applicable, by the officer or police staff in charge of showing the images to that person or in charge of the conditions under which that person sees the individual. The person must be asked to read and check the completed record and as applicable, confirm that it is correctly and accurately reflects the part they played in the viewing (see *Note 3H*).

Part (c) Recognition by uncontrolled viewing of films, photographs and images

D:3.38 This Part applies when, for the purpose of identifying and tracing suspects, films and photographs of incidents or other images are: **A-126b**
(a) shown to the public (which may include police officers and police staff as well as members of the public) through the national or local media or any social media networking site; or
(b) circulated through local or national police communication systems for viewing by police officers and police staff; and
the viewing is not formally controlled and supervised as set out in Part B.

D:3.39 A copy of the relevant material released to the national or local media for showing as described in sub-paragraph 3.38(a), shall be kept. The suspect or their solicitor shall be allowed to view such material before any eye-witness identification procedure under paragraphs 3.5 to 3.10, 3.21 or 3.23 of Part A are carried out, provided it is practicable and would not unreasonably delay the investigation. This paragraph does not affect any separate requirement under the Criminal Procedure and Investigations Act 1996 to retain material in connection with criminal investigations that might apply to sub-paragraphs 3.38(a) and (b).

D:3.40 Each eye-witness involved in any eye-witness identification procedure under paragraphs 3.5 to 3.10, 3.21 or 3.23 shall be asked, *after they have taken part,* whether they have seen any film, photograph or image relating to the offence or any description of the suspect which has been broadcast or published as described in paragraph 3.38(a) and their reply recorded. If they have, they should be asked to give details of the circumstances and subject to the eye-witness's recollection, the record described in paragraph 3.41 should be completed.

D:3.41 As soon as practicable after an individual (member of the public, police officer or police staff) indicates in response to a viewing that they may have information relating to the identity and whereabouts of anyone they have seen in that viewing, arrangements should be made to ensure that they are asked to give details of the circumstances and, subject to the individual's recollection, a record of the circumstances and conditions under which the viewing took place is made. This record shall be made in accordance with the provisions of paragraph 3.36 insofar as they can be applied to the viewing in question (see *Note 3H*).

Notes for guidance

D:3AA The eye-witness identification procedures in Part A should not be used to test whether a witness can recognise a person as someone they know and would be able to give evidence of recognition along the lines that "On (describe date, time, location and circumstances) I saw an image of an individual who I recognised as AB." In these cases, the procedures in Part B shall apply if the viewing is controlled and the procedure in Part C shall apply if the viewing is not controlled. **A-127**

D:3ZA In paragraph 3.5(a)(i), examples of physical changes or differences that the identification officer may wish to consider include hair style and colour, weight, facial hair, wearing or removal of spectacles and tinted contact lenses, facial injuries, tattoos and makeup.

D:3A Except for the provisions of Annex E, para.1, a police officer who is a witness for the purposes of this part of the Code is subject to the same principles and procedures as a civilian witness.

D:3B When an eye-witness attending an identification procedure has previously been shown photographs, or been shown or provided with computerised or artist's composite likenesses, or similar likenesses or pictures, it is the officer in charge of the investigation's responsibility to make the identification officer aware of this.

D:3C The purpose of paragraph 3.19 is to avoid or reduce delay in arranging identification procedures by enabling the required information and warnings, see sub-paragraphs 3.17(ix) and 3.17(xii), to be given at the earliest opportunity.

D:3D Paragraph 3.21 would apply when a known suspect becomes "unavailable" and thereby delays or frustrates arrangements for obtaining identification evidence. It also applies when a suspect refuses or fails to take part in a video identification, an identification parade or a group identification, or refuses or fails to take part in the only practicable options from that list. It enables any suitable images of the suspect, moving or still, which are available or can be obtained, to be used in an identification procedure. Examples include images from custody and other CCTV systems and from visually recorded interview records, see Code F, Note for guidance 2D.

D:3E When it is proposed to show photographs to a witness in accordance with Annex E, it is the responsibility of the officer in charge of the investigation to confirm to the officer responsible for supervising and directing the showing, that the first description of the suspect given by that eye-witness has been recorded. If this description has not been recorded, the procedure under Annex E must be postponed, see Annex E, para. 2.

D:3F The admissibility and value of identification evidence obtained when carrying out the procedure under paragraph 3.2 may be compromised if:

(a) before a person is identified, the eye-witness' attention is specifically drawn to that person; or

(b) the suspect's identity becomes known before the procedure.

D:3G The admissibility and value of evidence of recognition obtained when carrying out the procedures in Part B may be compromised if, before the person is recognised, the witness who has claimed to know them is given or is made, or becomes aware of, information about the person which was not previously known to them personally but which they have purported to rely on to support their claim that the person is in fact known to them.

D:3H It is important that the record referred to in paragraphs 3.36 and 3.41 is made as soon as practicable after the viewing and whilst it is fresh in the mind of the individual who makes the recognition.

D:4 Identification by fingerprints and footwear impressions

(a) Taking fingerprints in connection with a criminal investigation

(a) General

A-128 D:4.1 References to "fingerprints" means any record, produced by any method, of the skin pattern and other physical characteristics or features of a person's:

(i) fingers; or

(ii) palms.

(b) Action

D:4.2 A person's fingerprints may be taken in connection with the investigation of an offence only with their consent or if paragraph 4.3 applies. If the person is at a police station, consent must be in writing.

D:4.3 PACE, s.61, provides powers to take fingerprints without consent from any person aged ten or over as follows:

(a) under section 61(3), from a person detained at a police station in consequence of being arrested for a recordable offence, see *Note 4A*, if they have not had their fingerprints taken in the course of the investigation of the offence unless those previously taken fingerprints are not a complete set or some or all of those fingerprints are not of sufficient quality to allow satisfactory analysis, comparison or matching.

(b) under section 61(4), from a person detained at a police station who has been charged with a recordable offence, see *Note 4A*, or informed they will be reported for such an offence if they have not had their fingerprints taken in the course of the investigation of the offence unless those previously taken fingerprints are not a complete set or some or all of those fingerprints are not of sufficient quality to allow satisfactory analysis, comparison or matching.

(c) under section 61(4A), from a person who has been bailed to appear at a court or police station if the person:

  (i) has answered to bail for a person whose fingerprints were taken previously and there are reasonable grounds for believing they are not the same person; or

  (ii) who has answered to bail claims to be a different person from a person whose fingerprints were previously taken;

and in either case, the court or an officer of inspector rank or above, authorises the fingerprints to be taken at the court or police station (an inspector's authority may be given in writing or orally and confirmed in writing, as soon as practicable);

(ca) under section 61(5A) from a person who has been arrested for a recordable offence and released if the person:

  (i) is on bail and has not had their fingerprints taken in the course of the investigation of the offence, or;

  (ii) has had their fingerprints taken in the course of the investigation of the offence, but they do not constitute a complete set or some, or all, of the fingerprints are not of sufficient quality to allow satisfactory analysis, comparison or matching.

(cb) under section 61(5B) from a person not detained at a police station who has been charged with a recordable offence or informed they will be reported for such an offence if:
- (i) they have not had their fingerprints taken in the course of the investigation; or
- (ii) their fingerprints have been taken in the course of the investigation of the offence but either:
  - they do not constitute a complete set or some, or all, of the fingerprints are not of sufficient quality to allow satisfactory analysis, comparison or matching; or
  - the investigation was discontinued but subsequently resumed and, before the resumption, their fingerprints were destroyed pursuant to section 63D(3).

(d) under section 61(6), from a person who has been:
- (i) convicted of a recordable offence; or
- (ii) given a caution in respect of a recordable offence (see *Note 4A*) which, at the time of the caution, the person admitted;

if, since being convicted or cautioned:
- their fingerprints have not been taken; or
- their fingerprints which have been taken do not constitute a complete set or some, or all, of the fingerprints are not of sufficient quality to allow satisfactory analysis, comparison or matching;

and in either case, an officer of inspector rank or above is satisfied that taking the fingerprints is necessary to assist in the prevention or detection of crime and authorises the taking;

(e) under section 61(6A) from a person a constable reasonably suspects is committing or attempting to commit, or has committed or attempted to commit, any offence if either:
- (i) the person's name is unknown to, and cannot be readily ascertained by, the constable; or
- (ii) the constable has reasonable grounds for doubting whether a name given by the person as their name is their real name.

Note: fingerprints taken under this power are not regarded as having been taken in the course of the investigation of an offence.

[See *Note 4C*]

(f) under section 61(6D) from a person who has been convicted outside England and Wales of an offence which if committed in England and Wales would be a qualifying offence as defined by PACE, section 65A (see *Note 4AB*) if:
- (i) the person's fingerprints have not been taken previously under this power or their fingerprints have been so taken on a previous occasion but they do not constitute a complete set or some, or all, of the fingerprints are not of sufficient quality to allow satisfactory analysis, comparison or matching; and
- (ii) a police officer of inspector rank or above is satisfied that taking fingerprints is necessary to assist in the prevention or detection of crime and authorises them to be taken.

D:4.4 PACE, s.63A(4) and Sched. 2A provide powers to:

(a) make a requirement (in accordance with Annex G) for a person to attend a police station to have their fingerprints taken in the exercise of one of the following powers (described in paragraph 4.3 above) within certain periods as follows:
- (i) section 61(5A)—Persons arrested for a recordable offence and released, see paragraph 4.3(ca): In the case of a person whose fingerprints were taken in the course of the investigation but those fingerprints do not constitute a complete set or some, or all, of the fingerprints are not of sufficient quality, the requirement may not be made more than six months from the day the investigating officer was informed that the fingerprints previously taken were incomplete or below standard. In the case of a person whose fingerprints were destroyed prior to the resumption of the investigation, the requirement may not be made more than six months from the day on which the investigation resumed.
- (ii) section 61(5B)—Persons not detained at a police station charged etc. with a recordable offence, see paragraph 4.3(cb): the requirement may not be made more than six months from:
  - the day the person was charged or informed that they would be reported, if fingerprints have not been taken in the course of the investigation of the offence; or
  - the day the investigating officer was informed that the fingerprints previously taken were incomplete or below standard, if fingerprints have been taken in the course of

the investigation but those fingerprints do not constitute a complete set or some, or all, of the fingerprints are not of sufficient quality; or

- the day on which the investigation was resumed, in the case of a person whose fingerprints were destroyed prior to the resumption of the investigation.

(iii) section 61(6)—Persons convicted or cautioned for a recordable offence in England and Wales, see paragraph 4.3(d): where the offence for which the person was convicted or cautioned is a qualifying offence (see *Note 4AB*), there is no time limit for the exercise of this power. Where the conviction or caution is for a recordable offence which is not a qualifying offence, the requirement may *not* be made more than two years from:

- in the case of a person who has not had their fingerprints taken since the conviction or caution, the day on which the person was convicted or cautioned, or, if later, the day on which Schedule 2A came into force (March 7, 2011), ; or
- in the case of a person whose fingerprints have been taken in the course of the investigation but those fingerprints do not constitute a complete set or some, or all, of the fingerprints are not of sufficient quality, the day on which an officer from the force investigating the offence was informed that the fingerprints previously taken were incomplete or below standard, or, if later, the day on which Schedule 2A came into force (March 7, 2011).

(iv) section 61(6D)—A person who has been convicted of a qualifying offence (see *Note 4AB*) outside England and Wales, see paragraph 4.3(g): there is no time limit for making the requirement.

Note: A person who has had their fingerprints taken under any of the powers in section 61 mentioned in paragraph 4.3 on two occasions in relation to any offence may not be required under Schedule 2A to attend a police station for their fingerprints to be taken again under section 61 in relation to that offence, unless authorised by an officer of inspector rank or above. The fact of the authorisation and the reasons for giving it must be recorded as soon as practicable.

(b) arrest, without warrant, a person who fails to comply with the requirement.

D:4.5 A person's fingerprints may be taken, as above, electronically.

D:4.6 Reasonable force may be used, if necessary, to take a person's fingerprints without their consent under the powers as in paragraphs 4.3 and 4.4.

D:4.7 Before any fingerprints are taken:

(a) without consent under any power mentioned in paragraphs 4.3 and 4.4 above, the person must be informed of:

(i) the reason their fingerprints are to be taken;

(ii) the power under which they are to be taken; and

(iii) the fact that the relevant authority has been given if any power mentioned in paragraph 4.3(c), (d) or (f) applies.

(b) with or without consent at a police station or elsewhere, the person must be informed:

(i) that their fingerprints may be subject of a speculative search against other fingerprints, see *Note 4B*; and

(ii) that their fingerprints may be retained in accordance with Annex F, Part (a) unless they were taken under the power mentioned in paragraph 4.3(e) when they must be destroyed after they have being [*sic*] checked (see *Note 4C*).

(c) Documentation

D:4.8A A record must be made as soon as practicable after the fingerprints are taken, of:

- the matters in paragraph 4.7(a)(i) to (iii) and the fact that the person has been informed of those matters; and
- the fact that the person has been informed of the matters in paragraph 4.7(b)(i) and (ii).

The record must be made in the person's custody record if they are detained at a police station when the fingerprints are taken.

D:4.8 If force is used, a record shall be made of the circumstances and those present.

D:4.9 [*Not used.*]

(b) Not used.

D:4.10 [*Not used.*]
D:4.11 [*Not used.*]
D:4.12 [*Not used.*]
D:4.13 [*Not used.*]
D:4.14 [*Not used.*]
D:4.15 [*Not used.*]

(c) Taking footwear impressions in connection with a criminal investigation

(a) Action

D:4.16 Impressions of a person's footwear may be taken in connection with the investigation of an offence only with their consent or if paragraph 4.17 applies. If the person is at a police station consent must be in writing. **A-129**

D:4.17 PACE, s.61A, provides power for a police officer to take footwear impressions without consent from any person over the age of ten years who is detained at a police station:

(a) in consequence of being arrested for a recordable offence, see *Note 4A*; or if the detainee has been charged with a recordable offence, or informed they will be reported for such an offence; and

(b) the detainee has not had an impression of their footwear taken in the course of the investigation of the offence unless the previously taken impression is not complete or is not of sufficient quality to allow satisfactory analysis, comparison or matching (whether in the case in question or generally).

D:4.18 Reasonable force may be used, if necessary, to take a footwear impression from a detainee without consent under the power in paragraph 4.17.

D:4.19 Before any footwear impression is taken with, or without, consent as above, the person must be informed:

(a) of the reason the impression is to be taken;

(b) that the impression may be retained and may be subject of a speculative search against other impressions, see *Note 4B*, unless destruction of the impression is required in accordance with Annex F, Pt B.

(b) Documentation

D:4.20 A record must be made, as soon as possible, of the reason for taking a person's footwear impressions without consent. If force is used, a record shall be made of the circumstances and those present.

D:4.21 A record shall be made when a person has been informed under the terms of paragraph 4.19(b), of the possibility that their footwear impressions may be subject of a speculative search.

Notes for guidance

D:4A References to "recordable offences" in this code relate to those offences for which convictions or cautions may be recorded in national police records. See PACE, s.27(4). The recordable offences current at the time when this Code was prepared, are any offences which carry a sentence of imprisonment on conviction (irrespective of the period, or the age of the offender or actual sentence passed) as well as the non-imprisonable offences under the Vagrancy Act 1824 ss.3 and 4 (begging and persistent begging), the Street Offences Act 1959, s.1 (loitering or soliciting for purposes of prostitution), the Road Traffic Act 1988, s.25 (tampering with motor vehicles), the Criminal Justice and Public Order Act 1994, s.167 (touting for hire car services) and others listed in the National Police Records (Recordable Offences) Regulations 2000 as amended.

D:4AB A qualifying offence is one of the offences specified in PACE, s.65A. These include offences which involve the use or threat of violence or unlawful force against persons, sexual offences, offences against children and other offences, for example:

- *murder, false imprisonment, kidnapping contrary to Common law*
- *manslaughter, conspiracy to murder, threats to kill, wounding with intent to cause grievous bodily harm (GBH), causing GBH and assault occasioning actual bodily harm contrary to the Offences Against the Person Act 1861;*
- *criminal possession or use of firearms contrary to sections 16 to 18 of the Firearms Act 1968;*
- *robbery, burglary and aggravated burglary contrary to sections 8, 9 or 10 of the Theft Act 1968 or an offence under section 12A of that Act involving an accident which caused a person's death;*
- *criminal damage required to be charged as arson contrary to section 1 of the Criminal Damage Act 1971;*
- *taking, possessing and showing indecent photographs of children contrary to section 1 of the Protection of Children Act 1978;*
- *rape, sexual assault, child sex offences, exposure and other offences contrary to the Sexual Offences Act 2003.*

D:4B Fingerprints, footwear impressions or a DNA sample (and the information derived from it) taken from a person arrested on suspicion of being involved in a recordable offence, or charged with such an offence, or informed they will be reported for such an offence, may be subject of a speculative search. This means the fingerprints, footwear impressions or DNA sample may be checked against other fingerprints, footwear impressions and DNA records held by, or on behalf of, the police and other law enforcement authorities in, or outside, the UK, or held in connection with, or as a result of, an investigation of an offence inside or outside the UK.

D:4C The power under section 61(6A) of PACE described in paragraph 4.3(e) allows fingerprints of a suspect who has not been arrested, and whose name is not known or cannot be ascertained, or who gave a doubtful name, to be taken in connection with any offence (whether recordable or not) using a mobile device and then checked on the street against the database containing the national fingerprint collection. Fingerprints taken under this power cannot be retained after they have been checked. The results may make an arrest for the suspected offence based on the name condition unnecessary (see Code G, para. 2.9(a)) and enable the offence to be disposed of without arrest, for example, by summons/charging by post, penalty notice or words of advice. If arrest for a non-recordable offence is necessary for any other reasons, this power may also be exercised at the station. Before the power is exercised, the officer should:

- *inform the person of the nature of the suspected offence and why they are suspected of committing it.*
- *give them a reasonable opportunity to establish their real name before deciding that their name is unknown and cannot be readily ascertained or that there are reasonable grounds to doubt that a name they have given is their real name.*
- *as applicable, inform the person of the reason why their name is not known and cannot be readily ascertained or of the grounds for doubting that a name they have given is their real name, including, for example, the reason why a particular document the person has produced to verify their real name, is not sufficient.*

D:5 Examinations to establish identity and the taking of photographs

(a) Detainees at police stations

(a) Searching or examination of detainees at police stations

A-130 D:5.1 PACE, s.54A(1), allows a detainee at a police station to be searched or examined or both, to establish:

(a) whether they have any marks, features or injuries that would tend to identify them as a person involved in the commission of an offence and to photograph any identifying marks, see paragraph 5.5; or

(b) their identity, see *Note 5A*.

A person detained at a police station to be searched under a stop and search power, see Code A, is not a detainee for the purposes of these powers.

D:5.2 A search and/or examination to find marks under s.54A(1)(a) may be carried out without the detainee's consent, see paragraph 2.12, only if authorised by an officer of at least inspector rank when consent has been withheld or it is not practicable to obtain consent, see *Note 5D*.

D:5.3 A search or examination to establish a suspect's identity under section 54A(1)(b) may be carried out without the detainee's consent, see paragraph 2.12, only if authorised by an officer of at least inspector rank when the detainee has refused to identify themselves or the authorising officer has reasonable grounds for suspecting the person is not who they claim to be.

D:5.4 Any marks that assist in establishing the detainee's identity, or their identification as a person involved in the commission of an offence, are identifying marks. Such marks may be photographed with the detainee's consent, see paragraph 2.12; or without their consent if it is withheld or it is not practicable to obtain it, see *Note 5D*.

D:5.5 A detainee may only be searched, examined and photographed under section 54A, by a police officer of the same sex.

D:5.6 Any photographs of identifying marks, taken under section 54A, may be used or disclosed only for purposes related to the prevention or detection of crime, the investigation of offences or the conduct of prosecutions by, or on behalf of, police or other law enforcement and prosecuting authorities inside, and outside, the UK. After being so used or disclosed, the photograph may be retained but must not be used or disclosed except for these purposes, see *Note 5B*.

D:5.7 The powers, as in paragraph 5.1, do not affect any separate requirement under the Criminal Procedure and Investigations Act 1996 to retain material in connection with criminal investigations.

D:5.8 Authority for the search and/or examination for the purposes of paragraphs 5.2 and 5.3 may be given orally or in writing. If given orally, the authorising officer must confirm it in writing as soon as practicable. A separate authority is required for each purpose which applies.

D:5.9 If it is established a person is unwilling to co-operate sufficiently to enable a search and/or examination to take place or a suitable photograph to be taken, an officer may use reasonable force to:

(a) search and/or examine a detainee without their consent; and

(b) photograph any identifying marks without their consent.

D:5.10 The thoroughness and extent of any search or examination carried out in accordance with the powers in section 54A must be no more than the officer considers necessary to achieve the required purpose. Any search or examination which involves the removal of more than the person's outer clothing shall be conducted in accordance with Code C, Annex A, para. 11.

D:5.11 An intimate search may not be carried out under the powers in s.54A.

(b) Photographing detainees at police stations and other persons elsewhere than at a police station

D:5.12 Under PACE, s.64A, an officer may photograph: A-131

(a) any person whilst they are detained at a police station; and

(b) any person who is elsewhere than at a police station and who has been:

(i) arrested by a constable for an offence;

(ii) taken into custody by a constable after being arrested for an offence by a person other than a constable;

(iii) made subject to a requirement to wait with a community support officer under paragraph 2(3) or (3B) of Schedule 4 to the Police Reform Act 2002;

(iiia) given a direction by a constable under section 27 of the Violent Crime Reduction Act 2006.

(iv) given a penalty notice by a constable in uniform under Chapter 1 of Part 1 of the Criminal Justice and Police Act 2001, a penalty notice by a constable under section 444A of the Education Act 1996, or a fixed penalty notice by a constable in uniform under section 54 of the Road Traffic Offenders Act 1988;

(v) given a notice in relation to a relevant fixed penalty offence (within the meaning of paragraph 1 of Schedule 4 to the Police Reform Act 2002) by a community support officer by virtue of a designation applying that paragraph to him;

(vi) given a notice in relation to a relevant fixed penalty offence (within the meaning of paragraph 1 of Schedule 5 to the Police Reform Act 2002) by an accredited person by virtue of accreditation specifying that that paragraph applies to him; or

(vii) given a direction to leave and not return to a specified location for up to 48 hours by a police constable (under section 27 of the Violent Crime Reduction Act 2006).

D:5.12A Photographs taken under PACE, s.64A:

(a) may be taken with the person's consent, or without their consent if consent is withheld or it is not practicable to obtain their consent, see *Note 5E*; and

(b) may be used or disclosed only for purposes related to the prevention or detection of crime, the investigation of offences or the conduct of prosecutions by, or on behalf of, police or other law enforcement and prosecuting authorities inside and outside the United Kingdom or the enforcement of any sentence or order made by a court when dealing with an offence. After being so used or disclosed, they may be retained but can only be used or disclosed for the same purposes. See *Note 5B*.

D:5.13 The officer proposing to take a detainee's photograph may, for this purpose, require the person to remove any item or substance worn on, or over, all, or any part of, their head or face. If they do not comply with such a requirement, the officer may remove the item or substance.

D:5.14 If it is established the detainee is unwilling to co-operate sufficiently to enable a suitable photograph to be taken and it is not reasonably practicable to take the photograph covertly, an officer may use reasonable force, see *Note 5F*.

(a) to take their photograph without their consent; and

(b) for the purpose of taking the photograph, remove any item or substance worn on, or over, all, or any part of, the person's head or face which they have failed to remove when asked.

D:5.15 For the purposes of this code, a photograph may be obtained without the person's consent by making a copy of an image of them taken at any time on a camera system installed anywhere in the police station.

(c) Information to be given

D:5.16 When a person is searched, examined or photographed under the provisions as in paragraph 5.1 and 5.12, or their photograph obtained as in paragraph 5.15, they must be informed of the: A-132

(a) purpose of the search, examination or photograph;

(b) grounds on which the relevant authority, if applicable, has been given; and

(c) purposes for which the photograph may be used, disclosed or retained.

This information must be given before the search or examination commences or the photograph is taken, except if the photograph is:

(i) to be taken covertly;

(ii) obtained as in paragraph 5.15, in which case the person must be informed as soon as practicable after the photograph is taken or obtained.

(d) Documentation

D:5.17 A record must be made when a detainee is searched, examined, or a photograph of the person, or any identifying marks found on them, are [*sic*] taken. The record must include the:

(a) identity, subject to paragraph 2.18, of the officer carrying out the search, examination or taking the photograph;
(b) purpose of the search, examination or photograph and the outcome;
(c) detainee's consent to the search, examination or photograph, or the reason the person was searched, examined or photographed without consent;
(d) giving of any authority as in paragraphs 5.2 and 5.3, the grounds for giving it and the authorising officer.

D:5.18 If force is used when searching, examining or taking a photograph in accordance with this section, a record shall be made of the circumstances and those present.

(b) Persons at police stations not detained

A-133 D:5.19 When there are reasonable grounds for suspecting the involvement of a person in a criminal offence, but that person is at a police station *voluntarily* and not detained, the provisions of paragraphs 5.1 to 5.18 should apply, subject to the modifications in the following paragraphs.

D:5.20 References to the "person being detained" and to the powers mentioned in paragraph 5.1 which apply only to detainees at police stations shall be omitted.

D:5.21 Force may not be used to:
(a) search and/or examine the person to:
 (i) discover whether they have any marks that would tend to identify them as a person involved in the commission of an offence; or
 (ii) establish their identity, see *Note 5A*;
(b) take photographs of any identifying marks, see paragraph 5.4; or
(c) take a photograph of the person.

D:5.22 Subject to paragraph 5.24, the photographs of persons or of their identifying marks which are not taken in accordance with the provisions mentioned in paragraphs 5.1 or 5.12, must be destroyed (together with any negatives and copies) unless the person:
(a) is charged with, or informed they may be prosecuted for, a recordable offence;
(b) is prosecuted for a recordable offence;
(c) is cautioned for a recordable offence or given a warning or reprimand in accordance with the Crime and Disorder Act 1998 for a recordable offence; or
(d) gives informed consent, in writing, for the photograph or image to be retained as in paragraph 5.6.

D:5.23 When paragraph 5.22 requires the destruction of any photograph, the person must be given an opportunity to witness the destruction or to have a certificate confirming the destruction provided they so request the certificate within five days of being informed the destruction is required.

D:5.24 Nothing in paragraph 5.22 affects any separate requirement under the Criminal Procedure and Investigations Act 1996 to retain material in connection with criminal investigations.

Notes for guidance

A-134 *D:5A The conditions under which fingerprints may be taken to assist in establishing a person's identity, are described in section 4.*

D:5B Examples of purposes related to the prevention or detection of crime, the investigation of offences or the conduct of prosecutions include:
(a) checking the photograph against other photographs held in records or in connection with, or as a result of, an investigation of an offence to establish whether the person is liable to arrest for other offences;
(b) when the person is arrested at the same time as other people, or at a time when it is likely that other people will be arrested, using the photograph to help establish who was arrested, at what time and where;
(c) when the real identity of the person is not known and cannot be readily ascertained or there are reasonable grounds for doubting a name and other personal details given by the person, are their real name and personal details. In these circumstances, using or disclosing the photograph to help to establish or verify their real identity or determine whether they are liable to arrest for some other offence, e.g. by checking it against other photographs held in records or in connection with, or as a result of, an investigation of an offence;
(d) when it appears any identification procedure in section 3 may need to be arranged for which the person's photograph would assist;
(e) when the person's release without charge may be required, and if the release is:
 (i) on bail to appear at a police station, using the photograph to help verify the person's identity when they answer their bail and if the person does not answer their bail, to assist in arresting them; or
 (ii) without bail, using the photograph to help verify their identity or assist in locating them for the purposes of serving them with a summons to appear at court in criminal proceedings;

(f) when the person has answered to bail at a police station and there are reasonable grounds for doubting they are the person who was previously granted bail, using the photograph to help establish or verify their identity;

(g) when the person arrested on a warrant claims to be a different person from the person named on the warrant and a photograph would help to confirm or disprove their claim;

(h) when the person has been charged with, reported for, or convicted of, a recordable offence and their photograph is not already on record as a result of (a) to (f) or their photograph is on record but their appearance has changed since it was taken and the person has not yet been released or brought before a court.

D:5C There is no power to arrest a person convicted of a recordable offence solely to take their photograph. The power to take photographs in this section applies only where the person is in custody as a result of the exercise of another power, e.g. arrest for fingerprinting under PACE, Sched. 2A, para. 17.

D:5D Examples of when it would not be practicable to obtain a detainee's consent, see paragraph 2.12, to a search, examination or the taking of a photograph of an identifying mark include:

(a) when the person is drunk or otherwise unfit to give consent;

(b) when there are reasonable grounds to suspect that if the person became aware a search or examination was to take place or an identifying mark was to be photographed, they would take steps to prevent this happening, e.g. by violently resisting, covering or concealing the mark etc and it would not otherwise be possible to carry out the search or examination or to photograph any identifying mark;

(c) in the case of a juvenile, if the parent or guardian cannot be contacted in sufficient time to allow the search or examination to be carried out or the photograph to be taken.

D:5E Examples of when it would not be practicable to obtain the person's consent, see paragraph 2.12, to a photograph being taken include:

(a) when the person is drunk or otherwise unfit to give consent;

(b) when there are reasonable grounds to suspect that if the person became aware a photograph, suitable to be used or disclosed for the use and disclosure described in paragraph 5.6, was to be taken, they would take steps to prevent it being taken, e.g. by violently resisting, covering or distorting their face etc, and it would not otherwise be possible to take a suitable photograph;

(c) when, in order to obtain a suitable photograph, it is necessary to take it covertly; and

(d) in the case of a juvenile, if the parent or guardian cannot be contacted in sufficient time to allow the photograph to be taken.

D:5F The use of reasonable force to take the photograph of a suspect elsewhere than at a police station must be carefully considered. In order to obtain a suspect's consent and cooperation to remove an item of religious headwear to take their photograph, a constable should consider whether in the circumstances of the situation the removal of the headwear and the taking of the photograph should be by an officer of the same sex as the person. It would be appropriate for these actions to be conducted out of public view (see paragraph 1.1 and Note 1A).

D:6 Identification by body samples and impressions

(a) General

D:6.1 References to: **A-135**

(a) an "intimate sample" mean a dental impression or sample of blood, semen or any other tissue fluid, urine, or pubic hair, or a swab taken from any part of a person's genitals or from a person's body orifice other than the mouth;

(b) a "non-intimate sample" means:

(i) a sample of hair, other than pubic hair, which includes hair plucked with the root, see *Note 6A*;

(ii) a sample taken from a nail or from under a nail;

(iii) a swab taken from any part of a person's body other than a part from which a swab taken would be an intimate sample;

(iv) saliva;

(v) a skin impression which means any record, other than a fingerprint, which is a record, in any form and produced by any method, of the skin pattern and other physical characteristics or features of the whole, or any part of, a person's foot or of any other part of their body.

(b) Action

(a) Intimate samples

D:6.2 PACE, s.62, provides that intimate samples may be taken under: **A-136**

(a) section 62(1), from a person in police detention only:

(i) if a police officer of inspector rank or above has reasonable grounds to believe such an impression or sample will tend to confirm or disprove the suspect's involvement in a recordable offence, see *Note 4A*, and gives authorisation for a sample to be taken; and

(ii) with the suspect's written consent;

(b) section 62(1A), from a person not in police detention but from whom two or more nonintimate samples have been taken in the course of an investigation of an offence and the samples, though suitable, have proved insufficient if:

(i) a police officer of inspector rank or above authorises it to be taken; and

(ii) the person concerned gives their written consent. See *Notes 6B* and *6C*

(c) section 62(2A), from a person convicted outside England and Wales of an offence which if committed in England and Wales would be qualifying offence [*sic*] as defined by PACE, s.65A (see *Note 4AB*) from whom two or more non-intimate samples taken under section 63(3E) (see paragraph 6.6(h) have proved insufficient if:

(i) a police officer of inspector rank or above is satisfied that taking the sample is necessary to assist in the prevention or detection of crime and authorises it to be taken; and

(ii) the person concerned gives their written consent.

D:6.2A PACE, s.63A(4) and Sched. 2A provide powers to:

(a) make a requirement (in accordance with Annex G) for a person to attend a police station to have an intimate sample taken in the exercise of one of the following powers (see paragraph 6.2) :

(i) section 62(1A)—Persons from whom two or more non-intimate samples have been taken and proved to be insufficient, see paragraph 6.2(b): There is no time limit for making the requirement.

(ii) section 62(2A)—Persons convicted outside England and Wales from whom two or more non-intimate samples taken under section 63(3E) (see paragraph 6.6(g)have proved insufficient, see paragraph 6.2(c): There is no time limit for making the requirement.

(b) arrest without warrant a person who fails to comply with the requirement

D:6.3 Before a suspect is asked to provide an intimate sample, they must be:

(a) informed:

(i) of the reason, including the nature of the suspected offence (except if taken under paragraph 6.2(c) from a person convicted outside England and Wales).

(ii) that authorisation has been given and the provisions under which given;

(iii) that a sample taken at a police station may be subject of a speculative search;

(b) warned that if they refuse without good cause their refusal may harm their case if it comes to trial, see *Note 6D.* If the suspect is in police detention and not legally represented, they must also be reminded of their entitlement to have free legal advice, see Code C, para. 6.5, and the reminder noted in the custody record. If paragraph 6.2(b) applies and the person is attending a station voluntarily, their entitlement to free legal advice as in Code C, para. 3.21 shall be explained to them.

D:6.4 Dental impressions may only be taken by a registered dentist. Other intimate samples, except for samples of urine, may only be taken by a registered medical practitioner or registered nurse or registered paramedic.

(b) Non-intimate samples

A-137 D:6.5 A non-intimate sample may be taken from a detainee only with their written consent or if paragraph 6.6 applies.

D:6.6 A non-intimate sample may be taken from a person without the appropriate consent in the following circumstances:

(a) under section 63(2A) from a person who is in police detention as a consequence of being arrested for a recordable offence and who has not had a non-intimate sample of the same type and from the same part of the body taken in the course of the investigation of the offence by the police or they have had such a sample taken but it proved insufficient;

(b) under section 63(3) from a person who is being held in custody by the police on the authority of a court if an officer of at least the rank of inspector authorises it to be taken. An authorisation may be given:

(i) if the authorising officer has reasonable grounds for suspecting the person of involvement in a recordable offence and for believing that the sample will tend to confirm or disprove that involvement, and

(ii) in writing or orally and confirmed in writing, as soon as practicable;

but an authorisation may not be given to take from the same part of the body a further non-intimate sample consisting of a skin impression unless the previously taken impression proved insufficient;

(c) under section 63(3ZA) from a person who has been arrested for a recordable offence and released if:
 (i) in the case of a person who is on bail, they have not had a sample of the same type and from the same part of the body taken in the course of the investigation of the offence, or;
 (ii) in any case, the person has had such a sample taken in the course of the investigation of the offence, but either:
 - it was not suitable or proved insufficient; or
 - the investigation was discontinued but subsequently resumed and before the resumption, any DNA profile derived from the sample was destroyed and the sample itself was destroyed pursuant to section 63R(4), (5) or (12);

(d) under section 63(3A), from a person (whether or not in police detention or held in custody by the police on the authority of a court) who has been charged with a recordable offence or informed they will be reported for such an offence if the person:
 (i) has not had a non-intimate sample taken from them in the course of the investigation of the offence; or
 (ii) has had a sample so taken, but it was not suitable or proved insufficient, see *Note 6B*; or
 (iii) has had a sample taken in the course of the investigation of the offence and the sample has been destroyed and in proceedings relating to that offence there is a dispute as to whether a DNA profile relevant to the proceedings was derived from the destroyed sample;

(e) under section 63(3B), from a person who has been:
 (i) convicted of a recordable offence; or
 (ii) given a caution in respect of a recordable offence which, at the time of the caution, the person admitted;

 if, since their conviction or caution a non-intimate sample has not been taken from them or a sample which has been taken since then was not suitable or proved insufficient and in either case, an officer of inspector rank or above, is satisfied that taking the fingerprints is necessary to assist in the prevention or detection of crime and authorises the taking;

(f) under section 63(3C) from a person to whom section 2 of the Criminal Evidence (Amendment) Act 1997 applies (persons detained following acquittal on grounds of insanity or finding of unfitness to plead);

(g) under section 63(3E) from a person who has been convicted outside England and Wales of an offence which if committed in England and Wales would be a qualifying offence as defined by PACE, section 65A (see *Note 4AB*) if:
 (i) a non-intimate sample has not been taken previously under this power or unless a sample was so taken but was not suitable or proved insufficient; and
 (ii) a police officer of inspector rank or above is satisfied that taking a sample is necessary to assist in the prevention or detection of crime and authorises it to be taken.

D:6.6A PACE, s.63A(4) and Sched. 2A provide powers to:

(a) make a requirement (in accordance with Annex G) for a person to attend a police station to have a non-intimate sample taken in the exercise of one of the following powers (see paragraph 6.6 above) within certain time limits as follows:
 (i) section 63(3ZA)—Persons arrested for a recordable offence and released, see paragraph 6.6(c): In the case of a person from whom a non-intimate sample was taken in the course of the investigation but that sample was not suitable or proved insufficient, the requirement may not be made more than six months from the day the investigating officer was informed that the sample previously taken was not suitable or proved insufficient. In the case of a person whose DNA profile and sample was destroyed prior to the resumption of the investigation, the requirement may not be made more than six months from the day on which the investigation resumed.
 (ii) section 63(3A)—Persons charged etc. with a recordable offence, see paragraph 6.6(d): The requirement may not be made more than six months from:
 - the day the person was charged or informed that they would be reported, if a sample has not been taken in the course of the investigation;
 - the day the investigating officer was informed that the sample previously taken was not suitable or proved insufficient, if a sample has been taken in the course of the investigation but the sample was not suitable or proved insufficient; or
 - the day on which the investigation was resumed, in the case of a person whose DNA profile and sample were destroyed prior to the resumption of the investigation.
 (iii) section 63(3B)—Person convicted or cautioned for a recordable offence in England and

Wales, see paragraph 6.6(e): Where the offence for which the person was convicted etc is also a qualifying offence (see *Note 4AB*), there is no time limit for the exercise of this power. Where the conviction etc was for a recordable offence that is *not* a qualifying offence, the requirement may not be made more than two years from:

- in the case of a person whose sample has not been taken since they were convicted or cautioned, the day the person was convicted or cautioned, or, if later, the day Schedule 2A came into force (March 7, 2011); or
- in the case of a person whose sample has been taken but was not suitable or proved insufficient, the day an officer from the force investigating the offence was informed that the sample previously taken was not suitable or proved insufficient or, if later, the day Schedule 2A came into force (March 7, 2011).

(iv) section 63(3E)—A person who has been convicted of qualifying offence (see *Note 4AB*) outside England and Wales, see paragraph 6.6(h): there is no time limit for making the requirement.

Note: A person who has had a non-intimate sample taken under any of the powers in section 63 mentioned in paragraph 6.6 on two occasions in relation to any offence may not be required under Schedule 2A to attend a police station for a sample to be taken again under section 63 in relation to that offence, unless authorised by an officer of inspector rank or above. The fact of the authorisation and the reasons for giving it must be recorded as soon as practicable.

(b) arrest, without warrant, a person who fails to comply with the requirement.

D:6.7 Reasonable force may be used, if necessary, to take a non-intimate sample from a person without their consent under the powers mentioned in paragraph 6.6.

D:6.8 Before any non-intimate sample is taken:

(a) without consent under any power mentioned in paragraphs 6.6 and 6.6A, the person must be informed of:
   (i) the reason for taking the sample;
   (ii) the power under which the sample is to be taken;
   (iii) the fact that the relevant authority has been given if any power mentioned in paragraph 6.6(b), (e) or (g) applies, including the nature of the suspected offence (except if taken under paragraph 6.6(e) from a person convicted or cautioned, or under paragraph 6.6(g) if taken from a person convicted outside England and Wales;

(b) with or without consent at a police station or elsewhere, the person must be informed:
   (i) that their sample or information derived from it may be subject of a speculative search against other samples and information derived from them, see *Note 6E* and
   (ii) that their sample and the information derived from it may be retained in accordance with Annex F, Part (a).

(c) Removal of clothing

D:6.9 When clothing needs to be removed in circumstances likely to cause embarrassment to the person, no person of the opposite sex who is not a registered medical practitioner or registered health care professional shall be present, (unless in the case of a juvenile, mentally disordered or mentally vulnerable person, that person specifically requests the presence of an appropriate adult of the opposite sex who is readily available) nor shall anyone whose presence is unnecessary. However, in the case of a juvenile, this is subject to the overriding proviso that such a removal of clothing may take place in the absence of the appropriate adult only if the juvenile signifies in their presence, that they prefer the adult's absence and they agree.

(c) Documentation

D:6.10 A record must be made as soon as practicable after the sample is taken of:

- The matters in paragraph 6.8(a)(i) to (iii) and the fact that the person has been informed of those matters; and
- The fact that the person has been informed of the matters in paragraph 6.8(b)(i) and (ii).

D:6.10A If force is used, a record shall be made of the circumstances and those present.

D:6.11 A record must be made of a warning given as required by paragraph 6.3.

Notes for guidance

A-138 *D:6A When hair samples are taken for the purpose of DNA analysis (rather than for other purposes such as making a visual match), the suspect should be permitted a reasonable choice as to what part of the body the hairs are taken from. When hairs are plucked, they should be plucked individually, unless the suspect prefers otherwise and no more should be plucked than the person taking them reasonably considers necessary for a sufficient sample.*

D:6B(a) An insufficient sample is one which is not sufficient either in quantity or quality to provide information for a particular form of analysis, such as DNA analysis. A sample may also be insufficient if enough information cannot be obtained from it by analysis because of loss, destruction, damage or contamination of the sample or as a result of an earlier, unsuccessful attempt at analysis.

(b) An unsuitable sample is one which, by its nature, is not suitable for a particular form of analysis.

D:6C Nothing in paragraph 6.2 prevents intimate samples being taken for elimination purposes with the consent of the person concerned but the provisions of paragraph 2.12 relating to the role of the appropriate adult, should be applied. Paragraph 6.2(b) does not, however, apply where the non-intimate samples were previously taken under the Terrorism Act 2000, Sched. 8, para. 10.

D:6D In warning a person who is asked to provide an intimate sample as in paragraph 6.3, the following form of words may be used:

> *"You do not have to provide this sample/allow this swab or impression to be taken, but I must warn you that if you refuse without good cause, your refusal may harm your case if it comes to trial."*

D:6E Fingerprints or a DNA sample and the information derived from it taken from a person arrested on suspicion of being involved in a recordable offence, or charged with such an offence, or informed they will be reported for such an offence, may be subject of a speculative search. This means they may be checked against other fingerprints and DNA records held by, or on behalf of, the police and other law enforcement authorities in or outside the UK or held in connection with, or as a result of, an investigation of an offence inside or outside the UK.

See Annex F regarding the retention and use of fingerprints and samples taken with consent for elimination purposes.

D:6F Samples of urine and non-intimate samples taken in accordance with sections 63B and 63C of PACE may not be used for identification purposes in accordance with this Code. See Code C, Note for guidance 17D.

ANNEX A

Video Identification

(a) General

D:1. The arrangements for obtaining and ensuring the availability of a suitable set of images to be used in a video identification must be the responsibility of an identification officer (see paragraph 3.11 of this code) who has no direct involvement with the case. **A-139**

D:2. The set of images must include the suspect and at least eight other people who, so far as possible, and subject to paragraph 7, resemble the suspect in age, general appearance and position in life. Only one suspect shall appear in any set unless there are two suspects of roughly similar appearance, in which case they may be shown together with at least twelve other people.

D:2A If the suspect has an unusual physical feature, e.g., a facial scar, tattoo or distinctive hairstyle or hair colour which does not appear on the images of the other people that are available to be used, steps may be taken to:

(a) conceal the location of the feature on the images of the suspect and the other people; or

(b) replicate that feature on the images of the other people.

For these purposes, the feature may be concealed or replicated electronically or by any other method which it is practicable to use to ensure that the images of the suspect and other people resemble each other. The identification officer has discretion to choose whether to conceal or replicate the feature and the method to be used.

D:2B If the identification officer decides that a feature should be concealed or replicated, the reason for the decision and whether the feature was concealed or replicated in the images shown to any eye-witness shall be recorded.

D:2C If the eye-witness requests to view any image where an unusual physical feature has been concealed or replicated without the feature being concealed or replicated, the identification officer has discretion to allow the eye-witness to view such image(s) if they are available.

D:3. The images used to conduct a video identification shall, as far as possible, show the suspect and other people in the same positions or carrying out the same sequence of movements. They shall also show the suspect and other people under identical conditions unless the identification officer reasonably believes:

(a) because of the suspect's failure or refusal to co-operate or other reasons, it is not practicable for the conditions to be identical; and

(b) any difference in the conditions would not direct an eye-witness' attention to any individual image.

D:4. The reasons identical conditions are not practicable shall be recorded on forms provided for the purpose.

D:5. Provision must be made for each person shown to be identified by number.

D:6. If police officers are shown, any numerals or other identifying badges must be concealed. If a prison inmate is shown, either as a suspect or not, then either all, or none of, the people shown should be in prison clothing.

A-140 D:7. The suspect or their solicitor, friend, or appropriate adult must be given a reasonable opportunity to see the complete set of images before it is shown to any eye-witness. If the suspect has a reasonable objection to the set of images or any of the participants, the suspect shall be asked to state the reasons for the objection. Steps shall, if practicable, be taken to remove the grounds for objection. If this is not practicable, the suspect and/or their representative shall be told why their objections cannot be met and the objection, the reason given for it and why it cannot be met shall be recorded on forms provided for the purpose. The requirement in paragraph 2 that the images of the other people 'resemble' the suspect does not require the images to be identical or extremely similar (see *Note A1*).

D:8. Before the images are shown in accordance with paragraph 7, the suspect or their solicitor shall be provided with details of the first description of the suspect by any eye-witnesses who are to attend the video identification. When a broadcast or publication is made, as in paragraph 3.38(a), the suspect or their solicitor must also be allowed to view any material released to the media by the police for the purpose of recognising or tracing the suspect, provided it is practicable and would not unreasonably delay the investigation.

D:9. No unauthorised people may be present when the video identification is conducted. The suspect's solicitor, if practicable, shall be given reasonable notification of the time and place the video identification is to be conducted. The suspect's solicitor may only be present at the video identification on request and with the prior agreement of the identification officer, if the officer is satisfied that the solicitor's presence will not deter or distract any eye-witness from viewing the images and making an identification. If the identification officer is not satisfied and does not agree to the request, the reason must be recorded. The solicitor must be informed of the decision and the reason for it. and that they may then make representations about why they should be allowed to be present. The representations may be made orally or in writing, in person or remotely by electronic communication and must be recorded. These representations must be considered by an officer of at least the rank of inspector who is not involved with the investigation and responsibility for this may not be delegated under paragraph 3.11. If, after considering the representations, the officer is satisfied that the solicitor's presence will deter or distract the eye-witness, the officer shall inform the solicitor of the decision and reason for it and ensure that any response by the solicitor is also recorded. If allowed to be present, the solicitor is not entitled to communicate in any way with an eye-witness during the procedure but this does not prevent the solicitor from communicating with the identification officer. The suspect may not be present when the images are shown to any eye-witness and is not entitled to be informed of the time and place the video identification procedure is to be conducted. The video identification procedure itself shall be recorded on video with sound. The recording must show all persons present within the sight or hearing of the eye-witness whilst the images are being viewed and must include what the eye-witness says and what is said to them by the identification officer and by any other person present at the video identification procedure. A supervised viewing of the recording of the video identification procedure by the suspect and/or their solicitor may be arranged on request, at the discretion of the investigating officer. Where the recording of the video identification procedure is to be shown to the suspect and/or their solicitor, the investigating officer may arrange for anything in the recording that might allow the eye-witness to be identified to be concealed if the investigating officer considers that this is justified (see *Note A2*). In accordance with paragraph 2.18, the investigating officer may also arrange for anything in that recording that might allow any police officers or police staff to be identified to be concealed.

(b) Conducting the video identification

A-141 D:10. The identification officer is responsible for making the appropriate arrangements to make sure, before they see the set of images, eye-witnesses are not able to communicate with each other about the case, see any of the images which are to be shown, see, or be reminded of, any photograph or description of the suspect or be given any other indication as to the suspect's identity, or overhear an eye-witness who has already seen the material. There must be no discussion with the eye-witness about the composition of the set of images and they must not be told whether a previous eye-witness has made any identification.

D:11. Only one eye-witness may see the set of images at a time. Immediately before the images are shown, the eye-witness shall be told that the person they saw on a specified earlier occasion may, or may not, appear in the images they are shown and that if they cannot make an identification, they should say so. The eye-witness shall be advised that at any point, they may ask to see a particular part of the set of images or to have a particular image frozen for them to study. Furthermore, it should be pointed out to the eye-witness that there is no limit on how many times they can view the whole set of images or any part of them. However, they should be asked not to make any decision as to whether the person they saw is on the set of images until they have seen the whole set at least twice.

D:12. Once the eye-witness has seen the whole set of images at least twice and has indicated that they do not want to view the images, or any part of them, again, the eye-witness shall be asked to say whether the individual they saw in person on a specified earlier occasion has been shown and, if so, to identify them by number of the image. The eye-witness will then be shown that image to confirm the identification, see paragraph 17.

D:13. Care must be taken not to direct the eye-witness' attention to any one individual image or give any indication of the suspect's identity. Where an eye-witness has previously made an identification by photographs, or a computerised or artist's composite or similar likeness, they must not be reminded of such a photograph or composite likeness once a suspect is available for identification by other means in accordance with this code. Nor must the eyewitness be reminded of any description of the suspect.

D:13A. If after the video identification procedure has ended, the eye-witness informs any police officer or police staff involved in the post-viewing arrangements that they wish to change their decision about their identification, or they have not made an identification when in fact they could have made one, an accurate record of the words used by the eye-witness and of the circumstances immediately after the procedure ended, shall be made. If the eyewitness has not had an opportunity to communicate with other people about the procedure, the identification officer has the discretion to allow the eye-witness a second opportunity to make an identification by repeating the video identification procedure using the same images but in different positions.

D:14. After the procedure, action required in accordance with paragraph 3.40 applies.

(c) Image security and destruction

D:15. Arrangements shall be made for all relevant material containing sets of images used for specific identification procedures to be kept securely and their movements accounted for. In particular, no-one involved in the investigation shall be permitted to view the material prior to it being shown to any witness.

D:16. As appropriate, paragraph 3.30 or 3.31 applies to the destruction or retention of relevant sets of images.

(d) Documentation

D:17. A record must be made of all those participating in, or seeing, the set of images whose names are known to the police.

D:18. A record of the conduct of the video identification must be made on forms provided for the purpose. This shall include anything said by the witness about any identifications or the conduct of the procedure and any reasons it was not practicable to comply with any of the provisions of this Code governing the conduct of video identifications. This record is in addition to any statement that is taken from any eye-witness after the procedure.

Note for guidance

D:A1 The purpose of the video identification is to test the eye-witness' ability to distinguish the suspect from others and it would not be a fair test if all the images shown were identical or extremely similar to each other. The identification officer is responsible for ensuring that the images shown are suitable for the purpose of this test.

D:A2 The purpose of allowing the identity of the eye-witness to be concealed is to protect them in cases when there is information that suspects or their associates, may threaten the witness or cause them harm or when the investigating officer considers that special measures may be required to protect their identity during the criminal process.

ANNEX B

Identification parades

(a) General

D:1. A suspect must be given a reasonable opportunity to have a solicitor or friend present, and the suspect shall be asked to indicate on a second copy of the notice whether or not they wish to do so. **A-142**

D:2. An identification parade may take place either in a normal room or one equipped with a screen permitting witnesses to see members of the identification parade without being seen. The procedures for the composition and conduct of the identification parade are the same in both cases, subject to paragraph 8 (except that an identification parade involving a screen may take place only when the suspect's solicitor, friend or appropriate adult is present or the identification parade is recorded on video).

D:3. Before the identification parade takes place, the suspect or their solicitor shall be provided with details of the first description of the suspect by any witnesses who are attending the identification parade. When a broadcast or publication is made as in paragraph 3.38(a), the suspect or their solicitor should also be allowed to view any material released to the media by the police for the purpose of identifying and tracing the suspect, provided it is practicable to do so and would not unreasonably delay the investigation.

(b) Identification parades involving prison inmates

D:4. If a prison inmate is required for identification, and there are no security problems about the person leaving the establishment, they may be asked to participate in an identification parade or video identification.

D:5. An identification parade may be held in a Prison Department establishment but shall be conducted, as far as practicable under normal identification parade rules. Members of the public shall make up the identification parade unless there are serious security, or control, objections to their admission to the establishment. In such cases, or if a group or video identification is arranged within the establishment, other inmates may participate. If an inmate is the suspect, they are not required to wear prison clothing for the identification parade unless the other people taking part are other inmates in similar clothing, or are members of the public who are prepared to wear prison clothing for the occasion.

(c) Conduct of the identification parade

A-143 D:6. Immediately before the identification parade, the suspect must be reminded of the procedures governing its conduct and cautioned in the terms of Code C, paras 10.5 or 10.6, as appropriate.

D:7. All unauthorised people must be excluded from the place where the identification parade is held.

D:8. Once the identification parade has been formed, everything afterwards, in respect of it, shall take place in the presence and hearing of the suspect and any interpreter, solicitor, friend or appropriate adult who is present (unless the identification parade involves a screen, in which case everything said to, or by, any witness at the place where the identification parade is held, must be said in the hearing and presence of the suspect's solicitor, friend or appropriate adult or be recorded on video).

D:9. The identification parade shall consist of at least eight people (in addition to the suspect) who, so far as possible, resemble the suspect in age, height, general appearance and position in life. Only one suspect shall be included in an identification parade unless there are two suspects of roughly similar appearance, in which case they may be paraded together with at least twelve other people. In no circumstances shall more than two suspects be included in one identification parade and where there are separate identification parades, they shall be made up of different people.

D:10. If the suspect has an unusual physical feature, e.g., a facial scar, tattoo or distinctive hairstyle or hair colour which cannot be replicated on other members of the identification parade, steps may be taken to conceal the location of that feature on the suspect and the other members of the identification parade if the suspect and their solicitor, or appropriate adult, agree. For example, by use of a plaster or a hat, so that all members of the identification parade resemble each other in general appearance.

D:11. When all members of a similar group are possible suspects, separate identification parades shall be held for each unless there are two suspects of similar appearance when they may appear on the same identification parade with at least twelve other members of the group who are not suspects. When police officers in uniform form an identification parade any numerals or other identifying badges shall be concealed.

D:12. When the suspect is brought to the place where the identification parade is to be held, they shall be asked if they have any objection to the arrangements for the identification parade or to any of the other participants in it and to state the reasons for the objection. The suspect may obtain advice from their solicitor or friend, if present, before the identification parade proceeds. If the suspect has a reasonable objection to the arrangements or any of the participants, steps shall, if practicable, be taken to remove the grounds for objection. When it is not practicable to do so, the suspect shall be told why their objections cannot be met and the objection, the reason given for it and why it cannot be met, shall be recorded on forms provided for the purpose.

D:13. The suspect may select their own position in the line, but may not otherwise interfere with the order of the people forming the line. When there is more than one witness, the suspect must be told, after each witness has left the room, that they can, if they wish, change position in the line. Each position in the line must be clearly numbered, whether by means of a number laid on the floor in front of each identification parade member or by other means.

D:14. Appropriate arrangements must be made to make sure, before witnesses attend the identification parade, they are not able to: **A-144**

- (i) communicate with each other about the case or overhear a witness who has already seen the identification parade;
- (ii) see any member of the identification parade;
- (iii) see, or be reminded of, any photograph or description of the suspect or be given any other indication as to the suspect's identity; or
- (iv) see the suspect before or after the identification parade.

D:15. The person conducting a witness to an identification parade must not discuss with them the composition of the identification parade and, in particular, must not disclose whether a previous witness has made any identification.

D:16. Witnesses shall be brought in one at a time. Immediately before the witness inspects the identification parade, they shall be told the person they saw on a specified earlier occasion may, or may not, be present and if they cannot make an identification, they should say so. The witness must also be told they should not make any decision about whether the person they saw is on the identification parade until they have looked at each member at least twice.

D:17. When the officer or police staff (see paragraph 3.11) conducting the identification procedure is satisfied the witness has properly looked at each member of the identification parade, they shall ask the witness whether the person they saw on a specified earlier occasion is on the identification parade and, if so, to indicate the number of the person concerned, see paragraph 28.

D:18. If the witness wishes to hear any identification parade member speak, adopt any specified posture or move, they shall first be asked whether they can identify any person(s) on the identification parade on the basis of appearance only. When the request is to hear members of the identification parade speak, the witness shall be reminded that the participants in the identification parade have been chosen on the basis of physical appearance only. Members of the identification parade may then be asked to comply with the witness' request to hear them speak, see them move or adopt any specified posture.

D:19. If the witness requests that the person they have indicated remove anything used for the purposes of paragraph 10 to conceal the location of an unusual physical feature, that person may be asked to remove it. **A-145**

D:20. If the witness makes an identification after the identification parade has ended, the suspect and, if present, their solicitor, interpreter or friend shall be informed. When this occurs, consideration should be given to allowing the witness a second opportunity to identify the suspect.

D:21 After the procedure, action required in accordance with paragraph 3.40 applies.

D:22. When the last witness has left, the suspect shall be asked whether they wish to make any comments on the conduct of the identification parade.

(d) Documentation

D:23. A video recording must normally be taken of the identification parade. If that is impracticable, a colour photograph must be taken. A copy of the video recording or photograph shall be supplied, on request, to the suspect or their solicitor within a reasonable time.

D:24. As appropriate, paragraph 3.30 or 3.31, should apply to any photograph or video taken as in paragraph 23.

D:25. If any person is asked to leave an identification parade because they are interfering with its conduct, the circumstances shall be recorded.

D:26. A record must be made of all those present at an identification parade whose names are known to the police.

D:27. If prison inmates make up an identification parade, the circumstances must be recorded.

D:28. A record of the conduct of any identification parade must be made on forms provided for the purpose. This shall include anything said by the witness or the suspect about any identifications or the conduct of the procedure, and any reasons it was not practicable to comply with any of this Code's provisions.

ANNEX C

Group identification

(a) General

D:1. The purpose of this annex is to make sure, as far as possible, group identifications follow the **A-146** principles and procedures for identification parades so the conditions are fair to the suspect in the way they test the witness' ability to make an identification.

D:2. Group identifications may take place either with the suspect's consent and co-operation or covertly without their consent.

D:3. The location of the group identification is a matter for the identification officer, although the officer may take into account any representations made by the suspect, appropriate adult, their solicitor or friend.

D:4. The place where the group identification is held should be one where other people are either passing by or waiting around informally, in groups such that the suspect is able to join them and be capable of being seen by the witness at the same time as others in the group. For example people leaving an escalator, pedestrians walking through a shopping centre, passengers on railway and bus stations, waiting in queues or groups or where people are standing or sitting in groups in other public places.

D:5. If the group identification is to be held covertly, the choice of locations will be limited by the places where the suspect can be found and the number of other people present at that time. In these cases, suitable locations might be along regular routes travelled by the suspect, including buses or trains or public places frequented by the suspect.

A-147 D:6. Although the number, age, sex, race and general description and style of clothing of other people present at the location cannot be controlled by the identification officer, in selecting the location the officer must consider the general appearance and numbers of people likely to be present. In particular, the officer must reasonably expect that over the period the witness observes the group, they will be able to see, from time to time, a number of others whose appearance is broadly similar to that of the suspect.

D:7. A group identification need not be held if the identification officer believes, because of the unusual appearance of the suspect, none of the locations it would be practicable to use, satisfy the requirements of paragraph 6 necessary to make the identification fair.

D:8. Immediately after a group identification procedure has taken place (with or without the suspect's consent), a colour photograph or video should be taken of the general scene, if practicable, to give a general impression of the scene and the number of people present. Alternatively, if it is practicable, the group identification may be video recorded.

D:9. If it is not practicable to take the photograph or video in accordance with paragraph 8, a photograph or film of the scene should be taken later at a time determined by the identification officer if the officer considers it practicable to do so.

D:10. An identification carried out in accordance with this code remains a group identification even though, at the time of being seen by the witness, the suspect was on their own rather than in a group.

D:11. Before the group identification takes place, the suspect or their solicitor shall be provided with details of the first description of the suspect by any witnesses who are to attend the identification. When a broadcast or publication is made, as in paragraph 3.38(a), the suspect or their solicitor should also be allowed to view any material released by the police to the media for the purposes of identifying and tracing the suspect, provided that it is practicable and would not unreasonably delay the investigation.

D:12. After the procedure, action required in accordance with paragraph 3.40 applies.

(b) Identification with the consent of the suspect

A-148 D:13. A suspect must be given a reasonable opportunity to have a solicitor or friend present. They shall be asked to indicate on a second copy of the notice whether or not they wish to do so.

D:14. The witness, the person carrying out the procedure and the suspect's solicitor, appropriate adult, friend or any interpreter for the witness, may be concealed from the sight of the individuals in the group they are observing, if the person carrying out the procedure considers this assists the conduct of the identification.

D:15. The person conducting a witness to a group identification must not discuss with them the forthcoming group identification and, in particular, must not disclose whether a previous witness has made any identification.

D:16. Anything said to, or by, the witness during the procedure about the identification should be said in the presence and hearing of those present at the procedure.

D:17. Appropriate arrangements must be made to make sure, before witnesses attend the group identification, they are not able to:

(i) communicate with each other about the case or overhear a witness who has already been given an opportunity to see the suspect in the group;
(ii) see the suspect; or
(iii) see, or be reminded of, any photographs or description of the suspect or be given any other indication of the suspect's identity.

D:18. Witnesses shall be brought one at a time to the place where they are to observe the group. Immediately before the witness is asked to look at the group, the person conducting the procedure shall tell them that the person they saw on a specified earlier occasion may, or may not, be in the group and that if they cannot make an identification, they should say so. The witness shall be asked to observe the group in which the suspect is to appear. The way in which the witness should do this will depend on whether the group is moving or stationary.

Moving group

D:19. When the group in which the suspect is to appear is moving, e.g. leaving an escalator, the provisions of paragraphs 20 to 24 should be followed. **A-149**

D:20. If two or more suspects consent to a group identification, each should be the subject of separate identification procedures. These may be conducted consecutively on the same occasion.

D:21. The person conducting the procedure shall tell the witness to observe the group and ask them to point out any person they think they saw on the specified earlier occasion.

D:22. Once the witness has been informed as in paragraph 21 the suspect should be allowed to take whatever position in the group they wish.

D:23. When the witness points out a person as in paragraph 21 they shall, if practicable, be asked to take a closer look at the person to confirm the identification. If this is not practicable, or they cannot confirm the identification, they shall be asked how sure they are that the person they have indicated is the relevant person.

D:24. The witness should continue to observe the group for the period which the person conducting the procedure reasonably believes is necessary in the circumstances for them to be able to make comparisons between the suspect and other individuals of broadly similar appearance to the suspect as in paragraph 6.

Stationary groups

D:25. When the group in which the suspect is to appear is stationary, e.g. people waiting in a queue, the provisions of paragraphs 26 to 29 should be followed. **A-150**

D:26. If two or more suspects consent to a group identification, each should be subject to separate identification procedures unless they are of broadly similar appearance when they may appear in the same group. When separate group identifications are held, the groups must be made up of different people.

D:27. The suspect may take whatever position in the group they wish. If there is more than one witness, the suspect must be told, out of the sight and hearing of any witness, that they can, if they wish, change their position in the group.

D:28. The witness shall be asked to pass along, or amongst, the group and to look at each person in the group at least twice, taking as much care and time as possible according to the circumstances, before making an identification. Once the witness has done this, they shall be asked whether the person they saw on the specified earlier occasion is in the group and to indicate any such person by whatever means the person conducting the procedure considers appropriate in the circumstances. If this is not practicable, the witness shall be asked to point out any person they think they saw on the earlier occasion.

D:29. When the witness makes an indication as in paragraph 28, arrangements shall be made, if practicable, for the witness to take a closer look at the person to confirm the identification. If this is not practicable, or the witness is unable to confirm the identification, they shall be asked how sure they are that the person they have indicated is the relevant person.

All cases

D:30. If the suspect unreasonably delays joining the group, or having joined the group, deliberately conceals themselves [*sic*] from the sight of the witness, this may be treated as a refusal to co-operate in a group identification. **A-151**

D:31. If the witness identifies a person other than the suspect, that person should be informed what has happened and asked if they are prepared to give their name and address. There is no obligation upon any member of the public to give these details. There shall be no duty to record any details of any other member of the public present in the group or at the place where the procedure is conducted.

D:32. When the group identification has been completed, the suspect shall be asked whether they wish to make any comments on the conduct of the procedure.

D:33. If the suspect has not been previously informed, they shall be told of any identifications made by the witnesses.

(c) Group Identification without the suspect's consent

A-152 D:34. Group identifications held covertly without the suspect's consent should, as far as practicable, follow the rules for conduct of group identification by consent.

D:35. A suspect has no right to have a solicitor, appropriate adult or friend present as the identification will take place without the knowledge of the suspect.

D:36. Any number of suspects may be identified at the same time.

(d) Identifications in police stations

D:37. Group identifications should only take place in police stations for reasons of safety, security or because it is not practicable to hold them elsewhere.

D:38. The group identification may take place either in a room equipped with a screen permitting witnesses to see members of the group without being seen, or anywhere else in the police station that the identification officer considers appropriate.

D:39. Any of the additional safeguards applicable to identification parades should be followed if the identification officer considers it is practicable to do so in the circumstances.

(e) Identifications involving prison inmates

A-153 D:40. A group identification involving a prison inmate may only be arranged in the prison or at a police station.

D:41. When a group identification takes place involving a prison inmate, whether in a prison or in a police station, the arrangements should follow those in paragraphs 37 to 39. If a group identification takes place within a prison, other inmates may participate. If an inmate is the suspect, they do not have to wear prison clothing for the group identification unless the other participants are wearing the same clothing.

(f) Documentation

D:42 When a photograph or video is taken as in paragraph 8 or 9, a copy of the photograph or video shall be supplied on request to the suspect or their solicitor within a reasonable time.

D:43. Paragraph 3.30 or 3.31, as appropriate, shall apply when the photograph or film taken in accordance with paragraph 8 or 9 includes the suspect.

D:44. A record of the conduct of any group identification must be made on forms provided for the purpose. This shall include anything said by the witness or suspect about any identifications or the conduct of the procedure and any reasons why it was not practicable to comply with any of the provisions of this Code governing the conduct of group identifications.

ANNEX D

Confrontation by an eye-witness

A-154 D:1. Before the confrontation takes place, the eye-witness must be told that the person they saw on a specified earlier occasion may, or may not, be the person they are to confront and that if they are not that person, then the witness should say so.

D:2. Before the confrontation takes place the suspect or their solicitor shall be provided with details of the first description of the suspect given by any eye-witness who is to attend. When a broadcast or publication is made, as in paragraph 3.38(a), the suspect or their solicitor should also be allowed to view any material released to the media for the purposes of recognising or tracing the suspect, provided it is practicable to do so and would not unreasonably delay the investigation.

D:3. Force may not be used to make the suspect's face visible to the eye-witness.

D:4. Confrontation must take place in the presence of the suspect's solicitor, interpreter or friend unless this would cause unreasonable delay.

D:5. The suspect shall be confronted independently by each eye-witness, who shall be asked "Is this the person?". If the eye-witness identifies the person but is unable to confirm the identification, they shall be asked how sure they are that the person is the one they saw on the earlier occasion.

D:6. The confrontation should normally take place in the police station, either in a normal room or one equipped with a screen permitting the eye-witness to see the suspect without being seen. In both cases, the procedures are the same except that a room equipped with a screen may be used only when the suspect's solicitor, friend or appropriate adult is present or the confrontation is recorded on video.

D:7. After the procedure, action required in accordance with paragraph 3.40 applies.

ANNEX E

Showing photographs to eye-witnesses

D:1. An officer of sergeant rank or above shall be responsible for supervising and directing the showing of photographs. The actual showing may be done by another officer or police staff, see paragraph 3.11. **A-155**

D:2. The supervising officer must confirm the first description of the suspect given by the eyewitness has been recorded before they are shown the photographs. If the supervising officer is unable to confirm the description has been recorded they shall postpone showing the photographs.

D:3. Only one eye-witness shall be shown photographs at any one time. Each witness shall be given as much privacy as practicable and shall not be allowed to communicate with any other eye-witness in the case.

D:4. The eye-witness shall be shown not less than twelve photographs at a time, which shall, as far as possible, all be of a similar type.

D:5. When the eye-witness is shown the photographs, they shall be told the photograph of the person they saw on a specified earlier occasion may, or may not, be amongst them and if they cannot make an identification, they should say so. The eye-witness shall also be told they should not make a decision until they have viewed at least twelve photographs. The eye-witness shall not be prompted or guided in any way but shall be left to make any selection without help.

D:6. If an eye-witness makes an identification from photographs, unless the person identified is otherwise eliminated from enquiries or is not available, other eye-witnesses shall not be shown photographs. But both they, and the eye-witness who has made the identification, shall be asked to attend a video identification, an identification parade or group identification unless there is no dispute about the suspect's identification.

D:7. If the eye-witness makes a selection but is unable to confirm the identification, the person showing the photographs shall ask them how sure they are that the photograph they have indicated is the person they saw on the specified earlier occasion. **A-156**

D:8. When the use of a computerised or artist's composite or similar likeness has led to there being a known suspect who can be asked to participate in a video identification, appear on an identification parade or participate in a group identification, that likeness shall not be shown to other potential eye-witnesses.

D:9. When an eye-witness attending a video identification, an identification parade or group identification has previously been shown photographs or computerised or artist's composite or similar likeness (and it is the responsibility of the officer in charge of the investigation to make the identification officer aware that this is the case), the suspect and their solicitor must be informed of this fact before the identification procedure takes place.

D:10. None of the photographs shown shall be destroyed, whether or not an identification is made, since they may be required for production in court. The photographs shall be numbered and a separate photograph taken of the frame or part of the album from which the eye-witness made an identification as an aid to reconstituting it.

(b) Documentation

D:11. Whether or not an identification is made, a record shall be kept of the showing of photographs on forms provided for the purpose. This shall include anything said by the eye-witness about any identification or the conduct of the procedure, any reasons it was not practicable to comply with any of the provisions of this Code governing the showing of photographs and the name and rank of the supervising officer. **A-157**

D:12. The supervising officer shall inspect and sign the record as soon as practicable.

ANNEX F

Fingerprints, Samples and Footwear Impressions—Destruction and Speculative Searches

Part A: Fingerprints and samples

Paragraphs 1 to 12 summarise and update information which is available at: **A-158**
https://www.gov.uk/government/publications/protection-of-freedoms-act-2012-dna-and-fingerprint-provisions/protection-of-freedoms-act-2012-how-dna-and-fingerprint-evidence-is-protected-in-law

DNA samples

D:1. A DNA sample is an individual's biological material, containing all of their genetic information. The Act requires all DNA samples to be destroyed within 6 months of being taken. This allows sufficient time for the sample to be analysed and a DNA profile to be produced for use on the database.

D:2. The only exception to this is if the sample is or may be required for disclosure as evidence, in which case it may be retained for as long as this need exists under the Criminal Procedure and Investigations Act 1996.

DNA profiles and fingerprints

D:3. A DNA profile consists of a string of 16 pairs of numbers and 2 letters (XX for women, XY for men) to indicate gender. This number string is stored on the National DNA Database (NDNAD). It allows the person to be identified if they leave their DNA at a crime scene.

D:4. Fingerprints are usually scanned electronically from the individual in custody and the images stored on IDENT1, the national fingerprint database.

Retention Periods: Fingerprints and DNA profiles

D:5. The retention period depends on the outcome of the investigation of the recordable offence in connection with which the fingerprints and DNA samples was taken, the age of the person at the time the offence was committed and whether the *recordable* offence is a qualifying offence and whether it is an excluded offence (See Table Notes (a) to (c)) , as follows:

Table - Retention periods

(a) Convictions

Age when offence committed	*Outcome*	*Retention Period*
Any age	Convicted or given a caution or youth caution for a recordable offence which is also a qualifying offence	Indefinite
18 or over	Convicted or given a caution for a recordable offence which is NOT a qualifying offence	Indefinite
Under 18	Convicted or given a youth caution for a recordable offence which is NOT a qualifying offence.	1st conviction or youth caution - 5 years plus length of any prison sentence. Indefinite if prison sentence 5 years or more 2nd conviction or youth caution: indefinite

(b) Non-convictions

Age when offence committed	*Outcome*	*Retention Period*
Any age	Charged but not convicted of a recordable qualifying offence.	3 years plus a 2-year extension if granted by a District Judge (or indefinite if the individual has a previous conviction for a recordable offence which is not excluded)
Any age	Arrested for, but not charged with, a recordable qualifying offence	3 years if granted by the Biometrics Commissioner plus a 2-year extension if granted by a District Judge (or indefinite if the individual has a previous conviction for a recordable

Age when offence committed	*Outcome*	*Retention Period*
		offence which is not excluded)
Any age	Arrested for or charged with a recordable offence which is not a qualifying offence.	Indefinite if the person has a previous conviction for a recordable offence which is not excluded otherwise NO RETENTION)
18 or over	Given Penalty Notice for Disorder for recordable offence	2 years

Table notes:

(a) *A "recordable" offence is one for which the police are required to keep a record. Generally speaking, these are imprisonable offences; however, it also includes a number of nonimprisonable offences such as begging and taxi touting. The police are not able to take or retain the DNA or fingerprints of an individual who is arrested for an offence which is not recordable.*

(b) *A "qualifying" offence is one listed under section 65A of the Police and Criminal Evidence Act 1984 (the list comprises sexual, violent, terrorism and burglary offences).*

(c) *An "excluded" offence is a recordable offence which is not a qualifying offence, was committed when the individual was under 18, for which they received a sentence of fewer than 5 years imprisonment and is the only recordable offence for which the person has been convicted*

Speculative searches

D:6. Where the retention framework above requires the deletion of a person's DNA profile and fingerprints, the Act first allows a *speculative search* of their DNA and fingerprints against DNA and fingerprints obtained from crime scenes which are stored on NDNAD and IDENT1. Once the speculative search has been completed, the profile and fingerprints are deleted unless there is a match, in which case they will be retained for the duration of any investigation and thereafter in accordance with the retention framework (e.g. if that investigation led to a conviction for a qualifying offence, they would be retained indefinitely).

Extensions of retention period

D:7. For qualifying offences, PACE allows chief constables to apply for extensions to the given retention periods for DNA profiles and fingerprints if considered necessary for prevention or detection of crime.

D:8. Section 20 of the Protection of Freedoms Act 2012 established the independent office of Commissioner for the Retention and Use of Biometric Material ("the 'Biometrics Commissioner'). For details, see *https://www.gov.uk/government/organisations/biometricscommissioner.*

D:9. Where an individual is arrested for, but not charged with, a qualifying offence, their DNA profile and fingerprint record will normally be deleted. However, the police can apply to the Biometrics Commissioner for permission to retain their DNA profile and fingerprint record for a period of 3 years. The application must be made within 28 days of the decision not to proceed with a prosecution.

D:10. If the police make such an application, the Biometrics Commissioner would first give both them and the arrested individual an opportunity to make written representations and then, taking into account factors including the age and vulnerability of the victim(s) of the alleged offences, and their relationship to the suspect, make a decision on whether or not retention is appropriate.

D:11. If after considering the application, the Biometrics Commissioner decides that retention is not appropriate, the DNA profile and fingerprint record in question must be destroyed.

D:12. If the Biometrics Commissioner agrees to allow retention, the police will be able to retain that individual's DNA profile and fingerprint record for a period of 3 years from the date the samples were taken. At the end of that period, the police will be able to apply to a District Judge (magistrates' courts) for a single 2 year extension to the retention period. If the application is rejected, the force must then destroy the DNA profile and fingerprint record.

Part B: Footwear impressions

D:13. Footwear impressions taken in accordance with section 61A of PACE (see paragraphs 4.16

to 4.21) may be retained for as long as is necessary for purposes related to the prevention or detection of crime, the investigation of an offence or the conduct of a prosecution.

Part C: Fingerprints, samples and footwear impressions taken in connection with a criminal investigation from a person not suspected of committing the offence under investigation for elimination purposes.

A-159 D:14. When fingerprints, footwear impressions or DNA samples are taken from a person in connection with an investigation and the person is *not suspected of having committed the offence*, see *Note F1*, they must be destroyed as soon as they have fulfilled the purpose for which they were taken unless:

(a) they were taken for the purposes of an investigation of an offence for which a person has been convicted; and

(b) fingerprints, footwear impressions or samples were also taken from the convicted person for the purposes of that investigation.

However, subject to paragraph 14, the fingerprints, footwear impressions and samples, and the information derived from samples, may not be used in the investigation of any offence or in evidence against the person who is, or would be, entitled to the destruction of the fingerprints, footwear impressions and samples, see *Note F2.*

D:15. The requirement to destroy fingerprints, footwear impressions and DNA samples, and information derived from samples and restrictions on their retention and use in paragraph 14 do not apply if the person gives their written consent for their fingerprints, footwear impressions or sample to be retained and used after they have fulfilled the purpose for which they were taken, see *Note F1.*

This consent can be withdrawn at any time.

D:16. When a person's fingerprints, footwear impressions or sample are to be destroyed:

(a) any copies of the fingerprints and footwear impressions must also be destroyed; and

(b) neither the fingerprints, footwear impressions, the sample, or any information derived from the sample, may be used in the investigation of any offence or in evidence against the person who is, or would be, entitled to its destruction.

Notes for guidance

A-160 *D:F1 Fingerprints, footwear impressions and samples given voluntarily for the purposes of elimination play an important part in many police investigations. It is, therefore, important to make sure innocent volunteers are not deterred from participating and their consent to their fingerprints, footwear impressions and DNA being used for the purposes of a specific investigation is fully informed and voluntary. If the police or volunteer seek to have the fingerprints, footwear impressions or samples retained for use after the specific investigation ends, it is important the volunteer's consent to this is also fully informed and voluntary. The volunteer must be told that they may withdraw their consent at any time.*

The consent must be obtained in writing using current nationally agreed forms provided for police use according to the purpose for which the consent is given. This purpose may be either:

- *DNA/fingerprints/footwear impressions - to be used only for the purposes of a specific investigation; or*
- *DNA/fingerprints/footwear impressions - to be used in the specific investigation and retained by the police for future use.*

To minimise the risk of confusion:

- *if a police officer or member of police staff has any doubt about:*
  - *how the consent forms should be completed and signed, or*
  - *whether a consent form they propose to use and refer to is fully compliant with the current nationally agreed form,*

  the relevant national police helpdesk (for DNA or fingerprints) should be contacted.
- *in each case, the meaning of consent should be explained orally and care taken to ensure the oral explanation accurately reflects the contents of the written form the person is to be asked to sign.*

A-161 *D:F2 The provisions for the retention of fingerprints, footwear impressions and samples in paragraph 15 allow for all fingerprints, footwear impressions and samples in a case to be available for any subsequent miscarriage of justice investigation.*

ANNEX G

Requirement for a person to attend a police station for fingerprints and samples (paragraphs 4.4, 6.2a and 6.6a).

A-161a D:1. A requirement under Schedule 2A for a person to attend a police station to have fingerprints or samples taken:

(a) must give the person a period of at least seven days within which to attend the police station; and

(b) may direct them to attend at a specified time of day or between specified times of day.

D:2. When specifying the period and times of attendance, the officer making the requirements must consider whether the fingerprints or samples could reasonably be taken at a time when the person is required to attend the police station for any other reason. See *Note G1.*

D:3. An officer of the rank of inspector or above may authorise a period shorter than 7 days if there is an urgent need for person's fingerprints or sample for the purposes of the investigation of an offence. The fact of the authorisation and the reasons for giving it must be recorded as soon as practicable.

D:4. The constable making a requirement and the person to whom it applies may agree to vary it so as to specify any period within which, or date or time at which, the person is to attend. However, variation shall not have effect for the purposes of enforcement, unless it is confirmed by the constable in writing.

Notes for guidance

D:G1 The specified period within which the person is to attend need not fall within the period allowed (if applicable) for making the requirement. **A-161b**

D:G2 To justify the arrest without warrant of a person who fails to comply with a requirement, (see paragraphs 4.4(b) and 6.7(b) above), the officer making the requirement, or confirming a variation, should be prepared to explain how, when and where the requirement was made or the variation was confirmed and what steps were taken to ensure the person understood what to do and the consequences of not complying with the requirement.

(6) Tape-recording of interviews

The text that follows is of the version of the code that came into force on 31 July 2018: see above, Appendix A-1. **A-162**

For further details of the application of the code, and as to the commencement of the governing legislation, see § 15-236 of the main work.

E. CODE OF PRACTICE ON AUDIO RECORDING INTERVIEWS WITH SUSPECTS

Commencement—transitional arrangements

This Code applies to interviews carried out after 00.00 on 31 July 2018, notwithstanding that the interview may have commenced before that time. **A-162a**

E:1 General

E:1.0 The procedures in this Code must be used fairly, responsibly, with respect for the people to whom they apply and without unlawful discrimination. Under the Equality Act 2010, section 149 (Public Sector Equality Duty), police forces must, in carrying out their functions, have due regard to the need to eliminate unlawful discrimination, harassment, victimisation and any other conduct which is prohibited by that Act, to advance equality of opportunity between people who share a relevant protected characteristic and people who do not share it, and to foster good relations between those persons. The Equality Act also makes it unlawful for police officers to discriminate against, harass or victimise any person on the grounds of the 'protected characteristics' of age, disability, gender reassignment, race, religion or belief, sex and sexual orientation, marriage and civil partnership, pregnancy and maternity, when using their powers. See *Note 1B.* **A-163**

E:1.1 This Code of Practice must be readily available for consultation by:

- police officers
- police staff
- detained persons
- members of the public.

E:1.2 The *Notes for guidance* included are not provisions of this Code. They form guidance to police officers and others about its application and interpretation.

E:1.3 Nothing in this Code shall detract from the requirements of Code C, the Code of Practice for the detention, treatment and questioning of persons by police officers.

E:1.4 The interviews and other matters to which this Code applies are described in section 2. This Code does not apply to the conduct and recording in England and Wales, of:

- interviews of persons detained under section 41 of, or Schedule 7 to, the Terrorism Act 2000, and
- post-charge questioning of persons authorised under section 22 of the Counter-Terrorism Act 2008.

These must be video recorded with sound in accordance with the provisions of the separate Code of Practice issued under paragraph 3 of Schedule 8 to the Terrorism Act 2000 and under section 25 of the Counter-Terrorism Act 2008. If, during the course of an interview or questioning under this Code, it becomes apparent that the interview or questioning should be conducted under that separate Code, the interview should only continue in accordance with that Code.

Note: The provisions of this Code and Code F which govern the conduct and recording of interviews *do not apply* to interviews with, or taking statements from, witnesses.

E:1.5 In this Code:

- "appropriate adult" has the same meaning as in Code C, *paragraph 1.7.*
- "vulnerable person" has the same meaning as described in Code C *paragraph 1.13(d).*
- "solicitor" has the same meaning as in Code C, *paragraph 6.12.*
- "interview" has the same meaning as in *Code C, paragraph 11.1A.*

E:1.5A The provisions of this Code which require interviews with suspects to be audio recorded and the provisions of Code F which permit simultaneous visual recording provide safeguards:

- for suspects against inaccurate recording of the words used in questioning them and of their demeanour during the interview; and;
- for police interviewers against unfounded allegations made by, or on behalf of, suspects about the conduct of the interview and what took place during the interview which might otherwise appear credible.

Recording of interviews must therefore be carried out openly to instil confidence in its reliability as an impartial and accurate record of the interview.

E:1.5B The provisions of Code C:

- *sections 10 and 11,* and the applicable *Notes for guidance* apply to the conduct of interviews to which this Code applies.
- *paragraphs 11.7 to 11.14* apply only when a written record is needed.

E:1.5C Code C, *paragraphs 10.10, 10.11* and *Annex C* describe the restriction on drawing adverse inferences from an arrested suspect's failure or refusal to say anything about their involvement in the offence when interviewed or after being charged or informed they may be prosecuted, and how it affects the terms of the caution and determines if and by whom a special warning under sections 36 and 37 of the Criminal Justice and Public Order Act 1994 can be given.

A-164 E:1.6 In this Code:

(a) in relation to the place where an interview of a suspect to which this Code or (as the case may be) Code F, applies, is conducted and recorded (see *Note 1A*):

(i) "authorised" in relation to the recording devices described in (ii) and (iii), means any such device that the chief officer has authorised interviewers under their direction and control to use to record the interview in question at the place in question, provided that the interviewer in question has been trained to set up and operate the device, in compliance with the manufacturer's instructions and subject to the operating procedures required by the chief officer;

(ii) "removable recording media device" means a recording device which, when set up and operated in accordance with the manufacturer's instructions and the operating procedures required by the chief officers, uses removable, physical recording media (such as magnetic tape, optical disc or solid state memory card) for the purpose of making a clear and accurate, audio recording or (as the case may be) audio-visual recording, of the interview in question which can then be played back and copied using that device or any other device. A sign or indicator on the device which is visible to the suspect must show when the device is recording;

(iii) "secure digital recording network device" means a recording device which, when set up and operated in accordance with the manufacturer's instructions and the operating procedures required by the chief officers, enables a clear and accurate original audio recording or (as the case may be) audio-visual recording, of the interview in question, to be made and stored using non-removable storage, as a digital file or a series of such files that can be securely transferred by a wired or wireless connection to a remote secure network file server system (which may have cloud based storage) which ensures that access to interview recordings for all purposes is strictly controlled and is restricted to those whose access, either generally or in specific cases, is necessary. Examples of access include playing back the whole or part of any original recording and making one or more copies of, the whole or part of that original recording. A sign or indicator on the device which is visible to the suspect must show when the device is recording.

(b) "designated person" means a person other than a police officer, who has specified powers and duties conferred or imposed on them by designation under section 38 or 39 of the Police Reform Act 2002.

(c) any reference to a police officer includes a designated person acting in the exercise or performance of the powers and duties conferred or imposed on them by their designation.

E:1.7 Section 2 of this Code sets out the requirement that an authorised recording device, if available, must be used to record a suspect interview and when such a device cannot be used, it allows a 'relevant officer' (see *paragraph 2.3(c)*) to decide that the interview is to be recorded in writing in accordance with Code C. For detained suspects, the 'relevant officer' is the custody officer and for voluntary interviews, the officer is determined according to the type of offence (indictable or summary only) and where the interview takes place (police station or elsewhere). Provisions in sections 3 and 4 deal with the conduct and recording of interviews according to the type of authorised recording device used. Section 3 applies to *removable recording media devices* (see *paragraph 1.6(a)(i)*) and section 4 applies to *secure digital recording network devices* (see *paragraph 1.6(a)(ii)*). The Annex applies when a voluntary interview is conducted elsewhere than at a police station about one of the four offence types specified in the Annex. For such interviews, the relevant officer is the interviewer.

E:1.8 Nothing in this Code prevents the custody officer, or other officer given custody of the detainee, from allowing police staff who are not designated persons to carry out individual procedures or tasks at the police station if the law allows. However, the officer remains responsible for making sure the procedures and tasks are carried out correctly in accordance with this Code. Any such police staff must be:

(a) a person employed by a police force and under the control and direction of the Chief Officer of that force; or

(b) employed by a person with whom a police force has a contract for the provision of services relating to persons arrested or otherwise in custody.

E:1.9 Designated persons and other police staff must have regard to any relevant provisions of the Codes of Practice.

E:1.10 References to pocket book shall include any official report book or electronic recording device issued to police officers or police staff that enables a record required to be made by any provision of this Code (but which is not an audio record to which *paragraph 2.1* applies) to be made and dealt with in accordance with that provision. References in this Code to written records, forms and signatures include electronic records and forms and electronic confirmation that identifies the person making the record or completing the form.

Chief officers must be satisfied as to the integrity and security of the devices, records and forms to which this paragraph applies and that use of those devices, records and forms satisfies relevant data protection legislation.

E:1.11 References to a custody officer include those performing the functions of a custody officer as in *paragraph 1.9* of Code C.

E:1.12 *Not used.*

E:1.13 Nothing in this Code requires the identity of officers or police staff conducting interviews to be recorded or disclosed if the interviewer reasonably believes recording or disclosing their name might put them in danger. In these cases, the officers and staff should use warrant or other identification numbers and the name of their police station. Such instances and the reasons for them shall be recorded in the custody record or the interviewer's pocket book. (See *Note 1C*.)

Notes for guidance

E:1A An interviewer who is not sure, or has any doubt, about whether a place or location elsewhere than a police station is suitable for carrying out an interview of a juvenile or vulnerable person, using a particular recording device, should consult an officer of the rank of sergeant or above for advice. See Code C paragraphs 3.21, 3.22 and Note 3I **A-165**

E:1B In paragraph 1.0, under the Equality Act 2010, section 149, the 'relevant protected characteristics' are: age, disability, gender reassignment, pregnancy and maternity, race, religion/belief, and sex and sexual orientation. For further detailed guidance and advice on the Equality Act, see: https://www.gov.uk/guidance/equality-act-2010-guidance.

E:1C The purpose of paragraph 1.13 is to protect those involved in serious organised crime investigations or arrests of particularly violent suspects when there is reliable information that those arrested or their associates may threaten or cause harm to those involved. In cases of doubt, an officer of the rank of inspector or above should be consulted.

E:1D Attention is drawn to the provisions set out in Code C about the matters to be considered when deciding whether a detained person is fit to be interviewed.

E:2 Interviews and other matters to be audio recorded under this Code

(a) Requirement to use authorised audio-recording device when available

E:2.1 Subject to *paragraph 2.3*, if an authorised recording device (see *paragraph 1.6(a)*) in working **A-166** order *and* an interview room or other location (see *Note 1A*) suitable for that device to be used, are available, then that device shall be used to record the following matters:

(a) any interview with a person cautioned in accordance with Code C, *section 10* in respect of any *summary* offence or any *indictable* offence, which includes any offence triable either way, when:

(i) that person (the suspect) is questioned about their involvement or suspected involvement in that offence and they have not been charged or informed they may be prosecuted for that offence; and

(ii) exceptionally, further questions are put to a person about any offence *after* they have been charged with, or told they may be prosecuted for, that offence (see Code C, *paragraph 16.5 and Note 2C*).

(b) when a person who has been charged with, or informed they may be prosecuted for, any offence, is told about any written statement or interview with another person and they are handed a true copy of the written statement or the content of the interview record is brought to their attention in accordance with Code C, *paragraph 16.4 and Note 2D.*

See *Note 2A*

E:2.2 The whole of each of the matters described in *paragraph 2.1* shall be audio-recorded, including the taking and reading back of any statement as applicable.

E:2.3 A written record of the matters described in *paragraph 2.1(a)* and *(b)* shall be made in accordance with Code C, *section 11,* only if,

(a) an authorised recording device (see *paragraph 1.6(a)*) in working order is *not available*; or

(b) such a device is available but a location suitable for using that device to make the audio recording of the matter in question is not available; and

(c) the 'relevant officer' described in *paragraph 2.4* considers on reasonable grounds, that the proposed interview or (as the case may be) continuation of the interview or other action, should not be delayed until an authorised recording device in working order and a suitable interview room or other location become available (see *Note 2E*) and decides that a written record shall be made;

(d) if in accordance with *paragraph 3.9,* the suspect or the appropriate adult on their behalf, objects to the interview being audibly recorded and the 'relevant officer' described in *paragraph 2.4,* after having regard to the nature and circumstances of the objections (see *Note 2F*), decides that a written record shall be made;

(e) in the case of a detainee who refuses to go into or remain in a suitable interview room and in accordance with Code C *paragraphs 12.5* and *12.11,* the custody officer directs that interview be conducted in a cell and considers that an authorised recording device cannot be safely used in the cell.

Note: When the suspect appears to have a hearing impediment, this paragraph does not affect the separate requirement in *paragraphs 3.7* and *4.4* for the interviewer to make a written note of the interview at the same time as the audio recording.

(b) Meaning of 'relevant officer'

A-167 E:2.4 In *paragraph 2.3(c)*:

(a) if the person to be interviewed is arrested elsewhere than at a police station for an offence and before they arrive at a police station, an urgent interview in accordance with *Code C paragraph 11.1* is necessary to avert one or more of the risks mentioned in *sub-paragraphs (a)* to *(c)* of that paragraph, the "relevant officer" means the *interviewer,* who may or may not be the arresting officer, who must have regard to the time, place and urgency of the proposed interview.

(b) if the person in question has been taken to a police station after being arrested elsewhere for an offence or is arrested for an offence whilst at a police station after attending voluntarily and is detained at that police station or elsewhere in the charge of a constable, the "relevant officer" means the *custody officer at the station where the person's detention* was last authorised. The custody officer must have regard to the nature of the investigation and in accordance with *Code C paragraph 1.1,* ensure that the detainee is dealt with expeditiously, and released as soon as the need for their detention no longer applies.

(c) In the case of a voluntary interview (see *Code C paragraph 3.21* to *3.22*) which takes place:

(i) at a police station and the offence in question is an indictable offence, the "relevant officer" means *an officer of the rank of sergeant or above,* in consultation with the investigating officer;

(ii) at a police station and the offence in question is a summary offence, the "relevant officer" means the *interviewer* in consultation with the investigating officer if different,

(iii) elsewhere than at a police station and the offence is one of the four indictable offence types which satisfy the conditions in Part 1 of the Annex to this Code, the "relevant officer" means *the interviewer* in consultation with the investigating officer, if different.

(iv) elsewhere than at a police station and the offence in question is an indictable offence which is not one of the four indictable offence types which satisfy the conditions in Part 1 of the Annex to this Code, the "relevant officer" means an *officer of the rank of sergeant or above*, in consultation with the investigating officer.

(v) elsewhere than at a police station and the offence in question is a summary only offence, the "relevant officer" means *the interviewer* in consultation with the investigating officer, if different.

See *Note 2B -Summary table - relevant officer for voluntary interviews*

(c) Duties of the 'relevant officer' and the interviewer

E:2.5 When, in accordance with *paragraph 2.3*, a written record is made: **A-168**

(a) the relevant officer must:

(i) record the reasons for not making an audio recording and the date and time the decision in *paragraph 2.3(c)* or (as applicable) *paragraph 2.3(d)* was made; and

(ii) ensure that the suspect is informed that a written record will be made;

(b) the interviewer must ensure that the written record includes:

(i) the date and time the decision in *paragraph 2.3(c)* or (as applicable) *paragraph 2.3(d)* was made, who made it and where the decision is recorded, and

(ii) the fact that the suspect was informed.

(c) the written record shall be made in accordance with Code C, *section 11*;

See *Note 2B*

(d) Remote monitoring of interviews

E:2.6 If the interview room or other location where the interview takes place is equipped with facilities that enable audio recorded interviews to be remotely monitored as they take place, the interviewer must ensure that suspects, their legal representatives and any appropriate adults are fully aware of what this means and that there is no possibility of privileged conversations being listened to. With this in mind, the following safeguards should be applied: **A-169**

(a) The remote monitoring system should only be able to operate when the audio recording device has been turned on.

(b) The equipment should incorporate a light, clearly visible to all in the interview room, which is automatically illuminated as soon as remote monitoring is activated.

(c) Interview rooms and other locations fitted with remote monitoring equipment must contain a notice, prominently displayed, referring to the capacity for remote monitoring and to the fact that the warning light will illuminate whenever monitoring is taking place.

(d) At the beginning of the interview, the interviewer must explain the contents of the notice to the suspect and if present, to the solicitor and appropriate adult and that explanation should itself be audio recorded.

(e) The fact that an interview, or part of an interview, was remotely monitored should be recorded in the suspect's custody record or, if the suspect is not in detention, the interviewer's pocket book. That record should include the names of the officers doing the monitoring and the purpose of the monitoring (e.g. for training, to assist with the investigation, etc.)

(e) Use of live link - Interviewer not present at the same station as the detainee

E:2.7 Code C *paragraphs 12.9A* and *12.9B* set out the conditions which, if satisfied allow a suspect in police detention to be interviewed using a live link by a police officer who is not present at the police station where the detainee is held. These provisions also set out the duties and responsibilities of the custody officer, the officer having physical custody of the suspect and the interviewer and the modifications that apply to ensure that any such interview is conducted and audio recorded in accordance with this Code or (as the case may be) visually recorded in accordance with Code F. **A-170**

Notes for guidance

E:2A Nothing in this Code is intended to preclude audio-recording at police discretion at police stations or elsewhere when persons are charged with, or told they may be prosecuted for, an offence or they respond after being so charged or informed. **A-170a**

E:2B A decision made in accordance with paragraph 2.3 not to audio-record an interview for any reason may be the subject of comment in court. The 'relevant officer' responsible should be prepared to justify that decision.

Table: Summary of paragraph 2.4(c) - relevant officer for voluntary interviews:

	Location of voluntary interview	*Offence type*	*Relevant Officer*
(i)	*Police station*	*Any indictable offence.*	*Sergeant or above+*
(ii)	*Police station*	*Any summary only offence*	*Interviewer+*
(iii)	*Elsewhere than at a police station*	*Indictable offence type defined by the Annex.*	*Interviewer+*
(iv)	*Elsewhere than at a police station*	*Indictable offence type not defined by the Annex.*	*Sergeant or above+*
(v)	*Elsewhere than at a police station*	*Summary only.*	*Interviewer+*

+ = in consultation with the investigating officer.

E:2C Code C sets out the circumstances in which a suspect may be questioned about an offence after being charged with it.

E:2D Code C sets out the procedures to be followed when a person's attention is drawn after charge, to a statement made by another person. One method of bringing the content of an interview with another person to the notice of a suspect may be to play them a recording of that interview. The person may not be questioned about the statement or interview record unless this is allowed in accordance with paragraph 16.5 of Code C.

E:2E A voluntary interview should be arranged for a time and place when it can be audio recorded and enable the safeguards and requirements set out in Code C paragraphs 3.21 to 3.22B to be implemented. It would normally be reasonable to delay the interview to enable audio recording unless the delay to do so would be likely to compromise the outcome of the interview or investigation, for example if there are grounds to suspect that the suspect would use the delay to fabricate an innocent explanation, influence witnesses or tamper with other material evidence.

E:2F Objections for the purpose of paragraphs 2.3(d) and 3.9 are meant to apply to objections based on the suspect's genuine and honestly held beliefs and to allow officers to exercise their discretion to decide that a written interview record is to be made according to the circumstances surrounding the suspect and the investigation. Objections that appear to be frivolous with the intentions of frustrating or delaying the investigation would not be relevant.

E:3 Interview recording using removable recording media device

(a) Recording and sealing master recordings - general

A-171 E:3.1 When using an authorised *removable recording media* device (see *paragraph 1.6(a)(i)*), one recording, the master recording, will be sealed in the suspect's presence. A second recording will be used as a working copy. The master recording is any of the recordings made by a multi-deck/drive machine or the only recording made by a single deck/drive machine. The working copy is one of the other recordings made by a multi-deck/drive machine or a copy of the master recording made by a single deck/drive machine.

E:3.2 The purpose of sealing the master recording before it leaves the suspect's presence is to establish their confidence that the integrity of the recording is preserved. If a single deck/drive machine is used the working copy of the master recording must be made in the suspect's presence and without the master recording leaving their sight. The working copy shall be used for making further copies if needed.

(b) Commencement of interviews

A-172 E:3.3 When the suspect is brought into the interview room or arrives at the location where the interview is to take place, the interviewer shall, without delay but in the suspect's sight, unwrap or open the new recording media, load the recording device with new recording media and set it to record.

E:3.4 The interviewer must point out the sign or indicator which shows that the recording equipment is activated and is recording (see *paragraph 1.6(a)(i)*) and shall then:

(a) tell the suspect that the interview is being audibly recorded using an authorised *removable recording media* device and outline the recording process (see *Note 3A*);
(b) subject to *paragraph 1.13*, give their name and rank and that of any other interviewer present;
(c) ask the suspect and any other party present, e.g. the appropriate adult, a solicitor or interpreter, to identify themselves (see *Note 3A*);
(d) state the date, time of commencement and place of the interview;
(e) tell the suspect that:

- they will be given a copy of the recording of the interview in the event that they are charged or informed that they will be prosecuted but if they are not charged or informed that they will be prosecuted they will only be given a copy as agreed with the police or on the order of a court; and
- they will be given a written notice at the end of the interview setting out their right to a copy of the recording and what will happen to the recording and;

(f) if equipment for remote monitoring of interviews as described in *paragraph 2.6* is installed, explain the contents of the notice to the suspect, solicitor and appropriate adult as required by *paragraph 2.6(d)* and point out the light that illuminates automatically as soon as remote monitoring is activated.

E:3.5 Any person entering the interview room after the interview has commenced shall be invited by the interviewer to identify themselves for the purpose of the audio recording and state the reason why they have entered the interview room.

E:3.6 The interviewer shall:

- caution the suspect, see Code C *section 10*; and
- if they are detained, remind them of their entitlement to free legal advice, see Code C, *paragraph 11.2*; or
- if they are not detained under arrest, explain this and their entitlement to free legal advice (see Code C, *paragraph 3.21*) and ask the suspect to confirm that they agree to the voluntary interview proceeding (see Code C *paragraph 3.22A*).

E:3.7 The interviewer shall put to the suspect any significant statement or silence, see Code C, *paragraph 11.4*.

(c) Interviews with suspects who appear to have a hearing impediment

E:3.8 If the suspect appears to have a hearing impediment, the interviewer shall make a written note of the interview in accordance with Code C, at the same time as audio recording it in accordance with this Code. (See *Notes 3B* and *3C*.) **A-173**

(d) Objections and complaints by the suspect

E:3.9 If the suspect or an appropriate adult on their behalf, objects to the interview being audibly recorded either at the outset, during the interview or during a break, the interviewer shall explain that the interview is being audibly recorded and that this Code requires the objections to be recorded on the audio recording. When any objections have been audibly recorded or the suspect or appropriate adult have refused to have their objections recorded, the relevant officer shall decide in accordance with *paragraph 2.3(d)* (which requires the officer to have regard to the nature and circumstances of the objections) whether a written record of the interview or its continuation, is to be made and that audio recording should be turned off. Following a decision that a written record is to be made, the interviewer shall say they are turning off the recorder and shall then make a written record of the interview as in Code C, *section 11*. If, however, following a decision that a written record is not to be made, the interviewer may proceed to question the suspect with the audio recording still on. This procedure also applies in cases where the suspect has previously objected to the interview being visually recorded, see Code F *paragraph 2.7*, and the investigating officer has decided to audibly record the interview. (See *Notes 2F* and *3D*.) **A-174**

E:3.10 If in the course of an interview a complaint is made by or on behalf of the person being questioned concerning the provisions of this or any other Codes, or it comes to the interviewer's notice that the person may have been treated improperly, the interviewer shall act as in Code C, *paragraph 12.9*. (See *Notes 3E* and *3F*.)

E:3.11 If the suspect indicates they want to tell the interviewer about matters not directly connected with the offence of which they are suspected and they are unwilling for these matters to be audio recorded, the suspect should be given the opportunity to tell the interviewer about these matters after the conclusion of the formal interview.

(e) Changing recording media

E:3.12 When the recorder shows the recording media only has a short time left to run, the interviewer shall so inform the person being interviewed and round off that part of the interview. If the interviewer leaves the room for a second set of recording media, the suspect shall not be left unattended. The interviewer will remove the recording media from the recorder and insert the new recording media which shall be unwrapped or opened in the suspect's presence. The recorder should be set to record on the new media. To avoid confusion between the recording media, the interviewer shall mark the media with an identification number immediately after it is removed from the recorder.

(f) Taking a break during interview

A-175 E:3.13 When a break is taken, the fact that a break is to be taken, the reason for it and the time shall be recorded on the audio recording.

E:3.14 When the break is taken and the interview room vacated by the suspect, the recording media shall be removed from the recorder and the procedures for the conclusion of an interview followed, see *paragraph 3.19*.

E:3.15 When a break is a short one and both the suspect and an interviewer remain in the interview room, the recording may be stopped. There is no need to remove the recording media and when the interview recommences the recording should continue on the same recording media. The time the interview recommences shall be recorded on the audio recording.

E:3.16 After any break in the interview the interviewer must, before resuming the interview, remind the person being questioned of their right to legal advice if they have not exercised it and that they remain under caution or, if there is any doubt, give the caution in full again. (See *Note 3G*.)

(g) Failure of recording equipment

A-176 E:3.17 If there is an equipment failure which can be rectified quickly, e.g. by inserting new recording media, the interviewer shall follow the appropriate procedures as in *paragraph 3.12*. When the recording is resumed the interviewer shall explain what happened and record the time the interview recommences. However, if it is not possible to continue recording using the same recording device or by using a replacement device, the interview should be audio-recorded using a secure digital recording network device as in *paragraph 4.1*, if the necessary equipment is available. If it is not available, the interview may continue and be recorded in writing in accordance with *paragraph 2.3* as directed by the 'relevant officer'. (See *Note 3H*.)

(h) Removing recording media from the recorder

A-177 E:3.18 Recording media which is removed from the recorder during the interview shall be retained and the procedures in *paragraph 3.12* followed.

(i) Conclusion of interview

A-178 E:3.19 At the conclusion of the interview, the suspect shall be offered the opportunity to clarify anything they have said and asked if there is anything they want to add.

E:3.20 At the conclusion of the interview, including the taking and reading back of any written statement, the time shall be recorded and the recording shall be stopped. The interviewer shall seal the master recording with a master recording label and treat it as an exhibit in accordance with force standing orders. The interviewer shall sign the label and ask the suspect and any third party present during the interview to sign it. If the suspect or third party refuse to sign the label an officer of at least the rank of inspector, or if not available the custody officer, or if the suspect has not been arrested, a sergeant, shall be called into the interview room and asked, subject to *paragraph 1.13*, to sign it.

E:3.21 The suspect shall be handed a notice which explains:

- how the audio recording will be used;
- the arrangements for access to it;
- that if they are charged or informed they will be prosecuted, a copy of the audio recording will be supplied as soon as practicable or as otherwise agreed between the suspect and the police or on the order of a court.

(j) After the interview

A-179 E:3.22 The interviewer shall make a note in their pocket book that the interview has taken place and that it was audibly recorded, the time it commenced, its duration and date and identification number of the master recording (see *Note 3I*).

E:3.23 If no proceedings follow in respect of the person whose interview was recorded, the recording media must be kept securely as in *paragraph 3.22* and *Note 3J*.

(k) Master Recording security

(i) General

A-179a E:3.24 The officer in charge of each police station at which interviews with suspects are recorded or as the case may be, where recordings of interviews carried out elsewhere than at a police station are held, shall make arrangements for master recordings to be kept securely and their movements accounted for on the same basis as material which may be used for evidential purposes, in accordance with force standing orders. (See *Note 3J.*)

(ii) Breaking master recording seal for criminal proceedings

E:3.25 A police officer has no authority to break the seal on a master recording which is required for criminal trial or appeal proceedings. If it is necessary to gain access to the master recording, the police officer shall arrange for its seal to be broken in the presence of a representative of the Crown Prosecution Service. The defendant or their legal adviser should be informed and given a reasonable opportunity to be present. If the defendant or their legal representative is present they shall be invited to re-seal and sign the master recording. If either refuses or neither is present this should be done by the representative of the Crown Prosecution Service. (See *Notes 3K* and *3L.*) **A-179b**

(iii) Breaking master recording seal: other cases

E:3.26 The chief officer of police is responsible for establishing arrangements for breaking the seal of the master copy where no criminal proceedings result, or the criminal proceedings to which the interview relates, have been concluded and it becomes necessary to break the seal. These arrangements should be those which the chief officer considers are reasonably necessary to demonstrate to the person interviewed and any other party who may wish to use or refer to the interview record that the master copy has not been tampered with and that the interview record remains accurate. (See *Note 3M.*) **A-179c**

E:3.27 Subject to *paragraph 3.29*, a representative of each party must be given a reasonable opportunity to be present when the seal is broken and the master recording copied and resealed.

E:3.28 If one or more of the parties is not present when the master copy seal is broken because they cannot be contacted or refuse to attend or *paragraph 3.29* applies, arrangements should be made for an independent person such as a custody visitor, to be present. Alternatively, or as an additional safeguard, arrangements should be made to visually record the procedure.

E:3.29 *Paragraph 3.28* does not require a person to be given an opportunity to be present when;

- (a) it is necessary to break the master copy seal for the proper and effective further investigation of the original offence or the investigation of some other offence; and
- (b) the officer in charge of the investigation has reasonable grounds to suspect that allowing an opportunity might prejudice such an investigation or criminal proceedings which may be brought as a result or endanger any person. (See *Note 3N.*)

(iv) Documentation

E:3.30 When the master recording seal is broken, a record must be made of the procedure followed, including the date, time, place and persons present. **A-179d**

Notes for guidance

Commencement of interviews (paragraph 3.3)

E:3A When outlining the recording process, the interviewer should refer to paragraph 1.6(a)(ii) and (iii) and briefly describe how the recording device being used is operated and how recordings are made. For the purpose of voice identification the interviewer should ask the suspect and any other people present to identify themselves. **A-179e**

Interviews with suspects who appear to have a hearing impediment (paragraph 3.8)

E:3B This provision is to give a person who is deaf or has impaired hearing equivalent rights of access to the full interview record as far as this is possible using audio recording.

E:3C The provisions of Code C on interpreters for suspects who do not appear to speak or understand English or who appear to have a hearing or speech impediment, continue to apply.

Objections and complaints by the suspect (paragraph 3.9)

E:3D The relevant officer should be aware that a decision to continue recording against the wishes of the suspect may be the subject of comment in court.

E:3E If the custody officer, or in the case of a person who has not been arrested, a sergeant, is called to deal with the complaint, the recorder should, if possible, be left on until the officer has entered the room and spoken to the person being interviewed. Continuation or termination of the interview should be at the interviewer's discretion pending action by an inspector under Code C, paragraph 9.2.

E:3F If the complaint is about a matter not connected with this Code or Code C, the decision to continue is at the interviewer's discretion. When the interviewer decides to continue the interview, they shall tell the suspect that at the conclusion of the interview, the complaint will be brought to the attention of the custody officer, or in the case of a person who has not been arrested, a sergeant. When the interview is concluded the interviewer must, as soon as practicable, inform the custody officer or, as the case may be, the sergeant, about the existence and nature of the complaint made.

E:3G In considering whether to caution again after a break, the interviewer should bear in mind that they may have to satisfy a court that the person understood that they were still under caution when the interview resumed. The interviewer should also remember that it may be necessary to show to the court that nothing occurred during a break or between interviews which influenced the suspect's recorded evidence. After a break or at the beginning of a subsequent interview, the interviewer should consider summarising on the record the reason for the break and confirming this with the suspect.

Failure of recording equipment (paragraph 3.17)

E:3H Where the interview is being recorded and the media or the recording equipment fails the interviewer should stop the interview immediately. Where part of the interview is unaffected by the error and is still accessible on the media, that part shall be copied and sealed in the suspect's presence as a master copy and the interview recommenced using new equipment/media as required. Where the content of the interview has been lost in its entirety, the media should be sealed in the suspect's presence and the interview begun again. If the recording equipment cannot be fixed and no replacement is immediately available, subject to paragraph 2.3, the interview should be recorded in accordance with Code C, section 11.

E:3I Any written record of an audio recorded interview should be made in accordance with current national guidelines for police officers, police staff and CPS prosecutors concerned with the preparation, processing and submission of prosecution files.

Master Recording security (paragraphs 3.24 to 3.30)

E:3J This section is concerned with the security of the master recording sealed at the conclusion of the interview. Care must be taken of working copy recordings because their loss or destruction may lead unnecessarily to the need to access master recordings.

Breaking master recording seal for criminal proceedings (paragraph 3.25)

E:3K If the master recording has been delivered to the crown court for their keeping after committal for trial the crown prosecutor will apply to the chief clerk of the crown court centre for the release of the recording for unsealing by the crown prosecutor.

E:3L Reference to the Crown Prosecution Service or to the crown prosecutor in this part of the Code should be taken to include any other body or person with a statutory responsibility for the proceedings for which the police recorded interview is required.

Breaking master recording seal: other cases (paragraphs 3.26 to 3.29)

E:3M The most common reasons for needing access to master copies that are not required for criminal proceedings arise from civil actions and complaints against police and civil actions between individuals arising out of allegations of crime investigated by police.

E:3N Paragraph 3.29(b) could apply, for example, when one or more of the outcomes or likely outcomes of the investigation might be; (i) the prosecution of one or more of the original suspects; (ii) the prosecution of someone previously not suspected, including someone who was originally a witness, and (iii) any original suspect being treated as a prosecution witness and when premature disclosure of any police action, particularly through contact with any parties involved, could lead to a real risk of compromising the investigation and endangering witnesses.

E:4 Interview recording using secure digital recording network device

(a) General

A-179f E:4.1 An authorised secure digital recording network device (see *paragraph 1.6(a)(iii)* does not use removable media and this section specifies the provisions which will apply when such a device is used. For ease of reference, it repeats in full some of the provisions of section 3 that apply to both types of recording device.

(b) Commencement of interviews

A-179g E:4.2 When the suspect is brought into the interview room or arrives at the location where the interview is to take place, the interviewer shall without delay and in the sight of the suspect, switch on the recording equipment and in accordance with the manufacturer's instructions start recording.

E:4.3 The interviewer must point out the sign or indicator which shows that the recording equipment is activated and is recording (see *paragraph 1.6(a)(iii)*) and shall then:

(a) tell the suspect that the interview is being audibly recorded using an authorised *secure digital recording network device* and outline the recording process (see *Note 3A*);

(b) subject to *paragraph 1.13*, give their name and rank and that of any other interviewer present;
(c) ask the suspect and any other party present, e.g. the appropriate adult, a solicitor or interpreter, to identify themselves (see *Note 3A*);
(d) state the date, time of commencement and place of the interview; and
(e) inform the person that:
  - they will be given access to the recording of the interview in the event that they are charged or informed that they will be prosecuted but if they are not charged or informed that they will be prosecuted they will only be given access as agreed with the police or on the order of a court; and
  - they will be given a written notice at the end of the interview setting out their rights to access the recording and what will happen to the recording.

(f) If equipment for remote monitoring of interviews as described in *paragraph 2.6* is installed, explain the contents of the notice to the suspect, solicitor and appropriate adult as required by *paragraph 2.6(d)* and point out the light that illuminates automatically as soon as remote monitoring is activated.

E:4.4 *Paragraphs 3.5* to *3.7* apply.

(c) Interviews with suspects who appear to have a hearing impediment

E:4.5 *Paragraph 3.8* applies. **A-179h**

(d) Objections and complaints by the suspect

E:4.6 *Paragraphs 3.9, 3.10* and *3.11* apply. **A-179i**

(e) Taking a break during interview

E:4.7 When a break is taken, the fact that a break is to be taken, the reason for it and the time shall be recorded on the audio recording. The recording shall be stopped and the procedures in *paragraphs 4.11* and *4.12* for the conclusion of interview followed. **A-179j**

E:4.8 When the interview recommences the procedures in *paragraphs 4.2* to *4.3* for commencing an interview shall be followed to create a new file to record the continuation of the interview. The time the interview recommences shall be recorded on the audio recording.

E:4.9 After any break in the interview the interviewer must, before resuming the interview, remind the person being questioned of their right to legal advice if they have not exercised it and that they remain under caution or, if there is any doubt, give the caution in full again (see *Note 3G*).

(f) Failure of recording equipment

E:4.10 If there is an equipment failure which can be rectified quickly, e.g. by commencing a new secure digital network recording using the same device or a replacement device, the interviewer shall follow the appropriate procedures as in *paragraphs 4.7 to 4.9 (Taking a break during interview)*. When the recording is resumed, the interviewer shall explain what happened and record the time the interview recommences. However, if it is not possible to continue recording on the same device or by using a replacement device, the interview should be audio-recorded on removable media as in *paragraph 3.3*, if the necessary equipment is available. If it is not available, the interview may continue and be recorded in writing in accordance with *paragraph 2.3* as directed by the 'relevant officer'. (See *Note 3H*.) **A-179k**

(g) Conclusion of interview

E:4.11 At the conclusion of the interview, the suspect shall be offered the opportunity to clarify anything he or she has said and asked if there is anything they want to add. **A-179l**

E:4.12 At the conclusion of the interview, including the taking and reading back of any written statement:
(a) the time shall be orally recorded.
(b) the suspect shall be handed a notice (see *Note 4A*) which explains:
  - how the audio recording will be used
  - the arrangements for access to it
  - that if they are charged or informed that they will be prosecuted, they will be given access to the recording of the interview either electronically or by being given a copy on removable recording media, but if they are not charged or informed that they will prosecuted, they will only be given access as agreed with the police or on the order of a court.

(c) the suspect must be asked to confirm that he or she has received a copy of the notice at *sub-paragraph (b)* above. If the suspect fails to accept or to acknowledge receipt of the notice, the interviewer will state for the recording that a copy of the notice has been provided to the suspect and that he or she has refused to take a copy of the notice or has refused to acknowledge receipt.

(d) the time shall be recorded and the interviewer shall ensure that the interview record is saved to the device in the presence of the suspect and any third party present during the interview and notify them accordingly. The interviewer must then explain that the record will be transferred securely to the remote secure network file server (see *paragraph 4.15*). If the equipment is available to enable the record to be transferred there and then in the suspect's presence, then it should be so transferred. If it is transferred at a later time, the time and place of the transfer must be recorded. The suspect should then be informed that the interview is terminated.

(h) After the interview

A-179m E:4.13 The interviewer shall make a note in their pocket book that the interview has taken place and that it was audibly recorded, time it commenced, its duration and date and the identification number, filename or other reference for the recording (see *Note 3I*).

E:4.14 If no proceedings follow in respect of the person whose interview was recorded, the

(i) Security of secure digital network interview records

A-179n E:4.15 The recordings are first saved locally on the device before being transferred to the remote network file server system (see *paragraph 1.6(a)(iii)*). The recording remains on the local device until the transfer is complete. If for any reason the network connection fails, the recording will be transferred when the network connection is restored (see *paragraph 4.12(d)*). The interview record files are stored in read only form on non-removable storage devices, for example, hard disk drives, to ensure their integrity.

E:4.16 Access to interview recordings, including copying to removable media, must be strictly controlled and monitored to ensure that access is restricted to those who have been given specific permission to access for specified purposes when this is necessary. For example, police officers and CPS lawyers involved in the preparation of any prosecution case, persons interviewed if they have been charged or informed they may be prosecuted and their legal representatives.

Note for guidance

A-179o *E:4A The notice at paragraph 4.12(b) above should provide a brief explanation of the secure digital network and how access to the recording is strictly limited. The notice should also explain the access rights of the suspect, their legal representative, the police and the prosecutor to the recording of the interview. Space should be provided on the form to insert the date, the identification number, filename or other reference for the interview recording. recordings must be kept securely as in paragraphs 4.15 and 4.16.*

ANNEX

Paragraph 2.4(c)(iii) - Four Indictable Offence Types for which the Interviewer may Decide to Make a Written Record of a Voluntary Interview Elsewhere than at a Police Station when an Authorised Audio Recording Device Cannot be Used.

[See *Notes 2* and *3*]

Part 1: Four specified indictable offence types–two conditions

A-179p E:1. The *first* condition is that the *indictable* offence in respect of which the person has been cautioned is *one* of the following:

(a) Possession of a controlled drug contrary to section 5(2) of the Misuse of Drugs Act 1971 if the drug is cannabis as defined by that Act and in a form commonly known as herbal cannabis or cannabis resin (see *Note 5*);

(b) Possession of a controlled drug contrary to section 5(2) of the Misuse of Drugs Act 1971 if the drug is khat as defined by that Act (see *Note 5*);

(c) Retail theft (shoplifting) contrary to section 1 of the Theft Act 1968 (see *Note 6*); and

(d) Criminal damage to property contrary to section 1(1) of the Criminal Damage Act 1971 (see *Note 6*), and in this paragraph, the reference to each of the above offences applies to an attempt to commit that offence as defined by section 1 of the Criminal Attempts Act 1981.

E:2. The *second* condition is that:

(a) where the person has been cautioned in respect of an offence described in *paragraph 1(a)* (Possession of herbal cannabis or cannabis resin) or *paragraph 1(b)* (Possession of khat), the requirements of *paragraphs 3* and *4* are satisfied; or

(b) where the person has been cautioned in respect of an offence described in *paragraph 1(c)* (Retail theft), the requirements of *paragraphs 3* and *5* are satisfied; or

(c) where the person has been cautioned in respect of an offence described in *paragraph 1(d)* (criminal damage), the requirements of *paragraphs 3* and *6* are satisfied.

E:3. The requirements of this paragraph that apply to all four offences described in *paragraph 1* are that:

(i) with regard to the person suspected of committing the offence:
- they appear to be aged 18 or over;
- there is no reason to suspect that they are a vulnerable person for whom an appropriate adult is required (see *paragraph 1.5* of this Code);
- they do *not* appear to be unable to understand what is happening because of the effects of drink, drugs or illness, ailment or condition;
- they do *not* require an interpreter in accordance with *Code C section 13*; and
- in accordance with Code G (Arrest), their arrest is *not* necessary in order to investigate the offence;

(ii) it appears that the commission of the offence:
- has *not* resulted in any injury to any person;
- has *not* involved any realistic threat or risk of injury to any person; and
- has *not* caused any *substantial* financial or material loss to the private property of any individual; and

(iii) the person is not being interviewed about any other offence.

See *Notes 3* and *8*.

E:4. The requirements of this paragraph that apply to the offences described in *paragraph 1(a)* (possession of herbal cannabis or cannabis resin) and *paragraph 1(b)* (possession of khat) are that a police officer who is experienced in the recognition of the physical appearance, texture and smell of herbal cannabis, cannabis resin or (as the case may be) khat, is able to say that the substance which has been found in the suspect's possession by that officer or, as the case may be, by any other officer not so experienced and trained:

(i) is a controlled drug being either herbal cannabis, cannabis resin or khat; and

(ii) the quantity of the substance found is consistent with personal use by the suspect and does not provide any grounds to suspect an intention to supply others.

See *Note 5*.

E:5. The requirements of this paragraph that apply to the offence described in *paragraph 1(c)* (retail theft), are that it appears to the officer:

(i) that the value of the property stolen does not exceed £100 inclusive of VAT;

(ii) that the stolen property has been recovered and remains fit for sale unless the items stolen comprised drink or food and have been consumed; and

(iii) that the person suspected of stealing the property is not employed (whether paid or not) by the person, company or organisation to which the property belongs.

See *Note 3*.

E:6. The requirements of this paragraph that apply to the offence described in *paragraph 1(d)* (Criminal damage), are that it appears to the officer:

(i) that the value of the criminal damage does not exceed £300; and

(ii) that the person suspected of damaging the property is not employed (whether paid or not) by the person, company or organisation to which the property belongs.

See *Note 3*.

Part 2: Other provisions applicable to all interviews to which this Annex applies

E:7. *Paragraphs 3.21* to *3.22B* of Code C set out the responsibilities of the interviewing officer for ensuring compliance with the provisions of Code C that apply to the conduct and recording of voluntary interviews to which this Annex applies. See *Note 7*. **A-179q**

E:8. If it appears to the interviewing officer that before the conclusion of an interview, any of the requirements in *paragraphs 3 to 6* of *Part 1* that apply to the offence in question described in *paragraph 1* of Part 1 have ceased to apply; this Annex shall cease to apply. The person being interviewed must be so informed and a break in the interview must be taken. The reason must be recorded in the written interview record and the continuation of the interview shall be audio recorded in accordance with section 2 of this Code. For the purpose of the continuation, the provisions of *paragraphs 3.3* and *4.2* (Commencement of interviews) shall apply. See *Note 8*.

Notes for guidance

A-179r *E:1 Not used.*

E:2 The purpose of allowing the interviewer to decide that a written record is to be made is to support the policy which gives police in England and Wales options for dealing with lowlevel offences quickly and non-bureaucratically in a proportionate manner. Guidance for police about these options is available at: https://www.app.college.police.uk/app-content/prosecution-and-case-management/justice-outcomes/.

E:3 A decision in relation to a particular indictable offence that the conditions and requirements in this Annex are satisfied is an operational matter for the interviewing officer according to all the particular circumstances of the case. These circumstances include the outcome of the officer's investigation at that time and any other matters that are relevant to the officer's consideration as to how to deal with the matter.

E:4 Not used.

E:5 Under the Misuse of Drugs Act 1971 as at the date this Code comes into force:

(a) cannabis includes any part of the cannabis plant but not mature stalks and seeds separated from the plant, cannabis resin and cannabis oil, but paragraph 1(a) applies only to the possession of herbal cannabis and cannabis resin; and

(b) khat includes the leaves, stems and shoots of the plant.

E:6 The power to issue a Penalty Notice for Disorder (PND) for an offence contrary to section 1 of the Theft Act 1968 applies when the value of the goods stolen does not exceed £100 inclusive of VAT. The power to issue a PND for an offence contrary to section 1(1) of the Criminal Damage Act 1971 applies when the value of the damage does not exceed £300.

E:7 The provisions of Code C that apply to the conduct and recording of voluntary interviews to which this Annex applies are described in paragraphs 3.21 to 3.22B of Code C. They include the suspect's right to free legal advice, the provision of information about the offence before the interview (see Code C paragraph 11.1A) and the right to interpretation and translation (see Code C section 13). These and other rights and entitlements are summarised in the notice that must be given to the suspect.

E:8 The requirements in paragraph 3 of Part 1 will cease to apply if, for example during the course of an interview, as a result of what the suspect says or other information which comes to the interviewing officer's notice:

- *it appears that the suspect:*
  - *is aged under 18;*
  - *does require an appropriate adult;*
  - *is unable to appreciate the significance of questions and their answers;*
  - *is unable to understand what is happening because of the effects of drink, drugs or illness, ailment or condition; or*
  - *requires an interpreter; or*
- *the police officer decides that the suspect's arrest is now necessary (see Code G).*

(7) Visual recording of interviews

A-180 The text that follows is of the version of the code that came into force on 31 July 2018: see above, Appendix A-1.

As at 10 September 2018, there was no requirement on any police force to make visual recordings of interviews, but police officers who choose to make such recordings will still be required to have regard to the provisions of this code.

F. CODE OF PRACTICE ON VISUAL RECORDINGS WITH SOUND OF INTERVIEWS WITH SUSPECTS

Commencement—transitional arrangements

A-180a This contents of this Code should be considered if an interviewer proposes to make a visual recording with sound of an interview with a suspect after 00.00 on 31 July 2018.

There is no statutory requirement under PACE to visually record interviews.

F:1 General

A-181 F:1.0 The procedures in this Code must be used fairly, responsibly, with respect for the people to whom they apply and without unlawful discrimination. Under the Equality Act 2010, section 149

(Public Sector Equality Duty), police forces must, in carrying out their functions, have due regard to the need to eliminate unlawful discrimination, harassment, victimisation and any other conduct which is prohibited by that Act, to advance equality of opportunity between people who share a relevant protected characteristic and people who do not share it, and to foster good relations between those persons. The Equality Act also makes it unlawful for police officers to discriminate against, harass or victimise any person on the grounds of the 'protected characteristics' of age, disability, gender reassignment, race, religion or belief, sex and sexual orientation, marriage and civil partnership, pregnancy and maternity, when using their powers. See *Note 1C.*

F:1.1 This Code of Practice must be readily available for consultation by police officers and other police staff, detained persons and members of the public.

F:1.2 The *Notes for guidance* included are not provisions of this code. They form guidance to police officers and others about its application and interpretation.

F:1.3 Nothing in this Code shall detract from the requirements of Code C, the Code of Practice for the detention, treatment and questioning of persons by police officers.

F:1.4 The interviews and matters to which this Code applies and provisions that govern the conduct and recording of those interviews and other matters are described in section 2.

Note: The provisions of this Code and Code E which govern the conduct and recording of interviews *do not apply* to interviews with, or taking statements from, witnesses.

F:1.5 *Not used.*

F:1.5A The provisions of Code E which require interviews with suspects to be audio recorded and the provisions of this Code which permit simultaneous visual recording provide safeguards:

- for suspects against inaccurate recording of the words used in questioning them and of their demeanour during the interview; and
- for police interviewers against unfounded allegations made by, or on behalf of, suspects about the conduct of the interview and what took place during the interview which might otherwise appear credible.

The visual recording of interviews must therefore be carried out openly to instil confidence in its reliability as an impartial and accurate record of the interview.

F:1.6 *Not used.*

F:1.6A *Not used.*

F:1.7 *Not used.*

F:1.8 *Not used.*

Notes for guidance

F:1A Not used. **A-182**

F:1B Not used.

F:1C In paragraph 1.0, under the Equality Act 2010, section 149, the 'relevant protected characteristics' are: age, disability, gender reassignment, pregnancy and maternity, race, religion/belief, and sex and sexual orientation. For further detailed guidance and advice on the Equality Act, see: https://www.gov.uk/guidance/equality-act-2010-guidance.

F:2. When interviews and matters to which Code F applies may be visually recorded with sound and provisions for their conduct and recording

(a) General

F:2.1 For the purpose of this Code, a visual recording with sound means an audio recording of an interview or other matter made in accordance with the requirement in *paragraph 2.1* of the Code of Practice on audio recording interviews with suspects (Code E) (see *Note 2A*) during which a *simultaneous* visual recording is made which shows the suspect, the interviewer and those in whose presence and hearing the audio recording was made. **A-183**

F:2.2 There is no statutory requirement to make a visual recording, however, the provisions of this Code shall be followed on any occasion that the 'relevant officer' described in *Code E paragraph 2.4* considers that a visual recording of any matters mentioned in *paragraph 2.1* should be made. Having regard to the safeguards described in *paragraph 1.5A,* examples of occasions when the relevant officer is likely to consider that a visual recording should be made include when:

(a) the suspect (whether or not detained) requires an appropriate adult;
(b) the suspect or their solicitor or appropriate adult requests that the interview be recorded visually;
(c) the suspect or other person whose presence is necessary is deaf or deaf/blind or speech impaired and uses sign language to communicate;
(d) the interviewer anticipates that when asking the suspect about their involvement in the of-

fence concerned, they will invite the suspect to demonstrate their actions or behaviour at the time or to examine a particular item or object which is handed to them;

(e) the officer in charge of the investigation believes that a visual recording with sound will assist in the conduct of the investigation, for example, when briefing other officers about the suspect or matters coming to light during the course of the interview; and

(f) the authorised recording device that would be used in accordance with *paragraph 2.1 of Code E* incorporates a camera and creates a combined audio and visual recording and does not allow the visual recording function to operate independently of the audio recording function.

F:2.3 For the purpose of making such a visual recording, the provisions of Code E and the relevant *Notes for guidance* shall apply equally to visual recordings with sound as they do to audio-only recordings, subject to the additional provisions in *paragraphs 2.5* to *2.12* below which apply exclusively to visual recordings. (See *Note 2E.*)

F:2.4 This Code does not apply to the conduct and recording in England and Wales, of:

- interviews of persons detained under section 41 of, or Schedule 7 to, the Terrorism Act 2000, and
- post-charge questioning of persons authorised under section 22 of the Counter-Terrorism Act 2008.

These must be video recorded with sound in accordance with the provisions of the separate Code of Practice issued under paragraph 3 of Schedule 8 to the Terrorism Act 2000 and under section 25 of the Counter-Terrorism Act 2008. If, during the course of an interview or questioning being visually recorded under this Code, it becomes apparent that the interview or questioning should be conducted under that separate Code, the interview should only continue in accordance with that Code (see *Code E paragraph 1.4*).

(b) Application of Code E–additional provisions that apply to visual recording with sound.

(i) General

A-184 F:2.5 Before visual recording commences, the interviewer must inform the suspect that in accordance with *paragraph 2.2*, a visual recording is being made and explain the visual and audio recording arrangements. If the suspect is a juvenile or a vulnerable person (see Code C, *paragraphs 1.4, 1.5* and *1.13(d)*), the information and explanation must be provided or (as the case may be) provided again, in the presence of the appropriate adult.

F:2.6 The device used to make the visual recording at the same time as the audio recording (see *paragraph 2.1*) must ensure coverage of as much of the room or location where the interview takes place as it is practically possible to achieve whilst the interview takes place (see *Note 2B*).

F:2.7 In cases to which *paragraph 1.13* of Code E (disclosure of identity of officers or police staff conducting interviews) applies:

(a) the officers and staff may have their backs to the visual recording device; and

(b) when in accordance with Code E *paragraph 3.21* or *4.12* as they apply to this Code, arrangements are made for the suspect to have access to the visual recording, the investigating officer may arrange for anything in the recording that might allow the officers or police staff to be identified to be concealed.

F:2.8 Following a decision made by the relevant officer in accordance with *paragraph 2.2* that an interview or other matter mentioned in *paragraph 2.1* above should be *visually recorded*, the relevant officer may decide that the interview is not to be visually recorded if it no longer appears that a visual recording should be made or because of a fault in the recording device. However, a decision not to make a *visual recording* does not detract in any way from the requirement for the interview to be *audio recorded* in accordance with *paragraph 2.1 of Code E.* (See *Note 2C.*)

F:2.9 The provisions in Code E *paragraph 2.6* for remote monitoring of interviews shall apply to visually recorded interviews.

(ii) Objections and complaints by the suspect about visual recording

A-185 F:2.10 If the suspect or an appropriate adult on their behalf objects to the interview being visually recorded either at the outset or during the interview or during a break in the interview, the interviewer shall explain that the visual recording is being made in accordance with *paragraph 2.2* and that this Code requires the objections to be recorded on the visual recording. When any objections have been recorded or the suspect or the appropriate adult have refused to have their objections recorded visually, the relevant officer shall decide in accordance with *paragraph 2.8* and having regard to the nature and circumstances of the objections, whether visual recording should be turned off (see *Note 2D*). Following a decision that visual recording should be turned off, the interviewer shall say that they are turning off the *visual* recording. The audio recording required to be maintained in accordance with Code E shall continue and the interviewer shall ask the person to record their objections to the interview being *visually* recorded on the audio recording. If the relevant officer considers that visual recording should not be turned off, the interviewer may proceed to question the suspect with the visual recording still on. If the suspect also objects to the interview being audio recorded, *paragraph 3.9* of Code E will apply if a removable recording media device (see Code E *paragraph 1.6(a)(ii)*) is being used) and *paragraph 4.6* of Code E will apply if a secure digital recording device (see Code E *paragraph 1.6(a)(iii)*) is being used.

F:2.11 If the suspect indicates that they wish to tell the interviewer about matters not directly connected with the offence of which they are suspected and that they are unwilling for these matters to be visually recorded, the suspect should be given the opportunity to tell the interviewer about these matters after the conclusion of the formal interview.

(ii) Failure of visual recording device

F:2.12 If there is a failure of equipment and it is not possible to continue visual recording using the same type of recording device (i.e. a removable recording media device as in Code E *paragraph 1.6(a)(ii)* or a secure digital recording network device as in Code E *paragraph 1.6(a)(iii)*) or by using a replacement device of either type, the relevant officer may decide that the interview is to continue without being visually recorded. In these circumstances, the continuation of the interview must be conducted and recorded in accordance with the provisions of Code E (See *Note 2F.*) **A-186**

Notes for guidance

F:2A Paragraph 2.1 of Code E describes the requirement that authorised audio-recording devices are to be used for recording interviews and other matters. **A-186a**

F:2B Interviewers will wish to arrange that, as far as possible, visual recording arrangements are unobtrusive. It must be clear to the suspect, however, that there is no opportunity to interfere with the recording equipment or the recording media.

F:2C A decision made in accordance with paragraph 2.8 not to record an interview visually for any reason may be the subject of comment in court. The 'relevant officer' responsible should therefore be prepared to justify that decision.

F:2D Objections for the purpose of paragraph 2.10 are meant to apply to objections based on the suspect's genuine and honestly held beliefs and to allow officers to exercise their discretion to decide whether a visual recording is to be made according to the circumstances surrounding the suspect and the investigation. Objections that appear to be frivolous with the intentions of frustrating or delaying the investigation would not be relevant.

F:2E The visual recording made in accordance with this Code may be used for eye-witness identification procedures to which paragraph 3.21 and Annex E of Code D apply.

F:2F Where the interview is being visually recorded and the media or the recording device fails, the interviewer should stop the interview immediately. Where part of the interview is unaffected by the error and is still accessible on the media or on the network device, that part shall be copied and sealed in the suspect's presence as a master copy or saved as a new secure digital network recording as appropriate. The interview should then be recommenced using a functioning recording device and new recording media as appropriate. Where the media content of the interview has been lost in its entirety, the media should be sealed in the suspect's presence and the interview begun again. If the visual recording equipment cannot be fixed and a replacement device is not immediately available, the interview should be audio recorded in accordance with Code E.

F:2G The relevant officer should be aware that a decision to continue visual recording against the wishes of the suspect may be the subject of comment in court.

[The next paragraph is A-203.]

(8) Statutory power of arrest

The first version of Code G came into force on 1 January 2006, to coincide with the commencement of the substantial changes to the provisions of the PACE Act 1984 relating to the powers of arrest of police constables. As from that date, all offences became arrestable offences, but the lawfulness of an arrest by a constable for an offence became dependent on the constable having "reasonable grounds for believing that for any of the reasons mentioned in subsection (5) [of section 24] it is necessary to arrest the person in question". For the substituted section 24, see § 15-183 in the main work. **A-203**

A revised code G came into force on 12 November 2012 (see A-1).

G. CODE OF PRACTICE FOR THE STATUTORY POWER OF ARREST BY POLICE OFFICERS

Commencement

This code applies to any arrest made by a police officer after 00.00 on 12 November 2012. **A-203a**

G:1 Introduction

A-204 G:1.1 This code of practice deals with statutory power of police to arrest a person who is involved, or suspected of being involved, in a criminal offence. The power of arrest must be used fairly, responsibly, with respect for people suspected of committing offences and without unlawful discrimination. The Equality Act 2010 makes it unlawful for police officers to discriminate against, harass or victimise any person on the grounds of the "protected characteristics" of age, disability, gender reassignment, race, religion or belief, sex and sexual orientation, marriage and civil partnership, pregnancy and maternity when using their powers. When police forces are carrying out their functions they also have a duty to have regard to the need to eliminate unlawful discrimination, harassment and victimisation and to take steps to foster good relations.

G:1.2 The exercise of the power of arrest represents an obvious and significant interference with the right to liberty and security under Article 5 of the European Convention on Human Rights set out in Part I of Schedule 1 to the Human Rights Act 1998.

G:1.3 The use of the power must be fully justified and officers exercising the power should consider if the necessary objectives can be met by other, less intrusive means. Absence of justification for exercising the power of arrest may lead to challenges should the case proceed to court. It could also lead to civil claims against police for unlawful arrest and false imprisonment. When the power of arrest is exercised it is essential that it is exercised in a non-discriminatory and proportionate manner which is compatible with the right to liberty under Article 5. See *Note 1B*.

G:1.4 Section 24 of the Police and Criminal Evidence Act 1984 (as substituted by section 110 of the Serious Organised Crime and Police Act 2005) provides the statutory power for a constable to arrest without warrant for all offences. If the provisions of the Act and this code are not observed, both the arrest and the conduct of any subsequent investigation may be open to question.

G:1.5 This code of practice must be readily available at all police stations for consultation by police officers and police staff, detained persons and members of the public.

G:1.6 The notes for guidance are not provisions of this code.

G:2 Elements of arrest under section 24 PACE

A-205 G:2.1 A lawful arrest requires two elements:

a person's involvement or suspected involvement or attempted involvement in the commission of a criminal offence; and

reasonable grounds for believing that the person's arrest is necessary.

Both elements must be satisfied, and it can never be necessary to arrest a person unless there are reasonable grounds to suspect them of committing an offence.

G:2.2 The arrested person must be informed that they have been arrested, even if this fact is obvious, and of the relevant circumstances of the arrest in relation to both the above elements. The custody officer must be informed of these matters on arrival at the police station. See paragraphs 2.9, 3.3 and *Note 3* and Code C, para. 3.4.

(a) "Involvement in the commission of an offence"

A-206 G:2.3 A constable may arrest without warrant in relation to any offence (see *Notes 1* and *1A*) anyone:

- who is about to commit an offence or is in the act of committing an offence;
- whom the officer has reasonable grounds for suspecting is about to commit an offence or to be committing an offence;
- whom the officer has reasonable grounds to suspect of being guilty of an offence which he or she has reasonable grounds for suspecting has been committed;
- anyone [*sic*] who is guilty of an offence which has been committed or anyone whom the officer has reasonable grounds for suspecting to be guilty of that offence.

G:2.3A There must be some reasonable, objective grounds for the suspicion, based on known facts and information which are relevant to the likelihood the offence has been committed and the person liable to arrest committed it. See *Notes 2* and *2A*.

(b) Necessity criteria

A-207 G:2.4 The power of arrest is only exercisable if the constable has reasonable grounds for believing that it is necessary to arrest the person. The statutory criteria for what may constitute necessity are set out in paragraph 2.9 and it remains an operational decision at the discretion of the constable to decide:

- which one or more of the necessity criteria (if any) applies to the individual; and

- if any of the criteria do apply, whether to arrest, grant street bail after arrest, report for summons or for charging by post, issue a penalty notice or take any other action that is open to the officer.

G:2.5 In applying the criteria, the arresting officer has to be satisfied that at least one of the reasons supporting the need for arrest is satisfied.

G:2.6 Extending the power of arrest to all offences provides a constable with the ability to use that power to deal with any situation. However, applying the necessity criteria requires the constable to examine and justify the reason or reasons why a person needs to be arrested or (as the case may be) further arrested, for an offence for the custody officer to decide whether to authorise their detention for that offence. See *Note 2C*.

G:2.7 The criteria in paragraph 2.9 below which are set out in section 24 of PACE, as substituted by section 110 of the Serious Organised Crime and Police Act 2005, are exhaustive. However, the circumstances that may satisfy those criteria remain a matter for the operational discretion of individual officers. Some examples are given to illustrate what those circumstances might be and what officers might consider when deciding whether arrest is necessary.

G:2.8 In considering the individual circumstances, the constable must take into account the situation of the victim, the nature of the offence, the circumstances of the suspect and the needs of the investigative process.

G:2.9 When it is practicable to tell a person why their arrest is necessary (as required by paragraphs 2.2, 3.3 and *Note 3*), the constable should outline the facts, information and other circumstances which provide the grounds for believing that their arrest is necessary and which the officer considers satisfy one or more of the statutory criteria in sub-paragraphs (a) to (f), namely: **A-208**

(a) to enable the name of the person in question to be ascertained (in the case where the constable does not know, and cannot readily ascertain, the person's name, or has reasonable grounds for doubting whether a name given by the person as his name is his real name):
an officer might decide that a person's name cannot be readily ascertained if they fail or refuse to give it when asked, particularly after being warned that failure or refusal is likely to make their arrest necessary (see *Note 2D*); grounds to doubt a name given may arise if the person appears reluctant or hesitant when asked to give their name or to verify the name they have given;
where mobile fingerprinting is available and the suspect's name cannot be ascertained or is doubted, the officer should consider using the power under section 61(6A) of PACE (see Code D, para. 4.3(e)) to take and check the fingerprints of a suspect as this may avoid the need to arrest solely to enable their name to be ascertained;

(b) correspondingly as regards the person's address:
an officer might decide that a person's address cannot be readily ascertained if they fail or refuse to give it when asked, particularly after being warned that such a failure or refusal is likely to make their arrest necessary (see *Note 2D*); grounds to doubt an address given may arise if the person appears reluctant or hesitant when asked to give their address or is unable to provide verifiable details of the locality they claim to live in;
when considering reporting to consider summons or charging by post as alternatives to arrest, an address would be satisfactory if the person will be at it for a sufficiently long period for it to be possible to serve them with the summons or requisition and charge; or, that some other person at that address specified by the person will accept service on their behalf; when considering issuing a penalty notice, the address should be one where the person will be in the event of enforcement action if the person does not pay the penalty or is convicted and fined after a court hearing;

(c) to prevent the person in question:
  (i) causing physical injury to himself or any other person; this might apply where the suspect has already used or threatened violence against others and it is thought likely that they may assault others if they are not arrested (see *Note 2D*);
  (ii) suffering physical injury; this might apply where the suspect's behaviour and actions are believed likely to provoke, or have provoked, others to want to assault the suspect unless the suspect is arrested for their own protection (see *Note 2D*);
  (iii) causing loss or damage to property; this might apply where the suspect is a known persistent offender with a history of serial offending against property (theft and criminal damage) and it is thought likely that they may continue offending if they are not arrested;
  (iv) committing an offence against public decency (only applies where members of the public going about their normal business cannot reasonably be expected to avoid the person in question); this might apply when an offence against public decency is being committed in a place to which the public have access and is likely to be repeated in

that or some other public place at a time when the public are likely to encounter the suspect (see *Note 2D*);

(v) causing an unlawful obstruction of the highway; this might apply to any offence where its commission causes an unlawful obstruction which it is believed may continue or be repeated if the person is not arrested, particularly if the person has been warned that they are causing an obstruction (see *Note 2D*);

(d) to protect a child or other vulnerable person from the person in question; this might apply when the health (physical or mental) or welfare of a child or vulnerable person is likely to be harmed or is at risk of being harmed, if the person is not arrested in cases where it is not practicable and appropriate to make alternative arrangements to prevent the suspect from having any harmful or potentially harmful contact with the child or vulnerable person;

(e) to allow the prompt and effective investigation of the offence or of the conduct of the person in question (see *Note 2E*); this may arise when it is thought likely that unless the person is arrested and then either taken in custody to the police station or granted "street bail" to attend the station later (see *Note 2J*), further action considered necessary to properly investigate their involvement in the offence would be frustrated, unreasonably delayed or otherwise hindered and therefore be impracticable; examples of such actions include:

(i) interviewing the suspect on occasions when the person's voluntary attendance is not considered to be a practicable alternative to arrest, because for example:
- it is thought unlikely that the person would attend the police station voluntarily to be interviewed;
- it is necessary to interview the suspect about the outcome of other investigative action for which their arrest is necessary, see (ii) to (v) below;
- arrest would enable the special warning to be given in accordance with Code C, paras 10.10 and 10.11 when the suspect is found:
  - in possession of incriminating objects, or at a place where such objects are found;
  - at or near the scene of the crime at or about the time it was committed;
- the person has made false statements and/or presented false evidence;
- it is thought likely that the person:
  - may steal or destroy evidence;
  - may collude or make contact with, co-suspects or conspirators;
  - may intimidate or threaten or make contact with, witnesses;

(see *Notes 2F* and *2G*);

(ii) when considering arrest in connection with the investigation of an indictable offence (see *Note 6*), there is a need:
- to enter and search without a search warrant any premises occupied or controlled by the arrested person or where the person was when arrested or immediately before arrest;
- to prevent the arrested person from having contact with others;
- to detain the arrested person for more than 24 hours before charge;

(iii) when considering arrest in connection with any recordable offence and it is necessary to secure or preserve evidence of that offence by taking fingerprints, footwear impressions or samples from the suspect for evidential comparison or matching with other material relating to that offence, for example, from the crime scene (see *Note 2H*);

(iv) when considering arrest in connection with any offence and it is necessary to search, examine or photograph the person to obtain evidence (see *Note 2H*);

(v) when considering arrest in connection with an offence to which the statutory Class A drug testing requirements in Code C, section 17, apply, to enable testing when it is thought that drug misuse might have caused or contributed to the offence (see *Note 2I*);

(f) to prevent any prosecution for the offence from being hindered by the disappearance of the person in question; this may arise when it is thought that:
- if the person is not arrested they are unlikely to attend court if they are prosecuted;
- the address given is not a satisfactory address for service of a summons or a written charge and requisition to appear at court because the person will not be at it for a sufficiently long period for the summons or charge and requisition to be served and no other person at that specified address will accept service on their behalf.

G:3 Information to be given on arrest

(a) Cautions—when a caution must be given

A-209 G:3.1 Code C, paras 10.1 and 10.2, set out the requirement for a person whom there are grounds to suspect of an offence (see *Note 2*) to be cautioned before being questioned or further questioned about an offence.

G:3.2 [*Not used.*]

G:3.3 A person who is arrested, or further arrested, must be informed at the time if practicable, or if not, as soon as it becomes practicable thereafter, that they are under arrest and of the grounds and reasons for their arrest (see paragraphs [*sic*] 2.2 and *Note 3*).

G:3.4 A person who is arrested, or further arrested, must be cautioned unless:

(a) it is impracticable to do so by reason of their condition or behaviour at the time;

(b) they have already been cautioned immediately prior to arrest as in paragraph 3.1.

(b) Terms of the caution (taken from Code C, section 10)

G:3.5 The caution, which must be given on arrest, should be in the following terms: **A-210**

> "*You do not have to say anything. But it may harm your defence if you do not mention when questioned something which you later rely on in court. Anything you do say may be given in evidence.*".

Where the use of the Welsh language is appropriate, a constable may provide the caution directly in Welsh in the following terms:

> "*Does dim rhaid i chi ddweud dim byd. Ond gall niweidio eich amddiffyniad os na fyddwch chi'n sôn, wrth gael eich holi, am rywbeth y byddwch chi'n dibynnu arno nes ymlaen yn y Llys. Gall unrhyw beth yr ydych yn ei ddweud gael ei roi fel tystiolaeth.*".

See *Note 4*.

G:3.6 Minor deviations from the words of any caution given in accordance with this code do not constitute a breach of this code, provided the sense of the relevant caution is preserved. See *Note 5*.

G:3.7 *Not used.*

G:4 Records of arrest

(a) General

G:4.1 The arresting officer is required to record in his pocket book or by other methods used for recording information: **A-211**

- the nature and circumstances of the offence leading to the arrest;
- the reason or reasons why arrest was necessary;
- the giving of the caution; and
- anything said by the person at the time of arrest.

G:4.2 Such a record should be made at the time of the arrest unless impracticable to do. If not made at that time, the record should then be completed as soon as possible thereafter.

G:4.3 On arrival at the police station or after being first arrested at the police station, the arrested person must be brought before the custody officer as soon as practicable and a custody record must be opened in accordance with section 2 of Code C. The information given by the arresting officer on the circumstances and reason or reasons for arrest shall be recorded as part of the custody record. Alternatively, a copy of the record made by the officer in accordance with paragraph 4.1 above shall be attached as part of the custody record. See paragraph 2.2 and Code C, paras 3.4 and 10.3.

G:4.4 The custody record will serve as a record of the arrest. Copies of the custody record will be provided in accordance with paragraphs 2.4 and 2.4A of Code C and access for inspection of the original record in accordance with paragraph 2.5 of Code C.

(b) Interviews and arrests

G:4.5 Records of interviews, significant statements or silences will be treated in the same way as set out in sections 10 and 11 of Code C and in Codes E and F (audio and visual recording of interviews).

Notes for guidance

G:1 For the purposes of this code, "offence" means any statutory or common law offence for which a person may be tried by a magistrates' court or the Crown Court and punished if convicted. [The note then gives examples of statutory and common law offences.] **A-212**

G:1A This code does not apply to powers of arrest conferred on constables under any arrest warrant, for example, a warrant issued under the Magistrates' Courts Act 1980, ss.1 or 13, or the Bail Act 1976, s.7(1), or to the powers of constables to arrest without warrant other than under section 24 of PACE for an offence. These other powers to arrest without warrant do not depend on the arrested person committing any specific offence and include:

- *PACE, s.46A, arrest of person who fails to answer police bail to attend police station or is suspected of breaching any condition of that bail for the custody officer to decide whether they should be kept in police detention which applies whether or not the person commits an offence under section 6 of the Bail Act 1976 (e.g. failing without reasonable cause to surrender to custody);*
- *Bail Act 1976, s.7(3), arrest of person bailed to attend court who is suspected of breaching, or is believed likely to breach, any condition of bail to take them to court for bail to be re-considered;*
- *Children and Young Persons Act 1969, s.32(1A) (absconding) - arrest to return the person to the place where they are required to reside;*
- *Immigration Act 1971, Sched. 2, to arrest a person liable to examination to determine their right to remain in the U.K.;*
- *Mental Health Act 1983, s.136 to remove person suffering from mental disorder to place of safety for assessment;*
- *Prison Act 1952, s.49, arrest to return person unlawfully at large to the prison, etc., where they are liable to be detained;*
- *Road Traffic Act 1988, s.6D, arrest of driver following the outcome of a preliminary roadside test requirement to enable the driver to be required to provide an evidential sample;*
- *common law power to stop or prevent a breach of the peace—after arrest a person aged 18 or over may be brought before a justice of the peace court to show cause why they should not be bound over to keep the peace - not criminal proceedings.*

G:1B Juveniles should not be arrested at their place of education unless this is unavoidable. When a juvenile is arrested at their place of education, the principal or their nominee must be informed (from Code C, Note 11D).

G:2 Facts and information relevant to a person's suspected involvement in an offence should not be confined to those which tend to indicate the person has committed or attempted to commit the offence. Before making a decision to arrest, a constable should take account of any facts and information that are available, including claims of innocence made by the person, that might dispel the suspicion.

G:2A Particular examples of facts and information which might point to a person's innocence and may tend to dispel suspicion include those which relate to the statutory defence provided by the Criminal Law Act 1967, s.3(1) which allows the use of reasonable force in the prevention of crime or making an arrest and the common law of self-defence. This may be relevant when a person appears, or claims, to have been acting reasonably in defence of themselves or others or to prevent their property or the property of others from being stolen, destroyed or damaged, particularly if the offence alleged is based on the use of unlawful force, e.g. a criminal assault. When investigating allegations involving the use of force by school staff, the power given to all school staff under the Education and Inspections Act 2006, s.93, to use reasonable force to prevent their pupils from committing any offence, injuring persons, damaging property or prejudicing the maintenance of good order and discipline may be similarly relevant. The Association of Chief Police Officers and the Crown Prosecution Service have published joint guidance to help the public understand the meaning of reasonable force and what to expect from the police and CPS in cases which involve claims of self-defence. Separate advice for school staff on their powers to use reasonable force is available from the Department for Education.

G:2B If a constable who is dealing with an allegation of crime and considering the need to arrest becomes an investigator for the purposes of the Code of Practice under the Criminal Procedure and Investigations Act 1996, the officer should, in accordance with paragraph 3.5 of that code, "pursue all reasonable lines of inquiry, whether these point towards or away from the suspect. What is reasonable in each case will depend on the particular circumstances."

G:2C For a constable to have reasonable grounds for believing it necessary to arrest, he or she is not required to be satisfied that there is no viable alternative to arrest. However, it does mean that in all cases, the officer should consider that arrest is the practical, sensible and proportionate option in all the circumstances at the time the decision is made. This applies equally to a person in police detention after being arrested for an offence who is suspected of involvement in a further offence and the necessity to arrest them for that further offence is being considered.

G:2D Although a warning is not expressly required, officers should if practicable, consider whether a warning which points out their offending behaviour, and explains why, if they do not stop, the resulting consequences may make their arrest necessary. Such a warning might:

- *if heeded, avoid the need to arrest, or*
- *if it is ignored, support the need to arrest and also help prove the mental element of certain offences, for example, the person's intent or awareness, or help to rebut a defence that they were acting reasonably.*

A person who is warned that they may be liable to arrest if their real name and address cannot be ascertained, should be given a reasonable opportunity to establish their real name and address before deciding that either or both are unknown and cannot be readily ascertained or that there are reasonable grounds to doubt that a name and address they have given is their real name and address. They should be told why their name is not known and cannot be readily ascertained and (as the case may be) of the grounds for doubting that a name and address they have given is their real name and address, including, for example, the reason why a particular document the person has produced to verify their real name and/or address, is not sufficient.

G:2E The meaning of "prompt" should be considered on a case by case basis taking account of all the circumstances. It indicates that the progress of the investigation should not be delayed to the extent that it would adversely affect the effectiveness of the investigation. The arresting officer also has discretion to release the arrested person on "street bail" as an alternative to taking the person directly to the station (see Note 2J).

G:2F An officer who believes that it is necessary to interview the person suspected of committing the offence must then consider whether their arrest is necessary in order to carry out the interview. The officer is not required to interrogate the suspect to determine whether they will attend a police station voluntarily to be interviewed but they must consider whether the suspect's voluntary attendance is a practicable alternative for carrying out the interview. If it is, then arrest would not be necessary. Conversely, an officer who considers this option but is not satisfied that it is a practicable alternative, may have reasonable grounds for deciding that the arrest is necessary at the outset "on the street". Without such considerations, the officer would not be able to establish that arrest was necessary in order to interview.

Circumstances which suggest that a person's arrest "on the street" would not be necessary to interview them might be where the officer:

- *is satisfied as to their identity and address and that they will attend the police station voluntarily to be interviewed, either immediately or by arrangement at a future date and time; and*
- *is not aware of any other circumstances which indicate that voluntary attendance would not be a practicable alternative (see paragraph 2.9(e)(i) to (v)).*

When making arrangements for the person's voluntary attendance, the officer should tell the person:

- *that to properly investigate their suspected involvement in the offence they must be interviewed under caution at the police station, but in the circumstances their arrest for this purpose will not be necessary if they attend the police station voluntarily to be interviewed;*
- *that if they attend voluntarily, they will be entitled to free legal advice before, and to have a solicitor present at, the interview;*
- *that the date and time of the interview will take account of their circumstances and the needs of the investigation; and*
- *that if they do not agree to attend voluntarily at a time which meets the needs of the investigation, or having so agreed, fail to attend, or having attended, fail to remain for the interview to be completed, their arrest will be necessary to enable them to be interviewed.*

G:2G When the person attends the police station voluntarily for interview by arrangement as in Note 2F above, their arrest on arrival at the station prior to interview would only be justified if:

- *new information coming to light after the arrangements were made indicates that from that time, voluntary attendance ceased to be a practicable alternative and the person's arrest became necessary; and*
- *it was not reasonably practicable for the person to be arrested before they attended the station.*

If a person who attends the police station voluntarily to be interviewed decides to leave before the interview is complete, the police would at that point be entitled to consider whether their arrest was necessary to carry out the interview. The possibility that the person might decide to leave during the interview is therefore not a valid reason for arresting them before the interview has commenced (see Code C, para. 3.21).

G:2H The necessity criteria do not permit arrest solely to enable the routine taking, checking (speculative searching) and retention of fingerprints, samples, footwear impressions and photographs when there are no prior grounds to believe that checking and comparing the fingerprints, etc., or taking a photograph would provide relevant evidence of the person's involvement in the offence concerned or would help to ascertain or verify their real identity.

G:2I The necessity criteria do not permit arrest for an offence solely because it happens to be one of the statutory drug testing "trigger offences" (see Code C, Note 17E) when there is no suspicion that Class A drug misuse might have caused or contributed to the offence.

G:2J Having determined that the necessity criteria have been met and having made the arrest, the officer can then consider the use of street bail on the basis of the effective and efficient progress of the investigation of the offence in question. It gives the officer discretion to compel the person to attend a police station at a date/ time that best suits the overall needs of the particular investigation. Its use is not confined to dealing with child care issues or allowing officers to attend to more urgent operational duties and granting street bail does not retrospectively negate the need to arrest.

G:3 An arrested person must be given sufficient information to enable them to understand they have been deprived of their liberty and the reason they have been arrested, as soon as practicable after the arrest, e.g. when a person is arrested on suspicion of committing an offence they must be informed of the nature of the suspected offence and when and where it was committed. The suspect must also be informed of the reason or reasons why arrest is considered necessary. Vague or technical language should be avoided. When explaining why one or more of the arrest criteria apply, it is not necessary to disclose any specific details that might undermine or otherwise adversely affect any investigative processes. An example might be the conduct of a formal interview when prior disclosure of such details might give the suspect an opportunity to fabricate an innocent explanation or to otherwise conceal lies from the interviewer.

G:4 Nothing in this code requires a caution to be given or repeated when informing a person not under arrest they may be prosecuted for an offence. However, a court will not be able to draw any inferences under the Criminal Justice and Public Order Act 1994, s.34, if the person was not cautioned.

G:5 If it appears a person does not understand the caution, the person giving it should explain it in their own words.

G:6 Certain powers available as the result of an arrest - for example, entry and search of premises, detention without charge beyond 24 hours, holding a person incommunicado and delaying access to legal advice - only apply in respect of indictable offences and are subject to the specific requirements on authorisation as set out in PACE and the relevant code of practice.

(9) Detention, treatment and questioning of terrorist suspects

A-213 The Police and Criminal Evidence Act 1984 (Code of Practice C and Code of Practice H) Order 2006 (SI 2006/1938) provided for a revised Code C, and for a new Code H (on detention, treatment and questioning by police officers of persons under section 41 of, and Schedule 8 to, the Terrorism Act 2000), to come into operation on 25 July 2006. The new codes were consequential upon the commencement of the provisions of the Terrorism Act 2006, which were concerned with the 28-day detention of those arrested under section 41 of the 2000 Act. Whereas Code C had previously regulated the detention, treatment and questioning of those detained following arrest under section 41, from that date onwards these matters were regulated by Code H. Code C was revised so as to remove references to detention under the 2000 Act. The new Code H largely mirrored the provisions of Code C, but with various differences.

A revised Code H came into force on 10 July 2012, and further revisions came into force on 27 October 2013, 2 June 2014, 23 February 2017 and 31 July 2018.

The text that follows is that of a further revision that came into force on 21 August 2019 (as to which, see above, A-1).

H. CODE OF PRACTICE IN CONNECTION WITH THE DETENTION, TREATMENT AND QUESTIONING BY POLICE OFFICERS OF PERSONS UNDER SECTION 41 OF, AND SCHEDULE 8 TO, THE TERRORISM ACT 2000

POLICE AND CRIMINAL EVIDENCE ACT 1984 CODE H REVISED

CODE OF PRACTICE IN CONNECTION WITH: THE DETENTION, TREATMENT AND QUESTIONING BY POLICE OFFICERS OF PERSONS IN POLICE DETENTION UNDER SECTION 41 OF, AND SCHEDULE 8 TO, THE TERRORISM ACT 2000

THE TREATMENT AND QUESTIONING BY POLICE OFFICERS OF DETAINED PERSONS IN RESPECT OF WHOM AN AUTHORISATION TO QUESTION AFTER CHARGE HAS BEEN GIVEN UNDER SECTION 22 OF THE COUNTER-TERRORISM ACT 2008

Commencement - Transitional Arrangements

A-214 This Code applies to people detained under the terrorism provisions after 00:00 on 21 August 2019 notwithstanding that their period of detention may have commenced before that time.

H:1 General

A-214a H:1.0 The powers and procedures in this Code must be used fairly, responsibly, with respect for the people to whom they apply and without unlawful discrimination. Under the Equality Act 2010, section 149 (Public sector Equality Duty), police forces must, in carrying out their functions, have due regard to the need to eliminate unlawful discrimination, harassment, victimisation and any other conduct which is prohibited by that Act, to advance equality of opportunity between people who share a relevant protected characteristic and people who do not share it, and to foster good relations between those persons. The Equality Act also makes it unlawful for police officers to discriminate against, harass or victimise any person on the grounds of the 'protected characteristics' of age, disability, gender reassignment, race, religion or belief, sex and sexual orientation, marriage and civil partnership, pregnancy and maternity, when using their powers. See *Notes 1A* and *1AA.*

H:1.1 This Code of Practice applies to, and *only* to:

(a) persons in police detention after being arrested under section 41 of the Terrorism Act 2000 (TACT) and detained under section 41 of, or Schedule 8 to that Act and *not charged,* and

(b) detained persons in respect of whom an authorisation has been given under section 22 of the Counter-Terrorism Act 2008 (post-charge questioning of terrorist suspects) to interview them in which case, section 15 of this Code will apply.

H:1.2 The provisions in PACE Code C apply when a person:

(a) is in custody *otherwise* than as a result of being arrested under section 41 of TACT or detained for examination under Schedule 7 to TACT (see *paragraph 1.4*);
(b) is charged with an offence, or
(c) is being questioned about any offence after being charged with that offence *without* an authorisation being given under section 22 of the Counter-Terrorism Act 2008.

See *Note 1N*.

H:1.3 In this Code references to an offence and to a person's involvement or suspected involvement in an offence where the person has not been charged with an offence, include being concerned, or suspected of being concerned, in the commission, preparation or instigation of acts of terrorism.

H:1.4 The Code of Practice issued under paragraph 6 of Schedule 14 to TACT applies to persons detained for examination under Schedule 7 to TACT. See *Note 1N*.

H:1.5 All persons in custody must be dealt with expeditiously, and released as soon as the need for detention no longer applies.

H:1.6 There is no provision for bail under TACT before or after charge. See *Note 1N*.

H:1.7 An officer must perform the assigned duties in this Code as soon as practicable. An officer will not be in breach of this Code if delay is justifiable and reasonable steps are taken to prevent unnecessary delay. The custody record shall show when a delay has occurred and the reason. See *Note 1H*.

H:1.8 This Code of Practice must be readily available at all police stations for consultation by: **A-214b**

- police officers;
- police staff;
- detained persons;
- members of the public.

H:1.9 The provisions of this Code:

- include the *Annexes*;
- do not include the *Notes for Guidance*.

H:1.10 If at any time an officer has any reason to suspect that a person of any age may be vulnerable (see *paragraph 1.17(d)*) in the absence of clear evidence to dispel that suspicion, that person shall be treated as such for the purposes of this Code and to establish whether any such reason may exist in relation to a person suspected of committing an offence (see *paragraph 10.1* and *Note 10A*), the custody officer in the case of a detained person, or the officer investigating the offence in the case of a person who has not been arrested or detained, shall take, or cause to be taken, (see *paragraph 3.5* and *Note 3I*) the following action:

(a) reasonable enquiries shall be made to ascertain what information is available that is relevant to any of the factors described in *paragraph 1.17(d)* as indicating that the person may be vulnerable might apply;
(b) a record shall be made describing whether any of those factors appear to apply and provide any reason to suspect that the person may be vulnerable or (as the case may be) may not be vulnerable; and
(c) the record mentioned in sub-paragraph (b) shall be made available to be taken into account by police officers, police staff and any others who, in accordance with the provisions of this or any other Code, are required or entitled to communicate with the person in question. This would include any solicitor, appropriate adult and health care professional and is particularly relevant to communication for the purpose of interviewing and questioning after charge (see *sections 11, 12* and *15*), live link interpretation (see *paragraph 13.12*) and reviews and extensions of detention (see *section 14*).

See *Notes 1G, 1GA, 1GB* and *1GC*.

H:1.11 Anyone who appears to be under 18 shall, in the absence of clear evidence that they are older, be treated as a juvenile for the purposes of this Code. **A-214c**

H:1.11A *Not used*.

H:1.12 If a person appears to be blind, seriously visually impaired, deaf, unable to read or speak or has difficulty orally because of a speech impediment, they shall be treated as such for the purposes of this Code in the absence of clear evidence to the contrary.

H:1.13 "The appropriate adult" means, in the case of a:

(a) juvenile:
  (i) the parent, guardian or, if the juvenile is in the care of a local authority or voluntary organisation, a person representing that authority or organisation (see *Note 1B*);
  (ii) a social worker of a local authority (see *Note 1C*);
  (iii) failing these, some other responsible adult aged 18 or over who is *not*:
    ~ a police officer;
    ~ employed by the police;

~ under the direction or control of the chief officer of a police force;
~ a person who provides services under contractual arrangements (but without being employed by the chief officer of a police force), to assist that force in relation to the discharge of its chief officer's functions,

whether or not they are on duty at the time.

See *Note 1F*.

(b) a person who is vulnerable: See *paragraph 1.10* and *Note 1D*

(i) a relative, guardian or other person responsible for their care or custody;

(ii) someone experienced in dealing with vulnerable persons but who is *not*:

~ a police officer;
~ employed by the police;
~ under the direction or control of the chief officer of a police force;
~ a person who provides services under contractual arrangements (but without being employed by the chief officer of a police force), to assist that force in relation to the discharge of its chief officer's functions,

whether or not they are on duty at the time;

(iii) failing these, some other responsible adult aged 18 or over who is other than a person described in the bullet points in sub-paragraph (b)(ii) above.

See *Note 1F*.

A-214d H:1.13A The role of the appropriate adult is to safeguard the rights, entitlements and welfare of juveniles and vulnerable persons (see *paragraphs 1.10* and *1.11* to whom the provisions of this and any other Code of Practice apply. For this reason, the appropriate adult is expected, amongst other things, to:

- support, advise and assist them when, in accordance with this Code or any other Code of Practice, they are given or asked to provide information or participate in any procedure;
- observe whether the police are acting properly and fairly to respect their rights and entitlements, and inform an officer of the rank of inspector or above if they consider that they are not;
- assist them to communicate with the police whilst respecting their right to say nothing unless they want to as set out in the terms of the caution see *paragraphs 10.5* and *10.5*);
- help them understand their rights and ensure that those rights are protected and respected (see *paragraphs 3.17, 3.18, 6.6, and 11.10.*

H:1.14 If this Code requires a person be given certain information, they do not have to be given it if at the time they are incapable of understanding what is said, are violent or may become violent or in urgent need of medical attention, but they must be given it as soon as practicable.

H:1.15 References to a custody officer include any police officer who for the time being, is performing the functions of a custody officer.

H:1.16 When this Code requires the prior authority or agreement of an officer of at least inspector or superintendent rank, that authority may be given by a sergeant or chief inspector authorised by section 107 of PACE to perform the functions of the higher rank under TACT.

H:1.17 In this Code:

(a) "designated person" means a person other than a police officer, who has specified powers and duties conferred or imposed on them by designation under section 38 or 39 of the Police Reform Act 2002;

(b) reference to a police officer includes a designated person acting in the exercise or performance of the powers and duties conferred or imposed on them by their designation.

(c) if there is doubt as to whether the person should be treated, or continue to be treated, as being male or female in the case of:

(i) a search or other procedure to which this Code applies which may only be carried out or observed by a person of the *same* sex as the detainee; or

(ii) any other procedure which requires action to be taken or information to be given that depends on whether the person is to be treated as being male or female;

then the gender of the detainee and other parties concerned should be established and recorded in line with Annex I of this Code.

(d) 'vulnerable' applies to any person who, because of their mental health condition or mental disorder (see *Notes 1G* and *1GB*):

(i) may have difficulty understanding or communicating effectively about the full implications for them of any procedures and processes connected with:

- their arrest and detention at a police station or elsewhere;
- the exercise of their rights and entitlements.

(ii) does not appear to understand the significance of what they are told, of questions they are asked or of their replies.

(iii) appears to be particularly prone to:
- becoming confused and unclear about their position;
- providing unreliable, misleading or incriminating information without knowing or wishing to do so;
- accepting or acting on suggestions from others without consciously knowing or wishing to do so; or
- readily agreeing to suggestions or proposals without any protest or question.

H:1.18 Designated persons are entitled to use reasonable force as follows: **A-214e**

(a) when exercising a power conferred on them which allows a police officer exercising that power to use reasonable force, a designated person has the same entitlement to use force; and

(b) at other times when carrying out duties conferred or imposed on them that also entitle them to use reasonable force, for example:
- when at a police station carrying out the duty to keep detainees for whom they are responsible under control and to assist any other police officer or designated person to keep any detainee under control and to prevent their escape.
- when securing, or assisting any other police officer or designated person in securing, the detention of a person at a police station.
- when escorting, or assisting any other police officer or designated person in escorting, a detainee within a police station.
- for the purpose of saving life or limb; or
- preventing serious damage to property.

H:1.19 Nothing in this Code prevents the custody officer, or other police officer or designated person (see *paragraph 1.17(a)*) given custody of the detainee by the custody officer, from allowing another person (see (a) and (b) below) to carry out individual procedures or tasks at the police station if the law allows. However, the officer or designated person given custody remains responsible for making sure the procedures and tasks are carried out correctly in accordance with the Codes of Practice (see *paragraph 3.5* and *Note 3I*). The other person who is allowed to carry out the procedures or tasks must be someone who *at that time*, is:

(a) under the direction and control of the chief officer of the force responsible for the police station in question; or

(b) providing services under contractual arrangements (but without being employed by the chief officer the police force), to assist a police force in relation to the discharge of its chief officer's functions.

H:1.20 Designated persons and others mentioned in sub-paragraphs (a) and (b) of *paragraph 1.19* must have regard to any relevant provisions of this Code.

H:1.21 In any provision of this or any other Code of Practice which allows or requires police officers or police staff to make a record in their report book, the references to report book shall include any official report book or electronic recording device issued to them that enables the record in question to be made and dealt with in accordance with that provision. References in this and any other Code to written records, forms and signatures include electronic records and forms and electronic confirmation that identifies the person making the record or completing the form.

Chief officers must be satisfied as to the integrity and security of the devices, records and forms to which this paragraph applies and that use of those devices, records and forms satisfies relevant data protection legislation.

Notes for Guidance

H:1A This Code applies specifically to people detained under terrorism legislation. See PACE Code C (Detention) for detailed provisions and guidance that apply to persons who attend police stations and other locations voluntarily to assist with an investigation. **A-214f**

H:1AA In paragraph 1.0, under the Equality Act 2010, section 149, the 'relevant protected characteristics' are age, disability, gender reassignment, pregnancy and maternity, race, religion/belief and sex and sexual orientation. For further detailed guidance and advice on the Equality Act, see: https://www.gov.uk/guidance/equality-act-2010-guidance.

H:1B A person, including a parent or guardian, should not be an appropriate adult if they:
- *are:*
  - *suspected of involvement in the offence or involvement in the commission, preparation or instigation of acts of terrorism;*
  - *the victim; a witness;*
  - *involved in the investigation.*
- *received admissions prior to attending to act as the appropriate adult.*

Note: If a juvenile's parent is estranged from the juvenile, they should not be asked to act as the appropriate adult if the juvenile expressly and specifically objects to their presence.

H:1C If a juvenile admits an offence to, or in the presence of, a social worker or member of a youth offending team other than during the time that person is acting as the juvenile's appropriate adult, another appropriate adult should be appointed in the interest of fairness.

H:1D In the case of someone who is vulnerable, it may be more satisfactory if the appropriate adult is someone experienced or trained in their care rather than a relative lacking such qualifications. But if the person prefers a relative to a better qualified stranger or objects to a particular person their wishes should, if practicable, be respected.

H:1E A detainee should always be given an opportunity, when an appropriate adult is called to the police station, to consult privately with a solicitor in the appropriate adult's absence if they want. An appropriate adult is not subject to legal privilege.

H:1F An appropriate adult who is not a parent or guardian in the case of a juvenile, or a relative, guardian or carer in the case of a vulnerable person, must be independent of the police as their role is to safeguard the rights and entitlements of a detained person. Additionally, a solicitor or independent custody visitor who is present at the police station and acting in that capacity may not be the appropriate adult.

H:1G An adult may be vulnerable as a result of a having a mental health condition or mental disorder. Similarly, simply because an individual does not have, or is not known to have, any such condition or disorder, does not mean that they are not vulnerable for the purposes of this Code. It is therefore important that the custody officer in the case of a detained person considers, on a case by case basis whether any of the factors described in paragraph 1.17(d) might apply to the person in question. In doing so, the officer must take into account the particular circumstances of the individual and how the nature of the investigation might affect them and bear in mind that juveniles, by virtue of their age will always require an appropriate adult.

A-214g *H:1GA For the purposes of paragraph 1.10(a), examples of relevant information that may be available include:*

- *the behaviour of the adult or juvenile;*
- *the mental health and capacity of the adult or juvenile;*
- *what the adult or juvenile says about themselves;*
- *information from relatives and friends of the adult or juvenile;*
- *information from police officers and staff and from police records;*
- *information from health and social care (including liaison and diversion services) and other professionals who know, or have had previous contact with, the individual and may be able to contribute to assessing their need for help and support from an appropriate adult. This includes contacts and assessments arranged by the police or at the request of the individual or (as applicable) their appropriate adult or solicitor.*

H:1GB The Mental Health Act 1983 Code of Practice at page 26 describes the range of clinically recognised conditions which can fall with the meaning of mental disorder for the purpose of paragraph 1.17(d). The Code is published here: https://www.gov.uk/government/publications/code-of-practice-mental-health-act-1983.

H:1GC When a person is under the influence of drink and/or drugs, it is not intended that they are to be treated as vulnerable and requiring an appropriate adult for the purpose of unless other information indicates that any of the factors described in paragraph 1.17(d) may apply to that person. When the person has recovered from the effects of drink and/or drugs, they should be re-assessed in accordance with paragraph 1.10.

H:1H Paragraph 1.7 is intended to cover delays which may occur in processing detainees e.g. if:

- *a large number of suspects are brought into the station simultaneously to be placed in custody;*
- *interview rooms are all being used;*
- *there are difficulties contacting an appropriate adult, solicitor or interpreter.*

H:1I The custody officer must remind the appropriate adult and detainee about the right to legal advice and record any reasons for waiving it in accordance with section 6.

H:1J Not used

H:1K This Code does not affect the principle that all citizens have a duty to help police officers to prevent crime and discover offenders. This is a civic rather than a legal duty; but when police officers are trying to discover whether, or by whom, offences have been committed, they are entitled to question any person from whom they think useful information can be obtained, subject to the restrictions imposed by this Code. A person's declaration that they are unwilling to reply does not alter this entitlement.

H:1L If a person is moved from a police station to receive medical treatment, or for any other reason, the period of detention is still calculated from the time of arrest under section 41 of TACT (or, if a person was being detained under TACT Schedule 7 when arrested, from the time at which the examination under Schedule 7 began).

H:1M Under Paragraph 1 of Schedule 8 to TACT, all police stations are designated for detention of persons arrested under section 41 of TACT. Paragraph 4 of Schedule 8 requires that the constable who arrests a person under section 41 takes them as soon as practicable to the police station which the officer considers is "most appropriate".

H:1N The powers under Part IV of PACE to detain and release on bail (before or after charge) a person arrested under section 24 of PACE for any offence (see PACE Code G (Arrest)) do not apply to persons whilst they are detained under the terrorism powers following their arrest/detention under section 41 of, or Schedule 7 to,

TACT. If when the grounds for detention under these powers cease the person is arrested under section 24 of PACE for a specific offence, the detention and bail provisions of PACE will apply and must be considered from the time of that arrest.

H:1O Not used.

H:1P Not used.

H:2 Custody records

H:2.1 When a person is: A-215

- brought to a police station following arrest under TACT section 41,
- arrested under TACT section 41 at a police station having attended there voluntarily,
- brought to a police station and there detained to be questioned in accordance with an authorisation under section 22 of the Counter-Terrorism Act 2008 (post-charge questioning) (see *Notes 15A* and *15B*), or
- at a police station and there detained when authority for post-charge questioning is given under section 22 of the Counter-Terrorism Act 2008 (see *Notes 15A* and *15B*),

they should be brought before the custody officer as soon as practicable after their arrival at the station or, if appropriate, following the authorisation of post-charge questioning or following arrest after attending the police station voluntarily *see Note 3H*. A person is deemed to be "at a police station" for these purposes if they are within the boundary of any building or enclosed yard which forms part of that police station.

H:2.2 A separate custody record must be opened as soon as practicable for each person described in *paragraph 2.1*. All information recorded under this Code must be recorded as soon as practicable in the custody record unless otherwise specified. Any audio or video recording made in the custody area is not part of the custody record.

H:2.3 If any action requires the authority of an officer of a specified rank, this must be noted in the custody record, subject to *paragraph 2.8*.

H:2.3A If a person is arrested under TACT, section 41 and taken to a police station as a result of a search in the exercise of any stop and search power to which PACE Code A (Stop and search) or the 'search powers code' issued under TACT applies, the officer carrying out the search is responsible for ensuring that the record of that stop and search is made as part of the person's custody record. The custody officer must then ensure that the person is asked if they want a copy of the search record and if they do, that they are given a copy as soon as practicable. The person's entitlement to a copy of the search record which is made as part of their custody record is in addition to, and does not affect, their entitlement to a copy of their custody record or any other provisions of section 2 (Custody records) of this Code. See Code A *paragraph 4.2B* and the TACT search powers code *paragraph 5.3.5*).

H:2.4 The custody officer is responsible for the custody record's accuracy and completeness and for making sure the record or copy of the record accompanies a detainee if they are transferred to another police station. The record shall show the: A-215a

- time and reason for transfer;
- time a person is released from detention.

H:2.5 The detainees solicitor and appropriate adult must be permitted to inspect the detainee's custody record as soon as practicable after their arrival at the station and at any other time whilst the person is detained.

On request, the detainee, their solicitor and appropriate adult must be allowed to inspect the following records, as promptly as is practicable at any time whilst the person is detained:

(a) The information about the circumstances and reasons for the detainee's arrest as recorded in the custody record in accordance with *paragraph 3.4*. This applies to any further reasons which come to light and are recorded whilst the detainee is detained;

(b) The record of the grounds for each authorisation to keep the person in custody. The authorisations to which this applies are the same as those described in *paragraph 2* of *Annex M* of this Code.

Access to the custody record for the purposes of this paragraph must be arranged and agreed with the custody officer and may not unreasonably interfere with the custody officer's duties or the justifiable needs of the investigation. A record shall be made when access is allowed. This access is in addition to the requirements in *paragraphs 3.4(b), 11.1* and *14.0* to provide information about the reasons for arrest and detention and in *14.4A* to give the detainee written information about the grounds for continued detention when an application for a warrant of further detention (or for an extension of such a warrant) is made.

H:2.6 When a detainee leaves police detention or is taken before a court they, their legal representative or appropriate adult shall be given, on request, a copy of the custody record as soon as practicable. This entitlement lasts for 12 months after release.

H:2.7 The detainee, appropriate adult or legal representative shall be permitted to inspect the original custody record once the detained person is no longer being held under the provisions of TACT section 41 and Schedule 8 or being questioned after charge as authorised under section 22 of the Counter-Terrorism Act 2008 (see *section 15*), provided they give reasonable notice of their request. Any such inspection shall be noted in the custody record.

H:2.8 All entries in custody records must be timed and identified by the maker. Nothing in this Code requires the identity of officers or other police staff to be recorded or disclosed in the case of enquiries linked to the investigation of terrorism. In these cases, they shall use their warrant or other identification numbers and the name of their police station, *see Note 2A*. Records entered on computer shall be timed and contain the operator's identification.

H:2.9 The fact and time of any detainee's refusal to sign a custody record, when asked in accordance with this Code, must be recorded.

Note for Guidance

A-215b *H:2A The purpose of paragraph 2.8 is to protect those involved in terrorist investigations or arrests of terrorist suspects from the possibility that those arrested, their associates or other individuals or groups may threaten or cause harm to those involved.*

H:3 Initial action

(a) Detained persons - normal procedure

A-216 H:3.1 When a person to whom paragraph 2.1 applies is at a police station, the custody officer must make sure the person is told clearly about:

(a) the following continuing rights which may be exercised at any stage during the period in custody:
  (i) their right to consult privately with a solicitor and that free independent legal advice is available as in *section 6*;
  (ii) their right to have someone informed of their arrest as in *section 5*;
  (iii) their right to consult this Code of Practice (see *Note 3D*);
  (iv) their right to medical help as in *section 9*;
  (v) their right to remain silent as set out in the caution (see *section 10*); and
  (vi) if applicable, their right to interpretation and translation (see *paragraph 3.14*) and the right to communication with their High Commission, Embassy or Consulate (see *paragraph 3.14A*).

(b) their right to be informed about why they have been arrested and detained on suspicion of being involved in the commission, preparation or instigation of acts of terrorism in accordance with *paragraphs 2.5, 3.4* and *11.1A* of this Code.

A-216a H:3.2 The detainee must also be given a written notice, which contains information:

(a) to allow them to exercise their rights by setting out:
  (i) their rights under paragraph 3.1 (subject to *paragraphs 3.14* and *3.14A*);
  (ii) the arrangements for obtaining legal advice, see *section 6*;
  (iii) their right to a copy of the custody record as in *paragraph 2.6*;
  (iv) the caution in the terms prescribed in *section 10*;
  (v) their rights to:
    - information about the reasons and grounds for their arrest and detention and (as the case may be) any further grounds and reasons that come to light whilst they are in custody;
    - to have access to records and documents which are essential to effectively challenging the lawfulness of their arrest and detention;

    as required in accordance with *paragraphs 2.4, 2.4A, 2.5, 3.4, 11.1, 14.0* and *15.7A(c)* of this Code and *paragraph 3.3* of *Code G;*
  (vi) the maximum period for which they may be kept in police detention without being charged, when detention must be reviewed and when release is required.
  (vii) their right to communicate with their High Commission Embassy or Consulate in accordance with *section 7* of this Code, see *paragraph 3.14A*;
  (xiii)their right to medical assistance in accordance with *section 9* of this Code
  (xi) their right, if they are prosecuted, to have access to the evidence in the case in accordance with the Criminal Procedure and Investigations Act 1996, the Attorney General's Guidelines on Disclosure and the common law and the Criminal Procedure Rules; and

(b) briefly setting out their entitlements while in custody, by:

(i) mentioning:
- the provisions relating to the conduct of interviews;
- the circumstances in which an appropriate adult should be available to assist the detainee and their statutory rights to make representations whenever the need for their detention is reviewed.

(ii) listing the entitlements in this Code, concerning
- reasonable standards of physical comfort;
- adequate food and drink;
- access to toilets and washing facilities, clothing, medical attention, and exercise when practicable;
- personal needs relating to health, hygiene and welfare concerning the provision of menstrual and any other health, hygiene and welfare products needed by the detainee in question and speaking about these in private to a member of the custody staff (see *paragraphs 9.4A* and *9.4B*).

See *Note 3A*

H:3.2A The detainee must be given an opportunity to read the notice and shall be asked to sign the custody record to acknowledge receipt of the notices. Any refusal must be recorded on the custody record.

H:3.3 *Not used.*

H:3.3A An audio version of the notice and an 'easy read' illustrated version should also be provided if they are available (see *Note 3A*).

H:3.4 **A-216b**

(a) The custody officer shall:
- record that the person was arrested under section 41 of TACT and the reason(s) for the arrest on the custody record. See *paragraph 10.2 and Note 3G*
- note on the custody record any comment the detainee makes in relation to the arresting officer's account but shall not invite comment. If the arresting officer is not physically present when the detainee is brought to a police station, the arresting officer's account must be made available to the custody officer remotely or by a third party on the arresting officer's behalf;
- note any comment the detainee makes in respect of the decision to detain them but shall not invite comment;
- not put specific questions to the detainee regarding their involvement in any offence (see *paragraph 1.3*), nor in respect of any comments they may make in response to the arresting officer's account or the decision to place them in detention. *See paragraphs 14.1* and *14.2* and *Notes 3H, 14A* and *14B*. Such an exchange is likely to constitute an interview as in *paragraph 11.1* and require the associated safeguards in *section 11.*

Note: This sub-paragraph also applies to any further reasons and grounds for detention which come to light whilst the person is detained.

See *paragraph 11.8A* in respect of unsolicited comments.

If the first review of detention is carried out at this time, see *paragraphs 14.1* and *14.2*, and Part II of Schedule 8 to the Terrorism Act 2000 in respect of action by the review officer.

(b) Documents and materials which are essential to effectively challenging the lawfulness the detainee's arrest and detention must be made available to the detainee or their solicitor. Documents and material will be "essential" for this purpose if they are capable of undermining the reasons and grounds which make the detainee's arrest and detention necessary. The decision about what needs to be disclosed for the purpose of this requirement rests with the custody officer in consultation with the investigating officer who has the knowledge of the documents and materials in a particular case necessary to inform that decision (see *Note 3G*). A note should be made in the detainee's custody record of the fact that action has been taken under this sub-paragraph and when. The investigating officer should make a separate note of what has been made available in a particular case. This also applies for the purposes of *section 14*, see *paragraph 14.0.*

H:3.5 The custody officer or other custody staff as directed by the custody officer shall: **A-216c**

(a) ask the detainee, whether at this time, they:
   (i) would like legal advice, see *paragraph 6.4*;
   (ii) want someone informed of their detention, see *section 5*;

(b) ask the detainee to sign the custody record to confirm their decisions in respect of (*a*);

(c) determine whether the detainee:
   (i) is, or might be, in need of medical treatment or attention, see *section 9*;
   (ii) is a juvenile and/or vulnerable and therefore requires an appropriate adult (see *paragraphs 1.10, 1.11* and *3.17*);

(iia) wishes to speak in private with a member of the custody staff who may be of the same sex about any matter concerning their personal needs relating to health, hygiene and welfare (see *paragraph 9.4A*);

(iii) requires

- help to check documentation (see *paragraph 3.21*);
- an interpreter (see *paragraph 3.14* and *Note 13B*).

(ca) if the detainee is a female aged 18 or over, ask if they require or are likely to require any menstrual products whilst they are in custody (see *paragraph 9.4B*). For girls under 18, see *paragraph 3.21A*;

(d) record the decision and actions taken as applicable in respect of (*c*) and (ca).

Where any duties under this paragraph have been carried out by custody staff at the direction of the custody officer, the outcomes shall, as soon as practicable, be reported to the custody officer who retains overall responsibility for the detainee's care and safe custody and ensuring it complies with this Code. See *Note 3I*.

H:3.6 When the needs mentioned in *paragraph 3.5(c)* are being determined, the custody officer is responsible for initiating an assessment to consider whether the detainee is likely to present specific risks to custody staff, any individual who may have contact with detainee (e.g. legal advisers, medical staff), or themselves. This risk assessment must include the taking of reasonable steps to establish the detainee's identity and to obtain information about the detainee that is relevant to their safe custody, security and welfare and risks to others. Such assessments should therefore always include a check on the Police National Computer (PNC), to be carried out as soon as practicable, to identify any risks that have been highlighted in relation to the detainee. Although such assessments are primarily the custody officer's responsibility, it will be necessary to obtain information from other sources, especially the investigation team *see Note 3E*, the arresting officer or an appropriate healthcare professional, see *paragraph 9.15*. Other records held by or on behalf of the police and other UK law enforcement authorities that might provide information relevant to the detainee's safe custody, security and welfare and risk to others and to confirming their identity should also be checked. Reasons for delaying the initiation or completion of the assessment must be recorded.

H:3.7 Chief officers should ensure that arrangements for proper and effective risk assessments required by *paragraph 3.6* are implemented in respect of all detainees at police stations in their area.

H:3.8 Risk assessments must follow a structured process which clearly defines the categories of risk to be considered and the results must be incorporated in the detainee's custody record. The custody officer is responsible for making sure those responsible for the detainee's custody are appropriately briefed about the risks. The content of any risk assessment and any analysis of the level of risk relating to the person's detention is not required to be shown or provided to the detainee or any person acting on behalf of the detainee. If no specific risks are identified by the assessment, that should be noted in the custody record. See *Note 3F* and *paragraph 9.15*.

A-216d H:3.8A The content of any risk assessment and any analysis of the level of risk relating to the person's detention is not required to be shown or provided to the detainee or any person acting on behalf of the detainee. But information should not be withheld from any person acting on the detainee's behalf, for example, an appropriate adult, solicitor or interpreter, if to do so might put that person at risk.

H:3.9 Custody officers are responsible for implementing the response to any specific risk assessment, which should include for example:

- reducing opportunities for self harm;
- calling an appropriate healthcare professional;
- increasing levels of monitoring or observation;
- reducing the risk to those who come into contact with the detainee.

See *Note 3F*

H:3.10 Risk assessment is an ongoing process and assessments must always be subject to review if circumstances change.

H:3.11 If video cameras are installed in the custody area, notices shall be prominently displayed showing cameras are in use. Any request to have video cameras switched off shall be refused.

H:3.12 A constable, prison officer or other person authorised by the Secretary of State may take any steps which are reasonably necessary for:

(a) photographing the detained person;
(b) measuring the person, or
(c) identifying the person.

H:3.13 *Paragraph 3.12* concerns the power in TACT Schedule 8 Paragraph 2. The power in TACT Schedule 8 Paragraph 2 does not cover the taking of fingerprints, intimate samples or non-intimate samples, which is covered *in* TACT Schedule 8 paragraphs 10 to 15.

(b) Detained persons - special groups

A-216e H:3.14 If the detainee appears to be someone who does not speak or understand English or who has a hearing or speech impediment the custody officer must ensure:

(a) that without delay, arrangements (see *paragraph 13.1ZA*) are made for the detainee to have the assistance of an interpreter in the action under *paragraphs 3.1* to *3.5*. If the person appears to have a hearing or speech impediment, the reference to "interpreter" includes appropriate assistance necessary to comply with *paragraphs 3.1 to 3.5*. See *paragraph 13.1C* if the detainee is in Wales. See *section 13* and *Note 13B*;
(b) that in addition to the rights set out in *paragraph 3.1(i)* to *(iii)*, the detainee is told clearly about their right to interpretation and translation;
(c) that the written notice given to the detainee in accordance with *paragraph 3.2* is in a language the detainee understands and includes the right to interpretation and translation together with information about the provisions in *section 13* and Annex K, which explain how the right applies (see *Note 3A*); and
(d) that if the translation of the notice is not available, the information in the notice is given through an interpreter and a written translation provided without undue delay

H:3.14A If the detainee is a citizen of an independent Commonwealth country or a national of a foreign country, including the Republic of Ireland, the custody officer must ensure that in addition to the rights set out in *paragraph 3.1(i)* to *(v)*, they are informed as soon as practicable about their rights of communication with their High Commission, Embassy or Consulate set out in *section 7*. This right must be included in the written notice given to the detainee in accordance with *paragraph 3.2*.

H:3.15 If the detainee is a juvenile, the custody officer must, if it is practicable, ascertain the identity of a person responsible for their welfare. That person:

- may be:
  - the parent or guardian;
  - if the juvenile is in local authority or voluntary organisation care, or is otherwise being looked after under the Children Act 1989, a person appointed by that authority or organisation to have responsibility for the juvenile's welfare;
  - any other person who has, for the time being, assumed responsibility for the juvenile's welfare.
- must be informed as soon as practicable that the juvenile has been arrested, why they have been arrested and where they are detained. This right is in addition to the juvenile's right in *section 5* not to be held incommunicado. See *Note 3C*.

H:3.16 If a juvenile is known to be subject to a court order under which a person or organisation is given any degree of statutory responsibility to supervise or otherwise monitor them, reasonable steps must also be taken to notify that person or organisation (the 'responsible officer'). The responsible officer will normally be a member of a Youth Offending Team, except for a curfew order which involves electronic monitoring when the contractor providing the monitoring will normally be the responsible officer.

H:3.17 If the detainee is a juvenile or a vulnerable person, the custody officer must, as soon as practicable, ensure that: **A-216f**

- the detainee is informed of the decision that an appropriate adult is required and the reason for that decision (see *paragraph 3.5(c)(ii)* and;
- the detainee is advised:
  - of the duties of the appropriate adult as described in *paragraph 1.13A*; and
  - that they can consult privately with the appropriate adult at any time.
- the appropriate adult, who in the case of a juvenile may or may not be a person responsible for their welfare, as in *paragraph 3.15*, is informed of:
  - the grounds for their detention;
  - their whereabouts; and
- the attendance of the appropriate adult at the police station to see the detainee is secured.

H:3.18 If the appropriate adult is:

- already at the police station, the provisions of *paragraphs 3.1* to *3.5* must be complied with in the appropriate adult's presence;
- not at the station when these provisions are complied with, they must be complied with again in the presence of the appropriate adult when they arrive,

and a copy of the notice given to the detainee in accordance with *paragraph 3.2*, shall also be given to the appropriate adult if they wish to have a copy.

H:3.18A The custody officer must ensure that at the time the copy of the notice is given to the appropriate adult, or as soon as practicable thereafter, the appropriate adult is advised of the duties of the appropriate adult as described in *paragraph 1.13A*.

H:3.19 *Not used.*

H:3.20 If the detainee, or appropriate adult on the detainee's behalf, asks for a solicitor to be called to give legal advice, the provisions of *section 6* apply. (see *paragraph 6.6* and *Note 3K*).

H:3.21 If the detainee is blind, seriously visually impaired or unable to read, the custody officer shall make sure their solicitor, relative, appropriate adult or some other person likely to take an interest in them and not involved in the investigation is available to help check any documentation. When this Code requires written consent or signing the person assisting may be asked to sign instead, if the detainee prefers. This paragraph does not require an appropriate adult to be called solely to assist in checking and signing documentation for a person who is not a juvenile, or vulnerable (see *paragraph 3.17* and *Note 13C*).

H:3.21A The Children and Young Persons Act 1933, section 31, requires that arrangements must be made for ensuring that a girl under the age of 18, while detained in a police station, is under the care of a woman. The custody officer must ensure that the woman under whose care the girl is, makes the enquiries and provides the information concerning personal needs relating to their health, hygiene and welfare described in *paragraph 9.4A* and menstrual products described in *paragraph 9.4B*. See *Note 3J*. Section 31 also requires that arrangements must be made to prevent any person under 18 while being detained in a police station, from associating with an adult charged with any offence, unless that adult is a relative or the adult is jointly charged with the same offence as the person under 18.

(c) Documentation

A-216g H:3.22 The grounds for a person's detention shall be recorded, in the person's presence if practicable.

H:3.23 Action taken under *paragraphs 3.14* to *3.21A* shall be recorded.

(d) Requirements for suspects to be informed of certain rights

A-216h H:3.24 The provisions of this section identify the information which must be given to suspects who have been arrested under section 41of the Terrorism Act and cautioned in accordance with *section 10 of this Code*. It includes information required by EU Directive 2012/13 on the right to information in criminal proceedings. If a complaint is made by or on behalf of such a suspect that the information and (as the case may be) access to records and documents has not been provided as required, the matter shall be reported to an inspector to deal with as a complaint for the purposes of *paragraph 9.3*, or *paragraph 12.10* if the challenge is made during an interview. This would include, for example:

- not informing them of their rights (see *paragraph 3.1*);
- not giving them a copy of the Notice (see *paragraph 3.2(a)*)
- not providing an opportunity to read the notice (see *paragraph 3.2A*)
- not providing the required information (see *paragraphs 3.2(a), 3.14(b)* and, *3.14A*;
- not allowing access to the custody record (see *paragraph 2.5*);
- not providing a translation of the Notice (see *paragraph 3.14(c)* and *(d)*);

Notes for Guidance

A-216i *H:3A For access to the currently available notices, including 'easy-read' versions, see https://www.gov.uk/notice-of-rights-and-entitlements-a-persons-rights-in-police-detention.*

H:3B Not used.

H:3C If the juvenile is in local authority or voluntary organisation care but living with their parents or other adults responsible for their welfare, although there is no legal obligation to inform them, they should normally be contacted, as well as the authority or organisation unless they are suspected of involvement in the offence concerned. Even if the juvenile is not living with their parents, consideration should be given to informing them.

H:3D The right to consult this or other relevant Codes of Practice does not entitle the person concerned to delay unreasonably any necessary investigative or administrative action whilst they do so. Examples of action which need not be delayed unreasonably include:

- *searching detainees at the police station;*
- *taking fingerprints or non-intimate samples without consent for evidential purposes.*

H:3E The investigation team will include any officer involved in questioning a suspect, gathering or analysing evidence in relation to the offences of which the detainee is suspected of having committed. Should a custody officer require information from the investigation team, the first point of contact should be the officer in charge of the investigation.

H:3F The Detention and Custody Authorised Professional Practice (APP) produced by the College of Policing (see http://www.app.college.police.uk) provides more detailed guidance on risk assessments and identifies key risk areas which should always be considered.

H:3G Arrests under TACT section 41 can only be made where an officer has reasonable grounds to suspect that the individual concerned is a "terrorist". This differs from the constable's power of arrest for all offences under PACE, section 24, in that it need not be linked to a specific offence. There may also be circumstances where an arrest under TACT is made on the grounds of sensitive information which cannot be disclosed. In such circumstances, the grounds for arrest may be given in terms of the interpretation of a "terrorist" set out in TACT section 40(1)(a) or (b).

H:3H For the purpose of arrests under TACT section 41, the review officer is responsible for authorising detention (see paragraphs 14.1 and 14.2, and Notes 14A and 14B). The review officer's role is explained in TACT Schedule 8 Part II. A person may be detained after arrest pending the first review, which must take place as soon as practicable after the person's arrest.

H:3I A custody officer or other officer who, in accordance with this Code, allows or directs the carrying out of any task or action relating to a detainee's care, treatment, rights and entitlements by another officer or any other person must be satisfied that the officer or person concerned is suitable, trained and competent to carry out the task or action in question.

H:3J Guidance for police officers and police staff on the operational application of section 31 of the Children and Young Persons Act 1933 has been published by the College of Policing and is available at: https://www.app.college.police.uk/app-content/detention-and-custody-2/detainee-care/children-and-young-persons/#girls.

H:3K The purpose of the provisions at paragraphs 3.20 and 6.6 is to protect the rights of juvenile and vulnerable persons who may not understand the significance of what is said to them. They should always be given an opportunity, when an appropriate adult is called to the police station, to consult privately with a solicitor in the absence of the appropriate adult if they want.

H:4 Detainee's property

(a) Action

H:4.1 The custody officer is responsible for: **A-217**

(a) ascertaining what property a detainee:

(i) has with them when they come to the police station, either on first arrival at the police station or any subsequent arrivals at a police station in connection with that detention;

(ii) might have acquired for an unlawful or harmful purpose while in custody.

(b) the safekeeping of any property taken from a detainee which remains at the police station.

The custody officer may search the detainee or authorise their being searched to the extent they consider necessary, provided a search of intimate parts of the body or involving the removal of more than outer clothing is only made as in *Annex A*. A search may only be carried out by an officer of the same sex as the detainee. See *Note 4A* and *Annex I.*

H:4.2 Subject to *paragraph 4.3A,* detainees may retain clothing and personal effects at their own risk unless the custody officer considers they may use them to cause harm to themselves or others, interfere with evidence, damage property, effect an escape or they are needed as evidence. In this event, the custody officer may withhold such articles as they consider necessary and must tell the detainee why.

H:4.3 Personal effects are those items a detainee may lawfully need, use or refer to while in detention but do not include cash and other items of value.

H:4.3A For the purposes of *paragraph 4.2,* the reference to clothing and personal effects shall be treated as including menstrual and any other health, hygiene and welfare products needed by the detainee in question (see *paragraphs 9.4A* and *9.4B*) and a decision to withhold any such products must be subject to a further specific risk assessment.

(b) Documentation

H:4.4 It is a matter for the custody officer to determine whether a record should be made of the property a detained person has with him or had taken from him on arrest (*see Note 4D*). Any record made is not required to be kept as part of the custody record but the custody record should be noted as to where such a record exists and that record shall be treated as being part of the custody record for the purpose of this Code of Practice (see *paragraphs 2.4, 2.5* and *2.7*). Whenever a record is made the detainee shall be allowed to check and sign the record of property as correct. Any refusal to sign shall be recorded. **A-217a**

H:4.5 If a detainee is not allowed to keep any article of clothing or personal effects, the reason must be recorded.

Notes for Guidance

H:4A PACE, Section 54(1) and paragraph 4.1 require a detainee to be searched when it is clear the custody officer will have continuing duties in relation to that detainee or when that detainee's behaviour or offence makes an inventory appropriate. They do not require every detainee to be searched, e.g. if it is clear a person will only be detained for a short period and is not to be placed in a cell, the custody officer may decide not to search them. In such a case the custody record will be endorsed 'not searched', paragraph 4.4 will not apply, and the detainee will **A-217b** *be invited to sign the entry. If the detainee refuses, the custody officer will be obliged to ascertain what property they have in accordance with paragraph 4.1.*

H:4B Paragraph 4.4 does not require the custody officer to record on the custody record property in the detainee's possession on arrest if, by virtue of its nature, quantity or size, it is not practicable to remove it to the police station.

H:4C Paragraph 4.4 does not require items of clothing worn by the person to be recorded unless withheld by the custody officer as in paragraph 4.2.

H:4D Section 43(2) of TACT allows a constable to search a person who has been arrested under section 41 to discover whether they have anything in their possession that may constitute evidence that they are a terrorist.

H:5 Right not to be held incommunicado

(a) Action

A-218 H:5.1 Any person to whom this Code applies who is held in custody at a police station or other premises may, on request, have one named person who is a friend, relative or a person known to them who is likely to take an interest in their welfare informed at public expense of their whereabouts as soon as practicable. If the person cannot be contacted the detainee may choose up to two alternatives. If they cannot be contacted, the person in charge of detention or the investigation has discretion to allow further attempts until the information has been conveyed. See *Notes 5D* and *5E.*

H:5.2 The exercise of the above right in respect of each person nominated may be delayed only in accordance with *Annex B.*

H:5.3 The above right may be exercised each time a detainee is taken to another police station or returned to a police station having been previously transferred to prison. This Code does not afford such a right to a person on transfer to a prison, where a detainee's rights will be governed by Prison Rules, see *Annex J paragraph 4.*

H:5.4 If the detainee agrees, they may at the custody officer's discretion, receive visits from friends, family or others likely to take an interest in their welfare, or in whose welfare the detainee has an interest. Custody Officers should liaise closely with the investigation team (*see Note 3E*) to allow risk assessments to be made where particular visitors have been requested by the detainee or identified themselves to police. In circumstances where the nature of the investigation means that such requests can not be met, consideration should be given, in conjunction with a representative of the relevant scheme, to increasing the frequency of visits from independent visitor schemes. See *Notes 5B and 5C.*

H:5.5 If a friend, relative or person with an interest in the detainee's welfare enquires about their whereabouts, this information shall be given if the suspect agrees and *Annex B* does not apply. See *Note 5E.*

H:5.6 The detainee shall be given writing materials, on request, and allowed to telephone one person for a reasonable time, see *Notes 5A* and *5F.* Either or both these privileges may be denied or delayed if an officer of inspector rank or above considers sending a letter or making a telephone call may result in any of the consequences in *Annex B paragraphs 1* and 2, particularly in relation to the making of a telephone call in a language which an officer listening to the call (see paragraph 5.7) does not understand. See *Note 5G.*

Nothing in this paragraph permits the restriction or denial of the rights in *paragraphs 5.1* and *6.1.*

H:5.7 Before any letter or message is sent, or telephone call made, the detainee shall be informed that what they say in any letter, call or message (other than in a communication to a solicitor) may be read or listened to and may be given in evidence. A telephone call may be terminated if it is being abused *see Note 5G.* The costs can be at public expense at the custody officer's discretion.

H:5.8 Any delay or denial of the rights in this section should be proportionate and should last no longer than necessary.

(b) Documentation

A-218a H:5.9 A record must be kept of any:

(a) request made under this section and the action taken;
(b) letters, messages or telephone calls made or received or visit received;
(c) refusal by the detainee to have information about them given to an outside enquirer, or any refusal to see a visitor. The detainee must be asked to countersign the record accordingly and any refusal recorded.

Notes for Guidance

A-218b *H:5A A person may request an interpreter to interpret a telephone call or translate a letter.*

H:5B At the custody officer's discretion and subject to the detainee's consent, visits should be allowed when possible, subject to sufficient personnel being available to supervise a visit and any possible hindrance to the investigation. Custody Officers should bear in mind the exceptional nature of prolonged TACT detention and consider the potential benefits that visits may bring to the health and welfare of detainees who are held for extended periods.

H:5C Official visitors should be given access following consultation with the officer who has overall responsibility for the investigation provided the detainee consents, and they do not compromise safety or security or unduly delay or interfere with the progress of an investigation. Official visitors should still be required to provide appropriate identification and subject to any screening process in place at the place of detention. Official visitors may include:

- *An accredited faith representative;*
- *Members of either House of Parliament;*
- *Public officials needing to interview the prisoner in the course of their duties;*
- *Other persons visiting with the approval of the officer who has overall responsibility for the investigation;*
- *Consular officials visiting a detainee who is a national of the country they represent subject to section 7 of this Code.*

Visits from appropriate members of the Independent Custody Visitors Scheme should be dealt with in accordance with the separate Code of Practice on Independent Custody Visiting.

H:5D If the detainee does not know anyone to contact for advice or support or cannot contact a friend or relative, the custody officer should bear in mind any local voluntary bodies or other organisations that might be able to help. Paragraph 6.1 applies if legal advice is required.

H:5E In some circumstances it may not be appropriate to use the telephone to disclose information under paragraphs 5.1 and 5.5.

H:5F The telephone call at paragraph 5.6 is in addition to any communication under paragraphs 5.1 and 6.1. Further calls may be made at the custody officer's discretion.

H:5G The nature of terrorism investigations means that officers should have particular regard to the possibility of suspects attempting to pass information which may be detrimental to public safety, or to an investigation.

H:6 Right to legal advice

(a) Action

H:6.1 Unless *Annex B* applies, all detainees must be informed that they may at any time consult and communicate privately with a solicitor, whether in person, in writing or by telephone, and that free independent legal advice is available from the duty solicitor. Where an appropriate adult is in attendance, they must also be informed of this right. See *paragraph 3.1, Note 1I, Notes 6B* and *6J* **A-219**

H:6.2 A poster advertising the right to legal advice must be prominently displayed in the charging area of every police station. See *Note 6G.*

H:6.3 No police officer should, at any time, do or say anything with the intention of dissuading any person who is entitled to legal advice in accordance with this Code, from obtaining legal advice. See *Note 6ZA.*

H:6.4 The exercise of the right of access to legal advice may be delayed exceptionally only as in *Annex B.* Whenever legal advice is requested, and unless *Annex B* applies, the custody officer must act without delay to secure the provision of such advice. If, on being informed or reminded of this right, the detainee declines to speak to a solicitor in person, the officer should point out that the right includes the right to speak with a solicitor on the telephone (see *paragraph 5.6*). If the detainee continues to waive this right the officer should ask them why and any reasons should be recorded on the custody record or the interview record as appropriate. Reminders of the right to legal advice must be given as in *paragraphs 3.5, 11.3* and *5 of Annex K* of this Code and PACE Code D on the Identification of Persons by Police Officers, *paragraphs 3.17(ii)* and *6.3.* Once it is clear a detainee does not want to speak to a solicitor in person or by telephone they should cease to be asked their reasons. See *Note 6J.*

H:6.5 An officer of the rank of Commander or Assistant Chief Constable or above may give a direction under TACT Schedule 8 paragraph 9 that a detainee may only consult a solicitor within the sight and hearing of a qualified officer. Such a direction may only be given if the officer has reasonable grounds to believe that if it were not, it may result in one of the consequences set out in TACT Schedule 8 paragraph 8(4) or (5)(c). See *Annex B paragraph 3 and Note 6I.* A "qualified officer" means a police officer who:

(a) is at least the rank of inspector;
(b) is of the uniformed branch of the force of which the officer giving the direction is a member, and
(c) in the opinion of the officer giving the direction, has no connection with the detained person's case.

Officers considering the use of this power should first refer to Home Office *Circular 40/2003*.

A-219a H:6.6 In the case of a person who is a juvenile or is vulnerable, an appropriate adult should consider whether legal advice from a solicitor is required. If such a detained person wants to exercise the right to legal advice, the appropriate action should be taken and should not be delayed until the appropriate adult arrives. If the person indicates that they do not want legal advice, the appropriate adult has the right to ask for a solicitor to attend if this would be in the best interests of the person and must be so informed. In this case, action to secure the provision of advice if so requested by the appropriate adult shall be taken without delay in the same way as when requested by the person. However, the person cannot be forced to see the solicitor if they are adamant that they do not wish to do so.

H:6.7 A detainee who wants legal advice may not be interviewed or continue to be interviewed until they have received such advice unless:

(a) *Annex B* applies, when the restriction on drawing adverse inferences from silence in *Annex C* will apply because the detainee is not allowed an opportunity to consult a solicitor; or

(b) an officer of superintendent rank or above has reasonable grounds for believing that:

(i) the consequent delay might:

- lead to interference with, or harm to, evidence connected with an offence;
- lead to interference with, or physical harm to, other people;
- lead to serious loss of, or damage to, property;
- lead to alerting other people suspected of having committed an offence but not yet arrested for it;
- hinder the recovery of property obtained in consequence of the commission of an offence.

See *Note 6A*

(ii) when a solicitor, including a duty solicitor, has been contacted and has agreed to attend, awaiting their arrival would cause unreasonable delay to the process of investigation.

Note: In these cases the restriction on drawing adverse inferences from silence in *Annex C* will apply because the detainee is not allowed an opportunity to consult a solicitor.

(c) the solicitor the detainee has nominated or selected from a list:

(i) cannot be contacted;

(ii) has previously indicated they do not wish to be contacted; or

(iii) having been contacted, has declined to attend; and

- the detainee has been advised of the Duty Solicitor Scheme but has declined to ask for the duty solicitor;
- in these circumstances the interview may be started or continued without further delay provided an officer of inspector rank or above has agreed to the interview proceeding.

Note: The restriction on drawing adverse inferences from silence in *Annex C* will not apply because the detainee is allowed an opportunity to consult the duty solicitor;

(d) the detainee changes their mind, about wanting legal advice or (as the case may be) about wanting a solicitor present at the interview, and states that they no longer wish to speak to a solicitor. In these circumstances the interview may be started or continued without delay provided that:

(i) an officer of inspector rank or above:

- speaks to the detainee to enquire about the reasons for their change of mind (see *Note 6J*), and
- makes, or directs the making of, reasonable efforts to ascertain the solicitor's expected time of arrival and to inform the solicitor that the suspect has stated that they wish to change their mind and the reason (if given);

(ii) the detainee's reason for their change of mind (if given) and the outcome of the action in (i) are recorded in the custody record;

(iii) the detainee, after being informed of the outcome of the action in (i) above, confirms in writing that they want the interview to proceed without speaking or further speaking to a solicitor or (as the case may be) without a solicitor being present and do not wish to wait for a solicitor by signing an entry to this effect in the custody record;

(iv) an officer of inspector rank or above is satisfied that it is proper for the interview to proceed in these circumstances and:

- gives authority in writing for the interview to proceed and if the authority is not recorded in the custody record, the officer must ensure that the custody record shows the date and time of the authority and where it is recorded; and
- takes or directs the taking of, reasonable steps to inform the solicitor that the author-

ity has been given and the time when the interview is expected to commence and records or causes to be recorded, the outcome of this action in the custody record.

(v) When the interview starts and the interviewer reminds the suspect of their right to legal advice (see *paragraph 11.3*) and the Code of Practice issued under paragraph 3 of Schedule 8 to the Terrorism Act 2000 for the video recording with sound of interviews, the interviewer shall then ensure that the following is recorded in the interview record made in accordance with that Code:

- confirmation that the detainee has changed their mind about wanting legal advice or (as the case may be) about wanting a solicitor present and the reasons for it if given;
- the fact that authority for the interview to proceed has been given and, subject to *paragraph 2.8*, the name of the authorising officer;
- that if the solicitor arrives at the station before the interview is completed, the detainee will be so informed without delay and *a break will be taken* to allow them to speak to the solicitor if they wish, unless *paragraph 6.7(a)* applies, and
- that at any time during the interview, the detainee may again ask for legal advice and that if they do, a break will be taken to allow them to speak to the solicitor, unless *paragraph 6.7(a), (b), or (c)* applies.

Note: In these circumstances the restriction on drawing adverse inferences from silence in *Annex C* will not apply because the detainee is allowed an opportunity to consult a solicitor if they wish.

H:6.8 If *paragraph 6.7(a)* applies, where the reason for authorising the delay ceases to apply, there may be no further delay in permitting the exercise of the right in the absence of a further authorisation unless *paragraph 6.7(b), (c)* or *(d)* applies. If *paragraph 6.7(b)(i)* applies, once sufficient information has been obtained to avert the risk, questioning must cease until the detainee has received legal advice unless *paragraph 6.7(a), (b)(ii), (c)* or *(d)* applies. **A-219b**

H:6.9 A detainee who has been permitted to consult a solicitor shall be entitled on request to have the solicitor present when they are interviewed unless one of the exceptions in *paragraph 6.7* applies.

H:6.10 The solicitor may only be required to leave the interview if their conduct is such that the interviewer is unable properly to put questions to the suspect. See *Notes 6C and 6D.*

H:6.11 If the interviewer considers a solicitor is acting in such a way, they will stop the interview and consult an officer not below superintendent rank, if one is readily available, and otherwise an officer not below inspector rank not connected with the investigation. After speaking to the solicitor, the officer consulted will decide if the interview should continue in the presence of that solicitor. If they decide it should not, the suspect will be given the opportunity to consult another solicitor before the interview continues and that solicitor given an opportunity to be present at the interview. *See Note 6D.*

H:6.12 The removal of a solicitor from an interview is a serious step and, if it occurs, the officer of superintendent rank or above who took the decision will consider if the incident should be reported to the Solicitors Regulatory Authority. If the decision to remove the solicitor has been taken by an officer below superintendent rank, the facts must be reported to an officer of superintendent rank or above, who will similarly consider whether a report to the Solicitors Regulatory Authority would be appropriate. When the solicitor concerned is a duty solicitor, the report should be both to the Solicitors Regulatory Authority and to the Legal Aid Agency.

H:6.13 "Solicitor" in this Code means:

- a solicitor who holds a current practising certificate;
- an accredited or probationary representative included on the register of representatives maintained by the Legal Aid Agency.

H:6.14 An accredited or probationary representative sent to provide advice by, and on behalf of, a solicitor shall be admitted to the police station for this purpose unless an officer of inspector rank or above considers such a visit will hinder the investigation and directs otherwise. Hindering the investigation does not include giving proper legal advice to a detainee as in *Note 6C.* Once admitted to the police station, *paragraphs 6.7* to *6.11* apply. **A-219c**

H:6.15 In exercising their discretion under *paragraph 6.14*, the officer should take into account in particular:

- whether:
  - ˜ the identity and status of an accredited or probationary representative have been satisfactorily established;
  - ˜ they are of suitable character to provide legal advice,
- any other matters in any written letter of authorisation provided by the solicitor on whose behalf the person is attending the police station. See *Note 6E.*

H:6.16 If the inspector refuses access to an accredited or probationary representative or a decision is taken that such a person should not be permitted to remain at an interview, the inspector must notify the solicitor on whose behalf the representative was acting and give them an opportunity to make alternative arrangements. The detainee must be informed and the custody record noted.

H:6.17 If a solicitor arrives at the station to see a particular person, that person must, unless *Annex B* applies, be so informed whether or not they are being interviewed and asked if they would like to see the solicitor. This applies even if the detainee has declined legal advice or, having requested it, subsequently agreed to be interviewed without receiving advice. The solicitor's attendance and the detainee's decision must be noted in the custody record.

(b) Documentation

A-219d H:6.18 Any request for legal advice and the action taken shall be recorded.

H:6.19 A record shall be made in the interview record if a detainee asks for legal advice and an interview is begun either in the absence of a solicitor or their representative, or they have been required to leave an interview.

Notes for Guidance

A-219e *H:6ZA No police officer or police staff shall indicate to any suspect, except to answer a direct question, that the period for which they are liable to be detained, or the time taken to complete the interview, might be reduced:*

- if they do not ask for legal advice or do not want a solicitor present when they are interviewed; or
- if after asking for legal advice, they change their mind about wanting it or (as the case may be) wanting a solicitor present when they are interviewed and agree to be interviewed without waiting for a solicitor.

H:6A In considering if paragraph 6.7(b) applies, the officer should, if practicable, ask the solicitor for an estimate of how long it will take to come to the station and relate this to the time detention is permitted, the time of day (i.e. whether the rest period under paragraph 12.2 is imminent) and the requirements of other investigations. If the solicitor is on their way or is to set off immediately, it will not normally be appropriate to begin an interview before they arrive. If it appears necessary to begin an interview before the solicitor's arrival, they should be given an indication of how long the police would be able to wait so there is an opportunity to make arrangements for someone else to provide legal advice. Nothing within this section is intended to prevent police from ascertaining immediately after the arrest of an individual whether a threat to public safety exists (see paragraph 11.2).

H:6B A detainee has a right to free legal advice and to be represented by a solicitor. This Note for Guidance explains the arrangements which enable detainees to whom this Code applies to obtain legal advice. An outline of these arrangements is also included in the Notice of Rights and Entitlements given to detainees in accordance with paragraph 3.2.

The detainee can ask for free advice from a solicitor they know or if they do not know a solicitor or the solicitor they know cannot be contacted, from the duty solicitor.

To arrange free legal advice, the police should telephone the Defence Solicitor Call Centre (DSCC). The call centre will contact either the duty solicitor or the solicitor requested by the detainee as appropriate.

When a detainee wants to pay for legal advice themselves:

- *the DSCC will contact a solicitor of their choice on their behalf;*
- *they should be given an opportunity to consult a specific solicitor or another solicitor from that solicitor's firm. If this solicitor is not available, they may choose up to two alternatives. If these alternatives are not available, the custody officer has discretion to allow further attempts until a solicitor has been contacted and agreed to provide advice;*
- *they are entitled to a private consultation with their chosen solicitor on the telephone or the solicitor may decide to come to the police station;*
- *if their chosen solicitor cannot be contacted, the DSCC may still be called to arrange free legal advice.*

Apart from carrying out duties necessary to implement these arrangements, an officer must not advise the suspect about any particular firm of solicitors.

H:6C The solicitor's only role in the police station is to protect and advance the legal rights of their client. On occasions this may require the solicitor to give advice which has the effect of the client avoiding giving evidence which strengthens a prosecution case. The solicitor may intervene in order to seek clarification, challenge an improper question to their client or the manner in which it is put, advise their client not to reply to particular questions, or if they wish to give their client further legal advice. Paragraph 6.9 only applies if the solicitor's approach or conduct prevents or unreasonably obstructs proper questions being put to the suspect or the suspect's response being recorded. Examples of unacceptable conduct include answering questions on a suspect's behalf or providing written replies for the suspect to quote.

H:6D An officer who takes the decision to exclude a solicitor must be in a position to satisfy the court the decision was properly made. In order to do this they may need to witness what is happening.

H:6E If an officer of at least inspector rank considers a particular solicitor or firm of solicitors is persistently sending probationary representatives who are unsuited to provide legal advice, they should inform an officer of at least superintendent rank, who may wish to take the matter up with the Solicitors Regulatory Authority.

H:6F Subject to the constraints of Annex B, a solicitor may advise more than one client in an investigation if they wish. Any question of a conflict of interest is for the solicitor under their professional code of conduct. If, however, waiting for a solicitor to give advice to one client may lead to unreasonable delay to the interview with another, the provisions of paragraph 6.7(b) may apply.

H:6G In addition to a poster in English, a poster or posters containing translations into Welsh, the main minority ethnic languages and the principal European languages should be displayed wherever they are likely to be helpful and it is practicable to do so.

H:6H Not used

H:6I Whenever a detainee exercises their right to legal advice by consulting or communicating with a solicitor, they must be allowed to do so in private. This right to consult or communicate in private is fundamental. Except as allowed by the Terrorism Act 2000, Schedule 8, paragraph 9, if the requirement for privacy is compromised because what is said or written by the detainee or solicitor for the purpose of giving and receiving legal advice is overheard, listened to, or read by others without the informed consent of the detainee, the right will effectively have been denied. When a detainee speaks to a solicitor on the telephone, they should be allowed to do so in private unless a direction under Schedule 8, paragraph 9 of the Terrorism Act 2000 has been given or this is impractical because of the design and layout of the custody area, or the location of telephones. However, the normal expectation should be that facilities will be available, unless they are being used, at all police stations to enable detainees to speak in private to a solicitor either face to face or over the telephone.

H:6J A detainee is not obliged to give reasons for declining legal advice and should not be pressed to do so.

H:7 Citizens of independent Commonwealth countries or foreign nationals

(a) Action

H:7.1 A detainee who is a citizen of an independent Commonwealth country or a national of a foreign country, including the Republic of Ireland, has the right, upon request, to communicate at any time with the appropriate High Commission, Embassy or Consulate. That detainee must be informed as soon as practicable of this right and asked if they want to have their High Commission, Embassy or Consulate told of their whereabouts and the grounds for their detention. Such a request should be acted upon as soon as practicable. See *Note 7A*. **A-220**

H:7.2 A detainee who is a citizen of a country with which a bilateral consular convention or agreement is in force requiring notification of arrest, must also be informed that subject to *paragraph 7.4*, notification of their arrest will be sent to the appropriate High Commission, Embassy or Consulate as soon as practicable, whether or not they request it. A list of the countries to which this requirement currently applies and contact details for the relevant High Commissions, Embassies and Consulates can be obtained from the Consular Directorate of the Foreign and Commonwealth Office (FCO) as follows:

- from the FCO web pages:
  - *https://gov.uk/government/publications/table-of-consular-conventions-and-mandatory-notification-obligations*, and
  - *https://www.gov.uk/government/publications/foreign-embassies-in-the-uk*
- by telephone to 020 7008 3100,
- by email to *fcocorrespondence@fco.gov.uk*.
- by letter to the Foreign and Commonwealth Office, King Charles Street, London, SW1A 2AH.

H:7.3 Consular officers may, if the detainee agrees, visit one of their nationals in police detention to talk to them and, if required, to arrange for legal advice. Such visits shall take place out of the hearing of a police officer.

H:7.4 Notwithstanding the provisions of consular conventions, if the detainee claims that they are a refugee or have applied or intend to apply for asylum the custody officer must ensure that UK Visas and Immigration (UKVI) (formerly the UK Border Agency) are informed as soon as practicable of the claim. UKVI will then determine whether compliance with relevant international obligations requires notification of arrest to be sent and will inform the custody officer as to what action police need to take.

(b) Documentation

H:7.5 A record shall be made: **A-220a**

- when a detainee is informed of their rights under this section and of any requirement in paragraph 7.2;
- of any communications with a High Commission, Embassy or Consulate, and

- of any communications with UKVI about a detainee's claim to be a refugee or to be seeking asylum and the resulting action taken by police.

Note for Guidance

A-220b *H:7A The exercise of the rights in this section may not be interfered with even though Annex B applies.*

H:8 Conditions of detention

(a) Action

A-221 H:8.1 So far as it is practicable, not more than one detainee should be detained in each cell. See *Note 8E.*

H:8.2 Cells in use must be adequately heated, cleaned and ventilated. They must be adequately lit, subject to such dimming as is compatible with safety and security to allow people detained overnight to sleep. No additional restraints shall be used within a locked cell unless absolutely necessary and then only restraint equipment, approved for use in that force by the chief officer, which is reasonable and necessary in the circumstances having regard to the detainee's demeanour and with a view to ensuring their safety and the safety of others. If a detainee is deaf or a vulnerable person, particular care must be taken when deciding whether to use any form of approved restraints.

H:8.3 Blankets, mattresses, pillows and other bedding supplied shall be of a reasonable standard and in a clean and sanitary condition.

H:8.4 Access to toilet and washing facilities must be provided. This must take account of the dignity of the detainee. *See Note 8F.*

H:8.5 If it is necessary to remove a detainee's clothes for the purposes of investigation, for hygiene, health reasons or cleaning, removal shall be conducted with proper regard to the dignity, sensitivity and vulnerability of the detainee and replacement clothing of a reasonable standard of comfort and cleanliness shall be provided. A detainee may not be interviewed unless adequate clothing has been offered.

H:8.6 At least two light meals and one main meal should be offered in any 24-hour period. See *Note 8B.* Drinks should be provided at meal times and upon reasonable request between meals. Whenever necessary, advice shall be sought from the appropriate healthcare professional, see *Note 9A,* on medical and dietary matters. As far as practicable, meals provided shall offer a varied diet and meet any specific dietary needs or religious beliefs the detainee may have. Detainees should also be made aware that the meals offered meet such needs. The detainee may, at the custody officer's discretion, have meals supplied by their family or friends at their expense. See *Note 8A.*

H:8.7 Brief outdoor exercise shall be offered daily if practicable. Where facilities exist, indoor exercise shall be offered as an alternative if outside conditions are such that a detainee can not be reasonably expected to take outdoor exercise (e.g., in cold or wet weather) or if requested by the detainee or for reasons of security. S*ee Note 8C.*

H:8.8 Where practicable, provision should be made for detainees to practice religious observance. Consideration should be given to providing a separate room which can be used as a prayer room. The supply of appropriate food and clothing, and suitable provision for prayer facilities, such as uncontaminated copies of religious books, should also be considered. *See Note 8D.*

H:8.9 A juvenile shall not be placed in a cell unless no other secure accommodation is available and the custody officer considers it is not practicable to supervise them if they are not placed in a cell or that a cell provides more comfortable accommodation than other secure accommodation in the station. A juvenile may not be placed in a cell with a detained adult.

H:8.10 Police stations should keep a reasonable supply of reading material available for detainees, including but not limited to, the main religious texts. *See Note 8D.* Detainees should be made aware that such material is available and reasonable requests for such material should be met as soon as practicable unless to do so would:

(i) interfere with the investigation; or

(ii) prevent or delay an officer from discharging his statutory duties, or those in this Code.

If such a request is refused on the grounds of (i) or (ii) above, this should be noted in the custody record and met as soon as possible after those grounds cease to apply.

(b) Documentation

A-221a H:8.11 A record must be kept of replacement clothing and meals offered.

H:8.11A If a juvenile is placed in a cell, the reason must be recorded.

H:8.12 The use of any restraints on a detainee whilst in a cell, the reasons for it and, if appropriate, the arrangements for enhanced supervision of the detainee whilst so restrained, shall be recorded. See *paragraph 3.9*

Notes for Guidance

H:8A In deciding whether to allow meals to be supplied by family or friends, the custody officer is entitled to take account of the risk of items being concealed in any food or package and the officer's duties and responsibilities under food handling legislation. If an officer needs to examine food or other items supplied by family and friends before deciding whether they can be given to the detainee, he should inform the person who has brought the item to the police station of this and the reasons for doing so. **A-221b**

H:8B Meals should, so far as practicable, be offered at recognised meal times, or at other times that take account of when the detainee last had a meal.

H:8C In light of the potential for detaining individuals for extended periods of time, the overriding principle should be to accommodate a period of exercise, except where to do so would hinder the investigation, delay the detainee's release or charge, or it is declined by the detainee.

H:8D Police forces should consult with representatives of the main religious communities to ensure the provision for religious observance is adequate, and to seek advice on the appropriate storage and handling of religious texts or other religious items.

H:8E The Detention and Custody Authorised Professional Practice (APP) produced by the College of Policing (see http://www.app.college.police.uk) provides more detailed guidance on matters concerning detainee healthcare and treatment and associated forensic issues which should be read in conjunction with sections 8 and 9 of this Code.

H:8F In cells subject to CCTV monitoring, privacy in the toilet area should be ensured by any appropriate means and detainees should be made aware of this when they are placed in the cell. If a detainee or appropriate adult on their behalf, expresses doubts about the effectiveness of the means used, reasonable steps should be taken to allay those doubts, for example, by explaining or demonstrating the means used.

H:9 Care and treatment of detained persons

(a) General

H:9.1 Notwithstanding other requirements for medical attention as set out in this section, detainees who are held for more than 96 hours must be visited by an appropriate healthcare professional at least once every 24 hours. **A-222**

H:9.2 Nothing in this section prevents the police from calling an appropriate healthcare professional, to examine a detainee for the purposes of obtaining evidence relating to any offence in which the detainee is suspected of being involved. See *Note 9A*.

H:9.3 If a complaint is made by, or on behalf of, a detainee about their treatment since their arrest, or it comes to notice that a detainee may have been treated improperly, a report must be made as soon as practicable to an officer of inspector rank or above not connected with the investigation. If the matter concerns a possible assault or the possibility of the unnecessary or unreasonable use of force, an appropriate healthcare professional must also be called as soon as practicable.

H:9.4 Detainees should be visited at least every hour. If no reasonably foreseeable risk was identified in a risk assessment, see *paragraphs 3.6* to *3.10*, there is no need to wake a sleeping detainee. Those suspected of being under the influence of drink or drugs or both or of having swallowed drugs, see *Note 9C*, or whose level of consciousness causes concern must, subject to any clinical directions given by the appropriate healthcare professional, see *paragraph 9.15*:

- be visited and roused at least every half hour;
- have their condition assessed as in *Annex H*;
- and clinical treatment arranged if appropriate.

See *Notes 9B, 9C* and *9G*

H:9.4A As soon as practicable after arrival at the police station, each detainee must be given an opportunity to speak in private with a member of the custody staff who if they wish may be of the *same* sex as the detainee (see *paragraph 1.17(c)*), about any matter concerning the detainee's personal needs relating to their health, hygiene and welfare that might affect or concern them whilst in custody. If the detainee wishes to take this opportunity, the necessary arrangements shall be made as soon as practicable. In the case of a juvenile or vulnerable person, the appropriate adult must be involved in accordance with *paragraph 3.17* and in the case of a girl under 18, see *paragraph 3.20A*. (See *Note 9CB*).

[*3.21A*]

H:9.4B Each female detainee aged 18 or over shall be asked in private if possible and at the earliest opportunity, if they require or are likely to require any menstrual products whilst they are in custody. They must also be told that they will be provided free of charge and that replacement products are available. At the custody officer's discretion, detainees may have menstrual products supplied by their family or friends at their expense (see *Note 9CC*). For girls under 18, see *paragraph 3.21A*.

H:9.5 When arrangements are made to secure clinical attention for a detainee, the custody officer must make sure all relevant information which might assist in the treatment of the detainee's condition is made available to the responsible healthcare professional. This applies whether or not the healthcare professional asks for such information. Any officer or police staff with relevant information must inform the custody officer as soon as practicable.

(b) Clinical treatment and attention

A-222a H:9.6 The custody officer must make sure a detainee receives appropriate clinical attention as soon as reasonably practicable if the person:

(a) appears to be suffering from physical illness; or
(b) is injured; or
(c) appears to be suffering from a mental disorder; or
(d) appears to need clinical attention

H:9.7 This applies even if the detainee makes no request for clinical attention and whether or not they have already received clinical attention elsewhere. If the need for attention appears urgent, e.g. when indicated as in *Annex H*, the nearest available healthcare professional or an ambulance must be called immediately.

H:9.8 The custody officer must also consider the need for clinical attention as set out in *Note 9C* in relation to those suffering the effects of alcohol or drugs.

H:9.9 If it appears to the custody officer, or they are told, that a person brought to a station under arrest may be suffering from an infectious disease or condition, the custody officer must take reasonable steps to safeguard the health of the detainee and others at the station. In deciding what action to take, advice must be sought from an appropriate healthcare professional. See *Note 9D*. The custody officer has discretion to isolate the person and their property until clinical directions have been obtained.

H:9.10 If a detainee requests a clinical examination, an appropriate healthcare professional must be called as soon as practicable to assess the detainee's clinical needs. If a safe and appropriate care plan cannot be provided, the appropriate healthcare professional's advice must be sought. The detainee may also be examined by a medical practitioner of their choice at their expense.

H:9.11 If a detainee is required to take or apply any medication in compliance with clinical directions prescribed before their detention, the custody officer must consult the appropriate healthcare professional before the use of the medication. Subject to the restrictions in *paragraph 9.12*, the custody officer is responsible for the safekeeping of any medication and for making sure the detainee is given the opportunity to take or apply prescribed or approved medication. Any such consultation and its outcome shall be noted in the custody record.

A-222b H:9.12 No police officer may administer or supervise the self-administration of medically prescribed controlled drugs of the types and forms listed in the Misuse of Drugs Regulations 2001, Schedule 2 or 3. A detainee may only self-administer such drugs under the personal supervision of the registered medical practitioner authorising their use or other appropriate healthcare professional. The custody officer may supervise the self-administration of, or authorise other custody staff to supervise the self-administration of, drugs listed in Schedule 4 or 5 if the officer has consulted the appropriate healthcare professional authorising their use and both are satisfied self-administration will not expose the detainee, police officers or anyone else to the risk of harm or injury.

H:9.13 When appropriate healthcare professionals administer drugs or authorise the use of other medications, or consult with the custody officer about allowing self administration of drugs listed in Schedule 4 or 5, it must be within current medicines legislation and the scope of practice as determined by their relevant regulatory body.

H:9.14 If a detainee has in their possession, or claims to need, medication relating to a heart condition, diabetes, epilepsy or a condition of comparable potential seriousness then, even though *paragraph 9.6* may not apply, the advice of the appropriate healthcare professional must be obtained.

H:9.15 Whenever the appropriate healthcare professional is called in accordance with this section to examine or treat a detainee, the custody officer shall ask for their opinion about:

- any risks or problems which police need to take into account when making decisions about the detainee's continued detention;
- when to carry out an interview if applicable; and
- the need for safeguards.

H:9.16 When clinical directions are given by the appropriate healthcare professional, whether orally or in writing, and the custody officer has any doubts or is in any way uncertain about any aspect of the directions, the custody officer shall ask for clarification. It is particularly important that directions concerning the frequency of visits are clear, precise and capable of being implemented. See *Note 9E*.

(c) Documentation

A-222c H:9.17 A record must be made in the custody record of:

(a) the arrangements made for an examination by an appropriate healthcare professional under *paragraph 9.3* and of any complaint reported under that paragraph together with any relevant remarks by the custody officer;
(b) any arrangements made in accordance with *paragraph 9.6*;
(c) any request for a clinical examination under *paragraph 9.10* and any arrangements made in response;
(d) the injury, ailment, condition or other reason which made it necessary to make the arrangements in (*a*) to (*c*); See *Note 9F*
(e) any clinical directions and advice, including any further clarifications, given to police by a healthcare professional concerning the care and treatment of the detainee in connection with any of the arrangements made in (*a*) to (*c*); See *Notes 9D* and *9E*
(f) if applicable, the responses received when attempting to rouse a person using the procedure in *Annex H*. See *Note 9G*.

H:9.18 If a healthcare professional does not record their clinical findings in the custody record, the record must show where they are recorded. See *Note 9F*. However, information which is necessary to custody staff to ensure the effective ongoing care and well being of the detainee must be recorded openly in the custody record, see *paragraph 3.8* and *Annex G, paragraph 7*.

H:9.19 Subject to the requirements of *Section 4*, the custody record shall include:

- a record of all medication a detainee has in their possession on arrival at the police station;
- a note of any such medication they claim to need but do not have with them.

Notes for Guidance

H:9A A "healthcare professional" means a clinically qualified person working within the scope of practice as determined by their relevant statutory regulatory body. Whether a healthcare professional is 'appropriate' depends on the circumstances of the duties they carry out at the time. **A-222d**

H:9B Whenever possible detained juveniles and vulnerable persons should be visited more frequently.

H:9C A detainee who appears drunk or behaves abnormally may be suffering from illness, the effects of drugs or may have sustained injury, particularly a head injury which is not apparent. A detainee needing or dependent on certain drugs, including alcohol, may experience harmful effects within a short time of being deprived of their supply. In these circumstances, when there is any doubt, police should always act urgently to call an appropriate healthcare professional or an ambulance. Paragraph 9.6 does not apply to minor ailments or injuries which do not need attention. However, all such ailments or injuries must be recorded in the custody record and any doubt must be resolved in favour of calling the appropriate healthcare professional.

H:9CB Matters concerning personal needs to which paragraph 9.4A applies include any requirement for menstrual products incontinence products and colostomy appliances, where these needs have not previously been identified (see paragraph 3.5(c)). It also enables adult women to speak in private to a female officer about their requirements for menstrual products if they decline to respond to the more direct enquiry envisaged under paragraph 9.4B. This contact should be facilitated at any time, where possible.

H:9CC Detailed guidance for police officers and staff concerning menstruating female detainees in police custody is included in the College of Policing Authorised Professional Practice (APP).

H:9D It is important to respect a person's right to privacy and information about their health must be kept confidential and only disclosed with their consent or in accordance with clinical advice when it is necessary to protect the detainee's health or that of others who come into contact with them.

H:9E The custody officer should always seek to clarify directions that the detainee requires constant observation or supervision and should ask the appropriate healthcare professional to explain precisely what action needs to be taken to implement such directions.

H:9F Paragraphs 9.17 and 9.18 do not require any information about the cause of any injury, ailment or condition to be recorded on the custody record if it appears capable of providing evidence of an offence.

H:9G The purpose of recording a person's responses when attempting to rouse them using the procedure in Annex H is to enable any change in the individual's consciousness level to be noted and clinical treatment arranged if appropriate.

H:10 Cautions

(a) When a caution must be given

H:10.1 A person whom there are grounds to suspect of an offence, see *Note 10A*, must be cautioned before any questions about an offence, or further questions if the answers provide the grounds for suspicion, are put to them if either the suspect's answers or silence, (i.e. failure or refusal to answer or answer satisfactorily) may be given in evidence to a court in a prosecution. **A-223**

H:10.2 A person who is arrested, or further arrested, must be informed at the time if practicable or, if not, as soon as it becomes practicable thereafter, that they are under arrest and of the grounds and reasons for their arrest, see paragraph 3.4, *Note 3G* and *Note 10B*.

H:10.3 As required by section 3 of PACE Code G, a person who is arrested, or further arrested, must also be cautioned unless:

(a) it is impracticable to do so by reason of their condition or behaviour at the time; or
(b) they have already been cautioned immediately prior to arrest as in *paragraph 10.1*.

(b) Terms of the cautions

A-223a H:10.4 The caution which must be given:

(a) on arrest;
(b) on all other occasions before a person is charged or informed they may be prosecuted; see *PACE Code C, section 16*, and
(c) before post-charge questioning under section 22 of the Counter-Terrorism Act 2008 (see *section 15.9*),

should, unless the restriction on drawing adverse inferences from silence applies, see *Annex C*, be in the following terms:

> "You do not have to say anything. But it may harm your defence if you do not mention when questioned something which you later rely on in Court. Anything you do say may be given in evidence."

Where the use of the Welsh Language is appropriate, a constable may provide the caution directly in Welsh in the following terms:

> "*Does dim rhaid i chi ddweud dim byd. Ond gall niweidio eich amddiffyniad os na fyddwch chi'n sôn, wrth gael eich holi, am rywbeth y byddwch chi'n dibynnu arno nes ymlaen yn y Llys. Gall unrhyw beth yr ydych yn ei ddweud gael ei roi fel tystiolaeth.*"

See *Note 10F*

H:10.5 *Annex C, paragraph 2* sets out the alternative terms of the caution to be used when the restriction on drawing adverse inferences from silence applies.

H:10.6 Minor deviations from the words of any caution given in accordance with this Code do not constitute a breach of this Code, provided the sense of the relevant caution is preserved. See *Note 10C.*

H:10.7 After any break in questioning under caution, the person being questioned must be made aware they remain under caution. If there is any doubt the relevant caution should be given again in full when the interview resumes. See *Note 10D.*

H:10.8 When, despite being cautioned, a person fails to co-operate or to answer particular questions which may affect their immediate treatment, the person should be informed of any relevant consequences and that those consequences are not affected by the caution. Examples are when a person's refusal to provide:

- their name and address when charged may make them liable to detention;
- particulars and information in accordance with a statutory requirement.

(c) Special warnings under the Criminal Justice and Public Order Act 1994, sections 36 and 37

A-223b H:10.9 When a suspect interviewed at a police station or authorised place of detention after arrest fails or refuses to answer certain questions, or to answer satisfactorily, after due warning, see *Note 10E*, a court or jury may draw such inferences as appear proper under the Criminal Justice and Public Order Act 1994, sections 36 and 37. Such inferences may only be drawn when:

(a) the restriction on drawing adverse inferences from silence, see *Annex C*, does not apply; and
(b) the suspect is arrested by a constable and fails or refuses to account for any objects, marks or substances, or marks on such objects found:
  - on their person;
  - in or on their clothing or footwear;
  - otherwise in their possession; or
  - in the place they were arrested;
(c) the arrested suspect was found by a constable at a place at or about the time the offence for which that officer has arrested them is alleged to have been committed, and the suspect fails or refuses to account for their presence there.

When the restriction on drawing adverse inferences from silence applies, the suspect may still be asked to account for any of the matters in (*b*) or (*c*) but the special warning described in *paragraph 10.10* will not apply and must not be given.

H:10.10 For an inference to be drawn when a suspect fails or refuses to answer a question about one of these matters, or to answer it satisfactorily, the suspect must first be told in ordinary language:

(a) what offence is being investigated;
(b) what fact they are being asked to account for;
(c) this fact may be due to them taking part in the commission of the offence;
(d) a court may draw a proper inference if they fail or refuse to account for this fact; and
(e) a record is being made of the interview and it may be given in evidence if they are brought to trial.

(d) Juveniles and vulnerable persons

H:10.10A The information required in *paragraph 10.10* must not be given to a suspect who is a juvenile or a vulnerable person unless the appropriate adult is present. **A-223c**

H:10.11 If a juvenile or a vulnerable person is cautioned in the absence of the appropriate adult, the caution must be repeated in the adult's presence.

H:10.11A *Not used.*

(e) Documentation

H:10.12 A record shall be made when a caution is given under this section, either in the interviewer's pocket book or in the interview record. **A-223d**

Notes for Guidance

H:10A There must be some reasonable, objective grounds for the suspicion, based on known facts or information which are relevant to the likelihood the offence has been committed and the person to be questioned committed it. **A-223e**

H:10B An arrested person must be given sufficient information to enable them to understand that they have been deprived of their liberty and the reason they have been arrested, e.g. when a person is arrested on suspicion of committing an offence they must be informed of the suspected offence's nature, when and where it was committed, see Note 3G. The suspect must also be informed of the reason or reasons why the arrest is considered necessary. Vague or technical language should be avoided.

H:10C If it appears a person does not understand the caution, the person giving it should explain it in their own words.

H:10D It may be necessary to show to the court that nothing occurred during an interview break or between interviews which influenced the suspect's recorded evidence. After a break in an interview or at the beginning of a subsequent interview, the interviewer should summarise the reason for the break and confirm this with the suspect.

H:10E The Criminal Justice and Public Order Act 1994, sections 36 and 37 apply only to suspects who have been arrested by a constable or an officer of Revenue and Customs and are given the relevant warning by the police or Revenue and Customs officer who made the arrest or who is investigating the offence. They do not apply to any interviews with suspects who have not been arrested.

H:10F Nothing in this Code requires a caution to be given or repeated when informing a person not under arrest they may be prosecuted for an offence. However, a court will not be able to draw any inferences under the Criminal Justice and Public Order Act 1994, section 34, if the person was not cautioned.

H:11 Interviews - general

(a) Action

H:11.1 An interview in this Code is the questioning of a person arrested on suspicion of being a terrorist which, under *paragraph 10.1*, must be carried out under caution. Whenever a person is interviewed they and their solicitor must be informed of the grounds for arrest, and given sufficient information to enable them to understand the nature of their suspected involvement in the commission, preparation or instigation of acts of terrorism (see *paragraph 3.4(a)*) in order to allow for the effective exercise of the rights of the defence. However, whilst the information must always be sufficient information for the person to understand the nature of their suspected involvement in the commission, preparation or instigation of acts of terrorism, this does not require the disclosure of details at a time which might prejudice the terrorism investigation (*see Note 3G*). The decision about what needs to be disclosed for the purpose of this requirement therefore rests with the investigating officer who has sufficient knowledge of the case to make that decision. The officer who discloses the information shall make a record of the information disclosed and when it was disclosed. This record may be made in the interview record, in the officer's report book or other form provided for this purpose. See *Note 11ZA*. **A-224**

H:11.2 Following the arrest of a person under *section 41 TACT*, that person must not be interviewed about the relevant offence except at a place designated for detention under *paragraph 1 of Schedule 8 to the Terrorism Act 2000*, unless the consequent delay would be likely to:

(a) lead to:
- interference with, or harm to, evidence connected with an offence;
- interference with, or physical harm to, other people; or
- serious loss of, or damage to, property;

(b) lead to alerting other people suspected of committing an offence but not yet arrested for it; or

(c) hinder the recovery of property obtained in consequence of the commission of an offence.

Interviewing in any of these circumstances shall cease once the relevant risk has been averted or the necessary questions have been put in order to attempt to avert that risk.

H:11.3 Immediately prior to the commencement or re-commencement of any interview at a designated place of detention, the interviewer should remind the suspect of their entitlement to free legal advice and that the interview can be delayed for legal advice to be obtained, unless one of the exceptions in *paragraph 6.7* applies. It is the interviewer's responsibility to make sure all reminders are recorded in the interview record.

A-224a H:11.4 At the beginning of an interview the interviewer, after cautioning the suspect, see *section 10,* shall put to them any significant statement or silence which occurred in the presence and hearing of a police officer or other police staff before the start of the interview and which have not been put to the suspect in the course of a previous interview. See *Note 11A.* The interviewer shall ask the suspect whether they confirm or deny that earlier statement or silence and if they want to add anything.

H:11.5 A significant statement is one which appears capable of being used in evidence against the suspect, in particular a direct admission of guilt. A significant silence is a failure or refusal to answer a question or answer satisfactorily when under caution, which might, allowing for the restriction on drawing adverse inferences from silence, see *Annex C,* give rise to an inference under the Criminal Justice and Public Order Act 1994, Part III.

H:11.6 No interviewer may try to obtain answers or elicit a statement by the use of oppression. Except as in *paragraph 10.8,* no interviewer shall indicate, except to answer a direct question, what action will be taken by the police if the person being questioned answers questions, makes a statement or refuses to do either. If the person asks directly what action will be taken if they answer questions, make a statement or refuse to do either, the interviewer may inform them what action the police propose to take provided that action is itself proper and warranted.

H:11.7 The interview or further interview of a person about an offence with which that person has not been charged or for which they have not been informed they may be prosecuted, must cease when:

(a) the officer in charge of the investigation is satisfied all the questions they consider relevant to obtaining accurate and reliable information about the offence have been put to the suspect, this includes allowing the suspect an opportunity to give an innocent explanation and asking questions to test if the explanation is accurate and reliable, e.g. to clear up ambiguities or clarify what the suspect said;

(b) the officer in charge of the investigation has taken account of any other available evidence; and

(c) the officer in charge of the investigation, or in the case of a detained suspect, the custody officer, see *PACE Code C paragraph 16.1,* reasonably believes there is sufficient evidence to provide a realistic prospect of conviction for that offence. See *Note 11B.*

(b) Interview records

A-224b H:11.8 Interviews of a person detained under *section 41 of, or Schedule 8 to, TACT* must be video recorded with sound in accordance with the Code of Practice issued under *paragraph 3 of Schedule 8 to the Terrorism Act 2000,* or in the case of post-charge questioning authorised under *section 22 of the Counter-Terrorism Act 2008,* the Code of Practice issued under section 25 of that Act.

H:11.8A A written record shall be made of any comments made by a suspect, including unsolicited comments, which are outside the context of an interview but which might be relevant to the offence. Any such record must be timed and signed by the maker. When practicable the suspect shall be given the opportunity to read that record and to sign it as correct or to indicate how they consider it inaccurate. See *Note 11E.*

(c) Juveniles and vulnerable persons

A-224c H:11.9 A juvenile or vulnerable person must not be interviewed regarding their involvement or suspected involvement in a criminal offence or offences, or asked to provide or sign a written statement under caution or record of interview, in the absence of the appropriate adult unless *paragraphs 11.2* or *11.11* to *11.13* apply. See *Note 11C.*

H:11.10 If an appropriate adult is present at an interview, they shall be informed:

- that they are not expected to act simply as an observer; and
- that the purpose of their presence is to:
  - advise the person being interviewed;
  - observe whether the interview is being conducted properly and fairly;
  - facilitate communication with the person being interviewed.

See *paragraph 1.13A.*

H:11.10A The appropriate adult may be required to leave the interview if their conduct is such that the interviewer is unable properly to put questions to the suspect. This will include situations where the appropriate adult's approach or conduct prevents or unreasonably obstructs proper questions being put to the suspect or the suspect's responses being recorded (see *Note 11F*). If the interviewer considers an appropriate adult is acting in such a way, they will stop the interview and consult an officer not below superintendent rank, if one is readily available, and otherwise an officer not below inspector rank not connected with the investigation. After speaking to the appropriate adult, the officer consulted must remind the adult that their role under *paragraph 11.10* does not allow them to obstruct proper questioning and give the adult an opportunity to respond. The officer consulted will then decide if the interview should continue without the attendance of that appropriate adult. If they decide it should, another appropriate adult must be obtained before the interview continues, unless the provisions of *paragraph 11.11* below apply.

(d) Vulnerable suspects - urgent interviews at police stations

H:11.11 The following interviews may take place only if an officer of superintendent rank or above considers delaying the interview will lead to the consequences in *paragraph 11.2(a)* to *(c)*, and is satisfied the interview would not significantly harm the person's physical or mental state (see *Annex G*): **A-224d**

(a) an interview of a detained juvenile or vulnerable person without the appropriate adult being present (see *Note 11C*);

(b) an interview of anyone other than in *(a)* who appears unable to:
- appreciate the significance of questions and their answers; or
- understand what is happening because of the effects of drink, drugs or any illness, ailment or condition;

(c) an interview without an interpreter having been arranged, of a detained person whom the custody officer has determined requires an interpreter (see *paragraphs 3.5(c)(ii)* and *3.14*) which is carried out by an interviewer speaking the suspect's own language or (as the case may be) otherwise establishing effective communication which is sufficient to enable the necessary questions to be asked and answered in order to avert the consequences. See *paragraphs 13.2* and *13.5*.

H:11.12 These interviews may not continue once sufficient information has been obtained to avert the consequences in *paragraph 11.2(a)* to *(c)*.

H:11.13 A record shall be made of the grounds for any decision to interview a person under *paragraph 11.11.*

Notes for Guidance

H:11ZA The requirement in paragraph 11.1 for a suspect to be given sufficient information about the nature of their suspected involvement in the commission, preparation or instigation of acts of terrorism offence applies prior to the interview and whether or not they are legally represented. What is sufficient will depend on the circumstances of the case, but it should normally include, as a minimum, a description of the facts relating to the suspected involvement that are known to the officer, including the time and place in question. This aims to avoid suspects being confused or unclear about what they are supposed to have done and to help an innocent suspect to clear the matter up more quickly. **A-224e**

H:11A Paragraph 11.4 does not prevent the interviewer from putting significant statements and silences to a suspect again at a later stage or a further interview.

H:11B The Criminal Procedure and Investigations Act 1996 Code of Practice, paragraph 3.4 states 'In conducting an investigation, the investigator should pursue all reasonable lines of enquiry, whether these point towards or away from the suspect. What is reasonable will depend on the particular circumstances.' Interviewers should keep this in mind when deciding what questions to ask in an interview.

H:11C Although juveniles or vulnerable persons are often capable of providing reliable evidence, they may, without knowing or wishing to do so, be particularly prone in certain circumstances to providing information that may be unreliable, misleading or self-incriminating. Special care should always be taken when questioning such a person, and the appropriate adult should be involved if there is any doubt about a person's age, mental state or capacity. Because of the risk of unreliable evidence it is also important to obtain corroboration of any facts admit-

ted whenever possible. Because of the risks, which the presence of the appropriate adult is intended to minimise, officers of superintendent rank or above should exercise their discretion under paragraph 11.11(a) to authorise the commencement of an interview in the appropriate adult's absence only in exceptional cases, if it is necessary to avert one or more of the specified risks in paragraph 11.2.

H:11D Consideration should be given to the effect of extended detention on a detainee and any subsequent information they provide, especially if it relates to information on matters that they have failed to provide previously in response to similar questioning (see *Annex G*).

H:11E Significant statements described in paragraph 11.4 will always be relevant to the offence and must be recorded. When a suspect agrees to read records of interviews and other comments and sign them as correct, they should be asked to endorse the record with, e.g. 'I agree that this is a correct record of what was said' and add their signature. If the suspect does not agree with the record, the interviewer should record the details of any disagreement and ask the suspect to read these details and sign them to the effect that they accurately reflect their disagreement. Any refusal to sign should be recorded.

H:11F The appropriate adult may intervene if they consider it is necessary to help the suspect understand any question asked and to help the suspect to answer any question. Paragraph 11.10A only applies if the appropriate adult's approach or conduct prevents or unreasonably obstructs proper questions being put to the suspect or the suspect's response being recorded. Examples of unacceptable conduct include answering questions on a suspect's behalf or providing written replies for the suspect to quote. An officer who takes the decision to exclude an appropriate adult must be in a position to satisfy the court the decision was properly made. In order to do this they may need to witness what is happening and give the suspect's solicitor (if they have one) who witnessed what happened, an opportunity to comment.

H:12 Interviews in police stations

(a) Action

A-225 H:12.1 If a police officer wants to interview or conduct enquiries which require the presence of a detainee, the custody officer is responsible for deciding whether to deliver the detainee into the officer's custody. An investigating officer who is given custody of a detainee takes over responsibility for the detainee's care and treatment for the purposes of this Code until they return the detainee to the custody officer when they must report the manner in which they complied with the Code whilst having custody of the detainee.

H:12.2 Except as below, in any period of 24 hours a detainee must be allowed a continuous period of at least 8 hours for rest, free from questioning, travel or any interruption in connection with the investigation concerned. This period should normally be at night or other appropriate time which takes account of when the detainee last slept or rested. If a detainee is arrested at a police station after going there voluntarily, the period of 24 hours runs from the time of their arrest (or, if a person was being detained under TACT Schedule 7 when arrested, from the time at which the examination under Schedule 7 began) and not the time of arrival at the police station. The period may not be interrupted or delayed, except:

(a) when there are reasonable grounds for believing not delaying or interrupting the period would:
  (i) involve a risk of harm to people or serious loss of, or damage to, property;
  (ii) delay unnecessarily the person's release from custody; or
  (iii) otherwise prejudice the outcome of the investigation;
(b) at the request of the detainee, their appropriate adult or legal representative;
(c) when a delay or interruption is necessary in order to:
  (i) comply with the legal obligations and duties arising under *section 14*; or
  (ii) to take action required under *section 9* or in accordance with medical advice.

If the period is interrupted in accordance with *(a)*, a fresh period must be allowed. Interruptions under *(b)* and *(c)* do not require a fresh period to be allowed.

H:12.3 Before a detainee is interviewed the custody officer, in consultation with the officer in charge of the investigation and appropriate healthcare professionals as necessary, shall assess whether the detainee is fit enough to be interviewed. This means determining and considering the risks to the detainee's physical and mental state if the interview took place and determining what safeguards are needed to allow the interview to take place. The custody officer shall not allow a detainee to be interviewed if the custody officer considers it would cause significant harm to the detainee's physical or mental state. Vulnerable suspects listed at *paragraph 11.11* shall be treated as always being at some risk during an interview and these persons may not be interviewed except in accordance with *paragraphs 11.11* to *11.13*.

H:12.4 As far as practicable interviews shall take place in interview rooms which are adequately heated, lit and ventilated.

A-225a H:12.5 A suspect whose detention without charge has been authorised under TACT Schedule 8, because the detention is necessary for an interview to obtain evidence of the offence for which they have been arrested, may choose not to answer questions but police do not require the suspect's consent or agreement to interview them for this purpose. If a suspect takes steps to prevent themselves being questioned or further questioned, e.g. by refusing to leave their cell to go to a suitable interview room or by trying to leave the interview room, they shall be advised that their consent or agreement to be interviewed is not required. The suspect shall be cautioned as in *section 10,* and informed if they fail or refuse to co-operate, the interview may take place in the cell and that their failure or refusal to co-operate may be given in evidence. If they refuse and the custody officer considers, on reasonable grounds, that the interview should not be delayed, the custody officer has discretion to direct that the interview be conducted in a cell. The suspect shall then be invited to co-operate and go into the interview room.

H:12.6 People being questioned or making statements shall not be required to stand.

H:12.7 Before the interview commences each interviewer shall, subject to the qualification at *paragraph 2.8,* identify themselves and any other persons present to the interviewee.

H:12.8 Breaks from interviewing should be made at recognised meal times or at other times that take account of when an interviewee last had a meal. Short refreshment breaks shall be provided at approximately two hour intervals, subject to the interviewer's discretion to delay a break if there are reasonable grounds for believing it would:

(i) involve a:
- risk of harm to people;
- serious loss of, or damage to, property;

(ii) unnecessarily delay the detainee's release;

(iii) otherwise prejudice the outcome of the investigation.

See *Note 12B*

H:12.9 During extended periods where no interviews take place, because of the need to gather further evidence or analyse existing evidence, detainees and their legal representative shall be informed that the investigation into the relevant offence remains ongoing. If practicable, the detainee and legal representative should also be made aware in general terms of any reasons for long gaps between interviews. Consideration should be given to allowing visits, more frequent exercise, or for reading or writing materials to be offered *see paragraph 5.4, section 8 and Note 12C.*

H:12.10 If during the interview a complaint is made by or on behalf of the interviewee concerning the provisions of any of the Codes, or it comes to the interviewer's notice that the interviewee may have been treated improperly, the interviewer should:

(i) record the matter in the interview record; and

(ii) inform the custody officer, who is then responsible for dealing with it as in *section 9.*

(b) Documentation

H:12.11 A record must be made of the: **A-225b**
- time a detainee is not in the custody of the custody officer, and why;
- reason for any refusal to deliver the detainee out of that custody.

H:12.12 A record shall be made of:
- the reasons it was not practicable to use an interview room; and
- any action taken as in *paragraph 12.5.*

The record shall be made on the custody record or in the interview record for action taken whilst an interview record is being kept, with a brief reference to this effect in the custody record.

H:12.13 Any decision to delay a break in an interview must be recorded, with reasons, in the interview record.

H:12.14 All written statements made at police stations under caution shall be written on forms provided for the purpose.

H:12.15 All written statements made under caution shall be taken in accordance with *Annex D.* Before a person makes a written statement under caution at a police station they shall be reminded about the right to legal advice. See *Note 12A.*

Notes for Guidance

H:12A It is not normally necessary to ask for a written statement if the interview was recorded in accordance with the Code of Practice issued under TACT Schedule 8 Paragraph 3. Statements under caution should normally be taken in these circumstances only at the person's express wish. A person may however be asked if they want to make such a statement. **A-225c**

H:12B Meal breaks should normally last at least 45 minutes and shorter breaks after two hours should last at least 15 minutes. If the interviewer delays a break in accordance with paragraph 12.8 and prolongs the interview, a longer break should be provided. If there is a short interview, and another short interview is contemplated, the length of the break may be reduced if there are reasonable grounds to believe this is necessary to avoid any of the consequences in paragraph 12.8(i) to (iii).

H:12C Consideration should be given to the matters referred to in paragraph 12.9 after a period of over 24 hours without questioning. This is to ensure that extended periods of detention without an indication that the investigation remains ongoing do not contribute to a deterioration of the detainee's well-being.

H:13 Interpreters

(a) General

A-226 H:13.1 Chief officers are responsible for making arrangements (see *paragraph 13.1ZA*) to provide appropriately qualified independent persons to act as interpreters and to provide translations of essential documents for detained suspects who, in accordance with *paragraph 3.5(c)(ii),* the custody officer has determined require an interpreter.

If the suspect has a hearing or speech impediment, references to 'interpreter' and 'interpretation' in this Code include appropriate assistance necessary to establish effective communication with that person. See *paragraph 13.1C* if the detainee is in Wales.

H:13.1ZA References in *paragraph 13.1* above and elsewhere in this Code (see *paragraphs 3.14(a), 13.2, 13.3, 13.5, 13.6, 13.9, 13.10A, 13.10D* and *13.11 below* and in any other Code, to making arrangements for an interpreter to assist a suspect, mean making arrangements for the interpreter to be *physically* present in the same location as the suspect *unless* the provisions in *paragraph 13.12* below, and Part 1 of *Annex L,* allow live-link interpretation to be used.

H:13.1A The arrangements must comply with the minimum requirements set out in Directive 2010/64/EU of the European Parliament and of the Council of 20 October 2010 on the right to interpretation and translation in criminal proceedings (see *Note 13A*). The provisions of this Code implement the requirements for those to whom this Code applies. These requirements include the following:

- That the arrangements made and the quality of interpretation and translation provided shall be sufficient to '*safeguard the fairness of the proceedings, in particular by ensuring that suspected or accused persons have knowledge of the cases against them and are able to exercise their right of defence*'. This term which is used by the Directive means that the suspect must be able to understand their position and be able to communicate effectively with police officers, interviewers, solicitors and appropriate adults as provided for by this and any other Code in the same way as a suspect who can speak and understand English who does not have a hearing or speech impediment and who would not require an interpreter. See *paragraphs 13.12* to *13.14* and *Annex L* for application to live-link interpretation
- The provision of a written translation of all documents considered essential for the person to exercise their right of defence and to '*safeguard the fairness of the proceedings*' as described above. For the purposes of this Code, this includes any decision to authorise a person to be detained and details of any offence(s) with which the person has been charged or for which they have been told they may be prosecuted, see *Annex K.*
- Procedures to help determine:
  - ˜ whether a suspect can speak and understand English and needs the assistance of an interpreter (*see paragraph 13.1* and *Notes 13B* and *13C*); and
  - ˜ whether another interpreter should be called or another translation should be provided when a suspect complains about the quality of either or both (see *paragraphs 13.10A* and *13.10C*).

H:13.1B All reasonable attempts should be made to make the suspect understand that interpretation and translation will be provided at public expense.

H:13.1C With regard to persons in Wales, nothing in this or any other Code affects the application of the Welsh Language Schemes produced by police and crime commissioners in Wales in accordance with the Welsh Language Act 1993. See paragraphs *3.14 and 13.1.*

(b) Interviewing suspects - foreign languages

A-226a H:13.2 Unless *paragraphs 11.2 or 11.11(c)* apply, a suspect who for the purposes of this Code requires an interpreter because they do not appear to speak or understand English (see *paragraphs 3.5(c)(ii)* and *3.14*) must not be interviewed unless arrangements are made for a person capable of interpreting to assist the suspect to understand and communicate.

H:13.3 If a person who is a juvenile or a vulnerable person is interviewed and the person acting as the appropriate adult, does not appear to speak or understand English, arrangements must be made for an interpreter to assist communication between the between the person, the appropriate adult and the interviewer, unless the interview is urgent and *paragraphs 11.2 or 11.11(c)* apply.

H:13.4 In the case of a person making a statement under caution to a police officer or other police staff other than in English:

(a) the interpreter shall record the statement in the language it is made;
(b) the person shall be invited to sign it;
(c) an official English translation shall be made in due course.

See *paragraphs 13.12* to *13.14* and *Annex L* for application to live-link interpretation.

(c) Interviewing suspects who have a hearing or speech impediment

H:13.5 Unless *paragraphs 11.2* or *11.11(c)* (urgent interviews) apply, a suspect who for the purposes of this Code requires an interpreter or other appropriate assistance to enable effective communication with them because they appear to have a hearing or speech impediment (see *paragraphs 3.5(c)(ii)* and *3.14*) must not be interviewed without arrangements having been made to provide an independent person capable of interpreting or of providing other appropriate assistance. **A-226b**

H:13.6 An interpreter should also be arranged if a person who is a juvenile or a vulnerable person is interviewed and the person who is present as the appropriate adult appears to have a hearing or speech impediment, unless the interview is urgent and *paragraphs 11.2* or *11.11(c)* apply.

H:13.7 *Not used*

(d) Additional rules for detained persons

H:13.8 *Not used.* **A-226c**

H:13.9 If *paragraph 6.1* applies and the detainee cannot communicate with the solicitor because of language, hearing or speech difficulties, arrangements must be made for an interpreter to enable communication. A police officer or any other police staff may not be used for this purpose.

H:13.10 After the custody officer has determined that a detainee requires an interpreter (see *paragraph 3.5(c)(ii)*) and following the initial action in *paragraphs 3.1 to 3.5*, arrangements must also be made for an interpreter to explain:

- the grounds and reasons for any authorisation of their detention under the provisions of the Terrorism Act 2000 or the Counter Terrorism Act 2008 (post-charge questioning) to which this Code applies; and
- any information about the authorisation given to them by the authorising officer or (as the case may be) the court and which is recorded in the custody record.

See *sections 14* and *15* of this Code.

H:13.10A If a detainee complains that they are not satisfied with the quality of interpretation, the custody officer or (as the case may be) the interviewer, is responsible for deciding whether to make arrangements for a different interpreter in accordance with the procedures set out in the arrangements made by the chief officer, *see paragraph 13.1A.*

(e) Translations of essential documents

H:13.10B Written translations, oral translations and oral summaries of essential documents in a language the detainee understands shall be provided in accordance with Annex K (Translations of documents and records). **A-226d**

H:13.10C If a detainee complains that they are not satisfied with the quality of the translation, the custody officer or (as the case may be) the interviewer, is responsible for deciding whether a further translation should be provided in accordance with the procedures set out in the arrangements made by the chief officer, see *paragraph 13.1A.*

(f) Decisions not to provide interpretation and translation.

H:13.10D If a suspect challenges a decision: **A-226e**

- made by the custody officer in accordance with this Code (see *paragraph 3.5(c)(ii)*) that they do not require an interpreter, or
- made in accordance with *paragraphs 13.10A, 13.10B* or *13.10C* not to make arrangements to provide a different interpreter or another translation or not to translate a requested document,

the matter shall be reported to an inspector to deal with as a complaint for the purposes of *paragraph 9.3* or *12.10* if the challenge is made during an interview.

(g) Documentation

H:13.11 The following must be recorded in the custody record or as applicable, interview record: **A-226f**

(a) Action taken to arrange for an interpreter, including the live-link requirements in *Annex L* as applicable;

(b) Action taken when a detainee is not satisfied about the standard of interpretation or translation provided, see *paragraphs 13.10A* and *13.10C*;
(c) When an urgent interview is carried out in accordance with *paragraph 13.2* or *13.5* in the absence of an interpreter;
(d) When a detainee has been assisted by an interpreter for the purpose of providing or being given information or being interviewed;
(e) Action taken in accordance with Annex K when:
- a written translation of an essential document is provided;
- an oral translation or oral summary of an essential document is provided instead of a written translation and the authorising officer's reason(s) why this would not prejudice the fairness of the proceedings (see *Annex K, paragraph 3*);
- a suspect waives their right to a translation of an essential document (see *Annex K, paragraph 4*);
- when representations that a document which is not included in the table is essential and that a translation should be provided are refused and the reason for the refusal (see *Annex K, paragraph 8*).

(h) Live-link interpretation

A-226g H:13.12 In this section and in *Annex L*, "live-link interpretation" means an arrangement to enable communication between the suspect and an interpreter who is not *physically* present with the suspect. The arrangement must ensure that anything said by any person in the suspect's presence and hearing can be interpreted in the same way as if the interpreter was physically present at that time. The communication must be by audio *and* visual means for the purpose of an interview, and for all other purposes it may be *either*; by audio and visual means, or by audio means *only*, as follows:

(a) **Audio and visual communication** This is required for interviews conducted and recorded in accordance with the Code of Practice for the video recording with sound, of interviews of persons detained under *section 41 of the Terrorism Act 2000* and of persons for whom an authorisation to question after charge has been given under *section 22 of the Counter-Terrorism act 2008* (see *Note 13D*). In these each of these cases, the interview must be video recorded with sound and during that interview, live link interpretation must *enable*:
  (i) the suspect, the interviewer, solicitor, appropriate adult and any other person *physically* present with the suspect at any time during the interview and an interpreter who is not *physically* present, to *see* and *hear* each other; and
  (ii) the interview to be conducted and recorded in accordance with the relevant provisions of the Code, subject to the modifications in *Part 2 of Annex L*.
(b) **Audio and visual or audio without visual communication.** This applies to communication for the purposes of any provision of this Code except as described in (a), which requires or permits information to be given to, sought from, or provided by a suspect, whether orally or in writing, which would include communication between the suspect and their solicitor and/or appropriate adult, and for these cases, live link interpretation must:
  (i) *enable* the suspect, the person giving or seeking that information, any other person *physically* present with the suspect at that time and an interpreter who is not so present, to either *see* and *hear* each other, or to *hear without seeing* each other (for example by using a telephone); and
  (ii) enable that information to be given to, sought from, or provided by, the suspect in accordance with the provisions of this Code that apply to that information, as modified for the purposes of the live-link, by *Part 2 of Annex L*.

H:13.12A The requirement in *sub-paragraphs 13.12(a)(ii)* and *(b)(ii)*, that live-link interpretation must enable compliance with the relevant provisions of the specified Codes, means that the arrangements must provide for any written or electronic record of what the suspect says in their own language which is made by the interpreter, to be securely transmitted without delay so that the suspect can be invited to read, check and if appropriate, sign or otherwise confirm that the record is correct or make corrections to the record.

H:13.13 Chief officers must be satisfied that live-link interpretation used in their force area for the purposes of *paragraphs 13.12(a)* and *(b)*, provides for accurate and secure communication with the suspect. This includes ensuring that at any time during which live link interpretation is being used, a person cannot see, hear or otherwise obtain access to any communications between the suspect and interpreter or communicate with the suspect or interpreter unless so authorised or allowed by the custody officer or in the case of an interview, the interviewer and that as applicable, the confidentiality of any private consultation between a suspect and their solicitor and appropriate adult (see *paragraphs 13.2A, 13.6* and *13.9*) is maintained. See *Annex L paragraph 4*.

Notes for Guidance

A-226h *H:13A Chief officers have discretion when determining the individuals or organisations they use to provide* *interpretation and translation services for their forces provided that these services are compatible with the requirements of the Directive. One example which chief officers may wish to consider is the Ministry of Justice commercial agreements for interpretation and translation services.*

H:13B A procedure for determining whether a person needs an interpreter might involve a telephone interpreter service or using cue cards or similar visual aids which enable the detainee to indicate their ability to speak and understand English and their preferred language. This could be confirmed through an interpreter who could also assess the extent to which the person can speak and understand English.

H:13C There should also be a procedure for determining whether a suspect who requires an interpreter requires assistance in accordance with paragraph 3.20 to help them check and if applicable, sign any documentation.

H:13D The Code of Practice referred to in paragraph 13.12, is available here: https://www.gov.uk/government/publications/terrorism-act-2000-video-recording-code-of-practice.

H:14 Reviews and Extensions of Detention under the Terrorism Act 2000

(a) General

H:14.0 The requirement in *paragraph 3.4(b)* that documents and materials essential to challenging the lawfulness the detainee's arrest and detention must be made available to the detainee or their solicitor, applies for the purposes of this section. **A-227**

H:14.1 The powers and duties of the review officer are in the Terrorism Act 2000, Schedule 8, Part II. See *Notes 14A and 14B.* A review officer should carry out their duties at the police station where the detainee is held and be allowed such access to the detainee as is necessary to exercise those duties.

H:14.2 For the purposes of reviewing a person's detention, no officer shall put specific questions to the detainee:

- regarding their involvement in any offence; or
- in respect of any comments they may make:
  - ~ when given the opportunity to make representations; or
  - ~ in response to a decision to keep them in detention or extend the maximum period of detention.

Such an exchange could constitute an interview as in *paragraph 11.1* and would be subject to the associated safeguards in *section 11.*

H:14.3 If detention is necessary for longer than 48 hours from the time of arrest or, if a person was being detained under *TACT Schedule 7,* from the time at which the examination under Schedule 7 began, a police officer of at least superintendent rank, or a Crown Prosecutor may apply for a warrant of further detention or for an extension or further extension of such a warrant under *paragraph 29* or (as the case may be) *36 of Part III of Schedule 8 to the Terrorism Act 2000.* See *Note 14C.*

H:14.4 When an application is made for a warrant as described in paragraph 14.3, the detained person and their representative must be informed of their rights in respect of the application. These include:

(i) the right to a written notice of the application (s*ee paragraph 14.4*);
(ii) the right to make oral or written representations to the judicial authority / High Court judge about the application;
(iii) the right to be present and legally represented at the hearing of the application, unless specifically excluded by the judicial authority / High Court judge;
(iv) their right to free legal advice (see *section 6* of this Code).

H:14.4A TACT Schedule 8 paragraph 31 requires the notice of the application for a warrant of further detention to be provided before the judicial hearing of the application for that warrant and that the notice must include:

(a) notification that the application for a warrant has been made;
(b) the time at which the application was made;
(c) the time at which the application is to be heard;
(d) the grounds on which further detention is sought.

A notice must also be provided each time an application is made to extend or further extend an existing warrant.

(b) Transfer of persons detained for more than 14 days to prison

H:14.5 If the *Detention of Terrorists Suspects (Temporary Extension) Bill* is enacted and in force, a High Court judge may extend or further extend a warrant of further detention to authorise a person to be detained beyond a period of 14 days from the time of their arrest (or if they were being detained under *TACT Schedule 7,* from the time at which their examination under *Schedule 7* began). **A-227a**

The provisions of *Annex J* will apply when a warrant of further detention is so extended or further extended.

H:14.6 *Not used.*

H:14.7 *Not used.*

H:14.8 *Not used.*

H:14.9 *Not used.*

H:14.10 *Not used.*

(c) Documentation

A-227b H:14.11 It is the responsibility of the officer who gives any reminders as at *paragraph 14.4*, to ensure that these are noted in the custody record, as well any comments made by the detained person upon being told of those rights.

H:14.12 The grounds for, and extent of, any delay in conducting a review shall be recorded.

H:14.13 Any written representations shall be retained.

H:14.14 A record shall be made as soon as practicable about the outcome of each review and, if applicable, the grounds on which the review officer authorises continued detention. A record shall also be made as soon as practicable about the outcome of an application for a warrant of further detention or its extension.

H:14.15 *Not used.*

Notes for Guidance

A-227c *H:14A TACT Schedule 8 Part II sets out the procedures for review of detention up to 48 hours from the time of arrest under TACT section 41 (or if a person was being detained under TACT Schedule 7, from the time at which the examination under Schedule 7 began). These include provisions for the requirement to review detention, postponing a review, grounds for continued detention, designating a review officer, representations, rights of the detained person and keeping a record. The review officer's role ends after a warrant has been issued for extension of detention under Part III of Schedule 8.*

H:14B A review officer may authorise a person's continued detention if satisfied that detention is necessary:

(a) to obtain relevant evidence whether by questioning the person or otherwise;

(b) to preserve relevant evidence;

(c) while awaiting the result of an examination or analysis of relevant evidence;

(d) for the examination or analysis of anything with a view to obtaining relevant evidence;

(e) pending a decision to apply to the Secretary of State for a deportation notice to be served on the detainee, the making of any such application, or the consideration of any such application by the Secretary of State;

(f) pending a decision to charge the detainee with an offence.

H:14C Applications for warrants to extend detention beyond 48 hours, may be made for periods of 7 days at a time (initially under TACT Schedule 8 paragraph 29, and extensions thereafter under TACT Schedule 8, paragraph 36), up to a maximum period of 14 days (or 28 days if the Detention of Terrorists Suspects (Temporary Extension) Bill) is enacted and in force) from the time of their arrest (or if they were being detained under TACT Schedule 7, from the time at which their examination under Schedule 7 began). Applications may be made for shorter periods than 7 days, which must be specified. The judicial authority or High Court judge may also substitute a shorter period if they feel a period of 7 days is inappropriate.

H:14D Unless Note 14F applies, applications for warrants that would take the total period of detention up to 14 days or less should be made to a judicial authority, meaning a District Judge (Magistrates' Court) designated by the Lord Chief Justice to hear such applications.

H:14E If by virtue of the relevant provisions described in Note 14C being enacted the maximum period of detention is extended to 28 days, any application for a warrant which would take the period of detention beyond 14 days from the time of arrest (or if a person was being detained under TACT Schedule 7, from the time at which the examination under Schedule 7 began), must be made to a High Court Judge.

H:14F If, when the Detention of Terrorists Suspects (Temporary Extension) Bill is enacted and in force, an application is made to a High Court judge for a warrant which would take detention beyond 14 days and the High Court judge instead issues a warrant for a period of time which would not take detention beyond 14 days, further applications for extension of detention must also be made to a High Court judge, regardless of the period of time to which they refer.

H:14G Not used.

H:14H An officer applying for an order under TACT Schedule 8 paragraph 34 to withhold specified information on which they intend to rely when applying for a warrant of further detention or the extension or further extension of such a warrant, may make the application for the order orally or in writing. The most appropriate method of application will depend on the circumstances of the case and the need to ensure fairness to the detainee.

H:14I After hearing any representations by or on behalf of the detainee and the applicant, the judicial authority or High Court judge may direct that the hearing relating to the extension of detention under Part III of Schedule 8 is to take place using video conferencing facilities. However, if the judicial authority requires the detained person to be physically present at any hearing, this should be complied with as soon as practicable. Paragraph 33(4) to (9) of TACT Schedule 8 govern the hearing of applications via video-link or other means.

H:14J Not used.

H:14K Not used.

H:15 Charging and post-charge questioning in terrorism cases

(a) Charging

H:15.1 Charging of detained persons is covered by PACE and guidance issued under PACE by the Director of Public Prosecutions. Decisions to charge persons to whom this Code (H) applies, the charging process and related matters are subject to section 16 of PACE Code C. **A-228**

(b) Post-charge questioning

H:15.2 Under *section 22 of the Counter-Terrorism Act 2008*, a judge of the Crown Court may authorise the questioning of a person about an offence for which they have been charged, informed that they may be prosecuted or sent for trial, if the offence: **A-228a**

- is a terrorism offence as set out in *section 27 of the Counter-Terrorism Act 2008*; or
- is an offence which appears to the judge to have a terrorist connection. See *Note 15C.*

The decision on whether to apply for such questioning will be based on the needs of the investigation. There is no power to detain a person solely for the purposes of post-charge questioning. A person can only be detained whilst being so questioned (whether at a police station or in prison) if they are already there in lawful custody under some existing power. If at a police station the contents of *sections 8* and *9* of this Code must be considered the minimum standards of treatment for such detainees.

H:15.3 The Crown Court judge may authorise the questioning if they are satisfied that:

- further questioning is necessary in the interests of justice;
- the investigation for the purposes of which the further questioning is being proposed is being conducted diligently and expeditiously; and
- the questioning would not interfere unduly with the preparation of the person's defence to the charge or any other criminal charge that they may be facing.

See *Note 15E*

H:15.4 The judge authorising questioning may specify the location of the questioning.

H:15.5 The judge may only authorise a period up to a maximum of 48 hours before further authorisation must be sought. The 48 hour period would run continuously from the commencement of questioning. This period must include breaks in questioning in accordance with *paragraphs 8.6* and *12.2* of this Code (see *Note 15B*).

H:15.6 Nothing in this Code shall be taken to prevent a suspect seeking a voluntary interview with the police at any time.

H:15.7 For the purposes of this section, any reference in *sections 6, 10, 11, 12* and *13* of this Code to:

- "suspect" means the person in respect of whom an authorisation has been given under section 22 of the Counter-Terrorism Act 2008 (post-charge questioning of terrorist suspects) to interview them;
- "interview" means post-charge questioning authorised under section 22 of the Counter-Terrorism Act 2008;
- "offence" means an offence for which the person has been charged, informed that they may be prosecuted or sent for trial and about which the person is being questioned; and
- "place of detention" means the location of the questioning specified by the judge (see *paragraph 15.4*),

and the provisions of those sections apply (as appropriate), to such questioning (whether at a police station or in prison) subject to the further modifications in the following paragraphs:

Right to legal advice

H:15.8 In *section 6* of this Code, for the purposes of post-charge questioning: **A-228b**

- access to a solicitor may not be delayed under Annex B; and
- *paragraph 6.5* (direction that a detainee may only consult a solicitor within the sight and hearing of a qualified officer) does not apply.

Cautions

A-228c H:15.9 In *section 10* of this Code, unless the restriction on drawing adverse inferences from silence applies (see paragraph 15.10), for the purposes of post-charge questioning, the caution must be given in the following terms before any such questions are asked:

> "*You do not have to say anything. But it may harm your defence if you do not mention when questioned something which you later rely on in Court. Anything you do say may be given in evidence.*"

Where the use of the Welsh Language is appropriate, a constable may provide the caution directly in Welsh in the following terms:

> "*Does dim rhaid i chi ddweud dim byd. Ond gall niweidio eich amddiffyniad os na fyddwch chi'n sôn, wrth gael eich holi, am rywbeth y byddwch chi'n dibynnu arno nes ymlaen yn y Llys. Gall unrhyw beth yr ydych yn ei ddweud gael ei roi fel tystiolaeth.*"

H:15.10 The only restriction on drawing adverse inferences from silence, see *Annex C*, applies in those situations where a person has asked for legal advice and is questioned before receiving such advice in accordance with paragraph 6.7(b).

Interviews

A-228d H:15.11 In *section 11*, for the purposes of post-charge questioning, whenever a person is questioned, they must be informed of the offence for which they have been charged or informed that they may be prosecuted, or that they have been sent for trial and about which they are being questioned.

H:15.12 *Paragraph 11.2* (place where questioning may take place) does not apply to post-charge questioning.

Recording post-charge questioning

A-228e H:15.13 All interviews must be video recorded with sound in accordance with the separate Code of Practice issued under section 25 of the Counter-Terrorism Act 2008 for the video recording with sound of post-charge questioning authorised under section 22 of the Counter-Terrorism Act 2008 (see *paragraph 11.8*).

Notes for Guidance

A-228f *H:15A If a person is detained at a police station for the purposes of post-charge questioning, a custody record must be opened in accordance with section 2 of this Code. The custody record must note the power under which the person is being detained, the time at which the person was transferred into police custody, their time of arrival at the police station and their time of being presented to the custody officer.*

H:15B The custody record must note the time at which the interview process commences. This shall be regarded as the relevant time for any period of questioning in accordance with paragraph 15.5 of this Code.

H:15C Where reference is made to 'terrorist connection' in paragraph 15.2, this is determined in accordance with section 30 of the Counter-Terrorism Act 2008. Under section 30 of that Act a court must in certain circumstances determine whether an offence has a terrorist connection. These are offences under general criminal law which may be prosecuted in terrorism cases (for example explosives-related offences and conspiracy to murder). An offence has a terrorist connection if the offence is, or takes place in the course of, an act of terrorism or is committed for the purposes of terrorism (section 98 of the Act). Normally the court will make the determination during the sentencing process, however for the purposes of post-charge questioning, a Crown Court Judge must determine whether the offence could have a terrorist connection.

H:15D The powers under section 22 of the Counter-Terrorism Act 2008 are separate from and additional to the normal questioning procedures within this code. Their overall purpose is to enable the further questioning of a terrorist suspect after charge. They should not therefore be used to replace or circumvent the normal powers for dealing with routine questioning.

H:15E Post-charge questioning has been created because it is acknowledged that terrorist investigations can be large and complex and that a great deal of evidence can come to light following the charge of a terrorism suspect. This can occur, for instance, from the translation of material or as the result of additional investigation. When considering an application for post-charge questioning, the police must 'satisfy' the judge on all three points under paragraph 15.3. This means that the judge will either authorise or refuse an application on the balance of whether the conditions in paragraph 15.3 are all met. It is important therefore, that when making the application, to consider the following questions:

- *What further evidence is the questioning expected to provide?*
- *Why was it not possible to obtain this evidence before charge?*
- *How and why was the need to question after charge first recognised?*

- *How is the questioning expected to contribute further to the case?*
- *To what extent could the time and place for further questioning interfere with the preparation of the person's defence (for example if authorisation is sought close to the time of a trial)?*
- *What steps will be taken to minimise any risk that questioning might interfere with the preparation of the person's defence?*

This list is not exhaustive but outlines the type of questions that could be relevant to any asked by a judge in considering an application.

H:16 Testing persons for the presence of specified Class A drugs

H:16.1 The provisions for drug testing under section 63B of PACE (as amended by section 5 of the Criminal Justice Act 2003 and section 7 of the Drugs Act 2005), do not apply to persons to whom this Code applies. Guidance on these provisions can be found in section 17 of PACE Code C. **A-229**

ANNEX A: INTIMATE AND STRIP SEARCHES

A Intimate search

H:1. An intimate search consists of the physical examination of a person's body orifices other than the mouth. The intrusive nature of such searches means the actual and potential risks associated with intimate searches must never be underestimated. **A-229a**

(a) Action

H:2. Body orifices other than the mouth may be searched if authorised by an officer of inspector rank or above who has reasonable grounds for believing that the person may have concealed on themselves anything which they could and might use to cause physical injury to themselves or others at the station and the officer has reasonable grounds for believing that an intimate search is the only means of removing those items. **A-229b**

H:3. Before the search begins, a police officer or designated detention officer, must tell the detainee:

(a) that the authority to carry out the search has been given;

(b) the grounds for giving the authorisation and for believing that the article cannot be removed without an intimate search.

H:4. An intimate search may only be carried out by a registered medical practitioner or registered nurse, unless an officer of at least inspector rank considers this is not practicable, in which case a police officer may carry out the search. See *Notes A1* to *A5*.

H:5. Any proposal for a search under *paragraph 2* to be carried out by someone other than a registered medical practitioner or registered nurse must only be considered as a last resort and when the authorising officer is satisfied the risks associated with allowing the item to remain with the detainee outweigh the risks associated with removing it. See *Notes A1* to *A5*.

H:6. An intimate search at a police station of a juvenile or a vulnerable person may take place only in the presence of an appropriate adult of the same sex (see *Annex I*), unless the detainee specifically requests a particular adult of the opposite sex who is readily available. In the case of a juvenile the search may take place in the absence of the appropriate adult only if the juvenile signifies in the presence of the appropriate adult they do not want the adult present during the search and the adult agrees. A record shall be made of the juvenile's decision and signed by the appropriate adult.

H:7. When an intimate search under *paragraph 2* is carried out by a police officer, the officer must be of the same sex as the detainee (see *Annex I*). A minimum of two people, other than the detainee, must be present during the search. Subject to *paragraph 6*, no person of the opposite sex who is not a medical practitioner or nurse shall be present, nor shall anyone whose presence is unnecessary. The search shall be conducted with proper regard to the dignity, sensitivity and vulnerability of the detainee including in particular, their health, hygiene and welfare needs to which *paragraphs 9.4A* and *9.4B* apply.

(b) Documentation

H:8. In the case of an intimate search under paragraph 2, the following shall be recorded as soon as practicable, in the detainee's custody record: **A-229c**

- the authorisation to carry out the search;
- the grounds for giving the authorisation;
- the grounds for believing the article could not be removed without an intimate search;

- which parts of the detainee's body were searched;
- who carried out the search;
- who was present;
- the result.

H:9. If an intimate search is carried out by a police officer, the reason why it was impracticable for a registered medical practitioner or registered nurse to conduct it must be recorded.

B Strip search

A-229d H:10. A strip search is a search involving the removal of more than outer clothing. In this Code, outer clothing includes shoes and socks.

(a) Action

A-229e H:11. A strip search may take place only if it is considered necessary to remove an article which a detainee would not be allowed to keep, and the officer reasonably considers the detainee might have concealed such an article. Strip searches shall not be routinely carried out if there is no reason to consider that articles are concealed.

The conduct of strip searches

A-229f H:12. When strip searches are conducted:

(a) a police officer carrying out a strip search must be the same sex as the detainee (see *Annex I*);

(b) the search shall take place in an area where the detainee cannot be seen by anyone who does not need to be present, nor by a member of the opposite sex (see *Annex I*) except an appropriate adult who has been specifically requested by the detainee;

(c) except in cases of urgency, where there is risk of serious harm to the detainee or to others, whenever a strip search involves exposure of intimate body parts, there must be at least two people present other than the detainee, and if the search is of a juvenile or a vulnerable person, one of the people must be the appropriate adult. Except in urgent cases as above, a search of a juvenile may take place in the absence of the appropriate adult only if the juvenile signifies in the presence of the appropriate adult that they do not want the adult to be present during the search and the adult agrees. A record shall be made of the juvenile's decision and signed by the appropriate adult. The presence of more than two people, other than an appropriate adult, shall be permitted only in the most exceptional circumstances;

(d) the search shall be conducted with proper regard to the dignity, sensitivity and vulnerability of the detainee in these circumstances including in particular, their health, hygiene and welfare needs to which *paragraphs 9.4A* and *9.4B* apply. Every reasonable effort shall be made to secure the detainee's co-operation, maintain their dignity and minimise embarrassment. Detainees who are searched shall not normally be required to remove all their clothes at the same time, e.g. a person should be allowed to remove clothing above the waist and redress before removing further clothing;

(e) if necessary to assist the search, the detainee may be required to hold their arms in the air or to stand with their legs apart and bend forward so a visual examination may be made of the genital and anal areas provided no physical contact is made with any body orifice;

(f) if articles are found, the detainee shall be asked to hand them over. If articles are found within any body orifice other than the mouth, and the detainee refuses to hand them over, their removal would constitute an intimate search, which must be carried out as in *Part A*;

(g) a strip search shall be conducted as quickly as possible, and the detainee allowed to dress as soon as the procedure is complete.

(b) Documentation

A-229g H:13. A record shall be made on the custody record of a strip search including the reason it was considered necessary, those present and any result.

Notes for Guidance

A-229h *H:A1 Before authorising any intimate search, the authorising officer must make every reasonable effort to persuade the detainee to hand the article over without a search. If the detainee agrees, a registered medical practitioner or registered nurse should whenever possible be asked to assess the risks involved and, if necessary, attend to assist the detainee.*

H:A2 If the detainee does not agree to hand the article over without a search, the authorising officer must carefully review all the relevant factors before authorising an intimate search. In particular, the officer must consider whether the grounds for believing an article may be concealed are reasonable.

H:A3 If authority is given for a search under paragraph 2, a registered medical practitioner or registered nurse shall be consulted whenever possible. The presumption should be that the search will be conducted by the registered medical practitioner or registered nurse and the authorising officer must make every reasonable effort to persuade the detainee to allow the medical practitioner or nurse to conduct the search.

H:A4 A constable should only be authorised to carry out a search as a last resort and when all other approaches have failed. In these circumstances, the authorising officer must be satisfied the detainee might use the article for one or more of the purposes in paragraph 2 and the physical injury likely to be caused is sufficiently severe to justify authorising a constable to carry out the search.

H:A5 If an officer has any doubts whether to authorise an intimate search by a constable, the officer should seek advice from an officer of superintendent rank or above.

ANNEX B: DELAY IN NOTIFICATION OF ARREST AND WHEREABOUTS OR ALLOWING ACCESS TO LEGAL ADVICE FOR PERSONS DETAINED UNDER THE TERRORISM ACT 2000.

A DELAYS under TACT Schedule 8

H:1. The rights as in *sections 5* or *6*, may be delayed if the person is detained under the Terrorism Act 2000, section 41, has not yet been charged with an offence and an officer of superintendent rank or above has reasonable grounds for believing the exercise of either right will have one of the following consequences: **A-229i**

(a) interference with or harm to evidence of a serious offence,
(b) interference with or physical injury to any person,
(c) the alerting of persons who are suspected of having committed a serious offence but who have not been arrested for it,
(d) the hindering of the recovery of property obtained as a result of a serious offence or in respect of which a forfeiture order could be made under section 23,
(e) interference with the gathering of information about the commission, preparation or instigation of acts of terrorism,
(f) the alerting of a person and thereby making it more difficult to prevent an act of terrorism, or
(g) the alerting of a person and thereby making it more difficult to secure a person's apprehension, prosecution or conviction in connection with the commission, preparation or instigation of an act of terrorism.

H:2. These rights may also be delayed if the officer has reasonable grounds for believing that:

(a) the detained person has benefited from his criminal conduct (to be decided in accordance with Part 2 of the Proceeds of Crime Act 2002), and
(b) the recovery of the value of the property constituting the benefit will be hindered by—
  (i) informing the named person of the detained person's detention (in the case of an authorisation under paragraph 8(1)(a) of Schedule 8 to TACT), or
  (ii) the exercise of the right under paragraph 7 (in the case of an authorisation under paragraph 8(1)(b) of Schedule 8 to TACT).

H:3. Authority to delay a detainee's right to consult privately with a solicitor may be given only if the authorising officer has reasonable grounds to believe the solicitor the detainee wants to consult will, inadvertently or otherwise, pass on a message from the detainee or act in some other way which will have any of the consequences specified under paragraph 8 of Schedule 8 to the Terrorism Act 2000. In these circumstances, the detainee must be allowed to choose another solicitor. See *Note B3*.

H:4. If the detainee wishes to see a solicitor, access to that solicitor may not be delayed on the grounds they might advise the detainee not to answer questions or the solicitor was initially asked to attend the police station by someone else. In the latter case the detainee must be told the solicitor has come to the police station at another person's request, and must be asked to sign the custody record to signify whether they want to see the solicitor.

H:5. The fact the grounds for delaying notification of arrest may be satisfied does not automatically mean the grounds for delaying access to legal advice will also be satisfied.

H:6. These rights may be delayed only for as long as is necessary but not beyond 48 hours from the time of arrest (or if a person was being detained under TACT Schedule 7, from the time at which the examination under Schedule 7 began). If the above grounds cease to apply within this time the detainee must as soon as practicable be asked if they wish to exercise either right, the custody record noted accordingly, and action taken in accordance with the relevant section of this Code.

H:7. A person must be allowed to consult a solicitor for a reasonable time before any court hearing.

B Documentation

A-229j H:8. The grounds for action under this Annex shall be recorded and the detainee informed of them as soon as practicable.

H:9. Any reply given by a detainee under *paragraph 6* must be recorded and the detainee asked to endorse the record in relation to whether they want to receive legal advice at this point.

C Cautions and special warnings

A-229k H:10. When a suspect detained at a police station is interviewed during any period for which access to legal advice has been delayed under this Annex, the court or jury may not draw adverse inferences from their silence.

Notes for Guidance

A-229l *H:B1 Even if Annex B applies in the case of a juvenile, or a or a vulnerable person, action to inform the appropriate adult and the person responsible for a juvenile's welfare, if that is a different person, must nevertheless be taken as in paragraph 3.15 and 3.17.*

H:B2 In the case of Commonwealth citizens and foreign nationals, see Note 7A.

H:B3 A decision to delay access to a specific solicitor is likely to be a rare occurrence and only when it can be shown the suspect is capable of misleading that particular solicitor and there is more than a substantial risk that the suspect will succeed in causing information to be conveyed which will lead to one or more of the specified consequences.

ANNEX C: RESTRICTION ON DRAWING ADVERSE INFERENCES FROM SILENCE AND TERMS OF THE CAUTION WHEN THE RESTRICTION APPLIES

(a) The restriction on drawing adverse inferences from silence

A-230 H:1. The Criminal Justice and Public Order Act 1994, sections 34, 36 and 37 as amended by the Youth Justice and Criminal Evidence Act 1999, section 58 describe the conditions under which adverse inferences may be drawn from a person's failure or refusal to say anything about their involvement in the offence when interviewed, after being charged or informed they may be prosecuted. These provisions are subject to an overriding restriction on the ability of a court or jury to draw adverse inferences from a person's silence. This restriction applies:

(a) to any detainee at a police station who, before being interviewed, see *section 11* or being charged or informed they may be prosecuted, see *section 15*, has:
  - (i) asked for legal advice, see *section 6, paragraph 6.1*;
  - (ii) not been allowed an opportunity to consult a solicitor, including the duty solicitor, as in this Code; and
  - (iii) not changed their mind about wanting legal advice, see *section 6, paragraph 6.7(d)*.

  Note the condition in (ii) will:
  - apply when a detainee who has asked for legal advice is interviewed before speaking to a solicitor as in *section 6, paragraph 6.6(a)* or *(b)*;
  - not apply if the detained person declines to ask for the duty solicitor, see *section 6, paragraphs 6.7(b)* and *(c)*.

(b) to any person who has been charged with, or informed they may be prosecuted for, an offence who:
  - (i) has had brought to their notice a written statement made by another person or the content of an interview with another person which relates to that offence, see PACE Code C *section 16, paragraph 16.4*;
  - (ii) is interviewed about that offence, see PACE Code C *section 16, paragraph 16.5*; or
  - (iii) makes a written statement about that offence, see *Annex D paragraphs 4* and *9*,

  unless post-charge questioning has been authorised in accordance with section 22 of the Counter-Terrorism Act 2008, in which case the restriction will apply only if the person has asked for legal advice, see *section 6, paragraph 6.1*, and is questioned before receiving such advice in accordance with *paragraph* 6.7(b). See *paragraph 15.11*.

(b) Terms of the caution when the restriction applies

A-230a H:2. When a requirement to caution arises at a time when the restriction on drawing adverse inferences from silence applies, the caution shall be:

'*You do not have to say anything, but anything you do say may be given in evidence.*'

Where the use of the Welsh Language is appropriate, the caution may be used directly in Welsh in the following terms:

'*Does dim rhaid i chi ddweud dim byd, ond gall unrhyw beth yr ydych chi'n ei ddweud gael ei roi fel tystiolaeth.*'

H:3. Whenever the restriction either begins to apply or ceases to apply after a caution has already been given, the person shall be re-cautioned in the appropriate terms. The changed position on drawing inferences and that the previous caution no longer applies shall also be explained to the detainee in ordinary language. See *Note C1*.

Notes for Guidance

H:C1 The following is suggested as a framework to help explain changes in the position on drawing adverse inferences if the restriction on drawing adverse inferences from silence: **A-230b**

(a) *begins to apply:*

'*The caution you were previously given no longer applies. This is because after that caution:*
(i) *you asked to speak to a solicitor but have not yet been allowed an opportunity to speak to a solicitor. See paragraph 1(a); or*
(ii) *you have been charged with/informed you may be prosecuted. See paragraph 1(b).*

'*This means that from now on, adverse inferences cannot be drawn at court and your defence will not be harmed just because you choose to say nothing. Please listen carefully to the caution I am about to give you because it will apply from now on. You will see that it does not say anything about your defence being harmed.*'

(b) *ceases to apply before or at the time the person is charged or informed they may be prosecuted, see paragraph 1(a);*

'*The caution you were previously given no longer applies. This is because after that caution you have been allowed an opportunity to speak to a solicitor. Please listen carefully to the caution I am about to give you because it will apply from now on. It explains how your defence at court may be affected if you choose to say nothing.*'

ANNEX D: WRITTEN STATEMENTS UNDER CAUTION

(a) Written by a person under caution

H:1. A person shall always be invited to write down what they want to say. **A-230c**

H:2. A person who has not been charged with, or informed they may be prosecuted for, any offence to which the statement they want to write relates, shall:

(a) unless the statement is made at a time when the restriction on drawing adverse inferences from silence applies, see Annex C, be asked to write out and sign the following before writing what they want to say:

'*I make this statement of my own free will. I understand that I do not have to say anything but that it may harm my defence if I do not mention when questioned something which I later rely on in court. This statement may be given in evidence.*';

(b) if the statement is made at a time when the restriction on drawing adverse inferences from silence applies, be asked to write out and sign the following before writing what they want to say;

'*I make this statement of my own free will. I understand that I do not have to say anything. This statement may be given in evidence.*'

H:3. When a person, on the occasion of being charged with or informed they may be prosecuted for any offence, asks to make a statement which relates to any such offence and wants to write it they shall:

(a) unless the restriction on drawing adverse inferences from silence, see Annex C, applied when they were so charged or informed they may be prosecuted, be asked to write out and sign the following before writing what they want to say:

'*I make this statement of my own free will. I understand that I do not have to say anything but that it may harm my defence if I do not mention when questioned something which I later rely on in court. This statement may be given in evidence.*';

(b) if the restriction on drawing adverse inferences from silence applied when they were so charged or informed they may be prosecuted, be asked to write out and sign the following before writing what they want to say:

'*I make this statement of my own free will. I understand that I do not have to say anything. This statement may be given in evidence.*'

H:4. When a person who has already been charged with or informed they may be prosecuted for any offence, asks to make a statement which relates to any such offence and wants to write it they shall be asked to write out and sign the following before writing what they want to say:

'*I make this statement of my own free will. I understand that I do not have to say anything. This statement may be given in evidence.*';

H:5. Any person writing their own statement shall be allowed to do so without any prompting except a police officer or other police staff may indicate to them which matters are material or question any ambiguity in the statement.

(b) Written by a police officer or other police staff

A-230d H:6. If a person says they would like someone to write the statement for them, a police officer, or other police staff shall write the statement.

H:7. If the person has not been charged with, or informed they may be prosecuted for, any offence to which the statement they want to make relates they shall, before starting, be asked to sign, or make their mark, to the following:

(a) unless the statement is made at a time when the restriction on drawing adverse inferences from silence applies, see *Annex C*:

'*I, ..., wish to make a statement. I want someone to write down what I say. I understand that I do not have to say anything but that it may harm my defence if I do not mention when questioned something which I later rely on in court. This statement may be given in evidence.*';

(b) if the statement is made at a time when the restriction on drawing adverse inferences from silence applies:

'*I, ..., wish to make a statement. I want someone to write down what I say. I understand that I do not have to say anything. This statement may be given in evidence.*'

H:8. If, on the occasion of being charged with or informed they may be prosecuted for any offence, the person asks to make a statement which relates to any such offence they shall before starting be asked to sign, or make their mark to, the following:

(a) unless the restriction on drawing adverse inferences from silence applied, see *Annex C*, when they were so charged or informed they may be prosecuted:

'*I, ..., wish to make a statement. I want someone to write down what I say. I understand that I do not have to say anything but that it may harm my defence if I do not mention when questioned something which I later rely on in court. This statement may be given in evidence.*';

(b) if the restriction on drawing adverse inferences from silence applied when they were so charged or informed they may be prosecuted:

'*I, ..., wish to make a statement. I want someone to write down what I say. I understand that I do not have to say anything. This statement may be given in evidence.*'

H:9. If, having already been charged with or informed they may be prosecuted for any offence, a person asks to make a statement which relates to any such offence they shall before starting, be asked to sign, or make their mark to:

'*I, ..., wish to make a statement. I want someone to write down what I say. I understand that I do not have to say anything. This statement may be given in evidence.*'

H:10. The person writing the statement must take down the exact words spoken by the person making it and must not edit or paraphrase it. Any questions that are necessary, e.g. to make it more intelligible, and the answers given must be recorded at the same time on the statement form.

H:11. When the writing of a statement is finished the person making it shall be asked to read it and to make any corrections, alterations or additions they want. When they have finished reading they shall be asked to write and sign or make their mark on the following certificate at the end of the statement:

'I have read the above statement, and I have been able to correct, alter or add anything I wish. This statement is true. I have made it of my own free will.'

H:12. If the person making the statement cannot read, or refuses to read it, or to write the above mentioned certificate at the end of it or to sign it, the person taking the statement shall read it to them and ask them if they would like to correct, alter or add anything and to put their signature or make their mark at the end. The person taking the statement shall certify on the statement itself what has occurred.

ANNEX E: SUMMARY OF PROVISIONS RELATING TO VULNERABLE PERSONS

H:1. If at any time an officer has reason to suspect that a person of any age may be vulnerable (see *paragraph 1.17(d)*), in the absence of clear evidence to dispel that suspicion in the absence of clear evidence to dispel that suspicion, that person shall be treated as such for the purposes of this Code and to establish whether any such reason may exist in relation to a person suspected of committing an offence (see *paragraph 10.1* and *Note 10A*), the custody officer shall take, or cause to be taken (see *paragraph 3.5* and *Note 3I*) the following action: **A-230e**

(a) reasonable enquiries shall be made to ascertain what information is available that is relevant to any of the factors described in *paragraph 1.17(d)* as indicating that the person may be vulnerable might apply;
(b) a record shall be made describing whether any of those factors appear to apply and provide any reason to suspect that the person may be vulnerable or (as the case may be) may not be vulnerable; and
(c) the record mentioned in sub-paragraph (b) shall be made available to be taken into account by police officers, police staff and any others who, in accordance with the provisions of this or any other Code, are required or entitled to communicate with the person in question. This would include any solicitor, appropriate adult and health care professional and is particularly relevant to communication for the purpose of interviewing and questioning after charge (see *sections 11, 12* and *15*), live link interpretation (see *paragraph 13.12*) and reviews and extensions of detention (see *section 14*).

See *Notes 1G, E4, E5* and *E6*.

H:2. In the case of a person who is vulnerable, "the appropriate adult" means:

(i) a relative, guardian or other person responsible for their care or custody;
(ii) someone experienced in dealing with vulnerable persons but who is not:
  ~ a police officer;
  ~ employed by the police;
  ~ under the direction or control of the chief officer of a police force;
  ~ a person who provides services under contractual arrangements (but without being employed by the chief officer of a police force), to assist that force in relation to the discharge of its chief officer's functions,

  whether or not they are on duty at the time.
(iii) failing these, some other responsible adult aged 18 or over who is other than a person described in the bullet points in *sub-paragraph (ii)* above.

See *paragraph 1.13(b)* and *Note 1D*

H:2A The role of the appropriate adult is to safeguard the rights, entitlements and welfare of 'vulnerable persons' (see *paragraph 1*) to whom the provisions of this and any other Code of Practice apply. For this reason, the appropriate adult is expected, amongst other things, to:

- support, advise and assist them when in accordance with this code or any other Code of Practice they are given or asked to provide information or participate in any procedure;
- observe whether the police are acting properly and fairly to respect their rights and entitlements , and inform an officer of the rank of inspector or above if they consider that they are not;
- assist them to communicate with the police whilst respecting their right to say nothing unless they want to as set out in the terms of the caution see *paragraphs 10.5* and *10.5*);
- help them to understand their rights and ensure that those rights are protected and respected.

See *paragraph 1.13A*.

H:3. If the detention of a person who is vulnerable is authorised by the review officer (see *paragraphs 14.1* and *14.2* and *Notes 14A* and *14B*), the custody officer must as soon as practicable inform the appropriate adult of the grounds for detention and the person's whereabouts, and secure **A-230f** the attendance of the appropriate adult at the police station to see the detainee. If the appropriate adult:

- is already at the station when information is given as in *paragraphs 3.1* to *3.5* the information must be given in their presence;
- is not at the station when the provisions of *paragraph 3.1* to *3.5* are complied with these provisions must be complied with again in their presence once they arrive.

See *paragraphs 3.15* to *3.16*

H:4. If the appropriate adult, having been informed of the right to legal advice, considers legal advice should be taken, the provisions of *section 6* apply as if the vulnerable person had requested access to legal advice. See *paragraphs 3.20, 6.6* and *Note E1.*

H:5. The custody officer must make sure a person receives appropriate clinical attention as soon as reasonably practicable if the person appears to be suffering from a mental disorder or in urgent cases immediately call the nearest appropriate healthcare professional or an ambulance. See *paragraphs 9.6* and *9.8.* See Code C *paragraphs 9.5* and *9.6* which when a person is detained under the Mental Health Act 1983, sections 135 and 136, as amended by the Policing and Crime Act 2017.

H:6. If a vulnerable person is cautioned in the absence of the appropriate adult, the caution must be repeated in the appropriate adult's presence. See *paragraph 10.11.*

H:7. A vulnerable person must not be interviewed or asked to provide or sign a written statement in the absence of the appropriate adult unless the provisions of *paragraphs 11.2* or *11.11* to *11.13* apply. Questioning in these circumstances may not continue in the absence of the appropriate adult once sufficient information to avert the risk has been obtained. A record shall be made of the grounds for any decision to begin an interview in these circumstances. See *paragraphs 11.2, 11.9* and *11.11* to *11.13*

H:8. If the appropriate adult is present at an interview, they shall be informed they are not expected to act simply as an observer and the purposes of their presence are to:

- advise the interviewee
- observe whether or not the interview is being conducted properly and fairly
- facilitate communication with the interviewee

See *paragraph 11.10.*

H:9. If the custody officer charges a vulnerable person with an offence or takes such other action as is appropriate when there is sufficient evidence for a prosecution this must be carried out in the presence of the appropriate adult if they are at the police station. A copy of the written notice embodying any charge must be given to the appropriate adult. See *PACE Code C Section 16.*

H:10. An intimate or strip search of a vulnerable person may take place only in the presence of the appropriate adult of the same sex, unless the detainee specifically requests the presence of a particular adult of the opposite sex. A strip search may take place in the absence of an appropriate adult only in cases of urgency when there is a risk of serious harm to the detainee or others. See *Annex A, paragraphs 6* and *12(c)*

H:11. Particular care must be taken when deciding whether to use any form of approved restraints on a vulnerable person in a locked cell. See *paragraph 8.2*

Notes for Guidance

A-230g *H:E1 The purpose of the provision at paragraph 3.20 and 6.6 is to protect the rights of a vulnerable person who does not understand the significance of what is said to them. A vulnerable person should always be given an opportunity, when an appropriate adult is called to the police station, to consult privately with a solicitor in the absence of the appropriate adult if they want.*

H:E2 Although vulnerable persons are often capable of providing reliable evidence, they may, without knowing or wanting to do so, be particularly prone in certain circumstances to provide information that may be unreliable, misleading or self-incriminating. Special care should always be taken when questioning such a person, and the appropriate adult should be involved if there is any doubt about a person's mental state or capacity. Because of the risk of unreliable evidence, it is important to obtain corroboration of any facts admitted whenever possible.

H:E3 Because of the risks referred to in Note E2, which the presence of the appropriate adult is intended to minimise, officers of superintendent rank or above should exercise their discretion to authorise the commencement of an interview in the appropriate adult's absence only in exceptional cases, if it is necessary to avert one or more of the specified risks in paragraph 11.2. See *paragraphs 11.2 and 11.11 to 11.13.*

H:E4 For the purposes of Annex E paragraph 1, examples of relevant information that may be available include:

- *the behaviour of the adult or juvenile;*
- *the mental health and capacity of the adult or juvenile;*
- *what the adult or juvenile says about themselves;*
- *information from relatives and friends of the adult or juvenile;*
- *information from police officers and staff and from police records;*

- *information from health and social care (including liaison and diversion services) and other professionals who know, or have had previous contact with, the individual and may be able to contribute to assessing their need for help and support from an appropriate adult. This includes contacts and assessments arranged by the police or at the request of the individual or (as applicable) their appropriate adult or solicitor.*

H:E5 The Mental Health Act 1983 Code of Practice at page 26 describes the range of clinically recognised conditions which can fall with the meaning of mental disorder for the purpose of paragraph 1.17(d). The Code is published here: https://www.gov.uk/government/publications/code-of-practice-mental-health-act-1983.

H:E6 When a person is under the influence of drink and/or drugs, it is not intended that they are to be treated as vulnerable and requiring an appropriate adult for the purpose of unless other information indicates that any of the factors described in paragraph 1.17(d) may apply to that person. When the person has recovered from the effects of drink and/or drugs, they should be re-assessed in accordance with Annex E paragraph 1.

ANNEX F

Not used **A-230h**

ANNEX G: FITNESS TO BE INTERVIEWED

H:1. This Annex contains general guidance to help police officers and healthcare professionals assess whether a detainee might be at risk in an interview. **A-230i**

H:2. A detainee may be at risk in an interview if it is considered that:

(a) conducting the interview could significantly harm the detainee's physical or mental state;

(b) anything the detainee says in the interview about their involvement or suspected involvement in the offence about which they are being interviewed *might* be considered unreliable in subsequent court proceedings because of their physical or mental state.

H:3. In assessing whether the detainee should be interviewed, the following must be considered:

(a) how the detainee's physical or mental state might affect their ability to understand the nature and purpose of the interview, to comprehend what is being asked and to appreciate the significance of any answers given and make rational decisions about whether they want to say anything;

(b) the extent to which the detainee's replies may be affected by their physical or mental condition rather than representing a rational and accurate explanation of their involvement in the offence;

(c) how the nature of the interview, which could include particularly probing questions, might affect the detainee.

H:4. It is essential healthcare professionals who are consulted consider the functional ability of the detainee rather than simply relying on a medical diagnosis, e.g. it is possible for a person with severe mental illness to be fit for interview.

H:5. Healthcare professionals should advise on the need for an appropriate adult to be present, whether reassessment of the person's fitness for interview may be necessary if the interview lasts beyond a specified time, and whether a further specialist opinion may be required.

H:6. When healthcare professionals identify risks they should be asked to quantify the risks. They should inform the custody officer:

- whether the person's condition:
  - ~ is likely to improve;
  - ~ will require or be amenable to treatment; and
- indicate how long it may take for such improvement to take effect.

H:7. The role of the healthcare professional is to consider the risks and advise the custody officer of the outcome of that consideration. The healthcare professional's determination and any advice or recommendations should be made in writing and form part of the custody record.

H:8. Once the healthcare professional has provided that information, it is a matter for the custody officer to decide whether or not to allow the interview to go ahead and if the interview is to proceed, to determine what safeguards are needed. Nothing prevents safeguards being provided in addition to those required under the Code. An example might be to have an appropriate healthcare professional present during the interview, in addition to an appropriate adult, in order constantly to monitor the person's condition and how it is being affected by the interview.

ANNEX H: DETAINED PERSON: OBSERVATION LIST

H:1. If any detainee fails to meet any of the following criteria, an appropriate healthcare professional or an ambulance must be called. **A-230j**

H:2. When assessing the level of rousability, consider:

Rousability - can they be woken?

- go into the cell
- call their name
- shake gently

Response *to questions* - can they give appropriate answers to questions such as:

- What's your name?
- Where do you live?
- Where do you think you are?

Response to commands - can they respond appropriately to commands such as:

- Open your eyes!
- Lift one arm, now the other arm!

H:3. Remember to take into account the possibility or presence of other illnesses, injury, or mental condition; a person who is drowsy and smells of alcohol may also have the following:

- Diabetes
- Epilepsy
- Head injury
- Drug intoxication or overdose
- Stroke

ANNEX I: ESTABLISHING GENDER OF PERSONS FOR THE PURPOSE OF SEARCHING AND CERTAIN OTHER PROCEDURES

A-230k H:1. Certain provisions of this and other PACE Codes explicitly state that searches and other procedures may only be carried out by, or in the presence of, persons of the same sex as the person subject to the search or other procedure or require action to be taken or information to be given which depends on whether the detainee is treated as being male or female. See *Note I1.*

H:2. All such searches, procedures and requirements must be carried out with courtesy, consideration and respect for the person concerned. Police officers should show particular sensitivity when dealing with transgender individuals (including transsexual persons) and transvestite persons (see *Notes I2, I3 and I4*).

(a) Consideration

A-230l H:3. In law, the gender (and accordingly the sex) of an individual is their gender as registered at birth, unless they have been issued with a Gender Recognition Certificate (GRC) under the Gender Recognition Act 2004 (GRA), in which case the person's gender is their acquired gender. This means that if the acquired gender is the male gender, the person's sex becomes that of a man and, if it is the female gender, the person's sex becomes that of a woman) and they must be treated as their acquired gender.

H:4. When establishing whether the person concerned should be treated as being male or female for the purposes of these searches, procedures and requirements, the following approach which is designed to maintain their dignity, minimise embarrassment and secure their cooperation should be followed:

(a) The person must not be asked whether they have a GRC (see *paragraph 8*);

(b) If there is no doubt as to as to whether the person concerned should be treated as being male or female, they should be dealt with as being of that sex.

(c) If at any time (including during the search or carrying out the procedure or requirement) there is doubt as to whether the person should be treated, or continue to be treated, as being male or female:

(i) the person should be asked what gender they consider themselves to be. If they express a preference to be dealt with as a particular gender, they should be asked to indicate and confirm their preference by signing the custody record or, if a custody record has not been opened, the search record or the officer's notebook. Subject to (ii) below, the person should be treated according to their preference except with regard to the requirements to provide *that* person with information concerning menstrual products and their personal needs relating to health, hygiene and welfare described in *paragraph 3.21A* (if aged under 18) and *paragraphs 9.4A* and *9.4B* (if aged 18 or over). In these cases, a person whose confirmed preference is to be dealt with as being male should be asked in private whether they wish to speak in private with a member of the custody staff of a gender of their choosing about the provision of menstrual products and their personal needs, notwithstanding their confirmed preference (see *Note I3A*);

(ii) if there are grounds to doubt that the preference in (i) accurately reflects the person's predominant lifestyle, for example, if they ask to be treated as woman but documents and other information make it clear that they live predominantly as a man, or vice versa, they should be treated according to what appears to be their predominant lifestyle and not their stated preference;

(iii) If the person is unwilling to express a preference as in (i) above, efforts should be made to determine their predominant lifestyle and they should be treated as such. For example, if they appear to live predominantly as a woman, they should be treated as being female; except with regard to the requirements to provide *that* person with information concerning menstrual products and their personal needs relating to health, hygiene and welfare described in *paragraph 3.21A* (if aged under 18) and *paragraphs 9.4A* and *9.4B* (if aged 18 or over). In these cases, a person whose predominant lifestyle has been determined to be male should be asked in private whether they wish to speak in private with a member of the custody staff of a gender of their choosing about the provision of menstrual products and their personal needs, notwithstanding their determined predominant lifestyle (see *Note I3A*); or

(iv) if none of the above apply, the person should be dealt with according to what reasonably appears to have been their sex as registered at birth.

H:5. Once a decision has been made about which gender an individual is to be treated as, each officer responsible for the search, procedure or requirement should where possible be advised before the search or procedure starts of any doubts as to the person's gender and the person informed that the doubts have been disclosed. This is important so as to maintain the dignity of the person and any officers concerned.

(b) Documentation

H:6. The person's gender as established under *paragraph 4(c)(i)* to *(iv)* above must be recorded in the person's custody record, or if a custody record has not been opened, on the search record or in the officer's notebook. **A-230m**

H:7. Where the person elects which gender they consider themselves to be under *paragraph 4(b)(i)* but following *4(b)(ii)* is not treated in accordance with their preference, the reason must be recorded in the search record, in the officer's notebook or, if applicable, in the person's custody record.

(c) Disclosure of information

H:8. Section 22 of the GRA defines any information relating to a person's application for a GRC or to a successful applicant's gender before it became their acquired gender as 'protected information'. Nothing in this Annex is to be read as authorising or permitting any police officer or any police staff who has acquired such information when acting in their official capacity to disclose that information to any other person in contravention of the GRA. Disclosure includes making a record of 'protected information' which is read by others. **A-230n**

Notes for Guidance

H:I1 Provisions to which paragraph 1 applies include: **A-230o**

- *In Code C; paragraphs 3.20A, 4.1 and Annex A paragraphs 5, 6, 11 and 12 (searches, strip and intimate searches of detainees under sections 54 and 55 of PACE) and 9.3B;*
- *In Code A; paragraphs 2.8 and 3.6 and Note 4;*
- *In Code D; paragraph 5.5 and Note 5F (searches, examinations and photographing of detainees under section 54A of PACE) and paragraph 6.9 (taking samples);*
- *In Code H; paragraphs 3.21A, 4.1 and Annex A paragraphs 6, 7 and 12 (searches, strip and intimate searches under sections 54 and 55 of PACE of persons arrested under section 41 of the Terrorism Act 2000) and 9.4B.*

H:I2 While there is no agreed definition of transgender (or trans), it is generally used as an umbrella term to describe people whose gender identity (self-identification as being a woman, man, neither or both) differs from the sex they were registered as at birth. The term includes, but is not limited to, transsexual people.

H:I3 Transsexual means a person who is proposing to undergo, is undergoing or has undergone a process (or part of a process) for the purpose of gender reassignment which is a protected characteristic under the Equality Act 2010 (see paragraph 1.0), by changing physiological or other attributes of their sex. This includes aspects of gender such as dress and title. It would apply to a woman making the transition to being a man and a man making the transition to being a woman, as well as to a person who has only just started out on the process of gender reassignment and to a person who has completed the process. Both would share the characteristic of gender reassignment with each having the characteristics of one sex, but with certain characteristics of the other sex.

H:I3A The reason for the exception is to modify the same sex/gender approach for searching to acknowledge the possible needs of transgender individuals in respect of menstrual products and other personal needs relating to health, hygiene and welfare and ensure that they are not overlooked.

H:14 Transvestite means a person of one gender who dresses in the clothes of a person of the opposite gender. However, a transvestite does not live permanently in the gender opposite to their birth sex.

H:15 Chief officers are responsible for providing corresponding operational guidance and instructions for the deployment of transgender officers and staff under their direction and control to duties which involve carrying out, or being present at, any of the searches and procedures described in paragraph 1. The guidance and instructions must comply with the Equality Act 2010 and should therefore complement the approach in this Annex.

ANNEX J: TRANSFER OF PERSONS DETAINED FOR MORE THAN 14 DAYS TO PRISON

A-230p H:1. When a warrant of further detention is extended or further extended by a High Court judge to authorise a person's detention beyond a period of 14 days from the time of their arrest (or if they were being detained under TACT Schedule 7, from the time at which their examination under Schedule 7 began), the person must be transferred from detention in a police station to detention in a designated prison as soon as is practicable after the warrant is issued, unless:

(a) the detainee specifically requests to remain in detention at a police station and that request can be accommodated, or

(b) there are reasonable grounds to believe that transferring the detainee to a prison would:

(i) significantly hinder a terrorism investigation;

(ii) delay charging of the detainee or their release from custody, or

(iii) otherwise prevent the investigation from being conducted diligently and expeditiously.

Any grounds in (b)(i) to (iii) above which are relied upon for not transferring the detainee to prison must be presented to the senior judge as part of the application for the extension or further extension of the warrant. See *Note J1*.

H:2. If at any time during which a person remains in detention at a police station under the warrant, the grounds at (b)(i) to (iii) cease to apply, the person must be transferred to a prison as soon as practicable.

H:3. Police should maintain an agreement with the National Offender Management Service (NOMS) that stipulates named prisons to which individuals may be transferred under this paragraph. This should be made with regard to ensuring detainees are moved to the most suitable prison for the purposes of the investigation and their welfare, and should include provision for the transfer of male, female and juvenile detainees. Police should ensure that the Governor of a prison to which they intend to transfer a detainee is given reasonable notice of this. Where practicable, this should be no later than the point at which a warrant is applied for that would take the period of detention beyond 14 days.

H:4. Following a detainee's transfer to a designated prison, their detention will be governed by the terms of Schedule 8 to TACT 2000 and the Prison Rules and this Code of Practice will not apply during any period that the person remains in prison detention. The Code will once more apply if the person is transferred back from prison detention to police detention. In order to enable the Governor to arrange for the production of the detainee back into police custody, police should give notice to the Governor of the relevant prison as soon as possible of any decision to transfer a detainee from prison back to a police station. Any transfer between a prison and a police station should be conducted by police and this Code will be applicable during the period of transit. *See Note 2J*. A detainee should only remain in police custody having been transferred back from a prison, for as long as is necessary for the purpose of the investigation.

H:5. The investigating team and custody officer should provide as much information as necessary to enable the relevant prison authorities to provide appropriate facilities to detain an individual. This should include, but not be limited to:

(i) medical assessments

(ii) security and risk assessments

(iii) details of the detained person's legal representatives

(iv) details of any individuals from whom the detained person has requested visits, or who have requested to visit the detained person.

H:6. Where a detainee is to be transferred to prison, the custody officer should inform the detainee's legal adviser beforehand that the transfer is to take place (including the name of the prison). The custody officer should also make all reasonable attempts to inform:

- family or friends who have been informed previously of the detainee's detention; and
- the person who was initially informed of the detainee's detention in accordance with *paragraph 5.1*.

H:7. Any decision not to transfer a detained person to a designated prison under paragraph *1*, must be recorded, along with the reasons for this decision. If a request under paragraph *1(a)* is not accommodated, the reasons for this should also be recorded.

Notes for Guidance

A-230q *H:J1 Transfer to prison is intended to ensure that individuals who are detained for extended periods of time are held in a place designed for longer periods of detention than police stations. Prison will provide detainees with a greater range of facilities more appropriate to longer detention periods.*

H:J2 This Code will only apply as is appropriate to the conditions of detention during the period of transit. There is obviously no requirement to provide such things as bed linen or reading materials for the journey between prison and police station.

ANNEX K: DOCUMENTS AND RECORDS TO BE TRANSLATED

H:1. For the purposes of Directive 2010/64/EU of the European Parliament and of the Council of 20 October 2010 and this Code, essential documents comprise records required to be made in accordance with this Code which are relevant to decisions to deprive a person of their liberty, to any charge and to any record considered necessary to enable a detainee to defend themselves in criminal proceedings and safeguard the fairness of the proceedings. Passages of essential documents which are not relevant need not be translated. See *Note K1*. **A-230r**

H:2. The documents considered essential for the purposes of this Code and for which (subject to paragraphs 3 to 7) written translations must be created are the records made in accordance with this Code of the grounds and reasons for any authorisation of a suspects detention under the provisions of the Terrorism Act 2000 or the Counter Terrorism Act 2008 (post-charge questioning) to which this Code applies as they are described and referred to in the suspect's custody record. Translations should be created as soon as practicable after the authorisation has been recorded and provided as soon as practicable thereafter, whilst the person is detained or after they have been released (see *Note K3*). See *paragraphs 13.12* to *13.14* and *Annex L* for application to live-link interpretation.

H:3. The custody officer may authorise an oral translation or oral summary of the documents to be provided (through an interpreter) instead of a written translation. Such an oral translation or summary may only be provided if it would not prejudice the fairness of the proceedings by in any way adversely affecting or otherwise undermining or limiting the ability of the suspect in question to understand their position and to communicate effectively with police officers, interviewers, solicitors and appropriate adults with regard to their detention and the investigation of the offence in question and to defend themselves in the event of criminal proceedings. The quantity and complexity of the information in the document should always be considered and specific additional consideration given if the suspect is a vulnerable or is a juvenile. The reason for the decision must be recorded (see *paragraph 13.11(e)*).

H:4. Subject to *paragraphs 5* to *7* below, a suspect may waive their right to a written translation of the essential documents described in the table but only if they do so voluntarily after receiving legal advice or having full knowledge of the consequences and give their unconditional and fully informed consent in writing (see *paragraph 9*).

H:5. The suspect may be asked if they wish to waive their right to a written translation and before giving their consent, they must be reminded of their right to legal advice and asked whether they wish to speak to a solicitor.

H:6. No police officer or police staff should do or say anything with the intention of persuading a suspect who is entitled to a written translation of an essential document to waive that right. See *Notes K2 and K3*.

H:7. For the purpose of the waiver:

(a) the consent of a vulnerable person is only valid if the information about the circumstances under which they can waive the right and the reminder about their right to legal advice mentioned in *paragraphs 3* to *5* and their consent is given in the presence of the appropriate adult, and the appropriate adult also agrees.

(b) the consent of a juvenile is only valid if their parent's or guardian's consent is also obtained unless the juvenile is under 14, when their parent's or guardian's consent is sufficient in its own right and the information and reminder mentioned in *sub paragraph (a)* above and their consent is also given in the presence of the appropriate adult (who may or may not be a parent or guardian).

H:8. The detainee, their solicitor or appropriate adult may make representations to the custody officer that a document which is not included in the table is essential and that a translation should be provided. The request may be refused if the officer is satisfied that the translation requested is not essential for the purposes described in *paragraph 1* above.

H:9. If the custody officer has any doubts about:

- providing an oral translation or summary of an essential document instead of a written translation (see *paragraph 3*);
- whether the suspect fully understands the consequences of waiving their right to a written translation of an essential document (see *paragraph 4*); or
- about refusing to provide a translation of a requested document (see *paragraph 7*),

the officer should seek advice from an inspector or above.

Documentation

A-230s H:10. Action taken in accordance with this Annex shall be recorded in the detainee's custody record or interview record as appropriate (see *Code H paragraph 13.11(e)*).

Note for Guidance

A-230t *H:K1 It is not necessary to disclose information in any translation which is capable of undermining or otherwise adversely affecting any investigative processes, for example, by enabling the suspect to fabricate an innocent explanation or to conceal lies from the interviewer.*

H:K2 No police officer or police staff shall indicate to any suspect, except to answer a direct question whether the period for which they are liable to be detained, or if not detained, the time taken to complete the interview, might be reduced:

- if they do not ask for legal advice before deciding whether they wish to waive their right to a written translation of an essential document; or
- if they decide to waive their right to a written translation of an essential document.

H:K3 There is no power under TACT to detain a person or to delay their release solely to create and provide a written translation of any essential document.

ANNEX L: LIVE-LINK INTERPRETATION (PARA. 13.12)

Part 1: When the physical presence of the interpreter is not required.

A-230u H:1. EU Directive 2010/64 (see *paragraph 13.1*), Article 2(6) provides "Where appropriate, communication technology such as videoconferencing, telephone or the Internet may be used, unless the physical presence of the interpreter is required in order to safeguard the fairness of the proceedings." This Article permits, but does not require the use of a live-link, and the following provisions of this Annex determine whether the use of a live-link is appropriate in any particular case.

H:2. Decisions in accordance with this Annex that the physical presence of the interpreter is not required and to permit live-link interpretation, must be made on a case by case basis. Each decision must take account of the age, gender and vulnerability of the suspect, the nature and circumstances of the terrorism investigation and the impact on the suspect according to the particular purpose(s) for which the suspect requires the assistance of an interpreter and the time(s) when that assistance is required (see *Note L1*). For this reason, the custody officer must consider whether the ability of the particular suspect, to communicate confidently and effectively for the purpose in question (see *paragraph 3*) is likely to be adversely affected or otherwise undermined or limited if the interpreter is not physically present and live-link interpretation is used. Although a suspect for whom an appropriate adult is required may be more likely to be adversely affected as described, it is important to note that a person who does not require an appropriate adult may also be adversely impacted by the use of live-link interpretation.

H:3. Examples of purposes referred to in *paragraph 2* include:

(a) understanding and appreciating their position having regard to any information given to them, or sought from them, in accordance with this or any other Code of Practice which, in particular, include:
- the caution (see *paragraphs C10.1* and *10.12*).
- the special warning (see *paragraphs 10.9* to *10.11*).
- information about their suspected involvement in the commission, preparation or instigation of acts of terrorism offence (see *paragraphs 10.3, 11.1* and *Note 11ZA*).
- the grounds and reasons for detention (see *paragraphs 13.10* and *13.10A*).
- the translation of essential documents (see *paragraph 13.10B* and *Annex L*).
- their rights and entitlements (see *paragraph 3.14*).
- intimate and non-intimate searches of detained persons at police stations.
- provisions and procedures that apply to taking fingerprints, samples and photographs from persons detained for the purposes of a terrorism investigation.

(b) understanding and seeking clarification from the interviewer of questions asked during an interview that must be video recorded with sound (see *paragraph 7*) and of anything else that is said by the interviewer and answering the questions.

(c) consulting privately with their solicitor and (if applicable) the appropriate adult (see *paragraphs 3.18, 13.3, 13.6* and *13.9*):
(i) to help decide whether to answer questions put to them during interview; and
(ii) about any other matter concerning their detention and treatment whilst in custody.

(d) communicating with practitioners and others who have some formal responsibility for, or an interest in, the health and welfare of the suspect. Particular examples include appropriate healthcare professionals (see *section 9* of this Code) and Independent Custody Visitors.

H:4. If the custody officer is satisfied that for a particular purpose as described in *paragraphs 2 and 3 above,* the live-link interpretation *would not* adversely affect or otherwise undermine or limit the suspect's ability to communicate confidently and effectively for *that* purpose, they must so inform the suspect, their solicitor and (if applicable) the appropriate adult. At the same time, the operation of live-link interpretation must be explained and demonstrated to them, they must be advised of the chief officer's obligations concerning the security of live-link communications under *paragraph 13.13* (see *Note L2*) and they must be asked if they wish to make representations that live-link interpretation should not be used or if they require more information about the operation of the arrangements. They must also be told that at any time live-link interpretation is in use, they may make representations to the custody officer or interviewer that its operation should cease and that the physical presence of an interpreter should be arranged.

When the authority of an inspector is required

H:5. If representations are made that live-link interpretation should not be used, or that at anytime live-link interpretation is in use, its operation should cease and the physical presence of an interpreter arranged and the custody officer is unable to allay the concerns raised, live-link interpretation may not be used, or (as the case may be) continue to be used, *unless* authorised in writing by an officer of the rank of inspector or above, in accordance with *paragraph 6.* **A-230v**

H:6. Authority may be given if the officer is satisfied that for the purpose(s) in question at the time an interpreter is required, live-link interpretation is necessary and justified. In making this decision, the officer must have regard to:

(a) the circumstances of the suspect;
(b) the nature and seriousness of the offence;
(c) the requirements of the investigation, including its likely impact on both the suspect and any victim(s);
(d) the representations made by the suspect, their solicitor and (if applicable) the appropriate adult that live-link interpretation should not be used (see *paragraph 5*);
(e) the availability of a suitable interpreter to be *physically* present compared with the availability of a suitable interpreter for live-link interpretation (see *Note L3*); and
(f) the risk if the interpreter is not *physically* present, evidence obtained using live-link interpretation might be excluded in subsequent criminal proceedings.
(g) the likely impact on the suspect and the investigation of any consequential delay to arrange for the interpreter to be *physically* present with the suspect.

H:7. The separate Code of Practice that governs the conduct and recording of interviews of persons detained at a police station under section 41 of the Terrorism Act 2000 (TACT) and of persons in respect of whom an authorisation to question after charge has been given under section 22 of the Counter-Terrorism Act 2008 requires those interviews to be video recorded with sound. This will require the visual record to show the live-link interpretation arrangements and the interpreter as seen and experienced by the suspect during the interview (see *Note L4*).

Documentation

H:8. A record must be made of the actions, decisions, authorisations and outcomes arising from the requirements of this Annex. This includes representations made in accordance with *paragraphs 4* and *7.* **A-230w**

Part 2: Modifications for live-link interpretation

H:9. The following modification shall apply for the purposes of live-link interpretation: **A-230x**

(a) **Code H paragraph 13.4:** For sub-paragraph (b), *substitute*: "A clear legible copy of the complete statement shall be sent without delay via the live-link to the interviewer. The interviewer, after confirming with the suspect that the copy is legible and complete, shall invite the suspect to sign it. The interviewer is responsible for ensuring that that the signed copy and the original record made by the interpreter are retained with the case papers for use in evidence if required and must advise the interpreter of their obligation to keep the original record securely for that purpose.";
(b) **Code of Practice for video recording interviews with sound – paragraph 4.4** At the beginning of the paragraph *insert*: "Before the interview commences, the operation of live-link interpretation shall be explained and demonstrated to the suspect, their solicitor and appropriate adult, unless it has been previously explained and demonstrated (see Code H Annex L *paragraph 4*)."

(c) **Code for video recording interviews with sound - paragraph 4.22 (signing master recording label)** After the *third sentence*, insert, "If live-link interpretation has been used, the interviewer should ask the interpreter to observe the removal and sealing of the master recording and to confirm in writing that they have seen it sealed and signed by the interviewer. A clear legible copy of the confirmation signed by the interpreter must be sent via the livelink to the interviewer. The interviewer is responsible for ensuring that the original confirmation and the copy are retained with the case papers for use in evidence if required, and must advise the interpreter of their obligation to keep the original confirmation securely for that purpose."

Notes for Guidance

A-230y *H:L1 For purposes other than an interview, audio-only live-link interpretation, for example by telephone (see Code H paragraph 13.12(b)) may provide an appropriate option until an interpreter is physically present or audio-visual live-link interpretation becomes available. A particular example would be the initial action required when a detained suspect arrives at a police station to inform them of, and to explain, the reasons for their arrest and detention and their various rights and entitlements. Another example would be to inform the suspect by telephone, that an interpreter they will be able to see and hear is being arranged. In these circumstances, telephone live-link interpretation may help to allay the suspect's concerns and contribute to the completion of the risk assessment (see Code H paragraph 3.6).*

H:L2 The explanation and demonstration of live-link interpretation is intended to help the suspect, solicitor and appropriate adult make an informed decision on whether to agree to its use and to allay any concerns they may have.

H:L3 Factors affecting availability of a suitable interpreter will include the location of the police station and the language and type of interpretation (oral or sign language) required.

H:L4 The Code of Practice referred to in paragraphs 7 and 9, is available here: https://www.gov.uk/government/publications/terrorism-act-2000-video-recording-code-of-practice.

B. UNDER THE CRIMINAL PROCEDURE AND INVESTIGATIONS ACT 1996

(1) As to the recording and retention by the police of material obtained during an investigation and its supply to the prosecutor

Introduction

★A-231 Pursuant to sections 23 and 25 of the 1996 Act (§§ 12-97, 12-98 in the main work), the Secretary of State has prepared and published codes of practice governing the action the police must take in recording and retaining material obtained in the course of a criminal investigation and regulating its supply to the prosecutor for a decision on disclosure.

A revised version of the code of practice (set out below) came into force on 31 December 2020: Criminal Procedure and Investigations Act 1996 (Code of Practice) Order 2020 (SI 2020/1330). The revised code replaces that given effect by the Criminal Procedure and Investigations Act 1996 (Code of Practice) Order 2015 (SI 2015/861) and implements various changes recommended by the Attorney General's Review of the efficiency and effectiveness of disclosure in the criminal justice system (2018).

CRIMINAL PROCEDURE AND INVESTIGATIONS ACT 1996 CODE OF PRACTICE UNDER PART II

Preamble

★A-232 This code of practice is issued under Part II of the Criminal Procedure and Investigations Act 1996 ('the Act'). It sets out the manner in which police officers are to record, retain and reveal to the prosecutor material obtained in a criminal investigation and which may be relevant to the investigation, and related matters.

1. Introduction

★A-232a 1.1 This code of practice applies in respect of criminal investigations conducted by police officers which begin on or after the day on which this code comes into effect. Persons other than police officers who are charged with the duty of conducting an investigation as defined in the Act are to have regard to the relevant provisions of the code, and should take these into account in applying their own operating procedures.

1.2 This code does not apply to persons who are not charged with the duty of conducting an investigation as defined in the Act.

1.3 Nothing in this code applies to material intercepted in obedience to a warrant issued under section 2 of the Interception of Communications Act 1985 or section 5 of the Regulation of Investigatory Powers Act 2000, or to any copy of that material as defined in section 10 of the 1985 Act or section 15 of the 2000 Act and by sections of the Investigatory Powers Act 2016.

1.4 This code extends only to England and Wales.

2. Definitions

2.1 In this code:

1. *a criminal investigation* is an investigation conducted by police officers with a view to it being ascertained whether a person should be charged with an offence, or whether a person charged with an offence is guilty of it. This will include: ★A-233
   - investigations into crimes that have been committed;
   - investigations whose purpose is to ascertain whether a crime has been committed, with a view to the possible institution of criminal proceedings; and
   - investigations which begin in the belief that a crime may be committed, for example when the police keep premises or individuals under observation for a period of time, with a view to the possible institution of criminal proceedings;
2. charging a person with an offence includes prosecution by way of summons or postal requisition;
3. *an investigator* is any police officer involved in the conduct of a criminal investigation. All investigators have a responsibility for carrying out the duties imposed on them under this code, including in particular recording information, and retaining records of information and other material;
4. the *officer in charge of an investigation* is the police officer responsible for directing a criminal investigation. They are also responsible for ensuring that proper procedures are in place for recording information, and retaining records of information and other material, in the investigation;
5. the *disclosure officer* is the person responsible for examining material retained by the police during the investigation; revealing material to the prosecutor during the investigation and any criminal proceedings resulting from it, and certifying that they have done this; and disclosing material to the accused at the request of the prosecutor;
6. the *prosecutor* is the authority responsible for the conduct, on behalf of the Crown, of criminal proceedings resulting from a specific criminal investigation;
7. *material* is material of any kind, including information and objects, which is obtained or inspected in the course of a criminal investigation and which may be relevant to the investigation. This includes not only material coming into the possession of the investigator (such as documents seized in the course of searching premises) but also material generated by them (such as interview records); ★A-233a
8. material may be *relevant to an investigation* if it appears to an investigator, or to the officer in charge of an investigation, or to the disclosure officer, that it has some bearing on any offence under investigation or any person being investigated, or on the surrounding circumstances of the case, unless it is incapable of having any impact on the case;
9. *sensitive material* is material, the disclosure of which the disclosure officer believes would give rise to a real risk of serious prejudice to an important public interest;
10. references to *prosecution disclosure* are to the duty of the prosecutor under sections 3 and 7A of the Act to disclose material which is in their possession or which they have inspected in pursuance of this code, and which might reasonably be considered capable of undermining the case against the accused, or of assisting the case for the accused;
11. references to the disclosure of material to a person accused of an offence include references to the disclosure of material to their legal representative;
12. references to police officers and to the chief officer of police include those employed in a police force as defined in section 3(3) of the Prosecution of Offences Act 1985.

3. General responsibilities

3.1 The functions of the investigator, the officer in charge of an investigation and the disclosure officer are separate. Whether they are undertaken by one, two or more persons will depend on the complexity of the case and the administrative arrangements within each police force. Where they are undertaken by more than one person, close consultation between them is essential to the effective performance of the duties imposed by this code. ★A-234

3.2 In any criminal investigation, one or more deputy disclosure officers may be appointed to assist the disclosure officer, and a deputy disclosure officer may perform any function of a disclosure officer as defined in paragraph 2.1.

3.3 The chief officer of police for each police force is responsible for putting in place arrangements to ensure that in every investigation the identity of the officer in charge of an investigation and the disclosure officer is recorded. The chief officer of police for each police force shall ensure that disclosure officers and deputy disclosure officers have sufficient skills and authority, commensurate with the complexity of the investigation, to discharge their functions effectively. An individual must not be appointed as disclosure officer, or continue in that role, if that is likely to result in a conflict of interest, for instance, if the disclosure officer is the victim of the alleged crime which is the subject of the investigation. The advice of a more senior officer must always be sought if there is doubt as to whether a conflict of interest precludes an individual acting as disclosure officer. If thereafter the doubt remains, the advice of a prosecutor should be sought.

★A-234a 3.4 The officer in charge of an investigation may delegate tasks to another investigator, to civilians employed by the police force, or to other persons participating in the investigation under arrangements for joint investigations, but they remain responsible for ensuring that these have been carried out and for accounting for any general policies followed in the investigation. In particular, it is an essential part of their duties to ensure that all material which may be relevant to an investigation is retained, and either made available to the disclosure officer or (in exceptional circumstances) revealed directly to the prosecutor.

3.5 In conducting an investigation, the investigator should pursue all reasonable lines of inquiry, whether these point towards or away from the suspect. What is reasonable in each case will depend on the particular circumstances. It is a matter for the investigator, with the assistance of the prosecutor if required, to decide what constitutes a reasonable line of inquiry in each case.

3.6 If the officer in charge of an investigation believes that other persons may be in possession of material that may be relevant to the investigation, and if this has not been obtained under paragraph 3.5 above, they should ask the disclosure officer to inform them of the existence of the investigation and to invite them to retain the material in case they receive a request for its disclosure. The disclosure officer should inform the prosecutor that they may have such material. However, the officer in charge of an investigation is not required to make speculative enquiries of other persons; there must be some reason to believe that they may have relevant material. That reason may come from information provided to the police by the accused or from other inquiries made or from some other source.

3.7 If, during a criminal investigation, the officer in charge of an investigation or disclosure officer for any reason no longer has responsibility for the functions falling to them, either their supervisor or the police officer in charge of criminal investigations for the police force concerned must assign someone else to assume that responsibility. That person's identity must be recorded, as with those initially responsible for these functions in each investigation.

4. Recording of information

★A-235 4.1 If material which may be relevant to the investigation consists of information which is not recorded in any form, the officer in charge of an investigation must ensure that it is recorded in a durable or retrievable form.

4.2 Where it is not practicable to retain the initial record of information because it forms part of a larger record which is to be destroyed, its contents should be transferred as a true record to a durable and more easily-stored form before that happens.

4.3 Negative information is often relevant to an investigation. If it may be relevant it must be recorded. An example might be a number of people present in a particular place at a particular time who state that they saw nothing unusual.

4.4 Where information which may be relevant is obtained, it must be recorded at the time it is obtained or as soon as practicable after that time. This includes, for example, information obtained in house-to-house enquiries, although the requirement to record information promptly does not require an investigator to take a statement from a potential witness where it would not otherwise be taken.

5. Retention of material

(a) Duty to retain material

★A-236 5.1 The investigator must retain material obtained in a criminal investigation which may be relevant to the investigation. Material may be photographed, video-recorded, captured digitally or otherwise retained in the form of a copy rather than the original at any time, if the original is perishable; the original was supplied to the investigator rather than generated by them and is to be returned to its owner; or the retention of a copy rather than the original is reasonable in all the circumstances.

5.2 Where material has been seized in the exercise of the powers of seizure conferred by the Police and Criminal Evidence Act 1984, the duty to retain it under this code is subject to the provisions on the retention of seized material in section 22 of that Act.

5.3 If the officer in charge of an investigation becomes aware as a result of developments in the case that material previously examined but not retained (because it was not thought to be relevant) may now be relevant to the investigation, they should, wherever practicable, take steps to obtain it or ensure that it is retained for further inspection or for production in court if required.

5.4 The duty to retain material includes in particular the duty to retain material falling into the following categories: ★A-236a

- Records which are derived from tapes or recordings of telephone messages (for example, 999 calls) containing descriptions of an alleged offence or offender;
- Any incident logs relating to the allegation;
- Contemporaneous records of the incident, such as:
  - crime reports and crime report forms;
  - an investigation log;
  - any record or note made by an investigator (including police notebook entries and other handwritten notes) on which they later make a statement or which relates to contact with suspects, victims or witnesses;
  - an account of an incident or information relevant to an incident noted by an investigator in manuscript or electronically;
  - records of actions carried out by officers (such as house-to-house interviews, CCTV or forensic enquiries) noted by a police officer in manuscript or electronically;
  - CCTV footage, or other imagery, of the incident in action;
- The defendant's custody record or voluntary attendance record;
- Any previous accounts made by a complainant or any other witnesses;
- Interview records (written records, or audio or video tapes, of interviews with actual or potential witnesses or suspects);
- Any material casting doubt on the reliability of a witness e.g. relevant previous convictions and relevant cautions of any prosecution witnesses and any co-accused;
- Final versions of witness statements (and draft versions where their content differs from the final version), including any exhibits mentioned (unless these have been returned to their owner on the understanding that they will be produced in court if required);
- Material relating to other suspects in the investigation;
- Communications between the police and experts such as forensic scientists, reports of work carried out by experts, and schedules of scientific material prepared by the expert for the investigator, for the purposes of criminal proceedings;
- Records of the first description of a suspect by each potential witness who purports to identify or describe the suspect, whether or not the description differs from that of subsequent descriptions by that or other witnesses.

5.5 The duty to retain material where it may be relevant to the investigation also includes in particular the duty to retain any material which may satisfy the test for prosecution disclosure in the Act, such as: ★A-236b

- information provided by an accused person which indicates an explanation for the offence with which they have been charged;
- any material casting doubt on the reliability of a confession;
- any material casting doubt on the reliability of a prosecution witness.

5.6 The duty to retain material falling into these categories does not extend to items which are purely ancillary to such material and possess no independent significance (for example, duplicate copies of records or reports).

(b) Length of time for which material is to be retained

5.7 All material which may be relevant to the investigation must be retained until a decision is taken whether to institute proceedings against a person for an offence. ★A-236c

5.8 If a criminal investigation results in proceedings being instituted, all material which may be relevant must be retained at least until the accused is acquitted or convicted or the prosecutor decides not to proceed with the case.

5.9 Where the accused is convicted, all material which may be relevant must be retained at least until:

- the convicted person is released from custody, or discharged from hospital, in cases where the court imposes a custodial sentence or a hospital order;

- six months from the date of conviction, in all other cases.

If the court imposes a custodial sentence or hospital order and the convicted person is released from custody or discharged from hospital earlier than six months from the date of conviction, all material which may be relevant must be retained at least until six months from the date of conviction.

5.10 If an appeal against conviction is in progress when the release or discharge occurs, or at the end of the period of six months specified in paragraph 5.9, all material which may be relevant must be retained until the appeal is determined. Similarly, if the Criminal Cases Review Commission is considering an application at that point in time, all material which may be relevant must be retained at least until the Commission decides not to refer the case to the Court.

6. Preparation of material for prosecutor

(a) Schedules of unused material

★A-237 6.1 The officer in charge of the investigation, the disclosure officer or an investigator may seek advice from the prosecutor about whether any particular item of material may be relevant to the investigation.

6.2 Material which may be relevant to an investigation and has been retained in accordance with this code, and which the disclosure officer believes will not form part of the prosecution case, must be listed on the appropriate schedule of unused material.

6.3 The disclosure officer must ensure that the appropriate schedule of unused material is prepared in the following circumstances:

- the accused is charged with an offence which is triable only on indictment;
- the accused is charged with an offence which is triable either way, and it is considered that the case is likely to be tried on indictment;
- the accused is charged with an either-way offence that is likely to remain in the magistrates' court, and it is considered that they are likely to plead not guilty;
- the accused is charged with a summary offence and it is considered that they are likely to plead not guilty.

6.4 Where, however, the accused is charged with a summary offence or an either-way offence, and it is considered that they are likely to plead guilty (e.g. because they have admitted the offence), a schedule is *not* required unless a not guilty plea is subsequently entered or indicated.

6.5 Irrespective of the anticipated plea, the Common Law test for disclosure requires material to be disclosed if there is material known to the disclosure officer that might assist the defence with the early preparation of their case or at a bail hearing (for example, a key prosecution witness has relevant previous convictions or a witness has withdrawn their statement). A note must be made on the case summary for the prosecutor of any such material, which must be revealed to the prosecutor who will review it and consider whether it is disclosable. Where there is no such material, a certificate to that effect must be completed.

★A-237a 6.6 Material in the following list (which where it exists will have been retained or recorded in accordance with paragraph 5.4) is likely to include information which meets the test for prosecution disclosure. This material must therefore, subject to the exception at 6.4 above, be scheduled and provided to the prosecutor. In reviewing this material, disclosure officers and prosecutors are to start with a presumption that it is likely to meet the disclosure test, although the material will need to be carefully considered and the disclosure test applied before a decision is made:

a) records which are derived from tapes or recordings of telephone messages (for example 999 calls) containing descriptions of an alleged offence or offender;
b) any incident logs relating to the allegation;
c) contemporaneous records of the incident, such as:
   - crime reports and crime report forms;
   - an investigation log;
   - any record or note made by an investigator (including police notebook entries and other handwritten notes) on which they later make a statement or which relates to contact with suspects, victims or witnesses;
   - an account of an incident or information relevant to an incident noted by an investigator in manuscript or electronically;
   - records of actions carried out by officers (such as house-to-house interviews, CCTV or forensic enquiries) noted by a police officer in manuscript or electronically;
   - CCTV footage, or other imagery, of the incident in action;
d) the defendant's custody record or voluntary attendance record;
e) any previous accounts made by a complainant or by any other witnesses;
f) interview records (written records, or audio or video tapes, of interviews with actual or potential witnesses or suspects);

g) any material casting doubt on the reliability of a witness e. g. relevant previous convictions and relevant cautions of any prosecution witnesses and any co-accused.

This material must be listed on the schedule by the disclosure officer in addition to all other material which may be relevant to an investigation; it is likely that some of this material will need to be redacted (see 6.12).

(b) Way in which material is to be listed on schedule

6.7 Material which the disclosure officer does not believe is sensitive must be listed on a schedule of non-sensitive material, which must include a statement that the disclosure officer does not believe the material is sensitive. Where there is sensitive unused material, see para 6.13 below. **★A-237b**

6.8 The disclosure officer should ensure, subject to paras 6.10-6.11 below, that each item of material is listed separately on the schedule, and is numbered consecutively (which may include numbering by volume and sub-volume).

6.9 The description of each item should make clear the nature of the item and should contain sufficient detail to enable the prosecutor to decide whether they need to inspect the material before deciding whether or not it should be disclosed.

6.10 In some investigations it may be disproportionate to list each item of material separately. These may be listed in a block or blocks and described by quantity and generic title.

6.11 Even if some material is listed in a block, the disclosure officer must ensure that any items among that material which might satisfy the test for prosecution disclosure are listed and described individually.

(c) Redaction of sensitive material

6.12 The disclosure officer should redact any sensitive information contained in material that is likely to satisfy the test for prosecution disclosure. The disclosure officer should also redact any personal, confidential information in material that is to be disclosed. Such could include a person's date of birth, address, email address and phone number. **★A-237c**

6.13 Any material which is believed to be sensitive must be listed on a schedule of sensitive material. If there is no sensitive material, the disclosure officer must record this fact on a schedule of sensitive material, or otherwise so indicate.

6.14 Subject to paragraph 6.15 below, the disclosure officer must list on a sensitive schedule any material the disclosure of which they believe would give rise to a real risk of serious prejudice to an important public interest, and the reason for that belief. The schedule must include a statement that the disclosure officer believes the material is sensitive. Depending on the circumstances, examples of such material may include the following, among others:

- material relating to national security;
- material received from the intelligence and security agencies;
- material relating to intelligence from foreign sources which reveals sensitive intelligence gathering methods;
- material given in confidence;
- material relating to the identity or activities of informants, or undercover police officers, or witnesses, or other persons supplying information to the police who may be in danger if their identities are revealed;
- material revealing the location of any premises or other place used for police surveillance, or the identity of any person allowing a police officer to use them for surveillance;
- material revealing, either directly or indirectly, techniques and methods relied upon by a police officer in the course of a criminal investigation, for example covert surveillance techniques, or other methods of detecting crime;
- material whose disclosure might facilitate the commission of other offences or hinder the prevention and detection of crime;
- material upon the strength of which search warrants were obtained;
- material containing details of persons taking part in identification parades;
- material supplied to an investigator during a criminal investigation which has been generated by an official of a body concerned with the regulation or supervision of bodies corporate or of persons engaged in financial activities, or which has been generated by a person retained by such a body;
- material supplied to an investigator during a criminal investigation which relates to a child or young person and which has been generated by a local authority social services department, an Area Child Protection Committee or other party contacted by an investigator during the investigation;

• material relating to the private life of a witness.

★A-237d 6.15 In exceptional circumstances, where an investigator considers that material is so sensitive that its revelation to the prosecutor by means of an entry on the sensitive schedule is inappropriate, the existence of the material must be revealed to the prosecutor separately. This will apply only where compromising the material would be likely to lead directly to the loss of life, or directly threaten national security.

6.16 In such circumstances, the responsibility for informing the prosecutor lies with the investigator who knows the detail of the sensitive material. The investigator should act as soon as is reasonably practicable after the file containing the prosecution case is sent to the prosecutor. The investigator must also ensure that the prosecutor is able to inspect the material so that they can assess whether it is disclosable and, if so, whether it needs to be brought before a court for a ruling on disclosure.

7. Revelation of material to prosecutor

★A-238 7.1 Where cases have been charged on the Full Code Test and it is anticipated that the defendant will plead not guilty, the disclosure officer should provide the schedules concerning unused material to the prosecutor at the same time as submitting the case file.

7.2 In all other cases the disclosure officer must provide the schedules as soon as possible after a not guilty plea has been either indicated or entered.

7.3 The disclosure officer should draw the attention of the prosecutor to any material an investigator has retained (including material to which paragraph 6.15 applies) which it is considered may satisfy the test for prosecution disclosure in the Act, explaining the reasons for coming to that view.

7.4 The disclosure officer must give the prosecutor a copy of any such material (unless it has already been supplied as part of the file containing the material for the prosecution case), together with any material which falls into the following categories:

- information provided by an accused person which indicates an explanation for the offence with which they has been charged;
- any material casting doubt on the reliability of a confession;
- any material casting doubt on the reliability of a prosecution witness.

7.5 The disclosure officer must give the prosecutor a copy of any material which has been scheduled in accordance with paragraph 6.6, indicating whether it is, or is not, considered to satisfy the test for prosecution disclosure, and in either case explaining the reasons for coming to that view.

7.6 The disclosure officer must comply with a request from the prosecutor to be allowed to inspect material which has not already been copied to them. If the prosecutor asks to be provided with a copy of such material it should be provided, except where (having consulted the officer in charge of the investigation) the disclosure officer believes that the material is too sensitive to be copied and can only be inspected.

7.7 If material consists of information which is recorded other than in writing, whether it should be given to the prosecutor in its original form as a whole, or by way of relevant extracts recorded in the same form, or in the form of a transcript, is a matter for agreement between the disclosure officer and the prosecutor.

8. Subsequent action by disclosure officer

★A-239 8.1 At the time when a schedule of non-sensitive material is prepared, the disclosure officer may not know exactly what material will form the case against the accused. In addition, the prosecutor may not have given advice about the likely relevance of particular items of material. Once these matters have been determined, the disclosure officer must give the prosecutor, where necessary, an amended schedule listing any additional material:

- which may be relevant to the investigation,
- which does not form part of the case against the accused,
- which is not already listed on the schedule, and
- which they believe is not sensitive,

unless they are informed in writing by the prosecutor that the prosecutor intends to disclose the material to the defence.

8.2 Section 7A of the Act imposes a continuing duty on the prosecutor, for the duration of criminal proceedings against the accused, to disclose material which satisfies the test for disclosure (subject to public interest considerations). To enable this to be done, any new material coming to light should be treated in the same way as the earlier material.

8.3 In particular, after a defence statement has been given, or details of the issues in dispute have been recorded on the Preparation for Effective Trial form or the Plea and Trial Preparation Hearing form, the disclosure officer must look again at the material which has been retained and must draw the attention of the prosecutor to any material which might reasonably be considered capable of undermining the case for the prosecution against the accused or of assisting the case for the accused; and must reveal it to them in accordance with paragraphs 7.4 and 7.5 above.

9. Certification by disclosure officer

9.1 The disclosure officer must certify to the prosecutor that, to the best of their knowledge and belief, all relevant material which has been retained and made available to them has been revealed to the prosecutor in accordance with this code. They must sign and date the disclosure officer certificate. It will be necessary to certify not only at the time when the schedule and accompanying material is submitted to the prosecutor, and when relevant material which has been retained is reconsidered after the accused has given a defence statement, but also whenever a schedule is otherwise given or material is otherwise revealed to the prosecutor. **★A-239a**

10. Disclosure of material to accused

10.1 A prosecutor must review the schedules of unused material provided by the disclosure officer and endorse the schedule to indicate whether each item of material does or does not meet the test for disclosure. If any of the material does meet the test for disclosure, the prosecutor should record the reason for this decision. **★A-240**

10.2 A prosecutor must additionally review any material provided by the disclosure officer under paragraph 6.6 (*material likely to meet the test for disclosure*). The prosecutor must endorse the schedule to indicate whether the material does or does not meet the test for disclosure, and must record the reason for the decision.

10.3 When a prosecutor provides material to the defence in accordance with the obligation under section 3 or section 7A of the Criminal Procedure and Investigations Act 1996, the prosecutor must at the same time provide the schedule of non-sensitive material to the defence.

10.4 Other than early disclosure under Common Law, in the magistrates' court the schedule (and any relevant unused material to be disclosed under it) must be disclosed to the accused either:

- at the hearing where a not guilty plea is entered, or
- as soon as possible following a formal indication from the accused or representative that a not guilty plea will be entered at the hearing.

In the Crown Court, initial disclosure should if possible be served prior to the Plea and Trial Preparation Hearing (PTPH). Where this has not been done, it should be served as soon as possible after that hearing and in accordance with any direction made by the Court.

10.5 If material has been copied to the prosecutor, and it is to be disclosed, whether it is disclosed by the prosecutor or the disclosure officer is a matter of agreement between the two of them. **★A-241**

10.6 If material has not already been copied to the prosecutor, and they request its disclosure to the accused on the ground that:

- it satisfies the test for prosecution disclosure, **or**
- the court has ordered its disclosure after considering an application from the accused,

the disclosure officer must disclose it to the accused.

10.7 The disclosure officer must disclose material to the accused either by giving them a copy or by allowing them to inspect it. If the accused person asks for a copy of any material which they have been allowed to inspect, the disclosure officer must supply it, unless in the opinion of the disclosure officer that is either not practicable (for example because the material consists of an object which cannot be copied, or because the volume of material is so great), or not desirable (for example because the material is a statement by a child witness in relation to a sexual offence).

10.8 If material which the accused has been allowed to inspect consists of information which is recorded other than in writing, whether it should be given to the accused in its original form or in the form of a transcript is a matter for the discretion of the disclosure officer. If the material is transcribed, the disclosure officer must ensure that the transcript is certified to the accused as a true record of the material which has been transcribed.

10.9 If a court concludes that an item of sensitive material satisfies the prosecution disclosure test and that the interests of the defence outweigh the public interest in withholding disclosure, it will be necessary to disclose the material if the case is to proceed. This does not mean that sensitive documents must always be disclosed in their original form: for example, the court may agree that sensitive details still requiring protection should be blocked out, or that documents may be summarised, or that the prosecutor may make an admission about the substance of the material under section 10 of the Criminal Justice Act 1967.

(2) As to the practice for arranging and conducting interviews of witnesses notified by the accused

Introduction

As from 1 May 2010, a new code of practice entitled "Code of Practice for Arranging and **A-241a**

Conducting Interviews of Witnesses Notified by the Accused", which was prepared under section 21A of the CPIA 1996, was brought into force by the Criminal Procedure and Investigations Act 1996 (Code of Practice for Interviews of Witnesses Notified by Accused) Order 2010 (SI 2010/1223).

CODE OF PRACTICE FOR ARRANGING AND CONDUCTING INTERVIEWS OF WITNESSES NOTIFIED BY THE ACCUSED

Preamble

A-241b This code of practice is issued under section 21A of the Criminal Procedure and Investigations Act 1996 ("the Act"). It sets out guidance that police officers and other persons charged with investigating offences must follow if they arrange or conduct interviews of proposed witnesses whose details are disclosed to the prosecution by an accused person pursuant to the disclosure provisions in Part I of the Act.

Introduction

A-241c 1.1 Part I of the Act sets out rules governing disclosure of information in the course of criminal proceedings by both the prosecution and persons accused of offences to which that Part of the Act applies.

1.2. Sections 5 and 6 of the Act provide for accused persons to give defence statements to the prosecution and to the court and section 6A sets out what those defence statements must contain. Section 6A(2) requires that any defence statement that discloses an alibi must give particulars of it, including prescribed details of any witness who the accused believes is able to give evidence in support of the alibi and any information the accused has which may assist in identifying or finding such a witness.

1.3. Section 6C of the Act requires the accused to give to the prosecutor and the court a notice indicating whether he intends to call any witnesses at trial and giving details of those witnesses.

1.4. This code of practice sets out guidance that police officers and other persons charged with investigating offences must have regard to when they are arranging and conducting interviews of proposed witnesses identified in a defence statement given under section 6A(2) of the Act or a notice given under section 6C of the Act.

Definitions

A-241d 2. In this code:–

- *the accused* means a person mentioned in section 1(1) or (2) of the Act;
- "an appropriate person" means:
  - (a) in the case of a witness under the age of 18:
    - (i) the parent, guardian or, if the witness is in local authority or voluntary organisation care, or is otherwise being looked after under the Children Act 1989, a person representing that authority or organisation; or
    - (ii) a social worker of a local authority; or
    - (iii) failing these, some other responsible person aged 18 or over who is not a police officer or employed by the police; and
  - (b) in the case of a witness who is mentally disordered or mentally vulnerable:
    - (i) a relative, guardian or other person responsible for the witness's care or custody; or
    - (ii) someone experienced in dealing with mentally disordered or mentally vulnerable people but who is not a police officer or employed by the police; or
    - (iii) failing these, some other responsible person aged 18 or over who is not a police officer or employed by the police.
- *an investigator* is a police officer or any other person charged with the duty of investigating offences.
- *a witness* is a potential witness identified by an accused person either:
  - in a defence statement under section 6A(2) of the Act as being a witness that he believes is able to give evidence in support of an alibi disclosed in the statement; or
  - in a notice given to the court and the prosecutor under section 6C of the Act as being a person that he intends to call as a witness at his trial.

Arrangement of the interview

Information to be provided to the witness before any interview may take place

A-241e 3.1. If an investigator wishes to interview a witness, the witness must be asked whether he consents to being interviewed and informed that:

- an interview is being requested following his identification by the accused as a proposed witness under section 6A(2) or section 6C of the Act;
- he is not obliged to attend the proposed interview;
- he is entitled to be accompanied by a solicitor at the interview (but nothing in this code of practice creates any duty on the part of the Legal Services Commission to provide funding for any such attendance); and
- a record will be made of the interview and he will subsequently be sent a copy of the record.

3.2. If the witness consents to being interviewed, the witness must be asked:

- whether he wishes to have a solicitor present at the interview;
- whether he consents to a solicitor attending the interview on behalf of the accused, as an observer; and
- whether he consents to a copy of the record being sent to the accused. If he does not consent, the witness must be informed that the effect of disclosure requirements in criminal proceedings may nevertheless require the prosecution to disclose the record to the accused (and any co-accused) in the course of the proceedings.

Information to be provided to the accused before any interview may take place

4.1. The investigator must notify the accused or, if the accused is legally represented in the proceedings, the accused's representatives: **A-241f**

- that the investigator requested an interview with the witness;
- whether the witness consented to the interview; and
- if the witness consented to the interview, whether the witness also consented to a solicitor attending the interview on behalf of the accused, as an observer.

4.2. If the accused is not legally represented in the proceedings, and if the witness consents to a solicitor attending the interview on behalf of the accused, the accused must be offered the opportunity, a reasonable time before the interview is held, to appoint a solicitor to attend it.

Identification of the date, time and venue for the interview

5. The investigator must nominate a reasonable date, time and venue for the interview and notify the witness of them and any subsequent changes to them. **A-241g**

Notification to the accused's solicitor of the date, time and venue of the interview

6. If the witness has consented to the presence of the accused's solicitor, the accused's solicitor must be notified that the interview is taking place, invited to observe, and provided with reasonable notice of the date, time and venue of the interview and any subsequent changes. **A-241h**

Conduct of the interview

The investigator conducting the interview

7. The identity of the investigator conducting the interview must be recorded. That person must have sufficient skills and authority, commensurate with the complexity of the investigation, to discharge his functions effectively. That person must not conduct the interview if that is likely to result in a conflict of interest, for instance, if that person is the victim of the alleged crime which is the subject of the proceedings. The advice of a more senior officer must always be sought if there is doubt as to whether a conflict of interest precludes an individual conducting the interview. If thereafter the doubt remains, the advice of a prosecutor must be sought. **A-241i**

Attendance of the accused's solicitor

8.1. The accused's solicitor may only attend the interview if the witness has consented to his presence as an observer. Provided that the accused's solicitor was given reasonable notice of the date, time and place of the interview, the fact that the accused's solicitor is not present will not prevent the interview from being conducted. If the witness at any time withdraws consent to the accused's solicitor being present at the interview, the interview may continue without the presence of the accused's solicitor. **A-241j**

8.2. The accused's solicitor may attend only as an observer.

Attendance of the witness's solicitor

9. Where a witness has indicated that he wishes to appoint a solicitor to be present, that solicitor must be permitted to attend the interview. **A-241k**

Attendance of any other appropriate person

A-241l 10. A witness under the age of 18 or a witness who is mentally disordered or otherwise mentally vulnerable must be interviewed in the presence of an appropriate person.

Recording of the interview

A-241m 11.1. An accurate record must be made of the interview, whether it takes place at a police station or elsewhere. The record must be made, where practicable, by audio recording or by visual recording with sound, or otherwise in writing. Any written record must be made and completed during the interview, unless this would not be practicable or would interfere with the conduct of the interview, and must constitute either a verbatim record of what has been said or, failing this, an account of the interview which adequately and accurately summarises it. If a written record is not made during the interview it must be made as soon as practicable after its completion. Written interview records must be timed and signed by the maker.

11.2 A copy of the record must be given, within a reasonable time of the interview, to:

(a) the witness; and

(b) if the witness consents, to the accused or the accused's solicitor.

II. ATTORNEY-GENERAL'S GUIDELINES

A. DISCLOSURE

Introduction

★A-242 On 2 October 2020 a revised version of the Attorney General's guidelines on disclosure was published. The new guidelines came into force on 31 December 2020. They substantially restructure the 2013 guidelines and contain new material including, in particular, new sections on sensitive material, pre-charge engagement and the disclosure of digital material. Annex C also contains a new template of a disclosure management document. It has now been confirmed that the new guidelines will come into force on 31 December 2020 (CLW/20/46/55).

Introduction

★A-243 These Guidelines are issued by the Attorney General for investigators, prosecutors and defence practitioners on the application of the disclosure regime contained in the Criminal Procedure and Investigations Act 1996 ('CPIA') Code of Practice Order 2020.

These Guidelines replace the existing Attorney General's Guidelines on Disclosure issued in 2013 and the Supplementary Guidelines on Digital Material issued in 2013, which is an annex to the general guidelines.

The Guidelines outline the high level principles which should be followed when the disclosure regime is applied throughout England and Wales. They are not designed to be an unequivocal statement of the law at any one time, nor are they a substitute for a thorough understanding of the relevant legislation, codes of practice, case law and procedure.

Important principles

★A-244

1. Every accused person has a right to a fair trial. This right is a fundamental part of our legal system and is guaranteed by Article 6 of the European Convention on Human Rights (ECHR). The disclosure process secures the right to a fair trial. ★A-244a

2. The statutory framework for criminal investigations and disclosure is contained in the Criminal Procedure and Investigations Act 1996 (the CPIA 1996). The CPIA 1996 is an important part of the system that ensures criminal investigations and trials are conducted in a fair, objective and thorough manner.

3. A fair trial does not require consideration of irrelevant material. It does not require irrelevant material to be obtained or reviewed. It should not involve spurious applications or arguments which aim to divert the trial process from examining the real issues before the court.

4. The statutory disclosure regime does not require the prosecutor to make available to the accused either neutral material or material which is adverse to the accused[1]. This material may be listed on the schedule, alerting the accused to its existence, but does not need to be disclosed: prosecutors should not disclose material which they are not required to, as this would overburden the participants in the trial process, divert attention away from the relevant issues and may lead to unjustifiable delays. **Disclosure should be completed in a thinking manner.**[2]**, in light of the issues in the case, and not simply as a schedule completing exercise.**[3]. Prosecutors need to think about what the case is about, what the likely issues for trial are going to be and how this affects the reasonable lines of inquiry, what material is relevant, and whether material meets the test for disclosure.

5. There will always be a number of participants in prosecutions and investigations. Communication within the prosecution team is vital to ensure that all disclosure issues are given sufficient atten- ★A-244b

---

[1] *R v H and others* [2004] UKHL 3, [2004] 2 AC 134 paragraphs [17] and [35].

[2] "Not undertaking the process in a mechanical manner...keeping the issues in mind...being alive to the countervailing points of view...considering the impact of disclosure decisions...keeping disclosure decisions under review". *R v Olu, Wilson and Brooks* [2010] EWCA Crim 2975, [2011] 1 Cr. App. R. 33 [42] - [44].

[3] *R v Olu, Wilson and Brooks* [2010] EWCA Crim 2975, [2011] 1 Cr. App. R. 33 [42] - [44].

tion by the right person. The respective roles of an investigator, the officer in charge of an investigation, disclosure officer, and prosecutor are set out in the CPIA Code.[4].

6. A full log of disclosure decisions and the reasons for those decisions must be kept on file and made available to the prosecution team. Any prosecutor must be able to see and understand previous disclosure decisions before carrying out their continuous review function.

7. The role of the reviewing lawyer is central to ensuring that all members of the prosecution team are aware of their role and their duties. Where prosecution advocates are instructed, they should be provided with clear written instructions about disclosure and provided with copies of any unused material which has been disclosed to the defence.

8. Investigators and disclosure officers must be fair and objective and must work together with prosecutors to ensure that disclosure obligations are met. Investigators and disclosure officers should be familiar with the CPIA Code of Practice.[5] - in particular their obligations to **retain and record** the relevant material, to **review** it and to **reveal** it to the prosecutor (see paragraphs 3-7 of the Code).

9. Investigators and disclosure officers should be deployed on cases which are commensurate with their training, skills and experience. The conduct of an investigation provides the foundation for the entire case, and may even impact on linked cases. The specific strategy and approach to disclosure that will be taken must always be considered at the start of each investigation.

10. Where there are a number of disclosure officers assigned to a case there should be a lead disclosure officer who is the focus for enquiries and whose responsibility it is to ensure that the investigator's disclosure obligations are complied with. Regular case conferences should be held, as required, to ensure that prosecutors are apprised of all relevant developments. Full records, including detailed minutes, should be kept of any such meetings. The parties involved should agree at the outset whose responsibility it will be to record the case conferences.

The balance between the right to a fair trial (Article 6 of the European Convention of Human Rights) and the right to private and family life (Article 8 of the European Convention of Human Rights)

★A-245 11. Investigators and prosecutors need to be aware of the delicate questions which arise when both the right to a fair trial and the privacy of complainants and witnesses are engaged.[6]

12. Fulfilling disclosure obligations is part of ensuring a fair trial in accordance with Article 6 of the ECHR. To comply with Article 6, during the course of an investigation, the investigator or prosecutor may decide that it is necessary to request and/or process personal or private information from a complainant or witness to pursue a reasonable line of inquiry; this includes, but is not limited to, digital material.

★A-245a 13. When seeking to obtain and review such material, investigators and prosecutors should be aware that these lines of inquiry may engage that individual's Article 8 rights and those rights in respect of other parties within that material. Such material may also include sensitive data.[7]. When seeking to satisfy their disclosure obligations in these circumstances, investigators and prosecutors should apply the following principles:

a. Collecting and/or processing personal or private material can only be done when in accordance with the law, strictly necessary.[8], and proportionate.

b. In order to be in accordance with the law and strictly necessary, an investigator must be pursuing a reasonable line of inquiry in seeking to obtain the material. What constitutes a reasonable line of inquiry may be informed by others, including the prosecutor and the defendant. Seeking the personal or private information of a complainant or witness will not be a reasonable line of inquiry in every case - an assessment of reasonableness is required (see below for an example).

c. The assessment of reasonableness must be made on a case-by-case basis and regard may be had to:
   (i) the prospect of obtaining relevant material; and
   (ii) what the perceived relevance of that material is, having regard to the identifiable facts and issues in the individual case;

d. If, by following a reasonable line of inquiry, it becomes necessary to obtain personal or private material, investigators will also need to consider:

---

[4] The CPIA Code (n2) paragraph 2.1.

[5] Ministry of Justice, *Criminal Procedure and Investigations Act 1996 Code of Practice* (2020) (the CPIA Code)

[6] Guidance is given by the Court of Appeal in *Bater-James and Mohammed* [2020] EWCA Crim 790

[7] See Section 35(8) of the Data Protection Act 2018 for data that requires sensitive processing

[8] The processing must relate to a pressing social need, and where the investigator or prosecutor cannot reasonably achieve it through less intrusive means. See Part 3 and Schedule 8 of the Data Protection Act 2018

(i) what review is required;
(ii) how the review of this material should be conducted;
(iii) what is the least intrusive method which will nonetheless secure relevant material;
(iv) are particular parameters for searching best suited to the identification of relevant material;
(v) is provision of the material in its entirety to the investigator strictly necessary; or alternatively, could the material be obtained from other sources, or by the investigator viewing and/or capturing the material in situ? An incremental approach should be taken to the degree of intrusion.

e. The rationale for pursuing the reasonable line of inquiry and the scope of the review it necessitates should be open and transparent. It should be capable of articulation by the investigator making the decision. It should provide the basis for:
(i) consultation with the prosecutor,
(ii) engagement with the defence and,
(iii) the provision of information to the witness about how their material is to be handled.

f. The refusal by a witness to provide private or personal material requires an investigator and prosecutor to consider the information the witness has been provided (and could be provided) with regard to the use of their personal material, the reasons for refusal, and how the trial process could address the absence of the material.

g. Disclosure of such material to the defence is in accordance with the law and necessary if, but only if, the material meets the disclosure test in the CPIA 1996. Personal information which does not meet this test but is contained within the material to be disclosed should be redacted.

h. Where there is a conflict between both of these rights, investigators and prosecutors should bear in mind that the right to a fair trial is an absolute right. Where prosecutors and investigators work within the framework provided by the CPIA, any unavoidable intrusion into privacy rights is likely to be justified, so long as any intrusion is no more than necessary.

For retention of data, see paragraphs 21-25 of Annex A on Digital Material and paragraph 5(a) and (b) of the Code.

Example

There will be cases where there is no requirement for the police to take the devices of a complainant/witness or others at all, and no requirement for any examination to be undertaken. ★A-245b

Examples of this could include sexual offences committed opportunistically against strangers, or historic allegations where there is considered to be no prospect that the complainant's phone will contain any material relevant to the period in which the conduct is said to have occurred and/or the complainant through age or other circumstances did not have access to a phone at that time.

However, decisions will depend on the facts of the case in question. For example, in the case of a sexual offence committed opportunistically against a stranger, a mobile phone could contain first complaint evidence. Investigators should always carefully consider what is relevant for the case in question.

A case might, for example, involve a complainant contacting the police to make an allegation of an offence against a person they had met that same day. The suspect may accept that they met the complainant but deny the allegation. The complainant and suspect communicated on a single medium. The investigator may consider it is a reasonable line of enquiry to view the messages from the day on which the two persons met as, before and after, they are highly likely to be relevant. They may contain material about what was expected or not expected when complainant and suspect met, the nature of their relationship, and the response after they met, all of which may cast light on the complainant's account and the suspect's account. That is unlikely to require the investigator taking custody of the phone or obtaining a large volume of data. If, by way of example and contrast, the complainant alleged coercive and controlling behaviour over a period of years, including manipulative conduct over various platforms, a larger quantity of data may be relevant and require review and retention by the investigator by different means.

The investigation

14. Consideration of disclosure issues is an integral part of an investigation and is not something that should be considered in isolation. ★A-246

15. Investigators should approach the investigation with a view to establishing what actually happened. They are to be fair and objective.

16. The following diagram illustrates how material that forms part of an investigation may be categorised and consequently treated. Further information on sensitive material can be found at paragraph 65.

★A-247

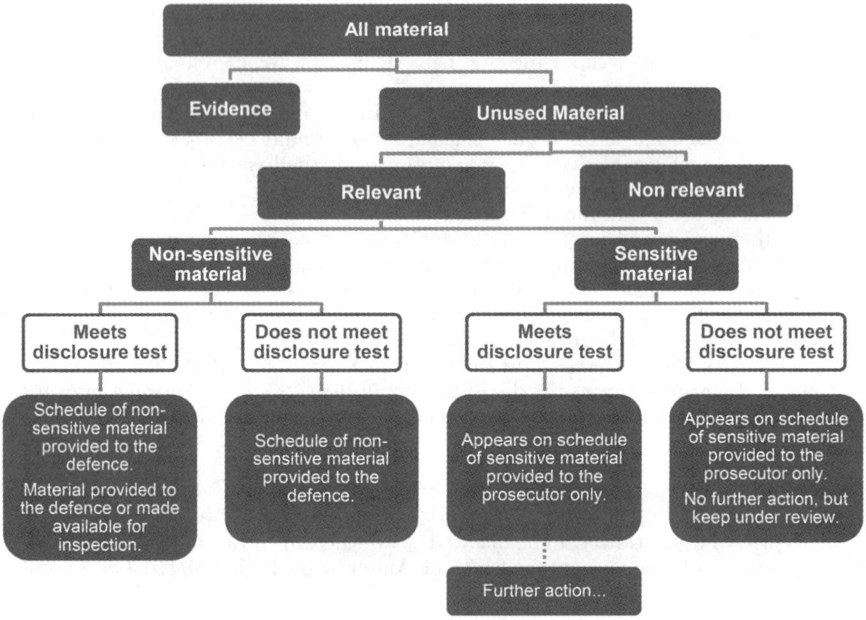

★A-248 17. Investigators should ensure that all reasonable lines of inquiry are investigated, whether they point towards or away from the suspect. What is 'reasonable' will depend on the context of the case. A fair investigation does not mean an endless investigation. Investigators and disclosure officers must give thought to defining, and articulating the limits of the scope of their investigations. When assessing what is reasonable, thought should be given to what is likely to be obtained as a result of the line of inquiry and how it can be obtained. An investigator may seek the advice of the prosecutor when considering which lines of inquiry should be pursued where appropriate.

18. When conducting an investigation, an investigator should always have in mind their obligation to retain and record all relevant material.[9]. Material which is presumed to meet the test for disclosure, as set out in paragraph 87 of these guidelines, must always be retained and recorded. All relevant material must be retained, whereas non-relevant material does not need to be retained.

The definition of relevant material

★A-249 Material may be relevant to an investigation if it appears to an investigator, or to the officer in charge of an investigation, or to the disclosure officer, that it has some bearing on any offence under investigation or any person being investigated, or on the surrounding circumstances of the case, unless it is incapable of having any impact on the case.[10].

★A-250 19. The decision as to relevance requires an exercise of judgment and, although some material may plainly be relevant or non-relevant, ultimately this requires a decision by the disclosure officer or investigator.

20. Disclosure officers and/or investigators must inspect, view, listen to, or search all relevant material. The disclosure officer must provide a personal declaration that this task has been completed. In some cases a detailed examination of every item of material seized would be disproportionate. In these cases the disclosure officer can apply search techniques using the principles contained in Annex A. Whatever the approach taken by disclosure officers in examining material, it is crucial that disclosure officers record their reasons for a particular approach in writing.

[9] The CPIA Code paragraphs 4 and 5
[10] The CPIA Code paragraph 2

21. Disclosure officers should seek the advice and assistance of prosecutors when in doubt as to their responsibility as early as possible. They must deal expeditiously with requests by the prosecutor for further information on material, which may lead to disclosure.

22. Where prosecutors have reason to believe that the disclosure officer has not inspected, viewed, listened to or searched relevant material, or has not done so sufficiently or has not articulated a reason for doing so, they should raise this issue with the disclosure officer and request that it is addressed. Prosecutors should also assist disclosure officers and investigators in defining the parameters of review and the methodology to be adopted. ★A-251

23. It may become apparent to an investigator that some material obtained in the course of an investigation, either because it was considered to be potentially relevant, or because it was inextricably linked to material that was relevant, is in fact incapable of impacting on the case.[11]. It is not necessary to retain such material. However, the investigator should also exercise considerable caution in reaching that conclusion. The investigator should be particularly mindful of the fact that some investigations continue over some time. Material that is incapable of impact may change over time and it may not be possible to foresee what the issues in the case will be. The advice of the prosecutor may be sought where necessary. Ultimately, however, the decision on whether to retain material is one for the investigator, and should always be based on their assessment of the relevance of the material and the likelihood of it having any impact on the case in future.

24. Prosecutors must be alert to the need to provide advice to and, where necessary, probe actions taken by the investigator to ensure that disclosure obligations are capable of being met. This should include advice on potential further reasonable lines of inquiry. There should be no aspects of an investigation about which prosecutors are unable to ask probing questions. ★A-251a

25. In some investigations it may be appropriate for the officer in charge of the investigation to seek engagement with the defence at the pre-charge stage. This is likely to be where it is possible that such engagement will lead to the defence volunteering additional information which may assist in identifying new lines of inquiry. Annex B sets out the process for any such pre-charge engagement.

Third party material

26. Third party material is material held by a person, organisation, or government department other than the investigator and prosecutor, either within the UK or outside the UK. Third parties are not directly involved in the case in question, but may hold information relevant to it. ★A-252

27. The CPIA Code and these guidelines make clear the obligation on the investigator to pursue all reasonable lines of inquiry in relation to material held by third parties within the UK.

28. It is for investigators, in consultation or discussion with prosecutors where appropriate, to pursue all reasonable lines of inquiry. Prosecutors can advise on additional reasonable lines of inquiry and should satisfy themselves that such reasonable lines of inquiry have been pursued.

29. If as a result of the duty to pursue all reasonable lines of inquiry, the investigator or prosecutor obtains or receives material from a third party, then it must be dealt with in accordance with the CPIA 1996, (i.e. the prosecutor must disclose material if it meets the disclosure tests, subject to any public interest immunity claim). The person who has an interest in the material (the third party) may make representations to the court concerning public interest immunity (see section 16 of the CPIA 1996).

30. Material not in the possession of an investigator or prosecutor falls outside the CPIA. In such cases these guidelines prescribe the approach to be taken to disclosure of material held by third parties.

Material held by Government departments

31. During an investigation or prosecution it may become apparent that a Government department or another Crown body has material that may be relevant to an issue in the case. ★A-253

32. The investigator or prosecutor should inform the Government department or Crown body at the earliest opportunity of the nature of the case and the relevant issues in the case, and ask whether it has any relevant material. They should assist the Government department or Crown body in understanding what may be relevant in the context of the case in question.

33. Crown Servants have a duty to support the administration of justice and should take reasonable steps to identify and consider such material. This extends to revealing to the investigator or prosecutor the extent of the searches conducted and the existence of any information which they

[11] The CPIA (section 23 (1))

believe may be relevant to the issues in the case, to supply them with that information unless it is protected to the issues in the case, and to supply them with that information unless it is protected in law, subject to legal professional privilege or attracts public interest immunity.

★A-253a 34. If access is denied to relevant material, the investigator or prosecutor should consider the reasons given by the Government department or Crown body and what, if any, further steps might be taken to obtain the material. The final decision on further steps rests with the prosecutor.

35. Investigators and prosecutors cannot be regarded to be in constructive possession of material held by Government departments or Crown bodies simply by virtue of their status as Government departments or Crown bodies.

36. The steps taken to identify and obtain relevant material held by a Government department or Crown body should be recorded by the investigator and the prosecutor.

37. Where appropriate, the defence should be informed of the steps taken to obtain material and the results of the line of inquiry.

Other domestic bodies

★A-254 38. An investigator, disclosure officer or a prosecutor may believe that a third party (for example a local authority, social services department, hospital, doctor, school, provider of forensic services, or CCTV operator) has material or information which might be relevant to the case. If so, then reasonable steps should be taken to secure and consider the material held by the third party where it appears that such material exists and that it may be relevant to an issue in the case.

39. The investigator, disclosure officer or prosecutor should follow the steps in paragraphs 32, 34 and 36 above when engaging with the relevant domestic body.

40. A third party has no obligation under the CPIA to reveal material to investigators or prosecutors. There is also no duty on the third party to retain material which may be relevant to the investigation and, in some circumstances, the third party may not be aware of the investigation or prosecution.

41. If access to the material is refused and, despite the reasons given for refusal of access, it is still believed that it is reasonable to seek production of the material or information and that the requirements of a witness summons.[12], .[13] are satisfied (or any other relevant power), then the prosecutor or investigator should apply for the summons causing a representative of the third party to produce the material to court.

42. When the third party material in question is personal data, investigators and prosecutors must refer to paragraphs 11 - 13 of these guidelines to ensure that there is no unjust intrusion of privacy.

43. Further guidance and best practice on obtaining third party material can be found in the Joint Protocol on Third Party Material and Chapter 5 of the *CPS Disclosure Manual.*

44. The defence should be informed of what steps have been taken to obtain material and what the results of the inquiry have been.

International enquiries

★A-255 45. The obligations under the CPIA Code to pursue all reasonable lines of inquiry apply to material held overseas.

46. Where it appears that there is relevant material, the investigator or prosecutor must take reasonable steps to obtain it, either informally or by making use of the powers contained in the Crime (International Co-operation) Act 2003, the Criminal Justice (European Investigation Order) Regulations 2017 and any international conventions.

47. There may be cases where a foreign state or court refuses to make the material available to the investigator or prosecutor. There may be other cases where the foreign state, though willing to show the material to investigators, will not allow the material to be copied or otherwise made available and the courts of the foreign state will not order its provision.

48. It is for these reasons that there is no absolute duty on the prosecutor to disclose relevant material held overseas by entities not subject to the jurisdiction of the courts in England and Wales. However, consideration should be given to whether the type of material believed to be held can be provided to the defence.

★A-255a 49. The obligation on the investigator and prosecutor under the CPIA Code is to take reasonable steps. Where investigators are allowed to examine the files of a foreign state but are not allowed to

[12] Criminal Procedure (Attendance of Witnesses) Act 1965, s2
[13] Magistrates Court Act 1980, s97

take copies, take notes or list the documents held, there is no breach by the prosecution in its duty of disclosure by reason of its failure to obtain such material, provided reasonable steps have been taken to try and obtain it. Prosecutors have a margin of consideration as to what steps are appropriate in the particular case, but prosecutors must be alive to their duties and there may be some circumstances where these duties cannot be met. Whether or not a prosecutor has taken reasonable steps is for the court to determine in each case if the matter is raised.

50. Where it is apparent during the investigation that there may be relevant material held overseas then investigators and prosecutors should consider engaging with the defence at the pre-charge stage, applying the principles contained in Annex B, to ensure that all reasonable lines of inquiry are followed.

51. It is important that the position taken in relation to any material held overseas is clearly set out in a document such as a disclosure management document (DMD) so that the court and the defence know what the position is. Further information on DMDs can be found below, at paragraph 92.

52. In the DMD, investigators and prosecutors must record and explain the situation and set out, insofar as they are permitted by the foreign state, such information as they can and the steps they have taken to obtain it.

53. The defence should be informed of what steps have been taken to obtain material and what the results of the enquiry have been.

Electronic material

54. The exponential increase in the use of technology in society means that many routine investigations are increasingly likely to have to engage with digital material of some form. It is not only in large and complex investigations where there may be large quantities of such material. When dealing with large quantities of digital material prosecutors and investigators should apply the principles contained in Annex A to these guidelines. **★A-256**

55. Where investigations involve a large quantity of digital material it may be impossible for investigators to examine every item of such material individually. Therefore there should be no expectation that this should happen. Investigators and disclosure officers will need to decide how best to pursue a reasonable line of inquiry in relation to the relevant digital material, and ensure that the extent and manner of the examination are appropriate to the issues in the case. In reaching any such decisions, investigators and disclosure officers must bear in mind the overriding obligation to ensure a fair trial of any suspect who is charged and the requirement to provide disclosure in the trial process.

56. Prosecutors and investigators must ensure that any line of inquiry pursued in relation to the digital devices of victims and witnesses are reasonable in the context of the likely issues in the case. Digital devices should not be obtained as a matter of course and the decision to obtain and examine a digital device will be a fact-specific decision to be made in each and every case.[14]. Where digital devices are obtained, if it becomes apparent that they do not contain relevant material they should be returned at the earliest opportunity.

57. Prosecutors should be consulted, where appropriate, to agree a strategy for dealing with digital material. This strategy should be set out in a disclosure management document (DMD) and shared with the defence at the appropriate time.

Revelation of material to a prosecutor

58. Prosecutors only have knowledge of the matters which are revealed to them by investigators and disclosure officers. The schedules are the means by which that revelation takes place. Therefore it is crucial that the schedules detail all of the relevant material and that the material is adequately described. This process will also enable defence practitioners to become appraised of relevant material at the appropriate stage of the investigation. More detail on what constitutes relevant material can be found here. **★A-257**

59. Schedules must be completed in a form which not only reveals sufficient information to the prosecutor, but which demonstrates a transparent and thinking approach to the disclosure exercise. The speed with which the schedule is produced should not reduce the quality of the material contained therein.

---

[14] *R v E*, [2018] EWCA 2426 (Crim)

60. Descriptions on the schedules must be clear and accurate and must contain sufficient detail to enable the prosecutor to make an informed decision on disclosure. Abbreviations and acronyms should be avoided as they risk significant material being overlooked.

★A-257a 61. Investigators and disclosure officers must ensure that material which is presumed to meet the test for disclosure, as set out in paragraph 87 of these guidelines and paragraph 6.6 of the CPIA Code, is placed on the schedules. The requirement to schedule this material is in addition to the requirement to schedule all other relevant unused material.

62. Where relevant unused material has been omitted from the schedule or where material is not described sufficiently, and the prosecutor asks the disclosure officer to rectify the schedule, the disclosure officer must comply with this request in a timely manner.

63. Disclosure officers must bring to the prosecutor's attention any material which is potentially capable of meeting the test for disclosure. This material should be provided to the prosecutor along with the reasons why it is thought to meet the test.

64. Disclosure officers must also draw material to the attention of the prosecutor for consideration where they have doubt as to whether it might reasonably be considered capable of undermining the prosecution case or of assisting the case for the accused.

Revelation of sensitive material

What is sensitive material?

★A-257b 65. Sensitive material is material that, if disclosed, would give rise to a *real* risk of *serious* prejudice to an *important* public interest. Investigators must ensure that all relevant unused sensitive material is retained, reviewed and revealed to the prosecutor. Sensitive material should be revealed to a prosecutor on a separate schedule to the non-sensitive material.

Examples of sensitive material can be found in paragraph 6.14 of the CPIA Code.

★A-257c 66. When making a decision about the sensitivity of an item, investigators should have regard to the types of material listed in paragraph 6.14 of the CPIA Code. The disclosure officer must ensure that the sensitive material schedule include the reasons why it is asserted that items on the schedule are considered sensitive.

67. Where a document contains a mix of sensitive and non-sensitive material, the sensitive material must be redacted, with a copy of the redacted document placed on the non-sensitive unused material schedule and the original placed on the sensitive schedule.

68. Investigators must ensure that the descriptions of sensitive unused material are sufficiently clear to enable the prosecutor to make an informed decision as to whether or not the material itself should be viewed, to the extent possible without compromising the confidentiality of the information.

69. Prosecutors must carefully review the sensitive unused material schedule in order to be satisfied that there are no omissions, that the items have been correctly identified as sensitive, and that the items are adequately described. If a prosecutor identifies that a schedule is inadequate, the investigator must provide an adequate schedule as soon as possible. This may involve items being moved from the sensitive unused material schedule to the non-sensitive unused material schedule.

The timing of revelation

★A-258 70. In order to support prosecutors' assessment of the impact of unused material on any proposed prosecution, it is essential that prosecutors are provided with the schedule of unused material at an early stage, as well as any material which the disclosure officer considers potentially capable of meeting the test for disclosure. This will allow for a thorough review of the case, and will enable the prosecutor to consider what the disclosure strategy should be.

71. The timing of revelation of material should be in accordance with paragraph 7.1 of the Code. The point at which the case file is submitted to the CPS will depend on the circumstances of the charging decision and on the anticipated plea:

a. Where the police are seeking a charging decision under the Full Code Test from the CPS, and it is anticipated that the defendant will plead not guilty, the unused material schedules should be provided to the prosecutor by the disclosure officer at the same time as seeking this charging decision.

b. Where the police have charged a suspect on the Full Code Test under the arrangements contained in the Director's Guidance on Charging, and a not guilty plea is anticipated, then the unused material schedule should be provided to the prosecutor at the point at which the case file is submitted to the CPS.

c. In all other cases the disclosure officer must provide the schedules as soon as possible after a not guilty plea has either been indicated or entered.

72. There may be instances where an investigator is seeking a charging decision on the Full Code Test and anticipating a not guilty plea, but where it is not feasible to provide the unused material schedules to the prosecutor at the same time as seeking a charging decision. This may be the case where an arrest is not planned, and the suspect cannot be bailed. **★A-258a**

73. For large and complex investigations, particularly those conducted by the Serious Fraud Office, it is recognised that the preparation of schedules continues beyond the point of charge due to the quantity and complexity of data to be analysed, and that it may not be feasible or necessary to provide the schedules at the same time that a charging decision is sought.

74. Disclosure officers should apply the criteria contained in the Director's Guidance on Charging when making a decision about a suspect's likely plea, and must follow any additional guidance provided by the prosecutor.

The charging decision

75. Prosecutors must ensure that all reasonable lines of inquiry likely to affect the application of the Full Code Test have been pursued before the Test is applied, unless the prosecutor is satisfied that any further evidence or material is unlikely to affect the application of the Full Code Test.[15]. The failure to pursue reasonable lines of inquiry may result in the application of the Full Code Test being deferred, or in a decision that the Test cannot be met. **★A-259**

76. If a decision is made to charge a case under the Threshold Test, then prosecutors and investigators need to be proactive in ensuring that any outstanding lines of inquiry are pursued and that the case is kept under continuous review.

Common law disclosure

77. A prosecutor's statutory duty of disclosure applies from the point of a not guilty plea in the magistrates' court and from the point a case is sent to the Crown Court.[16]. However prosecutors must also consider their duties under the common law, which apply at all stages of a case, from charge to sentence and post-conviction (see paragraphs 137 and 138), and regardless of anticipated or actual plea. **★A-260**

78. These duties may require the prosecutor to disclose material to the accused outside the statutory scheme in accordance with the interests of justice and fairness. An example of this is where it would assist the accused in the preparation of the defence case, prior to plea and regardless of anticipated plea. This would include material which would assist in the making of a bail application, material which may enable the accused to make an early application to stay the proceedings as an abuse of process, material which may enable the accused to make representations about the trial venue or a lesser charge, or material which would enable an accused to prepare for trial effectively.[17].

Initial disclosure

79. The defence must be provided with copies of, or access to, any prosecution material not previously disclosed, which might reasonably be considered capable of undermining the case for the prosecution against the accused, or of assisting the case for the accused.[18]. Paragraphs 100-107 of these Guidelines contain guidance as to when initial disclosure should be served. **★A-261**

80. In order for the prosecutor to comply with their duty of initial disclosure they must analyse the case for the prosecution, the defence case, and the likely trial issues. A prosecutor can anticipate the likely issues on the basis of information available (such as any explanation provided by the accused in interview).

81. The prosecutor must also encourage dialogue and prompt engagement with the defence about the likely issues for trial.

82. The defence are under a duty to engage with the prosecutor in order to aid understanding about the defence case and the likely issues for trial at this early stage. This engagement assists in ensuring compliance with the overriding objective of the Criminal Procedure Rules.[19]. [20].

---

[15] Crown Prosecution Service, *The Code for Crown Prosecutors* paragraph 4.3
[16] Criminal Procedure and Investigations Act 1996 (CPIA 1996), s1(1)(a) and (2)(cc)
[17] *R v DPP, ex p. Lee* [1999] 1 WLR 1950 [1962] - [1963]
[18] CPIA 1996, s3
[19] The Criminal Procedure Rules 2020 SI No. 759 (L.19) (the CrimPR), part 1
[20] *R v R and others* [2015] EWCA Crim 1941, [2016] 1 WLR 1872, paragraph [35]

83. Prosecutors must review schedules prepared by disclosure officers thoroughly at an early stage and must be alert to the possibility that relevant material may exist which has not been revealed to them or material included which should not have been. If no schedules are provided, if there are apparent omissions from the schedules, or if documents or other items are inadequately described or are unclear, the prosecutor must request properly completed schedules from the investigator. Investigators must comply with any such request. A log of such communications should be kept by the prosecutor.

★A-261a 84. In deciding whether material satisfies the disclosure test, consideration should include:

a. The use that might be made of it in cross-examination;
b. Its capacity to support submissions that could lead to:
    i. The exclusion of evidence;
    ii. A stay of proceedings, where the material is required to allow a proper application to be made;
    iii. A court or tribunal finding that any public authority had acted incompatibly with the accused's rights under the European Convention of Human Rights;
c. Its capacity to suggest an explanation or partial explanation of the accused's actions;
d. Its capacity to undermine the reliability or credibility of a prosecution witness;
e. The capacity of the material to have a bearing on scientific or medical evidence in the case.

85. Material relating to the accused's mental or physical health, intellectual capacity, or to any ill treatment which the accused may have suffered when in the investigator's custody is likely to meet the test for disclosure.

86. Material should not be viewed in isolation as, whilst items taken alone may not be reasonably considered capable of undermining the prosecution case or assisting the case for the accused, several items together can have that effect.

Material which is likely to meet the test for disclosure

★A-261b 87. The following material is likely to include information which meets the test for disclosure:

a) records which are derived from tapes or recordings of telephone messages (for example 999 calls) containing descriptions of an alleged offence or offender;
b) any incident logs relating to the allegation;
c) contemporaneous records of the incident, such as:
    - crime reports and crime report forms;
    - an investigation log;
    - any record or note made by an investigator (including police notebook entries and other handwritten notes) on which they later make a statement or which relates to contact with suspects, victims or witnesses;
    - an account of an incident or information relevant to an incident noted by an investigator in manuscript or electronically;
    - records of actions carried out by officers (such as house-to-house interviews, CCTV or forensic enquiries) noted by a police officer in manuscript or electronically;
    - CCTV footage, or other imagery, of the incident in action;
d) the defendant's custody record or voluntary attendance record;
e) any previous accounts made by a complainant or by any other witnesses;
f) interview records (written records, or audio or video tapes, of interviews with actual or potential witnesses or suspects);
g) any material casting doubt on the reliability of a witness e. g. relevant previous convictions and relevant cautions of any prosecution witnesses and any co-accused.

88. This list is reflected in paragraph 5.4 and 6.6 of the Code. This material, in addition to all other material which may be relevant to an investigation, must be **retained** and **listed** on the schedule by the investigator. It is likely that some of this material will need to be redacted (see paragraph 6(c) of the Code and paragraph 65 of these guidelines for redaction and revelation of sensitive material.)

89. As this material is likely to contain information which meets the test for disclosure, prosecutors should start their review of the material with a presumption that this material should be disclosed to the defence. However, in every instance the disclosure test should be applied in a thinking manner.

90. After applying the disclosure test, a prosecutor must record on the unused material schedule whether each item of this material does or does not meet the test for disclosure and they must record the reason for that decision.

91. This list of material is not intended to cause automatic disclosure – investigators and prosecutors should always apply the disclosure test and consider each list of material carefully in the context of the case in question.

Disclosure management document (DMD)

What is a disclosure management document?

92. A disclosure management document (DMD) outlines the strategy and approach taken in relation to disclosure and should be served to the defence and the court at an early stage. DMDs will require careful preparation and presentation which is tailored to the individual case. The investigator should provide information for use in the DMD and the prosecutor should prepare it. ★A-262

93. A DMD is a living document which should be amended in light of developments in the case and kept up to date as the case progresses. DMDs are intended to assist the court in case management and will also enable the defence to engage from an early stage with the prosecution's proposed approach to disclosure.

94. DMDs may set out:

a. Where prosecutors and investigators operate in an integrated office, an explanation as to how the disclosure responsibilities have been managed.
b. A brief summary of the prosecution case and a statement outlining how the prosecutor's general approach will comply with the CPIA 1996 regime and these guidelines
c. The prosecutor's understanding of the defence case, including information revealed during interview. The prosecutor may wish to explain their understanding of what is in dispute and what is not in dispute, the lines of inquiry that have been pursued in light of these issues, and specific disclosure decisions that have been taken.
d. An outline of the prosecution's general approach to disclosure, which may include detail relating to:
    i. The lines of inquiry pursued, particularly those which may assist the defence.
    ii. The timescales for disclosure and, where relevant, how the review of unused material has been prioritised.
    iii. The method and extent of examination of digital material, in accordance with the Annex A to these guidelines.
    iv. Any potential video footage.
    v. Any linked investigations, including an explanation of the nexus between investigations and any memoranda of understanding and disclosure agreements between investigators.
    vi. Any third party material, including the steps taken to obtain the material.
    vii. Any international material, including the steps taken to obtain the material.
    viii. Credibility of prosecution witnesses (including professional witnesses).

95. In cases heard in the magistrates' court and the youth court, prosecutors should always consider whether or not a disclosure management document (DMD) would be beneficial. DMDs are most likely to be beneficial in cases with the following features: ★A-262a

a. Substantial or complex third party material;
b. Digital material in which parameters of search, examination or analysis have been set;
c. Cases involving international enquiries;
d. Cases where there are linked operations;
e. Non-recent offending;
f. Cases involving material held or sought by the investigation that is susceptible to a claim of legal professional privilege.

96. DMDs should be prepared in all Crown Court cases.

97. In order for the prosecutor to complete a DMD at an early stage, the investigator should, at the point of or prior to charge, provide written details as to the lines of inquiry that have been pursued.

98. Where a DMD has been prepared, it should be served at the same time as initial disclosure.

99. An example template for a DMD is contained in Annex C.

The timing of initial disclosure

100. In all cases it is essential that the prosecution takes a grip on the case and its disclosure requirements at an early stage. Prosecutors must adopt a considered and appropriately resourced approach to providing initial disclosure. Initial disclosure in this context refers to the period post-charge; more detailed timings for this are set out below. ★A-263

Cases expected to be tried in the magistrates' courts

★A-263a 101. Where a case is charged on the Full Code Test and a not guilty plea is anticipated, initial disclosure should be served in advance of the first hearing.

102. Where a guilty plea was originally anticipated but a not guilty plea is entered then initial disclosure should be served as soon as possible after a not guilty plea is entered.

103. Where a case is charged on the Threshold Test, initial disclosure should be served as soon as possible after the Full Code Test is applied and in accordance with any order made by the court.

Cases sent to the Crown Court for trial

★A-263b 104. Where it is expected that the accused will maintain a not guilty plea, it is encouraged as a matter of best practice for initial disclosure to be served prior to the Plea and Trial Preparation Hearing (PTPH).

105. It is accepted that it may not be appropriate or possible to serve initial disclosure prior to the PTPH for cases charged on the Threshold Test. Where initial disclosure has not been served at the PTPH it should be served as soon as possible after that hearing and in accordance with any direction made by the court.

106. In cases prosecuted by the Serious Fraud Office, or other similarly large or complex cases, it is accepted that full initial disclosure may not be capable of being served prior to the PTPH. In such cases, best practice is to adopt a phased approach to disclosure, ensuring that robust judicial case management during Further Case Management Hearings, and in line with the Criminal Procedure Rules and Criminal Practice Directions, manages the on-going disclosure process. Utilising an initial DMD at the PTPH which outlines the intended plan for onwards staged disclosure of remaining materials and associated schedules, can be an effective mechanism for this approach and is to adopted where possible.

107. Nothing in these guidelines should undermine the established principles of the Better Case Management Framework.

Case management

★A-263c 108. In order for the statutory disclosure regime to work effectively all parties should ensure compliance with the Criminal Procedure Rules. The rules require the court to actively manage the case by identifying the real issues.[21]. Each party is obliged to assist the court with this duty.[22].

109. It is important that prosecutors keep a record of all correspondence which relates to disclosure and keep a record of any disclosure decisions made.

Magistrates' court

★A-263d 110. Following a not guilty plea being entered in the magistrates' court, the defence must ensure that the trial issues are clearly identified both in court and on the preparation for effective trial form. Prosecutors should ensure that any issues of dispute that are raised are noted on file. The preparation for effective trial form should be carefully reviewed, alongside the DMD (where this is exists). Consideration of any issues raised in court or on the form will assist in deciding whether any further material undermines the prosecution case or assists the accused.

Crown Court

★A-263e 111. A focus of the Plea and Trial Preparation Hearing (PTPH) must be on the disclosure strategy. This will involve the defence identifying the likely trial issues, a discussion of any additional lines of inquiry, and scrutiny of the DMD.

112. Prosecutors must ensure that the disclosure strategy and any disclosure decisions taken previously are reviewed in light of any issues raised at the PTPH and on the plea and trial preparation form.

113. Where the defence do not feel that the prosecution have adequately discharged their obligations then this must be brought to the court's attention at an early stage. The defence should be

---

[21] The CrimPR, rule 3.2(2)(a)
[22] The CrimPR, rule 3.3(1)(a)

proactive in ensuring that any issue is addressed, and must not delay raising these issues until a late stage in the proceedings. The DMD may be relevant in any challenge raised.

114. Where any party has not complied with their obligations, the court will consider giving any direction appropriate to ensure compliance and progression of the case.

Applications for non-disclosure in the public interest

115. The CPIA 1996 allows prosecutors to apply to the court for an order to withhold material which would otherwise fall to be disclosed if disclosure would give rise to a real risk of serious prejudice to an important public interest. Before making such an application, prosecutors should aim to disclose as much of the material as they properly can (for example, by giving the defence redacted or edited copies or summaries). Neutral material or material damaging to the defendant should not be disclosed, and should not be brought to the attention of the court. Only in truly borderline cases should the prosecution seek a judicial ruling on whether material in its possession should be disclosed. ★A-263f

116. Prior to the hearing, the prosecutor and the prosecution advocate must examine all material which is the subject matter of the application and make any necessary enquiries of the investigator. There is an additional duty of candour on the advocate at this hearing, given the defendant will not be present. In order to assist the court, it is best practice for the advocate to prepare a note that is either written in conjunction, or agreed with, the prosecutor and disclosure officer.

117. The investigator must also be frank with the prosecutor about the full extent of the sensitive material. Prior to or at the hearing the court must be provided with full and accurate information about the material.

118. The prosecutor and/or investigator should attend such applications. Section 16 of the CPIA 1996 allows a person claiming to have an interest in the sensitive material to apply to the court for the opportunity to be heard at the application.

119. The prosecutor should carefully consider the series of questions contained in paragraph 36 of *R v H and others* [2004] UKHL 3. These are the questions that the court must address before it makes a decision to withhold material. It is essential that these principles are scrupulously adhered to, to ensure that the procedure for examination of material in the absence of the accused is compliant with Article 6 of the ECHR. ★A-263g

120. If the prosecutor concludes that a fair trial cannot take place because material which satisfies the test for disclosure cannot be disclosed and that this cannot be remedied by an application for non-disclosure in the public interest, through altering the presentation of the case or by any other means, then they should not continue with the case.

The defence statement

121. Defence statements are an integral part of the statutory disclosure regime. A defence statement should help to focus the attention of the prosecutor, court and co-defendants on the relevant issues in order to identify material which may meet the test for disclosure. The defence must serve their defence statement in a timely manner, in accordance with any court directions made. ★A-264

122. There is no requirement for a defence statement to be served in the magistrates' court but it should be noted that if one is not provided the court does not have a power to hear an application for further prosecution disclosure under section 8 of the CPIA 1996.

123. Defence practitioners should ensure that defence statements are drafted in accordance with the requirements in the CPIA 1996.[23]. Defence statements should not make general and unspecified allegations in order to seek far reaching disclosure.[24] and should not describe the defence in ambiguous or limited terms (such as self-defence, mistaken identify, consent).

124. It is vital that prosecutors consider defence statements thoroughly. Prosecutors should challenge the lack of (in the Crown Court) or inadequate defence statements in writing, copying the document to the court and the defence and seeking directions from the court to require the provision of an adequate defence statement from the defence.

125. Prosecutors must send a copy of the defence statement to the investigator as soon as reasonably practicable after receipt and, at the same time, provide guidance to the disclosure officer about the key issues. The advice should contain guidance on whether any further reasonable lines of inquiry need to be pursued, guidance on what to look for when reviewing the unused material and guidance on what further material may need to be disclosed. On receipt of a defence statement, disclosure officers must re-review retained unused material and draw to the attention of the prosecu- ★A-264a

[23] CPIA 1996, s 6A
[24] *R v H and others*

tor any material which is potentially capable of meeting the test for disclosure and consider whether any further reasonable lines of inquiry need to be pursued. They should address the matters raised in guidance given by the prosecutor.

126. Defence requests for further disclosure should ordinarily only be answered by the prosecution if the request is relevant to, and directed to, an issue identified in the defence statement. If it is not, then a further or amended defence statement should be sought and obtained by the prosecutor before considering the request for further disclosure.

Continuing disclosure

★A-264b 127. The obligation of continuing disclosure is crucial and particular attention must be paid to understanding the significance of developments in the case on the unused material and earlier disclosure decisions. After service of initial disclosure, a prosecutor must keep under review whether or not there is prosecution material which might reasonably be considered capable of undermining the case for the prosecution against the accused, or of assisting the case for the accused, which has not been previously been disclosed. This obligation is a continuous one.[25], and it can be beneficial for it to take place in tranches, particularly in large and/or complex cases.

128. In particular, prosecutors should consider any issues raised by the defence at the first hearing in the magistrates' court or the PTPH in the Crown Court, as well as during any further hearings and after receipt of a defence statement. Any matters raised on the preparation for effective trial form or the PTPH form should also be carefully considered.

Applications for disclosure under Section 8 of the CPIA

★A-264c 129. An application for disclosure can only be made if the defence have provided an adequate defence statement.

130. Any application for disclosure must describe the material which is subject to the application and explain why there is reasonable cause to believe that the prosecutor has the material and why it meets the test for disclosure.

131. Prosecutors must carefully review any application for disclosure and consider whether any items described in the application meet the test for disclosure. This may require the prosecutor asking the disclosure officer for copies of the items or inspecting the items.

The trial

★A-264d 132. Prosecutors must ensure that advocates in court are provided with sufficient instructions regarding the disclosure strategy and any disclosure decisions taken.

133.

Prosecution advocates should ensure that all material which ought to be disclosed under the CPIA 1996 is disclosed to the defence. Prosecution advocates must ensure that they are fully informed about disclosure so that they are able to make decisions. Prosecution advocates must consider, in every case, whether they can be satisfied that they are in possession of all relevant documentation and that they have been fully instructed regarding disclosure matters. If the advocate considers that further information or action is required then written advice should be provided setting out the aspects that need clarification or action.

134. All decisions regarding disclosure must be kept under review until the conclusion of the trial, whenever possible in consultation with the reviewing prosecutor. The prosecution advocate must in every case specifically consider whether they can satisfactorily discharge the duty of continuing review on the basis of the material supplied already, or whether it is necessary to reconsider the unused material schedule and/or unused material.

135. Prosecution advocates must not abrogate their responsibility under the CPIA 1996 by disclosing material which does not pass the test for disclosure. This is especially so where it is proposed to disclose material engaging Article 8 rights.

136. There is no basis in practice or law for counsel-to-counsel disclosure. It is of critical importance that, even where prosecution counsel is advising and leading on disclosure, the duty to disclose material that meets the test for disclosure remains with the prosecutor. A record of material disclosed made must be kept, not least in the event of an appeal or a re-trial.

---

[25] CPIA 1996, s 7A

Material relevant to sentence

137. At sentence, the prosecutor should disclose any material which might reasonably be considered capable of ensuring fairness in the sentencing process. This material could include information which might mitigate the seriousness of the offence or the level of the defendant's involvement. ★A-264e

Post-conviction

138. Where, at any stage after the conclusion of the proceedings, material comes to light which might reasonably be considered capable of casting doubt upon the safety of the conviction, the prosecutor should disclose such material. ★A-264f

Confiscation Proceedings

139. The disclosure regime in the CPIA ceases to have effect post-conviction and the continuing duty of disclosure does not apply to confiscation proceedings (see section 7A(1)(b) of the CPIA). ★A-264g

140. Part 2 of the Proceeds of Crime Act 2002 provides the legislative scheme for confiscation in the Crown Court following a conviction. The prosecutor is required to set out relevant matters in accordance with Section 16 of the Proceeds of Crime Act 2002 apply and the disclosure requirements at common law also apply meaning that there may be a requirement to disclose material in the interests of justice and fairness in the proceedings.

ANNEX A -DIGITAL MATERIAL

A1. This annex is intended to supplement the Attorney General's Guidelines on Disclosure. It is not intended to be a detailed operational guide but is intended to set out a common approach to be adopted when seeking to obtain and handle digital material, whether that be from a suspect or from a complainant. This annex aims to set out how relevant material and consequently material satisfying the test for disclosure can best be identified, revealed and if necessary disclosed to the defence without imposing unrealistic or disproportionate demands on the investigator and prosecutor. This annex also seeks to recognise the considerations investigators and prosecutors should have when obtaining and handling sensitive personal information, in accordance with obligations under data protection legislation. ★A-265

A2. In cases involving large amounts of digital material, investigators should complete an investigation management document (IMD) which will inform the disclosure management document (DMD) that prosecutors should complete. The DMD allows prosecutors to be open and transparent with the defence and the court about how the prosecution has approached complying with its disclosure obligations in the specific context of the individual case.

A3. In cases where there may be a large amount of digital material, the investigator should consult the prosecutor, ideally before it is seized, and in turn they may consider seeking the advice of a digital forensic specialist on the strategy for the identification and review of digital material, including potential timings for this.

A4. The defence must also play their part in defining the real issues in the case. This is required by the overriding objective of the Criminal Procedure Rules.[26]. The defence should be invited by the prosecution at an early stage to participate in defining the scope of the reasonable searches that may be made of digital material in order to identify material that might reasonably be expected to undermine the prosecution case or assist the case for the defence.

A5. This approach enables the court to use its case management powers robustly to ensure that the prosecution's obligation of disclosure is discharged effectively.

General principles for investigators

A6. These general principles must be followed by investigators in handling and examining digital material.[27]: ★A-265a

a. No action should be taken which changes data on a device which may subsequently be relied upon in court.

[26] The CrimPR, part 1
[27] Association of Chief Police Officers, *ACPO Good Practice Guide for Digital Evidence* (2012), para 2.1

b. If it is necessary to access original data then that data should only be accessed by someone who is competent to do so and is able to explain the relevance and implications of their actions to a court.
c. An audit trail should be kept of all processes followed. Another practitioner should be able to follow the audit trail and achieve the same results.
d. The investigator in charge of the investigation has responsibility for ensuring that the law and these principles are followed.

A7. Where an investigator has reasonable grounds for believing that digital material may contain material subject to legal professional privilege then this may not be seized unless the provisions of the Criminal Justice and Police Act 2001 apply. This is addressed in more detail later on in this Annex.

A8. The legal obligations in relation to seizure, relevance and retention are found in the Police and Criminal Evidence Act 1984, the Criminal Justice and Police Act 2001 and the Criminal Procedure and Investigations Act 1996.

Obtaining devices by seizure or co-operation

★A-265b A9. Digital material may be seized from suspects using legal powers but this material may be obtained from suspects and witnesses with their cooperation as well. Before searching a suspect's premises where digital material is likely to be found, consideration must be given to:
a. What sort of material is likely to be found, and in what volume;
b. Whether it is likely that relevant material at the location will be able to be viewed and copied; and
c. What should be seized.

A10. Investigators will need to consider the practicalities of requesting/seizing digital devices, especially where there are a large number of devices. They will also need to consider the effect that taking possession/seizure will have on a business, organisation or individual; and where it is not feasible to obtain an image of the digital material, the likely timescale for returning the obtained items.

A11. In deciding whether to obtain and retain digital material, it is important that the investigator either complies with the procedure under the relevant statutory authority, relying on statutory powers or a search warrant, or obtains the owner's permission.

A12. When seeking to obtain digital material, whether from a suspect or a witness/complainant, investigators should be guided by the principles set out in paragraphs 11-13 in the Attorney General's Guidelines. Any intrusion into the personal and private lives of individuals should be carried out only where deemed necessary and using the least intrusive means possible to obtain the material required, adopting an incremental approach. Further guidance has been published by the CPS which has been endorsed by the Court of Appeal.[28]

★A-265c A13. A computer hard drive is a single storage entity. This means that if any digital material found on the hard drive can lawfully be obtained or seized, the computer hard drive may, if appropriate, be seized or imaged. In some circumstances investigators may wish to image specific folders, files or categories of data where it is feasible to do so without seizing the hard drive or other media. Digital material may also be contained across a number of digital devices and so more than one device may be required in order to access the information sought.

A14. Digital material must not be requested or seized if an investigator has reasonable grounds for believing it is subject to legal professional privilege, other than where sections 50 or 51 of the Criminal Justice and Police Act 2001 apply. If such material is seized it must be isolated from other seized material and any other investigation material in the possession of the investigation authority.

The Police and Criminal Evidence Act 1984

★A-265d A15. The Police and Criminal Evidence Act 1984 provides the power to seize anything from a suspect in the following circumstances:
a. Where a search has been authorised pursuant to a warrant - the search must fall within the scope of the warrant issued.[29];
b. After arrest.[30];

[28] CPS Guidance on '*Reasonable lines of Enquiry and Communications Evidence*' and '*Disclosure - Guidance on Communications Evidence*', endorsed in the case of *R v E* [2018] EWCA 2426 (Crim)
[29] The Police and Criminal Evidence Act 1984 (PACE 1984), s. 8
[30] PACE 1984, s 18

c. Where evidence or anything used in the commission of an offence is on a premises and it is necessary to seize it to prevent it being concealed, lost, altered or destroyed.[31].

A16. An image of the digital material may be taken at the location of the search. Where an image is taken the original does not need to be seized. Where it is not possible to image the digital material it will need to be removed from the location for examination elsewhere. This allows the investigator to seize and sift material for the purpose of identifying material which meets the test of retention.[32]. If digital material is seized in its original form, investigators must be prepared to copy or image the material for the owners of that material when reasonably practicable.[33].

The Criminal Justice and Police Act 2001

A17. The additional powers of seizure in sections 50 and 51 of the Criminal Justice and Police Act 2001 (CJPA 2001) only extend the scope of existing powers of search and seizure under the Police and Criminal Evidence Act 1984 and other specified statutory authorities.[34] where the relevant conditions and circumstances specified in the legislation apply. **★A-265e**

A18. Investigators must be careful to only exercise powers under the CJPA 2001 when it is necessary and to not remove any more material than is justified. The removal of large volumes of material, much of which may not ultimately be retainable, may have serious consequences for the owner of the material, particularly when they are involved in business or other commercial activities.

A19. A written notice must be given to the occupier of the premises where items are seized under sections 50 and 51.[35].

A20. Until material seized under the CJPA 2001 has been examined, it must be kept securely and separately from any material seized under other powers. Any such material must be examined as soon as reasonably practicable to determine which elements may be retained and which should be returned. Consideration should be given as to whether the person from whom the property was seized, or a person with interest in the property, should be given an opportunity of being present or represented at the examination.

Retention

A21. Where material is seized under the powers conferred by PACE 1984 the duty to retain it under the Code is subject to the provisions on retention under section 22 of PACE 1984. Material seized under sections 50 and 51 of the CJPA 2001 may be retained or returned in accordance with sections 53 to 58 of the CJPA 2001. Where material is obtained through co-operation and not using powers conferred on investigators by legislation, these principles should also be observed, including retaining the material for only as long as is necessary (see paragraph 5(b) of the Code). **★A-266**

A22. Retention is limited to evidence and relevant material (as defined in the CPIA Code). Where either evidence or relevant material is inextricably linked to non-relevant material which it is not reasonably practicable to separate from the other linked material without prejudicing the use of that other material in any investigation or proceedings, that material can also be retained.

A23. However, inextricably linked material must not be examined, imaged, copied or used for any purpose other than for providing the source of or the integrity of the linked material.

A24. There are four categories of material that may be retained: **★A-266a**

a. Material that is evidence or potential evidence in the case. Where material is retained for evidential purposes there will be a strong argument that the whole thing (or an authenticated image or copy) should be retained for the purpose of proving provenance and continuity.

b. Where evidential material has been retained, inextricably linked non-relevant material which it is not reasonably practicable to separate can also be retained (PACE Code B paragraph 7).

c. An investigator should retain material that is relevant to the investigation and required to be scheduled as unused material. This is broader than but includes the duty to retain material which may satisfy the test for prosecution disclosure. The general duty to retain relevant material is set out in the CPIA Code at paragraph 5.

d. Material which is inextricably linked to relevant unused material which of itself may not be relevant material. Such material should be retained (PACE Code B paragraph 7).

---

31 PACE 1984, s. 19

32 Special provision exists for investigators conducted by Her Majesty's Revenue and Customs in the application of their powers under PACE 1984 (see s. 114(2)(b) of PACE and the CJPA)

33 The Home Office, *PACE 1984 Codes of Practice Code B* (2013), para 7.17

34 Criminal Justice and Police Act 2001 (CJPA 2001), sch 1

35 CJPA 2001, s 52

A25. The balance of any digital material should be returned in accordance with sections 53-55 of the CJPA 2001 if seized under that Act.

Legal professional privilege

★A-266b A26. No digital material may be requested or seized which an investigator has reasonable grounds for believing to be subject to legal professional privilege (LPP), other than under the additional powers of seizure in the CJPA 2001.

A27. The CJPA 2001 enables an investigator to seize relevant items which contain LPP material where it is not reasonably practicable on the search premises to separate LPP material from non-LPP material.

A28. Where LPP material or material suspected of containing LPP is seized, it must be isolated from the other material which has been seized in the investigation. Where suspected LPP material is discovered when reviewing material, and it was not anticipated that this material existed, again it must be isolated from the other material and the steps outlined below taken. The prosecution will need to decide on a case by case basis if the material is LPP material or not - defence may be able to assist with this.

A29. Where material has been identified as potentially containing LPP it must be reviewed by a lawyer independent of the prosecuting authority. No member of the investigative or prosecution team involved in either the current investigation or, if the LPP material relates to other criminal proceedings, in those proceedings should have sight of or access to the LPP material.

★A-266c A30. If the material is voluminous, search terms or other filters may have to be used to identify the LPP material. If so this will also have to be done by someone independent and not connected with the investigation.

A31. It is essential that anyone dealing with LPP material maintains proper records showing the way in which the material has been handled and those who have had access to it, as well as decisions taken in relation to that material.

A32. LPP material can only be retained in specific circumstances in accordance with section 54 of the CJPA 2001. It can only be retained where the property which comprises the LPP material has been lawfully seized and it is not reasonably practicable for the item to be separated from the rest of the property without prejudicing the use of the rest of the property. LPP material which cannot be retained must be returned as soon as practicable after the seizure without waiting for the whole examination of the seized material.

Excluded and special procedure material

★A-266d A33. Similar principles to those that apply to LPP material apply to excluded or special procedure material.[36]. [37]. By way of example, this may include material a journalist holds in confidence from a source.

Encryption

★A-266e A34. Part III of the Regulation of Investigatory Powers Act 2000 (RIPA 2000) and the Investigation of Protected Electronic Information Code of Practice govern encryption.

A35. RIPA enables specified law enforcement agencies to compel individuals or companies to provide passwords or encryption keys for the purpose of rendering protected material readable. Failure to comply with RIPA 2000 Part III orders is a criminal offence. The Code of Practice provides guidance when exercising powers under RIPA, to require disclosure of protected electronic data in an intelligible form or to acquire the means by which protected electronic data may be accessed or put in an intelligible form.

Sifting and examination

★A-267 A36. In complying with its duty of disclosure, the prosecution should follow the procedure as outlined below.

A37. Where digital material is examined, the extent and manner of inspecting, viewing or listening will depend on the nature of the material and its form.

---

[36] CJPA 2001, s 55

[37] Special provision exists for investigators conducted by Her Majesty's Revenue and Customs in the application of their powers under PACE 1984 (see s. 114(2)(b) of PACE and the CJPA)

A38. It is important for investigators and prosecutors to remember that the duty under the CPIA Code is to "pursue all reasonable lines of inquiry including those that point away from the suspect".

A39. Lines of inquiry, of whatever kind, should be pursued only if they are reasonable in the context of the individual case. It is not the duty of the prosecution to comb through all the material in its possession (e.g. every word or byte of computer material) on the lookout for anything which might conceivably or speculatively undermine the case or assist the defence. The duty of the prosecution is to disclose material which might reasonably be considered capable of undermining its case or assisting the case for the accused which they become aware of, or to which their attention is drawn.

A40. In some cases, the sift may be conducted by an investigator and/or disclosure officer manually assessing the content of the computer or other digital material from its directory and determining which files are relevant and should be retained for evidence or unused material.

A41. In other cases, such an approach may not be feasible. Where there is a large volume of material, it is perfectly proper for the investigator and/or disclosure officer to search by sample, key words, or other appropriate search tools or analytical techniques to locate relevant passages, phrases and identifiers. For the avoidance of any doubt, mobile phones are capable of storing a large volume of material. Technology that takes the form of search tools which use unambiguous calculations to perform problem-solving operations, such as algorithms or predictive coding, are an acceptable method of examining and reviewing material for disclosure purposes. **★A-267a**

A42. In cases involving very large quantities of data, the person in charge of the investigation will develop a strategy setting out how the material should be analysed or searched to identify categories of data. This strategy may include an initial scoping exercise of the material obtained to ascertain the most effective strategy for reviewing relevant material. Any such strategy should be agreed with the prosecutor and communicated to the court and defence using a DMD

A43. Where search terms are to be used, investigators and prosecutors should consider whether engagement with the defence at the pre-charge stage would assist in the identification of relevant search terms. It will usually be appropriate to provide to the accused and their legal representative with a copy of the reasonable search terms used, or to be used, and to invite them to suggest any further reasonable search terms. If search terms are suggested which the investigator or prosecutor believes will not be productive, for example where the use of common words is likely to identify a mass of irrelevant material, the investigator or prosecutor should discuss the issues with the defence in order to agree sensible refinements.

A44. The digital strategy must be set out in an IMD and subsequently a DMD. This should include the details of any sampling techniques used (including key word searches) and how the material identified as a result was examined. **★A-267b**

A45. It may be necessary to carry out sampling and searches on more than one occasion, especially as there is a duty on the prosecutor to keep duties of disclosure under review. To comply with this duty, further sampling and searches may be appropriate (and should be considered) where:

a. Further evidence or unused material is obtained in the course of the investigation; and/or
b. The defence statement is served on the prosecutor; and/or
c. The defendant makes an application under section 8 of the CPIA 1996 for disclosure; and/or
d. The defendant requests that further sampling or searches be carried out (provided it is a reasonable line of inquiry).

Record keeping

A46. A record or log must be made of all digital material seized or imaged and subsequently retained as relevant to the investigation. **★A-267c**

A47. In cases involving large quantities of data where the person in charge of the investigation has developed a strategy setting out how the material should be analysed or searched to identify categories of data, a record should be made of the strategy and the analytical techniques used to search the data, including the software used. The record should include details of the person who has carried out the process and the date and time it was carried out. In such cases the strategy should record the reasons why certain categories have been searched for (such as names, companies, dates etc.).

A48. It is important that any searching or analytical processing of digital material, as well as the data identified by that process, is properly recorded. So far as is practicable, what is required is a record of the terms of the searches or processing that has been carried out. This means that in principle the following details may be recorded: **★A-267d**

a. A record of all searches carried out, including the date of each search and the person(s) who conducted it.

b. A record of all search words or terms used on each search. However, where it is impracticable to record each word or term it will usually be sufficient to record each broad category of search.
c. A log of the key judgements made while refining the search strategy in light of what is found, or deciding not to carry out further searches.
d. Where material relating to a "hit" is not examined, the decision not to examine should be explained in the record of examination or in a statement. For instance, a large number of "hits" may be obtained in relation to a particular search word or term, but material relating to the "hits" is not examined because they do not appear to be relevant to the investigation. Any subsequent refinement of the search terms and further hits should also be noted and explained as above.

A49. Just as it is not necessary for the investigator or prosecutor to produce records of every search made of hard copy material, it is not necessary to produce records of what may be many hundreds of searches or analyses that have been carried out on digitally stored material simply to demonstrate that these have been done. Instead, the investigator and the prosecutor should ensure that they are able to explain how the disclosure exercise has been approached and to give the accused or suspect's legal representative an opportunity to participate in defining the reasonable searches to be made, as described in the section on sifting/examination.

Scheduling

★A-267e A50. The disclosure officer should ensure that scheduling of relevant material is carried out in accordance with the CPIA Code of Practice. This may require each item of unused material to be listed separately on the unused material schedule and numbered consecutively (which may include numbering by volume and sub-volume). The description of each item should make clear the nature of the item and should contain sufficient detail to enable the prosecutor to decide whether they need to inspect the material before deciding whether or not it should be disclosed.

A51. It will generally be disproportionate in cases involving large quantities of digital data to list each item of material separately. Unless it is necessary or otherwise appropriate to separately list each item, the material should be listed in a block or blocks and described by quantity and generic title. Where the material is listed in a block or blocks, the search terms used and any items of material which might satisfy the disclosure test should be listed and described separately. In practical terms this will mean, where appropriate, cross referencing the schedules to the DMD.

A52. Where material has been listed in a block and metadata is available for the material within the block, consideration should be given to creating a file of that metadata and listing this separately and linked to the block listing to which it relates.

A53. Where continuation sheets of the unused material schedule are used, or additional schedules are sent subsequently, the item numbering must be, where possible, sequential to all other items on earlier schedules. This may include numbering by volume or sub-volume.

ANNEX B –PRE-CHARGE ENGAGEMENT

The scope of pre-charge engagement

★A-268 B1. These Guidelines are intended to assist prosecutors, investigators, suspects and suspect's legal representatives who wish to enter into discussions about an investigation at any time after the first PACE interview, up until the commencement of criminal proceedings.

B2. These Guidelines are not intended to cover discussions regarding pleas to an allegation of serious or complex fraud. Nor do they apply to formal agreements relating to the provision of information or evidence about the criminal activities of others. In such cases, where appropriate, the parties should refer to the relevant guidance and follow the advised procedures:

a. In cases of serious or complex fraud, see the Attorney General's Guidelines on Plea discussions in cases of serious or complex fraud.
b. In cases where the suspect wishes to enter into a formal agreement to provide information or evidence, see sections 71-75 of the Serious Organised Crime and Police Act (SOCPA) 2005 and the CPS legal guidance on SOCPA 2005 - Queen's Evidence.

What is pre-charge engagement?

★A-268a B3. Pre-charge engagement in these guidelines refers to voluntary engagement between the parties to an investigation after the first PACE interview, and before any suspect has been formally charged. Pre-charge engagement is a voluntary process and it may be terminated at any time. It does not refer to engagement between the parties to an investigation by way of further PACE interviews, and none of the guidance in this Annex is intended to apply to such circumstances. Should a defendant choose not to engage at this stage, that decision should not be held against him at a later stage in the proceedings.

B4. Pre-charge engagement may, among other things, involve:

a. Giving the suspect the opportunity to comment on any proposed further lines of inquiry.
b. Ascertaining whether the suspect can identify any other lines of inquiry.
c. Asking whether the suspect is aware of, or can provide access to, digital material that has a bearing on the allegation.
d. Discussing ways to overcome barriers to obtaining potential evidence, such as revealing encryption keys.
e. Agreeing any key word searches of digital material that the suspect would like carried out.
f. Obtaining a suspect's consent to access medical records.
g. The suspect identifying and providing contact details of any potential witnesses.
h. Clarifying whether any expert or forensic evidence is agreed and, if not, whether the suspect's representatives intend to instruct their own expert, including timescales for this.

B5. Pre-charge engagement is encouraged by the Code for Crown Prosecutors and may impact decisions as to charge.[38].

When is pre-charge engagement appropriate?

B6. It may take place whenever it is agreed between the parties that it may assist the investigation. Where a suspect is not yet represented, an investigator should take care to ensure that the suspect understands their right to legal advice before the pre charge engagement process commences. Sufficient time should be given to enable a suspect to access this advice if they wish to do so. ★A-268b

B7. Pre-charge engagement should not, however, be considered a replacement to a further interview with a suspect. Investigators and prosecutors should be conscious that adverse inferences under section 34 of the Criminal Justice and Public Order Act 1994 are not available at trial where a suspect failed to mention a fact when asked about a matter in pre-charge engagement. An adverse inference may only be drawn where the suspect failed to mention a fact while being questioned under caution by a constable trying to discover whether or by whom the offence had been committed. Moreover, investigators and prosecutors should be aware of the advantages of holding a further formal interview, including the fact that suspects will have been appropriately cautioned and that any answers given will be recorded.

B8. Accordingly, investigators and prosecutors should not seek to initiate, or agree to, pre-charge engagement in respect of matters where they are likely to seek to rely on the contents of the suspect's answers as evidence at trial. Pre-charge engagement should not therefore be used for putting new summaries of the case to the defence, and where deemed necessary such accounts should be put to the suspect in a further interview.

B9. A no comment interview does not preclude the possibility of pre-charge engagement. When taking into account paragraph 8 above, while a no comment interview may limit the scope of any such discussions, pre-charge engagement may still be pursued where appropriate, but consideration should be given to a further PACE interview with the suspect before there is any agreement to engage in pre-charge engagement. ★A-268c

B10. There are a number of potential benefits that may arise from pre-charge engagement:

a. Suspects who maintain their innocence will be aided by early identification of lines of inquiry which may lead to evidence or material that points away from the suspect or points towards another suspect.
b. Pre-charge engagement can help inform a prosecutor's charging decision. It might avoid a case being charged that would otherwise be stopped later in proceedings, when further information becomes available.
c. The issues in dispute may be narrowed, so that unnecessary inquiries are not pursued, and if a case is charged and proceeds to trial, it can be managed more efficiently.
d. Early resolution of a case may reduce anxiety and uncertainty for suspects and complainants.
e. The cost of the matter to the criminal justice system may be reduced, including potentially avoiding or mitigating the cost of criminal proceedings.

[38] *The Code for Crown Prosecutors*, paragraph 3.4.

Who may initiate and conduct pre-charge engagement?

★A-269 B11. Depending on the circumstances, it may be appropriate for an investigator, the prosecutor, the suspect's representative or an unrepresented suspect to initiate pre-charge engagement.

B12. When referring a case to a prosecutor, the investigator should inform the prosecutor if any pre-charge engagement has already taken place and should indicate if they believe pre-charge engagement would benefit the case.

B13. The prosecutor may advise the investigator to initiate and carry out pre-charge engagement, or do so themselves.

B14. In cases in which statutory time limits on charging apply, it will usually be more practical for the investigator, rather than the prosecutor, to initiate and conduct pre-charge engagement.

B15. Prosecutors and investigators should be alert to use pre-charge engagement as a means to frustrate or delay the investigation unnecessarily. Engagement should not be initiated or continued where this is apparent. In particular, pre-charge engagement is not intended to provide an opportunity for the suspect to make unfounded allegations against the complainant, so that the complainant becomes unjustly subject to investigation. Prosecutors and investigators should be alert to prevent this happening and investigators are not obliged to follow any line of inquiry suggested by the suspect's representative: a line of inquiry should be reasonable in the circumstances of the case. What is reasonable is a matter for an investigator to decide, with the assistance of a prosecutor if required. Refer to Annex A and paragraphs 11-13 for more guidance on reasonable lines of inquiry, particularly in relation to the obtaining of a complainant's mobile or other personal devices.

Information on pre-charge engagement

★A-270 B16. The investigator should provide information on pre-charge engagement to the suspect or their representative either before or after interview.

B17. The pre-charge engagement process should be explained orally or in writing, in simple terms.

B18. The explanation may include the aim and benefits of the process, any relevant timescales and a police point of contact to make any future representations at the pre-charge stage.

Conducting pre-charge engagement

★A-271 B19. Pre-charge engagement discussions may take place face to face or via correspondence.

B20. It need not always be undertaken via a formal process, but a written record should always be made and kept. For instance, the process may be initiated immediately after interview, when the investigator and suspect's representative may agree on the further lines of inquiry that have arisen from interview.

B21. However, in some circumstances the parties will require a more formal mechanism to enable them to begin the process at any stage post-interview and before charge. This may be done by the investigator, prosecutor or suspect's representative sending a letter of invitation to the other party, which:

a. Asks whether the other party wishes to enter into pre-charge engagement in accordance with these Guidelines.
b. Explains in what way the engagement may assist the investigation. The prosecutor or investigator may wish to include the information sought, or sought to be discussed.

Disclosure during PCE

★A-272 B22. Since pre-charge engagement takes place prior to the institution of any proceedings, the statutory disclosure rules will not be engaged. However, disclosure of unused material must be considered as part of the pre-charge engagement process, to ensure that the discussions are fair and that the suspect is not misled as to the strength of the prosecution case.

B23. Accordingly, before, during and after pre-charge engagement, the investigator/prosecutor should consider whether any further material, additional to that contained in the summary of the allegation, falls to be disclosed to the suspect. The investigator/prosecutor should at all stages bear in mind the potential need to cease pre-charge engagement and to put further evidence to the suspect in a PACE interview.

B24. As the suspect provides information during the process, the investigator/prosecutor should continually be alive to the potential need to make any further disclosure.

Recording the discussions

B25. A full written, signed record of the pre-charge engagement discussions should be made. ★A-273

B26. Additionally, the prosecutor and/or investigator should record every key action involved in the process, such as the provision of written information on pre-charge engagement to the suspect, any informal discussions with the suspect's representative about entering into the process, or any formal letter of invitation sent or received.

B27. A record should be made of all information provided by the suspect's representative, such as potential lines of inquiry, suggested key word searches of digital material and any witness details.

B28. The law may require the prosecutor to disclose any information provided by the suspect's representative to another party, including a defendant in criminal proceedings. ★A-274

B29. A record should also be made of all information and material provided to the suspect's representative, including any disclosure material.

B30. The prosecutor and investigator should ensure that the records of the pre-charge engagement are provided to each other. Information or material generated by the process will need to be assessed for evidential and disclosure purposes.

ANNEX C

Annex C (which is not reproduced in this work) provides a template disclosure management document (DMDs). ★A-275

B. ACCEPTANCE OF PLEAS

Introduction

The Attorney-General issued revised guidelines on the acceptance of pleas, which came into force on 1 December 2009. The principal changes were to Part C (basis of plea). Paragraph C.1 now makes it clear that in multi-handed cases, any bases of plea must be factually consistent with each other. Paragraph C.2 now states that a defence advocate must reduce an acceptable basis of plea to writing in all cases save for those in which the defendant has indicated that the guilty plea has been or will be tendered on the basis of the prosecution case (previously this was not necessary in cases where the issue was "simple"). Paragraph C.4 now additionally provides that, where the basis of plea differs in its implications for sentencing or the making of ancillary orders from the case originally outlined by the prosecution, the prosecution advocate must ensure that such differences are accurately reflected in the written record prior to showing it to the prosecuting authority. New paragraph C.6 provides that in all cases where it is likely to assist the court where the sentencing issues are complex or unfamiliar, the prosecution must add to the written outline of the case served upon the court a summary of the key considerations, taking the form of brief notes on (a) any statutory limitations, (b) any relevant sentencing authorities or guidelines, (c) the scope for any ancillary orders, and (d) the age of the defendant and information regarding any outstanding offences. Paragraph C.7 was new and clarifies that the prosecution are able to provide further written information where they think that it is likely to assist the judge or where the judge requests it. Old paragraph C.7 became new paragraph C.8, and was amended to ensure that the procedure to be followed where the prosecution advocate takes issue with all or part of the written basis of plea is in line with the then consolidated criminal practice direction. Old paragraph C.8 is now paragraph C.11. For the relevant provisions of *Criminal Practice Direction VII (Sentencing) B*, see below, Appendix B-417b et seq. A-276

ATTORNEY-GENERAL'S GUIDELINES ON THE ACCEPTANCE OF PLEAS AND THE PROSECUTOR'S ROLE IN THE SENTENCING EXERCISE

A. Foreword

A:1. Prosecutors have an important role in protecting the victim's interests in the criminal justice process, not least in the acceptance of pleas and the sentencing exercise. The basis of plea, particularly in a case that is not contested, is the vehicle through which the victim's voice is heard. Factual inaccuracies in pleas in mitigation cause distress and offence to victims, the families of victims and witnesses. This can take many forms but may be most acutely felt when the victim is dead and the family hears inaccurate assertions about the victim's character or lifestyle. Prosecution advocates are A-277 reminded that they are required to adhere to the standards set out in the Victim's Charter, which places the needs of the victim at the heart of the criminal justice process, and that they are subject to a similar obligation in respect of the Code of Practice for Victims of Crime.

A:2. The principle of fairness is central to the administration of justice. The implementation of Human Rights Act 1998 [*sic*] in October 2000 incorporated into domestic law the principle of fairness to the accused articulated in the European Convention on Human Rights. Accuracy and reasonableness of plea plays an important part in ensuring fairness both to the accused and to the victim.

A:3. The Attorney General's Guidelines on the Acceptance of Pleas issued on December 7, 2000 highlighted the importance of transparency in the conduct of justice. The basis of plea agreed by the parties in a criminal trial is central to the sentencing process. An illogical or unsupported basis of plea can lead to an unduly lenient sentence being passed and has a consequential effect where consideration arises as to whether to refer the sentence to the Court of Appeal under section 36 of the Criminal Justice Act 1988.

A:4. These Guidelines, which replace the Guidelines issued in October 2005, give guidance on how prosecutors should meet these objectives of protection of victims' interests and of securing fairness and transparency in the process. They take into account paragraphs IV.45.4 and following of the consolidated criminal practice direction, amended May 2009, and the guidance issued by the Court of Appeal (Criminal) Division [*sic*] in *Beswick* [1996] 1 Cr. App. R. 343, *Tolera* [1999] 1 Cr. App. R. 25 and *Underwood* [2005] 1 Cr. App. R 13. They complement the Bar Council Guidance on Written Standards for the Conduct of Professional Work issued with the 7th edition of the Code of Conduct for the Bar of England and Wales and the Law Society's Professional Conduct Rules. When considering the acceptance of a guilty plea prosecution advocates are also reminded of the need to apply "The Farquharson Guidelines on The Role and Responsibilities of the Prosecution Advocate".

A:5. The Guidelines should be followed by all prosecutors and those persons designated under section 7 of the Prosecution of Offences Act 1985 (designated caseworkers) and apply to prosecutions conducted in England and Wales.

B. General Principles

A-278 B:1. Justice in this jurisdiction, save in the most exceptional circumstances, is conducted in public. This includes the acceptance of pleas by the prosecution and sentencing.

B:2. The Code for Crown Prosecutors governs the prosecutor's decision-making prior to the commencement of the trial hearing and sets out the circumstances in which pleas to a reduced number of charges, or less serious charges, can be accepted.

B:3. When a case is listed for trial and the prosecution form the view that the appropriate course is to accept a plea before the proceedings commence or continue, or to offer no evidence on the indictment or any part of it, the prosecution should whenever practicable speak to the victim or the victim's family, so that the position can be explained. The views of the victim or the family may assist in informing the prosecutor's decision as to whether it is the [*sic*] public interest, as defined by the Code for Crown Prosecutors, to accept or reject the plea. The victim or victim's family should then be kept informed and decisions explained once they are made at court.

B:4. The appropriate disposal of a criminal case after conviction is as much a part of the criminal justice process as the trial of guilt or innocence. The prosecution advocate represents the public interest, and should be ready to assist the court to reach its decision as to the appropriate sentence. This will include drawing the court's attention to:

- any victim personal statement or other information available to the prosecution advocate as to the impact of the offence on the victim;
- where appropriate, to any evidence of the impact of the offending on a community;
- any statutory provisions relevant to the offender and the offences under consideration;
- any relevant sentencing guidelines and guideline cases; and
- the aggravating and mitigating factors of the offence under consideration.

The prosecution advocate may also offer assistance to the court by making submissions, in the light of all these factors, as to the appropriate sentencing range.

In all cases, it is the prosecution advocate's duty to apply for appropriate ancillary orders, such as anti-social behaviour orders and confiscation orders. When considering which ancillary orders to apply for, prosecution advocates must always have regard to the victim's needs, including the question of his or her future protection.

C. The Basis of Plea

C:1. The basis of a guilty plea must not be agreed on a misleading or untrue set of facts and must take proper account of the victim's interests. An illogical or insupportable basis of plea will inevitably result in the imposition of an inappropriate sentence and is capable of damaging public confidence in the criminal justice system. In cases involving multiple defendants the bases of plea for each defendant must be factually consistent with each other. A-279

C:2. When the defendant indicates an acceptable plea, the defence advocate should reduce the basis of the plea to writing. This must be done in all cases save for those in which the defendant has indicated that the guilty plea has been or will be tendered on the basis of the prosecution case.

C:3. The written basis of plea must be considered with great care, taking account of the position of any other relevant defendant where appropriate. The prosecution should not lend itself to any agreement whereby a case is presented to the sentencing judge on a misleading or untrue set of facts or on a basis that is detrimental to the victim's interests. There will be cases where a defendant seeks to mitigate on the basis of assertions of fact which are outside the scope of the prosecution's knowledge. A typical example concerns the defendant's state of mind. If a defendant wishes to be sentenced on this basis, the prosecution advocate should invite the judge not to accept the defendant's version unless he or she gives evidence on oath to be tested in cross-examination. Paragraph IV.45.14 of the consolidated criminal practice direction states that in such circumstances the defence advocate should be prepared to call the defendant and, if the defendant is not willing to testify, subject to any explanation that may be given, the judge may draw such inferences as appear appropriate.

C:4. The prosecution advocate should show the prosecuting authority any written record relating to the plea and agree with them the basis on which the case will be opened to the court. If, as may well be the case, the basis of plea differs in its implications for sentencing or the making of ancillary orders from the case originally outlined by the prosecution, the prosecution advocate must ensure that such differences are accurately reflected in the written record prior to showing it to the prosecuting authority.

C:5. It is the responsibility of the prosecution advocate thereafter to ensure that the defence advocate is aware of the basis on which the plea is accepted by the prosecution and the way in which the prosecution case will be opened to the court.

C:6. In all cases where it is likely to assist the court where the sentencing issues are complex or unfamiliar the prosecution must add to the written outline of the case which is served upon the court a summary of the key considerations. This should take the form of very brief notes on:

- any relevant statutory limitations;
- the names of any relevant sentencing authorities or guidelines;
- the scope for any ancillary orders (e.g. concerning anti-social behaviour, confiscation or deportation will need to be considered.

The outline should also include the age of the defendant and information regarding any outstanding offences.

C:7. It remains open to the prosecutor to provide further written information (for example to supplement and update the analysis at later stages of the case) where he or she thought that likely to assist the court, or if the judge requests it.

C:8. When the prosecution advocate has agreed the written basis of plea submitted by the defence advocate, he or she should endorse the document accordingly. If the prosecution advocate takes issue with all or part of the written basis of plea, the procedure set out in the consolidated criminal practice direction (and in Part 37.10(5) of the Criminal Procedure Rules) should be followed. The defendant's basis of plea must be set out in writing identifying what is in dispute; the court may invite the parties to make representations about whether the dispute is material to sentence; and if the court decides that it is a material dispute, the court will invite further representations or evidence as it may require and decide the dispute in accordance with the principles set out in *Newton*, 77 Cr. App. R.13, CA. The signed original document setting out the disputed factual matters should be made available to the trial judge and thereafter lodged with the court papers, as it will form part of the record of the hearing.

C:9. Where the basis of plea cannot be agreed and the discrepancy between the two accounts is such as to have a potentially significant effect on the level of sentence, it is the duty of the defence advocate so to inform the court before the sentencing process begins. There remains an overriding duty on the prosecution advocate to ensure that the sentencing judge is made aware of the discrepancy and of the consideration which must be given to holding a *Newton* hearing to resolve the issue. The court should be told where a derogatory reference to a victim, witness or third party is not accepted, even though there may be no effect on sentence.

C:10. As emphasised in paragraph IV.45.10 of the consolidated criminal practice direction, whenever an agreement as to the basis of plea is made between the prosecution and defence, any such agreement will be subject to the approval of the trial judge, who may of his or her own motion disregard the agreement and direct that a *Newton* hearing should be held to determine the proper basis on which sentence should be passed.

C:11. Where a defendant declines to admit an offence that he or she previously indicated should be taken into consideration, the prosecution advocate should indicate to the defence advocate and the court that, subject to further review, the offence may now form the basis of a new prosecution.

D. Sentence Indications

A-280 D:1. Only in the Crown Court may sentence indications be sought. Advocates there are reminded that indications as to sentence should not be sought from the trial judge unless issues between the prosecution and defence have been addressed and resolved. Therefore, in difficult or complicated cases, no less than seven days notice in writing of an intention to seek an indication should normally be given to the prosecution and the court. When deciding whether the circumstances of a case require such notice to be given, defence advocates are reminded that prosecutors should not agree a basis of plea unless and until the necessary consultation has taken place first with the victim and/or the victim's family and second, in the case of an independent prosecution advocate, with the prosecuting authority.

D:2. If there is no final agreement about the plea to the indictment, or the basis of plea, and the defence nevertheless proceeds to seek an indication of sentence, which the judge appears minded to give, the prosecution advocate should remind him or her of the guidance given in *Goodyear (Karl)* [2005] EWCA 888 [*sic*] that normally speaking an indication of sentence should not be given until the basis of the plea has been agreed or the judge has concluded that he or she can properly deal with the case without the need for a trial of the issue.

D:3. If an indication is sought, the prosecution advocate should normally enquire whether the judge is in possession of or has access to all the evidence relied on by the prosecution, including any victim personal statement, as well as any information about relevant previous convictions recorded against the defendant.

D:4. Before the judge gives the indication, the prosecution advocate should draw the judge's attention to any minimum or mandatory statutory sentencing requirements. Where the prosecution advocate would be expected to offer the judge assistance with relevant guideline cases or the views of the Sentencing Guidelines Council, he or she should invite the judge to allow them to do so. Where it applies, the prosecution advocate should remind the judge that the position [*sic*] of the Attorney General to refer any sentencing decision as unduly lenient is unaffected. In any event, the prosecution advocate should not say anything which may create the impression that the sentence indication has the support or approval of the Crown.

E. Pleas in Mitigation

A-281 E:1. The prosecution advocate must challenge any assertion by the defence in mitigation which is derogatory to a person's character (for instance, because it suggests that his or her conduct is or has been criminal, immoral or improper) and which is either false or irrelevant to proper sentencing considerations. If the defence advocate persists in that assertion, the prosecution advocate should invite the court to consider holding a *Newton* hearing to determine the issue.

E:2. The defence advocate must not submit in mitigation anything that is derogatory to a person's character without giving advance notice in writing so as to afford the prosecution advocate the opportunity to consider their position under paragraph E:1. When the prosecution advocate is so notified they must take all reasonable steps to establish whether the assertions are true. Reasonable steps will include seeking the views of the victim. This will involve seeking the views of the victim's family if the victim is deceased, and the victim's parents or legal guardian where the victim is a child. Reasonable steps may also include seeking the views of the police or other law enforcement authority, as appropriate. An assertion which is derogatory to a person's character will rarely amount to mitigation unless it has a causal connection to the circumstances of the offence or is otherwise relevant to proper sentencing considerations.

E:3. Where notice has not been given in accordance with paragraph E:2, the prosecution advocate must not acquiesce in permitting mitigation which is derogatory to a person's character. In such circumstances, the prosecution advocate should draw the attention of the court to the failure to give advance notice and seek time, and if necessary, an adjournment to investigate the assertion in the same way as if proper notice had been given. Where, in the opinion of the prosecution advocate, there are substantial grounds for believing that such an assertion is false or irrelevant to sentence, he or she should inform the court of their opinion and invite the court to consider making an order under section 58(8) of the Criminal Procedure and Investigations Act 1996, preventing publication of the assertion.

E:4. Where the prosecution advocate considers that the assertion is, if true, relevant to sentence, or the court has so indicated, he or she should seek time, and if necessary an adjournment, to establish whether the assertion is true. If the matter cannot be resolved to the satisfaction of the parties, the prosecution advocate should invite the court to consider holding a *Newton* hearing to determine the issue.

C. JURY CHECKS

Introduction

For the background to these guidelines, see § 4-275 in the main work. They were updated in November 2012. **A-282**

Attorney-General's Guidelines: Jury checks, unreported, 27 November 2012

1. The principles which are generally to be observed are: **A-283**

(a) that members of a jury should be selected at random from the panel,
(b) the Juries Act 1974 identifies those classes of persons who alone are either disqualified from or ineligible for service on a jury; no other class of person may be treated as disqualified or ineligible,
(c) the correct way for the Crown to seek to exclude a member of the panel from sitting as a juror is by the exercise in open court of the right to request a stand by or, if necessary, to challenge for cause.

2. Parliament has provided safeguards against jurors who may be corrupt or biased. In addition to the provision for majority verdicts, there is the sanction of a criminal offence for a disqualified person to serve on a jury. The omission of a disqualified person from the panel is a matter for court officials—they will check criminal records for the purpose of ascertaining whether or not a potential juror is a disqualified person.

3. There are, however, certain exceptional types of case of public importance for which the provisions as to majority verdicts and the disqualification of jurors may not be sufficient to ensure the proper administration of justice. In such cases it is in the interests of both justice and the public that there should be further safeguards against the possibility of bias and in such cases checks which go beyond the investigation of criminal records may be necessary. **A-284**

4. These classes of case may be defined broadly as (a) cases in which national security is involved and part of the evidence is likely to be heard *in camera*, and (b) security and terrorist cases in which a juror's extreme beliefs could prevent a fair trial.

5. The particular aspects of these cases which may make it desirable to seek extra precautions are:

(a) in security cases a danger that a juror, either voluntarily or under pressure, may make an improper use of evidence which, because of its sensitivity, has been given in camera,
(b) in both security and terrorist cases the danger that a juror's personal beliefs are so biased as to go beyond normally reflecting the broad spectrum of views and interests in the community to reflect the extreme views of sectarian interest or pressure group to a degree which might interfere with his fair assessment of the facts of the case or lead him to exert improper pressure on his fellow jurors.

6. In order to ascertain whether in exceptional circumstances of the above nature either of these factors might seriously influence a potential juror's impartial performance of his duties or his respecting the secrecy of evidence given *in camera*, it may be necessary to conduct a limited investigation of the panel. In general, such further investigation beyond one of criminal records made for disqualifications may only be made with the records of the police. However, a check may, additionally, be made against the records of the Security Service. No checks other than on these sources and no general inquiries are to be made save to the limited extent that they may be needed to confirm the identity of a juror about whom the initial check has raised serious doubts. **A-285**

7. No further investigation, as described in paragraph 6 above, should be made save with the personal authority of the Attorney-General on the application of the Director of Public Prosecutions and such checks are hereafter referred to as "authorised checks". When a chief officer of police or the prosecutor has reason to believe that it is likely that an authorised check may be desirable and proper in accordance with these guidelines, he should refer the matter to the Director of Public Prosecutions. In those cases in which the Director of Public Prosecutions believes authorised checks are both proportionate and necessary, the Director will make an application to the Attorney-General.

8. The Director of Public Prosecutions will provide the Attorney-General with all relevant information in support of the requested authorised checks. The Attorney-General will consider personally the request and, if appropriate, authorise the check.

9. The result of any authorised check will be sent to the Director of Public Prosecutions. The Director will then decide, having regard to the matters set out in paragraph 5 above, what information ought to be brought to the attention of prosecuting counsel. The Director will also provide the Attorney-General with the result of the authorised check.

A-286 **10.** Although the right of stand by and the decision to authorise checks are wholly within the discretion of the Attorney-General, when the Attorney-General has agreed to an authorised check being conducted, the Director of Public Prosecutions will write to the presiding judge for the area to advise him that this is being done.

11. No right of stand by should be exercised by counsel for the Crown on the basis of information obtained as a result of an authorised check save with the personal authority of the Attorney-General and unless the information is such as, having regard to the facts of the case and the offences charged, to afford strong reason for believing that a particular juror might be a security risk, be susceptible to improper approaches or be influenced in arriving at a verdict for the reasons given above.

12. Information revealed in the course of an authorised check must be considered in line with the normal rules on disclosure.

13. A record is to be kept by the Director of Public Prosecutions of the use made by counsel of the information passed to him and of the jurors stood by or challenged by the parties to the proceedings. A copy of this record is to be forwarded to the Attorney-General for the sole purpose of enabling him to monitor the operation of these guidelines.

A-287 **14.** No use of the information obtained as a result of an authorised check is to be made except as may be necessary in direct relation to or arising out of the trial for which the check was authorised. The information may, however, be used for the prevention of crime or as evidence in a future criminal prosecution, save that material obtained from the Security Service may only be used in those circumstances with the authority of the Security Service.

D. PROSECUTION'S RIGHT OF STAND BY

A-288 For the background to these guidelines, see §§ 4-304, 4-305 in the main work. They were updated in November 2012.

Attorney-General's Guidelines on the Exercise by the Crown of its Right of Stand By, unreported, 27 November 2012

A-289 **1.** Although the law has long recognised the right of the Crown to exclude a member of a jury panel from sitting as a juror by the exercise in open court of the right to request a stand by or, if necessary, by challenge for cause, it has been customary for those instructed to prosecute on behalf of the Crown to assert that right only sparingly and in exceptional circumstances. It is generally accepted that the prosecution should not use its right in order to influence the overall composition of a jury or with a view to tactical advantage.

2. The approach outlined above is founded on the principles that:

(a) the members of a jury should be selected at random from the panel subject to any rule of law as to right of challenge by the defence, and

(b) the Juries Act 1974 identifies those classes of persons who alone are disqualified from or ineligible for service on a jury. No other class of person may be treated as disqualified or ineligible.

3. The enactment by Parliament of section 118 of the Criminal Justice Act 1988 abolishing the right of defendants to remove jurors by means of peremptory challenge makes it appropriate that the Crown should assert its right to stand by only on the basis of clearly defined and restrictive criteria. Derogation from the principle that members of a jury should be selected at random should be permitted only where it is essential.

4. Primary responsibility for ensuring that an individual does not serve on a jury if he is not competent to discharge properly the duties of a juror rests with the appropriate court officer and, ultimately the trial judge. Current legislation provides, in sections 9 to 10 of the Juries Act 1974, fairly wide discretion to excuse, defer or discharge jurors.

5. The circumstances in which it would be proper for the Crown to exercise its right to stand by a member of a jury panel are:

(a) where a jury check authorised in accordance with the Attorney-General's guidelines on jury checks reveals information justifying exercise of the right to stand by in accordance with paragraph 11 of the guidelines ... and the Attorney-General personally authorises the exercise of the right to stand by; or

(b) where a person is about to be sworn as a juror who is manifestly unsuitable and the defence agree that, accordingly, the exercise by the prosecution of the right to stand by would be appropriate. An example of the sort of exceptional circumstances which might justify stand by is where it becomes apparent that, despite the provisions mentioned in paragraph 4 above, a juror selected for service to try a complex case is in fact illiterate.

E. CONSPIRACY TO DEFRAUD

The Attorney-General has issued guidance to prosecuting authorities in relation to charging a common law conspiracy to defraud instead of a substantive offence, contrary to the Fraud Act 2006, or a statutory conspiracy to commit a substantive offence, contrary to section 1 of the CLA 1977 (§ 33-2 in the main work); the prosecutor should consider (i) whether the conduct alleged falls within the ambit of a statutory offence, and (ii) whether such a charge or charges would adequately reflect the gravity of the alleged offending; as to (i), non-exhaustive examples of circumstances falling outside of the range of statutory offences, but within the ambit of the common law offence, are: (a) the dishonest obtaining of land or other property which cannot be stolen; (b) the dishonest infringement of another's right (e.g. the dishonest exploitation of another's patent); (c) an agreement involving an intention that the final offence be committed by someone outside the conspiracy; and (d) an agreement where the conspirators cannot be proved to have had the necessary degree of knowledge for the substantive offence to be perpetrated; as to (ii), prosecution for the common law offence may be more effective where the interests of justice can only be served by presenting an overall picture which could not be achieved by charging a series of substantive offences or statutory conspiracies (because of a large number of counts and/or the possibility of severed trials and evidence on one count being deemed inadmissible on another); where a case lawyer proposes to charge the common law offence, he must consider, and set out in the review note, how much such a charge would add to the amount of evidence likely to be called by the parties, the justification for using the charge, and why specific statutory offences are inadequate or otherwise inappropriate; a supervising lawyer experienced in fraud cases must also specifically approve the charge: *Attorney-General's guidance on the use of the common law offence of conspiracy to defraud*, unreported, 9 January 2007. **A-290**

F. PROSECUTOR'S ROLE IN APPLICATIONS FOR WITNESS ANONYMITY ORDERS

On 21 July 2008, the Attorney-General issued guidelines on the overarching principles which a prosecutor must consider when deciding whether to apply for witness anonymity orders under the Criminal Evidence (Witness Anonymity) Act 2008 (now the Coroners and Justice Act 2009, ss.86–97 (§§ 8-151 et seq. in the main work)). **A-291**

The guidance is in four parts (Part A (foreword), Part B (prosecutor's duties), Part C (applications by defendants) and Part D (appointment and role of special counsel)), and, to a large extent, highlights various provisions of the Act and restates elementary aspects of fairness at trial. Paragraph A2 makes clear that, given that the defendant's right to confront and challenge those who accuse him is an important aspect of a fair trial, making a witness anonymity order is a serious step which must only be taken where there are genuine grounds to believe that the conditions set out in the Act have been satisfied, which must be evaluated with care on the facts of each case. Paragraph B3 sets out the prosecutor's role, which prosecutors must approach in light of their overriding duties to be fair, independent and objective, and which includes a duty: (a) to examine with care and probe where appropriate, the material provided in support of the application and the evidential basis for it, and (b) to put before the court and to disclose to the defendant all material relevant to the application and the defence, including material which may undermine or qualify the prosecution case. Any such material is particularly relevant if credibility is in issue, for example, if there is a known link between the witness and defendant or a co-accused. Paragraph B4 explains that applications should only be authorised by prosecutors of an appropriately senior level. Paragraph D5 explains that a prosecutor making an application for an order must always be prepared to assist the court to consider whether the circumstances are such that exceptionally the appointment of special counsel may be called for, and, where appropriate, should draw to the attention of the court any aspect of the application which may be relevant to such appointment. Where the court decides to invite the Attorney-General to appoint special counsel, the prosecutor should (regardless of any steps taken by the court or any defendant) ensure that the Attorney-General's office is promptly notified and receives all information needed to take a decision as to whether to make such appointment. If special counsel is appointed, the prosecutor should then provide special counsel with open material made available to the accused regarding the application, and any other open material requested by special counsel. Closed or unredacted material which has been provided to the court should only be given to special counsel after open material has been provided and after special counsel has subsequently sought instructions from the defendant and his legal representative.

G. PLEA DISCUSSIONS IN CASES OF SERIOUS OR COMPLEX FRAUD

(1) Guidelines

A-292 On 18 March 2009, the Attorney-General issued guidelines setting out the process by which a prosecutor may discuss allegations of serious or complex fraud with a person whom he is prosecuting or expecting to prosecute.

ATTORNEY GENERAL'S GUIDELINES ON PLEA DISCUSSIONS IN CASES OF SERIOUS OR COMPLEX FRAUD

A. Foreword

A-293 A:1 These guidelines set out a process by which a prosecutor may discuss an allegation of serious or complex fraud with a person who he or she is prosecuting or expects to prosecute, or with that person's legal representative. They come into force on the 5th day of May 2009 and apply to plea discussions initiated on or after that date.

A:2 The guidelines will be followed by all prosecutors in England and Wales when conducting plea discussions in cases of serious or complex fraud. For the purposes of the guidelines, fraud means any financial, fiscal or commercial misconduct or corruption which is contrary to the criminal law. Fraud may be serious or complex if at least two of the following factors are present:

- the amount obtained or intended to be obtained is alleged to exceed £500,000;
- there is a significant international dimension;
- the case requires specialised knowledge of financial, commercial, fiscal or regulatory matters such as the operation of markets, banking systems, trusts or tax regimes;
- the case involves allegations of fraudulent activity against numerous victims;
- the case involves an allegation of substantial and significant fraud on a public body;
- the case is likely to be of widespread public concern;
- the alleged misconduct endangered the economic well-being of the United Kingdom, for example by undermining confidence in financial markets.

Taking account of these matters, it is for the prosecutor to decide whether or not a case is one of fraud, and whether or not it is serious or complex.

A:3 The decision whether a person should be charged with a criminal offence rests with the prosecutor. In selecting the appropriate charge or charges, the prosecutor applies principles set out in the Code for Crown Prosecutors ("the code"). Charges should reflect the seriousness and extent of the offending, give the court adequate sentencing powers and enable the case to be presented in a clear and simple way. The code also states that prosecutors should not go ahead with more charges to encourage a defendant to plead guilty to a few; equally, prosecutors should not charge a more serious offence to encourage a defendant to plead to a less serious one.

A:4 Once proceedings are instituted, the accused may plead guilty to all of the charges selected. If the defendant will plead guilty to some, but not all, of the charges or to a different, possibly less serious charge, the code states that a prosecutor is entitled to accept such pleas if he or she assesses that the court could still pass an adequate sentence. In taking these decisions the prosecutor also applies the Attorney General's Guidelines on the Acceptance of Pleas and the Prosecutor's Role in the Sentencing Exercise ("the acceptance of pleas guidelines") [A-259 et seq.].

A:5 The purpose of plea discussions is to narrow the issues in the case with a view to reaching a just outcome at the earliest possible time, including the possibility of reaching an agreement about acceptable pleas of guilty and preparing a joint submission as to sentence.

A:6 The potential benefits of plea discussions are that:

- early resolution of the case may reduce the anxiety and uncertainty for victims and witnesses, and provide earlier clarity for accused persons who admit their guilt (subject to the court's power to reject the agreement);
- the issues in dispute may be narrowed so that even if the case proceeds to trial, it can be managed more efficiently in accordance with rule 3.2 of the Criminal Procedure Rules 2005. If pleas are agreed, litigation can be kept to a minimum.

A:7 Where plea discussions take place prior to the commencement of proceedings, the charges brought by the prosecutor will reflect those agreed, rather than those that the prosecutor would necessarily have preferred if no agreement had been reached. Also, any criminal investigation may not be complete when these discussions take place. For these reasons it is important that the procedures followed should command public and judicial confidence; that any agreement reached is reasonable, fair and just; that there are safeguards to ensure that defendants are not under improper pressure to make admissions; and that there are proper records of discussions that have taken place.

A:8 The guidelines are not intended to prevent or discourage existing practices by which prosecutors and prosecuting advocates discuss cases with defence legal representatives after charge, in order to narrow the issues or to agree a basis of plea. Neither do they affect the existing practice of judicial sentence indications at the plea and case management hearing or later in accordance with the guidance in *Goodyear* [2005] 2 Cr. App. R. 20 (see also the acceptance of pleas guidelines). They complement, and do not detract from or replace, the code and the acceptance of pleas guidelines, or any other relevant guidance such as the Prosecutor's Pledge, the Victim's Charter and the Code of Practice for Victims of Crime.

A:9 Where a plea agreement is reached, it remains entirely a matter for the court to decide how to deal with the case.

B. General Principles

B:1 In conducting plea discussions and presenting a plea agreement to the court, the prosecutor must act openly, fairly and in the interests of justice. **A-294**

B:2 Acting in the interests of justice means ensuring that the plea agreement reflects the seriousness and extent of the offending, gives the court adequate sentencing powers, and enables the court, the public and the victims to have confidence in the outcome. The prosecutor must consider carefully the impact of a proposed plea or basis of plea on the community and the victim, and on the prospects of successfully prosecuting any other person implicated in the offending. The prosecutor must not agree to a reduced basis of plea which is misleading, untrue or illogical.

B:3 Acting fairly means respecting the rights of the defendant and of any other person who is being or may be prosecuted in relation to the offending. The prosecutor must not put improper pressure on a defendant in the course of plea discussions, for example by exaggerating the strength of the case in order to persuade the defendant to plead guilty, or to plead guilty on a particular basis.

B:4 Acting openly means being transparent with the defendant, the victim and the court. The prosecutor must:

- ensure that a full and accurate record of the plea discussions is prepared and retained;
- ensure that the defendant has sufficient information to enable him or her to play an informed part in the plea discussions;
- communicate with the victim before accepting a reduced basis of plea, wherever it is practicable to do so, so that the position can be explained; and
- ensure that the plea agreement placed before the court fully and fairly reflects the matters agreed. The prosecutor must not agree additional matters with the defendant which are not recorded in the plea agreement and made known to the court.

C. Initiating Plea Discussions

When and with whom discussions should be initiated and conducted

C:1 Where he or she believes it advantageous to do so, the prosecutor may initiate plea discussions with any person who is being prosecuted or investigated with a view to prosecution in connection with a serious or complex fraud, and who is legally represented. The prosecutor will not initiate plea discussions with a defendant who is not legally represented. If the prosecutor receives an approach from such a defendant, he or she may enter into discussions if satisfied that it is appropriate to do so. **A-295**

C:2 Where proceedings have not yet been instituted, the prosecutor should not initiate plea discussions until he or she and the investigating officer are satisfied that the suspect's criminality is known. This will not usually be the case until after the suspect has been interviewed under caution.

C:3 The prosecutor should be alert to any attempt by the defendant to use plea discussions as a means of delaying the investigation or prosecution, and should not initiate or continue discussions where the defendant's commitment to the process is in doubt. The prosecutor should ensure that the position is preserved during plea discussions by, for example, restraining assets in anticipation of the making of a confiscation order. Where a defendant declines to take part in plea discussions, the prosecutor should not make a second approach unless there is a material change in circumstances.

Invitation letter

C:4 In order to initiate the plea discussions, the prosecutor will send the defendant's representatives a letter which:

- asks whether the defence wish to enter into discussions in accordance with these guidelines; and
- sets a deadline for a response from the defence.

Terms and conditions letter

C:5 Where the defence agree to engage in plea discussions, the prosecutor should send them a letter setting out the way in which the discussions will be conducted. This letter should deal with:

- the confidentiality of information provided by the prosecutor and defendant in the course of the plea discussions;
- the use which may be made by the prosecutor of information provided by the defendant; and
- the practical means by which the discussions will be conducted.

Confidentiality and use of information

C:6 In relation to confidentiality, the prosecutor will indicate that he or she intends to provide an undertaking to the effect that the fact that the defendant has taken part in the plea discussions, and any information provided by the defence in the course of the plea discussions will be treated as confidential and will not be disclosed to any other party other than for the purposes of the plea discussions and plea agreement (applying these guidelines), or as required by law. The undertaking will make it clear that the law in relation to the disclosure of unused material may require the prosecutor to provide information about the plea discussions to another defendant in criminal proceedings.

C:7 The prosecutor will require the defendant's legal representative to provide an undertaking to the effect that information provided by the prosecutor in the course of the plea discussions will be treated as confidential and will not be disclosed to any other party, other than for the purposes of the plea discussion and plea agreement or as required by law.

C:8 In relation to the use of information, the prosecutor will indicate that he or she intends to undertake not to rely upon the fact that the defendant has taken part in the plea discussions, or any information provided by the defendant in the course of the discussions, as evidence in any prosecution of that defendant for the offences under investigation, should the discussions fail. However, this undertaking will make it clear that the prosecutor is not prevented from:

- relying upon a concluded and signed plea agreement as confession evidence or as admissions;
- relying upon any evidence obtained from enquiries made as a result of the provision of information by the defendant;
- relying upon information provided by the defendant as evidence against him or her in any prosecution for an offence other than the fraud which is the subject of the plea discussion and any offence which is consequent upon it, such as money laundering; and
- relying upon information provided by the defendant in a prosecution of any other person for any offence (so far as the rules of evidence allow).

C:9 In exceptional circumstances the prosecutor may agree to different terms regarding the confidentiality and use of information. However, the prosecutor must not surrender the ability to rely upon a concluded and signed plea agreement as evidence against the defendant. The prosecutor may reserve the right to bring other charges (additional to those to which the defendant has indicated a willingness to plead guilty) in specific circumstances, for example if substantial new information comes to light at a later stage, the plea agreement is rejected by the court, or the defendant fails to honour the agreement.

C:10 Until the issues of confidentiality and use of information have been agreed to the satisfaction of both parties, and the agreement reflected in signed undertakings, the prosecutor must not continue with the substantive plea discussions.

D. Conducting Plea Discussions

Statement of case

D:1 Where plea discussions take place prior to proceedings being instituted, the prosecutor will provide a statement of case to the defence. This is a written summary of the nature of the allegation against the suspect and the evidence which has been obtained, or is expected to be obtained, to support it. The statement of case should include a list of the proposed charges. Material in support of the statement of case may also be provided, whether or not in the form of admissible evidence. However, the prosecutor is not obliged to reveal to the suspect all of the information or evidence supporting his case, provided that this does not mislead the suspect to his or her prejudice. **A-296**

D:2 Where plea discussions are initiated after proceedings have been commenced, but before the prosecutor has provided the defence with a case summary or opening note, the prosecutor may provide a statement of case to assist the defendant in understanding the evidence and identifying the issues.

Unused material

D:3 These guidelines do not affect the prosecutor's existing duties in relation to the disclosure of unused material. Where plea discussions take place prior to the institution of proceedings, the prosecutor should ensure that the suspect is not misled as to the strength of the prosecution case. It will not usually be necessary to provide copies of unused material in order to do this.

Conducting and recording the discussions

D:4 Having provided the defence with the statement of case and supporting material, the parties will then be in a position to conduct the plea discussion proper. Whether this is done by correspondence, by face-to-face meetings or by a combination of the two is a matter for the parties to decide in the individual case.

D:5 It is essential that a full written record is kept of every key action and event in the discussion process, including details of every offer or concession made by each party, and the reasons for every decision taken by the prosecutor. Meetings between the parties should be minuted and the minutes agreed and signed. Particular care should be taken where the defendant is not legally represented. The prosecutor should only meet with a defendant who is not legally represented if the defendant agrees to the meeting being recorded, or to the presence of an independent third party.

Queen's evidence

D:6 If the defendant offers at any stage to provide information, or to give evidence about the criminal activities of others, any such offer will be dealt with in accordance with sections 71 to 75 of the Serious Organised Crime and Police Act 2005 ("SOCPA"), the judgment of the Court of Appeal in *P.*; *Blackburn* [2008] 2 Cr. App. R.(S.) 5 and the guidance agreed and issued by the Director of Public Prosecutions, the Director of the Serious Fraud Office and the Director of Revenue and Customs Prosecutions.

Discussion of pleas

D:7 In deciding whether or not to accept an offer by the defendant to plead guilty, the prosecutor will follow sections 7 and 10 of the code relating to the selection of charges and the acceptance of guilty pleas. The prosecutor should ensure that:

- the charges reflect the seriousness and extent of the offending;
- they give the court adequate powers to sentence and impose appropriate post-conviction orders;
- they enable the case to be presented in a clear and simple way (bearing in mind that many cases of fraud are necessarily complex);
- the basis of plea enables the court to pass a sentence that matches the seriousness of the offending, particularly if there are aggravating features;
- the interests of the victim, and where possible any views expressed by the victim, are taken into account when deciding whether it is in the public interest to accept the plea; and
- the investigating officer is fully appraised of developments in the plea discussions and his or her views are taken into account.

D:8 In reaching an agreement on pleas, the parties should resolve any factual issues necessary to allow the court to sentence the defendant on a clear, fair and accurate basis. Before agreeing to proposed pleas, the prosecutor should satisfy him or herself that the full code test as set out in the code will be made out in respect of each charge. In considering whether the evidential stage of the test will be met, the prosecutor should assume that the offender will sign a plea agreement amounting to an admission to the charge.

Discussion of sentence

D:9 Where agreement is reached as to pleas, the parties should discuss the appropriate sentence with a view to presenting a joint written submission to the court. This document should list the aggravating and mitigating features arising from the agreed facts, set out any personal mitigation available to the defendant, and refer to any relevant sentencing guidelines or authorities. In the light of all of these factors, it should make submissions as to the applicable sentencing range in the relevant guideline. The prosecutor must ensure that the submissions are realistic, taking full account of all relevant material and considerations.

D:10 The prosecutor should bear in mind all of the powers of the court, and seek to include in the joint submission any relevant ancillary orders. It is particularly desirable that measures should be included that achieve redress for victims (such as compensation orders) and protection for the public (such as directors' disqualification orders, serious crime prevention orders or financial reporting orders).

D:11 Due regard should be had to the court's asset recovery powers and the desirability of using these powers both as a deterrent to others and as a means of preventing the defendant from benefiting from the proceeds of crime or funding future offending. The Proceeds of Crime Act 2002 requires the Crown Court to proceed to the making of a confiscation order against a convicted defendant who has benefited from his criminal conduct where the prosecutor asks the court to do so, or the court believes that it is appropriate to do so. Fraud is an acquisitive crime, and the expectation in a fraud case should be that a confiscation order will be sought by the prosecutor reflecting the full benefit to the defendant. However, in doing so it is open to the prosecutor to take a realistic view of the likely approach of the court to the determination of any points in dispute (such as the interest of a third party in any property).

D:12 In the course of the plea discussions the prosecutor must make it clear to the defence that the joint submission as to sentence (including confiscation) is not binding on the court.

Liaison with another prosecutor or regulator

D:13 The prosecutor may become aware that another prosecuting authority or regulatory body (either in England and Wales or elsewhere) has an interest in the defendant. The prosecutor should liaise with the other agency, in accordance with the Prosecutors' Convention and any other relevant agreement or guidance. The other agency may wish to take part in the plea discussions, or they may authorise the prosecutor to discuss with the defendant the matters which they are interested in, with a view to resolving all matters in one plea agreement. The prosecutor should warn the defendant that a plea agreement will not bind any other agency which is not a party to it.

E. The Written Plea Agreement

A-297 E:1 All matters agreed between the prosecutor and the defence must be reduced to writing as a plea agreement and signed by both parties. The plea agreement will include:

- a list of the charges;
- a statement of the facts; and
- a declaration, signed by the defendant personally, to the effect that he or she accepts the stated facts and admits he or she is guilty of the agreed charges.

E:2 Any agreement under the SOCPA regarding the giving of assistance to the prosecutor by the defendant should be in a separate document accompanying the plea agreement.

E:3 Once a plea agreement is signed in a case where proceedings have not yet been commenced, the prosecutor will review the case in accordance with the code and, assuming the evidential stage of the full code test is satisfied on the basis of the signed plea agreement and the other available evidence, will arrange for proceedings to be instituted by summons or charge.

E:4 In advance of the defendant's first appearance in the Crown Court, the prosecutor should send the court sufficient material to allow the judge to understand the facts of the case and the history of the plea discussions, to assess whether the plea agreement is fair and in the interests of justice, and to decide the appropriate sentence. This will include:

- the signed plea agreement;
- a joint submission as to sentence and sentencing considerations;

- any relevant sentencing guidelines or authorities;
- all of the material provided by the prosecution to the defendant in the course of the plea discussions;
- any material provided by the defendant to the prosecution, such as documents relating to personal mitigation; and
- the minutes of any meetings between the parties and any correspondence generated in the plea discussions.

E:5 It will then be for the court to decide how to deal with the plea agreement. In particular, the court retains an absolute discretion as to whether or not it sentences in accordance with the joint submission from the parties.

F. Failure of Plea Discussions

F:1 There are several circumstances in which plea discussions may result in an outcome other than the defendant pleading guilty in accordance with a plea agreement. The prosecutor or the defendant may break off the discussions. They may be unable to reach an agreement. They may reach an agreement, but intervening events may lead the prosecutor to decide that proceedings should not be instituted. Proceedings may be instituted but the court may reject the plea agreement. The defendant may decline to plead guilty in accordance with the plea agreement, either as a result of a sentence indication given under the procedure set out in *Goodyear*, or for some other reason. **A-298**

F:2 If any of these situations arises, the prosecutor may wish for further enquiries to be made with a view to bringing or completing proceedings against the defendant. If proceedings have already been instituted, the prosecutor will use the appropriate means to delay them - either discontinuing under section 23 or 23A of the Prosecution of Offences Act 1985 or (if the indictment has already been preferred) applying for an adjournment or stay of the proceedings. The prosecutor and the defendant's representatives will continue to be bound by the preliminary undertakings made in relation to the confidentiality and use of information provided in the course of the plea discussions.

F:3 Where plea discussions have broken down for any reason, it will be rare that the prosecutor will wish to re-open them, but he or she may do so if there is a material change in circumstances which warrants it.

(2) Practice

See the *Criminal Practice Directions VII (Sentencing) B*, below, Appendix B-417b et seq. **A-299**

(3) Authorities

As to the limitations on prosecuting authorities' power to enter into agreements (with overseas authorities or a potential accused) as to how a case should be disposed of, see *Innospec Ltd*, § 1-467 in the main work. As to this case, see also § 5B-21 in the main work. **A-300**

In *Dougall* [2011] 1 Cr. App. R.(S.) 37, CA, it was said that a joint submission as to sentence pursuant to the Attorney-General's Guidelines on Plea Discussions in Cases of Serious or Complex Fraud, above, should recognise that it is the court alone that decides on sentence, should avoid advocacy of a particular outcome, and should confine itself to the appropriate range within which it is said the sentence should fall. As to this case, see also § 5A-102 in the main work.

H. ASSET RECOVERY POWERS OF PROSECUTING AUTHORITIES

The Attorney-General and the Home Secretary have issued joint guidance under section 2A of the POCA 2002 to the National Crime Agency, the DPP, the Director of Revenue and Customs Prosecutions, the Director of the Serious Fraud Office and the DPP for Northern Ireland directing them to consider using their civil asset recovery powers under the 2002 Act wherever proceeds of crime have been identified but it is not feasible to secure a conviction, or a conviction has been secured but no confiscation order made (para. 2). They must also consider whether the public interest might be better served by using these powers, rather than by instituting a criminal investigation or prosecution, whilst applying the principle that a criminal disposal will generally make the best contribution to the reduction of crime (para. 3). Paragraph 4 states that the factors listed in the Code for Crown Prosecutors (Appendix E-6) as being relevant to the question whether a prosecution would be in the public interest might also be relevant when considering at **A-301** any stage whether or not the civil recovery powers should be used; but it is emphasised that a potential defendant should not be able to escape an appropriate prosecution by the simple device of agreeing to a civil recovery order. Paragraph 5 contains a non-exhaustive list of circumstances in which use of the powers might be appropriate because it is not feasible to secure a conviction and paragraph 6 contains an equivalent list for where a conviction is feasible but where the public interest might be better served by use of these powers. Paragraph 8 sets out the ways in which the relevant authorities should seek to minimise any potential prejudice to a related or potential criminal investigation or proceedings, including through the disclosure of relevant information. Paragraph 9 confirms that the guidance does not prohibit (i) a criminal investigation being carried out by a law enforcement authority at the same time as a civil recovery and/or a tax investigation; (ii) civil recovery and/or tax proceedings being instituted where a criminal investigation by a law enforcement authority is being carried out at the same time into unrelated criminality (subjectto the duty set out in para. 8, above); or (iii) criminal proceedings being instituted or carried on by a prosecuting authority at the same time as a civil recovery and/or tax investigation is being carried out. However, paragraph 10 prohibits in all circumstances criminal and civil/tax proceedings being carried on at the same time in relation to the same criminality. Where criminal proceedings have been stayed by a court, or cannot progress (e.g. because the defendant has absconded), they are not being "carried on" for the purposes of this prohibition. Paragraph 11 sets out the circumstances in which a relevant authority may agree to accept a reduced sum in satisfaction of a civil recovery claim. For the full text of the guidance, see *http://www.attorneygeneral.gov.uk/Publications/Pages/AttorneyGeneralsGuidelines.aspx.*

APPENDIX B
Criminal Procedure Rules and Criminal Practice Directions

Criminal Procedure Rules 2020; Criminal Practice Directions (2015) (as amended) and Criminal Costs Practice Directions (2015)

(Appendix B and main work paragraph numbers are set out below. Main work paragraphs are shown in brackets.)

CRIMINAL PROCEDURE RULE	*PARAGRAPH NUMBERS*
Part 1 (The overriding objective)	
rr.1.1–1.3	B-1 (4-114)
Part 2 (Understanding and applying the rules and powers of authorised court officers)	
r.2.1	B-4 (2-159)
r.2.2	B-5 (2-160)
r.2.3	B-6 (2-161)
r.2.4	B-7
r.2.5	B-8
r.2.6	B-9
r.2.7	B-10
r.2.8	B-11
r.2.9	B-12
r.2.10	B-13
Part 3 (Case management)	
rr.3.1–3.4	B-14 (4-115)
rr.3.5–3.8	B-15 (4-116, 4-117)
rr.3.9–3.10	B-16 (4-117)
r.3.11	B-17 (12-47b)
r.3.12	B-18 (4-117)
r.3.13	B-19 (4-118)
rr.3.14-3.15	B-20 (4-119)
rr.3.16–3.18	B-21
r.3.19	B-22
r.3.20	B-23
rr.3.21-3.22	B-24 (4-120c, 4-139)
r.3.23	B-25 (4-139)
r.3.24	B-26 (4-140)
r.3.25	B-27 (4-140)
r.3.26	B-28 (4-140)
r.3.27	B-29 (4-120d)
r.3.28	B-30 (4-101a)
r.3.29	B-31 (4-120f)
r.3.30	B-32 (4-120f)
r.3.31	B-33 (4-120g)
r.3.32	B-34 (4-121)
r.3.33	B-35 (4-122)
r.3.34	B-36 (4-64)
Part 4 (Service of documents)	
r.4.1	B-101 (2-162)
r.4.2	B-102 (2-163)
r.4.3	B-103 (2-164)
r.4.4	B-104 (2-165)

CRIMINAL PROCEDURE RULE	*PARAGRAPH NUMBERS*
r.4.5	B-105 (2-166)
r.4.6	B-106 (2-167)
r.4.7	B-107 (2-168)
r.4.8	B-108 (2-169)
r.4.9	B-109 (2-170)
r.4.10	B-110 (2-171)
r.4.11	B-111 (2-172)
r.4.12	B-112 (2-173)
r.4.13	B-113 (2-174)
Part 5 (Forms and court records)	
r.5.1	B-114 (2-176)
r.5.2	B-115 (2-178)
r.5.3	B-116 (2-179)
r.5.4	B-117 (2-180)
r.5.5	B-118 (2-181)
r.5.6	B-119 (2-182)
r.5.7	B-120 (2-183)
r.5.8	B-121 (2-184)
r.5.9	B-122 (2-186)
Part 6 (Reporting, etc., restrictions)	
rr.6.1-6.3	B-137 (4-47)
rr.6.4-6.8	B-138 (4-48)
r.6.9	B-139 (4-49)
r.6.10	B-140 (28-76)
Part 7 (Starting a prosecution in a magistrates' court)	
r.7.1	B-155
r.7.2	B-156
r.7.3	B-157
r.7.4	B-158
Part 8 (Initial details of the prosecution case)	
r.8.1	B-161 (12-142)
r.8.2	B-162 (12-143)
r.8.3	B-163 (12-144)
r.8.4	B-164 (12-144)
Part 9 (Allocation and sending for trial)	
r.9.1	B-167
r.9.2	B-168
r.9.3	B-169
r.9.4	B-170
r.9.5	B-171
r.9.6	B-172
r.9.7	B-173
r.9.8	B-174
r.9.9	B-175
r.9.10	B-176
r.9.11	B-177

CRIMINAL PROCEDURE RULE	*PARAGRAPH NUMBERS*
r.9.12	B-178
r.9.13	B-179
r.9.14	B-180
Part 10 (The indictment)	
r.10.1	B-182
r.10.2	B-183
r.10.3	B-184
r.10.4	B-185
r.10.5	B-186
r.10.6	B-187
r.10.7	B-188
r.10.8	B-189
r.10.9	B-190
Part 11 (Deferred prosecution agreements)	
r.11.1	B-200 (1-383)
r.11.2	B-201 (1-384)
r.11.3	B-202 (1-385)
r.11.4	B-203 (1-386)
r.11.5	B-204 (1-387)
r.11.6	B-205 (1-388)
r.11.7	B-206 (1-389)
r.11.8	B-207 (1-390)
r.11.9	B-208 (1-391)
rr.11.10, 11.11	B-209 (1-392, 1-393)
Part 12 (Discontinuing a prosecution)	
rr.12.1–12.3	B-210
Part 13 (Warrants for arrest, detention or imprisonment)	
r.13.1	B-211
r.13.2	B-212
r.13.3	B-213
r.13.4	B-214
r.13.5	B-215
r.13.6	B-216
r.13.7	B-217
Part 14 (Bail and custody time limits)	
r.14.1	B-218 (3-118)
r.14.2	B-219 (3-119)
r.14.3	B-220 (3-120)
r.14.4	B-221 (3-121)
r.14.5	B-222 (3-122)
r.14.6	B-223 (3-123)
r.14.7	B-224 (3-124)
r.14.8	B-225 (3-125)
r.14.9	B-226 (3-126)
r.14.10	B-227 (3-127)
r.14.11	B-228 (3-128)

CRIMINAL PROCEDURE RULE	*PARAGRAPH NUMBERS*
r.14.12	B-229 (3-129)
r.14.13	B-230 (3-130)
r.14.14	B-231 (3-131)
r.14.15	B-232 (3-132)
r.14.16	B-235 (3-133)
r.14.17	B-236 (3-134)
r.14.18	B-237 (3-134a)
r.14.19	B-238 (3-134b)
r.14.20	B-239 (3-134c)
Part 15 (Disclosure)	
r.15.1	B-254 (12-103)
r.15.2	B-255 (12-104)
r.15.3	B-256 (12-105)
r.15.4	B-257 (12-112)
r.15.5	B-258 (12-113)
r.15.6	B-259 (12-114)
r.15.7	B-260 (12-115)
r.15.8	B-261 (12-116)
r.15.9	B-262 (12-117)
Part 16 (Written witness statements)	
r.16.1	B-264 (10-16)
r.16.2	B-265 (10-17)
r.16.3	B-266 (10-18)
r.16.4	B-267 (10-19)
Part 17 (Witness summonses, warrants and orders)	
r.17.1	B-273 (8-15)
r.17.2	B-274 (8-16)
r.17.3	B-275 (8-17)
r.17.4	B-276 (8-18)
r.17.5	B-277 (8-19)
r.17.6	B-278 (8-20)
r.17.7	B-279 (8-21)
r.17.8	B-280 (8-22)
Part 18 (Measures to help a witness or defendant to give evidence or otherwise participate)	
r.18.1	B-282 (8-118)
r.18.2	B-283 (8-119)
r.18.3	B-283a
r.18.4	B-284 (8-120)
r.18.5	B-285 (8-121)
r.18.6	B-286 (8-122)
r.18.7	B-287 (8-123)
r.18.8	B-289 (8-125)
r.18.9	B-290 (8-126)
r.18.10	B-291 (8-127)

CRIMINAL PROCEDURE RULE	*PARAGRAPH NUMBERS*
r.18.11	B-292 (8-128)
r.18.12	B-283 (8-129)
r.18.13	B-294 (8-130)
r.18.14	B-295 (8-131)
r.18.15	B-296 (8-132)
r.18.16	B-297 (8-133)
r.18.17	B-298 (8-134)
r.18.18	B-299 (8-135)
r.18.19	B-300 (8-136)
r.18.20	B-301 (8-137)
r.18.21	B-302 (8-138)
r.18.22	B-303 (8-139)
r.18.23	B-304 (8-140)
r.18.24	B-305 (8-141)
r.18.25	B-306 (8-142)
r.18.26	B-307 (8-143)
r.18.27	B-307a
r.18.28	B-307b
r.18.29	B-307c
r.18.30	B-307d
r.18.31	B-307e
r.18.32	B-307f
Part 19 (Expert evidence)	
r.19.1	B-338 (10-39)
r.19.2	B-339 (10-40)
r.19.3	B-340 (10-41)
r.19.4	B-341 (10-42)
r.19.5	B-342 (10-43)
r.19.6	B-343 (10-44)
r.19.7	B-344 (10-45)
r.19.8	B-345 (10-45a)
r.19.9	B-346 (10-46)
r.19.10	B-347 (10-46a)
Part 20 (Hearsay evidence)	
r.20.1	B-351 (11-52)
r.20.2	B-352 (11-53)
r.20.3	B-353 (11-54)
r.20.4	B-354 (11-55)
r.20.5	B-355 (11-56)
Part 21 (Evidence of bad character)	
r.21.1	B-356
r.21.2	B-357
r.21.3	B-358
r.21.4	B-359
r.21.5	B-360
r.21.6	B-361 (13-69)

CRIMINAL PROCEDURE RULE	*PARAGRAPH NUMBERS*
Part 22 (Evidence of a complainant's previous sexual behaviour)	
r.22.1	B-363 (8-302)
r.22.2	B-364 (8-303)
r.22.3	B-365 (8-304)
r.22.4	B-366 (8-305)
r.22.5	B-367 (8-306)
r.22.6	B-368 (8-307)
r.22.7	B-369 (8-308)
r.22.8	B-370 (8-309)
Part 23 (Restriction on cross-examination by a defendant)	
r.23.1	B-375 (8-275)
r.23.2	B-376 (8-276)
r.23.3	B-377 (8-277)
r.23.4	B-378 (8-278)
r.23.5	B-379 (8-279)
r.23.6	B-380 (8-280)
r.23.7	B-381 (8-281)
r.23.8	B-382 (8-282)
Part 24 (Trial and sentence in a magistrates' court)	
r.24.1	B-387
r.24.2	B-388
r.24.3	B-389
r.24.4	B-390
r.24.5	B-391
r.24.6	B-392
r.24.7	B-393
r.24.8	B-394
r.24.9	B-395
r.24.10	B-396
r.24.11	B-397
r.24.12	B-398
r.24.13	B-399
r.24.15	B-400
r.24.16	B-401
Part 25 (Trial and sentence in the Crown Court)	
rr.25.1, 25.2	B-415 (4-265a)
r.25.3	B-416 (4-265b)
r.25.4	B-417 (4-265c)
r.25.5	B-418 (4-254)
r.25.6	B-419 (4-265d)
rr.25.7, 25.8	B-420 (4-265e)
r.25.9	B-421 (4-265f)
r.25.10	B-422 (4-235)

CRIMINAL PROCEDURE RULE	*PARAGRAPH NUMBERS*
r.25.11	B-423 (8-68)
r.25.12	B-424 (10-19, 10-46b and 11-56a)
r.25.13	B-425 (10-8)
r.25.14	B-426 (4-265g)
r.25.15	B-427 (4-265h)
r.25.16	B-428 (5A-234)
r.25.17	B-429 (4-265j)
r.25.18	B-430 (2-16)
Part 26 (Jurors)	
r.26.1	B-433 (4-289)
r.26.2	B-434 (4-291)
r.26.3	B-435 (4-291b)
r.26.4	B-436 (4-291c)
r.26.5	B-437 (4-325c)
Part 27 (Retrial after acquittal)	
r.27.1	B-474 (4-199, 7-307a)
r.27.2	B-475 (4-200)
r.27.3	B-476 (7-307c)
r.27.4	B-477 (7-307d)
r.27.5	B-478 (7-307e)
r.27.6	B-479 (7-307f)
r.27.7	B-480 (7-307g)
Part 28 (Sentencing procedures in special cases)	
r.28.1	B-481
r.28.2	B-482 (5A-543)
r.28.3	B-483
r.28.4	B-484 (5A-1230, 5ASC-1435)
r.28.5	B-485
r.28.6	B-486
r.28.7	B-487 (5A-459, 5ASC-533)
r.28.8	B-488 (5A-1172, 5ASC-1377)
r.28.9	B-489 (5A-1173, 5ASC-1378)
r.28.10	B-490 (5A-216, 5ASC-258)
r.28.11	B-491 (5A-1246, 5ASC-1456)
Part 29 (Road traffic penalties)	
r.29.1	B-492
r.29.2	B-493
r.29.3	B-494
r.29.4	B-495
r.29.5	B-496
r.29.6	B-497
Part 30 (Enforcement of fines and other orders for payment)	
r.30.1	B-498
r.30.2	B-499
r.30.3	B-500

CRIMINAL PROCEDURE RULE	*PARAGRAPH NUMBERS*
r.30.4	B-501
r.30.5	B-502
r.30.6	B-503
r.30.7	B-504
r.30.8	B-505
r.30.9	B-506
Part 31 (Behaviour orders)	
r.31.1	B-508 (5A-793, 5ASC-913)
r.31.2	B-509 (5A-794, 5ASC-914)
r.31.3	B-510 (5A-795, 5ASC-915)
r.31.4	B-511 (5A-796, 5ASC-916)
r.31.5	B-512 (5A-797, 5ASC-917)
r.31.6	B-513 (5A-798, 5ASC-918)
r.31.7	B-514 (5A-799, 5ASC-919)
r.31.8	B-515 (5A-800, 5ASC-920)
r.31.9	B-518 (5A-803, 5ASC-923)
Part 32 (Breach, revocation and amendment of community and other orders)	
r.32.1	B-519 (5A-1280, 5ASC-1493)
r.32.2	B-520 (5A-1281, 5ASC-1494)
r.32.3	B-521 (5A-1282, 5ASC-1495)
r.32.4	B-522 (5A-1283, 5ASC-1496)
Part 33 (Confiscation and related proceedings)	
r.33.1	B-566 (5B-186)
r.33.2	B-567 (5B-187)
r.33.3	B-568 (5B-188)
r.33.4	B-569 (5B-189)
r.33.5	B-570 (5B-190)
r.33.6	B-571 (5B-191)
r.33.7	B-572 (5B-192)
r.33.8	B-573 (5B-193)
r.33.9	B-574 (5B-194)
r.33.10	B-575 (5B-195)
r.33.11	B-576 (5B-196)
r.33.12	B-577 (5B-197)
r.33.13	B-578 (5B-198)
r.33.14	B-579 (5B-199)
r.33.15	B-580 (5B-200)
r.33.16	B-581 (5B-201)
r.33.17	B-582 (5B-202)
r.33.18	B-583 (5B-203)
r.33.19	B-584 (5B-204)
r.33.20	B-585 (5B-205)
r.33.21	B-586 (5B-206)
r.33.22	B-587 (5B-207)
r.33.23	B-588 (5B-208)

CRIMINAL PROCEDURE RULE	*PARAGRAPH NUMBERS*
r.33.24	B-589 (5B-209)
r.33.25	B-590 (5B-210)
r.33.26	B-591 (5B-211)
r.33.27	B-592 (5B-212)
r.33.28	B-593 (5B-213)
r.33.29	B-594 (5B-214)
r.33.30	B-595 (5B-215)
r.33.31	B-596 (5B-216)
r.33.32	B-597 (5B-217)
rr.33.33–33.35	B-598 (5B-218, 5B-219, 5B-220)
r.33.36	B-599 (5B-221)
rr.33.37, 33.38	B-600 (5B-222, 5B-223)
r.33.39	B-601 (5B-224)
r.33.40	B-602 (5B-225)
r.33.41	B-603 (5B-226)
r.33.42	B-604 (5B-227)
rr.33.43, 33.44	B-605 (5B-228, 5B-229)
r.33.45	B-606 (5B-230)
r.33.46	B-607 (5B-231)
r.33.47	B-608 (5B-232)
r.33.48	B-609 (5B-233)
rr.33.49, 33.50	B-610 (5B-234, 5B-235)
r.33.51	B-611 (5B-236)
r.33.52	B-612 (5B-237)
r.33.53	B-613 (5B-238)
r.33.54	B-614 (5B-239)
r.33.55	B-615 (5B-240)
r.33.56	B-616 (5B-241)
r.33.57	B-617 (5B-242)
r.33.58	B-618 (5B-243)
r.33.59	B-619 (5B-244)
r.33.60	B-620 (5B-245)
r.33.61	B-621 (5B-246)
r.33.62	B-622 (5B-247)
r.33.63	B-623 (5B-248)
r.33.64	B-624 (5B-249)
r.33.65	B-625 (5B-250)
r.33.66	B-626 (5B-251)
r.33.67	B-627 (5B-252)
r.33.68	B-628 (5B-253)
r.33.69	B-629 (5B-254)
r.33.70	B-630 (5B-255)
Part 34 (Appeal to the Crown Court)	
r.34.1	B-631 (2-117)
r.34.2	B-632 (2-118)
r.34.3	B-633 (2-119)

CRIMINAL PROCEDURE RULE	*PARAGRAPH NUMBERS*
r.34.4	B-634 (2-120)
r.34.5	B-635 (2-121)
r.34.6	B-636 (2-122)
r.34.7	B-637 (2-123)
r.34.8	B-638 (2-124)
r.34.9	B-639 (2-111)
r.34.10	B-640 (2-126)
r.34.11	B-641 (2-8)
Part 35 (Appeal to the High Court by case stated)	
r.35.1	B-644
rr.35.2, 35.3	B-645 (7-18)
r.35.4	B-646
r.35.5	B-647
Part 36 (Appeal to the Court of Appeal: general rules)	
r.36.1	B-648 (7-366)
r.36.2	B-649 (7-367)
r.36.3	B-650 (7-368)
r.36.4	B-651 (7-369)
r.36.5	B-652 (7-370)
r.36.6	B-653 (7-371)
r.36.7	B-654 (7-372)
r.36.8	B-655 (7-373)
r.36.9	B-656 (7-374)
r.36.10	B-657 (7-375)
r.36.11	B-658 (7-376)
r.36.12	B-659 (7-377)
r.36.13	B-660 (7-185)
r.36.14	B-661 (7-186)
r.36.15	B-662 (7-222a)
Part 37 (Appeal to the Court of Appeal against ruling at a preparatory hearing)	
r.37.1	B-663 (7-315)
r.37.2	B-664 (7-316)
r.37.3	B-665 (7-317)
r.37.4	B-666 (7-318)
r.37.5	B-667 (7-319)
r.37.6	B-668 (7-320)
r.37.7	B-669 (7-321)
r.37.8	B-670 (7-322)
Part 38 (Appeal to the Court of Appeal against ruling adverse to the prosecution)	
r.38.1	B-671 (7-265)
r.38.2	B-672 (7-266)
r.38.3	B-673 (7-267)
r.38.4	B-674 (7-268)

CRIMINAL PROCEDURE RULE	*PARAGRAPH NUMBERS*
r.38.5	B-675 (7-269)
r.38.6	B-676 (7-270)
r.38.7	B-677 (7-271)
r.38.8	B-678 (7-272)
r.38.9	B-679 (7-273)
r.38.10	B-680 (7-274)
r.38.11	B-681 (7-275)
Part 39 (Appeal to the Court of Appeal about conviction or sentence)	
r.39.1	B-682 (7-380)
r.39.2	B-683 (7-381)
r.39.3	B-684 (7-382)
r.39.4	B-685 (7-383)
r.39.5	B-686 (7-159)
r.39.6	B-687 (7-203)
r.39.7	B-688 (7-386)
r.39.8	B-689 (7-177)
r.39.9	B-690 (7-178)
r.39.10	B-691 (7-179)
r.39.11	B-692 (7-194)
r.39.12	B-693 (7-195)
r.39.13	B-694 (7-150)
r.39.14	B-695 (7-115)
Part 40 (Appeal to the Court of Appeal about reporting or public access restriction)	
r.40.1	B-707 (7-326)
r.40.2	B-708 (7-327)
r.40.3	B-709 (7-328)
r.40.4	B-710 (7-329)
r.40.5	B-711 (7-330)
r.40.6	B-712 (7-331)
r.40.7	B-713 (7-332)
r.40.8	B-714 (7-333)
r.40.9	B-715 (7-334)
Part 41 (Reference to the Court of Appeal of point of law or unduly lenient sentencing)	
r.41.1	B-716 (7-453)
r.41.2	B-717 (7-454)
r.41.3	B-718 (7-455)
r.41.4	B-720 (7-456)
r.41.5	B-721 (7-457)
r.41.6	B-722 (7-458)
r.41.7	B-723 (7-459)
Part 42 (Appeal to the Court of Appeal in confiscation and related proceedings)	
r.42.1	B-724 (5B-274)
r.42.2	B-725 (5B-275)

CRIMINAL PROCEDURE RULE	*PARAGRAPH NUMBERS*
r.42.3	B-726 (5B-276)
r.42.4	B-727 (5B-277)
r.42.5	B-728 (5B-278)
r.42.6	B-729 (5B-279)
r.42.7	B-730 (5B-280)
r.42.8	B-731 (5B-281)
r.42.9	B-732 (5B-282)
r.42.10	B-733 (5B-283)
r.42.11	B-734 (5B-284)
r.42.12	B-735 (5B-285)
r.42.13	B-736 (5B-286)
r.42.14	B-737 (5B-287)
r.42.15	B-738 (5B-288)
r.42.16	B-739 (5B-289)
r.42.17	B-740 (5B-290)
r.42.18	B-741 (5B-291)
r.42.19	B-742 (5B-292)
r.42.20	B-743 (5B-293)
Part 43 (Appeal or reference to the Supreme Court)	
r.43.1	B-744 (7-400)
r.43.2	B-745 (7-401)
r.43.3	B-746 (7-402)
r.43.4	B-747 (7-403)
Part 44 (Reopening a case in a magistrates' court)	
r.44.1	B-748
r.44.2	B-749
r.44.3	B-750
Part 45 (Costs)	
r.45.1	B-752
r.45.2	B-753
r.45.3	B-754
r.45.4	B-755, (6-3)
r.45.5	B-756 (6-37)
r.45.6	B-757
r.45.7	B-758
r.45.8	B-759
r.45.9	B-760
r.45.10	B-761
r.45.11	B-762
r.45.12	B-763
r.45.13	B-764
r.45.14	B-765
Part 46 (Representatives)	
r.46.1	B-766 (2-187)
r.46.2	B-767 (4-68a)

CRIMINAL PROCEDURE RULE	PARAGRAPH NUMBERS
r.46.3	B-768 (6-180)
Part 47 (Investigation orders and warrants)	
r.47.1	B-769
r.47.2	B-770
r.47.3	B-771
r.47.4	B-772
r.47.5	B-773
r.47.6	B-774
r.47.7	B-775
r.47.8	B-776
r.47.9	B-777
r.47.10	B-778
r.47.11	B-779
r.47.12	B-780
r.47.13	B-781
r.47.14	B-782
r.47.15	B-783
r.47.16	B-784
r.47.17	B-785
r.47.18	B-786
r.47.19	B-787
r.47.20	B-788
r.47.21	B-789
r.47.22	B-790
r.47.23	B-791
r.47.24	B-792
r.47.25	B-793
r.47.26	B-794
r.47.27	B-795
r.47.28	B-796
r.47.29	B-797
r.47.30	B-798
r.47.31	B-799
r.47.32	B-800
r.47.33	B-801
r.47.34	B-802
r.47.35	B-803
r.47.36	B-804
r.47.37	B-805
r.47.38	B-806
r.47.39	B-807
r.47.40	B-808
r.47.41	B-809
r.47.42	B-810
r.47.43	B-811
r.47.44	B-812

CRIMINAL PROCEDURE RULE	*PARAGRAPH NUMBERS*
r.47.45	B-813
r.47.46	B-814
r.47.47	B-815
r.47.48	B-816
r.47.49	B-817
r.47.50	B-818
r.47.51	B-819
r.47.52	B-820
r.47.53	B-821
r.47.54	B-822
r.47.55	B-823
r.47.56	B-824
r.47.57	B-825
r.47.58	B-826
r.47.59	B-830 (26-42e)
r.47.60	B-831 (26-42f)
r.47.61	B-832 (26-42g)
r.47.62	B-833 (26-42h)
r.47.63	B-834
r.47.64	B-835
r.47.65	B-836
r.47.66	B-837
r.47.67	B-838
r.47.68	B-839
Part 48 (Contempt of court)	
r.48.1	B-846
r.48.2	B-847
r.48.3	B-848
r.48.4	B-849
r.48.5	B-850
r.48.6	B-851
r.48.7	B-852
r.48.8	B-853
r.48.9	B-854
r.48.10	B-855
r.48.11	B-856
r.48.12	B-857
r.48.13	B-858
r.48.14	B-859
r.48.15	B-860
r.48.16	B-861
r.48.17	B-862
Part 49 (International co-operation)	
r.49.1	B-866
r.49.2	B-867
r.49.3	B-868

CRIMINAL PROCEDURE RULE	*PARAGRAPH NUMBERS*
r.49.4	B-869
r.49.5	B-870
r.49.6	B-871
r.49.7	B-872
r.49.8	B-873
r.49.9	B-874
r.49.10	B-875
r.49.11	B-876
Part 50 (Extradition)	
r.50.1	B-883
r.50.2	B-884
r.50.3	B-885
r.50.4	B-886
r.50.5	B-887
r.50.6	B-888
r.50.7	B-889
r.50.8	B-890
r.50.9	B-891
r.50.10	B-892
r.50.11	B-893
r.50.12	B-894
r.50.13	B-895
r.50.14	B-896
r.50.15	B-897
r.50.16	B-898
r.50.17	B-899
r.50.18	B-900
r.50.19	B-901
r.50.20	B-902
r.50.21	B-903
r.50.22	B-904
r.50.23	B-905
r.50.24	B-906
r.50.25	B-907
r.50.26	B-908
r.50.27	B-909
r.50.28	B-910
r.50.29	B-911
r.50.30	B-912
r.50.31	B-913
r.50.32	B-914

Criminal Practice Directions (2015) (as amended) and Criminal Costs Practice Directions (2015)

(Appendix B and main work paragraph numbers are set out below. Main work paragraphs are shown in brackets.)

CRIMINAL PRACTICE DIRECTION	*PARAGRAPH NUMBERS*
CPD I (General matters) A	B-2
CPD I (General matters) 1A: The overriding objective	
1A.1-1A.3	B-3 (4-114a)
CPD I (General matters) 3A: Case management	
3A.1-3A.3	B-37 (4-120)
3A.4	B-38
3A.5, 3A.6	B-39
3A.7	B-40
3A.8	B-41
3A.9, 3A.10	B-42
3A.11	B-43
3A.12-3A.14	B-44 (12-144a)
3A.15	B-45
3A.16-3A.20	B-46 (4-123)
3A.21, 3A.22	B-47 (4-123a)
3A.23-3A.28	B-48 (4-120a)
Note to the Practice Direction	B-49 (4-123b)
CPD I (General matters) 3B: Pagination and indexing of served evidence	
3B.1-3B.5	B-50
CPD I (General matters) 3C: Abuse of process stay applications	
3C.1-3C.5	B-51 (4-101b)
CPD I (General matters) 3D: Vulnerable people in the courts	
3D.1-3D.8	B-52 (8-131e)
CPD I (General matters) 3E: Ground rules hearings to plan the questioning of a vulnerable witness or defendant	
3E.1-3E.6	B-53 (8-131f)
CPD I (General matters) 3F: Intermediaries	
3F.1-3F.3	B-54 (8-131g)
3F.4, 3F.5	B-55 (8-131h)
3F.6-3F.10	B-56 (8-131i)
3F.11-3F.18	B-57 (8-131j)
3F.19-3F.23	B-58 (8-131k)
3F.24-3F.26	B-59 (8-131l)
3F.27	B-60 (8-131m)
3F.28	B-61 (8-131n)
3F.29	B-62 (8-131o)
CPD I (General matters) 3G: Vulnerable defendants	
3G.1-3G.6	B-63 (4-162)
3G.7-3G.14	B-64 (4-163)
CPD I (General matters) 3H: Wales and the Welsh language: devolution issues	

CRIMINAL PRACTICE DIRECTION	*PARAGRAPH NUMBERS*
3H.1	B-65
CPD I (General matters) 3J: Wales and the Welsh language: applications for evidence to be given in Welsh	
3J.1	B-66
CPD I (General matters) 3K: Wales and the Welsh language: use of the Welsh language in courts in Wales	
3K.1	B-67
3K.2-3K.6	B-68
3K.7	B-69
3K.8	B-70
3K.9	B-71
3K.10-3K.13	B-72
3K.14	B-73
3K.15	B-74
3K.16	B-75
CPD I (General matters) 3L: Security of prisoners at court	
3L.1-3L.4	B-76 (3-232a)
3L.5, 3L.6	B-77 (3-232b)
3L.7-3L.10	B-78 (3-232c)
3L.11	B-79 (3-232d)
CPD I (General matters) 3M: Procedure for application for armed police presence in Crown Court and magistrates' court buildings	
3M.1-3M.3	B-80
3M.4	B-81
3M.5-3M.7	B-82
3M.8, 3M.9	B-83
3M.10-3M.14	B-84
3M.15-3M.19	B-85
3M.20, 3M.21	B-86
3M.22, 3M.23	B-87
3M.24, 3M.25	B-88
CPD I (General matters) 3N: Use of live link and telephone facilities	
3N.1-3N.12	B-89
3N.13-3N.15	B-90
3N.16	B-91
3N.17	B-92
CPD I (General matters) 3P: Commissioning medical reports	
3P.1-3.P.4	B-93
3P.5-3P.7	B-94
3P.8-3P.10	B-95
3P.11-3P.14	B-96
3P.15-3P.16	B-97

CRIMINAL PRACTICE DIRECTION	*PARAGRAPH NUMBERS*
Paragraphs 1, 2	B-148
Paragraphs 3, 4	B-149
Paragraphs 5, 6	B-150
Paragraph 7	B-151
Paragraphs 8-10	B-152
Paragraph 11	B-153
Paragraphs 12, 13	B-154
CPD II (Preliminary Proceedings) 7A: First court attendance after charge or detention	
7A.1-7A.4	B-159
7A.5-7A.8	B-160
CPD II (Preliminary proceedings) 8A: Defendant's record	
8A.1-8A.5	B-165 (12-145)
8A.6-8A.8	B-166 (12-146)
CPD II (Preliminary proceedings) 9A: Allocation (mode of trial)	
9A.1-9A.3	B-181 (1-114)
CPD II (Preliminary proceedings) 10A: Preparation and content of the indictment	
10A.1	B-191
10A.2	B-192
10A.3-10A.5	B-193
10A.6, 10A.7	B-194
10A.8, 10A.9	B-195
10A.9	B-196
10A.11-10A.14	B-197
10A.15-10A.20	B-198
CPD II (Preliminary proceedings) 10B: Voluntary bills of indictment	
10B.1-10B.6	B-199
CPD III (Custody and bail) 14A: Bail before sending for trial	
14A.1	B-240 (3-206a)
14A.2	B-241 (3-206b)
CPD III (Custody and bail) 14B: Bail: failure to surrender and trials in absence	
14B.1-14B.4	B-242 (3-39)
CPD III (Custody and bail) 14C: Failure to surrender to bail: consequences and penalties	
14C.1, 14C.2	B-243 (3-40)
14C.3, 14C.4	B-244 (3-41)
14C.5, 14C.6	B-245 (3-42)
14C.7-14C.10	B-246 (3-43)
14C.11-14C.12	B-247
14C.13-14C.15	B-248

CRIMINAL PRACTICE DIRECTION	*PARAGRAPH NUMBERS*
CPD III (Custody and bail) 14D: Relationship between the Bail Act offence and further remands on bail or in custody	
14D.1-14D.4	B-249 (3-44)
CPD III (Custody and bail) 14E: Trials in absence	
14E.1-14E.4	B-250
CPD III (Custody and bail) 14F: Forfeiture of monies lodged as security or pledged by a surety / estreatment of recognizances	
14F.1-14F.5	B-251 (3-53)
CPD III (Custody and bail) 14G: Bail during trial	
14G.1-14G.4	B-252 (3-204)
CPD III (Custody and bail) 14H: Crown Court judge's certification of fitness to appeal and applications to the Crown Court for bail pending appeal	
14H.1-14H.6	B-253 (7-38a)
CPD IV Disclosure 15A: Disclosure of unused material	
15A.1, 15A.2	B-263
CPD V (Evidence) 16A: Evidence by written statement	
16.A.1	B-268 (10-19a)
16A.2	B-269 (10-19b)
16A.3-16A.6	B-270 (10-19c)
CPD V (Evidence) 16B: Video recorded evidence in chief	
16B.1-16B.4	B-271 (8-131p)
CPD V (Evidence) 16C: Evidence of audio and video recorded interviews	
16C.1-16C.16	B-272 (15-238)
CPD V (Evidence) 17A: Wards of court and children subject to current family proceedings	
17A.1-17A.8	B-281 (8-60)
CPD V (Evidence) 18A: Measures to assist a witness or defendant to give evidence	
18A.1, 18A.2	B-308 (8-131q)
CPD V (Evidence) 18B: Witnesses giving evidence by live link	
18B.1-18B.5	B-309 (8-131r)
CPD V (Evidence) 18C: Visually recorded interviews: memory refreshing and watching a different time from the jury	
18C.1-18C.5	B-310 (8-131s)
CPD V (Evidence) 18D: Witness anonymity orders	

CRIMINAL PRACTICE DIRECTION	*PARAGRAPH NUMBERS*
18D.1, 18D.2	B-311 (8-167)
18D.3	B-312 (8-168)
18D.4	B-313 (8-169)
18D.5	B-314
18D.6, 18D.7	B-315
18D.8-18D.17	B-316
18D.18-18D.21	B-317
18D.22-18D.24	B-318
18D.25	B-319
CPD V (Evidence) 18E: Use of YJCEA 1999, s.28; pre-recording of cross-examination and re-examination for witnesses captured by YJCEA 1999, s.16	
18E.1-18E.7	B-320 (8-131t)
18E.8-18E.13	B-321 (8-131t)
18E.14-18E.16	B-322 (8-131u)
18E.17-18E.18	B-2323 (8-131u)
18E.19-18E.26	B-324 (8-131u)
18E.27-18E.31	B-325 (8-131v)
18E.32-18E.37	B-326 (8-131v)
18E.38-18E.44	B-327 (8-131w)
18E.45, 18E.46	B-328 (8-131w)
18E.47-18E.54	B-329 (8-131w)
18E.55-18E.57	B-330 (8-131x)
18E.58	B-331 (8-131x)
18E.59-18E.64	B-332 (8-131x)
18E.65-18E.67	B-333 (8-131x)
Annex, paras 1-5	B-334
Annex, para.6	B-335
Annex, paras 7-22	B-336
Annex (Court of Appeal guidance)	B-337
CPD V (Evidence) 19A: Expert evidence	
19.A.1-19A.	B-348 (10-46c)
CPD V (Evidence) 19B: Statements of understanding and declarations of truth in expert reports	
19B.1	B-349 (10-46d)
CPD V (Evidence) 19C: Pre-hearing discussion of expert evidence	
19C.1-19C.8	B-350 (10-46e)
CPD V (Evidence) 21A: Spent convictions	
21A.1-21A.3	B-362 (13-83)
CPD V (Evidence) 22A: Use of ground rules hearing when dealing with s.41 Youth Justice and Criminal Evidence Act 1999 (YJCEA 1999) evidence of complainant's previous sexual behaviour	
22A.1-22A.2	B-371

CRIMINAL PRACTICE DIRECTION	*PARAGRAPH NUMBERS*
22A.3-22A.4	B-372
22A.5-22A.7	B-373
22A.8	B-374
CPD V (Evidence) 23A: Cross-examination advocates	
23A.1-23A.2	B-383
23A.3-23A.5	B-384
23A.6-23A.7	B-385
23A.8-23A.10	B-386
CPD VI (Trial) 24A: Role of the justices' clerk/legal adviser	
24A.1-24A.18	B-402
CPD VI (Trial) 24B: Identification for the court of the issues in the case	
24B.1-24B.4	B-403
CPD VI Trial 24C: Trial adjournment in the magistrates' court	
24C.1-24C.4	B-404
24C.5-24C.9	B-405
24C.10-24C.13	B-406
24C.14-24C.15	B-407
24C.16	B-408
24C.17-24C.19	B-409
24C.20	B-410
24C.21-24C.22	B-411
24C.23-24C.26	B-412
24C.27-24C.29	B-413
24C.30-24C.32	B-414
CPD VI (Trial) 25A: Identification for the jury of the issues in the case	
25A.1-25A.6	B-431 (4-342, 4-343a)
CPD VI Trial 25B: Trial adjournment in the Crown Court	
25B.1-25B.3	B-432
CPD VI (Trial) 26A: Juries: introduction	
26A.1, 26A.2	B-438
CPD VI (Trial) 26B: Juries: preliminary matters arising before jury service commences	
26B.1-26B.4	B-439
CPD VI (Trial) 26C: Juries: eligibility	
26C.1-26C.10	B-440 (4-291a)
CPD VI (Trial) 26D: Juries: precautionary measures before swearing	
26D.1-26D.4	B-441 (4-291e)
CPD VI (Trial) 26E: Juries: swearing in jurors	
26E.1-26E.3	B-442 (4-306)

CRIMINAL PRACTICE DIRECTION	*PARAGRAPH NUMBERS*
CPD VI (Trial) 26F: Juries: ensuring an effective jury panel	
26F.1	B-442
CPD VI (Trial) 26G: Juries: preliminary instructions to jurors	
26G.1-26G.5	B-443 (4-325)
CPD VI (Trial) 26H: Juries: discharge of a juror for personal reasons	
26H.1-26H.3	B-444 (4-307a)
CPD VI (Trial) 26J): Juries: views	
26J.1	B-445 (4-111a)
CPD VI (Trial) 26K: Juries: directions, written materials and summing up	
26K.1	B-446
26K.2-26K.7	B-447
26K.8-26K.10	B-448
26K.11-26K.15	B-449 (4-418a)
26K.16-26K.18	B-450 (4-418c)
26K.19-26K.22	B-451 (4-430a)
CPD VI (Trial) 26L: Juries: jury access to exhibits and evidence in retirement	
26L.1-26L.3	B-452 (4-495a)
CPD VI (Trial) 26M: Juries: jury irregularities	
26M.1-26M.4	B-453 (4-308)
26M.5-26M.7	B-454 (4-308a)
26M.8, 26M.9	B-455 (4-308b)
26M.10-26M.13	B-456 (4-308c)
26M.14-26M.19	B-457 (4-308d)
26M.20, 26M.21	B-458 (4-308e)
26M.22, 26M.23	B-459 (4-308f)
26M.24-26M.26	B-460 (4-308g)
26M.27-26M.34	B-461 (4-308h)
26M.35-26M.40	B-462 (4-308i)
26M.41, 26M.42	B-463
26M.43-26M.46	B-464
26M.47-26M.51	B-465
26M.52	B-466
26M.53	B-467
26M.54-26M.56	B-468
26M.57, 26M.58	B-469
Contact details	B-470
CPD VI (Trial) 26N: Open justice	
26N.1	B-471 (4-107)
CPD VI (Trial) 26P: Defendant's right to give or not to give evidence	
26P.1-26P.5	B-472 (4-380)

CRIMINAL PRACTICE DIRECTION	*PARAGRAPH NUMBERS*
CPD VI (Trial) 26Q: Majority verdicts	
26Q.1-26Q.9	B-473 (4-510)
CPD VII (Sentencing) A: Pleas of guilty in the Crown Court	B-523
CPD VII (Sentencing) B: Determining the factual basis of sentence	
B.1-B.5	B-524
B.6	B-525
B.7-B.10	B-526
B.11-B.13	B-527
B.14	B-528
B.15-B.17	B-529
B.18-B.21	B-530
B.22-B.27	B-531
CPD VII (Sentencing) C: Indications of sentence: Goodyear	
C.1-C.8	B-532 (5A-129)
CPD VII (Sentencing) D: Facts to be stated on pleas of guilty	
D.1	B-533
CPD VII (Sentencing) E: Concurrent and consecutive sentences	
E.1-E.3	B-534 (5A-168)
CPD VII (Sentencing) F: Victim personal statements	
F.1-F.3	B-535 (5A-302)
CPD VII (Sentencing) G: Families bereaved by homicide and other criminal conduct	
G.1-G.3	B-536 (5A-303)
CPD VII (Sentencing) H: Community impact statements	
H.1-H.6	B-537 (5A-309)
CPD VII (Sentencing) I: Impact statements for businesses	
I.1-I.10	B-538 (5A-308)
CPD VII (Sentencing) J: Binding over orders and conditional discharges	
J.1	B-539 (5A-356)
J.2, J.3	B-540 (5A-357)
J.4	B-541 (5A-358)
J.5-J.7	B-542 (5A-359)
J.8, J.9	B-543 (5A-360)
J.10-J.12	B-544 (5A-361)
J.13-J.15	B-545 (5A-362)
J.16	B-546 (5A-363)
J.17, J.18	B-547 (5A-364)
J.19	B-548
J.20	B-549

CRIMINAL PRACTICE DIRECTION	*PARAGRAPH NUMBERS*
CPD VII (Sentencing) K: Committal for sentence	
K.1	B-550 (5A-217)
CPD VII (Sentencing) L: Imposition of life sentences	
L.1–L.5	B-551 (5A-715)
CPD VII (Sentencing) M: Mandatory life sentences	
M.1–M.14	B-552 (5A-786)
CPD VII (Sentencing) N: Transitional arrangements for sentences where the offence was committed before 18 December 2003	
N.1–N.10	B-553
N.11, N.12	B-554
N.13	B-555
N.14–N.18	B-556
N.19–N.21	B-557
CPD VII (Sentencing) P: Procedure for announcing the minimum term in open court	
P.1–P.3	B-558 (5A-787)
CPD VII (Sentencing) Q: Financial, etc. information required for sentencing	
Q.1–Q.6	B-559
CPD VII (Sentencing) R: Medical reports for sentencing purposes	
R.1–R.4	B-560
R.5–R.8	B-561
R.10–R.13	B-562
R.14–R.15	B-563
R.16	B-564
CPD VII (Sentencing) S: Variation of sentence	
S.1–S.4	B-565
CPD IX (Appeal) 34A: Appeals to the Crown Court	
34A.1–34A.3	B-642 (2-128a)
CPD IX (Appeal) 34B: Appeal to the Crown Court: information from the magistrates' court	
34B.1–34B.4	B-643
CPD IX (Appeal) 39A: Appeals against conviction and sentence—the provision of notice to the prosecution	
39A.1–39A.6	B-696 (7-202)
CPD IX (Appeal) 39B: Listing of appeals against conviction and sentence in the Court of Appeal Criminal Division (CACD)	
39B.1–39B.5	B-697 (7-190)

CRIMINAL PRACTICE DIRECTION	*PARAGRAPH NUMBERS*
CPD IX (Appeal) 39C: Appeal notices containing grounds of appeal	
39C.1-39C.4	B-698 (7-168a)
39C.5	B-699
39C.6	B-700
39C.7	B-701
CPD IX (Appeal) 39D: Respondents' notices	
39D.1	B-702
CPD IX (Appeal) 39E: Loss of time	
39E.1-39E.4	B-703
CPD IX (Appeal) 39F: Skeleton arguments	
39F.1-39F.4	B-704 (7-200)
CPD IX (Appeal) 39G: Criminal Appeal Office summaries	
39G.1-39G.7	B-705 (7-189)
CPD IX (Appeal) 39H: Criminal Appeal Office bundles & indexes for full court hearings	
39H.1-39H.4	B-706
CPD IX (Appeal) 44A: References to the European Court of Justice	
44A.1-44A.7	B-751 (7-466)
CPD XI Other proceedings 47A: Investigation orders and warrants	
47A.1-47A.5	B-840
CPD XI Other proceedings 47B: Investigation orders and warrants in the Crown Court	
47B.1	B-841
47B.2-47B.4	B-842
47B.5-47B.10	B-843
47B.11-47B.14	B-844
47B.15	B-845
CPD XI Other proceedings 48A: Contempt in the face of the magistrates' court	
48A.1	B-863
48A.2	B-864
48A.3	B-865
CPD XI Other proceedings 50A: Extradition: general matters and case management	
50A.1	B-915
50A.2-50A.5	B-916
CPD XI Other proceedings 50B: Management of appeal to the High Court	
50B.1, 50B.2	B-917
50B.3-50B.5	B-918
50B.6, 50B.7	B-919
50B.8-50B.10	B-920
50B.11-50B.14	B-921

CRIMINAL PRACTICE DIRECTION	*PARAGRAPH NUMBERS*
50B.15–50B.17	B-922
50B.18, 50B.19	B-923
50B.20	B-924
50B.21, 50B.22	B-925
50B.23–50B.26	B-926
50B.27, 50B.28	B-927
CPD XI Other proceedings 50C: Extradition: representation orders	
50C.1–50C.3	B-928
50C.4–50C.6	B-929
50C.7, 50C.8	B-930
CPD XI Other proceedings 50D: Extradition: applications, etc	
50D.1	B-931
50D.2, 50D.3	B-932
50D.4–50D.6	B-933
50D.7, 50D.8	B-934
50D.9–50D.14	B-935
50D.15	B-936
50D.16–50D.19	B-937
50D.20–50D.22	B-938
CPD XI Other proceedings 50E: Extradition: court papers	
50E.1–50E.7	B-939
50E.8–50E.12	B-940
CPD XI Other proceedings 50F: Extradition: consequences of non compliance with directions	
50F.1–50F.4	B-941
CPD XII (General application) A: Court dress	
A.1, A.2	B-942 (2-29)
CPD XII (General application) B: Modes of address and titles of judges and magistrates	
B.1, B.2	B-943 (2-14)
B.3	
CPD XII (General application) C: Availability of judgments given in the Court of Appeal and High Court	
C.1, C.2	B-945
C.3–C.7	B-946
C.8–C.12	B-947
C.13, C.14	B-948
CPD XII (General application) D: Citation of authority and provision of copies of judgments to the court	
D.1	B-949 (7-200a)
D.2–D.7	B-950 (7-200b)
D.8–D.10	B-951 (7-200c)

CRIMINAL PRACTICE DIRECTION	*PARAGRAPH NUMBERS*
D.11–D.13	B-952 (7-200d)
D.14–D.16	B-953 (7-200e)
D.17–D.20	B-954 (7-200f)
D.21–D.23	B-955 (7-200f)
CPD XII (General application) E: Preparation of Judgments: neutral citation	
E.1–E.6	B-956
CPD XII (General application) F: Citation of Hansard	
F.1, F.2	B-957 (9-38)
CPD XIII (Listing) A: Judicial responsibility for listing and key principles	
A.1, A.2	B-958 (2-22)
A.3, A.4	B-959 (2-22a)
A.5, A.6	B-960 (2-22b)
CPD XIII (Listing) B: Classification	
B.1	B-961 (2-22c)
B.2	B-962 (2-22d)
B.3	B-963 (2-22e)
CPD XIII (Listing) C: Referral of cases in the Crown Court to the resident judge and to the presiding judges	
C.1–C.3	B-964 (2-22f)
C.4–C.6	B-965 (2-22g)
C.7–C.10	B-966 (2-22h)
CPD XIII (Listing) D: Authorisation of judges	
D.1–D.4	B-967 (2-22i)
CPD XIII (Listing) E: Allocation of business within the Crown Court	
E.1–E.14	B-968 (2-22j)
CPD XIII (Listing) F: Listing of trials, custody time limits and transfer of cases	
F.1, F.2	B-969 (2-22k)
F.3	B-970 (2-22l)
F.4, F.5	B-971 (2-22m)
F.6, F.7	B-972 (2-22n)
F.8–F.10	B-973 (2-22o)
F.11–F.13	B-974 (2-22p)
CPD XIII (Listing) G: Listing of hearings other than trials	
G.1–G.5	B-975 (2-22q)
G.6, G.7	B-976 (2-22r)
G.8	B-977 (2-22s)
G.9, G.10	B-978 (2-22t)
G.11	B-979 (2-22u)
G.12	B-980
G.13–G.15	B-981

CRIMINAL PRACTICE DIRECTION	PARAGRAPH NUMBERS
CPD XIII (Listing) Annex 1: General principles for the deployment of the kudiciary in the magistrates' court	
Introduction	B-982
Paragraphs 1-7	B-983
CPD XIII (Listing) Annex 2: Sexual offences in the youth court	
Paragraphs 1-5	B-984
Paragraphs 6-10	B-985
Paragraph 11	B-986
CPD XIII (Listing) Annex 3: Cases involving very large fines in the magistrates' court	
Paragraphs 1-7	B-987
CPD XIII (Listing) Annex 4: The management of terrorism cases	
Paragraph 1	B-988
Paragraphs 2, 3	B-989
Paragraphs 4-8	B-990
Paragraphs 9-11	B-991
Paragraphs 12, 13	B-992
Paragraphs 14, 15	B-993
Paragraph 16	B-994
Paragraph 17	B-995
CPD XIII (Listing) Annex 5: Management of cases from the organised crime division of the Crown Prosecution Service	
Paragraphs 1, 2	B-996
Paragraph 3	B-997
Paragraphs 4-6	B-998
Paragraph 7	B-999
Paragraph 8	B-1000
Paragraph 9-11	B-1001
Criminal Costs Practice Direction (2015)	Appendix F

Criminal Procedure Rules 2020 (SI 2020/759), Pt 1

THE OVERRIDING OBJECTIVE

The overriding objective

1.1.–(1) The overriding objective of this procedural code is that criminal cases be dealt with justly. **★B-1**

(2) Dealing with a criminal case justly includes–

(a) acquitting the innocent and convicting the guilty;

(b) treating all participants with politeness and respect;

(c) dealing with the prosecution and the defence fairly;

(d) recognising the rights of a defendant, particularly those under Article 6 of the European Convention on Human Rights;

(e) respecting the interests of witnesses, victims and jurors and keeping them informed of the progress of the case;

(f) dealing with the case efficiently and expeditiously;

(g) ensuring that appropriate information is available to the court when bail and sentence are considered; and

(h) dealing with the case in ways that take into account—
  (i) the gravity of the offence alleged,
  (ii) the complexity of what is in issue,
  (iii) the severity of the consequences for the defendant and others affected, and
  (iv) the needs of other cases.

[This rule is printed as amended, with effect from 8 February 2021, by SI 2021/40, r.5]

The duty of the participants in a criminal case

1.2.—(1) Each participant, in the conduct of each case, must—
(a) prepare and conduct the case in accordance with the overriding objective;
(b) comply with these Rules, practice directions and directions made by the court; and
(c) at once inform the court and all parties of any significant failure (whether or not that participant is responsible for that failure) to take any procedural step required by these Rules, any practice direction or any direction of the court. A failure is significant if it might hinder the court in furthering the overriding objective.

(2) Anyone involved in any way with a criminal case is a participant in its conduct for the purposes of this rule.

The application by the court of the overriding objective

1.3. The court must further the overriding objective in particular when—
(a) exercising any power given to it by legislation (including these rules);
(b) applying any practice direction; or
(c) interpreting any rule or practice direction.

CPD I General Matters A

B-2 **A.1** The Lord Chief Justice has power, including power under section 74 of the Courts Act 2003 and Part 1 of Schedule 2 to the Constitutional Reform Act 2005, to give directions as to the practice and procedure of the criminal courts. The following directions are given accordingly.

A.2 These practice directions replace the *Criminal Practice Directions* given on 7th October, 2013 [2013] EWCA Crim. 1631; [2013] 1 W.L.R. 3164 as amended by the directions given on (i) 10th December, 2013 [2013] EWCA Crim. 2328; [2014] 1 W.L.R. 35, (ii) 23rd July, 2014 [2014] EWCA Crim. 1569; [2014] 1 W.L.R. 3001, (iii) 18th March, 2015 [2015] EWCA Crim. 430; [2015] 1 W.L.R. 1643 and (iv) 16th July, 2015 [2015] EWCA Crim. 1253; [2015] 1 W.L.R. 3582.

A.3 Annexes D and E to the *Consolidated Criminal Practice Direction* of 8th July, 2002, [2002] 1 W.L.R. 2870; [2002] 2 Cr. App. R. 35, as amended, which set out forms for use in connection with the Criminal Procedure Rules, remain in force. See also para. I 5A of these practice directions.

A.4 These practice directions supplement many, but not all, parts of the Criminal Procedure Rules, and include other directions about practice and procedure in the courts to which they apply. They are to be known as the *Criminal Practice Directions* 2015. They come into force on 5th October, 2015. They apply to all cases in all the criminal courts of England and Wales from that date.

A.5 Consequent on the rearrangement of the Criminal Procedure Rules in the Criminal Procedure Rules 2015, S.I. 2015/1490:
(a) the content of these practice directions is arranged to correspond; within each division of these directions the paragraphs are numbered to correspond with the associated part of the *Criminal Procedure Rules* 2015; compared with the criminal practice directions given in 2013, as amended, the numbering and content of some divisions is amended consequentially, as shown in this table:

Derivations	
Divisions of 2015 Directions	*Divisions of 2013 Directions*
I General matters	I General matters; II Preliminary proceedings 16A - C
II Preliminary proceedings	II Preliminary proceedings 9A, 10A, 14A - B
III Custody and bail	III Custody and bail
IV Disclosure	IV Disclosure
V Evidence	V Evidence
VI Trial	VI Trial
VII Sentencing	VII Sentencing

Derivations	
VIII Confiscation and related proceedings [empty]	VIII Confiscation and related proceedings [empty]
IX Appeal	X Appeal
X Costs [Criminal Costs Practice Direction]	XI Costs [Criminal Costs Practice Direction]
XI Other proceedings	II Preliminary proceedings 6A, 17A - F; IX Contempt of court
XII General application	XII General application
XIII Listing	XIII Listing

(b) the text of these practice directions is amended:

(i) to bring up to date the cross-references to the Criminal Procedure Rules and to other paragraphs of these directions which that text contains, and

(ii) to adopt the abbreviation of references to the Criminal Procedure Rules ("CrimPR") for which rule 2.3(2) of the Criminal Procedure Rules 2015 provides.

A.6 In all other respects, the content of the *Criminal Practice Directions* 2015 reproduces that of the *Criminal Practice Directions* 2013, as amended.

CPD I General Matters 1A: The overriding objective

1A.1 The presumption of innocence and an adversarial process are essential features of English and Welsh legal tradition and of the defendant's right to a fair trial. But it is no part of a fair trial that questions of guilt and innocence should be determined by procedural manoeuvres. On the contrary, fairness is best served when the issues between the parties are identified as early and as clearly as possible. As Lord Justice Auld noted, a criminal trial is not a game under which a guilty defendant should be provided with a sporting chance. It is a search for truth in accordance with the twin principles that the prosecution must prove its case and that a defendant is not obliged to inculpate himself, the object being to convict the guilty and acquit the innocent. **B-3**

1A.2 Further, it is not just for a party to obstruct or delay the preparation of a case for trial in order to secure some perceived procedural advantage, or to take unfair advantage of a mistake by someone else. If courts allow that to happen it damages public confidence in criminal justice. The rules and the practice directions, taken together, make it clear that courts must not allow it to happen.

1A.3 The Criminal Procedure Rules and the Criminal Practice Directions are the law. Together they provide a code of current practice that is binding on the courts to which they are directed, and which promotes the consistent administration of justice. Participants must comply with the Rules and Practice Direction, and directions made by the court, and so it is the responsibility of the courts and those who participate in cases to be familiar with, and to ensure that these provisions are complied with.

Criminal Procedure Rules 2020 (SI 2020/759), Pt 2

Understanding and Applying the Rules and Powers of Authorised Court Officers

When the Rules apply

2.1.—(1) In general, Criminal Procedure Rules apply— **★B-4**

(a) in all criminal cases in magistrates' courts and in the Crown Court;

(b) in extradition cases in the High Court; and

(c) in all cases in the criminal division of the Court of Appeal.

(2) If a rule applies only in one or some of those courts, the rule makes that clear.

(3) These Rules apply on and after 5th October, 2020, but unless the court otherwise directs, they do not affect a right or duty existing under the Criminal Procedure Rules 2015.

(4) The following rules temporarily have effect as described beneath, subject to paragraphs (5) and (6) of this rule—

(a) in this Part, rules 2.2 (Definitions), 2.7 (Exercise of functions of the Crown Court) and 2.8 (Exercise of functions of a magistrates' court) as if they were amended by rule 5 of the Criminal Procedure (Amendment No. 2) (Coronavirus) Rules 2020 ('the Coronavirus Rules');

(b) in Part 3 (Case management)—

(i) rules 3.2 (The duty of the court), 3.3 (The duty of the parties) and 3.5 (The court's case management powers) as if they were amended by rule 6(a), (b) and (c) respectively of the Coronavirus Rules,

(ii) rule 3.8 (Case preparation and progression) as if it were amended by rule 6(d) of the Coronavirus Rules (which amended rule 3.9 of the Criminal Procedure Rules 2015), and

(iii) rule 3.10 (Directions for commissioning medical reports, other than for sentencing purposes) as if it were amended by rule 6(e) of the Coronavirus Rules (which amended rule 3.28 of the Criminal Procedure Rules 2015);

(c) in Part 5 (Forms and court records), rule 5.4 (Duty to make records) as if it were amended by rule 7 of the Coronavirus Rules;

(d) in Part 14 (Bail and custody time limits), rule 14.18 (Exercise of court's powers: extension of live link bail) as if it were amended by rule 8 of the Coronavirus Rules;

(e) in Part 18 (Measures to assist a witness or defendant to give evidence)—

(i) the heading to the Part as if it were amended by rule 9(a) of the Coronavirus Rules,

(ii) rules 18.1 (When this Part applies), 18.2 (Meaning of 'witness'), 18.4 (Decisions and reasons), 18.23 (Exercise of court's powers), 18.24 (Content of application for a live link direction), 18.25 (Application to discharge a live link direction, etc.) and 18.26 (Representations in response) as if they were amended by rule 9(b) to (h) respectively of the Coronavirus Rules, and

(iii) the note at the end of the Part as if it were amended by rule 9(i) of the Coronavirus Rules;

(f) in Part 24 (Trial and sentence in a magistrates' court), rule 24.11 (Procedure if the court convicts) as if it were amended by rule 10 of the Coronavirus Rules;

(g) in Part 25 (Trial and sentence in the Crown Court), rule 25.16 (Procedure if the court convicts) as if it were amended by rule 11 of the Coronavirus Rules;

(h) in Part 28 (Sentencing procedures in special cases), rule 28.8 (Directions for commissioning medical reports for sentencing purposes) as if it were amended by rule 12 of the Coronavirus Rules;

(i) in Part 47 (Investigation orders and warrants) the rules listed in rule 13 of the Coronavirus Rules as if they were amended by that rule; and

(j) in Part 50 (Extradition), rules 50.3 (Exercise of magistrates' court's powers) and 50.17 (Exercise of High Court's powers) as if they were amended by rule 14 of the Coronavirus Rules.

(5) The temporary amendments to rules 3.10 (Directions for commissioning medical reports, other than for sentencing purposes) and 28.8 (Directions for commissioning medical reports for sentencing purposes) to which paragraph (4) of this rule refers cease to have effect when paragraph 6 of Schedule 8 to the Coronavirus Act 2020 expires.

(6) The other temporary amendments to which paragraph (4) of this rule refers cease to have effect when section 53 (and Schedule 23), section 54 (and Schedule 24) and section 55 (and Schedule 25) of the Coronavirus Act 2020 expire.

[This rule is printed as amended, with effect from 8 February 2021, by SI 2021/40, r.30(a). The modifications are also subjected to further modifications by r.10 of SI 2021/40 the effect of which are reproduced where relevant.]

Definitions

B-5 **2.2.**—(1) In these rules, unless the context makes it clear that something different is meant:

"advocate" means a person who is entitled to exercise a right of audience in the court under section 13 of the Legal Services Act 2007;

"authorised court officer" has the meaning given by rule 2.4

;

"business day" means any day except Saturday, Sunday, Christmas Day, Boxing Day, Good Friday, Easter Monday or a bank holiday;

"court" means a tribunal with jurisdiction over criminal cases. It includes a judge, recorder, District Judge (Magistrates' Court), lay justice and, when exercising their judicial powers, the Registrar of Criminal Appeals, and an authorised court officer;

"court officer" means the appropriate member of the staff of a court;

"justices' legal adviser" means a person authorised under section 28 of the Courts Act 2003 to give advice about law to justices' of the peace;

"legal representative" means:

(i) the person for the time being named as a party's representative in any legal aid representation order made under section 16 of the Legal Aid, Sentencing and Punishment Offenders Act 2012 [§ 6-120 in the main work], or

(ii) subject to that, the person named as a party's representative in any notice for the time being given under rule 46.2 (notice of appointment, etc. of legal representative: general rules), provided that person is entitled to conduct litigation in the court under section 13 of the Legal Services Act 2007;

"live link" means an arrangement by which a person can see and hear, and be seen and heard by, the court when that person is not in the courtroom;

['live link' means a live video link or a live audio link and:

(i) 'live video link' means a live television link or other arrangement by which a person taking part in a hearing can see and hear, and be seen and heard by, everyone else who is taking part and who is not in the same place as that person,

(ii) 'live audio link' means a live telephone link or other arrangement by which a person taking part in a hearing can hear, and be heard by, everyone else who is taking part and who is not in the same place as that person;]

"Practice Direction" means the Lord Chief Justice's Criminal Practice Directions, as amended, and "Criminal Costs Practice Direction" means the Lord Chief Justice's Practice Direction (Costs in Criminal Proceedings), as amended;

"public interest ruling" means a ruling about whether it is in the public interest to disclose prosecution material under sections 3(6), 7A(8) or 8(5) of the Criminal Procedure and Investigations Act 1996 [ibid., §§ 12-58, 12-74, 12-76]; and

"Registrar" means the Registrar of Criminal Appeals or a court officer exercising a function of the Registrar.

(2) Definitions of some other expressions are in the rules in which they apply.

[This rule is also subject to temporary modification by r.5(a) of the Criminal Procedure (Amendment No. 2) (Coronavirus) Rules 2020 (SI 2020/417) - the insertion of the text in square brackets and omission of the italicised text. These temporary modifications cease when ss.53, 54 and 55 (and Schs. 23, 24 and 25) of the Coronavirus Act 2020 expire.]

References to legislation, including these rules

2.3.–(1) In these rules, where a rule refers to an Act of Parliament or to subordinate legislation by title and year, subsequent references to that Act or to that legislation in the rule are shortened: so, for example, after a reference to the Criminal Procedure and Investigations Act 1996 that Act is called "the 1996 Act"; and after a reference to the Criminal Procedure and Investigations Act 1996 (Defence Disclosure Time Limits) Regulations 2011 those Regulations are called "the 2011 Regulations". **B-6**

(2) In the courts in which these rules apply–

(a) unless the context makes it clear that something different is meant, a reference to the Criminal Procedure Rules, without reference to a year, is a reference to the Criminal Procedure Rules in force at the date on which the event concerned occurs or occurred;

(b) a reference to the Criminal Procedure Rules may be abbreviated to "CrimPR"; and

(c) a reference to a Part or rule in the Criminal Procedure Rules may be abbreviated to, for example, "CrimPR Part 3" or "CrimPR 3.5".

Exercise of court's functions by authorised court officers: general rules

2.4.–(1) This rule and rules 2.5, 2.6, 2.7, 2.8 and 2.9 provide for the exercise of relevant judicial functions within the meaning of section 67A of the Courts Act 2003– **B-7**

(a) in a court in which these Rules apply; and

(b) by a person authorised for the purpose by the Lord Chief Justice under section 67B of that Act.

(2) In this rule and in rules 2.5, 2.6, 2.7, 2.8 and 2.9–

(a) "authorised court officer" means any such person; and

(b) a reference to an authorised court officer who is legally qualified is a reference to one who has such qualifications as are for the time being prescribed by regulations made under section 28(3) of the Courts Act 2003.

(3) No court officer may–

(a) authorise a person's committal to prison;

(b) authorise a person's arrest (but that exclusion does not apply to the issue of a warrant of arrest, whether or not endorsed for bail, to secure that a person attends court proceedings relating to an offence of which the person has been accused or convicted in a case in which no objection is made by or on behalf of that person to the issue of the warrant);

(c) grant or withhold bail, except to the extent that rule 2.6 or rule 2.8 allows;
(d) adjudicate on guilt, or on the act or omission with which a defendant is charged, except to the extent of—
  (i) acquitting a defendant against whom the prosecutor offers no evidence,
  (ii) convicting a defendant who pleads guilty, or
  (iii) giving a prosecutor permission to withdraw a case;
(e) determine the admissibility of evidence;
(f) set ground rules for the conduct of questioning where rule 3.8(6), (7) (directions for the appropriate treatment and questioning of a witness or the defendant) applies;
(g) make findings of fact for the purpose of sentence, defer or pass sentence, impose a penalty or commit a defendant to the Crown Court for sentence;
(h) make an order for a party or other person to pay costs, unless that party or person agrees;
(i) make any other order consequent upon acquittal, conviction or a finding that the accused did the act or made the omission charged, except to the extent that rule 2.8 allows;
(j) vary, discharge, remit, remove, revoke, review or suspend a sentence, penalty or other order consequent on acquittal or conviction, except to the extent that rule 2.8 allows;
(k) order the search, confiscation, restraint, detention or seizure of property except to the extent that rule 2.8 allows;
(l) determine an appeal or reference to an appeal court, or an application for permission to appeal or refer, except to the extent that rule 2.6 allows; or
(m) determine an allegation of contempt of court.

(4) An authorised court officer may exercise a relevant judicial function for which rule 2.5, 2.6, 2.7, 2.8 or 2.9 provides—
(a) only subject to the same conditions as apply to its exercise by the court or person whose function it is; and
(b) where a party affected by the exercise of that function is entitled to make representations before its exercise, only if each such party has had a reasonable opportunity to make such representations—
  (i) in writing, or
  (ii) at a hearing (whether or not that party in fact attends).

(5) Unless the context makes it clear that something different is meant, provision in rule 2.5, 2.6, 2.7, 2.8 or 2.9 permitting the exercise of a relevant judicial function by an authorised court officer includes a power to decline to exercise that function.

Exercise of functions of the Court of Appeal

B-8 **2.5.**—(1) This rule provides for the exercise by an authorised court officer of relevant judicial functions of—
(a) the criminal division of the Court of Appeal; and
(b) the Registrar of Criminal Appeals.

(2) Subject to rule 2.4, an authorised court officer may exercise—
(a) any function of the criminal division of the Court of Appeal that may be exercised by the Registrar of Criminal Appeals; and
(b) any other judicial function of the Registrar.

(3) Where an authorised court officer exercises a function of the court—
(a) the same provision as that made by section 31A(4) or section 31C(3), as the case may be, of the Criminal Appeal Act 1968(4) applies as if that function had been exercised by the Registrar; and
(b) rule 36.5 (Renewing an application refused by a judge or the Registrar) applies.

Exercise of functions of the High Court

B-9 **2.6.**—(1) This rule provides for the exercise by an authorised court officer of relevant judicial functions of the High Court in relation to its jurisdiction under the Extradition Act 2003.

(2) An authorised court officer may exercise any such function of the High Court to which the rules in Section 3 of Part 50 apply (Extradition; Appeal to the High Court), subject to—
(a) rule 2.4; and
(b) paragraph (3) of this rule.

(3) No court officer may—
(a) grant or withhold bail;
(b) impose or vary a condition of bail; or

(c) reopen a decision which determines an appeal or an application for permission to appeal, unless paragraph (4) applies.

(4) If making a decision to which the parties have agreed in writing, an authorised court officer may–

(a) give or refuse permission to appeal;
(b) determine an appeal;
(c) grant or withhold bail; or
(d) impose or vary a condition of bail.

(5) Paragraph (6) of this rule–

(a) applies where a party wants a judge to reconsider a decision made by an authorised court officer; but
(b) does not apply where such an officer agrees to postpone the date on which the required period for extradition begins under section 36(3) of the Extradition Act 2003.

(6) Such a party must–

(a) apply for such a reconsideration as soon as reasonably practicable, and in any event no later than the earlier of–
 (i) the next hearing before a judge, or
 (ii) the fifth business day after the date on which notice of the decision is served on the applicant;
(b) unless the application is made at a hearing, serve the application on–
 (i) the court officer, and
 (ii) each other party (if any) affected by the decision; and
(c) in the application–
 (i) specify the decision in issue,
 (ii) explain why it is appropriate for the decision to be reconsidered and what decision the applicant thinks would be appropriate, and
 (iii) ask for a hearing, if one is wanted, and explain why it is needed.

(7) The judge may determine the application–

(a) at a hearing (which may be in public or private), or without a hearing and
(b) in the absence of–
 (i) the applicant,
 (ii) each other party (if any) affected by the decision.

(8) But the judge must not determine the application in the absence of an affected party unless that party has had–

(a) such notice as the nature and urgency of the application permits; and
(b) a reasonable opportunity to make representations.

Exercise of functions of the Crown Court

2.7.–(1) This rule provides for the exercise by an authorised court officer of relevant judicial functions of the Crown Court in a criminal cause or matter. **B-10**

(2) Subject to rule 2.4 and to paragraph (3) of this rule, an authorised court officer may–

(a) determine an application to extend a time limit set by a rule or by a judge, including a time limit for the conduct of confiscation proceedings, unless the effect would be–
 (i) to affect the date of any hearing that has been fixed, including a trial, or
 (ii) significantly to affect the progress of the case in any other way;
(b) give a live link direction under section 57B, 57E or 57F of the Crime and Disorder Act 1998 *(Use of live link at preliminary hearings where accused is in custody; Use of live link in sentencing hearings; Use of live link in certain enforcement hearings)* [(Use of live link at preliminary hearings; Use of live link in sentencing hearings; Use of live link in enforcement hearings)]; and
(c) exercise the court's functions listed in rule 23.2 (Appointment of advocate to cross-examine witness) and select such an advocate as that rule describes (but a court officer may not decline to select such an advocate where that rule applies).

(3) An authorised court officer may not exercise a function of the court in a case in which a judge so directs.

(4) Paragraph (5) of this rule applies where a party or an advocate appointed under rule 23.2 (Appointment of advocate to cross-examine witness) wants a judge to reconsider a decision made by an authorised court officer.

(5) Such a party or advocate must–

(a) apply for such a reconsideration as soon as reasonably practicable, and in any event no later than the earlier of—
  (i) the next hearing before a judge, or
  (ii) the tenth business day after the date on which notice of the decision is served on the applicant;
(b) unless the application is made at a hearing, serve the application on—
  (i) the court officer, and
  (ii) each other party (if any) affected by the decision; and
(c) in the application—
  (i) specify the decision in issue,
  (ii) explain why it is appropriate for the decision to be reconsidered and what decision the applicant thinks would be appropriate, and
  (iii) ask for a hearing, if one is wanted, and explain why it is needed.

(6) The judge may determine the application—
(a) at a hearing (which may be in public or private), or without a hearing;
(b) in the absence of—
  (i) the applicant,
  (ii) each other party (if any) affected by the decision.

(7) But the judge must not determine the application in the absence of an affected party unless that party has had—
(a) such notice as the nature and urgency of the application permits; and
(b) a reasonable opportunity to make representations.

[This rule is also subject to temporary modification by virtue of r.5(b) of the Criminal Procedure (Amendment No. 2) (Coronavirus) Rules 2020 (SI 2020/417) - the insertion of the text in square brackets and omission of the italicised text. These temporary modifications cease when ss.53, 54 and 55 (and Schs. 23, 24 and 25) of the Coronavirus Act 2020 expire.]

Exercise of functions of a magistrates' court

B-11 **2.8.**—(1) This rule provides for the exercise by an authorised court officer of relevant judicial functions of a magistrates' court in a criminal cause or matter.

(2) Subject to rule 2.4 and to paragraph (12) of this rule, an authorised court officer may—
(a) fix, cancel or vary the date, time or place for a hearing, including a trial, or adjourn a hearing;
(b) adjourn, remit or transfer proceedings from one local justice area to another;
(c) determine an application to extend a time limit set by a rule or by the court, unless the effect would be—
  (i) to affect the date of any hearing that has been fixed, including a trial, or
  (ii) significantly to affect the progress of the case in any other way;
(d) issue a summons at the request of a public prosecutor, or under section 16B of the Magistrates' Courts Act 1980 (Cases not tried in accordance with section 16A) or section 83 of that Act (Process for securing attendance of offender);
(e) give a prosecutor permission to withdraw a case;
(f) grant bail where the defendant already is on bail and—
  (i) the conditions, if any, to which that bail is subject will remain the same, or
  (ii) bail conditions will be varied or imposed with both parties' agreement;
(g) give consent for another magistrates' court to deal with a defendant for an offence in respect of which the defendant, when an adult, was discharged conditionally;
(h) order a convicted defendant to produce his or her driving licence;
(i) require a statement of the defendant's assets and other financial circumstances;
(j) amend an attendance centre order to—
  (i) vary the day or hour specified in that order for the defendant's first attendance, or
  (ii) substitute an alternative centre;
(k) amend the local justice area or responsible officer named in an order of the court;
(l) amend a sentence or order by requiring it to be completed in Northern Ireland or Scotland;
(m) extend the time for service of a statutory declaration to which applies—
  (i) rule 44.2 (Statutory declaration of ignorance of proceedings), or
  (ii) rule 29.4 (Statutory declaration to avoid fine after fixed penalty notice);
(n) fix a later time at which a defendant must attend court for the purposes of an enquiry or

hearing under section 82 of the Magistrates' Courts Act 1980 (Restriction on power to impose imprisonment for default);

(o) conduct a means enquiry;

(p) make a collection order;

(q) issue a warrant of control;

(r) extend the time for payment of a fine or sum to which Part 30 (Enforcement of fines and other orders for payment) applies;

(s) vary an order for the payment by instalments of such a fine or sum;

(t) make a transfer of fine order;

(u) make a disclosure order under section 125CA Magistrates' Courts Act 1980 (Power to make disclosure order) for the purposes of securing the execution of a warrant;

(v) make an attachment of earnings order;

(w) make or withdraw an application for deductions to be made from a defendant's benefit payments; and

(x) take any step listed in paragraph 38 of Schedule 5 to the Courts Act 2003 (range of further steps available against defaulters).

(3) In addition to the functions listed in paragraph (2), subject to rule 2.4 and to paragraph (12) of this rule an authorised court officer who is legally qualified may exercise the other functions of a magistrates' court listed in paragraphs (4) to (11).

(4) In connection with the rules about general matters (Parts 1 to 6)—

(a) exercising the powers to which section 50 of the Crime and Disorder Act 1998 (Early administrative hearings) refers, where that section applies and subject to the restrictions that it contains;

(b) giving, varying or revoking a live link direction under Part IIIA of the Crime and Disorder Act 1998 *(Live links for accused's attendance at certain preliminary, sentencing and other hearings)* [(Live links in preliminary, sentencing and enforcement hearings)];

(c) determining an application to extend a time limit set by a rule or by the court;

(d) giving, varying or revoking an order for separate or joint trials in respect of two or more defendants or two or more offences, if all parties agree;

(e) giving, varying or revoking directions for the conduct of proceedings, including—

(i) the timetable for the case,

(ii) the attendance of the parties,

(iii) the service of documents (including summaries of any legal arguments relied on by the parties),

(iv) the manner in which evidence is to be given, insofar as this rule makes no other provision and except the making, varying or revocation of a witness anonymity order;

(f) determining an application under rule 5.7(5) (supply to a party of information or documents from records or case materials; information to which paragraph (4) of that rule does not apply) where—

(i) rule 5.7(6) applies (information about the grounds on which an order was made, or a warrant was issued, in the absence of the party or person applying for that information), and

(ii) no notice of objection under that paragraph is given within the time for which that paragraph provides;

(g) imposing a reporting restriction under section 45 of the Youth Justice and Criminal Evidence Act 1999 (identity of a person under 18) where there is no objection to the order;

(h) giving permission for proceedings to be recorded; and

(i) asking a court security officer to remove a person from a courtroom.

(5) In connection with the rules about preliminary proceedings (Parts 7 to 12)—

(a) issuing a summons and giving directions for service;

(b) under section 4 of the Summary Jurisdiction (Process) Act 1881, endorsing a summons or warrant issued by a court in Scotland;

(c) giving a prosecutor permission to withdraw a charge;

(d) dismissing a prosecution where the prosecutor offers no evidence;

(e) amending a charge; and

(f) sending a defendant to the Crown Court for trial where the only condition for sending is—

(i) that prescribed by section 51(2)(a), of the Crime and Disorder Act 1998 (offence triable only on indictment other than one in respect of which notice is given under section 51B or 51C of that Act), or

(ii) the service of a notice under section 51B or 51C of that Act (prosecutor's notice requiring sending for trial in a case of serious or complex fraud or a case in which a child is to be called as a witness).

(6) In connection with the rules about custody and bail (Parts 13 and 14)—

(a) issuing or withdrawing a warrant for a person's arrest to secure that the person attends court proceedings relating to an offence of which the person has been accused or convicted in a case in which no objection is made by or on behalf of that person to the issue of the warrant; and

(b) granting bail where—

(i) the defendant is present,

(ii) the prosecutor agrees to the grant of bail, and

(iii) the conditions, if any, to which that bail will be subject will remain the same as before, or will be varied or imposed with the parties' agreement.

(7) In connection with the rules about evidence (Parts 16 to 23)—

(a) requiring a person who has made a written statement to attend before the court to give evidence;

(b) issuing a witness summons and giving directions for its service; and

(c) exercising the court's functions listed in rule 23.2 (Appointment of advocate to cross-examine witness) and appointing such an advocate as that rule describes (but a court officer may not decline to appoint such an advocate where that rule applies).

(8) In connection with the rules about trial (Parts 24 to 27)—

(a) convicting a defendant who has pleaded guilty;

(b) requesting a pre-sentence report where a defendant pleads guilty; and

(c) directing the commissioning of a medical report.

(9) In connection with the rules about appeal (Parts 34 to 44)—

(a) stating a case for the opinion of the High Court where the decision under appeal was made by an authorised court officer; and

(b) requiring the appellant to enter into a recognizance under section 114 of the Magistrates' Courts Act 1980 on an application to state a case for the opinion of the High Court.

(10) In connection with the rules about costs (Part 45)—

(a) making or varying an order for a party to pay costs, if both parties agree;

(b) making or varying an order for another person to pay costs, if that person agrees; and

(c) making a costs order to which rule 45.4 (Costs out of central funds) applies.

(11) In connection with the rules about other proceedings (Parts 46 to 50)—

(a) making a legal aid representation order on an appeal against a refusal of legal aid (but a court officer may not decline to make such an order); and

(b) determining an application for a change of legal representative.

(12) An authorised court officer who is not a justices' legal adviser may not exercise a function of the court in a case in which a District Judge (Magistrates' Courts), a lay justice or a justices' legal adviser so directs.

[This rule is subject to temporary modification by virtue of r.5(c) the Criminal Procedure (Amendment No. 2) (Coronavirus) Rules 2020 (SI 2020/417) - the insertion of the text in square brackets and omission of the italicised text. These temporary modifications cease when ss.53, 54 and 55 (and Schs. 23, 24 and 25) of the Coronavirus Act 2020 expire.]

Exercise of functions of a District Judge (Magistrates' Courts) in extradition cases

B-12 **2.9.**—(1) This rule provides for the exercise by an authorised court officer of relevant judicial functions of a District Judge (Magistrates' Courts) in a case to which Part 50 (Extradition) applies.

(2) Subject to rule 2.4, an authorised court officer who is legally qualified may—

(a) fix, cancel or vary the date, time or place for a hearing, including an extradition hearing;

(b) determine an application to extend a time limit set by a rule or by the court, unless the effect would be—

(i) to affect the date of any hearing that has been fixed, including an extradition hearing, or

(ii) significantly to affect the progress of the case in any other way.

(3) An authorised court officer who is not a justices' legal adviser may not exercise a function of the court in a case in which a District Judge (Magistrates' Courts) or a justices' legal adviser so directs.

Court's power to extend time under rule 2.6 or rule 2.7

B-13 **2.10.**—(1) The court may extend (even after it has expired) a time limit under rule 2.6 (Exercise of functions of the High Court) or rule 2.7 (Exercise of functions of the Crown Court).

(2) A party who wants an extension of time must–

(a) apply when serving the application for which it is needed; and

(b) explain the delay.

Criminal Procedure Rules 2020 (SI 2020/759), Pt 3

Case Management

General rules

When this Part applies

3.1.–(1) Rules 3.1 to 3.15 apply to the management of each case in a magistrates' court and in the Crown Court (including an appeal to the Crown Court) until the conclusion of that case. ★B-14

(1) Rules 3.16 to 3.18 apply in a magistrates' court unless–

(a) the court sends the defendant for trial in the Crown Court; or

(b) the case is one to which rule 24.8 or rule 24.9 applies (Written guilty plea: special rules; Single justice procedure: special rules).

(2) Rules 3.19 to 3.34 apply where–

(a) the defendant is sent to the Crown Court for trial;

(b) a High Court or Crown Court judge gives permission to serve a draft indictment; or

(c) the Court of Appeal orders a retrial.

The duty of the court

3.2–(1) The court must further the overriding objective by actively managing the case.

(2) Active case management includes–

(a) the early identification of the real issues;

(b) the early identification of the needs of witnesses;

(c) achieving certainty as to what must be done, by whom, and when, in particular by the early setting of a timetable for the progress of the case;

(d) monitoring the progress of the case and compliance with directions;

(e) ensuring that evidence, whether disputed or not, is presented in the shortest and clearest way;

(f) discouraging delay, dealing with as many aspects of the case as possible on the same occasion, and avoiding unnecessary hearings;

(g) encouraging the participants to co-operate in the progression of the case; and

(h) making use of technology.

(3) The court must actively manage the case by giving any direction appropriate to the needs of that case as early as possible.

[(4) Where appropriate live links are available, making use of technology for the purposes of this rule includes giving a live link direction–

(a) for the conduct of any hearing by live link under a power to which the rules in Part 18 apply (Measures to help a person give evidence or otherwise participate); and

(b) whether an application for such a direction is made or not.]

(4) Where appropriate live links are available, making use of technology for the purposes of this rule includes directing the use of such facilities, whether an application for such a direction is made or not–

(a) for the conduct of a pre-trial hearing, including a pre-trial case management hearing;

(b) for the defendant's attendance at such a hearing–

where the defendant is in custody, or where the defendant is not in custody and wants to attend by live link, but

only if the court is satisfied that the defendant can participate effectively by such means, having regard to all the circumstances including whether the defendant is represented or not; and

(c) for receiving evidence under one of the powers to which the rules in Part 18 apply (Measures to assist a witness or defendant to give evidence).

(5) Where appropriate telephone facilities are available, making use of technology for the purposes of this rule includes directing the use of such facilities, whether an application for such a direction is made or not, for the conduct of a pre-trial case management hearing–

(a) if telephone facilities are more convenient for that purpose than live links;

(b) unless at that hearing the court expects to take the defendant's plea; and

(c) only if–

the defendant is represented, or
exceptionally, the court is satisfied that the defendant can participate effectively by such means without a representative.

[This rule is subject to temporary modification by r.6(a) of the Criminal Procedure (Amendment No.2) (Coronavirus) Rules 2020 (SI 2020/417) - insertion of text in square brackets and omission of italicised text. These temporary modifications cease when ss.53, 54 and 55 (and Schs. 23, 24 and 25) of the Coronavirus Act 2020 expire.]

The duty of the parties

3.3—(1) Each party must—
- (a) actively assist the court in fulfilling its duty under rule 3.2, without or if necessary with a direction; and
- (b) apply for a direction if needed to further the overriding objective.

(2) Active assistance for the purposes of this rule includes—
- (a) at the beginning of the case, communication between the prosecutor and the defendant at the first available opportunity and in any event no later than the beginning of the day of the first hearing;
- (b) after that, communication between the parties and with the court officer until the conclusion of the case;
- (c) by such communication establishing, among other things—
  - (i) whether the defendant is likely to plead guilty or not guilty,
  - (ii) what is agreed and what is likely to be disputed,
  - (iii) what information, or other material, is required by one party of another, and why, and
  - (iv) what is to be done, by whom, and when (without or if necessary with a direction);
- (d) reporting on that communication to the court—
  - (i) at the first hearing, and
  - (ii) after that, as directed by the court;
- (e) alerting the court to any reason why—
  - (i) a direction should not be made in any of the circumstances listed in rule 3.2(4) or (5) (The duty of the court: use of live link *or telephone* facilities), or
  - (ii) such a direction should be varied or revoked.
- (f) alerting the court to any potential impediment to the defendant's effective participation in the trial; and
- (g) alerting the court to any related family proceedings or anticipated such proceedings as soon as reasonably practicable after becoming aware of them.

[This rule is subject to temporary modification by r.6(b) of the Criminal Procedure (Amendment No.2) (Coronavirus) Rules 2020 (SI 2020/417) - omission of italicised text. These temporary modifications cease when ss.53, 54 and 55 (and Schs. 23, 24 and 25) of the Coronavirus Act 2020 expire. The rule is also printed as amended, with effect from 8 February 2021, by SI 2021/40, r.6(a).]

Case progression officers and their duties

3.4—(1) At the beginning of the case each party must, unless the court otherwise directs—
- (a) nominate someone responsible for progressing that case; and
- (b) tell other parties and the court who that is and how to contact that person.

(2) In fulfilling its duty under rule 3.2, the court must where appropriate—
- (a) nominate a court officer responsible for progressing the case; and
- (b) make sure the parties know who that is and how to contact that court officer.

(3) In this Part a person nominated under this rule is called a case progression officer.

(4) A case progression officer must—
- (a) monitor compliance with directions;
- (b) make sure that the court is kept informed of events that may affect the progress of that case;
- (c) make sure that he or she can be contacted promptly about the case during ordinary business hours;
- (d) act promptly and reasonably in response to communications about the case; and
- (e) if he or she will be unavailable, appoint a substitute to fulfil his or her duties and inform the other case progression officers.

The court's case management powers

★B-15 **3.5**—(1) In fulfilling its duty under rule 3.2 the court may give any direction and take any step actively to manage a case unless that direction or step would be inconsistent with legislation, including these Rules.

(2) In particular, the court may–

(a) nominate a judge, magistrate or justices' legal adviser to manage the case;

(b) give a direction on its own initiative or on application by a party;

(c) ask or allow a party to propose a direction;

[(d) receive applications, notices, representations and information by letter, by live link, by email or by any other means of electronic communication, and conduct a hearing by live link or other such electronic means;]

(d) receive applications, notices, representations and information by letter, by telephone, by live link, by email or by any other means of electronic communication, and conduct a hearing by live link, telephone or other such electronic means;

(e) give a direction–

(i) at a hearing, in public or in private, or

(ii) without a hearing;

(f) fix, postpone, bring forward, extend, cancel or adjourn a hearing;

(g) shorten or extend (even after it has expired) a time limit fixed by a direction;

(h) require that issues in the case should be–

(i) identified in writing,

(ii) determined separately, and decide in what order they will be determined;

(i) specify the consequences of failing to comply with a direction.

(j) request information from a court dealing with family proceedings by–

(i) making the request itself, or

(ii) directing the court officer or a party to make the request on the criminal court's behalf; and

(k) supply information to a court dealing with family proceedings as if an application had been made under rule 5.8(7) (Supply to the public, including reporters, of information about cases) by–

(i) supplying the information itself, or

(ii) directing the court officer or a party to supply that information on the criminal court's behalf.

(3) A magistrates' court may give a direction that will apply in the Crown Court if the case is to continue there.

(4) The Crown Court may give a direction that will apply in a magistrates' court if the case is to continue there.

(5) Any power to give a direction under this Part includes a power to vary or revoke that direction.

(6) If a party fails to comply with a rule or a direction, the court may–

(a) fix, postpone, bring forward, extend, cancel or adjourn a hearing;

(b) exercise its powers to make a costs order; and

(c) impose such other sanction as may be appropriate.

[This rule is subject to temporary modification by r.6(c) of the Criminal Procedure (Amendment No.2) (Coronavirus) Rules 2020 (SI 2020/417) - insertion of text in square brackets and omission of italicised text. These temporary modifications cease when ss.53, 54 and 55 (and Schs. 23, 24 and 25) of the Coronavirus Act 2020 expire. It is also printed as amended, with effect from 8 February 2021, by SI 2021/40, r.6(b).]

Application to vary a direction

3.6–(1) A party may apply to vary a direction if–

(a) the court gave it without a hearing;

(b) the court gave it at a hearing in that party's absence; or

(c) circumstances have changed.

(2) A party who applies to vary a direction must–

(a) apply as soon as practicable after becoming aware of the grounds for doing so; and

(b) give as much notice to the other parties as the nature and urgency of the application permits.

Agreement to vary a time limit fixed by a direction

3.7–(1) The parties may agree to vary a time limit fixed by a direction, but only if–

(a) the variation will not–

affect the date of any hearing that has been fixed, or
significantly affect the progress of the case in any other way;

(b) the court has not prohibited variation by agreement; and

(c) the court's case progression officer is promptly informed.

(2) The court's case progression officer must refer the agreement to the court if in doubt that the condition in paragraph (1)(a) is satisfied.

Case preparation and progression

3.8—(1) At every hearing, if a case cannot be concluded there and then the court must give directions so that it can be concluded at the next hearing or as soon as possible after that.

(2) At every hearing the court must, where relevant—

(a) if the defendant is absent, decide whether to proceed nonetheless;

(b) take the defendant's plea (unless already done) or if no plea can be taken then find out whether the defendant is likely to plead guilty or not guilty;

(c) set, follow or revise a timetable for the progress of the case, which may include a timetable for any hearing including the trial or (in the Crown Court) the appeal;

(d) in giving directions, ensure continuity in relation to the court and to the parties' representatives where that is appropriate and practicable; and

(e) where a direction has not been complied with, find out why, identify who was responsible, and take appropriate action.

(3) In order to prepare for the trial, the court must take every reasonable step—

(a) to encourage and to facilitate the attendance of witnesses when they are needed; and

(b) to facilitate the participation of any person, including the defendant.

(4) Facilitating the participation of the defendant includes finding out whether the defendant needs interpretation because—

(a) the defendant does not speak or understand English; or

(b) the defendant has a hearing or speech disorder.

(5) Where the defendant needs interpretation—

(a) the court officer must arrange for interpretation to be provided at every hearing which the defendant is due to attend;

(b) interpretation may be by an intermediary where the defendant has a speech disorder, without the need for a defendant's evidence direction;

(c) on application or on its own initiative, the court may require a written translation to be provided for the defendant of any document or part of a document, unless—
translation of that document, or part, is not needed to explain the case against the defendant, or
the defendant agrees to do without and the court is satisfied that the agreement is clear and voluntary and that the defendant has had legal advice or otherwise understands the consequences; and

(d) on application by the defendant, the court must give any direction which the court thinks appropriate, including a direction for interpretation by a different interpreter, where—
no interpretation is provided,
no translation is ordered or provided in response to a previous application by the defendant, or
the defendant complains about the quality of interpretation or of any translation.

(6) Facilitating the participation of any person includes giving directions for the appropriate treatment and questioning of a witness or the defendant, especially where the court directs that such questioning is to be conducted through an intermediary.

(7) Where directions for appropriate treatment and questioning are required, the court must—

(a) invite representations by the parties and by any intermediary; and

(b) set ground rules for the conduct of the questioning, which rules may include—
a direction relieving a party of any duty to put that party's case to a witness or a defendant in its entirety,
directions about the manner of questioning,
directions about the duration of questioning,
if necessary, directions about the questions that may or may not be asked,
directions about the means by which any intermediary may intervene in questioning, if necessary,
where there is more than one defendant, the allocation among them of the topics about which a witness may be asked, and

directions about the use of models, plans, body maps or similar aids to help communicate a question or an answer.

[(8) Facilitating the participation of any person includes giving a live link direction under a power to which the rules in Part 18 apply (Measures to help a person give evidence or otherwise participate)—

(a) where appropriate live links are available;

(b) for a witness or the defendant to give evidence by live link, subject to the requirements listed in rule 18.23 (Exercise of court's powers) and in rule 18.24 (Content of application for a live link direction);

(c) for a person to attend a hearing by live link when not giving evidence, subject to those requirements; and

(d) whether an application for such a direction is made or not.]]

[This rule is subject to temporary modification by r.6(d) of the Criminal Procedure (Amendment No.2) (Coronavirus) Rules 2020 (SI 2020/417) - insertion of text in square brackets. These temporary modifications cease when ss.53, 54 and 55 (and Schs. 23, 24 and 25) of the Coronavirus Act 2020 expire.]

Ground rules hearing

3.9—(1) This rule applies where the court exercises the powers to which rule 3.8(6) and (7) apply (directions for appropriate treatment and questioning of a witness or defendant). **B-16**

(2) At a pre-trial case management hearing convened for the purpose—

(a) the parties and any intermediary must—
attend, unless the court otherwise directs, and
actively assist the court in setting ground rules and giving directions;

(b) the court must—
discuss proposed ground rules and directions with the parties and any intermediary,
set ground rules for the conduct of questioning of the witness or defendant, as applicable, and
give such other directions as may be required to facilitate the effective participation of that witness or defendant; and

(c) despite rule 3.14(b) (court officer's duty to make a record of directions), the court may require the parties—
to make a record of those ground rules and directions, and
to serve that record on each other, on any intermediary and on the court officer.

(3) In setting such ground rules and giving such directions, the court must have regard to—

(a) any intermediary's report;

(b) the parties' representations; and

(c) such other information or advice as the court requires.

(4) The ground rules for questioning set by the court may include any listed in rule 3.8(7)(b).

(5) The directions given by the court may include any about—

(a) the timetable for the submission of proposed questions;

(b) the timetable for the trial, including the taking of breaks during proceedings;

(c) seating arrangements in the court room for the defendant, the defendant's advocate and legal representative, any intermediary and any parent, guardian or other companion of the defendant; and

(d) any explanation to be given to the jury, if there is one, of—
the witness' or the defendant's communication needs and behaviour, as applicable, and
the role of the intermediary, if there is one.

Directions for commissioning medical reports, other than for sentencing purposes

3.10—(1) This rule applies where, because of a defendant's suspected mental ill-health—

(a) a magistrates' court requires expert medical opinion about the potential suitability of a hospital order under section 37(3) of the Mental Health Act 1983 (hospital order without convicting the defendant);

(b) the Crown Court requires expert medical opinion about the defendant's fitness to participate at trial, under section 4 of the Criminal Procedure (Insanity) Act 1964; or

(c) a magistrates' court or the Crown Court requires expert medical opinion to help the court determine a question of intent or insanity,

other than such opinion introduced by a party.

(2) A court may exercise the power to which this rule applies on its own initiative having regard to—

(a) an assessment of the defendant's health by a mental health practitioner acting independently of the parties to assist the court;
(b) representations by a party; or
(c) observations by the court.

(3) A court that requires expert medical opinion to which this rule applies must—
(a) identify each issue in respect of which the court requires such opinion and any legislation applicable;
(b) specify the nature of the expertise likely to be required for giving such opinion;
(c) identify each party or participant by whom a commission for such opinion must be prepared, who may be—
(i) a party (or party's representative) acting on that party's own behalf,
(ii) a party (or party's representative) acting on behalf of the court, or
(iii) the court officer acting on behalf of the court;
(d) where there are available to the court arrangements with the National Health Service under which an assessment of a defendant's mental health may be prepared, give such directions as are needed under those arrangements for obtaining the expert report or reports required;
(e) where no such arrangements are available to the court, or they will not be used, give directions for the commissioning of an expert report or expert reports, including—
(i) such directions as can be made about supplying the expert or experts with the defendant's medical records,
(ii) directions about the other information, about the defendant and about the offence or offences alleged to have been committed by the defendant, which is to be supplied to each expert, and
(iii) directions about the arrangements that will apply for the payment of each expert;
(f) set a timetable providing for—
(i) the date by which a commission is to be delivered to each expert,
(ii) the date by which any failure to accept a commission is to be reported to the court,
(iii) the date or dates by which progress in the preparation of a report or reports is to be reviewed by the court officer, and
(iv) the date by which each report commissioned is to be received by the court; and
(g) identify the person (each person, if more than one) to whom a copy of a report is to be supplied, and by whom.

(4) A commission addressed to an expert must—
(a) identify each issue in respect of which the court requires expert medical opinion and any legislation applicable;
(b) include—
(i) the information required by the court to be supplied to the expert,
(ii) details of the timetable set by the court, and
(iii) details of the arrangements that will apply for the payment of the expert;
(c) identify the person (each person, if more than one) to whom a copy of the expert's report is to be supplied; and
(d) request confirmation that the expert from whom the opinion is sought—
(i) accepts the commission, and
(ii) will adhere to the timetable.

Hearing to inform the court of sensitive material

B-17 **3.11**—(1) This rule applies where the prosecutor has, or is aware of, material—
(a) the revelation of which to the public or to the defendant the prosecutor thinks would give rise to a real risk of serious prejudice to an important public interest;
(b) to which the prosecutor does not think the obligation to disclose prosecution material applies, under Part I of the Criminal Procedure and Investigations Act 1996; but
(c) of the existence of which the prosecutor thinks it necessary to inform the court to avoid—
(i) potential unfairness to the defendant in the conduct of the trial,
(ii) potential prejudice to the fair management of the trial, or
(iii) potential prejudice to that public interest.

(2) Such a prosecutor must—
(a) ask for a hearing so to inform the court; and
(b) notify the defendant of that request only to such extent, if any, and at such time, if at all, as the court directs.

(3) At or before the hearing the prosecutor must–
(a) explain–
(i) why the hearing is necessary, and
(ii) why it is necessary for the hearing to take place in the defendant's absence;
(b) explain to what extent, if any, and when, if at all, the defendant should be informed–
(i) of the hearing, and
(ii) of the material of which the prosecutor wants to inform the court; and
(c) provide or describe the material to the court–
(i) only to the extent needed to achieve the purpose for which the hearing is convened, and
(ii) in such manner as the court directs.
(4) Unless the court otherwise directs–
(a) any such hearing–
(i) must be in private, and
(ii) must take place in the defendant's absence;
(b) the court officer must not give notice to anyone other than the prosecutor of–
(i) the court's decision on the request for a hearing,
(ii) the arrangements for any such hearing, and
(iii) any directions given at such a hearing; and
(c) the court officer may–
(i) keep any written representations or material received under this rule, or
(ii) arrange for the whole or any part to be kept by some other appropriate person, subject to any conditions that the court may impose.

Readiness for trial or appeal

3.12–(1) This rule applies to a party's preparation for trial or appeal, and in this rule and rule 3.13 'trial' includes any hearing at which evidence will be introduced. **B-18**
(2) In fulfilling the duty under rule 3.3, each party must–
(a) comply with directions given by the court;
(b) take every reasonable step to make sure that party's witnesses will attend when they are needed;
(c) make appropriate arrangements to present any written or other material; and
(d) promptly inform the court and the other parties of anything that may–
(i) affect the date or duration of the trial or appeal, or
(ii) significantly affect the progress of the case in any other way.
(3) The court may require a party to give a certificate of readiness.

Conduct of a trial or an appeal

3.13 In order to manage a trial or an appeal, the court– **B-19**
(a) must establish, with the active assistance of the parties, what are the disputed issues;
(b) must consider setting a timetable that–
(i) takes account of those issues and of any timetable proposed by a party, and
(ii) may limit the duration of any stage of the hearing;
(c) may require a party to identify–
(i) which witnesses that party wants to give evidence in person,
(ii) the order in which that party wants those witnesses to give their evidence,
(iii) whether that party requires an order compelling the attendance of a witness,
(iv) what arrangements are desirable to facilitate the giving of evidence by a witness,
(v) what arrangements are desirable to facilitate the participation of any other person, including the defendant,
(vi) what written evidence that party intends to introduce,
(vii) what other material, if any, that person intends to make available to the court in the presentation of the case, and
(viii) whether that party intends to raise any point of law that could affect the conduct of the trial or appeal; and
(d) may limit–
(i) the examination, cross-examination or re-examination of a witness, and
(ii) the duration of any stage of the hearing.

Duty of court officer

B-20 **3.14** The court officer must—

(a) where a person is entitled or required to attend a hearing, give as much notice as reasonably practicable to—

(i) that person, and

(ii) that person's custodian (if any); and

(b) where the court gives directions, promptly make a record available to the parties.

Court's power to vary requirements under this Part

3.15—(1) The court may—

(a) shorten or extend (even after it has expired) a time limit set by this Part; and

(b) allow an application or representations to be made orally.

(2) A person who wants an extension of time must—

(a) apply when serving the application or representations for which it is needed; and

(b) explain the delay.

Preparation for trial in a Magistrates' Court

Pre-trial hearings in a magistrates' court: general rules

★B-21 **3.16**—(1) A magistrates' court—

(a) must conduct a preparation for trial hearing unless—

(i) the court sends the defendant for trial in the Crown Court, or

(ii) the case is one to which rule 24.8 or rule 24.9 applies (Written guilty plea: special rules; Single justice procedure: special rules); and

(b) may conduct a further pre-trial case management hearing (and if necessary more than one such hearing) only where—

(i) the court anticipates a guilty plea,

(ii) it is necessary to conduct such a hearing in order to give directions for an effective trial, or

(iii) such a hearing is required to set ground rules for the conduct of the questioning of a witness or defendant.

(2) At a preparation for trial hearing the court must give directions for an effective trial.

(3) At a preparation for trial hearing, if the defendant is present the court must—

(a) satisfy itself that there has been explained to the defendant, in terms the defendant can understand (with help, if necessary), that the defendant will receive credit for a guilty plea;

(b) take the defendant's plea or if no plea can be taken then find out whether the defendant is likely to plead guilty or not guilty; and

(c) unless the defendant pleads guilty, satisfy itself that there has been explained to the defendant, in terms the defendant can understand (with help, if necessary), that at the trial—

(i) the defendant will have the right to give evidence after the court has heard the prosecution case,

(ii) if the defendant does not attend, the trial is likely to take place in the defendant's absence, and

(iii) where the defendant is released on bail, failure to attend court when required is an offence for which the defendant may be arrested and punished and bail may be withdrawn.

(4) A pre-trial case management hearing must be in public, as a general rule, but all or part of the hearing may be in private if the court so directs.

(5) The court—

(a) at the first hearing in the case must require a defendant who is present to provide, in writing or orally, his or her name and date of birth; and

(b) at any subsequent hearing may require such a defendant to provide that information by those means.

[This rule is printed as amended, with effect from 8 February 2021, by SI 2021/40, r.6(d).]

Place of magistrates' court trial

3.17 The court officer must arrange for a magistrates' court trial to take place in a courtroom provided by the Lord Chancellor, unless—

(a) the court otherwise directs; or

(b) the case is one to which rule 24.9 (Single justice procedure: special rules) applies.

Use of Welsh language at magistrates' court trial

3.18 Where a magistrates' court trial takes place in Wales–

(a) any party or witness may use the Welsh language; and

(b) if practicable, at least one member of the court must be Welsh-speaking.

Preparation for trial in the Crown Court

Service of prosecution evidence

3.19–(1) This rule applies where– **B-22**

(a) a magistrates' court sends the defendant to the Crown Court for trial; and

(b) the prosecutor serves on the defendant copies of the documents containing the evidence on which the prosecution case relies.

(2) The prosecutor must at the same time serve copies of those documents on the Crown Court officer.

Application to dismiss offence sent for Crown Court trial

3.20–(1) This rule applies where a defendant wants the Crown Court to dismiss an offence sent for trial there. **B-23**

(2) The defendant must–

(a) apply in writing–

(i) not more than 20 business days after service of the prosecution evidence, and

(ii) before the defendant's arraignment under rule 3.32 (Arraigning the defendant on the indictment);

(b) serve the application on–

(i) the Crown Court officer, and

(ii) each other party; and

(c) in the application–

(i) explain why the prosecution evidence would not be sufficient for the defendant to be properly convicted,

(ii) ask for a hearing, if the defendant wants one, and explain why it is needed,

(iii) identify any witness whom the defendant wants to call to give evidence in person, with an indication of what evidence the witness can give,

(iv) identify any material already served that the defendant thinks the court will need to determine the application, and

(v) include any material not already served on which the defendant relies.

(3) A prosecutor who opposes the application must–

(a) serve notice of opposition, not more than 10 business days after service of the defendant's notice, on–

(i) the Crown Court officer, and

(ii) each other party; and

(b) in the notice of opposition–

(i) explain the grounds of opposition,

(ii) ask for a hearing, if the prosecutor wants one, and explain why it is needed,

(iii) identify any witness whom the prosecutor wants to call to give evidence in person, with an indication of what evidence the witness can give,

(iv) identify any material already served that the prosecutor thinks the court will need to determine the application, and

(v) include any material not already served on which the prosecutor relies.

(4) The court may determine an application under this rule–

(a) at a hearing, in public or in private, or without a hearing; and

(b) in the absence of–

(i) the defendant who made the application, and

(ii) the prosecutor, if the prosecutor has had at least 10 business days in which to serve notice opposing the application.

(5) The court may–

(a) shorten or extend (even after it has expired) a time limit under this rule; and

(b) allow a witness to give evidence in person even if that witness was not identified in the defendant's application or in the prosecutor's notice.

Pre-trial hearings in the Crown Court: general rules

3.21–(1) The Crown Court– **★B-24**

(a) may, and in some cases must, conduct a preparatory hearing where rule 3.22 (Preparatory hearing) applies;
(b) must conduct a plea and trial preparation hearing; and
(c) may conduct a further pre-trial case management hearing (and if necessary more than one such hearing) only where—
 (i) the court anticipates a guilty plea,
 (ii) it is necessary to conduct such a hearing in order to give directions for an effective trial, or
 (iii) such a hearing is required to set ground rules for the conduct of the questioning of a witness or defendant.

(2) At the plea and trial preparation hearing the court must—
(a) satisfy itself that there has been explained to the defendant, in terms the defendant can understand (with help, if necessary), that the defendant will receive credit for a guilty plea;
(b) take the defendant's plea in accordance with rule 3.32 (Arraigning the defendant on the indictment) or if no plea can be taken then find out whether the defendant is likely to plead guilty or not guilty;
(c) unless the defendant pleads guilty, satisfy itself that there has been explained to the defendant, in terms the defendant can understand (with help, if necessary), that at the trial—
 (i) the defendant will have the right to give evidence after the court has heard the prosecution case,
 (ii) if the defendant does not attend, the trial may take place in the defendant's absence,
 (iii) if the trial takes place in the defendant's absence, the judge may inform the jury of the reason for that absence, and
 (iv) where the defendant is released on bail, failure to attend court when required is an offence for which the defendant may be arrested and punished and bail may be withdrawn; and
(d) give directions for an effective trial.

(3) A pre-trial case management hearing—
(a) must be in public, as a general rule, but all or part of the hearing may be in private if the court so directs; and
(b) must be recorded, in accordance with rule 5.5 (Recording and transcription of proceedings in the Crown Court).

(4) Where the court determines a pre-trial application in private, it must announce its decision in public.

(5) The court—
(a) at the first hearing in the Crown Court must require a defendant who is present—
 (i) to provide, in writing or orally, his or her name and date of birth, or
 (ii) to confirm that information by those means, where the information was given to the magistrates' court which sent the defendant for trial; and
(b) at any subsequent hearing may require such a defendant to provide or confirm that information by those means.

[This rule is printed as amended, with effect from 8 February 2021, by SI 2021/40, r.6(d).]

Preparatory hearing

3.22—(1) This rule applies where the Crown Court—
(a) can order a preparatory hearing, under—
 (i) section 7 of the Criminal Justice Act 1987 (cases of serious or complex fraud), or
 (ii) section 29 of the Criminal Procedure and Investigations Act 1996 (other complex, serious or lengthy cases);
(b) must order such a hearing, to determine an application for a trial without a jury, under—
 (i) section 44 of the Criminal Justice Act 2003(danger of jury tampering), or
 (ii) section 17 of the Domestic Violence, Crime and Victims Act 2004(trial of sample counts by jury, and others by judge alone); and
(c) must order such a hearing, under section 29 of the 1996 Act, where section 29(1B) or (1C) applies (cases in which a terrorism offence is charged, or other serious cases with a terrorist connection).

(2) The court may decide whether to order a preparatory hearing—
(a) on an application or on its own initiative;
(b) at a hearing (in public or in private), or without a hearing; and

(c) in a party's absence, if that party–
(i) applied for the order, or
(ii) has had at least 10 business days in which to make representations.

Application for preparatory hearing

3.23–(1) A party who wants the court to order a preparatory hearing must– **B-25**
(a) apply in writing–
(i) as soon as reasonably practicable, and in any event
(ii) not more than 10 business days after the defendant pleads not guilty; and
(b) serve the application on–
(i) the court officer, and
(ii) each other party.
(2) The applicant must either–
(a) if relevant, explain what legislation requires the court to order a preparatory hearing; or
(b) explain–
(i) what makes the case complex or serious, or makes the trial likely to be long,
(ii) why a substantial benefit will accrue from a preparatory hearing, and
(iii) why the court's ordinary powers of case management are not adequate.
(3) A prosecutor who wants the court to order a trial without a jury must explain–
(a) where the prosecutor alleges a danger of jury tampering–
(i) what evidence there is of a real and present danger that jury tampering would take place,
(ii) what steps, if any, reasonably might be taken to prevent jury tampering, and
(iii) why, notwithstanding such steps, the likelihood of jury tampering is so substantial as to make it necessary in the interests of justice to order such a trial; or
(b) where the prosecutor proposes trial without a jury on some counts on the indictment–
(i) why a trial by jury involving all the counts would be impracticable,
(ii) how the counts proposed for jury trial can be regarded as samples of the others, and
(iii) why it would be in the interests of justice to order such a trial.

Application for non-jury trial containing information withheld from a defendant

3.24–(1) This rule applies where– **B-26**
(a) the prosecutor applies for an order for a trial without a jury because of a danger of jury tampering; and
(b) the application includes information that the prosecutor thinks ought not be revealed to a defendant.
(2) The prosecutor must–
(a) omit that information from the part of the application that is served on that defendant;
(b) mark the other part to show that, unless the court otherwise directs, it is only for the court; and
(c) in that other part, explain why the prosecutor has withheld that information from that defendant.
(3) The hearing of an application to which this rule applies–
(a) must be in private, unless the court otherwise directs; and
(b) if the court so directs, may be, wholly or in part, in the absence of a defendant from whom information has been withheld.
(4) At the hearing of an application to which this rule applies–
(a) the general rule is that the court will receive, in the following sequence–
(i) representations first by the prosecutor and then by each defendant, in all the parties' presence, and then
(ii) further representations by the prosecutor, in the absence of a defendant from whom information has been withheld; but
(b) the court may direct other arrangements for the hearing.
(5) Where, on an application to which this rule applies, the court orders a trial without a jury–
(a) the general rule is that the trial will be before a judge other than the judge who made the order; but
(b) the court may direct other arrangements.

Representations in response to application for preparatory hearing

3.25–(1) This rule applies where a party wants to make representations about– **B-27**

(a) an application for a preparatory hearing; or
(b) an application for a trial without a jury.

(2) Such a party must—
(a) serve the representations on—
(i) the court officer, and
(ii) each other party;
(b) do so not more than 10 business days after service of the application; and
(c) ask for a hearing, if that party wants one, and explain why it is needed.

(3) Where representations include information that the person making them thinks ought not be revealed to another party, that person must—
(a) omit that information from the representations served on that other party;
(b) mark the information to show that, unless the court otherwise directs, it is only for the court; and
(c) with that information include an explanation of why it has been withheld from that other party.

(4) Representations against an application for an order must explain why the conditions for making it are not met.

Commencement of preparatory hearing

B-28 **3.26** At the beginning of a preparatory hearing, the court must—
(a) announce that it is such a hearing; and
(b) take the defendant's plea under rule 3.32 (Arraigning the defendant on the indictment), unless already done.

Defence trial advocate

B-29 **3.27**—(1) The defendant must notify the court officer of the identity of the intended defence trial advocate—
(a) as soon as practicable, and in any event no later than the day of the plea and trial preparation hearing; and
(b) in writing, or orally at that hearing.

(2) The defendant must notify the court officer in writing of any change in the identity of the intended defence trial advocate as soon as practicable, and in any event not more than 5 business days after that change.

Application to stay case for abuse of process

B-30 **3.28**—(1) This rule applies where a defendant wants the Crown Court to stay the case on the grounds that the proceedings are an abuse of the court, or otherwise unfair.

(2) Such a defendant must—
(a) apply in writing—
(i) as soon as practicable after becoming aware of the grounds for doing so,
(ii) at a pre-trial hearing, unless the grounds for the application do not arise until trial, and
(iii) in any event, before the defendant pleads guilty or the jury (if there is one) retires to consider its verdict at trial;
(b) serve the application on—
(i) the court officer, and
(ii) each other party; and
(c) in the application—
(i) explain the grounds on which it is made,
(ii) include, attach or identify all supporting material,
(iii) specify relevant events, dates and propositions of law, and
(iv) identify any witness the applicant wants to call to give evidence in person.

(3) A party who wants to make representations in response to the application must serve the representations on—
(a) the court officer; and
(b) each other party,

not more than 10 business days after service of the application.

Application for joint or separate trials, etc.

B-31 **3.29**—(1) This rule applies where a party wants the Crown Court to order—

(a) the joint trial of–
offences charged by separate indictments, or
defendants charged in separate indictments;
(b) separate trials of offences charged by the same indictment;
(c) separate trials of defendants charged in the same indictment; or
(d) the deletion of a count from an indictment.

(2) Such a party must–
(a) apply in writing–
(i) as soon as practicable after becoming aware of the grounds for doing so, and
(ii) before the trial begins, unless the grounds for the application do not arise until trial;
(b) serve the application on–
(i) the court officer, and
(ii) each other party; and
(c) in the application–
(i) specify the order proposed, and
(ii) explain why it should be made.

(3) A party who wants to make representations in response to the application must serve the representations on–
(a) the court officer; and
(b) each other party,
not more than 10 business days after service of the application.

(4) Where the same indictment charges more than one offence, the court may exercise its power to order separate trials of those offences if of the opinion that–
(a) the defendant otherwise may be prejudiced or embarrassed in his or her defence (for example, where the offences to be tried together are neither founded on the same facts nor form or are part of a series of offences of the same or a similar character); or
(b) for any other reason it is desirable that the defendant should be tried separately for any one or more of those offences.

Order for joint or separate trials, or amendment of the indictment

3.30–(1) This rule applies where the Crown Court makes an order– **B-32**
(a) on an application to which rule 3.29 (Application for joint or separate trials, etc.) applies; or
(b) amending an indictment in any other respect.

(2) Unless the court otherwise directs, the court officer must endorse any paper copy of each affected indictment made for the court with–
(a) a note of the court's order; and
(b) the date of that order.

Application for indication of sentence

3.31–(1) This rule applies where a defendant wants the Crown Court to give an indication of the maximum sentence that would be passed if a guilty plea were entered when the indication is sought. **B-33**

(2) Such a defendant must–
(a) apply in writing as soon as practicable; and
(b) serve the application on–
(i) the court officer, and
(ii) the prosecutor.

(3) The application must–
(a) specify–
(i) the offence or offences to which it would be a guilty plea, and
(ii) the facts on the basis of which that plea would be entered; and
(b) include the prosecutor's agreement to, or representations on, that proposed basis of plea.

(4) The prosecutor must–
(a) provide information relevant to sentence, including–
(i) any previous conviction of the defendant, and the circumstances where relevant, and
(ii) any statement of the effect of the offence on the victim, the victim's family or others; and
(b) identify any other matter relevant to sentence, including–
(i) the legislation applicable,
(ii) any sentencing guidelines, or guideline cases, and

(iii) aggravating and mitigating factors.

(5) The hearing of the application—

(a) may take place in the absence of any other defendant; and

(b) must be attended by—

(i) the applicant defendant's legal representatives (if any), and

(ii) the prosecution advocate.

Arraigning the defendant on the indictment

B-34 **3.32**—(1) In order to take the defendant's plea, the Crown Court must—

(a) obtain the prosecutor's confirmation, in writing or orally—

(i) that the indictment (or draft indictment, as the case may be) sets out a statement of each offence that the prosecutor wants the court to try and such particulars of the conduct constituting the commission of each such offence as the prosecutor relies upon to make clear what is alleged, and

(ii) of the order in which the prosecutor wants the defendants' names to be listed in the indictment, if the prosecutor proposes that more than one defendant should be tried at the same time;

(b) ensure that the defendant is correctly identified by the indictment or draft indictment;

(c) satisfy itself that there has been explained to the defendant, in terms the defendant can understand (with help, if necessary), each allegation against him or her; and

(d) in respect of each count—

(i) read the count aloud to the defendant, or arrange for it to be read aloud or placed before the defendant in writing,

(ii) ask whether the defendant pleads guilty or not guilty to the offence charged by that count, and

(iii) take the defendant's plea.

(2) Where a count is read which is substantially the same as one already read aloud, then only the materially different details need be read aloud.

(3) Where a count is placed before the defendant in writing, the court must summarise its gist aloud.

(4) In respect of each count in the indictment—

(a) if the defendant declines to enter a plea, the court must treat that as a not guilty plea unless rule 25.10 applies (Defendant unfit to plead);

(b) if the defendant pleads not guilty to the offence charged by that count but guilty to another offence of which the court could convict on that count—

(i) if the prosecutor and the court accept that plea, the court must treat the plea as one of guilty of that other offence, but

(ii) otherwise, the court must treat the plea as one of not guilty; and

(c) if the defendant pleads a previous acquittal or conviction of the offence charged by that count—

(i) the defendant must identify that acquittal or conviction in writing, explaining the basis of that plea, and

(ii) the court must exercise its power to decide whether that plea disposes of that count.

(5) In a case in which a magistrates' court sends the defendant for trial, the Crown Court must take the defendant's plea—

(a) not less than 10 business days after the date on which that sending takes place, unless the parties otherwise agree; and

(b) not more than 80 business days after that date, unless the court otherwise directs (either before or after that period expires).

Place of Crown Court trial

B-35 **3.33**—(1) Unless the court otherwise directs, the court officer must arrange for a Crown Court trial to take place in a courtroom provided by the Lord Chancellor.

(2) The court officer must arrange for the court and the jury (if there is one) to view any place required by the court.

Use of Welsh language at Crown Court trial

B-36 **3.34** Where a Crown Court trial will take place in Wales and a participant wishes to use the Welsh language—

(a) that participant must serve notice on the court officer, or arrange for such a notice to be served on that participant's behalf—

(i) at or before the plea and trial preparation hearing, or
(ii) in accordance with any direction given by the court; and
(b) if such a notice is served, the court officer must arrange for an interpreter to attend.

CPD I General Matters 3A: Case management (as amended by Criminal Practice Directions 2015 (Amendment No. 11) [2020] EWCA Crim 1347, Lord Burnett CJ)

3A.1 CrimPR 1.1(2)(e) requires that cases be dealt with efficiently and expeditiously. CrimPR 3.2 requires the court to further the overriding objective by actively managing the case, for example: **B-37**

a) when dealing with an offence which is triable only on indictment the court must ask the defendant whether he or she intends to plead guilty at the Crown Court (CrimPR 9.7(5));
b) on a guilty plea, the court must pass sentence at the earliest opportunity, in accordance with CrimPR 24.11(9)(a) (magistrates' courts) and 25.16(7)(a) (the Crown Court).

3A.2 Given these duties, magistrates' courts and the Crown Court therefore will proceed as described in paragraphs 3A.3 to 3A.28 below. The parties will be expected to have prepared in accordance with CrimPR 3.3(1) to avoid unnecessary and wasted hearings. They will be expected to have communicated with each other by the time of the first hearing; to report to the court on that communication at the first hearing; and to continue thereafter to communicate with each other and with the court officer, in accordance with CrimPR 3.3(2).

3A.3 There is a Preparation for Effective Trial form for use in the magistrates' courts, and a Plea and Trial Preparation Hearing form for use in the Crown Court, each of which must be used as appropriate in connection with CrimPR, Pt 3: see para. 5A.2 .... Versions of those forms in pdf and Word, together with guidance notes, are available on the Criminal Procedure Rules pages of the Ministry of Justice website.

Case Progression and Trial Preparation in Magistrates' Courts

3A.4 CrimPR 8.3 applies in all cases and requires the prosecutor to serve: **B-38**

i. a summary of the circumstances of the offence;
ii. any account given by the defendant in interview, whether contained in that summary or in another document;
iii. any written witness statement or exhibit that the prosecutor then has available and considers material to plea or to the allocation of the case for trial or sentence;
iv. a list of the defendant's criminal record, if any; and
v. any available statement of the effect of the offence on a victim, a victim's family or others.

The details must include sufficient information to allow the defendant and the court at the first hearing to take an informed view:

i. on plea;
ii. on venue for trial (if applicable);
iii. for the purposes of case management; or
iv. for the purposes of sentencing (including committal for sentence, if applicable).

Defendant in custody

3A.5 If the defendant has been detained in custody after being charged with an offence which is indictable only or triable either way, at the first hearing a magistrates' court will proceed at once with the allocation of the case for trial, where appropriate, and, if so required, with the sending of the defendant to the Crown Court for trial. The court will be expected to ask for and record any indication of plea and issues for trial to assist the Crown Court. **B-39**

3A.6 If the offence charged is triable only summarily, or if at that hearing the case is allocated for summary trial, the court will forthwith give such directions as are necessary, either (on a guilty plea) to prepare for sentencing, or for a trial.

Defendant on bail

3A.7 If the defendant has been released on bail after being charged, the case must be listed for the first hearing 14 days after charge, or the next available court date thereafter when the prosecutor anticipates a guilty plea which is likely to be sentenced in the magistrates' court. In cases where there is an anticipated not guilty plea or the case is likely to be sent or committed to the Crown Court for either trial or sentence, then it must be listed for the first hearing 28 days after charge or the next available court date thereafter. **B-40**

Guilty plea in the magistrates' courts

3A.8 Where a defendant pleads guilty or indicates a guilty plea in a magistrates' court the court should consider whether a pre-sentence report - a stand down report if possible - is necessary. **B-41**

Guilty plea in the Crown Court

B-42 **3A.9** Where a magistrates' court is considering committal for sentence or the defendant has indicated an intention to plead guilty in a matter which is to be sent to the Crown Court, the magistrates' court should request the preparation of a pre-sentence report for the Crown Court's use if the magistrates' court considers that:

(a) there is a realistic alternative to a custodial sentence; or
(b) the defendant may satisfy the criteria for classification as a dangerous offender; or
(c) there is some other appropriate reason for doing so.

3A.10 When a magistrates' court sends a case to the Crown Court for trial and the defendant indicates an intention to plead guilty at the Crown Court, then that magistrates' court must set a date for a Plea and Trial Preparation Hearing at the Crown Court, in accordance with CrimPR 9.7(5)(a)(i).

Case sent for Crown Court trial: no indication of guilty plea

B-43 **3A.11** In any case sent to the Crown Court for trial, other than one in which the defendant indicates an intention to plead guilty, the magistrates' court must set a date for a Plea and Trial Preparation Hearing, in accordance with CrimPR 9.7(5)(a)(ii). The Plea and Trial Preparation Hearing must be held within 28 days of sending, unless the standard directions of the presiding judges of the circuit direct otherwise. Paragraph 3A.16 below additionally applies to the arrangements for such hearings. A magistrates' court may give other directions appropriate to the needs of the case, in accordance with CrimPR 3.5(3), and in accordance with any standard directions issued by the presiding judges of the circuit.

Defendant on bail: anticipated not guilty plea

B-44 **3A.12** Where the defendant has been released on bail after being charged, and where the prosecutor does not anticipate a guilty plea at the first hearing in a magistrates' court, then it is essential that the initial details of the prosecution case that are provided for that first hearing are sufficient to assist the court, in order to identify the real issues and to give appropriate directions for an effective trial (regardless of whether the trial is to be heard in the magistrates' court or the Crown Court). In these circumstances, unless there is good reason not to do so, the prosecution should make available the following material in advance of the first hearing in the magistrates' court:

(a) a summary of the circumstances of the offence(s) including a summary of any account given by the defendant in interview;
(b) statements and exhibits that the prosecution has identified as being of importance for the purpose of plea or initial case management, including any relevant CCTV that would be relied upon at trial and any streamlined forensic report;
(c) details of witness availability, as far as they are known at that hearing;
(d) defendant's criminal record;
(e) victim personal statements if provided;
(f) an indication of any medical or other expert evidence that the prosecution is likely to adduce in relation to a victim or the defendant;
(g) any information as to special measures, bad character or hearsay, where applicable.

3A.13 In addition to the material required by CrimPR, Pt 8, the information required by the Preparation for Effective Trial form must be available to be submitted at the first hearing, and the parties must complete that form, in accordance with the guidance published with it. Where there is to be a contested trial in a magistrates' court, that form includes directions and a timetable that will apply in every case unless the court otherwise orders.

3A.14 Nothing in paragraph 3A.12-3A.13 shall preclude the court from taking a plea pursuant to CrimPR 3.9(2)(b) at the first hearing and for the court to case manage as far as practicable under Part 3 CrimPR.

Exercise of magistrates' court's powers

B-45 **3A.15** In accordance with CrimPR 9.1, sections 49, 51(13) and 51A(11) of the CDA 1998 [§§ 1-24, 1-25 in the main work], and sections 17E, 18(5) and 24D of the MCA 1980 [ibid., §§ 1-62, 1-64, 1-87 in the main work a single justice can:

a) allocate and send for trial;
b) take an indication of a guilty plea (but not pass sentence);
c) take a not guilty plea and give directions for the preparation of trial including:
    i. timetable for the proceedings;
    ii. the attendance of the parties;
    iii. the service of documents;
    iv. the manner in which evidence is to be given.

Case Progression and Trial Preparation in the Crown Court

Plea and Trial Preparation Hearing

B-46 **3A.16** In a case in which a magistrates' court has directed a Plea and Trial Preparation Hearing, the period which elapses between sending for trial and the date of that hearing must be consistent within each circuit. In every case, the time allowed for the conduct of the Plea and Trial Preparation Hearing must be sufficient for effective trial preparation. It is expected in every case that an indictment will be lodged at least 7 days in advance of the hearing. Please see the Note to the Practice Direction.

3A.17 In a case in which the defendant, not having done so before, indicates an intention to plead guilty to his representative after being sent for trial but before the Plea and Trial Preparation Hearing, the defence representative will notify the Crown Court and the prosecution forthwith. The court will ensure there is sufficient time at the Plea and Trial Preparation Hearing for sentence and a judge should at once request the preparation of a pre-sentence report if it appears to the court that either:

(a) there is a realistic alternative to a custodial sentence; or
(b) the defendant may satisfy the criteria for classification as a dangerous offender; or
(c) there is some other appropriate reason for doing so.

3A.18 If at the Plea and Trial Preparation Hearing the defendant pleads guilty and no presentence report has been prepared, if possible the court should obtain a stand down report.

3A.19 Where the defendant was remanded in custody after being charged and was sent for trial without initial details of the prosecution case having been served, then at least 7 days before the Plea and Trial Preparation Hearing the prosecutor should serve, as a minimum, the material identified in paragraph 3A.12 above. If at the Plea and Trial Preparation Hearing the defendant does not plead guilty, the court will be expected to identify the issues in the case and give appropriate directions for an effective trial. Please see the Note to the Practice Direction.

3A.20 At the Plea and Trial Preparation Hearing, in addition to the material required by paragraph 3A.12 above, the prosecutor must serve sufficient evidence to enable the court to case manage effectively without the need for a further case management hearing, unless the case falls within paragraph 3A.21. In addition, the information required by the Plea and Trial Preparation Hearing form must be available to the court at that hearing, and it must have been discussed between the parties in advance. The prosecutor must provide details of the availability of likely prosecution witnesses so that a trial date can immediately be arranged if the defendant does not plead guilty.

Further case management hearing

3A.21 In accordance with CrimPR 3.13(1)(c), after the Plea and Trial Preparation Hearing there will be no further case management hearing before the trial unless: **B-47**

(i) a condition listed in that rule is met; and
(ii) the court so directs, in order to further the overriding objective.

The directions to be given at the Plea and Trial Preparation Hearing therefore may include a direction for a further case management hearing, but usually will do so only in one of the following cases:

(a) Class 1 cases;
(b) Class 2 cases which carry a maximum penalty of 10 years or more;
(c) cases involving death by driving (whether dangerous or careless), or death in the workplace;
(d) cases involving a vulnerable witness;
(e) cases in which the defendant is a child or otherwise under a disability, or requires special assistance;
(f) cases in which there is a corporate or unrepresented defendant;
(g) cases in which the expected trial length is such that a further case management hearing is desirable and any case in which the trial is likely to last longer than four weeks;
(h) cases in which expert evidence is to be introduced;
(i) cases in which a party requests a hearing to enter a plea;
(j) cases in which an application to dismiss or stay has been made;
(k) cases in which arraignment has not taken place, whether because of an issue relating to fitness to plead, or abuse of process or sufficiency of evidence, or for any other reason;
(l) cases in which there are likely to be linked criminal and care directions in accordance with the 2013 Protocol;
(m) cases in which a substantial quantity of unused prosecution material has been disclosed, or will be disclosed, or in which the disclosure of such material raises complex questions of law or procedure.

3A.22 If a further case management hearing is directed, a defendant in custody will not usually be expected to attend in person, unless the court otherwise directs.

Compliance hearing

3A.23 If a party fails to comply with a case management direction, that party may be required to attend the court to explain the failure. Unless the court otherwise directs a defendant in custody will not usually be expected to attend. See paras 3A.26-3A.28 below. **B-48**

Conduct of case progression hearings

3A.24 As far as possible, case progression should be managed without a hearing in the courtroom, using electronic communication in accordance with CrimPR 3.5(2)(d). Court staff should be nominated to conduct case progression as part of their role, in accordance with CrimPR 3.4(2). To aid effective communication the prosecution and defence representative should notify the court and provide details of who shall be dealing with the case at the earliest opportunity.

COMPLETION OF EFFECTIVE TRIAL MONITORING FORM

3A.25 It is imperative that the Effective Trial Monitoring form (as devised and issued by Her Majesty's Courts and Tribunals Service) is accurately completed by the parties for all cases that have been listed for trial. Advocates must engage with the process by providing the relevant details and completing the form.

COMPLIANCE COURTS

3A.26 To ensure effective compliance with directions of the courts made in accordance with the Criminal Procedure Rules and the overriding objective, courts should maintain a record whenever a party to the proceedings has failed to comply with a direction made by the court. The parties may have to attend a hearing to explain any lack of compliance.

3A.27 These hearings may be conducted by live link facilities or via other electronic means, as the court may direct.

3A.28 It will be for the presiding judges, resident judge and justices' clerks to decide locally how often compliance courts should be held, depending on the scale and nature of the problem at each court centre.

NOTE TO THE PRACTICE DIRECTION

B-49 In 3A.16 and 3A.19 the reference to "at least 7 days" in advance of the hearing is necessitated by the fact that, for the time being, different circuits have different timescales for the Plea and Trial Preparation Hearing. Had this not been so, the paragraphs would have been drafted forward from the date of sending rather than backwards from the date of the Plea and Trial Preparation Hearing.

CPD I General Matters 3B: Pagination and indexing of served evidence

B-50 **3B.1** The following directions apply to matters before the Crown Court, where—

(a) there is an application to prefer a bill of indictment in relation to the case;

(b) a person is sent for trial under section 51 of the CDA 1998 [§ 1-24 in the main work] ..., to the service of copies of the documents containing the evidence on which the charge or charges are based under paragraph 1 of Schedule 3 to that Act [ibid., § 1-36]; or

(c) a defendant wishes to serve evidence.

3B.2 A party who serves documentary evidence in the Crown Court should:

(a) paginate each page in any bundle of statements and exhibits sequentially;

(b) provide an index to each bundle of statements produced including the following information:

(i) the name of the case;
(ii) the author of each statement;
(iii) the start page number of the witness statement;
(iv) the end page number of the witness statement;

(c) provide an index to each bundle of documentary and pictorial exhibits produced, including the following information:

(i) the name of the case;
(ii) the exhibit reference;
(iii) a short description of the exhibit;
(iv) the start page number of the exhibit;
(v) the end page number of the exhibit;
(vi) where possible, the name of the person producing the exhibit should be added.

3B.3 Where additional documentary evidence is served, a party should paginate following on from the last page of the previous bundle or in a logical and sequential manner. A party should also provide notification of service of any amended index.

3B.4 The prosecution must ensure that the running total of the pages of prosecution evidence is easily identifiable on the most recent served bundle of prosecution evidence.

3B.5 For the purposes of these directions, the number of pages of prosecution evidence served on the court includes all (a) witness statements; (b) documentary and pictorial exhibits; (c) records of interviews with the defendant; and (d) records of interviews with other defendants which form part of the served prosecution documents or which are included in any notice of additional evidence, but does not include any document provided on CD-ROM or by other means of electronic communication.

CPD I General Matters 3C: Abuse of process stay applications (as amended by Criminal Practice Directions 2015 (Amendment No. 6), unreported, 22 March 2018, Lord Burnett CJ)

3C.1 In all cases where a defendant in the Crown Court proposes to make an application to stay an indictment on the ground of abuse of process, written notice of such application must be given to the prosecuting authority and to any co-defendant as soon as practicable after the defendant becomes aware of the grounds for doing so and not later than 14 days before the date fixed or warned for trial ("the relevant date"). Such notice must (a) give the name of the case and the indictment number; (b) state the fixed date or the warned date as appropriate; (c) specify the nature of the application; (d) set out in numbered sub-paragraphs the grounds on which the application is to be made; (e) be copied to the chief listing officer at the court centre where the case is due to be heard. **B-51**

3C.2 Any co-defendant who wishes to make a like application must give a like notice not later than seven days before the relevant date, setting out any additional grounds relied upon.

3C.3 In relation to such applications, the following automatic directions shall apply: (a) the advocate for the applicant(s) must lodge with the court and serve on all other parties a skeleton argument in support of the application, at least five clear working days before the relevant date; if reference is to be made to any document not in the existing trial documents, a paginated and indexed bundle of such documents is to be provided with the skeleton argument; (b) the advocate for the prosecution must lodge with the court and serve on all other parties a responsive skeleton argument at least two clear working days before the relevant date, together with a supplementary bundle if appropriate.

3C.4 Paragraphs XII D.17 to D.23 of these Practice Directions set out the general requirements for skeleton arguments. All skeleton arguments must specify any propositions of law to be advanced (together with the authorities relied on in support, with paragraph references to passages relied upon), and, where appropriate, include a chronology of events and a list of dramatis personae. In all instances where reference is made to a document, the reference in the trial documents or supplementary bundle is to be given.

3C.5 The above time limits are minimum time limits. In appropriate cases the court will order longer lead times. To this end in all cases where defence advocates are, at the time of the preliminary hearing or as soon as practicable after the case has been sent, considering the possibility of an abuse of process application, this must be raised with the judge dealing with the matter, who will order a different timetable if appropriate, and may wish, in any event, to give additional directions about the conduct of the application. If the trial judge has not been identified, the matter should be raised with the resident judge.

CPD I General Matters 3D: Vulnerable people in the courts

3D.1 In respect of eligibility for special measures, "vulnerable" and "intimidated" witnesses are defined in sections 16 and 17 of the YJCEA 1999 ...; "vulnerable" includes those under 18 years of age and people with a mental disorder or learning disability; a physical disorder or disability; or who are likely to suffer fear or distress in giving evidence because of their own circumstances or those relating to the case. **B-52**

3D.2 However, many other people giving evidence in a criminal case, whether as a witness or defendant, may require assistance: the court is required to take "every reasonable step" to encourage and facilitate the attendance of witnesses and to facilitate the participation of any person, including the defendant (r.3.9(3)(a) and (b)). This includes enabling a witness or defendant to give their best evidence, and enabling a defendant to comprehend the proceedings and engage fully with his defence. The pre-trial and trial process should, so far as necessary, be adapted to meet those ends. Regard should be had to the welfare of a young defendant as required by section 44 of the CYPA 1933 [§ 5A-947, 5ASC-1073 in the main work], and generally to Parts 1 and 3 of the Criminal Procedure Rules ....

3D.3 Under Part 3 of the rules, the court must identify the needs of witnesses at an early stage (r.3.2(2)(b)) and may require the parties to identify arrangements to facilitate the giving of evidence and participation in the trial (r.3.11(c)(iv) and (v). There are various statutory special measures that the court may utilise to assist a witness in giving evidence. Part 18 of the rules gives the procedures to be followed. Courts should note the "primary rule" which requires the court to give a direction for a special measure to assist a child witness or qualifying witness and that in such cases an application to the court is not required (r.18.9).

3D.4 Court of Appeal decisions on this subject include ... *Cox* [2012] EWCA Crim 549; [2012] 2

Cr. App. R. 6, *Wills* [2011] EWCA Crim 1938; [2012] 1 Cr. App. R. 2, and *E* [2011] EWCA Crim 3028; [2012] Crim L.R. 563.

3D.5 In *Wills*, the court endorsed the approach taken by the report of the *Advocacy Training Council (ATC) "Raising the Bar: the Handling of Vulnerable Witnesses, Victims and Defendants in Court" (2011)*. The report includes and recommends the use of "toolkits" to assist advocates as they prepare to question vulnerable people at court: *http://advocacytrainingcouncil.org/images/word/raisingthebar.pdf*.

3D.6 Further toolkits are available through the advocate's gateway which is managed by the ATC's management committee: *http://www.theadvocatesgateway.org/*.

3D.7 These toolkits represent best practice. Advocates should consult and follow the relevant guidance whenever they prepare to question a young or otherwise vulnerable witness or defendant. Judges may find it helpful to refer advocates to this material and to use the toolkits in case management.

3D.8 "Achieving Best Evidence in Criminal Proceedings" (Ministry of Justice 2011) describes best practice in preparation for the investigative interview and trial: *http://www.cps.gov.uk/publications/docs/best_evidence_in_criminal_proceedings.pdf*.

CPD I General Matters 3E: Ground rules hearings to plan the questioning of a vulnerable witness or defendant

B-53 **3E.1** The judiciary is responsible for controlling questioning. Over-rigorous or repetitive cross-examination of a child or vulnerable witness should be stopped. Intervention by the judge, magistrates or intermediary (if any) is minimised if questioning, taking account of the individual's communication needs, is discussed in advance and ground rules are agreed and adhered to.

3E.2 Discussion of ground rules is required in all intermediary trials where they must be discussed between the judge or magistrates, advocates and intermediary before the witness gives evidence. The intermediary must be present but is not required to take the oath (the intermediary's declaration is made just before the witness gives evidence).

3E.3 Discussion of ground rules is good practice, even if no intermediary is used, in all young witness cases and in other cases where a witness or defendant has communication needs. Discussion before the day of trial is preferable to give advocates time to adapt their questions to the witness's needs. It may be helpful for a trial practice note of boundaries to be created at the end of the discussion. The judge may use such a document in ensuring that the agreed ground rules are complied with.

3E.4 All witnesses, including the defendant and defence witnesses, should be enabled to give the best evidence they can. In relation to young and/or vulnerable people, this may mean departing radically from traditional cross-examination. The form and extent of appropriate cross-examination will vary from case to case. For adult non-vulnerable witnesses an advocate will usually put his case so that the witness will have the opportunity of commenting upon it and/or answering it. When the witness is young or otherwise vulnerable, the court may dispense with the normal practice and impose restrictions on the advocate "putting his case" where there is a risk of a young or otherwise vulnerable witness failing to understand, becoming distressed or acquiescing to leading questions. Where limitations on questioning are necessary and appropriate, they must be clearly defined. The judge has a duty to ensure that they are complied with and should explain them to the jury and the reasons for them. If the advocate fails to comply with the limitations, the judge should give relevant directions to the jury when that occurs and prevent further questioning that does not comply with the ground rules settled upon in advance. Instead of commenting on inconsistencies during cross-examination, following discussion between the judge and the advocates, the advocate or judge may point out important inconsistencies after (instead of during) the witness's evidence. The judge should also remind the jury of these during summing up. The judge should be alert to alleged inconsistencies that are not in fact inconsistent, or are trivial.

3E.5 If there is more than one defendant, the judge should not permit each advocate to repeat the questioning of a vulnerable witness. In advance of the trial, the advocates should divide the topics between them, with the advocate for the first defendant leading the questioning, and the advocate(s) for the other defendant(s) asking only ancillary questions relevant to their client's case, without repeating the questioning that has already taken place on behalf of the other defendant(s).

3E.6 In particular in a trial of a sexual offence, "body maps" should be provided for the witness's use. If the witness needs to indicate a part of the body, the advocate should ask the witness to point to the relevant part on the body map. In sex cases, judges should not permit advocates to ask the witness to point to a part of the witness's own body. Similarly, photographs of the witness's body should not be shown around the court while the witness is giving evidence.

CPD I General Matters 3F: Intermediaries (as substituted by Criminal Practice Directions 2015 (Amendment No. 1) [2016] EWCA Crim 97, Lord Thomas CJ; and subsequently amended by Criminal Practice Directions 2015 (Amendment No.7) [2018] EWCA Crim 1760, Lord Burnett CJ)

Role and functions of intermediaries in criminal courts

3F.1 Intermediaries facilitate communication with witnesses and defendants who have communication needs. Their primary function is to improve the quality of evidence and aid understanding between the court, the advocates and the witness or defendant. For example, they commonly advise on the formulation of questions so as to avoid misunderstanding. On occasion, they actively assist and intervene during questioning. The extent to which they do so (if at all) depends on factors such as the communication needs of the witness or defendant, and the skills of the advocates in adapting their language and questioning style to meet those needs. **B-54**

3F.2 Intermediaries are independent of parties and owe their duty to the court. The court and parties should be vigilant to ensure they act impartially and their assistance to witnesses and defendants is transparent. It is however permissible for an advocate to have a private consultation with an intermediary when formulating questions (although control of questioning remains the overall responsibility of the court).

3F.3 Further information is in Intermediaries: Step by Step (Toolkit 16; The Advocate's Gateway, 2015) and chapter 5 of the Equal Treatment Bench Book (Judicial College, 2013).

Links to publications

- *http://www.theadvocatesgateway.org/images/toolkits/16intermediariesstepbystep060315.pdf*
- *http://www.judiciary.gov.uk/wp-content/uploads/2013/11/5-children-and-vulnerable-adults.pdf*

Assessment

3F.4 The process of appointment should begin with assessment by an intermediary and a report. The report will make recommendations to address the communication needs of the witness or defendant during trial. **B-55**

3F.5 In light of the scarcity of intermediaries, the appropriateness of assessment must be decided with care to ensure their availability for those witnesses and defendants who are most in need. The decision should be made on an individual basis, in the context of the circumstances of the particular case.

Intermediaries for prosecution and defence witnesses

3F.6 Intermediaries are one of the special measures available to witnesses under the YJCEA 1999. Witnesses deemed vulnerable in accordance with the criteria in [section 16] are eligible for the assistance of an intermediary when giving evidence pursuant to [section 29]. These provisions do not apply to defendants. **B-56**

3F.7 An application for an intermediary to assist a witness when giving evidence must be made in accordance with Part 18 of the Criminal Procedure Rules. In addition, where an intermediary report is available (see 3F.4 above), it should be provided with the application

3F.8 The Witness Intermediary Scheme (WIS) operated by the National Crime Agency identifies intermediaries for witnesses and may be used by the prosecution and defence. The WIS is contactable at wit@nca.x.gsi.gov.uk / 0845 000 5463. An intermediary appointed through the WIS is defined as a "registered intermediary" and matched to the particular witness based on expertise, location and availability. Registered intermediaries are accredited by the WIS and bound by Codes of Practice and Ethics issued by the Ministry of Justice (which oversees the WIS).

3F.9 Having identified a registered intermediary, the WIS does not provide funding. The party appointing the registered intermediary is responsible for payment at rates specified by the Ministry of Justice.

3F.10 Further information is in the Registered Intermediaries Procedural Guidance Manual (Ministry of Justice, 2015) and Intermediaries: Step by Step (see 3F.3 above).

Link to publication

- *http://www.theadvocatesgateway.org/images/procedures/registered-intermediaryprocedural-guidance-manual.pdf*

Intermediaries for defendants

3F.11 Statutory provisions providing for defendants to be assisted by an intermediary when giving evidence (where necessary to ensure a fair trial) are not in force (because s.104 [of the] Coroners and Justice Act 2009, which would insert ss.33BA and 33BB into the YJCEA 1999 [§§ 8-109, 8-110 in the main work], has yet to be commenced). **B-57**

3F.12 The court may direct the appointment of an intermediary to assist a defendant in reliance on its inherent powers (*C v Sevenoaks Youth Court* [2009] EWHC 3088 (Admin)). There is however no presumption that a defendant will be so assisted and, even where an intermediary would improve the trial process, appointment is not mandatory (*Cox* [2012] EWCA Crim 549). The court should adapt the trial process to address a defendant's communication needs (*Cox* [2012] EWCA Crim 549). It will rarely exercise its inherent powers to direct appointment of an intermediary but where a defendant is vulnerable or for some other reason experiences communication or hearing difficulties, such that he or she needs more help to follow the proceedings than her or his legal representatives readily can give having regard to their other functions on the defendant's behalf, then the court should consider sympathetically any application for the defendant to be accompanied throughout the trial by a support worker or other appropriate companion who can provide that assistance. This is consistent with CrimPR 3.9(3)(b) (see paragraph 3D.2 above); consistent with the observations in *Cox* (see paragraph 3D.4 above), *R. (OP) v Ministry of Justice* [2014] EWHC 1944 (Admin) and *Rashid* [2017] EWCA Crim 2; and consistent with the arrangements contemplated at paragraph 3G.8 below.

3F.13 The court may exercise its inherent powers to direct appointment of an intermediary to assist a defendant giving evidence or for the entire trial. Terms of appointment are for the court and there is no illogicality in restricting the appointment to the defendant's evidence (*R.* [2015] EWCA Crim 1870), when the "most pressing need" arises ([*R. (O.P.) v Secretary of State for Justice* [2015] 1 Cr. App. R. 7, DC]). Directions to appoint an intermediary for a defendant's evidence will thus be rare, but for the entire trial extremely rare, keeping in mind paragraph 3F.12 above.

3F.14 An application for an intermediary to assist a defendant must be made in accordance with Part 18 of the Criminal Procedure Rules. In addition, where an intermediary report is available (see 3F.4 above), it should be provided with the application.

3F.15 The WIS is not presently available to identify intermediaries for defendants (although in [*R. (O.P.) v Secretary of State for Justice*], the Ministry of Justice was ordered to consider carefully whether it were justifiable to refuse equal provision to witnesses and defendants with respect to their evidence). "Non-registered intermediaries" (intermediaries appointed other than through the WIS) must therefore be appointed for defendants. Although training is available, there is no accreditation process for non-registered intermediaries and rates of payment are unregulated.

3F.16 Arrangements for funding of intermediaries for defendants depend on the stage of the appointment process. Where the defendant is publicly funded, an application should be made to the Legal Aid Agency for prior authority to fund a pre-trial assessment. If the application is refused, an application may be made to the court to use its inherent powers to direct a pre-trial assessment and funding thereof. Where the court uses its inherent powers to direct assistance by an intermediary at trial (during evidence or for the entire trial), court staff are responsible for arranging payment from central funds. Internal guidance for court staff is in Guidance for HMCTS Staff: Registered and Non-Registered Intermediaries for Vulnerable Defendants and Non-Vulnerable Defence and Prosecution Witnesses (Her Majesty's Courts and Tribunals Service, 2014).

3F.17 The court should be satisfied that a non-registered intermediary has expertise suitable to meet the defendant's communication needs.

3F.18 Further information is in Intermediaries: Step by Step (see 3F.3 above).

Ineffective directions for intermediaries to assist defendants

B-58 **3F.19** Directions for intermediaries to help defendants may be ineffective due to general unavailability, lack of suitable expertise, or non-availability for the purpose directed (for example, where the direction is for assistance during evidence, but an intermediary will only accept appointment for the entire trial).

3F.20 Intermediaries may contribute to the administration of justice by facilitating communication with appropriate defendants during the trial process. A trial will not be rendered unfair because a direction to appoint an intermediary for the defendant is ineffective. "It would, in fact, be a most unusual case for a defendant who is fit to plead to be so disadvantaged by his condition that a properly brought prosecution would have to be stayed" because an intermediary with suitable expertise is not available for the purpose directed by the court (*Cox*).

3F.21 Faced with an ineffective direction, it remains the court's responsibility to adapt the trial process to address the defendant's communication needs, as was the case prior to the existence of intermediaries (*Cox*). In such a case, a ground rules hearing should be convened to ensure every reasonable step is taken to facilitate the defendant's participation in accordance with [rule 3.9 of the Criminal Procedure Rules]. At the hearing, the court should make new, further and / or alternative directions. This includes setting ground rules to help the defendant follow proceedings and (where applicable) to give evidence.

3F.22 For example, to help the defendant follow proceedings the court may require evidence to be adduced by simple questions, with witnesses being asked to answer in short sentences. Regular breaks may assist the defendant's concentration and enable the defence advocate to summarise the evidence and take further instructions.

3F.23 Further guidance is available in publications such as Ground Rules Hearings and the Fair

Treatment of Vulnerable People in Court (Toolkit 1; The Advocate's Gateway, 2015) and General Principles from Research – Planning to Question a Vulnerable Person or Someone with Communication Needs (Toolkit 2(a); The Advocate's Gateway, 2015). In the absence of an intermediary, these publications include information on planning how to manage the participation and questioning of the defendant, and the formulation of questions to avert misunderstanding (for example, by avoiding "long and complicated questions...posed in a leading or 'tagged' manner" (*Wills* [2012] 1 Cr. App. R. 2, CA).

Links to publications

- *http://www.theadvocatesgateway.org/images/toolkits/1groundruleshearingsandthefairtreatmentofvulnerablepeopleincourt060315.pdf*
- *http://www.theadvocatesgateway.org/images/toolkits/2generalprinciplesfromresearchpolicyandguidance-planningtoquestionavulnerablepersonorsomeonewithcommunicationneeds141215.pdf*

Intermediaries for witnesses and defendants under 18

3F.24 Communication needs (such as short attention span, suggestibility and reticence in relation to authority figures) are common to many witnesses and defendants under 18. Consideration should therefore be given to the communication needs of all children and young people appearing in the criminal courts and to adapting the trial process to address any such needs. Guidance is available in publications such as Planning to Question a Child or Young Person (Toolkit 6; The Advocate's Gateway, 2015) and Effective Participation of Young Defendants (Toolkit 8; The Advocate's Gateway, 2013). **B-59**

Links to publications

- *http://www.theadvocatesgateway.org/images/toolkits/6planningtoquestionachildoryoungperson141215.pdf*
- *http://www.theadvocatesgateway.org/images/toolkits/8YoungDefendants211013.pdf*

3F.25 For the reasons set out in 3F.5 above, the appropriateness of an intermediary assessment for witnesses and defendants under 18 must be decided with care. Whilst there is no presumption that they will be assessed by an intermediary (to evaluate their communication needs prior to trial) or assisted by an intermediary at court (for example, if / when giving evidence), the decision should be made on an individual basis in the context of the circumstances of the particular case.

3F.26 Assessment by an intermediary should be considered for witnesses and defendants under 18 who seem liable to misunderstand questions or to experience difficulty expressing answers, including those who seem unlikely to be able to recognise a problematic question (such as one that is misleading or not readily understood), and those who may be reluctant to tell a questioner in a position of authority if they do not understand.

Attendance at ground rules hearing

3F.27 Where the court directs questioning will be conducted through an intermediary, [rule 3.9 of the Criminal Procedure Rules] requires the court to set ground rules. The intermediary should be present at the ground rules hearing to make representations in accordance with [rule] 3.9(7)(a). **B-60**

Listing

3F.28 Where the court directs an intermediary will attend the trial, their dates of availability should be provided to the court. It is preferable that such trials are fixed rather than placed in warned lists. **B-61**

Photographs of court facilities

3F.29 Resident judges in the Crown Court or the chief clerk or other responsible person in the magistrates' courts should, in consultation with HMCTS managers responsible for court security matters, develop a policy to govern under what circumstances photographs or other visual recordings may be made of court facilities, such as a live link room, to assist vulnerable or child witnesses to familiarise themselves with the setting, so as to be enabled to give their best evidence. For example, a photograph may provide a helpful reminder to a witness whose court visit has taken place sometime earlier. Resident judges should tend to permit photographs to be taken for this purpose by intermediaries or supporters, subject to whatever restrictions the resident judge or responsible person considers to be appropriate, having regard to the security requirements of the court. **B-62**

CPD I General Matters 3G: Vulnerable defendants

Before the trial, sentencing or appeal

3G.1 If a vulnerable defendant, especially one who is young, is to be tried jointly with one who is not, the court should consider at the plea and case management hearing, or at a case management **B-63**

hearing in a magistrates' court, whether the vulnerable defendant should be tried on his own, but should only so order if satisfied that a fair trial cannot be achieved by use of appropriate special measures or other support for the defendant. If a vulnerable defendant is tried jointly with one who is not, the court should consider whether any of the modifications set out in this direction should apply in the circumstances of the joint trial and, so far as practicable, make orders to give effect to any such modifications.

3G.2 It may be appropriate to arrange that a vulnerable defendant should visit, out of court hours and before the trial, sentencing or appeal hearing, the courtroom in which that hearing is to take place so that he can familiarise him or herself with it.

3G.3 Where an intermediary is being used to help the defendant to communicate at court, the intermediary should accompany the defendant on his or her pre-trial visit. The visit will enable the defendant to familiarise him or herself with the layout of the court, and may include matters such as: where the defendant will sit, either in the dock or otherwise; court officials (what their roles are and where they sit); who else might be in the court, for example those in the public gallery and press box; the location of the witness box; basic court procedure; and the facilities available in the court.

3G.4 If the defendant's use of the live link is being considered, he or she should have an opportunity to have a practice session.

3G.5 If any case against a vulnerable defendant has attracted or may attract widespread public or media interest, the assistance of the police should be enlisted to try and ensure that the defendant is not, when attending the court, exposed to intimidation, vilification or abuse. Section 41 of the CJA 1925 prohibits the taking of photographs of defendants and witnesses (among others) in the court building or in its precincts, or when entering or leaving those precincts. A direction reminding media representatives of the prohibition may be appropriate. The court should also be ready at this stage, if it has not already done so, where relevant to make a reporting restriction under section 39 of the CYPA 1933 or, on an appeal to the Crown Court from a youth court, to remind media representatives of the application of section 49 of that Act.

3G.6 The provisions of the practice direction accompanying Part 6 should be followed.

The trial, sentencing or appeal hearing

B-64 **3G.7** Subject to the need for appropriate security arrangements, the proceedings should, if practicable, be held in a courtroom in which all the participants are on the same or almost the same level.

3G.8 Subject again to the need for appropriate security arrangements, a vulnerable defendant, especially if he is young, should normally, if he wishes, be free to sit with members of his family or others in a like relationship, and with some other suitable supporting adult such as a social worker, and in a place which permits easy, informal communication with his legal representatives. The court should ensure that a suitable supporting adult is available throughout the course of the proceedings.

3G.9 It is essential that at the beginning of the proceedings, the court should ensure that what is to take place has been explained to a vulnerable defendant in terms he or she can understand and, at trial in the Crown Court, it should ensure in particular that the role of the jury has been explained. It should remind those representing the vulnerable defendant and the supporting adult of their responsibility to explain each step as it takes place and, at trial, explain the possible consequences of a guilty verdict and credit for a guilty plea. The court should also remind any intermediary of the responsibility to ensure that the vulnerable defendant has understood the explanations given to him/her. Throughout the trial the court should continue to ensure, by any appropriate means, that the defendant understands what is happening and what has been said by those on the bench, the advocates and witnesses.

3G.10 A trial should be conducted according to a timetable which takes full account of a vulnerable defendant's ability to concentrate. Frequent and regular breaks will often be appropriate. The court should ensure, so far as practicable, that the whole trial is conducted in clear language that the defendant can understand and that evidence in chief and cross-examination are conducted using questions that are short and clear. The conclusions of the "ground rules" hearing should be followed, and advocates should use and follow the "toolkits" as discussed above (*Criminal Practice Direction I (General matters) 3D*).

3G.11 A vulnerable defendant who wishes to give evidence by live link, in accordance with section 33A of the YJCEA 1999 [§ 8-106 in the main work], may apply for a direction to that effect; the procedure in rules 18.14 to 18.17 should be followed. Before making such a direction, the court must be satisfied that it is in the interests of justice to do so and that the use of a live link would enable the defendant to participate more effectively as a witness in the proceedings. The direction will need to deal with the practical arrangements to be made, including the identity of the person or persons who will accompany him or her.

3G.12 In the Crown Court, the judge should consider whether robes and wigs should be worn, and should take account of the wishes of both a vulnerable defendant and any vulnerable witness. It is generally desirable that those responsible for the security of a vulnerable defendant who is in custody, especially if he or she is young, should not be in uniform, and that there should be no recognisable police presence in the courtroom save for good reason.

3G.13 The court should be prepared to restrict attendance by members of the public in the courtroom to a small number, perhaps limited to those with an immediate and direct interest in the outcome. The court should rule on any challenged claim to attend. However, facilities for reporting the proceedings (subject to any restrictions under s.39 or 49 of the CYPA 1933) must be provided. The court may restrict the number of reporters attending in the courtroom to such number as is judged practicable and desirable. In ruling on any challenged claim to attend in the courtroom for the purpose of reporting, the court should be mindful of the public's general right to be informed about the administration of justice.

3G.14 Where it has been decided to limit access to the courtroom, whether by reporters or generally, arrangements should be made for the proceedings to be relayed, audibly and if possible visually, to another room in the same court complex to which the media and the public have access if it appears that there will be a need for such additional facilities. Those making use of such a facility should be reminded that it is to be treated as an extension of the courtroom and that they are required to conduct themselves accordingly.

CPD I General Matters 3H: Wales and the Welsh language: devolution issues

3H.1 These are the subject of *Practice Direction: (Supreme Court) (Devolution Issues)* [1999] 1 W.L.R. 1592; [1999] 3 All E.R. 466; [1999] 2 Cr. App. R. 486, to which reference should be made. **B-65**

CPD I General Matters 3J: Wales and the Welsh language: applications for evidence to be given in Welsh

3J.1 If a defendant in a court in England asks to give or call evidence in the Welsh language, the case should not be transferred to Wales. In ordinary circumstances, interpreters can be provided on request. **B-66**

CPD I General Matters 3K: Wales and the Welsh language: use of the Welsh language in courts in Wales

3K.1 The purpose of this direction is to reflect the principle of the Welsh Language Act 1993 that, in the administration of justice in Wales, the English and Welsh languages should be treated on a basis of equality. **B-67**

General

3K.2 It is the responsibility of the legal representatives in every case in which the Welsh language may be used by any witness or party, or in any document which may be placed before the court, to inform the court of that fact, so that appropriate arrangements can be made for the listing of the case. **B-68**

3K.3 Any party or witness is entitled to use Welsh in a magistrates' court in Wales without giving prior notice. Arrangements will be made for hearing such cases in accordance with the "Magistrates' Courts' Protocol for Listing Cases where the Welsh Language is used" (January 2008) which is available on the judiciary's website: *http://www.judiciary.gov.uk/NR/exeres/57AD4763-F265-47B9-8A35-0442E08160E6*. See also r.24.14.

3K.4 If the possible use of the Welsh language is known at the time of sending or appeal to the Crown Court, the court should be informed immediately after sending or when the notice of appeal is lodged. Otherwise, the court should be informed as soon as the possible use of the Welsh language becomes known.

3K.5 If costs are incurred as a result of failure to comply with these directions, a wasted costs order may be made against the defaulting party and / or his legal representatives.

3K.6 The law does not permit the selection of jurors in a manner which enables the court to discover whether a juror does or does not speak Welsh, or to secure a jury whose members are bilingual, to try a case in which the Welsh language may be used.

Preliminary and Plea and Case Management Hearings

3K.7 An advocate in a case in which the Welsh language may be used must raise that matter at the preliminary and/or the plea and case management hearing and endorse details of it on the advocates' questionnaire, so that appropriate directions may be given for the progress of the case. **B-69**

Listing

3K.8 The listing officer, in consultation with the resident judge, should ensure that a case in which the Welsh language may be used is listed— **B-70**

(a) wherever practicable before a Welsh speaking judge, and
(b) in a court in Wales with simultaneous translation facilities.

Interpreters

B-71 **3K.9** Whenever an interpreter is needed to translate evidence from English into Welsh or from Welsh into English, the court listing officer in whose court the case is to be heard shall contact the Welsh Language Unit who will ensure the attendance of an accredited interpreter.

Jurors

B-72 **3K.10** The jury bailiff, when addressing the jurors at the start of their period of jury service, shall inform them that each juror may take an oath or affirm in Welsh or English as he wishes.

3K.11 After the jury has been selected to try a case, and before it is sworn, the court officer swearing in the jury shall inform the jurors in open court that each juror may take an oath or affirm in Welsh or English as he wishes. A juror who takes the oath or affirms in Welsh should not be asked to repeat it in English.

3K.12 Where Welsh is used by any party or witness in a trial, an accredited interpreter will provide simultaneous translation from Welsh to English for the jurors who do not speak Welsh. There is no provision for the translation of evidence from English to Welsh for a Welsh speaking juror.

3K.13 The jury's deliberations must be conducted in private with no other person present and therefore no interpreter may be provided to translate the discussion for the benefit of one or more of the jurors.

Witnesses

B-73 **3K.14** When each witness is called, the court officer administering the oath or affirmation shall inform the witness that he may be sworn or affirm in Welsh or English, as he wishes. A witness who takes the oath or affirms in Welsh should not be asked to repeat it in English.

Opening / Closing of Crown Courts

B-74 **3K.15** Unless it is not reasonably practicable to do so, the opening and closing of the court should be performed in Welsh and English.

Role of liaison judge

B-75 **3K.16** If any question or problem arises concerning the implementation of these directions, contact should in the first place be made with the liaison judge for the Welsh language through the Wales Circuit Office: HMCTS WALES / GLITEM CYMRU, 3rd Floor, Churchill House / 3ydd Llawr Ty Churchill, Churchill Way / Ffordd Churchill, Cardiff / Caerdydd, CF10 2HH029 2067 8300.

CPD I General Matters 3L: Security of prisoners at court

B-76 **3L.1** High-risk prisoners identified to the court as presenting a significant risk of escape, violence in court or danger to those in the court and its environs, and to the public at large, will as far as possible, have administrative and remand appearances listed for disposal by way of live link. They will have priority for the use of video equipment.

3L.2 In all other proceedings that require the appearance in person of a high-risk prisoner, the proceedings will be listed at an appropriately secure court building and in a court with a secure (enclosed or ceiling-high) dock.

3L.3 Where a secure dock or live link is not available the court will be asked to consider an application for additional security measures, which may include: (a) the use of approved restraints (but see below at para. 3L.6); (b) the deployment of additional escort staff; (c) securing the court room for all or part of the proceedings; (d) in exceptional circumstances, moving the hearing to a prison.

3L.4 National Offender Management Service ("NOMS") will be responsible for providing the assessment of the prisoner and it is accepted that this may change at short notice. NOMS must provide notification to the listing officer of all Category A prisoners, those on the escape list and restricted status prisoners or other prisoners who have otherwise been assessed as presenting a significant risk of violence or harm. There is a presumption that all prisoners notified as high-risk will be allocated a hearing by live link and/or secure dock facilities. Where the court cannot provide a secure listing, the reasons should be provided to the establishment so that alternative arrangements can be considered.

Applications for use of approved restraints

3L.5 It is the duty of the court to decide whether a prisoner who appears before them should appear in restraints or not. Their decision must comply with the requirements of the ECHR, particularly Article 3, which prohibits degrading treatment: see *Raninen v. Finland*, 26 E.H.R.R. 563. **B-77**

3L.6 No prisoner should be handcuffed in court unless there are reasonable grounds for apprehending that he will be violent or will attempt to escape. If an application is made, it must be entertained by the court and a ruling must be given. The defence should be given the opportunity to respond to the application: proceeding in the absence of the defendant or his representative may give rise to an issue under Article 6.1 of the Convention [§ 16-72 in the main work]: *Rollinson*, 161 J.P. 107. If an application is to be made *ex parte* then that application should be made *inter partes* and the defence should be given an opportunity to respond.

Additional security measures

3L.7 It may be in some cases that additional dock officers are deployed to mitigate the risk that a prisoner presents. When the nature of the risk is so serious that increased deployment will be insufficient or would in itself be so obtrusive as to prejudice a fair trial, then the court may be required to consider the following measures: (a) reconsider the case for a live link hearing, including transferring the case to a court where the live link is available; (b) transfer the case to an appropriately secure court; (c) the use of approved restraints on the prisoner for all or part of the proceedings; (d) securing the court room for all or part of the proceedings; and (e) the use of (armed) police in the court building. **B-78**

3L.8 The establishment seeking the additional security measures will submit a court management directions form setting out the evidence of the prisoner's identified risk of escape or violence and requesting the court's approval of security measures to mitigate that risk. This must be sent to the listing officer along with current, specific and credible evidence that the security measures are both necessary and proportionate to the identified risk and that the risk cannot be managed in any other way.

3L.9 If the court is asked to consider transfer of the case, then this must be in accordance with *Criminal Practice Direction XIII (Listing) F*, paras 11-13 in the main work]. The listing officer will liaise with the establishment, prosecution and the defence to ensure the needs of the witnesses are taken into account.

3L.10 The judge who has conduct of the case must deal with any application for the use of restraints or any other security measure and will hear representations from the Crown Prosecution Service and the defence before proceeding. The application will only be granted if: (a) there are good grounds for believing that the prisoner poses a significant risk of trying to escape from the court (beyond the assumed motivation of all prisoners to escape) and/or risk of serious harm towards those persons in court or the public generally should an escape attempt be successful; and (b) where there is no other viable means of preventing escape or serious harm.

High-risk prisoners giving evidence from the witness box

3L.11 High-risk prisoners giving evidence from the witness box may pose a significant security risk. In circumstances where such prisoners are required to move from a secure dock to an insecure witness box, an application may be made for the court to consider the use of additional security measures including: (a) the use of approved restraints; (b) the deployment of additional escort staff or police in the courtroom or armed police in the building (the decision to deploy an armed escort is for the chief inspector of the relevant borough: the decision to allow the armed escort in or around the court room is for the senior presiding judge [see Criminal Practice Direction I (General matters) 3M]); (c) securing the courtroom for all or part of the proceedings; (d) giving evidence from the secure dock; and (e) use of live link if the prisoner is not the defendant. **B-79**

CPD I General Matters 3M: Procedure for applications for armed police presence in Crown Courts and magistrates' court buildings (as substituted by Criminal Practice Directions 2015 (Amendment No. 2) [2016] EWCA Crim 1714, Lord Thomas CJ and subsequently amended by Criminal Practice Directions 2015 (Amendment No. 11) [2020] EWCA Crim 1347, Lord Burnett CJ)

3M.1 This practice direction sets out the procedure for the making and handling of applications for authorisation for the presence of armed police officers within the precincts of any Crown Court and magistrates' court buildings at any time. It applies to an application to authorise the carriage of firearms or tasers in court for security purposes. It does not apply to officers who are carrying CS spray or PAVA incapacitant spray, which is included in the standard equipment issued to officers in some forces and therefore no separate authorisation is required for its carriage in court. Likewise, no separate authorisation is required for officers carrying tasers as part of their standard personal **★B-80**

protection equipment where they are attending court on routine court business or to give evidence. If, however, the carrying of tasers is part of a tactical deployment for security purposes then an application must be made in accordance with the following provisions to ensure the court is aware of the arrangements sought.

3M.2 This practice direction applies to all cases in England and Wales in which a police unit intends to request authorisation for the presence of armed police officers in the Crown Court or in the magistrates' court buildings at any time and including during the delivery of prisoners to court.

3M.3 This practice direction allows applications to be made for armed police presence in the Royal Courts of Justice.

Emergency situations

B-81 **3M.4** This practice direction does not apply in an emergency situation. In such circumstances, the police must be able to respond in a way in which their professional judgment deems most appropriate.

Designated court centres

B-82 **3M.5** Applications may only be made for armed police presence in the designated Crown Court and magistrates' court centres (see below). This list may be revised from time to time in consultation with the Association of Chief Police Officers (ACPO) and HMCTS. It will be reviewed at least every five years in consultation with ACPO armed police secretariat and the presiding judges.

3M.6 The Crown Court centres designated for firearms deployment are:

(a) Northern Circuit: Carlisle, Chester, Liverpool, Preston, Manchester Crown Square & Manchester Minshull Street.

(b) North Eastern Circuit: Bradford, Leeds, Newcastle upon Tyne, Sheffield, Teesside and Kingston-upon-Hull.

(c) Western Circuit: Bristol, Winchester and Exeter.

(d) South Eastern Circuit (not including London): Canterbury, Chelmsford, Ipswich, Luton, Maidstone, Norwich, Reading and St Albans.

(e) South Eastern Circuit (London only): Central Criminal Court, Woolwich, Kingston and Snaresbrook.

(f) Midland Circuit: Birmingham, Northampton, Nottingham and Leicester.

(g) Wales Circuit: Cardiff, Swansea and Caernarfon.

3M.7 The magistrates' courts designated for firearms deployment are: South Eastern Circuit (London only): Westminster Magistrates' Court and Belmarsh Magistrates' Court.

Preparatory work prior to applications in all cases

B-83 **3M.8** Prior to the making of any application for armed transport of prisoners or the presence of armed police officers in the court building, consideration must be given to making use of prison video link equipment to avoid the necessity of prisoners' attendance at court for the hearing in respect of which the application is to be made.

3M.9 Notwithstanding their designation, each requesting officer will attend the relevant court before an application is made to ensure that there have been no changes to the premises and that there are no circumstances that might affect security arrangements.

Applying in the Royal Courts of Justice

B-84 **3M.10** All applications should be sent to the listing office of the division in which the case is due to appear. The application should be sent by email if possible and must be on the standard form.

3M.11 The listing office will notify the head of division, providing a copy of the email and any supporting evidence. The head of division may ask to see the senior police office [*sic*] concerned.

3M.12 The head of division will consider the application. If it is refused, the application fails and the police must be notified.

3M.13 In the absence of the head of division, the application should be considered by the vice-president of the division.

3M.14 The relevant court office will be notified of the decision and that office will immediately inform the police by telephone. The decision must then be confirmed in writing to the police.

Applying to the Crown Court

B-85 **3M.15** All applications should be sent to the cluster manager and should be sent by email if possible and must be on the standard form.

3M.16 The cluster manager will notify the presiding judge on the circuit and the resident judge by email, providing a copy of the form and any supporting evidence. The presiding judge may ask to see the senior police officer concerned.

3M.17 The presiding judge will consider the application. If it is refused the application fails and the police must be informed.

3M.18 If the presiding judge approves the application it should be forwarded to the secretary in the senior presiding judge's office. The senior presiding judge will make the final decision. The presiding judge will receive written confirmation of that decision.

3M.19 The presiding judge will notify the cluster manager and the resident judge of the decision. the cluster manager will immediately inform the police of the decision by telephone. The decision must then be confirmed in writing to the police.

Urgent applications to the Crown Court

3M.20 If the temporary deployment of armed police arises as an urgent issue and a case would otherwise have to be adjourned; or if the trial judge is satisfied that there is a serious risk to public safety, then the resident judge will have a discretion to agree such deployment without having obtained the consent of a presiding judge or the senior presiding judge. In such a case: **B-86**

(a) the resident judge should assess the facts and agree the proposed solution with a police officer of at least superintendent level; that officer should agree the approach with the firearms division of the police;

(b) if the proposed solution involves the use of armed police officers, the resident judge must try to contact the presiding judge and/or the senior presiding judge by email and telephone; the cluster manager should be informed of the situation;

(c) if the resident judge cannot obtain a response from the presiding judge or the senior presiding judge, the resident judge may grant the application if satisfied:
  (i) that the application is necessary;
  (ii) that without such deployment there would be a significant risk to public safety; and
  (iii) that the case would have to be adjourned at significant difficulty or inconvenience.

3M.21 The resident judge must keep the position under continual review, to ensure that it remains appropriate and necessary. The resident judge must make continued efforts to contact the presiding judge and the senior presiding judge to notify them of the full circumstances of the authorisation.

Applying to the magistrates' courts

3M.22 All applications should be directed, by email if possible, to the office of the Chief Magistrate, at Westminster Magistrates' Court and must be on the standard form. **B-87**

3M.23 The Chief Magistrate should consider the application and, if approved, it should be forwarded to the senior presiding judge's office. The senior presiding judge will make the final decision. The Chief Magistrate will receive written confirmation of that decision and will then notify the requesting police officer and, where authorisation is given, the affected magistrates' court of the decision.

Urgent applications in the magistrates' courts

3M.24 If the temporary deployment of armed police arises as an urgent issue and a case would otherwise have to be adjourned; or if the Chief Magistrate is satisfied that there is a serious risk to public safety, then the Chief Magistrate will have a discretion to agree such deployment without having obtained the consent of the senior presiding judge. In such a case: **B-88**

(a) the Chief Magistrate should assess the facts and agree the proposed solution with a police officer of at least superintendent level; that officer should agree the approach with the firearms division of the police;

(b) if the proposed solution involves the use of armed police officers, the Chief Magistrate must try to contact the senior presiding judge by email and telephone; the cluster manager should be informed of the situation;

(c) if the Chief Magistrate cannot obtain a response from the senior presiding judge, the Chief Magistrate may grant the application if satisfied:
  (i) that the application is necessary;
  (ii) that without such deployment there would be a significant risk to public safety; and
  (iii) that the case would have to be adjourned at significant difficulty or inconvenience.

3M.25 The Chief Magistrate must keep the position under continual review, to ensure that it remains appropriate and necessary. The Chief Magistrate must make continued efforts to contact the senior presiding judge to notify him of the full circumstances of the authorisation.

CPD I General Matters 3N: Use of live link and telephone facilities (as inserted by Criminal Practice Directions 2015 (Amendment No. 3) [2017] EWCA Crim 30, Lord Thomas CJ; and subsequently amended by Criminal Practice Directions 2015 (Amendment No.7) [2018] EWCA Crim 1760, Lord Burnett CJ and Criminal Practice Directions 2015 (Amendment No. 11) [2020] EWCA Crim 1347, Lord Burnett CJ)

3N.1 Where it is lawful and in the interests of justice to do so, courts should exercise their statu- **B-89**

tory and other powers to conduct hearings by live link or telephone. This is consistent with the Criminal Procedure Rules and with the recommendations of the President of the Queen's Bench Division's *Review of Efficiency in Criminal Proceedings* published in January 2015. Save where legislation circumscribes the court's jurisdiction, the breadth of that jurisdiction is acknowledged by CrimPR 3.5(1), (2)(d).

3N.2 It is the duty of the court to make use of technology actively to manage the case: CrimPR 3.2(1), (2)(h). That duty includes an obligation to give directions for the use of live links and telephone facilities in the circumstances listed in CrimPR 3.2(4) and (5) (pre-trial hearings, including pre-trial case management hearings). Where the court directs that evidence is to be given by live link, and especially where such a direction is given on the court's own initiative, it is essential that the decision is communicated promptly to the witness: CrimPR 18.4. Contrary to a practice adopted by some courts, none of those rules or other provisions require the renewal of a live link direction merely because a trial has had to be postponed or adjourned. Once made, such a direction applies until it is discharged by the court, having regard to the relevant statutory criteria.

3N.3 It is the duty of the parties to alert the court to any reason why live links or telephones should not be used where CrimPR 3.2 otherwise would oblige the court to do so; and, where a direction for the use of such facilities has been made, it is the duty of the parties as soon as practicable to alert the court to any reason why that direction should be varied (CrimPR 3.3(2)(e) and 3.6).

3N.4 The word "appropriate" in CrimPR 3.2(4) and (5) is not a term of art. It has the ordinary English meaning of "fitting", or "suitable". Whether the facilities available to the court in any particular case can be considered appropriate is a matter for the court, but plainly to be appropriate such facilities must work, at the time at which they are required; all participants must be able to hear and, in the case of a live link, see each other clearly; and there must be no extraneous noise, movement or other distraction suffered by a participant, or transmitted by a participant to others. What degree of protection from accidental or deliberate interception should be considered appropriate will depend upon the purpose for which a live link or telephone is to be used. If it is to participate in a hearing which is open to the public anyway, then what is communicated by such means is by definition public and the use of links such as Skype or Facetime, which are not generally considered secure from interception, may not be objectionable. If it is to participate in a hearing in private, and especially one at which sensitive information will be discussed - for example, on an application for a search warrant - then a more secure service is likely to be required.

3N.5 There may be circumstances in which the court should not require the use of live link or telephone facilities despite their being otherwise appropriate at a pre-trial hearing. In every case, in deciding whether any such circumstances apply, the court will keep in mind that, for the purposes of what may be an essentially administrative hearing, it may be compatible with the overriding objective to proceed in the defendant's absence altogether, especially if he or she is represented, unless, exceptionally, a rule otherwise requires. The principle that the court always must consider proceeding in a defendant's absence is articulated in CrimPR 3.9(2)(a). Where at a pre-trial hearing bail may be under consideration, the provisions of CrimPR 14.2 will be relevant.

3N.6 Such circumstances will include any case in which the defendant's effective participation cannot be achieved by his or her attendance by such means, and CrimPR 3.2(4) and (5) except such cases from the scope of the obligation which that rule otherwise imposes on the court. That exception may apply where (this list is not exhaustive) the defendant has a disorder or disability, including a hearing, speech or sight impediment, or has communication needs to which the use of a live link or telephone is inimical (whether or not those needs are such as to require the appointment of an intermediary); or where the defendant requires interpretation and effective interpretation cannot be provided by live link or telephone, as the case may be. In deciding whether to require a defendant to attend a first hearing in a magistrates' court by live link from a police station, the court should take into account any views expressed by the defendant, the terms of any mental health or other medical assessment of the defendant carried out at the police station, and all other relevant information and representations available. No single factor is determinative, but the court must keep in mind the terms of section 57C(6A) of the Crime and Disorder Act 1998 (Use of live link at preliminary hearings where accused is at police station) which provides that 'A live link direction under this section may not be given unless the court is satisfied that it is not contrary to the interests of justice to give the direction.'

3N.7 Finally, that exception sometimes may apply where the defendant's attendance in person at a pre-trial hearing will facilitate communication with his or her legal representatives. The court should not make such an exception merely to allow client and representatives to meet if that meeting can and should be held elsewhere. However, there will be cases in which defence representatives reasonably need to meet with a defendant, to take his or her instructions or to explain events to him or her, either shortly before or immediately after a pre-trial hearing and in circumstances in which that meeting cannot take place effectively by live link.

3N.8 Nothing prohibits the member or members of a court from conducting a pre-trial hearing by attending by live link or telephone from a location distant from all the other participants. Despite the conventional view that the venue for a court hearing is the court room in which that hearing has been arranged to take place, the Criminal Procedure Rules define "court" as "a tribunal with jurisdiction over criminal cases. It includes a judge, recorder, District Judge (Magistrates' Court), lay justice and, when exercising their judicial powers, the Registrar of Criminal Appeals, a justices' clerk or assistant clerk." Neither CrimPR 3.25 (place of trial), which applies in the Crown Court, nor CrimPR 24.14 (place of trial), which applies in magistrates' courts, each of which requires proceedings to take place in a courtroom provided by the Lord Chancellor, applies for the purposes of a pre-trial hearing. Thus for the purposes of such a hearing there is no legal obstacle to the judge, magistrate or magistrates conducting it from elsewhere, with other participants assembled in a courtroom from which the member or members of the court are physically absent. In principle, nothing prohibits the conduct of a pre-trial hearing by live link or telephone with each participant, including the member or members of the court, in a different location (an arrangement sometimes described as a "virtual hearing"). This is dependent upon there being means by which that hearing can be witnessed by the public - for example, by public attendance at a courtroom or other venue from which the participants all can be seen and heard (if by live link), or heard (if by telephone). The principle of open justice to which paragraph 3N.17 refers is relevant.

3N.9 Sections 57A to 57F of the CDA 1998 [§§ 3-226 et seq. in the main work] allow a defendant who is in custody to enter a plea by live link, and allow for such a defendant who attends by live link to be sentenced. In appropriate circumstances, the court may allow a defendant who is not in custody to enter a plea by live link; but the same considerations as apply to sentencing in such a case will apply: see para. 3N.13 beneath.

3N.10 The CDA 1998 does not allow for the attendance by live link at a contested trial of a defendant who is in custody. The court may allow a defendant who wishes to do so to observe all or part of his or her trial by live link, whether she or he is in custody or not, but (a) such a defendant cannot lawfully give evidence by such means unless he or she satisfies the criteria prescribed by section 33A of the YJCEA 1999 [ibid., § 8-106] and the court so orders under that section (see also CrimPR 18.14 - 18.17); (b) a defendant who is in custody and who observes the trial by live link is not present, as a matter of law, and the trial must be treated as taking place in his or her absence, she or he having waived the right to attend; and (c) a defendant who has refused to attend his or her trial when required to do so, or who has absconded, must not be permitted to observe the proceedings by live link.

3N.11 Paragraphs I 3D to 3G inclusive of these practice directions (vulnerable people in the courts; ground rules hearings to plan the questioning of a vulnerable witness or defendant; intermediaries; vulnerable defendants) contain directions relevant to the use of a live link as a special measure for a young or otherwise vulnerable witness, or to facilitate the giving of evidence by a defendant who is likewise young or otherwise vulnerable, within the scope of the YJCEA 1999. Defence representatives and the court must keep in mind that special measures under the 1999 Act and CrimPR, Pt 18, including the use of a live link, are available to defence as well as to prosecution witnesses who meet the statutory criteria. Defence representatives should always consider whether their witnesses would benefit from giving evidence by live link and should apply for a direction if appropriate, either at the case management hearing or as soon as possible thereafter. A defence witness should be afforded the same facilities and treatment as a prosecution witness, including the same opportunity to make a pre-trial visit to the court building in order to familiarise himself or herself with it. Where a live link is sought as a special measure for a young or vulnerable witness or defendant, CrimPR 18.10 and 18.15 respectively require, among other things, that the applicant must identify someone to accompany that witness or defendant while they give evidence; must name the person, if possible; and must explain why that person would be an appropriate companion for that witness. The court must ensure that directions are given accordingly when ordering such a live link. Witness Service volunteers are available to support all witnesses, prosecution and defence, if required.

3N.12 Under sections 57A and 57D or 57E of the CDA 1998 [ibid., §§ 3-226, 3-229, 3-230] the court may pass sentence on a defendant in custody who attends by live link. The court may allow a defendant who is not in custody and who wishes to attend his or her sentencing by live link to do so, and may receive representations (but not evidence) from her or him by such means. Factors of which the court will wish to take account in exercising its discretion include, in particular, the penalty likely to be imposed; the importance of ensuring that the explanations of sentence required by CrimPR 24.11(9), in magistrates' courts, and in the Crown Court by CrimPR 25.16(7), can be given satisfactorily, for the defendant, for other participants and for the public, including reporters; and the preferences of the maker of any victim personal statement which is to be read aloud or played pursuant to paragraph VII F.3(c) of these practice directions.

Youth defendants

3N.13 In the youth court or when a youth is appearing in the magistrates' court or the Crown **B-90**

Court, it will usually be appropriate for the youth to be produced in person at court. This is to ensure that the court can engage properly with the youth and that the necessary level of engagement can be facilitated with the youth offending team worker, defence representative and/or appropriate adult responsible for the youth's care. The court should deal with any application for use of a live-link on a case-by-case basis, after consultation with the parties and the youth offending team. Such hearings that may be appropriate, include, onward remand hearings at which there is no bail application or case management hearings, particularly if the youth is already serving a custodial sentence.

3N.14 It rarely will be appropriate for a youth to be sentenced over a live link. However, notwithstanding the court's duties of engagement with a youth, the overriding welfare principle and the statutory responsibility of the youth offending worker to explain the sentence to the youth, after consultation with the parties and the youth offending team, there may be circumstances in which it may be appropriate to sentence a youth over the live-link:

(a) if the youth is already serving a custodial sentence and the sentence to be imposed by the court is bound to be a further custodial sentence, whether concurrent or consecutive;

(b) if the youth is already serving a custodial sentence and the court is minded to impose a non-custodial sentence which will have no material impact on the sentence being served;

(c) the youth is being detained in a secure establishment at such a distance from the court that the travelling time from one to the other will be significant so as to materially affect the welfare of the youth;

(d) the youth's condition - whether mental or otherwise - is so disturbed that his or her production would be a significant detriment to his or her welfare.

3N.15 Arrangements must be made in advance of any live link hearing to enable the youth offending worker to be at the secure establishment where the youth is in custody. In the event that such arrangements are not practicable, the youth offending worker must have sufficient access to the youth via the live link booth before and after the hearing.

Conduct of participants

B-91 **3N.16** Where a live link is used, the immediate vicinity of the device by which a person attends becomes, temporarily, part of the courtroom for the purposes of that person's participation. That person, and any advocate or legal representative, custodian, court officer, intermediary or other companion, whether immediately visible to the court or not, becomes a participant for the purposes of CrimPR 1.2(2) and is subject to the court's jurisdiction to regulate behaviour in the courtroom. The substance and effect of this direction must be drawn to the attention of all such participants.

Open justice and records of proceedings

B-92 **3N.17** The principle of open justice to which CrimPR 6.2(1) gives effect applies as strongly where electronic means of communication are used to conduct a hearing as it applies in other circumstances. Open justice is the principal means by which courts are kept under scrutiny by the public. It follows that where a participant attends a hearing in public by live link or telephone then that person's participation must be, as nearly as may be, equally audible and, if applicable, equally visible to the public as it would be were he or she physically present. Where electronic means of communication are used to conduct a hearing, records of the event must be maintained in the usual way: CrimPR 5.4. In the Crown Court, this includes the recording of the proceedings: CrimPR 5.5.

CPD I General Matters 3P: Commissioning medical reports (as inserted by Criminal Practice Directions 2015 (Amendment No.7) [2018] EWCA Crim 1760, Lord Burnett CJ)

General observations

B-93 **3P.1** CrimPR 24.3 and 25.10 concern procedures to be followed in magistrates' courts and in the Crown Court respectively where there is doubt about a defendant's mental health and, in the Crown Court, the defendant's capacity to participate in a trial. CrimPR 3.28 governs the procedure where, on the court's own initiative, a magistrates' court requires expert medical opinion about the potential suitability of a hospital order under section 37(3) of the Mental Health Act 1983 (hospital order without convicting the defendant), the Crown Court requires such opinion about the defendant's fitness to participate at trial, under section 4 of the Criminal Procedure (Insanity) Act 1964, or either a magistrates' court or the Crown Court requires such opinion to help the court determine a question of intent or insanity.

3P.2 Rule 3.28 governs the procedure to be followed where a report is commissioned at the instigation of the court. It is not a substitute for the prompt commissioning of a report or reports by a party or party's representatives where expert medical opinion is material to that party's case. In particular, those representing a defendant may wish to obtain a medical report or reports wholly independently of the court. Nothing in these directions, therefore, should be read as discouraging a party from commissioning a medical report before the case comes before the court, where that party believes such a report to be material to an issue in the case and where it is possible promptly to commission it. However, where a party has commissioned such a report then if that report has not been received by the time the court gives directions for preparation for trial, and if the court agrees that it seems likely that the report will be material to what is in issue, then when giving directions for trial the court should include a timetable for the reception of that report and should give directions for progress to be reviewed at intervals, adopting the timetable set out in these directions with such adaptations as are needed.

3P.3 In assessing the likely materiality of an expert medical report to help the court assess a defendant's health and capacity at the time of the alleged offence or the time of trial, or both, the court will be assisted by the parties' representations; by the views expressed in any assessment that may already have been prepared; and by the views of practitioners in local criminal justice mental health services, whose assistance is available to the court under local liaison arrangements.

3P.4 Where the court requires the assistance of such a report then it is essential that there should be (i) absolute clarity about who is expected to do what, by when, and at whose expense; and (ii) judicial directions for progress with that report to be monitored and reviewed at prescribed intervals, following a timetable set by the court which culminates in the consideration of the report at a hearing. This is especially important where the report in question is a psychiatric assessment of the defendant for the preparation of which specific expertise may be required which is not readily available and because in some circumstances a second such assessment, by another medical practitioner, may be required.

Timetable for the commissioning, preparation and consideration of a report or reports

3P.5 CrimPR 3.28 requires the court to set a timetable appropriate to the case for the preparation and reception of a report. That timetable must not be in substitution for the usual timetable for preparation for trial but must instead be incorporated within the trial preparation timetable. The fact that a medical report is to be obtained, whether that is commissioned at a party's instigation or on the court's own initiative, is never a reason to postpone a preparation for trial or a plea and trial preparation hearing, or to decline to give the directions needed for preparation for trial. It follows that a trial date must be set and other directions given in the usual way. **B-94**

3P.6 In setting the timetable for obtaining a report or reports the court will take account of such representations and other information that it receives, including information about the anticipated availability and workload of medical practitioners with the appropriate expertise. However, the timetable ought not be a protracted one. It is essential to keep in mind the importance of maintaining progress: in recognition of the defendant's rights and with respect for the interests of victims and witnesses, as required by CrimPR Part 1 (the overriding objective). In a magistrates' court account must be taken, too, of section 11 of the Powers of Criminal Courts (Sentencing) Act 2000, which limits the duration of each remand pending the preparation of a report to 3 weeks, where the defendant is to be in custody, and to 4 weeks if the defendant is to be on bail.

3P.7 Subject, therefore, to contrary judicial direction the timetable set by the court should require:

(a) the convening of a further pre-trial case management hearing to consider the report and its implications for the conduct of the proceedings no more than 6 - 8 weeks after the court makes its request in a magistrates' court, and no more than 10 - 12 weeks after the request in the Crown Court (at the end of Stage 2 of the directions for pre-trial preparation in the Crown Court);

(b) the prompt identification of an appropriate medical practitioner or practitioners, if not already identified by the court, and the despatch of a commission or commissions accordingly, within 2 business days of the court's decision to request a report;

(c) acknowledgement of a commission by its recipient, and acceptance or rejection of that commission, within 5 business days of its receipt;

(d) enquiries by court staff to confirm that the commission has been received, and to ascertain the action being taken in response, in the event that no acknowledgement is received within 10 business days of its despatch;

(e) delivery of the report within 5 weeks of the despatch of the commission;

(f) enquiries into progress by court staff in the event that no report is received within 5 weeks of the despatch of the commission.

3P.8 The further pre-trial case management hearing that is convened for the court to consider the report should not be adjourned before it takes place save in exceptional circumstances and then only by explicit judicial direction the reasons for which must be recorded. If by the time of that hearing the report is available, as usually should be the case, then at that hearing the court can be expected to determine the issue in respect of which the report was commissioned and give further directions accordingly. If by that time, exceptionally, the report is not available then the court should take the opportunity provided by that hearing to enquire into the reasons, give such directions as are **B-95**

appropriate, and if necessary adjourn the hearing to a fixed date for further consideration then. Where it is known in advance of that hearing that the report will not be available in time, the hearing may be conducted by live link or telephone: subject, in the defendant's case, to the same considerations as are identified at paragraph 3N.6 of these Practice Directions. However, it rarely will be appropriate to dispense altogether with that hearing, or to make enquiries and give further directions without any hearing at all, in view of the arrangements for monitoring and review that the court already will have directed and which, by definition therefore, thus far will have failed to secure the report's timely delivery.

3P.9 Where a requirement of the timetable set by the court is not met, or where on enquiry by court staff it appears that the timetable is unlikely to be met, and in any instance in which a medical practitioner who accepts a commission asks for more time, then court staff should not themselves adjust the timetable or accede to such a request but instead should seek directions from an appropriate judicial authority. Subject to local judicial direction, that will be, in the Crown Court, the judge assigned to the case or the resident judge and, in a magistrates' court, a District Judge (Magistrates' Courts) or justice of the peace assigned to the case, or the Justices' Clerk, an assistant clerk or other senior legal adviser. Even if the timetable is adjusted in consequence:

(a) the further pre-trial case management hearing convened to consider the report rarely should be adjourned before it takes place: see paragraph 3O.13 above;

(b) directions should be given for court staff henceforth to make regular enquiries into progress, at prescribed intervals of not more than 2 weeks, and to report the outcome to an appropriate judicial authority who will decide what further directions, if any, to give.

3P.10 Any adjournment of a hearing convened to consider the report should be to a specific date: the hearing should not be adjourned generally, or to a date to be set in due course. The adjournment of such a hearing should not be for more than a further 6 - 8 weeks save in the most exceptional circumstances; and no more than one adjournment of the hearing should be allowed without obtaining written or oral representations from the commissioned medical practitioner explaining the reasons for the delay.

Commissioning a report

B-96 **3P.11** Guidance entitled 'Good practice guidance: commissioning, administering and producing psychiatric reports for sentencing' prepared for and published by the Ministry of Justice and HM Courts and Tribunals Service in September 2010 contains material that will assist court staff and those who are asked to prepare such reports: *http://www.ohrn.nhs.uk/resource/policy/GoodPracticeGuidePsychReports.pdf* The guidance includes standard forms of letters of instruction and other documents.

3P.12 CrimPR 3.28 requires the commissioner of a report to explain why the court seeks the report and to include relevant information about the circumstances. The HMCTS Guidance contains forms for judicial use in the instruction of court staff, and guidance to court staff on the preparation of letters of instruction, where a report is required for sentencing purposes. Those forms and that guidance can be adapted for use where the court requires a report on the defendant's fitness to participate, in the Crown Court, or in a magistrates' court requires a report for the purposes of section 37(3) of the Mental Health Act 1983.

3P.13 The commission should invite a practitioner who is unable to accept it promptly to nominate a suitably qualified substitute, if possible, and to transfer the commission to that person, reporting the transfer when acknowledging the court officer's letter. It is entirely appropriate for the commission to draw the recipient's attention to CrimPR 1.2 (the duty of the participants in a criminal case) and to CrimPR 19.2(1)(b) (the obligation of an expert witness to comply with directions made by a court and at once to inform the court of any significant failure, by the expert or another, to take any step required by such a direction).

3P.14 Where the relevant legislation requires a second psychiatric assessment by a second medical practitioner, and where no commission already has been addressed to a second such practitioner, the commission may invite the person to whom it is addressed to nominate a suitably qualified second person and to pass a copy of the commission to that person forthwith.

Funding arrangements

B-97 **3P.15** Where a medical report has been, or is to be, commissioned by a party then that party is responsible for arranging payment of the fees incurred, even though the report is intended for the court's use. That must be made clear in that party's commission.

3P.16 Where a medical report is requested by the court and commissioned by a party or by court staff at the court's direction then the commission must include (i) confirmation that the fees will be paid by HMCTS, (ii) details of how, and to whom, to submit an invoice or claim for fees, and (iii) notice of the prescribed rates of fees and of any legislative or other criteria applicable to the calculation of the fees that may be paid.

Remand in custody

3P.17 Where the defendant who is to be examined will be remanded in custody then notice that directions have been given for a medical report or reports to be prepared must be included in the information given to the defendant's custodian, to ensure that the preparation of the report or reports can be facilitated. This is especially important where bail is withheld on the ground that it would be otherwise impracticable to complete the required report, and in particular where that is the only ground for withholding bail. **B-98**

CPD I General matters 3Q: Failure to comply with requirement to give name, date of birth and nationality (as inserted by Criminal Practice Directions 2015 (Amendment No.10) [2020] EWCA Crim 605, Lord Burnett CJ)

3Q.1 Section 86A of the Courts Act 2003 requires a magistrates' court and the Crown Court to require a defendant to provide his or her name, date of birth and nationality in the circumstances and at the times set out in CrimPR 3.13(5) and 3.27(5). Section 86A(3) of the Act makes it an offence for the defendant without reasonable excuse to fail to comply with such a requirement, whether by providing false or incomplete information or by providing no information. A person guilty of such an offence is liable on summary conviction to imprisonment for a term not exceeding 6 months, or to a fine, or both. It follows that a prosecution for failure to comply with a section 86A requirement may be brought by any of the procedures for which CrimPR Part 7 provides (Starting a prosecution in a magistrates' court) in the same way as any other allegation of a summary offence. **B-99**

3Q.2 It does not follow, however, that every such allegation first must be reported to the police. Where the defendant's conduct evinces guilt, especially if the defendant refuses altogether to give the information required, such conduct undermines the administration of justice and the authority of the court. In principle, it should be dealt with at once. Section 86A(6) of the Act provides that, 'The criminal court before which a person is required to provide his or her name, date of birth and nationality may deal with any suspected offence under subsection (3) at the same time as dealing with the offence for which the person was already before the court'. In such a case, therefore, a magistrates' court may invite the prosecutor to institute proceedings orally, there and then, pursuant to section 1 of the Magistrates' Courts Act 1980 and CrimPR Part 7, and may there and then try the alleged offence in accordance with the rules in CrimPR Part 24 (Trial and sentence in a magistrates' court). A defendant should be allowed a reasonable opportunity to reflect and to take legal advice, from a duty solicitor if the defendant has no legal representative in the prosecution for the main offence. After that, unless the defendant then pleads guilty the prosecutor must call such evidence as may be convenient and sufficient, in the prosecutor's view, formally to prove the allegation; and the defendant may present evidence, for example of reasonable excuse, and may make representations in accordance with those rules.

3Q.3 Given that the Act expressly contemplates a prompt determination by the court before which there occurs an ostensible failure to comply with a section 86A requirement, rarely will it be necessary or appropriate to adjourn the trial of that allegation to a differently constituted court unless there emerges such a dispute of fact about what has occurred in the sight and hearing of the court as to disqualify the first bench from determining that dispute with perceived impartiality. In that rare event the trial of the allegation must be heard, the same day, by a different bench.2 In any other event the constitution before whom the alleged offence under section 86A(3) has occurred usually should try the allegation, usually the same day.

3Q.4 If in the circumstances contemplated in the preceding paragraph a different bench convicts the defendant of the section 86A(3) offence, and if the defendant is convicted by the first bench of the offence for which the defendant was already before the court, then the court which passes sentence for that main offence should pass sentence also under section 86A(3). However, an offence under section 86A(3) is one that stands apart from the proceedings in the course of which it was committed the seriousness of which can be reflected by an appropriate and, generally, separate penalty.

3Q.5 Whether an alleged contravention of a section 86A requirement is dealt with the same day or later, after investigation by the police, no member of the court before whom the alleged contravention occurs should participate in the proceedings as the complainant or as a witness. Nor will it be appropriate to invite the defendant's representative, if any, to give evidence of what that representative may have witnessed in the court room. It is unexceptionable for court staff, including a legal adviser in a magistrates' court, to be asked to give evidence of what has taken place.

3Q.6 The offence contrary to section 86A(3) of the 2003 Act is one to which the time limit imposed by section 127 of the Magistrates' Courts Act 1980 applies, namely that a magistrates' court may not try an information unless that information was laid within 6 months from the time when the offence was committed. Where the court does not adopt the procedure described in paragraphs 3Q.2 and 3Q.3 above the alleged offence must be reported promptly to allow it to be investigated and, if appropriate, prosecuted in time.

CPD I General matters 3R: Hearing to inform the court of sensitive material (as inserted by Criminal Practice Directions 2015 (Amendment No.10) [2020] EWCA Crim 605, Lord Burnett CJ)

B-100 **3R.1** CrimPR 3.29 (Hearing to inform the court of sensitive material) governs the procedure that must be followed where a prosecutor has, or is aware of, sensitive material to which the prosecutor does not think the obligation to disclose applies but of the existence of which the prosecutor thinks it necessary to inform the court in order to mitigate the risks listed in that rule.

3R.2 Examples of such material were given by the Court of Appeal in *R v Ali* [2019] EWCA Crim 1527. Examples include information about the activities of a defendant or witness, or about a person to whom the evidence in the case refers, or information to the effect that the prosecution evidence omits matters irrelevant to the trial, derived from observations, for example, which is of sensitivity in some other respect. These are, however, only examples and other material may come within the scope of the rule.

3R.3 In the Crown Court a hearing to which rule 3.29 applies must be recorded: CrimPR 5.5 (Recording and transcription of proceedings in the Crown Court). It is very likely that the hearing will be conducted in private (see CrimPR 3.29(4)) and very likely that it will take place in a private room rather than in the courtroom. The recording therefore should be made using a suitable and suitably secure device, and it should be stored securely. In some circumstances that may require arrangements for the storage of the recording to be dealt with in accordance with CrimPR 3.29(4)(c)(ii) (storage by an appropriate person other than the court officer). Such storage arrangements are likely also to apply to any written material provided to the court under CrimPR 3.29(3)(c).

Criminal Procedure Rules 2020 (SI 2020/759), Pt 4

When this Part applies

B-101 **4.1.**—(1) The rules in this Part apply—

(a) to the service of every document in a case to which these rules apply; and

(b) for the purposes of section 12 of the Road Traffic Offenders Act 1988, to the service of a requirement to which that section applies.

(2) The rules apply subject to any special rules in other legislation (including other parts of these rules) or in the Practice Direction.

(3) In this Part, 'the relevant court office' means—

(a) in relation to a case in a magistrates' court or in the Crown Court, an office—

(i) at which that court's business is administered, and

(ii) the address or electronic address of which is advertised by the Lord Chancellor at the date of service as that at which that type of document must be served;

(b) in relation to an application to a High Court judge for permission to serve a draft indictment—

(i) in London, the Queen's Bench Listing Office, Royal Courts of Justice, Strand, London WC2A 2LL,

(ii) elsewhere, the office at which court staff administer the business of any court then constituted of a High Court judge, and

(iii) in either case, the electronic address which is advertised by the Lord Chancellor at the date of service as that at which such an application must be served;

(c) in relation to an extradition appeal case in the High Court—

(i) the Administrative Court Office, Royal Courts of Justice, Strand, London WC2A 2LL, and

(ii) the electronic address which is advertised by the Lord Chancellor at the date of service as that at which that type of document must be served; and

(d) where the recipient is the Registrar of Criminal Appeals—

(i) the Criminal Appeal Office, Royal Courts of Justice, Strand, London WC2A 2LL, and

(ii) the electronic address which is advertised by the Lord Chancellor at the date of service as that at which that type of document must be served.

Methods of service

B-102 **4.2.**—(1) A document may be served by any of the methods described in rules 4.3 to 4.6 (subject to rules 4.7 and 4.10), or in rule 4.8.

(2) Where a document may be served by electronic means under rule 4.6, the general rule is that the person serving it must use that method.

Service by handing over a document

B-103 **4.3.**—(1) A document may be served on—

(a) an individual by handing it to him or her;
(b) a corporation by handing it to a person holding a senior position in that corporation;
(c) an individual or corporation who is legally represented in the case by handing it to that legal representative;
(d) the prosecution by handing it to the prosecutor or to the prosecution representative; and
(e) the court officer or the Registrar of Criminal Appeals by handing it to a court officer with authority to accept it at the relevant court office.

(2) If an individual is under 18, a copy of a document served under paragraph (1)(a) must be handed to his or her parent, or another appropriate adult, unless no such person is readily available.

(3) Unless the court otherwise directs, for the purposes of paragraph (1)(c) or (d) (service by handing a document to a party's representative) "representative" includes an advocate appearing for that party at a hearing.

Service by leaving or posting a document

4.4.–(1) A document may be served by addressing it to the person to be served and leaving it at the appropriate address for service under this rule, or by sending it to that address by first class post or by the equivalent of first class post. **B-104**

(2) The address for service under this rule on–
(a) an individual is an address where it is reasonably believed that he or she will receive it;
(b) a corporation is its principal office, and if there is no readily identifiable principal office then any place where it carries on its activities or business;
(c) an individual or corporation who is legally represented in the case is that legal representative's office;
(d) the prosecution is the prosecutor's office;
(e) the court officer or the Registrar of Criminal Appeals is the relevant court office.

Service by document exchange

4.5.–(1) This rule applies where– **B-105**
(a) the person to be served–
(i) has given a document exchange (DX) box number, and
(ii) has not refused to accept service by DX; or
(b) the person to be served is legally represented in the case and the legal representative has given a DX box number.

(2) A document may be served by–
(a) addressing it to that person or legal representative, as appropriate, at that DX box number; and
(b) leaving it at–
(i) the document exchange at which the addressee has that DX box number, or
(ii) a document exchange at which the person serving it has a DX box number.

(3) Where the person to be served under this rule is the court officer, the address for service is the relevant court office.

Service by electronic means

4.6.–(1) This rule applies where– **B-106**
(a) the person to be served–
(i) has given an electronic address and has not refused to accept service at that address, or
(ii) is given access to an electronic address at which a document may be deposited and has not refused to accept service by the deposit of a document at that address; or
(b) the person to be served is legally represented in the case and the legal representative–
(i) has given an electronic address, or
(ii) is given access to an electronic address at which a document may be deposited.

(2) A document may be served–
(a) by sending it by electronic means to the address which the recipient has given; or
(b) by depositing it at an address to which the recipient has been given access and–
(i) in every case, making it possible for the recipient to read the document, or view or listen to its content, as the case may be,
(ii) unless the court otherwise directs, making it possible for the recipient to make and keep an electronic copy of the document, and
(iii) notifying the recipient of the deposit of the document (which notice may be given by electronic means).

(3) Where the person to be served under this rule is the court officer, the address for service is the relevant court office.

(4) Where a document is served under this rule the person serving it need not provide a paper copy as well.

Documents that must be served by specified methods

B-107 **4.7.**—(1) An application or written statement, and notice, under rule 48.9 alleging contempt of court may be served—

(a) on an individual, only under rule 4.3(1)(a) (by handing it to him or her); and

(b) on a corporation, only under rule 4.3(1)(b) (by handing it to a person holding a senior position in that corporation).

(2) For the purposes of section 12 of the Road Traffic Offenders Act 1988, a notice of a requirement under section 172 of the Road Traffic Act 1988 [§ 32-185 in the main work] or under section 112 of the Road Traffic Regulation Act 1984 to identify the driver of a vehicle may be served—

(a) on an individual, only by post under rule 4.4(1) and (2)(a); and

(b) on a corporation, only by post under rule 4.4(1) and (2)(b).

Service by person in custody

B-108 **4.8.**—(1) A person in custody may serve a document by handing it to the custodian addressed to the person to be served.

(2) The custodian must—

(a) endorse it with the time and date of receipt;

(b) record its receipt; and

(c) forward it promptly to the addressee.

Service by another method

B-109 **4.9.**—(1) The court may allow service of a document by a method—

(a) other than those described in rules 4.3 to 4.6 and in rule 4.8; and

(b) other than one specified by rule 4.7, where that rule applies.

(2) An order allowing service by another method must specify—

(a) the method to be used; and

(b) the date on which the document will be served.

Documents that may not be served on a legal representative

B-110 **4.10.** Unless the court otherwise directs, service on a party's legal representative of any of the following documents is not service of that document on that party—

(a) a summons, requisition, single justice procedure notice or witness summons;

(b) notice of an order under section 25 of the Road Traffic Offenders Act 1988;

(c) a notice of registration under section 71(6) of that Act;

(d) notice of a hearing to review the postponement of the issue of a warrant of detention or imprisonment under section 77(6) of the Magistrates' Courts Act 1980;

(e) notice under section 86 of that Act of a revised date to attend a means inquiry;

(f) any notice or document served under Part 14 (bail and custody time limits);

(g) notice under rule 24.15(a) of when and where an adjourned hearing will resume;

(h) notice under rule 28.5(3) of an application to vary or discharge a compensation order;

(i) notice under rule 28.10(2)(c) of the location of the sentencing or enforcing court;

(j) a collection order, or notice requiring payment, served under rule 30.2(a); or

(k) an application or written statement, and notice, under rule 48.9 alleging contempt of court.

Date of service

B-111 **4.11.**—(1) A document served under rule 4.3 or rule 4.8 is served on the day it is handed over.

(2) Unless something different is shown, a document served on a person by any other method is served—

(a) in the case of a document left at an address, on the next business day after the day on which it was left;

(b) in the case of a document sent by first class post or by the equivalent of first class post, on the second business day after the day on which it was posted or despatched;

(c) in the case of a document served by document exchange, on the second business day after the day on which it was left at a document exchange allowed by rule 4.5;

(d) in the case of a document served by electronic means—

(i) on the day on which it is sent under rule 4.6(2)(a), if that day is a business day and if it is sent by no later than 2.30pm that day (4.30pm that day, in an extradition appeal case in the High Court, or 5pm that day if it is an application for permission to refer a sentencing case to which Part 41 (Reference to the Court of Appeal of point of law or unduly lenient sentencing) applies),

(ii) on the day on which notice of its deposit is given under rule 4.6(2)(b), if that day is a business day and if that notice is given by no later than 2.30pm that day (4.30pm that day, in an extradition appeal case in the High Court, or 5pm that day if it is an application for permission to refer a sentencing case to which Part 41 (Reference to the Court of Appeal of point of law or unduly lenient sentencing) applies), or

(iii) otherwise, on the next business day after it was sent or such notice was given; and

(e) in any case, on the day on which the addressee responds to it, if that is earlier.

(3) Unless something different is shown, a document produced by a computer system for dispatch by post is to be taken as having been sent by first class post, or by the equivalent of first class post, to the addressee on the business day after the day on which it was produced.

(4) Where a document is served on or by the court officer, "business day" does not include a day on which the court offce is closed.

Proof of service

4.12. The person who serves a document may prove that by signing a certificate explaining how and when it was served. **B-112**

Court's power to give directions about service

4.13.—(1) The court may specify the time as well as the date by which a document must be— **B-113**

(a) served under rule 4.3 (service by handing over a document) or rule 4.8 (service by person in custody); or

(b) sent or deposited by electronic means, if it is served under rule 4.6.

(2) The court may treat a document as served if the addressee responds to it even if it was not served in accordance with the rules in this Part.

Criminal Procedure Rules 2020 (SI 2020/759), Pt 5

Forms and Court Records

Forms

Applications, etc. by forms or electronic means

5.1.—(1) This rule applies where a rule, a practice direction or the court requires a person to— **B-114**

(a) make an application or give a notice;

(b) supply information for the purposes of case management by the court; or

(c) supply information needed for other purposes by the court.

(2) Unless the court otherwise directs, such a person must—

(a) use such electronic arrangements as the court officer may make for that purpose, in accordance with those arrangements; or

(b) if no such arrangements have been made, use the appropriate form set out in the Practice Direction or the Criminal Costs Practice Direction, in accordance with those directions.

Forms in Welsh

5.2.—(1) Any Welsh language form set out in the Practice Direction, or in the Criminal Costs Practice Direction, is for use in connection with proceedings in courts in Wales. **B-115**

(2) Both a Welsh form and an English form may be contained in the same document.

(3) Where only a Welsh form, or only the corresponding English form, is served—

(a) the following words in Welsh and English must be added: "Darperir y ddogfen hon yn Gymraeg / Saesneg os bydd arnoch ei heisiau. Dylech wneud cais yn ddi-oed i (swyddog y llys) (rhodder yma'r cyfeiriad) This document will be provided in Welsh / English if you require it. You should apply immediately to (the court officer) (address)"; and

(b) the court officer, or the person who served the form, must, on request, supply the corresponding form in the other language to the person served.

Signature of forms

5.3.—(1) This rule applies where a form provides for its signature. **B-116**

(2) Unless other legislation otherwise requires, or the court otherwise directs, signature may be by any written or electronic authentication of the form by, or with the authority of, the signatory.

Court records

Duty to make records

B-117 **5.4.**—(1) For each case, as appropriate, the court officer must record, by such means as the Lord Chancellor directs—

(a) each charge or indictment against the defendant;
(b) the defendant's plea to each charge or count;
(c) each acquittal, conviction, sentence, determination, direction or order;
(d) each decision about bail;
(e) the power exercised where the court commits or adjourns the case to another court—
  (i) for sentence, or
  (ii) for the defendant to be dealt with for breach of a community order, a deferred sentence, a conditional discharge, or a suspended sentence of imprisonment, imposed by that other court;
(f) the court's reasons for a decision, where legislation requires those reasons to be recorded;
(g) any appeal;
(h) each party's presence or absence at each hearing;
(i) any consent that legislation requires before the court can proceed with the case, or proceed to a decision;
(j) in a magistrates' court—
  (i) any indication of sentence given in connection with the allocation of a case for trial, and
  (ii) the registration of a fixed penalty notice for enforcement as a fine, and any related endorsement on a driving record;
(k) in the Crown Court, any request for assistance or other communication about the case received from a juror;
(l) the identity of—
  (i) the prosecutor,
  (ii) the defendant,
  (iii) any other applicant to whom these rules apply,
  (iv) any interpreter or intermediary,
  (v) the parties' legal representatives, if any, *and*
  (vi) the judge, magistrate or magistrates, justices' legal adviser or other person who made each recorded decision; [and]
  [(vii) each person who takes part in a hearing by live link;]
(m) where a defendant is entitled to attend a hearing, any agreement by the defendant to waive that right; and
(n) where interpretation is required for a defendant, any agreement by that defendant to do without the written translation of a document.

(2) Such records must include—

(a) each party's and representative's address, including any electronic address and telephone number available;
(b) the defendant's date of birth, if available; and
(c) the date of each event and decision recorded.

[This rule is subject to temporary modification by virtue of r.7 of the Criminal Procedure (Amendment No. 2) (Coronavirus) Rules 2020 (SI 2020/417)- insertion of words in square brackets and omission of italicised text. These temporary modifications cease when ss.53, 54 and 55 (and Schs. 23, 24 and 25) of the Coronavirus Act 2020 expire.]

Recording and transcription of proceedings in the Crown Court

B-118 **5.5.**—(1) Where someone may appeal to the Court of Appeal, the court officer must—

(a) arrange for the recording of the proceedings in the Crown Court, unless the court otherwise directs; and
(b) arrange for the transcription of such a recording if—
  (i) the Registrar wants such a transcript, or
  (ii) anyone else wants such a transcript (but that is subject to the restrictions in paragraph (2)).

(2) Unless the court otherwise directs, a person who transcribes a recording of proceedings under such arrangements—

(a) may only supply a transcript of a recording of a hearing in private to–
 (i) the Registrar, or
 (ii) an individual who was present at that hearing;
(b) if the recording of a hearing in public contains information to which reporting restrictions apply, may only supply a transcript containing that information to–
 (i) the Registrar, or
 (ii) a recipient to whom that supply will not contravene those reporting restrictions; but
(c) subject to paragraph (2)(a) and (b), must supply any person with any transcript for which that person asks–
 (i) in accordance with the transcription arrangements made by the court officer, and
 (ii) on payment by that person of any fee prescribed.

(3) A party who wants to hear a recording of proceedings must–
(a) apply–
 (i) in writing to the Registrar, if an appeal notice has been served where Part 36 applies (appeal to the Court of Appeal: general rules), or
 (ii) orally or in writing to the Crown Court officer;
(b) explain the reasons for the request; and
(c) pay any fee prescribed.

(4) If the Crown Court or the Registrar so directs, the Crown Court officer must allow that party to hear a recording of–
(a) a hearing in public; and
(b) a hearing in private, if the applicant was present at that hearing.

Custody of case materials

5.6. Unless the court otherwise directs, in respect of each case the court officer may– **B-119**
(a) keep any evidence, application, representation or other material served by the parties; or
(b) arrange for the whole or any part to be kept by some other appropriate person, subject to–
 (i) any condition imposed by the court, and
 (ii) the rules in Part 34 (appeal to the Crown Court) and Part 36 (appeal to the Court of Appeal: general rules) about keeping exhibits pending any appeal.

Supply to a party of information or documents from records or case materials

5.7.–(1) This rule– **B-120**
(a) applies where–
 (i) a party wants information, or a copy of a document, from records or case materials kept by the court officer (for example, in case of loss, or to establish what is retained), or
 (ii) a person affected by an order made, or warrant issued, by the court wants such information or such a copy; but
(b) does not apply to–
 (i) a recording arranged under rule 5.5 (Recording and transcription of proceedings in the Crown Court),
 (ii) a copy of such a recording, or
 (ii) a transcript of such a recording.

(2) Such a party must–
(a) apply to the court officer;
(b) specify the information or document required; and
(c) pay any fee prescribed.

(3) The application–
(a) may be made orally, giving no reasons, if paragraph (4) requires the court officer to supply the information or document requested; but
(b) must be in writing, unless the court otherwise permits, and must explain for what purpose the information is required, in any other case.

(4) The court officer must supply to the applicant party or person–
(a) a copy of any document served by, or on, that party or person (but not of any document not so served); and
(b) by word of mouth, or in writing, as requested–
 (i) information that was received from that party or person in the first place,
 (ii) information about the terms of any direction or order directed to that party or person, or made on an application by that party or person, or at a hearing in public, and

(iii) information about the outcome of the case.

(5) If the court so permits, the court officer must supply to the applicant party or person, by word of mouth or in writing, as requested, information that paragraph (4) does not require the court officer to supply.

(6) Where the information requested is about the grounds on which an order was made, or a warrant was issued, in the absence of the party or person applying for that information—

(a) that party or person must also serve the request on the person who applied for the order or warrant;

(b) if the person who applied for the order or warrant objects to the supply of the information requested, that objector must—

(i) give notice of the objection not more than 10 business days after service of the request (or within any longer period allowed by the court),

(ii) serve that notice on the court officer and on the party or person requesting the information, and

(iii) if the objector wants a hearing, explain why one is needed;

(c) the court may determine the application for information at a hearing (which must be in private unless the court otherwise directs), or without a hearing; and

(d) the court must not permit the information requested to be supplied unless the person who applied for the order or warrant has had at least 10 business days (or any longer period allowed by the court) in which to make representations.

(7) A notice of objection under paragraph (6) must explain—

(a) whether the objection is to the supply of any part of the information requested, or only to the supply of a specified part, or parts, of it;

(b) whether the objection is to the supply of the information at any time, or only to its supply before a date or event specified by the objector; and

(c) the grounds of the objection.

(8) Where a notice of objection under paragraph (6) includes material that the objector thinks ought not be revealed to the party or person applying for information, the objector must—

(a) omit that material from the notice served on that party or person;

(b) mark the material to show that it is only for the court; and

(c) with that material include an explanation of why it has been withheld.

(9) Where paragraph (8) applies—

(a) a hearing of the application may take place, wholly or in part, in the absence of the party or person applying for information; and

(b) at any such hearing, the general rule is that the court must consider, in the following sequence—

(i) representations first by the party or person applying for information and then by the objector, in the presence of both, and then

(ii) further representations by the objector, in the absence of that party or person but the court may direct other arrangements for the hearing.

Supply to the public, including reporters, of information about cases

B-121 **5.8.**—(1) This rule—

(a) requires the supply and publication of information about cases with regard to the importance of—

(i) dealing with criminal cases in public, and

(ii) allowing a public hearing to be reported to the public;

(b) applies where a member of the public, including a reporter, wants information about a case from the court officer;

(c) requires the court officer to publish information about cases due to be considered by the court; but

(d) does not apply to—

(i) a recording arranged under rule 5.5 (Recording and transcription of proceedings in the Crown Court),

(ii) a copy of such a recording, or

(ii) a transcript of such a recording.

(2) A person who wants information about a case from the court officer must—

(a) apply to the court officer;

(b) specify the information requested; and

(c) pay any fee prescribed.

(3) The application–

(a) may be made orally, giving no reasons, if–

(i) paragraph (4) requires the court officer to supply the information requested, and

(ii) the information is to be supplied only by word of mouth; but

(b) must be in writing, unless the court otherwise permits, and must explain for what purpose the information is required, in any other case.

(4) The court officer must supply to the applicant–

(a) any information listed in paragraph (6), if–

(i) the information is available to the court officer,

(ii) the supply of the information is not prohibited by a reporting restriction, and

(iii) the trial has not yet concluded, or the verdict was not more than 6 months ago; and

(b) details of any reporting or access restriction ordered by the court.

(5) The court officer must supply that information–

(a) by word of mouth; or

(b) in writing, including by–

(i) written certificate or extract, or

(ii) such arrangements as the Lord Chancellor directs.

(6) The information that paragraph (4) requires the court officer to supply is–

(a) the date of any hearing in public, unless any party has yet to be notified of that date;

(b) each alleged offence and any plea entered;

(c) the court's decision at any hearing in public, including any decision about–

(i) bail, or

(ii) the committal, sending or transfer of the case to another court;

(d) whether the case is under appeal;

(e) the outcome of the case;

(f) the identity of–

(i) the prosecutor,

(ii) the defendant,

(iii) the parties' representatives, including their addresses, and

(iv) the judge, magistrate or magistrates, or justices' legal adviser by whom a decision at a hearing in public was made; and

(g) such other information about the case as is required by arrangements made under paragraph (5)(b)(ii).

(7) If the court so directs, the court officer must–

(a) supply to the applicant, by word of mouth or in writing (including by written certificate or extract), other information about the case; or

(b) allow the applicant to inspect or copy a document, or part of a document, containing information about the case.

(8) The court may determine an application to which paragraph (7) applies–

(a) at a hearing, in public or in private; or

(b) without a hearing.

(9) Where a case is due to be heard in public, the court officer must–

(a) publish the information listed in paragraph (10) if–

(i) the information is available to the court officer, and

(ii) the publication of the information is not prohibited by a reporting restriction; and

(b) publish that information for no longer than 5 business days–

(i) by notice displayed somewhere prominent in the vicinity of a court room in which the hearing is due to take place, and

(ii) by such arrangements as the Lord Chancellor directs, including arrangements for publication by electronic means, but only to the extent needed to comply with paragraph (1)(a).

(10) The information that paragraph (9) requires the court officer to publish is–

(a) the date, time and place of the hearing;

(b) the identity of the defendant; and

(c) such other information as it may be practicable to publish concerning–

(i) the type of hearing,

(ii) the identity of the prosecutor,

(iii) the identity of the court,
(iv) the offence or offences alleged, and
(v) whether any reporting restriction applies.

(11) Where a case is ready to be tried without a hearing under rule 24.9 (Single justice procedure: special rules), the court officer must—
(a) publish the information listed in paragraph (12) if—
(i) the information is available to the court officer, and
(ii) the publication of the information is not prohibited by a reporting restriction; and
(b) publish that information for no longer than 5 business days—
(i) by such arrangements as the Lord Chancellor directs, including arrangements for publication by electronic means, but
(ii) only to the extent needed to comply with paragraph (1)(a).

(12) The information that paragraph (11) requires the court officer to publish is—
(a) the identity of the defendant;
(b) the identity of the prosecutor;
(c) the offence or offences alleged; and
(d) whether any reporting restriction applies.

Supply of written certificate or extract from records for use in evidence, etc.

B-122 **5.9.**—(1) This rule applies where legislation—
(a) allows a certificate of conviction or acquittal, or an extract from records kept by the court officer, to be introduced in evidence in criminal proceedings; or
(b) requires such a certificate or extract to be supplied by the court officer to a specified person for a specified purpose.

(2) A person who wants such a certificate or extract must—
(a) apply in writing to the court officer;
(b) specify the certificate or extract required;
(c) explain under what legislation and for what purpose it is required; and
(d) pay any fee prescribed.

(3) If the application satisfies the requirements of that legislation, the court officer must supply the certificate or extract requested—
(a) to a party; and
(b) unless the court otherwise directs, to any other applicant.

CPD I General Matters 5A: Forms

B-123 **5A.1** The forms at Annex D to the *Consolidated Criminal Practice Direction* [2002] 1 W.L.R. 2870, or forms to that effect, are to be used in the criminal courts, in accordance with rule 5.1.

5A.2 The forms at Annex E to that practice direction, the case management forms, must be used in the criminal courts, in accordance with that rule.

5A.3 The table at the beginning of each of those annexes lists the forms and:
(a) shows the rule in connection with which each applies;
(b) describes each form.

5A.4 The forms may be amended or withdrawn from time to time, or new forms added, under the authority of the Lord Chief Justice.

CPD I General Matters 5B: Access to information held by the court (as amended by Criminal Practice Directions 2015 (Amendment No. 6), unreported, 22 March 2018, Lord Burnett CJ)

B-124 **5B.1** Open justice, as Lord Justice Toulson re-iterated in the case of *R (Guardian News and Media Ltd) v City of Westminster Magistrates' Court* [2012] EWCA Civ 420, [2013] QB 618, is a "principle at the heart of our system of justice and vital to the rule of law". There are exceptions but these "have to be justified by some even more important principle." However, the practical application of that undisputed principle, and the proper balancing of conflicting rights and principles, call for careful judgments to be made. The following is intended to provide some assistance to courts making decisions when asked to provide the public, including journalists, with access to or copies of information and documents held by the court, or when asked, exceptionally, to forbid the supply of transcripts that otherwise would have been supplied. It is not a prescriptive list, as the court will have to consider all the circumstances of each individual case.

5B.2 It remains the responsibility of the recipient of information or documents to ensure that they comply with any and all restrictions such as reporting restrictions (see Pt 16 and the accompanying practice direction).

5B.3 For the purposes of this direction, the word document includes images in photographic, digital including DVD format, video, CCTV or any other form.

5B.4 Certain information can and should be provided to the public on request, subject to any restrictions, such as reporting restrictions, imposed in that particular case. CrimPR 5.5 governs the supply of transcript of a recording of proceedings in the Crown Court. CrimPR 5.8(4) and 5.8(6) read together specify the information that the court officer will supply to the public; an oral application is acceptable and no reason need be given for the request. There is no requirement for the court officer to consider the non-disclosure provisions of the Data Protection Act 1998 as the exemption under section 35 applies to all disclosure made under 'any enactment ... or by the order of a court', which includes under the Criminal Procedure Rules.

5B.5 If the information sought is neither transcript nor listed at CrimPR 5.8(6), rule 5.8(7) will apply, and the provision of information is at the discretion of the court. The following guidance is intended to assist the court in exercising that discretion.

5B.6 A request for access to documents used in a criminal case should first be addressed to the party who presented them to the court or who, in the case of a written decision by the court, received that decision. Prosecuting authorities are subject to the Freedom of Information Act 2000 and the Data Protection Act 1998 and their decisions are susceptible to review.

5B.7 If the request is from a journalist or media organisation, note that there is a protocol between the NPCC, the CPS and the media entitled 'Publicity and the Criminal Justice System':

www.cps.gov.uk/publications/agencies/mediaprotocol.html
www.cps.gov.uk/publication/publicity-and-criminal-justice-system

There is additionally a protocol made under CrimPR 5.8(5)(b) between the media and HMCTS:

www.newsmediauk.org/write/MediaUploads/PDF%20Docs/Protocol_for_Sharing_Court_Documents.pdf

This Practice Direction does not affect the operation of those protocols. Material should generally be sought under the relevant protocol before an application is made to the court.

5B.8 An application to which rule 5.8(7) applies must be made in accordance with rule 5.8; it must be in writing, unless the court permits otherwise, and "must explain for what purpose the information is required." A clear, detailed application, specifying the name and contact details of the applicant, whether or not he ... represents a media organisation, and setting out the reasons for the application and to what use the information will be put, will be of most assistance to the court. Applicants should state if they have requested the information under a protocol and include any reasons given for the refusal. Before considering such an application, the court will expect the applicant to have given notice of the request to the parties.

5B.9 The court will consider each application on its own merits. The burden of justifying a request for access rests on the applicant. Considerations to be taken into account will include: (i) whether or not the request is for the purpose of contemporaneous reporting; a request after the conclusion of the proceedings will require careful scrutiny by the court; (ii) the nature of the information or documents being sought; (iii) the purpose for which they are required; (iv) the stage of the proceedings at the time when the application is made; (v) the value of the documents in advancing the open justice principle, including enabling the media to discharge its role, which has been described as a "public watchdog", by reporting the proceedings effectively; (vi) any risk of harm which access to them may cause to the legitimate interests of others; and (vii) any reasons given by the parties for refusing to provide the material requested and any other representations received from the parties. Further, all of the principles below are subject to any specific restrictions in the case. Courts should be aware that the risk of providing a document may reduce after a particular point in the proceedings, and when the material requested may be made available.

Documents read aloud in their entirety

5B.10 If a document has been read aloud to the court in its entirety, it should usually be provided on request, unless to do so would be disruptive to the court proceedings or place an undue burden on the court, the advocates or others. It may be appropriate and convenient for material to be provided electronically, if this can be done securely. **B-125**

5B.11 Documents likely to fall into this category are: (i) opening notes; (ii) statements agreed under section 9 of the CJA 1967 [§ 10-14 in the main work], including experts' reports, if read in their entirety; (iii) admissions made under section 10 of the CJA 1967 [§ 10-7 in the main work].

Documents treated as read aloud in their entirety

5B.12 A document treated by the court as if it had been read aloud in public, though in fact it has been neither read nor summarised aloud, should generally be made available on request. The burden on the court, the advocates or others in providing the material should be considered, but the presumption in favour of providing the material is greater when the material has only been treated as having been read aloud. Again, subject to security considerations, it may be convenient for the material to be provided electronically. **B-126**

5B.13 Documents likely to fall into this category include:
i. Skeleton arguments
ii. Written submissions
iii. Written decisions by the court

Documents read aloud in part or summarised aloud

B-127 **5B.14** Open justice requires only access to the part of the document that has been read aloud. If a member of the public requests a copy of such a document, the court should consider whether it is proportionate to order one of the parties to produce a suitably redacted version. If not, access to the document is unlikely to be granted; however, open justice will generally have been satisfied by the document having been read out in court.

5B.15 If the request comes from an accredited member of the press (see "Access by reporters" below), there may be circumstances in which the court orders that a copy of the whole document be shown to the reporter, or provided, subject to the condition that those matters that had not been read out to the court may not be used or reported. A breach of such an order would be treated as a contempt of court.

5B.16 Documents in this category are likely to include section 9 statements that are edited.

Jury bundles and exhibits (including video footage shown to the jury)

B-128 **5B.17** The court should consider:

(i) whether access to the specific document is necessary to understand or effectively to report the case;
(ii) the privacy of third parties, such as the victim (in some cases, the reporting restriction imposed by s.1 of the Judicial Proceedings (Regulation of Reports) Act 1926 will apply (indecent or medical matter));
(iii) whether the reporting of anything in the document may be prejudicial to a fair trial in this or another case, in which case whether it may be necessary to make an order under section 4(2) of the Contempt of Court Act 1981 [§ 28-65 in the main work].

The court may order one of the parties to provide a copy of certain pages (or parts of the footage), but these should not be provided electronically.

Statements of witnesses who give oral evidence

B-129 **5B.18** A witness statement does not become evidence unless it is agreed under section 9 of the CJA 1967 [§ 10-14 in the main work] and presented to the court. Therefore the statements of witnesses who give oral evidence, including ABE interview and transcripts and experts' reports, should not usually be provided. Open justice is generally satisfied by public access to the court.

Confidential documents

B-130 **5B.19** A document the content of which, though relied upon by the court, has not been communicated to the public or reporters, nor treated as if it had been, is likely to have been supplied in confidence and should be treated accordingly. This will apply even if the court has made reference to the document or quoted from the document. There is most unlikely to be a sufficient reason to displace the expectation of confidentiality ordinarily attaching to a document in this category, and it would be exceptional to permit the inspection or copying by a member of the public or of the media of such a document. The rights and legitimate interests of others are likely to outweigh the interests of open justice with respect these documents.

5B.20 Documents in this category are likely to include: (i) pre-sentence reports; (ii) medical reports; (iii) victim personal statements; (iv) reports and summaries for confiscation.

Prohibitions against the provision of information

B-131 **5B.21** Statutory provisions may impose specific prohibitions against the provision of information. Those most likely to be encountered are listed in the note to rule 5.8 and include the Rehabilitation of Offenders Act 1974, section 18 of the CPIA 1996 ("unused material" disclosed by the prosecution) [§ 12-91 in the main work], sections 33, 34 and 35 of the LASPOA 2012 (privileged information furnished to the Legal Aid Agency) and reporting restrictions generally.

5B.22 Reports of allocation or sending proceedings are restricted by section 52A of the CDA 1998 [§ 1-33 in the main work], so that only limited information, as specified in the statute, may be reported, whether it is referred to in the courtroom or not. The magistrates' court has power to order that the restriction shall not apply; if any defendant objects the court must apply the interests of justice test as specified in section 52A. The restriction ceases to apply either after all defendants indicate a plea of guilty, or after the conclusion of the trial of the last defendant to be tried. If the case does not result in a guilty plea, a finding of guilt or an acquittal, the restriction does not lift automatically and an application must be made to the court.

5B.23 Extradition proceedings have some features in common with committal proceedings, but no automatic reporting restrictions apply.

5B.24 Public interest immunity and the rights of a defendant, witnesses and victims under Article 6 and 8 of the ECHR [§§ 16-72, 16-137 in the main work] may also restrict the power to release material to third parties.

Other documents

5B.25 The following table indicates the considerations likely to arise on an application to inspect or copy other documents. **B-132**

Document	*Considerations*
Charge sheet/Indictment	The alleged offence(s) will have been read aloud in court, and their terms must be supplied under CrimPR 5.8(4)
Material disclosed under CPIA 1996	To the extent that the content is deployed at trial, it becomes public at that hearing. Otherwise, it is a criminal offence for it to be disclosed: section 18 of the 1996 Act [§ 12-91 in the main work].
Written notices, applications, replies (including any application for representation)	To the extent that evidence is introduced, or measures taken, at trial, the content becomes public at that hearing. A statutory prohibition against disclosure applies to an application for representation: sections 33, 34 and 35 of the LASPO Act 2012.
Written decisions by the court, other than those read aloud in public or treated as if so read	Such decisions should usually be provided, subject to the criteria listed in CrimPR 5.8(4)(a) (and see also paragraph 5B.31 below).
Sentencing remarks	Sentencing remarks should usually be provided to the accredited Press, if the judge was reading from a prepared script which was handed out immediately afterwards; if not, then permission for a member of the accredited Press to obtain a transcript should usually be given (see also paragraphs 5B.26 and 29 below).
Official recordings/Transcript	See CrimPR 5.5. See CrimPR 5.5 (and see also paragraphs 5B.32 to 36 below).

Access by reporters

5B.26 Under Part 5 of the rules, the same procedure applies for applications for access to information by reporters as to other members of the public. However, if the application is made by legal representatives instructed by the media, or by an accredited member of the media, who is able to produce in support of the application a valid press card (*http://www.ukpresscardauthority.co.uk/*) then there is a greater presumption in favour of providing the requested material, in recognition of the press' role as "public watchdog" in a democratic society (*Observer and Guardian v U.K.*, 14 E.H.R.R. 153). The general principle in those circumstances is that the court should supply documents and information unless there is a good reason not to in order to protect the rights or legitimate interests of others and the request will not place an undue burden on the court (*R. (Guardian News and Media Ltd) v City of Westminster Magistrates' Court (Article 19 intervening)* at [87]). Subject to that, the paragraphs above relating to types of documents should be followed. **B-133**

5B.27 Court staff should usually verify the authenticity of cards, checking the expiry date on the card and where necessary may consider telephoning the number on the reverse of the card to verify the card holder. Court staff may additionally request sight of other identification if necessary to ensure that the card holder has been correctly identified. The supply of information under rule 5.8(7) is at the discretion of the court, and court staff must ensure that they have received a clear direction from the court before providing any information or material under rule 5.8(7) to a member of the public, including to the accredited media or their legal representatives.

5B.28 Opening notes and skeleton arguments or written submissions, once they have been placed before the court, should usually be provided to the media. If there is no opening note, permission for the media to obtain a transcript of the prosecution opening should usually be given (see below). It may be convenient for copies to be provided electronically by counsel, provided that the documents are kept suitably secure. The media are expected to be aware of the limitations on the use to which such material can be put, for example that legal argument held in the absence of the jury must not be reported before the conclusion of the trial.

5B.29 The media should also be able to obtain transcripts of hearings held in open court directly from the transcription service provider, on payment of any required fee. The service providers commonly require the judge's authorisation before they will provide a transcript, as an additional verification to ensure that the correct material is released and reporting restrictions are noted. However, responsibility for compliance with any restriction always rests with the person receiving the information or material: see *Criminal Practice Direction I (General Matters) 6B*.

5B.30 It is not for the judge to exercise an editorial judgment about "the adequacy of the material already available to the paper for its journalistic purpose" *(R. (Guardian News and Media Ltd) v City of Westminster Magistrates' Court (Article 19 intervening)* at [82]), but the responsibility for complying with the Contempt of Court Act 1981 and any and all restrictions on the use of the material rests with the recipient.

Written decisions

B-134 **5B.31** Where the Criminal Procedure Rules allow for a determination without a hearing there may be occasions on which it furthers the overriding objective to deliver the court's decision to the parties in writing, without convening a public hearing at which that decision will be pronounced: on an application for costs made at the conclusion of a trial, for example. If the only reason for delivering a decision in that way is to promote efficiency and expedition and if no other consideration arises then usually a copy of the decision should be provided in response to any request once the decision is final. However, had the decision been announced in public then the criteria in CrimPR 5.8(4)(a) would have applied to the supply of information by the court officer; and ordinarily those same criteria should be applied by the court, therefore. Moreover, where considerations other than efficiency and expedition have influenced the court's decision to reach a determination without convening a hearing then those same considerations may be inimical to the supply of the written decision to any applicant other than a party. Reporting restrictions may be relevant, for example; as may the considerations listed in paragraph 5B.9 above. In such a case the court should consider supplying a redacted version of the decision in response to a request by anyone who is not a party; or it may be appropriate to give the decision in terms that can be supplied to the public, supplemented by additional reasons provided only to the parties.

Transcript

B-135 **5B.32** CrimPR 5.5 does not require an application to the court for transcript, nor does the rule anticipate recourse to the court for a judicial decision about the supply of transcript in any but unusual circumstances. Ordinarily it is the rule itself that determines the circumstances in which the transcriber of a recording may or may not supply transcript to an applicant.

5B.33 Where reporting restrictions apply to information contained in the recording from which the transcript is prepared then unless the court otherwise directs it is for the transcriber to redact that transcript where redaction is necessary to permit its supply to that applicant. Having regard to the terms of the statutes that impose reporting restrictions, however, it is unlikely that redaction will be required frequently. Statutory restrictions prohibit publication 'to the public at large or any section of the public', or some comparable formulation. They do not ordinarily prohibit a publication constituted only of the supply of transcript to an individual applicant. However, any reporting restrictions will continue to apply to a recipient of transcript, and where they apply the recipient must be alerted to them by the endorsement on the transcript of a suitable warning notice, to this or the like effect:

> "WARNING: reporting restrictions may apply to the contents transcribed in this document, particularly if the case concerned a sexual offence or involved a child. Reporting restrictions prohibit the publication of the applicable information to the public or any section of the public, in writing, in a brwhere the court can give, vary or discharge a direction (a "defendant's evidenceoadcast or by means of the internet, including social media. Anyone who receives a copy of this transcript is responsible in law for making sure that applicable restrictions are not breached. A person who breaches a reporting restriction is liable to a fine and/or imprisonment. For guidance on whether reporting restrictions apply, and to what information, ask at the court office or take legal advice."

5B.34 Exceptionally, court staff may invite the court to direct that transcript must be redacted before it is supplied to an applicant, or that transcript must not be supplied to an applicant pending the supply of further information or assurances by that applicant, or at all, in exercise of the judicial discretion to which CrimPR 5.5(2) refers. Circumstances giving rise to concern may include, for example, the occurrence of events causing staff reasonably to suspect that an applicant intends or is likely to disregard a reporting restriction that applies, despite the warning notice endorsed on the transcript, or reasonably to suspect that an applicant has malicious intentions towards another person. Given that the proceedings will have taken place in public, despite any such suspicions cogent and compelling reasons will be required to deny a request for transcript of such proceedings and the onus rests always on the court to justify such a denial, not on the applicant to justify the request. Even where there are reasons to suspect a criminal intent, the appropriate course may be to direct that the police be informed of those reasons rather than to direct that the transcript be withheld. Nevertheless, it may be appropriate in such a case to direct that an application for the transcript should be made which complies with paragraph 5B.8 above (even though that paragraph does not apply); and then for the court to review that application with regard to the considerations listed in paragraph 5B.9 above (but the usual burden of justifying a request under that paragraph does not apply).

5B.35 Some applicants for transcript may be taken to be aware of the significance of reporting restrictions, where they apply, and, by reason of such an applicant's statutory or other public or quasi-public functions, in any event unlikely to contravene any such restriction. Such applicants include public authorities within the meaning of section 6 of the Human Rights Act 1998 (a definition which extends to government departments and their agencies, local authorities, prosecuting authorities, and institutions such as the Parole Board and the Sentencing Council) and include public or private bodies exercising disciplinary functions in relation to practitioners of a regulated profession such as doctors, lawyers, accountants, etc. It would be only in the most exceptional circumstances that a court might conclude that any such body should not receive unredacted transcript of proceedings in public, irrespective of whether reporting restrictions do or do not apply.

5B.36 The rule imposes no time limit on a request for the supply of transcript. The assumption is that transcript of proceedings in public in the Crown Court will continue to be available for as long as relevant records are maintained by the Lord Chancellor under the legislation to which CrimPR 5.4 refers.

CPD I General Matters 5C: Issue of medical certificates

5C.1 Doctors will be aware that medical notes are normally submitted by defendants in criminal proceedings as justification for not answering bail. Medical notes may also be submitted by witnesses who are due to give evidence and jurors. **B-136**

5C.2 If a medical certificate is accepted by the court, this will result in cases (including contested hearings and trials) being adjourned rather than the court issuing a warrant for the defendant's arrest without bail. Medical certificates will also provide the defendant with sufficient evidence to defend a charge of failure to surrender to bail.

5C.3 However, a court is not absolutely bound by a medical certificate. The medical practitioner providing the certificate may be required by the court to give evidence. Alternatively the court may exercise its discretion to disregard a certificate which it finds unsatisfactory: *Ealing Magistrates' Court, ex p. Burgess*, 165 J.P. 82, DC.

5C.4 Circumstances where the court may find a medical certificate unsatisfactory include:

(a) where the certificate indicates that the defendant is unfit to attend work (rather than to attend court);

(b) where the nature of the defendant's ailment (e.g. a broken arm) does not appear to be capable of preventing his attendance at court;

(c) where the defendant is certified as suffering from stress/anxiety/depression and there is no indication of the defendant recovering within a realistic timescale.

5C.5 It therefore follows that the minimum standards a medical certificate should set out are:

(a) the date on which the medical practitioner examined the defendant;

(b) the exact nature of the defendant's ailments

(c) if it is not self-evident, why the ailment prevents the defendant attending court;

(d) an indication as to when the defendant is likely to be able to attend court, or a date when the current certificate expires.

5C.6 Medical practitioners should be aware that when issuing a certificate to a defendant in criminal proceedings they make themselves liable to being summonsed to court to give evidence about the content of the certificate, and they may be asked to justify their statements.

Criminal Procedure Rules 2020 (SI 2020/759), Pt 6

Reporting, Etc. Restrictions

General rules

When this Part applies

6.1.—(1) This Part applies where the court can— **B-137**

(a) impose a restriction on—

(i) reporting what takes place at a public hearing, or
(ii) public access to what otherwise would be a public hearing;
(b) vary or remove a reporting or access restriction that is imposed by legislation;
(c) withhold information from the public during a public hearing;
(d) order a trial in private; or
(e) allow there to take place during a hearing—
(i) sound recording, or
(ii) communication by electronic means.

(2) This Part does not apply to arrangements required by legislation, or directed by the court, in connection with—
(a) sound recording during a hearing, or the transcription of such a recording; or
(b) measures to assist a witness or defendant to give evidence.

Exercise of court's powers to which this Part applies

6.2.—(1) When exercising a power to which this Part applies, as well as furthering the overriding objective, in accordance with rule 1.3, the court must have regard to the importance of—
(a) dealing with criminal cases in public; and
(b) allowing a public hearing to be reported to the public.

(2) The court may determine an application or appeal under this Part—
(a) at a hearing, in public or in private; or
(b) without a hearing.

(3) But the court must not exercise a power to which this Part applies unless each party and any other person directly affected—
(a) is present; or
(b) has had an opportunity—
(i) to attend, or
(ii) to make representations.

Court's power to vary requirements under this Part

6.3.—(1) The court may—
(a) shorten or extend (even after it has expired) a time limit under this Part;
(b) require an application to be made in writing instead of orally;
(c) consider an application or representations made orally instead of in writing; and
(d) dispense with a requirement to—
(i) give notice, or
(ii) serve an application.

(2) Someone who wants an extension of time must—
(a) apply when making the application or representations for which it is needed; and
(b) explain the delay.

Reporting and access restrictions

Reporting and access restrictions

B-138 **6.4.**—(1) This rule applies where the court can—
(a) impose a restriction on—
(i) reporting what takes place at a public hearing, or
(ii) public access to what otherwise would be a public hearing; or
(b) withhold information from the public during a public hearing.

(2) Unless other legislation otherwise provides, the court may do so—
(a) on application by a party; or
(b) on its own initiative.

(3) A party who wants the court to do so must—
(a) apply as soon as reasonably practicable;
(b) notify—
(i) each other party, and
(ii) such other person (if any) as the court directs;
(c) specify the proposed terms of the order, and for how long it should last;
(d) explain—
(i) what power the court has to make the order, and

(ii) why an order in the terms proposed is necessary;

(e) where the application is for a reporting direction under section 45A of the Youth Justice and Criminal Evidence Act 1999 (power to restrict reporting of criminal proceedings for lifetime of witnesses and victims under 18), explain—

(i) how the circumstances of the person whose identity is concerned meet the conditions prescribed by that section, having regard to the factors which that section lists; and

(ii) why such a reporting direction would be likely to improve the quality of any evidence given by that person, or the level of co-operation given by that person to any party in connection with the preparation of that party's case, taking into account the factors listed in that section; and

(f) where the application is for a reporting direction under section 46 of the Youth Justice and Criminal Evidence Act 1999 (power to restrict reports about certain adult witnesses in criminal proceedings), explain—

(i) how the witness is eligible for assistance, having regard to the factors listed in that section, and

(ii) why such a reporting direction would be likely to improve the quality of the witness' evidence, or the level of co-operation given by the witness to the applicant in connection with the preparation of the applicant's case, taking into account the factors which that section lists.

Varying or removing restrictions

6.5.—(1) This rule applies where the court can vary or remove a reporting or access restriction.

(2) Unless other legislation otherwise provides, the court may do so—

(a) on application by a party or person directly affected; or

(b) on its own initiative.

(3) A party or person who wants the court to do so must—

(a) apply as soon as reasonably practicable;

(b) notify—

(i) each other party, and

(ii) such other person (if any) as the court directs;

(c) specify the restriction; and

(d) explain, as appropriate, why it should be varied or removed.

(4), (5) [*Appeals from magistrates' courts under the Education Act 2002, s.141F(7) (relating to restrictions on reporting alleged offences by teachers).*]

Trial in private

6.6.—(1) This rule applies where the court can order a trial in private.

(2) A party who wants the court to do so must—

(a) apply in writing not less than 5 business days before the trial is due to begin; and

(b) serve the application on—

(i) the court officer, and

(ii) each other party.

(3) The applicant must explain—

(a) the reasons for the application;

(b) how much of the trial the applicant proposes should be in private; and

(c) why no measures other than trial in private will suffice, such as—

(i) reporting restrictions,

(ii) an admission of facts,

(iii) the introduction of hearsay evidence,

(iv) a direction for a special measure under section 19 of the Youth Justice and Criminal Evidence Act 1999,

(v) a witness anonymity order under section 86 of the Coroners and Justice Act 2009, or

(vi) arrangements for the protection of a witness.

(4) Where the application includes information that the applicant thinks ought not be revealed to another party, the applicant must—

(a) omit that information from the part of the application that is served on that other party;

(b) mark the other part to show that, unless the court otherwise directs, it is only for the court; and

(c) in that other part, explain why the applicant has withheld that information from that other party.

(5) The court officer must at once—
(a) display notice of the application somewhere prominent in the vicinity of the courtroom; and
(b) give notice of the application to reporters by such other arrangements as the Lord Chancellor directs.
(6) The application must be determined at a hearing which—
(a) must be in private, unless the court otherwise directs;
(b) if the court so directs, may be, wholly or in part, in the absence of a party from whom information has been withheld; and
(c) in the Crown Court, must be after the defendant is arraigned but before the jury is sworn.
(7) At the hearing of the application—
(a) the general rule is that the court must consider, in the following sequence—
(i) representations first by the applicant and then by each other party, in all the parties' presence, and then
(ii) further representations by the applicant, in the absence of a party from whom information has been withheld; but
(b) the court may direct other arrangements for the hearing.
(8) The court must not hear a trial in private until—
(a) the business day after the day on which it orders such a trial, or
(b) the disposal of any appeal against, or review of, any such order, if later.

Representations in response

6.7.—(1) This rule applies where a party, or person directly affected, wants to make representations about an application or appeal.
(2) Such a party or person must—
(a) serve the representations on—
(i) the court officer,
(ii) the applicant,
(iii) each other party, and
(iv) such other person (if any) as the court directs;
(b) do so as soon as reasonably practicable after notice of the application; and
(c) ask for a hearing, if that party or person wants one, and explain why it is needed.
(3) Representations must—
(a) explain the reasons for any objection; and
(b) specify any alternative terms proposed.

Order about restriction or trial in private

6.8.—(1) This rule applies where the court—
(a) orders, varies or removes a reporting or access restriction; or
(b) orders a trial in private.
(2) The court officer must—
(a) record the court's reasons for the decision; and
(b) as soon as reasonably practicable, arrange for notice of the decision to be—
(i) displayed somewhere prominent in the vicinity of the courtroom, and
(ii) communicated to reporters by such other arrangements as the Lord Chancellor directs.

Sound recording and electronic communication

B-139 **6.9.**—(1) This rule applies where the court can give permission to—
(a) bring into a hearing for use, or use during a hearing, a device for—
(i) recording sound, or
(ii) communicating by electronic means; or
(b) publish a sound recording made during a hearing.
(2) The court may give such permission—
(a) on application; or
(b) on its own initiative.
(3) A person who wants the court to give such permission must—
(a) apply as soon as reasonably practicable;
(b) notify—
(i) each party, and

(ii) such other person (if any) as the court directs; and
(c) explain why the court should permit the use or publication proposed.

(4) As a condition of the applicant using such a device, the court may direct arrangements to minimise the risk of its use–
(a) contravening a reporting restriction;
(b) disrupting the hearing; or
(c) compromising the fairness of the hearing, for example by affecting–
(i) the evidence to be given by a witness, or
(ii) the verdict of a jury.

(5) Such a direction may require that the device is used only–
(a) in a specified part of the courtroom;
(b) for a specified purpose;
(c) for a purpose connected with the applicant's activity as a member of a specified group, for example representatives of news-gathering or reporting organisations; or
(d) at a specified time, or in a specified way.

Forfeiture of unauthorised sound recording

6.10.–(1) This rule applies where someone without the court's permission– **B-140**
(a) uses a device for recording sound during a hearing; or
(b) publishes a sound recording made during a hearing.

(2) The court may exercise its power to forfeit the device or recording–
(a) on application by a party, or on its own initiative; and
(b) provisionally, despite rule 6.2(3), to allow time for representations.

(3) A party who wants the court to forfeit a device or recording must–
(a) apply as soon as reasonably practicable;
(b) notify–
(i) as appropriate, the person who used the device, or who published the recording, and
(ii) each other party; and
(c) explain why the court should exercise that power.

CPD I General Matters 6A: Unofficial sound recording of proceedings

6A.1 [Summarises s.9(1)(a)-(c) and (4) of the Contempt of Court Act 1981 (§ 28-74 in the main work).] **B-141**

6A.2 The discretion given to the court to grant, withhold or withdraw leave to use equipment for recording sound or to impose conditions as to the use of the recording is unlimited, but the following factors may be relevant to its exercise:
(a) the existence of any reasonable need on the part of the applicant for leave, whether a litigant or a person connected with the press or broadcasting, for the recording to be made;
(b) the risk that the recording could be used for the purpose of briefing witnesses out of court;
(c) any possibility that the use of the recorder would disturb the proceedings or distract or worry any witnesses or other participants.

6A.3 Consideration should always be given whether conditions as to the use of a recording made pursuant to leave should be imposed. The identity and role of the applicant for leave and the nature of the subject-matter of the proceedings may be relevant to this.

6A.4 The particular restriction imposed by section 9(1)(b) applies in every case, but may not be present to the mind of every applicant to whom leave is given. It may, therefore, be desirable on occasion for this provision to be drawn to the attention of those to whom leave is given.

6A.5 The transcript of a permitted recording is intended for the use of the person given leave to make it and is not intended to be used as, or to compete with, the official transcript mentioned in section 9(4).

6A.6 Where a contravention of section 9(1) is alleged, the procedure in section 2 of Part 48 of the Rules should be followed. Section 9(3) of the 1981 Act [§ 28-74 in the main work] permits the court to "order the instrument, or any recording made with it, or both, to be forfeited". The procedure at CrimPR 6.10 should be followed.

CPD I General Matters 6B: Restrictions on reporting proceedings

6B.1 Open justice is an essential principle in the criminal courts but the principle is subject to some statutory restrictions. These restrictions are either automatic or discretionary. Guidance is provided in the joint publication, Reporting Restrictions in the Criminal Courts issued by the **B-142**

Judicial College, the Newspaper Society, the Society of Editors and the Media Lawyers Association. The current version is the fourth edition and has been updated to be effective from May 2015. [*Editorial note: a revised version was issued in May, 2016.*]

6B.2 Where a restriction is automatic no order can or should be made in relation to matters falling within the relevant provisions. However, the court may, if it considers it appropriate to do so, give a reminder of the existence of the automatic restriction. The court may also discuss the scope of the restriction and any particular risks in the specific case in open court with representatives of the press present. Such judicial observations cannot constitute an order binding on the editor or the reporter although it is anticipated that a responsible editor would consider them carefully before deciding what should be published. It remains the responsibility of those reporting a case to ensure that restrictions are not breached.

6B.3 Before exercising its discretion to impose a restriction the court must follow precisely the statutory provisions under which the order is to be made, paying particular regard to what has to be established, by whom and to what standard.

6B.4 Without prejudice to the above paragraph, certain general principles apply to the exercise of the court's discretion:

(a) the court must have regard to Parts 6 and 18 of the Criminal Procedure Rules;

(b) the court must keep in mind the fact that every order is a departure from the general principle that proceedings shall be open and freely reported;

(c) before making any order the court must be satisfied that the purpose of the proposed order cannot be achieved by some lesser measure, e.g. the grant of special measures, screens or the clearing of the public gallery (usually subject to a representative/s of the media remaining);

(d) the terms of the order must be proportionate so as to comply with Article 10 [of the] ECHR (freedom of expression) [§ 16-157 in the main work];

(e) no order should be made without giving other parties to the proceedings and any other interested party, including any representative of the media, an opportunity to make representations;

(f) any order should provide for any interested party who has not been present or represented at the time of the making of the order to have permission to apply within a limited period, e.g. 24 hours;

(g) the wording of the order is the responsibility of the judge or bench making the order; it must be in precise terms and, if practicable, agreed with the advocates.

(h) the order must be in writing and must state:

    (i) the power under which it is made;

    (ii) its precise scope and purpose; and

    (iii) the time at which it shall cease to have effect, if appropriate;

(i) the order must specify, in every case, whether or not the making or terms of the order may be reported or whether this itself is prohibited; such a report could cause the very mischief which the order was intended to prevent.

6B.5 A series of template orders have been prepared by the Judicial College and are available as an appendix to the Crown Court Bench Book Companion; these template orders should generally be used.

6B.6 A copy of the order should be provided to any person known to have an interest in reporting the proceedings and to any local or national media who regularly report proceedings in the court.

6B.7 Court staff should be prepared to answer any enquiry about a specific case; but it is and will remain the responsibility of anyone reporting a case to ensure that no breach of any order occurs and the onus rests on such person to make enquiry in case of doubt.

CPD I General Matters 6C: Use of live text-based forms of communication (including Twitter) from court for the purposes of fair and accurate reporting

B-143 **6C.1** This part clarifies the use which may be made of live text-based communications, such as mobile email, social media (including Twitter) and internet-enabled laptops in and from courts throughout England and Wales. For the purpose of this part these means of communication are referred to, compendiously, as "live text-based communications". It is consistent with the legislative structure which:

(a) prohibits:

    (i) the taking of photographs in court (s.41 of the CJA 1925);

    (ii) the use of sound recording equipment in court unless the leave of the judge has first been obtained (s.9 of the Contempt of Court Act 1981 [§ 28-74 in the main work]); and

(b) requires compliance with the strict prohibition rules created by sections 1, 2 and 4 of the Contempt of Court Act 1981 [§§ 28-55, 28-56 and 28-65 in the main work] in relation to the reporting of court proceedings.

General Principles

6C.2 The judge has an overriding responsibility to ensure that proceedings are conducted consistently, with the proper administration of justice, and to avoid any improper interference with its processes. **B-144**

6C.3 A fundamental aspect of the proper administration of justice is the principle of open justice. Fair and accurate reporting of court proceedings forms part of that principle. The principle is, however, subject to well-known statutory and discretionary exceptions. Two such exceptions are the prohibitions, set out in paragraph 6C.1(a), on photography in court and on making sound recordings of court proceedings.

6C.4 The statutory prohibition on photography in court, by any means, is absolute. There is no judicial discretion to suspend or dispense with it. Any equipment which has photographic capability must not have that function activated.

6C.5 Sound recordings are also prohibited unless, in the exercise of its discretion, the court permits such equipment to be used. In criminal proceedings, some of the factors relevant to the exercise of that discretion are contained in paragraph 6A.2. The same factors are likely to be relevant when consideration is being given to the exercise of this discretion in civil or family proceedings.

Use of Live Text-Based Communications: General Considerations

6C.6 The normal, indeed almost invariable, rule has been that mobile phones must be turned off in court. There is however no statutory prohibition on the use of live text-based communications in open court. **B-145**

6C.7 Where a member of the public, who is in court, wishes to use live text-based communications during court proceedings an application for permission to activate and use, in silent mode, a mobile phone, small laptop or similar piece of equipment, solely in order to make live text-based communications of the proceedings will need to be made. The application may be made formally or informally (for instance by communicating a request to the judge through court staff).

6C.8 It is presumed that a representative of the media or a legal commentator using live textbased communications from court does not pose a danger of interference to the proper administration of justice in the individual case. This is because the most obvious purpose of permitting the use of live text-based communications would be to enable the media to produce fair and accurate reports of the proceedings. As such, a representative of the media or a legal commentator who wishes to use live text-based communications from court may do so without making an application to the court.

6C.9 When considering, either generally on its own motion, or following a formal application or informal request by a member of the public, whether to permit live text-based communications, and if so by whom, the paramount question for the judge will be whether the application may interfere with the proper administration of justice.

6C.10 In considering the question of permission, the factors listed in paragraph 6A.2 are likely to be relevant.

6C.11 Without being exhaustive, the danger to the administration of justice is likely to be at its most acute in the context of criminal trials e.g., where witnesses who are out of court may be informed of what has already happened in court and so coached or briefed before they then give evidence, or where information posted on, for instance, Twitter about inadmissible evidence may influence members of the jury. However, the danger is not confined to criminal proceedings; in civil and sometimes family proceedings, simultaneous reporting from the courtroom may create pressure on witnesses, by distracting or worrying them.

6C.12 It may be necessary for the judge to limit live text-based communications to representatives of the media for journalistic purposes but to disallow its use by the wider public in court. That may arise if it is necessary, for example, to limit the number of mobile electronic devices in use at any given time because of the potential for electronic interference with the court's own sound recording equipment, or because the widespread use of such devices in court may cause a distraction in the proceedings.

6C.13 Subject to these considerations, the use of an unobtrusive, hand-held, silent piece of modern equipment, for the purposes of simultaneous reporting of proceedings to the outside world as they unfold in court, is generally unlikely to interfere with the proper administration of justice.

6C.14 Permission to use live text-based communications from court may be withdrawn by the court at any time.

CPD I General matters 6D: Taking notes in court (as inserted by Criminal Practice Directions 2015 (Amendment No. 1) [2016] EWCA Crim 98, Lord Thomas CJ)

6D.1 As long as it does not interfere with the proper administration of justice, anyone who at- **B-146**

tends a court hearing may quietly take notes, on paper or by silent electronic means. If that person is a participant, including an expert witness who is in the courtroom under CrimPR 24.4(2)(a)(ii) or 25.11(2)(a)(ii), note taking may be an essential aid to that person's own or (if they are a representative) to their client's effective participation. If that person is a reporter or a member of the public, attending a hearing to which, by definition, they have been admitted, note taking is a feature of the principle of open justice. The permission of the court is not required, and the distinctions between members of the public and others which are drawn at paragraphs 6C.7 and 6C.8 of these practice directions do not apply.

6D.2 However, where there is reason to suspect that the taking of notes may be for an unlawful purpose, or that it may disrupt the proceedings, then it is entirely proper for court staff to make appropriate enquiries, and ultimately it is within the power of the court to prohibit note taking by a specified individual or individuals in the court room if that is necessary and proportionate to prevent unlawful conduct. If, for example, there is reason to believe that notes are being taken in order to influence the testimony of a witness who is due to give evidence, perhaps by briefing that witness on what another witness has said, then because such conduct is unlawful (it is likely to be in contempt of court, and it may constitute a perversion of the course of justice) it is within the court's power to prohibit such note taking. If there is reason to believe that what purports to be taking notes with an electronic device is in fact the transmission of live text-based communications from court without the permission required by paragraph 6C.7 of these practice directions, or where permission to transmit such communications has been withdrawn under paragraph 6C.14, then that, too, would constitute grounds for prohibiting the taking of such notes.

6D.3 The existence of a reporting restriction, without more, is not a sufficient reason to prohibit note taking (though it may need to be made clear to those who take notes that the reporting restriction affects how much, if any, of what they have noted may be communicated to anyone else). However, if there is reason to believe that notes are being taken in order to facilitate the contravention of a reporting restriction then that, too, would constitute grounds for prohibiting such note taking.

CPD I General matters 6E: Access to courts (as inserted by Criminal Practice Directions 2015 (Amendment No.9) [2019] EWCA Crim 1603, Lord Burnett CJ)

Proceedings before the Crown Court

B-147 **6E.1** The right of the public to access court rooms to observe proceedings is a fundamental part of open justice, and good practice will ensure that the public are able to view proceedings quietly, and without causing interruption, as far as is possible.

6E.2 However, as observed in *R (O'Connor) v Aldershot Magistrates' Court* [2017] 1 WLR 2833 "The right to attend a public court hearing and to enter the court building for that purpose is not unqualified." The court has an inherent power to restrict public access to the courtroom where it is necessary to do so in the interests of justice, for example to prevent disorder.

6E.3 During criminal proceedings in a Crown Court there are some specific parts of proceedings whereby it may be appropriate for a judge to restrict movement in the public gallery. As observed by Bean LJ in *R (on the application of Ewing) v Isleworth Crown Court* [2019] EWHC 288 (Admin) this is to ensure that during "these sensitive moments, generally of brief duration, it is necessary for the court to be still so that the process can take place without distraction and in a manner which preserves the dignity and solemnity of the proceedings". It is expected that during the following parts of the proceedings, access may be restricted to prevent comings and goings in the public gallery:

I. Arraignment;
II. Empanelling and swearing in of the jury;
III. Oath taking or affirmation;
IV. Return of verdict by a jury;
V. Passing of sentence by a Judge.

6E.4 In the *Ewing* judgment the Administrative Court made clear that it would be unlawful to issue a blanket policy that restricted access during other parts of the proceedings. Unless the judge has specifically directed restrictions to access to the public gallery for good reason in a particular case, then at all other times, it is expected that the public can enter and leave the courtroom as they require, provided they do so quietly and without disrupting proceedings.

CPD I General matters: Annex: Guidance on establishing and using live link and telephone facilities for criminal court hearings (as inserted by Criminal Practice Directions 2015 (Amendment No. 3) [2017] EWCA Crim 30, Lord Thomas CJ)

B-148 **1** This guidance supplements paragraph I 3N of these practice directions on the use of live link and telephone facilities to conduct a hearing or receive evidence in a criminal court.

2 This guidance deals with many of the practical considerations that arise in connection with setting up and using live link and telephone facilities. However, it does not contain detailed instructions about how to use particular live link or telephone equipment at particular locations (how to turn the equipment on; how, and exactly when, to establish a connection between the courtroom and the other location; etc.) because details vary from place to place and cannot practicably all be contained in general guidance. Those details will be made available locally to those who need them. Nor does this guidance contain detailed instructions about the individual responsibilities of court staff, police officers and prison staff because those are matters for court managers, chief constables and H.M. prison governors.

Installation of live link and telephone facilities in the courtroom

3 Everyone in the courtroom must be able to hear and, in the case of a live link, see clearly those who attend by live link or telephone; and the equipment in the courtroom must allow those who attend by live link or telephone to hear, and in the case of a live link see, all the participants in the courtroom. If more than one person is to attend by live link or telephone simultaneously then the equipment must be capable of accommodating them all. (These requirements of course are subject to any special or other measures which a court in an individual case may direct to prevent a witness seeing, or being seen by, the defendant or another participant, or members of the public.) **B-149**

4 Some of the considerations that apply to the installation and use of equipment in other locations will apply in a courtroom, too. They are set out in the following paragraphs. In the case of a live link, attention will need to be given to lighting and to making sure that those attending by live link can see and hear clearly what takes place in the courtroom without being distracted by the movement of court staff, legal representatives or members of the public, or by noise inside the courtroom. The sensitivity and positioning of the courtroom microphones may mean that even the movement of papers, or the operation of keyboards, while barely audible inside the courtroom itself, is clearly audible and distracting to a witness or defendant attending by live link or telephone.

Installation and use of live link and telephone facilities in a live link room

5 Paragraph 6 applies to the installation and use of equipment in a building or in a vehicle which is to be used regularly for giving evidence by live link. It applies to a room within the court building, but separated from the courtroom itself, from which a witness can give evidence by live link; it applies to such a room at a police station or elsewhere which has been set aside for regular use for such a purpose; and it applies to a van or other vehicle which has been adapted for use as a mobile live link room. However, that paragraph does not apply to the courtroom itself; it does not apply to a place from which a witness gives evidence, or a participant takes part in the proceedings, by live link or telephone, if that place is not regularly used for such a purpose (but see para. 7 beneath); and it does not apply in a prison or other place of detention (as to which, see para. 12 beneath). The objective is to ensure that anyone who participates by live link or telephone is conscious of the gravity of the occasion and of the authority of the court, and realises that they are required to conduct themselves in the same respectful manner as if they were physically present in a courtroom. **B-150**

6 A live link room should have the following features:

(a) the room should be an appropriate size, neither too small nor too large;

(b) the room should have suitable lighting, whether natural or electric; any windows may need blinds or curtains fitted that can be adjusted in accordance with the weather conditions outside and to ensure privacy;

(c) there should be a sign or other means of making clear to those outside the room when the room is in use;

(d) arrangements should be made to ensure that nobody in the vicinity of the room is able to hear the evidence being given inside, unless the court otherwise directs (for example, to allow a witness's family to watch the witness's evidence on a supplementary screen in a nearby waiting room, as if they were seeing and hearing that evidence by live link in the courtroom);

(e) arrangements should be made to minimise the risk of disruption to the proceedings by noise outside the room; such noise will distract the witness and may be audible and distracting to the court;

(f) the room should be provided with appropriate and comfortable seating for the witness and, where the witness is a civilian witness, seating for a Witness Service or other companion; a waiting area/room adjacent to the live link room may be required for any other persons attending with the witness; there must be adequate accommodation, support and, where appropriate, security within the premises for witnesses; if both prosecution and defence witnesses attend the same facility, they should wait in separate rooms; it may be inappropriate for defence witnesses to give evidence in police premises (for example in a trial for assaulting a police officer) and in that case parties and the court should identify an alternative venue such as a court building (not necessarily the location of the hearing), or arrange for evidence to be given from elsewhere by Skype, etc; care must be taken to ensure that all witnesses, whether prosecution or defence, are afforded the same assistance, respect and security;

(g) the equipment installed (monitor, microphone and camera, or cameras) in the room must be good enough to ensure that both the picture and sound quality from the room to the court, and from the court to the room, is fit for purpose; the link must enable all in the courtroom to see and hear the witness clearly and it must enable the witness to see and hear clearly all participants in the courtroom;

(h) unless the court otherwise directs, the witness usually will sit to take the oath or affirm and to give evidence; the camera(s) must be positioned to ensure that the witness's face and demeanour can be seen whether he or she sits or stands;

(i) the wall behind the witness, and thus in view of the camera, should be a pale neutral colour (beige and light green/blue are most suitable) and there should be no pictures or notices displayed on that wall;

(j) the royal coat of arms may be displayed to remind witnesses and others that when in use the room is part of the courtroom;

(k) a notice should be displayed that reminds users of the live link to conduct themselves in the same manner as if they were present in person in the courtroom, and to remind them that while using the live link they are subject to the court's jurisdiction to regulate behaviour in the courtroom;

(l) the room should be supplied with the same oath and affirmation cards and holy books as are available in a courtroom; the guidance for the taking of oaths and the making of affirmations which applies in a courtroom applies equally in a live link room; holy books must be treated with the utmost respect and stored with appropriate care;

(m) unless court or other staff are on hand to operate the live link or telephone equipment, clear instructions for users must be in the live link room explaining how, and when, to establish a connection to the courtroom.

Provision and use of live link and telephone facilities elsewhere

B-151 **7** Where a witness gives evidence by live link, or a participant takes part in proceedings by live link or telephone, otherwise than from an established live link room, the objective remains the same as explained in paragraph 5 above. In accordance with that objective, the spirit of the requirements for a live link room should be followed as far as is reasonably practicable; but of course the court will not expect adherence to the letter of those requirements where, for example, a witness who is seriously ill but still able to testify is willing to do so from his or her sick bed, or a doctor or other expert witness is to testify by live link from her or his office. In any such case it is essential that the parties anticipate the arrangements and directions that may be required. Of particular and obvious importance is the need for arrangements that will exclude audible and visible interruptions during the proceedings, and the need for adequate clarity of communication between the remote location and the courtroom.

Conduct of hearings by live link or telephone

B-152 **8** Before live link or telephone equipment is to be used to conduct a hearing, court staff must make sure that the equipment is in working order and that the essential criteria listed in paragraph I 3N.4 of the practice directions ("appropriate" facilities) are met.

9 If a witness who gives evidence by live link produces exhibits, the court must be asked to give appropriate directions during preparation for trial. In most cases the parties can be expected to agree the identity of the exhibit, whatever else is in dispute. In the absence of agreement, documentary exhibits, copies of which have been provided under CrimPR 24.13 (magistrates' court trial) or CrimPR 25.17 (Crown Court trial), and other exhibits which are clearly identifiable by reference to their features and which have been delivered by someone else to the court, may be capable of production by a witness who is using a live link.

10 Where a witness who gives evidence by live link is likely to be referred to exhibits or other material while he or she does so, whether or not as the producer of an exhibit, the court must be asked to give directions during preparation for trial to facilitate such a reference: for example, by requiring the preparation of a paginated and indexed trial bundle which will be readily accessible to the witness, on paper or in electronic form, as well as available to those who are in the courtroom. It is particularly important to make sure that documents and images which are to be displayed by electronic means in the courtroom will be accessible to the witness too. It is unlikely that the live link equipment will be capable of displaying sufficiently clearly to the witness images displayed only on a screen in the courtroom; and likely to be necessary to arrange for those images to be displayed also at the location from which the witness gives evidence, or made available to him or her by some other means. It is likewise important that there should be readily accessible to the witness, on paper or in electronic form, a copy of his or her witness statement (to which she or he may be referred under CrimPR 24.4(5), in a magistrates' court, or under CrimPR 25.11(5), in the Crown Court) and transcript of his or her ABE interview, if applicable.

Conduct of those attending by live link or telephone: practical considerations

11 A person who gives evidence by live link, or who participates by live link or telephone, must behave exactly as if he or she were in the courtroom, addressing the court and the other participants in the proper manner and observing the appropriate social conventions, remembering that she or he will be heard, and if using a live link seen, as if physically present. A practical application of the rules and social conventions governing a participant's behaviour requires, among other things, the following: **B-153**

(i) in the case of a professional participant, including a police officer, lawyer or expert witness:

(a) a participant should prepare themselves to communicate with the court with adequate time in hand, and especially where it will be necessary first to establish the live link or telephone connection with the court;

(b) on entering a live link room a participant should ensure that those outside are made aware that the room is in use, to avoid being interrupted while in communication with the court

(c) a participant should ensure that they have the means to communicate with court staff by some means other than the proposed live link or telephone equipment, in case the equipment they plan to use should fail; they should have to hand an alternative contact number for the court and, if using a mobile phone for the purpose, they should ensure that it is fully charged;

(d) immediately before using the live link or telephone equipment to communicate with the court the person using that equipment and any other person in the live link room must as a general rule switch off any mobile telephone or other device which might interfere with that equipment or interrupt the proceedings; if the device is essential to giving evidence (for example, an electronic notebook), or if it is the only available means of communication with court staff should the other equipment fail, then every effort must be made to minimise the risk of interference, for example by switching a mobile telephone to silent and by placing electronic devices at a distance from the microphone;

(e) a person who gives evidence by live link, or who takes part in the proceedings for some other purpose by live link, must dress as they would if attending by physical presence in the courtroom;

(f) each person in a live link room, whether he or she can be seen by the court or not, and each person present where a telephone conference or loudspeaker facility is in use, must identify themselves clearly to the court;

(g) a person who participates by telephone otherwise than from a room specially equipped for that purpose must take care to ensure that they cannot be interrupted while in communication with the court and that no extraneous noise will be audible so as to distract that participant or the court;

(h) a person who participates by telephone in a call to which he or she, the court and others all contribute must take care to speak clearly and to avoid interrupting in such a way as to prevent any other participant hearing what is said; particular care is required where a participant uses a hands-free or other loudspeaker phone;

(i) a witness who gives evidence by live link may take with him or her into the live link room a copy of her or his written witness statement and (if a police officer) his or her notebook; while giving evidence the witness must place the statement or notes face down, or otherwise out of sight, unless the court gives permission to refer to it; the witness must take the statement or notes away when leaving the live link room;

(j) where successive witnesses are due to give evidence about the same events by live link, and especially where they are due to do so from the same live link room; where the events in question are controversial; or where there is any suggestion that arrangements are required to guard against the accidental or deliberate contamination of a witness's evidence by communication with one who has already given evidence, then the court must be asked to give directions accordingly; subject to those directions, the usual arrangement should be that a witness who has been released should remain in sight of the court, by means of the live link, in the live link room while the next witness enters, and then should leave, so that the court will be able to see that no inappropriate communication between the two has occurred;

(ii) in the case of any other participant:
(a) the preparation of any live link room and the use of the equipment will be the responsibility of court staff, or of the staff present at that live link room if it is outside the court building; where the participant is a witness giving evidence pursuant to a special measures direction, detailed arrangements will have been made accordingly;
(b) mobile telephones and other devices that might interfere with the live link or telephone equipment must be switched off;
(c) a witness or other participant should take care to speak clearly and to avoid interrupting or making a sound which prevents another participant hearing what is said, especially where a hands-free or other loudspeaker phone is in use;
(d) the party who calls a witness, or the witness supporter, or court or other staff, as the case may be, must supply the witness with all he or she may need for the purpose of giving evidence, in accordance with the relevant rules and practice directions; this may, and usually will, include a copy of the witness's statement, in case it becomes necessary to ask him or her to refer to it, and copies of any exhibits or other material to which he or she may be asked to refer: see also para. 10 above.

Prison to court video links

B-154 **12** The objective of the guidance in the preceding paragraphs applies. It is essential that the authority and gravity of the proceedings is respected, by defendants and by their custodians. Detailed instructions are contained in the information issued jointly by the National Offender Management Service and by H.M. Courts and Tribunals Service, with which prison and court staff must familiarise themselves. The principles set out in that guidance correspond with those of the criminal practice directions, as elaborated in this guidance.

13 Where a defendant in custody attends court by live link it is likely that he or she will need to communicate with his or her representatives before and after the hearing, using the live link or by telephone. Arrangements will be required to allow that to take place.

14 Court staff are reminded that a live link to a prison establishment is a means of communication with the defendant. It does not provide an alternative means of formal communication with that establishment and it may not be used in substitution for service on that establishment of those notices and orders required to be served by the Criminal Procedure Rules.

Criminal Procedure Rules 2020 (SI 2020/759), Pt 7

Starting a Prosecution in a magistrates' court

When this Part applies

B-155 **7.1.**—(1) This Part applies in a magistrates' court where—
(a) a prosecutor wants the court to issue a summons or warrant under section 1 of the Magistrates' Courts Act 1980;
(b) a prosecutor with the power to do so issues—
(i) a written charge and requisition, or
(ii) a written charge and single justice procedure notice under section 29 of the Criminal Justice Act 2003;
(c) a person who is in custody is charged with an offence; or
(d) the prosecutor alleges an offence against a defendant who is due to attend, or attends, the court in response to another allegation.

(2) In this Part, "authorised prosecutor" means a prosecutor authorised under section 29 of the Criminal Justice Act 2003 to issue a written charge and requisition or single justice procedure notice.

Application for summons, etc.

B-156 **7.2.**—(1) A prosecutor who wants the court to issue a summons must—
(a) serve on the court officer a written application; or
(b) unless other legislation prohibits this, present an application orally to the court, with a written statement of the allegation or allegations made by the prosecutor.

(2) A prosecutor who wants the court to issue a warrant must—
(a) serve on the court officer—
(i) a written application, or
(ii) a copy of a written charge that has been issued; or
(b) present to the court either of those documents.

(3) An application for the issue of a summons or warrant must—
(a) set out the allegation or allegations made by the applicant in terms that comply with rule

7.3(1) (Allegation of offence in application or charge); and
(b) demonstrate—
(i) that the application is made in time, if legislation imposes a time limit, and
(ii) that the applicant has the necessary consent, if legislation requires it.

(4) As well as complying with paragraph (3), an application for the issue of a warrant must—
(a) demonstrate that the offence or offences alleged can be tried in the Crown Court;
(b) demonstrate that the offence or offences alleged can be punished with imprisonment; or
(c) concisely outline the applicant's grounds for asserting that the defendant's address is not sufficiently established for a summons to be served.

(5) Paragraph (6) applies unless the prosecutor is—
(a) a public authority within the meaning of section 17 of the Prosecution of Offences Act 1985; or
(b) a person acting—
(i) on behalf of such an authority, or
(ii) in that person's capacity as an official appointed by such an authority.

(6) Where this paragraph applies, as well as complying with paragraph (3), and with paragraph (4) if applicable, an application for the issue of a summons or warrant must—
(a) concisely outline the grounds for asserting that the defendant has committed the alleged offence or offences;
(b) disclose—
(i) details of any previous such application by the same applicant in respect of any allegation now made, and
(ii) details of any current or previous proceedings brought by another prosecutor in respect of any allegation now made; and
(c) include a statement that to the best of the applicant's knowledge, information and belief—
(i) the allegations contained in the application are substantially true,
(ii) the evidence on which the applicant relies will be available at the trial,
(iii) the details given by the applicant under paragraph (6)(b) are true, and
(iv) the application discloses all the information that is material to what the court must decide.

(7) Where the statement required by paragraph (6)(c) is made orally—
(a) the statement must be on oath or affirmation, unless the court otherwise directs; and
(b) the court must arrange for a record of the making of the statement.

(8) An authorised prosecutor who issues a written charge must notify the court officer immediately.

(9) A single document may contain—
(a) more than one application; or
(b) more than one written charge.

(10) Where an offence can be tried only in a magistrates' court, then unless other legislation otherwise provides—
(a) a prosecutor must serve an application for the issue of a summons or warrant on the court officer or present it to the court; or
(b) an authorised prosecutor must issue a written charge,
not more than 6 months after the offence alleged.

(11) Where an offence can be tried in the Crown Court then—
(a) a prosecutor must serve an application for the issue of a summons or warrant on the court officer or present it to the court; or
(b) an authorised prosecutor must issue a written charge,
within any time limit that applies to that offence.

(12) The court may determine an application to issue or withdraw a summons or warrant—
(a) without a hearing, as a general rule, or at a hearing (which must be in private unless the court otherwise directs);
(b) in the absence of—
(i) the prosecutor,
(ii) the defendant; and
(c) with or without representations by the defendant.

(13) If the court so directs, a party to an application to issue or withdraw a summons or warrant may attend a hearing by live link or telephone.

Allegation of offence

B-157 **7.3.**—(1) An allegation of an offence in an application for the issue of a summons or warrant or in a charge must contain—

(a) a statement of the offence that—

(i) describes the offence in ordinary language, and

(ii) identifies any legislation that creates it; and

(b) such particulars of the conduct constituting the commission of the offence as to make clear what the prosecutor alleges against the defendant, including the value of any damage or theft alleged where that value is known and where it affects the exercise of the court's powers.

(2) More than one incident of the commission of the offence may be included in the allegation if those incidents taken together amount to a course of conduct having regard to the time, place or purpose of commission.

(3) Where rule 7.1(1)(d) applies (additional allegation in existing prosecution), the prosecutor must—

(a) set out the additional allegation in terms that comply with paragraph (1);

(b) as soon as practicable—

(i) serve the additional allegation on the court officer and the defendant, or

(ii) present the additional allegation orally to the court, with a written statement of that allegation;

(c) demonstrate that the allegation is made in time, if legislation imposes a time limit; and

(d) demonstrate that the prosecutor has the necessary consent, if legislation requires it.

Summons, warrant and requisition

B-158 **7.4.**—(1) A summons, warrant or requisition may be issued in respect of more than one offence.

(2) A summons or requisition must—

(a) contain notice of when and where the defendant is required to attend the court;

(b) specify each offence in respect of which it is issued;

(c) in the case of a summons, identify—

(i) the court that issued it, unless that is otherwise recorded by the court officer, and

(ii) the court office for the court that issued it; and

(d) in the case of a requisition, identify the person under whose authority it is issued.

(3) A summons may be contained in the same document as an application for the issue of that summons.

(4) A requisition may be contained in the same document as a written charge.

(5) Where the court issues a summons—

(a) the prosecutor must—

(i) serve it on the defendant, and

(ii) notify the court officer; or

(b) the court officer must—

(i) serve it on the defendant, and

(ii) notify the prosecutor.

(6) Where an authorised prosecutor issues a requisition that prosecutor must—

(a) serve on the defendant—

(i) the requisition, and

(ii) the written charge; and

(b) serve a copy of each on the court officer.

(7) Unless it would be inconsistent with other legislation, a replacement summons or requisition may be issued without a fresh application or written charge where the one replaced—

(a) was served under rule 4.4 (Service by leaving or posting a document); but

(b) is shown not to have been received by the addressee.

(8) A summons or requisition issued to a defendant under 18 may require that defendant's parent or guardian to attend the court with the defendant, or a separate summons or requisition may be issued for that purpose.

CPD II Preliminary Proceedings 7A: First court attendance after charge or detention (as inserted by Criminal Practice Directions 2015 (Amendment No.10) [2020] EWCA Crim 605, Lord Burnett CJ; and subsequently amended by Criminal Practice Directions 2015 (Amendment No. 11) [2020] EWCA Crim 1347, Lord Burnett CJ)

B-159 **7A.1** A defendant who has been kept in police detention after being charged with an offence must be brought before a magistrates' court as soon as practicable and in any event no later than the first subsequent court sitting: section 46 of the Police and Criminal Evidence Act 1984. If no magistrates' court is due to sit on the day on which the defendant is charged, or on the next day which is not a Sunday, Christmas Day or Good Friday, then the Act requires the police custody officer to inform the court's designated officer of the defendant's detention, and requires the designated officer to arrange for a magistrates' court to sit.

7A.2 The 1984 Act thus imposes duties on the police and on HM Courts and Tribunals Service. *In R (on the application of H (A Child)) v Clerk to Teesside Justices* [2000] 10 WLUK 532 the High Court observed, "it is incumbent on justices and their clerks, however busy their courts may be, to ensure that they are able to receive persons in custody up to the end of normal court hours, at least, in order to comply with section 46 ..., unless some exceptional circumstance intervenes to make that impossible in any particular case".

7A.3 To comply with those duties arrangements must be made to allow courts to receive such defendants during the course of a sitting day if the available time allows for the hearing of all cases to be concluded by 4.30pm, or later if, and only if, some disability or vulnerability of the defendant so requires. In practice, to allow sufficient time for consultation with a legal representative and for the subsequent hearing, the defendant must have been brought to the court building, or given access to a live link to the court, by no later than 3.30pm. To that end, Judicial Business Groups must ensure that effective practical arrangements have been made between police forces, HMCTS, the Crown Prosecution Service and prisoner escort contractors for the prompt transmission of information about defendants held for production before the court.

7A.4 On a Saturday or bank holiday normal court hours may differ from court to court based on likely caseload. Those hours must be determined by the HMCTS Head of Legal Operations in consultation with the judiciary and other agencies. In accordance with the court's observations in the Teesside Justices' Clerk case, all magistrates' courts should sit until at least 11.30 a.m. to receive defendants to whom these directions apply unless arrangements have been made for such defendants to be dealt with by another court, either by attendance in person or by live link.

7A.5 For the purposes of section 46 of the 1984 Act the designated officer is the HMCTS Director of Operations, by whom the exercise of that statutory function is delegated to members of court staff. When informing such a delegate of a defendant's detention the police custody officer must at the same time supply the following, usually by electronic means: **B-160**

(a) confirmation that:
  - (i) the defendant has been charged,
  - (ii) the case file is complete and available,
  - (iii) any interpreter required is available,
  - (iv) any appropriate adult or local authority officer responsible for the defendant's care has been notified and is available,
  - (v) the defendant's legal representative has been notified and is available, and
  - (vi) the CPS or other relevant prosecuting authority has been notified;

(b) the custody officer's proposal for the means by which the defendant should attend court, whether by live link or in person, and, if the latter, then whether by police transport or by prisoner escort contractor transport; and

(c) details of:
  - (i) any physical or mental disability or other vulnerability (whether by reason of age or other circumstance) of the defendant of which police officers are aware, in particular where any such might be thought to make the use of live link inappropriate, and
  - (ii) the expected time of arrival at court, if the defendant is to be brought to court in person.

No court should be expected to hear a case in respect of which such information is missing or incomplete, or in respect of which such arrangements have not been made.

7A.6 The designated officer's delegates must liaise with staff at the court buildings to which defendants in police detention may be brought. Each such delegate must be sufficiently experienced to be able to assess, swiftly and accurately, the availability of courts sitting in those buildings, and of sufficient seniority to take the decisions required by these directions. Each must be in a position to assess (i) the availability of court members, of legal advisers, of prosecutors and of the other staff needed to deal with an unexpected case, (ii) the potential effect of an unexpected case on other cases awaiting hearing that day, including the risk of a less urgent case being adjourned, perhaps not for the first time, in consequence of accommodating the unexpected hearing, (iii) the likely length of the unexpected hearing, and (iv) the significance of the age and any disability or other vulnerability of the unexpected defendant.

7A.7 The delegate to whom a police custody officer reports a defendant's detention must decide whether, and if so how, when and where, to accommodate that defendant's case within the period to which paragraph 7A.3 or 7A.4 refers, having regard to the availability and content of the information to which paragraph 7A.5 refers and to the considerations listed in paragraph 7A.6. The decision must be informed by the views of those court members and legal advisers who may be affected, as listing is a judicial responsibility and function. It may be necessary for the delegate to take such steps as arranging for the unexpected case to be heard by live link; reorganising courts sitting in the court building to which the defendant is due to be brought; adjourning other cases; calling upon additional resources; or making arrangements with the delegate at another court building for the unexpected case to be heard by a court sitting there, by live link if appropriate. It may be necessary for the court that hears the unexpected case to impose a timetable for representations or to restrict the decisions that will be taken immediately. If it will not be possible to hear within the period to which paragraph 7A.3 or 7A.4 refers every case due to be heard that day at the court building to which the defendant is to be brought then every effort must be made to ensure that the cases of all defendants in custody, whether in that court building or attending by live link, still can be heard within that period. The delegate for that building must ensure that the police, the staff responsible for the court's own cells and the relevant prisoner escort contractor all are aware of the arrangements that have been made. If the prosecuting authority is not the CPS then that delegate must ensure that that other authority will arrange for a representative to attend, in person or by live link, to assist the court.

7A.8 If after conducting the assessment required by paragraph 7A.6 and taking the steps to which paragraph 7A.7 refers the designated officer's delegate finds it impossible to accommodate an unexpected case within the period to which paragraph 7A.3 or 7A.4 refers then arrangements must be made to hear the case on the next sitting day and the police custody officer must promptly be so informed.

Criminal Procedure Rules 2020 (SI 2020/759), Pt 8

Initial Details of the Prosecution Case

When this part applies

B-161 **8.1.** This Part applies in a magistrates' court.

Providing initial details of the prosecution case

B-162 **8.2.**—(1) The prosecutor must serve initial details of the prosecution case on the court officer—

(a) as soon as practicable; and

(b) in any event, no later than the beginning of the day of the first hearing.

(2) Where a defendant requests those details, the prosecutor must serve them on the defendant—

(a) as soon as practicable; and

(b) in any event, no later than the beginning of the day of the first hearing.

(3) Where a defendant does not request those details, the prosecutor must make them available to the defendant at, or before, the beginning of the day of the first hearing.

Content of initial details

B-163 **8.3.** Initial details of the prosecution case must include—

(a) where, immediately before the first hearing in the magistrates' court, the defendant was in police custody for the offence charged—

(i) a summary of the circumstances of the offence, and

(ii) the defendant's criminal record, if any; or

(b) where paragraph (a) does not apply—

(i) a summary of the circumstances of the offence,

(ii) any account given by the defendant in interview, whether contained in that summary or in another document,

(iii) any written witness statement or exhibit that the prosecutor then has available and considers material to plea, or to the allocation of the case for trial, or to sentence,

(iv) the defendant's criminal record, if any, and

(v) any available statement of the effect of the offence on a victim, a victim's family or others.

Use of initial details

B-164 **8.4.**—(1) This rule applies where-

(a) the prosecutor wants to introduce information contained in a document listed in rule 8.3; and

(b) the prosecutor has not

(i) served that document on the defendant, or

(ii) made that information available to the defendant.

(2) The court must not allow the prosecutor to introduce that information unless the court first allows the defendant sufficient time to consider it.

CPD II Preliminary Proceedings 8A: Defendant's record

Copies of record

8A.1 The defendant's record (previous convictions, cautions, reprimands, etc) may be taken into **B-165**
account when the court decides not only on sentence but also, for example, about bail, or when allocating a case for trial. It is therefore important that up to date and accurate information is available.

Previous convictions must be provided as part of the initial details of the prosecution case under Part 8 of the rules.

8A.2 The record should usually be provided in the following format:

Personal details and summary of convictions and cautions – Police National Computer ["PNC"] Court / Defence / Probation Summary Sheet;

Previous convictions – PNC Court / Defence / Probation printout, supplemented by Form MG16 if the police force holds convictions not shown on PNC;

Recorded cautions – PNC Court / Defence / Probation printout, supplemented by Form MG17 if the police force holds cautions not shown on PNC.

8A.3 The defence representative should take instructions on the defendant's record and if the defence wish to raise any objection to the record, this should be made known to the prosecutor immediately.

8A.4 It is the responsibility of the prosecutor to ensure that a copy of the defendant's record has been provided to the probation service.

8A.5 Where following conviction a custodial order is made, the court must ensure that a copy is attached to the order sent to the prison.

Additional information

8A.6 In the Crown Court, the police should also provide brief details of the circumstances of the **B-166**
last three similar convictions and / or of convictions likely to be of interest to the court, the latter being judged on a case-by-case basis.

8A.7 Where the current alleged offence could constitute a breach of an existing sentence such as a suspended sentence, community order or conditional discharge, and it is known that that sentence is still in force then details of the circumstances of the offence leading to the sentence should be included in the antecedents. The detail should be brief and include the date of the offence.

8A.8 On occasions the PNC printout provided may not be fully up to date. It is the responsibility of the prosecutor to ensure that all of the necessary information is available to the court and the probation service and provided to the defence. Oral updates at the hearing will sometimes be necessary, but it is preferable if this information is available in advance.

Criminal Procedure Rules 2020 (SI 2020/759), Pt 9

Allocation and Sending for Trial

General rules

When this Part applies

9.1.–(1) This Part applies to the allocation and sending of cases for trial under– **B-167**

(a) sections 17A to 26 of the Magistrates' Courts Act 1980; and

(b) sections 50A to 52 of the Crime and Disorder Act 1998.

(2) Rules 9.6 and 9.7 apply in a magistrates' court where the court must, or can, send a defendant to the Crown Court for trial, without allocating the case for trial there.

(3) Rules 9.8 and 9.14 apply in a magistrates' court where the court must allocate the case to a magistrates' court or to the Crown Court for trial.

Exercise of magistrates' court's powers

9.2.–(1) This rule applies to the exercise of the powers to which rules 9.6 to 9.14 apply. **B-168**

(2) The general rule is that the court must exercise its powers at a hearing in public, but it may exercise any power it has to–

(a) withhold information from the public; or

(b) order a hearing in private.

(3) The general rule is that the court must exercise its powers in the defendant's presence, but it may exercise the powers to which the following rules apply in the defendant's absence on the conditions specified–

(a) where rule 9.8 (adult defendant: request for plea), rule 9.9 (adult defendant: guilty plea) or rule 9.13 (young defendant) applies, if—
(i) the defendant is represented, and
(ii) the defendant's disorderly conduct makes his or her presence in the courtroom impracticable; and
(b) where rule 9.10 (adult defendant: not guilty plea) or rule 9.11 (adult defendant: allocation for magistrates' court trial) applies, if—
(i) the defendant is represented and waives the right to be present, or
(ii) the defendant's disorderly conduct makes his or her presence in the courtroom impracticable.

(4) The court may exercise its power to adjourn—
(a) if either party asks; or
(b) on its own initiative.

(5) Where the court on the same occasion deals with two or more offences alleged against the same defendant, the court must deal with those offences in the following sequence—
(a) any to which rule 9.6 applies (prosecutor's notice requiring Crown Court trial);
(b) any to which rule 9.7 applies (sending for Crown Court trial, without allocation there), in this sequence—
(i) any the court must send for trial, then
(ii) any the court can send for trial; and
(c) any to which rule 9.14 applies (allocation for Crown Court trial).

(6) Where the court on the same occasion deals with two or more defendants charged jointly with an offence that can be tried in the Crown Court then in the following sequence—
(a) the court must explain, in terms each defendant can understand (with help, if necessary), that if the court sends one of them to the Crown Court for trial then the court must send for trial in the Crown Court, too, any other of them—
(i) who is charged with the same offence as the defendant sent for trial, or with an offence which the court decides is related to that offence,
(ii) who does not wish to plead guilty to each offence with which he or she is charged, and
(iii) (if that other defendant is under 18, and the court would not otherwise have sent him or her for Crown Court trial) where the court decides that sending is necessary in the interests of justice even if the court by then has decided to allocate that other defendant for magistrates' court trial; and
(b) the court may ask the defendants questions to help it decide in what order to deal with them.

(7) After following paragraph (5), if it applies, where the court on the same occasion—
(a) deals with two or more defendants charged jointly with an offence that can be tried in the Crown Court;
(b) allocates any of them to a magistrates' court for trial; and
(c) then sends another one of them to the Crown Court for trial,

the court must deal again with each one whom, on that occasion, it has allocated for magistrates' court trial.

Matters to be specified on sending for trial

B-169 **9.3.**—(1) Where the court sends a defendant to the Crown Court for trial, it must specify—
(a) each offence to be tried;
(b) in respect of each, the power exercised to send the defendant for trial for that offence; and
(c) the Crown Court centre at which the trial will take place.

(2) In a case in which the prosecutor serves a notice to which rule 9.6(1)(a) applies (notice requiring Crown Court trial in a case of serious or complex fraud), the court must specify the Crown Court centre identified by that notice.

(3) In any other case, in deciding the Crown Court centre at which the trial will take place, the court must take into account—
(a) the convenience of the parties and witnesses;
(b) how soon a suitable courtroom will be available; and
(c) the directions on the allocation of Crown Court business contained in the Practice Direction.

Duty of justices' legal adviser

B-170 **9.4.**—(1) This rule applies—

(a) only in a magistrates' court; and
(b) unless the court–
(i) includes a District Judge (Magistrates' Courts), and
(ii) otherwise directs.

(2) On the court's behalf, a justices' legal adviser may–
(a) read the allegation of the offence to the defendant;
(b) give any explanation and ask any question required by the rules in this Part; and
(c) make any announcement required by the rules in this Part, other than an announcement of–
(i) the court's decisions about allocation and sending,
(ii) any indication by the court of likely sentence, or
(iii) sentence.

(3) A justices' legal adviser must–
(a) assist an unrepresented defendant;
(b) give the court such advice as is required to enable it to exercise its powers; and
(c) if required, attend the members of the court outside the courtroom to give such advice, but inform the parties of any advice so given.

Duty of magistrates' court officer

9.5.–(1) The magistrates' court officer must– **B-171**
(a) serve notice of a sending for Crown Court trial on–
(i) the Crown Court officer, and
(ii) the parties;
(b) in that notice record–
(i) the matters specified by the court under rule 9.3 (matters to be specified on sending for trial),
(ii) any decision by the defendant under rule 9.7 (Sending for Crown Court trial) to require Crown Court trial for low-level shoplifting,
(iii) any indication given by the defendant under rule 9.7 of intended guilty plea,
(iv) any decision by the defendant under rule 9.11 (Adult defendant: allocation to magistrates' court for trial) to decline magistrates' court trial, and
(v) the date on which any custody time limit will expire;
(c) record any indication of likely sentence to which rule 9.11 applies; and
(d) give the court such other assistance as it requires.

(2) The magistrates' court officer must include with the notice served on the Crown Court officer–
(a) the initial details of the prosecution case served by the prosecutor under rule 8.2;
(b) a record of any–
(i) listing or case management direction affecting the Crown Court,
(ii) direction about reporting restrictions,
(iii) decision about bail, for the purposes of section 5 of the Bail Act 1976 [§ 3-28 in the main work],
(iv) recognizance given by a surety, or
(v) representation order; and
(c) if relevant, any available details of any–
(i) interpreter,
(ii) intermediary, or
(iii) other supporting adult, where the defendant is assisted by such a person.

Sending without allocation for Crown Court trial

Prosecutor's notice requiring Crown Court trial

9.6.–(1) This rule applies where a prosecutor with power to do so requires a magistrates' court to send for trial in the Crown Court– **B-172**
(a) a case of serious or complex fraud; or
(b) a case which will involve a child witness.

(2) The prosecutor must serve notice of that requirement–
(a) on the magistrates' court officer and on the defendant; and
(b) before trial in a magistrates' court begins under Part 24 (trial and sentence in a magistrates'

court).

(3) The notice must identify—

(a) the power on which the prosecutor relies; and

(b) the Crown Court centre at which the prosecutor wants the trial to take place.

(4) The prosecutor—

(a) must, when choosing a Crown Court centre, take into account the matters listed in rule 9.3(3) (court deciding to which Crown Court centre to send a case); and

(b) may change the centre identified before the case is sent for trial.

Sending for Crown Court trial

B-173 **9.7.**—(1) This rule applies where a magistrates' court must, or can, send a defendant to the Crown Court for trial without first allocating the case for trial there.

(2) The court must read the allegation of the offence to the defendant.

(3) The court must explain, in terms the defendant can understand (with help, if necessary)—

(a) the allegation, unless it is self-explanatory;

(b) that the offence is one for which the court, as appropriate—

(i) must send the defendant to the Crown Court for trial because the offence is one which can only be tried there or because the court for some other reason is required to send that offence for trial,

(ii) may send the defendant to the Crown Court for trial if the magistrates' court decides that the offence is related to one already sent for trial there, or

(iii) (where the offence is low-value shoplifting and the defendant is 18 or over) must send the defendant to the Crown Court for trial if the defendant wants to be tried there; and

(c) that reporting restrictions apply, which the defendant may ask the court to vary or remove.

(4) In the following sequence, the court must then—

(a) invite the prosecutor to—

(i) identify the court's power to send the defendant to the Crown Court for trial for the offence, and

(ii) make representations about any ancillary matters, including bail and directions for the management of the case in the Crown Court;

(b) invite the defendant to make representations about—

(i) the court's power to send the defendant to the Crown Court, and

(ii) any ancillary matters;

(c) (where the offence is low-value shoplifting and the defendant is 18 or over) offer the defendant the opportunity to require trial in the Crown Court; and

(d) decide whether or not to send the defendant to the Crown Court for trial.

(5) If the court sends the defendant to the Crown Court for trial, it must—

(a) ask whether the defendant intends to plead guilty in the Crown Court and—

(i) if the answer is "yes", make arrangements for the Crown Court to take the defendant's plea as soon as possible, or

(ii) if the defendant does not answer, or the answer is "no", make arrangements for a case management hearing in the Crown Court; and

(b) give any other ancillary directions.

Allocation for magistrates' court or Crown Court trial

Adult defendant: request for plea

B-174 **9.8.**—(1) This rule applies where—

(a) the defendant is 18 or over; and

(b) the court must decide whether a case is more suitable for trial in a magistrates' court or in the Crown Court.

(2) The court must read the allegation of the offence to the defendant.

(3) The court must explain, in terms the defendant can understand (with help, if necessary)—

(a) the allegation, unless it is self-explanatory;

(b) that the offence is one which can be tried in a magistrates' court or in the Crown Court;

(c) that the court is about to ask whether the defendant intends to plead guilty;

(d) that if the answer is "yes", then the court must treat that as a guilty plea and must sentence the defendant, or commit the defendant to the Crown Court for sentence;

(e) that if the defendant does not answer, or the answer is "no", then–
(i) the court must decide whether to allocate the case to a magistrates' court or to the Crown Court for trial,
(ii) the value involved may require the court to order trial in a magistrates' court (where the offence is one to which section 22 of the Magistrates' Courts Act 1980 applies [§ 1-77 in the main work]), and
(iii) if the court allocates the case to a magistrates' court for trial, the defendant can nonetheless require trial in the Crown Court (unless the offence is one to which section 22 of the Magistrates' Courts Act 1980 applies and the value involved requires magistrates' court trial); and
(f) that reporting restrictions apply, which the defendant may ask the court to vary or remove.
(4) The court must then ask whether the defendant intends to plead guilty.

Adult defendant: guilty plea

9.9.–(1) This rule applies where– **B-175**
(a) rule 9.8 applies; and
(b) the defendant indicates an intention to plead guilty.
(2) The court must exercise its power to deal with the case–
(a) as if the defendant had just pleaded guilty at trial in a magistrates' court; and
(b) in accordance with rule 24.11 (procedure if the court convicts).

Adult defendant: not guilty plea

9.10.–(1) This rule applies where– **B-176**
(a) rule 9.8 applies; and
(b) the defendant–
(i) indicates an intention to plead not guilty, or
(ii) gives no indication of intended plea.
(2) In the following sequence, the court must then–
(a) where the offence is one to which section 22 of the Magistrates' Courts Act 1980 applies, explain in terms the defendant can understand (with help, if necessary) that–
(i) if the court decides that the value involved clearly is less than £5,000, the court must order trial in a magistrates' court,
(ii) if the court decides that it is not clear whether that value is more or less than £5,000, then the court will ask whether the defendant agrees to be tried in a magistrates' court, and
(iii) if the answer to that question is "yes", then the court must order such a trial and if the defendant is convicted then the maximum sentence is limited;
(b) invite the prosecutor to–
(i) identify any previous convictions of which it can take account, and
(ii) make representations about how the court should allocate the case for trial, including representations about the value involved, if relevant;
(c) invite the defendant to make such representations; and
(d) where the offence is one to which section 22 of the Magistrates' Courts Act 1980 applies–
(i) if it is not clear whether the value involved is more or less than £5,000, ask whether the defendant agrees to be tried in a magistrates' court,
(ii) if the defendant's answer to that question is "yes", or if that value clearly is less than £5,000, order a trial in a magistrates' court,
(iii) if the defendant does not answer that question, or the answer is "no", or if that value clearly is more than £5,000, apply paragraph (2)(e); and
(e) exercise its power to allocate the case for trial, taking into account–
(i) the adequacy of a magistrates' court's sentencing powers,
(ii) any representations by the parties, and
(iii) any allocation guidelines issued by the Sentencing Council.

Adult defendant: allocation for magistrates' court trial

9.11.–(1) This rule applies where– **B-177**
(a) rule 9.10 applies; and
(b) the court allocates the case to a magistrates' court for trial.
(2) The court must explain, in terms the defendant can understand (with help, if necessary) that–

(a) the court considers the case more suitable for trial in a magistrates' court than in the Crown Court;
(b) if the defendant is convicted at a magistrates' court trial, then in some circumstances the court may commit the defendant to the Crown Court for sentence;
(c) if the defendant does not agree to a magistrates' court trial, then the court must send the defendant to the Crown Court for trial; and
(d) before deciding whether to accept magistrates' court trial, the defendant may ask the court for an indication of whether a custodial or non-custodial sentence is more likely in the event of a guilty plea at such a trial, but the court need not give such an indication.

(3) If the defendant asks for such an indication of sentence and the court gives such an indication—
(a) the court must then ask again whether the defendant intends to plead guilty;
(b) if, in answer to that question, the defendant indicates an intention to plead guilty, then the court must exercise its power to deal with the case—
(i) as if the defendant had just pleaded guilty to an offence that can be tried only in a magistrates' court, and
(ii) in accordance with rule 24.11 (procedure if the court convicts); and
(c) if, in answer to that question, the defendant indicates an intention to plead not guilty, or gives no indication of intended plea, in the following sequence the court must then—
(i) ask whether the defendant agrees to trial in a magistrates' court,
(ii) if the defendant's answer to that question is "yes", order such a trial, and
(iii) if the defendant does not answer that question, or the answer is "no", apply rule 9.14.

(4) If the defendant asks for an indication of sentence but the court gives none, or if the defendant does not ask for such an indication, in the following sequence the court must then—
(a) ask whether the defendant agrees to trial in a magistrates' court;
(b) if the defendant's answer to that question is "yes", order such a trial; and
(c) if the defendant does not answer that question, or the answer is "no", apply rule 9.14.

Adult defendant: prosecutor's application for Crown Court trial

B-178 **9.12.**—(1) This rule applies where—
(a) rule 9.11 applies;
(b) the defendant agrees to trial in a magistrates' court; but
(c) the prosecutor wants the court to exercise its power to send the defendant to the Crown Court for trial instead.

(2) The prosecutor must—
(a) apply before trial in a magistrates' court begins under Part 24 (trial and sentence in a magistrates' court); and
(b) notify—
(i) the defendant, and
(ii) the magistrates' court officer.

(3) The court must determine an application to which this rule applies before it deals with any other pre-trial application.

Young defendant

B-179 **9.13.**—(1) This rule applies where—
(a) the defendant is under 18; and
(b) the court must decide whether to send the defendant for Crown Court trial instead of ordering trial in a youth court.

(2) The court must read the allegation of the offence to the defendant.

(3) The court must explain, in terms the defendant can understand (with help, if necessary)—
(a) the allegation, unless it is self-explanatory;
(b) that the offence is one which can be tried in the Crown Court instead of in a youth court;
(c) that the court is about to ask whether the defendant intends to plead guilty;
(d) that if the answer is "yes", then the court must treat that as a guilty plea and must sentence the defendant, or commit the defendant to the Crown Court for sentence;
(e) that if the defendant does not answer, or the answer is "no", then the court must decide whether to send the defendant for Crown Court trial instead of ordering trial in a youth court; and
(f) that reporting restrictions apply, which the defendant may ask the court to vary or remove.

(4) The court must then ask whether the defendant intends to plead guilty.

(5) If the defendant's answer to that question is "yes", the court must exercise its power to deal with the case–

(a) as if the defendant had just pleaded guilty at a trial in a youth court; and

(b) in accordance with rule 24.11 (procedure if the court convicts).

(6) If the defendant does not answer that question, or the answer is "no", in the following sequence the court must then–

(a) invite the prosecutor to make representations about whether Crown Court or youth court trial is more appropriate;

(b) invite the defendant to make such representations; and

(c) exercise its power to allocate the case for trial, taking into account–

(i) the offence and the circumstances of the offence,

(ii) the suitability of a youth court's sentencing powers,

(iii) where the defendant is jointly charged with an adult, whether it is necessary in the interests of justice for them to be tried together in the Crown Court, and

(iv) any representations by the parties.

Allocation and sending for Crown Court trial

9.14.–(1) This rule applies where– **B-180**

(a) under rule 9.10 or rule 9.13, the court allocates the case to the Crown Court for trial;

(b) under rule 9.11, the defendant does not agree to trial in a magistrates' court; or

(c) under rule 9.12, the court grants the prosecutor's application for Crown Court trial.

(2) In the following sequence, the court must–

(a) invite the prosecutor to make representations about any ancillary matters, including bail and directions for the management of the case in the Crown Court;

(b) invite the defendant to make any such representations; and

(c) exercise its powers to–

(i) send the defendant to the Crown Court for trial, and

(ii) give any ancillary directions.

CPD II Preliminary Proceedings 9A: Allocation (mode of trial) (as substituted by Criminal Practice Directions 2015 (Amendment No. 2), unreported, 16 November 2016, Lord Thomas CJ)

9A.1 Courts must follow the Sentencing Council's guideline on allocation (mode of trial) when deciding whether or not to send defendants charged with "either-way" offences for trial in the Crown Court under section 51(1) of the CDA 1998 [§ 1-24 in the main work]. **B-181**

Criminal Procedure Rules 2020 (SI 2020/759), Pt 10

The Indictment

When this Part applies

10.1. This Part applies where–

(a) a magistrates' court sends a defendant to the Crown Court for trial under section 51 or section 51A of the Crime and Disorder Act 1998; **B-182**

(b) a prosecutor wants a High Court judge's permission to serve a draft indictment;

(c) the Crown Court approves a proposed indictment under paragraph 2 of Schedule 17 to the Crime and Courts Act 2013 and rule 11.4 (deferred prosecution agreements: application to approve the terms of an agreement);

(d) a prosecutor wants to re-institute proceedings in the Crown Court under section 22B of the Prosecution of Offences Act 1985; or

(e) the Court of Appeal orders a retrial, under section 8 of the Criminal Appeal Act 1968 or under section 77 of the Criminal Justice Act 2003.

The indictment: general rules

10.2.–(1) The indictment on which the defendant is arraigned under rule 3.32 (arraigning the defendant on the indictment) must be in writing and must contain, in a paragraph called a "count"– **B-183**

(a) a statement of the offence charged that–

(i) describes the offence in ordinary language, and

(ii) identifies any legislation that creates it; and

(b) such particulars of the conduct constituting the commission of the offence as to make clear what the prosecutor alleges against the defendant.

(2) More than one incident of the commission of the offence may be included in a count if those incidents taken together amount to a course of conduct having regard to the time, place or purpose of commission.

(3) The counts must be numbered consecutively.

(4) An indictment may contain—

(a) any count charging substantially the same offence as one for which the defendant was sent for trial;

(b) any count contained in a draft indictment served with the permission of a High Court judge or at the direction of the Court of Appeal; and

(c) any other count charging an offence that the Crown Court can try and which is based on the prosecution evidence that has been served, including a summary offence to which section 40 of the Criminal Justice Act 1988 applies.

(5) For the purposes of section 2 of the Administration of Justice (Miscellaneous Provisions) Act 1933—

(a) a draft indictment constitutes a bill of indictment; and

(b) the draft, or bill, is preferred before the Crown Court and becomes the indictment—

(i) where rule 10.3 applies (draft indictment generated electronically on sending for trial), immediately before the first count (or the only count, if there is only one) is read to or placed before the defendant to take the defendant's plea under rule 3.24(1)(d),

(ii) when the prosecutor serves the draft indictment on the Crown Court officer, where rule 10.4 (draft indictment served by the prosecutor after sending for trial), rule 10.5 (draft indictment served by the prosecutor with a High Court judge's permission), rule 10.7 (draft indictment served by the prosecutor on re-instituting proceedings) or rule 10.8 (draft indictment served by the prosecutor at the direction of the Court of Appeal) applies, or

(iii) when the Crown Court approves the proposed indictment, where rule 10.6 applies (draft indictment approved by the Crown Court with deferred prosecution agreement).

(6) An indictment must be in one of the forms set out in the Practice Direction unless—

(a) rule 10.3 applies; or

(b) the Crown Court otherwise directs.

(7) Unless the Crown Court otherwise directs, the court officer must—

(a) endorse any paper copy of the indictment made for the court with—

(i) a note to identify it as a copy of the indictment, and

(ii) the date on which the draft indictment became the indictment under paragraph (5); and

(b) where rule 10.4, 10.5, 10.7 or 10.8 applies, serve a copy of the indictment on all parties.

(8) The Crown Court may extend the time limit under rule 10.4, 10.5, 10.7 or 10.8, even after it has expired.

Draft indictment generated electronically on sending for trial

B-184 **10.3.**—(1) Unless the Crown Court otherwise directs before the defendant is arraigned, this rule applies where—

(a) a magistrates' court sends a defendant to the Crown Court for trial;

(b) the magistrates' court officer serves on the Crown Court officer the notice required by rule 9.5 (duty of magistrates' court officer); and

(c) by means of such electronic arrangements as the court officer may make for the purpose, there is presented to the Crown Court as a count—

(i) each allegation of an indictable offence specified in the notice, and

(ii) each allegation specified in the notice to which section 40 of the Criminal Justice Act 1988 applies (specified summary offences founded on the prosecution evidence).

(2) Where this rule applies—

(a) each such allegation constitutes a count;

(b) the allegation or allegations so specified together constitute a draft indictment;

(c) before the draft indictment so constituted is preferred before the Crown Court under rule 10.2(5)(b)(i) the prosecutor may substitute for any count an amended count to the same effect and charging the same offence;

(d) if under rule 3.19 (service of prosecution evidence) the prosecutor has served copies of the documents containing the evidence on which the prosecution case relies then, before the draft indictment is preferred before the Crown Court under rule 10.2(5)(b)(i), the prosecu-

tor may substitute or add–
(i) any count charging substantially the same offence as one specified in the notice, and
(ii) any other count charging an offence which the Crown Court can try and which is based on the prosecution evidence so served; and
(e) a prosecutor who substitutes or adds a count under paragraph (2)(c) or (d) must serve that count on the Crown Court officer and the defendant.

Draft indictment served by the prosecutor after sending for trial

10.4.–(1) This rule applies where– **B-185**
(a) a magistrates' court sends a defendant to the Crown Court for trial; and
(b) rule 10.3 (draft indictment generated electronically on sending for trial) does not apply

(2) The prosecutor must serve a draft indictment on the Crown Court officer not more than 20 business days after serving under rule 3.19 (service of prosecution evidence) copies of the documents containing the evidence on which the prosecution case relies.

Draft indictment served by the prosecutor with a High Court judge's permission

10.5.–(1) This rule applies where– **B-186**
(a) the prosecutor applies to a High Court judge under rule 10.9 (application to a High Court judge for permission to serve a draft indictment); and
(b) the judge gives permission to serve a proposed indictment.

(2) Where this rule applies–
(a) that proposed indictment constitutes the draft indictment; and
(b) the prosecutor must serve the draft indictment on the Crown Court officer not more than 20 business days after the High Court judge's decision.

Draft indictment approved with deferred prosecution agreement

10.6.–(1) This rule applies where– **B-187**
(a) the prosecutor applies to the Crown Court under rule 11.4 (deferred prosecution agreements: application to approve the terms of an agreement); and
(b) the Crown Court approves the proposed indictment served with that application.

(2) Where this rule applies, that proposed indictment constitutes the draft indictment.

Draft indictment served by the prosecutor on re-instituting proceedings

10.7.–(1) This rule applies where the prosecutor wants to re-institute proceedings in the Crown Court under section 22B of the Prosecution of Offences Act 1985. **B-188**

(2) The prosecutor must serve a draft indictment on the Crown Court officer not more than 3 months after the proceedings were stayed under section 22(4) of that Act.

Draft indictment served by the prosecutor at the direction of the Court of Appeal

10.8.–(1) This rule applies where the Court of Appeal orders a retrial. **B-189**

(2) The prosecutor must serve a draft indictment on the Crown Court officer not more than 28 days after that order.

Application to a High Court judge for permission to serve a draft indictment

10.9.–(1) This rule applies where a prosecutor wants a High Court judge's permission to serve a draft indictment. **B-190**

(2) Such a prosecutor must–
(a) apply in writing;
(b) serve the application on–
(i) the court officer, and
(ii) the proposed defendant, unless the judge otherwise directs; and
(c) ask for a hearing, if the prosecutor wants one, and explain why it is needed.

(3) The application must–
(a) attach–
(i) the proposed indictment,
(ii) copies of the documents containing the evidence on which the prosecutor relies, including any written witness statement or statements complying with rule 16.2 (content of written witness statement) and any documentary exhibit to any such statement,
(iii) a copy of any indictment on which the defendant already has been arraigned, and
(iv) if not contained in such an indictment, a list of any offence or offences for which the defendant already has been sent for trial;

(b) include—
(i) a concise statement of the circumstances in which, and the reasons why, the application is made, and
(ii) a concise summary of the evidence contained in the documents accompanying the application, identifying each passage in those documents said to evidence each offence alleged by the prosecutor and relating that evidence to each count in the proposed indictment; and
(c) contain a statement that, to the best of the prosecutor's knowledge, information and belief—
(i) the evidence on which the prosecutor relies will be available at the trial, and
(ii) the allegations contained in the application are substantially true
unless the application is made by or on behalf of the Director of Public Prosecutions or the Director of the Serious Fraud Office.

(4) A proposed defendant served with an application who wants to make representations to the judge must—
(a) serve the representations on the court officer and on the prosecutor;
(b) do so as soon as practicable, and in any event with in such period as the judge directs; and
(c) ask for a hearing, if the proposed defendant wants one, and explain why it is needed.

(5) The judge may determine the application—
(a) without a hearing, or at a hearing in public or in private; and
(b) with or without receiving the oral evidence of any proposed witness.

(6) At any hearing, if the judge so directs a statement required by paragraph (3)(c) must be repeated on oath or affirmation.

(7) If the judge gives permission to serve a draft indictment, the decision must be recorded in writing and endorsed on, or annexed to, the proposed indictment.

CPD II Preliminary Proceedings 10A: Preparation and content of the indictment (as substituted by Criminal Practice Directions 2015 (Amendment No. 2), unreported, 16 November 2016, Lord Thomas CJ and amended by Criminal Practice Directions 2015 (Amendment No. 6), unreported, 22 March 2018, Lord Burnett CJ)

Preferring the indictment

B-191 **10A.1** Section 2 of the Administration of Justice (Miscellaneous Provisions) Act 1933 [§§ 1-328, 1-348 in the main work] allows Criminal Procedure Rules to "make provision ... as to the manner in which and the time at which bills of indictment are to be preferred". CrimPR 10.2(5) lists the events which constitute preferment for the purposes of that Act. Where a defendant is contemplating an application to the Crown Court to dismiss an offence sent for trial, under the provisions to which CrimPR 9.16 applies, or where the prosecutor is contemplating discontinuance, under the provisions to which CrimPR, Pt 12, applies, the parties and the court must be astute to the effect of the occurrence of those events: the right to apply for dismissal is lost if the defendant is arraigned, and the right to discontinue is lost if the indictment is preferred.

Printing and signature of indictment

B-192 **10A.2** Neither section 2 of the Administration of Justice (Miscellaneous Provisions) Act 1933 nor the Criminal Procedure Rules require an indictment to be printed or signed. Section 2(1) of the Act was amended by section 116 of the Coroners and Justice Act 2009 to remove the requirement for signature. For the potential benefit of the Criminal Appeal Office, CrimPR 10.2(7) requires only that any paper copy of the indictment which for any reason in fact is made for the court must be endorsed with a note to identify it as a copy of the indictment, and with the date on which the indictment came into being. For the same reason, CrimPR 3.22 requires only that any paper copy of an indictment which in fact has been made must be endorsed with a note of the order and of its date where the court makes an order for joint or separate trials affecting that indictment or makes an order for the amendment of that indictment in any respect.

Content of indictment; joint and separate trials

B-193 **10A.3** The rule has been abolished which formerly required an indictment containing more than one count to include only offences founded on the same facts, or offences which constitute all or part of a series of the same or a similar character. However, if an indictment charges more than one offence, and if at least one of those offences does not meet those criteria, then CrimPR 3.21(4) cites that circumstance as an example of one in which the court may decide to exercise its power to order separate trials under section 5(3) of the Indictments Act 1915 [§ 1-249 in the main work]. It is for the court to decide which allegations, against whom, should be tried at the same time, having regard to the prosecutor's proposals, the parties' representations, the court's powers under the 1915 Act (see also CrimPR 3.21(4)) and the overriding objective. Where necessary the court should be invited to exercise those powers. It is generally undesirable for a large number of counts to be tried at the same time and the prosecutor may be required to identify a selection of counts on which the trial should proceed, leaving a decision to be taken later whether to try any of the remainder.

10A.4 Where an indictment contains substantive counts and one or more related conspiracy counts, the court will expect the prosecutor to justify their joint trial. Failing justification, the prosecutor should be required to choose whether to proceed on the substantive counts or on the conspiracy counts. In any event, if there is a conviction on any counts that are tried, then those that have not been proceeded with can remain on the file marked "not to be proceeded with without the leave of the court or the Court of Appeal". In the event that a conviction is later quashed on appeal, the remaining counts can be tried.

10A.5 There is no rule of law or practice which prohibits two indictments being in existence at the same time for the same offence against the same person and on the same facts. However, the court will not allow the prosecutor to proceed on both indictments. They cannot be tried together and the court will require the prosecutor to elect the one on which the trial will proceed. Where different defendants have been separately sent for trial for offences which properly may be tried together then it is permissible to join in one indictment counts based on the separate sendings for trial even if an indictment based on one of them already exists.

Draft indictment generated electronically on sending for trial

10A.6 CrimPR 10.3 applies where court staff have introduced arrangements for the charges sent for trial to be presented in the Crown Court as the counts of a draft indictment without the need for those charges to be rewritten and served a second time on the defendant and on the court office. Where such arrangements are introduced, court users will be informed (and the fact will become apparent on the sending for trial). **B-194**

10A.7 Now that there is no restriction on the counts that an indictment may contain (see para. 10A.3 above), and given the Crown Court's power, and in some cases obligation, to order separate trials, few circumstances will arise in which the court will wish to exercise the discretion conferred by rule 10.3(1) to direct that the rule will not apply, thus discarding such an electronically generated draft indictment. The most likely such circumstance to arise would be in a case in which prosecution evidence emerging soon after sending requires such a comprehensive amendment of the counts as to make it more convenient to all participants for the prosecutor to prepare and serve under CrimPR 10.4 a complete new draft indictment than to amend the electronically generated draft.

Draft indictment served by the prosecutor

10A.8 CrimPR 10.4 applies after sending for trial wherever CrimPR 10.3 does not. It requires the prosecutor to prepare a draft indictment and serve it on the Crown Court officer, who by CrimPR 10.2(7)(b) then must serve it on the defendant. In most instances service will be by electronic means, usually by making use of the Crown Court digital case system to which the prosecutor will upload the draft (which at once then becomes the indictment, under s.2 of the Administration of Justice (Miscellaneous Provisions) Act 1933 and CrimPR 10.2(5)(b)(ii)). **B-195**

10A.9 The prosecutor's time limit for service of the draft indictment under CrimPR 10.4 is 28 days after serving under CrimPR 9.15 the evidence on which the prosecution case relies. The Crown Court may extend that time limit, under CrimPR 10.2(8). However, under paragraph CrimPD I 3A.16 of these practice directions the court will expect that in every case a draft indictment will be served at least 7 days before the plea and trial preparation hearing, whether the time prescribed by the rule will have expired or not.

Amending the content of the indictment

10A.10 Where the prosecutor wishes to substitute or add counts to a draft indictment, or to invite the court to allow an indictment to be amended, so that the draft indictment, or indictment, will charge offences which differ from those with which the defendant first was charged, the defendant should be given as much notice as possible of what is proposed. It is likely that the defendant will need time to consider his or her position and advance notice will help to avoid delaying the proceedings. **B-196**

Multiple offending: count charging more than one incident

10A.11 CrimPR 10.2(2) allows a single count to allege more than one incident of the commission of an offence in certain circumstances. Each incident must be of the same offence. The circumstances in which such a count may be appropriate include, but are not limited to, the following: **B-197**

(a) the victim on each occasion was the same, or there was no identifiable individual victim as, for example, in a case of the unlawful importation of controlled drugs or of money laundering;

(b) the alleged incidents involved a marked degree of repetition in the method employed or in their location, or both;
(c) the alleged incidents took place over a clearly defined period, typically (but not necessarily) no more than about a year;
(d) in any event, the defence is such as to apply to every alleged incident. Where what is in issue differs between different incidents, a single "multiple incidents" count will not be appropriate (though it may be appropriate to use two or more such counts according to the circumstances and to the issues raised by the defence).

10A.12 Even in circumstances such as those set out above, there may be occasions on which a prosecutor chooses not to use such a count, in order to bring the case within section 75(3)(a) of the PCA 2002 (criminal lifestyle established by conviction of three or more offences in the same proceedings [§ 5B-152 in the main work]): for example, because section 75(2)(c) of that Act does not apply (criminal lifestyle established by an offence committed over a period of at least six months). Where the prosecutor proposes such a course, it is unlikely that CrimPR, Pt 1 (the overriding objective) will require an indictment to contain a single "multiple incidents" count in place of a larger number of counts, subject to the general principles set out at paragraph 10A.3.

10A.13 For some offences, particularly sexual offences, the penalty for the offence may have changed during the period over which the alleged incidents took place. In such a case, additional "multiple incidents" counts should be used so that each count only alleges incidents to which the same maximum penalty applies.

10A.14 In other cases, such as sexual or physical abuse, a complainant may be in a position only to give evidence of a series of similar incidents without being able to specify when or the precise circumstances in which they occurred. In these cases, a "multiple incidents" count may be desirable. If on the other hand, the complainant is able to identify particular incidents of the offence by reference to a date or other specific event, but alleges that in addition there were other incidents which the complainant is unable to specify, then it may be desirable to include separate counts for the identified incidents and a "multiple incidents" count or counts alleging that incidents of the same offence occurred "many" times. Using a "multiple incidents" count may be an appropriate alternative to using "specimen" counts in some cases where repeated sexual or physical abuse is alleged. The choice of count will depend on the particular circumstances of the case and should be determined bearing in mind the implications for sentencing set out in *Canavan*; *Kidd*; *Shaw* [1998] 1 Cr. App. R. 79, CA. In *A* [2015] 2 Cr. App. R.(S.) 12, the Court of Appeal reviewed the circumstances in which a mixture of multiple incident and single incident counts might be appropriate where the prosecutor alleged sustained sexual abuse.

Multiple offending: trial by jury and then by judge alone

B-198 **10A.15** Under sections 17 to 21 of the Domestic Violence, Crime and Victims Act 2004 [§§ 4-338 et seq. in the main work], the court may order that the trial of certain counts will be by jury in the usual way and, if the jury convicts, that other associated counts will be tried by judge alone. The use of this power is likely to be appropriate where justice cannot be done without charging a large number of separate offences and the allegations against the defendant appear to fall into distinct groups by reference to the identity of the victim, by reference to the dates of the offences, or by some other distinction in the nature of the offending conduct alleged.

10A.16 In such a case, it is essential to make clear from the outset the association asserted by the prosecutor between those counts to be tried by a jury and those counts which it is proposed should be tried by judge alone, if the jury convict on the former. A special form of indictment is prescribed for this purpose.

10A.17 An order for such a trial may be made only at a preparatory hearing. It follows that where the prosecutor intends to invite the court to order such a trial it will normally be appropriate to proceed as follows. A draft indictment in the form appropriate to such a trial should be served with an application under CrimPR 3.15 for a preparatory hearing. This will ensure that the defendant is aware at the earliest possible opportunity of what the prosecutor proposes and of the proposed association of counts in the indictment.

10A.18 At the start of the preparatory hearing, the defendant should be arraigned on all counts in Part One of the indictment. Arraignment on Part Two need not take place until after there has been either a guilty plea to, or finding of guilt on, an associated count in Part One of the indictment.

10A.19 If the prosecutor's application is successful, the prosecutor should prepare an abstract of the indictment, containing the counts from Part One only, for use in the jury trial. Preparation of such an abstract does not involve "amendment" of the indictment. It is akin to where a defendant pleads guilty to certain counts in an indictment and is put in the charge of the jury on the remaining counts only.

10A.20 If the prosecutor's application for a two stage trial is unsuccessful, the prosecutor may apply to amend the indictment to remove from it any counts in Part Two which would make jury trial on the whole indictment impracticable and to revert to a standard form of indictment. It will be a matter for the court whether arraignment on outstanding counts takes place at the preparatory hearing, or at a future date.

CPD II Preliminary Proceedings 10B: Voluntary bills of indictment (as substituted by Criminal Practice Directions 2015 (Amendment No. 1), unreported, 23 March 2016, Lord Thomas CJ)

10B.1 Section 2(2)(b) of the Administration of Justice (Miscellaneous Provisions) Act 1933 [§ 1-328 in the main work] and paragraph 2(6) of Schedule 3 to the CDA 1998 [ibid., § 1-37 et seq.] allow the preferment of a bill of indictment by the direction or with the consent of a judge of the High Court. Bills so preferred are known as "voluntary bills". **B-199**

10B.2 Applications for such consent must comply with CrimPR 10.3.

10B.3 Those requirements should be complied with in relation to each defendant named in the indictment for which consent is sought, whether or not it is proposed to prefer any new count against him or her.

10B.4 The preferment of a voluntary bill is an exceptional procedure. Consent should only be granted where good reason to depart from the normal procedure is clearly shown and only where the interests of justice, rather than considerations of administrative convenience, require it.

10B.5 Prosecutors must follow the procedures prescribed by the rule unless there are good reasons for not doing so, in which case prosecutors must inform the judge that the procedures have not been followed and seek leave to dispense with all or any of them. Judges should not give leave to dispense unless good reasons are shown.

10B.6 A judge to whom application for consent to the preferment of a documents [sic] submitted by the prosecutor and any written submissions made by the prospective defendant, and may properly seek any necessary amplification [*sic*]. CrimPR 10.3(4)(b) allows the judge to set a timetable for representations. The judge may invite oral submissions from either party, or accede to a request for an opportunity to make oral submissions, if the judge considers it necessary or desirable to receive oral submissions in order to make a sound and fair decision on the application. Any such oral submissions should be made on notice to the other party and in open court unless the judge otherwise directs.

Criminal Procedure Rules 2020 (SI 2020/759), Pt 11

Deferred Prosecution Agreements

When this Part applies

11.1.–(1) This Part applies to proceedings in the Crown Court under Schedule 17 to the Crime and Courts Act 2013. **B-200**

(2) In this Part–

(a) "agreement" means a deferred prosecution agreement under paragraph 1 of that Schedule;

(b) "prosecutor" means a prosecutor designated by or under paragraph 3 of that Schedule; and

(c) "defendant" means the corporation, partnership or association with whom the prosecutor proposes to enter, or enters, an agreement.

Exercise of court's powers

11.2.–(1) The court must determine an application to which this Part applies at a hearing, which– **B-201**

(a) must be in private, under rule 11.3 (application to approve a proposal to enter an agreement);

(b) may be in public or private, under rule 11.4 (application to approve the terms of an agreement), rule 11.6 (application to approve a variation of the terms of an agreement) or rule 11.9 (application to postpone the publication of information by the prosecutor); and

(c) must be in public, under rule 11.5 (application on breach of agreement) or rule 11.7 (application to lift suspension of prosecution), unless the court otherwise directs.

(2) If at a hearing in private to which rule 11.4 or rule 11.6 applies the court approves the agreement or the variation proposed, the court must announce its decision and reasons at a hearing in public.

(3) The court must not determine an application under rule 11.3, rule 11.4 or rule 11.6 unless–

(a) both parties are present;

(b) the prosecutor provides the court with a written declaration that, for the purposes of the application–

(i) the investigator enquiring into the alleged offence or offences has certified that no

information has been supplied which the investigator knows to be inaccurate, misleading or incomplete, and
(ii) the prosecutor has complied with the prosecution obligation to disclose material to the defendant; and
(c) the defendant provides the court with a written declaration that, for the purposes of the application—
(i) the defendant has not supplied any information which the defendant knows to be inaccurate, misleading or incomplete, and
(ii) the individual through whom the defendant makes the declaration has made reasonable enquiries and believes the defendant's declaration to be true.
(4) The court must not determine an application under rule 11.5 or rule 11.7—
(a) in the prosecutor's absence; or
(b) in the absence of the defendant, unless the defendant has had at least 20 business days in which to make representations.
(5) If the court approves a proposal to enter an agreement—
(a) the general rule is that any further application to which this Part applies must be made to the same judge; but
(b) the court may direct other arrangements.
(6) The court may adjourn a hearing—
(a) if either party asks, or on its own initiative; and
(b) in particular, if the court requires more information about—
(i) the facts of an alleged offence,
(ii) the terms of a proposal to enter an agreement, or of a proposed agreement or variation of an agreement, or
(iii) the circumstances in which the prosecutor wants the court to decide whether the defendant has failed to comply with the terms of an agreement.
(7) The court may—
(a) hear an application under rule 11.4 immediately after an application under rule 11.3, if the court approves a proposal to enter an agreement; and
(b) hear an application under rule 11.7 immediately after an application under rule 11.5, if the court terminates an agreement.

Application to approve a proposal to enter an agreement

B-202 **11.3.**—(1) This rule applies where a prosecutor wants the court to approve a proposal to enter an agreement.
(2) The prosecutor must—
(a) apply in writing after the commencement of negotiations between the parties but before the terms of agreement have been settled; and
(b) serve the application on—
(i) the court officer, and
(ii) the defendant.
(3) The application must—
(a) identify the parties to the proposed agreement;
(b) attach a proposed indictment setting out such of the offences listed in Part 2 of Schedule 17 to the Crime and Courts Act 2013 as the prosecutor is considering;
(c) include or attach a statement of facts proposed for inclusion in the agreement, which must give full particulars of each alleged offence, including details of any alleged financial gain or loss;
(d) include any information about the defendant that would be relevant to sentence in the event of conviction for the offence or offences;
(e) specify the proposed expiry date of the agreement;
(f) describe the proposed terms of the agreement, including details of any—
(i) monetary penalty to be paid by the defendant, and the time within which any such penalty is to be paid,
(ii) compensation, reparation or donation to be made by the defendant, the identity of the recipient of any such payment and the time within which any such payment is to be made,
(iii) surrender of profits or other financial benefit by the defendant, and the time within which any such sum is to be surrendered,

(iv) arrangement to be made in relation to the management or conduct of the defendant's business,
(v) co-operation required of the defendant in any investigation related to the offence or offences,
(vi) other action required of the defendant,
(vii) arrangement to monitor the defendant's compliance with a term,
(viii) consequence of the defendant's failure to comply with a term, and
(ix) prosecution costs to be paid by the defendant, and the time within which any such costs are to be paid;

(g) in relation to those terms, explain how they comply with—
(i) the requirements of the code issued under paragraph 6 of Schedule 17 to the Crime and Courts Act 2013, and
(ii) any sentencing guidelines or guideline cases which apply;

(h) contain or attach the defendant's written consent to the proposal; and
(i) explain why—
(i) entering into an agreement is likely to be in the interests of justice, and
(ii) the proposed terms of the agreement are fair, reasonable and proportionate.

(4) If the proposed statement of facts includes assertions that the defendant does not admit, the application must—
(a) specify the facts that are not admitted; and
(b) explain why that is immaterial for the purposes of the proposal to enter an agreement.

Application to approve the terms of an agreement

11.4.—(1) This rule applies where— B-203
(a) the court has approved a proposal to enter an agreement on an application under rule 11.3; and
(b) the prosecutor wants the court to approve the terms of the agreement.

(2) The prosecutor must—
(a) apply in writing as soon as practicable after the parties have settled the terms; and
(b) serve the application on—
(i) the court officer, and
(ii) the defendant.

(3) The application must—
(a) attach the agreement;
(b) indicate in what respect, if any, the terms of the agreement differ from those proposed in the application under rule 11.3;
(c) contain or attach the defendant's written consent to the agreement;
(d) explain why—
(i) the agreement is in the interests of justice, and
(ii) the terms of the agreement are fair, reasonable and proportionate;
(e) attach a draft indictment, charging the defendant with the offence or offences the subject of the agreement; and
(f) include any application for the hearing to be in private.

(4) If the court approves the agreement and the draft indictment, the court officer must—
(a) endorse any paper copy of the indictment made for the court with—
(i) a note to identify it as the indictment approved by the court, and
(ii) the date of the court's approval; and
(b) treat the case as if it had been suspended by order of the court.

Application on breach of agreement

11.5.—(1) This rule applies where— B-204
(a) the prosecutor believes that the defendant has failed to comply with the terms of an agreement; and
(b) the prosecutor wants the court to decide—
(i) whether the defendant has failed to comply, and
(ii) if so, whether to terminate the agreement, or to invite the parties to agree proposals to remedy that failure.

(2) The prosecutor must—
(a) apply in writing, as soon as practicable after becoming aware of the grounds for doing so; and

(b) serve the application on—
(i) the court officer, and
(ii) the defendant.

(3) The application must—
(a) specify each respect in which the prosecutor believes the defendant has failed to comply with the terms of the agreement, and explain the reasons for the prosecutor's belief; and
(b) attach a copy of any document containing evidence on which the prosecutor relies.

(4) A defendant who wants to make representations in response to the application must serve the representations on—
(a) the court officer; and
(b) the prosecutor,
not more than 20 business days after service of the application.

Application to approve a variation of the terms of an agreement

B-205 **11.6.**—(1) This rule applies where the parties have agreed to vary the terms of an agreement because—
(a) on an application under rule 11.5 (application on breach of agreement), the court has invited them to do so; or
(b) variation of the agreement is necessary to avoid a failure by the defendant to comply with its terms in circumstances that were not, and could not have been, foreseen by either party at the time the agreement was made.

(2) The prosecutor must—
(a) apply in writing, as soon as practicable after the parties have settled the terms of the variation; and
(b) serve the application on—
(i) the court officer, and
(ii) the defendant.

(3) The application must—
(a) specify each variation proposed;
(b) contain or attach the defendant's written consent to the variation;
(c) explain why—
(i) the variation is in the interests of justice, and
(ii) the terms of the agreement as varied are fair, reasonable and proportionate; and
(d) include any application for the hearing to be in private.

Application to lift suspension of prosecution

B-206 **11.7.**—(1) This rule applies where—
(a) the court terminates an agreement before its expiry date; and
(b) the prosecutor wants the court to lift the suspension of the prosecution that applied when the court approved the terms of the agreement.

(2) The prosecutor must—
(a) apply in writing, as soon as practicable after the termination of the agreement; and
(b) serve the application on—
(i) the court officer, and
(ii) the defendant.

(3) A defendant who wants to make representations in response to the application must serve the representations on—
(a) the court officer; and
(b) the prosecutor,
not more than 20 business days after service of the application.

Notice to discontinue prosecution

B-207 **11.8.**—(1) This rule applies where an agreement expires—
(a) on its expiry date, or on a date treated as its expiry date; and
(b) without having been terminated by the court.

(2) The prosecutor must—
(a) as soon as practicable give notice in writing discontinuing the prosecution on the indictment approved by the court under rule 11.4 (application to approve the terms of an agreement); and

(b) serve the notice on–
(i) the court officer, and
(ii) the defendant.

Application to postpone the publication of information by the prosecutor

11.9.–(1) This rule applies where the prosecutor– B-208
(a) makes an application under rule 11.4 (application to approve the terms of an agreement), rule 11.5 (application on breach of agreement) or rule 11.6 (application to approve a variation of the terms of an agreement);
(b) decides not to make an application under rule 11.5, despite believing that the defendant has failed to comply with the terms of the agreement; or
(c) gives a notice under rule 11.8 (notice to discontinue prosecution).

(2) A party who wants the court to order that the publication of information by the prosecutor about the court's or the prosecutor's decision should be postponed must–
(a) apply in writing, as soon as practicable and in any event before such publication occurs;
(b) serve the application on–
(i) the court officer, and
(ii) the other party; and
(c) in the application–
(i) specify the proposed terms of the order, and for how long it should last, and
(ii) explain why an order in the terms proposed is necessary.

Duty of court officer, etc.

11.10.–(1) Unless the court otherwise directs, the court officer must– B-209
(a) arrange for the recording of proceedings on an application to which this Part applies; and
(b) arrange for the transcription of such a recording if–
(i) a party wants such a transcript, or
(ii) anyone else wants such a transcript (but that is subject to the restrictions in paragraph (2)).

(2) Unless the court otherwise directs, a person who transcribes a recording of proceedings under such arrangements–
(a) must not supply anyone other than a party with a transcript of a recording of–
(i) a hearing in private, or
(ii) a hearing in public to which reporting restrictions apply; but
(b) subject to that, must supply any person with any transcript for which that person asks–
(i) in accordance with the transcription arrangements made by the court officer, and
(ii) on payment by that person of any fee prescribed.

(3) The court officer must not identify either party to a hearing in private under rule 11.3 (application to approve a proposal to enter an agreement) or rule 11.4 (application to approve the terms of an agreement)–
(a) in any notice displayed in the vicinity of the courtroom; or
(b) in any other information published by the court officer.

Court's power to vary requirements under this Part

11.11.–(1) The court may–
(a) shorten or extend (even after it has expired) a time limit under this Part; and
(b) allow there to be made orally–
(i) an application under rule 11.4 (application to approve the terms of an agreement), or
(ii) an application under rule 11.7 (application to lift suspension of prosecution)
where the court exercises its power under rule 11.2(7) to hear one application immediately after another.

(2) A party who wants an extension of time must–
(a) apply when serving the application or notice for which it is needed; and
(b) explain the delay.

Criminal Procedure Rules 2020 (SI 2020/759), Pt 12

Discontinuing a Prosecution

When this Part applies

12.1–(1) This Part applies where– B-210

(a) the Director of Public Prosecutions can discontinue a case in a magistrates' court, under section 23 of the Prosecution of Offences Act 1985; or
(b) the Director of Public Prosecutions, or another public prosecutor, can discontinue a case sent for trial in the Crown Court, under section 23A of the Prosecution of Offences Act 1985.
(2) In this Part, "prosecutor" means one of those authorities.

Discontinuing a case

12.2–(1) A prosecutor exercising a power to which this Part applies must serve notice on–
(a) the court officer;
(b) the defendant; and
(c) any custodian of the defendant.
(2) Such a notice must–
(a) identify–
(i) the defendant and each offence to which the notice relates,
(ii) the person serving the notice, and
(iii) the power that that person is exercising; and
(b) explain–
(i) in the copy of the notice served on the court officer, the reasons for discontinuing the case,
(ii) that the notice brings the case to an end,
(iii) if the defendant is in custody for any offence to which the notice relates, that the defendant must be released from that custody, and
(iv) if the notice is under section 23 of the 1985 Act, that the defendant has a right to require the case to continue.
(3) Where the defendant is on bail, the court officer must notify–
(a) any surety; and
(b) any person responsible for monitoring or securing the defendant's compliance with a condition of bail.

Defendant's notice to continue

12.3–(1) This rule applies where a prosecutor serves a notice to discontinue under section 23 of the 1985 Act.
(2) A defendant who wants the case to continue must serve notice–
(a) on the court officer; and
(b) not more than 25 business days after service of the notice to discontinue.
(3) If the defendant serves such a notice, the court officer must–
(a) notify the prosecutor; and
(b) refer the case to the court.

Criminal Procedure Rules 2020 (SI 2020/759), Pt 13

WARRANTS FOR ARREST, DETENTION OR IMPRISONMENT

When this Part applies

B-211 **13.1.**–(1) This Part applies where the court can issue a warrant for arrest, detention or imprisonment.
(2) In this Part, 'defendant' means anyone against whom such a warrant is issued.

Terms of a warrant for arrest

B-212 **13.2.**– A warrant for arrest must require each person to whom it is directed to arrest the defendant and–
(a) bring the defendant to a court–
(i) specified in the warrant, or
(ii) required or allowed by law; or
(b) release the defendant on bail (with conditions or without) to attend court at a date, time and place–
(i) specified in the warrant, or
(ii) to be notified by the court.

Terms of a warrant for detention or imprisonment

B-213 **13.3.**–(1) A warrant for detention or imprisonment must–

(a) require each person to whom it is directed to detain the defendant and–
(i) take the defendant to any place specified in the warrant or required or allowed by law, and
(ii) deliver the defendant to the custodian of that place; and
(b) require that custodian to detain the defendant, as ordered by the court, until in accordance with the law–
(i) the defendant is delivered to the appropriate court or place, or
(ii) the defendant is released.

(2) Where a magistrates' court remands a defendant to police detention under section 128(7) or section 136 of the Magistrates' Courts Act 1980, or to customs detention under section 152 of the Criminal Justice Act 1988, the warrant it issues must–
(a) be directed, as appropriate, to–
(i) a constable, or
(ii) an officer of Her Majesty's Revenue and Customs; and
(b) require that constable or officer to detain the defendant–
(i) for a period (not exceeding the maximum permissible) specified in the warrant, or
(ii) until in accordance with the law the defendant is delivered to the appropriate court or place.

(3) Where a magistrates' court sentences a defendant to imprisonment or detention and section 11(3) of the Magistrates' Courts Act 1980 applies (custodial sentence imposed in the defendant's absence), the warrant it issues must–
(a) require each person to whom the warrant is directed–
(i) to arrest the defendant and bring him or her to a court specified in the warrant, and
(ii) unless the court then otherwise directs, after that to act as required by paragraph (1)(a) of this rule; and
(b) require the custodian to whom the defendant is delivered in accordance with that paragraph to act as required by paragraph (1)(b) of this rule.

Information to be included in a warrant

13.4.–(1) A warrant must identify– B-214
(a) each person to whom it is directed;
(b) the defendant against whom it was issued;
(c) the reason for its issue;
(d) the court that issued it, unless that is otherwise recorded by the court officer; and
(e) the court office for the court that issued it.

(2) A warrant for detention or imprisonment must contain a record of any decision by the court under–
(a) section 91 of the Legal Aid, Sentencing and Punishment of Offenders Act 2012 (remands of children otherwise than on bail), including in particular–
(i) whether the defendant must be detained in local authority accommodation or youth detention accommodation,
(ii) the local authority designated by the court,
(iii) any requirement imposed by the court on that authority,
(iv) any condition imposed by the court on the defendant, and
(v) the reason for any such requirement or condition;
(b) section 80 of the Magistrates' Courts Act 1980 (application of money found on defaulter to satisfy sum adjudged); or
(c) section 82(1) or (4) of the 1980 Act (conditions for issue of a warrant).

(3) A warrant for detention or imprisonment must include such an indication of the defendant's physical and mental health as may be needed to alert those to whom the warrant is directed–
(a) to any vulnerability of the defendant; and
(b) to any risk to others that may be posed by the defendant.

(4) The indication required by paragraph (3) may be given by reference to an accompanying document.

(5) A warrant that contains an error is not invalid, as long as–
(a) it was issued in respect of a lawful decision by the court; and
(b) it contains enough information to identify that decision.

Execution of a warrant

13.5.–(1) A warrant may be executed– B-215

(a) by any person to whom it is directed; or
(b) if the warrant was issued by a magistrates' court, by anyone authorised to do so by section 125 (warrants), 125A (civilian enforcement officers) or 125B (execution by approved enforcement agency) of the Magistrates' Courts Act 1980.

(2) The person who executes a warrant must—
(a) explain, in terms the defendant can understand, what the warrant requires, and why;
(b) show the defendant the warrant, if that person has it; and
(c) if the defendant asks—
(i) arrange for the defendant to see the warrant, if that person does not have it, and
(ii) show the defendant any written statement of that person's authority required by section 125A or 125B of the 1980 Act.

(3) The person who executes a warrant of arrest that requires the defendant to be released on bail must—
(a) make a record of—
(i) the defendant's name,
(ii) the reason for the arrest,
(iii) the defendant's release on bail, and
(iv) when and where the warrant requires the defendant to attend court; and
(b) serve the record on—
(i) the defendant, and
(ii) the court officer.

(4) The person who executes a warrant of detention or imprisonment must—
(a) take the defendant—
(i) to any place specified in the warrant, or
(ii) if that is not immediately practicable, to any other place at which the defendant may be lawfully detained (and the warrant then has effect as if it specified that place);
(b) obtain a receipt from the custodian; and
(c) notify the court officer that the defendant has been taken to that place.

Warrants that cease to have effect on payment

B-216 **13.6.**—(1) This rule applies to a warrant issued by a magistrates' court under any of the following provisions of the Magistrates' Courts Act 1980—
(a) section 76 (enforcement of sums adjudged to be paid);
(b) section 83 (process for securing attendance of offender);
(c) section 86 (power of magistrates' court to fix day for appearance of offender at means inquiry, etc.); or
(d) section 136 (committal to custody overnight at police station for non-payment of sum adjudged by conviction).

(2) The warrant no longer has effect if—
(a) the sum in respect of which the warrant was issued is paid to the person executing it;
(b) that sum is offered to, but refused by, that person; or
(c) that person is shown a receipt for that sum given by—
(i) the court officer, or
(ii) the authority to which that sum is due.

Warrant issued when the court is closed

B-217 **13.7.**—(1) This rule applies where the court issues a warrant when the court office is closed.

(2) The applicant for the warrant must, not more than 72 hours later, serve on the court officer—
(a) a copy of the warrant; and
(b) any written material that was submitted to the court.

Criminal Procedure Rules 2020 (SI 2020/759), Pt 14

Bail and Custody Time Limits

General rules

When this Part applies

★B-218 **14.1.**—(1) This Part applies where a magistrates' court or the Crown Court can—
(a) grant or withhold bail, or impose or vary a condition of bail; and

(b) where bail has been withheld, extend a custody time limit.

(2) Rules 14.18, 14.19 and 14.20 apply where a magistrates' court can authorise an extension of the period for which a defendant is released on bail before being charged with an offence.

(3) In this part, "defendant" includes a person who has been granted bail by a police officer.

[This rule is printed as amended, with effect from 8 February 2021, by SI 2021/40, r.8(a).]

Exercise of court's powers: general

14.2.–(1) The court must not make a decision to which this Part applies unless– B-219

(a) each party to the decision and any surety directly affected by the decision–

(i) is present, or

(ii) has had an opportunity to make representations;

(b) on an application for bail by a defendant who is absent and in custody, the court is satisfied that the defendant–

(i) has waived the right to attend, or

(ii) was present when a court withheld bail in the case on a previous occasion and has been in custody continuously since then;

(c) on a prosecutor's appeal against a grant of bail, application to extend a custody time limit or appeal against a refusal to extend such a time limit–

(i) the court is satisfied that a defendant who is absent has waived the right to attend, or

(ii) the court is satisfied that it would be just to proceed even though the defendant is absent; and

(d) the court is satisfied that sufficient time has been allowed–

(i) for the defendant to consider the information provided by the prosecutor under rule 14.5(2), and

(ii) for the court to consider the parties representations and make the decision required.

(2) The court may make a decision to which this Part applies at a hearing, in public or in private.

(3) The court may determine without a hearing an application to vary a condition of bail if–

(a) the parties to the application have agreed the terms of the variation proposed; or

(b) on an application by a defendant, the court determines the application no sooner than the fifth business day after the application was served.

(4) The court may adjourn a determination to which this Part applies, if that is necessary to obtain information sufficient to allow the court to make the decision required.

(5) At any hearing at which the court makes one of the following decisions, the court must announce in terms the defendant can understand (with help, if necessary), and by reference to the circumstances of the defendant and the case, its reasons for–

(a) withholding bail, or imposing or varying a bail condition;

(b) granting bail, where the prosecutor opposed the grant; or

(c) where the defendant is under 18–

(i) imposing or varying a bail condition when ordering the defendant to be detained in local authority accommodation, or

(ii) ordering the defendant to be detained in youth detention accommodation.

(6) At any hearing at which the court grants bail, the court must–

(a) tell the defendant where and when to surrender to custody; or

(b) arrange for the court officer to give the defendant, as soon as practicable, notice of where and when to surrender to custody.

(7) This rule does not apply on an application to a magistrates' court to authorise an extension of pre-charge bail.

Duty of justices' legal adviser

14.3.–(1) This rule applies– B-220

(a) only in a magistrates' court; and

(b) unless the court–

(i) includes a District Judge (Magistrates' Courts), and

(ii) otherwise directs.

(2) A justices' legal adviser must–

(a) assist an unrepresented defendant;

(b) give the court such advice as is required to enable it to exercise its powers; and

(c) if required, attend the members of the court outside the courtroom to give such advice, but inform the parties of any advice so given.

General duties of court officer

★B-221 **14.4.**—(1) The court officer must arrange for a note or other record to be made of—
(a) the parties' representations about bail; and
(b) the court's reasons for a decision—
(i) to withhold bail, or to impose or vary a bail condition,
(ii) to grant bail, where the prosecutor opposed the grant, or
(iii) on an application to which rule 14.19 applies (application to authorise extension of pre-charge bail).

(2) The court officer must serve notice of a decision about bail on—
(a) the defendant (but, in the Crown Court, only where the defendant's legal representative asks for such a notice, or where the defendant has no legal representative);
(b) the prosecutor (but only where the court granted bail, the prosecutor opposed the grant, and the prosecutor asks for such a notice);
(c) a party to the decision who was absent when it was made;
(d) a surety who is directly affected by the decision;
(e) the defendant's custodian, where the defendant is in custody and the decision requires the custodian—
(i) to release the defendant (or will do so, if a requirement ordered by the court is met), or
(ii) to transfer the defendant to the custody of another custodian; and
(f) the court officer for any other court at which the defendant is required by that decision to surrender to custody.

(3) Where the court postpones the date on which a defendant who is on bail must surrender to custody, the court officer must serve notice of the postponed date on—
(a) the defendant; and
(b) any surety.

(4) Where a magistrates' court withholds bail in a case to which section 5(6A) of the Bail Act 1976 applies (remand in custody after hearing full argument on an application for bail), the court officer must serve on the defendant a certificate that the court heard full argument.

(5) Where the court determines without a hearing an application to which rule 14.19 applies (application to authorise extension of pre-charge bail), the court officer must—
(a) if the court allows the application, notify the applicant; and
(b) if the court refuses the application, notify the applicant and the defendant.

[This rule is printed as amended, with effect from 8 February 2021, by SI 2021/40, r.8(c).]

Bail

Prosecutor's representations about bail

B-222 **14.5.**—(1) This rule applies whenever the court can grant or withhold bail.

(2) The prosecutor must as soon as practicable—
(a) provide the defendant with all the information in the prosecutor's possession which is material to what the court must decide; and
(b) provide the court with the same information.

(3) A prosecutor who opposes the grant of bail must specify—
(a) each exception to the general right to bail on which the prosecutor relies; and
(b) each consideration that the prosecutor thinks relevant.

(4) A prosecutor who wants the court to impose a condition on any grant of bail must—
(a) specify each condition proposed; and
(b) explain what purpose would be served by such a condition.

Reconsideration of police bail by magistrates' court

B-223 **14.6.**—(1) This rule applies where—
(a) a party wants a magistrates' court to reconsider a bail decision by a police officer after the defendant is charged with an offence; and
(b) a defendant wants a magistrates' court to reconsider a bail condition imposed by a police officer before the defendant is charged with an offence.

(2) An application under this rule must be made to—
(a) the magistrates' court to whose custody the defendant is under a duty to surrender, if any; or

(b) any magistrates' court acting for the police officer's local justice area, in any other case.

(3) The applicant party must–

(a) apply in writing; and

(b) serve the application on–

(i) the court officer,

(ii) the other party, and

(iii) any surety affected or proposed.

(4) The application must–

(a) specify–

(i) the decision that the applicant wants the court to make,

(ii) each offence charged, or for which the defendant was arrested, and

(iii) the police bail decision to be reconsidered and the reasons given for it;

(b) explain, as appropriate–

(i) why the court should grant bail itself, or withdraw it, or impose or vary a condition, and

(ii) if the applicant is the prosecutor, what material information has become available since the police bail decision was made;

(c) propose the terms of any suggested condition of bail; and

(d) if the applicant wants an earlier hearing than paragraph (7) requires, ask for that, and explain why it is needed.

(5) A prosecutor who applies under this rule must serve on the defendant, with the application, notice that the court has power to withdraw bail and, if the defendant is absent when the court makes its decision, order the defendant's arrest.

(6) A party who opposes an application must–

(a) so notify the court officer and the applicant at once; and

(b) serve on each notice of the reasons for opposition.

(7) Unless the court otherwise directs, the court officer must arrange for the court to hear the application as soon as practicable and in any event–

(a) if it is an application to withdraw bail, no later than the second business day after it was served; and

(b) in any other case, no later than the fifth business day after it was served.

(8) The court may–

(a) vary or waive a time limit under this rule;

(b) allow an application to be in a different form to one set out in the Practice Direction; and

(c) if rule 14.2 allows, determine without a hearing an application to vary a condition.

Notice of application to consider bail

14.7.–(1) This rule applies where– B-224

(a) in a magistrates' court–

(i) a prosecutor wants the court to withdraw bail granted by the court, or to impose or vary a condition of such bail, or

(ii) a defendant wants the court to reconsider such bail before the next hearing in the case; and

(b) in the Crown Court–

(i) a party wants the court to grant bail that has been withheld, or to withdraw bail that has been granted, or to impose a new bail condition or to vary a present one, or

(ii) a prosecutor wants the court to consider whether to grant or withhold bail, or impose or vary a condition of bail, under section 88 or section 89 of the Criminal Justice Act 2003 (bail and custody in connection with an intended application to the Court of Appeal to which Part 27 (retrial after acquittal) applies).

(2) Such a party must–

(a) apply in writing;

(b) serve the application on–

(i) the court officer,

(ii) the other party, and

(iii) any surety affected or proposed; and

(c) serve the application not less than 2 business days before any hearing in the case at which the applicant wants the court to consider it, if such a hearing is already due.

(3) The application must–

(a) specify—
  (i) the decision that the applicant wants the court to make,
  (ii) each offence charged, and
  (iii) each relevant previous bail decision and the reasons given for each;
(b) if the applicant is a defendant, explain—
  (i) as appropriate, why the court should not withhold bail, or why it should vary a condition, and
  (ii) what further information or legal argument, if any, has become available since the most recent previous bail decision was made;
(c) if the applicant is the prosecutor, explain—
  (i) as appropriate, why the court should withdraw bail, or impose or vary a condition, and
  (ii) what material information has become available since the most recent previous bail decision was made;
(d) propose the terms of any suggested condition of bail; and
(e) if the applicant wants an earlier hearing than paragraph (6) requires, ask for that, and explain why it is needed.

(4) A prosecutor who applies under this rule must serve on the defendant, with the application, notice that the court has power to withdraw bail and, if the defendant is absent when the court makes its decision, order the defendant's arrest.

(5) A party who opposes an application must—
(a) so notify the court officer and the applicant at once; and
(b) serve on each notice of the reasons for opposition.

(6) Unless the court otherwise directs, the court officer must arrange for the court to hear the application as soon as practicable and in any event—
(a) if it is an application to grant or withdraw bail, no later than the second business day after it was served; and
(b) if it is an application to impose or vary a condition, no later than the fifth business day after it was served.

(7) The court may—
(a) vary or waive a time limit under this rule;
(b) allow an application to be in a different form to one set out in the Practice Direction, or to be made orally; and
(c) if rule 14.2 allows, determine without a hearing an application to vary a condition.

Defendant's application or appeal to the Crown Court after magistrates' court bail decision

B-225 **14.8.**—(1) This rule applies where a defendant wants to—
(a) apply to the Crown Court for bail after a magistrates' court has withheld bail; or
(b) appeal to the Crown Court after a magistrates' court has refused to vary a bail condition as the defendant wants.

(2) The defendant must—
(a) apply to the Crown Court in writing as soon as practicable after the magistrates' court's decision; and
(b) serve the application on—
  (i) the Crown Court officer,
  (ii) the magistrates' court officer,
  (iii) the prosecutor, and
  (iv) any surety affected or proposed.

(3) The application must—
(a) specify—
  (i) the decision that the applicant wants the Crown Court to make, and
  (ii) each offence charged;
(b) explain—
  (i) as appropriate, why the Crown Court should not withhold bail, or why it should vary the condition under appeal, and
  (ii) what further information or legal argument, if any, has become available since the magistrates' court's decision;
(c) propose the terms of any suggested condition of bail; and
(d) if the applicant wants an earlier hearing than paragraph (6) requires, ask for that, and explain why it is needed; and

(e) on an application for bail, attach a copy of the certificate of full argument served on the defendant under rule 14.4(4).

(4) The magistrates' court officer must as soon as practicable serve on the Crown Court officer—

(a) a copy of the note or record made under rule 14.4(1) in connection with the magistrates' court's decision; and

(b) the date of the next hearing, if any, in the magistrates' court.

(5) A prosecutor who opposes the application must—

(a) so notify the Crown Court officer and the defendant at once; and

(b) serve on each notice of the reasons for opposition.

(6) Unless the Crown Court otherwise directs, the court officer must arrange for the court to hear the application or appeal as soon as practicable and in any event no later than the business day after it was served.

(7) The Crown Court may vary a time limit under this rule.

Prosecutor's appeal against grant of bail

14.9.—(1) This rule applies where a prosecutor wants to appeal— B-226

(a) to the Crown Court against a grant of bail by a magistrates' court, in a case in which the defendant has been charged with, or convicted of, an offence punishable with imprisonment; or

(b) to the High Court against a grant of bail—

(i) by a magistrates' court, in an extradition case, or

(ii) by the Crown Court, in a case in which the defendant has been charged with, or convicted of, an offence punishable with imprisonment (but not in a case in which the Crown Court granted bail on an appeal to which paragraph (1)(a) applies).

(2) The prosecutor must tell the court which has granted bail of the decision to appeal—

(a) at the end of the hearing during which the court granted bail; and

(b) before the defendant is released on bail.

(3) The court which has granted bail must exercise its power to remand the defendant in custody pending determination of the appeal.

(4) The prosecutor must serve an appeal notice—

(a) on the court officer for the court which has granted bail and on the defendant; and

(b) not more than 2 hours after telling that court of the decision to appeal.

(5) The appeal notice must specify—

(a) each offence with which the defendant is charged;

(b) the decision under appeal;

(c) the reasons given for the grant of bail; and

(d) the grounds of appeal.

(6) On an appeal to the Crown Court, the magistrates' court officer must, as soon as practicable, serve on the Crown Court officer—

(a) the appeal notice;

(b) a copy of the note or record made under rule 14.4(1) (record of bail decision); and

(c) notice of the date of the next hearing in the court which has granted bail.

(7) If the Crown Court so directs, the Crown Court officer must arrange for the defendant to be assisted by the Official Solicitor in a case in which the defendant—

(a) has no legal representative; and

(b) asks for such assistance.

(8) On an appeal to the Crown Court, the Crown Court officer must arrange for the court to hear the appeal as soon as practicable and in any event no later than the second business day after the appeal notice was served.

(9) The prosecutor—

(a) may abandon an appeal to the Crown Court without the court's permission, by serving a notice of abandonment, signed by or on behalf of the prosecutor, on—

(i) the defendant,

(ii) the Crown Court officer, and

(iii) the magistrates' court officer

before the hearing of the appeal begins; but

(b) after the hearing of the appeal begins, may only abandon the appeal with the Crown Court's permission.

(10) The court officer for the court which has granted bail must instruct the defendant's custodian

to release the defendant on the bail granted by that court, subject to any condition or conditions of bail imposed, if—

(a) the prosecutor fails to serve an appeal notice within the time to which paragraph (4) refers; or

(b) the prosecutor serves a notice of abandonment under paragraph (9).

Consideration of bail in a murder case

B-227 **14.10.**—(1) This rule applies in a case in which—

(a) the defendant is charged with murder; and

(b) the Crown Court has not yet considered bail.

(2) The magistrates' court officer must arrange with the Crown Court officer for the Crown Court to consider bail as soon as practicable and in any event no later than the second business day after—

(a) a magistrates' court sends the defendant to the Crown Court for trial; or

(b) the first hearing in the magistrates' court, if the defendant is not at once sent for trial.

Condition of residence

B-228 **14.11.**—(1) The defendant must notify the prosecutor of the address at which the defendant will live and sleep if released on bail with a condition of residence—

(a) as soon as practicable after the institution of proceedings, unless already done; and

(b) as soon as practicable after any change of that address.

(2) The prosecutor must help the court to assess the suitability of an address proposed as a condition of residence.

Electronic monitoring requirements

B-229 **14.12.**—(1) This rule applies where the court imposes electronic monitoring requirements, where available, as a condition of bail.

(2) The court officer must—

(a) inform the person responsible for the monitoring ("the monitor") of—

(i) the defendant's name, and telephone number if available,

(ii) each offence with which the defendant is charged,

(iii) details of the place at which the defendant's presence must be monitored,

(iv) the period or periods during which the defendant's presence at that place must be monitored, and

(v) if fixed, the date on which the defendant must surrender to custody;

(b) inform the defendant and, where the defendant is under 16, an appropriate adult, of the monitor's identity and the means by which the monitor may be contacted; and

(c) notify the monitor of any subsequent—

(i) variation or termination of the electronic monitoring requirements, or

(ii) fixing or variation of the date on which the defendant must surrender to custody.

Accommodation or support requirements

B-230 **14.13.**—(1) This rule applies where the court imposes as a condition of bail a requirement, where available, that the defendant must—

(a) reside in accommodation provided for that purpose by, or on behalf of, a public authority; or

(b) receive bail support provided by, or on behalf of, a public authority.

(2) The court officer must—

(a) inform the person responsible for the provision of any such accommodation or support ("the service provider") of—

(i) the defendant's name, and telephone number if available,

(ii) each offence with which the defendant is charged,

(iii) details of the requirement,

(iv) any other bail condition, and

(v) if fixed, the date on which the defendant must surrender to custody;

(b) inform the defendant and, where the defendant is under 16, an appropriate adult, of—

(i) the service provider's identity and the means by which the service provider may be contacted, and

(ii) the address of any accommodation in which the defendant must live and sleep; and

(c) notify the service provider of any subsequent—

(i) variation or termination of the requirement,

(ii) variation or termination of any other bail condition, and
(iii) fixing or variation of the date on which the defendant must surrender to custody.

Requirement for a surety or payment, etc.

14.14.–(1) This rule applies where the court imposes as a condition of bail a requirement for– **B-231**

(a) a surety;
(b) a payment; or
(c) the surrender of a document or thing.

(2) The court may direct how such a condition must be met.

(3) Unless the court otherwise directs, if any such condition or direction requires a surety to enter into a recognizance–

(a) the recognizance must specify–
(i) the amount that the surety will be required to pay if the purpose for which the recognizance is entered is not fulfilled, and
(ii) the date, or the event, upon which the recognizance will expire;
(b) the surety must enter into the recognizance in the presence of–
(i) the court officer,
(ii) the defendant's custodian, where the defendant is in custody, or
(iii) someone acting with the authority of either; and
(c) the person before whom the surety enters into the recognizance must at once serve a copy on–
(i) the surety, and
(ii) as appropriate, the court officer and the defendant's custodian.

(4) Unless the court otherwise directs, if any such condition or direction requires someone to make a payment, or surrender a document or thing–

(a) that payment, document or thing must be made or surrendered to–
(i) the court officer,
(ii) the defendant's custodian, where the defendant is in custody, or
(iii) someone acting with the authority of either; and
(b) the court officer or the custodian, as appropriate, must serve immediately on the other a statement that the payment, document or thing has been made or surrendered.

(5) The custodian must release the defendant when each requirement ordered by the court has been met.

Forfeiture of a recognizance given by a surety

14.15.–(1) This rule applies where the court imposes as a condition of bail a requirement that a surety enter into a recognizance and, after the defendant is released on bail– **B-232**

(a) the defendant fails to surrender to custody as required, or
(b) it appears to the court that the surety has failed to comply with a condition or direction.

(2) The court officer must serve notice on–

(a) the surety; and
(b) each party to the decision to grant bail,

of the hearing at which the court will consider the forfeiture of the recognizance.

(3) The court must not forfeit the recognizance less than 5 business days after service of notice under paragraph (2).

[The next paragraph is B-235.]

Application to extend a custody time limit

14.16.–(1) This rule applies where the prosecutor gives notice of application to extend a custody time limit. **★B-235**

(2) The court officer must arrange for the court to hear that application as soon as practicable after the expiry of–

(a) 5 days from the giving of notice, in the Crown Court; or
(b) 2 days from the giving of notice, in a magistrates' court.

(3) The court may shorten a time limit under this rule.

[This rule is printed as re-numbered, with effect from 8 February 2021, by SI 2021/40, r.8(f).]

Appeal against custody time limit decision

14.17.–(1) This rule applies where– **★B-236**

(a) a defendant wants to appeal to the Crown Court against a decision by a magistrates' court to extend a custody time limit; or
(b) a prosecutor wants to appeal to the Crown Court against a decision by a magistrates' court to refuse to extend a custody time limit.

(2) The appellant must serve an appeal notice—
(a) on—
(i) the other party to the decision,
(ii) the Crown Court officer, and
(iii) the magistrates' court officer;
(b) in a defendant's appeal, as soon as practicable after the decision under appeal; and
(c) in a prosecutor's appeal—
(i) as soon as practicable after the decision under appeal, and
(ii) before the relevant custody time limit expires.

(3) The appeal notice must specify—
(a) each offence with which the defendant is charged;
(b) the decision under appeal;
(c) the date on which the relevant custody time limit will expire;
(d) on a defendant's appeal, the date on which the relevant custody time limit would have expired but for the decision under appeal; and
(e) the grounds of appeal.

(4) The Crown Court officer must arrange for the Crown Court to hear the appeal as soon as practicable and in any event no later than the second business day after the appeal notice was served.

(5) The appellant—
(a) may abandon an appeal without the Crown Court's permission, by serving a notice of abandonment, signed by or on behalf of the appellant, on—
(i) the other party,
(ii) the Crown Court officer, and
(iii) the magistrates' court officer
before the hearing of the appeal begins; but
(b) after the hearing of the appeal begins, may only abandon the appeal with the Crown Court's permission.

[This rule is printed as re-numbered, with effect from 8 February 2021, by SI 2021/40, r.8(f).]

Extension of Bail before Charge

Exercise of court's powers: extension of pre-charge bail

★B-237 **14.18.**—(1) The court must determine an application to which rule 14.19 (application to authorise extension of pre-charge bail) applies—
(a) without a hearing, subject to paragraph (2); and
(b) as soon as practicable, but as a general rule no sooner than the fifth business day after the application was served.

(2) The court must determine an application at a hearing where—
(a) if the application succeeds, its effect will be to extend the period for which the defendant is on bail to less than 12 months from the day after the defendant's arrest for the offence and the court considers that the interests of justice require a hearing;
(b) if the application succeeds, its effect will be to extend that period to more than 12 months from that day and the applicant or the defendant asks for a hearing; or
(c) it is an application to withhold information from the defendant and the court considers that the interests of justice require a hearing.

(3) Any hearing must be in private.

(4) Subject to rule 14.20 (application to withhold information from the defendant), at a hearing the court may determine an application in the absence of—
(a) the applicant; and
(b) the defendant, if the defendant has had at least 5 business days in which to make representations.

(5) If the court so directs, a party to an application may attend a hearing by live link *or telephone.*

(6) The court must not authorise an extension of the period for which a defendant is on bail before being charged unless—
(a) the applicant states, in writing or orally, that to the best of the applicant's knowledge and belief—

(i) the application discloses all the information that is material to what the court must decide, and
(ii) the content of the application is true; or
(b) the application includes a statement by an investigator of the suspected offence that to the best of that investigator's knowledge and belief those requirements are met.

(7) Where the statement required by paragraph (6) is made orally–
(a) the statement must be on oath or affirmation, unless the court otherwise directs; and
(b) the court must arrange for a record of the making of the statement.

(8) The court may shorten or extend (even after it has expired) a time limit imposed by this rule or by rule 14.19 (application to authorise extension of pre-charge bail).

[This rule is subject to temporary modification by virtue of r.8 of the Criminal Procedure (Amendment No. 2) (Coronavirus) Rules 2020 (SI 2020/417)- omission of italicised text in para.(5). These temporary modifications cease when ss.53, 54 and 55 (and Schs. 23, 24 and 25) of the Coronavirus Act 2020 expire. It is printed as re-numbered and amended, with effect from 8 February 2021, by SI 2021/40, r.8(f) and (g).]

Application to authorise extension of pre-charge bail

14.19.–(1) This rule applies where an applicant wants the court to authorise an extension of the period for which a defendant is released on bail before being charged with an offence. ★B-238

(2) The applicant must–
(a) apply in writing before the date on which the defendant's pre-charge bail is due to end;
(b) demonstrate that the applicant is entitled to apply as a constable, a member of staff of the Financial Conduct Authority, a member of the Serious Fraud Office or a Crown Prosecutor;
(c) serve the application on–
(i) the court officer, and
(ii) the defendant; and
(d) serve on the defendant, with the application, a form of response notice for the defendant's use.

(3) The application must specify–
(a) the offence or offences for which the defendant was arrested;
(b) the date on which the defendant's pre-charge bail began;
(c) the date and period of any previous extension of that bail;
(d) the date on which that bail is due to end;
(e) the conditions of that bail; and
(f) if different, the bail conditions which are to be imposed if the court authorises an extension, or further extension, of the period for which the defendant is released on pre-charge bail.

(4) The application must explain–
(a) the grounds for believing that, as applicable–
(i) further investigation is needed of any matter in connection with the offence or offences for which the defendant was released on bail, or
(ii) further time is needed for making a decision as to whether to charge the defendant with that offence or those offences;
(b) the grounds for believing that, as applicable–
(i) the investigation into the offence or offences for which the defendant was released on bail is being conducted diligently and expeditiously, or
(ii) the decision as to whether to charge the defendant with that offence or those offences is being made diligently and expeditiously; and
(c) the grounds for believing that the defendant's further release on bail is necessary and proportionate in all the circumstances having regard, in particular, to any conditions of bail imposed.

(5) The application must–
(a) indicate whether the applicant wants the court to authorise an extension of the defendant's bail for 3 months or for 6 months; and
(b) if for 6 months, explain why the investigation is unlikely to be completed or the charging decision made, as the case may be, within 3 months.

(6) The application must explain why it was not made earlier where–
(a) the application is made before the date on which the defendant's bail is due to end; but
(b) it is not likely to be practicable for the court to determine the application before that date.

(7) A defendant who objects to the application must—
(a) serve notice on—
(i) the court officer, and
(ii) the applicant,
not more than 5 business days after service of the application; and
(b) in the notice explain the grounds of the objection.

[This rule is printed as re-numbered, with effect from 8 February 2021, by SI 2021/40, r.8(f).]

Application to withhold information from the defendant

★B-239 **14.20.**—(1) This rule applies where an application to authorise an extension of pre-charge bail includes an application to withhold information from the defendant.

(2) The applicant must—
(a) omit that information from the part of the application that is served on the defendant;
(b) mark the other part to show that, unless the court otherwise directs, it is only for the court; and
(c) in that other part, explain the grounds for believing that the disclosure of that information would have one or more of the following results—
(i) evidence connected with an indictable offence would be interfered with or harmed,
(ii) a person would be interfered with or physically injured,
(iii) a person suspected of having committed an indictable offence but not yet arrested for the offence would be alerted, or
(iv) the recovery of property obtained as a result of an indictable offence would be hindered.

(3) At any hearing of an application to which this rule applies—
(a) the court must first determine the application to withhold information, in the defendant's absence and that of any legal representative of the defendant; and
(b) if the court allows the application to withhold information, then in the following sequence—
(i) the court must consider representations first by the applicant and then by the defendant, in the presence of both, and
(ii) the court may consider further representations by the applicant in the defendant's absence and that of any legal representative of the defendant, if satisfied that there are reasonable grounds for believing that information withheld from the defendant would be disclosed during those further representations.

(4) If the court refuses an application to withhold information from the defendant, the applicant may withdraw the application to authorise an extension of pre-charge bail.

[This rule is printed as re-numbered, with effect from 8 February 2021, by SI 2021/40, r.8(f).]

CPD III Custody and Bail 14A: Bail before sending for trial

B-240 **14A.1** Before the Crown Court can deal with an application under rule 14.8 by a defendant after a magistrates' court has withheld bail, it must be satisfied that the magistrates' court has issued a certificate, under section 5(6A) of the Bail Act 1976 [§ 3-28 in the main work], that it heard full argument on the application for bail before it refused the application.

The certificate of full argument is produced by the magistrates' court's computer system, Libra, as part of the GENORD (General Form of Order). Two hard copies are produced, one for the defence and one for the prosecution. Some magistrates' courts may also produce a manual certificate which will usually be available from the justices' legal adviser at the conclusion of the hearing; the GENORD may not be produced until the following day. Under rule 14.4(4), the magistrates' court officer will provide the defendant with a certificate that the court heard full argument. However, it is the responsibility of the defence, as the applicant in the Crown Court, to ensure that a copy of the certificate ... is provided to the Crown Court as part of the application (r.14.8(3)(e)). The applicant's solicitors should attach a copy of the certificate to the bail application form. If the certificate is not enclosed with the application form, it will be difficult to avoid some delay in listing.

Venue

B-241 **14A.2** Applications should be made to the court to which the defendant will be, or would have been, sent for trial. In the event of an application in a purely summary case, it should be made to the Crown Court centre which normally receives class 3 work. The hearing will be listed as a chambers matter unless a judge has directed otherwise.

CPD III Custody and Bail 14B: Bail: failure to surrender and trials in absence

B-242 **14B.1** The failure of defendants to comply with the terms of their bail by not surrendering, or not doing so at the appointed time, undermines the administration of justice and disrupts proceedings. The resulting delays impact on victims, witnesses and other court users and also waste costs. A defendant's failure to surrender affects not only the case with which he ... is concerned, but also the court's ability to administer justice more generally, by damaging the confidence of victims, witnesses and the public in the effectiveness of the court system and the judiciary. It is, therefore, most important that defendants who are granted bail appreciate the significance of the obligation to surrender to custody in accordance with the terms of their bail and that courts take appropriate action, if they fail to do so.

14B.2 A defendant who will be unable for medical reasons to attend court in accordance with his ... bail must obtain a certificate from his ... general practitioner or another appropriate medical practitioner such as the doctor with care of the defendant at a hospital. This should be obtained in advance of the hearing and conveyed to the court through the defendant's legal representative. In order to minimise the disruption to the court and to others, particularly witnesses if the case is listed for trial, the defendant should notify the court through his legal representative as soon as his inability to attend court becomes known.

14B.3 Guidance has been produced by the British Medical Association and the CPS on the roles and responsibilities of medical practitioners when issuing medical certificates in criminal proceedings. Judges and magistrates should seek to ensure that this guidance is followed. However, it is a matter for each individual court to decide whether, in any particular case, the issued certificate should be accepted. Without a medical certificate or if an unsatisfactory certificate is provided, the court is likely to consider that the defendant has failed to surrender to bail.

14B.4 If a defendant fails to surrender ...there are at least four courses of action for the courts to consider taking:–

(a) imposing penalties for the failure to surrender [see the definitive sentencing guideline, § S-9 et seq.];
(b) revoking bail or imposing more stringent conditions;
(c) conducting trials in the absence of the defendant; and
(d) ordering that some or all of any sums of money lodged with the court as a security or pledged by a surety as a condition on the grant of bail be forfeit.

CPD III Custody and Bail 14C: Failure to surrender to bail: consequences and penalties

Initiating proceedings–bail granted by a police officer

14C.1 When a person has been granted bail by a police officer to attend court and subsequently fails to surrender ..., the decision whether to initiate proceedings for a section 6(1) or ... (2) [§ 3-31 in the main work] offence will be for the police/prosecutor and proceedings are commenced in the usual way. **B-243**

14C.2 The offence in this form is a summary offence .... The offence should be dealt with on the first appearance after arrest, unless an adjournment is necessary, as it will be relevant in considering whether to grant bail again.

Initiating proceedings–bail granted by a court

14C.3 Where a person has been granted bail by a court and subsequently fails to surrender on arrest that person should normally be brought as soon as appropriate before the court at which the proceedings in respect of which bail was granted are to be heard. (There is no requirement to lay an information within the time limit for a Bail Act offence where bail was granted by the court.) **B-244**

14C.4 Given that bail was granted by a court, it is more appropriate that the court itself should initiate the proceedings by its own motion although the prosecutor may invite the court to take proceedings, if the prosecutor considers proceedings are appropriate.

Timing of disposal

14C.5 Courts should not, without good reason, adjourn the disposal of a section 6(1) or ... (2) ... offence ... until the conclusion of the proceedings in respect of which bail was granted but should deal with defendants as soon as is practicable. In deciding what is practicable, the court must take into account when the proceedings in respect of which bail was granted are expected to conclude, the seriousness of the offence for which the defendant is already being prosecuted, the type of penalty that might be imposed for the Bail Act offence and the original offence, as well as any other relevant circumstances. **B-245**

14C.6 If the Bail Act offence is adjourned alongside the substantive proceedings, then it is still necessary to consider imposing a separate penalty at the trial. In addition, bail should usually be revoked in the meantime. Trial in the absence of the defendant is not a penalty for the Bail Act offence and a separate penalty may be imposed for the Bail Act offence.

Conduct of proceedings

14C.7 Proceedings under section 6 ... may be conducted either as a summary offence or as a **B-246**

criminal contempt of court. Where proceedings are commenced by the police or prosecutor, the prosecutor will conduct the proceedings and, if the matter is contested, call the evidence. Where the court initiates proceedings, with or without an invitation from the prosecutor, the court may expect the assistance of the prosecutor, such as in cross-examining the defendant, if required.

14C.8 The burden of proof is on the defendant to prove that he had reasonable cause for his failure to surrender ... (s.6(3)).

14C.9, 14C.10 [Sentencing for a Bail Act offence: see § Appendix S-9 et seq.]

Arrest for breach of bail

B-247 **14C.11** A defendant who has been released on bail but subsequently arrested for breach of a bail condition, or for failure to surrender to the court, actual or anticipated, must be brought before a magistrates' court (or a Crown Court judge, if the defendant is charged with murder) as soon as practicable and in any event within 24 hours of arrest. This does not apply to a defendant who is arrested within 24 hours of the next court hearing which that defendant is due to attend: such a defendant must be produced at that hearing instead. The period of 24 hours does not include Sunday, Christmas Day or Good Friday: see section 7 of the Bail Act 1976.

14C.12 Paragraphs II 7A.2 to 7A.8 of these Practice Directions apply to such a defendant as they do to one charged and brought before the court under section 46 of the Police and Criminal Evidence Act 1984, except for the requirements listed at paragraph II 7A.5(a)(i) and (ii) (requirements for confirmation of charge and preparation of case file), which must be read as if they required confirmation that (i) the allegation or allegations of breach of bail have been reduced to writing, and (ii) that allegation or those allegations, and any supporting documents, are complete and available. If the requirements of paragraph 7A.5, as thus read, are met, then the court before which the defendant is brought should take all the appropriate next steps in the case, including the taking of the defendant's plea; allocation and sending for trial, if applicable; and, if possible, sentencing; and should do so even if the defendant had been released on bail by a different court.

Voluntary attendance at a court after failure to attend

B-248 **14C.13** The court may consider taking any of the following courses of action where (i) a defendant has failed to attend a court at the appointed time, (ii) a warrant has been issued for the defendant's arrest for that failure, and (iii) the defendant subsequently attends voluntarily at some other time, or indicates a wish to do so, for example by making telephone enquiries of court staff:

(a) if the defendant is present, the court may arrange for the execution there and then of the warrant;

(b) if the defendant is present, the court may deal there and then with the case as if consequent on the execution of the warrant;

(c) the court may arrange a resumed hearing in the defendant's case at the next convenient opportunity, while warning the defendant that the warrant remains liable to be executed in the meantime; and

(d) the court may withdraw the warrant and arrange a resumed hearing in the defendant's case at the next convenient opportunity. The court should not withdraw an outstanding warrant unless the defendant provides evidence of an established current residential address, a telephone number and, if available, an email or other established electronic address.

14C.14 If an outstanding warrant is executed there and then, or if the court decides to deal at once with the defendant as if consequent on arrest, then paragraphs 14C.11 and 14C.12 apply and, consequently, paragraphs II 7A.2 to 7A.8 of these Practice Directions. However, if the defendant has not been arrested then the designated officer's delegate is under no such statutory duty as otherwise would apply to make efforts to accommodate the defendant's case and no step should be taken that disadvantages other cases awaiting hearing that day. In particular, it is only in exceptional circumstances that efforts should be made to accommodate a defendant who attends voluntarily and unexpectedly at a court building on any day other than a weekday on which a court is sitting at that building, or later than 12 noon on any such day.

14C.15 If an outstanding warrant for the defendant's arrest for failure to attend is either executed or withdrawn, court staff must ensure that this is recorded promptly in national police records.

CPD III Custody and Bail 14D: Relationship between the Bail Act offence and further remands on bail or in custody

B-249 **14D.1** The court at which the defendant is produced should, where practicable and legally permissible, arrange to have all outstanding cases brought before it (including those from different courts) for the purpose of progressing matters and dealing with the question of bail. This is likely to be practicable in the magistrates' court where cases can easily be transferred from one magistrates' court to another. Practice is likely to vary in the Crown Court. If the defendant appears before a different court, for example because he is charged with offences committed in another area, and it is not practicable for all matters to be concluded by that court then the defendant may be remanded on bail or in custody, if appropriate, to appear before the first court for the outstanding offences to be dealt with.

14D.2 When a defendant has been convicted of a Bail Act offence, the court should review the remand status of the defendant, including the conditions of that bail, in respect of all outstanding proceedings against the defendant.

14D.3 Failure by the defendant to surrender or a conviction for failing to surrender to bail in connection with the main proceedings will be significant factors weighing against the re-granting of bail.

14D.4 Whether or not an immediate custodial sentence has been imposed for the Bail Act offence, the court may, having reviewed the defendant's remand status, also remand the defendant in custody in the main proceedings.

CPD III Custody and Bail 14E: Trials in absence (as amended by Criminal Practice Directions 2015 (Amendment No. 8) [2019] EWCA Crim 495, Lord Burnett CJ)

14E.1 Paragraphs VI 24C and 25B of these Practice Directions (Trial adjournment in magistrates' courts; Trial adjournment in the Crown Court) include guidance on the circumstances in which the court should proceed with or adjourn a trial from which the defendant absents himself or herself voluntarily. **B-250**

CPD III Custody and Bail 14F: Forfeiture of monies lodged as security or pledged by a surety/ estreatment of recognizances

14F.1 A surety undertakes to forfeit a sum of money if the defendant fails to surrender as required. Considerable care must be taken to explain that obligation and the consequences before a surety is taken. This system ... has great antiquity. It is immensely valuable. A court concerned that a defendant will fail to surrender will not normally know that defendant personally, nor indeed much about him. When members of the community who do know the defendant say they trust him to surrender and are prepared to stake their own money on that trust, that can have a powerful influence on the decision of the court as to whether or not to grant bail. There are two important side-effects. The first is that the surety will keep an eye on the defendant, and report to the authorities if there is a concern that he will abscond. In those circumstances, the surety can withdraw. The second is that a defendant will be deterred from absconding by the knowledge that if he does so then his family or friends who provided the surety will lose their money. In the experience of the courts, it is comparatively rare for a defendant to fail to surrender when meaningful sureties are in place. **B-251**

14F.2 Any surety should have the opportunity to make representations to the defendant to surrender himself, in accordance with their obligations.

14F.3 The court should not wait or adjourn a decision on estreatment of sureties or securities until such time, if any, that the bailed defendant appears before the court. It is possible that any defendant who apparently absconds may have a defence of reasonable cause to the allegation of failure to surrender. If that happens, then any surety or security estreated would be returned. The reason for proceeding is that the defendant may never surrender, or may not surrender for many years. The court should still consider the sureties' obligations if that happens. Moreover, the longer the matter is delayed the more probable it is that the personal circumstances of the sureties will change.

14F.4 The court should follow the procedure at rule 14.15 of the Criminal Procedure Rules. Before the court makes a decision, it should give the sureties the opportunity to make representations, either in person, through counsel or by statement.

14F.5 The court has discretion to forfeit the whole sum, part only of the sum, or to remit the sum. The starting point is that the surety is forfeited in full. It would be unfortunate if this valuable method of allowing a defendant to remain at liberty were undermined. Courts would have less confidence in the efficacy of sureties. It is also important to note that a defendant who absconds without in any way forewarning his sureties does not thereby release them from any or all of their responsibilities. Even if a surety does his best, he remains liable for the full amount, except at the discretion of the court. However, all factors should be taken into account and the following are noted for guidance only:

(i) the presence or absence of culpability is a factor, but is not in itself a reason to reduce or set aside the obligations entered into by the surety;
(ii) the means of a surety, and in particular changed means, are relevant;
(iii) the court should forfeit no more than is necessary, in public policy, to maintain the integrity and confidence of the system of taking sureties.

CPD III Custody and Bail 14G: Bail during trial

B-252 **14G.1** The following should be read subject to the Bail Act 1976.

14G.2 Once a trial has begun the further grant of bail, whether during the short adjournment or overnight, is in the discretion of the trial judge or trial bench. It may be a proper exercise of this discretion to refuse bail during the short adjournment if the accused cannot otherwise be segregated from witnesses and jurors.

14G.3 An accused who was on bail while on remand should not be refused bail during the trial unless, in the opinion of the court, there are positive reasons to justify this refusal. Such reasons might include:

(a) that a point has been reached where there is a real danger that the accused will abscond, either because the case is going badly for him, or for any other reason;

(b) that there is a real danger that he may interfere with witnesses, jurors or co-defendants.

14G.4 Once the jury has returned a guilty verdict or a finding of guilt has been made, a further renewal of bail should be decided in the light of the gravity of the offence, any friction between codefendants and the likely sentence to be passed in all the circumstances of the case.

CPD III Custody and Bail 14H: Crown Court judge's certificaton of fitness to appeal and applications to the Crown Court for bail pending appeal

B-253 **14H.1** The trial or sentencing judge may grant a certificate of fitness for appeal (see, e.g., ss.1(2)(b) and 11(1A) of the CAA 1968 [§§ 7-37, 7-125 in the main work]); the judge ... should only certify cases in exceptional circumstances. The ... judge should use the Criminal Appeal Office Form C (Crown Court Judge's Certificate of fitness for appeal) which is available to court staff on the HMCTS intranet.

14H.2 The judge may well think it right to encourage the defendant's advocate to submit to the court, and serve on the prosecutor, before the hearing of the application, a draft of the grounds of appeal which he will ask the judge to certify on Form C.

14H.3 The first question for the judge is then whether there exists a particular and cogent ground of appeal. If there is no such ground, there can be no certificate; and if there is no certificate there can be no bail. A judge should not grant a certificate with regard to sentence merely in the light of mitigation to which he has, in his opinion, given due weight, nor in regard to conviction on a ground where he considers the chance of a successful appeal is not substantial. The judge should bear in mind that, where a certificate is refused, application may be made to the Court of Appeal for leave to appeal and for bail; it is expected that certificates will only be granted in exceptional circumstances.

14H.4 Defence advocates should note that the effect of a grant of a certificate is to remove the need for leave to appeal to be granted by the Court of Appeal. It does not in itself commence the appeal. The completed Form C will be sent by the Crown Court to the Criminal Appeal Office; it is not copied to the parties. The procedures in Part 39 of the Criminal Procedure Rules should be followed.

14H.5 Bail pending appeal ... may be granted by the ... judge if they have certified the case as fit for appeal (see s.81(1)(f) and (1B) of the Senior Courts Act 1981 [§ 3-208 in the main work]). Bail can only be granted in the Crown Court within 28 days of the conviction or sentence which is to be the subject of the appeal and may not be granted if an application for bail has already been made to the Court of Appeal. The procedure for bail to be granted by a judge of the Crown Court pending an appeal is governed by Part 14 of the Criminal Procedure Rules. The ... judge should use the Criminal Appeal Office Form BC (Crown Court Judge's Order granting bail) which is available to court staff on the HMCTS intranet.

14H.6 The length of the period which might elapse before the hearing of any appeal is not relevant to the grant of a certificate; but, if the judge does decide to grant a certificate, it may be one factor in the decision whether or not to grant bail. If bail is granted, the judge should consider imposing a condition of residence in line with the practice in the Court of Appeal.

Criminal Procedure Rules 2020 (SI 2020/759), Pt 15

Disclosure

When this Part applies

B-254 **15.1.** This Part applies in a magistrates' court and in the Crown Court where Parts I and II of the Criminal Procedure and Investigations Act 1996 apply.

Prosecution disclosure

B-255 **15.2.**—(1) This rule applies in the Crown Court where, under section 3 of the Criminal Procedure and Investigations Act 1996, the prosecutor–

(a) discloses prosecution material to the defendant; or

(b) serves on the defendant a written statement that there is no such material to disclose.

(2) The prosecutor must at the same time so inform the court officer.

Prosecutor's application for public interest ruling

15.3.–(1) This rule applies where– **B-256**

(a) without a court order, the prosecutor would have to disclose material; and

(b) the prosecutor wants the court to decide whether it would be in the public interest to disclose it.

(2) The prosecutor must–

(a) apply in writing for such a decision; and

(b) serve the application on–

(i) the court officer,

(ii) any person who the prosecutor thinks would be directly affected by disclosure of the material, and

(iii) the defendant, but only to the extent that serving it on the defendant would not disclose what the prosecutor thinks ought not be disclosed.

(3) The application must–

(a) describe the material, and explain why the prosecutor thinks that–

(i) it is material that the prosecutor would have to disclose,

(ii) it would not be in the public interest to disclose that material, and

(iii) no measure such as the prosecutor's admission of any fact, or disclosure by summary, extract or edited copy, adequately would protect both the public interest and the defendant's right to a fair trial;

(b) omit from any part of the application that is served on the defendant anything that would disclose what the prosecutor thinks ought not be disclosed (in which case, paragraph (4) of this rule applies); and

(c) explain why, if no part of the application is served on the defendant.

(4) Where the prosecutor serves only part of the application on the defendant, the prosecutor must–

(a) mark the other part, to show that it is only for the court; and

(b) in that other part, explain why the prosecutor has withheld it from the defendant.

(5) Unless already done, the court may direct the prosecutor to serve an application on–

(a) the defendant; and

(b) any other person who the court considers would be directly affected by the disclosure of the material.

(6) The court must determine the application at a hearing which–

(a) must be in private, unless the court otherwise directs; and

(b) if the court so directs, may take place, wholly or in part, in the defendant's absence.

(7) At a hearing at which the defendant is present–

(a) the general rule is that the court must consider, in the following sequence–

(i) representations first by the prosecutor and any other person served with the application, and then by the defendant, in the presence of them all, and then

(ii) further representations by the prosecutor and any such other person in the defendant's absence; but

(b) the court may direct other arrangements for the hearing.

(8) The court may only determine the application if satisfied that it has been able to take adequate account of–

(a) such rights of confidentiality as apply to the material; and

(b) the defendant's right to a fair trial.

(9) Unless the court otherwise directs, the court officer–

(a) must not give notice to anyone other than the prosecutor–

(i) of the hearing of an application under this rule, unless the prosecutor served the application on that person, or

(ii) of the court's decision on the application; and

(b) may–

(i) keep a written application or representations, or

(ii) arrange for the whole or any part to be kept by some other appropriate person, subject to any conditions that the court may impose.

Defence disclosure

B-257 **15.4.**—(1) This rule applies where—

(a) under section 5 or 6 of the Criminal Procedure and Investigations Act 1996, the defendant gives a defence statement; and

(b) under section 6C of the 1996 Act, the defendant gives a defence witness notice.

(2) The defendant must serve such a statement or notice on—

(a) the court officer; and

(b) the prosecutor.

Defendant's application for prosecution disclosure

B-258 **15.5.**—(1) This rule applies where the defendant—

(a) has served a defence statement given under the Criminal Procedure and Investigations Act 1996; and

(b) wants the court to require the prosecutor to disclose material.

(2) The defendant must serve an application on—

(a) the court officer; and

(b) the prosecutor.

(3) The application must—

(a) describe the material that the defendant wants the prosecutor to disclose;

(b) explain why the defendant thinks there is reasonable cause to believe that—

(i) the prosecutor has that material, and

(ii) it is material that the Criminal Procedure and Investigations Act 1996 requires the prosecutor to disclose; and

(c) ask for a hearing, if the defendant wants one, and explain why it is needed.

(4) The court may determine an application under this rule—

(a) at a hearing, in public or in private; or

(b) without a hearing.

(5) The court must not require the prosecutor to disclose material unless the prosecutor—

(a) is present; or

(b) has had at least 10 business days in which to make representations.

Review of public interest ruling

B-259 **15.6.**—(1) This rule applies where the court has ordered that it is not in the public interest to disclose material that the prosecutor otherwise would have to disclose, and—

(a) the defendant wants the court to review that decision; or

(b) the Crown Court reviews that decision on its own initiative.

(2) Where the defendant wants the court to review that decision, the defendant must—

(a) serve an application on—

(i) the court officer, and

(ii) the prosecutor; and

(b) in the application—

(i) describe the material that the defendant wants the prosecutor to disclose, and

(ii) explain why the defendant thinks it is no longer in the public interest for the prosecutor not to disclose it.

(3) The prosecutor must serve any such application on any person who the prosecutor thinks would be directly affected if that material were disclosed.

(4) The prosecutor, and any such person, must serve any representations on—

(a) the court officer; and

(b) the defendant, unless to do so would in effect reveal something that either thinks ought not be disclosed.

(5) The court may direct—

(a) the prosecutor to serve any such application on any person who the court considers would be directly affected if that material were disclosed; and

(b) the prosecutor and any such person to serve any representations on the defendant.

(6) The court must review a decision to which this rule applies at a hearing which—

(a) must be in private, unless the court otherwise directs; and

(b) if the court so directs, may take place, wholly or in part, in the defendant's absence.

(7) At a hearing at which the defendant is present—

(a) the general rule is that the court must consider, in the following sequence—

(i) representations first by the defendant, and then by the prosecutor and any other person served with the application, in the presence of them all, and then
(ii) further representations by the prosecutor and any such other person in the defendant's absence; but
(b) the court may direct other arrangements for the hearing.

(8) The court may only conclude a review if satisfied that it has been able to take adequate account of—
(a) such rights of confidentiality as apply to the material; and
(b) the defendant's right to a fair trial.

Defendant's application to use disclosed material

15.7.—(1) This rule applies where a defendant wants the court's permission to use disclosed prosecution material— **B-260**
(a) otherwise than in connection with the case in which it was disclosed; or
(b) beyond the extent to which it was displayed or communicated publicly at a hearing.
(2) The defendant must serve an application on—
(a) the court officer; and
(b) the prosecutor.
(3) The application must—
(a) specify what the defendant wants to use or disclose; and
(b) explain why.
(4) The court may determine an application under this rule—
(a) at a hearing, in public or in private; or
(b) without a hearing.
(5) The court must not permit the use of such material unless—
(a) the prosecutor has had at least 20 business days in which to make representations; and
(b) the court is satisfied that it has been able to take adequate account of any rights of confidentiality that may apply to the material.

Unauthorised use of disclosed material

15.8.—(1) This rule applies where a person is accused of using disclosed prosecution material in contravention of section 17 of the Criminal Procedure and Investigations Act 1996 [§ 12-88 in the main work]. **B-261**

(2) A party who wants the court to exercise its power to punish that person for contempt of court must comply with the rules in Part 48 (contempt of court).

(3) The court must not exercise its power to forfeit material used in contempt of court unless—
(a) the prosecutor; and
(b) any other person directly affected by the disclosure of the material, is present, or has had at least 10 business days in which to make representations.

Court's power to vary requirements under this Part

15.9. The court may— **B-262**
(a) shorten or extend (even after it has expired) a time limit under this Part;
(b) allow a defence statement or a defence witness notice to be in a different written form to one set out in the Practice Direction, as long as it contains what the Criminal Procedure and Investigations Act 1996 requires;
(c) allow an application under this Part to be in a different form to one set out in the Practice Direction, or to be presented orally; and
(d) specify the period within which—
(i) any application under this Part must be made, or
(ii) any material must be disclosed, on an application to which rule 15.5 applies (defendant's application for prosecution disclosure).

CPD IV Disclosure 15A: Disclosure of unused material

15A.1 Disclosure is a vital part of the preparation for trial, both in the magistrates' courts and in the Crown Court. All parties must be familiar with their obligations, in particular under the Criminal Procedure and Investigations Act 1996 as amended and the Code issued under that Act, and must comply with the relevant judicial protocol and guidelines from the Attorney-General. These documents have recently been revised and the new guidance will be issued shortly as Judicial Protocol on **B-263**

the Disclosure of Unused Material in Criminal Cases [Appendix N-52 et seq.] and the Attorney-General's Guidelines on Disclosure [Appendix A-242a et seq.]. The new documents should be read together as complementary, comprehensive guidance. They will be available electronically on the respective websites.

15A.2 In addition, certain procedures are prescribed under CrimPR Part 15 and these should be followed. The notes to Part 15 contain a useful summary of the requirements of the CPIA 1996 as amended.

Criminal Procedure Rules 2020 (SI 2020/759), Pt 16

Written Witness Statements

When this Part applies

B-264 **16.1.**—(1) This Part applies where a party wants to introduce a written statement in evidence under section 9 of the Criminal Justice Act 1967.

Content of written statement

B-265 **16.2.** The statement must contain—

(a) at the beginning—
  (i) the witness' name, and
  (ii) the witness' age, if under 18;
(b) a declaration by the witness that—
  (i) it is true to the best of the witness' knowledge and belief, and
  (ii) the witness knows that if it is introduced in evidence, then it would be an offence wilfully to have stated in it anything that the witness knew to be false or did not believe to be true;
(c) if the witness cannot read the statement, a signed declaration by someone else that that person read it to the witness; and
(d) the witness' signature.

Reference to exhibit

B-266 **16.3** Where the statement refers to a document or object as an exhibit, it must identify that document or object clearly.

Written witness statement in evidence

B-267 **16.4.**—(1) A party who wants to introduce in evidence a written statement must—

(a) before the hearing at which that party wants to introduce it, serve a copy of the statement on—
  (i) the court officer, and
  (ii) each other party; and
(b) at or before that hearing, serve on the court officer the statement or an authenticated copy.

(2) If that party relies on only part of the statement, that party must mark the copy in such a way as to make that clear.

(3) A prosecutor must serve on a defendant, with the copy of the statement, a notice—

(a) of the right to object to the introduction of the statement in evidence instead of the witness giving evidence in person;
(b) of the time limit for objecting under this rule; and
(c) that if the defendant does not object in time, the court—
  (i) can nonetheless require the witness to give evidence in person, but
  (ii) may decide not to do so.

(4) A party served with a written witness statement who objects to its introduction in evidence must—

(a) serve notice of the objection on—
  (i) the party who served it, and
  (ii) the court officer; and
(b) serve the notice of objection not more than 5 business days after service of the statement unless—
  (i) the court extends that time limit, before or after the statement was served,
  (ii) rule 24.8 (written guilty plea: special rules) applies, in which case the time limit is the later of 5 business days after service of the statement or 5 business days before the hearing date, or

(iii) rule 24.9 (single justice procedure: special rules) applies, in which case the time limit is 15 business days after service of the statement.

(5) The court may exercise its power to require the witness to give evidence in person—
(a) on application by any party; or
(b) on its own initiative.

(6) A party entitled to receive a copy of a statement may waive that entitlement by so informing—
(a) the party who would have served it; and
(b) the court.

CPD V Evidence 16A: Evidence by written statement

16A.1 Where the prosecution proposes to tender written statements in evidence under section 9 of the CJA 1967 [§ 10-14 in the main work], it will frequently be necessary for certain statements to be edited. This will occur either because a witness has made more than one statement whose contents should conveniently be reduced into a single, comprehensive statement, or where a statement contains inadmissible, prejudicial or irrelevant material. Editing of statements must be done by a crown prosecutor (or by a legal representative, if any, of the prosecutor if the case is not being conducted by the CPS) and not by a police officer. **B-268**

Composite statements

16A.2 A composite statement giving the combined effect of two or more earlier statements must be prepared in compliance with the requirements of section 9 of the 1967 Act and must then be signed by the witness. **B-269**

Editing single statements

16A.3 There are two acceptable methods of editing single statements. They are: **B-270**

(a) by marking copies of the statement in a way which indicates the passages on which the prosecution will not rely; this merely indicates that the prosecution will not seek to adduce the evidence so marked; the original signed statement to be tendered to the court is not marked in any way; the marking on the copy statement is done by lightly striking out the passages to be edited, so that what appears beneath can still be read, or by bracketing, or by a combination of both; it is not permissible to produce a photocopy with the deleted material obliterated, since this would be contrary to the requirement that the defence and the court should be served with copies of the signed original statement; whenever the striking out / bracketing method is used, it will assist if the following words appear at the foot of the frontispiece or index to any bundle of copy statements to be tendered: *"The prosecution does not propose to adduce evidence of those passages of the attached copy statements which have been struck out and / or bracketed (nor will it seek to do so at the trial unless a notice of further evidence is served).";*

(b) by obtaining a fresh statement, signed by the witness, which omits the offending material, applying the procedure for composite statements above.

16A.4 In most cases where a single statement is to be edited, the striking out/bracketing method will be the more appropriate, but the taking of a fresh statement is preferable in the following circumstances. (a) When a police (or other investigating) officer's statement contains details of interviews with more suspects than are eventually charged, a fresh statement should be prepared and signed omitting all details of interview with those not charged except, in so far as it is relevant, for the bald fact that a certain named person was interviewed at a particular time, date and place. (b) When a suspect is interviewed about more offences than are eventually made the subject of charges, a fresh statement should be prepared and signed, omitting all questions and answers about the uncharged offences unless either they might appropriately be taken into consideration, or evidence about those offences is admissible on the charges preferred. It may, however, be desirable to replace the omitted questions and answers with a phrase such as: "After referring to some other matters, I then said ... ", so as to make it clear that part of the interview has been omitted. (c) A fresh statement should normally be prepared and signed if the only part of the original on which the prosecution is relying is only a small proportion of the whole, although it remains desirable to use the alternative method if there is reason to believe that the defence might itself wish to rely, in mitigation or for any other purpose, on at least some of those parts which the prosecution does not propose to adduce. (d) When the passages contain material which the prosecution is entitled to withhold from disclosure to the defence.

16A.5 Prosecutors should also be aware that, where statements are to be tendered under section 9 of the 1967 Act in the course of summary proceedings, there will be a need to prepare fresh statements excluding inadmissible or prejudicial material, rather than using the striking out or bracketing method.

16A.6 Whenever a fresh statement is taken from a witness and served in evidence, the earlier, unedited statement(s) becomes unused material and should be scheduled and reviewed for disclosure to the defence in the usual way.

CPD V Evidence 16B: Video recorded evidence in chief

B-271 **16B.1** [The procedure for making an application for leave to admit into evidence video recorded evidence in chief under section 27 of the Youth Justice and Criminal Evidence Act 1999 is given in CrimPR Part 18.]

16B.2 Where a court, on application by a party to the proceedings or of its own motion, grants leave to admit a video recording in evidence under section 27(1) ..., it may direct that any part of the recording be excluded (s.27(2) and (3)). When such direction is given, the party who made the application to admit the video recording must edit the recording in accordance with the judge's directions and send a copy of the edited recording to the appropriate officer of the Crown Court and to every other party to the proceedings.

16B.3 Where a video recording is to be adduced during proceedings before the Crown Court, it should be produced and proved by the interviewer, or any other person who was present at the interview with the witness at which the recording was made. The applicant should ensure that such a person will be available for this purpose, unless the parties have agreed to accept a written statement in lieu of attendance by that person.

16B.4 Once a trial has begun, if, by reason of faulty or inadequate preparation or for some other cause, the procedures set out above have not been properly complied with and an application is made to edit the video recording, thereby necessitating an adjournment for the work to be carried out, the court may, at its discretion, make an appropriate award of costs.

CPD V Evidence 16C: Evidence of audio and video recorded interviews

B-272 **16C.1** The interrogation of suspects is primarily governed by Code C [Appendix A-39 et seq.] ... Under that code, interviews must normally be contemporaneously recorded. Under ... Code E [Appendix A-162 et seq.], interviews conducted at a police station concerning an indictable offence must normally be audio-recorded. In practice, most interviews are audio-recorded under Code E, or video-recorded under Code F, and it is best practice to do so. The questioning of terrorism suspects is governed ... by Code H [Appendix A-213 et seq.].

16C.2 Where a record of the interview is to be prepared, this should be in accordance with the current national guidelines, as envisaged by Note 5A of Code E.

16C.3 If the prosecution wishes to rely on the defendant's interview in evidence, the prosecution should seek to agree the record with the defence. Both parties should have received a copy of the audio or video recording, and can check the record against the recording. The record should be edited (see below) if inadmissible matters are included within it and, in particular if the interview is lengthy, the prosecution should seek to shorten it by editing or summary.

16C.4 If the record is agreed there is usually no need for the audio or video recording to be played in court. It is a matter for the discretion of the ... judge, but usual practice is for edited copies of the record to be provided to the court, and to the jury if there is one, and for the prosecution advocate to read the interview with the interviewing officer or the officer in the case, as part of the officer's evidence in chief, the officer reading the interviewer and the advocate reading the defendant and defence representative. In the magistrates' court, the Bench sometimes retire to read the interview themselves, and the document is treated as if it had been read aloud in court. This is permissible, but rule 24.5 should be followed.

16C.5 Where the prosecution intends to adduce the interview in evidence, and agreement between the parties has not been reached about the record, sufficient notice must be given to allow consideration of any amendment to the record, or the preparation of any transcript of the interview, or any editing of a recording for the purpose of playing it in court. To that end, the following practice should be followed:

(a) where the defence is unable to agree a record of interview or transcript (where one is already available) the prosecution should be notified at latest at the Plea and Case Management Hearing ("PCMH"), with a view to securing agreement to amend; the notice should specify the part to which objection is taken, or the part omitted which the defence consider should be included; a copy of the notice should be supplied to the court within the period specified above; the PCMH form inquires about the admissibility of the defendant's interview and shortening by editing or summarising for trial;

(b) if agreement is not reached and it is proposed that the audio or video recording or part of it be played in court, notice should be given to the prosecution by the defence as ordered at the PCMH, in order that the advocates for the parties may agree those parts of the audio or video recording that should not be adduced and that arrangements may be made, by editing or in some other way, to exclude that material; a copy of the notice should be supplied to the court;

(c) notice of any agreement reached should be supplied to the court by the prosecution, as soon as is practicable.

16C.6 Alternatively, if, the prosecution advocate proposes to play the audio or video recording or part of it, the prosecution should at latest at the PCMH, notify the defence and the court. The defence should notify the prosecution and the court within 14 days of receiving the notice, if they object to the production of the audio or video recording on the basis that a part of it should be excluded. If the objections raised by the defence are accepted, the prosecution should prepare an edited recording, or make other arrangements to exclude the material part; and should notify the court of the arrangements made.

16C.7 If the defendant wishes to have the audio or video recording or any part of it played to the court, the defence should provide notice to the prosecution and the court at latest at the PCMH. The defence should also, at that time, notify the prosecution of any proposals to edit the recording and seek the prosecution's agreement to those amendments.

16C.8 Whenever editing or amendment of a record of interview or of an audio or video recording or of a transcript takes place, the following general principles should be followed:

(i) where a defendant has made a statement which includes an admission of one or more other offences, the portion relating to other offences should be omitted unless it is or becomes admissible in evidence;

(ii) where the statement of one defendant contains a portion which exculpates him ... and partly implicates a co-defendant in the trial, the defendant making the statement has the right to insist that everything relevant which is exculpatory goes before the jury; in such a case the judge must be consulted about how best to protect the position of the co-defendant.

16C.9 If it becomes necessary for either party to access the master copy of the audio or video recording, they should give notice to the other party and follow the procedure in ... Code E at section 6.

16C.10 If there is a challenge to the integrity of the master recording, notice and particulars should be given to the court and to the prosecution by the defence as soon as is practicable. The court may then, at its discretion, order a case management hearing or give such other directions as may be appropriate.

16C.11 If an audio or video recording is to be adduced during proceedings before the Crown Court, it should be produced and proved in a witness statement by the interviewing officer or any other officer who was present at the interview at which the recording was made. The prosecution should ensure that the witness is available to attend court if required by the defence in the usual way.

16C.12 It is the responsibility of the prosecution to ensure that there is a person available to operate any audio or video equipment needed during the course of the proceedings. Subject to their other responsibilities, the court staff may be able to assist.

16C.13 If either party wishes to present audio or video evidence, that party must ensure, in advance of the hearing, that the evidence is in a format that is compatible with the court's equipment, and that the material to be used does in fact function properly in the relevant court room.

16C.14 In order to avoid the necessity for the court to listen to or watch lengthy or irrelevant material before the relevant part of a recording is reached, counsel shall indicate to the equipment operator those parts of a recording which it may be necessary to play. Such an indication should, so far as possible, be expressed in terms of the time track or other identifying process used by the interviewing police force and should be given in time for the operator to have located those parts by the appropriate point in the trial.

16C.15 Once a trial has begun, if, by reason of faulty preparation or for some other cause, the procedures above have not been properly complied with, and an application is made to amend the record of interview or transcript or to edit the recording, as the case may be, thereby making necessary an adjournment for the work to be carried out, the court may make at its discretion an appropriate award of costs.

16C.16 Where a case is listed for hearing on a date which falls within the time limits set out above, it is the responsibility of the parties to ensure that all the necessary steps are taken to comply with this Practice Direction within such shorter period as is available.

Criminal Procedure Rules 2020 (SI 2020/759), Pt 17

Witness Summonses, Warrants and Orders

When this Part applies

17.1.—(1) This Part applies in magistrates' courts and in the Crown Court where— **B-273**

(a) a party wants the court to issue a witness summons, warrant or order under—
(i) section 97 of the Magistrates' Courts Act 1980,
(ii) paragraph 4 of Schedule 3 to the Crime and Disorder Act 1998,
(iii) section 2 of the Criminal Procedure (Attendance of Witnesses) Act 1965, or
(iv) section 7 of the Bankers' Books Evidence Act 1879;
(b) the court considers the issue of such a summons, warrant or order on its own initiative as if a party had applied; or
(c) one of those listed in rule 17.7 wants the court to withdraw such a summons, warrant or order.

(2) A reference to a "witness" in this Part is a reference to a person to whom such a summons, warrant or order is directed.

Issue etc. of summons, warrant or order with or without a hearing

B-274 **17.2.**—(1) The court may issue or withdraw a witness summons, warrant or order with or without a hearing.

(2) A hearing under this Part must be in private unless the court otherwise directs.

Application for summons, warrant or order: general rules

B-275 **17.3.**—(1) A party who wants the court to issue a witness summons, warrant or order must apply as soon as practicable after becoming aware of the grounds for doing so.

(2) A party applying for a witness summons or order must—
(a) identify the proposed witness;
(b) explain—
(i) what evidence the proposed witness can give or produce,
(ii) why it is likely to be material evidence, and
(iii) why it would be in the interests of justice to issue a summons, order or warrant as appropriate.

(3) A party applying for an order to be allowed to inspect and copy an entry in bank records must—
(a) identify the entry;
(b) explain the purpose for which the entry is required; and
(c) propose—
(i) the terms of the order, and
(ii) the period within which the order should take effect, if 3 days from the date of service of the order would not be appropriate.

(4) The application may be made orally unless—
(a) rule 17.5 applies; or
(b) the court otherwise directs.

(5) The applicant must serve any order made on the witness to whom, or the bank to which, it is directed.

Written application: form and service

B-276 **17.4.**—(1) An application in writing under rule 17.3 must be in the form set out in the Practice Direction, containing the same declaration of truth as a witness statement.

(2) The party applying must serve the application—
(a) in every case, on the court officer and as directed by the court; and
(b) as required by rule 17.5, if that rule applies.

Application for summons to produce a document, etc.: special rules

B-277 **17.5.**—(1) This rule applies to an application under rule 17.3 for a witness summons requiring the proposed witness—
(a) to produce in evidence a document or thing; or
(b) to give evidence about information apparently held in confidence,
that relates to another person.

(2) The application must be in writing in the form required by rule 17.4.

(3) The party applying must serve the application—
(a) on the proposed witness, unless the court otherwise directs; and
(b) on one or more of the following, if the court so directs—
(i) a person to whom the proposed evidence relates, and
(ii) another party.

(4) The court must not issue a witness summons where this rule applies unless–
(a) everyone served with the application has had at least 10 business days in which to make representations, including representations about whether there should be a hearing of the application before the summons is issued; and
(b) the court is satisfied that it has been able to take adequate account of the duties and rights, including rights of confidentiality, of the proposed witness and of any person to whom the proposed evidence relates.

(5) This rule does not apply to an application for an order to produce in evidence a copy of an entry in bank records.

Application for summons to produce a document, etc.: court's assessment of relevance and confidentiality

17.6.–(1) This rule applies where a person served with an application for a witness summons requiring the proposed witness to produce in evidence a document or thing objects to its production on the ground that– **B-278**
(a) it is not likely to be material evidence; or
(b) even if it is likely to be material evidence, the duties or rights, including rights of confidentiality, of the proposed witness or of any person to whom the document or thing relates outweigh the reasons for issuing a summons.

(2) The court may require the proposed witness to make the document or thing available for the objection to be assessed.

(3) The court may invite–
(a) the proposed witness or any representative of the proposed witness; or
(b) a person to whom the document or thing relates or any representative of such a person,
to help the court assess the objection.

Application to withdraw a summons, warrant or order

17.7.–(1) The court may withdraw a witness summons, warrant or order if one of the following applies for it to be withdrawn– **B-279**
(a) the party who applied for it, on the ground that it is no longer is needed;
(b) the witness, on the grounds that he was not aware of any application for it and–
(i) he cannot give or produce evidence likely to be material evidence, or
(ii) even if he can, his duties or rights, including rights of confidentiality, or those of any person to whom the evidence relates, outweigh the reasons for the issue of the summons, warrant or order; or
(c) any person to whom the proposed evidence relates, on the grounds that he was not aware of any application for it and–
(i) that evidence is not likely to be material evidence, or
(ii) even if it is, his duties or rights, including rights of confidentiality, or those of the witness, outweigh the reasons for the issue of the summons, warrant or order.

(2) A person applying under the rule must–
(a) apply in writing as soon as practicable after becoming aware of the grounds for doing so, explaining why he wants the summons, warrant or order to be withdrawn; and
(b) serve the application on the court officer and as appropriate on–
(i) the witness,
(ii) the party who applied for the summons, warrant or order, and
(iii) any other person who he knows was served with the application for the summons, warrant or order.

(3) Rule 17.6 applies to an application under this rule that concerns a document or thing to be produced in evidence.

Court's power to vary requirements under this Part

17.8.–(1) The court may– **B-280**
(a) shorten or extend (even after it has expired) a time limit under this Part; and
(b) where a rule or direction requires an application under this Part to be in writing, allow that application to be made orally instead.

(2) Someone who wants the court to allow an application to be made orally under paragraph (1)(b) of this rule must–
(a) give as much notice as the urgency of his application permits to those on whom he would otherwise have served an application in writing; and
(b) in doing so explain the reasons for the application and for wanting the court to consider it orally.

CPD V Evidence 17A: Wards of court and children subject to current family proceedings

B-281 **17A.1** Where police wish to interview a child who is subject to current family proceedings, leave of the Family Court is only required where such an interview may lead to a child disclosing information confidential to those proceedings and not otherwise available to the police under Working Together to Safeguard Children (March 2013), a guide to inter-agency working to safeguard and promote the welfare of children: *www.workingtogetheronline.co.uk/chapters/contents.html.*

17A.2 Where exceptionally the child to be interviewed or called as a witness in criminal proceedings is a ward of court then the leave of the court which made the wardship order will be required.

17A.3 Any application for leave in respect of any such child must be made to the court in which the relevant family proceedings are continuing and must be made on notice to the parents, any actual carer (e.g. relative or foster parent) and, in care proceedings, to the local authority and the guardian. In private proceedings the family court reporter (if appointed) should be notified.

17A.4 If the police need to interview the child without the knowledge of another party (usually a parent or carer), they may make the application for leave without giving notice to that party.

17A.5 Where leave is given the order should ordinarily give leave for any number of interviews that may be required. However, anything beyond that actually authorised will require a further application.

17A.6 Exceptionally the police may have to deal with complaints by or allegations against such a child immediately without obtaining the leave of the court as, for example:

(a) a serious offence against a child (like rape) where immediate medical examination and collection of evidence is required; or

(b) where the child is to be interviewed as a suspect.

When any such action is necessary, the police should, in respect of each and every interview, notify the parents and other carer (if any) and the family court reporter (if appointed). In care proceedings the local authority and guardian should be notified. The police must comply with all relevant codes of practice when conducting any such interview.

17A.7 The Family Court should be appraised of the position at the earliest reasonable opportunity by one of the notified parties and should thereafter be kept informed of any criminal proceedings.

17A.8 No evidence or document in the family proceedings or information about the proceedings should be disclosed into criminal proceedings without the leave of the Family Court.

Criminal Procedure Rules 2020 (SI 2020/759), Pt 18

MEASURES TO HELP A WITNESS OR DEFENDANT TO GIVE EVIDENCE OR OTHERWISE PARTICIPATE

General rules

When this Part applies

★B-282 **18.1.** This Part applies—

(a) where the court can give a direction (a "special measures direction"), under section 19 of the Youth Justice and Criminal Evidence Act 1999, on an application or on its own initiative, for any of the following measures—

(i) preventing a witness from seeing the defendant (section 23 of the 1999 Act),

(ii) allowing a witness to give evidence by live link (section 24 of the 1999 Act),

(iii) hearing a witness' evidence in private (section 25 of the 1999 Act),

(iv) dispensing with the wearing of wigs and gowns (section 26 of the 1999 Act),

(v) admitting video recorded evidence (sections 27 and 28 of the 1999 Act),

(vi) questioning a witness through an intermediary (section 29 of the 1999 Act),

(vii) using a device to help a witness communicate (section 30 of the 1999 Act);

(b) where the court can vary or discharge such a direction, under section 20 of the 1999 Act;

(c) where the court can give, vary or discharge a direction (a "defendant's evidence direction") for a defendant to give evidence—

(i) by live link, under section 33A of the 1999 Act, or

(ii) through an intermediary, under sections 33BA and 33BB of the 1999 Act;

(d) where the court can—

(i) make a witness anonymity order, under section 86 of the Coroners and Justice Act 2009 , or

(ii) vary or discharge such an order, under section 91, 92 or 93 of the 2009 Act;

[(e) where the court can give, vary or rescind a direction (a 'live link direction'), on an application or on its own initiative, for a witness, defendant or other person to take part in a hearing by live link under—

the Criminal Justice Act 2003;]

(e) *where the court can give or discharge a direction (a "live link direction"), on an application or on its own initiative, for a witness to give evidence by live link under–*
 (i) *section 32 of the Criminal Justice Act 1988, or*
 (ii) *sections 51 and 52 of the Criminal Justice Act 2003;*

(f) where the court can–
 (i) appoint an intermediary to facilitate a defendant's effective participation in that defendant's trial, when the defendant gives evidence or at any other time, or
 (ii) vary or discharge such an appointment; and

(g) where the court can exercise any other power it has to give, make, vary, rescind, discharge or revoke a direction for a measure to help a witness to give evidence or to help a defendant to participate in that defendant's trial.

[This rule is also subject to temporary modification by virtue of r.19(b) of the Criminal Procedure (Amendment No. 2) (Coronavirus) Rules 2020 (SI 2020/417) (as modified by r.10(a) of SI 2021/40)- insertion of text in square brackets and omission of italicised text. These temporary modifications cease when ss.53, 54 and 55 (and Schs. 23, 24 and 25) of the Coronavirus Act 2020 expire. The rule is also printed as amended, with effect from 5 April 2021, by SI 2021/40, r.9(b).]

Meaning of "witness"

18.2. In this Part, "witness" means anyone (other than a defendant) for whose benefit an application, direction or order is made. **B-283**

Meaning of 'intermediary' and 'intermediary's report'

18.3. In this Part **★B-283a**

(a) 'intermediary' means a person who is–
 (i) approved by the court for the purposes of section 29 of the Youth Justice and Criminal Evidence Act 1999 (Examination of witness through intermediary),
 (ii) approved by the court for the purposes of section 33BA of the 1999 Act (Examination of accused through intermediary),
 (iii) asked to assess a defendant's communication needs, or
 (iv) appointed by the court to facilitate a defendant's effective participation in the trial, when the defendant gives evidence or at any other time, where otherwise that defendant's communication needs would impede such participation; and

(b) a reference to 'an intermediary's report' means a report by such a person which complies with rule 18.32.

[This rule is printed as inserted, with effect from 5 April 2021, by SI 2021/40, r.9(f).]

Making an application for a direction or order

18.4. A party who wants the court to exercise its power to give or make a direction or order must– **★B-284**

(a) apply in writing as soon as reasonably practicable, and in any event, not more than–
 (i) 20 business days after the defendant pleads not guilty, in a magistrates' court, or
 (ii) 10 business days after the defendant pleads not guilty, in the Crown Court; and

(b) serve the application on–
 (i) the court officer, and
 (ii) each other party.

[This rule is printed as re-numbered, with effect from 5 April 2021, by SI 2021/40, r.9(e).]

Decisions and reasons

18.5.–(1) A party who wants to introduce the evidence of a witness who is the subject of an application, direction or order must– **★B-285**

(a) inform the witness of the court's decision as soon as reasonably practicable; and

(b) explain to the witness the arrangements that as a result will be made for him or her to give evidence.

(2) The court must–

(a) promptly determine an application; and

(b) allow a party sufficient time to comply with the requirements of–
 (i) paragraph (1), and
 (ii) the code of practice issued under section 32 of the Domestic Violence, Crime and

Victims Act 2004.

(3) The court must announce, at a hearing in public before the witness gives evidence or the defendant's trial begins (as the case may be), the reasons for a decision–

(a) to give, make, vary or discharge a direction or order; or

(b) to refuse to do so.

[(3) The court must announce, at a hearing in public before the witness gives evidence or the defendant's trial begins (as the case may be), the reasons for a decision–

(a) to give, make, vary or discharge–

(i) a special measures direction for a witness, or

(ii) a direction to help a defendant to participate in that defendant's trial; or

(b) to refuse to do so.

(4) Where the court can give, vary or rescind a live link direction the court must–

(a) announce the reasons for a decision not to give such a direction; and

(b) in the case of a live link direction for a sentencing hearing, announce the reasons for a decision to rescind that direction.

(5) Where the court gives a direction for everyone taking part in a hearing to do so by live link the court must announce the reasons for a decision–

(a) not to direct that the proceedings are to be broadcast, within the meaning of section 85A of the Courts Act 2003 (Enabling the public to see and hear proceedings); or

(b) not to direct that a recording of the proceedings is to be made, within the meaning of that section of that Act.]

[This rule is subject to temporary modification effected by SI 2021/40, r.10 (replacing temporary modifications given effect by SI 2020/417, r.9(d)) - insertion of text in square brackets and omission of italicised text. These temporary modifications cease when ss.53, 54 and 55 (and Schs. 23, 24 and 25) of the Coronavirus Act 2020 expire. This rule is also printed as re-numbered and amended, with effect from 5 April 2021, by SI 2021/40, r.9(e) and (h).]

Court's power to vary requirements under this Part

★B-286 **18.6.**–(1) The court may–

(a) shorten or extend (even after it has expired) a time limit under this Part; and

(b) allow an application or representations to be made in a different form to one set out in the Practice Direction, or to be made orally.

(2) A person who wants an extension of time must–

(a) apply when serving the application or representations for which it is needed; and

(b) explain the delay.

[This rule is printed as re-numbered, with effect from 5 April 2021, by SI 2021/40, r.9(e).]

Custody of documents

★B-287 **18.7.** Unless the court otherwise directs, the court officer may–

(a) keep a written application or representations; or

(b) arrange for the whole or any part to be kept by some other appropriate person, subject to any conditions that the court may impose.

[This rule is printed as re-numbered, with effect from 5 April 2021, by SI 2021/40, r.9(e).]

[The next paragraph is B-289.]

Special measures directions

Exercise of court's powers

B-289 **18.8.** The court may decide whether to give, vary or discharge a special measures direction–

(a) at a hearing, in public or in private, or without a hearing; and

(b) in a party's absence, if that party–

(i) applied for the direction, variation or discharge, or

(ii) has had at least 10 business days in which to make representations.

Special measures direction without application

B-290 **18.9.**–(1) This rule applies where–

(a) a party notifies the court that a witness is eligible for assistance under section 16 or section

17 of the Youth Justice and Criminal Evidence Act 1999;
(b) the notice is given at–
(i) a preparation for trial hearing in a magistrates' court, or
(ii) a plea and trial preparation hearing in the Crown Court; and
(c) no other party opposes the giving of a special measures direction for the benefit of that witness.

(2) The court may exercise its power to give a special measures direction without requiring an application under rule 18.10.

(3) The party who gives the notice must–
(a) provide any information that the court may need to assess–
(i) the measure or measures likely to maximise so far as practicable the quality of the witness' evidence, and
(ii) the witness' own views; and
(b) where a direction provides for video recorded evidence to be admitted under section 27 or section 28 of the Youth Justice and Criminal Evidence Act 1999, as soon as reasonably practicable serve such evidence on–
(i) the court officer, and
(ii) each other party.

Content of application for a special measures direction

18.10. An applicant for a special measures direction must– **B-291**
(a) explain how the witness is eligible for assistance;
(b) explain why special measures would be likely to improve the quality of the witness' evidence;
(c) propose the measure or measures that in the applicant's opinion would be likely to maximise so far as practicable the quality of that evidence;
(d) report any views that the witness has expressed about–
(i) his or her eligibility for assistance,
(ii) the likelihood that special measures would improve the quality of his or her evidence, and
(iii) the measure or measures proposed by the applicant;
(e) in a case in which a child witness or a qualifying witness does not want the primary rule to apply, provide any information that the court may need to assess the witness' views;
(f) in a case in which the applicant proposes that the witness should give evidence by live link–
(i) identify someone to accompany the witness while the witness gives evidence,
(ii) name that person, if possible, and
(iii) explain why that person would be an appropriate companion for the witness, including the witness' own views;
(g) in a case in which the applicant proposes the admission of video recorded evidence, identify–
(i) the date and duration of the recording, and
(ii) which part the applicant wants the court to admit as evidence, if the applicant does not want the court to admit all of it;
(h) attach any other material on which the applicant relies; and
(i) if the applicant wants a hearing, ask for one, and explain why it is needed.

Application to vary or discharge a special measures direction

18.11.–(1) A party who wants the court to vary or discharge a special measures direction must– **B-292**
(a) apply in writing, as soon as reasonably practicable after becoming aware of the grounds for doing so; and
(b) serve the application on–
(i) the court officer, and
(ii) each other party.

(2) The applicant must–
(a) explain what material circumstances have changed since the direction was given (or last varied, if applicable);
(b) explain why the direction should be varied or discharged; and
(c) ask for a hearing, if the applicant wants one, and explain why it is needed.

Application containing information withheld from another party

18.12.–(1) This rule applies where– **B-293**

(a) an applicant serves an application for a special measures direction, or for its variation or discharge; and
(b) the application includes information that the applicant thinks ought not be revealed to another party.

(2) The applicant must—
(a) omit that information from the part of the application that is served on that other party;
(b) mark the other part to show that, unless the court otherwise directs, it is only for the court; and
(c) in that other part, explain why the applicant has withheld that information from that other party.

(3) Any hearing of an application to which this rule applies—
(a) must be in private, unless the court otherwise directs; and
(b) if the court so directs, may be, wholly or in part, in the absence of a party from whom information has been withheld.

(4) At any hearing of an application to which this rule applies—
(a) the general rule is that the court must consider, in the following sequence—
(i) representations first by the applicant and then by each other party, in all the parties' presence, and then
(ii) further representations by the applicant, in the absence of a party from whom information has been withheld; but
(b) the court may direct other arrangements for the hearing.

Representations in response

B-294 **18.13.**—(1) This rule applies where a party wants to make representations about—
(a) an application for a special measures direction;
(b) an application for the variation or discharge of such a direction; or
(c) a direction, variation or discharge that the court proposes on its own initiative.

(2) Such a party must—
(a) serve the representations on—
(i) the court officer, and
(ii) each other party;
(b) do so not more than 10 business days after, as applicable—
(i) service of the application, or
(ii) notice of the direction, variation or discharge that the court proposes; and
(c) ask for a hearing, if that party wants one, and explain why it is needed.

(3) Where representations include information that the person making them thinks ought not be revealed to another party, that person must—
(a) omit that information from the representations served on that other party;
(b) mark the information to show that, unless the court otherwise directs, it is only for the court; and
(c) with that information include an explanation of why it has been withheld from that other party.

(4) Representations against a special measures direction must explain, as appropiate—
(a) why the witness is not eligible for assistance; or
(b) if the witness is eligible for assistance, why—
(i) no special measure would be likely to improve the quality of the witness' evidence,
(ii) the proposed measure or measures would not be likely to maximise so far as practicable the quality of the witness' evidence, or
(iii) the proposed measure or measures might tend to inhibit the effective testing of that evidence; and
(c) in a case in which the admission of video recorded evidence is proposed, why it would not be in the interests of justice for the recording, or part of it, to be admitted as evidence.

(5) Representations against the variation or discharge of a special measures direction must explain why it should not be varied or discharged.

Defendant's evidence directions

Exercise of court's powers

B-295 **18.14.** The court may decide whether to give, vary or discharge a defendant's evidence direction—

(a) at a hearing, in public or in private, or without a hearing; and
(b) in a party's absence, if that party–
(i) applied for the direction, variation or discharge, or
(ii) has had at least 10 business days in which to make representations.

Content of application for a defendant's evidence direction

18.15. An applicant for a defendant's evidence direction must– **B-296**
(a) explain how the proposed direction meets the conditions prescribed by the Youth Justice and Criminal Evidence Act 1999;
(b) in a case in which the applicant proposes that the defendant give evidence by live link–
(i) identify a person to accompany the defendant while the defendant gives evidence, and
(ii) explain why that person is appropriate; and
(c) ask for a hearing, if the applicant wants one, and explain why it is needed.

Application to vary or discharge a defendant's evidence direction

18.16.–(1) A party who wants the court to vary or discharge a defendant's evidence direction must– **B-297**
(a) apply in writing, as soon as reasonably practicable after becoming aware of the grounds for doing so; and
(b) serve the application on–
(i) the court officer, and
(ii) each other party.

(2) The applicant must–
(a) on an application to discharge a live link direction, explain why it is in the interests of justice to do so;
(b) on an application to discharge a direction for an intermediary, explain why it is no longer necessary in order to ensure that the defendant receives a fair trial;
(c) on an application to vary a direction for an intermediary, explain why it is necessary for the direction to be varied in order to ensure that the defendant receives a fair trial; and
(d) ask for a hearing, if the applicant wants one, and explain why it is needed.

Representations in response

18.17.–(1) This rule applies where a party wants to make representations about– **B-298**
(a) an application for a defendant's evidence direction;
(b) an application for the variation or discharge of such a direction; or
(c) a direction, variation or discharge that the court proposes on its own initiative.

(2) [*Identical to r.18.13(2), § B-294.*]

(3) Representations against a direction, variation or discharge must explain why the conditions prescribed by the Youth Justice and Criminal Evidence Act 1999 are not met.

Witness anonymity orders

Exercise of court's powers

18.18.–(1) The court may decide whether to make, vary or discharge a witness anonymity order– **B-299**
(a) at a hearing (which must be in private, unless the court otherwise directs), or without a hearing (unless any party asks for one); and
(b) in the absence of a defendant.

(2) The court must not exercise its power to make, vary or discharge a witness anonymity order, or to refuse to do so–
(a) before or during the trial, unless each party has had an opportunity to make representations;
(b) on an appeal by the defendant to which applies Part 34 (appeal to the Crown Court) or Part 39 (appeal to the Court of Appeal about conviction or sentence), unless in each party's case–
(i) that party has had an opportunity to make representations, or
(ii) the appeal court is satisfied that it is not reasonably practicable to communicate with that party; or
(c) after the trial and any such appeal are over, unless in the case of each party and the witness–
(i) each has had an opportunity to make representations, or
(ii) the court is satisfied that it is not reasonably practicable to communicate with that party or witness.

Content and conduct of application for a witness anonymity order

B-300 **18.19.**—(1) An applicant for a witness anonymity order must—

(a) include in the application nothing that might reveal the witness' identity;

(b) describe the measures proposed by the applicant;

(c) explain how the proposed order meets the conditions prescribed by section 88 of the Coroners and Justice Act 2009 [§ 8-175 in the main work];

(d) explain why no measures other than those proposed will suffice, such as—

(i) an admission of the facts that would be proved by the witness,

(ii) an order restricting public access to the trial,

(iii) reporting restrictions, in particular under section 46 of the Youth Justice and Criminal Evidence Act 1999 [ibid., § 4-33] or under section 39 of the Children and Young Persons Act 1933,

(iv) a direction for a special measure under section 19 of the Youth Justice and Criminal Evidence Act 1999 [ibid., § 8-78],

(v) introduction of the witness' written statement as hearsay evidence, under section 116 of the Criminal Justice Act 2003 [ibid., § 11-15], or

(vi) arrangements for the protection of the witness;

(e) attach to the application—

(i) a witness statement setting out the proposed evidence, edited in such a way as not to reveal the witness' identity,

(ii) where the prosecutor is the applicant, any further prosecution evidence to be served, and any further prosecution material to be disclosed under the Criminal Procedure and Investigations Act 1996, similarly edited, and

(iii) any defence statement that has been served, or as much information as may be available to the applicant that gives particulars of the defence; and

(f) ask for a hearing, if the applicant wants one.

(2) At any hearing of the application, the applicant must—

(a) identify the witness to the court, unless at the prosecutor's request the court otherwise directs; and

(b) present to the court, unless it otherwise directs—

(i) the unedited witness statement from which the edited version has been prepared,

(ii) where the prosecutor is the applicant, the unedited version of any further prosecution evidence or material from which an edited version has been prepared, and

(iii) such further material as the applicant relies on to establish that the proposed order meets the conditions prescribed by section 88 of the 2009 Act.

(3) At any such hearing—

(a) the general rule is that the court must consider, in the following sequence—

(i) representations dirst by the applicant and then by each other party, in all the parties' presence, and then

(ii) information withheld from a defendant, and further representations by the applicant, in the absence of any (or any other) defendant; but

(b) the court may direct other arrangements for the hearing.

(4) Before the witness gives evidence, the applicant must identify the witness to the court—

(a) if not already done;

(b) without revealing the witness' identity to any other party or person; and

(c) unless at the prosecutor's request the court otherwise directs.

Duty of court officer to notify the Director of Public Prosecutions

B-301 **18.20.** The court officer must notify the Director of Public Prosecutions of an application, unless the prosecutor is, or acts on behalf of, a public authority.

Application to vary or discharge a witness anonymity order

B-302 **18.21.**—(1) A party who wants the court to vary or discharge a witness anonymity order, or a witness who wants the court to do so when the case is over, must—

(a) apply in writing, as soon as reasonably practicable after becoming aware of the grounds for doing so; and

(b) serve the application on—

(i) the court officer, and

(ii) each other party.

(2) The applicant must–

(a) explain what material circumstances have changed since the order was made (or last varied, if applicable);

(b) explain why the order should be varied or discharged, taking account of the conditions for making an order; and

(c) ask for a hearing, if the applicant wants one.

(3) Where an application includes information that the applicant thinks might reveal the witness' identity, the applicant must–

(a) omit that information from the application that is served on a defendant;

(b) mark the information to show that it is only for the court and the prosecutor (if the prosecutor is not the applicant); and

(c) with that information include an explanation of why it has been withheld.

(4) Where a party applies to vary or discharge a witness anonymity order after the trial and any appeal are over, the party who introduced the witness' evidence must serve the application on the witness.

Representations in response

18.22.–(1) This rule applies where a party or, where the case is over, a witness, wants to make representations about– **B-303**

(a) an application for a witness anonymity order;

(b) an application for the variation or discharge of such an order; or

(c) a variation or discharge that the court proposes on its own initiative.

(2) Such a party or witness must–

(a) serve the representations on–

(i) the court officer, and

(ii) each other party;

(b) do so not more than 10 business days days after, as applicable–

(i) service of the application, or

(ii) notice of the variation or discharge that the court proposes; and

(c) ask for a hearing, if that party or witness wants one.

(3) Where representations include information that the person making them thinks might reveal the witness' identity, that person must–

(a) omit that information from the representations served on a defendant;

(b) mark the information to show that it is only for the court (and for the prosecutor, if relevant); and

(c) with that information include an explanation of why it has been withheld.

(4) Representations against a witness anonymity order must explain why the conditions for making the order are not met.

(5) Representations against the variation or discharge of such an order must explain why it would not be appropriate to vary or discharge it, taking account of the conditions for making an order.

(6) A prosecutor's representations in response to an application by a defendant must include all information available to the prosecutor that is relevant to the conditions and considerations specified by sections 88 and 89 of the Coroners and Justice Act 2009 [§§ 8-175, 8-176 in the main work].

Live link directions

Exercise of court's powers

***18.23.** The court may decide whether to give or discharge a live link direction–* **B-304**

(a) at a hearing, in public or in private, or without a hearing; and

(b) in a party's absence, if that party–

(i) applied for the direction or discharge, or

(ii) has had at least 10 business days days in which to make representations in response to an application by another party.

[18.23.–(1) The court may exercise its power to give, vary or rescind a live link direction–

(a) at a hearing, in public or in private, or without a hearing; and

(b) without requiring an application under rule 18.24 (Content of application for a live link direction).

(2) Whether it acts on an application or on its own initiative, the court must not–

(a) give or vary such a direction in contravention of a prohibition or limitation imposed by the

Crime and Disorder Act 1998 or the Criminal Justice Act 2003; or

(b) give, vary or rescind such a direction—

(i) in the absence of any party and (if applicable) any representative of the youth offending team whose functions are exercisable in relation to a defendant unless the absentee has had an opportunity to make representations, and

(ii) without first satisfying itself that the requirements of the Crime and Disorder Act 1998 or the Criminal Justice Act 2003 which apply are met.

(3) Where the court gives a direction for everyone taking part in a hearing to do so by live link the court may exercise its power under section 85A of the Courts Act 2003 (Enabling the public to see and hear proceedings) to direct that—

(a) the proceedings are to be broadcast, within the meaning of that section of that Act; and

(b) a recording of the proceedings is to be made, within the meaning of that section.]

[This rule is subject to temporary substitution by virtue of the Criminal Procedure (Amendment No. 2) (Coronavirus) Rules 2020 (SI 2020/417). The text in square brackets is the rule as substituted, and the italicised text is the previous version of the rule. The temporary substitution ceases when ss.53, 54 and 55 (and Schs. 23, 24 and 25) of the Coronavirus Act 2020 expire.]

Content of application for a live link direction

★B-305 **18.24—** *An applicant for a live link direction must–*

(a) *unless the court otherwise directs, identify the place from which the witness will give evidence;*

(b) *if that place is in the United Kingdom, explain why it would be in the interests of the efficient or effective administration of justice for the witness to give evidence by live link;*

(c) *if the applicant wants the witness to be accompanied by another person while giving evidence–*

(i) *name that person, if possible, and*

(ii) *explain why it is appropriate for the witness to be accompanied;*

(d) *ask for a hearing, if the applicant wants one, and explain why it is needed.*

[An applicant for a live link direction must—

(a) identify the power that the applicant wants the court to exercise;

(b) specify the hearing or hearings in respect of which the applicant wants the direction to apply;

(c) identify each person to whom the applicant wants the direction to apply and specify—

(i) each one whom the applicant wants to give evidence by live link, and

(ii) each one whom the applicant wants to take part by live link without giving evidence;

(d) in respect of each such person, specify the type of live link proposed (either video or audio);

(e) unless the court otherwise directs, identify the place from which each such person will take part if the direction is given;

(f) identify any material circumstances relating to—

(i) the availability of the proposed participant by live link,

(ii) any potential need for that participant to attend in person, not by live link,

(iii) any views which that participant may have expressed,

(iv) the suitability of the facilities at the place from which that participant would take part by live link if the direction were given, and

(v) that participant's ability to take part effectively if the direction were given, including in particular, if that participant is the defendant, whether he or she will be represented at the hearing in respect of which the direction is proposed;

(g) if the proposed direction is for a person to give evidence by live link, identify any material circumstances relating to—

(i) the importance to the hearing of that person's evidence, and

(ii) any potential for the proposed direction to inhibit a party from effectively testing that evidence;

(h) explain why it is in the interests of justice for each proposed participant by live link to take part by those means;

(i) if the applicant wants a witness to be accompanied by another person while giving evidence—

(i) name that person, if possible, and

(ii) explain why it is appropriate for that witness to be accompanied; and

(j) ask for a hearing of the application, if the applicant wants one, and explain why it is needed.]

[This rule is subject to temporary modification by virtue of r.9(f) of the Criminal Procedure (Amendment No. 2) (Coronavirus) Rules 2020 (SI 2020/417)- insertion of text in square brackets and omission of italicised text. These temporary modifications cease when ss.53, 54 and 55 (and Schs. 23, 24 and 25) of the Coronavirus Act 2020 expire. It is also printed as amended, with effect from 5 April 2021, by SI 2021/40, r.9(i).]

Application to discharge [vary or rescind] *a live link direction*

18.25.—(1) A party who wants the court to *discharge* [vary or rescind] *a live link direction must*– ★B-306

(a) apply in writing, as soon as reasonably practicable after becoming aware of the grounds for doing so; and

(b) serve the application on–

(i) the court officer, and

(ii) each other party.

(2) The applicant must–

(a) explain what material circumstances have changed since the direction was given;

(b) explain why it is in the interests of justice to *discharge* [vary or rescind] *the direction; and*

(c) ask for a hearing, if the applicant wants one, and explain why it is needed.

[This rule is subject to temporary modification by virtue of r.9(g) of the Criminal Procedure (Amendment No. 2) (Coronavirus) Rules 2020 (SI 2020/417) - substitution of title and insertion of words in square brackets for italicised words. These temporary modifications cease when ss.53, 54 and 55 (and Schs. 23, 24 and 25) of the Coronavirus Act 2020 expire. This rule is also printed as amended, with effect from 5 April 2021, by SI 2021/40, r.9(j).]

Representations in response

18.26.—(1) This rule applies where a party wants to make representations about an application for a live link direction or for the [variation or rescission] *of such a direction.* B-307

(2) Such a party must–

(a) serve the representations on–

(i) the court officer, and

(ii) each other party;

(b) do so not more than 10 business days after service of the application; and

(c) ask for a hearing, if that party wants one, and explain why it is needed.

(3) Representations against a direction or discharge must explain, as applicable, why the conditions prescribed by the Criminal Justice Act 1988 or the Criminal Justice Act 2003 are not met.

[(3) Representations must explain why the requirements of the Crime and Disorder Act 1998 or the Criminal Justice Act 2003, as applicable, are not met.]

[This rule is subject to temporary modification by virtue of r.9(h) of the Criminal Procedure (Amendment No. 2) (Coronavirus) Rules 2020 (SI 2020/417) - insertion of text in square brackets and omission of italicised text. These temporary modifications cease when ss.53, 54 and 55 (and Schs. 23, 24 and 25) of the Coronavirus Act 2020 expire.]

Intermediary for a Defendant

Appointment of intermediary to facilitate a defendant's participation

18.27.—(1) The court must exercise its power to appoint an intermediary to facilitate a defendant's effective participation in the trial where– ★B-307a

(a) the defendant's ability to participate is likely to be diminished by reason of–

(i) age, if the defendant is under 18, or

(ii) mental disorder (as defined in section 1(2) of the Mental Health Act 1983), a significant impairment of intelligence and social functioning, or a physical disability or disorder; and

(b) the appointment is necessary for that purpose.

(2) In determining whether such an appointment is necessary, who to appoint and the duration or purpose of the appointment, the court must have regard to–

(a) the defendant's communication needs as reported to the court;

(b) the recommendations in any intermediary's report received by the court;

(c) any views that the defendant has expressed about–

(i) receiving the assistance of an intermediary,

(ii) other measures or arrangements to facilitate the defendant's effective participation in the trial;

(d) the likely impact of the defendant's age, if under 18, level of intellectual ability or social functioning on the ability to–

(i) give evidence, and
(ii) understand what is said and done by the court and other participants;
(e) the likely impact on such participation and on such understanding of any mental disorder or other significant impairment of intelligence or social functioning;
(f) the adequacy of arrangements for questioning the defendant in the absence of an intermediary;
(g) any assistance that the defendant has received in the past—
(i) while giving evidence in legal proceedings,
(ii) while being questioned during the investigation of an alleged offence, or
(iii) as a defendant in a criminal case;
(h) any assessment of the defendant's health by a mental health practitioner acting independently of the parties to assist the court;
(i) any expert medical opinion that the court may have received; and
(j) any other matter that the court thinks relevant.

(3) The court may exercise its power to appoint an intermediary—
(a) for the duration of every hearing that the defendant is due to attend;
(b) for the duration of any specified such hearing or hearings, or for the duration of a specified part of such a hearing; or
(c) for a specified purpose during a hearing.

(4) Unless the court otherwise directs, the appointment of an intermediary extends to facilitating the defendant's communication with that defendant's legal representatives for the duration and for the purpose of the appointment.

(5) The court may decide whether to appoint an intermediary to facilitate a defendant's effective participation in the trial and whether to vary or discharge any such appointment—
(a) on application or on the court's own initiative;
(b) at a hearing, in public or in private, or without a hearing; and
(c) in a party's absence, if that party—
(i) applied for the appointment, variation or discharge, or
(ii) has had at least 10 business days in which to make representations.

(6) The court must not exercise its power to vary or discharge a direction for the appointment of an intermediary unless satisfied that—
(a) since the direction was made—
(i) the defendant's communication needs have changed materially, or
(ii) any other material circumstance has changed materially; and
(b) the defendant will be able to participate effectively in the trial despite the variation or discharge of the direction.

[This rule is printed as inserted, with effect from 5 April 2021, by SI 2021/40, r.9(k).]

Application to vary or discharge the appointment of an intermediary for a defendant

★B-307b **18.28.**—(1) A party who wants the court to vary or discharge the appointment of an intermediary to facilitate a defendant's effective participation in the trial must—
(a) apply in writing, as soon as reasonably practicable after becoming aware of the grounds for doing so; and
(b) serve the application on—
(i) the court officer, and
(ii) each other party.

(2) The applicant must—
(a) explain how the criteria listed in rule 18.27(7) are met (variation or discharge of appointment); and
(b) ask for a hearing, if the applicant wants one, and explain why it is needed.

[This rule is printed as inserted, with effect from 5 April 2021, by SI 2021/40, r.9(k).]

Representations in response to application or proposal

★B-307c **18.29.**—(1) This rule applies where a party wants to make representations about—
(a) an application or proposal for the appointment of an intermediary to facilitate a defendant's effective participation in the trial; or
(b) an application or proposal for the variation or discharge of such an appointment.

(2) Such a party must—

(a) serve the representations on–
(i) the court officer, and
(ii) each other party;
(b) do so not more than 10 business days after, as applicable–
(i) service of the application, or
(ii) notice of the appointment, variation or discharge that the court proposes; and
(c) ask for a hearing, if that party wants one, and explain why it is needed.

(3) Representations against such an appointment, variation or discharge must explain why the criteria that apply are not met.

[This rule is printed as inserted, with effect from 5 April 2021, by SI 2021/40, r.9(k).]

Duties of Intermediaries

Intermediary's duty to the court

18.30.–(1) This rule applies to an intermediary who accepts– ★B-307d
(a) approval by the court for the purposes of section 29 of the Youth Justice and Criminal Evidence Act 1999 (Examination of witness through intermediary);
(b) approval by the court for the purposes of section 33BA of the 1999 Act (Examination of accused through intermediary); or
(c) appointment by the court to facilitate a defendant's effective participation in the trial, when the defendant gives evidence or at any other time.

(2) The intermediary must help the court to achieve the overriding objective–
(a) to the best of the intermediary's skill and understanding by–
(i) communicating to the witness or defendant (as the case may be) questions put to them,
(ii) communicating to the questioner and the court the replies, and
(iii) explaining such questions and answers so that they can be understood;
(b) by assessing continually the witness' or the defendant's (as the case may be) ability to participate effectively and intervening if necessary;
(c) where the intermediary is appointed to facilitate a defendant's effective participation, by explaining to the defendant, in terms the defendant can understand, what is said and done by the court and other participants; and
(d) by actively assisting the court in fulfilling its duties under rule 3.2 (Case management; The duty of the court) and rule 3.9 (Case management; Ground rules hearing), in particular by–
(i) complying with directions made by the court, and
(ii) at once informing the court of any significant failure (by the intermediary or another) to take any step required by such a direction.

(3) This duty overrides any obligation to the witness or to the defendant (as the case may be), or to the person by whom the intermediary is paid.

[This rule is printed as inserted, with effect from 5 April 2021, by SI 2021/40, r.9(k).]

Declaration by intermediary

18.31.–(1) This rule applies where– ★B-307e
(a) a video recorded interview with a witness is conducted through an intermediary; or
(b) the court directs the examination of a witness or defendant through an intermediary.

(2) The intermediary must make a declaration–
(a) before such an interview begins; and
(b) before the examination begins (even if such an interview with the witness was conducted through the same intermediary).

(3) The declaration must be in these terms, or in any corresponding terms that the intermediary declares to be binding–

"I swear by Almighty God [*or* I solemnly, sincerely and truly declare and affirm] that I shall faithfully communicate questions and answers and make true explanation of all matters and things required of me according to the best of my skill and understanding."

[This rule is printed as inserted, with effect from 5 April 2021, by SI 2021/40, r.9(k).]

Content of intermediary's report

18.32.–(1) An intermediary's report must, in every case– ★B-307f

(a) give details of the intermediary's qualifications, relevant experience and any accreditation;
(b) identify the commissioner of the report;
(c) identify those from whom the intermediary has obtained information material to the report;
(d) list the documents received or inspected by the intermediary which contained such information and give an indication of their content;
(e) give the date or dates on which the intermediary met the witness or defendant, as the case may be, for the purpose of preparing the report;
(f) describe the nature and duration of the intermediary's assessment, or assessments, of the witness or defendant;
(g) by reference to examples drawn from the intermediary's assessment of the witness or defendant explain why in this particular case intermediary assistance is necessary;
(h) include an evaluation of—
  (i) the impact of any condition or conditions which, whether in isolation or together, may adversely affect the witness' or the defendant's ability to communicate, and
  (ii) the extent, if any, to which that impact may be exacerbated by the trial;
(i) if the intermediary is not able to reach an evaluation without qualifying it, state the qualification;
(j) report the views of the witness or defendant, as the case may be, on receiving the assistance of an intermediary;
(k) include in a summary of the intermediary's conclusions any recommendation, with reasons, for—
  (i) the approval or appointment of an intermediary,
  (ii) the manner and duration of any questioning of the witness or defendant, as the case may be, and
  (iii) arrangements for the way in which the intermediary, if approved or appointed, should participate; and
(l) contain a statement that the intermediary—
  (i) understands an intermediary's duty to the court, and
  (ii) will comply with that duty if approved or appointed.

(2) Where the intermediary is asked to evaluate a defendant's communication needs the report must also—
(a) include an evaluation of the extent to which any measures or arrangements beside the appointment of an intermediary will facilitate the defendant's effective participation in the trial; and
(b) in the summary of the intermediary's conclusions include any recommendation, with reasons, for—
  (i) the duration and purpose of any appointment of an intermediary, and
  (ii) other measures or arrangements to help the defendant to participate effectively in the trial.

[This rule is printed as inserted, with effect from 5 April 2021, by SI 2021/40, r.9(k).]

CPD V Evidence 18A: Measures to assist a witness or defendant to give evidence

B-308 **18A.1** For special measures applications, the procedures at Part 18 should be followed. However, assisting a vulnerable witness to give evidence is not merely a matter of ordering the appropriate measure. Further directions about vulnerable people in the courts, ground rules hearings and intermediaries are given in the practice direction accompanying Part 3.

18A.2 Special measures need not be considered or ordered in isolation. The needs of the individual witness should be ascertained, and a combination of special measures may be appropriate. For example, if a witness who is to give evidence by live link wishes, screens can be used to shield the live link screen from the defendant and the public, as would occur if screens were being used for a witness giving evidence in the court room.

CPD V Evidence 18B: Witnesses giving evidence by live link

B-309 **18B.1** A special measures direction for the witness to give evidence by live link may also provide for a specified person to accompany the witness (r.18.10(f)). In determining who this should be, the court must have regard to the wishes of the witness. The presence of a supporter is designed to provide emotional support to the witness, helping reduce the witness's anxiety and stress and contributing to the ability to give best evidence. It is preferable for the direction to be made well before the trial begins and to ensure that the designated person is available on the day of the witness's testimony so as to provide certainty for the witness.

18B.2 An increased degree of flexibility is appropriate as to who can act as supporter. This can be anyone known to and trusted by the witness who is not a party to the proceedings and has no detailed knowledge of the evidence in the case. The supporter may be a member of the witness service but need not be an usher or court official. Someone else may be appropriate.

18B.3 The usher should continue to be available both to assist the witness and the witness supporter, and to ensure that the court's requirements are properly complied with in the live link room.

18B.4 In order to be able to express an informed view about special measures, the witness is entitled to practise speaking using the live link (and to see screens in place). Simply being shown the room and equipment is inadequate for this purpose.

18B.5 If, with the agreement of the court, the witness has chosen not to give evidence by live link but to do so in the court room, it may still be appropriate for a witness supporter to be selected in the same way, and for the supporter to sit alongside the witness while the witness is giving evidence.

CPD V Evidence 18C: Visually recorded interviews: memory refreshing and watching at a different time from the jury (as amended by Criminal Practice Directions 2015 (Amendment No. 6), unreported, 22 March 2018, Lord Burnett CJ)

18C.1 Witnesses are entitled to refresh their memory from their statement or visually recorded interview. The court should enquire at the PCMH or other case management hearing about arrangements for memory refreshing. The witness's first viewing of the visually recorded interview can be distressing or distracting. It should not be seen for the first time immediately before giving evidence. Depending upon the age and vulnerability of the witness several competing issues have to be considered and it may be that the assistance of the intermediary is needed to establish exactly how memory refreshing should be managed. **B-310**

18C.2 If the interview is ruled inadmissible, the court must decide what constitutes an acceptable alternative method of memory refreshing.

18C.3 Decisions about how, when and where refreshing should take place should be court-led and made on a case-by-case basis in respect of each witness. General principles to be addressed include:

(i) the venue for viewing; the delicate balance between combining the court familiarisation visit and watching the DVD, and having them on two separate occasions, needs to be considered in respect of each witness as combining the two may lead to "information overload"; refreshing need not necessarily take place within the court building but may be done, for example, at the police ABE suite;

(ii) requiring that any viewing is monitored by a person (usually the officer in the case) who will report to the court about anything said by the witness;

(iii) whether it is necessary for the witness to see the DVD more than once for the purpose of refreshing; the court will need to ask the advice of the intermediary, if any, with respect to this;

(iv) arrangements, if the witness will not watch the DVD at the same time as the trial bench or judge and jury, for the witness to watch it before attending to be cross-examined (depending upon their ability to retain information this may be the day before).

18C.4 There is no legal requirement that the witness should watch the interview at the same time as the trial bench or jury. Increasingly, this is arranged to occur at a different time, with the advantages that breaks can be taken as needed without disrupting the trial, and cross-examination starts while the witness is fresh. An intermediary may be present to facilitate communication but should not act as the independent person designated to take a note and report to the court if anything is said.

18C.5 Where the viewing takes place at a different time from that of the trial bench or jury, the witness is sworn (or promises) just before cross-examination and, unless the judge otherwise directs:

(a) it is good practice for the witness to be asked by the prosecutor, (or the judge/magistrate if they so direct), in appropriate language if, and when, he or she has watched the recording of the interview;

(b) if, in watching the recording of the interview or otherwise the witness has indicated that there is something he or she wishes to correct or to add then it is good practice for the prosecutor (or the judge/magistrate if they so direct) to deal with that before cross-examination provided that proper notice has been given to the defence.

CPD V Evidence 18D: Witness anonymity orders (as amended by Criminal Practice Directions 2015 (Amendment No.7) [2018] EWCA Crim 1760, Lord Burnett CJ)

18D.1 [*Recites that this direction supplements the Coroners and Justice Act 2009, s.87 and rr.18.18-18.22.*] **B-311**

18D.2 As the Court of Appeal stated in *Mayers* [2008] EWCA Crim 2989; [2009] 1 Cr. App. R. 30 and emphasised again in *Donovan and Kafunda* [2012] EWCA Crim 2749, "a witness anonymity order is to be regarded as a special measure of the last practicable resort". In making such an application, the prosecution's obligations of disclosure "go much further than the ordinary duties of disclosure" (*Mayers*); reference should be made to the Judicial Protocol on Disclosure (Appendix N-52 et seq.): see the practice direction accompanying Part 15.

Case Management

B-312 **18D.3** Where such an application is proposed, with the parties' active assistance the court should set a realistic timetable, in accordance with the duties imposed by rules 3.2 and 3.3. Where possible, the trial judge should determine the application, and any hearing should be attended by the parties' trial advocates.

Service of Evidence and Disclosure of Prosecution Material Pending an Application

B-313 **18D.4** Where the prosecutor proposes an application for a witness anonymity order it is not necessary for that application to have been determined before the proposed evidence is served. In most cases an early indication of what that evidence will be if an order is made will be consistent with a party's duties under rules 1.2 and 3.3. The prosecutor should serve with the other prosecution evidence a witness statement setting out the proposed evidence, redacted in such a way as to prevent disclosure of the witness' identity, as permitted by section 87(4) ... . Likewise the prosecutor should serve with other prosecution material disclosed under the CPIA 1996 any such material appertaining to the witness, similarly redacted.

The Application

B-314 **18D.5** An application for a witness anonymity order should be made as early as possible and within the period for which rule 18.3 provides. The application, and any hearing of it, must comply with the requirements of that rule and with those of rule 18.19. In accordance with rules 1.2 and 3.3, the applicant must provide the court with all available information relevant to the considerations to which the Act requires a court to have regard.

Response to the Application

B-315 **18D.6** A party upon whom an application for a witness anonymity order is served must serve a response in accordance with rule 18.22. That period may be extended or shortened in the court's discretion: r.18.5.

18D.7 To avoid the risk of injustice, a respondent, whether the prosecution or a defendant, must actively assist the court. If not already done, a respondent defendant should serve a defence statement under section 5 or 6 of the CPIA 1996 [§§ 12-62, 12-63 in the main work], so that the court is fully informed of what is in issue. When a defendant makes an application for a witness anonymity order the prosecutor should consider the continuing duty to disclose material under section 7A of the CPIA 1996 [§ 12-74 in the main work]; therefore a prosecutor's response should include confirmation that that duty has been considered. Great care should be taken to ensure that nothing disclosed contains anything that might reveal the witness' identity. A respondent prosecutor should provide the court with all available information relevant to the considerations to which the Act requires a court to have regard, whether or not that information falls to be disclosed under the 1996 Act.

Determination of the Application

B-316 **18D.8** All parties must have an opportunity to make oral representations to the court on an application for a witness anonymity order: s.87(6) ... . However, a hearing may not be needed if none is sought: r.18.18(1)(a). Where, for example, the witness is an investigator who is recognisable by the defendant but known only by an assumed name, and there is no likelihood that the witness' credibility will be in issue, then the court may indicate a provisional decision and invite representations within a defined period, usually 14 days, including representations about whether there should be a hearing. In such a case, where the parties do not object the court may make an order without a hearing. Or where the court provisionally considers an application to be misconceived, an applicant may choose to withdraw it without requiring a hearing. Where the court directs a hearing of the application then it should allow adequate time for service of the representations in response.

18D.9 The hearing of an application for a witness anonymity order usually should be in private: CrimPR 18.18(1)(a), and before the trial judge wherever possible. The court has power to hear a party in the absence of a defendant and that defendant's representatives: section 87(7) of the Act and rule 18.18(1)(b). In the Crown Court, a recording of the proceedings will be made, in accordance with CrimPR 5.5. The Crown Court officer must treat such a recording in the same way as the recording of an application for a public interest ruling. It must be kept in secure conditions, and the arrangements made by the Crown Court officer for any transcription must impose restrictions that correspond with those under CrimPR 5.5(2).

18D.10 Where confidential supporting information is presented to the court before the last stage of the hearing, the court may prefer not to read that information until that last stage.

18D.11 The court may adjourn the hearing at any stage, and should do so if its duty under rule 3.2 so requires.

18D.12 On a prosecutor's application, the court is likely to be assisted by the attendance of a senior investigator or other person of comparable authority who is familiar with the case.

18D.13 During the last stage of the hearing it is essential that the court test thoroughly the information supplied in confidence in order to satisfy itself that the conditions prescribed by the Act are met. At that stage, if the court concludes that this is the only way in which it can satisfy itself as to a relevant condition or consideration, exceptionally it may invite the applicant to present the proposed witness to be questioned by the court. Any such questioning should be carried out at such a time, and the witness brought to the court in such a way, as to prevent disclosure of his ... identity.

18D.14 The court may ask the Attorney-General to appoint special counsel to assist. However, it must be kept in mind that, "Such an appointment will always be exceptional, never automatic; a course of last and never first resort. It should not be ordered unless and until the trial judge is satisfied that no other course will adequately meet the overriding requirement of fairness to the defendant": *H.* [2004] UKHL 3; [2004] 2 A.C. 134. Whether to accede to such a request is a matter for the Attorney-General, and adequate time should be allowed for the consideration of such a request.

18D.15 The Court of Appeal in *Mayers* "emphasised that all three conditions, A, B and C, must be met before the jurisdiction to make a witness anonymity order arises. Each is mandatory. Each is distinct." The court also noted that if there is more than one anonymous witness in a case any link, and the nature of any link, between the witnesses should be investigated: "questions of possible improper collusion between them, or cross-contamination of one another, should be addressed."

18D.16 Following a hearing the court should announce its decision ... in the parties' presence and in public: r.18.4(2). The court should give such reasons as it is possible to give without revealing the witness' identity. In the Crown Court, the court will be conscious that reasons given in public may be reported and reach the jury. Consequently, the court should ensure that nothing in its decision or its reasons could undermine any warning it may give jurors under section 90(2) [§ 8-177 in the main work] ... . A record of the reasons must be kept. In the Crown Court, the announcement of those reasons will be recorded.

18D.17 Where the court makes a witness anonymity order, it is essential that the measures to be taken are clearly specified in a written record of that order approved by the court and issued on its behalf. An order made in a magistrates' court must be recorded in the court register, in accordance with rule 5.4.

Order

18D.18 Should the judge grant the anonymity then the following should be considered by the judge with the assistance of the court staff, so that the practical arrangements (confidentially recorded) are in place to ensure that the witness's anonymity is not compromised: B-317

i. Any pre-trial visit by the anonymous witness;
ii. How the witness will enter and leave the court building;
iii. Where the witness will wait until they give evidence;
iv. Provision for prosecution counsel to speak to the anonymous witness at court before they give evidence;
v. Provision for the anonymous witness to see their statement or view their ABEs;
vi. How the witness will enter and leave the court room;
vii. Provisions to disguise the identity of the anonymous witness whilst they give evidence (voice modulation and screens);
viii. Provisions for the anonymous witness to have any breaks required;
ix. Provisions to protect the anonymity of the witness in the event of an emergency such as a security alert.

18D.19 Self-evidently, the written record of the order must not disclose the identity of the witness to whom it applies. However, it is essential that there be maintained some means of establishing a clear correlation between witness and order, and especially where in the same proceedings witness anonymity orders are made in respect of more than one witness, specifying different measures in respect of each. Careful preservation of the application for the order, including the confidential part, ordinarily will suffice for this purpose.

18D.20 Should the application for anonymity be refused, consideration will be given as to whether the witness to whom the application related can be compelled to give evidence despite any risk to their safely and what special measures could support them to give their evidence.

Discharge or Variation of the Order

B-318 **18D.21** Section 91 [§ 8-178 in the main work] ... allows the court to discharge or vary a witness anonymity order: on application, if there has been a material change of circumstances since the order was made or since any previous variation of it; or on its own initiative. Rule 18.21 allows the parties to apply for the variation of a pre-trial direction where circumstances have changed.

18D.22 The court should keep under review the question of whether the conditions for making an order are met. In addition, consistently with the parties' duties under rules 1.2 and 3.3, it is incumbent on each, and in particular on the applicant for the order, to keep the need for it under review.

18D.23 Where the court considers the discharge or variation of an order, the procedure that it adopts should be appropriate to the circumstances. As a general rule, that procedure should approximate to the procedure for determining an application for an order. The court may need to hear further representations by the applicant for the order in the absence of a respondent defendant and that defendant's representatives.

18D.24 If retained by the court, confidential material must be stored in secure conditions by the court officer. Alternatively, subject to such directions as the court may give, such material may be committed to the safe-keeping of the applicant or any other appropriate person in exercise of the powers conferred by rule 18.6. If the material is released to any such person, the court should ensure that it will be available to the court at trial.

Arrangements at Trial

B-319 **18D.25** At trial the greatest possible care must be taken to ensure that nothing will compromise the witness' anonymity. Detailed arrangements may have been proposed by the applicant under CrimPR 18.19(1)(b) and directed by the court on determining the application for the order. Such arrangements must take account of the layout of the courtroom and of the means of access for the witness, for the defendant or defendants, and for members of the public. The risk of a chance encounter between the witness and someone who may recognise him or her, either then or subsequently, must be rigorously excluded. Subject to contrary direction by the trial judge, the court staff and those accompanying the witness must adopt necessary measures to ensure that the witness is neither seen nor heard by anyone whose observation would, or might, render nugatory the court's order. Further HMCTS guidance for court staff can be found in Guidance for Criminal Courts for England and Wales for Anonymous/Protected Witnesses.

CPD V Evidence 18E: Use of s.28 Youth Justice and Criminal Evidence Act 1999; pre-recording of cross-examination and re-examination for witnesses captured by s.16 YJCEA 1999 (as inserted by Criminal Practice Directions 2015 (Amendment No. 5), [2017] EWCA Crim 1076, Lord Thomas CJ; and subsequently amended by Criminal Practice Directions 2015 (Amendment No. 11) [2020] EWCA Crim 1347, Lord Burnett CJ)

B-320 **18E1** When section 28 of the Youth Justice and Criminal Evidence Act 1999 (s.28 YJCEA 1999 [§ 8-98 in the main work]) is bought into force by statutory instrument for a particular Crown Court, under that S.I., a witness will be eligible for special measures under s.28 if—

i. he or she is under the age of 18 at the time of the special measures determination; or
ii. he or she suffers from a mental disorder within the meaning of the MHA 1983, or has a significant impairment of intelligence and social functioning, or has a physical disability or a physical disorder, and the quality of his or her evidence is likely to be diminished as a consequence.

18E.2 This process is governed by the Criminal Procedure Rules and careful attention should be paid to the court's case management powers and the obligations on the parties. Advocates should also refer to the annex of [*sic*] this practice direction which contains further detailed guidance on ground rules hearings.

18E.3 The resident judge may appoint a judicial lead from full time judges at the court centre who will be responsible for monitoring and supervision of the scheme. The Plea and Trial Preparation Hearing (PTPH) must be conducted by a full time judge authorised by the resident judge to sit on that class of case and who has been authorised to deal with s.28 YJCEA 1999 cases by the resident judge.

18E.4 Reference should be made to the joint protocol agreed between the police and the Crown Prosecution Service.

18E.5 Witnesses eligible for special measures under s.28 YJCEA 1999 should be identified by the police. The police and Crown Prosecution Service should discuss, with the witness or with the witness' parent or carer, special measures available and the witness' needs, such that the most appropriate package of special measures can be identified. This may include use of a registered intermediary (see Criminal Practice Directions 2015 (CPD) General matters 3D: Vulnerable people in the courts and 3F: Intermediaries).

18E.6 For access to special measures under s.28 YJCEA 1999, the witness' interview must be recorded in accordance with the Achieving Best Evidence ("ABE") guidance which is available on the Ministry of Justice website.

18E.7 For timetabling of the case, it is imperative that the investigators and prosecutor commence the disclosure process at the start of the investigation. The *Judicial Protocol on Disclosure of Unused Material in Criminal Proceedings* (November 2013) must be followed, and if applicable, the *2013 Protocol and Good Practice Model on Disclosure of information in cases of alleged child abuse and linked criminal and care directions.* Local Implementation Teams (LITs) should encourage all appropriate agencies to endorse and follow both the Protocol and the Good Practice Model. LITs should monitor compliance and issues should initially be raised at the LITs.

The First Hearing in the Magistrates' Court

18E.8 Initial details of the prosecution case must be served in accordance with Part 8 of the Rules. **B-321**

18E.9 The prosecutor must formally notify the court at the first hearing that the case is eligible for special measures under s.28 YJCEA 1999.

18E.10 At the hearing the court must follow Part 9 of the Rules (allocation) and refer to the Sentencing Council's guideline on allocation. This practice direction applies only where the defendant indicates a not guilty plea or does not indicate a plea, and the case is sent for trial in the Crown Court, either with or without allocation.

18E.11 If the case is to be sent to the Crown Court, the prosecutor should inform the court and the defence if not already notified that the prosecution will seek special measures including under s.28 YJCEA 1999.

18E.12 In any case that is sent to the Crown Court for trial in which the prosecution has notified the court of its intention to make an application for special measures under s.28 YJCEA 1999 the timetable is that as established by the Better Case Management initiative. The court must be mindful of its duties under Parts 1 and 3 of the Rules to manage the case effectively. Wherever the Crown Prosecution Service will seek a s.28 YJCEA 1999 special measures direction this should, where possible, be listed for PTPH within 28 days of the date of sending from the magistrates' court. Section 10.2 of *A protocol between the Association of Chief Police Officers, the Crown Prosecution Service and Her Majesty's Courts and Tribunals Service to expedite cases involving witnesses under 10 years* does not apply.

18E.13 From the point of grant of the s.28 YJCEA special measures application, timescales provided by section 8.6 of *A protocol between the Association of Chief Police Officers, the Crown Prosecution Service and Her Majesty's Courts and Tribunals Service to expedite cases involving witnesses under 10 years* will cease to apply and the case should be managed in accordance with the timescales established in this practice direction.

Before the PTPH Hearing in the Crown Court

18E.14 On being notified of the sending of the case by the magistrates' court, the case should be flagged as a s.28 case and referred to the resident judge or the judicial lead at that Crown Court, according to instructions issued by the resident judge. **B-322**

18E.15 A transcript of the ABE interview and the application for special measures, including under s.28 YJCEA 1999, must be served on the court and defence at least 7 days prior to the PTPH. The report of any registered intermediary must be served with the application for special measures.

18E.16 Any defence representations about the application for special measures must be served within 14 days of service of the application, and thus within 14 days of the first hearing at the magistrates' court, in accordance with rule 18.13.

Plea and Trial Preparation Hearing

18E.17 The s.28 YJCEA 1999 part of the PTPH form should, on enquiry of the parties, be completed by the judge during the hearing. Orders should be recorded on the form, and uploaded onto the Digital Case System (DCS) as the record of orders made by the court. Any unrepresented defendant should be served with a paper copy of the orders. **B-323**

18E.18 A plea should be taken and recorded and the defence required to identify the issues. The detail of a defence statement is not required at this stage, but the defence should identify the core issues in dispute.

The Application

B-324 **18E.19** The judge may hear submissions from the advocates and will rule on the application. If it is refused (see the assumptions to be applied by the courts in s.21 and s.22 of the YJCEA 1999 [§§ 8-82, 8-84 in the main work]), this practice direction ceases to apply.

18E.20 If the application is granted, the judge should make orders and give directions for preparation for the recorded cross-examination and re-examination hearing and advance preparation for the trial, including for disclosure of unused material. The correct and timely application of the CPIA 1996 will be vital and close attention should be paid to the *2013 Protocol and Good Practice Model on Disclosure* (November 2013), above.

18E.21 The orders made are likely to include:

i. service of the prosecution evidence within 50 days of sending;
ii. directions for service of defence witness requirements;
iii. service of initial disclosure under the CPIA 1996, as soon as reasonably practical; in this context, this should be interpreted as being simultaneous with the service of the prosecution evidence, i.e. within 50 days of sending for both bail and custody cases; this will be within 3 weeks of the PTPH;
iv. orders on disclosure material [*sic*] held by a third party;
v. service of the defence statement; under the CPIA 1996, this must be served within 28 days of the prosecutor serving or purporting to serve initial disclosure;
vi. any editing of the ABE interview;
vii. fixing a date for a ground rules hearing, about one week prior to the recorded cross-examination and re-examination hearing (see CPD General matters 3E: Ground rules hearings to plan questioning of a vulnerable witness or defendant);
viii. service of the Ground Rules Hearing Form by the defence advocate;
ix. making arrangements for the witness to refresh his or her memory by viewing the recorded examination-in-chief ("ABE interview") (see CPD Evidence 18C: Visually recorded interviews: memory refreshing and watching at a different time from the jury);
x. making arrangements for the recorded cross-examination and re-examination hearing under s.28, including fixing a date, time and location;
xi. other special measures;
xii. directions for any further directions hearing whether at the conclusion of the recorded cross-examination and re-examination hearing or subsequently;
xiii. fixing a date for trial.

18E.22 The timetable should ensure the prosecution evidence and initial disclosure are served swiftly. The ground rules hearing will usually be soon after the deadline for service of the defence statement, the recorded cross-examination and re-examination hearing about one week later. However, there must be time afforded for any further disclosure of unused material following service of the defence statement and for determination of any application under s.8 of the CPIA 1996 [§ 12-76 in the main work]. Subject to judicial discretion applications for extensions of time for service of disclosure by either party should generally be refused.

18E.23 Where the defendant may be unfit to plead, a timetable for s.28 should usually still be set, taking into account extra time needed for the obtaining of medical reports, save in cases where it is indicated that it is unlikely that there would be a trial if the defendant is found fit.

18E.24 As far as possible, without diminishing the defendant's right to a fair trial, the timing and duration of the recorded cross-examination should take into account the needs of the witness. For a young child, the hearing should usually be in the morning and conclude before lunch time.

18E.25 An application for a witness summons to obtain material held by a third party, should be served in advance of the PTPH and determined at that hearing, or as soon as reasonably practicable thereafter. The timetable should accommodate any consequent hearings or applications, but it is imperative parties are prompt to obtain third party disclosure material. The prosecution must make the court and the defence aware of any difficulty as soon as it arises. As noted above, the *2013 Protocol and Good Practice Model on Disclosure of information in cases of alleged child abuse and linked criminal and care directions hearings* should be followed, if applicable. Engagement with the protocol is to be overseen by LITs. A single point of contact in each relevant agency can facilitate speedy disclosure.

18E.26 The needs of other witnesses should not be neglected. Witness and intermediary availability dates should be available for the PTPH.

Pior to Ground Rules and Hearing Under Section 28

B-325 **18E.27** It is imperative parties abide by orders made at the PTPH, including the completion and service of the Ground Rules Hearing Form by the defence advocate. Delays or failures must be reported to the judge as soon as they arise; this is the responsibility of each legal representative. If ordered, the lead lawyer for the prosecution and defence must provide a weekly update to the court case progression officer, copied to the judge and parties, detailing the progress and any difficulties or delays in complying with orders. The court may order a further case management hearing if necessary.

18E.28 Any applications under s.100 of the CJA 2003 (non-defendant's bad character [§ 13-19 in the main work]) or under s.41 of the YJCEA 1999 (evidence or cross-examination about complainant's sexual behaviour [§ 8-285 in the main work]) or any other application which may affect the cross-examination must be made promptly, and responses submitted in time for the judge to rule on the application at the ground rules hearing. Parts 21 and 22 of the Rules apply to applications under s.100 and s.41 respectively.

18E.29 The witness' court familiarisation visit must take place, including an opportunity to practise on the live link/recording facilities, see the Code of Practice for Victims of Crime, October 2013, Chap. 3, para. 1.22. The witness must have the opportunity to view his or her ABE interview to refresh his or her memory. It may or may not be appropriate for this to take place on the day of the court visit: CPD Evidence 18C must be followed.

18E.30 When the court has deemed that the case is suitable for the witness to give evidence from a remote site then a familiarisation visit should take place at that site. At the ground rules hearing the judge and advocates should consider appropriate arrangements for them to talk to the witness before the cross examination hearing.

18E.31 Applications to vary or discharge a special measures declaration must comply with Rule 18.11. Although the need for prompt action will make case preparation tight.

Ground Rules Hearing

18E.32 Advocates should master the toolkits available through the Advocate's Gateway. These provide guidance on questioning a vulnerable witness (see CPD General matters 3D and the annex to this practice direction). **B-326**

18E.33 Any appointed registered intermediary must attend the ground rules hearing (see CPD General matters 3E.2).

18E.34 The defence advocate at the ground rules hearing must be she or he who will conduct the recorded cross-examination. See listing and allocation below on continuity of counsel and release from other cases.

18E.35 Topics for discussion and agreement at the ground rules hearing will depend on the individual needs of the witness, and an intermediary may provide advance indications. CPD General matters 3E must be followed. Topics that will need discussion in every case will include:

i. the overall length of cross-examination;
ii. cross-examination by a single advocate in a multi-handed case;
iii. any restrictions on the advocate's usual duty to "put the defence case".

18E.36 It may be helpful to discuss at this stage how any limitations on questioning will be explained to the jury.

18E.37 At the ground rules hearing, the judge should:

i. rule on any application under s.100 of the CJA 2003 or s.41 of the YJCEA 1999, or other applications that may affect the cross-examination;
ii. decide how the witness may view exhibits or documents;
iii. review progress in complying with orders made at the preliminary hearing and make any necessary orders.

Recording of Cross-examination and Re-examination: Hearing Under s.28

18E.38 At the hearing, the witness will be cross-examined and re-examined, if required, via the live link from the court room to the witness suite (unless provision has been made for the use of a remote link) and the examination will be recorded. It is the responsibility of the designated court clerk to ensure in advance that all of the equipment is working and to contact the provider's Service Desk if support is required. Any other special measures must be in place and any intermediary or supporter should sit in the live link room with the witness. The intermediary's role is transparent and therefore must be visible and audible to the judge and advocates at the cross-examination and in the subsequent replaying. **B-327**

18E.39 The judge, advocates and parties, including the defendant will usually assemble in the court room for the hearing. In some cases the judge and advocates may be in the witness suite with the witness, for example when questioning a very young child or where the witness has a particular communication need. The court will decide this on a case-by-case basis. The defendant should be able to communicate with his or her representatives and should be able to hear the witness via the live link and see the proceedings: s.28(2). Whether the witness is screened or not will depend on the other special measures ordered, for example screens may have been ordered under s.23 YJCEA 1999.

18E.40 On the admission of the public or media to the hearing, please see below.

18E.41 At the conclusion of the hearing, the judge will issue further orders, such as for the editing of the recorded cross-examination and may set a timetable for progress.

18E.42 Under s.28(4) YJCEA 1999, the judge, on application of any parties or on the court's own motion may direct that the recorded examination is not admitted into evidence, despite any previous direction. Such direction must be given promptly, preferably immediately after the conclusion of the examination

18E.43 Without exception, editing of the ABE interview/examination-in-chief or recorded cross-examination is precluded without an order of the court.

18E.44 The ability to record simultaneously from a court and a witness room and to play back the recording at trial will be provided in all Crown Courts [*sic*] as an additional facility within the existing Justice Video Service (JVS). Courts will book recording slots with the service desk who will launch the recording at the scheduled time when the court is ready. Recordings will be stored in a secure data centre with backup and resiliency, for authorised access.

After the Recording

B-328 **18E.45** Following the recording the judge should review compliance with orders and progress towards preparation for trial, make any further orders necessary and confirm the date of the trial. Any further orders made by the judge should be recorded and uploaded onto the relevant section of the DCS.

18E.46 If the defendant enters a guilty plea, the judge should proceed towards sentence, making any appropriate orders, such as for a Pre-Sentence Report and setting a date for sentencing. Any reduction for a guilty plea shall reflect the day of the recorded cross-examination as the first day of trial; the Sentencing Council guideline on guilty plea reductions should be applied.

Preparation for Trial

B-329 **18E.47** Parties must notify the court promptly if any difficulties arise or any orders are not complied with. The court may order a further case management hearing (FCMH).

18E.48 In accordance with orders, either after recorded cross-examination or at the FCMH, necessary editing of the ABE interview/examination-in-chief and/or the recorded cross-examination must be done only on the order of the court. Any editing must be done promptly.

18E.49 Recorded cross-examinations and re-examinations will be stored securely by the service provider so as to be accessible to the advocates and the court. It will not usually be necessary to obtain a transcript of the recorded cross-examination, but if it is difficult to comprehend, a transcript should be obtained and served. The ground rules hearing form outlines questions to the witness that might be completed electronically by the judge during cross-examination forming a contemporaneous note of the hearing, served on the parties as an agreed record.

18E.50 Editing, authorised by the judge, is to be submitted by the court to the service desk, who produce an edited copy. The master and all edited copy versions are retained in the secure data centre from where they can be accessed. Courts book playback timeslots with the service desk for the trial date. The court may authorise parties to view playback at JVS endpoints, by submitting a request form to the service desk. Access for those so authorised is via the Quickcode (recording ID) and a security PIN (password) on the courtroom touch panel or remote control.

18E.51 No further cross-examination or re-examination of the witness may take place unless the criteria in section 28(6) are satisfied and the judge makes a further special measures direction under section 28(5). Any such further examination must be recorded via live link as described above.

18E.52 Section 28(6) of the YJCEA 1999 provides as follows:

"(6) The court may only give such a further direction if it appears to the court—
(a) that the proposed cross-examination is sought by a party to the proceedings as a result of that party having become aware, since the time when the original recording was made in pursuance of subsection (1), of a matter which that party could not with reasonable diligence have ascertained by then, or
(b) that for any other reason it is in the interests of justice to give the further direction.".

18E.53 Any application under section 28(5) must be in writing and be served on the court and the prosecution at least 28 days before the date of trial. The application must specify:

i. the topics on which further cross-examination is sought;

ii. the material or matter of which the defence has become aware since the original recording;
iii. why it was not possible for the defence to have obtained the material or ascertained the matter earlier; and
iv. the expected impact on the issues before the court at trial.

18E.54 The prosecution should respond in writing within 7 days of the application. The judge may determine the application on the papers or order a hearing. Any further cross-examination ordered must be recorded via live link in advance of the trial and served on the court and the parties.

Trial

18E.55 In accordance with the judge's directions, the ABE interview/examination-in-chief and the recorded cross-examination and re-examination, edited as directed, should be played to the jury at the appropriate point within the trial. **B-330**

18E.56 The jury should not usually receive transcripts of the recordings, and if they do these should be removed from the jury as soon as the recording has been played (see CPD Trial 26L.2).

18E.57 If the matter was not addressed at the ground rules hearing, the judge should discuss with the advocates how any limitations on questioning should be explained to the jury before summing-up.

After Conclusion of Trial

18E.58 Immediately after the trial, the ABE interview/examination-in-chief and the recorded cross-examination and re-examination should be stored securely on the cloud. **B-331**

Listing and Allocation

18E.59 Advocates: it is the responsibility of the defence advocate, on accepting the brief, to ensure that he or she is available for both the ground rules hearing and the hearing under section 28; continuity at trial is obligatory except in exceptional circumstances. The judge and list office will make whatever reasonable arrangements are possible to achieve this, assisted by the resident judge where necessary. **B-332**

18E.60 When the timetable for the case is being set, advocates must have their up to date availability with them (in so far as is possible). When an advocate who is part-heard in another trial at a different Crown Court centre finds themselves in difficulties in attending either the ground rules hearing, s.28 hearing itself or the trial where s.28 has been utilised, they must inform the resident judges of both courts as soon as practicable. The resident judges must resolve any conflict with the advocate's availability. The starting point should be that the case involving s.28 hearing takes priority. However, due consideration should also be given to custody time limits, other issues which make either case particularly complex or sensitive, high profile cases and anything else that the judges should take into consideration in the interests of justice.

18E.61 Judicial: all PTPHs must be listed before judges who have been authorised to deal with s.28 cases by the resident judge at the relevant court centre. The nominated lead judge (if there is one) or resident judge may allocate individual cases to one of the judges in the court centre identified to deal with the case if necessary. The resident judge, lead judge or allocated judge may make directions in the case if required.

18E.62 It is essential that the ground rules hearing and the s.28 YJCEA 1999 hearing are before the same judge. Once the s.28 hearing has taken place, any judge, in accordance with CPD XIII Listing E, including recorders, can deal with the trial.

18E.63 LITs should be established with all relevant agencies represented by someone of sufficient seniority. Their task will be to monitor the operation of the scheme and compliance with this practice direction and other relevant protocols.

18E.64 Listing: due to the limited availability of recording facilities, the hearing held under section 28 must take precedence over other hearings. Section 28 hearings should be listed as the first matter in the morning and will usually conclude before lunch time. Ground rules hearings may be held at any time, including towards the end of the court day, to accommodate the advocates and intermediary (if there is one) and to minimise disruption to other trials.

Public, Including Media Access, and Reporting Restrictions

18E.65 Open justice is an essential principle of the common law. However, certain automatic statutory restrictions may apply, and the judge may consider it appropriate in the specific circumstances of a case to make an order applying discretionary restrictions. CPD Preliminary proceedings 16B must be followed and the templates published by the Judicial College (available on **B-333**

LMS) should be used. The parties to the proceedings, and interested parties such as the media, should have the opportunity to make representations before an order is made.

18E.66 The statutory powers most likely to be available to the judge are listed below. The judge should consider the specific statutory requirements necessary for the making of the particular order carefully, and the order made must be in writing.

a) *Provisions to exclude the public from hearings:*
   i. section 37 of the CYPA 1933 [§ 4-11 in the main work], applicable to witnesses under 18;
   ii. section 25 of the YJCEA 1999 [ibid., § 8-89], applicable to the evidence of a child or vulnerable adult in sexual offences cases.

b) *Automatic reporting restrictions:*
   i. section 1 of the Sexual Offences (Amendment) Act 1992 [ibid., § 20-19], applicable to the complainant in any sex offence case.

c) *Discretionary reporting restrictions:*
   i. section 45 of the YJCEA 1999 [ibid., § 4-27], applicable to under 18s concerned in criminal proceedings;
   ii. section 46 of the YJCEA 1999 [ibid., § 4-33], applicable to an adult witness whose evidence would be diminished by fear or distress.

d) *Postponement of fair and accurate reports*
   under section 4(2) of the Contempt of Court Act 1981 [ibid., § 28-65].

18E.67 Note that public access to information held by the court is now the subject of rule 5.8 and CPD General matters 5B that must be followed.

Annex for Section 28 Ground Rules Hearings at the Crown Court when Dealing with Witnesses Under s.16 YJCEA 1999

Introduction

B-334 **1.** This annex is designed to assist all advocates in their preparation for cross-examination of vulnerable witnesses.

2. Adherence to the principles below will avoid interruption during the pre-recorded cross-examination and reduce any ordered editing.

3. Issues concerning the vulnerable witness and the nature of the cross-examination will be addressed by the judge at the Ground Rules Hearing (GRH).

4. In appropriate cases and in particular where the witness is of very young years or suffers from a disability or disorder it is expected that the advocate will have prepared his or her cross-examination in writing for consideration by the court.

5. It is thus incumbent on the defence to ensure that full instructions have been taken prior to the GRH.

Required preparation prior to the GRH

B-335 **6.** All advocates should be familiar with the relevant toolkits, available through the Advocates' Gateway *www.theadvocatesgateway.org/toolkits* which provide guidance on questioning a vulnerable witness. A synopsis of this guidance, which advocates should have read prior to any GRH, is included in this annex.

Attendance at, and procedure during, the GRH

B-336 **7.** In preparation for trial, courts must take every reasonable step to facilitate the participation of witnesses and defendants (CPR 3.8(4)(d)). The court should order that the defendant attends the GRH.

8. The defence advocate must complete and submit the Ground Rules Hearing form by the time and date ordered at the PTPH.

9. The hearing facilitates the judge's duty to control questioning if and when necessary.

10. The hearing enables the court to ensure its process is adapted to enable the witness to give his or her best evidence whilst ensuring the defendant's right to a fair trial is not diminished. Accordingly the ground rules and the nature of the questioning of the witness by the advocate (and limitations imposed if necessary in accordance with principles above) will be discussed.

11. Prior to the hearing it is necessary for both advocates and the judge to have viewed the ABE evidence.

12. The judge will state what ground rules will apply. The advocates must comply with them.

13. Any intermediary must attend the GRH. It is the responsibility of those instructing the intermediary to ensure this.

14. The defendant's advocate attending the hearing must be the same advocate who will be conducting the recorded cross-examination (and the subsequent trial, if any).

15. Any intermediary for the witness should only be warned for the GRH and the section 28 hearing they are assisting with. An intermediary should not be instructed unless available to attend the GRH and the section 28 hearings ordered by the court.

16. Topics for discussion and agreement at the GRH will depend on the individual needs of the witness. CPD I General Matters 3E must be followed.

17. Topics of discussion at the hearing will include the length of cross-examination and any restrictions on the advocate's usual duty to "put the defence case". As was made plain by the Vice President of the Court of Appeal Criminal Division in *Lubemba*; *P. (J.)* [2015] 1 Cr. App. R. 12, advocates cannot insist upon any supposed right "to put one's case" or previous inconsistent statements to a vulnerable witness. If there is a right to "put one's case" it must be modified for young or vulnerable witnesses. It is perfectly possible to ensure the jury are made aware of the defence case and of significant inconsistencies without intimidation or distressing a witness. It is expected that all advocates will be familiar with and have read this case.

18. At the GRH counsel need to agree with the judge how and when the matters referred to in paragraph 11 will be explained to the jury. This explanation will normally be done by the judge, but may exceptionally, and only with the permission of the judge, be explained by counsel. If there is no agreement the judge will rule on it.

19. A section 28 Defence GRH form should be completed as far as possible prior to attendance at the GRH before the judge.

20. Rulings will be made on any application under section 100 of the CJA 2003 or section 41 of the YJCEA 1999, and on any other application that may affect the conduct of the cross examination. Any ruling will be included in the trial practice note.

21. A review will take place of the progress made by the parties in complying with the orders made at the PTPH and the court will make any other necessary orders.

22. Additional information can be found in the Inns of Court College of Advocacy training document "Advocacy and the vulnerable: 20 principles of questioning" at the following link:
www.icca.ac.uk/images/download/advocacy-and-the-vulnerable/20-principles-of-questioning.pdf

This document is part of a suite of training materials available to assist advocates in dealing with questioning vulnerable victims in the criminal justice system.

Court of Appeal guidance

In a series of decisions the Court of Appeal has made it clear that there has to be a different and fresh approach to the cross-examination of, in particular, children of tender years, and witnesses who are vulnerable as a result of mental incapacity. The following propositions have support in decisions on appeal (*B.* [2010] EWCA Crim 4); *F. (J.R.)* [2013] EWCA Crim 424; *Wills (Practice Note)* [2011] EWCA Crim 1938; *E.* [2011] EWCA Crim 3028; *Watts* [2010] EWCA Crim. 1824; *W. and M.*, [2010] EWCA Crim. 1926); **B-337**

> "The reality of questioning children of tender years is that direct challenge that he or she is wrong or lying could lead to confusion and, worse, to capitulation which the child does not, in reality, accept.
>
> Capitulation is not a consequence of unreliability but a function of the youngster's age. Experience has shown that young children are scared of disagreeing with a mature adult whom they do not wish to confront
>
> It is common, in the trial of an adult, to hear, once the nursery slopes of cross-examination have been skied, the assertion 'You were never punched or kicked, as you have suggested, were you?'
>
> It was precisely that approach which the court is anxious to avoid. Such an approach risks confusion in the minds of the witness whose evidence was bound to take centre stage, and it is difficult to see how it can be helpful. We struggle to understand how the defendant's right to a fair trial was in any way compromised simply because Mr X was not allowed to ask the question 'Simon did not punch you in the way you suggest?'"
>
> "The overriding objective. The Criminal Procedure Rules objective is that criminal cases be dealt with justly. Dealing with a criminal case justly includes dealing with the case efficiently and expeditiously in ways that take account of the gravity of the offence alleged and the complexity of what is in issue.
>
> In our collective experience the age of a witness is not determinative of his or her ability to give truthful and accurate evidence. Like adults some children will provide truthful and accurate testimony, and some will not. However children are not miniature adults, but children, and to be treated for what they are, not what they will, in the years ahead, grow to be.
>
> There is undoubtedly a danger of a child witness wishing simply to please

There is undoubtedly a danger of a child witness assenting to what is put rather than disagreeing during the questioning process in an endeavour to bring that process to a speedier conclusion.

It is particularly important in the case of a child witness to keep a question short and simple, and even more important than it is with an adult witness to avoid questions which are rolled up and contain, inadvertently two or three questions at once. It is generally recognised that, particularly with child witnesses, short and untagged questions are best at eliciting the evidence. By untagged we mean questions that do not contain a statement of the answer which is sought. That said, when it comes to directly contradicting a particular statement and inviting the witness to face a directly contradictory suggestion, it may often be difficult to examine otherwise.

No doubt if a way can be found of engaging the witness to tell the story, and the content then differs from what had been said before, that will be a yet better indication that the original account is wrong. But that is difficult to achieve and indeed may itself have the disadvantage of prolonging the child's time giving evidence. Even then there may be no guarantee as to which account is the more reliable.

Most of the questions which produced the answers which were chiefly relied upon, unlike many others, constituted the putting of direct suggestions with an indication of the answer 'this happened didn't it?' Or 'this didn't happen, did it?' The consequence of that is that it can be very difficult to tell whether the child is truly changing her account or simply taking the line of least resistance.

At the same time the right of the defendant to a fair trial must be undiminished. When the issue is whether the child is lying or mistaken, when claiming that the defendant behaved indecently towards him or her, it should not be over problematic for the advocate to formulate short, simple questions, which put the essential elements of the defendant's case to the witness, and fully ventilate before the jury the areas of evidence which bear on the child's credibility.

Aspects of evidence which undermine or are believed to undermine the child's credibility must, of course, be revealed to the jury. However it is not necessarily appropriate for them to form the subject matter of detailed cross-examination of the child, and the advocate may have to forego much of the kind of contemporary cross-examination which consists of no more than comment on matters which will be before the jury, in any event, from different sources.

Notwithstanding some of the difficulties; when all is said and done, the witness whose cross-examination is in contemplation is a child, sometimes very young, and it should not take very lengthy cross examination to demonstrate, when it is the case, that the child may indeed be fabricating, or fantasising, or imagining, or reciting a well-rehearsed untruthful script, learned by rote; or simply just suggestible, or contaminated by or in collusion with others to make false allegations, or making assertions in language which is beyond his or her level of comprehension; and are therefore likely to be derived from another source. Comment on the evidence, including comment on evidence which may bear adversely on the credibility of the child, should be addressed after the child has finished giving evidence.

Clear limitations have to be imposed on the cross-examination of vulnerable young complainants."

Criminal Procedure Rules 2020 (SI 2020/759), Pt 19

Expert Evidence

When this Part applies

B-338 **19.1**—(1) This Part applies where a party wants to introduce expert opinion evidence.

(2) A reference to an "expert" in this part is a reference to a person who is required to give or prepare expert evidence for the purpose of criminal proceedings, including evidence required to determine fitness to plead or for the purpose of sentencing.

Expert's duty to the court

B-339 **19.2.**—(1) An expert must help the court to achieve the overriding objective—

(a) by giving opinion which is—

(i) objective and unbiased, and

(ii) within the expert's area or areas of expertise; and

(b) by actively assisting the court in fulfilling its duty of case management under rule 3.2, in

particular by–
(i) complying with directions made by the court, and
(ii) at once informing the court of any significant failure (by the expert or another) to take any step required by such a direction.

(2) This duty overrides any obligation to the person from whom the expert receives instructions or by whom the expert is paid.

(3) This duty includes obligations–
(a) to define the expert's area or areas of expertise–
(i) in the expert's report, and
(ii) when giving evidence in person;
(b) when giving evidence in person, to draw the court's attention to any question to which the answer would be outside the expert's area or areas of expertise;
(c) to inform all parties and the court if the expert's opinion changes from that contained in a report served as evidence or given in a statement; and
(d) to disclose to the party for whom the expert's evidence is commissioned anything–
(i) of which the expert is aware, and
(ii) of which that party, if aware of it, would be required to give notice under rule 19.3(3)(c).

Introduction of expert evidence

19.3.–(1) A party who wants another party to admit as fact a summary of an expert's conclusions must serve that summary– **B-340**
(a) on the court officer and on each party from whom that admission is sought; and
(b) as soon as practicable after the defendant whom it affects pleads not guilty.

(2) A party on whom such a summary is served must–
(a) serve a response stating–
(i) which, if any, of the expert's conclusions are admitted as fact, and
(ii) where a conclusion is not admitted, what are the disputed issues concerning that conclusion; and
(b) serve the response–
(i) on the court officer and on the party who served the summary, and
(ii) as soon as practicable, and in any event not more than 10 business days after service of the summary.

(3) A party who wants to introduce expert evidence otherwise than as admitted fact must–
(a) serve a report by the expert which complies with rule 19.4 on–
(i) the court officer, and
(ii) each other party;
(b) serve the report as soon as practicable, and in any event with any application in support of which that party relies on that evidence;
(c) serve with the report notice of anything of which the party serving it is aware which might reasonably be thought capable of–
(i) undermining the reliability of the expert's opinion, or
(ii) detracting from the credibility or impartiality of the expert; and
(d) if another party so requires, give that party a copy of, or a reasonable opportunity to inspect–
(i) a record of any examination, measurement, test or experiment on which the expert's findings and opinion are based, or that were carried out in the course of reaching those findings and opinion, and
(ii) anything on which any such examination, measurement, test or experiment was carried out.

(4) Unless the parties otherwise agree or the court directs, a party may not–
(a) introduce expert evidence if that party has not complied with paragraph (3); or
(b) introduce in evidence an expert report if the expert does not give evidence in person.

Content of expert's report

19.4. Where rule 19.3(3) applies, an expert's report must– **B-341**
(a) give details of the expert's qualifications, relevant experience and accreditation;
(b) give details of any literature or other information which the expert has relied on in making the report;

(c) contain a statement setting out the substance of all facts given to the expert which are material to the opinions expressed in the report, or upon which those opinions are based;
(d) make clear which of the facts stated in the report are within the expert's own knowledge;
(e) where the expert has based an opinion or inference on a representation of fact or opinion made by another person for the purposes of criminal proceedings (for example, as to the outcome of an examination, measurement, test or experiment)—
(i) identify the person who made that representation to the expert,
(ii) give the qualifications, relevant experience and any accreditation of that person, and
(iii) certify that that person had personal knowledge of the matters stated in that representation;
(f) where there is a range of opinion on the matters dealt with in the report—
(i) summarise the range of opinion, and
(ii) give reasons for the expert's own opinion;
(g) if the expert is not able to give an opinion without qualification, state the qualification;
(h) include such information as the court may need to decide whether the expert's opinion is sufficiently reliable to be admissible as evidence;
(i) contain a summary of the conclusions reached;
(j) contain a statement that the expert understands an expert's duty to the court, and has complied and will continue to comply with that duty; and
(k) contain the same declaration of truth as a witness statement.

Expert to be informed of service of report

B-342 **19.5.** A party who serves on another party or on the court a report by an expert must, at once, inform that expert of that fact.

Pre-hearing discussion of expert evidence

B-343 **19.6.**—(1) This rule applies where more than one party wants to introduce expert evidence.

(2) The court may direct the experts to—
(a) discuss the expert issues in the proceedings; and
(b) prepare a statement for the court of the matters on which they agree and disagree, giving their reasons.

(3) Except for that statement, the content of that discussion must not be referred to without the court's permission.

(4) A party may not introduce expert evidence without the court's permission if the expert has not complied with a direction under this rule.

Court's power to direct that evidence is to be given by a single joint expert

B-344 **19.7.**—(1) Where more than one defendant wants to introduce expert evidence on an issue at trial, the court may direct that the evidence on that issue is to be given by one expert only.

(2) Where the co-defendants cannot agree who should be the expert, the court may—
(a) select the expert from a list prepared or identified by them; or
(b) direct that the expert be selected in another way.

Instructions to a single joint expert

B-345 **19.8.**—(1) Where the court gives a direction under rule 19.7 for a single joint expert to be used, each of the co-defendants may give instructions to the expert.

(2) A co-defendant who gives instructions to the expert must, at the same time, send a copy of the instructions to each other co-defendant.

(3) The court may give directions about—
(a) the payment of the expert's fees and expenses; and
(b) any examination, measurement, test or experiment which the expert wishes to carry out.

(4) The court may, before an expert is instructed, limit the amount that can be paid by way of fees and expenses to the expert.

(5) Unless the court otherwise directs, the instructing co-defendants are jointly and severally liable for the payment of the expert's fees and expenses.

Application to withhold information from another party

B-346 **19.9.**—(1) This rule applies where—
(a) a party introduces expert evidence under rule 19.3(3);
(b) the evidence omits information which it otherwise might include because the party introducing it thinks that that information ought not be revealed to another party; and

(c) the party introducing the evidence wants the court to decide whether it would be in the public interest to withhold that information.

(2) The party who wants to introduce the evidence must–

(a) apply for such a decision; and

(b) serve the application on–

(i) the court officer, and

(ii) the other party, but only to the extent that serving it would not reveal what the applicant thinks ought to be withheld.

(3) The application must–

(a) identify the information;

(b) explain why the applicant thinks that it would be in the public interest to withhold it; and

(c) omit from the part of the application that is served on the other party anything that would reveal what the applicant thinks ought to be withheld.

(4) Where the applicant serves only part of the application on the other party, the applicant must–

(a) mark the other part, to show that it is only for the court; and

(b) in that other part, explain why the applicant has withheld it from the other party.

(5) The court may–

(a) direct the applicant to serve on the other party any part of the application which has been withheld; and

(b) determine the application at a hearing or without a hearing.

(6) Any hearing of an application to which this rule applies–

(a) must be in private, unless the court otherwise directs; and

(b) if the court so directs, may be, wholly or in part, in the absence of the party from whom information has been withheld.

(7) At any hearing of an application to which this rule applies–

(a) the general rule is that the court must consider, in the following sequence–

(i) representations first by the applicant and then by the other party, in both parties' presence, and then

(ii) further representations by the applicant, in the absence of the party from whom information has been withheld; but

(b) the court may direct other arrangements for the hearing.

Court's power to vary requirements under this Part

19.10–(1) The court may extend (even after it has expired) a time limit under this Part. **B-347**

(2) A party who wants an extension of time must–

(a) apply when serving the report, summary or notice for which it is required; and

(b) explain the delay.

CPD V Evidence 19A: Expert evidence (as amended by Criminal Practice Directions 2015 (Amendment No. 8) [2019] EWCA Crim 495, Lord Burnett CJ)

19A.1 Expert opinion evidence is admissible in criminal proceedings at common law if, in summary, (i) it is relevant to a matter in issue in the proceedings; (ii) it is needed to provide the court with information likely to be outside the court's own knowledge and experience; and (iii) the witness is competent to give that opinion. **B-348**

19A.2 [*Summarises the CJA 1988, s.30 [§ 10-35 in the main work], and the Criminal Procedure Rules 2015, Pt 19.*]

19A.3 [*Refers to the non-implementation of a Law Commission proposal for the enactment of a statutory test for admissibility.*] The common law, therefore, remains the source of the criteria by reference to which the court must assess the admissibility and weight of such evidence; and rule 19.4 ... lists those matters with which an expert's report must deal, so that the court can conduct an adequate such assessment.

19A.4 In ... [*Dlugosz; Pickering; S. (M.D.)* [2013] 1 Cr. App. R. 32], the Court of Appeal observed (at [11]): "It is essential to recall the principle which is applicable, namely in determining the issue of admissibility, the court must be satisfied that there is a sufficiently reliable scientific basis for the evidence to be admitted. If there is then the court leaves the opposing views to be tested before the jury." Nothing at common law precludes assessment by the court of the reliability of anexpert opinion by reference to substantially similar factors to those the Law Commission recommended as conditions of admissibility, and courts are encouraged actively to enquire into such factors.

19A.5 Therefore factors which the court may take into account in determining the reliability of expert opinion, and especially of expert scientific opinion, include:

(a) the extent and quality of the data on which the expert's opinion is based, and the validity of the methods by which they were obtained;

(b) if the expert's opinion relies on an inference from any findings, whether the opinion properly explains how safe or unsafe the inference is (whether by reference to statistical significance or in other appropriate terms);

(c) if the expert's opinion relies on the results of the use of any method (for instance, a test, measurement or survey), whether the opinion takes proper account of matters, such as the degree of precision or margin of uncertainty, affecting the accuracy or reliability of those results;

(d) the extent to which any material upon which the expert's opinion is based has been reviewed by others with relevant expertise (for instance, in peer-reviewed publications), and the views of those others on that material;

(e) the extent to which the expert's opinion is based on material falling outside the expert's own field of expertise;

(f) the completeness of the information which was available to the expert, and whether the expert took account of all relevant information in arriving at the opinion (including information as to the context of any facts to which the opinion relates);

(g) if there is a range of expert opinion on the matter in question, where in the range the expert's own opinion lies and whether the expert's preference has been properly explained; and

(h) whether the expert's methods followed established practice in the field and, if they did not, whether the reason for the divergence has been properly explained.

19A.6 In addition, in considering reliability, and especially the reliability of expert scientific opinion, the court should be astute to identify potential flaws in such opinion which detract from its reliability, such as:

(a) being based on a hypothesis which has not been subjected to sufficient scrutiny (including, where appropriate, experimental or other testing), or which has failed to stand up to scrutiny;

(b) being based on an unjustifiable assumption;

(c) being based on flawed data;

(d) relying on an examination, technique, method or process which was not properly carried out or applied, or was not appropriate for use in the particular case; or

(e) relying on an inference or conclusion which has not been properly reached.

19A.7 To assist in the assessment described above, CrimPR 19.3(3)(c) requires a party who introduces expert evidence to give notice of anything of which that party is aware which might reasonably be thought capable of undermining the reliability of the expert's opinion, or detracting from the credibility or impartiality of the expert; and CrimPR 19.2(3)(d) requires the expert to disclose to that party any such matter of which the expert is aware. Examples of matters that should be disclosed pursuant to those rules include (this is not a comprehensive list), both in relation to the expert and in relation to any corporation or other body with which the expert works, as an employee or in any other capacity:

(a) any fee arrangement under which the amount or payment of the expert's fees is in any way dependent on the outcome of the case (see also the declaration required by paragraph 19B.1 of these directions);

(b) any conflict of interest of any kind, other than a potential conflict disclosed in the expert's report (see also the declaration required by paragraph 19B.1 of these directions);

(c) adverse judicial comment;

(d) any case in which an appeal has been allowed by reason of a deficiency in the expert's evidence;

(e) any adverse finding, disciplinary proceedings or other criticism by a professional, regulatory or registration body or authority, including the Forensic Science Regulator;

(f) any such adverse finding or disciplinary proceedings against, or other such criticism of, others associated with the corporation or other body with which the expert works which calls into question the quality of that corporation's or body's work generally;

(g) conviction of a criminal offence in circumstances that suggest:

  (i) a lack of respect for, or understanding of, the interests of the criminal justice system (for example, perjury; acts perverting or tending to pervert the course of public justice),

  (ii) dishonesty (for example, theft or fraud), or

  (iii) a lack of personal integrity (for example, corruption or a sexual offence);

(h) lack of an accreditation or other commitment to prescribed standards where that might be expected;
(i) a history of failure or poor performance in quality or proficiency assessments;
(j) a history of lax or inadequate scientific methods;
(k) a history of failure to observe recognised standards in the expert's area of expertise;
(l) a history of failure to adhere to the standards expected of an expert witness in the criminal justice system.

19A.8 In a case in which an expert, or a corporation or body with which the expert works, has been criticised without a full investigation, for example by adverse comment in the course of a judgment, it would be reasonable to expect those criticised to supply information about the conduct and conclusions of any independent investigation into the incident, and to explain what steps, if any, have been taken to address the criticism.

19A.9 The rules require disclosure of that of which the expert, or the party who introduces the expert evidence, is aware. The rules do not require persistent or disproportionate enquiry, and courts will recognise that there may be occasions on which neither the expert nor the party has been made aware of criticism. Nevertheless, where matters ostensibly within the scope of the disclosure obligations come to the attention of the court without their disclosure by the party who introduces the evidence then that party, and the expert, should expect a searching examination of the circumstances by the court; and, subject to what emerges, the court may exercise its power under section 81 of the Police and Criminal Evidence Act 1984 or section 20 of the Criminal Procedure and Investigations Act 1996 to exclude the expert evidence.

CPD V Evidence 19B: Statements of understanding and declarations of truth in expert reports (as inserted by Criminal Practice Directions 2015 (Amendment No. 2), unreported, 16 November 2016, Lord Thomas CJ, and as amended by Criminal Practice Directions 2015 (Amendment No. 4), unreported, 28 March 2017, Lord Thomas CJ)

19B.1 The statement and declaration required by CrimPR 19.4(j), (k) should be in the following terms, or in terms substantially the same as these: **B-349**

"I (name) DECLARE THAT:

1. I understand that my duty is to help the court to achieve the overriding objective by giving independent assistance by way of objective, unbiased opinion on matters within my expertise, both in preparing reports and giving oral evidence. I understand that this duty overrides any obligation to the party by whom I am engaged or the person who has paid or is liable to pay me. I confirm that I have complied with and will continue to comply with that duty.
2. I confirm that I have not entered into any arrangement where the amount or payment of my fees is in any way dependent on the outcome of the case.
3. I know of no conflict of interest of any kind, other than any which I have disclosed in my report.
4. I do not consider that any interest which I have disclosed affects my suitability as an expert witness on any issues on which I have given evidence.
5. I will advise the party by whom I am instructed if, between the date of my report and the trial, there is any change in circumstances which affect my answers to points 3 and 4 above.
6. I have shown the sources of all information I have used.
7. I have exercised reasonable care and skill in order to be accurate and complete in preparing this report.
8. I have endeavoured to include in my report those matters, of which I have knowledge or of which I have been made aware, that might adversely affect the validity of my opinion. I have clearly stated any qualifications to my opinion.
9. I have not, without forming an independent view, included or excluded anything which has been suggested to me by others including my instructing lawyers.
10. I will notify those instructing me immediately and confirm in writing if for any reason my existing report requires any correction or qualification.
11. I understand that:
    (a) my report will form the evidence to be given under oath or affirmation;
    (b) the court may at any stage direct a discussion to take place between experts;
    (c) the court may direct that, following a discussion between the experts, a statement should be prepared showing those issues which are agreed and those issues which are not agreed, together with the reasons;

(d) I may be required to attend court to be cross-examined on my report by a cross-examiner assisted by an expert;
(e) I am likely to be the subject of public adverse criticism by the judge if the court concludes that I have not taken reasonable care in trying to meet the standards set out above.

12. I have read Part 19 of the Criminal Procedure Rules and I have complied with its requirements.
13. I confirm that I have acted in accordance with the the code of practice or conduct for experts of my discipline, namely [*identify the code*].
14. [For experts instructed by the prosecution only] I confirm that I have read guidance contained in a booklet known as *Disclosure: Experts' Evidence and Unused Material* which details my role and documents my responsibilities, in relation to revelation as an expert witness. I have followed the guidance and recognise the continuing nature of my responsibilities of disclosure. In accordance with my duties of disclosure, as documented in the guidance booklet, I confirm that:
(a) I have complied with my duties to record, retain and reveal material in accordance with the CPIA 1996, as amended;
(b) I have compiled an index of all material; I will ensure that the index is updated in the event I am provided with or generate additional material;
(c) in the event my opinion changes on any material issue, I will inform the investigating officer, as soon as reasonably practicable and give reasons.

I confirm that the contents of this report are true to the best of my knowledge and belief and that I make this report knowing that, if it is tendered in evidence, I would be liable to prosecution if I have wilfully stated anything which I know to be false or that I do not believe to be true."

CPD V Evidence 19C: Pre-hearing discussion of expert evidence (as inserted by Criminal Practice Directions 2015 (Amendment No. 2), unreported, 16 November 2016, Lord Thomas CJ)

B-350 **19C.1** To assist the court in the preparation of the case for trial, parties must consider, with their experts, at an early stage, whether there is likely to be any useful purpose in holding an experts' discussion and, if so, when. Under CrimPR 19.6 such pre-trial discussions are not compulsory unless directed by the court. However, such a direction is listed in the magistrates' courts' Preparation for Effective Trial form and in the Crown Court Plea and Trial Preparation Hearing form as one to be given by default, and therefore the court can be expected to give such a direction in every case unless persuaded otherwise. Those standard directions include a timetable to which the parties must adhere unless it is varied.

19C.2 The purpose of discussions between experts is to agree and narrow issues and in particular to identify:
(a) the extent of the agreement between them;
(b) the points of and short reasons for any disagreement;
(c) action, if any, which may be taken to resolve any outstanding points of disagreement; and
(d) any further material issues not raised and the extent to which these issues are agreed.

19C.3 Where the experts are to meet, that meeting conveniently may be conducted by telephone conference or live link; and experts' meetings always should be conducted by those means where that will avoid unnecessary delay and expense.

19C.4 Where the experts are to meet, the parties must discuss and if possible agree whether an agenda is necessary, and if so attempt to agree one that helps the experts to focus on the issues which need to be discussed. The agenda must not be in the form of leading questions or hostile in tone. The experts may not be required to avoid reaching agreement, or to defer reaching agreement, on any matter within the experts' competence.

19C.5 If the legal representatives do attend:
(a) they should not normally intervene in the discussion, except to answer questions put to them by the experts or to advise on the law; and
(b) the experts may if they so wish hold part of their discussions in the absence of the legal representatives.

19C.6 A statement must be prepared by the experts dealing with paragraphs 19C.2(a)-(d) above. Individual copies of the statements must be signed or otherwise authenticated by the experts, in manuscript or by electronic means, at the conclusion of the discussion, or as soon thereafter as practicable, and in any event within 5 business days. Copies of the statements must be provided to the parties no later than 10 business days after signing.

19C.7 Experts must give their own opinions to assist the court and do not require the authority of the parties to sign a joint statement. The joint statement should include a brief re-statement that the experts recognise their duties, which should be in the following terms, or in terms substantially the same as these:

"We each DECLARE THAT:

1. We individually here re-state the expert's declaration contained in our respective reports that we understand our overriding duties to the court, have complied with them and will continue to do so.
2. We have neither jointly nor individually been instructed to, nor has it been suggested that we should, avoid reaching agreement, or defer reaching agreement, on any matter within our competence."

19C.8 If an expert significantly alters an opinion, the joint statement must include a note or addendum by that expert explaining the change of opinion.

Criminal Procedure Rules 2020 (SI 2020/759), Pt 20

Hearsay Evidence

When this part applies

20.1. This Part applies in a magistrates' court and in the Crown Court where a party wants to introduce hearsay evidence within the meaning of section 114 of the Criminal Justice Act 2003. **B-351**

Notice to introduce hearsay evidence

20.2.–(1) This rule applies where a party wants to introduce hearsay evidence for admission under any of the following sections of the Criminal Justice Act 2003– **B-352**

(a) section 114(1)(d) (evidence admissible in the interests of justice);
(b) section 116 (evidence where a witness is unavailable);
(c) section 117(1)(c) (evidence in a statement prepared for the purposes of criminal proceedings); or
(d) section 121 (multiple hearsay).

(2) That party must–

(a) serve notice on–
  (i) the court officer, and
  (ii) each other party;
(b) in the notice–
  (i) identify the evidence that is hearsay,
  (ii) set out any facts on which that party relies to make the evidence admissible,
  (iii) explain how that party will prove those facts if another party disputes them, and
  (iv) explain why the evidence is admissible; and
(c) attach to the notice any statement or other document containing the evidence that has not already been served.

(3) A prosecutor who wants to introduce such evidence must serve the notice not more than–

(a) 20 business days after the defendant pleads not guilty, in a magistrates' court; or
(b) 10 business days after the defendant pleads not guilty, in the Crown Court.

(4) A defendant who wants to introduce such evidence must serve the notice as soon as reasonably practicable.

(5) A party entitled to receive a notice under this rule may waive that entitlement by so informing–

(a) the party who would have served it; and
(b) the court.

Opposing the introduction of hearsay evidence

20.3.–(1) This rule applies where a party objects to the introduction of hearsay evidence. **B-353**

(2) That party must–

(a) apply to the court to determine the objection;
(b) serve the application on–
  (i) the court officer, and
  (ii) each other party;
(c) serve the application as soon as reasonably practicable, and in any event not more than 10 business days after–
  (i) service of notice to introduce the evidence under rule 20.2,

(ii) service of the evidence to which that party objects, if no notice is required by that rule, or
(iii) the defendant pleads not guilty
whichever of those events happens last; and
(d) in the application, explain—
(i) which, if any, facts set out in a notice under rule 20.2 that party disputes,
(ii) why the evidence is not admissible,
(iii) any other objection to the evidence.
(3) The court—
(a) may determine an application—
(i) at a hearing, in public or in private, or
(ii) without a hearing;
(b) must not determine the application unless the party who served the notice—
(i) is present, or
(ii) has had a reasonable opportunity to respond;
(c) may adjourn the application; and
(d) may discharge or vary a determination where it can do so under—
(i) section 8B of the Magistrates' Courts Act 1980 (ruling at pre-trial hearing in a magistrates' court), or
(ii) section 9 of the Criminal Justice Act 1987, or section 31 or 40 of the Criminal Procedure and Investigations Act 1996 (ruling at preparatory or other pre-trial hearing in the Crown Court).

Unopposed hearsay evidence

B-354 **20.4.**—(1) This rule applies where—
(a) a party has served notice to introduce hearsay evidence under rule 20.2; and
(b) no other party has applied to the court to determine an objection to the introduction of the evidence.
(2) The court must treat the evidence as if it were admissible by agreement.

Court's power to vary requirements under this part

B-355 **20.5.**—(1) The court may—
(a) shorten or extend (even after it has expired) a time limit under this part;
(b) allow an application or notice to be in a different form to one set out in the Practice Direction, or to be made or given orally; and
(c) dispense with the requirement for notice to introduce hearsay evidence.
(2) A party who wants an extension of time must—
(a) apply when serving the application or notice for which it is needed; and
(b) explain the delay.

Criminal Procedure Rules 2020 (SI 2020/759), Pt 21

Evidence of Bad Character

When this Part applies

B-356 **21.1.** This Part applies in a magistrates' court and in the Crown Court where a party wants to introduce evidence of bad character within the meaning of section 98 of the Criminal Justice Act 2003.

Content of application or notice

B-357 **21.2.**—(1) A party who wants to introduce evidence of bad character must—
(a) make an application under rule 21.3, where it is evidence of a non-defendant's bad character; or
(b) give notice under rule 21.4, where it is evidence of a defendant's bad character.
(2) An application or notice must—
(a) set out the facts of the misconduct on which that party relies,
(b) explain how that party will prove those facts (whether by certificate of conviction, other official record, or other evidence), if another party disputes them, and
(c) explain why the evidence is admissible.

Application to introduce evidence of a non-defendant's bad character

B-358 **21.3.**—(1) This rule applies where a party wants to introduce evidence of the bad character of a person other than the defendant.

(2) That party must serve an application to do so on–
(a) the court officer; and
(b) each other party.
(3) The applicant must serve the application–
(a) as soon as reasonably practicable; and in any event
(b) not more than 10 business days after the prosecutor discloses material on which the application is based (if the prosecutor is not the applicant).
(4) A party who objects to the introduction of the evidence must–
(a) serve notice on–
(i) the court officer, and
(ii) each other party
not more than 10 business days after service of the application; and
(b) in the notice explain, as applicable–
(i) which, if any, facts of the misconduct set out in the application that party disputes,
(ii) what, if any, facts of the misconduct that party admits instead,
(iii) why the evidence is not admissible, and
(iv) any other objection to the application.
(5) The court–
(a) may determine an application–
(i) at a hearing, in public or in private, or
(ii) without a hearing;
(b) must not determine the application unless each party other than the applicant–
(i) is present, or
(ii) has had at least 10 business days in which to serve a notice of objection;
(c) may adjourn the application; and
(d) may discharge or vary a determination where it can do so under–
(i) section 8B of the Magistrates' Courts Act 1980 (ruling at pre-trial hearing in a magistrates' court), or
(ii) section 9 of the Criminal Justice Act 1987, or section 31 or 40 of the Criminal Procedure and Investigations Act 1996) (ruling at preparatory or other pre-trial hearing in the Crown Court).

Notice to introduce evidence of a defendant's bad character

21.4.–(1) This rule applies where a party wants to introduce evidence of a defendant's bad character. **B-359**
(2) A prosecutor or co-defendant who wants to introduce such evidence must serve notice on–
(a) the court officer; and
(b) each other party.
(3) A prosecutor must serve any such notice not more than–
(a) 10 business days after the defendant pleads not guilty, in a magistrates' court; or
(b) 10 business days after the defendant pleads not guilty, in the Crown Court.
(4) A co-defendant must serve any such notice–
(a) as soon as reasonably practicable; and in any event
(b) not more than 10 business days after the prosecutor discloses material on which the notice is based.
(5) A party who objects to the introduction of the evidence identified by such a notice must–
(a) apply to the court to determine the objection;
(b) serve the application on–
(i) the court officer, and
(ii) each other party
not more than 10 business days after service of the notice; and
(c) in the application explain, as applicable–
(i) which, if any, facts of the misconduct set out in the notice that party disputes,
(ii) what, if any, facts of the misconduct that party admits instead,
(iii) why the evidence is not admissible,
(iv) why it would be unfair to admit the evidence, and
(v) any other objection to the notice.
(6) The court–

(a) may determine such an application—
(i) at a hearing, in public or in private, or
(ii) without a hearing;
(b) must not determine the application unless the party who served the notice—
(i) is present, or
(ii) has had a reasonable opportunity to respond;
(c) may adjourn the application; and
(d) may discharge or vary a determination where it can do so under—
(i) section 8B of the Magistrates' Courts Act 1980 (ruling at pre-trial hearing in a magistrates' court), or
(ii) section 9 of the Criminal Justice Act 1987, or section 31 or 40 of the Criminal Procedure and Investigations Act 1996 (ruling at preparatory or other pre-trial hearing in the Crown Court).

(7) A party entitled to receive such a notice may waive that entitlement by so informing—
(a) the party who would have served it; and
(b) the court.

(8) A defendant who wants to introduce evidence of his or her own bad character must—
(a) give notice, in writing or orally—
(i) as soon as reasonably practicable, and in any event
(ii) before the evidence is introduced, either by the defendant or in reply to a question asked by the defendant of another party's witness in order to obtain that evidence; and
(b) in the Crown Court, at the same time give notice (in writing, or orally) of any direction about the defendant's character that the defendant wants the court to give the jury under rule 25.14 (directions to the jury and taking the verdict).

Reasons for decisions

B-360 **21.5.** The court must announce at a hearing in public (but in the absence of the jury, if there is one) the reasons for a decision—
(a) to admit evidence as evidence of bad character, or to refuse to do so; or
(b) to direct an acquittal or a retrial under section 107 of the Criminal Justice Act 2003.

Court's power to vary requirements under this Part

B-361 **21.6.**—(1) The court may—
(a) shorten or extend (even after it has expired) a time limit under this Part;
(b) allow an application or notice to be in a different form to one set out in the Practice Direction, or to be made or given orally; and
(c) dispense with a requirement for notice to introduce evidence of a defendant's bad character.

(2) A party who wants an extension of time must—
(a) apply when serving the application or notice for which it is needed; and
(b) explain the delay.

CPD V Evidence 21A: Spent convictions

B-362 **21A.1** The effect of section 4(1) of the Rehabilitation of Offenders Act 1974 [§ 13-85 in the main work] is that a person who has become a rehabilitated person for the purpose of the Act in respect of a conviction ... shall be treated for all purposes in law as a person who has not committed, or been charged with or prosecuted for, or convicted of or sentenced for, the offence or offences which were the subject of that conviction.

21A.2 Section 4(1) ... does not apply, however, to evidence given in criminal proceedings: s.7(2)(a) [§ 13-89 in the main work]. During the trial of a criminal charge, reference to previous convictions (and therefore to spent convictions) can arise in a number of ways. The most common is when a bad character application is made under the CJA 2003. When considering bad character applications ...regard should always be had to the general principles of the [1974 Act].

21A.3 On conviction, the court must be provided with a statement of the defendant's record for the purposes of sentence. The record supplied should contain all previous convictions, but those which are spent should, so far as practicable, be marked as such. No one should refer in open court to a spent conviction without the authority of the judge, which authority should not be given unless the interests of justice so require. When passing sentence the judge should make no reference to a spent conviction unless it is necessary to do so for the purpose of explaining the sentence to be passed.

Criminal Procedure Rules 2020 (SI 2020/759), Pt 22

Evidence Of A Complainant's Previous Sexual Behaviour

When this Part applies

22.1. This Part applies in a magistrates' court and in the Crown Court where– **B-363**

(a) section 41 of the Youth Justice and Criminal Evidence Act 1999 prohibits the introduction of evidence or cross-examination about any sexual behaviour of the complainant of a sexual offence; and

(b) despite that prohibition, a defendant wants to introduce such evidence or to cross-examine a witness about such behaviour.

Exercise of court's powers

22.2. The court– **B-364**

(a) must determine an application under rule 22.4 (Application for permission to introduce evidence or cross-examine)–
  (i) at a hearing in private, and
  (ii) in the absence of the complainant;

(b) must not determine the application unless–
  (i) each party other than the applicant is present, or has had at least 10 business days in which to make representations, and
  (ii) the court is satisfied that it has been able to take adequate account of the complainant's rights;

(c) may adjourn the application; and

(d) may discharge or vary a determination where it can do so under–
  (i) section 8B of the Magistrates' Courts Act 1980 (ruling at pre-trial hearing in a magistrates' court), or
  (ii) section 9 of the Criminal Justice Act 1987, or section 31 or 40 of the Criminal Procedure and Investigations Act 1996 (ruling at preparatory or other pre-trial hearing in the Crown Court).

Decisions and reasons

22.3.–(1) A prosecutor who wants to introduce the evidence of a complainant in respect of whom the court allows the introduction of evidence or cross-examination about any sexual behaviour must– **B-365**

(a) inform the complainant of the court's decision as soon as reasonably practicable; and

(b) explain to the complainant any arrangements that as a result will be made for him or her to give evidence.

(2) The court must–

(a) promptly determine an application; and

(b) allow the prosecutor sufficient time to comply with the requirements of–
  (i) paragraph (1), and
  (ii) the code of practice issued under section 32 of the Domestic Violence, Crime and Victims Act 2004.

(3) The court must announce at a hearing in public–

(a) the reasons for a decision to allow or refuse an application under rule 22.4; and

(b) if it allows such an application, the extent to which evidence may be introduced or questions asked.

Application for permission to introduce evidence or cross-examine

22.4.–(1) A defendant who wants to introduce evidence or cross-examine a witness about any sexual behaviour of the complainant must– **B-366**

(a) serve an application for permission to do so on–
  (i) the court officer, and
  (ii) each other party; and

(b) serve the application–
  (i) as soon as reasonably practicable after becoming aware of the grounds for doing so, and in any event
  (ii) not more than 10 business days after the prosecutor discloses material on which the application is based.

(2) The application must–

(a) identify the issue to which the defendant says the complainant's sexual behaviour is relevant;
(b) give particulars of—
(i) any evidence that the defendant wants to introduce, and
(ii) any questions that the defendant wants to ask;
(c) identify the exception to the prohibition in section 41 of the Youth Justice and Criminal Evidence Act 1999 on which the defendant relies; and
(d) give the name and date of birth of any witness whose evidence about the complainant's sexual behaviour the defendant wants to introduce.

Application containing information withheld from another party

B-367 **22.5.**—(1) This rule applies where—
(a) an applicant serves an application under rule 22.4 (Application for permission to introduce evidence or cross-examine); and
(b) the application includes information that the applicant thinks ought not be revealed to another party.
(2) The applicant must—
(a) omit that information from the part of the application that is served on that other party;
(b) mark the other part to show that, unless the court otherwise directs, it is only for the court; and
(c) in that other part, explain why the applicant has withheld that information from that other party.
(3) If the court so directs, the hearing of an application to which this rule applies may be, wholly or in part, in the absence of a party from whom information has been withheld.
(4) At the hearing of an application to which this rule applies—
(a) the general rule is that the court must consider, in the following sequence—
(i) representations first by the applicant and then by each other party, in all the parties' presence, and then
(ii) further representations by the applicant, in the absence of a party from whom information has been withheld; but
(b) the court may direct other arrangements for the hearing.

Representations in response

B-368 **22.6.**—(1) This rule applies where a party wants to make representations about—
(a) an application under rule 22.4 (Application for permission to introduce evidence or cross-examine); or
(b) a proposed variation or discharge of a decision allowing such an application.
(2) Such a party must—
(a) serve the representations on—
(i) the court officer, and
(ii) each other party; and
(b) do so not more than 10 business days after, as applicable—
(i) service of the application, or
(ii) notice of the proposal to vary or discharge.
(3) Where representations include information that the person making them thinks ought not be revealed to another party, that person must—
(a) omit that information from the representations served on that other party;
(b) mark the information to show that, unless the court otherwise directs, it is only for the court; and
(c) with that information include an explanation of why it has been withheld from that other party.
(4) Representations against an application under rule 22.4 must explain the grounds of objection.
(5) Representations against the variation or discharge of a decision must explain why it should not be varied or discharged.

Special measures, etc. for a witness

★B-369 **22.7.**—(1) This rule applies where the court allows an application under rule 22.4 (Application for permission to introduce evidence or cross-examine).
(2) Despite the time limits in rule 18.4 (Making an application for a direction or order)—
(a) a party may apply not more than 10 business days after the court's decision for a special measures direction or for the variation of an existing special measures direction; and

(b) the court may shorten the time for opposing that application.

(3) Where the court allows the cross-examination of a witness, the court must give directions for the appropriate treatment and questioning of that witness in accordance with rule 3.8(6) and (7) (setting ground rules for the conduct of questioning).

[This rule is printed as amended, with effect from 5 April 2021, by SI 2021/40, r.30(b).]

Court's power to vary requirements under this Part

22.8. The court may shorten or extend (even after it has expired) a time limit under this Part. **B-370**

Criminal Practice Direction V (Evidence) 22A: Use of ground rules hearing when dealing with s.41 Youth Justice and Criminal Evidence Act 1999 (YJCEA 1999) evidence of complainant's previous sexual behaviour (as inserted by Criminal Practice Directions 2015 (Amendment No. 6), unreported, 22 March 2018, Lord Burnett CJ)

The application

22A.1 When a defendant wishes to introduce evidence, or cross-examine about the previous sexual behaviour of the complainant, then it is imperative that the timetable and procedure as laid down in the Criminal Procedure Rules Part 22 is followed. The application must be submitted in writing as soon as reasonably practicable and not more than 14 days after the prosecutor has disclosed material on which the application is based. Should the prosecution wish to make any representations then these should be served on the court and other parties not more than 14 days after receiving the application. **B-371**

22A.2 The application must clearly state the issue to which the defendant says the complainant's sexual behaviour is relevant and the reasons why it should be admitted. It must outline the evidence which the defendant wants to introduce and articulate the questions which it is proposed should be asked. The application must identify the statutory exception to the prohibition in s.41 YJCEA 1999 [§ 8-285 in the main work] on which the defendant relies and give the name and date of birth of any witness whose evidence about the complainant's sexual behaviour the defendant wants to introduce.

The hearing

22A.3 When determining the application, the judge should examine the questions with the usual level of scrutiny expected at a ground rules hearing. For each question that it is sought to put to a witness, or evidence it is sought to adduce, the defence should identify clearly for the judge the suggested relevance it has to an issue in the case. In order for the judge to rule on which evidence can be adduced or questions put, the defence must set out individual questions for the judge; merely identifying a topic is not sufficient for this type of application. The judge should make it clear that if the application is granted then no other questions on this topic will be allowed to be asked, unless with the express permission of the court. **B-372**

22A.4 The application should be dealt with in private and in the absence of the complainant, but the judge must state in open court, without the jury or complainant present, the reasons for the decision, and if leave is granted, the extent of the questions or evidence that is allowed.

Late applications

22A.5 Late applications should be considered with particular scrutiny especially if there is a suggestion of tactical thinking behind the timing of the application and/or when the application is based on material that has been available for some time. If consideration of a late application has the potential to disrupt the timetabling of witnesses, then the judge will need to take account of the potential impact of delay upon a witness who is due to give evidence. If necessary, the judge may defer consideration of any such application until later in the trial **B-373**

22A.6 By analogy, following the approach adopted by the Court of Appeal in *R v Musone* [2007] 1 W.L.R. 2467, the trial judge is entitled to refuse the application where (s)he is satisfied that the applicant is seeking to manipulate the court process so as to prevent the respondent from being able to prepare an adequate response. This may be the only remedy available to the court to ensure that the fairness of the trial is upheld and will be particularly relevant when the application is made on the day of trial.

22A.7 Where the application has been granted in good time before the trial, the complainant is entitled to be made aware that such evidence is part of the defence case.

At the trial

22A.8 Advocates should be reminded that the questioning must be conducted in an appropriate manner. Any aggressive, repetitive and oppressive questioning will be stopped by the judge. Judges should intervene and stop any attempts to refer to evidence that might have been adduced under s 41, but for which no leave has been given and/or should have formed the basis of a s41 application, **B-374**

but did not do so. When evidence about the complainant's previous sexual behaviour is referred to without an application, the judge may be required to consider whether the impact of that happening is so prejudicial to the overall fairness of the trial that the trial should be stopped and a re-trial should be ordered, should the impact not be capable of being ameliorated by way of jury direction.

Criminal Procedure Rules 2020 (SI 2020/759), Pt 23

RESTRICTION ON CROSS-EXAMINATION BY A DEFENDANT

General rules

When this Part applies

B-375 **23.1.** This Part applies where—

(a) a defendant may not cross-examine in person a witness because of section 34 or section 35 of the Youth Justice and Criminal Evidence Act 1999 (complainants in proceedings for sexual offences; child complainants and other child witnesses); or

(b) the court can prohibit a defendant from cross-examining in person a witness under section 36 of that Act (direction prohibiting accused from cross-examining particular witness).

Appointment of advocate to cross-examine witness

B-376 **23.2.**—(1) This rule applies where a defendant may not cross-examine in person a witness in consequence of—

(a) the prohibition imposed by section 34 or section 35 of the Youth Justice and Criminal Evidence Act 1999; or

(b) a prohibition imposed by the court under section 36 of the 1999 Act.

(2) The court must, as soon as practicable, explain in terms the defendant can understand (with help, if necessary)—

(a) the prohibition and its effect;

(b) that if the defendant will not be represented by a lawyer with a right of audience in the court for the purposes of the case then the defendant is entitled to arrange for such a lawyer to cross-examine the witness on his or her behalf;

(c) that the defendant must notify the court officer of the identity of any such lawyer, with details of how to contact that person, by no later than a date set by the court; and

(d) that if the defendant does not want to make such arrangements, or if the defendant gives no such notice by that date, then—

(i) the court must decide whether it is necessary in the interests of justice to appoint such a lawyer to cross-examine the witness in the defendant's interests, and

(ii) if the court decides that that is necessary, the court will appoint a lawyer chosen by the court who will not be responsible to the defendant .

(3) Having given those explanations, the court must—

(a) ask whether the defendant wants to arrange for a lawyer to cross-examine the witness, and set a date by when the defendant must notify the court officer of the identity of that lawyer if the answer to that question is "yes"; and

(b) if the answer to that question is "no", or if by the date set the defendant has given no such notice—

(i) decide whether it is necessary in the interests of justice for the witness to be cross-examined by an advocate appointed to represent the defendant's interests, and

(ii) if the court decides that that is necessary, give directions for the appointment of such an advocate.

(4) The court may give the explanations and ask the questions required by this rule—

(a) at a hearing, in public or in private; or

(b) without a hearing, by written notice to the defendant.

(5) The court may extend (even after it has expired) the time limit that it sets under paragraph (3)(a)—

(a) on application by the defendant; or

(b) on its own initiative.

(6) Paragraphs (7), (8), (9) and (10) apply where the court appoints an advocate.

(7) The directions that the court gives under paragraph (3)(b)(ii) must provide for the supply to the advocate of a copy of—

(a) all material served by one party on the other, whether before or after the advocate's appointment, to which applies—

(i) Part 8 (Initial details of the prosecution case),
(ii) in the Crown Court, rule 9.19 (service of prosecution evidence in a case sent for trial),
(iii) Part 16 (Written witness statements),
(iv) Part 19 (Expert evidence),
(v) Part 20 (Hearsay evidence),
(vi) Part 21 (Evidence of bad character), or
(vii) Part 22 (Evidence of a complainant's previous sexual behaviour);

(b) any material disclosed, given or served, whether before or after the advocate's appointment, which is–
(i) prosecution material disclosed to the defendant under section 3 (Initial duty of prosecutor to disclose) [§ 12-58 in the main work] or section 7A (Continuing duty of prosecutor to disclose) of the Criminal Procedure and Investigations Act 1996 [§ 12-74 in the main work],
(ii) a defence statement given by the defendant under section 5 (Compulsory disclosure by accused) [§ 12-62 in the main work] or section 6 (Voluntary disclosure by accused) of the 1996 Act [§ 12-63 in the main work],
(iii) a defence witness notice given by the defendant under section 6C of that Act (Notification of intention to call defence witnesses) [§ 12-68 in the main work], or
(iv) an application by the defendant under section 8 of that Act (Application by accused for disclosure) [§ 12-76 in the main work];

(c) any case management questionnaire prepared for the purposes of the trial or, as the case may be, the appeal; and

(d) all case management directions given by the court for the purposes of the trial or the appeal.

(8) Where the defendant has given a defence statement–
(a) section 8(2) of the Criminal Procedure and Investigations Act 1996 [§ 12-76 in the main work] is modified to allow the advocate, as well as the defendant, to apply for an order for prosecution disclosure under that subsection if the advocate has reasonable cause to believe that there is prosecution material concerning the witness which is required by section 7A of the Act [§ 12-74 in the main work] to be disclosed to the defendant and has not been; and
(b) rule 15.5 (Defendant's application for prosecution disclosure) applies to an application by the advocate as it does to an application by the defendant.

(9) Before receiving evidence the court must establish, with the active assistance of the parties and of the advocate, and in the absence of any jury in the Crown Court–
(a) what issues will be the subject of the advocate's cross-examination; and
(b) whether the court's permission is required for any proposed question, for example where Part 21 or Part 22 applies.

(10) The appointment terminates at the conclusion of the cross-examination of the witness.

Application to prohibit cross-examination

Exercise of court's powers

23.3.–(1) The court may decide whether to impose or discharge a prohibition against cross-sexamination under section 36 of the Youth Justice and Criminal Evidence Act 1999– **B-377**
(a) at a hearing, in public or in private, or without a hearing; and
(b) in a party's absence, if that party–
(i) applied for the prohibition or discharge, or
(ii) has had at least 10 business days in which to make representations.

(2) The court must announce, at a hearing in public before the witness gives evidence, the reasons for a decision–
(a) to impose or discharge such a prohibition; or
(b) to refuse to do so.

Application to prohibit cross-examination

23.4.–(1) This rule applies where under section 36 of the Youth Justice and Criminal Evidence Act 1999 the prosecutor wants the court to prohibit the cross-examination of a witness by a defendant in person. **B-378**

(2) The prosecutor must–
(a) apply in writing, as soon as reasonably practicable after becoming aware of the grounds for doing so; and

(b) serve the application on—
(i) the court officer,
(ii) the defendant who is the subject of the application, and
(iii) any other defendant, unless the court otherwise directs.

(3) The application must—
(a) report any views that the witness has expressed about whether he or she is content to be cross-examined by the defendant in person;
(b) identify—
(i) the nature of the questions likely to be asked, having regard to the issues in the case,
(ii) any relevant behaviour of the defendant at any stage of the case, generally and in relation to the witness,
(iii) any relationship, of any nature, between the witness and the defendant,
(iv) any other defendant in the case who is subject to such a prohibition in respect of the witness, and
(v) any special measures direction made in respect of the witness, or for which an application has been made;
(c) explain why the quality of evidence given by the witness on cross-examination—
(i) is likely to be diminished if no such prohibition is imposed, and
(ii) would be likely to be improved if it were imposed; and
(d) explain why it would not be contrary to the interests of justice to impose the prohibition.

Application to discharge prohibition imposed by the court

B-379 **23.5.**—(1) A party who wants the court to discharge a prohibition against cross-examination which the court imposed under section 36 of the Youth Justice and Criminal Evidence Act 1999 must—
(a) apply in writing, as soon as reasonably practicable after becoming aware of the grounds for doing so; and
(b) serve the application on—
(i) the court officer, and
(ii) each other party.

(2) The applicant must—
(a) explain what material circumstances have changed since the prohibition was imposed; and
(b) ask for a hearing, if the applicant wants one, and explain why it is needed.

Application containing information withheld from another party

B-380 **23.6.**—(1) This rule applies where—
(a) an applicant serves an application for the court to impose a prohibition against crossexamination, or for the discharge of such a prohibition; and
(b) the application includes information that the applicant thinks ought not be revealed to another party.

(2) The applicant must—
(a) omit that information from the part of the application that is served on that other party;
(b) mark the other part to show that, unless the court otherwise directs, it is only for the court; and
(c) in that other part, explain why the applicant has withheld that information from that other party.

(3) Any hearing of an application to which this rule applies—
(a) must be in private, unless the court otherwise directs; and
(b) if the court so directs, may be, wholly or in part, in the absence of a party from whom information has been withheld.

(4) At any hearing of an application to which this rule applies—
(a) the general rule is that the court must consider, in the following sequence—
(i) representations first by the applicant and then by each other party, in all the parties' presence, and then
(ii) further representations by the applicant, in the absence of a party from whom information has been withheld; but
(b) the court may direct other arrangements for the hearing.

Representations in response

B-381 **23.7.**—(1) This rule applies where a party wants to make representations about—

(a) an application under rule 23.4 for a prohibition against cross-examination;
(b) an application under rule 23.5 for the discharge of such a prohibition; or
(c) a prohibition or discharge that the court proposes on its own initiative.

(2) Such a party must–
(a) serve the representations on–
(i) the court officer, and
(ii) each other party;
(b) do so not more than 1 after, as applicable–
(i) service of the application, or
(ii) notice of the prohibition or discharge that the court proposes; and
(c) ask for a hearing, if that party wants one, and explain why it is needed.

(3) Representations against a prohibition must explain in what respect the conditions for imposing it are not met.

(4) Representations against the discharge of a prohibition must explain why it should not be discharged.

(5) Where representations include information that the person making them thinks ought not be revealed to another party, that person must–
(a) omit that information from the representations served on that other party;
(b) mark the information to show that, unless the court otherwise directs, it is only for the court; and
(c) with that information include an explanation of why it has been withheld from that other party.

Court's power to vary requirements

23.8.–(1) The court may– **B-382**
(a) shorten or extend (even after it has expired) a time limit under rule 23.4 (application to prohibit cross-examination), rule 23.5 (application to discharge prohibition imposed by the court) or rule 23.7 (representations in response); and
(b) allow an application or representations required by any of those rules to be made in a different form to one set out in the Practice Direction, or to be made orally.

(2) A person who wants an extension of time must–
(a) apply when serving the application or representations for which it is needed; and
(b) explain the delay.

Criminal Practice Direction V (Evidence) 23A: Cross-examination advocates (as inserted by Criminal Practice Directions 2015 (Amendment No. 6), unreported, 22 March 2018, Lord Burnett CJ)

Provisional appointment of advocate

23A.1 At the first hearing in the court in the case, and in a Magistrates' court in particular, there may be occasions on which a defendant has engaged no legal representative, within the meaning of the Criminal Procedure Rules, for the purposes of the case generally, but still intends to do so - for example, where he or she has made an application for legal aid which has yet to be determined. Where the defendant nonetheless has identified a prospective legal representative who has a right of audience in the court; where the court is satisfied that that representative will be willing to cross-examine the relevant witness or witnesses in the interests of the defendant should it transpire that the defendant will not be represented for the purposes of the case generally; and if the court is in a position there and then to make, contingently, the decision required by section 38(3) of the Youth Justice and Criminal Evidence Act 1999 [§ 8-273] in the main work] ('the court must consider whether it is necessary in the interests of justice for the witness to be cross-examined by a legal representative appointed to represent the interests of the accused'); then the court may appoint that representative under section 38(4) of the 1999 Act contingently, the appointment to come into effect only if, and when, it is established that the defendant will not be represented for the purposes of the case generally. **B-383**

23A.2 Where such a provisional appointment is made it is essential that the role and status of the representative is clearly established at the earliest possible opportunity. The court's directions under CrimPR 23.2(3) should require the defendant to notify the court officer, by the date set by the court, whether:

(i) the defendant will be represented by a legal representative for the purposes of the case generally, and if so by whom (in which event the court's provisional appointment has no effect);

(ii) the defendant will not be represented for the purposes of the case generally, but the defendant and the legal representative provisionally appointed by the court remain content with that provisional appointment (in which event the court's provisional appointment takes effect); or

(iii) the defendant will not be represented for the purposes of the case generally, but will arrange for a lawyer to cross-examine the relevant witness or witnesses on his or her behalf, giving that lawyer's name and contact details.

If in the event the defendant fails to give notice by the due date then, unless it is apparent that she or he will, in fact, be represented for the purposes of the case generally, the court may decide to confirm the provisional appointment and proceed accordingly.

Supply of case papers

B-384 **23A.3** For the advocate to fulfil the duty imposed by the appointment, and to achieve a responsible, professional and appropriate treatment both of the defendant and of the witness, it is essential for the advocate to establish what is in issue. To that end, it is likewise essential for the advocate to have been supplied with the material listed in CrimPR 23.2(7).

23A.4 In the Crown Court, much of this this can be achieved most conveniently by giving the advocate access to the Crown Court Digital Case System. However, material disclosed by the prosecutor to the defendant under section 3 or section 7A of the Criminal Procedure and Investigations Act 1996 [§§ 12-58 and 12-74 in the main work] is not stored in that system and therefore must be supplied to the advocate either by the defendant or by the prosecutor. In the latter case, the prosecutor reasonably may omit from the copies supplied to the advocate any material that can have no bearing on the cross-examination for which the advocate has been appointed - the medical or social services records of another witness, for example.

23A.5 In a magistrates' court, pending the introduction of comparable electronic arrangements:

i. in some instances the advocate may have received the relevant material at a point at which he or she was acting as the defendant's legal representative subject to a restriction on the purpose or duration of that appointment notified under CrimPR 46.2(5) - for example, pending the outcome of an application for legal aid.

ii. in some instances the defendant may be able to provide spare copies of relevant material. Where that material has been disclosed by the prosecutor under section 3 or section 7A of the Criminal Procedure and Investigations Act 1996 then its supply to the advocate by the defendant is permitted by section 17(2)(a) of the 1996 Act (exception to the prohibition against further disclosure where that further disclosure is 'in connection with the proceedings for whose purposes [the defendant] was given the object or allowed to inspect it') [§ 12-88 in the main work].

iii. in some instances the prosecutor may be able to supply the relevant material, or some of it, at no, or minimal, expense by electronic means.

iv. in the event that, unusually, none of those sources of supply is available, then the court's directions under CrimPR 23.2(3) should require the court officer to provide copies from the court's own records, as if the advocate were a party and had applied under CrimPR 5.7.

Obtaining information and observations from the defendant

B-385 **23A.6** Advocates and courts should keep in mind section 38(5) of the 1999 Act [§ 8-273 in the main work], which provides 'A person so appointed shall not be responsible to the accused.' The advocate therefore cannot and should not take instructions from the defendant, in the usual sense; and to avoid any misapprehension in that respect, either by the defendant or by others, some advocates may prefer to avoid direct oral communication with the defendant before, and even perhaps during, the trial.

23A.7 However, as remarked above at paragraph 23A.3, for the advocate to fulfil the duty imposed by the appointment it is essential for him or her to establish what is in issue; which may require communication with the defendant both before and at the trial as well as a thorough examination of the case papers. CrimPR 23.2(7)(a) in effect requires the advocate to have identified the issues on which the cross-examination of the witness is expected to proceed before the court begins to receive prosecution evidence, and to have taken part in their discussion with the court. To that end, communication with the defendant may be necessary.

Extent of cross-examination advocate's appointment

B-386 **23A.8** In *Abbas v Crown Prosecution Service* [2015] EWHC 579 (Admin); [2015] 2 Cr. App. R. 11 the Divisional Court observed:

> "The role of a section 38 advocate is, undoubtedly, limited to the proper performance of their duty as a cross examiner of a particular witness. Sections 36 and 38 are all about protecting

vulnerable witnesses from cross examination by the accused. Therefore, it should not be thought that an advocate appointed under section 38 has a free ranging remit to conduct the trial on the accused's behalf. Their professional duty and their statutory duty would be to ensure that they are in a position properly to conduct the cross examination. Their duties might include therefore applications to admit bad character of the witness and or applications for disclosure of material relevant to the cross examination. That is as far as one can go. All these matters must be entirely fact specific. The important thing to note is that the section 38 advocate must ensure that s/he performs his/her duties in accordance with the words of the statute.

It means also that their appointment comes to an end, under section 38, at the conclusion of the cross examination, save to the extent that the court otherwise determines. Technically the lawyer no longer has a role in the proceedings thereafter. However, if the lawyer is prepared to stay and assist the defendant on a pro bono basis, I see nothing in the Act and no logical reason why the court should oblige them to leave. The advocate may well prove beneficial to the efficient and fair resolution of the proceedings.

The aim of the legislation as I have said is simply to stop the accused cross examining the witness. It is not to prevent the person appointed to cross examine from playing any other part in the trial."

23A.9 Advocates will be alert to, and courts should keep in mind, the extent of the remuneration available to a cross-examination advocate, in assessing the amount of which the court has only a limited role: see section 19(3) of the Prosecution of Offences Act 1985, which empowers the Lord Chancellor to make regulations authorising payments out of central funds 'to cover the proper fee or costs of a legal representative appointed under section 38(4) of the Youth Justice and Criminal Evidence Act 1999 and any expenses properly incurred in providing such a person with evidence or other material in connection with his appointment', and also sections 19(3ZA) and 20(1A)(d) of the 1985 Act and the Costs in Criminal Cases (General) Regulations 1986, as amended.

23A.10 Advocates and courts must be alert, too, to the possibility that were an advocate to agree to represent a defendant generally at trial, for no payment save that to which such regulations entitled him or her, then the statutory condition precedent for the appointment might be removed and the appointment in consequence withdrawn.

Criminal Procedure Rules 2020 (SI 2020/759), Pt 24

Trial and Sentence in a Magistrates' Court

When this Part applies

24.1.–(1) This Part applies in a magistrates' court where the court tries a case or the defendant pleads guilty. **B-387**

(2) Where the defendant is under 18, in this Part–

(a) a reference to convicting the defendant includes a reference to finding the defendant guilty of an offence; and

(b) a reference to sentence includes a reference to an order made on a finding of guilt.

General rules

24.2.–(1) Where this Part applies– **B-388**

(a) the general rule is that the hearing must be in public; but

(b) the court may exercise any power it has to

(i) impose reporting restrictions.

(ii) withhold information from the public, or

(iii) order a hearing in private; and

(c) unless the court otherwise directs, only the following may attend a hearing in a youth court–

(i) the parties and their legal representatives,

(ii) a defendant's parents, guardian or other supporting adult.

(iii) a witness.

(iv) anyone else directly concerned in the case, and

(v) a representative of a news-gathering or reporting organisation.

(2) Unless already done, the justices' legal adviser or the court must–

(a) read the allegation of the offence to the defendant;

(b) explain, in terms the defendant can understand (with help, if necessary)–

(i) the allegation, and
(ii) what the procedure at the hearing will be;
(c) ask whether the defendant has been advised about the potential effect on sentence of a guilty plea;
(d) ask whether the defendant pleads guilty or not guilty; and
(e) take the defendant's plea.

(3) The court may adjourn the hearing
(a) at any stage, to the same or to another magistrates' court; or
(b) to a youth court, where the court is not itself a youth court and the defendant is under 18.

(4) Paragraphs (1) and (2) of this rule do not apply where the court tries a case under rule 24.9 (single justice procedure: special rules)

Procedure on plea of not guilty

B-389 **24.3.**—(1) This rule applies—
(a) if the defendant has—
(i) entered a plea of not guilty, or
(ii) not entered a plea; or
(b) if, in either case, it appears to the court that there may be grounds for making a hospital order without convicting the defendant.

(2) If a not guilty plea was taken on a previous occasion, the justices' legal adviser or the court must ask the defendant to confirm that plea.

(3) In the following sequence—
(a) the prosecutor may summarise the prosecution case, concisely identifying the relevant law, outlining the facts and indicating the matters likely to be in dispute;
(b) to help the members of the court to understand the case and resolve any issue in it, the court may invite the defendant concisely to identify what is in issue;
(c) the prosecutor must introduce the evidence on which the prosecution case relies;
(d) at the conclusion of the prosecution case, on the defendant's application or on its own initiative, the court—
(i) may acquit on the ground that the prosecution evidence is insufficient for any reasonable court properly to convict, but
(ii) must not do so unless the prosecutor has had an opportunity to make representations;
(e) the justices' legal adviser or the court must explain, in terms the defendant can understand (with help, if necessary)—
(i) the right to give evidence, and
(ii) the potential effect of not doing so at all, or of refusing to answer a question while doing so;
(f) the defendant may introduce evidence;
(g) a party may introduce further evidence if it is then admissible (for example, because it is in rebuttal of evidence already introduced);
(h) the prosecutor may make final representations in support of the prosecution case, where—
(i) the defendant is represented by a legal representative, or
(ii) whether represented or not, the defendant has introduced evidence other than his or her own; and
(i) the defendant may make final representations in support of the defence case.

(4) Where a party wants to introduce evidence or make representations after that party's opportunity to do so under paragraph (3), the court—
(a) may refuse to receive any such evidence or representations; and
(b) must not receive any such evidence or representations after it has announced its verdict.

(5) If the court—
(a) convicts the defendant; or
(b) makes a hospital order instead of doing so,
it must give sufficient reasons to explain its decision.

(6) If the court acquits the defendant, it may—
(a) give an explanation of its decision; and
(b) exercise any power it has to make—
(i) a behaviour order, or
(ii) a costs order.

Evidence of a witness in person

24.4.–(1) This rule applies where a party wants to introduce evidence by calling a witness to give that evidence in person. **B-390**

(2) Unless the court otherwise directs–

(a) a witness waiting to give evidence must not wait inside the courtroom, unless that witness is–

(i) a party, or

(ii) an expert witness;

(b) a witness who gives evidence in the courtroom must do so from the place provided for that purpose; and

(c) a witness' address must not be announced unless it is relevant to an issue in the case.

(3) Unless other legislation otherwise provides, before giving evidence a witness must take an oath or affirm.

(4) In the following sequence–

(a) the party who calls a witness must ask questions in examination-in-chief;

(b) every other party may ask questions in cross-examination; and

(c) the party who called the witness may ask questions in re-examination.

(5) If other legislation so permits, at any time while giving evidence a witness may refer to a record of that witness' recollection of events.

(6) The justices' legal adviser or the court may–

(a) ask a witness questions; and in particular

(b) where the defendant is not represented, ask any question necessary in the defendant's interests.

Evidence of a witness in writing

24.5.–(1) This rule applies where a party wants to introduce in evidence the written statement of a witness to which applies– **B-391**

(a) Part 16 (written witness statements);

(b) Part 19 (expert evidence); or

(c) Part 20 (hearsay evidence).

(2) If the court admits such evidence–

(a) the court must read the statement; and

(b) unless the court otherwise directs, if any member of the public, including any reporter, is present, each relevant part of the statement must be read or summarised aloud.

Evidence by admission

24.6. (1) This rule applies where– **B-392**

(a) a party introduces in evidence a fact admitted by another party; or

(b) parties jointly admit a fact.

(2) Unless the court otherwise directs, a written record must be made of the admission.

Procedure on plea of guilty

24.7.–(1) This rule applies if– **B-393**

(a) the defendant pleads guilty; and

(b) the court is satisfied that the plea represents a clear acknowledgement of guilt.

(2) The court may convict the defendant without receiving evidence.

Written guilty plea: special rules

24.8.–(1) This rule applies where– **B-394**

(a) the offence alleged–

(i) can be tried only in a magistrates' court, and

(ii) is not one specified under section 12(1)(a) of the Magistrates' Courts Act 1980.

(b) the defendant is at least 16 years old;

(c) the prosecutor has served on the defendant–

(i) the summons or requisition.

(ii) the material listed in paragraph (2) on which the prosecutor relies to set out the facts of the offence,

(iii) the material listed in paragraph (3) on which the prosecutor relies to provide the court with information relevant to sentence,

(iv) a notice that the procedure set out in this rule applies, and
(v) a notice for the defendant's use if the defendant wants to plead guilty without attending court; and
(d) the prosecutor has served on the court officer—
(i) copies of those documents, and
(ii) a certificate of service of those documents on the defendant.

(2) The material that the prosecutor must serve to set out the facts of the offence is—
(a) a summary of the evidence on which the prosecution case is based;
(b) any—
(i) written witness statement to which Part 16 (written witness statements) applies, or
(ii) document or extract setting out facts; or
(c) any combination of such a summary, statement, document or extract.

(3) The material that the prosecutor must serve to provide information relevant to sentence is—
(a) details of any previous conviction of the defendant which the prosecutor considers relevant, other than any conviction listed in the defendant's driving record;
(b) if applicable, a notice that the defendant's driving record will be made available to the court; and
(c) a notice containing or describing any other information about the defendant, relevant to sentence. which will be made available to the court.

(4) A defendant who wants to plead guilty without attending court must, before the hearing date specified in the summons or requisition—
(a) serve a notice of guilty plea on the court officer; and
(b) include with that notice—
(i) any representations that the defendant wants the court to consider, and
(ii) a statement of the defendant's assets and other financial circumstances.

(5) A defendant who wants to withdraw such a notice must notify the court officer in writing before the hearing date.

(6) If the defendant does not withdraw the notice before the hearing date, then on or after that date—
(a) to establish the facts of the offence and other information about the defendant relevant to sentence, the court may take account only of—
(i) information contained in a document served by the prosecutor under paragraph (1),
(ii) any previous conviction listed in the defendant's driving record, where the offence is under the Road Traffic Regulation Act 1984, the Road Traffic Act 1988, the Road Traffic (Consequential Provisions) Act 1988 or the Road Traffic (Driver Licensing and Information Systems) Act 1989,
(iii) any other information about the defendant, relevant to sentence, of which the prosecutor served notice under paragraph (1), and
(iv) any representations and any other information served by the defendant under paragraph (4)

and rule 24.11(3) to (9) inclusive must be read accordingly;
(b) unless the court otherwise directs, the prosecutor need not attend; and
(c) the court may accept such a guilty plea and pass sentence in the defendant's absence.

(7) With the defendant's agreement, the court may deal with the case in the same way as under paragraph (6) where the defendant is present and
(a) has served a notice of guilty plea under paragraph (4); or
(b) pleads guilty there and then.

Single justice procedure: special rules

B-395 **24.9.**—(1) This rule applies where—
(a) the offence alleged—
(i) can be tried only in a magistrates' court, and
(ii) is not one punishable with imprisonment;
(b) the defendant is at least 18 years old;
(c) the prosecutor has served on the defendant—
(i) a written charge,
(ii) the material listed in paragraph (2) on which the prosecutor relies to set out the facts of the offence,
(iii) the material listed in paragraph (3) on which the prosecutor relies to provide the court with information relevant to sentence,

(iv) a notice that the procedure set out in this rule applies,
(v) a notice for the defendant's use if the defendant wants to plead guilty,
(vi) a notice for the defendant's use if the defendant wants to plead guilty but wants the case dealt with at a hearing by a court comprising more than one justice, and
(vii) a notice for the defendant's use if the defendant wants to plead not guilty; and
(d) the prosecutor has served on the court officer–
(i) copies of those documents, and
(ii) a certificate of service of those documents on the defendant.

(2) The material that the prosecutor must serve to set out the facts of the offence is–
(a) a summary of the evidence on which the prosecution case is based;
(b) any–
(i) written witness statement to which Part 16 (written witness statements) applies, or
(ii) document or extract setting out facts; or
(c) any combination of such a summary, statement, document or extract.

(3) The material that the prosecutor must serve to provide information relevant to sentence is–
(a) details of any previous conviction of the defendant which the prosecutor considers relevant, other than any conviction listed in the defendant's driving record;
(b) if applicable, a notice that the defendant's driving record will be made available to the court; and
(c) a notice containing or describing any other information about the defendant, relevant to sentence, which will be made available to the court.

(4) Not more 15 business days after service on the defendant of the documents listed in paragraph (1)(c)–
(a) a defendant who wants to plead guilty must serve a notice to that effect on the court officer and include with that notice–
(i) any representations that the defendant wants the court to consider, and
(ii) a statement of the defendant's assets and other financial circumstances;
(b) a defendant who wants to plead guilty but wants the case dealt with at a hearing by a court comprising more than one justice must serve a notice to that effect on the court officer; and
(c) a defendant who wants to plead not guilty must serve a notice to that effect on the court officer.

(5) If within 15 business days of service on the defendant of the documents listed in paragraph (l)(c) the defendant serves a notice to plead guilty under paragraph (4)(a)–
(a) the court officer must arrange for the court to deal with the case in accordance with that notice; and
(b) the time for service of any other notice under paragraph (4) expires at once.

(6) If within 15 business days of service on the defendant of the documents listed in paragraph (l)(c) the defendant wants to withdraw a notice which he or she has served under paragraph (4)(b) (notice to plead guilty at a hearing) or under paragraph (4)(c) (notice to plead not guilty), the defendant must–
(a) serve notice of that withdrawal on the court officer; and
(b) serve any substitute notice under paragraph (4).

(7) Paragraph (8) applies where by the date of trial the defendant has not–
(a) served notice under paragraph (4)(b) or (c) of wanting to plead guilty at a hearing, or wanting to plead not guilty; or
(b) given notice to that effect under section 16B(2) of the Magistrates' Courts Act 1980.

(8) Where this paragraph applies–
(a) the court may try the case in the parties' absence and without a hearing;
(b) the court may accept any guilty plea of which the defendant has given notice under paragraph (4)(a); and
(c) to establish the facts of the offence and other information about the defendant relevant to sentence, the court may take account only of–
(i) information contained in a document served by the prosecutor under paragraph (1),
(ii) any previous conviction listed in the defendant's driving record, where the offence is under the Road Traffic Regulation Act 1984, the Road Traffic Act 1988, the Road Traffic (Consequential Provisions) Act 1988 or the Road Traffic (Driver Licensing and Information Systems) Act 1989,
(iii) any other information about the defendant, relevant to sentence, of which the prosecutor served notice under paragraph (1), and

(iv) any representations and any other information served by the defendant under paragraph (4)(a)

and rule 24.11(3) to (9) inclusive must be read accordingly.

(9) Paragraph (10) applies where—

(a) the defendant serves on the court officer a notice under paragraph (4)(b) or (c); or

(b) the court which tries the defendant under paragraph (8) adjourns the trial for the defendant to attend a hearing by a court comprising more than one justice.

(10) Where this paragraph applies, the court must exercise its power to issue a summons and—

(a) the rules in Part 7 apply (starting a prosecution in a magistrates' court) as if the prosecutor had just served an application for a summons to be issued in the same terms as the written charge;

(b) the rules in Part 8 (initial details of the prosecution case) apply as if the documents served by the prosecutor under paragraph (1) had been served under that Part; and

(c) except for rule 24.8 (written guilty plea: special rules) and this rule, the rules in this Part apply.

Application to withdraw a guilty plea

B-396 **24.10.**—(1) This rule applies where the defendant wants to withdraw a guilty plea.

(2) The defendant must apply to do so—

(a) as soon as practicable after becoming aware of the reasons for doing so; and

(b) before sentence.

(3) Unless the court otherwise directs, the application must be in writing and the defendant must serve it on—

(a) the court officer; and

(b) the prosecutor.

(4) The application must—

(a) explain why it would be unjust not to allow the defendant to withdraw the guilty plea,

(b) identify—

(i) any witness that the defendant wants to call, and

(ii) any other proposed evidence; and

(c) say whether the defendant waives legal professional privilege, giving any relevant name and date.

Procedure if the court convicts

B-397 **24.11.**—(1) This rule applies if the court convicts the defendant.

(2) The court—

(a) may exercise its power to require—

(i) a statement of the defendant's assets and other financial circumstances,

(ii) a pre-sentence report; and

(b) may (and in some circumstances must) remit the defendant to a youth court for sentence where—

(i) the defendant is under 18, and

(ii) the convicting court is not itself a youth court.

(3) The prosecutor must—

(a) summarise the prosecution case, if the sentencing court has not heard evidence;

(b) identify any offence to be taken into consideration in sentencing;

(c) provide information relevant to sentence, including any statement of the effect of the offence on the victim, the victim's family or others; and

(d) where it is likely to assist the court, identify any other matter relevant to sentence including—

(i) the legislation applicable,

(ii) any sentencing guidelines, or guideline cases,

(iii) aggravating and mitigating features affecting the defendant's culpability and the harm which the offence caused, was intended to cause or might forseeably have caused, and

(iv) the effect of such of the information listed in paragraph (2)(a) as the court may need to take into account.

(4) The defendant must provide details of financial circumstances—

(a) in any form required by the court officer and

(b) by any date directed by the court or by the court officer.

(5) Where the defendant pleads guilty but wants to be sentenced on a different basis to that disclosed by the prosecution case—

(a) the defendant must set out that basis in writing, identifying what is in dispute;
(b) the court may invite the parties to make representations about whether the dispute is material to sentence; and
(c) if the court decides that it is a material dispute, the court must—
  (i) invite such further representations or evidence as it may require, and
  (ii) decide the dispute.

(6) Where the court has power to order the endorsement of the defendant's driving record, or power to order the defendant to be disqualified from driving—
(a) if other legislation so permits, a defendant who wants the court not to exercise that power must introduce the evidence or information on which the defendant relies;
(b) the prosecutor may introduce evidence; and
(c) the parties may make representations about that evidence or information.

(7) Before the court passes sentence—
(a) the court must—
  (i) give the defendant an opportunity to make representations and introduce evidence relevant to sentence, and
  (ii) where the defendant is under 18, give the defendant's parents, guardian or other supporting adult, if present, such an opportunity as well; and
(b) the justices' legal adviser or the court must elicit any further information relevant to sentence that the court may require.

(8) If the court requires more information, it may exercise its power to adjourn the hearing for not more than—
(a) 3 weeks at a time, if the defendant will be in custody; or
(b) 4 weeks at a time.

(9) When the court has taken into account all the evidence, information and any report available, the court must—
(a) as a general rule, pass sentence there and then;
(b) when passing sentence, explain the reasons for deciding on that sentence, unless neither the defendant nor any member of the public, including any reporter, is present;
(c) when passing sentence, explain to the defendant its effect, the consequences of failing to comply with any order or pay any fine, and any power that the court has to vary or review the sentence, unless—
  (i) the defendant is absent, or
  (ii) the defendant's ill-health or disorderly conduct makes such an explanation impracticable;
(d) give any such explanation in terms the defendant, if present, can understand (with help, if necessary); and
(e) consider exercising any power it has to make a costs or other order.

(10) Despite the general rule—
(a) the court must adjourn the hearing if the defendant is absent, the case started with a summons, requisition or single justice procedure notice, and either—
  (i) the court considers passing a custodial sentence (where it can do so), or
  (ii) the court considers imposing a disqualification (unless it has already adjourned the hearing to give the defendant an opportunity to attend); and
(b) the court may exercise any power it has to—
  (i) commit the defendant to the Crown Court for sentence (and in some cases it must do so), or
  (ii) defer sentence for up to 6 months.

Procedure where a party is absent

24.12.—(1) This rule— **B-398**
(a) applies where a party is absent; but
(b) does not apply where—
  (i) the defendant has served a notice of guilty plea under rule 24.8 (written guilty plea: special rules), or
  (ii) the court tries a case under rule 24.9 (single justice procedure: special rules).

(2) Where the prosecutor is absent, the court may—
(a) if it has received evidence, deal with the case as if the prosecutor were present; and
(b) in any other case—

(i) enquire into the reasons for the prosecutor's absence, and
(ii) if satisfied there is no good reason, exercise its power to dismiss the allegation.

(3) Where the defendant is absent the general rule is that the court must proceed as if the defendant were present and had pleaded not guilty (unless a plea already has been taken), but the general rule—

(a) does not apply if the defendant is under 18;
(b) is subject to the court being satisfied that—
(i) any summons or requisition was served on the defendant a reasonable time before the hearing, or
(ii) in a case in which the hearing has been adjourned, the defendant had reasonable notice of where and when it would resume; and
(c) is subject to rule 24.11(10)(a) (restrictions on passing sentence in the defendant's absence).

(4) Where the defendant is absent, the court—

(a) must exercise its power to issue a warrant for the defendant's arrest and detention in the terms required by rule 13.3(3) (Terms of a warrant for detention or imprisonment), if it passes a custodial sentence; and
(b) may exercise its power to issue a warrant for the defendant's arrest in any other case, if it does not apply the general rule in paragraph (3)(a) of this rule about proceeding in the defendant's absence.

[This rule is printed as amended by the Criminal Procedure (Amendment) Rules 2018 (SI 2018/132).]

Provision of documents for the court

B-399 **24.13.**—(1) A party who introduces a document in evidence, or who otherwise uses a document in presenting that party's case, must provide a copy for—

(a) each other party;
(b) any witness that party wants to refer to that document;
(c) the court; and
(d) the justices' legal adviser.

(2) Unless the court otherwise directs, on application or on its own initiative, the court officer must provide for the court—

(a) any copy received under paragraph (1) before the hearing begins; and
(b) a copy of the court officer's record of—
(i) information supplied by each party for the purposes of case management, including any revision of information previously supplied,
(ii) each pre-trial direction for the management of the case,
(iii) any pre-trial decision to admit evidence,
(iv) any pre-trial direction about the giving of evidence, and
(v) any admission to which rule 24.6 applies.

(3) Where rule 24.8 (written guilty plea: special rules) applies, the court officer must provide for the court—

(a) each document served by the prosecutor under rule 24.8(1)(d);
(b) the defendant's driving record, where the offence is under the Road Traffic Regulation Act 1984, the Road Traffic Act 1988 the Road Traffic (Consequential Provisions) Act 1988 or the Road Traffic (Driver Licensing and Information Systems) Act 1989;
(c) any other information about the defendant, relevant to sentence, of which the prosecutor served notice under rule 24.8(1); and
(d) the notice of guilty plea and any representations and other information served by the defendant under rule 24.8(4).

(4) Where the court tries a case under rule 24.9 (single justice procedure: special rules), the court officer must provide for the court—

(a) each document served by the prosecutor under rule 24.9(l)(d);
(b) the defendant's driving record, where the offence is under the Road Traffic Regulation Act 1984, the Road Traffic Act 1988, the Road Traffic (Consequential Provisions) Act 1988 or the Road Traffic (Driver Licensing and Information Systems) Act 1989;
(c) any other information about the defendant, relevant to sentence, of which the prosecutor served notice under rule 24.9(1); and
(d) any notice, representations and other information served by the defendant under rule 24.9(4)(a).

Duty of justices' legal adviser

24.14.–(1) A justices' legal adviser must attend the court and carry out the duties listed in this rule, as applicable, unless the court– **B-400**

(a) includes a District Judge (magistrates' courts); and

(b) otherwise directs.

(2) A justices' legal adviser must–

(a) before the hearing begins, by reference to what is provided for the court under rule 24.13 (provision of documents for the court) draw the court's attention to–

(i) what the prosecutor alleges,

(ii) what the parties say is agreed,

(iii) what the parties say is in dispute, and

(iv) what the parties say about how each expects to present the case, especially where that may affect its duration and timetabling;

(b) whenever necessary, give the court legal advice and–

(i) if necessary, attend the members of the court outside the courtroom to give such advice, but

(ii) inform the parties (if present) of any such advice given outside the courtroom; and

(c) assist the court, where appropriate, in the formulation of its reasons and the recording of those reasons.

(3) A justices' legal adviser must–

(a) assist an unrepresented defendant; and

(b) assist the court by–

(i) making a note of the substance of any oral evidence or representations, to help the court recall that information,

(ii) if the court rules inadmissible part of a written statement introduced in evidence, marking that statement in such a way as to make that clear,

(iii) ensuring that an adequate record is kept of the court's decisions and the reasons for them, and

(iv) making any announcement, other than of the verdict or sentence.

(4) Where the defendant has served a notice of guilty plea to which rule 24.8 (written guilty plea: special rules) applies, a justices' legal adviser must–

(a) unless the court otherwise directs, if any member of the public, including any reporter, is present, read aloud to the court–

(i) the material on which the prosecutor relies to set out the facts of the offence and to provide information relevant to sentence (or summarise any written statement included in that material, if the court so directs), and

(ii) any written representations by the defendant; and

(b) otherwise, draw the court's attention to–

(i) what the prosecutor alleges, and any significant features of the material listed in paragraph (4)(a)(i), and

(ii) any written representations by the defendant.

(5) Where the court tries a case under rule 24.9 (single justice procedure: special rules), a justices' legal adviser must draw the court's attention to–

(a) what the prosecutor alleges, and any significant features of the material on which the prosecutor relies to prove the alleged offence and to provide information relevant to sentence; and

(b) any representations served by the defendant.

Duty of court officer and custodian

24.15. (1) The court officer must– **★B-401**

(a) serve on each party notice of where and when an adjourned hearing will resume, unless–

(i) the party was present when that was arranged,

(ii) the defendant has served a notice of guilty plea to which rule 24.8 (written guilty plea: special rules) applies, and the adjournment is for not more than 4 weeks, or

(iii) the court tries a case under rule 24.9 (single justice procedure: special rules), and the adjourned trial will resume under that rule;

(b) if the reason for the adjournment was to postpone sentence, include that reason in any such notice to the defendant;

(c) unless the court otherwise directs, make available to the parties any written report to which rule 24.11 (procedure if the court convicts) applies;

(d) where the court has ordered a defendant to provide information under section 25 of the Road Traffic Offenders Act 1988, serve on the defendant notice of that order unless the defendant was present when it was made;

(e) serve on the prosecutor—

(i) any notice of guilty plea to which rule 24.8 (written guilty plea: special rules) applies; and

(ii) any declaration served under rule 44.2 (statutory declaration of ignorance of proceedings) that the defendant did not know about the case;

(f) serve on the prosecutor notice of any hearing date arranged in consequence of such a declaration, unless—

(i) the prosecutor was present when that was arranged, or

(ii) the court otherwise directs;

(g) serve on the prosecutor—

(i) notice of any hearing date arranged in consequence of the issue of a summons under rule 37.9 (single justice procedure: special rules), and in that event

(ii) any notice served by the defendant under rule 37.9(2)(b) or (c);

(h) record the court's reasons for not proceeding in the defendant's absence where rule 24.12(3)(a) applies; and

(i) give the court such other assistance as it requires.

(2) Where the court passes a sentence of immediate imprisonment or detention, or orders a suspended sentence of imprisonment to take effect, by this rule—

(a) the court requires the defendant to provide, in writing or orally, his or her nationality; and

(b) the custodian must obtain that information and record it.

[This rule is printed as amended, with effect from 8 February 2021, by SI 2021/40, r.12(c).]

CPD VI Trial 24A: Role of the justices' clerk/legal adviser

B-402 **24A.1** The role of the justices' clerk/legal adviser is a unique one, which carries with it independence from direction when undertaking a judicial function and when advising magistrates. These functions must be carried out in accordance with the Bangalore Principles of Judicial Conduct (judicial independence, impartiality, integrity, propriety, ensuring fair treatment and competence and diligence). More specifically, duties must be discharged in accordance with the relevant professional Code of Conduct and the Legal Adviser Competence Framework.

24A.2 A justices' clerk is responsible for:

(a) the legal advice tendered to the justices within the area;

(b) the performance of any of the functions set out below by any member of his staff acting as justices' legal adviser;

(c) ensuring that competent advice is available to justices when the justices' clerk is not personally present in court; and

(d) ensuring that advice given at all stages of proceedings and powers exercised (including those delegated to justices' legal advisers) take into account the court's duty to deal with cases justly and actively to manage the case.

24A.3 Where a person other than the justices' clerk (a justices' legal adviser), who is authorised to do so, performs any of the functions referred to in this direction, he or she will have the same duties, powers and responsibilities as the justices' clerk. The justices' legal adviser may consult the justices' clerk, or other person authorised by the justices' clerk for that purpose, before tendering advice to the bench. If the justices' clerk or that person gives any advice directly to the bench, he or she should give the parties or their advocates an opportunity of repeating any relevant submissions, prior to the advice being given.

24A.4 When exercising judicial powers, a justices' clerk or legal adviser is acting in exactly the same capacity as a magistrate. The justices' clerk may delegate powers to a justices' legal adviser in accordance with the relevant statutory authority. The scheme of delegation must be clear and in writing, so that all justices' legal advisers are certain of the extent of their powers. Once a power is delegated, judicial discretion in an individual case lies with the justices' legal adviser exercising the power. When exercise of a power does not require the consent of the parties, a justices' clerk or legal adviser may deal with and decide a contested issue or may refer that issue to the court

24A.5 It shall be the responsibility of the justices' clerk or legal adviser to provide the justices with any advice they require to perform their functions justly, whether or not the advice has been requested, on:

(a) questions of law;

(b) questions of mixed law and fact;
(c) matters of practice and procedure;
(d) the process to be followed at sentence and the matters to be taken into account, together with the range of penalties and ancillary orders available, in accordance with the relevant sentencing guidelines;
(e) any relevant decisions of the superior courts or other guidelines;
(f) the appropriate decision-making structure to be applied in any given case; and
(g) other issues relevant to the matter before the court.

24A.6 In addition to advising the justices, it shall be the justices' legal adviser's responsibility to assist the court, where appropriate, as to the formulation of reasons and the recording of those reasons.

24A.7 The justices' legal adviser has a duty to assist an unrepresented defendant, see CrimPR 9.4(3)(a), 14.3(2)(a) and 24.15(3)(a), in particular when the court is making a decision on allocation, bail, at trial and on sentence.

24A.8 Where the court must determine allocation, the legal adviser may deal with any aspect of the allocation hearing save for the decision on allocation, indication of sentence and sentence.

24A.9 When a defendant acting in person indicates a guilty plea, the legal adviser must explain the procedure and inform the defendant of their right to address the court on the facts and to provide details of their personal circumstances in order that the court can decide the appropriate sentence.

24A.10 When a defendant indicates a not guilty plea but has not completed the relevant sections of the Magistrates' Courts Trial Preparation Form, the legal adviser must either ensure that the Form is completed or, in appropriate cases, assist the court to obtain and record the essential information on the form.

24A.11 Immediately prior to the commencement of a trial, the legal adviser must summarise for the court the agreed and disputed issues, together with the way in which the parties propose to present their cases. If this is done by way of pre-court briefing, it should be confirmed in court or agreed with the parties.

24A.12 A justices' clerk or legal adviser must not play any part in making findings of fact, but may assist the bench by reminding them of the evidence, using any notes of the proceedings for this purpose, and clarifying the issues which are agreed and those which are to be determined.

24A.13 A justices' clerk or legal adviser may ask questions of witnesses and the parties in order to clarify the evidence and any issues in the case. A legal adviser has a duty to ensure that every case is conducted justly.

24A.14 When advising the justices, the justices' clerk or legal adviser, whether or not previously in court, should:
(a] ensure that he is aware of the relevant facts; and
(b) provide the parties with an opportunity to respond to any advice given.

24A.15 At any time, justices are entitled to receive advice to assist them in discharging their responsibilities. If they are in any doubt as to the evidence which has been given, they should seek the aid of their legal adviser, referring to his notes as appropriate. This should ordinarily be done in open court Where the justices request their adviser to join them in the retiring room, this request should be made in the presence of the parties in court Any legal advice given to the justices other than in open court should be clearly stated to be provisional; and the adviser should subsequently repeat the substance of the advice in open court and give the parties the opportunity to make any representations they wish on that provisional advice. The legal adviser should then state in open court whether the provisional advice is confirmed or, if it is varied, the nature of the variation.

24A.16 The legal adviser is under a duty to assist unrepresented parties, whether defendants or not to present their case, but must do so without appearing to become an advocate for the party concerned. The legal adviser should also ensure that members of the court are aware of obligations under the Victims' Code.

24A.17 The role of legal advisers in fine default proceedings, or any other proceedings for the enforcement of financial orders, obligations or penalties, is to assist the court They must not act in an adversarial or partisan manner, such as by attempting to establish wilful refusal or neglect or any other type of culpable behaviour, to offer an opinion on the facts, or to urge a particular course of action upon the justices. The expectation is that a legal adviser will ask questions of the defaulter to elicit information which the justices will require to make an adjudication, such as the explanation for the default A legal adviser may also advise the justices as to the options open to them in dealing with the case.

24A.18 The performance of a legal adviser is subject to regular appraisal. For that purpose the appraiser may be present in the justices' retiring room. The content of the appraisal is confidential, but the fact that an appraisal has taken place, and the presence of the appraiser in the retiring room, should be briefly explained in open court

CPD VI Trial 24B: Identification for the court of the issues in the case (as inserted by Criminal Practice Direction 2015 (Amendment No. 1) unreported, 23 March 2016, Lord Thomas CJ and as amended by Criminal Practice Direction 2015 (Amendment No. 8) [2019] EWCA Crim 495, Lord Burnett CJ)

B-403 **24B.1** CrimPR 3.11(a) requires the court, with the active assistance of the parties, to establish what are the disputed issues in order to manage the trial. To that end, the purpose of the prosecutor's summary of the prosecution case is to explain briefly, in the prosecutor's own terms, what the case is about, including any relevant legislation or case law relevant to the particular case. It will not usually be necessary, or helpful, to present a detailed account of all the prosecution evidence due to be introduced.

24B.2 CrimPR 24.3(3)(b) provides for a defendant, or his or her advocate, immediately after the prosecution opening to set out the issues in the defendant's own terms, if invited to do so by the court The purpose of any such identification of issues is to provide the court with focus as to what it is likely to be called upon to decide, so that the members of the court will be alert to those issues from the outset and can evaluate the prosecution evidence that they hear accordingly.

24B.3 The parties should keep in mind that in most cases, the members of the court already will be aware of what has been declared to be in issue. The court will have access to any written admissions and to information supplied for the purposes of case management: CrimPR 24.13(2). The court's legal adviser will have drawn the court's attention to what is alleged and to what is understood to be in dispute: CrimPR 24.15(2). If a party has nothing of substance to add to that then he or she should say so. The requirement to be concise will be enforced and the exchange with the court properly may be confined to enquiry and confirmation that the court's understanding of those allegations and issues is correct. Nevertheless, for the defendant to be offered an opportunity to identify issues at this stage may assist even if all he or she wishes to announce, or confirm, is that the prosecution is being put to proof.

24B.4 The identification of issues at the case management stage will have been made without the risk that they would be used at trial as statements of the defendant admissible in evidence against the defendant provided the advocate follows the letter and the spirit of the Criminal Procedure Rules. The court may take the view that a party is not acting in the spirit of the Criminal Procedure Rules in seeking to ambush the other party or raising late and technical legal arguments that were not previously raised as issues. No party that seeks to ambush the other at trial should derive an advantage from such a course of action. The court may also take the view that a defendant is not acting in the spirit of the Criminal Procedure Rules if he or she refuses to identify the issues and puts the prosecutor to proof at the case management stage. In both such circumstances the court may limit the proceedings on the day of trial in accordance with CrimPR 3.11(d). In addition any significant divergence from the issues identified at case management at this late stage may well result in the exercise of the court's powers under CrimPR 3.5(6), the powers to impose sanctions.

CPD VI Trial 24C: Trial adjournment in the magistrates' court

B-404 **24C.1** Courts are entitled to expect the parties and other participants to adhere to CrimPR 1.2 (The duty of the participants in a criminal case) and to prepare accordingly for the trial to proceed on the date arranged. The court will expect communication between the parties and with the court regarding any issues which are likely to affect the effectiveness of any trial: CrimPR 3.2(2)(b)-(e). In particular, any revision of the information provided in the preparation for effective trial form must be reported to the court and each other party well in advance of the trial, not at trial or shortly before; and in considering any application to adjourn a trial the court will regard as especially significant any failure in this respect. Any communication should clearly identify the issue and any direction sought and should require reference to a legal adviser or case progression officer. The parties and other participants are entitled to expect the court and its staff to adhere to CrimPR 1.3 (The application by the court of the overriding objective) and to conduct its business accordingly. If relevant Criminal Procedure Rules, Criminal Practice Directions and judicial directions for trial preparation are followed, an effective trial on the date arranged will be the result.

24C.2 In some circumstances during preparation for trial it will become apparent to a party that a trial will not be required. It is in the interests of victims, witnesses, defendants, the court and legal representatives that these decisions are made at the earliest opportunity and that the other party, or parties, and the court are notified immediately. The requirements for an application to vacate a trial fixture are set out at paragraphs 24C.30 to 24C.32 beneath.

24C.3 Where a defendant who previously has pleaded not guilty decides to enter a guilty plea, notice of that decision, and the basis of plea, should be given to the prosecution and court as soon as possible so that a decision can be taken about the need for witnesses to attend (but caution should be exercised before the witnesses' attendance is dispensed with, and usually it will be advisable to set a date for the plea to be taken in advance of the date already set for trial). The sooner that notice of such a plea is given, the greater the reduction in sentence the defendant can expect. The court will expect an explanation for the change of plea to assess the level of credit to be applied.

24C.4 Where a party is unable to comply with a direction within the time set by the court, and that failure will have implications for preparation by another party or for the likelihood of the trial proceeding within the time allocated, the party concerned should advise each other party and the court immediately of the failure and of the anticipated date for compliance: CrimPR 1.2(1)(c) and 3.10(2)(d). Parties are encouraged to communicate with each other to agree alternative dates consistent with maintaining the trial fixture: CrimPR 3.7.

Application to adjourn on day of trial

General principles

24C.5 The court is entitled to expect that trials will start on time with all case management issues dealt with in advance of the trial date. Early engagement between the parties and communication with the court should mean that it is rare for applications to adjourn trials to be made on the day of trial, except in circumstances that could not have been foreseen. However, there will be occasions on which, on the day set for trial, the court is invited without prior warning to adjourn to another day in consequence of an event or events said to make it unjust to proceed as planned; and in some circumstances it may have been necessary to arrange to hear a contested application to adjourn a trial on the very date on which that trial is due to begin (though before making such arrangements the court should have kept in mind the need to make time available for other cases, too, where the time available for the trial will be abbreviated by the time required to hear the application to adjourn it). **B-405**

24C.6 Section 10 of the Magistrates' Courts Act 1980 confers a discretionary power to adjourn, and see also CrimPR 24.2(3). The following directions codify and restate procedural principles established in a long line of judgments of the senior courts, to some of which they refer. Therefore these directions supersede those judgments and it is to these directions that magistrates' courts must refer in the first instance.

24C.7 The starting point is that the trial should proceed. The basic approach was explained by Gross LJ in *Director of Public Prosecutions v Petrie* [2015] EWHC 48 (Admin):

> "... successive initiatives ... have repeatedly exhorted the magistracy and District Bench to case manage robustly and to resist the granting of adjournments. Although there are of course instances where the interests of justice require the grant of an adjournment, this should be a course of last rather than first resort - and after other alternatives have been considered. ... It is essential that parties to proceedings in a magistrates' court should proceed on the basis of a need to get matters right first time; any suggestion of a culture readily permitting an opportunity to correct failures of preparation should be firmly dispelled."

24C.8 A magistrates' court may keep in mind that, if appropriate, the court's decision may be reopened (see CrimPR 24.18), and that avenues of appeal by way of rehearing or of review are open to the parties, including in a case in which it is later discovered that the court has acted on a material mistake of fact (see *R. (Director of Public Prosecutions) v Sunderland Magistrates' Court*; *R. (Kharaghan) v City of London Magistrates' Court* [2018] EWHC 229 (Admin)). The court should not be deterred from a prompt and robust determination therefore. Only if there are compelling reasons for doing so will the High Court interfere with the court's exercise of its discretion.

24C.9 In general, the relevant principles relating to trial adjournment are these:

- the court's duty is to deal justly with the case, which includes doing justice between the parties.
- the court must have regard to the need for expedition. Delay is generally inimical to the interests of justice and brings the criminal justice system into disrepute. Proceedings in a magistrates' court should be simple and speedy.
- applications for adjournments should be rigorously scrutinised and the court must have a clear reason for adjourning. To do this, the court must review the history of the case.
- where the prosecutor asks for an adjournment the court must consider not only the interest of the defendant in getting the matter dealt with without delay but also the public interest in ensuring that criminal charges are adjudicated upon thoroughly, with the guilty convicted as well as the innocent acquitted.
- with a more serious charge the public interest that there be a trial will carry greater weight. It is, however, reasonable for the court to expect that parties should have given especially careful attention to the preparation of trials involving serious offences or where the trial has significant implications for victims or witnesses.
- where the defendant asks for an adjournment the court must consider whether he or she will be able to present the defence fully without and, if not, the extent to which his or her ability to do so is compromised.

- the court must consider the consequences of an adjournment and its impact on the ability of witnesses and defendants accurately to recall events.
- the impact of adjournment on other cases. The relisting of one case almost inevitably delays or displaces the hearing of others. The length of the hearing and the extent of delay in other cases will need to be considered.

The relevance of fault

B-406 **24C.10** As the starting point is that the trial should proceed, a consequence of doing so without adjournment may be that the prosecutor is unable to prove the prosecution case, or that the defendant is unable to explore an issue. That may be a just consequence of inadequate preparation. Even in the absence of fault on the part of either party it may not be in the interests of justice to adjourn, notwithstanding that an imperfect trial may be the result.

24C.11 The reason why the adjournment is required should be examined and if it arises through the fault of the applicant for that adjournment then that weighs against its grant, carrying weight in accordance with the gravity of the fault. For the purposes of this paragraph, the prosecutor and those who investigated the case usually should be treated as one.

24C.12 If the applicant was at fault, was it serious? A fault will be serious if the relevant act or omission has been repeated, especially where it has caused a previous adjournment, or where there is no reasonable explanation for that act or omission. The more serious the default, the less willing the court will be to adjourn.

24C.13 Where a party has been at fault, did the other party, if aware of it, draw attention to that fault promptly and explicitly? CrimPR 1.2(1)(c) imposes a collective responsibility on participants promptly to draw attention to a significant failure to take a required procedural step. CrimPR 3.10(2)(d) requires each party promptly to inform the court and the other parties of anything that may affect the date or duration of the trial or significantly affect the progress of the case in any other way. If no such action has been taken by a party who could have done so then the court may look less favourably on any application by that same party to adjourn, and especially if that application reasonably might have been made before the trial date.

Length of adjournment

B-407 **24C.14** Were an adjournment granted, for how long would it need to be? The shorter the necessary adjournment, the less objectionable it will be - although much will depend on the ability of the court to accommodate it without undue impact on other cases. Courts must make every effort to make the adjournment as short as possible, for example by using time vacated by another trial or by conducting the hearing at another court house. In some cases it may be possible to achieve a just outcome by a short adjournment to later on the same day.

24C.15 If the reason for the application to adjourn is that the applicant party seeks more time in which to raise or explore an issue, has that party reasonable grounds for its late identification despite the requirements of CrimPR 3.3(1) read with 3.2(2) (early identification of issues)? In the absence of such grounds, that failure will constitute a fault for the purposes of these directions.

Particular grounds of applications to adjourn trials

B-408 **24C.16** The following paragraphs identify some particular factors which may need to be taken into account in addition to those identified in paragraphs 24C.5 - 24C15.

Absence of defendant

B-409 **24C.17** If a defendant has attained the age of 18 years, the court shall proceed in his absence unless it appears to the court to be contrary to the interests of justice to do so: section 11 of the Magistrates' Courts Act 1980. In marked contrast to the position in the Crown Court, in magistrates' courts proceeding in the absence of a defendant is the default position where the defendant is aware of the date of trial and no acceptable reason is offered for that absence. The court is not obliged to investigate if no reason is offered. In assessing where the interests of justice lie the court will take into account all factors, including such reasons for absence as may be offered; the reliability of the information supplied in support of those reasons; the date on which the reasons for absence became known to the defendant; and what action the defendant thereafter took in response. Where the defendant provides a medical note to excuse his or her non-attendance the court must consider 5C of these Practice Directions (issue of medical certificates) and give reasons if deciding to proceed notwithstanding.

24C.18 If the court does not proceed to trial in the absence of the defendant it is required by the 1980 Act to give its reasons, which must be specific to the case: section 11(7), and see also CrimPR 24.16(h).

24C.19 Where a defendant is under 18, there is no presumption that the court should proceed in absence. In deciding whether it is in the interests of justice to proceed the court should take into account:

- that trial in absence can and sometimes does result in acquittal and that it is in nobody's interests to delay an acquittal;
- that if convicted the defendant can ask that the conviction be re-opened in the interests of justice, for example if absence was involuntary;
- that if convicted the defendant has a right to a rehearing on appeal to the Crown Court;
- the age, vulnerability, or experience of the defendant;
- whether a parent or guardian is present, whether a parent or guardian ordinarily would be required to attend and whether such a person has attended a previous hearing;
- the interests of any co-defendant in the case proceeding;
- the interests of witnesses who have attended, including the age of any such witness;
- the nature of the evidence and whether memories of relevant evidence are liable to fade;
- how soon an adjourned trial can be accommodated in the court list. When proceeding in absence or adjourning the court must give its reasons.

Absence of witness

24C.20 Where the court is asked to adjourn because a witness has failed to attend, the court must: **B-410**

- rigorously investigate the steps taken to secure that witness' attendance, the reasons given for absence and the likelihood of the witness attending should the case be adjourned;
- consider the relevance of the witness to the case, and whether the witness' statement can be agreed or admitted, in whole or part, as hearsay, including under section 114(1)(d) of the Criminal Justice Act 2003 ;
- in the case of a defence witness, consider whether proper notice has been given of the intention to call that witness;
- consider whether an absent witness can be heard later in the trial;
- where other witnesses have attended and the court has determined that the absent witness is required, consider hearing those witnesses who are present and adjourning the case part-heard, provided the next hearing can be held conveniently in a matter of days or weeks, not months, to avoid having to recall all the witnesses.

Failure to serve evidence in time

24C.21 It should rarely be the case that an application to adjourn based on a failure to serve evidence is made on the day of trial. The court is entitled to expect that evidence will have been served in good time and in accordance with the directions of the court. The court should consider whether the party who complains of the failure had drawn attention to it: CrimPR 1.2(1)(c) and 3.10(2)(d), and see paragraphs 24C.10 - 24C.13 above. **B-411**

24C.22 The court must conduct a rigorous inquiry into the nature of the evidence and must consider whether any of what is sought has been served, and if so when; the volume and the significance of what is sought; and the time likely to be needed for its consideration. In particular, the court must satisfy itself that any material still sought is relevant and that the party seeking it has a right to it. In some circumstances a failure to serve evidence can be addressed by refusing to admit it instead of by adjourning the trial to allow it to be served: see *Boardman* [2015] EWCA Crim 175; [2015] 1 Cr. App. R. 33; [2015] Crim. L.R. 451.

Failure to comply with disclosure obligations

24C.23 The parties' disclosure obligations arise from the Criminal Procedure and Investigations Act 1996. The procedure to comply with those duties is set out at CrimPR Part 15. Disclosure is not a trial issue. It should have been resolved by the parties complying with their statutory obligations and with the Rules in advance of the trial. **B-412**

24C.24 Where a defendant complains of a prosecution failure to disclose material that ought to have been disclosed the court must first establish whether either party is applying for an adjournment as a result. If an adjournment is sought, the court should consider whether the matter can be resolved by the giving of disclosure immediately. If it cannot, the court should consider whether the parties have complied with their obligations under CrimPR 3.3 and under the provisions listed in paragraph 24C.1 above, and should consider the relevance of fault.

24C.25 If the prosecutor has complied or purported to comply with his or her initial disclosure obligations, no further material is disclosable and consequently no application to adjourn should be entertained unless the defendant has served a defence statement in accordance with section 6 of the Criminal Procedure and Investigations Act 1996 and CrimPR 15.4.

24C.26 If the defendant has served a defence statement and asks for further disclosure, in consequence of the prosecutor's allegedly inadequate response or in consequence of a failure to respond at all, the court has no power to entertain an application for that further disclosure unless it is made pursuant to section 8 of the Criminal Procedure and Investigations Act 1996 and CrimPR 15.5. The court should consider hearing such an application immediately, provided that there is sufficient time available for the application itself and then for the defence to consider any material disclosed in consequence of it.

MANAGING TRIALS WITHIN AVAILABLE COURT TIME

B-413 **24C.27** Where there is a risk of a trials being adjourned for lack of court time the court or legal adviser must assess the priority to be assigned to each trial listed for hearing that day based on the needs of the parties, whether the case has been adjourned before and the seriousness of the offence; giving priority to any cases in which the defendant is in custody by reason only of a trial due to be heard that day. Where more than one court is sitting to deal with trials, liaison between courtrooms should occur to determine the potential for all listed trials to be heard through movement of cases. Where a case is moved from one courtroom to another and as a result is assigned to a different advocate, the court must allow the fresh advocate adequate time in which to prepare. Courts should always begin a trial by reviewing the need for witnesses and the timetable set during pre-trial case management. The court will be slow to adjourn a trial until it is clear that all other trials assessed as having an equal or higher priority for hearing that day will be effective.

24C.28 The court is entitled to expect that parties will present their case within the time set during pre-trial case management. In entertaining additional applications for which no time has been allowed the court must keep in mind the expectation that the trial will be completed within the allocated time with minimal impact on other cases.

24C.29 While it is preferable to complete a trial on the date allocated, there will be occasions on which it is appropriate to adjourn part-heard, particularly where it is possible to hear the majority of witnesses. If necessary future listings will be moved to accommodate the hearing.

APPLICATIONS TO VACATE TRIALS

B-414 **24C.30** To make the best use of the court's and the parties' time it is expected that applications to vacate trials will be made promptly and in writing, in advance of the date of trial. Any application should be served on each other party at the same time as it is served on the court. As a general rule, such an application will be dealt with outside the courtroom under CrimPR 3.5. An application to vacate a trial will be considered in accordance with the same principles as those identified in paragraphs 24C.5 - 24C.26 of these Directions.

24C.31 Given the binding nature of any decision on an application to vacate and refix a trial, absent a change of circumstances, it is incumbent on the parties to provide full and accurate information to the court to enable it to assess where the interests of justice lie: see *R. (on the application of F and another) v Knowsley Magistrates Court* [2006] EWHC 695 (Admin); *R. (Jones) v South East Surrey Local Justice Area* [2010] EWHC 916 (Admin), (2010) 174 JP 342; *DPP v Woods* [2017] EWHC 1070 (Admin). Any application should, as a minimum, include (as should, as appropriate, any response):

- the reason for the application;
- a chronology of the case, recording the dates of compliance with any directions and of communication between the parties;
- an assessment of the interests of justice, addressing the factors identified in these Practice Directions and indicating the likely effect should the court conclude that the trial should proceed on the date fixed;
- any restrictions on the future availability of witnesses;
- any likely changes to the number of witnesses or the way in which the evidence will be presented and any impact on the trial time estimate.

24C.32 On receipt of an application each other party should serve that party's response on the court and on the applicant within 2 business days unless the court otherwise directs. Any request for the matter to be determined at a hearing should be served with the application to vacate the trial or with the response to that application, as the case may be, together with the reasons for that request, to enable the court to decide whether a hearing is needed.

Criminal Procedure Rules 2020 (SI 2020/759), Pt 25

TRIAL AND SENTENCE IN THE CROWN COURT

When this Part applies

★B-415 **25.1.** This Part applies in the Crown Court where the court tries a case or the defendant pleads guilty.

General powers and requirements

25.2.—(1) Where this Part applies, the general rule is that—

(a) the trial must be in public, but that is subject to the court's power to–
  (i) impose a restriction on reporting what takes place at a public hearing, or public access to what otherwise would be a public hearing,
  (ii) withhold information from the public during a public hearing, or
  (iii) order a trial in private;
(b) the court must not proceed if the defendant is absent, unless the court is satisfied that–
  (i) the defendant has waived the right to attend, and
  (ii) the trial will be fair despite the defendant's absence; and
(c) the court must not sentence the defendant to imprisonment or detention unless–
  (i) the defendant has a legal representative,
  (ii) the defendant has been sentenced to imprisonment or detention on a previous occasion in the United Kingdom, or
  (iii) the defendant could have been represented under legal aid but is not because section 226(7), (8) of the Sentencing Act 2020 applies to him or her.

(2) Before proceeding to trial the court must–
(a) obtain the prosecutor's confirmation, in writing or orally, that the indictment on which the defendant is about to be tried sets out–
  (i) a statement of each offence that the prosecutor wants the court to try, and
  (ii) such particulars of the conduct constituting the commission of each such offence as the prosecutor relies upon to make clear what is alleged;
(b) ensure that the defendant is correctly identified by that indictment;
(c) satisfy itself that there has been explained to the defendant, in terms the defendant can understand (with help, if necessary), each allegation in that indictment against him or her; and
(d) invite any objection to the terms or validity of that indictment.

(3) The court may adjourn the trial at any stage

[This rule is printed as amended, with effect from 8 February 2021, by SI 2021/40, r.13(a).]

Application for ruling on procedure, evidence or other question of law

25.3.–(1) This rule applies to an application– **B-416**
(a) about–
  (i) case management, or any other question of procedure, or
  (ii) the introduction or admissibility of evidence, or any other question of law; and
(b) that has not been determined before the trial begins.

(2) The application is subject to any other rule that applies to it (for example, as to the time and form in which the application must be made).

(3) Unless the court otherwise directs, the application must be made, and the court's decision announced, in the absence of the jury (if there is one).

Procedure on plea of guilty

25.4.–(1) This rule applies if– **B-417**
(a) the defendant pleads guilty to an offence; and
(b) the court is satisfied that the plea represents a clear acknowledgement of guilt.

(2) The court need not receive evidence unless rule 25.16(4) applies (determination of facts for sentencing).

Application to vacate a guilty plea

25.5.–(1) This rule applies where a party wants the court to vacate a guilty plea. **B-418**

(2) Such a party must–
(a) apply in writing–
  (i) as soon as practicable after becoming aware of the grounds for doing so, and
  (ii) in any event, before the final disposal of the case, by sentence or otherwise; and
(b) serve the application on–
  (i) the court officer, and
  (ii) the prosecutor.

(3) Unless the court otherwise directs, the application must–
(a) explain why it would be unjust for the guilty plea to remain unchanged;
(b) indicate what, if any, evidence the applicant wishes to call;
(c) identify any proposed witness; and

(d) indicate whether legal professional privilege is waived, specifying any material name and date.

Selecting the jury

B-419 **25.6.**—(1) This rule—

(a) applies where—

(i) the defendant pleads not guilty,

(ii) the defendant declines to enter a plea and the court treats that as a not guilty plea, or

(iii) the court determines that the defendant is not fit to be tried; but

(b) does not apply where—

(i) the court orders a trial without a jury because of a danger of jury tampering or where jury tampering appears to have taken place, or

(ii) the court tries without a jury counts on an indictment after a trial of sample counts with a jury.

(2) The court must select a jury to try the case from the panel, or part of the panel, of jurors summoned by the Lord Chancellor to attend at that time and place.

(3) Where it appears that too few jurors to constitute a jury will be available from among those so summoned, the court—

(a) may exercise its own power to summon others in the court room, or in the vicinity, up to the number likely to be required, and add their names to the panel summoned by the Lord Chancellor; but

(b) must inform the parties, if they are absent when the court exercises that power.

(4) The court must select the jury by drawing at random each juror's name from among those so summoned and—

(a) announcing each name so drawn; or

(b) announcing an identifying number assigned by the court officer to that person, where the court is satisfied that that is necessary.

(5) If too few jurors to constitute a jury are available from the panel after all their names have been drawn, the court may—

(a) exercise its own power to summon others in the court room, or in the vicinity, up to the number required; and

(b) announce—

(i) the name of each person so summoned, or

(ii) an identifying number assigned by the court officer to that person, where the court is satisfied that that is necessary.

(6) The jury the court selects—

(a) must comprise no fewer than 12 jurors; and

(b) may comprise as many as 14 jurors to begin with, where the court expects the trial to last for more than 4 weeks.

(7) Where the court selects a jury comprising more than 12 jurors, the court must explain to them that—

(a) the purpose of selecting more than 12 jurors to begin with is to fill any vacancy or vacancies caused by the discharge of any of the first 12 before the prosecution evidence begins;

(b) any such vacancy or vacancies will be filled by the extra jurors in order of their selection from the panel;

(c) the court will discharge any extra juror or jurors remaining by no later than the beginning of the prosecution evidence; and

(d) any juror who is discharged for that reason then will be available to be selected for service on another jury, during the period for which that juror has been summoned.

(8) Each of the 12 or more jurors the court selects—

(a) must take an oath or affirm; and

(b) becomes a full jury member until discharged.

(9) The oath or affirmation must be in these terms, or in any corresponding terms that the juror declares to be binding on him or her—

"I swear by Almighty God [or I do solemnly, sincerely and truly declare and affirm] that I will faithfully try the defendant and give a true verdict according to the evidence.".

Discharging jurors

B-420 **25.7.**—(1) The court may exercise its power to discharge a juror at any time—

(a) after the juror completes the oath or affirmation; and

(b) before the court discharges the jury.

(2) No later than the beginning of the prosecution evidence, if the jury then comprises more than 12 jurors the court must discharge any in excess of 12 in reverse order of their selection from the panel.

(3) The court may exercise its power to discharge the jury at any time–

(a) after each juror has completed the oath or affirmation; and

(b) before the jury has delivered its verdict on each offence charged in the indictment.

(4) The court must exercise its power to discharge the jury when, in respect of each offence charged in the indictment, either–

(a) the jury has delivered its verdict on that offence; or

(b) the court has discharged the jury from reaching a verdict.

Objecting to jurors

25.8.–(1) A party who objects to the panel of jurors must serve notice explaining the objection on the court officer and on the other party before the first juror's name or number is drawn.

(2) A party who objects to the selection of an individual juror must–

(a) tell the court of the objection–

(i) after the juror's name or number is announced, and

(ii) before the juror completes the oath or affirmation; and

(b) explain the objection.

(3) A prosecutor who exercises the prosecution right without giving reasons to prevent the court selecting an individual juror must announce the exercise of that right before the juror completes the oath or affirmation.

(4) The court must determine an objection under paragraph (1) or (2)–

(a) at a hearing, in public or in private; and

(b) in the absence of the jurors, unless the court otherwise directs.

Procedure on plea of not guilty

25.9.–(1) This rule applies where– B-421

(a) the defendant pleads not guilty; or

(b) the defendant declines to enter a plea and the court treats that as a not guilty plea.

(2) In the following sequence–

(a) where there is a jury, the court must–

(i) inform the jurors of each offence charged in the indictment to which the defendant pleads not guilty, and

(ii) explain to the jurors that it is their duty, after hearing the evidence, to decide whether the defendant is guilty or not guilty of each offence;

(b) the prosecutor may summarise the prosecution case, concisely outlining the facts and the matters likely to be in dispute;

(c) where there is a jury, to help the jurors to understand the case and resolve any issue in it the court may–

(i) invite the defendant concisely to identify what is in issue, if necessary in terms approved by the court, and

(ii) if the defendant declines to do so, direct that the jurors be given a copy of any defence statement served under rule 15.4 (defence disclosure), edited if necessary to exclude any reference to inappropriate matters or to matters evidence of which would not be admissible;

(d) the prosecutor must introduce the evidence on which the prosecution case relies;

(e) subject to paragraph (3), at the end of the prosecution evidence, on the defendant's application or on its own initiative, the court–

(i) may direct the jury (if there is one) to acquit on the ground that the prosecution evidence is insufficient for any reasonable court properly to convict, but

(ii) must not do so unless the prosecutor has had an opportunity to make representations;

(f) subject to paragraph (4), at the end of the prosecution evidence, the court must ask whether the defendant intends to give evidence in person and, if the answer is "no", then the court must satisfy itself that there has been explained to the defendant, in terms the defendant can understand (with help, if necessary)–

(i) the right to give evidence in person, and

(ii) that if the defendant does not give evidence in person, or refuses to answer a question while giving evidence, the court may draw such inferences as seem proper;

(g) the defendant may summarise the defence case, if he or she intends to call at least one witness other than him or herself to give evidence in person about the facts of the case;
(h) in this order (or in a different order, if the court so directs) the defendant may—
  (i) give evidence in person,
  (ii) call another witness, or witnesses, to give evidence in person, and
  (iii) introduce any other evidence;
(i) a party may introduce further evidence if it is then admissible (for example, because it is in rebuttal of evidence already introduced);
(j) the prosecutor may make final representations, where—
  (i) the defendant has a legal representative,
  (ii) the defendant has called at least one witness, other than the defendant him or herself, to give evidence in person about the facts of the case, or
  (iii) the court so permits; and
(k) the defendant may make final representations.

(3) Paragraph (2)(e) does not apply in relation to a charge of murder, manslaughter, attempted murder, or causing harm contrary to section 18 or 20 of the Offences against the Person Act 1861 until the court has heard all the evidence (including any defence evidence), where the defendant is charged with—
(a) any of those offences; and
(b) an offence of causing or allowing a child or vulnerable adult to die or to suffer serious physical harm, contrary to section 5 of the Domestic Violence, Crime and Victims Act 2004.

(4) Paragraph (2)(f) does not apply where it appears to the court that, taking account of all the circumstances, the defendant's physical or mental condition makes it undesirable for the defendant to give evidence in person.

(5) Where there is more than one defendant, this rule applies to each in the order their names appear in the indictment, or in an order directed by the court.

(6) Unless the jury (if there is one) has retired to consider its verdict, the court may allow a party to introduce evidence, or make representations, after that party's opportunity to do so under paragraph (2).

(7) Unless the jury has already reached a verdict on a count, the court may exercise its power to—
(a) discharge the jury from reaching a verdict on that count;
(b) direct the jury to acquit the defendant on that count; or
(c) invite the jury to convict the defendant, if the defendant pleads guilty to the offence charged by that count.

Defendant unfit to plead

B-422 **25.10.**—(1) This rule applies where—
(a) it appears to the court, on application or on its own initiative, that the defendant may not be fit to be tried; and
(b) the defendant has not by then been acquitted of each offence charged by the indictment.

(2) The court—
(a) must exercise its power to decide, without a jury, whether the defendant is fit to be tried; but
(b) may postpone the exercise of that power until immediately before the opening of the defence case.

(3) Where the court determines that the defendant is not fit to be tried—
(a) the court must exercise its power to appoint a person to put the case for the defence, taking account of all the circumstances and in particular—
  (i) the willingness and suitability (including the qualifications and experience) of that person,
  (ii) the nature and complexity of the case,
  (iii) any advantage of continuity of representation, and
  (iv) the defendant's wishes and needs;
(b) the court must select a jury, if none has been selected yet; and
(c) rule 25.9 (procedure on plea of not guilty) applies, if the steps it lists have not already been taken, except that—
  (i) everything which that rule requires to be done by the defendant may be done instead by the person appointed to put the case for the defence,
  (ii) under rule 25.9(2)(a), the court must explain to the jurors that their duty is to decide

whether or not the defendant did the act or made the omission charged as an offence, not whether the defendant is guilty of that offence, and
(iii) rule 25.9(2)(e) does not apply (warning of consequences of defendant not giving evidence).

Evidence of a witness in person

25.11–(1) This rule applies where a party wants to introduce evidence by calling a witness to give that evidence in person. **B-423**

(2) Unless the court otherwise directs–
(a) a witness waiting to give evidence must not wait inside the courtroom, unless that witness is–
(i) a party, or
(ii) an expert witness;
(b) a witness who gives evidence in the courtroom must do so from the place provided for that purpose; and
(c) a witness' address–
(i) must not be given in public unless the address is relevant to an issue in the case, and
(ii) may be given in writing to the court, parties and jury.

(3) Unless other legislation otherwise provides, before giving evidence a witness must take an oath or affirm.

(4) In the following sequence–
(a) the party who calls a witness may ask questions in examination-in-chief;
(b) if the witness gives evidence for the prosecution–
(i) the defendant, if there is only one, may ask questions in cross-examination, or
(ii) subject to the court's directions, each defendant, if there is more than one, may ask such questions, in the order their names appear in the indictment or as directed by the court;
(c) if the witness gives evidence for a defendant–
(i) subject to the court's directions, each other defendant, if there is more than one, may ask questions in cross-examination, in the order their names appear in the indictment or as directed by the court, and
(ii) the prosecutor may ask such questions; and
(d) the party who called the witness may ask questions in re-examination arising out of any cross-examination.

(5) If other legislation so permits, at any time while giving evidence a witness may refer to a record of that witness' recollection of events.

(6) The court may–
(a) ask a witness questions; and in particular
(b) where the defendant is not represented, ask a witness any question necessary in the defendant's interests.

Evidence of witness in writing

25.12.–(1) This rule applies where a party wants to introduce in evidence the written statement of a witness to which applies– **B-424**
(a) Part 16 (written witness statements);
(b) Part 19 (expert evidence); or
(c) Part 20 (hearsay evidence).

(2) If the court admits such evidence each relevant part of the statement must be read or summarised aloud, unless the court otherwise directs.

Evidence by admission

25.13.–(1) This rule applies where– **B-425**
(a) a party introduces in evidence a fact admitted by another party; or
(b) parties jointly admit a fact.

(2) Unless the court otherwise directs, a written record must be made of the admission.

Directions to the jury and taking the verdict

25.14.–(1) This rule applies where there is a jury. **B-426**

(2) The court must give the jury directions about the relevant law at any time at which to do so will assist jurors to evaluate the evidence.

(3) After following the sequence in rule 25.9 (procedure on plea of not guilty), the court must—
(a) summarise for the jury, to such extent as is necessary, the evidence relevant to the issues they must decide;
(b) give the jury such questions, if any, as the court invites jurors to answer in coming to a verdict;
(c) direct the jury to retire to consider its verdict;
(d) if necessary, recall the jury—
(i) to answer jurors' questions, or
(ii) to give directions, or further directions, about considering and delivering its verdict or verdicts, including, if appropriate, directions about reaching a verdict by a majority;
(e) in a case in which the jury is required to return a single verdict—
(i) recall the jury (unless already recalled) when it informs the court that it has reached its verdict, and
(ii) direct the delivery of that verdict there and then;
(f) in a case in which the jury is required to return two or more verdicts—
(i) recall the jury (unless already recalled) when it informs the court that it has reached a verdict or verdicts, and
(ii) ask the jury whether its members all agree on every verdict required;
(g) if the answer to that question is 'yes', direct the delivery of each of those verdicts there and then; and
(h) if the answer to that question is 'no'—
(i) direct the delivery there and then of any unanimous verdict that has been reached, or
(ii) postpone the taking of any such verdict while the jury considers each other verdict required.

(4) The court may give the jury directions, questions or other assistance in writing.

(5) When the court directs the jury to deliver its verdict or verdicts, the court must ask the foreman chosen by the jury, in respect of each count—
(a) whether the jury has reached a verdict on which all the jurors agree;
(b) if so, whether that verdict is guilty or not guilty;
(c) if not, where the jury has deliberated for at least 2 hours and if the court decides to invite a majority verdict, then—
(i) whether at least 10 (of 11 or 12 jurors), or 9 (of 10 jurors), agreed on a verdict,
(ii) if so, is that verdict guilty or not guilty, and
(iii) if (and only if) such a verdict is guilty, how many jurors agreed to that verdict and how many disagreed.

(6) Where evidence has been given that the defendant was insane, so as not to be responsible for the act or omission charged as the offence, then under paragraph (5)(b) the court must ask whether the jury's verdict is guilty, not guilty, or not guilty by reason of insanity.

Conviction or acquittal without a jury

B-427 **25.15.**—(1) This rule applies where—
(a) the court tries the case without a jury; and
(b) after following the sequence in rule 25.9 (procedure on plea of not guilty).

(2) In respect of each count, the court must give reasons for its decision to convict or acquit.

Procedure if the court convicts

B-428 **25.16.**—(1) This rule applies where, in respect of any count in the indictment—
(a) the defendant pleads guilty; or
(b) the court convicts the defendant.

(2) The court may exercise its power—
(a) if the defendant is an individual—
(i) to require a pre-sentence report,
(ii) to commission a medical report,
(iii) to require a statement of the defendant's assets and other financial circumstances;
(b) if the defendant is a corporation, to require such information as the court directs about the defendant's corporate structure and financial resources;
(c) to adjourn sentence pending—
(i) receipt of any such report, statement or information,
(ii) the verdict in a related case.

(3) The prosecutor must–
(a) summarise the prosecution case, if the sentencing court has not heard evidence;
(b) identify in writing any offence that the prosecutor proposes should be taken into consideration in sentencing;
(c) provide information relevant to sentence, including–
(i) any previous conviction of the defendant, and the circumstances where relevant,
(ii) any statement of the effect of the offence on the victim, the victim's family or others; and
(d) identify any other matter relevant to sentence, including–
(i) the legislation applicable,
(ii) any sentencing guidelines, or guideline cases,
(iii) aggravating and mitigating features affecting the defendant's culpability and the harm which the offence caused, was intended to cause or might forseeably have caused, and
(iv) the effect of such of the information listed in paragraph (2) as the court may need to take into account.

(4) Where the defendant pleads guilty, the court may give directions for determining the facts on the basis of which sentence must be passed if–
(a) the defendant wants to be sentenced on a basis agreed with the prosecutor; or
(b) in the absence of such agreement, the defendant wants to be sentenced on the basis of different facts to those disclosed by the prosecution case.

(5) Where the court has power to order the endorsement of the defendant's driving record, or power to order the defendant to be disqualified from driving–
(a) if other legislation so permits, a defendant who wants the court not to exercise that power must introduce the evidence or information on which the defendant relies;
(b) the prosecutor may introduce evidence; and
(c) the parties may make representations about that evidence or information.

(6) Before passing sentence–
(a) the court must give the defendant an opportunity to make representations and introduce evidence relevant to sentence;
(b) where the defendant is under 18, the court may give the defendant's parents, guardian or other supporting adult, if present, such an opportunity as well; and
(c) if the court requires more information, it may exercise its power to adjourn the hearing.

(7) When the court has taken into account all the evidence, information and any report available, the court must–
(a) as a general rule, pass sentence at the earliest opportunity;
(b) when passing sentence–
(i) explain the reasons,
(ii) explain to the defendant its effect, the consequences of failing to comply with any order or pay any fine, and any power that the court has to vary or review the sentence, unless the defendant is absent or the defendant's ill-health or disorderly conduct makes such an explanation impracticable, and
(iii) give any such explanation in terms the defendant, if present, can understand (with help, if necessary); and
(c) deal with confiscation, costs and any civil behaviour order.

(8) The general rule is subject to the court's power to defer sentence for up to 6 months.

Provision of documents for the court

25.17.–(1) Unless the court otherwise directs, a party who introduces a document in evidence, or who otherwise uses a document in presenting that party's case, must provide a copy for– **B-429**
(a) each other party;
(b) any witness that party wants to refer to the document; and
(c) the court.

(2) If the court so directs, a party who introduces or uses a document for such a purpose must provide a copy for the jury.

(3) Unless the court otherwise directs, on application or on its own initiative, the court officer must provide for the court–
(a) any copy received under paragraph (1) before the trial begins; and
(b) a copy of the court officer's record of–
(i) information supplied by each party for the purposes of case management, including any revision of information previously supplied,

(ii) each pre-trial direction for the management of the case,
(iii) any pre-trial decision to admit evidence,
(iv) any pre-trial direction about the giving of evidence, and
(v) any admission to which rule 25.13 (evidence by admission) applies; and
(c) any other document served on the court officer for the use of the court.

Duty of court officer and custodian

★B-430 **25.18.** (1) The court officer must—
(a) serve on each party notice of where and when an adjourned hearing will resume, unless that party was present when that was arranged;
(b) if the reason for the adjournment was to postpone sentence, include that reason in any such notice to the defendant;
(c) unless the court otherwise directs, make available to the parties any written report to which rule 25.16(2) applies (pre-sentence and medical reports);
(d) where the court has ordered a defendant to provide information under section 25 of the Road Traffic Offenders Act 1988, serve on the defendant notice of that order unless the defendant was present when it was made;
(e) give the court such other assistance as it requires, including—
(i) selecting jurors from the panel summoned by the Lord Chancellor, under rule 25.6 (selecting the jury),
(ii) taking the oaths or affirmations of jurors and witnesses, under rules 25.6 and 25.11 (evidence of a witness in person),
(iii) informing the jurors of the offence or offences charged in the indictment, and of their duty, under rule 25.9 (procedure on plea of not guilty),
(iv) recording the date and time at which the court gives the jury oral directions under rule 25.14(2) (directions about the law),
(v) recording the date and time at which the court gives the jury any written directions, questions or other assistance under rule 25.14(4), and
(vi) asking the jury foreman to deliver the verdict under rule 25.14(5).

(2) Where the court passes a sentence of immediate imprisonment or detention, or orders a suspended sentence of imprisonment to take effect, by this rule—
(a) the court requires the defendant to provide, in writing or orally, his or her nationality; and
(b) the custodian must obtain that information and record it.

[This rule is printed as amended, with effect from 8 February 2021, by SI 2021/40, r.13(c).]

CPD VI Trial 25A: Identification for the jury of the issues in the case (as inserted by Criminal Practice Directions 2015 (Amendment No. 1), unreported, 23 March 2016, Lord Thomas CJ)

B-431 **25A.1** CrimPR 3.11(a) requires the court, with the active assistance of the parties, to establish what are the disputed issues in order to manage the trial. To that end, prosecution opening speeches are invaluable. They set out for the jury the principal issues in the trial, and the evidence which is to be introduced in support of the prosecution case. They should clarify, not obfuscate. The purpose of the prosecution opening is to help the jury understand what the case concerns, not necessarily to present a detailed account of all the prosecution evidence due to be introduced.

25A.2 CrimPR 25.9(2)(c) provides for a defendant, or his or her advocate, to set out the issues in the defendant's own terms (subject to superintendence by the court), immediately after the prosecution opening. Any such identification of issues at this stage is not to be treated as a substitute for or extension of the summary of the defence case which can be given later, under CrimPR 25.9(2)(g). Its purpose is to provide the jury with focus as to the issues that they are likely to be called upon to decide, so that jurors will be alert to those issues from the outset and can evaluate the prosecution evidence that they hear accordingly. For that purpose, the defendant is not confined to what is included in the defence statement (though any divergence from the defence statement will expose the defendant to adverse comment or inference), and for the defendant to take the opportunity at this stage to identify the issues may assist even if all he or she wishes to announce is that the prosecution is being put to proof.

25A.3 To identify the issues for the jury at this stage also provides an opportunity for the judge to give appropriate directions about the law; for example, as to what features of the prosecution evidence they should look out for in a case in which what is in issue is the identification of the defendant by an eye witness. Giving such directions at the outset is another means by which the jury can be helped to focus on the significant features of the evidence, in the interests of a fair and effective trial.

25A.4 A defendant is not entitled to identify issues at this stage by addressing the jury unless the court invites him or her to do so. Given the advantages described above, usually the court should extend such an invitation but there may be circumstances in which, in the court's judgment, it furthers the overriding objective not to do so. Potential reasons for denying the defendant the opportunity at this stage to address the jury about the issues include (i) that the case is such that the issues are apparent; (ii) that the prosecutor has given a fair, accurate and comprehensive account of the issues in opening, rendering repetition superfluous; and (iii) where the defendant is not represented, that there is a risk of the defendant, at this early stage, inflicting injustice on him or herself by making assertions to the jury to such an extent, or in such a manner, as is unfairly detrimental to his or her subsequent standing.

25A.5 Whether or not there is to be a defence identification of issues, and, if there is, in what manner and in what terms it is to be presented to the jury, are questions that must be resolved in the absence of the jury and that should be addressed at the opening of the trial.

25A.6 Even if invited to identify the issues by addressing the jury, the defendant is not obliged to accept the invitation. However, where the court decides that it is important for the jury to be made aware of what the defendant has declared to be in issue in the defence statement then the court may require the jury to be supplied with copies of the defence statement, edited at the court's direction if necessary, in accordance with section 6E(4) of the CPIA 1996 [§ 12-71 in the main work].

CPD VI Trial 25B: Trial adjournment in the Crown Court (inserted by Criminal Practice Directions 2015 (Amendment No. 8) [2019] EWCA Crim 495, Lord Burnett CJ)

25B.1 A defendant has a right, in general, to be present and to be represented at his trial. **B-432**
However, a defendant may choose not to exercise those rights, such as by voluntarily absenting himself and failing to instruct his lawyers adequately so that they can represent him.

25B.2 The court has a discretion as to whether a trial should take place or continue in the defendant's absence and must exercise its discretion with due regard for the interests of justice. The overriding concern must be to ensure that such a trial is as fair as circumstances permit and leads to a just outcome. If the defendant's absence is due to involuntary illness or incapacity it would very rarely be right to exercise the discretion in favour of commencing or continuing the trial.

25B.3 Proceeding in the absence of a defendant is a step which ought normally to be taken only if it is unavoidable. The court must exercise its discretion as to whether a trial should take place or continue in the defendant's absence with the utmost care and caution. Due regard should be had to the judgment of Lord Bingham in *Jones (Anthony William)* [2002] UKHL 5, [2003] 1 A.C. 1, [2002] 2 Cr. App. R. 9. Circumstances to be taken into account before proceeding include:

i) the conduct of the defendant,
ii) the disadvantage to the defendant,
iii) the public interest, taking account of the inconvenience and hardship to witnesses, and especially to any complainant, of a delay; if the witnesses have attended court and are ready to give evidence, that will weigh in favour of continuing with the trial,
iv) the effect of any delay,
v) whether the attendance of the defendant could be secured at a later hearing, and
vii) the likely outcome if the defendant is found guilty.

Even if the defendant is voluntarily absent, it is still generally desirable that he or she is represented.

Criminal Procedure Rules 2020 (SI 2020/759), Pt 26

Jurors

Appeal against officer's refusal to excuse or postpone jury service

26.1.—(1) This rule applies where a person summoned for jury service in the Crown Court, the **B-433**
High Court or the County Court wants to appeal against a refusal by an officer on the Lord Chancellor's behalf—

(a) to excuse that person from such service; or
(b) to postpone the date on which that person is required to attend for such service.

(2) The appellant must appeal to the court to which the appellant has been summoned.

(3) The appellant must—

(a) apply in writing, as soon as reasonably practicable; and
(b) serve the application on the court officer.

(4) The application must—

(a) attach a copy of—
(i) the jury summons, and

(ii) the refusal to excuse or postpone which is under appeal; and

(b) explain why the court should excuse the appellant from jury service, or postpone its date, as appropriate.

(5) The court to which the appeal is made—

(a) may extend the time for appealing, and may allow the appeal to be made orally;

(b) may determine the appeal at a hearing in public or in private, or without a hearing;

(c) may adjourn any hearing of the appeal; but

(d) must not determine an appeal unless the appellant has had a reasonable opportunity to make representations in person.

Excusal from jury service by court

B-434 **26.2.** At any time before a juror completes the oath or affirmation, the court may exercise its power to excuse him or her from jury service for lack of capacity to act effectively as a juror because of an insufficient understanding of English—

(a) on the court's own initiative, or where the court officer refers the juror to the court; and

(b) after enquiry of the juror.

Provision of information for jurors

B-435 **26.3.** The court officer must arrange for each juror to receive—

(a) by such means as the Lord Chancellor directs, general information about jury service and about a juror's responsibilities;

(b) written notice of the prohibitions against—

(i) research by a juror into the case,

(ii) disclosure by a juror of any such research to another juror during the trial,

(iii) conduct by a juror which suggests that that juror intends to try the case otherwise than on the evidence, and

(iv) disclosure by a juror of the deliberations of the jury; and

(c) written warning that breach of those prohibitions is an offence, for which the penalty is imprisonment or a fine or both, and may be a contempt of court.

Assessment of juror's availability for long trial, etc.

B-436 **26.4.**—(1) The court may invite each member of a panel of jurors to provide such information, by such means and at such a time as the court directs, about—

(a) that juror's availability to try a case expected to last for longer than the juror had expected to serve; and

(b) any association of that juror with, or any knowledge by that juror of—

(i) a party or witness, or

(ii) any other person, or any place, of significance to the case.

(2) Where jurors provide information under this rule, the court may postpone the selection of the jury to try a case to allow each juror an opportunity to review and amend that information before that selection.

(3) Using that information, the court may exercise its power to excuse a juror from selection as a member of the jury to try a case, but the court must not—

(a) excuse a juror without allowing the parties an opportunity to make representations; or

(b) refuse to excuse a juror without allowing that juror such an opportunity.

Surrender of electronic communication devices by jurors

B-437 **26.5.**—(1) This rule applies where the court can order the members of a jury to surrender for a specified period any electronic communication devices that they possess.

(2) The court may make such an order—

(a) on application; or

(b) on its own initiative.

(3) A party who wants the court to make such an order must—

(a) apply as soon as reasonably practicable;

(b) notify each other party;

(c) specify for what period any device should be surrendered; and

(d) explain why—

(i) the proposed order is necessary or expedient in the interest of justice, and

(ii) the terms of the proposed order are a proportionate means of safeguarding those interests.

CPD VI Trial 26A: Juries: introduction

26A.1 Jury service is an important public duty which individual members of the public are chosen at random to undertake. As the Court has acknowledged: "Jury service is not easy; it never has been. It involves a major civic responsibility" (*Thompson* [2010] 2 Cr. App. R. 27, CA (per Lord Judge CJ (at [9]))). B-438

Provision of information to prospective jurors

26A.2 HMCTS provide every person summoned as a juror with information about the role and responsibilities of a juror. Prospective jurors are provided with a pamphlet, "Your Guide to Jury Service", and may also view the film "Your Role as a Juror" online at anytime on the Ministry of Justice YouTube site *www.youtube.com/watch?v=JP7slp-X9Pc.* There is also information at *https://www.gov.uk/jury-service/overview.*

CPD VI Trial 26B: Juries: Preliminary matters arising before jury service commences

26B.1 The effect of section 321 of the CJA 2003 was to remove certain categories of persons from those previously ineligible for jury service (the judiciary and others concerned with the administration of justice) and certain other categories ceased to be eligible for excusal as of right (such as Members of Parliament and medical professionals). The normal presumption is that everyone, unless ineligible or disqualified, will be required to serve when summoned to do so. B-439

Excusal and deferral

26B.2 The jury summoning officer is empowered to defer or excuse individuals in appropriate circumstances and in accordance with the HMCTS Guidance for summoning officers when considering deferral and excusal applications (2009): *http://www.official-documents.gov.uk/document/other/9780108508400/9780108508400.pdf*

Appeals from officer's refusal to excuse or postpone jury service

26B.3 CrimPR 26.1 governs the procedure for a person's appeal against a summoning officer's decision in relation to excusal or deferral of jury service.

Provision of information at court

26B.4 The court officer is expected to provide relevant further information to jurors on their arrival in the court centre.

CPD VI Trial 26C: Juries: eligibility

English language ability

26C.1 Under the Juries Act 1974, s.10 [§ 4-273 in the main work], a person summoned for jury service who applies for excusal on the grounds of insufficient understanding of English may, where necessary, be brought before the judge. B-440

26C.2 The court may exercise its power to excuse any person from jury service for lack of capacity to act effectively as a juror because of an insufficient understanding of English.

26C.3 The judge has the discretion to stand down jurors who are not competent to serve by reason of a personal disability: *Mason* (1980) 71 Cr. App. R. 157; *Jalil* [2008] EWCA Crim 2910; [2009] 2 Cr. App. R.(S.) 40.

Jurors with professional and public service commitments

26C.4 The legislative change in the CJA 2003 means that more individuals are eligible to serve as jurors, including those previously excused as of right or ineligible. Judges need to be vigilant to the need to exercise their discretion to adjourn a trial, excuse or discharge a juror should the need arise.

26C.5 Whether or not an application has already been made to the jury summoning officer for deferral or excusal, it is also open to the person summoned to apply to the court to be excused. Such applications must be considered with common sense and according to the interests of justice. An explanation should be required for an application being much later than necessary.

Serving police officers, prison officers or employees of prosecuting agencies

26C.6 A judge should always be made aware at the stage of jury selection if any juror in waiting is in these categories. The juror summons warns jurors in these categories that they will need to alert court staff.

26C.7 In the case of police officers an inquiry by the judge will have to be made to assess whether a police officer may serve as a juror. Regard should be had to: whether evidence from the police is in dispute in the case and the extent to which that dispute involves allegations made against the police;

whether the potential juror knows or has worked with the officers involved in the case; whether the potential juror has served or continues to serve in the same police units within the force as those dealing with the investigation of the case or is likely to have a shared local service background with police witnesses in a trial.

26C.8 In the case of a serving prison officer summoned to a court, the judge will need to inquire whether the individual is employed at a prison linked to that court or is likely to have special knowledge of any person involved in a trial.

26C.9 The judge will need to ensure that employees of prosecuting authorities do not serve on a trial prosecuted by the prosecuting authority by which they are employed. They can serve on a trial prosecuted by another prosecuting authority: *Abdroikov* [§ 4-266 in the main work]; *Hanif v U.K.* [§ 7-89 in the main work]; *L. (L.)* [§ 4-293 in the main work]. Similarly, a serving police officer can serve where there is no particular link between the court and the station where the police officer serves.

26C.10 Potential jurors falling into these categories should be excused from jury service unless there is a suitable alternative court/trial to which they can be transferred.

CPD VI Trial 26D: Juries: precautionary measures before swearing

B-441 **26D.1** There should be a consultation with the advocates as to the questions, if any, it may be appropriate to ask potential jurors. Topics to be considered include: (a) the availability of jurors for the duration of a trial that is likely to run beyond the usual period for which jurors are summoned; (b) whether any juror knows the defendant or parties to the case; (c) whether potential jurors are so familiar with any locations that feature in the case that they may have, or come to have, access to information not in evidence; (d) in cases where there has been any significant local or national publicity, whether any questions should be asked of potential jurors.

26D.2 Judges should however exercise caution. At common law a judge has a residual discretion to discharge a particular juror who ought not to be serving, but this discretion can only be exercised to prevent an individual juror who is not competent from serving. It does not include a discretion to discharge a jury drawn from particular sections of the community or otherwise to influence the overall composition of the jury. However, if there is a risk that there is widespread local knowledge of the defendant or a witness in a particular case, the judge may, after hearing submissions from the advocates, decide to exclude jurors from particular areas to avoid the risk of jurors having or acquiring personal knowledge of the defendant or a witness.

Length of trial

26D.3 Where the length of the trial is estimated to be significantly longer than the normal period of jury service, it is good practice for the trial judge to enquire whether the potential jurors on the jury panel foresee any difficulties with the length and if the judge is satisfied that the jurors' concerns are justified, he may say that they are not required for that particular jury. This does not mean that the judge must excuse the juror from sitting at that court altogether, as it may well be possible for the juror to sit on a shorter trial at the same court.

Juror with potential connection to the case or parties

26D.4 Where a juror appears on a jury panel, it will be appropriate for a judge to excuse the juror from that particular case where the potential juror is personally concerned with the facts of the particular case, or is closely connected with a prospective witness. Judges need to exercise due caution as noted above.

CPD VI Trial 26E: Juries: swearing in jurors

Swearing jury for trial

B-442 **26E.1** All jurors shall be sworn or affirm. All jurors shall take the oath or affirmation in open court in the presence of one another. If, as a result of the juror's delivery of the oath or affirmation, a judge has concerns that a juror has such difficulties with language comprehension or reading ability that might affect that juror's capacity to undertake his or her duties, bearing in mind the likely evidence in the trial, the judge should make appropriate inquiry of that juror.

Form of oath or affirmation

26E.2 Each juror should have the opportunity to indicate to the court the Holy Book on which he or she wishes to swear. The precise wording will depend on his or her faith as indicated to the court.

26E.3 Any person who prefers to affirm shall be permitted to make a solemn affirmation instead. The wording of the affirmation is: "I do solemnly, sincerely and truly declare and affirm that I will faithfully try the defendant and give a true verdict according to the evidence."

CPD VI Trial 26F: Juries: ensuring an effective jury panel

Adequacy of numbers

26F.1 By section 6 of the Juries Act 1974 , if it appears to the court that a jury to try any issue before the court will be, or probably will be, incomplete, the court may, if the court thinks fit, require any persons who are in, or in the vicinity of, the court, to be summoned (without any written notice) for jury service up to the number needed (after allowing for any who may not be qualified under section 1 of the Act, and for excusals and challenges) to make up a full jury.

CPD VI Trial 26G: Juries: preliminary instructions to jurors (as amended by Criminal Practice Directions 2015 (Amendment No. 5), unreported, 26 July 2017, Lord Thomas CJ)

26G.1 After the jury has been sworn and the defendant has been put in charge the judge will want to give directions to the jury on a number of matters. B-443

26G.2 Jurors can be expected to follow the instructions diligently. As the Privy Council stated in *Taylor (Bonnett) v The Queen* [2013] 2 Cr. App. R. 18:

> "The assumption must be that the jury understood and followed the direction that they were given: ... the experience of trial judges is that juries perform their duty according to law. ... [T]he law proceeds on the footing that the jury, acting in accordance with the instructions given to them by the trial judge, will render a true verdict in accordance with the evidence. To conclude otherwise would be to underrate the integrity of the system of trial by jury and the effect on the jury of the instructions by the trial judge."

At the start of the trial

26G.3 Trial judges should instruct the jury on general matters which will include the time estimate for the trial and normal sitting hours. The jury will always need clear guidance on the following:

(i) the need to try the case only on the evidence and remain faithful to their oath or affirmation;

(ii) the prohibition on internet searches for matters related to the trial, issues arising or the parties;

(iii) the importance of not discussing any aspect of the case with anyone outside their own number or allowing anyone to talk to them about it, whether directly, by telephone, through internet facilities such as Facebook or Twitter or in any other way;

(iv) the importance of taking no account of any media reports about the case;

(v) the collective responsibility of the jury; as Lord Judge C.J. made clear in *Thompson* [2010] 2 Cr. App. R. 27: "[T]here is a collective responsibility for ensuring that the conduct of each member is consistent with the jury oath and that the directions of the trial judge about the discharge of their responsibilities are followed. The collective responsibility of the jury for its own conduct must be regarded as an integral part of the trial itself.";

(vi) the need to bring any concerns, including concerns about the conduct of other jurors, to the attention of the judge at the time, and not to wait until the case is concluded; the point should be made that, unless that is done while the case is continuing, it may not be possible to deal with the problem at all.

Subsequent reminder of the jury instructions

26G.4 Judges should consider reminding jurors of these instructions as appropriate at the end of each day and in particular when they separate after retirement.

26G.5 Following the judge's direction to the jury, each member of the jury must be provided with a copy of the notice "Your Legal Responsibilities as a Juror". This notice outlines what is required of the juror during and after their time on the jury. It is not a substitute for the judge's direction, but is designed to reinforce what the judge has outlined in the direction. The court clerk should ensure a record is made of service of the notice. Jurors are advised to keep their copy of the notice with their summons and at the end of the trial, they are allowed to retain it for future information.

CPD VI Trial 26H: Juries: discharge of a juror for personal reasons

26H.1 Where a juror unexpectedly finds him or herself in difficult professional or personal circumstances during the course of the trial, the juror should be encouraged to raise such problems with the trial judge. This might apply, for example, to a parent whose childcare arrangements unexpectedly fail, or a worker who is engaged in the provision of services the need for which can be critical, or a Member of Parliament who has deferred their jury service to an apparently more convenient time, but is unexpectedly called back to work for a very important reason. Such difficulties would normally be raised through a jury note in the normal manner. B-444

26H.2 In such circumstances, the judge must exercise his or her discretion according to the interests of justice and the requirements of each individual case. The judge must decide for him or herself whether the juror has presented a sufficient reason to interfere with the course of the trial. If the juror has presented a sufficient reason, in longer trials it may well be possible to adjourn for a short period in order to allow the juror to overcome the difficulty.

26H.3 In shorter cases, it may be more appropriate to discharge the juror and to continue the trial with a reduced number of jurors. The power to do this is implicit in section 16(1) of the Juries Act 1974 [§ 4-311 in the main work]. In unusual cases (such as an unexpected emergency arising overnight) a juror need not be discharged in open court. The good administration of justice depends on the cooperation of jurors, who perform an essential public service. All such applications should be dealt with sensitively and sympathetically and the trial judge should always seek to meet the interests of justice without unduly inconveniencing any juror.

CPD VI Trial 26J: Juries: views

B-445 **26J.1** In each case in which it is necessary for the jury to view a location, the judge should produce ground rules for the view, after discussion with the advocates. The rules should contain details of what the jury will be shown and in what order and who, if anyone, will be permitted to speak and what will be said. The rules should also make provision for the jury to ask questions and receive a response from the judge, following submissions from the advocates, while the view is taking place.

CPD VI Trial 26K: Juries: directions, written materials and summing up (as inserted by Criminal Practice Directions 2015 (Amendment No. 1), unreported, 23 March 2016, Lord Thomas CJ)

Overview

B-446 **26K.1** Sir Brian Leveson's Review of Efficiency in Criminal Proceedings 2015 contained recommendations to improve the efficiency of jury trials including:

- early provision of appropriate directions;
- provision of a written route to verdict;
- provision of a split summing up (a summing up delivered in two parts – the first part prior to the closing speeches and the second part afterwards); and
- streamlining the summing up to help the jury focus on the issues.

The purpose of this practice direction, and the associated criminal procedure rules, is to give effect to these recommendations.

Record-keeping

B-447 **26K.2** Full and accurate record-keeping is essential to enable the Registrar of Criminal Appeals to obtain transcripts in the event of an application or appeal to the Court of Appeal ....

26K.3 A court officer is required to record the date and time at which the court provides directions and written materials (CrimPR 25.18(e)(iv)-(v)).

26K.4 The judge should ensure that a court officer (such as a court clerk or usher) is present in court to record the information listed in paragraph 26K.5.

26K.5 A court officer should clearly record the:

- date, time and subject of submissions and rulings relating to directions and written materials;
- date, time and subject of directions and written materials provided prior to the summing up; and
- date and time of the summing up, including both parts of a split summing up.

26K.6 A court officer should retain a copy of written materials on the court file or database.

26K.7 The parties should also record the information listed in paragraph 26K.5 and retain a copy of written materials. Where relevant to a subsequent application or appeal to the Court of Appeal ..., the information listed in paragraph 26K.5 should be provided in the notice of appeal, and any written materials should be identified.

Early provision of appropriate directions

B-448 **26K.8** The court is required to provide directions about the relevant law at any time that will assist the jury to evaluate the evidence (CrimPR 25.14(2)). The judge may provide an early direction prior to any evidence being called, prior to the evidence to which it relates or shortly thereafter.

26K.9 Where the judge decides it will assist the jury in their approach to the evidence and/ or evaluating the evidence as they hear it, an early direction should be provided.

26K.10 For example:

- where identification is in issue, an early *Turnbull* direction is [see §§ 14-2 et seq. in the main work] likely to assist the jury in approaching the evidence with the requisite caution; and by having the relevant considerations in mind when listening to the evidence;

- where special measures are to be used and/ or ground rules will restrict the manner and scope of questioning, an early explanation may assist the jury in their approach to the evidence;
- an early direction may also assist the jury, by having the relevant approach, considerations and/ or test in mind, when listening to–
  - expert witnesses; and
  - evidence of bad character;
  - hearsay;
  - interviews of co-defendants; and
  - evidence involving legal concepts such as knowledge, dishonesty, consent, recklessness, conspiracy, joint enterprise, attempt, self-defence, excessive force, voluntary intoxication and duress.

Written route to verdict

26K.11 A route to verdict, which poses a series of questions that lead the jury to the appropriate verdict, may be provided by the court (CrimPR 25.14(3)(b)). Each question should tailor the law to the issues and evidence in the case. **B-449**

26K.12 Save where the case is so straightforward that it would be superfluous to do so, the judge should provide a written route to verdict. It may be presented (on paper or digitally) in the form of text, bullet points, a flowchart or other graphic.

Other written materials

26K.13 Where the judge decides it will assist the jury, written materials should be provided. They may be presented (on paper or digitally) in the form of text, bullet points, a table, a flowchart or other graphic.

26K.14 For example, written materials may assist the jury in relation to a complex direction or where the case involves a complex chronology, competing expert evidence or differing descriptions of a suspect.

26K.15 Such written materials may be prepared by the judge or the parties at the direction of the judge. Where prepared by the parties at the direction of the judge, they will be subject to the judge's approval.

Split summing up and provision of appropriate directions prior to closing speeches

26K.16 Where the judge decides it will assist the jury when listening to the closing speeches, a split summing up should be provided. For example, the provision of appropriate directions prior to the closing speeches may avoid repetitious explanations of the law by the advocates. **B-450**

26K.17 By way of illustration, such directions may include:

- functions of the judge and jury;
- burden and standard of proof;
- separate consideration of counts;
- separate consideration of defendants;
- elements of offence(s);
- defence(s);
- route to verdict;
- circumstantial evidence; and
- inferences from silence.

Closing speeches

26K.18 The advocates closing speeches should be consistent with any directions and route to verdict already provided by the judge.

Summing up

26K.19 Prior to beginning or resuming the summing up at the conclusion of the closing speeches, the judge should briefly list (without repeating) any directions provided earlier in the trial. The purpose of this requirement is to provide a definitive account of all directions for the benefit of the Registrar of Criminal Appeals and the Court of Appeal (...), in the event of an application or appeal. **B-451**

26K.20 The court is required to summarise the evidence relevant to the issues to such extent as is necessary (CrimPR 25.14(3)(a))).

26K.21 To assist the jury to focus on the issues during retirement, save where the case is so straightforward that it would be superfluous to do so, the judge should provide:

- a reminder of the issues;
- a summary of the nature of the evidence relating to each issue;
- a balanced account of the points raised by the parties; and

- any outstanding directions.

It is not necessary for the judge to recount all relevant evidence or to rehearse all of the significant points raised by the parties.

26K.22 At the conclusion of the summing up, the judge should provide final directions to the jury on the need:

- for unanimity (in respect of each count and defendant, where relevant);
- to dismiss any thoughts of majority verdicts until further direction; and
- to select a juror to chair their discussions and speak on their behalf to the court.

CPD VI Trial 26L: Juries: jury access to exhibits and evidence in retirement

B-452 **26L.1** At the end of the summing up it is also important that the judge informs the jury that any exhibits they wish to have will be made available to them.

26L.2 Judges should invite submissions from the advocates as to what material the jury should retire with and what material before them should be removed, such as the transcript of an ABE interview (which should usually be removed from the jury as soon as the recording has been played.)

26L.3 Judges will also need to inform the jury of the opportunity to view certain audio, DVD or CCTV evidence that has been played (excluding, for example ABE interviews). If possible, it may be appropriate for the jury to be able to view any such material in the jury room alone, such as on a sterile laptop, so that they can discuss it freely; this will be a matter for the judge's discretion, following discussion with counsel.

CPD VI Trial 26M: Juries: jury irregularities

B-453 **26M.1** This practice direction replaces the protocol regarding jury irregularities issued by the President of the Queen's Bench Division in November 2012, and the subsequent practice direction, in light of sections 20A to 20D of the Juries Act 1974 [§§ 28-41a et seq. in the main work] and the associated repeal of section 8 of the Contempt of Court Act 1981 (confidentiality of jury's deliberations) [ibid., § 28-73].

26M.2 A jury irregularity is anything that may prevent one or more jurors from remaining faithful to their oath or affirmation to "faithfully try the defendant and give a true verdict according to the evidence." Jury irregularities take many forms. Some are clear-cut such as a juror conducting research about the case or an attempt to suborn or intimidate a juror. Others are less clear-cut - for example, when there is potential bias or friction between jurors.

26M.3 A jury irregularity may involve contempt of court and / or the commission of an offence by or in relation to a juror.

26M.4 Under the previous version of this practice direction, the Crown Court required approval from the Vice-President of the Court of Appeal (Criminal Division) (CACD) prior to providing a juror's details to the police for the purposes of an investigation into a jury irregularity. Such approval is no longer required. Provision of a juror's details to the police is now a matter for the Crown Court.

Jury Irregularity During Trial

B-454 **26M.5** A jury irregularity that comes to light during a trial may impact on the conduct of the trial. It may also involve contempt of court and / or the commission of an offence by or in relation to a juror. The primary concern of the judge should be the impact on the trial.

26M.6 A jury irregularity should be drawn to the attention of the judge in the absence of the jury as soon as it becomes known.

26M.7 When the judge becomes aware of a jury irregularity, the judge should follow the procedure set out below:

STEP 1: Consider isolating juror(s)
STEP 2: Consult with advocates
STEP 3: Consider appropriate provisional measures (which may include surrender / seizure of electronic communications devices and taking defendant into custody)
STEP 4: Seek to establish basic facts of jury irregularity
STEP 5: Further consult with advocates
STEP 6: Decide what to do in relation to conduct of trial
STEP 7: Consider ancillary matters (contempt in face of court and / or commission of criminal offence)

STEP 1: Consider isolating juror(s)

B-455 **26M.8** The judge should consider whether the juror(s) concerned should be isolated from the rest of the jury, particularly if the juror(s) may have conducted research about the case.

26M.9 If two or more jurors are concerned, the judge should consider whether they should also be isolated from each other, particularly if one juror has made an accusation against another.

STEP 2: Consult with advocates

26M.10 The judge should consult with the advocates and invite submissions about appropriate provisional measures (Step 3) and how to go about establishing the basic facts of the jury irregularity (Step 4). **B-456**

26M.11 The consultation should be conducted

- in open court;
- in the presence of the defendant; and
- with all parties represented

unless there is good reason not to do so.

26M.12 If the jury irregularity involves a suspicion about the conduct of the defendant or another party, there may be good reason for the consultation to take place in the absence of the defendant or the other party. There may also be good reason for it to take place in private. If so, the proper location is in the court room, with DARTS recording, rather than in the judge's room.

26M.13 If the jury irregularity relates to the jury's deliberations, the judge should warn all those present that it is an offence to disclose, solicit or obtain information about a jury's deliberations (s.20D(1) of the Juries Act 1974 [§ 28-41d in the main work] - see paras 26M.35 to 26M.38 regarding the offence and exceptions). This would include disclosing information about the jury's deliberations divulged in court during consultation with the advocates (Step 2 and Step 5) or when seeking to establish the basic facts of the jury irregularity (Step 4). The judge should emphasise that the advocates, court staff and those in the public gallery would commit the offence by explaining to another what is said in court about the jury's deliberations.

STEP 3: Consider appropriate provisional measures

26M.14 The judge should consider appropriate provisional measures which may include surrender / seizure of electronic communications devices and taking the defendant into custody. **B-457**

Surrender / seizure of electronic communications devices

26M.15 The judge should consider whether to make an order under section 15A(1) of the Juries Act 1974 [§ 4-325b in the main work] requiring the juror(s) concerned to surrender electronic communications devices, such as mobile telephones or smart phones.

26M.16 Having made an order for surrender, the judge may require a court security officer to search a juror to determine whether the juror has complied with the order. Section 54A of the Courts Act 2003 contains the court security officer's powers of search and seizure.

26M.17 Section 15A(5) of the Juries Act 1974 provides that it is contempt of court for a juror to fail to surrender an electronic communications device in accordance with an order for surrender (see paras 26M.29 to 26M.30 regarding the procedure for dealing with such a contempt).

26M.18 Any electronic communications device surrendered or seized under these provisions should be kept safe by the court until returned to the juror or handed to the police as evidence.

Taking defendant into custody

26M.19 If the defendant is on bail, and the jury irregularity involves a suspicion about the defendant's conduct, the judge should consider taking the defendant into custody. If that suspicion involves an attempt to suborn or intimidate a juror, the defendant should be taken into custody.

STEP 4: Seek to establish basic facts of jury irregularity

26M.20 The judge should seek to establish the basic facts of the jury irregularity for the purpose of determining how to proceed in relation to the conduct of the trial. The judge's enquiries may involve having the juror(s) concerned write a note of explanation and / or questioning the juror(s). The judge may enquire whether the juror(s) feel able to continue and remain faithful to their oath or affirmation. If there is questioning, each juror should be questioned separately, in the absence of the rest of the jury, unless there is good reason not to do so. **B-458**

26M.21 In accordance with paragraphs 26M.10 to 26M.13, the enquiries should be conducted in open court; in the presence of the defendant; and with all parties represented unless there is good reason not to do so.

STEP 5: Further consult with advocates

26M.22 The judge should further consult with the advocates and invite submissions about how to proceed in relation to the conduct of the trial and what should be said to the jury (Step 6). **B-459**

26M.23 In accordance with paragraphs 26M.10 to 26M.13, the consultation should be conducted in open court; in the presence of the defendant; and with all parties represented unless there is good reason not to do so.

STEP 6: Decide what to do in relation to conduct of trial

B-460 **26M.24** When deciding how to proceed, the judge may take time to reflect.

26M.25 Considerations may include the stage the trial has reached. The judge should be alert to attempts by the defendant or others to thwart the trial. In cases of potential bias, the judge should consider whether a fair minded and informed observer would conclude that there was a real possibility that the juror(s) or jury would be biased (*Porter v Magill* [2002] 2 A.C. 357, HL).

26M.26 In relation to the conduct of the trial, there are three possibilities:

1. Take no action and continue with the trial
   If so, the judge should consider what, if anything, to say to the jury. For example, the judge may reassure the jury nothing untoward has happened or remind them their verdict is a decision of the whole jury and that they should try to work together. Anything said should be tailored to the circumstances of the case.
2. Discharge the juror(s) concerned and continue with the trial
   If so, the judge should consider what to say to the discharged juror(s) and the jurors who remain. All jurors should be warned not to discuss what has happened.
3. Discharge the whole jury
   If so, the judge should consider what to say to the jury and they should be warned not to discuss what has happened.

If the judge is satisfied that jury tampering has taken place, depending on the circumstances, the judge may continue the trial without a jury (s.46(3) of the CJA 2003 [§ 4-333 in the main work]) or order a new trial without a jury (s.46(5) of the CJA 2003). Alternatively, the judge may re-list the trial. If there is a real and present danger of jury tampering in the new trial, the prosecution may apply for a trial without a jury (s.44 of the CJA 2003 [§ 4-330 in the main work]).

STEP 7: Consider ancillary matters

B-461 **26M.27** A jury irregularity may also involve contempt in the face of the court and / or the commission of a criminal offence. The possibilities include the following:

- contempt in the face of the court by a juror;
- an offence by a juror or a non-juror under the Juries Act 1974 (ss.20-20D [§§ 28-41 et seq. in the main work]);
- an offence by juror or a non-juror other than under the Juries Act 1974 (examples are given).

Contempt in the face of the court by a juror

26M.28 If a juror commits contempt in the face of the court, the juror's conduct may also constitute an offence. If so, the judge should decide whether to deal with the juror summarily under the procedure for contempt in the face of the court or refer the matter to the Attorney-General's office or the police (see paras 26M.31 and 26M.33).

26M.29 In the case of a minor and clear contempt in the face of the court, the judge may deal with the juror summarily. The judge should follow the procedure in CrimPR 48.5 to 48.8. The judge should also have regard to the practice direction regarding contempt of court issued in March 2015 (Practice Direction: Committal for Contempt of Court - Open Court) [§ 28-118b in the main work], which emphasises the principle of open justice in relation to proceedings for contempt before all courts.

26M.30 If a juror fails to comply with an order for surrender of an electronic communications device (see paras 26M.15 to 26M.18), the judge should deal with the juror summarily following the procedure for contempt in the face of the court.

Offence by a juror or non-juror under the Juries Act 1974

26M.31 If it appears that an offence under the Juries Act 1974 may have been committed by a juror or non-juror (and the matter has not been dealt with summarily under the procedure for contempt in the face of the court), the judge should contact the Attorney-General's office to consider a police investigation, setting out the position neutrally. The officer in the case should not be asked to investigate. Contact details for the Attorney-General's office are set out at the end of this practice direction.

26M.32 If relevant to an investigation, any electronic communications device surrendered or seized pursuant to an order for surrender should be passed to the police as soon as practicable.

Offence by a juror or non-juror other than under the Juries Act 1974

26M.33 If it appears that an offence, other than an offence under the Juries Act 1974, may have been committed by a juror or non-juror (and the matter has not been dealt with summarily under the procedure for contempt in the face of the court), the judge or a member of court staff should contact the police setting out the position neutrally. The officer in the case should not be asked to investigate.

26M.34 If relevant to an investigation, any electronic communications device surrendered or seized pursuant to an order for surrender should be passed to the police as soon as practicable.

Other Matters to Consider

• *Jury deliberations*

26M.35 In light of the offence of disclosing, soliciting or obtaining information about a jury's deliberations (s.20D(1) of the Juries Act 1974 [§ 28-41 in the main work]), great care is required if a jury irregularity relates to the jury's deliberations. **B-462**

26M.36 During the trial, there are exceptions to this offence that enable the judge (and only the judge) to:

- seek to establish the basic facts of a jury irregularity involving the jury's deliberations (Step 4); and
- disclose information about the jury's deliberations to the Attorney-General's office if it appears that an offence may have been committed (Step 7).

26M.37 With regard to seeking to establish the basic facts of a jury irregularity involving the jury's deliberations (Step 4), it is to be noted that during the trial it is not an offence for the judge to disclose, solicit or obtain information about the jury's deliberations for the purposes of dealing with the case (ss.20E(2)(a) and 20G(1) of the Juries Act 1974 [§§ 28-41e, 28-41g in the main work]).

26M.38 With regard to disclosing information about the jury's deliberations to the Attorney-General's office if it appears that an offence may have been committed (Step 7), it is to be noted that during the trial:

- it is not an offence for the judge to disclose information about the jury's deliberations for the purposes of an investigation by a relevant investigator into whether an offence or contempt of court has been committed by or in relation to a juror (s.20E(2)(b) of the Juries Act 1974); and
- a relevant investigator means a police force or the Attorney-General (s.20E(5) of the Juries Act 1974).

• *Minimum number of jurors*

26M.39 If it is decided to discharge one or more jurors (Step 6), a minimum of nine jurors must remain if the trial is to continue (s.16(1) of the Juries Act 1974 [§ 4-311 in the main work]).

• *Preparation of statement by judge*

26M.40 If a jury irregularity occurs, and the trial continues, the judge should have regard to the remarks of Lord Hope in *Connors and Mirza* [2004] 1 A.C. 1118, HL (at [127], [128]), and consider whether to prepare a statement that could be used in an application for leave to appeal or an appeal relating to the jury irregularity.

Jury Irregularity after Jury Discharged

26M.41 A jury irregularity that comes to light after the jury has been discharged may involve the commission of an offence by or in relation to a juror. It may also provide a ground of appeal. **B-463**

26M.42 A jury irregularity after the jury has been discharged may come to the attention of the:

- trial judge or court
- Registrar of Criminal Appeals (the Registrar)
- prosecution
- defence.

• *Role of the trial judge or court*

26M.43 The judge has no jurisdiction in relation to a jury irregularity that comes to light after the jury has been discharged (*Thompson* [2010] 2 Cr. App. R. 27, CA). The jury will be deemed to have been discharged when all verdicts on all defendants have been delivered or when the jury has been discharged from giving all verdicts on all defendants. **B-464**

26M.44 The judge will be functus officio in relation to a jury irregularity that comes to light during an adjournment between verdict and sentence. The judge should proceed to sentence unless there is good reason not to do so.

26M.45 In practice, a jury irregularity often comes to light when the judge or court receives a communication from a former juror.

26M.46 If a jury irregularity comes to the attention of a judge or court after the jury has been discharged, and regardless of the result of the trial, the judge or a member of court staff should contact the Registrar setting out the position neutrally. Any communication from a former juror should be forwarded to the Registrar.

Contact details for the Registrar are set out at the end of this practice direction.

• *Role of the Registrar*

26M.47 If a jury irregularity comes to the attention of the Registrar after the jury has been **B-465**

discharged, and regardless of the result of the trial, the Registrar should consider if it appears that an offence may have been committed by or in relation to a juror. The Registrar should also consider if there may be a ground of appeal.

26M.48 When deciding how to proceed, particularly in relation to a communication from a former juror, the Registrar may seek the direction of the Vice-President of the Court of Appeal (Criminal Division) (CACD) or another judge of the CACD in accordance with instructions from the Vice-President.

26M.49 If it appears that an offence may have been committed by or in relation to a juror, the Registrar should contact the private offence of the Director of Public Prosecutions to consider a police investigation.

26M.50 If there may be a ground of appeal, the Registrar should inform the defence.

26M.51 If a communication from a former juror is not of legal significance, the Registrar should respond explaining that no action is required. An example of such a communication is if it is restricted to a general complaint about the verdict from a dissenting juror or an expression of doubt or second thoughts.

• *Role of the prosecution*

B-466 **26M.52** If a jury irregularity comes to the attention of the prosecution after the jury has been discharged, which may provide a ground of appeal, they should notify the defence in accordance with their duties to act fairly and assist in the administration of justice (*Makin* [2004] EWCA Crim. 1607, (2004) 148 S.J. 821).

• *Role of the defence*

B-467 **26M.53** If a jury irregularity comes to the attention of the defence after the jury has been discharged, which provides an arguable ground of appeal, an application for leave to appeal may be made.

• *Jury deliberations*

B-468 **26M.54** In light of the offence of disclosing, soliciting or obtaining information about a jury's deliberations (s.20D(1) of the Juries Act 1974 [§ 28-41d in the main work]), great care is required if a jury irregularity relates to the jury's deliberations.

26M.55 After the jury has been discharged, there are exceptions to this offence that enable a judge, a member of court staff, the Registrar, the prosecution and the defence to disclose information about the jury's deliberations if it appears that an offence may have been committed by or in relation to a juror or if there may be a ground of appeal.

26M.56 For example, it is to be noted that:

- after the jury has been discharged, it is not an offence for a person to disclose information about the jury's deliberations to defined persons if the person reasonably believes that an offence or contempt of court may have been committed by or in relation to a juror or the conduct of a juror may provide grounds of appeal (s.20F(1), (2) of the Juries Act 1974 [§ 28-41f in the main work]);
- the defined persons to whom such information may be disclosed are a member of a police force, a judge of the CACD, the Registrar, a judge where the trial took place or a member of court staff where the trial took place who would reasonably be expected to disclose the information only to one of the aforementioned defined persons (s.20F(2) of the Juries Act 1974);
- after the jury has been discharged, it is not an offence for a judge of the CACD or the Registrar to disclose information about the jury's deliberations for the purposes of an investigation by a relevant investigator into whether an offence or contempt of court has been committed by or in relation to a juror or the conduct of a juror may provide grounds of appeal (s.20F(4) of the Juries Act 1974);
- a relevant investigator means a police force, the Attorney-General, the Criminal Cases Review Commission (CCRC) or the CPS (s.20F(10) of the Juries Act 1974).

• *Investigation by the Criminal Cases Review Commission (CCRC)*

B-469 **26M.57** If an application for leave to appeal, or an appeal, includes a ground of appeal relating to a jury irregularity, the Registrar may refer the case to the full court to decide whether to direct the CCRC to conduct an investigation under section 23A of the CAA 1968.

26M.58 If the court directs the CCRC to conduct an investigation, directions should be given as to the scope of the investigation.

Contact Details

B-470 Attorney General's Office

Contempt.SharedMailbox@attorneygeneral.gsi.gov.uk
Telephone: 020 7271 2492
The Registrar
penny.donnelly@hmcts.x.gsi.gov.uk (Secretary) or
criminalappealoffice.generaloffice@hmcts.gsi.gov.uk
Telephone: 020 7947 6103 (Secretary) or 020 7947 6011

CPD VI Trial 26N: Open justice

26N.1 There must be freedom of access between advocate and judge. Any discussion must, however, be between the judge and the advocates on both sides. If an advocate is instructed by a solicitor who is in court, he or she, too, should be allowed to attend the discussion. This freedom of access is important because there may be matters calling for communication or discussion of such a nature that the advocate cannot, in the client's interest, mention them in open court, e.g. the advocate, by way of mitigation, may wish to tell the judge that reliable medical evidence shows that the defendant is suffering from a terminal illness and may not have long to live. It is imperative that, so far as possible, justice must be administered in open court. Advocates should, therefore, only ask to see the judge when it is felt to be really necessary. The judge must be careful only to treat such communications as private where, in the interests of justice, this is necessary. Where any such discussion takes place it should be recorded, preferably by audio recording. **B-471**

CPD VI Trial 26P: Defendant's right to give or not to give evidence (as amended by Criminal Practice Directions 2015 (Amendment No. 9) [2019] EWCA Crim 1603, Lord Burnett CJ)

26P.1 At the conclusion of the evidence for the prosecution, section 35(2) of the CJPOA 1994 [§ 4-377 in the main work] requires the court to satisfy itself that the defendant is aware that the stage has been reached at which evidence can be given for the defence and that the defendant's failure to give evidence, or if he does so his failure to answer questions, without a good reason, may lead to inferences being drawn against him. **B-472**

If the accused is legally represented

26P.2 After the close of the prosecution case, if the defendant's representative requests a brief adjournment to advise his client on this issue the request should, ordinarily, be granted. When appropriate the judge should, in the presence of the jury, inquire of the representative in these terms:

> "Have you advised your client that the stage has now been reached at which he may give evidence and, if he chooses not to do so or, having been sworn, without good cause refuses to answer any question, the jury may draw such inferences as appear proper from his failure to do so?"

26P.3 If the representative replies to the judge that the defendant has been so advised, then the case shall proceed. If counsel replies that the defendant has not been so advised, then the judge shall direct the representative to advise his client of the consequences and should adjourn briefly for this purpose, before proceeding further.

If the defendant is not legally represented

26P.4 If the defendant is not represented, the judge shall, at the conclusion of the evidence for the prosecution, in the absence of the jury, indicate what he will say to him in the presence of the jury and ask if he understands and whether he would like a brief adjournment to consider his position.

26P.5 When appropriate, and in the presence of the jury, the judge should say to the defendant:

> 'Now is your chance to give evidence if you choose to do so. If you do give evidence it will be on oath [or affirmation], and you will be cross-examined like any other witness. If you do not give evidence the jury may hold it against you. If you do give evidence but refuse without good reason to answer the questions the jury may, as I have just explained, hold that against you. Do you now intend to give evidence?'

CPD VI Trial 26Q: Majority verdicts (as amended by Criminal Practice Directions 2015 (Amendment No. 5) [2017] EWCA Crim 1076, Lord Thomas CJ)

26Q.1 It is very important that all those trying indictable offences should, so far as possible, adopt a uniform practice when complying with section 17 of the Juries Act 1974 [§ 4-509 in the main work], both in directing the jury in summing-up and also in receiving the verdict or giving further directions after retirement. So far as the summing-up is concerned, it is inadvisable for the judge, and indeed for advocates, to attempt an explanation of the section for fear that the jury will be **B-473**

confused. Before the jury retires, however, the judge should direct the jury in some such words as the following:

"As you may know, the law permits me, in certain circumstances, to accept a verdict which is not the verdict of you all. Those circumstances have not as yet arisen, so that when you retire I must ask you to reach a verdict upon which each one of you is agreed. Should, however, the time come when it is possible for me to accept a majority verdict, I will give you a further direction."

26Q.2 Thereafter the practice should be as follows. Should the jury return before two hours and ten minutes since the last member of the jury left the jury box to go to the jury room (or such longer time as the judge thinks reasonable) has elapsed (see s.17(4)), they should be asked: (a) "Have you reached a verdict upon which you are all agreed? Please answer Yes or No"; (b) (i) if unanimous, "What is your verdict?"; (ii) if not unanimous, the jury should be sent out again for further deliberation with a further direction to arrive if possible at a unanimous verdict.

26Q.3 Should the jury return (whether for the first time or subsequently) or be sent for after the two hours and ten minutes (or the longer period) has elapsed, questions (a) and (b)(i) in the paragraph above should be put to them and, if it appears that they are not unanimous, they should be asked to retire once more and told that they should continue to endeavour to reach a unanimous verdict but that, if they cannot, the judge will accept a majority verdict as in section 17(1).

26Q.4 When the jury finally return, they should be asked: (a) "Have at least ten (or nine as the case may be) of you agreed upon your verdict?"; (b) if "Yes", "What is your verdict? Please answer only Guilty or Not Guilty"; (c) (i) if "Not Guilty", accept the verdict without more ado; (ii) if "Guilty", "Is that the verdict of you all or by a majority?"; (d) if "Guilty" by a majority, "How many of you agreed to the verdict and how many dissented?"

26Q.5 At whatever stage the jury return, before question (a) is asked, the senior officer of the court present shall state in open court, for each period when the jury was out of court for the purpose of considering their verdict(s), the time at which the last member of the jury left the jury box to go to the jury room and the time of their return to the jury box; and will additionally state in open court the total of such periods.

26Q.6 The reason why section 17(3) is confined to a majority verdict of guilty, and for the somewhat complicated procedure set out above, is to prevent it being known that a verdict of "Not Guilty" is a majority verdict. If the final direction continues to require the jury to arrive, if possible, at a unanimous verdict and the verdict is received as specified, it will not be known for certain that the acquittal is not unanimous.

26Q.7 Where there are several counts (or alternative verdicts) left to the jury the above practice will, of course, need to be adapted to the circumstances. The procedure will have to be repeated in respect of each count (or alternative verdict), the verdict being accepted in those cases where the jury are unanimous and the further direction being given in cases in which they are not unanimous. The judge may exercise discretion in deciding when to record the unanimous verdict; the circumstances of the case may dictate that it is more desirable to give the majority direction before the recording of any unanimous verdicts. If so, then instead of being asked about each count in turn, the jury should be asked "Have you reached verdicts upon which you are all agreed in respect of all defendants and/or all counts?"

26Q.8 Should the jury in the end be unable to agree on a verdict by the required majority, the judge in his discretion will either ask them to deliberate further, or discharge them.

26Q.9 Section 17 will, of course, apply also to verdicts other than "Guilty" or "Not Guilty", e.g. to special verdicts under the Criminal Procedure (Insanity) Act 1964 [§§ 4-231 et seq. in the main work], following a finding by the judge that the defendant is unfit to be tried, and special verdicts on findings of fact. Accordingly in such cases the questions to jurors will have to be suitably adjusted.

Criminal Procedure Rules 2020 (SI 2020/759), Pt 27

Retrial after Acquittal

General

When this Part applies

B-474 **27.1.**—(1) Rule 27.2 applies where, under section 54 of the Criminal Procedure and Investigations Act 1996, the Crown Court or a magistrates' court can certify for the High Court that interference or intimidation has been involved in proceedings leading to an acquittal.

(2) Rules 27.3 to 27.7 apply where, under section 77 of the Criminal Justice Act 2003, the Court of Appeal can—

(a) quash an acquittal for a serious offence and order a defendant to be retried; or
(b) order that an acquittal outside the United Kingdom is no bar to the defendant being tried

in England and Wales,
if there is new and compelling evidence and it is in the interests of justice to make the order.

Application for certificate to allow order for retrial

Application for certificate
27.2.–(1) This rule applies where– B-475
(a) a defendant has been acquitted of an offence;
(b) a person has been convicted of one of the following offences involving interference with or intimidation of a juror or a witness (or potential witness) in any proceedings which led to the defendant's acquittal–
(i) perverting the course of justice,
(ii) intimidation etc. of witnesses, jurors and others under section 51(1) of the Criminal Justice and Public Order Act 1994, or
(iii) aiding, abetting, counselling, procuring, suborning or inciting another person to commit an offence under section 1 of the Perjury Act 1911; and
(c) the prosecutor wants the court by which that person was convicted to certify for the High Court that there is a real possibility that, but for the interference or intimidation, the defendant would not have been acquitted.
(2) The prosecutor must–
(a) apply in writing as soon as practicable after that person's conviction; and
(b) serve the application on–
(i) the court officer, and
(ii) the defendant who was acquitted, if the court so directs.
(3) The application must–
(a) give details, with relevant facts and dates, of–
(i) the conviction for interference or intimidation, and
(ii) the defendant's acquittal; and
(b) explain–
(i) why there is a real possibility that, but for the interference or intimidation, the defendant would not have been acquitted, and
(ii) why it would not be contrary to the interests of justice to prosecute the defendant again for the offence of which he or she was acquitted, despite any lapse of time or other reason.
(4) The court may–
(a) extend the time limit under paragraph (2);
(b) allow an application to be in a different form to one set out in the Practice Direction, or to be made orally; and
(c) determine an application under this rule–
(i) at a hearing, in private or in public; or
(ii) without a hearing.
(5) If the court gives a certificate, the court officer must serve it on–
(a) the prosecutor; and
(b) the defendant who was acquitted.

Application to Court of Appeal to quash acquittal and order retrial

Application for reporting restriction pending application for order for retrial
27.3.–(1) This rule applies where– B-476
(a) no application has been made under rule 27.4 (application for order for retrial);
(b) an investigation by officers has begun into an offence with a view to an application under that rule; and
(c) the Director of Public Prosecutions wants the Court of Appeal to make, vary or remove an order for a reporting restriction under section 82 of the Criminal Justice Act 2003 (restrictions on publication in the interests of justice).
(2) The Director must–
(a) apply in writing; and
(b) serve the application on–
(i) the Registrar, and
(ii) the defendant, unless the court otherwise directs.

(3) The application must, as appropriate—
(a) explain why the Director wants the court to direct that it need not be served on the defendant until the application under rule 27.4 is served;
(b) specify the proposed terms of the order, and for how long it should last;
(c) explain why an order in the terms proposed is necessary; and
(d) explain why an order should be varied or removed.

Application for order for retrial

B-477 **27.4.**—(1) This rule applies where—
(a) a defendant has been acquitted—
(i) in the Crown Court, or on appeal from the Crown Court, of an offence listed in Part 1 of Schedule 5 to the Criminal Justice Act 2003 (qualifying offences), or
(ii) in proceedings elsewhere than in the United Kingdom of an offence under the law of that place, if what was alleged would have amounted to or included one of those listed offences; and
(b) with the Director of Public Prosecutions' written consent, a prosecutor wants the Court of Appeal to make an order, as the case may be—
(i) quashing the acquittal in the Crown Court and ordering the defendant to be retried for the offence, or
(ii) declaring whether the acquittal outside the United Kingdom is a bar to the defendant's trial in England and Wales and, if it is, whether that acquittal shall not be such a bar.
(2) Such a prosecutor must—
(a) apply in writing;
(b) serve the application on the Registrar; and
(c) not more than 2 business days later serve on the defendant who was acquitted—
(i) the application, and
(ii) a notice charging the defendant with the offence, unless the defendant has already been arrested and charged under section 87 of the Criminal Justice Act 2003 (arrest, under warrant or otherwise, and charge).
(3) The application must—
(a) give details, with relevant facts and dates, of the defendant's acquittal;
(b) explain—
(i) what new and compelling evidence there is against the defendant, and
(ii) why in all the circumstances it would be in the interests of justice for the court to make the order sought;
(c) include or attach any application for the following, with reasons—
(i) an order under section 80(6) of the Criminal Justice Act 2003 (procedure and evidence) for the production of any document, exhibit or other thing which in the prosecutor's opinion is necessary for the determination of the application,
(ii) an order under that section for the attendance before the court of any witness who would be a compellable witness at the trial the prosecutor wants the court to order, or
(iii) an order for a reporting restriction under section 82 of the Criminal Justice Act 2003 (restrictions on publication in the interests of justice); and
(d) attach—
(i) written witness statements of the evidence on which the prosecutor relies as new and compelling evidence against the defendant,
(ii) relevant documents from the trial at which the defendant was acquitted, including a record of the offence or offences charged and of the evidence given, and
(iii) any other document or thing that the prosecutor thinks the court will need to decide the application.

Respondent's notice

B-478 **27.5.**—(1) A defendant on whom a prosecutor serves an application may serve a respondent's notice, and must do so if the defendant wants to make representations to the court.
(2) Such a defendant must serve the respondent's notice on—
(a) the Registrar; and
(b) the prosecutor,
not more than 20 business days after service of the application.
(3) The respondent's notice must—

(a) give the date on which the respondent was served with the prosecutor's application;
(b) summarise any relevant facts not contained in that application;
(c) explain the defendant's grounds for opposing that application;
(d) include or attach any application for the following, with reasons–
(i) an extension of time within which to serve the respondent's notice,
(ii) bail pending the hearing of the prosecutor's application, if the defendant is in custody,
(iii) a direction to attend in person any hearing that the defendant could attend by live link, if the defendant is in custody,
(iv) an order under section 80(6) of the Criminal Justice Act 2003 (procedure and evidence) for the production of any document, exhibit or other thing which in the defendant's opinion is necessary for the determination of the prosecutor's application, or
(v) an order under that section for the attendance before the court of any witness who would be a compellable witness at the trial the prosecutor wants the court to order; and
(e) attach or identify any other document or thing that the defendant thinks the court will need to decide the application.

Application to Crown Court for summons or warrant

27.6.–(1) This rule applies where– B-479
(a) the prosecutor has served on the Registrar an application under rule 27.4 (application for order for retrial);
(b) the defendant is not in custody as a result of arrest under section 88 of the Criminal Justice Act 2003 (bail and custody before application); and
(c) the prosecutor wants the Crown Court to issue–
(i) a summons requiring the defendant to appear before the Court of Appeal at the hearing of the prosecutor's application, or
(ii) a warrant for the defendant's arrest
under section 89 of the 2003 Act (bail and custody before hearing).
(2) The prosecutor must–
(a) apply in writing; and
(b) serve the application on the Crown Court officer.
(3) The application must–
(a) explain what the case is about, including a brief description of the defendant's acquittal, the new evidence and the stage that the application to the Court of Appeal has reached;
(b) specify–
(i) the decision that the prosecutor wants the Crown Court to make,
(ii) each offence charged, and
(iii) any relevant previous bail decision and the reasons given for it; and
(c) propose the terms of any suggested condition of bail.

Application of other rules about procedure in the Court of Appeal

27.7. On an application under rule 27.4 (application for order for retrial)– B-480
(a) the rules in Part 36 (appeal to the Court of Appeal: general rules) apply with the necessary modifications;
(b) rules 39.8, 39.9 and 39.10 (bail and bail conditions in the Court of Appeal) apply as if the references in those rules to appeal included references to an application under rule 27.4; and
(c) rule 39.14 (renewal or setting aside of order for retrial) applies as if the reference to section 7 of the Criminal Appeal Act 1968 were a reference to section 84 of the Criminal Justice Act 2003 (retrial).

Criminal Procedure Rules 2020 (SI 2020/759), Pt 28

Sentencing Procedures in Special Cases

Reasons for not following usual sentencing requirements

28.1.–(1) This rule applies where the court decides– B-481
(a) not to follow a relevant sentencing guideline;
(b) not to make, where it could–

(i) a reparation order (unless it passes a custodial or community sentence),
(ii) a compensation order,
(iii) a slavery and trafficking reparation order, or
(iv) a travel restriction order;

(c) not to order, where it could—
(i) that a suspended sentence of imprisonment is to take effect,
(ii) the endorsement of the defendant's driving record, or
(iii) the defendant's disqualification from driving, for the usual minimum period or at all; or

(d) to pass a lesser sentence than it otherwise would have passed because the defendant has assisted, or has agreed to assist, an investigator or prosecutor in relation to an offence.

(2) The court must explain why it has so decided, when it explains the sentence that it has passed.

(3) Where paragraph (1)(d) applies, the court must arrange for such an explanation to be given to the defendant and to the prosecutor in writing, if the court thinks that it would not be in the public interest to explain in public.

Notice of requirements of suspended sentence and community, etc. orders

B-482 **28.2.**—(1) This rule applies where the court—
(a) makes a suspended sentence order;
(b) imposes a requirement under—
(i) a community order,
(ii) a youth rehabilitation order, or
(iii) a suspended sentence order; or
(c) orders the defendant to attend meetings with a supervisor.

(2) The court officer must notify—
(a) the defendant of—
(i) the length of the sentence suspended by a suspended sentence order, and
(ii) the period of the suspension;
(b) the defendant and, where the defendant is under 14, an appropriate adult, of—
(i) any requirement or requirements imposed, and
(ii) the identity of any responsible officer or supervisor, and the means by which that person may be contacted;
(c) any responsible officer or supervisor, and, where the defendant is under 14, the appropriate qualifying officer (if that is not the responsible officer), of—
(i) the defendant's name, address and telephone number (if available),
(ii) the offence or offences of which the defendant was convicted, and
(iii) the requirement or requirements imposed; and
(d) the person affected, where the court imposes a requirement—
(i) for the protection of that person from the defendant, or
(ii) requiring the defendant to reside with that person.

(3) If the court imposes an electronic monitoring requirement, the monitor of which is not the responsible officer, the court officer must—
(a) notify the defendant and, where the defendant is under 16, an appropriate adult, of the monitor's name, and the means by which the monitor may be contacted; and
(b) notify the monitor of—
(i) the defendant's name, address and telephone number (if available),
(ii) the offence or offences of which the defendant was convicted,
(iii) the place or places at which the defendant's presence must be monitored,
(iv) the period or periods during which the defendant's presence there must be monitored, and
(v) the identity of the responsible officer, and the means by which that officer may be contacted.

Notification requirements

B-483 **28.3.**—(1) This rule applies where, on a conviction, sentence or order, legislation requires the defendant—
(a) to notify information to the police; or
(b) to be included in a barred list.

(2) The court must tell the defendant that such requirements apply, and under what legislation.

Variation of sentence

28.4.–(1) This rule– B-484

(a) applies where a magistrates' court or the Crown Court can vary or rescind a sentence or order, other than an order to which rule 44.3 applies (setting aside a conviction or varying a costs etc. order); and

(b) authorises the Crown Court, in addition to its other powers, to do so within the period of 56 days beginning with another defendant's acquittal or sentencing where–

(i) defendants are tried separately in the Crown Court on the same or related facts alleged in one or more indictments, and

(ii) one is sentenced before another is acquitted or sentenced.

(2) The court–

(a) may exercise its power–

(i) on application by a party, or on its own initiative,

(ii) at a hearing, in public or in private, or without a hearing; and

(b) must announce, at a hearing in public–

(i) a decision to vary or rescind a sentence or order, or to refuse to do so, and

(ii) the reasons for that decision.

(3) A party who wants the court to exercise that power must–

(a) apply in writing as soon as reasonably practicable after–

(i) the sentence or order that that party wants the court to vary or rescind, or

(ii) where paragraph (1)(b) applies, the other defendant's acquittal or sentencing;

(b) serve the application on–

(i) the court officer, and

(ii) each other party; and

(c) in the application–

(i) explain why the sentence should be varied or rescinded,

(ii) specify the variation that the applicant proposes, and

(iii) if the application is late, explain why.

(4) The court must not exercise its power in the defendant's absence unless–

(a) the court makes a variation–

(i) which is proposed by the defendant, or

(ii) the effect of which is that the defendant is no more severely dealt with under the sentence as varied than before; or

(b) the defendant has had an opportunity to make representations at a hearing (whether or not the defendant in fact attends).

(5) The court may–

(a) extend (even after it has expired) the time limit under paragraph (3), unless the court's power to vary or rescind the sentence cannot be exercised; and

(b) allow an application to be made orally.

(6) For the purposes of the announcement required by paragraph (2)(b), the court need not comprise the same member or members as the court by which the decision to be announced was made.

Application to vary or discharge a compensation, etc. order

28.5.–(1) This rule applies where on application by the defendant a magistrates' court can vary or B-485
discharge–

(a) a compensation order; or

(b) a slavery and trafficking reparation order.

(2) A defendant who wants the court to exercise that power must–

(a) apply in writing as soon as practicable after becoming aware of the grounds for doing so;

(b) serve the application on the magistrates' court officer;

(c) where the order was made in the Crown Court, serve a copy of the application on the Crown Court officer; and

(d) in the application, specify the order that the defendant wants the court to vary or discharge and explain (as applicable)–

(i) what civil court finding shows that the injury, loss or damage was less than it had appeared to be when the order was made,

(ii) in what circumstances the person for whose benefit the order was made has recovered the property for the loss of which it was made,

(iii) why a confiscation order, unlawful profit order or slavery and trafficking reparation order makes the defendant now unable to pay compensation or reparation in full, or

(iv) in what circumstances the defendant's means have been reduced substantially and unexpectedly, and why they seem unlikely to increase for a considerable period.

(3) The court officer must serve a copy of the application on the person for whose benefit the order was made.

(4) The court must not vary or discharge the order unless—

(a) the defendant, and the person for whose benefit it was made, each has had an opportunity to make representations at a hearing (whether or not either in fact attends); and

(b) where the order was made in the Crown Court, the Crown Court has notified its consent.

Application to remove, revoke or suspend a disqualification or restriction

B-486 **28.6.**—(1) This rule applies where, on application by the defendant, the court can remove, revoke or suspend a disqualification or restriction included in a sentence (except a disqualification from driving).

(2) A defendant who wants the court to exercise such a power must —

(a) apply in writing, no earlier than the date on which the court can exercise the power;

(b) serve the application on the court officer; and

(c) in the application—

(i) specify the disqualification or restriction, and

(ii) explain why the defendant wants the court to remove, revoke or suspend it.

(3) The court officer must serve a copy of the application on the chief officer of police for the local justice area.

Application for a restitution order by the victim of a theft

B-487 **28.7.**—(1) This rule applies where, on application by the victim of a theft, the court can order a defendant to give that person goods obtained with the proceeds of goods stolen in that theft.

(2) A person who wants the court to exercise that power if the defendant is convicted must—

(a) apply in writing as soon as practicable (without waiting for the verdict);

(b) serve the application on the court officer; and

(c) in the application—

(i) identify the goods, and

(ii) explain why the applicant is entitled to them.

(3) The court officer must serve a copy of the application on each party.

(4) The court must not determine the application unless the applicant and each party has had an opportunity to make representations at a hearing (whether or not each in fact attends).

(5) The court may—

(a) extend (even after it has expired) the time limit under paragraph (2); and

(b) allow an application to be made orally.

Directions for commissioning medical reports for sentencing purposes

B-488 **28.8.**—(1) This rule applies where for sentencing purposes the court requires—

(a) a medical examination of the defendant and a report; or

(b) information about the arrangements that could be made for the defendant where the court is considering—

(i) a hospital order, or

(ii) a guardianship order.

(2) The court must—

(a) identify each issue in respect of which the court requires expert medical opinion and the legislation applicable;

(b) specify the nature of the expertise likely to be required for giving such opinion;

(c) identify each party or participant by whom a commission for such opinion must be prepared, who may be—

(i) a party (or party's representative) acting on that party's own behalf,

(ii) a party (or party's representative) acting on behalf of the court, or

(iii) the court officer acting on behalf of the court;

(d) where there are available to the court arrangements with the National Health Service under which an assessment of a defendant's mental health may be prepared, give such directions as are needed under those arrangements for obtaining the expert report or reports required;

(e) where no such arrangements are available to the court, or they will not be used, give directions for the commissioning of an expert report or expert reports, including–
(i) such directions as can be made about supplying the expert or experts with the defendant's medical records,
(ii) directions about the other information, about the defendant and about the offence or offences alleged to have been committed by the defendant, which is to be supplied to each expert, and
(iii) directions about the arrangements that will apply for the payment of each expert;
(f) set a timetable providing for–
(i) the date by which a commission is to be delivered to each expert,
(ii) the date by which any failure to accept a commission is to be reported to the court,
(iii) the date or dates by which progress in the preparation of a report or reports is to be reviewed by the court officer, and
(iv) the date by which each report commissioned is to be received by the court; and
(g) identify the person (each person, if more than one) to whom a copy of a report is to be supplied, and by whom.
(3) A commission addressed to an expert must–
(a) identify each issue in respect of which the court requires expert medical opinion and the legislation applicable;
(b) include–
(i) the information required by the court to be supplied to the expert,
(ii) details of the timetable set by the court, and
(iii) details of the arrangements that will apply for the payment of the expert;
(c) identify the person (each person, if more than one) to whom a copy of the expert's report is to be supplied; and
(d) request confirmation that the expert from whom the opinion is sought–
(i) accepts the commission, and
(ii) will adhere to the timetable.

Information to be supplied on committal to custody or admission to hospital or guardianship

28.9.–(1) This rule applies where the court– **B-489**
(a) orders the defendant's committal to custody on withholding bail or on sentencing;
(b) orders the defendant's detention and treatment in hospital; or
(c) makes a guardianship order.

(2) Where paragraph (1)(a) applies, unless the court otherwise directs the court officer must, as soon as practicable, serve on or make available to the custodian any psychiatric, psychological or other medical report about the defendant received by the court for the purposes of the case.

(3) Where paragraph (1)(b) or (c) applies, unless the court otherwise directs the court officer must, as soon as practicable, serve on or make available to (as applicable) the hospital or the guardian–
(a) a record of the court's order;
(b) such information as the court has received that appears likely to assist in treating or otherwise dealing with the defendant, including information about–
(i) the defendant's mental condition,
(ii) the defendant's other circumstances, and
(iii) the circumstances of the offence.

Information to be supplied on committal for sentence, etc.

28.10.–(1) This rule applies where a magistrates' court or the Crown Court convicts the defendant and– **B-490**
(a) commits or adjourns the case to another court–
(i) for sentence, or
(ii) for the defendant to be dealt with for breach of a deferred sentence, a conditional discharge, or a suspended sentence of imprisonment, imposed by that other court;
(b) deals with a deferred sentence, a conditional discharge, or a suspended sentence of imprisonment, imposed by another court; or
(c) makes an order that another court is, or may be, required to enforce.

(2) Unless the convicting court otherwise directs, the court officer must, as soon as practicable–
(a) where paragraph (1)(a) applies, arrange the transmission from the convicting to the other court of a record of any relevant–

- (i) certificate of conviction,
- (ii) magistrates' court register entry,
- (iii) decision about bail, for the purposes of section 5 of the Bail Act 1976 [§ 3-28 in the main work],
- (iv) note of evidence,
- (v) statement or other document introduced in evidence,
- (vi) medical or other report,
- (vii) representation order or application for such order, and
- (viii) interim driving disqualification;

(b) where paragraph (1)(b) or (c) applies, arrange—

- (i) the transmission from the convicting to the other court of notice of the convicting court's order, and
- (ii) the recording of that order at the other court;

(c) in every case, notify the defendant and, where the defendant is under 14, an appropriate adult, of the location of the other court.

Application to review sentence because of assistance given or withheld

B-491 **28.11.**—(1) This rule applies where the Crown Court can reduce or increase a sentence on application by a prosecutor in a case in which—

(a) since being sentenced, the defendant has assisted, or has agreed to assist, an investigator or prosecutor in relation to an offence; or

(b) since receiving a reduced sentence for agreeing to give such assistance, the defendant has failed to do so.

(2) A prosecutor who wants the court to exercise that power must—

(a) apply in writing as soon as practicable after becoming aware of the grounds for doing so;

(b) serve the application on—

- (i) the court officer, and
- (ii) the defendant; and

(c) in the application—

- (i) explain why the sentence should be reduced, or increased, as appropriate, and
- (ii) identify any other matter relevant to the court's decision, including any sentencing guideline or guideline case.

(3) The general rule is that the application must be determined by the judge who passed the sentence, unless that judge is unavailable.

(4) The court must not determine the application in the defendant's absence unless the defendant has had an opportunity to make representations at a hearing (whether or not the defendant in fact attends).

Criminal Procedure Rules 2020 (SI 2020/759), Pt 29

Road Traffic Penalties

Representations about obligatory disqualification or endorsement

B-492 **29.1.**—(1) This rule applies—

(a) where the court—

- (i) convicts the defendant of an offence involving obligatory disqualification from driving and section 34(1) of the Road Traffic Offenders Act 1988 (disqualification for certain offences [§ 32-249 in the main work]) applies,
- (ii) convicts the defendant of an offence where section 35 of the 1988 Act (disqualification for repeated offences [ibid., § 32-264]) applies, or
- (iii) convicts the defendant of an offence involving obligatory endorsement of the defendant's driving record and section 44 of the 1988 Act (orders for endorsement [ibid., § 32-292]) applies;

(b) unless the defendant is absent.

(a) where paragraph (1)(a)(i) applies (obligatory disqualification under section 34)—

- (i) that the court must order the defendant to be disqualified from driving for a minimum of 12 months (or 2 or 3 years, as the case may be, according to the offence and the defendant's driving record), unless the court decides that there are special reasons to order disqualification for a shorter period, or not to order disqualification at all, and
- (ii) if applicable, that the period of disqualification will be reduced by at least 3 months

if, by no later than 2 months before the end of the reduced period, the defendant completes an approved driving course;

(2) The court must explain, in terms the defendant can understand (with help, if necessary)—

(b) where paragraph (1)(a)(ii) applies (disqualification under section 35)—

(i) that the court must order the defendant to be disqualified from driving for a minimum of 6 months (or 1 or 2 years, as the case may be, according to the defendant's driving record), unless, having regard to all the circumstances, the court decides to order disqualification for a shorter period, or not to order disqualification at all, and

(ii) that circumstances of which the court cannot take account in making its decision are any that make the offence not a serious one; hardship (other than exceptional hardship); and any that during the last 3 years already have been taken into account by a court when ordering disqualification for less than the usual minimum period, or not at all, for repeated driving offences;

(c) where paragraph (1)(a)(iii) applies (obligatory endorsement), that the court must order the endorsement of the defendant's driving record unless the court decides that there are special reasons not to do so; and

(d) in every case, as applicable—

(i) that the court already has received representations from the defendant about whether any such special reasons or mitigating circumstances apply and will take account of them, or

(ii) that the defendant may make such representations now, on oath or affirmation.

(3) Unless the court already has received such representations from the defendant, before it applies rule 24.11 (magistrates' court procedure if the court convicts) or rule 25.16 (Crown Court procedure if the court convicts), as the case may be, the court must—

(a) ask whether the defendant wants to make any such representations; and

(b) if the answer to that question is "yes", require the defendant to take an oath or affirm and make them.

Application to remove a disqualification from driving

29.2.—(1) This rule applies where, on application by the defendant, the court can remove a disqualification from driving. **B-493**

(2) A defendant who wants the court to exercise that power must—

(a) apply in writing, no earlier than the date on which the court can exercise the power;

(b) serve the application on the court officer; and

(c) in the application—

(i) specify the disqualification that the defendant wants the court to remove, and

(ii) explain why.

(3) The court officer must serve a copy of the application on the chief officer of police for the local justice area.

Information to be supplied on order for endorsement of driving record, etc.

29.3.—(1) This rule applies where the court— **B-494**

(a) convicts the defendant of an offence involving obligatory endorsement, and orders there to be endorsed on the defendant's driving record (and on any counterpart licence, if other legislation requires)—

(i) particulars of the conviction,

(ii) particulars of any disqualification from driving that the court imposes, and

(iii) the penalty points to be attributed to the offence;

(b) disqualifies the defendant from driving for any other offence; or

(c) suspends or removes a disqualification from driving.

(2) The court officer must, as soon as practicable, serve on the Secretary of State notice that includes details of—

(a) where paragraph (1)(a) applies—

(i) the local justice area in which the court is acting,

(ii) the dates of conviction and sentence,

(iii) the offence, and the date on which it was committed,

(iv) the sentence, and

(v) the date of birth, and sex, of the defendant, where those details are available;

(b) where paragraph (1)(b) applies—

(i) the date and period of the disqualification, and

(ii) the power exercised by the court; and

(c) where paragraph (1)(c) applies—

(i) the date and period of the disqualification,

(ii) the date and terms of the order for its suspension or removal,

(iii) the power exercised by the court, and

(iv) where the court suspends the disqualification pending appeal, the court to which the defendant has appealed.

Statutory declaration to avoid fine after fixed penalty notice

B-495 **29.4.**—(1) This rule applies where—

(a) a chief officer of police, or the Secretary of State, serves on the magistrates' court officer a certificate registering, for enforcement as a fine, a sum payable by a defendant after failure to comply with a fixed penalty notice;

(b) the court officer notifies the defendant of the registration; and

(c) the defendant makes a statutory declaration with the effect that there become void—

(i) the fixed penalty notice, or any associated notice sent to the defendant as owner of the vehicle concerned, and

(ii) the registration and any enforcement proceedings.

(2) The defendant must serve that statutory declaration not more than 21 days after service of notice of the registration, unless the court extends that time limit.

(3) The court officer must—

(a) serve a copy of the statutory declaration on the person by whom the certificate was registered;

(b) cancel any endorsement on the defendant's driving record (and on any counterpart licence, if other legislation requires); and

(c) notify the Secretary of State of any such cancellation.

(4) A court officer may take the statutory declaration to which this rule refers if that officer—

(a) is a justices' legal adviser; or

(b) is nominated for the purpose by such a legal adviser.

Application for declaration about a course or programme certificate decision

B-496 **29.5.**—(1) This rule applies where the court can declare unjustified—

(a) a course provider's failure or refusal to give a certificate of the defendant's satisfactory completion of an approved course; or

(b) a programme provider's giving of a certificate of the defendant's failure fully to participate in an approved programme.

(2) A defendant who wants the court to exercise that power must—

(a) apply in writing, not more than 20 business days after—

(i) the date by which the defendant was required to complete the course, or

(ii) the giving of the certificate of failure fully to participate in the programme;

(b) serve the application on the court officer; and

(c) in the application, specify the course or programme and explain (as applicable)—

(i) that the course provider has failed to give a certificate,

(ii) where the course provider has refused to give a certificate, why the defendant disagrees with the reasons for that decision, or

(iii) where the programme provider has given a certificate, why the defendant disagrees with the reasons for that decision.

(3) The court officer must serve a copy of the application on the course or programme provider.

(4) The court must not determine the application unless the defendant, and the course or programme provider, each has had an opportunity to make representations at a hearing (whether or not either in fact attends).

Appeal against recognition of foreign driving disqualification

B-497 **29.6.**—(1) This rule applies where—

(a) a Minister gives a disqualification notice under section 57 of the Crime (International Co operation) Act 2003; and

(b) the person to whom it is given wants to appeal under section 59 of the Act to a magistrates' court.

(2) That person ("the appellant") must serve an appeal notice on —

(a) the court officer, at a magistrates' court in the local justice area in which the appellant lives; and

(b) the Minister, at the address given in the disqualification notice.

(3) The appellant must serve the appeal notice within the period for which section 59 of the 2003 Act provides.

(4) The appeal notice must–

(a) attach a copy of the disqualification notice;

(b) explain which of the conditions in section 56 of the 2003 Act is not met, and why section 57 of the Act therefore does not apply; and

(c) include any application to suspend the disqualification, under section 60 of the Act.

(5) The Minister may serve a respondent's notice, and must do so if–

(a) the Minister wants to make representations to the court; or

(b) the court so directs.

(6) The Minister must–

(a) unless the court otherwise directs, serve any such respondent's notice not more than 10 business days after–

(i) the appellant serves the appeal notice, or

(ii) a direction to do so; and

(b) in any such respondent's notice–

(i) identify the grounds of opposition on which the Minister relies,

(ii) summarise any relevant facts not already included in the disqualification and appeal notices, and

(iii) identify any other document that the Minister thinks the court will need to decide the appeal (and serve any such document with the notice).

(7) Where the court determines an appeal, the general rule is that it must do so at a hearing (which must be in public, unless the court otherwise directs).

(8) The court officer must serve on the Minister–

(a) notice of the outcome of the appeal;

(b) notice of any suspension of the disqualification; and

(c) the appellant's driving licence, if surrendered to the court officer.

Criminal Procedure Rules 2020 (SI 2020/759), Pt 30

Enforcement of Fines and other Orders for Payment

When this Part applies

30.1.–(1) This Part applies where a magistrates' court can enforce payment of– **B-498**

(a) a fine, or a sum that legislation requires the court to treat as a fine; or

(b) any other sum that a court has ordered to be paid–

(i) on a conviction, or

(ii) on the forfeiture of a surety.

(2) Rules 30.7 to 30.9 apply where the court, or a fines officer, issues a warrant for an enforcement agent to take control of a defendant's goods and sell them, using the procedure in Schedule 12 to the Tribunals, Courts and Enforcement Act 2007.

(3) In this Part–

(a) 'defendant' means anyone liable to pay a sum to which this Part applies;

(b) 'payment terms' means by when, and by what (if any) instalments, such a sum must be paid.

Exercise of court's powers

30.2.– The court must not exercise its enforcement powers unless– **B-499**

(a) the court officer has served on the defendant any collection order or other notice of–

(i) the obligation to pay,

(ii) the payment terms, and

(iii) how and where the defendant must pay; and

(b) the defendant has failed to comply with the payment terms.

Duty to give receipt

30.3.–(1) This rule applies where the defendant makes a payment to– **B-500**

(a) the court officer specified in an order or notice served under rule 30.2;

(b) another court officer;
(c) any—
(i) custodian of the defendant,
(ii) supervisor appointed to encourage the defendant to pay, or
(iii) responsible officer appointed under a community sentence or a suspended sentence of imprisonment; or
(d) a person executing a warrant to which rule 13.6 (warrants for arrest, detention or imprisonment that cease to have effect on payment) or this Part applies.

(2) The person receiving the payment must—
(a) give the defendant a receipt, unless the method of payment generates an independent record (for example, a bank record); and
(b) as soon as practicable transmit the payment to the court officer specified in an order or notice served under rule 30.2, if the recipient is not that court officer.

Appeal against decision of fines officer

B-501 **30.4.**—(1) This rule applies where—
(a) a collection order is in force;
(b) a fines officer makes a decision under one of these paragraphs of Schedule 5 to the Courts Act 2003—
(i) paragraph 22 (Application to fines officer for variation of order or attachment of earnings order, etc.),
(ii) paragraph 31 (Application to fines officer for variation of reserve terms), or
(iii) paragraph 37 (Functions of fines officer in relation to defaulters: referral or further steps notice); and
(c) the defendant wants to appeal against that decision.

(2) Unless the court otherwise directs, the defendant must—
(a) appeal in writing not more than 10 business days after the decision;
(b) serve the appeal on the court officer; and
(c) in the appeal—
(i) explain why a different decision should be made, and
(ii) specify the decision that the defendant proposes.

(3) Where the court determines an appeal, the general rule is that it must do so at a hearing.

Application to reduce a fine, vary payment terms or remit a courts charge

★B-502 **30.5.**—(1) This rule applies where—
(a) no collection order is in force and the defendant wants the court to—
(i) reduce the amount of a fine, or
(ii) vary payment terms; or
(b) the defendant, a fines officer or an enforcement agent wants the court to remit a criminal courts charge.

(2) Unless the court otherwise directs, such a defendant, fines officer or enforcement agent must—
(a) apply in writing;
(b) serve the application on the court officer;
(c) if the application is to reduce a fine or vary payment terms, explain—
(i) what relevant circumstances have not yet been considered by the court, and
(ii) why the fine should be reduced, or the payment terms varied; and
(d) if the application is to remit a criminal courts charge, explain—
(i) how the circumstances meet the time limits and other conditions in section 50 of the Sentencing Act 2020, and
(ii) why the charge should be remitted.

(3) The court may determine an application—
(a) at a hearing, which may be in public or in private; or
(b) without a hearing.

[This rule is printed as amended, with effect from 8 February 2021, by SI 2021/40, r.16(a).]

Claim to avoid fine after penalty notice

B-503 **30.6.**—(1) This rule applies where—
(a) a chief officer of police serves on the magistrates' court officer a certificate registering, for

enforcement as a fine, a sum payable by a defendant after failure to comply with a penalty notice; and

(b) the court or a fines officer enforces the fine.

(2) A defendant who claims not to be the person to whom the penalty notice was issued must, unless the court otherwise directs—

(a) make that claim in writing; and

(b) serve it on the court officer.

(3) The court officer must—

(a) notify the chief officer of police by whom the certificate was registered; and

(b) refer the case to the court.

(4) Where such a claim is made—

(a) the general rule is that the court must adjourn the enforcement for 28 days and fix a hearing; but

(b) the court may make a different order.

(5) At any such hearing, the chief officer of police must introduce any evidence to contradict the defendant's claim.

Information to be included in a warrant of control

30.7.—(1) A warrant must identify— **B-504**

(a) each person to whom it is directed;

(b) the defendant against whom it was issued;

(c) the sum for which it was issued and the reason that sum is owed;

(d) the court or fines officer who issued it, unless that is otherwise recorded by the court officer; and

(e) the court office for the court or fines officer who issued it.

(2) A person to whom a warrant is directed must record on it the date and time at which it is received.

(3) A warrant that contains an error is not invalid, as long as—

(a) it was issued in respect of a lawful decision by the court or fines officer; and

(b) it contains enough information to identify that decision.

Warrant of control: application by enforcement agent for extension of time, etc.

30.8.—(1) This rule applies where an enforcement agent wants the court to exercise a power under Schedule 12 to the Tribunals, Courts and Enforcement Act 2007, or under regulations made under that Schedule, to— **B-505**

(a) shorten or extend a time limit;

(b) give the agent authority to—

(i) enter premises which the agent would not otherwise have authority to enter,

(ii) enter or remain on premises at a time at which the agent would not otherwise have authority to be there,

(iii) use reasonable force, in circumstances in which the agent would not otherwise have authority to use such force,

(iv) sell goods by a method which the agent would not otherwise have authority to use, or

(v) recover disbursements which the agent would not otherwise have authority to recover; or

(c) specify the manner in which goods which have not been sold must be disposed of.

(2) Such an enforcement agent must—

(a) apply in writing;

(b) serve the application on the court officer; and

(c) pay any fee prescribed.

(3) The application must—

(a) identify the power that the agent wants the court to exercise;

(b) explain how the conditions for the exercise of that power are satisfied, including any condition that requires the agent to give another person notice of the application;

(c) specify those persons, if any, to whom the agent has given notice in accordance with such a condition; and

(d) propose the terms of the order that the agent wants the court to make;

(4) A person to whom the enforcement agent has given notice of an application and who wants to make representations to the court must—

(a) serve the representations on—
(i) the court officer,
(ii) the enforcement agent, and
(iii) any other person to whom the enforcement agent gave notice;
(b) do so as soon as reasonably practicable and in any event within such period as the court directs; and
(c) in the representations, propose the terms of the order that that person wants the court to make, and explain why.

(5) The court—
(a) must not determine an application unless any person to whom the enforcement agent gave notice—
(i) is present, or
(ii) has had a reasonable opportunity to respond; but
(b) subject to that, may determine an application—
(i) at a hearing, which must be in private unless the court otherwise directs, or
(ii) without a hearing.

Warrant of control: application to resolve dispute

B-506 **30.9.**—(1) This rule applies where a defendant's goods are sold using the procedure in Schedule 12 to the Tribunals, Courts and Enforcement Act 2007 and there is a dispute about—
(a) what share of the proceeds of those goods should be paid by the enforcement agent to a co-owner; or
(b) the fees or disbursements sought or recovered by the enforcement agent out of the proceeds.

(2) An enforcement agent, a defendant or a co-owner who wants the court to resolve the dispute must—
(a) apply in writing as soon as practicable after becoming aware of the grounds for doing so;
(b) serve the application on
(i) the court officer,
(ii) each other party to the dispute, and
(iii) any other co-owner; and
(c) pay any fee prescribed.

(3) The application must—
(a) identify the warrant of control;
(b) specify the goods sold, the proceeds, and the fees and disbursements sought or recovered by the enforcement agent;
(c) identify the power that the applicant wants the court to exercise;
(d) specify the persons served with the application;
(e) explain the circumstances of the dispute; and
(f) propose the terms of the order that the applicant wants the court to make.

(4) A person served with an application who wants to make representations to the court must—
(a) serve the representations on—
(i) the court officer,
(ii) the applicant, and
(iii) any other person on whom the application was served;
(b) do so as soon as reasonably practicable and in any event within such period as the court directs; and
(c) in the representations, propose the terms of the order that that person wants the court to make, and explain why.

(5) The court—
(a) must determine an application at a hearing, which must be in private unless the court otherwise directs; but
(b) must not determine an application unless each party—
(i) is present, or
(ii) has had a reasonable opportunity to attend.

[The next paragraph is B-508.]

Criminal Procedure Rules 2020 (SI 2020/759), Pt 31

Behaviour Orders

When this part applies

31.1.–(1) This Part applies where a magistrates' court or the Crown Court can make, vary or revoke a civil order– **B-508**

(a) as well as, or instead of, passing a sentence, or in any other circumstances in which other legislation allows the court to make such an order; and

(b) that requires someone to do, or not do, something.

(2) A reference to a "behaviour order" in this part is a reference to any such order.

(3) A reference to "hearsay evidence" in this part is a reference to evidence consisting of hearsay within the meaning of section 1(2) of the Civil Evidence Act 1995.

[This rule is printed as amended, with effect from 8 February 2021, by SI 2021/40, r.17(a).]

Behaviour orders: general rules

31.2.–(1) The court must not make a behaviour order unless the person to whom it is directed has had an opportunity– **★B-509**

(a) to consider–

(i) what order is proposed and why, and

(ii) the evidence in support; and

(b) to make representations at a hearing (whether or not that person in fact attends).

(2) That restriction does not apply to making an interim behaviour order, but unless other legislation otherwise provides such an order has no effect unless the person to whom it is directed–

(a) is present when it is made; or

(b) is handed a document recording the order not more than 5 business days after it is made.

(3) Where the court decides not to make, where it could–

(a) a football banning order; or

(b) a parenting order, after a person under 16 is convicted of an offence, the court must announce, at a hearing in public, the reasons for its decision.

[This rule is printed as amended, with effect from 8 February 2021, by SI 2021/40, r.17(b).]

Application for behaviour order and notice of terms of proposed order: special rules

31.3.–(1) This rule applies where– **★B-510**

(a) a prosecutor wants the court to make one of the following orders if the defendant is convicted–

(i) an anti-social behaviour order (but this rule does not apply to an application for an interim anti-social behaviour order),

(ii) a serious crime prevention order,

(iii) a criminal behaviour order;

(iv) a prohibition order; or

(v) a knife crime prevention order;

(b) a prosecutor proposes, on the prosecutor's initiative or at the court's request, a sexual harm prevention order if the defendant is convicted; or

(c) a prosecutor proposes a restraining order whether the defendant is convicted or acquitted.

(2) Where paragraph (1)(a) applies (order on application) the prosecutor must serve a notice of intention to apply for such an order on–

(a) the court officer;

(b) the defendant against whom the prosecutor wants the court to make the order; and

(c) any person on whom the order would be likely to have a significant adverse effect,

as soon as practicable (without waiting for the verdict).

(3) A notice under paragraph (2) must–

(a) summarise the relevant facts;

(b) identify the evidence on which the prosecutor relies in support;

(c) attach any written statement that the prosecutor has not already served; and

(d) specify the order that the prosecutor wants the court to make.

(4) A defendant served with a notice under paragraph (2) must–

(a) serve notice of any evidence on which the defendant relies on–

(i) the court officer, and

(ii) the prosecutor,

as soon as practicable (without waiting for the verdict); and

(b) in the notice, identify that evidence and attach any written statement that has not already been served.

(5) Where paragraph (1)(b) (sexual harm prevention order proposed) applies, the prosecutor must—

(a) serve a draft order on the court officer and on the defendant not less than 2 business days before the hearing at which the order may be made; and

(b) in the draft order specify those prohibitions which the prosecutor proposes as necessary for the purpose of—

(i) protecting the public or any particular members of the public from sexual harm from the defendant, or

(ii) protecting children or vulnerable adults generally, or any particular children or vulnerable adults, from sexual harm from the defendant outside the United Kingdom.

(6) Where paragraph (1)(c) applies (restraining order proposed), the prosecutor must—

(a) serve a draft order on the court officer and on the defendant as soon as practicable (without waiting for the verdict); and

(b) in the draft order specify—

(i) those prohibitions which, if the defendant is convicted, the prosecutor proposes for the purpose of protecting a person from conduct which amounts to harassment or will cause fear of violence, or

(ii) those prohibitions which, if the defendant is acquitted, the prosecutor proposes as necessary to protect a person from harassment by the defendant.

(7) Where the prosecutor wants the court to make an anti-social behaviour order, a criminal behaviour order or a prohibition order, the rules about special measures directions in Part 18 (measures to assist a witness or defendant to give evidence) apply, but—

(a) the prosecutor must apply when serving a notice under paragraph (2); and

(b) the time limits in rule 18.4(a) do not apply.

[This rule is printed as amended, with effect from 8 February 2021, by SI 2021/40, r.17(c).]

Evidence to assist the court: special rules

B-511 **31.4.**—(1) This rule applies where the court can make on its own initiative—

(a) a football banning order;

(b) a restraining order; or

(c) an anti-social behaviour order.

(2) A party who wants the court to take account of evidence not already introduced must—

(a) serve notice on—

(i) the court officer, and

(ii) every other party,

as soon as practicable (without waiting for the verdict); and

(b) in the notice, identify that evidence; and

(c) attach any written statement containing such evidence.

Application to vary or revoke behaviour order

B-512 **31.5.**—(1) The court may vary or revoke a behaviour order if—

(a) the legislation under which it is made allows the court to do so; and

(b) one of the following applies—

(i) the prosecutor,

(ii) the person to whom the order is directed,

(iii) any other person protected or affected by the order,

(iv) the relevant authority or responsible officer,

(v) the relevant Chief Officer of Police,

(vi) the Director of Public Prosecutions, or

(vii) the Director of the Serious Fraud Office.

(2) A person applying under this rule must—

(a) apply in writing as soon as practicable after becoming aware of the grounds for doing so, explaining—

(i) what material circumstances have changed since the order was made, and

(ii) why the order should be varied or revoked as a result; and

(b) serve the application on–
(i) the court officer,
(ii) as appropriate, the prosecutor or defendant, and
(iii) any other person listed in paragraph (1)(b), if the court so directs.

(3) A party who wants the court to take account of any particular evidence before making its decision must, as soon as practicable–
(a) serve notice on–
(i) the court officer,
(ii) as appropriate, the prosecutor or defendant, and
(iii) any other person listed in paragraph (1)(b) on whom the court directed the application to be served; and
(b) in that notice identify the evidence and attach any written statement that has not already been served.

(4) The court may decide an application under this rule with or without a hearing.

(5) But the court must not–
(a) dismiss an application under this rule unless the applicant has had an opportunity to make representations at a hearing (whether or not the applicant in fact attends); or
(b) allow an application under this rule unless everyone required to be served, by this rule or by the court, has had at least 10 business days in which to make representations, including representations about whether there should be a hearing.

(6) The court officer must–
(a) serve the application on any person, if the court so directs; and
(b) give notice of any hearing to–
(i) the applicant, and
(ii) any person required to be served, by this rule or by the court.

Notice of hearsay evidence

31.6.–(1) A party who wants to introduce hearsay evidence must– **B-513**
(a) serve notice on–
(i) the court officer, and
(ii) every other party directly affected; and
(b) in that notice–
(i) explain that it is a notice of hearsay evidence,
(ii) identify that evidence,
(iii) identify the person who made the statement which is hearsay, or explain why if that person is not identified, and
(iv) explain why that person will not be called to give oral evidence.

(2) A party may serve one notice under this rule in respect of more than one notice [*sic*] and more than one witness.

Cross-examination of maker of hearsay statement

31.7.–(1) This rule applies where a party wants the court's permission to cross-examine a person who made a statement which another party wants to introduce as hearsay. **B-514**

(2) The party who wants to cross-examine that person must–
(a) apply in writing, with reasons, not more than 5 business days after service of the notice of hearsay evidence; and
(b) serve the application on–
(i) the court officer,
(ii) the party who served the hearsay evidence notice, and
(iii) every party on whom the hearsay evidence notice was served.

(3) The court may decide an application under this rule with or without a hearing.

(4) But the court must not–
(a) dismiss an application under this rule unless the applicant has had an opportunity to make representations at a hearing (whether or not the applicant in fact attends); or
(b) allow an application under this rule unless everyone served with the application has had at least 5 business days in which to make representations, including representations about whether there should be a hearing.

Credibility and consistency of maker of hearsay statement

31.8.–(1) This rule applies where a party wants to challenge the credibility or consistency of a person who made a statement which another party wants to introduce as hearsay. **B-515**

(2) The party who wants to challenge the credibility or consistency of that person must—
(a) serve notice of intention to do so on—
(i) the court officer, and
(ii) the party who served the notice of hearsay evidence
not more than 5 business days after service of that hearsay evidence notice; and
(b) in the notice, identify any statement or other material on which that party relies.
(3) The party who served the hearsay notice—
(a) may call that person to give oral evidence instead; and
(b) if so, must serve notice of intention to do so on—
(i) the court officer, and
(ii) every party on whom the hearsay notice was served
not more than 5 business days after service of the notice under paragraph (2).

[The next paragraph is B-518.]

Court's power to vary requirements under this part

★B-518 **31.9.** Unless other legislation otherwise provides, the court may—
(a) shorten a time limit or extend it (even after it has expired);
(b) allow a notice or application to be given in a different form, or presented orally.

[This rule is printed as re-numbered, with effect from 8 February 2021, by SI 2021/40, r.17(e).]

Criminal Procedure Rules 2020 (SI 2020/759), Pt 32

BREACH, REVOCATION AND AMENDMENT OF COMMUNITY AND OTHER ORDERS

When this Part applies

★B-519 **32.1.** This Part applies where—
(a) the person responsible for a defendant's compliance with an order to which applies—
(i) Schedule 5, 7, 10 or 16 to the Sentencing Act 2020, or
(ii) the Schedule to the Street Offences Act 1959
wants the court to deal with that defendant for failure to comply;
(b) one of the following wants the court to exercise any power it has to revoke or amend such an order—
(i) the responsible officer or supervisor,
(ii) the defendant, or
(iii) where the legislation allows, a person affected by the order; or
(c) the court considers exercising on its own initiative any power it has to revoke or amend such an order.

[This rule is printed as amended, with effect from 8 February 2021, by SI 2021/40, r.18(a).]

Application by responsible officer or supervisor

B-520 **32.2.**—(1) This rule applies where—
(a) the responsible officer or supervisor wants the court to—
(i) deal with a defendant for failure to comply with an order to which this Part applies, or
(ii) revoke or amend such an order; or
(b) the court considers exercising on its own initiative any power it has to—
(i) revoke or amend such an order, and
(ii) summon the defendant to attend for that purpose.

(2) Rules 7.2 to 7.4, which deal, among other things, with starting a prosecution in a magistrates' court, apply—
(a) as if—
(i) a reference in those rules to an allegation of an offence included a reference to an allegation of failure to comply with an order to which this Part applies, and
(ii) a reference to the prosecutor included a reference to the responsible officer or supervisor; and
(b) with the necessary consequential modifications.

Application by defendant or person affected

B-521 **32.3.**—(1) This rule applies where—

(a) the defendant wants the court to exercise any power it has to revoke or amend an order to which this Part applies; or
(b) where the legislation allows, a person affected by such an order wants the court to exercise any such power.
(2) That defendant, or person affected, must—
(a) apply in writing, explaining why the order should be revoked or amended; and
(b) serve the application on—
(i) the court officer,
(ii) the responsible officer or supervisor, and
(iii) as appropriate, the defendant or the person affected.

Procedure on application by responsible officer or supervisor
32.4.—(1) Except for rules 24.8 (written guilty plea: special rules) and 24.9 (single justice procedure: special rules), the rules in Part 24, which deal with the procedure at a trial in a magistrates' court, apply— **B-522**
(a) as if—
(i) a reference in those rules to an allegation of an offence included a reference to an allegation of failure to comply with an order to which this Part applies,
(ii) a reference to the court's verdict included a reference to the court's decision to revoke or amend such an order, or to exercise any other power it has to deal with the defendant, and
(iii) a reference to the court's sentence included a reference to the exercise of any such power; and
(b) with the necessary consequential modifications.
(2) The court officer must serve on each party any order revoking or amending an order to which this Part applies.

CPD VII Sentencing A: Pleas of guilty in the Crown Court

A.1 Prosecutors and Prosecution Advocates should be familiar with and follow the Attorney General's Guidelines on the Acceptance of Pleas and the Prosecutor's Role in the Sentencing Exercise. **B-523**

CPD VII Sentencing B: Determining the factual basis of sentence

Where a guilty plea is offered to less than the whole indictment and the prosecution is minded to accept pleas tendered to some counts or to lesser alternative counts.

B.1 In some cases, defendants wishing to plead guilty will simply plead guilty to all charges on the basis of the facts as alleged and opened by the prosecution, with no dispute as to the factual basis or the extent of offending. Alternatively a defendant may plead guilty to some of the charges brought; in such a case, the judge will consider whether that plea represents a proper plea on the basis of the facts set out by the papers. **B-524**

B.2 Where the prosecution advocate is considering whether to accept a plea to a lesser charge, the advocate may invite the judge to approve the proposed course of action. In such circumstances, the advocate must abide by the decision of the judge.

B.3 If the prosecution advocate does not invite the judge to approve the acceptance by the prosecution of a lesser charge, it is open to the judge to express his or her dissent with the course proposed and invite the advocate to reconsider the matter with those instructing him or her.

B.4 In any proceedings where the judge is of the opinion that the course proposed by the advocate may lead to serious injustice, the proceedings may be adjourned to allow the following procedure to be followed:
(a) as a preliminary step, the prosecution advocate must discuss the judge's observations with the Chief Crown Prosecutor or the senior prosecutor of the relevant prosecuting authority as appropriate, in an attempt to resolve the issue;
(b) where the issue remains unresolved, the Director of Public Prosecutions or the Director of the relevant prosecuting authority should be consulted;
(c) in extreme circumstances the judge may decline to proceed with the case until the prosecuting authority has consulted with the Attorney General, as may be appropriate.

B.5 Prior to entering a plea of guilty, a defendant may seek an indication of sentence under the procedure set out in *Goodyear* [2005] EWCA Crim 888, [2005] 1 W.L.R. 2532, [2005] 2 Cr. App. R. 20; see below.

Where a guilty plea is offered on a limited basis

B.6 A defendant may put forward a plea of guilty without accepting all of the facts as alleged by **B-525**

the prosecution. The basis of plea offered may seek to limit the facts or the extent of the offending for which the defendant is to be sentenced. Depending on the view taken by the prosecution, and the content of the offered basis, the case will fall into one of the following categories:

(a) a plea of guilty upon a basis of plea agreed by the prosecution and defence;

B-526 **B.7** The prosecution may reach an agreement with the defendant as to the factual basis on which the defendant will plead guilty, often known as an "agreed basis of plea". It is always subject to the approval of the court, which will consider whether it adequately and appropriately reflects the evidence as disclosed on the papers, whether it is fair and whether it is in the interests of justice.

B.8 *Underwood* [2004] EWCA Crim 2256, [2005] 1 Cr. App. R. 13, [2005] 1 Cr. App. R.(S.) 90 outlines the principles to be applied where the defendant admits that he or she is guilty, but disputes the basis of offending alleged by the prosecution:

(a) The prosecution may accept and agree the defendant's account of the disputed facts or reject it in its entirety, or in part. If the prosecution accepts the defendant's basis of plea, it must ensure that the basis of plea is factually accurate and enables the sentencing judge to impose a sentence appropriate to reflect the justice of the case;
(b) In resolving any disputed factual matters, the prosecution must consider its primary duty to the court and must not agree with or acquiesce in an agreement which contains material factual disputes;
(c) If the prosecution does accept the defendant's basis of plea, it must be reduced to writing, be signed by advocates for both sides, and made available to the judge prior to the prosecution's opening;
(d) An agreed basis of plea that has been reached between the parties should not contain matters which are in dispute and any aspects upon which there is not agreement should be clearly identified;
(e) On occasion, the prosecution may lack the evidence positively to dispute the defendant's account, for example, where the defendant asserts a matter outside the knowledge of the prosecution. Simply because the prosecution does not have evidence to contradict the defendant's assertions does not mean those assertions should be agreed. In such a case, the prosecution should test the defendant's evidence and submissions by requesting a *Newton* hearing (*Newton* (1982) 77 Cr. App. R. 13, (1982) 4 Cr. App. R.(S.) 388), following the procedure set out below.
(f) If it is not possible for the parties to resolve a factual dispute when attempting to reach a plea agreement under this part, it is the responsibility of the prosecution to consider whether the matter should proceed to trial, or to invite the court to hold a *Newton* hearing as necessary.

B.9 *Underwood* emphasises that, whether or not pleas have been "agreed", the judge is not bound by any such agreement and is entitled of his or her own motion to insist that any evidence relevant to the facts in dispute (or upon which the judge requires further evidence for whatever reason) should be called. Any view formed by the prosecution on a proposed basis of plea is deemed to be conditional on the judge's acceptance of the basis of plea.

B.10 A judge is not entitled to reject a defendant's basis of plea absent a *Newton* hearing unless it is determined by the court that the basis is manifestly false and as such does not merit examination by way of the calling of evidence or alternatively the defendant declines the opportunity to engage in the process of the *Newton* hearing whether by giving evidence on his own behalf or otherwise.

(b) a plea of guilty on a basis signed by the defendant but in respect of which there is no or only partial agreement by the prosecution

B-527 **B.11** Where the defendant pleads guilty, but disputes the basis of offending alleged by the prosecution and agreement as to that has not been reached, the following procedure should be followed:

(a) The defendant's basis of plea must be set out in writing, identifying what is in dispute and must be signed by the defendant;
(b) The prosecution must respond in writing setting out their alternative contentions and indicating whether or not they submit that a *Newton* hearing is necessary;
(c) The court may invite the parties to make representations about whether the dispute is material to sentence; and
(d) If the court decides that it is a material dispute, the court will invite such further representations or evidence as it may require and resolve the dispute in accordance with the principles set out in *Newton*.

B.12 Where the disputed issue arises from facts which are within the exclusive knowledge of the defendant and the defendant is willing to give evidence in support of his case, the defence advocate should be prepared to call the defendant. If the defendant is not willing to testify, and subject to any explanation which may be given, the judge may draw such inferences as appear appropriate.

B.13 The decision whether or not a *Newton* hearing is required is one for the judge. Once the decision has been taken that there will be a *Newton* hearing, evidence is called by the parties in the usual way and the criminal burden and standard of proof applies. Whatever view has been taken by the prosecution, the prosecutor should not leave the questioning to the judge, but should assist the court by exploring the issues which the court wishes to have explored. The rules of evidence should be followed as during a trial, and the judge should direct himself appropriately as the tribunal of fact. Paragraphs 6 to 10 of *Underwood* provide additional guidance regarding the *Newton* hearing procedure.

(c) a plea of guilty on a basis that contains within it matters that are purely mitigation and which do not amount to a contradiction of the prosecution case

B.14 A basis of plea should not normally set out matters of mitigation but there may be circumstances where it is convenient and sensible for the document outlining a basis to deal with facts closely aligned to the circumstances of the offending which amount to mitigation and which may need to be resolved prior to sentence. The resolution of these matters does not amount to a *Newton* hearing properly so defined and in so far as facts fall to be established the defence will have to discharge the civil burden in order to do so. The scope of the evidence required to resolve issues that are purely matters of mitigation is for the court to determine. **B-528**

(d) Cases involving serious fraud - a plea of guilty upon a basis of plea agreed by the prosecution and defence accompanied by joint submissions as to sentence

B.15 This section applies when the prosecution and the defendant(s) to a matter before the Crown Court involving allegations of serious or complex fraud have agreed a basis of plea and seek to make submissions to the court regarding sentence. **B-529**

B.16 Guidance for prosecutors regarding the operation of this procedure is set out in the 'Attorney General's Guidelines on Plea Discussions in Cases of Serious or Complex Fraud', which came into force on 5 May 2009 and is referred to in this direction as the "Attorney General's Plea Discussion Guidelines".

B.17 In this part -

(a) "a plea agreement" means a written basis of plea agreed between the prosecution and defendant(s) in accordance with the principles set out in *Underwood*, supported by admissible documentary evidence or admissions under section 10 of the Criminal Justice Act 1967;

(b) "a sentencing submission" means sentencing submissions made jointly by the prosecution and defence as to the appropriate sentencing authorities and applicable sentencing range in the relevant sentencing guideline relating to the plea agreement;

(c) "serious or complex fraud" includes, but is not limited to, allegations of fraud where two or more of the following are present:

- (i) the amount obtained or intended to be obtained exceeded £500,000;
- (ii) there is a significant international dimension;
- (iii) the case requires specialised knowledge of financial, commercial, fiscal or regulatory matters such as the operation of markets, banking systems, trusts or tax regimes;
- (iv) the case involves allegations of fraudulent activity against numerous victims;
- (v) the case involves an allegation of substantial and significant fraud on a public body;
- (vi) the case is likely to be of widespread public concern;
- (vii) the alleged misconduct endangered the economic well-being of the United Kingdom, for example by undermining confidence in financial markets.

Procedure

B.18 The procedure regarding agreed bases of plea outlined above, applies with equal rigour to the acceptance of pleas under this procedure. However, because under this procedure the parties will have been discussing the plea agreement and the charges from a much earlier stage, it is vital that the judge is fully informed of all relevant background to the discussions, charges and the eventual basis of plea. **B-530**

B.19 Where the defendant has not yet appeared before the Crown Court, the prosecutor must send full details of the plea agreement and sentencing submission(s) to the court, at least 7 days in advance of the defendant's first appearance. Where the defendant has already appeared before the Crown Court, the prosecutor must notify the court as soon as is reasonably practicable that a plea agreement and sentencing submissions under the Attorney General's Plea Discussion Guidelines are to be submitted. The court should set a date for the matter to be heard, and the prosecutor must send full details of the plea agreement and sentencing submission(s) to the court as soon as practicable, or in accordance with the directions of the court.

B.20 The provision to the judge of full details of the plea agreement requires sufficient information to be provided to allow the judge to understand the facts of the case and the history of the plea discussions, to assess whether the plea agreement is fair and in the interests of justice, and to decide the appropriate sentence. This will include, but is not limited to:

(i) the plea agreement;
(ii) the sentencing submission(s);
(iii) all of the material provided by the prosecution to the defendant in the course of the plea discussions;
(iv) relevant material provided by the defendant, for example documents relating to personal mitigation; and
(v) the minutes of any meetings between the parties and any correspondence generated in the plea discussions.

The parties should be prepared to provide additional material at the request of the court.

B.21 The court should at all times have regard to the length of time that has elapsed since the date of the occurrence of the events giving rise to the plea discussions, the time taken to interview the defendant, the date of charge and the prospective trial date (if the matter were to proceed to trial) so as to ensure that its consideration of the plea agreement and sentencing submissions does not cause any unnecessary further delay.

Status of plea agreement and joint sentencing submissions

B-531 **B.22** Where a plea agreement and joint sentencing submissions are submitted, it remains entirely a matter for the court to decide how to deal with the case. The judge retains the absolute discretion to refuse to accept the plea agreement and to sentence otherwise than in accordance with the sentencing submissions made under the Attorney General's Plea Discussion Guidelines.

B.23 Sentencing submissions should draw the court's attention to any applicable range in any relevant guideline, and to any ancillary orders that may be applicable. Sentencing submissions should not include a specific sentence or agreed range other than the ranges set out in sentencing guidelines or authorities.

B.24 Prior to pleading guilty in accordance with the plea agreement, the defendant(s) may apply to the court for an indication of the likely maximum sentence under the procedure set out below (a '*Goodyear* indication').

B.25 In the event that the judge indicates a sentence or passes a sentence which is not within the submissions made on sentencing, the plea agreement remains binding.

B.26 If the defendant does not plead guilty in accordance with the plea agreement, or if a defendant who has pleaded guilty in accordance with a plea agreement, successfully applies to withdraw his plea under CrimPR 25.5, the signed plea agreement may be treated as confession evidence, and may be used against the defendant at a later stage in these or any other proceedings. Any credit for a timely guilty plea may be lost. The court may exercise its discretion under section 78 of the Police and Criminal Evidence Act 1984 to exclude any such evidence if it appears to the court that, having regard to all the circumstances, including the circumstances in which the evidence was obtained, the admission of the evidence would have such an adverse effect on the fairness of the proceedings that the court ought not to admit it.

B.27 Where a defendant has failed to plead guilty in accordance with a plea agreement, the case is unlikely to be ready for trial immediately. The prosecution may have been commenced earlier than it otherwise would have been, in reliance upon the defendant's agreement to plead guilty. This is likely to be a relevant consideration for the court in deciding whether or not to grant an application to adjourn or stay the proceedings to allow the matter to be prepared for trial in accordance with the protocol on the 'Control and Management of Heavy Fraud and other Complex Criminal Cases', or as required.

CPD VII Sentencing C: Indications of sentence: Goodyear

B-532 **C.1** Prior to pleading guilty, it is open to a defendant in the Crown Court to request from the judge an indication of the maximum sentence that would be imposed if a guilty plea were to be tendered at that stage in the proceedings, in accordance with the guidance in *Goodyear* [2005] EWCA Crim 888, [2005] 1 W.L.R. 2532, [2005] 2 Cr. App. R. 20. The defence should notify the court and the prosecution of the intention to seek an indication in advance of any hearing.

C.2 Attention is drawn to the guidance set out in paragraphs 53 and following of *Goodyear*. The objective of the *Goodyear* guidelines is to safeguard against the creation or appearance of judicial pressure on a defendant. Any advance indication given should be the maximum sentence if a guilty plea were to be tendered at that stage of the proceedings only; the judge should not indicate the maximum possible sentence following conviction by a jury after trial. The judge should only give a *Goodyear* indication if one is requested by the defendant, although the judge can, in an appropriate case, remind the defence advocate of the defendant's entitlement to seek an advance indication of sentence.

C.3 Whether to give a *Goodyear* indication, and whether to give reasons for a refusal, is a matter for the discretion of the judge, to be exercised in accordance with the principles outlined by the Court of Appeal in that case. Such indications should normally not be given if there is a dispute as to the basis of plea unless the judge concludes that he or she can properly deal with the case without the need for a *Newton* hearing. If there is a basis of plea agreed by the prosecution and defence, it must be reduced into writing and a copy provided to the judge. As always, any basis of plea will be subject to the approval of the court. In cases where a dispute arises, the procedure in *Underwood* should be followed prior to the court considering a sentence indication further, as set out above. The judge should not become involved in negotiations about the acceptance of pleas or any agreed basis of plea, nor should a request be made for an indication of the different sentences that might be imposed if various different pleas were to be offered.

C.4 There should be no prosecution opening nor should the judge hear mitigation. However, during the sentence indication process the prosecution advocate is expected to assist the court by ensuring that the court has received all of the prosecution evidence, any statement from the victim about the impact of the offence, and any relevant previous convictions. Further, where appropriate, the prosecution should provide references to the relevant statutory powers of the court, relevant sentencing guidelines and authorities, and such other assistance as the court requires.

C.5 Attention is drawn to paragraph 70(d) of *Goodyear* which emphasises that the prosecution "should not say anything which may create the impression that the sentence indication has the support or approval of the Crown." This prohibition against the Crown indicating its approval of a particular sentence applies in all circumstances when a defendant is being sentenced, including when joint sentencing submissions are made.

C.6 An indication, once given, is, save in exceptional circumstances (such as arose in *Newman* [2010] EWCA Crim 1566, [2011] 1 Cr. App. R.(S.) 68), binding on the judge who gave it, and any other judge, subject to overriding statutory obligations such as those following a finding of "dangerousness". In circumstances where a judge proposes to depart from a *Goodyear* indication this must only be done in a way that does not give rise to unfairness (see *Newman*). However, if the defendant does not plead guilty, the indication will not thereafter bind the court.

C.7 If the offence is a specified offence such that the defendant might be liable to an assessment of 'dangerousness' in accordance with the Criminal Justice Act 2003 it is unlikely that the necessary material for such an assessment will be available. The court can still proceed to give an indication of sentence, but should state clearly the limitations of the indication that can be given.

C.8 A *Goodyear* indication should be given in open court in the presence of the defendant but any reference to the hearing is not admissible in any subsequent trial; and reporting restrictions should normally be imposed.

CPD VII Sentencing D: Facts to be stated on pleas of guilty

D.1 To enable the press and the public to know the circumstances of an offence of which an accused has been convicted and for which he is to be sentenced, in relation to each offence to which an accused has pleaded guilty the prosecution shall state those facts in open court, before sentence is imposed. **B-533**

CPD VII Sentencing E: Concurrent and consecutive sentences

E.1 Where a court passes on a defendant more than one term of imprisonment, the court should state in the presence of the defendant whether the terms are to be concurrent or consecutive. Should this not be done, the court clerk should ask the court, before the defendant leaves court, to do so. **B-534**

E.2 If a defendant is, at the time of sentence, already serving two or more consecutive terms of imprisonment and the court intends to increase the total period of imprisonment, it should use the expression 'consecutive to the total period of imprisonment to which you are already subject' rather than 'at the expiration of the term of imprisonment you are now serving', as the defendant may not then be serving the last of the terms to which he is already subject.

E.3 The Sentencing Council has issued a definitive guideline on Totality which should be consulted. Under section 125(1) of the Coroners and Justice Act 2009, for offences committed after 6 April 2010, the guideline must be followed unless it would be contrary to the interests of justice to do so.

CPD VII Sentencing F: Victim personal statements

F.1 Victims of crime are invited to make a statement, known as a Victim Personal Statement **B-535**

('VPS'). The statement gives victims a formal opportunity to say how a crime has affected them. It may help to identify whether they have a particular need for information, support and protection. The court will take the statement into account when determining sentence. In some circumstances, it may be appropriate for relatives of a victim to make a VPS, for example where the victim has died as a result of the relevant criminal conduct. The revised Code of Practice for Victims of Crime, published on 29 October 2013 gives further information about victims' entitlements within the criminal justice system, and the duties placed on criminal justice agencies when dealing with victims of crime.

F.2 When a police officer takes a statement from a victim, the victim should be told about the scheme and given the chance to make a VPS. The decision about whether or not to make a VPS is entirely a matter for the victim; no pressure should be brought to bear on their decision, and no conclusion should be drawn if they choose not to make such a statement. A VPS or a further VPS may be made (in proper s.9 form, see below) at any time prior to the disposal of the case. It will not normally be appropriate for a VPS to be made after the disposal of the case; there may be rare occasions between sentence and appeal when a further VPS may be necessary, for example, when the victim was injured and the final prognosis was not available at the date of sentence. However, VPS after disposal should be confined to presenting up to date factual material, such as medical information, and should be used sparingly.

F.3 If the court is presented with a VPS the following approach, subject to the further guidance given by the Court of Appeal in *Perkins; Bennett; Hall* [2013] EWCA Crim 323, [2013] Crim. L.R. 533, should be adopted:

a) The VPS and any evidence in support should be considered and taken into account by the court, prior to passing sentence.

b) Evidence of the effects of an offence on the victim contained in the VPS or other statement, must be in proper form, that is a witness statement made under section 9 of the Criminal Justice Act 1967 or an expert's report; and served in good time upon the defendant's solicitor or the defendant, if he or she is not represented. Except where inferences can properly be drawn from the nature of or circumstances surrounding the offence, a sentencing court must not make assumptions unsupported by evidence about the effects of an offence on the victim. The maker of a VPS may be cross-examined on its content.

c) At the discretion of the court, the VPS may also be read aloud or played in open court, in whole or in part, or it may be summarised. If the VPS is to be read aloud, the court should also determine who should do so. In making these decisions, the court should take account of the victim's preferences, and follow them unless there is good reason not to do so; examples of this include the inadmissibility of the content or the potentially harmful consequences for the victim or others. Court hearings should not be adjourned solely to allow the victim to attend court to read the VPS. For the purposes of CPD I General matters 5B: Access to information held by the court, a VPS that is read aloud or played in open court in whole or in part should be considered as such, and no longer treated as a confidential document.

d) In all cases it will be appropriate for a VPS to be referred to in the course of the sentencing hearing and/or in the sentencing remarks.

e) The court must pass what it judges to be the appropriate sentence having regard to the circumstances of the offence and of the offender, taking into account, so far as the court considers it appropriate, the impact on the victim. The opinions of the victim or the victim's close relatives as to what the sentence should be are therefore not relevant, unlike the consequences of the offence on them. Victims should be advised of this. If, despite the advice, opinions as to sentence are included in the statement, the court should pay no attention to them.

CPD VII Sentencing G: Families bereaved by homicide and other criminal conduct

B-536 **G.1** In cases in which the victim has died as a result of the relevant criminal conduct, the victim's family is not a party to the proceedings, but does have an interest in the case. Bereaved families have particular entitlements under the Code of Practice for Victims of Crime. All parties should have regard to the needs of the victim's family and ensure that the trial process does not expose bereaved families to avoidable intimidation, humiliation or distress.

G.2 In so far as it is compatible with family members' roles as witnesses, the court should consider the following measures:

a) Practical arrangements being discussed with the family and made in good time before the trial, such as seating for family members in the courtroom; if appropriate, in an alternative area, away from the public gallery.

b) Warning being given to families if the evidence on a certain day is expected to be particularly distressing.

c) Ensuring that appropriate use is made of the scheme for Victim Personal Statements, in accordance with the paragraphs above.

G.3 The sentencer should consider providing a written copy of the sentencing remarks to the family after sentence has been passed. Sentencers should tend in favour of providing such a copy, unless there is good reason not to do so, and the copy should be provided as soon as is reasonably practicable after the sentencing hearing.

CPD VII Sentencing H: Community impact statements

H.1 A community impact statement may be prepared by the police to make the court aware of particular crime trends in the local area and the impact of these on the local community. **B-537**

H.2 Such statements must be in proper form, that is a witness statement made under section 9 of the Criminal Justice Act 1967 or an expert's report; and served in good time upon the defendant's solicitor or the defendant, if he is not represented.

H.3 The community impact statement and any evidence in support should be considered and taken into account by the court, prior to passing sentence. The statement should be referred to in the course of the sentencing hearing and/or in the sentencing remarks. Subject to the court's discretion, the contents of the statement may be summarised or read out in open court.

H.4 The court must pass what it judges to be the appropriate sentence having regard to the circumstances of the offence and of the offender, taking into account, so far as the court considers it appropriate, the impact on the local community. Opinions as to what the sentence should be are therefore not relevant. If, despite the advice, opinions as to sentence are included in the statement, the court should pay no attention to them.

H.5 Except where inferences can properly be drawn from the nature of or circumstances surrounding the offence, a sentencing court must not make assumptions unsupported by evidence about the effects of an offence on the local community.

H.6 It will not be appropriate for a Community Impact Statement to be made after disposal of the case but before an appeal.

CPD VII Sentencing I: Impact statements for businesses (substituted by Criminal Practice Directions 2015 (Amendment No. 8) [2019] EWCA Crim 495, Lord Burnett CJ)

I.1 Individual victims of crime are invited to make a statement, known as a Victim Personal Statement ('VPS'), see *CPD VII Sentencing F.* If a victim, or one of those others affected by a crime, is a business, enterprise or other body (including a charity or public body, for example a school or hospital), of any size, a nominated representative may make an Impact Statement for Business ('ISB'). The ISB gives a formal opportunity for the court to be informed how a crime has affected a business or other body. The court will take the statement into account when determining sentence. This does not prevent individual employees from making a VPS about the impact of the same crime on them as individuals. Indeed, the ISB should be about the impact on the business or other body exclusively, and the impact on any individual included within a VPS. **B-538**

I.2 When a police officer takes statements about the alleged offence, he or she should also inform the business or other body about the scheme. An ISB may be made to the police at that time, or the ISB template may be downloaded from *www.police.uk,* completed and emailed or posted to the relevant police contact. Guidance on how to complete the form is available on *www.police.uk* and on the CPS website. There is no obligation to make an ISB.

I.3 An ISB or an updated ISB may be made (in proper s.9 form, see below) at any time prior to the disposal of the case. It will not be appropriate for an ISB to be made after disposal of the case but before an appeal.

I.4 A business or other body wishing to make an ISB should consider carefully who to nominate as the representative to make the statement on its behalf. A person making an ISB on behalf of such a business or body, the nominated representative, must be authorised to do so on its behalf, either by nature of their position, such as a director or owner or a senior official, or by having been suitably authorised, such as by the owner or Board of Directors or governing body. The nominated representative must also be in a position to give admissible evidence about the impact of the crime on the business or body. This will usually be through first hand personal knowledge, or using business documents (as defined in section 117 of the Criminal Justice Act 2003). The most appropriate person will vary depending on the nature of the crime, and the size and structure of the business or other body and may for example include a manager, director, chief executive or shop owner.

I.5 If the nominated representative leaves the business before the case comes to court, he or she will usually remain the representative, as the ISB made by him or her will still provide the best evidence of the impact of the crime, and he or she could still be asked to attend court. Nominated representatives should be made aware of the on-going nature of the role at the time of making the ISB.

I.6 If necessary a further ISB may be provided to the police if there is a change in circumstances. This could be made by an alternative nominated representative. However, the new ISB will usually supplement, not replace, the original ISB and again must contain admissible evidence. The prosecutor will decide which ISB to serve on the defence as evidence, and any ISB that is not served in evidence will be included in the unused material and considered for disclosure to the defence.

I.7 The ISB must be made in proper form, that is as a witness statement made under section 9 of the Criminal Justice Act 1967 or an expert's report; and served in good time upon the defendant's solicitor or the defendant, if he or she is not represented. The maker of an ISB can be cross-examined on its content.

I.8 The ISB and any evidence in support should be considered and taken into account by the court, prior to passing sentence. The statement should be referred to in the course of the sentencing hearing and/or in the sentencing remarks. Subject to the court's discretion, the contents of the statement may be summarised or read out in open court; the views of the business or body should be taken into account in reaching a decision.

I.9 The court must pass what it judges to be the appropriate sentence having regard to the circumstances of the offence and of the offender, taking into account, so far as the court considers it appropriate, the impact on the victims and others affected, including any business or other corporate victim. Opinions as to what the sentence should be are therefore not relevant. If, despite the advice, opinions as to sentence are included in the statement, the court should pay no attention to them.

I.10 Except where inferences can properly be drawn from the nature of or circumstances surrounding the offence, a sentencing court must not make assumptions unsupported by evidence about the effects of an offence on a business or other body.

CPD VII Sentencing J: Binding over orders and conditional discharges

B-539 **J.1** This direction takes into account the judgments of the European Court of Human Rights in *Steel v United Kingdom* (1999) 28 E.H.R.R. 603, [1998] Crim. L.R. 893 and in *Hashman and Harrup v United Kingdom* (2000) 30 E.H.R.R. 241, [2000] Crim. L.R. 185. Its purpose is to give practical guidance, in the light of those two judgments, on the practice of imposing binding over orders. The direction applies to orders made under the court's common law powers, under the Justices of the Peace Act 1361, under section 1(7) of the Justices of the Peace Act 1968 and under section 115 of the Magistrates' Courts Act 1980. This direction also gives guidance concerning the court's power to bind over parents or guardians under section 150 of the Powers of Criminal Courts (Sentencing) Act 2000 and the Crown Court's power to bind over to come up for judgment. The court's power to impose a conditional discharge under section 12 of the Powers of Criminal Courts (Sentencing) Act 2000 is also covered by this direction.

Binding over to keep the peace

B-540 **J.2** Before imposing a binding over order, the court must be satisfied so that it is sure that a breach of the peace involving violence, or an imminent threat of violence, has occurred or that there is a real risk of violence in the future. Such violence may be perpetrated by the individual who will be subject to the order or by a third party as a natural consequence of the individual's conduct.

J.3 In light of the judgment in *Hashman*, courts should no longer bind an individual over "to be of good behaviour". Rather than binding an individual over to "keep the peace" in general terms, the court should identify the specific conduct or activity from which the individual must refrain.

Written order

B-541 **J.4** When making an order binding an individual over to refrain from specified types of conduct or activities, the details of that conduct or those activities should be specified by the court in a written order, served on all relevant parties. The court should state its reasons for the making of the order, its length and the amount of the recognisance. The length of the order should be proportionate to the harm sought to be avoided and should not generally exceed 12 months.

Evidence

B-542 **J.5** Sections 51 to 57 of the Magistrates' Courts Act 1980 set out the jurisdiction of the magistrates' court to hear an application made on complaint and the procedure which is to be followed. This includes a requirement under section 53 to hear evidence and the parties, before making any order. This practice should be applied to all cases in the magistrates' court and the Crown Court where the court is considering imposing a binding over order. The court should give the individual who would be subject to the order and the prosecutor the opportunity to make representations, both as to the making of the order and as to its terms. The court should also hear any admissible evidence the parties wish to call and which has not already been heard in the proceedings. Particularly careful consideration may be required where the individual who would be subject to the order is a witness in the proceedings.

J.6 Where there is an admission which is sufficient to found the making of a binding over order and / or the individual consents to the making of the order, the court should nevertheless hear sufficient representations and, if appropriate, evidence, to satisfy itself that an order is appropriate in all the circumstances and to be clear about the terms of the order.

J.7 Where there is an allegation of breach of a binding over order and this is contested, the court should hear representations and evidence, including oral evidence, from the parties before making a finding. If unrepresented and no opportunity has been given previously the court should give a reasonable period for the person said to have breached the binding over order to find representation.

Burden and standard of proof

J.8 The court should be satisfied so that it is sure of the matters complained of before a binding over order may be imposed. Where the procedure has been commenced on complaint, the burden of proof rests on the complainant. In all other circumstances, the burden of proof upon the prosecution. **B-543**

J.9 Where there is an allegation of breach of a binding over order, the court should be satisfied on the balance of probabilities that the defendant is in breach before making any order for forfeiture of a recognisance. The burden of proof shall rest on the prosecution.

Recognisance

J.10 The court must be satisfied on the merits of the case that an order for binding over is appropriate and should announce that decision before considering the amount of the recognisance. If unrepresented, the individual who is made subject to the binding over order should be told he has a right of appeal from the decision. **B-544**

J.11 When fixing the amount of recognisance, courts should have regard to the individual's financial resources and should hear representations from the individual or his legal representatives regarding finances.

J.12 A recognisance is made in the form of a bond giving rise to a civil debt on breach of the order.

Refusal to enter into a recognizance

J.13 If there is any possibility that an individual will refuse to enter a recognizance, the court should consider whether there are any appropriate alternatives to a binding over order (for example, continuing with a prosecution). Where there are no appropriate alternatives and the individual continues to refuse to enter into the recognisance, the court may commit the individual to custody. In the magistrates' court, the power to do so will derive from section 1(7) of the Justices of the Peace Act 1968 or, more rarely, from section 115(3) of the Magistrates' Courts Act 1980, and the court should state which power it is acting under; in the Crown Court, this is a common law power. **B-545**

J.14 Before the court exercises a power to commit the individual to custody, the individual should be given the opportunity to see a duty solicitor or another legal representative and be represented in proceedings if the individual so wishes. Public funding should generally be granted to cover representation. In the Crown Court this rests with the Judge who may grant a Representation Order.

J.15 In the event that the individual does not take the opportunity to seek legal advice, the court shall give the individual a final opportunity to comply with the request and shall explain the consequences of a failure to do so.

Antecedents

J.16 Courts are reminded of the provisions of section 7(5) of the Rehabilitation of Offenders Act 1974 which excludes from a person's antecedents any order of the court "with respect to any person other than on a conviction". **B-546**

Binding over to come up for judgment

J.17 If the Crown Court is considering binding over an individual to come up for judgment, the court should specify any conditions with which the individual is to comply in the meantime and not specify that the individual is to be of good behaviour. **B-547**

J.18 The Crown Court should, if the individual is unrepresented, explain the consequences of a breach of the binding over order in these circumstances.

Binding over of parent or guardian

J.19 Where a court is considering binding over a parent or guardian under section 150 of the Powers of Criminal Courts (Sentencing) Act 2000 to enter into a recognisance to take proper care of and exercise proper control over a child or young person, the court should specify the actions which the parent or guardian is to take. **B-548**

Security for good behaviour

J.20 Where a court is imposing a conditional discharge under section 12 of the Powers of Criminal **B-549**

Courts (Sentencing) Act 2000, it has the power, under section 12(6) to make an order that a person who consents to do so give security for the good behaviour of the offender. When making such an order, the court should specify the type of conduct from which the offender is to refrain.

CPD VII Sentencing K: Committal for sentence

B-550 **K.1** CrimPR 28.10 applies when a case is committed to the Crown Court for sentence and specifies the information and documentation that must be provided by the magistrates' court. On a committal for sentence any reasons given by the magistrates for their decision should be included with the documents. All of these documents should be made available to the judge in the Crown Court if the judge requires them, in order to decide before the hearing questions of listing or representation or the like. They will also be available to the court during the hearing if it becomes necessary or desirable for the court to see what happened in the lower court.

CPD VII Sentencing L: Imposition of life sentences

B-551 **L.1** Section 82A of the Powers of Criminal Courts (Sentencing) Act 2000 empowers a judge when passing a sentence of life imprisonment, where such a sentence is not fixed by law, to specify by order such part of the sentence ('the relevant part') as shall be served before the prisoner may require the Secretary of State to refer his case to the Parole Board. This is applicable to defendants under the age of 18 years as well as to adult defendants.

L.2 Thus the life sentence falls into two parts: (a) the relevant part, which consists of the period of detention imposed for punishment and deterrence, taking into account the seriousness of the offence, and (b) the remaining part of the sentence, during which the prisoner's detention will be governed by consideration of risk to the public.

L.3 The judge is not obliged by statute to make use of the provisions of section 82A when passing a life sentence. However, the judge should do so, save in the very exceptional case where the judge considers that the offence is so serious that detention for life is justified by the seriousness of the offence alone, irrespective of the risk to the public. In such a case, the judge should state this in open court when passing sentence.

L.4 In cases where the judge is to specify the relevant part of the sentence under section 82A, the judge should permit the advocate for the defendant to address the court as to the appropriate length of the relevant part. Where no relevant part is to be specified, the advocate for the defendant should be permitted to address the court as to the appropriateness of this course of action.

L.5 In specifying the relevant part of the sentence, the judge should have regard to the specific terms of section 82A and should indicate the reasons for reaching his decision as to the length of the relevant part.

CPD VII Sentencing M: Mandatory life sentences

B-552 **M.1** The purpose of this section is to give practical guidance as to the procedure for passing a mandatory life sentence under section 269 and Schedule 21 of the Criminal Justice Act 2003 ('the Act'). This direction also gives guidance as to the transitional arrangements under section 276 and Schedule 22 of the Act. It clarifies the correct approach to looking at the practice of the Secretary of State prior to December 2002 for the purposes of Schedule 22 of the Act, in the light of the judgment in *Sullivan, Gibbs, Elener and Elener* [2004] EWCA Crim 1762, [2005] 1 Cr. App. R. 3, [2005] 1 Cr. App. R.(S.) 67.

M.2 Section 269 came into force on 18 December 2003. Under section 269, all courts passing a mandatory life sentence must either announce in open court the minimum term the prisoner must serve before the Parole Board can consider release on licence under the provisions of section 28 of the Crime (Sentences) Act 1997 (as amended by section 275 of the Act), or announce that the seriousness of the offence is so exceptionally high that the early release provisions should not apply at all (a 'whole life order').

M.3 In setting the minimum term, the court must set the term it considers appropriate taking into account the seriousness of the offence. In considering the seriousness of the offence, the court must have regard to the general principles set out in Schedule 21 of the Act as amended and any guidelines relating to offences in general which are relevant to the case and not incompatible with the provisions of Schedule 21. Although it is necessary to have regard to such guidance, it is always permissible not to apply the guidance if a judge considers there are reasons for not following it. It is always necessary to have regard to the need to do justice in the particular case. However, if a court departs from any of the starting points given in Schedule 21, the court is under a duty to state its reasons for doing so (section 270(2)(b) of the Act).

M.4 Schedule 21 states that the first step is to choose one of five starting points: "whole life", 30 years, 25 years, 15 years or 12 years. Where the 15 year starting point has been chosen, judges should have in mind that this starting point encompasses a very broad range of murders. At paragraph 35 of *Sullivan*, the court found it should not be assumed that Parliament intended to raise all minimum terms that would previously have had a lower starting point, to 15 years.

M.5 Where the offender was 21 or over at the time of the offence, and the court takes the view that the murder is so grave that the offender ought to spend the rest of his life in prison, the appropriate starting point is a 'whole life order'. (paragraph 4(1) of Schedule 21). The effect of such an order is that the early release provisions in section 28 of the Crime (Sentences) Act 1997 will not apply. Such an order should only be specified where the court considers that the seriousness of the offence (or the combination of the offence and one or more other offences associated with it) is exceptionally high. Paragraph 4 (2) sets out examples of cases where it would normally be appropriate to take the 'whole life order' as the appropriate starting point.

M.6 Where the offender is aged 18 to 20 and commits a murder that is so serious that it would require a whole life order if committed by an offender aged 21 or over, the appropriate starting point will be 30 years. (Paragraph 5(2)(h) of Schedule 21).

M.7 Where a case is not so serious as to require a 'whole life order' but where the seriousness of the offence is particularly high and the offender was aged 18 or over when he committed the offence, the appropriate starting point is 30 years (paragraph 5(1) of Schedule 21). Paragraph 5 (2) sets out examples of cases where a 30 year starting point would normally be appropriate (if they do not require a 'whole life order').

M.8 Where the offender was aged 18 or over when he committed the offence, took a knife or other weapon to the scene intending to commit any offence or have it available to use as a weapon, and used it in committing the murder, the offence is normally to be regarded as sufficiently serious for an appropriate starting point of 25 years (paragraph 5A of Schedule 21).

M.9 Where the offender was aged 18 or over when he committed the offence and the case does not fall within paragraph 4 (1), 5 (1) or 5A(1) of Schedule 21, the appropriate starting point is 15 years (see paragraph 6).

M.10 18 to 20 year olds are only the subject of the 30-year, 25-year and 15-year starting points.

M.11 The appropriate starting point when setting a sentence of detention during Her Majesty's pleasure for offenders aged under 18 when they committed the offence is always 12 years (paragraph 7 of Schedule 21).

M.12 The second step after choosing a starting point is to take account of any aggravating or mitigating factors which would justify a departure from the starting point. Additional aggravating factors (other than those specified in paragraphs 4 (2), 5(2) and 5A) are listed at paragraph 10 of Schedule 21. Examples of mitigating factors are listed at paragraph 11 of Schedule 21. Taking into account the aggravating and mitigating features, the court may add to or subtract from the starting point to arrive at the appropriate punitive period.

M.13 The third step is that the court should consider the effect of section 143(2) of the Act in relation to previous convictions; section 143(3) of the Act where the offence was committed whilst the offender was on bail; and section 144 of the Act where the offender has pleaded guilty (paragraph 12 of Schedule 21). The court should then take into account what credit the offender would have received for a remand in custody under section 240 or 240ZA of the Act and/or for a remand on bail subject to a qualifying curfew condition under section 240A, but for the fact that the mandatory sentence is one of life imprisonment. Where the offender has been thus remanded in connection with the offence or a related offence, the court should have in mind that no credit will otherwise be given for this time when the prisoner is considered for early release. The appropriate time to take it into account is when setting the minimum term. The court should make any appropriate subtraction from the punitive period it would otherwise impose, in order to reach the minimum term.

CPD VII Sentencing N: Transitional arrangements for sentences where the offence was committed before 18 December 2003

N.1 Where the court is passing a sentence of mandatory life imprisonment for an offence committed before 18 December 2003, the court should take a fourth step in determining the minimum term in accordance with section 276 and Schedule 22 of the Act. **B-553**

N.2 The purpose of those provisions is to ensure that the sentence does not breach the principle of non-retroactivity, by ensuring that a lower minimum term would not have been imposed for the offence when it was committed. Before setting the minimum term, the court must check whether the proposed term is greater than that which the Secretary of State would probably have notified under the practice followed by the Secretary of State before December 2002.

N.3 The decision in *Sullivan, Gibbs, Elener and Elener* [2004] EWCA Crim 1762, [2005] 1 Cr. App. R. 3, [2005] 1 Cr. App. R.(S.) 67 gives detailed guidance as to the correct approach to this practice and judges passing mandatory life sentences where the murder was committed prior to 18 December 2003 are well advised to read that judgment before proceeding.

N.4 The practical result of that judgment is that in sentences where the murder was committed before 31 May 2002, the best guide to what would have been the practice of the Secretary of State is the letter sent to judges by Lord Bingham CJ on 10th February 1997, the relevant parts of which are set out below.

N.5 The practice of Lord Bingham, as set out in his letter of 10 February 1997, was to take 14 years as the period actually to be served for the 'average', 'normal' or 'unexceptional' murder. Examples of factors he outlined as capable, in appropriate cases, of mitigating the normal penalty were:

(1) Youth;
(2) Age (where relevant to physical capacity on release or the likelihood of the defendant dying in prison);
(3) [Intellectual disability or mental disorder];
(4) Provocation (in a non-technical sense), or an excessive response to a personal threat; (5) The absence of an intention to kill;
(6) Spontaneity and lack of premeditation (beyond that necessary to constitute the offence: e.g. a sudden response to family pressure or to prolonged and eventually insupportable stress);
(7) Mercy killing;
(8) A plea of guilty, or hard evidence of remorse or contrition.

N.6 Lord Bingham then listed the following factors as likely to call for a sentence more severe than the norm:

(1) Evidence of planned, professional, revenge or contract killing;
(2) The killing of a child or a very old or otherwise vulnerable victim;
(3) Evidence of sadism, gratuitous violence, or sexual maltreatment, humiliation or degradation before the killing;
(4) Killing for gain (in the course of burglary, robbery, blackmail, insurance fraud, etc.);
(5) Multiple killings;
(6) The killing of a witness, or potential witness, to defeat the ends of justice;
(7) The killing of those doing their public duty (policemen, prison officers, postmasters, firemen, judges, etc.);
(8) Terrorist or politically motivated killings;
(9) The use of firearms or other dangerous weapons, whether carried for defensive or offensive reasons;
(10) A substantial record of serious violence;
(11) Macabre attempts to dismember or conceal the body.

N.7 Lord Bingham further stated that the fact that a defendant was under the influence of drink or drugs at the time of the killing is so common he would be inclined to treat it as neutral. But in the not unfamiliar case in which a couple, inflamed by drink, indulge in a violent quarrel in which one dies, often against a background of longstanding drunken violence, then he would tend to recommend a term somewhat below the norm.

N.8 Lord Bingham went on to say that given the intent necessary for proof of murder, the consequences of taking life and the understandable reaction of relatives to the deceased, a substantial term will almost always be called for, save perhaps in a truly venial case of mercy killing. While a recommendation of a punitive term longer than, say, 30 years will be very rare indeed, there should not be any upper limit. Some crimes will certainly call for terms very well in excess of the norm.

N.9 For the purposes of sentences where the murder was committed after 31 May 2002 and before 18 December 2003, the judge should apply the Practice Statement handed down on 31 May 2002 reproduced at paragraphs N.10 to N.20 below.

N.10 This Statement replaces the previous single normal tariff of 14 years by substituting a higher and a normal starting point of respectively 16 (comparable to 32 years) and 12 years (comparable to 24 years). These starting points have then to be increased or reduced because of aggravating or mitigating factors such as those referred to below. It is emphasised that they are no more than starting points.

The normal starting point of 12 years

B-554 **N.11** Cases falling within this starting point will normally involve the killing of an adult victim, arising from a quarrel or loss of temper between two people known to each other. It will not have the characteristics referred to in paragraph N.13. Exceptionally, the starting point may be reduced because of the sort of circumstances described in the next paragraph.

N.12 The normal starting point can be reduced because the murder is one where the offender's culpability is significantly reduced, for example, because:-

(a) the case came close to the borderline between murder and manslaughter; or
(b) the offender suffered from mental disorder, or from a mental disability which lowered the degree of his criminal responsibility for the killing, although not affording a defence of diminished responsibility; or

(c) the offender was provoked (in a non-technical sense) such as by prolonged and eventually unsupportable stress; or
(d) the case involved an over-reaction in self-defence; or
(e) the offence was a mercy killing.

These factors could justify a reduction to 8/9 years (equivalent to 16/18 years).

The higher starting point of 15/16 years

N.13 The higher starting point will apply to cases where the offender's culpability was exceptionally high, or the victim was in a particularly vulnerable position. Such cases will be characterised by a feature which makes the crime especially serious, such as:- **B-555**

(a) the killing was 'professional' or a contract killing;
(b) the killing was politically motivated;
(c) the killing was done for gain (in the course of a burglary, robbery etc.);
(d) the killing was intended to defeat the ends of justice (as in the killing of a witness or potential witness);
(e) the victim was providing a public service;
(f) the victim was a child or was otherwise vulnerable;
(g) the killing was racially aggravated;
(h) the victim was deliberately targeted because of his or her religion or sexual orientation;
(i) there was evidence of sadism, gratuitous violence or sexual maltreatment, humiliation or degradation of the victim before the killing;
(j) extensive and/or multiple injuries were inflicted on the victim before death;
(k) the offender committed multiple murders.

Variation of the starting point

N.14 Whichever starting point is selected in a particular case, it may be appropriate for the trial judge to vary the starting point upwards or downwards, to take account of aggravating or mitigating factors, which relate to either the offence or the offender, in the particular case. **B-556**

N.15 Aggravating factors relating to the offence can include:

(a) the fact that the killing was planned;
(b) the use of a firearm;
(c) arming with a weapon in advance;
(d) concealment of the body, destruction of the crime scene and/or dismemberment of the body;
(e) particularly in domestic violence cases, the fact that the murder was the culmination of cruel and violent behaviour by the offender over a period of time.

N.16 Aggravating factors relating to the offender will include the offender's previous record and failures to respond to previous sentences, to the extent that this is relevant to culpability rather than to risk.

N.17 Mitigating factors relating to the offence will include:

(a) an intention to cause grievous bodily harm, rather than to kill;
(b) spontaneity and lack of pre-meditation.

N.18 Mitigating factors relating to the offender may include:

(a) the offender's age;
(b) clear evidence of remorse or contrition;
(c) a timely plea of guilty.

Very serious cases

N.19 A substantial upward adjustment may be appropriate in the most serious cases, for example, those involving a substantial number of murders, or if there are several factors identified as attracting the higher starting point present. In suitable cases, the result might even be a minimum term of 30 years (equivalent to 60 years) which would offer little or no hope of the offender's eventual release. In cases of exceptional gravity, the judge, rather than setting a whole life minimum term, can state that there is no minimum period which could properly be set in that particular case. **B-557**

N.20 Among the categories of case referred to in paragraph N.13, some offences may be especially grave. These include cases in which the victim was performing his duties as a prison officer at the time of the crime, or the offence was a terrorist or sexual or sadistic murder, or involved a young child. In such a case, a term of 20 years and upwards could be appropriate.

N.21 In following this guidance, judges should bear in mind the conclusion of the Court in Sullivan that the general effect of both these statements is the same. While Lord Bingham does not identify as many starting points, it is open to the judge to come to exactly the same decision irrespective of which was followed. Both pieces of guidance give the judge a considerable degree of discretion.

CPD VII Sentencing P: Procedure for announcing the minimum term in open court

P.1 Having gone through the three or four steps outlined above, the court is then under a duty, **B-558**

under section 270 of the Act, to state in open court, in ordinary language, its reasons for deciding on the minimum term or for passing a whole life order.

P.2 In order to comply with this duty, the court should state clearly the minimum term it has determined. In doing so, it should state which of the starting points it has chosen and its reasons for doing so. Where the court has departed from that starting point due to mitigating or aggravating features, it must state the reasons for that departure and any aggravating or mitigating features which have led to that departure. At that point, the court should also declare how much, if any, time is being deducted for time spent in custody and/or on bail subject to a qualifying curfew condition. The court must then explain that the minimum term is the minimum amount of time the prisoner will spend in prison, from the date of sentence, before the Parole Board can order early release. If it remains necessary for the protection of the public, the prisoner will continue to be detained after that date. The court should also state that where the prisoner has served the minimum term and the Parole Board has decided to direct release, the prisoner will remain on licence for the rest of his life and may be recalled to prison at any time.

P.3 Where the offender was 21 or over when he committed the offence and the court considers that the seriousness of the offence is so exceptionally high that a 'whole life order' is appropriate, the court should state clearly its reasons for reaching this conclusion. It should also explain that the early release provisions will not apply.

CPD VII Sentencing Q: Financial, etc. information required for sentencing

B-559 **Q.1** These directions supplement CrimPR 24.11 and 25.16, which set out the procedure to be followed where a defendant pleads guilty, or is convicted, and is to be sentenced. They are not concerned exclusively with corporate defendants, or with offences of an environmental, public health, health and safety or other regulatory character, but the guidance which they contain is likely to be of particular significance in such cases.

Q.2 The rules set out the prosecutor's responsibilities in all cases. Where the offence is of a character, or is against a prohibition, with which the sentencing court is unlikely to be familiar, those responsibilities are commensurately more onerous. The court is entitled to the greatest possible assistance in identifying information relevant to sentencing.

Q.3 In such a case, save where the circumstances are very straightforward, it is likely that justice will best be served by the submission of the required information in writing: see *Friskies Petcare (UK) Ltd* [2000] 2 Cr. App. R.(S.) 401. Though it is the prosecutor's responsibility to the court to prepare any such document, if the defendant pleads guilty, or indicates a guilty plea, then it is very highly desirable that such sentencing information should be agreed between the parties and jointly submitted. If agreement cannot be reached in all particulars, then the nature and extent of the disagreement should be indicated. If the court concludes that what is in issue is material to sentence, then it will give directions for resolution of the dispute, whether by hearing oral evidence or by other means. In every case, when passing sentence the sentencing court must make clear on what basis sentence is passed: in fairness to the defendant, and for the information of any other person, or court, who needs or wishes to understand the reasons for sentence.

Q.4 If so directed by or on behalf of the court, a defendant must supply accurate information about financial circumstances. In fixing the amount of any fine the court must take into account, amongst other considerations, the financial circumstances of the offender (whether an individual or other person) as they are known or as they appear to be. Before fixing the amount of fine when the defendant is an individual, the court must inquire into his financial circumstances. Where the defendant is an individual the court may make a financial circumstances order in respect of him. This means an order in which the court requires an individual to provide a statement as to his financial means, within a specified time. It is an offence, punishable with imprisonment, to fail to comply with such an order or for knowingly/recklessly furnishing a false statement or knowingly failing to disclose a material fact. The provisions of section 20A Criminal Justice Act 1991 apply to any person (thereby including a corporate organisation) and place the offender under a statutory duty to provide the court with a statement as to his financial means in response to an official request. There are offences for non-compliance, false statements or non-disclosure. It is for the court to decide how much information is required, having regard to relevant sentencing guidelines or guideline cases. However, by reference to those same guidelines and cases the parties should anticipate what the court will require, and prepare accordingly. In complex cases, and in cases involving a corporate defendant, the information required will be more extensive than in others. In the case of a corporate defendant, that information usually will include details of the defendant's corporate structure; annual profit and loss accounts, or extracts; annual balance sheets, or extracts; details of shareholders' receipts; and details of the remuneration of directors or other officers.

Q.5 In *F Howe and Son (Engineers) Ltd* [1999] 2 Cr App R (S) 37 the Court of Appeal observed:

"If a defendant company wishes to make any submission to the court about its ability to pay a fine it should supply copies of its accounts and any other financial information on which it intends to rely in good time before the hearing both to the court and to the prosecution. This will give the prosecution the opportunity to assist the court should the court wish it. Usually accounts need to be considered with some care to avoid reaching a superficial and perhaps erroneous conclusion. Where accounts or other financial information are deliberately not supplied the court will be entitled to conclude that the company is in a position to pay any financial penalty it is minded to impose. Where the relevant information is provided late it may be desirable for sentence to be adjourned, if necessary at the defendant's expense, so as to avoid the risk of the court taking what it is told at face value and imposing an inadequate penalty."

Q.6 In the case of an individual, the court is likewise entitled to conclude that the defendant is able to pay any fine imposed unless the defendant has supplied financial information to the contrary. It is the defendant's responsibility to disclose to the court such information relevant to his or her financial position as will enable it to assess what he or she reasonably can afford to pay. If necessary, the court may compel the disclosure of an individual defendant's financial circumstances. In the absence of such disclosure, or where the court is not satisfied that it has been given sufficient reliable information, the court will be entitled to draw reasonable inferences as to the offender's means from evidence it has heard and from all the circumstances of the case.

CPD VII Sentencing R: Medical reports for sentencing purposes (as inserted by Criminal Practice Directions 2015 (Amendment No. 7) [2018] EWCA Crim 1760, Lord Burnett CJ)

General observations

R.1 CrimPR 24.11 and 25.16 concern standard sentencing procedures in magistrates' courts and in the Crown Court respectively. CrimPR 28.8 deals with the obtaining of medical reports for sentencing purposes. **B-560**

R.2 Rule 28.8 governs the procedure to be followed where a report is commissioned at the instigation of the court. It is not a substitute for the prompt commissioning of a report or reports by a defendant or defendant's representatives where expert medical opinion is material to the defence case. In particular, the defendant's representatives may wish to obtain a medical report or reports wholly independently of the court. Nothing in these directions, therefore, should be read as discouraging the commissioning of a medical report before the case comes before the court, where such a report is expected to be material and where it is possible promptly to commission it. However, where such a report has been commissioned then if that report has not been received in time for sentencing and if the court agrees that it seems likely to be material, then the court should set a timetable for the reception of that report and should give directions for progress to be reviewed at intervals, adopting the timetable set out in these directions with such adaptations as are needed.

R.3 In assessing the likely materiality of an expert medical report for sentencing purposes the court will be assisted by the parties' representations; by the views expressed in any pre-sentence report that may have been prepared; and by the views of practitioners in local criminal justice mental health services, whose assistance is available to the court under local liaison arrangements.

R.4 Where the court requires the assistance of such a report then it is essential that there should be (i) absolute clarity about who is expected to do what, by when, and at whose expense; and (ii) judicial directions for progress with that report to be monitored and reviewed at prescribed intervals, following a timetable set by the court which culminates in the consideration of the report at a hearing. This is especially important where the report in question is a psychiatric assessment of the defendant for the preparation of which specific expertise may be required which is not readily available and because in some circumstances a second such assessment, by another medical practitioner, may be required.

Timetable for the commissioning, preparation and consideration of a report or reports

R.5 CrimPR 28.8 requires the court to set a timetable appropriate to the case for the preparation and reception of a report. In doing so the court will take account of such representations and other information that it receives, including information about the anticipated availability and workload of practitioners with the appropriate expertise. However, the timetable ought not be a protracted one. It is essential to keep in mind the importance of maintaining progress: in recognition of the defendant's rights and with respect for the interests of victims and witnesses, as required by CrimPR Part 1 (the overriding objective). In a magistrates' court account must be taken, too, of section 11 of the Powers of Criminal Courts (Sentencing) Act 2000, which limits the duration of each remand pending the preparation of a report to 3 weeks, where the defendant is to be in custody, and to 4 weeks if the defendant is to be on bail. **B-561**

R.6 Subject, therefore, to contrary judicial direction the timetable set by the court should require:

(a) the convening of a hearing to consider the report no more than 6 – 8 weeks after the court makes its request;

(b) the prompt identification of an appropriate medical practitioner or practitioners, if not already identified by the court, and the despatch of a commission or commissions accordingly, within 2 business days of the court's decision to request a report;
(c) acknowledgement of a commission by its recipient, and acceptance or rejection of that commission, within 5 business days of its receipt;
(d) enquiries by court staff to confirm that the commission has been received, and to ascertain the action being taken in response, in the event that no acknowledgement is received within 10 business days of its despatch;
(e) delivery of the report within 5 weeks of the despatch of the commission;
(f) enquiries into progress by court staff in the event that no report is received within 5 weeks of the despatch of the commission.

R.7 The hearing that is convened for the court to consider the report, at 6 - 8 weeks after the court requests that report, should not be adjourned before it takes place save in exceptional circumstances and then only by explicit judicial direction the reasons for which must be recorded. If by the time of that hearing the report is available, as usually should be the case, then at that hearing the court can be expected to determine the issue in respect of which the report was commissioned and pass sentence. If by that time, exceptionally, the report is not available then the court should take the opportunity provided by that hearing to enquire into the reasons, give such directions as are appropriate, and if necessary adjourn the hearing to a fixed date for further consideration then. Where it is known in advance of that hearing that the report will not be available in time, the hearing may be conducted by live link or telephone: subject, in the defendant's case, to the same considerations as are identified at paragraph I.3N.6 of these Practice Directions. However, it rarely will be appropriate to dispense altogether with that hearing, or to make enquiries and give further directions without any hearing at all, in view of the arrangements for monitoring and review that the court already will have directed and which, by definition therefore, thus far will have failed to secure the report's timely delivery.

R.8 Where a requirement of the timetable set by the court is not met, or where on enquiry by court staff it appears that the timetable is unlikely to be met, and in any instance in which a medical practitioner who accepts a commission asks for more time, then court staff should not themselves adjust the timetable or accede to such a request but instead should seek directions from an appropriate judicial authority. Subject to local judicial direction, that will be, in the Crown Court, the judge assigned to the case or the resident judge and, in a magistrates' court, a District Judge (Magistrates' Courts) or justice of the peace assigned to the case, or the Justices' Clerk, an assistant clerk or other senior legal adviser. Even if the timetable is adjusted in consequence:
(a) the hearing convened to consider the report (that is, the hearing set for no more than 6 - 8 weeks after the court made its request) rarely should be adjourned before it takes place: see paragraph R.13 above;
(b) directions should be given for court staff henceforth to make regular enquiries into progress, at intervals of not more than 2 weeks, and to report the outcome to an appropriate judicial authority who will decide what further directions, if any, to give.

R.9 Any adjournment of a hearing convened to consider the report should be to a specific date: the hearing should not be adjourned generally, or to a date to be set in due course. The adjournment of such a hearing should not be for more than a further 6 - 8 weeks save in the most exceptional circumstances; and no more than one adjournment of the hearing should be allowed without obtaining written or oral representations from the commissioned medical practitioner explaining the reasons for the delay.

Commissioning a report

B-562 **R.10** Guidance entitled '*Good practice guidance: commissioning, administering and producing psychiatric reports for sentencing*' prepared for and published by the Ministry of Justice and HM Courts and Tribunals Service in September 2010 contains material that will assist court staff and those who are asked to prepare such reports: *http://www.ohrn.nhs.uk/resource/policy/GoodPracticeGuidePsychReports.pdf*

That guidance includes standard forms of letters of instruction and other documents.

R.11 CrimPR 28.8 requires the commissioner of a report to explain why the court seeks the report and to include relevant information about the circumstances. The HMCTS Guidance contains forms for judicial use in the instruction of court staff, and guidance to court staff on the preparation of letters of instruction, where a report is required for sentencing purposes. Where a report is requested in a case involving manslaughter by reason of diminished responsibility, the report writer should have regard to the Sentencing Council's guideline on Manslaughter by reason of Diminished Responsibility. This should assist the report writer in providing the most helpful assessment to enable the court to determine the level of diminution involved in the case.

R.12 The commission should invite a practitioner who is unable to accept it promptly to nominate a suitably qualified substitute, if possible, and to transfer the commission to that person, reporting the transfer when acknowledging the court officer's letter. It is entirely appropriate for the commission to draw the recipient's attention to CrimPR 1.2 (the duty of the participants in a criminal case) and to CrimPR 19.2(1)(b) (the obligation of an expert witness to comply with directions made by a court and at once to inform the court of any significant failure, by the expert or another, to take any step required by such a direction).

R.13 Where the relevant legislation requires a second psychiatric assessment by a second medical practitioner, and where no commission already has been addressed to a second such practitioner, the commission may invite the person to whom it is addressed to nominate a suitably qualified second person and to pass a copy of the commission to that person forthwith.

Funding arrangements

R.14 Where a medical report has been, or is to be, commissioned by a party then that party is responsible for arranging payment of the fees incurred, even though the report is intended for the court's use. That must be made clear in that party's commission. **B-563**

R.15 Where a medical report is requested by the court and commissioned by a party or by court staff at the court's direction then the commission must include (i) confirmation that the fees will be paid by HMCTS, (ii) details of how, and to whom, to submit an invoice or claim for fees, and (iii) notice of the prescribed rates of fees and of any legislative or other criteria applicable to the calculation of the fees that may be paid.

Remand in custody

R.16 Where the defendant who is to be examined will be remanded in custody then notice that directions have been given for a medical report or reports to be prepared must be included in the information given to the defendant's custodian, to ensure that the preparation of the report or reports can be facilitated. This is especially important where bail is withheld on the ground that it would be otherwise impracticable to complete the required report, and in particular where that is the only ground for withholding bail. **B-564**

CPD VII Sentencing S: Variation of sentence (as inserted by Criminal Practice Directions 2015 (Amendment No. 9) [2019] EWCA Crim 1603, Lord Burnett CJ)

S.1 Under section 142 of the Magistrates' Courts Act 1980, in some circumstances a magistrates' court may vary or rescind a sentence or other order that it has imposed or made if that appears to be in the interests of justice. Under section 155 of the Powers of Criminal Courts (Sentencing) Act 2000 the Crown Court may vary or rescind a sentence or order which it has imposed or made, within a period of 56 days beginning with the date of that sentence or order, or beginning with the date of another defendant's acquittal or sentencing in some circumstances (see CrimPR 28.4(1)(b)). **B-565**

S.2 CrimPR 28.4(2) allows the court to exercise those powers at a hearing, in public or in private, or without a hearing. However, rule 28.4(4) confines the court's discretion to dispense with a hearing by requiring the defendant's presence, necessarily at a hearing, unless the variation is one proposed by the defendant, or the effect of the variation is such that the defendant is no more severely dealt with under the sentence as varied than before; or, if neither of those conditions is satisfied, where a hearing has been convened at which the defendant has had an opportunity to make representations, whether or not he or she in fact attends. Moreover, rule 28.4 requires service on the other party of any application to vary a sentence or order, in response to which that other party may wish to make such representations as general principles of law require to be heard. It follows that the circumstances in which a variation of sentence properly may be made without a hearing, consistently with the rule, will be confined to cases in which neither party objects to what is proposed and in which the consequences for the defendant of the variation will be neutral or benign.

S.3 In such a case usually there will be no other objection to the making of the variation without a hearing. Even in such a case, however, the court retains a discretion to convene a hearing, in the exercise of which discretion due regard must be had to the overriding objective and to the importance of dealing with criminal cases in public, in accordance with the principle of open justice. The application of that latter principle was described in *R v Cox* [2019] EWCA Crim 71; [2019] 4 WLR 88 at paragraphs 18 - 19 in these terms:

> "As stated in cases such *as R v Pinkerton* [2017] 1 Cr App R(S) 47 at [8] (a case where there in fact was a downward adjustment of a concurrent custodial sentence which did not impact on the overall sentence) such alterations should be done openly "so that justice may be seen to be done". Likewise, in *R v Warren* [2017] 2 Cr App R(S) 5, the general desirability of re-sentencing taking place in the presence of the defendant and in court was stressed. Accordingly, whilst it is easy to understand the attractions of administrative convenience ... and particularly perhaps where the sentencing judge is not a full-time judge based at a particular court centre, those administrative attractions should not be permitted routinely to prevail over the delivery of open justice."

In reaching its decision the court therefore will take into account each of the relevant factors listed in CrimPR 1.1, and will be astute to distinguish between, on the one hand, the completion of details or the correction of errors of a quasi-administrative character and, on the other, a variation of sentence in which the determination will be a matter of legitimate public interest.

S.4 In any event, the making of the decision and the reasons for that decision always must be announced at a public hearing, even if only briefly and even if the parties are absent on that occasion: CrimPR 28.4(2)(b). While the decision itself must be made, and the reasons for that decision formulated, by the sentencing court itself (section 142(1) of the 1980 Act; section 155(4) of the 2000 Act), the public announcement may be made by a differently constituted court if it would be impracticable for the sentencing court to sit in public for the purpose within a reasonable time.

Criminal Procedure Rules 2020 (SI 2020/759), Pt 33

Confiscation and Related Proceedings

General rules

Interpretation

B-566 **33.1.** In this Part:

"document" means anything in which information of any description is recorded;

"hearsay evidence" means evidence consisting of hearsay within the meaning of section 1(2) of the Civil Evidence Act 1995 [§ 11-58 in the main work];

"restraint proceedings" means proceedings under sections 42 and 58(2) and (3) of the Proceeds of Crime Act 2002 [ibid., §§ 5B-89, 5B-129 et seq.];

"receivership proceedings" means proceedings under sections 48, 49, 50, 51, 54(4), 59(2) and (3), 62 and 63 of the 2002 Act;

"witness statement" means a written statement signed by a person which contains the evidence, and only that evidence, which that person would be allowed to give orally; and

words and expressions used have the same meaning as in Part 2 of the 2002 Act.

Calculation of time

B-567 **33.2.**—(1) This rule shows how to calculate any period of time for doing any act which is specified by this Part for the purposes of any proceedings under Part 2 of the Proceeds of Crime Act 2002 or by an order of the Crown Court in restraint proceedings or receivership proceedings.

(2) A period of time expressed as a number of days shall be computed as clear days.

(3) In this rule "clear days" means that in computing the number of days—

(a) the day on which the period begins; and

(b) if the end of the period is defined by reference to an event, the day on which that event occurs,

are not included.

(4) Where the specified period is 5 days or less and includes a day which is not a business day that day does not count.

Court office closed

B-568 **33.3.** When the period specified by this Part, or by an order of the Crown Court under Part 2 of the Proceeds of Crime Act 2002, for doing any act at the court office falls on a day on which the office is closed, that act shall be in time if done on the next day on which the court office is open.

Application for registration of Scottish or Northern Ireland order

B-569 **33.4.**—(1) This rule applies to an application for registration of an order under article 6 of the Proceeds of Crime Act 2002 (enforcement in different parts of the United Kingdom) Order 2002.

(2) The application may be made without notice.

(3) The application must be in writing and may be supported by a witness statement which must—

(a) exhibit the order or a certified copy of the order; and

(b) to the best of the witness's ability, give full details of the realisable property located in England and Wales in respect of which the order was made and specify the person holding that realisable property.

(4) If the court registers the order, the applicant must serve notice of the registration on—

(a) any person who holds realisable property to which the order applies; and

(b) any other person whom the applicant knows to be affected by the order.

(5) The permission of the Crown Court under rule 33.10 (service outside the jurisdiction) is not required to serve the notice outside England and Wales.

Application to vary or set aside registration

33.5.—(1) An application to vary or set aside registration of an order under article 6 of the Proceeds of Crime Act 2002 (enforcement in different parts of the United Kingdom) Order 2002 may be made to the Crown Court by— **B-570**

(a) any person who holds realisable property to which the order applies; and

(b) any other person affected by the order.

(2) The application must be in writing and may be supported by a witness statement.

(3) The application and any witness statement must be lodged with the Crown Court.

(4) The application must be served on the person who applied for registration at least 7 days before the date fixed by the court for hearing the application, unless the Crown Court specifies a shorter period.

(5) No property in England and Wales may be realised in pursuance of the order before the Crown Court has decided the application.

Register of orders

33.6.—(1) The Crown Court must keep, under the direction of the Lord Chancellor, a register of the orders registered under article 6 of the Proceeds of Crime Act 2002 (enforcement in different parts of the United Kingdom) Order 2002. **B-571**

(2) The register must include details of any variation or setting aside of a registration under rule 33.5 and of any execution issued on a registered order.

(3) If the person who applied for registration of an order which is subsequently registered notifies the Crown Court that the court which made the order has varied or discharged the order, details of the variation or discharge, as the case may be, must be entered in the register.

Statements of truth

33.7.—(1) Any witness statement required to be served by this part must be verified by a statement of truth contained in the witness statement. **B-572**

(2) A statement of truth is a declaration by the person making the witness statement to the effect that the witness statement is true to the best of his knowledge and belief and that he made the statement knowing that, if it were tendered in evidence, he would be liable to prosecution if he wilfully stated in it anything which he knew to be false or did not believe to be true.

(3) The statement of truth must be signed by the person making the witness statement.

(4) If the person making the witness statement fails to verify the witness statement by a statement of truth, the Crown Court may direct that it shall not be admissible as evidence.

Use of witness statements for other purposes

33.8.—(1) Except as provided by this rule, a witness statement served in proceedings under Part 2 of the Proceeds of Crime Act 2002 may be used only for the purpose of the proceedings in which it is served. **B-573**

(2) Paragraph (1) does not apply if and to the extent that—

(a) the witness gives consent in writing to some other use of it;

(b) the Crown Court gives permission for some other use; or

(c) the witness statement has been put in evidence at a hearing held in public.

Service of documents

33.9.—(1) Rule 49.1 (notice required to accompany process served outside the United Kingdom and translations) shall not apply in restraint proceedings and receivership proceedings. **B-574**

(2) An order made in restraint proceedings or receivership proceedings may be enforced against the defendant or any other person affected by it notwithstanding that service of a copy of the order has not been effected in accordance with Part 4 if the Crown Court is satisfied that the person had notice of the order by being present when the order was made.

Service outside the jurisdiction

33.10.—(1) Where this Part requires a document to be served on someone who is outside England and Wales, it may be served outside England and Wales with the permission of the Crown Court. **B-575**

(2) Where a document is to be served outside England and Wales it may be served by any method permitted by the law of the country in which it is to be served.

(3) Nothing in this rule or in any court order shall authorise or require any person to do anything in the country where the document is to be served which is against the law of that country.

(4) Where this Part requires a document to be served a certain period of time before the date of a hearing and the recipient does not appear at the hearing, the hearing must not take place unless the Crown Court is satisfied that the document has been duly served.

Certificates of service

B-576 **33.11.**—(1) Where this Part requires that the applicant for an order in restraint proceedings or receivership proceedings serve a document on another person, the applicant must lodge a certificate of service with the Crown Court within 7 days of service of the document.

(2) The certificate must state—

(a) the method of service;

(b) the date of service; and

(c) if the document is served under rule 4.9 (service by another method), such other information as the court may require when making the order permitting service by that method.

(3) Where a document is to be served by the Crown Court in restraint proceedings and receivership proceedings and the court is unable to serve it, the court must send a notice of nonservice stating the method attempted to the party who requested service.

External requests and orders

B-577 **33.12.**—(1) The rules in this Part and in Part 42 (appeal to the Court of Appeal in confiscation and related proceedings) apply with the necessary modifications to proceedings under the Proceeds of Crime Act 2002 (External Requests and Orders) Order 2005 in the same way that they apply to corresponding proceedings under Part 2 of the Proceeds of Crime Act 2002.

(2) This table shows how provisions of the 2005 Order correspond with provisions of the 2002 Act.

Article of the Proceeds of Crime Act 2002 (External Requests and Orders) Order 2005	*Section of the Proceeds of Crime Act 2002*
8	41
9	42
10	43
11	44
15	48
16	49
17	58
23	31
27	50
28	51
41	62
42	63
44	65
45	66

Confiscation proceedings

Statements in connection with confiscation orders

B-578 **33.13.**—(1) This rule applies where—

(a) the court can make a confiscation order; and

(b) the prosecutor asks the court to make such an order, or the court decides to make such an order on its own initiative.

(2) Within such periods as the court directs—

(a) if the court so orders, the defendant must give such information, in such manner, as the court directs;

(b) the prosecutor must serve a statement of information relevant to confiscation on the court officer and the defendant; and

(c) if the court so directs—

(i) the defendant must serve a response notice on the court officer and the prosecutor, and

(ii) the parties must identify what is in dispute.

(3) Where it appears to the court that a person other than the defendant holds, or may hold, an interest in property held by the defendant which property is likely to be realised or otherwise used to satisfy a confiscation order—

(a) the court must not determine the extent of the defendant's interest in that property unless that other person has had a reasonable opportunity to make representations; and

(b) the court may order that other person to give such information, in such manner and within such a period, as the court directs.

(4) The court may–

(a) shorten or extend a time limit which it has set;

(b) vary, discharge or supplement an order which it has made; and

(c) postpone confiscation proceedings without a hearing.

(5) A prosecutor's statement of information must–

(a) identify the maker of the statement and show its date;

(b) identify the defendant in respect of whom it is served;

(c) specify the conviction which gives the court power to make the confiscation order, or each conviction if more than one;

(d) if the prosecutor believes the defendant to have a criminal lifestyle, include such matters as the prosecutor believes to be relevant in connection with deciding–

(i) whether the defendant has such a lifestyle,

(ii) whether the defendant has benefited from his or her general criminal conduct,

(iii) the defendant's benefit from that conduct, and

(iv) whether the court should or should not make such assumptions about the defendant's property as legislation permits;

(e) if the prosecutor does not believe the defendant to have a criminal lifestyle, include such matters as the prosecutor believes to be relevant in connection with deciding–

(i) whether the defendant has benefited from his or her particular criminal conduct, and

(ii) the defendant's benefit from that conduct; and

(f) in any case, include such matters as the prosecutor believes to be relevant in connection with deciding–

(i) whether to make a determination about the extent of the defendant's interest in property in which another person holds, or may hold, an interest, and

(ii) what determination to make, if the court decides to make one.

(6) A defendant's response notice must–

(a) indicate the extent to which the defendant accepts the allegations made in the prosecutor's statement of information; and

(b) so far as the defendant does not accept an allegation, give particulars of any matters on which the defendant relies,

in any manner directed by the court.

(7) The court must satisfy itself that there has been explained to the defendant, in terms the defendant can understand (with help, if necessary)–

(a) that if the defendant accepts to any extent an allegation in a prosecutor's statement of information, then the court may treat that as conclusive for the purposes of deciding whether the defendant has benefited from general or particular criminal conduct, and if so by how much;

(b) that if the defendant fails in any respect to comply with a direction to serve a response notice, then the court may treat that as acceptance of each allegation to which the defendant has not replied, except the allegation that the defendant has benefited from general or particular criminal conduct; and

(c) that if the defendant fails without reasonable excuse to comply with an order to give information, then the court may draw such inference as it believes is appropriate.

Application for compliance order

33.14.–(1) This rule applies where– **B-579**

(a) the prosecutor wants the court to make a compliance order after a confiscation order has been made; or

(b) the prosecutor or a person affected by a compliance order wants the court to vary or discharge the order.

(2) Such a prosecutor or person must–

(a) apply in writing; and

(b) serve the application on–

(i) the court officer, and

(ii) as appropriate, the prosecutor and any person who is affected by the compliance order (or who would be affected if it were made), unless the court otherwise directs.

(3) The application must–

(a) specify–
(i) the confiscation order, and
(ii) the compliance order, if it is an application to vary or discharge that order;
(b) if it is an application for a compliance order–
(i) specify each measure that the prosecutor proposes to ensure that the confiscation order is effective, including in particular any restriction or prohibition on the defendant's travel outside the United Kingdom, and
(ii) explain why each such measure is appropriate;
(c) if it is an application to vary or discharge a compliance order, as appropriate–
(i) specify any proposed variation, and
(ii) explain why it is appropriate for the order to be varied or discharged;
(d) attach any material on which the applicant relies;
(e) propose the terms of the order; and
(f) ask for a hearing, if the applicant wants one, and explain why it is needed.

(4) A person who wants to make representations about the application must–
(a) serve the representations on–
(i) the court officer, and
(ii) the applicant;
(b) do so as soon as reasonably practicable after service of the application;
(c) attach any material on which that person relies; and
(d) ask for a hearing, if that person wants one, and explain why it is needed.

(5) The court–
(a) may determine the application at a hearing (which must be in private unless the court otherwise directs), or without a hearing; and
(b) may dispense with service on any person of a prosecutor's application for a compliance order if, in particular–
(i) the application is urgent, or
(ii) there are reasonable grounds for believing that to give notice of the application would cause the dissipation of property that otherwise would be available to satisfy the confiscation order.

Application for reconsideration

B-580 **33.15.**–(1) This rule applies where the prosecutor wants the court, in view of fresh evidence–
(a) to consider making a confiscation order where the defendant was convicted but no such order was considered;
(b) to reconsider a decision that the defendant had not benefited from criminal conduct; or
(c) to reconsider a decision about the amount of the defendant's benefit.

(2) The application must–
(a) be in writing and give–
(i) the name of the defendant,
(ii) the date on which and the place where any relevant conviction occurred,
(iii) the date on which and the place where any relevant confiscation order was made or varied,
(iv) details of any slavery and trafficking reparation order made by virtue of any relevant confiscation order,
(v) the grounds for the application, and
(vi) an indication of the evidence available to support the application; and
(b) where the parties are agreed on the terms of the proposed order include, in one or more documents–
(i) a draft order in the terms proposed, and
(ii) evidence of the parties' agreement.

(3) The application must be served on–
(a) the court officer; and
(b) the defendant.

(4) The court–
(a) may determine the application without a hearing where the parties are agreed on the terms of the proposed order; but
(b) must determine the application at a hearing in any other case.

(5) Where this rule or the court requires the application to be heard, the court officer must arrange for the court to hear it no sooner than the eighth day after it was served unless the court otherwise directs.

Application for new calculation of available amount

33.16.–(1) This rule applies where the prosecutor or a receiver wants the court to make a new calculation of the amount available for confiscation. **B-581**

(2) The application–

(a) must be in writing and may be supported by a witness statement;

(b) must identify any slavery and trafficking reparation order made by virtue of the confiscation order; and

(c) where the parties are agreed on the terms of the proposed order, must include in one or more documents–

(i) a draft order in the terms proposed, and

(ii) evidence of the parties' agreement.

(3) The application and any witness statement must be served on the court officer.

(4) The application and any witness statement must be served on–

(a) the defendant;

(b) the receiver, if the prosecutor is making the application and a receiver has been appointed; and

(c) the prosecutor, if the receiver is making the application.

(5) The court–

(a) may determine the application without a hearing where the parties are agreed on the terms of the proposed order; but

(b) must determine the application at a hearing in any other case.

(6) Where this rule or the court requires the application to be heard, the court officer must arrange for the court to hear it no sooner than the eighth day after it was served unless the court otherwise directs.

Variation of confiscation order due to inadequacy of available amount

33.17.–(1) This rule applies where the defendant, the prosecutor or a receiver wants the court to vary a confiscation order because the amount available is inadequate. **B-582**

(2), (3) [*Identical to r.33.16(2), (3),B-581.*]

(4) The application and any witness statement must be served on–

(a) the prosecutor;

(b) the defendant, if the receiver is making the application; and

(c) the receiver, if the defendant is making the application and a receiver has been appointed.

(5), (6) [*Identical to r.33.16(5), (6),B-581.*]

Application by magistrates' court officer to discharge confiscation order

33.18.–(1) This rule applies where a magistrates' court officer wants the court to discharge a confiscation order because the amount available is inadequate or the sum outstanding is very small. **B-583**

(2) The application must be in writing and give details of–

(a) the confiscation order;

(b) any slavery and trafficking reparation order made by virtue of the confiscation order;

(c) the amount outstanding under the order; and

(d) the grounds for the application.

(3) The application must be served on–

(a) the defendant;

(b) the prosecutor; and

(c) any receiver.

(4) The court may determine the application without a hearing unless a person listed in paragraph (3) indicates, within 7 days after the application was served, that he or she would like to make representations.

(5) If the court makes an order discharging the confiscation order, the court officer must, at once, send a copy of the order to–

(a) the magistrates' court officer who applied for the order;

(b) the defendant;

(c) the prosecutor; and

(d) any receiver.

Application for variation of confiscation order made against an absconder

B-584 **33.19.**—(1) This rule applies where the defendant wants the court to vary a confiscation order made while the defendant was an absconder.

(2) The application must be in writing and supported by a witness statement which must give details of—

(a) the confiscation order;

(b) any slavery and trafficking reparation order made by virtue of the confiscation order;

(c) the circumstances in which the defendant ceased to be an absconder;

(d) the defendant's conviction of the offence or offences concerned; and

(e) the reason why the defendant believes the amount required to be paid under the confiscation order was too large.

(3) The application and witness statement must be served on the court officer.

(4) The application and witness statement must be served on the prosecutor at least 7 days before the date fixed by the court for hearing the application, unless the court specifies a shorter period.

Application for discharge of confiscation order made against an absconder

B-585 **33.20.**—(1) This rule applies where the defendant wants the court to discharge a confiscation order made while the defendant was an absconder and—

(a) the defendant since has been tried and acquitted of each offence concerned; or

(b) the prosecution has not concluded or is not to proceed.

(2) The application must be in writing and supported by a witness statement which must give details of—

(a) the confiscation order;

(b) the date on which the defendant ceased to be an absconder;

(c) the acquittal of the defendant if he or she has been acquitted of the offence concerned; and

(d) if the defendant has not been acquitted of the offence concerned—

(i) the date on which the defendant ceased to be an absconder,

(ii) the date on which the proceedings taken against the defendant were instituted and a summary of steps taken in the proceedings since then, and

(iii) any indication that the prosecutor does not intend to proceed against the defendant.

(3), (4) [*Identical to r.33.19(3), (4), B-584.*]

(5) If the court orders the discharge of the confiscation order, the court officer must serve notice on any other court responsible for enforcing the order.

Application for increase in term of imprisonment in default

B-586 **33.21.**—(1) This rule applies where—

(a) a court varies a confiscation order; and

(b) the prosecutor wants the court in consequence to increase the term of imprisonment to be served in default of payment.

(2) The application must be made in writing and give details of—

(a) the name and address of the defendant;

(b) the confiscation order;

(c) the grounds for the application; and

(d) the enforcement measures taken, if any.

(3) On receipt of the application, the court officer must—

(a) at once, send to the defendant and any other court responsible for enforcing the order, a copy of the application; and

(b) fix a time, date and place for the hearing and notify the applicant and the defendant of that time, date and place.

(4) If the court makes an order increasing the term of imprisonment in default, the court officer must, at once, send a copy of the order to—

(a) the applicant;

(b) the defendant;

(c) where the defendant is in custody at the time of the making of the order, the person having custody of the defendant; and

(d) any other court responsible for enforcing the order.

Compensation - general

B-587 **33.22.**—(1) This rule applies where a person who held realisable property wants the court to award compensation for loss suffered in consequence of anything done in relation to that property in connection with confiscation proceedings.

(2) The application must be in writing and may be supported by a witness statement.

(3) The application and any witness statement must be served on the court officer.

(4) The application and any witness statement must be served on–

(a) the person alleged to be in default; and

(b) the person or authority by whom the compensation would be payable,

at least 7 days before the date fixed by the court for hearing the application, unless the court directs otherwise.

Compensation - confiscation order made against absconder

33.23.–(1) This rule applies where– **B-588**

(a) the court varies or discharges a confiscation order made against an absconder;

(b) a person who held realisable property suffered loss as a result of the making of that confiscation order; and

(c) that person wants the court to award compensation for that loss.

(2) The application must be in writing and supported by a witness statement which must give details of–

(a) the confiscation order;

(b) the variation or discharge of the confiscation order;

(c) the realisable property to which the application relates; and

(d) the loss suffered by the applicant as a result of the confiscation order.

(3), (4) [*Identical to r.33.19(3), (4), B-584.*]

Payment of money held or detained in satisfaction of confiscation order

33.24.–(1) An order under section 67 of the Proceeds of Crime Act 2002 [§ 5B-138 in the main work] requiring the payment of money to a magistrates' court officer ("a payment order") shall– **B-589**

(a) be directed to–

(i) the bank or building society concerned, where the money is held in an account maintained with that bank or building society, or

(ii) the person on whose authority the money is detained, in any other case;

(b) name the person against whom the confiscation order has been made;

(c) state the amount which remains to be paid under the confiscation order;

(d) state the name and address of the branch at which the account in which the money ordered to be paid is held and the sort code of that branch, if the sort code is known;

(e) state the name in which the account in which the money ordered to be paid is held and the account number of that account, if the account number is known;

(f) state the amount which the bank or building society is required to pay to the court officer under the payment order;

(g) give the name and address of the court officer to whom payment is to be made; and

(h) require the bank or building society to make payment within a period of 7 days beginning on the day on which the payment order is made, unless it appears to the court that a longer or shorter period would be appropriate in the particular circumstances.

(2) In this rule "confiscation order" has the meaning given to it by section 88(6) of the Proceeds of Crime Act 2002.

Application to realise seized property

33.25.–(1) This rule applies where– **B-590**

(a) property is held by a defendant against whom a confiscation order has been made;

(b) the property has been seized by or produced to an officer; and

(c) an officer who is entitled to apply wants a magistrates' court–

(i) to make an order under section 67A of the Proceeds of Crime Act 2002 [ibid., § 5B-139] authorising the realisation of the property towards satisfaction of the confiscation order, or

(ii) to determine any storage, insurance or realisation costs in respect of the property which may be recovered under section 67B of the 2002 Act [ibid., § 5B-140].

(2) Such an officer must–

(a) apply in writing; and

(b) serve the application on–

(i) the court officer, and

(ii) any person whom the applicant believes would be affected by an order.

(3) The application must–

(a) specify the property;

(b) explain–

(i) the applicant's entitlement to apply,

(ii) how the proposed realisation meets the conditions prescribed by section 67A of the 2002 Act, and

(iii) how any storage, etc. costs have been calculated;

(c) attach any material on which the applicant relies; and

(d) propose the terms of the order.

(4) The court may–

(a) determine the application at a hearing, or without a hearing;

(b) consider an application made orally instead of in writing; and

(c) consider an application which has not been served on a person likely to be affected by an order.

(5) If the court authorises the realisation of the property, the applicant must–

(a) notify any person affected by the order who was absent when it was made; and

(b) serve on the court officer a list of those so notified.

Appeal about decision on application to realise seized property

B-591 **33.26.**–(1) This rule applies where on an application under rule 33.25 for an order authorising the realisation of property–

(a) a magistrates' court decides not to make such an order and an officer who is entitled to apply wants to appeal against that decision to the Crown Court, under section 67C(1) of the Proceeds of Crime Act 2002 [ibid., § 5B-141];

(b) a magistrates' court makes such an order and a person who is affected by that decision, other than the defendant against whom the confiscation order was made, wants to appeal against it to the Crown Court, under section 67C(2) of the 2002 Act; or

(c) a magistrates' court makes a decision about storage, etc. costs and an officer who is entitled to apply wants to appeal against that decision to the Crown Court, under section 67C(4) of the 2002 Act.

(2) The appellant must serve an appeal notice–

(a) on the Crown Court officer and on any other party; and

(b) not more than 21 days after the magistrates' court's decision, or, if applicable, service of notice under rule 33.25(5).

(3) The appeal notice must–

(a) specify the decision under appeal;

(b) where paragraph (1)(a) applies, explain why the property should be realised; and

(c) in any other case, propose the order that the appellant wants the court to make, and explain why.

(4) Rule 34.11 (constitution of the Crown Court) applies on such an appeal.

Application for direction about surplus proceeds

B-592 **33.27.**–(1) This rule applies where–

(a) on an application under rule 33.25, a magistrates' court has made an order authorizing an officer to realise property;

(b) an officer so authorised holds proceeds of that realisation;

(c) the confiscation order has been fully paid; and

(d) the officer, or a person who had or has an interest in the property represented by the proceeds, wants a magistrates' court or the Crown Court to determine under section 67D of the Proceeds of Crime Act 2002 [ibid., § 5B-142] –

(i) to whom the remaining proceeds should be paid, and

(ii) in what amount or amounts.

(2) Such a person must–

(a) apply in writing; and

(b) serve the application on–

(i) the court officer, and

(ii) as appropriate, the officer holding the proceeds, or any person to whom such proceeds might be paid.

(3) The application must–
(a) specify the property which was realised;
(b) explain the applicant's entitlement to apply;
(c) describe the distribution proposed by the applicant and explain why that is proposed;
(d) attach any material on which the applicant relies; and
(e) ask for a hearing, if the applicant wants one, and explain why it is needed.
(4) A person who wants to make representations about the application must–
(a) serve the representations on–
(i) the court officer,
(ii) the applicant, and
(iii) any other person to whom proceeds might be paid;
(b) do so as soon as reasonably practicable after service of the application;
(c) attach any material on which that person relies; and
(d) ask for a hearing, if that person wants one, and explain why it is needed.
(5) The court–
(a) must not determine the application unless the applicant and each person on whom it was served–
(i) is present, or
(ii) has had an opportunity to attend or to make representations; but
(b) subject to that, may determine the application–
(i) at a hearing (which must be in private unless the court otherwise directs), or without a hearing, and
(ii) in the absence of any party to the application.

Seizure and detention proceedings

Application for approval to seize property or to search

33.28.–(1) This rule applies where an officer who is entitled to apply wants the approval of a magistrates' court, under section 47G of the Proceeds of Crime Act 2002– **B-593**
(a) to seize property, under section 47C of that Act; or
(b) to search premises or a person or vehicle for property to be seized, under section 47D, 47E or 47F of that Act.
(2) Such an officer must–
(a) apply in writing; and
(b) serve the application on the court officer.
(3) The application must–
(a) explain–
(i) the applicant's entitlement to apply, and
(ii) how the proposed seizure meets the conditions prescribed by sections 47B, 47C and, if applicable, 47D, 47E or 47F of the 2002 Act;
(b) if applicable, specify any premises, person or vehicle to be searched;
(c) attach any material on which the applicant relies; and
(d) propose the terms in which the applicant wants the court to give its approval.
(4) The court–
(a) must determine the application–
(i) at a hearing, which must be in private unless the court otherwise directs, and
(ii) in the applicant's presence; but
(b) may consider an application made orally instead of in writing.

Application to extend detention period

33.29.–(1) This rule applies where an officer who is entitled to apply, or the prosecutor, wants a magistrates' court to make an order, under section 47M of the Proceeds of Crime Act 2002, extending the period for which seized property may be detained. **B-594**
(2) Such an officer or prosecutor must–
(a) apply in writing; and
(b) serve the application on–
(i) the court officer, and
(ii) any person whom the applicant believes would be affected by an order.
(3) The application must–

(a) specify—
(i) the property to be detained, and
(ii) whether the applicant wants it to be detained for a specified period or indefinitely;
(b) explain—
(i) the applicant's entitlement to apply, and
(ii) how the proposed detention meets the conditions prescribed by section 47M of the 2002 Act;
(c) attach any material on which the applicant relies; and
(d) propose the terms of the order.
(4) The court—
(a) must determine the application—
(i) at a hearing, which must be in private unless the court otherwise directs, and
(ii) in the applicant's presence;
(b) may—
(i) consider an application made orally instead of in writing,
(ii) require service of the application on the court officer after it has been heard, instead of before.
(5) If the court extends the period for which the property may be detained, the applicant must—
(a) notify any person affected by the order who was absent when it was made; and
(b) serve on the court officer a list of those so notified.

Application to vary or discharge order for extended detention

B-595 **33.30.**—(1) This rule applies where an officer who is entitled to apply, the prosecutor, or a person affected by an order to which rule 33.29 applies, wants a magistrates' court to vary or discharge that order, under section 47N of the Proceeds of Crime Act 2002.
(2) Such a person must—
(a) apply in writing; and
(b) serve the application on—
(i) the court officer, and
(ii) as appropriate, the applicant for the order, or any person affected by the order.
(3) The application must—
(a) specify the order and the property detained;
(b) explain—
(i) the applicant's entitlement to apply,
(ii) why it is appropriate for the order to be varied or discharged,
(iii) if applicable, on what grounds the court must discharge the order;
(c) attach any material on which the applicant relies;
(d) if applicable, propose the terms of any variation; and
(e) ask for a hearing, if the applicant wants one, and explain why it is needed.
(4) A person who wants to make representations about the application must—
(a) serve the representations on—
(i) the court officer, and
(ii) the applicant;
(b) do so as soon as reasonably practicable after service of the application;
(c) attach any material on which that person relies; and
(d) ask for a hearing, if that person wants one, and explain why it is needed.
(5) The court—
(a) must not determine the application unless the applicant and each person on whom it was served—
(i) is present, or
(ii) has had an opportunity to attend or to make representations; but
(b) subject to that, may determine the application—
(i) at a hearing (which must be in private unless the court otherwise directs), or without a hearing,
(ii) in the absence of any party to the application.

Appeal about property detention decision

B-596 **33.31.**—(1) This rule applies where—

(a) on an application under rule 33.29 for an order extending the period for which property may be detained–
(i) a magistrates' court decides not to make such an order, and
(ii) an officer who is entitled to apply for such an order, or the prosecutor, wants to appeal against that decision to the Crown Court under section 47O(1) of the Proceeds of Crime Act 2002; or
(b) on an application under rule 33.30 to vary or discharge an order under rule 33.29–
(i) a magistrates' court determines the application, and
(ii) a person who is entitled to apply under that rule wants to appeal against that decision to the Crown Court under section 47O(2) of the 2002 Act.

(2) The appellant must serve an appeal notice–
(a) on the Crown Court officer and on any other party; and
(b) not more than 21 days after the magistrates' court's decision, or, if applicable, service of notice under rule 33.29(5).

(3) The appeal notice must–
(a) specify the decision under appeal;
(b) where paragraph (1)(a) applies, explain why the detention period should be extended; and
(c) where paragraph (1)(b) applies, propose the order that the appellant wants the court to make, and explain why.

(4) Rule 34.11 (constitution of the Crown Court) applies on such an appeal.

Restraint and receivership proceedings: rules that apply generally

Taking control of goods and forfeiture

33.32.–(1) This rule applies to applications under sections 58(2) and (3) and 59(2) and (3) of the Proceeds of Crime Act 2002 [§§ 5B-129, 5B-130 in the main work] for leave of the Crown Court to take control of goods or levy distress against property, or to exercise a right of forfeiture by peaceable re-entry in relation to a tenancy, in circumstances where the property or tenancy is the subject of a restraint order or a receiver has been appointed in respect of the property or tenancy. **B-597**

(2) The application must be made in writing to the Crown Court.

(3) The application must be served on–
(a) the person who applied for the restraint order or the order appointing the receiver; and
(b) any receiver appointed in respect of the property or tenancy,

at least 7 days before the date fixed by the court for hearing the application, unless the Crown Court specifies a shorter period.

Joining of applications

33.33. An application for the appointment of a management receiver or enforcement receiver under rule 33.56 may be joined with– **B-598**
(a) an application for a restraint order under rule 33.51; and
(b) an application for the conferral of powers on the receiver under rule 33.57.

Applications to be dealt with in writing

33.34. Applications in restraint proceedings and receivership proceedings are to be dealt with without a hearing, unless the Crown Court orders otherwise.

Business in chambers

33.35. Restraint proceedings and receivership proceedings may be heard in chambers.

Power of court to control evidence

33.36.–(1) When hearing restraint proceedings and receivership proceedings, the Crown Court may control the evidence by giving directions as to– **B-599**
(a) the issues on which it requires evidence;
(b) the nature of the evidence which it requires to decide those issues; and
(c) the way in which the evidence is to be placed before the court.

(2) The court may use its power under this rule to exclude evidence that would otherwise be admissible.

(3) The court may limit cross-examination in restraint proceedings and receivership proceedings.

Evidence of witnesses

33.37.–(1) The general rule is that, unless the Crown Court orders otherwise, any fact which **B-600**

needs to be proved in restraint proceedings or receivership proceedings by the evidence of a witness is to be proved by their evidence in writing.

(2) Where evidence is to be given in writing under this rule, any party may apply to the Crown Court for permission to cross-examine the person giving the evidence.

(3) If the Crown Court gives permission under paragraph (2) but the person in question does not attend as required by the order, his evidence may not be used unless the court gives permission.

Witness summons

33.38.—(1) Any party to restraint proceedings or receivership proceedings may apply to the Crown Court to issue a witness summons requiring a witness to—

(a) attend court to give evidence; or

(b) produce documents to the court.

(2) Rule 17.3 (application for summons, warrant or order: general rules) applies to an application under this rule as it applies to an application under section 2 of the Criminal Procedure (Attendance of Witnesses) Act 1965 [§ 8-1 in the main work].

Hearsay evidence

B-601 **33.39.** Section 2(1) of the Civil Evidence Act 1995 (duty to give notice of intention to rely on hearsay evidence [ibid., § 11-59]) does not apply to evidence in restraint proceedings and receivership proceedings.

Disclosure and inspection of documents

B-602 **33.40.**—(1) This rule applies where, in the course of restraint proceedings or receivership proceedings, an issue arises as to whether property is realisable property.

(2) The Crown Court may make an order for disclosure of documents.

(3) Part 31 of the Civil Procedure Rules 1998 as amended from time to time shall have effect as if the proceedings were proceedings in the High Court.

Court documents

B-603 **33.41.**—(1) Any order which the Crown Court issues in restraint proceedings or receivership proceedings must—

(a) state the name and judicial title of the person who made it;

(b) bear the date on which it is made; and

(c) be sealed by the Crown Court.

(2) The Crown Court may place the seal on the order—

(a) by hand; or

(b) by printing a facsimile of the seal on the order whether electronically or otherwise.

(3) A document purporting to bear the court's seal shall be admissible in evidence without further proof.

Consent orders

B-604 **33.42.**—(1) This rule applies where all the parties to restraint proceedings or receivership proceedings agree the terms in which an order should be made.

(2) Any party may apply for a judgment or order in the terms agreed.

(3) The Crown Court may deal with an application under paragraph (2) without a hearing.

(4) Where this rule applies—

(a) the order which is agreed by the parties must be drawn up in the terms agreed;

(b) it must be expressed as being "By Consent"; and

(c) it must be signed by the legal representative acting for each of the parties to whom the order relates or by the party if he is a litigant in person.

(5) Where an application is made under this rule, then the requirements of any other rule as to the procedure for making an application do not apply.

Slips and omissions

B-605 **33.43.**—(1) The Crown Court may at any time correct an accidental slip or omission in an order made in restraint proceedings or receivership proceedings.

(2) A party may apply for a correction without notice.

Supply of documents from court records

33.44.—(1) No document relating to restraint proceedings or receivership proceedings may be supplied from the records of the Crown Court for any person to inspect or copy unless the Crown Court grants permission.

(2) An application for permission under paragraph (1) must be made on notice to the parties to the proceedings.

Disclosure of documents in criminal proceedings

33.45.–(1) This rule applies where– **B-606**

(a) proceedings for an offence have been started in the Crown Court and the defendant has not been either convicted or acquitted on all counts; and

(b) an application for a restraint order under section 42(1) of the Proceeds of Crime Act 2002 [§ 5B-89 in the main work] has been made.

(2) The judge presiding at the proceedings for the offence may be supplied from the records of the Crown Court with documents relating to restraint proceedings and any receivership proceedings.

(3) Such documents must not otherwise be disclosed in the proceedings for the offence.

Preparation of documents

33.46.–(1) Every order in restraint proceedings or receivership proceedings must be drawn up by the Crown Court unless– **B-607**

(a) the Crown Court orders a party to draw it up;

(b) a party, with the permission of the Crown Court, agrees to draw it up; or

(c) the order is made by consent under rule 33.42.

(2) The Crown Court may direct that–

(a) an order drawn up by a party must be checked by the Crown Court before it is sealed; or

(b) before an order is drawn up by the Crown Court, the parties must lodge an agreed statement of its terms.

(3) Where an order is to be drawn up by a party–

(a) he must lodge it with the Crown Court no later than 7 days after the date on which the court ordered or permitted him to draw it up so that it can be sealed by the Crown Court; and

(b) if he fails to lodge it within that period, any other party may draw it up and lodge it.

(4) Nothing in this rule shall require the Crown Court to accept a document which is illegible, has not been duly authorised, or is unsatisfactory for some other similar reason.

Order for costs

33.47.–(1) This rule applies where the Crown Court is deciding whether to make an order for costs in restraint proceedings or receivership proceedings. **B-608**

(2) The court has discretion as to–

(a) whether costs are payable by one party to another;

(b) the amount of those costs; and

(c) when they are to be paid.

(3) If the court decides to make an order about costs–

(a) the general rule is that the unsuccessful party must be ordered to pay the costs of the successful party; but

(b) the court may make a different order.

(4) In deciding what order (if any) to make about costs, the court must have regard to all of the circumstances, including–

(a) the conduct of all the parties; and

(b) whether a party has succeeded on part of an application, even if he has not been wholly successful.

(5) The orders which the court may make include an order that a party must pay–

(a) a proportion of another party's costs;

(b) a stated amount in respect of another party's costs;

(c) costs from or until a certain date only;

(d) costs incurred before proceedings have begun;

(e) costs relating to particular steps taken in the proceedings;

(f) costs relating only to a distinct part of the proceedings; and

(g) interest on costs from or until a certain date, including a date before the making of an order.

(6) Where the court would otherwise consider making an order under paragraph (5)(f), it must instead, if practicable, make an order under paragraph (5)(a) or (c).

(7) Where the court has ordered a party to pay costs, it may order an amount to be paid on account before the costs are assessed.

Assessment of costs

B-609 **33.48.**—(1) Where the Crown Court has made an order for costs in restraint proceedings or receivership proceedings it may either—

(a) make an assessment of the costs itself; or

(b) order assessment of the costs under rule 45.11.

(2) In either case, the Crown Court or the assessing authority, as the case may be, must—

(a) only allow costs which are proportionate to the matters in issue; and

(b) resolve any doubt which it may have as to whether the costs were reasonably incurred or reasonable and proportionate in favour of the paying party.

(3) The Crown Court or the assessing authority, as the case may be, is to have regard to all the circumstances in deciding whether costs were proportionately or reasonably incurred or proportionate and reasonable in amount.

(4) In particular, the Crown Court or the assessing authority must give effect to any orders which have already been made.

(5) The Crown Court or the assessing authority must also have regard to—

(a) the conduct of all the parties, including in particular, conduct before, as well as during, the proceedings;

(b) the amount or value of the property involved;

(c) the importance of the matter to all the parties;

(d) the particular complexity of the matter or the difficulty or novelty of the questions raised;

(e) the skill, effort, specialised knowledge and responsibility involved;

(f) the time spent on the application; and

(g) the place where and the circumstances in which work or any part of it was done.

Time for complying with an order for costs

B-610 **33.49.** A party to restraint proceedings or receivership proceedings must comply with an order for the payment of costs within 14 days of—

(a) the date of the order if it states the amount of those costs;

(b) if the amount of those costs is decided later under rule 45.11, the date of the assessing authority's decision; or

(c) in either case, such later date as the Crown Court may specify.

Application of costs rules

33.50. Rules 33.47, 33.48 and 33.49 do not apply to the assessment of costs in proceedings to the extent that section 11 of the Access to Justice Act 1999 applies and provisions made under that Act make different provision.

Restraint proceedings

Application for restraint order or ancillary order

B-611 **33.51.**—(1) This rule applies where the prosecutor, or an accredited financial investigator, makes an application under section 42 of the Proceeds of Crime Act 2002 [§ 5B-89 in the main work] for—

(a) a restraint order, under section 41(1) of the 2002 Act [ibid., § 5B-76]; or

(b) an ancillary order, under section 41(7) of that Act, for the purpose of ensuring that a restraint order is effective.

(2) The application may be made without notice if the application is urgent or if there are reasonable grounds for believing that giving notice would cause the dissipation of realisable property which is the subject of the application.

(3) An application for a restraint order must be in writing and supported by a witness statement which must—

(a) give the grounds for the application;

(b) to the best of the witness' ability, give full details of the realisable property in respect of which the applicant is seeking the order and specify the person holding that realisable property;

(c) include the proposed terms of the order.

(4) An application for an ancillary order must be in writing and supported by a witness statement which must—

(a) give the grounds for, and full details of, the application;

(b) include, if appropriate—

(i) any request for an order for disclosure of documents to which rule 33.40 applies

(disclosure and inspection of documents),
 (ii) the identity of any person whom the applicant wants the court to examine about the extent or whereabouts of realisable property,
 (iii) a list of the main questions that the applicant wants to ask any such person, and
 (iv) a list of any documents to which the applicant wants to refer such a person; and
(c) include the proposed terms of the order.

(5) An application for a restraint order and an application for an ancillary order may (but need not) be made at the same time and contained in the same documents.

(6) An application by an accredited financial investigator must include a statement that, under section 68 of the 2002 Act [ibid., § 5B-143], the applicant has authority to apply.

Restraint and ancillary orders

33.52.–(1) The Crown Court may make a restraint order subject to exceptions, including, but not limited to, exceptions for reasonable living expenses and reasonable legal expenses, and for the purpose of enabling any person to carry on any trade, business or occupation. **B-612**

(2) But the Crown Court must not make an exception for legal expenses where this is prohibited by section 41(4) of the Proceeds of Crime Act 2002.

(3) An exception to a restraint order may be made subject to conditions.

(4) The Crown Court must not require the applicant for a restraint order to give any undertaking relating to damages sustained as a result of the restraint order by a person who is prohibited from dealing with realisable property by the restraint order.

(5) The Crown Court may require the applicant for a restraint order to give an undertaking to pay the reasonable expenses of any person, other than a person who is prohibited from dealing with realisable property by the restraint order, which are incurred in complying with the restraint order.

(6) An order must include a statement that disobedience of the order, either by a person to whom the order is addressed, or by another person, may be contempt of court and the order must include details of the possible consequences of being held in contempt of court.

(7) Unless the Crown Court otherwise directs, an order made without notice has effect until the court makes an order varying or discharging it.

(8) The applicant for an order must–
(a) serve copies of the order and of the witness statement made in support of the application on the defendant and any person who is prohibited by the order from dealing with realisable property; and
(b) notify any person whom the applicant knows to be affected by the order of its terms.

Application for discharge or variation of restraint or ancillary order by a person affected by the order

33.53.–(1) This rule applies where a person affected by a restraint order makes an application to the Crown Court under section 42(3) of the Proceeds of Crime Act 2002 to discharge or vary the restraint order or any ancillary order made under section 41(7) of the Act. **B-613**

(2) The application must be in writing and may be supported by a witness statement.

(3) The application and any witness statement must be lodged with the Crown Court.

(4) The application and any witness statement must be served on the person who applied for the restraint order and any person who is prohibited from dealing with realisable property by the restraint order (if he is not the person making the application) at least 2 days before the date fixed by the court for hearing the application, unless the Crown Court specifies a shorter period.

Application for variation of restraint or ancillary order by the person who applied for the order

33.54.–(1) This rule applies where the applicant for a restraint order makes an application under section 42(3) of the Proceeds of Crime Act 2002 to the Crown Court to vary the restraint order or any ancillary order made under section 41(7) of the 2002 Act (including where the court has already made a restraint order and the applicant is seeking to vary the order in order to restrain further realisable property). **B-614**

(2) The application may be made without notice if the application is urgent or if there are reasonable grounds for believing that giving notice would cause the dissipation of realizable property which is the subject of the application.

(3) The application must be in writing and must be supported by a witness statement which must–
(a) give the grounds for the application;
(b) where the application is for the inclusion of further realisable property in a restraint order give full details, to the best of the witness's ability, of the realisable property in respect of which the applicant is seeking the order and specify the person holding that realisable property;

(c) where the application is to vary an ancillary order, include, if appropriate—
(i) any request for an order for disclosure of documents to which rule 33.40 applies (disclosure and inspection of documents),
(ii) the identity of any person whom the applicant wants the court to examine about the extent or whereabouts of realisable property,
(iii) a list of the main questions that the applicant wants to ask any such person, and
(iv) a list of any documents to which the applicant wants to refer such a person; and
(d) include the proposed terms of the variation.

(4) An application by an accredited financial investigator must include a statement that, under section 68 of the 2002 Act [§ 5B-143 in the main work], the applicant has authority to apply.

(5) The application and witness statement must be lodged with the Crown Court.

(6) Except where, under paragraph (2), notice of the application is not required to be served, the application and witness statement must be served on any person who is prohibited from dealing with realisable property by the restraint order at least 2 days before the date fixed by the court for hearing the application, unless the Crown Court specifies a shorter period.

(7) If the court makes an order for the variation of a restraint or ancillary order, the applicant must serve copies of the order and of the witness statement made in support of the application on—
(a) the defendant;
(b) any person who is prohibited from dealing with realisable property by the restraint order (whether before or after the variation); and
(c) any other person whom the applicant knows to be affected by the order.

Application for discharge of restraint or ancillary order by the person who applied for the order

B-615 **33.55.**—(1) This rule applies where the applicant for a restraint order makes an application under section 42(3) of the Proceeds of Crime Act 2002 to discharge the order or any ancillary order made under section 41(7) of the 2002 Act.

(2) The application may be made without notice.

(3) The application must be in writing and must state the grounds for the application.

(4) If the court makes an order for the discharge of a restraint or ancillary order, the applicant must serve copies of the order on—
(a) the defendant;
(b) any person who is prohibited from dealing with realisable property by the restraint order (whether before or after the discharge); and
(c) any other person whom the applicant knows to be affected by the order.

Receivership proceedings

Application for appointment of a management or an enforcement receiver

B-616 **33.56.**—(1) This rule applies to an application for the appointment of a management receiver under section 48(1) of the Proceeds of Crime Act 2002 [§ 5B-117 in the main work] and an application for the appointment of an enforcement receiver under section 50(1) of the 2002 Act [ibid., § 5B-121].

(2) The application may be made without notice if—
(a) the application is joined with an application for a restraint order under rule 33.51 (application for restraint order or ancillary order);
(b) the application is urgent; or
(c) there are reasonable grounds for believing that giving notice would cause the dissipation of realisable property which is the subject of the application.

(3) The application must be in writing and must be supported by a witness statement which must—
(a) give the grounds for the application;
(b) give full details of the proposed receiver;
(c) to the best of the witness' ability, give full details of the realisable property in respect of which the applicant is seeking the order and specify the person holding that realisable property;
(d) where the application is made by an accredited financial investigator, include a statement that, under section 68 of the 2002 Act [ibid., § 5B-143], the applicant has authority to apply; and
(e) if the proposed receiver is not a person falling within section 55(8) of the 2002 Act [ibid., § 5B-126] and the applicant is asking the court to allow the receiver to act—

(i) without giving security, or

(ii) before he has given security or satisfied the court that he has security in place, explain the reasons why that is necessary.

(4) Where the application is for the appointment of an enforcement receiver, the applicantn must provide the Crown Court with a copy of the confiscation order made against the defendant.

(5) The application and witness statement must be lodged with the Crown Court.

(6) Except where, under paragraph (2), notice of the application is not required to be served, the application and witness statement must be lodged with the Crown Court and served on–

(a) the defendant;

(b) any person who holds realisable property to which the application relates; and

(c) any other person whom the applicant knows to be affected by the application,

at least 7 days before the date fixed by the court for hearing the application, unless the Crown Court specifies a shorter period.

(7) If the court makes an order for the appointment of a receiver, the applicant must serve copies of the order and of the witness statement made in support of the application on–

(a) the defendant;

(b) any person who holds realisable property to which the order applies; and

(c) any other person whom the applicant knows to be affected by the order.

Application for conferral of powers on a management receiver or an enforcement receiver

33.57.–(1) This rule applies to an application for the conferral of powers on a management receiver under section 49(1) of the Proceeds of Crime Act 2002 [ibid., § 5B-119] or an enforcement receiver under section 51(1) of the 2002 Act [ibid., § 5B-122]. **B-617**

(2) The application may be made without notice if the application is to give the receiver power to take possession of property and–

(a) the application is joined with an application for a restraint order under rule 33.51 (application for restraint order or ancillary order);

(b) the application is urgent; or

(c) there are reasonable grounds for believing that giving notice would cause the dissipation of the property which is the subject of the application.

(3) The application must be made in writing and supported by a witness statement which must–

(a) give the grounds for the application;

(b) give full details of the realisable property in respect of which the applicant is seeking the order and specify the person holding that realisable property;

(c) where the application is made by an accredited financial investigator, include a statement that, under section 68 of the 2002 Act, the applicant has authority to apply; and

(d) where the application is for power to start, carry on or defend legal proceedings in respect of the property, explain–

(i) what proceedings are concerned, in what court, and

(ii) what powers the receiver will ask that court to exercise.

(4) Where the application is for the conferral of powers on an enforcement receiver, the applicant must provide the Crown Court with a copy of the confiscation order made against the defendant.

(5) The application and witness statement must be lodged with the Crown Court.

(6) Except where, under paragraph (2), notice of the application is not required to be served, the application and witness statement must be served on–

(a) the defendant;

(b) any person who holds realisable property in respect of which a receiver has been appointed or in respect of which an application for a receiver has been made;

(c) any other person whom the applicant knows to be affected by the application; and

(d) the receiver (if one has already been appointed),

at least 7 days before the date fixed by the court for hearing the application, unless the Crown Court specifies a shorter period.

(7) If the court makes an order for the conferral of powers on a receiver, the applicant must serve copies of the order on–

(a) the defendant;

(b) any person who holds realisable property in respect of which the receiver has been appointed; and

(c) any other person whom the applicant knows to be affected by the order.

Applications for discharge or variation of receivership orders, and applications for other orders

33.58.–(1) This rule applies to applications under section 62(3) of the Proceeds of Crime Act **B-618**

2002 [ibid., § 5B-133] for orders (by persons affected by the action of receivers) and applications under section 63(1) of the 2002 Act [ibid., § 5B-134] for the discharge or variation of orders relating to receivers.

(2) The application must be made in writing and lodged with the Crown Court.

(3) The application must be served on the following persons (except where they are the person making the application)—

(a) the person who applied for appointment of the receiver;

(b) the defendant;

(c) any person who holds realisable property in respect of which the receiver has been appointed;

(d) the receiver; and

(e) any other person whom the applicant knows to be affected by the application,

at least 7 days before the date fixed by the court for hearing the application, unless the Crown Court specifies a shorter period.

(4) If the court makes an order for the discharge or variation of an order relating to a receiver under section 63(2) of the 2002 Act, the applicant must serve copies of the order on any persons whom he knows to be affected by the order.

Sums in the hands of receivers

★B-619 **33.59.**—(1) This rule applies where the amount payable under a confiscation order has been fully paid and any sums remain in the hands of an enforcement receiver.

(2) The receiver must make an application to the Crown Court for directions as to the distribution of the sums in his hands.

(3) The application and any evidence which the receiver intends to rely on in support of the application must be served on—

(a) the defendant; and

(b) any other person who held (or holds) interests in any property realised by the receiver,

at least 7 days before the date fixed by the court for hearing the application, unless the Crown Court specifies a shorter period.

(4) If any of the provisions listed in paragraph (5) (provisions as to the vesting of funds in a trustee in bankruptcy) apply, then the Crown Court must make a declaration to that effect.

(5) These are the provisions—

(a) section 82 of the Bankruptcy (Scotland) Act 2016;

(b) section 306B of the Insolvency Act 1986; and

(c) article 279B of the Insolvency (Northern Ireland) Order 1989.

[This rule is printed as amended, with effect from 8 February 2021, by SI 2021/40, r.19.]

Security

B-620 **33.60.**—(1) This rule applies where the Crown Court appoints a receiver under section 48 or 50 of the Proceeds of Crime Act 2002 [ibid., §§ 5B-117, 5B-121] and the receiver is not a person falling within section 55(8) [ibid., § 5B-126] of the 2002 Act (and it is immaterial whether the receiver is a permanent or temporary member of staff or on secondment from elsewhere).

(2) The Crown Court may direct that before the receiver begins to act, or within a specified time, he must either—

(a) give such security as the Crown Court may determine; or

(b) file with the Crown Court and serve on all parties to any receivership proceedings evidence that he already has in force sufficient security,

to cover his liability for his acts and omissions as a receiver.

(3) The Crown Court may terminate the appointment of a receiver if he fails to—

(a) give the security; or

(b) satisfy the court as to the security he has in force,

by the date specified.

Remuneration

B-621 **33.61.**—(1) [*Identical to r.33.60(1), B-620.*]

(2) The receiver may only charge for his services if the Crown Court—

(a) so directs; and

(b) specifies the basis on which the receiver is to be remunerated.

(3) Unless the Crown Court orders otherwise, in determining the remuneration of the receiver, the Crown Court shall award such sum as is reasonable and proportionate in all the circumstances and which takes into account—

(a) the time properly given by him and his staff to the receivership;
(b) the complexity of the receivership;
(c) any responsibility of an exceptional kind or degree which falls on the receiver in consequence of the receivership;
(d) the effectiveness with which the receiver appears to be carrying out, or to have carried out, his duties; and
(e) the value and nature of the subject matter of the receivership.

(4) The Crown Court may refer the determination of a receiver's remuneration to be ascertained by the taxing authority of the Crown Court and rules 45.11 (assessment and reassessment) to 45.14 (application for an extension of time) shall have effect as if the taxing authority was ascertaining costs.

(5) A receiver appointed under section 48 of the 2002 Act is to receive his remuneration by realising property in respect of which he is appointed, in accordance with section 49(2)(d) of the 2002 Act [ibid., § 5B-119].

(6) A receiver appointed under section 50 of the 2002 Act is to receive his remuneration by applying to the magistrates' court officer for payment under section 55(4)(b) of the 2002 Act.

Accounts

33.62.–(1) The Crown Court may order a receiver appointed under section 48 or 50 of the Proceeds of Crime Act 2002 to prepare and serve accounts. **B-622**

(2) A party to receivership proceedings served with such accounts may apply for an order permitting him to inspect any document in the possession of the receiver relevant to those accounts.

(3) Any party to receivership proceedings may, within 14 days of being served with the accounts, serve notice on the receiver–
(a) specifying any item in the accounts to which he objects;
(b) giving the reason for such objection; and
(c) requiring the receiver within 14 days of receipt of the notice, either–
(i) to notify all the parties who were served with the accounts that he accepts the objection, or
(ii) if he does not accept the objection, to apply for an examination of the accounts in relation to the contested item.

(4) When the receiver applies for the examination of the accounts he must at the same time lodge with the Crown Court–
(a) the accounts; and
(b) a copy of the notice served on him under this section of the rule.

(5) If the receiver fails to comply with paragraph (3)(c) of this rule, any party to receivership proceedings may apply to the Crown Court for an examination of the accounts in relation to the contested item.

(6) At the conclusion of its examination of the accounts the court must certify the result.

Non-compliance by receiver

33.63.–(1) If a receiver appointed under section 48 or 50 of the Proceeds of Crime Act 2002 fails to comply with any rule, practice direction or direction of the Crown Court, the Crown Court may order him to attend a hearing to explain his non-compliance. **B-623**

(2) At the hearing, the Crown Court may make any order it considers appropriate, including–
(a) terminating the appointment of the receiver;
(b) reducing the receiver's remuneration or disallowing it altogether; and
(c) ordering the receiver to pay the costs of any party.

Statements, etc. relevant to making confiscation orders

33.64.–(1) Where a prosecutor or defendant– **B-624**
(a) serves on the magistrates' court officer any statement or other document under section 73 of the Criminal Justice Act 1988 in any proceedings in respect of an offence listed in Schedule 4 to that Act; or
(b) serves on the Crown Court officer any statement or other document under section 11 of the Drug Trafficking Act 1994 or section 73 of the 1988 Act in any proceedings in respect of a drug trafficking offence or in respect of an offence to which Part VI of the 1988 Act applies,

that party must serve a copy as soon as practicable on the defendant or the prosecutor, as the case may be.

(2) Any statement tendered by the prosecutor to the magistrates' court under section 73 of the 1988 Act or to the Crown Court under section 11(1) of the 1994 Act or section 73(1A) of the 1988 Act must include the following particulars—

(a) the name of the defendant;

(b) the name of the person by whom the statement is made and the date on which it was made;

(c) where the statement is not tendered immediately after the defendant has been convicted, the date on which and the place where the relevant conviction occurred; and

(d) such information known to the prosecutor as is relevant to the determination as to whether or not the defendant has benefited from drug trafficking or relevant criminal conduct and to the assessment of the value of any proceeds of drug trafficking or, as the case may be, benefit from relevant criminal conduct.

(3) Where, in accordance with section 11(7) of the 1994 Act or section 73(1C) of the 1988 Act, the defendant indicates in writing the extent to which he or she accepts any allegation contained within the prosecutor's statement, the defendant must serve a copy of that reply on the court officer.

(4) Expressions used in this rule have the same meanings as in the 1994 Act or, where appropriate, the 1988 Act.

Postponed determinations

B-625 **33.65.**—(1) Where an application is made by the defendant or the prosecutor—

(a) to a magistrates' court under section 72A(5)(a) of the Criminal Justice Act 1988 asking the court to exercise its powers under section 72A(4) of that Act; or

(b) to the Crown Court under section 3(5)(a) of the Drug Trafficking Act 1994 asking the court to exercise its powers under section 3(4) of that Act, or under section 72A(5)(a) of the 1988 Act asking the court to exercise its powers under section 72A(4) of the 1988 Act,

the application must be in writing and the applicant must serve a copy on the prosecutor or the defendant, as the case may be.

(2) A party served with a copy of an application under paragraph (1) must, within 28 days of the date of service, notify the applicant and the court officer, in writing, whether or not that party opposes the application, giving reasons for any opposition.

(3) After the expiry of the period referred to in paragraph (2), the court may determine an application under paragraph (1)—

(a) without a hearing; or

(b) at a hearing at which the parties may be represented.

Confiscation orders - revised assessments

B-626 **33.66.**—(1) Where the prosecutor makes an application under section 13, 14 or 15 of the Drug Trafficking Act 1994 or section 74A, 74B or 74C of the Criminal Justice Act 1988, the application must be in writing and a copy must be served on the defendant.

(2) The application must include the following particulars –

(a) the name of the defendant;

(b) the date on which and the place where any relevant conviction occurred;

(c) the date on which and the place where any relevant confiscation order was made or, as the case may be, varied;

(d) the grounds on which the application is made; and

(e) an indication of the evidence available to support the application.

Application to the Crown Court to discharge or vary order to make material available

B-627 **33.67.**—(1) Where an order under section 93H of the Criminal Justice Act 1988 (order to make material available) or section 55 of the Drug Trafficking Act 1994 (order to make material available [§ 15A-240 in the main work]) has been made by the Crown Court, any person affected by it may apply in writing to the court officer for the order to be discharged or varied, and on hearing such an application the court may discharge the order or make such variations to it as the court thinks fit.

(2) Subject to paragraph (3), where a person proposes to make an application under paragraph (1) for the discharge or variation of an order, that person must give a copy of the application, not later than 48 hours before the making of the application—

(a) to a constable at the police station specified in the order; or

(b) to the office of the appropriate officer who made the application, as specified in the order, in either case together with a notice indicating the time and place at which the application for discharge or variation is to be made.

(3) The court may direct that paragraph (2) need not be complied with if satisfied that the person making the application has good reason to seek a discharge or variation of the order as soon as possible and it is not practicable to comply with that paragraph.

(4) In this rule:

"constable" includes a person commissioned by the Commissioners for Her Majesty's Revenue and Customs;

"police station" includes a place for the time being occupied by Her Majesty's Revenue and Customs.

Application to the Crown Court for increase in term of imprisonment in default of payment

33.68.–(1) This rule applies to applications made, or that have effect as made, to the Crown Court under section 10 of the Drug Trafficking Act 1994 and section 75A of the Criminal Justice Act 1988 (interest on sums unpaid under confiscation orders). **B-628**

(2) Notice of an application to which this rule applies to increase the term of imprisonment or detention fixed in default of payment of a confiscation order by a person ("the defendant") must be made by the prosecutor in writing to the court officer.

(3) A notice under paragraph (2) shall–

(a) state the name and address of the defendant;

(b) specify the grounds for the application;

(c) give details of the enforcement measures taken, if any; and

(d) include a copy of the confiscation order.

(4) On receiving a notice under paragraph (2), the court officer must –

(a) forthwith send to the defendant and the magistrates' court required to enforce payment of the confiscation order under section 140(1) of the Powers of Criminal Courts (Sentencing) Act 2000, a copy of the said notice; and

(b) notify in writing the applicant and the defendant of the date, time and place appointed for the hearing of the application.

(5) Where the Crown Court makes an order pursuant to an application mentioned in paragraph (1) above, the court officer must send forthwith a copy of the order–

(a) to the applicant;

(b) to the defendant;

(c) where the defendant is at the time of the making of the order in custody, to the person having custody of him or her; and

(d) to the magistrates' court mentioned in paragraph (4)(a).

Drug trafficking - compensation on acquittal in the Crown Court

33.69. Where the Crown Court cancels a confiscation order under section 22(2) of the Drug Trafficking Act 1994, the Crown Court officer must serve notice to that effect on the High Court officer and on the court officer of the magistrates' court which has responsibility for enforcing the order. **B-629**

Contempt proceedings

Application to punish for contempt of court

33.70.–(1) This rule applies where a person is accused of disobeying– **B-630**

(a) a compliance order made for the purpose of ensuring that a confiscation order is effective;

(b) a restraint order; or

(c) an ancillary order made for the purpose of ensuring that a restraint order is effective.

(2) An applicant who wants the Crown Court to exercise its power to punish that person for contempt of court must comply with the rules in Part 48 (contempt of court).

Criminal Procedure Rules 2020 (SI 2020/759), Pt 34

Appeal to the Crown Court

When this Part applies

34.1.–(1) This Part applies where– **B-631**

(a) a defendant wants to appeal under–

(i) section 108 of the Magistrates' Courts Act 1980,

(ii) section 45 of the Mental Health Act 1983,

(iii) paragraph 10 of Schedule 3 to the Powers of Criminal Courts (Sentencing) Act 2000, or paragraphs 9(8) or 13(5) of Schedule 8 to the Criminal Justice Act 2003, or

(iv) section 42 of the Counter-Terrorism Act 2008;

(b) the Criminal Cases Review Commission refers a defendant's case to the Crown Court under section 11 of the Criminal Appeal Act 1995;

(c) a prosecutor wants to appeal under—
(i) section 14A(5A) of the Football Spectators Act 1989, or
(ii) section 147(3) of the Customs and Excise Management Act 1979; or
(d) a person wants to appeal under—
(i) section 1 of the Magistrates' Courts (Appeals from Binding Over Orders) Act 1956,
(ii) section 12(5) of the Contempt of Court Act 1981,
(iii) regulation 3C or 3H of the Costs in Criminal Cases (General) Regulations 1986,
(iv) section 22 of the Football Spectators Act 1989,
(v) section 10(4) or (5) of the Crime and Disorder Act 1998, or
(vi) section 28(5)(b) of the Offensive Weapons Act 2019

(2) A reference to an "appellant" in this Part is a reference to such a party or person.

Service of appeal and respondent's notices

B-632 **34.2.**—(1) An appellant must serve an appeal notice on—
(a) the magistrates' court officer; and
(b) every other party.

(2) The appellant must serve the appeal notice—
(a) as soon after the decision appealed against as the appellant wants; but
(b) not more than 15 business days after—
(i) sentence or the date sentence is deferred, whichever is earlier, if the appeal is against conviction or against a finding of guilt,
(ii) sentence, if the appeal is against sentence, or
(iii) the order or failure to make an order about which the appellant wants to appeal, in any other case.

(3) The appellant must serve with the appeal notice any application for the following, with reasons—
(a) an extension of the time limit under this rule, if the appeal notice is late;
(b) bail pending appeal, if the appellant is in custody; and
(c) the suspension of any disqualification imposed or order made in the case, where the magistrates' court or the Crown Court can order such a suspension pending appeal.

(4) Where both the magistrates' court and the Crown Court can grant bail or suspend a disqualification or order pending appeal, an application must indicate by which court the appellant wants the application determined.

(5) Where the appeal is against conviction or against a finding of guilt, unless the respondent agrees that the court should allow the appeal—
(a) the respondent must serve a respondent's notice on—
(i) the Crown Court officer; and
(ii) the appellant; and
(b) the respondent must serve that notice not more than 15 business days after service of the appeal notice.

Form of appeal and respondent's notices

B-633 **34.3.**—(1) The appeal notice must—
(a) specify—
(i) the conviction or finding of guilt,
(ii) the sentence, or
(iii) the order, or the failure to make an order, about which the appellant wants to appeal;
(b) summarise the issues;
(c) in an appeal against conviction or against a finding of guilt, to the best of the appellant's ability and to assist the court in fulfilling its duty under rule 3.2 (the court's duty of case management)—
(i) identify the witnesses who gave oral evidence in the magistrates' court,
(ii) identify the witnesses who gave written evidence in the magistrates' court,
(iii) identify the prosecution witnesses whom the appellant will want to question if they are called to give oral evidence in the Crown Court,
(iv) identify the likely defence witnesses,
(v) give notice of any special arrangements or other measures that the appellant thinks are needed for witnesses,
(vi) explain whether the issues in the Crown Court differ from the issues in the magistrates' court, and if so how, and

(vii) say how long the trial lasted in the magistrates' court and how long the appeal is likely to last in the Crown Court;

(d) in an appeal against a sentence, order or failure to make an order–

(i) identify any circumstances, report or other information of which the appellant wants the court to take account, and

(ii) explain the significance of those circumstances or that information to what is in issue;

(e) in an appeal against a finding that the appellant insulted someone or interrupted proceedings in the magistrates' court, attach–

(i) the magistrates' court's written findings of fact, and

(ii) the appellant's response to those findings;

(f) say whether the appellant has asked the magistrates' court to reconsider the case; and

(g) include a list of those on whom the appellant has served the appeal notice.

(2) A respondent's notice must–

(a) give the date on which the respondent was served with the appeal notice; and

(b) to assist the court in fulfilling its duty under rule 3.2–

(i) identify the witnesses who gave oral evidence in the magistrates' court,

(ii) identify the witnesses who gave written evidence in the magistrates' court,

(iii) identify the prosecution witnesses whom the respondent intends to call to give oral evidence in the Crown Court,

(iv) give notice of any special arrangements or other measures that the respondent thinks are needed for witnesses,

(v) explain whether the issues in the Crown Court differ from the issues in the magistrates' court, and if so how, and

(vi) say how long the trial lasted in the magistrates' court and how long the appeal is likely to last in the Crown Court.

(3) Paragraph (4) applies in an appeal against conviction or against a finding of guilt where in the magistrates' court a party to the appeal–

(a) introduced in evidence material to which applies–

(i) Part 16 (Written witness statements),

(ii) Part 19 (Expert evidence),

(iii) Part 20 (Hearsay evidence),

(iv) Part 21 (Evidence of bad character), or

(v) Part 22 (Evidence of a complainant's previous sexual behaviour); or

(b) made an application to which applies–

(i) Part 17 (Witness summonses, warrants and orders),

(ii) Part 18 (Measures to assist a witness or defendant to give evidence), or

(iii) Part 23 (Restriction on cross-examination by a defendant).

(4) If such a party wants to reintroduce that material or to renew that application in the Crown Court that party must include a notice to that effect in the appeal or respondent's notice, as the case may be.

Duty of magistrates' court officer

34.4.–(1) The magistrates' court officer must– B-634

(a) arrange for the magistrates' court to hear as soon as practicable any application to that court under rule 34.2(3)(c) (suspension of disqualification or order pending appeal); and

(b) as soon as practicable notify the Crown Court officer of the service of the appeal notice and make available to that officer–

(i) the appeal notice and any accompanying application served by the appellant,

(ii) details of the parties including their addresses, and

(iii) a copy of each magistrates' court register entry relating to the decision under appeal and to any application for bail or for the suspension of a disqualification or order pending appeal.

(2) Where the appeal is against conviction or against a finding of guilt, the magistrates' court officer must make available to the Crown Court officer as soon as practicable–

(a) all material served on the magistrate's court officer to which applies–

(i) Part 8 (Initial details of the prosecution case),

(ii) Part 16 (Written witness statements),

(iii) Part 17 (Witness summonses, warrants and orders),

(iv) Part 18 (Measures to assist a witness or defendant to give evidence),

(v) Part 19 (Expert evidence),
(vi) Part 20 (Hearsay evidence),
(vii) Part 21 (Evidence of bad character),
(viii) Part 22 (Evidence of a complainant's previous sexual behaviour), or
(ix) Part 23 (Restriction on cross-examination by a defendant);

(b) any case management questionnaire prepared for the purposes of the trial;
(c) all case management directions given by the magistrates' court for the purposes of the trial; and
(d) any other document, object or information for which the Crown Court officer asks.

(3) Where the appeal is against sentence, the magistrates' court officer must make available to the Crown Court officer as soon as practicable any report received for the purposes of sentencing.

(4) Unless the magistrates' court otherwise directs, the magistrates' court officer—

(a) must keep any document or object exhibited in the proceedings in the magistrates' court, or arrange for it to be kept by some other appropriate person, until at least—
(i) 6 weeks after the conclusion of those proceedings, or
(ii) the conclusion of any proceedings in the Crown Court that begin within that 6 weeks; but

(b) need not keep such a document if—
(i) the document that was exhibited is a copy of a document retained by the party who produced it, and
(ii) what was in evidence in the magistrates' court was the content of that document.

Duty of person keeping exhibit

B-635 **34.5.** A person who, under arrangements made by the magistrates' court officer, keeps a document or object exhibited in the proceedings in the magistrates' court must—

(a) keep that exhibit until—
(i) 6 weeks after the conclusion of those proceedings, or
(ii) the conclusion of any proceedings in the Crown Court that begin within that 6 weeks, unless the magistrates' court or the Crown Court otherwise directs; and

(b) provide the Crown Court with any such document or object for which the Crown Court officer asks, within such period as the Crown Court officer may require.

Reference by the Criminal Cases Review Commission

B-636 **34.6.**—(1) The Crown Court officer must, as soon as practicable, serve a reference by the Criminal Cases Review Commission on—

(a) the appellant;
(b) every other party; and
(c) the magistrates' court officer.

(2) The appellant may serve an appeal notice on—

(a) the Crown Court officer; and
(b) every other party,

not more than 15 business days later.

(3) The Crown Court must treat the reference as the appeal notice if the appellant does not serve an appeal notice.

Preparation for appeal

B-637 **34.7.**—(1) The Crown Court may conduct a preparation for appeal hearing (and if necessary more than one such hearing) where—

(a) it is necessary to conduct such a hearing in order to give directions for the effective determination of the appeal; or
(b) such a hearing is required to set ground rules for the conduct of the questioning of a witness or appellant.

(2) Where under rule 34.3(4) a party gives notice to reintroduce material or to renew an application first introduced or made in the magistrates' court—

(a) no other notice or application to the same effect otherwise required by these Rules need be served; and
(b) any objection served by the other party in the magistrates' court is treated as renewed unless within 15 business days that party serves notice withdrawing it.

(3) Paragraphs (4) and (5) apply where—

(a) the appeal is against conviction or against a finding of guilt;

(b) a party wants to introduce material or make an application under a Part of these Rules listed in rule 34.3(3); and

(c) that party gives no notice of reintroduction or renewal under rule 34.3(4) (whether because the conditions for giving such a notice are not met or for any other reason).

(4) Such a party must serve the material, notice or application required by that Part not more than 15 business days after service of the appeal notice.

(5) Subject to paragraph (4), the requirements of that Part apply (for example, as to the form in which a notice must be given or an application made and as to the time and form in which such a notice or application may be opposed).

Hearings and decisions

34.8.–(1) The Crown Court as a general rule must hear in public an appeal or reference to which this Part applies, but– **B-638**

(a) may order any hearing to be in private; and

(b) where a hearing is about a public interest ruling, must hold that hearing in private.

(2) The Crown Court officer must give as much notice as reasonably practicable of every hearing to–

(a) the parties;

(b) any party's custodian; and

(c) any other person whom the Crown Court requires to be notified.

(3) The Crown Court officer must serve every decision on–

(a) the parties;

(b) any other person whom the Crown Court requires to be served; and

(c) the magistrates' court officer and any party's custodian, where the decision determines an appeal.

(4) But where a hearing or decision is about a public interest ruling, the Crown Court officer must not–

(a) give notice of that hearing to; or

(b) serve that decision on,

anyone other than the prosecutor who applied for that ruling, unless the court otherwise directs.

Abandoning an appeal

34.9.–(1) The appellant– **B-639**

(a) may abandon an appeal without the Crown Court's permission, by serving a notice of abandonment on–

(i) the magistrates' court officer,

(ii) the Crown Court officer, and

(iii) every other party

before the hearing of the appeal begins; but

(b) after the hearing of the appeal begins, may only abandon the appeal with the Crown Court's permission.

(2) A notice of abandonment must be signed by or on behalf of the appellant.

(3) Where an appellant who is on bail pending appeal abandons an appeal–

(a) the appellant must surrender to custody as directed by the magistrates' court officer; and

(b) any conditions of bail apply until then.

Court's power to vary requirements under this Part

34.10. The Crown Court may– **B-640**

(a) shorten or extend (even after it has expired) a time limit under this Part;

(b) allow an appellant to vary an appeal notice that that appellant has served;

(c) direct that an appeal notice be served on any person;

(d) allow an appeal notice or a notice of abandonment to be in a different form to one set out in the Practice Direction, or to be presented orally.

Constitution of the Crown Court

34.11. (1) On the hearing of an appeal the general rule is that– **B-641**

(a) the Crown Court must comprise–

(i) a judge of the High Court, a Circuit judge, a Recorder or a qualifying judge advocate, and

(ii) no less than two and no more than four justices of the peace, none of whom took part in the decision under appeal; and

(b) if the appeal is from a youth court, each justice of the peace must be qualified to sit as a member of a youth court

(2) Despite the general rule—

(a) the Crown Court may include only one justice of the peace if—

(i) the presiding judge decides that otherwise the start of the appeal hearing will be delayed unreasonably, or

(ii) one or more of the justices of the peace who started hearing the appeal is absent; and

(b) the Crown Court may comprise only a judge of the High Court, a Circuit judge, a Recorder or a qualifying judge advocate if—

(i) the appeal is against conviction, under section 108 of the Magistrates' Courts Act 1980, and

(ii) the respondent agrees that the court should allow the appeal, under section 48(2) of the Senior Courts Act 1981 [§ 2-114 in the main work].

(3) Before the hearing of an appeal begins and after that hearing ends—

(a) the Crown Court may comprise only a judge of the High Court, a Circuit judge, a Recorder or a qualifying judge advocate; and

(b) so constituted, the court may, among other things, exercise the powers to which apply—

(i) the rules in this Part and in Part 3 (Case management), and

(ii) rule 35.2 (stating a case for the opinion of the High Court, or refusing to do so).

CPD IX Appeal 34A: Appeals to the Crown Court (as amended by Criminal Practice Directions 2015 (Amendment No. 7) [2018] EWCA Crim 1760, Lord Burnett CJ)

B-642 **34A.1** On an appeal against conviction CrimPR 34.3 requires the appellant and respondent to supply information needed for the effective case management of the appeal, but allows the Crown Court to relieve the appellant - not the respondent - of that obligation, in whole or part.

34A.2 The court is most likely to exercise that discretion in an appellant's favour where he or she is not represented and is unable, without assistance, to provide reliable such information. The notes to the standard form of appeal notice invite the appellant to answer the relevant questions in that form to the extent that he or she is able, explaining that while the appellant may not be able to answer all those questions nevertheless any answers that can be given will assist in making arrangements for the hearing of the appeal. Where an appellant uses the prescribed form of easy read appeal notice the court usually should assume that the appellant will not be able to supply case management information, and that form contains no questions corresponding with those in the standard appeal notice. In such a case relevant information will be supplied by the respondent in the respondent's notice and may be gleaned from material obtained from magistrates' court records by Crown Court staff.

CPD IX Appeal 34B: Appeal to the Crown Court: information from the magistrates' court (as inserted by Criminal Practice Directions 2015 (Amendment No. 7) [2018] EWCA Crim 1760, Lord Burnett CJ)

B-643 **34B.1** CrimPR 34.4 applies when a defendant appeals to the Crown Court against conviction or sentence and specifies the information and documentation that must be made available by the magistrates' court.

34B.2 In all cases magistrates' court staff must ensure that Crown Court staff are notified of the appeal as soon as practicable: CrimPR 34.4(2)(b). In most cases Crown Court staff will be able to obtain the other information required by CrimPR 34.4(3) or (4) by direct access to the electronic records created by magistrates' court staff. However, if such access is not available then alternative arrangements must be made for the transfer of such information to Crown Court staff by electronic means. Paper copies of documents should be created and sent only as a last resort.

34B.3 On an appeal against conviction, the reasons given by the magistrates for their decision should not be included with the documents; the appeal hearing is not a review of the magistrates' court's decision but a re-hearing. There is no requirement for the Notice of Appeal form to be redacted in any way; the judge and magistrates presiding over the rehearing will base their decision on the evidence presented during the rehearing itself.

34B.4 On an appeal solely against sentence, the magistrates' court's reasons and factual finding leading to the finding of guilt should be included, but any reasons for the sentence imposed should be omitted as the Crown Court will be conducting a fresh sentencing exercise. Whilst reasons for the sentence imposed are not necessary for the rehearing, the Notice of Appeal form may include references to the sentence that is being appealed. There is no requirement to redact this before the form is given to the judge and magistrates hearing the appeal.

Criminal Procedure Rules 2020 (SI 2020/759), Pt 35

APPEAL TO THE HIGH COURT BY CASE STATED

When this Part applies

35.1.– This Part applies where a person wants to appeal to the High Court by case stated– **B-644**

(a) under section 111 of the Magistrates' Courts Act 1980 [§ 2-108 in the main work], against a decision of a magistrates' court; or

(b) under section 28 of the Senior Courts Act 1981 [ibid., § 7-2], against a decision of the Crown Court.

Application to state a case

35.2.–(1) A party who wants the court to state a case for the opinion of the High Court must– **B-645**

(a) apply in writing, not more than 21 days after the decision against which the applicant wants to appeal; and

(b) serve the application on–

(i) the court officer, and

(ii) each other party.

(2) The application must–

(a) specify the decision in issue;

(b) specify the proposed question or questions of law or jurisdiction on which the opinion of the High Court will be asked; (c) indicate the proposed grounds of appeal; and

(d) include or attach any application for the following, with reasons–

(i) if the application is to the Crown Court, an extension of time within which to apply to state a case,

(ii) bail pending appeal, or

(iii) the suspension of any disqualification imposed in the case, where the court can order such a suspension pending appeal.

(3) A party who wants to make representations about the application must–

(a) serve the representations on–

(i) the court officer, and

(ii) each other party; and

(b) do so not more than 10 business days after service of the application.

(4) The court may determine the application without a hearing.

(5) If the court decides not to state a case, the court officer must serve on each party–

(a) notice of that decision; and

(b) the court's written reasons for that decision, if not more than 15 business days later the applicant asks for those reasons.

Preparation of case stated

35.3–(1) This rule applies where the court decides to state a case for the opinion of the High Court.

(2) The court officer must serve on each party notice of–

(a) the decision to state a case, and

(b) any recognizance ordered by the court.

(3) Unless the court otherwise directs, not more than 15 business days after the court's decision to state a case–

(a) in a magistrates court, the court officer must serve a draft case on each party; or

(b) in the Crown Court, the applicant must serve a draft case on the court officer and each other party.

(4) The draft case must–

(a) specify the decision in issue;

(b) specify the question(s) of law or jurisdiction on which the opinion of the High Court will be asked;

(c) include a succinct summary of–

(i) the nature and history of the proceedings,

(ii) the court's relevant findings of fact, and
(iii) the relevant contentions of the parties; and
(d) if a question is whether there was sufficient evidence on which the court reasonably could reach a finding of fact—
(i) specify that finding, and
(ii) include a summary of the evidence on which the court reached that finding.

(5) Except to the extent that paragraph (4)(d) requires, the draft case must not include an account of the evidence received by the court.

(6) A party who wants to make representations about the content of the draft case, or to propose a revised draft, must—
(a) serve the representations, or revised draft, on—
(i) the court officer, and
(ii) each other party; and
(b) do so not more than 15 business days after service of the draft case.

(7) The court must state the case not more than 15 business days after the time for service of representations under paragraph (6) has expired.

(8) A case stated for the opinion of the High Court must—
(a) comply with paragraphs (4) and (5); and
(b) identify—
(i) the court that stated it, and
(ii) the court office for that court.

(9) The court officer must serve the case stated on each party.

Duty of justices' legal adviser

B-646 **35.4.**—(1) This rule applies—
(a) only in a magistrates' court; and
(b) unless the court—
(i) includes a District Judge (Magistrates' Courts), and
(ii) otherwise directs.

(2) A justices' legal adviser must—
(a) give the court legal advice; and
(b) if the court so requires, assist it by—
(i) preparing and amending the draft case, and
(ii) completing the case stated.

Court's power to vary requirements under this Part

B-647 **35.5.**—(1) The court may shorten or extend (even after it has expired) a time limit under this Part.

(2) A person who wants an extension of time must –
(a) apply when serving the application, representations or draft case for which it is needed; and
(b) explain the delay.

Criminal Procedure Rules 2020 (SI 2020/759), Pt 36

Appeal to the Court of Appeal: General Rules

When this Part applies

B-648 **36.1.**—(1) This Part applies to all the applications, appeals and references to the Court of Appeal to which Parts 37, 38, 39, 40, 41 and 43 apply.

(2) In this Part and in those, unless the context makes it clear that something different is meant "court" means the Court of Appeal or any judge of that court.

Case management in the Court of Appeal

B-649 **36.2.**—(1) The court and the parties have the same duties and powers as under Part 3 (case management).

(2) The Registrar—
(a) must fulfil the duty of active case management under rule 3.2; and
(b) in fulfilling that duty may exercise any of the powers of case management under—
(i) rule 3.5 (the court's general powers of case management),
(ii) rule 3.12(3) (requiring a certificate of readiness), and
(iii) rule 3.13 (requiring a party to identify intentions and anticipated requirements)

subject to the directions of the court.

(3) The Registrar must nominate a case progression officer under rule 3.4.

Power to vary requirements

36.3. The court or the Registrar may— **B-650**

(a) shorten a time limit or extend it (even after it has expired) unless that is inconsistent with other legislation;

(b) allow a party to vary any notice that that party has served;

(c) direct that a notice or application be served on any person; and

(d) allow a notice or application to be in a different form, or presented orally.

Application for extension of time

36.4. A person who wants an extension of time within which to serve a notice or make an application must— **B-651**

(a) apply for that extension of time when serving that notice or making that application; and

(b) give the reasons for the application for an extension of time.

Renewing an application refused by a judge or the Registrar

36.5.—(1) This rule applies where a party with the right to do so wants to renew— **B-652**

(a) to a judge of the Court of Appeal an application refused by the Registrar; or

(b) to the Court of Appeal an application refused by a judge of that court.

(2) That party must—

(a) renew the application in the form set out in the Practice Direction, signed by or on behalf of the applicant; and

(b) serve the renewed application on the Registrar not more than 10 business days after—

(i) the refusal of the application that the applicant wants to renew; or

(ii) the Registrar serves that refusal on the applicant, if the applicant was not present in person or by live link when the original application was refused.

Hearings

36.6.—(1) The general rule is that the Court of Appeal must hear in public— **B-653**

(a) an application, including an application for permission to appeal; and

(b) an appeal or reference,

but it may order any hearing to be in private.

(2) Where a hearing is about a public interest ruling that hearing must be in private unless the court otherwise directs.

(3) Where the appellant wants to appeal against an order restricting public access to a trial the court—

(a) may decide without a hearing—

(i) an application, including an application for permission to appeal, and

(ii) an appeal; but

(b) must announce its decision on such an appeal at a hearing in public.

(4) Where the appellant wants to appeal or to refer a case to the Supreme Court the court—

(a) may decide without a hearing an application—

(i) for permission to appeal or to refer a sentencing case, or

(ii) to refer a point of law; but

(b) must announce its decision on such an application at a hearing in open court.

(5) Where a party wants the court to reopen the determination of an appeal—

(a) the court—

(i) must decide the application without a hearing, as a general rule, but

(ii) may decide the application at a hearing; and

(b) need not announce its decision on such an application at a hearing in public.

such an application at a hearing in public.

(6) A judge of the Court of Appeal and the Registrar may exercise any of their powers—

(a) at a hearing in public or in private; or

(b) without a hearing.

Notice of hearings and decisions

36.7.—(1) The Registrar must give as much notice as reasonably practicable of every hearing to— **B-654**

(a) the parties;

(b) any party's custodian;
(c) any other person whom the court requires to be notified; and
(d) the Crown Court officer, where Parts 37, 38 or 40 apply.

(2) The Registrar must serve every decision on—
(a) the parties;
(b) any other person whom the court requires to be served; and
(c) the Crown Court officer and any party's custodian, where the decision determines an appeal or application for permission to appeal.

(3) But where a hearing or decision is about a public interest ruling, the Registrar must not—
(a) give notice of that hearing to; or
(b) serve that decision on,

anyone other than the prosecutor who applied for that ruling, unless the court otherwise directs.

Duty of Crown Court officer

★B-655 **36.8.**—(1) The Crown Court officer must—
(a) where electronic arrangements have been made to receive and store information and documents for the Crown Court, as soon as practicable ensure that all such material is available to the Registrar in accordance with those arrangements; and
(b) provide the Registrar with any document, object or information for which the Registrar asks, within such period as the Registrar may require.

(2) Where someone may appeal to the Court of Appeal, the Crown Court officer must keep any document or object exhibited in the proceedings in the Crown Court, or arrange for it to be kept by some other appropriate person, until—
(a) 6 weeks after the conclusion of those proceedings; or
(b) the conclusion of any appeal proceedings that begin within that 6 weeks,

unless the court, the Registrar or the Crown Court otherwise directs.

(3) Where Part 37 applies (appeal to the Court of Appeal against ruling at preparatory hearing), the Crown Court officer must as soon as practicable serve on the appellant a transcript or note of—
(a) each order or ruling against which the appellant wants to appeal; and
(b) the decision by the Crown Court judge on any application for permission to appeal.

(4) Where Part 38 applies (appeal to the Court of Appeal against ruling adverse to prosecution), the Crown Court officer must as soon as practicable serve on the appellant a transcript or note of—
(a) each ruling against which the appellant wants to appeal;
(b) the decision by the Crown Court judge on any application for permission to appeal; and
(c) the decision by the Crown Court judge on any request to expedite the appeal.

(5) Where Part 39 applies (appeal to the Court of Appeal about conviction or sentence), the Crown Court officer must as soon as practicable serve on or make available to the Registrar—
(a) any Crown Court judge's certificate that the case is fit for appeal;
(b) the decision on any application at the Crown Court centre for bail pending appeal;
(c) such of the Crown Court case papers as the Registrar requires; and
(d) such transcript of the Crown Court proceedings as the Registrar requires.

(6) Where Part 40 applies (appeal to the Court of Appeal regarding reporting or public access) and an order is made restricting public access to a trial, the Crown Court officer must—
(a) immediately notify the Registrar of that order, if the appellant has given advance notice of intention to appeal; and
(b) as soon as practicable provide the applicant for that order with a transcript or note of the application.

[This rule is printed as amended, with effect from 8 February 2021, by SI 2021/40, r.20.]

Duty of person transcribing proceedings in the Crown Court

B-656 **36.9.** A person who transcribes a recording of proceedings in the Crown Court under arrangements made by the Crown Court officer must provide the Registrar with any transcript for which the Registrar asks within such period as the Registrar may require.

Duty of person keeping exhibit

B-657 **36.10.** A person who under arrangements made by the Crown Court officer keeps a document or object exhibited in the proceedings in the Crown Court must—
(a) keep that exhibit until—
(i) 6 weeks after the conclusion of the Crown Court proceedings, or

(ii) the conclusion of any appeal proceedings that begin within that 6 weeks,
unless the court, the Registrar or the Crown Court otherwise directs; and
(b) provide the Registrar with any such document or object for which the Registrar asks within such period as the Registrar may require.

Registrar's duty to provide copy documents for appeal or reference

36.11. Unless the court otherwise directs, for the purposes of an appeal or reference– **B-658**
(a) the Registrar must–
(i) provide a party with a copy of any document or transcript held by the Registrar for such purposes, or
(ii) allow a party to inspect such a document or transcript on payment by that party of any charge fixed by the Treasury; but
(b) the Registrar must not provide a copy or allow the inspection of–
(i) a document provided only for the court and the Registrar, or
(ii) a transcript of a public interest ruling or of an application for such a ruling.

Declaration of incompatibility with a Convention right

36.12.–(1) This rule applies where a party– **B-659**
(a) wants the court to make a declaration of incompatibility with a Convention right under section 4 of the Human Rights Act 1998 [§ 16-19 in the main work]; or
(b) raises an issue that the Registrar thinks may lead the court to make such a declaration.
(2) The Registrar must serve notice on–
(a) the relevant person named in the list published under section 17(1) of the Crown Proceedings Act 1947; or
(b) the Treasury Solicitor, if it is not clear who is the relevant person.
(3) That notice must include or attach details of–
(a) the legislation affected and the Convention right concerned;
(b) the parties to the appeal; and
(c) any other information or document that the Registrar thinks relevant.
(4) A person who has a right under the 1998 Act to become a party to the appeal must–
(a) serve notice on–
(i) the Registrar, and
(ii) the other parties,
if that person wants to exercise that right; and
(b) in that notice–
(i) indicate the conclusion that that person invites the court to reach on the question of incompatibility, and
(ii) identify each ground for that invitation, concisely outlining the arguments in support.
(5) The court must not make a declaration of incompatibility–
(a) less than 15 business days after the Registrar serves notice under paragraph (2); and
(b) without giving any person who serves a notice under paragraph (4) an opportunity to make representations at a hearing.

Abandoning an appeal

36.13.–(1) This rule applies where an appellant wants to– **B-660**
(a) abandon–
(i) an application to the court for permission to appeal, or
(ii) an appeal; or
(b) reinstate such an application or appeal after abandoning it.
(2) The appellant–
(a) may abandon such an application or appeal without the court's permission by serving a notice of abandonment on–
(i) the Registrar, and
(ii) any respondent
before any hearing of the application or appeal; but
(b) at any such hearing, may only abandon that application or appeal with the court's permission.
(3) A notice of abandonment must be in the form set out in the Practice Direction, signed by or on behalf of the appellant.

(4) On receiving a notice of abandonment the Registrar must—
  (a) date it;
  (b) serve a dated copy on—
    (i) the appellant,
    (ii) the appellant's custodian, if any,
    (iii) the Crown Court officer, and
    (iv) any other person on whom the appellant or the Registrar served the appeal notice; and
  (c) treat the application or appeal as if it had been refused or dismissed by the Court of Appeal.

(5) An appellant who wants to reinstate an application or appeal after abandoning it must—
  (a) apply in writing, with reasons; and
  (b) serve the application on the Registrar.

Abandoning a ground of appeal or opposition

B-661 **36.14.**—(1) If the court gives permission to appeal then unless the court otherwise directs the decision indicates that—
  (a) the appellant has permission to appeal on every ground identified by the appeal notice; and
  (b) the court finds reasonably arguable each ground on which the appellant has permission to appeal.

(2) If the court gives permission to appeal but not on every ground identified by the appeal notice the decision indicates that—
  (a) at the hearing of the appeal the court will not consider representations that address any ground thus excluded from argument; and
  (b) an appellant who wants to rely on such an excluded ground needs the court's permission to do so.

(3) An appellant who wants to rely at the hearing of an appeal on a ground of appeal excluded from argument by a judge of the Court of Appeal when giving permission to appeal must—
  (a) apply for permission to do so, with reasons, and identify each such ground;
  (b) serve the application on—
    (i) the Registrar, and
    (ii) any respondent; and
  (c) serve the application not more than 10 business days after—
    (i) the giving of permission to appeal, or
    (ii) the Registrar serves notice of that decision on the applicant, if the applicant was not present in person or by live link when permission to appeal was given.

(4) Paragraph (5) applies where one of the following Parts applies—
  (a) Part 37 (Appeal to the Court of Appeal against ruling at preparatory hearing);
  (b) Part 38 (Appeal to the Court of Appeal against ruling adverse to prosecution);
  (c) Part 39 (Appeal to the Court of Appeal about conviction or sentence); or
  (d) Part 40 (Appeal to the Court of Appeal about reporting or public access restriction).

(5) An appellant who wants to rely on a ground of appeal not identified by the appeal notice must—
  (a) apply for permission to do so and identify each such ground;
  (b) in respect of each such ground—
    (i) explain why it was not included in the appeal notice, and
    (ii) where Part 39 applies, comply with rule 39.3(2);
  (c) serve the application on—
    (i) the Registrar, and
    (ii) any respondent; and
  (d) serve the application—
    (i) as soon as reasonably practicable, and in any event
    (ii) at the same time as serving any renewed application for permission to appeal which relies on that ground.

(6) Paragraph (7) applies where a party wants to abandon—
  (a) a ground of appeal on which that party has permission to appeal; or
  (b) a ground of opposition identified in a respondent's notice.

(7) Such a party must serve notice on—

(a) the Registrar; and
(b) each other party,
before any hearing at which that ground will be considered by the court.

Reopening the determination of an appeal
36.15.–(1) This rule applies where– B-662
(a) a party wants the court to reopen a decision which determines an appeal or reference to which this Part applies (including a decision on an application for permission to appeal or refer); or
(b) the Registrar refers such a decision to the court for the court to consider reopening it.
(2) Such a party must–
(a) apply in writing for permission to reopen that decision, as soon as practicable after becoming aware of the grounds for doing so; and
(b) serve the application on the Registrar.
(3) The application must–
(a) specify the decision which the applicant wants the court to reopen; and
(b) explain–
(i) why it is necessary for the court to reopen that decision in order to avoid real injustice,
(ii) how the circumstances are exceptional and make it appropriate to reopen the decision notwithstanding the rights and interests of other participants and the importance of finality,
(iii) why there is no alternative effective remedy among any potentially available, and
(iv) any delay in making the application.
(4) The Registrar–
(a) may invite a party's representations on–
(i) an application to reopen a decision, or
(ii) a decision that the Registrar has referred, or intends to refer, to the court; and
(b) must do so if the court so directs.
(5) A party invited to make representations must serve them on the Registrar within such period as the Registrar directs.
(6) The court must not reopen a decision to which this rule applies unless each other party has had an opportunity to make representations.

Criminal Procedure Rules 2020 (SI 2020/759), Pt 37

Appeal to the Court of Appeal Against a Ruling at a Preparatory Hearing

When this Part applies
37.1.–(1) This Part applies where a party wants to appeal under– B-663
(a) section 9(11) of the Criminal Justice Act 1987 [§ 7-309 in the main work] or section 35(1) of the Criminal Procedure and Investigations Act 1996 [ibid., §§ 4-137, 7-313]; or
(b) section 47(1) of the Criminal Justice Act 2003 [ibid., § 4-335].
(2) A reference to an "appellant" in this Part is a reference to such a party.

Service of appeal notice
37.2.–(1) An appellant must serve an appeal notice on– B-664
(a) the Crown Court officer;
(b) the Registrar; and
(c) every party directly affected by the order or ruling against which the appellant wants to appeal.
(2) The appellant must serve the appeal notice not more than 5 business days after–
(a) the order or ruling against which the appellant wants to appeal; or
(b) the Crown Court judge gives or refuses permission to appeal.

Form of appeal notice
37.3.–(1) An appeal notice must be in the form set out in the Practice Direction. ★B-665
(2) The appeal notice must–
(a) specify each order or ruling against which the appellant wants to appeal;
(b) identify each ground of appeal on which the appellant relies, numbering them consecutively (if there is more than one) and concisely outlining each argument in support;

(c) summarise the relevant facts;
(d) identify any relevant authorities;
(e) include or attach any application for the following, with reasons—
(i) permission to appeal, if the appellant needs the court's permission,
(ii) an extension of time within which to serve the appeal notice, and
(iii) a direction to attend in person a hearing that the appellant could attend by live link, if the appellant is in custody;
(f) include a list of those on whom the appellant has served the appeal notice;
(g) attach—
(i) a transcript or note of each order or ruling against which the appellant wants to appeal,
(ii) all relevant skeleton arguments considered by the Crown Court judge,
(iii) any written application for permission to appeal that the appellant made to the Crown Court judge,
(iv) a transcript or note of the decision by the Crown Court judge on any application for permission to appeal, and
(v) any other document or thing that the appellant thinks the court will need to decide the appeal and include or attach an electronic link to each such document that has been made available to the Registrar under rule 36.8(1)(a) (Duty of Crown Court officer); and
(h) include or attach—
(i) an electronic copy of any authority identified under paragraph (2)(d), or
(ii) if two or more such authorities are identified, electronic copies of each together in a single electronic document.

[This rule is printed as amended, with effect from 5 April 2021, by SI 2021/40, r.21(a).]

Crown Court judge's permission to appeal

B-666 **37.4.**—(1) An appellant who wants the Crown Court judge to give permission to appeal must—
(a) apply orally, with reasons, immediately after the order or ruling against which the appellant wants to appeal; or
(b) apply in writing and serve the application on—
(i) the Crown Court officer, and
(ii) every party directly affected by the order or ruling
not more than 2 business days after that order or ruling.

(2) A written application must include the same information (with the necessary adaptations) as an appeal notice.

Respondent's notice

★B-667 **37.5.**—(1) A party on whom an appellant serves an appeal notice may serve a respondent's notice, and must do so if—
(a) that party wants to make representations to the court; or
(b) the court so directs.

(2) Such a party must serve the respondent's notice on—
(a) the appellant;
(b) the Crown Court officer;
(c) the Registrar; and
(d) any other party on whom the appellant served the appeal notice.

(3) Such a party must serve the respondent's notice not more than 5 business days after—
(a) the appellant serves the appeal notice; or
(b) a direction to do so.

(4) The respondent's notice must be in the form set out in the Practice Direction.

(5) The respondent's notice must—
(a) give the date on which the respondent was served with the appeal notice;
(b) identify each ground of opposition on which the respondent relies, numbering them consecutively (if there is more than one), concisely outlining each argument in support and identifying the ground of appeal to which each relates;
(c) summarise any relevant facts not already summarised in the appeal notice;
(d) identify any relevant authorities;
(e) include or attach any application for the following, with reasons—

(i) an extension of time within which to serve the respondent's notice, or
(ii) a direction to attend in person any hearing that the respondent could attend by live link, if the respondent is in custody;

(f) identify any other document or thing that the respondent thinks the court will need to decide the appeal and include or attach an electronic link to each such document that has been made available to the Registrar under rule 36.8(1)(a) (Duty of Crown Court officer); and

(g) include or attach–
(i) an electronic copy of any authority identified under paragraph (5)(d), or
(ii) if two or more such authorities are identified, electronic copies of each together in a single electronic document.

[This rule is printed as amended, with effect from 5 April 2021, by SI 2021/40, r.21(b).]

Powers of Court of Appeal judge

37.6. A judge of the Court of Appeal may give permission to appeal as well as exercising the powers given by other legislation (including these rules). **B-668**

Renewing applications

37.7. Rule 36.5 (renewing an application refused by a judge or the Registrar) applies with a time limit of 5 business days. **B-669**

Right to attend hearing

37.8.–(1) A party who is in custody has a right to attend a hearing in public. **B-670**

(2) The court or the Registrar may direct that such a party is to attend a hearing by live link.

Criminal Procedure Rules 2020 (SI 2020/759), Pt 38

Appeal to the Court of Appeal Against Ruling Adverse to Prosecution

When this Part applies

38.1.–(1) This Part applies where a prosecutor wants to appeal under section 58(2) of the Criminal Justice Act 2003 [§ 7-247 in the main work]. **B-671**

(2) A reference to an "appellant" in this Part is a reference to such a prosecutor.

Decision to appeal

38.2.–(1) An appellant must tell the Crown Court judge of any decision to appeal– **B-672**

(a) immediately after the ruling against which the appellant wants to appeal; or
(b) on the expiry of the time to decide whether to appeal allowed under paragraph (2).

(2) If an appellant wants time to decide whether to appeal–

(a) the appellant must ask the Crown Court judge immediately after the ruling; and
(b) the general rule is that the judge must not require the appellant to decide there and then but instead must allow until the next business day.

Service of appeal notice

38.3.–(1) An appellant must serve an appeal notice on– **B-673**

(a) the Crown Court officer;
(b) the Registrar; and
(c) every defendant directly affected by the ruling against which the appellant wants to appeal.

(2) The appellant must serve the appeal notice not later than–

(a) the next business day after telling the Crown Court judge of the decision to appeal, if the judge expedites the appeal; or
(b) 5 business days after telling the Crown Court judge of that decision, if the judge does not expedite the appeal.

Form of appeal notice

38.4.–(1) An appeal notice must be in the form set out in the Practice Direction. **★B-674**

(2) The appeal notice must–

(a) specify each ruling against which the appellant wants to appeal;
(b) identify each ground of appeal on which the appellant relies, numbering them consecutively (if there is more than one) and concisely outlining each argument in support;
(c) summarise the relevant facts;

(d) identify any relevant authorities;
(e) include or attach any application for the following, with reasons—
(i) permission to appeal, if the appellant needs the court's permission,
(ii) an extension of time within which to serve the appeal notice,
(iii) expedition of the appeal, or revocation of a direction expediting the appeal;
(f) include a list of those on whom the appellant has served the appeal notice;
(g) attach—
(i) a transcript or note of each ruling against which the appellant wants to appeal,
(ii) all relevant skeleton arguments considered by the Crown Court judge,
(iii) any written application for permission to appeal that the appellant made to the Crown Court judge,
(iv) a transcript or note of the decision by the Crown Court judge on any application for permission to appeal,
(v) a transcript or note of the decision by the Crown Court judge on any request to expedite the appeal, and
(vi) any other document or thing that the appellant thinks the court will need to decide the appeal and include or attach an electronic link to each such document that has been made available to the Registrar under rule 36.8(1)(a) (Duty of Crown Court officer);
(h) include or attach—
(i) an electronic copy of any authority identified under paragraph (2)(d), or
(ii) if two or more such authorities are identified, electronic copies of each together in a single electronic document; and
(i) attach a form of respondent's notice for any defendant served with the appeal notice to complete if that defendant wants to do so.

[This rule is printed as amended, with effect from 5 April 2021, by SI 2021/40, r.22(a).]

Crown Court judge's permission to appeal

B-675 **38.5.**—(1) An appellant who wants the Crown Court judge to give permission to appeal must—
(a) apply orally, with reasons, immediately after the ruling against which the appellant wants to appeal; or
(b) apply in writing and serve the application on—
(i) the Crown Court officer, and
(ii) every defendant directly affected by the ruling
on the expiry of the time allowed under rule 38.2 to decide whether to appeal.

(2) A written application must include the same information (with the necessary adaptations) as an appeal notice.

(3) The Crown Court judge must allow every defendant directly affected by the ruling an opportunity to make representations.

(4) The general rule is that the Crown Court judge must decide whether or not to give permission to appeal on the day that the application for permission is made.

Expediting an appeal

B-676 **38.6.**—(1) An appellant who wants the Crown Court judge to expedite an appeal must ask, giving reasons, on telling the judge of the decision to appeal.

(2) The Crown Court judge must allow every defendant directly affected by the ruling an opportunity to make representations.

(3) The Crown Court judge may revoke a direction expediting the appeal unless the appellant has served the appeal notice.

Respondent's notice

★B-677 **38.7.**—(1) A defendant on whom an appellant serves an appeal notice may serve a respondent's notice, and must do so if—
(a) the defendant wants to make representations to the court; or
(b) the court so directs.

(2) Such a defendant must serve the respondent's notice on—
(a) the appellant;
(b) the Crown Court officer;
(c) the Registrar; and

(d) any other defendant on whom the appellant served the appeal notice.

(3) Such a defendant must serve the respondent's notice–

(a) not later than the next business day after–

(i) the appellant serves the appeal notice, or

(ii) a direction to do so

if the Crown Court judge expedites the appeal; or

(b) not more than 5 business days after–

(i) the appellant serves the appeal notice, or

(ii) a direction to do so

if the Crown Court judge does not expedite the appeal.

(4) The respondent's notice must be in the form set out in the Practice Direction.

(5) The respondent's notice must–

(a) give the date on which the respondent was served with the appeal notice;

(b) identify each ground of opposition on which the respondent relies, numbering them consecutively (if there is more than one), concisely outlining each argument in support and identifying the ground of appeal to which each relates;

(c) summarise any relevant facts not already summarised in the appeal notice;

(d) identify any relevant authorities;

(e) include or attach any application for the following, with reasons–

(i) an extension of time within which to serve the respondent's notice, or

(ii) a direction to attend in person any hearing that the respondent could attend by live link, if the respondent is in custody;

(f) identify any other document or thing that the respondent thinks the court will need to decide the appeal and include or attach an electronic link to each such document that has been made available to the Registrar under rule 36.8(1)(a) (Duty of Crown Court officer); and

(g) include or attach–

(i) an electronic copy of any authority identified under paragraph (5)(d), or

(ii) if two or more such authorities are identified, electronic copies of each together in a single electronic document.

[This rule is printed as amended, with effect from 5 April 2021, by SI 2021/40, r.22(b).]

Public interest ruling

38.8.–(1) This rule applies where the appellant wants to appeal against a public interest ruling. **B-678**

(2) The appellant must not serve on any defendant directly affected by the ruling–

(a) any written application to the Crown Court judge for permission to appeal; or

(b) an appeal notice

if the appellant thinks that to do so in effect would reveal something that the appellant thinks ought not be disclosed.

(3) The appellant must not include in an appeal notice–

(a) the material that was the subject of the ruling; or

(b) any indication of what sort of material it is

if the appellant thinks that to do so in effect would reveal something that the appellant thinks ought not be disclosed.

(4) The appellant must serve on the Registrar with the appeal notice an annex–

(a) marked to show that its contents are only for the court and the Registrar;

(b) containing whatever the appellant has omitted from the appeal notice, with reasons; and

(c) if relevant, explaining why the appellant has not served the appeal notice.

(5) Rules 38.5(3) and 38.6(2) do not apply.

Powers of Court of Appeal judge

38.9. A judge of the Court of Appeal may– **B-679**

(a) give permission to appeal;

(b) revoke a Crown Court judge's direction expediting an appeal; and

(c) where an appellant abandons an appeal, order a defendant's acquittal, his release from custody and the payment of his costs,

as well as exercising the powers given by other legislation (including these Rules).

Renewing applications

38.10. Rule 36.5 (renewing an application refused by a judge or the Registrar) applies with a time **B-680**

limit of 5 business days.

Right to attend hearing

B-681 **38.11.**—(1) A respondent who is in custody has a right to attend a hearing in public.

(2) The court or the Registrar may direct that such a respondent is to attend a hearing by live link.

Criminal Procedure Rules 2020 (SI 2020/759), Pt 39

APPEAL TO THE COURT OF APPEAL ABOUT CONVICTION OR SENTENCE

When this Part applies

★B-682 **39.1.**—(1) This Part applies where—

(a) a defendant wants to appeal under—
  (i) Part 1 of the Criminal Appeal Act 1968, or
  (ii) section 274(3) of the Criminal Justice Act 2003;
  (iii) paragraph 14 of Schedule 22 to the Criminal Justice Act 2003;
  (iv) section 42 of the Counter-Terrorism Act 2008;

(b) the Criminal Cases Review Commission refers a case to the Court of Appeal under section 9 of the Criminal Appeal Act 1995;

(c) a prosecutor wants to appeal to the Court of Appeal under section 14A(5A) of the Football Spectators Act 1989;

(d) a party wants to appeal under section 389 of the Sentencing Act 2020;

(e) a person found to be in contempt of court wants to appeal under section 13 of the Administration of Justice Act 1960 and section 18A of the Criminal Appeal Act 1968; or

(f) a person wants to appeal to the Court of Appeal under—
  (i) section 24 of the Serious Crime Act 2007,
  (ii) section 28(5)(a) of the Offensive Weapons Act 2019, or
  (iii) regulation 3C or 3H of the Costs in Criminal Cases (General) Regulations 1986.

(2) A reference to an "appellant" in this Part is a reference to such a party or person.

[This rule is printed as amended, with effect from 8 February 2021, by SI 2021/40, r.23(a).]

Service of appeal notice

B-683 **39.2.**—(1) The appellant must serve an appeal notice on the Registrar—

(a) not more than 28 days after—
  (i) the conviction, verdict, or finding,
  (ii) the sentence,
  (iii) the order (subject to paragraph (b)), or the failure to make an order, or
  (iv) the minimum term review decision under section 274(3) of, or paragraph 14 of Schedule 22 to, the Criminal Justice Act 2003 about which the appellant wants to appeal;

(b) not more than 15 business days after the order in a case in which the appellant appeals against a wasted or third party costs order; and

(c) not more than 20 business days after the Registrar serves notice that the Criminal Cases Review Commission has referred a conviction to the court.

(2) Unless the appeal notice includes grounds of appeal prepared by the person who was appointed to put the case for the defence under rule 25.10 (Defendant unfit to plead), paragraphs (3), (4) and (5) of this rule apply where the appeal is about—

(a) a finding of disability under section 4 of the Criminal Procedure (Insanity) Act 1964;

(b) a finding under section 4A of the 1964 Act that the defendant did the act or made the omission charged as an offence; or

(c) a hospital order, interim hospital order or supervision order made under section 5 or 5A of the 1964 Act.

(3) The Registrar must refer the appeal notice to a judge of the Court of Appeal for the judge to give or refuse to give procedural directions under section 31B of the Criminal Appeal Act 1968.

(4) The judge may—

(a) give such procedural directions as the case requires where the appeal notice includes grounds of appeal that the judge considers reasonably arguable; or

(b) refuse to give such directions, in any other case.

(5) Such procedural directions may include—

(a) a direction for the appointment of a person to put the case for the appellant on appeal;

(b) a direction to commission medical evidence; and
(c) a direction for the reference of the case to the judge again to give, or to refuse to give, further directions.

Form of appeal notice

39.3.–(1) An appeal notice must– **★B-684**

(a) specify–
  (i) the conviction, verdict, or finding,
  (ii) the sentence, or
  (iii) the order, or the failure to make an order
  about which the appellant wants to appeal;
(b) identify each ground of appeal on which the appellant relies (and see paragraph (2));
(c) identify the transcript that the appellant thinks the court will need, if the appellant wants to appeal against a conviction;
(d) identify the relevant sentencing powers of the Crown Court, if sentence is in issue;
(e) include or attach any application for the following, with reasons–
  (i) permission to appeal, if the appellant needs the court's permission,
  (ii) an extension of time within which to serve the appeal notice,
  (iii) bail pending appeal,
  (iv) a direction to attend in person a hearing that the appellant could attend by live link, if the appellant is in custody,
  (v) the introduction of evidence, including hearsay evidence and evidence of bad character,
  (vi) an order requiring a witness to attend court,
  (vii) a direction for special measures for a witness,
  (viii) a direction for special measures for the giving of evidence by the appellant, or
  (ix) the suspension of any disqualification imposed, or order made, in the case, where the Court of Appeal can order such a suspension pending appeal;
(f) identify any other document or thing that the appellant thinks the court will need to decide the appeal and include or attach an electronic link to each such document that has been made available to the Registrar under rule 36.8(1)(a) (Duty of Crown Court officer); and
(g) include or attach–
  (i) an electronic copy of any authority identified by the grounds of appeal (see paragraph (2)(f)), or
  (ii) if two or more such authorities are identified, electronic copies of each together in a single electronic document.

(2) The grounds of appeal must–
(a) include in no more than the first two pages a summary of the grounds that makes what then follows easy to understand;
(b) in each ground of appeal identify the event or decision to which that ground relates;
(c) in each ground of appeal summarise the facts relevant to that ground, but only to the extent necessary to make clear what is in issue;
(d) concisely outline each argument in support of each ground;
(e) number each ground consecutively, if there is more than one;
(f) identify any relevant authority and–
  (i) state the proposition of law that the authority demonstrates, and
  (ii) identify the parts of the authority that support that proposition; and
(g) where the Criminal Cases Review Commission refers a case to the court, explain how each ground of appeal relates (if it does) to the reasons for the reference.

[This rule is printed as amended, with effect from 5 April 2021, by SI 2021/40, r.23(b).]

Crown Court judge's certificate that case is fit for appeal.

39.4.–(1) An appellant who wants the Crown Court judge to certify that a case is fit for appeal must either– **B-685**

(a) apply orally, with reasons, immediately after there occurs–
  (i) the conviction, verdict, or finding,
  (ii) the sentence, or
  (iii) the order, or the failure to make an order
  about which the appellant wants to appeal; or

(b) apply in writing and serve the application on the Crown Court officer not more than 10 business days after that occurred.

(2) A written application must include the same information (with the necessary adaptations) as an appeal notice.

Reference by Criminal Cases Review Commission

B-686 **39.5.**—(1) The Registrar must serve on the appellant a reference by the Criminal Cases Review Commission.

(2) The court must treat that reference as the appeal notice if the appellant does not serve such a notice under rule 39.2.

Respondent's notice

★B-687 **39.6.**—(1) The Registrar—

(a) may serve an appeal notice on any party directly affected by the appeal; and

(b) must do so if the Criminal Cases Review Commission refers a conviction, verdict, finding or sentence to the court.

(2) Such a party may serve a respondent's notice, and must do so if—

(a) that party wants to make representations to the court; or

(b) the court or the Registrar so directs.

(3) Such a party must serve the respondent's notice on—

(a) the appellant;

(b) the Registrar; and

(c) any other party on whom the Registrar served the appeal notice.

(4) Such a party must serve the respondent's notice—

(a) not more than 10 business days after the Registrar serves—

(i) the appeal notice, or

(ii) a direction to do so; or

(b) not more than 20 business days after the Registrar serves notice that the Commission has referred a conviction.

(5) The respondent's notice must be in the form set out in the Practice Direction.

(6) The respondent's notice must—

(a) give the date on which the respondent was served with the appeal notice;

(b) identify each ground of opposition on which the respondent relies, numbering them consecutively (if there is more than one), concisely outlining each argument in support and identifying the ground of appeal to which each relates;

(c) identify the relevant sentencing powers of the Crown Court, if sentence is in issue;

(d) summarise any relevant facts not already summarised in the appeal notice;

(e) identify any relevant authorities;

(f) include or attach any application for the following, with reasons—

(i) an extension of time within which to serve the respondent's notice,

(ii) bail pending appeal,

(iii) a direction to attend in person a hearing that the respondent could attend by live link, if the respondent is in custody,

(iv) the introduction of evidence, including hearsay evidence and evidence of bad character,

(v) an order requiring a witness to attend court, or

(vi) a direction for special measures for a witness;

(g) identify any other document or thing that the respondent thinks the court will need to decide the appeal and include or attach an electronic link to each such document that has been made available to the Registrar under rule 36.8(1)(a) (Duty of Crown Court officer); and

(h) include or attach—

(i) an electronic copy of any authority identified under paragraph (6)(e), or

(ii) if two or more such authorities are identified, electronic copies of each together in a single electronic document.

[This rule is printed as amended, with effect from 5 April 2021, by SI 2021/40, r.23(c).]

Introducing evidence

B-688 **39.7.**—(1) The following Parts apply with such adaptations as the court or the Registrar may direct—

(a) Part 16 (written witness statements);
(b) Part 18 (measures to assist a witness or defendant to give evidence);
(c) Part 19 (expert evidence);
(d) Part 20 (hearsay evidence);
(e) Part 21 (evidence of bad character); and
(f) Part 22 (evidence of a complainant's previous sexual behaviour).

(2) But the general rule is that–
(a) a respondent who opposes an appellant's application or notice to which one of those Parts applies must do so in the respondent's notice, with reasons;
(b) an appellant who opposes a respondent's application or notice to which one of those Parts applies must serve notice, with reasons, on–
(i) the Registrar, and
(ii) the respondent
not more than 10 business days after service of the respondent's notice; and
(c) the court or the Registrar may give directions with or without a hearing.

(3) A party who wants the court to order the production of a document, exhibit or other thing connected with the proceedings must–
(a) identify that item; and
(b) explain–
(i) how it is connected with the proceedings,
(ii) why its production is necessary for the determination of the case, and
(iii) to whom it should be produced (the court, appellant or respondent, or any two or more of them).

(4) A party who wants the court to order a witness to attend to be questioned must–
(a) identify the proposed witness;
(b) explain–
(i) what evidence the proposed witness can give,
(ii) why that evidence is capable of belief,
(iii) if applicable, why that evidence may provide a ground for allowing the appeal,
(iv) on what basis that evidence would have been admissible in the case which is the subject of the application for permission to appeal or appeal, and
(v) why that evidence was not introduced in that case; and
(c) where the court can exercise a power to which Part 18 (Measures to assist a witness or defendant to give evidence) applies, provide any information that the court may need to assess–
(i) the measure or measures likely to maximise so far as practicable the quality of the witness' evidence, and
(ii) the witness' own views.

(5) Where the court orders a witness to attend to be questioned, the witness must attend the hearing of the application for permission to appeal or of the appeal, as applicable, unless the court otherwise directs.

(6) Where the court orders a witness to attend to be questioned before an examiner on the court's behalf, the court must identify the examiner and may give directions about–
(a) the time and place, or times and places, at which that questioning must be carried out;
(b) the manner in which that questioning must be carried out, in particular as to–
(i) the service of any report, statement or questionnaire in preparation for the questioning,
(ii) the sequence in which the parties may ask questions, and
(iii) if more than one witness is to be questioned, the sequence in which those witnesses may be questioned; and
(c) the manner in which, and when, a record of the questioning must be submitted to the court.

(7) Where the court orders the questioning of a witness before an examiner, the court may delegate to that examiner the giving of directions under paragraph (6)(a), (b) and (c).

Application for bail, or to suspend a disqualification or order, pending appeal or retrial

39.8.–(1) This rule applies where– ★B-689
(a) a party wants to make an application to the court about bail pending appeal or retrial; or
(b) an appellant wants to apply to the court to suspend a disqualification or order pending appeal.

(2) That party must serve an application in the form set out in the Practice Direction on—

(a) the Registrar, unless the application is with the appeal notice; and

(b) the other party.

(3) The court must not decide such an application without giving the other party an opportunity to make representations, including, in the case of a bail application, representations about any condition or surety proposed by the applicant.

[This rule is printed as amended, with effect from 8 February 2021, by SI 2021/40, r.23(d).]

Conditions of bail pending appeal or retrial

B-690 **39.9.**—(1) This rule applies where the court grants a party bail pending appeal or retrial subject to any condition that must be met before that party is released.

(2) The court may direct how such a condition must be met.

(3) The Registrar must serve a certificate in the form set out in the Practice Direction recording any such condition and direction on—

(a) that party;

(b) that party's custodian; and

(c) any other person directly affected by any such direction.

(4) A person directly affected by any such direction need not comply with it until the Registrar serves that person with that certificate.

(5) Unless the court otherwise directs, if any such condition or direction requires someone to enter into a recognizance it must be—

(a) in the form set out in the Practice Direction and signed before—

(i) the Registrar,

(ii) the custodian, or

(iii) someone acting with the authority of the Registrar or custodian;

(b) copied immediately to the person who enters into it; and

(c) served immediately by the Registrar on the appellant's custodian or vice versa, as appropriate.

(6) Unless the court otherwise directs, if any such condition or direction requires someone to make a payment, surrender a document or take some other step—

(a) that payment, document or step must be made, surrendered or taken to or before—

(i) the Registrar,

(ii) the custodian, or

(iii) someone acting with the authority of the Registrar or custodian; and

(b) the Registrar or the custodian, as appropriate, must serve immediately on the other a statement that the payment, document or step has been made, surrendered or taken, as appropriate.

(7) The custodian must release the appellant where it appears that any condition ordered by the court has been met.

(8) For the purposes of section 5 of the Bail Act 1976 (record of decision about bail [§ 3-28 in the main work]), the Registrar must keep a copy of—

(a) any certificate served under paragraph (3);

(b) a notice of hearing given under rule 36.7(1); and

(c) a notice of the court's decision served under rule 36.7(2).

(9) Where the court grants bail pending retrial the Registrar must serve on the Crown Court officer copies of the documents kept under paragraph (8).

Forfeiture of a recognizance given as a condition of bail

B-691 **39.10.**—(1) This rule applies where—

(a) the court grants a party bail pending appeal or retrial; and

(b) the bail is subject to a condition that that party provides a surety to guarantee that he will surrender to custody as required; but

(c) that party does not surrender to custody as required.

(2) The Registrar must serve notice on—

(a) the surety; and

(b) the prosecutor

of the hearing at which the court may order the forfeiture of the recognizance given by that surety.

(3) The court must not forfeit a surety's recognizance—

(a) less than 5 business days after the Registrar serves notice under paragraph (2); and

(b) without giving the surety an opportunity to make representations at a hearing.

Right to attend hearing

39.11. A party who is in custody has a right to attend a hearing in public unless— B-692

(a) it is a hearing preliminary or incidental to an appeal, including the hearing of an application for permission to appeal;

(b) it is the hearing of an appeal and the court directs that-

(i) the appeal involves a question of law alone, and

(ii) for that reason the appellant has no permission to attend; or

(c) that party is in custody in consequence of—

(i) a verdict of not guilty by reason of insanity, or

(ii) a finding of disability.

Power to vary determination of appeal against sentence

39.12.—(1) This rule applies where the court decides an appeal affecting sentence in a party's absence. B-693

(2) The court may vary such a decision if it did not take account of something relevant because that party was absent.

(3) A party who wants the court to vary such a decision must—

(a) apply in writing, with reasons; and

(b) serve the application on the Registrar not more than 5 business days after—

(i) the decision, if that party was represented at the appeal hearing, or

(ii) the Registrar serves the decision, if that party was not represented at that hearing.

Directions about re-admission to hospital on dismissal of appeal

39.13.—(1) This rule applies where— B-694

(a) an appellant subject to—

(i) an order under section 37(1) of the Mental Health Act 1983 (detention in hospital on conviction [§ 5A-1189 and 5ASC-1432 in the main work]), or

(ii) an order under section 5(2) of the Criminal Procedure (Insanity) Act 1964 (detention in hospital on finding of insanity or disability [ibid., §§ 4-239, 5A-1222 and 5ASC-1427])

has been released on bail pending appeal; and

(b) the court—

(i) refuses permission to appeal,

(ii) dismisses the appeal, or

(iii) affirms the order under appeal.

(2) The court must give appropriate directions for the appellant's—

(a) re-admission to hospital; and

(b) if necessary, temporary detention pending re-admission.

Renewal or setting aside of order for retrial

39.14.—(1) This rule applies where— B-695

(a) a prosecutor wants a defendant to be arraigned more than 2 months after the court ordered a retrial under section 7 of the Criminal Appeal Act 1968 [ibid., § 7-111]; or

(b) a defendant wants such an order set aside after 2 months have passed since it was made.

(2) That party must apply in writing, with reasons, and serve the application on—

(a) the Registrar; and

(b) the other party.

CPD IX Appeal 39A: Appeals against conviction and sentence—the provision of notice to the prosecution (as amended by Criminal Practice Directions 2015 (Amendment No. 5), unreported, 26 July 2017, Lord Thomas CJ)

39A.1 When an appeal notice served under rule 39.2 is received by the Registrar of Criminal Appeals, the registrar will notify the relevant prosecution authority, giving the case name, reference number and the trial or sentencing court. B-696

39A.2 If the court or the registrar directs, or invites, the prosecution authority to serve a respondent's notice under rule 39.6, prior to the consideration of leave, the registrar will also at that time serve on the prosecution authority the appeal notice containing the grounds of appeal and the transcripts, if available. If the prosecution authority is not directed or invited to serve a respondent's notice but wishes to do so, the authority should request the grounds of appeal and any existing transcript from the Criminal Appeal Office. Any respondent's notice received prior to the consideration of leave will be made available to the single judge.

39A.3 The Registrar of Criminal Appeals will notify the relevant prosecution authority in the event that:

(a) leave to appeal against conviction or sentence is granted by the single judge; or
(b) the single judge or the registrar refers an application for leave to appeal against conviction or sentence to the full court for determination; or
(c) there is to be a renewed application for leave to appeal against sentence only.

If the prosecution authority has not yet been served with the appeal notice and transcript, the registrar will serve these with the notification, and if leave is granted, the registrar will also serve the authority with the comments of the single judge.

39A.4 The prosecution should notify the registrar without delay if they wish to be represented at the hearing. The prosecution should note that the registrar will not delay listing to await a response from the prosecution as to whether they wish to attend. Prosecutors should note that occasionally, for example, where the single judge fixes a hearing date at short notice, the case may be listed very quickly.

39A.5 If the prosecution wishes to be represented at any hearing, the notification should include details of counsel instructed and a time estimate. An application by the prosecution to remove a case from the list for counsel's convenience, or to allow further preparation time, will rarely be granted.

39A.6 There may be occasions when the Court of Appeal ... will grant leave to appeal to an unrepresented applicant and proceed forthwith with the appeal in the absence of the appellant and counsel. The prosecution should not attend any hearing at which the appellant is unrepresented (*Nasteska v The former Yugoslav Republic of Macedonia (Application No.23152/05)*). As a court of review, the Court of Appeal ... would expect the prosecution to have raised any specific matters of relevance with the sentencing judge in the first instance.

39A.7 Where there is a renewed application for leave to appeal against a sentence imposed for an offence involving a fatality, the Crown Prosecution Service has indicated that it wishes to be represented at all sentence appeals in order to ensure that they are in a position, if appropriate, to make representations as to the impact of the offence upon the victim and their family. In those circumstances, if the court is minded to grant the application for leave to appeal the court should consider adjourning the hearing of the appeal to allow prosecution counsel to attend and for the victim's family to be notified and attend if they so wish.

CPD IX Appeal 39B: Listing of appeals against conviction and sentence in the Court of Appeal Criminal Division (CACD)

B-697 **39B.1** Arrangements for the fixing of dates for the hearing of appeals will be made by the Criminal Appeal Office Listing Officer, under the superintendence of the Registrar of Criminal Appeals who may give such directions as he deems necessary.

39B.2 Where possible, regard will be had to an advocate's existing commitments. However, in relation to the listing of appeals, the Court of Appeal takes precedence over all lower courts, including the Crown Court. Wherever practicable, a lower court will have regard to this principle when making arrangements to release an advocate to appear in the Court of Appeal. In case of difficulty the lower court should communicate with the Registrar. In general an advocate's commitment in a lower court will not be regarded as a good reason for failing to accept a date proposed for a hearing in the Court of Appeal.

39B.3 Similarly when the Registrar directs that an appellant should appear by video link, the prison must give precedence to video-links to the Court of Appeal over video-links to the lower courts, including the Crown Court.

39B.4 The copy of the Criminal Appeal Office summary provided to advocates will contain the summary writer's time estimate for the whole hearing including delivery of judgment. It will also contain a time estimate for the judges' reading time of the core material. The listing officer will rely on those estimates, unless the advocate for the appellant or the Crown provides different time estimates to the listing officer, in writing, within 7 days of the receipt of the summary by the advocate. Where the time estimates are considered by an advocate to be inadequate, or where the estimates have been altered because, for example, a ground of appeal has been abandoned, it is the duty of the advocate to inform the court promptly, in which event the Registrar will reconsider the time estimates and inform the parties accordingly.

39B.5 [*Provides for the following target times to run from receipt of an appeal by the listing officer as being ready for hearing: in the case of sentence appeals, 14 days from receipt by listing officer to fixing a hearing date, and 14 days from fixing the date to the date of hearing; in the case of conviction appeals, the corresponding times* *would be 21 and 42 days respectively; and, where a witness is to attend, the times would be 28 and 52 days respectively; where legal vacations impinge on those periods, they might be extended, and where expedition was required they might be abridged; and, for these purposes, "appeal" includes an application for leave to appeal which requires an oral hearing.*]

CPD IX Appeal 39C: Appeal notices containing grounds of appeal (as amended by Criminal Practice Directions 2015 (Amendment No. 1) [2016] EWCA Crim 97, Lord Thomas CJ; Criminal Practice Directions 2015 (Amendment No. 6) [2018] EWCA Crim 516, Lord Burnett CJ; and by Criminal Practice Directions 2015 (Amendment No. 7) [2018] EWCA Crim 1760, Lord Burnett CJ)

39C.1 The requirements for the service of notices of appeal and the time limits for doing so are as set out in Part 39 of the Criminal Procedure Rules. The court must be provided with an appeal notice as a single document which sets out the grounds of appeal. Advocates should not provide the court with an advice addressed to lay or professional clients. Any appeal notice or grounds of appeal served on the court will usually be provided to the respondent. **B-698**

39C.2 Advocates should not settle grounds unless they consider that they are properly arguable. Grounds should be carefully drafted; the court is not assisted by grounds of appeal which are not properly set out and particularised in accordance with CrimPR 39.3. The grounds must:

i. be concise; and
ii. be presented in A4 page size and portrait orientation, in not less than 12 point font and in 1.5 line spacing.

Appellants and advocates should keep in mind the powers of the court and the Registrar to return for revision, within a directed period, grounds that do not comply with the rule or with these directions, including grounds that are so prolix or diffuse as to render them incomprehensible. They should keep in mind also the court's powers to refuse permission to appeal on any ground that is so poorly presented as to render it unarguable and thus to exclude it from consideration by the court: see CrimPR 36.14. Should leave to amend the grounds be granted, it is most unlikely that further grounds will be entertained.

39C.3 Where the appellant wants to appeal against conviction, transcripts must be identified in accordance with CrimPR 39.3(1)(c). This includes specifying the date and time of transcripts in the notice of appeal. Accordingly, the date and time of the summing up should be provided, including both parts of a split summing-up. Where relevant, the date and time of additional transcripts (such as rulings or early directions) should be provided. Similarly, any relevant written materials (such as route to verdict) should be identified.

39C.4 Where the appellant wants to rely on a ground of appeal that is not identified by the appeal notice, an application under CrimPR 36.14(5) is required. In *James and Others* [2018] EWCA Crim 285 the Court of Appeal identified as follows the considerations that obtain and the criteria that the court will apply on any such application:

(a) as a general rule all the grounds of appeal that an appellant wishes to advance should be lodged with the appeal notice, subject to their being perfected on receipt of transcripts from the Registrar.
(b) the application for permission to appeal under section 31 of the Criminal Appeal Act 1968 is an important stage in the process. It may not be treated lightly or its determination in effect ignored merely because fresh representatives would have done or argued things differently to their predecessors. Fresh grounds advanced by fresh representatives must be particularly cogent.
(c) as well as addressing the factors material to the determination of an application for an extension of time within which to renew an application for permission to appeal, if that is required, on an application under CrimPR 36.14(5) the appellant or his or her representatives must address directly the factors which the court is likely to consider relevant when deciding whether to allow the substitution or addition of grounds of appeal. Those factors include (but this list is not exhaustive):
    (i) the extent of the delay in advancing the fresh ground or grounds;
    (ii) the reasons for that delay;
    (iii) whether the facts or issues the subject of the fresh ground were known to the appellant's representatives when they advised on appeal;
    (iv) the interests of justice and the overriding objective in Part 1 of the Criminal Procedure Rules.
(d) on the assumption that an appellant will have received advice on appeal from his or her trial advocate, who will have settled the grounds of appeal in the original appeal notice or who will have advised that there are no reasonably arguable grounds to challenge the safety of the conviction:

(i) fresh representatives should comply with the duty of due diligence explained in *McCook* [2014] EWCA Crim 734. Waiver of privilege by the appellant is very likely to be required.
(ii) once the trial lawyers have responded, the fresh representatives should again consider with great care their duty to the court and whether the proposed fresh grounds should be advanced as reasonably arguable and particularly cogent.
(iii) the Registrar will obtain, before the determination of the application under CrimPR 36.14(5), transcripts relevant to the fresh grounds and, where required, a respondents' notice relating to the fresh grounds.

(e) while an application under CrimPR 36.14(5) will not require "exceptional leave", and hence the demonstration of substantial injustice should it not be granted, the hurdle for the applicant is a high one nonetheless. Representatives should remind themselves of the provisions of paragraph 39C.2 above.
(f) permission to renew out of time an application for permission to appeal is not given unless the applicant can persuade the court that very good reasons exist. If that application to renew out of time is accompanied by an application to vary the grounds of appeal, the hurdle will be higher still.
(g) any application to substitute or add grounds will be considered by a fully constituted court and at a hearing, not on the papers.
(h) on any renewal of an application for permission to appeal accompanied by an application under CrimPR 36.14(5), if the court refuses those applications it has the power to make a loss of time order or an order for costs in line with *Gray and Others* [2014] EWCA Crim 2372. By analogy with *Kirk* [2015] EWCA Crim 1764 (where the court refused an extension of time) the court has the power to order payment of the costs of obtaining the respondent's notice and any additional transcripts.

DIRECT LODGEMENT

Direct Lodgement

B-699 **39C.5** With effect from 1st October 2018, Forms NG and Grounds of Appeal which are covered by Part 39 of the Criminal Procedure Rules (appeal to the Court of Appeal about conviction or sentence) are to be lodged directly with the Criminal Appeal Office and not with the Crown Court where the appellant was convicted or sentenced. This Practice Direction must be read alongside the detailed guidance notes that have been produced to accompany the new forms.

From this date the Crown Court will no longer accept Forms NG and will return them to the sender. Forms NG and Grounds of Appeal should only be lodged once. They should, where possible, be lodged by email. Applications should not be lodged directly onto the Digital Case System. Applications must be lodged at the following address: *criminalappealoffice.applications@hmcts.x.gsi.gov.uk*

If you do not have access to an email account, you should post Form NG and the Grounds of Appeal to:

The Registrar, Criminal Appeal Office, Royal Courts of Justice, Strand, London WC2A 2LL. Once an application has been effectively lodged, the Registrar will confirm receipt within 7 days.

Service

B-700 **39C.6** Legal representatives should make sure they provide their secure email address for the purposes of correspondence and service of document. The date of service for new applications lodged by email will be the day on which it is sent, if that day is a business day and if sent no later than 2:30pm on that day, otherwise the date of service will be on the next business day after it was sent.

Completing the Form NG

B-701 **39C.7** All applications must be compliant with the relevant Criminal Procedure Rules, particularly those in Part 39. A separate Form NG should be completed for each substantive application which is being made. Each application (conviction, sentence and confiscation order) has its own Form NG and must be drafted and lodged as a stand-alone application.

CPD IX Appeal 39D: Respondents' notices

B-702 **39D.1** The requirements for the service of respondents' notices and the time limits for doing so are as set out in CrimPR, Pt 39. Any respondent's notice served should be in accordance with CrimPR 39.6. The court does not require a response to the respondent's notice.

CPD IX Appeal 39E: Loss of time (as substituted by Criminal Practice Directions 2015 (Amendment No. 7) [2018] EWCA Crim 1760, Lord Burnett CJ)

B-703 **39E.1** Both the Court and the single judge have power, in their discretion, under the Criminal

Appeal Act 1968 sections 29 and 31, to direct that part of the time during which an applicant is in custody after lodging his notice of application for leave to appeal should not count towards sentence. When leave to appeal has been refused by the single judge, it is necessary to consider the reasons given by the single judge before making a decision whether to renew the application. Where an application devoid of merit has been refused by the single judge he may indicate that the Full Court should consider making a direction for loss of time on renewal of the application. However, the Full Court may make such a direction whether or not such an indication has been given by the single judge.

39E.2 The case of *Gray & Others* [2014] EWCA Crim 2372 makes clear "that unmeritorious renewal applications took up a wholly disproportionate amount of staff and judicial resources in preparation and hearing time. They also wasted significant sums of public money... The more time the Court of Appeal Office and the judges spent on unmeritorious applications, the longer the waiting times were likely to be....The only means the court has of discouraging unmeritorious applications which waste precious time and resources is by using the powers given to us by Parliament in the Criminal Appeal Act 1968 and the Prosecution of Offenders Act 1985.

39E.3 Further, applicants and counsel are reminded of the warning given by the Court of Appeal in *Hart and Others* [2006] EWCA Crim 3239, [2007] 1 Cr. App. R. 31, [2007] 2 Cr. App. R.(S.) 34 and should 'heed the fact that this court is prepared to exercise its power ... The mere fact that counsel has advised that there are grounds of appeal will not always be a sufficient answer to the question as to whether or not an application has indeed been brought which was totally without merit.'

39E.4 Where the Single Judge has not indicated that the Full Court should consider making a Loss of Time Order because the defendant has already been released, the case of *Terence Nolan* [2017] EWCA Crim 2449 indicates that the Single Judge should consider what, if any, costs have been incurred by the Registrar and the Prosecution and should make directions accordingly. Reference should be made to the relevant Costs Division of the Criminal Practice Direction.

CPD IX Appeal 39F: Skeleton arguments (as amended by Criminal Practice Directions 2015 (Amendment No. 6) [2018] EWCA Crim 516, Lord Burnett CJ and Criminal Practice Directions 2015 (Amendment No. 9) [2019] EWCA Crim 1603, Lord Burnett CJ)

39F.1 Advocates should always ensure that the court, and any other party as appropriate, has a ★B-704
single document containing all of the points that are to be argued. The appeal notice must comply with the requirements of CrimPR 39.3. In cases of an appeal against conviction, advocates must serve a skeleton argument when the appeal notice does not sufficiently outline the grounds of the appeal, particularly in cases where a complex or novel point of law has been raised. In an appeal against sentence it may be helpful for an advocate to serve a skeleton argument when a complex issue is raised."

39F.2 The appellant's skeleton argument, if any, must be served no later than 21 days before the hearing date, and the respondent's skeleton argument, if any, no later than 14 days before the hearing date, unless otherwise directed by the court.

39F.3 Paragraphs XII D.17 to D.23 of these Practice Directions set out the general requirements for skeleton arguments. A skeleton argument, if provided, should contain a numbered list of the points the advocate intends to argue, grouped under each ground of appeal, and stated in no more than one or two sentences. It should be as succinct as possible. Advocates should ensure that the correct Criminal Appeal Office number and the date on which the document was served appear at the beginning of any document and that their names are at the end.

39F.4 A skeleton argument must comply with the requirements of these Practice Directions and, if applicable, of the court. The Criminal Appeal Office may refuse to accept service of a document that fails to comply and instead return that document to the advocate for amendment.

CPD IX Appeal 39G: Criminal Appeal Office summaries

39G.1 To assist the court the Criminal Appeal Office prepares summaries of the cases coming B-705
before it. These are entirely objective and do not contain any advice about how the court should deal with the case or any view about its merits. They consist of two parts.

39G.2 Part I, which is provided to all of the advocates in the case, generally contains (a) particulars of the proceedings in the Crown Court, including representation and details of any co-accused, (b) particulars of the proceedings in the Court of Appeal (Criminal Division), (c) the facts of the case, as drawn from the transcripts, appeal notice, respondent's notice, witness statements and/or the exhibits, (d) the submissions and rulings, summing up and sentencing remarks. Should an advocate not want any factual material in his advice taken into account this should be stated in the advice.

39G.3 The contents of the summary are a matter for the professional judgment of the writer, but an advocate wishing to suggest any significant alteration to Part I should write to the Registrar of Criminal Appeals. If the registrar does not agree, the summary and the letter will be put to the court for decision. The court will not generally be willing to hear oral argument about the content of the summary.

39G.4 Advocates may show Part I of the summary to their professional or lay clients (but to no one else) if they believe it would help to check facts or formulate arguments, but summaries are not to be copied or reproduced without the permission of the Criminal Appeal Office; permission for this will not normally be given in cases involving children or sexual offences or where the Crown Court has made an order restricting reporting.

39G.5 Unless a judge of the High Court or the Registrar of Criminal Appeals gives a direction to the contrary in any particular case involving material of an explicitly salacious or sadistic nature, Part I will also be supplied to appellants who seek to represent themselves before the full court or who renew to the full court their applications for leave to appeal against conviction or sentence.

39G.6 Part II, which is supplied to the court alone, contains (a) a summary of the grounds of appeal and (b) in appeals against sentence (and applications for such leave), summaries of the antecedent histories of the parties and of any relevant pre-sentence, medical or other reports.

39G.7 All of the source material is provided to the court and advocates are able to draw attention to anything in it which may be of particular relevance.

CPD IX Appeal 39H: Criminal Appeal Office bundles & indexes for full court hearings (as inserted by Criminal Practice Directions 2015 (Amendment No. 9) [2019] EWCA Crim 1603, Lord Burnett CJ)

★B-706 **39H.1** To assist the full Court, the Criminal Appeal Office will, in most instances, prepare indexed bundles containing the documents and material which the Registrar considers necessary to understand and determine the appeal for each member of the constitution.

39H.2 The Registrar will not provide bundles where a party or the parties have been directed to prepare and lodge indexed bundles, or where an advocate has lodged indexed bundles of their own volition. Where an appellant who is not privately represented is directed to lodge indexed bundles, a Representation Order will usually be granted by the Court or the Registrar for this purpose.

39H.3 Where bundles are prepared by the Criminal Appeal Office, a copy of the index will be provided to the appellant, or if the appellant is represented, to the advocate. If the advocate or appellant considers that there is additional material which it is necessary to include in the bundle, they must notify the Registrar of this in writing.

39H.4 Where indexed bundles are lodged in response to a direction to do so, or of an advocate's own volition, unless otherwise directed, four copies of the indexed bundle should be lodged with the Registrar in good time before the hearing and in accordance with any direction as to the time by which they should be lodged. The bundles should contain only documents and material which are necessary for the proper understanding of, and determination of, the issues involved in the appeal. The index and order of documents / material in the bundles should follow the order of the Registrar's template *Index to Judge's Bundles* available from the Registrar on request.

Criminal Procedure Rules 2020 (SI 2020/759), Pt 40

Appeal to the Court of Appeal About Reporting or Public Access Restriction

When this Part applies

B-707 **40.1.**—(1) This Part applies where a person directly affected by an order to which section 159(1) of the Criminal Justice Act 1988 [§ 7-323 in the main work] applies wants to appeal against that order.

(2) A reference to an "appellant" in this Part is a reference to such a party.

Service of appeal notice

B-708 **40.2.**—(1) An appellant must serve an appeal notice on—

(a) the Crown Court officer;

(b) the Registrar;

(c) the parties; and

(d) any other person directly affected by the order against which the appellant wants to appeal.

(2) The appellant must serve the appeal notice not later than—

(a) the next business day after an order restricting public access to the trial; or

(b) 10 business days after an order restricting reporting of the trial.

Form of appeal notice

★B-709 **40.3.**—(1) An appeal notice must be in the form set out in the Practice Direction.

(2) The appeal notice must–

(a) specify the order against which the appellant wants to appeal;

(b) identify each ground of appeal on which the appellant relies, numbering them consecutively (if there is more than one) and concisely outlining each argument in support;

(c) summarise the relevant facts;

(d) identify any relevant authorities;

(e) include or attach, with reasons–

(i) an application for permission to appeal,

(ii) any application for an extension of time within which to serve the appeal notice,

(iii) any application for a direction to attend in person a hearing that the appellant could attend by live link, if the appellant is in custody,

(iv) any application for permission to introduce evidence, and

(v) a list of those on whom the appellant has served the appeal notice; and

(f) attach any document or thing that the appellant thinks the court will need to decide the appeal and include or attach an electronic link to each such document that has been made available to the Registrar under rule 36.8(1)(a) (Duty of Crown Court officer); and

(g) include or attach–

(i) an electronic copy of any authority identified under paragraph (2)(d), or

(ii) if two or more such authorities are identified, electronic copies of each together in a single electronic document.

[This rule is printed as amended, with effect from 5 April 2021, by SI 2021/40, r.24(a).]

Advance notice of appeal against order restricting public access

40.4.–(1) This rule applies where the appellant wants to appeal against an order restricting public access to a trial. **B-710**

(2) The appellant may serve advance written notice of intention to appeal against any such order that may be made.

(3) The appellant must serve any such advance notice–

(a) on–

(i) the Crown Court officer,

(ii) the Registrar,

(iii) the parties, and

(iv) any other person who will be directly affected by the order against which the appellant intends to appeal, if it is made; and

(b) not more than 5 business days after the Crown Court officer displays notice of the application for the order.

(4) The advance notice must include the same information (with the necessary adaptations) as an appeal notice.

(5) The court must treat that advance notice as the appeal notice if the order is made.

Duty of applicant for order restricting public access

40.5.–(1) This rule applies where the appellant wants to appeal against an order restricting public access to a trial. **B-711**

(2) The party who applied for the order must serve on the Registrar–

(a) a transcript or note of the application for the order; and

(b) any other document or thing that that party thinks the court will need to decide the appeal.

(3) That party must serve that transcript or note and any such other document or thing as soon as practicable after–

(a) the appellant serves the appeal notice; or

(b) the order, where the appellant served advance notice of intention to appeal.

Respondent's notice on appeal against reporting restriction

40.6.–(1) This rule applies where the appellant wants to appeal against an order restricting the reporting of a trial. **★B-712**

(2) A person on whom an appellant serves an appeal notice may serve a respondent's notice, and must do so if–

(a) that person wants to make representations to the court; or

(b) the court so directs.

(3) Such a person must serve the respondent's notice on–

(a) the appellant;
(b) Crown Court officer;
(c) the Registrar;
(d) the parties; and
(e) any other person on whom the appellant served the appeal notice.

(4) Such a person must serve the respondent's notice not more than 3 business days after—
(a) the appellant serves the appeal notice; or
(b) a direction to do so.

(5) The respondent's notice must be in the form set out in the Practice Direction.

(6) The respondent's notice must—
(a) give the date on which the respondent was served with the appeal notice;
(b) identify each ground of opposition on which the respondent relies, numbering them consecutively (if there is more than one), concisely outlining each argument in support and identifying the ground of appeal to which each relates;
(c) summarise any relevant facts not already summarised in the appeal notice;
(d) identify any relevant authorities;
(e) include or attach any application for the following, with reasons
 (i) an extension of time within which to serve the respondent's notice,
 (ii) a direction to attend in person any hearing that the respondent could attend by live link, if the respondent is in custody,
 (iii) permission to introduce evidence;
(f) identify any other document or thing that the respondent thinks the court will need to decide the appeal and include or attach an electronic link to each such document that has been made available to the Registrar under rule 36.8(1)(a) (Duty of Crown Court officer); and
(g) include or attach—
 (i) an electronic copy of any authority identified under paragraph (6)(d), or
 (ii) if two or more such authorities are identified, electronic copies of each together in a single electronic document.

[This rule is printed as amended, with effect from 5 April 2021, by SI 2021/40, r.24(b).]

Renewing applications

B-713 **40.7.** Rule 36.5 (Renewing an application refused by a judge or the Registrar) applies with a time limit of 5 business days.

Right to introduce evidence

B-714 **40.8.** No person may introduce evidence without the court's permission.

Right to attend hearing

B-715 **40.9.**—(1) A party who is in custody has a right to attend a hearing in public of an appeal against an order restricting the reporting of a trial.

(2) The court or the Registrar may direct that such a party is to attend a hearing by live link.

Criminal Procedure Rules 2020 (SI 2020/759), Pt 41

REFERENCE TO THE COURT OF APPEAL OF POINT OF LAW OR UNDULY LENIENT SENTENCING

When this Part applies

B-716 **41.1.** This Part applies where the Attorney General wants to—
(a) refer a point of law to the Court of Appeal under section 36 of the Criminal Justice Act 1972; or
(b) refer a sentencing case to the Court of Appeal under section 36 of the Criminal Justice Act 1988.

Service of notice of reference and application for permission

B-717 **41.2.**—(1) The Attorney General must serve any notice of reference and any application for permission to refer a sentencing case on—
(a) the Registrar; and
(b) the defendant.

(2) Where the Attorney General refers a point of law—

(a) the Attorney must give the Registrar details of–
(i) the defendant affected,
(ii) the date and place of the relevant Crown Court decision, and
(iii) the relevant verdict and sentencing; and
(b) the Attorney must give the defendant notice that–
(i) the outcome of the reference will not make any difference to the outcome of the trial, and
(ii) the defendant may serve a respondent's notice.

(3) Where the Attorney General applies for permission to refer a sentencing case, the Attorney must give the defendant notice that–
(a) the outcome of the reference may make a difference to that sentencing, and in particular may result in a more severe sentence; and
(b) the defendant may serve a respondent's notice.

(4) The Attorney General must serve an application for permission to refer a sentencing case on the Registrar not more than 28 days after the last of the sentences in that case.

Form of notice of reference and application for permission

41.3.–(1) A notice of reference and an application for permission to refer a sentencing case must give the year and number of that reference or that case. **★B-718**

(2) A notice of reference of a point of law must–
(a) specify the point of law in issue and indicate the opinion that the Attorney General invites the court to give;
(b) identify each ground for that invitation, numbering them consecutively (if there is more than one) and concisely outlining each argument in support;
(c) exclude any reference to the defendant's name and any other reference that may identify the defendant;
(d) summarise the relevant facts; and
(e) identify any relevant authorities.

(3) An application for permission to refer a sentencing case must–
(a) give details of–
(i) the defendant affected,
(ii) the date and place of the relevant Crown Court decision, and
(iii) the relevant verdict and sentencing;
(b) explain why that sentencing appears to the Attorney General unduly lenient, concisely outlining each argument in support; and
(c) include the application for permission to refer the case to the court.

(4) A notice of reference of a sentencing case must–
(a) include the same details and explanation as the application for permission to refer the case;
(b) summarise the relevant facts; and
(c) identify any relevant authorities.

(5) Where the court gives the Attorney General permission to refer a sentencing case, it may treat the application for permission as the notice of reference.

(6) A notice of reference must include or attach–
(a) an electronic link to each material document that has been made available to the Registrar under rule 36.8(1)(a) (Duty of Crown Court officer); and
(b) an electronic copy of any authority identified under paragraph (2)(e) or (4)(c), or if two or more such authorities are identified then electronic copies of each together in a single electronic document.

[This rule is printed as amended, with effect from 5 April 2021, by SI 2021/40, r.25(a).]

[The next paragraph is B-720.]

Respondent's notice

41.4.–(1) A defendant on whom the Attorney General serves a reference or an application for permission to refer a sentencing case may serve a respondent's notice, and must do so if– **★B-720**
(a) the defendant wants to make representations to the court; or
(b) the court so directs.

(2) Such a defendant must serve the respondent's notice on–

(a) the Attorney General; and
(b) the Registrar.

(3) Such a defendant must serve the respondent's notice—
(a) where the Attorney General refers a point of law, not more than 20 business days after—
(i) the Attorney serves the reference, or
(ii) a direction to do so; or
(b) where the Attorney General applies for permission to refer a sentencing case, not more than 10 business days after—
(i) the Attorney serves the application, or
(ii) a direction to do so.

(4) Where the Attorney General refers a point of law, the respondent's notice must—
(a) give the date on which the respondent was served with the notice of reference;
(b) identify each ground of opposition on which the respondent relies, numbering them consecutively (if there is more than one), concisely outlining each argument in support and identifying the Attorney General's ground or reason to which each relates;
(c) summarise any relevant facts not already summarised in the reference;
(d) identify any relevant authorities; and
(e) include or attach any application for the following, with reasons—
(i) an extension of time within which to serve the respondent's notice,
(ii) permission to attend a hearing that the respondent does not have a right to attend, or
(iii) a direction to attend in person a hearing that the respondent could attend by live link, if the respondent is in custody.

(5) Where the Attorney General applies for permission to refer a sentencing case, the respondent's notice must—
(a) give the date on which the respondent was served with the application;
(b) say if the respondent wants to make representations at the hearing of the application or reference; and
(c) include or attach any application for the following, with reasons—
(i) an extension of time within which to serve the respondent's notice,
(ii) permission to attend a hearing that the respondent does not have a right to attend, or
(iii) a direction to attend in person a hearing that the respondent could attend by live link, if the respondent is in custody.

(6) A notice of reference must include or attach—
(a) an electronic link to each material document that has been made available to the Registrar under rule 36.8(1)(a) (Duty of Crown Court officer); and
(b) an electronic copy of any authority identified under paragraph (4)(d), or if two or more such authorities are identified then electronic copies of each together in a single electronic document.

[This rule is printed as amended, with effect from 5 April 2021, by SI 2021/40, r.25(b).]

Variation or withdrawal of notice of reference or application for permission

B-721 **41.5.**—(1) This rule applies where the Attorney General wants to vary or withdraw—
(a) a notice of reference; or
(b) an application for permission to refer a sentencing case.

(2) The Attorney General—
(a) may vary or withdraw the notice or application without the court's permission by serving notice on—
(i) the Registrar, and
(ii) the defendant
before any hearing of the reference or application; but
(b) at any such hearing, may only vary or withdraw that notice or application with the court's permission.

Right to attend hearing

B-722 **41.6.**—(1) A respondent who is in custody has a right to attend a hearing in public unless it is a hearing preliminary or incidental to a reference, including the hearing of an application for permission to refer a sentencing case.

(2) The court or the Registrar may direct that such a respondent is to attend a hearing by live link.

Anonymity of defendant on reference of point of law

B-723 **41.7.** Where the Attorney General refers a point of law, the court must not allow anyone to identify the defendant during the proceedings unless the defendant gives permission.

Criminal Procedure Rules 2020 (SI 2020/759), Pt 42

Appeal to the Court of Appeal in Confiscation and Related Proceedings

General rules

Extension of time

42.1.–(1) An application to extend the time limit for giving notice of application for permission to appeal under Part 2 of the Proceeds of Crime Act 2002 must– **B-724**

(a) be included in the notice of appeal; and

(b) state the grounds for the application.

(2) The parties may not agree to extend any date or time limit set by this Part or by the Proceeds of Crime Act 2002 (Appeals under Part 2) Order 2003 [§§ 5B-256 et seq. in the main work].

Other applications

42.2. Rule 39.3(2)(h) (form of appeal notice) applies in relation to an application– **B-725**

(a) by a party to an appeal under Part 2 of the Proceeds of Crime Act 2002 that, under article 7 of the Proceeds of Crime Act 2002 (Appeals under Part 2) Order 2003, a witness be ordered to attend or that the evidence of a witness be received by the Court of Appeal; or

(b) by the defendant to be given permission by the court to be present at proceedings for which permission is required under article 6 of the 2003 Order,

as it applies in relation to applications under Part I of the Criminal Appeal Act 1968 and the form in which rule 39.3 requires notice to be given may be modified as necessary.

Examination of witness by court

42.3. Rule 36.7 (notice of hearings and decisions) applies in relation to an order of the court under article 7 of the Proceeds of Crime Act 2002 (Appeals under Part 2) Order 2003 to require a person to attend for examination as it applies in relation to such an order of the court under Part I of the Criminal Appeal Act 1968. **B-726**

Supply of documentary and other exhibits

42.4. Rule 36.11 (registrar's duty to provide copy documents for appeal or reference) applies in relation to an appellant or respondent under Part 2 of the Proceeds of Crime Act 2002 as it applies in relation to an appellant and respondent under Part I of the Criminal Appeal Act 1968. **B-727**

Registrar's power to require information from court of trial

42.5. The Registrar may require the Crown Court to provide the Court of Appeal with any assistance or information which it requires for the purposes of exercising its jurisdiction under Part 2 of the Proceeds of Crime Act 2002, the Proceeds of Crime Act 2002 (Appeals under Part 2) Order 2003 or this Part. **B-728**

Hearing by single judge

42.6. Rule 36.6(6) (hearings) applies in relation to a judge exercising any of the powers referred to in article 8 of the Proceeds of Crime Act 2002 (Appeals under Part 2) Order 2003 or the powers in rules 42.12(3) and (4) (respondent's notice), 42.15(2) (notice of appeal) and 42.16(6) (respondent's notice), as it applies in relation to a judge exercising the powers referred to in section 31(2) of the Criminal Appeal Act 1968. **B-729**

Determination by full court

42.7. Rule 36.5 (renewing an application refused by a judge or the Registrar) applies where a single judge has refused an application by a party to exercise in that party's favour any of the powers listed in article 8 of the Proceeds of Crime Act 2002 (Appeals under Part 2) Order 2003, or the power in rule 42.12(3) or (4) as it applies where the judge has refused to exercise the powers referred to in section 31(2) of the Criminal Appeal Act 1968 [ibid., § 7-233]. **B-730**

Notice of determination

42.8.–(1) This rule applies where a single judge or the Court of Appeal has determined an application or appeal under the Proceeds of Crime Act 2002 (Appeals under Part 2) Order 2003 or under Part 2 of the Proceeds of Crime Act 2002. **B-731**

(2) The Registrar must, as soon as practicable, serve notice of the determination on all of the parties to the proceedings.

(3) Where a single judge or the Court of Appeal has disposed of an application for permission to appeal or an appeal under section 31 of the 2002 Act [ibid., § 5B-64], the Registrar must also, as

soon as practicable, serve the order on a court officer of the court of trial and any magistrates' court responsible for enforcing any confiscation order which the Crown Court has made.

Record of proceedings and transcripts

B-732 **42.9.** Rule 5.5 (recording and transcription of proceedings in the Crown Court) and rule 36.9 (duty of person transcribing proceedings in the Crown Court) apply in relation to proceedings in respect of which an appeal lies to the Court of Appeal under Part 2 of the Proceeds of Crime Act 2002 as they apply in relation to proceedings in respect of which an appeal lies to the Court of Appeal under Part I of the Criminal Appeal Act 1968.

Appeal to the Supreme Court

B-733 **42.10.**—(1) An application to the Court of Appeal for permission to appeal to the Supreme Court under Part 2 of the Proceeds of Crime Act 2002 must be made—

(a) orally after the decision of the Court of Appeal from which an appeal lies to the Supreme Court; or

(b) in the form set out in the Practice Direction, in accordance with article 12 of the Proceeds of Crime Act 2002 (Appeals under Part 2) Order 2003 [ibid., § 5B-270] and served on the Registrar.

(2) The application may be abandoned at any time before it is heard by the Court of Appeal by serving notice in writing on the Registrar.

(3) Rule 36.6(6) (hearings) applies in relation to a single judge exercising any of the powers referred to in article 15 of the 2003 Order [ibid., § 5B-273], as it applies in relation to a single judge exercising the powers referred to in section 31(2) of the Criminal Appeal Act 1968.

(4) Rule 36.5 (renewing an application refused by a judge or the Registrar) applies where a single judge has refused an application by a party to exercise in that party's favour any of the powers listed in article 15 of the 2003 Order as they apply where the judge has refused to exercise the powers referred to in section 31(2) of the 1968 Act.

(5) The form in which rule 36.5(2) requires an application to be made may be modified as necessary.

Confiscation: appeal by prosecutor or by person with interest in property

Notice of appeal

B-734 **42.11.**—(1) Where an appellant wishes to apply to the Court of Appeal for permission to appeal under section 31 of the Proceeds of Crime Act 2002 [ibid., § 5B-64], the appellant must serve a notice of appeal in the form set out in the Practice Direction on—

(a) the Crown Court officer; and

(b) the defendant.

(2) When the notice of a prosecutor's appeal about a confiscation order is served on the defendant, it must be accompanied by a respondent's notice in the form set out in the Practice Direction for the defendant to complete and a notice which—

(a) informs the defendant that the result of an appeal could be that the Court of Appeal would increase a confiscation order already imposed, make a confiscation order itself or direct the Crown Court to hold another confiscation hearing;

(b) informs the defendant of any right under article 6 of the Proceeds of Crime Act 2002 (Appeals under Part 2) Order 2003 [ibid., § 5B-261] to be present at the hearing of the appeal, although in custody;

(c) invites the defendant to serve any notice on the Registrar—

  (i) to apply to the Court of Appeal for permission to be present at proceedings for which such permission is required under article 6 of the 2003 Order [ibid., § 5B-261], or

  (ii) to present any argument to the Court of Appeal on the hearing of the application or, if permission is given, the appeal, and whether the defendant wishes to present it in person or by means of a legal representative;

(d) draws to the defendant's attention the effect of rule 42.4 (supply of documentary and other exhibits); and

(e) advises the defendant to consult a solicitor as soon as possible.

(3) The appellant must provide the Crown Court officer with a certificate of service stating that the appellant has served the notice of appeal on the defendant in accordance with paragraph (1) or explaining why it has not been possible to do so.

Respondent's notice

B-735 **42.12.**—(1) This rule applies where a defendant is served with a notice of appeal under rule

42.11.

(2) If the defendant wishes to oppose the application for permission to appeal, the defendant must, not more than 10 business days after service of the notice of appeal, serve on the Registrar and on the appellant a notice in the form set out in the Practice Direction–

(a) stating the date on which the notice of appeal was served;

(b) summarising the defendant's response to the arguments of the appellant; and

(c) specifying the authorities which the defendant intends to cite.

(3) The time for giving notice under this rule may be extended by the Registrar, a single judge or by the Court of Appeal.

(4) Where the Registrar refuses an application under paragraph (3) for the extension of time, the defendant is entitled to have the application determined by a single judge.

(5) Where a single judge refuses an application under paragraph (3) or (4) for the extension of time, the defendant is entitled to have the application determined by the Court of Appeal.

Amendment and abandonment of appeal

42.13.–(1) The appellant may amend a notice of appeal served under rule 42.11 or abandon an appeal under section 31 of the Proceeds of Crime Act 2002– **B-736**

(a) without the permission of the court at any time before the Court of Appeal has begun hearing the appeal; and

(b) with the permission of the court after the Court of Appeal has begun hearing the appeal,

by serving notice in writing on the Registrar.

(2) Where the appellant serves a notice abandoning an appeal under paragraph (1), the appellant must send a copy of it to–

(a) the defendant;

(b) a court officer of the court of trial; and

(c) the magistrates' court responsible for enforcing any confiscation order which the Crown Court has made.

(3) Where the appellant serves a notice amending a notice of appeal under paragraph (1), the appellant must send a copy of it to the defendant.

(4) Where an appeal is abandoned under paragraph (1), the application for permission to appeal or appeal must be treated, for the purposes of section 85 of the 2002 Act (conclusion of proceedings [ibid., § 5B-165]), as having been refused or dismissed by the Court of Appeal.

Appeal about compliance, restraint or receivership order

Permission to appeal

42.14.–(1) Permission to appeal to the Court of Appeal under section 13B, section 43 or section 65 [ibid., §§ 5B-37, 5B-91, 5B-136] of the Proceeds of Crime Act 2002 may only be given where– **B-737**

(a) the Court of Appeal considers that the appeal would have a real prospect of success; or

(b) there is some other compelling reason why the appeal should be heard.

(2) An order giving permission to appeal may limit the issues to be heard and be made subject to conditions.

Notice of appeal

42.15.–(1) Where an appellant wishes to apply to the Court of Appeal for permission to appeal under section 13B, 43 or 65 of the Proceeds of Crime Act 2002 Act, the appellant must serve a notice of appeal in the form set out in the Practice Direction on the Crown Court officer. **B-738**

(2) Unless the Registrar, a single judge or the Court of Appeal directs otherwise, the appellant must serve the notice of appeal, accompanied by a respondent's notice in the form set out in the Practice Direction for the respondent to complete, on–

(a) each respondent;

(b) any person who holds realisable property to which the appeal relates; and

(c) any other person affected by the appeal,

as soon as practicable and in any event not later than 5 business days after the notice of appeal is served on the Crown Court officer.

(3) The appellant must serve the following documents with the notice of appeal–

(a) four additional copies of the notice of appeal for the Court of Appeal;

(b) four copies of any skeleton argument;

(c) one sealed copy and four unsealed copies of any order being appealed;

(d) four copies of any witness statement or affidavit in support of the application for permission to appeal;

(e) four copies of a suitable record of the reasons for judgment of the Crown Court; and

(f) four copies of the bundle of documents used in the Crown Court proceedings from which the appeal lies.

(4) Where it is not possible to serve all of the documents referred to in paragraph (3), the appellant must indicate which documents have not yet been served and the reasons why they are not currently available.

(5) The appellant must provide the Crown Court officer with a certificate of service stating that the notice of appeal has been served on each respondent in accordance with paragraph (2) and including full details of each respondent or explaining why it has not been possible to effect service.

Respondent's notice

B-739 **42.16.**—(1) This rule applies to an appeal under section 13B, 43 or 65 of the Proceeds of Crime Act 2002.

(2) A respondent may serve a respondent's notice on the Registrar.

(3) A respondent who—

(a) is seeking permission to appeal from the Court of Appeal; or

(b) wishes to ask the Court of Appeal to uphold the decision of the Crown Court for reasons different from or additional to those given by the Crown Court,

must serve a respondent's notice on the Registrar.

(4) A respondent's notice must be in the form set out in the Practice Direction and where the respondent seeks permission to appeal to the Court of Appeal it must be requested in the respondent's notice.

(5) A respondent's notice must be served on the Registrar not later than 10 business days after—

(a) the date the respondent is served with notification that the Court of Appeal has given the appellant permission to appeal; or

(b) the date the respondent is served with notification that the application for permission to appeal and the appeal itself are to be heard together.

(6) Unless the Registrar, a single judge or the Court of Appeal directs otherwise, the respondent serving a respondent's notice must serve the notice on the appellant and any other respondent—

(a) as soon as practicable; and

(b) in any event not later than 5 business days,

after it is served on the Registrar.

Amendment and abandonment of appeal

B-740 **42.17.**—(1) The appellant may amend a notice of appeal served under rule 42.15 or abandon an appeal under section 13B, 43 or 65 of the Proceeds of Crime Act 2002—

(a) without the permission of the court at any time before the Court of Appeal has begun hearing the appeal; and

(b) with the permission of the court after the Court of Appeal has begun hearing the appeal,

by serving notice in writing on the Registrar.

(2) Where the appellant serves a notice under paragraph (1), the appellant must send a copy of it to each respondent.

Stay

B-741 **42.18.** Unless the Court of Appeal or the Crown Court orders otherwise, an appeal under section 13B, 43 or 65 of the Proceeds of Crime Act 2002 does not operate as a stay of any order or decision of the Crown Court.

Striking out appeal notices and setting aside or imposing conditions on permission to appeal

B-742 **42.19.**—(1) The Court of Appeal may—

(a) strike out the whole or part of a notice of appeal served under rule 42.15; or

(b) impose or vary conditions upon which an appeal under section 13B, 43 or 65 of the Proceeds of Crime Act 2002 may be brought.

(2) The Court of Appeal may only exercise its powers under paragraph (1) where there is a compelling reason for doing so.

(3) Where a party is present at the hearing at which permission to appeal was given, that party may not subsequently apply for an order that the Court of Appeal exercise its powers under paragraph (1)(b).

Hearing of appeals

B-743 **42.20.**—(1) This rule applies to appeals under section 13B, 43 or 65 of the Proceeds of Crime Act

2002.

(2) Every appeal must be limited to a review of the decision of the Crown Court unless the Court of Appeal considers that in the circumstances of an individual appeal it would be in the interests of justice to hold a re-hearing.

(3) The Court of Appeal may allow an appeal where the decision of the Crown Court was–

(a) wrong; or

(b) unjust because of a serious procedural or other irregularity in the proceedings in the Crown Court.

(4) The Court of Appeal may draw any inference of fact which it considers justified on the evidence.

(5) At the hearing of the appeal a party may not rely on a matter not contained in that party's notice of appeal unless the Court of Appeal gives permission.

Criminal Procedure Rules 2020 (SI 2020/759), Pt 43

Appeal or Reference to the Supreme Court

When this Part applies

43.1.–(1) This Part applies where– **B-744**

(a) a party wants to appeal to the Supreme Court after–

(i) an application to the Court of Appeal to which Part 27 applies (retrial following acquittal), or

(ii) an appeal to the Court of Appeal to which applies Part 37 (appeal to the Court of Appeal against ruling at preparatory hearing), Part 38 (appeal to the Court of Appeal against ruling adverse to prosecution), or Part 39 (appeal to the Court of Appeal about conviction or sentence); or

(b) a party wants to refer a case to the Supreme Court after a reference to the Court of Appeal to which Part 41 applies (reference to the Court of Appeal of point of law or unduly lenient sentencing).

(2) A reference to an "appellant" in this Part is a reference to such a party.

Application for permission or reference

43.2.–(1) An appellant must– **B-745**

(a) apply orally to the Court of Appeal–

(i) for permission to appeal or to refer a sentencing case, or

(ii) to refer a point of law immediately after the court gives the reasons for its decision; or

(b) apply in writing and serve the application on the Registrar and every other party not more than–

(i) 14 days after the court gives the reasons for its decision if that decision was on a sentencing reference to which Part 41 applies (Attorney General's reference of sentencing case), or

(ii) 28 days after the court gives those reasons in any other case.

(2) An application for permission to appeal or to refer a sentencing case must–

(a) identify the point of law of general public importance that the appellant wants the court to certify is involved in the decision; and

(b) give reasons why–

(i) that point of law ought to be considered by the Supreme Court, and

(ii) the court ought to give permission to appeal.

(3) An application to refer a point of law must give reasons why that point ought to be considered by the Supreme Court.

(4) An application must include or attach any application for the following, with reasons–

(a) an extension of time within which to make the application for permission or for a reference, or

(b) bail pending appeal, or

(c) permission to attend any hearing in the Supreme Court, if the appellant is in custody.

(5) A written application must be in the form set out in the Practice Direction.

Determination of detention pending appeal, etc.

43.3. On an application for permission to appeal the Court of Appeal must– **B-746**

(a) decide whether to order the detention of a defendant who would have been liable to be detained but for the decision of the court; and

(b) determine any application for—
(i) bail pending appeal,
(ii) permission to attend any hearing in the Supreme Court, or
(iii) a representation order.

Bail pending appeal

B-747 **43.4.** Rules 39.8 (application for bail pending appeal or retrial), 39.9 (conditions of bail pending appeal or retrial) and 39.10 (forfeiture of a recognizance given as a condition of bail) apply.

Criminal Procedure Rules 2020 (SI 2020/759), Pt 44

Reopening a case in a Magistrates' Court

When this Part applies

B-748 **44.1.** (1) This Part applies in a magistrates' court where—
(a) under section 14 or section 16E of the Magistrates' Courts Act 1980, the defendant makes a statutory declaration of not having found out about the case until after the trial began; or
(b) under section 142 of the 1980 Act, the court can—
(i) set aside a conviction, or
(ii) vary or rescind a costs order, or an order to which Part 31 applies (Behaviour orders).

Statutory declaration of ignorance of proceedings

★B-749 **44.2.** (1) This rule applies where—
(a) the case started with—
(i) an application for a summons,
(ii) a written charge and requisition, or
(iii) a written charge and single justice procedure notice; and
(b) under section 14 or section 16E of the Magistrates' Courts Act 1980, the defendant makes a statutory declaration of not having found out about the case until after the trial began.

(2) The defendant must—
(a) serve such a declaration on the court officer—
(i) not more than 21 days after the date of finding out about the case, or
(ii) with an explanation for the delay, if serving it more than 21 days after that date; and
(b) serve with the declaration one of the following, as appropriate, if the case began with a written charge and single justice procedure notice—
(i) a notice under rule 24.9(4)(a) (notice of guilty plea), with any representations that the defendant wants the court to consider and a statement of the defendant's assets and other financial circumstances, as required by that rule,
(ii) a notice under rule 24.9(4)(b) (notice of intention to plead guilty at a hearing before a court comprising more than one justice), or
(iii) a notice under rule 24.9(4)(c) (notice of intention to plead not guilty).

(3) The court may extend that time limit, even after it has expired—
(a) at a hearing, in public or in private; or
(b) without a hearing.

(4) Where the defendant serves such a declaration, in time or with an extension of time in which to do so, and the case began with a summons or requisition—
(a) the court must treat the summons or requisition and all subsequent proceedings as void (but not the application for the summons or the written charge with which the case began);
(b) if the defendant is present when the declaration is served, the rules in Part 24 (Trial and sentence in a magistrates' court) apply as if the defendant had been required to attend the court on that occasion; and
(c) if the defendant is absent when the declaration is served—
(i) the rules in Part 7 apply (Starting a prosecution in a magistrates' court) as if the prosecutor had just served an application for a summons in the same terms as the original application or written charge;
(ii) the court may exercise its power to issue a summons in accordance with those rules; and
(iii) except for rule 24.8 (Written guilty plea: special rules), the rules in Part 24 then apply.

(5) Where the defendant serves such a declaration, in time or with an extension of time in which to do so, and the case began with a single justice procedure notice—

(a) the court must treat the single justice procedure notice and all subsequent proceedings as void (but not the written charge with which the case began);
(b) rule 24.9 (Single justice procedure: special rules) applies as if the defendant had served the notice required by paragraph (2)(b) of this rule within the time allowed by rule 24.9(4); and
(c) where that notice is under rule 24.9(4)(b) (notice of intention to plead guilty at a hearing before a court comprising more than one justice) or under rule 24.9(4)(c) (notice of intention to plead not guilty), then–
(i) if the defendant is present when the declaration is served, the rules in Part 24 apply as if the defendant had been required to attend the court on that occasion, or
(ii) if the defendant is absent when the declaration is served, paragraph (6) of this rule applies.

(6) Where this paragraph applies, the court must exercise its power to issue a summons and–
(a) the rules in Part 7 apply (Starting a prosecution in a magistrates' court) as if the prosecutor had just served an application for a summons in the same terms as the written charge;
(b) except for rule 24.8 (Written guilty plea: special rules) and rule 24.9 (Single justice procedure: special rules), the rules in Part 24 apply.

(7) A court officer may take the statutory declaration to which this rule refers if that officer–
(a) is a justices' legal adviser; or
(b) is nominated for the purpose by such a legal adviser.

[This rule is printed as amended, with effect from 8 February 2021, by SI 2021/40, r.26.]

Setting aside a conviction or varying a costs, etc. order

44.3. (1) This rule applies where under section 142 of the Magistrates' Courts Act 1980, the court can– **B-750**
(a) set aside a conviction, or
(b) vary or rescind–
(i) a costs order, or
(ii) an order to which Part 31 applies (Behaviour orders).

(2) The court may exercise its power–
(a) on application by a party, or on its own initiative; and
(b) at a hearing, in public or in private, or without a hearing.

(3) The court must not exercise its power in a party's absence unless–
(a) the court makes a decision proposed by that party;
(b) the court makes a decision to which that party has agreed in writing; or
(c) that party has had an opportunity to make representations at a hearing (whether or not that party in fact attends).

(4) A party who wants the court to exercise its power must–
(a) apply in writing as soon as reasonably practicable after the conviction or order that that party wants the court to set aside, vary or rescind;
(b) serve the application on–
(i) the court officer, and
(ii) each other party; and
(c) in the application–
(i) explain why, as appropriate, the conviction should be set aside, or the order varied or rescinded,
(ii) specify any variation of the order that the applicant proposes,
(iii) identify any witness that the defendant wants to call, and any other proposed evidence,
(iv) say whether the defendant waives legal professional privilege, giving any relevant name and date, and
(v) if the application is late, explain why.

(5) The court may–
(a) extend (even after it has expired) the time limit under paragraph (4), unless the court's power to set aside the conviction, or vary the order, can no longer be exercised; and
(b) allow an application to be made orally.

CPD IX Appeal 44A: References to the European Court of Justice

44A.1 Further to rule 44.3 of the Criminal Procedure Rules, the order containing the reference shall be filed with the Senior Master of the Queen's Bench Division of the High Court for onward **B-751**

transmission to the Court of Justice of the European Union. The order should be marked for the attention of Mrs Isaac and sent to the Senior Master, c/o Queen's Bench Division Associates Dept, Room WG03, Royal Courts of Justice, Strand, London, WC2A 2LL.

44A.2 There is no longer a requirement that the relevant court file be sent to the Senior Master. The parties should ensure that all appropriate documentation is sent directly to the European Court at the following address: The Registrar, Court of Justice of the European Union, Kirchberg, L-2925 Luxemburg.

44A.3 There is no prescribed form for use but the following details must be included in the back sheet to the order: (i) solicitor's full address; (ii) solicitor's and court references; (iii) solicitor's e-mail address.

44A.4 The European Court of Justice regularly updates its recommendation to national courts and tribunals in relation to the initiation of preliminary ruling proceedings. The current recommendation is 2012/C338/01: *http://eurlex.europa.eu/LexUriServ/LexUriServ.do?uri=OJ:C:2012:338:0001: 0006:EN:PDF.*

44A.5 The referring court may request the Court of Justice of the European Union to apply its urgent preliminary ruling procedure where the referring court's proceedings relate to a person in custody. For further information see Council Decision 2008/79/EC [2008] OJ L24/42: *http://eurlex.europa.eu/LexUriServ/LexUriServ.do?uri=OJ:L:2008:024:0042:0043:EN:PDF.*

44A.6 Any such request must be made in a document separate from the order or in a covering letter and must set out: (i) the matters of fact and law which establish the urgency; (ii) the reasons why the urgent preliminary ruling procedure applies; and (iii) in so far as possible, the court's view on the answer to the question referred to the Court of Justice of the European Union for a preliminary ruling.

44A.7 Any request to apply the urgent preliminary ruling procedure should be filed with the Senior Master as described above.

Criminal Procedure Rules 2020 (SI 2020/759), Pt 45

General

Costs

When this Part applies

B-752 **45.1.**—(1) This Part applies where the court can make an order about costs under—

- (a) Part II of the Prosecution of Offences Act 1985 and Part II, IIA or IIB of the Costs in Criminal Cases (General) Regulations 1986;
- (b) section 109 of the Magistrates' Courts Act 1980;
- (c) section 52 of the Senior Courts Act 1981 and rule 45.6 or rule 45.7;
- (d) section 8 of the Bankers Books Evidence Act 1879;
- (e) section 2C(8) of the Criminal Procedure (Attendance of Witnesses) Act 1965;
- (f) section 36(5) of the Criminal Justice Act 1972;
- (g) section 159(5) and Schedule 3, paragraph 11, of the Criminal Justice Act 1988;
- (h) section 14H(5) of the Football Spectators Act 1989;
- (i) section 4(7) of the Dangerous Dogs Act 1991;
- (j) Part 3 of the Serious Crime Act 2007 (Appeals under Section 24) Order 2008; or
- (k) Part 1 or 2 of the Extradition Act 2003.

(2) In this Part, "costs" means—

- (a) the fees payable to a legal representative;
- (b) the disbursements paid by a legal representative; and
- (c) any other expenses incurred in connection with the case.

Costs orders: general rules

B-753 **45.2.**—(1) The court must not make an order about costs unless each party and any other person directly affected—

- (a) is present; or
- (b) has had an opportunity—
  - (i) to attend, or
  - (ii) to make representations.

(2) The court may make an order about costs—

- (a) at a hearing in public or in private; or
- (b) without a hearing.

(3) In deciding what order, if any, to make about costs, the court must have regard to all the circumstances, including–
(a) the conduct of all the parties; and
(b) any costs order already made.
(4) If the court makes an order about costs, it must–
(a) specify who must, or must not, pay what, to whom; and
(b) identify the legislation under which the order is made, where there is a choice of powers.
(5) The court must give reasons if it–
(a) refuses an application for a costs order; or
(b) rejects representations opposing a costs order.
(6) If the court makes an order for the payment of costs–
(a) the general rule is that it must be for an amount that is sufficient reasonably to compensate the recipient for costs–
(i) actually, reasonably and properly incurred, and
(ii) reasonable in amount; but
(b) the court may order the payment of–
(i) a proportion of that amount,
(ii) a stated amount less than that amount,
(iii) costs from or until a certain date only,
(iv) costs relating only to particular steps taken, or
(v) costs relating only to a distinct part of the case.
(7) On an assessment of the amount of costs, relevant factors include–
(a) the conduct of all the parties;
(b) the particular complexity of the matter or the difficulty or novelty of the questions raised;
(c) the skill, effort, specialised knowledge and responsibility involved;
(d) the time spent on the case;
(e) the place where and the circumstances in which work or any part of it was done; and
(f) any direction or observations by the court that made the costs order.
(8) If the court orders a party to pay costs to be assessed under rule 45.11, it may order that party to pay an amount on account.
(9) An order for the payment of costs takes effect when the amount is assessed, unless the court exercises any power it has to order otherwise.

Court's power to vary requirements under Sections 2, 3 and 4

45.3.–(1) Unless other legislation provides, the court may– **B-754**
(a) extend a time limit for serving an application or representations under rules 45.4 to 45.10, even after it has expired; and
(b) consider an application or representations–
(i) made in a different form to one set out in the Practice Direction, or
(ii) made orally instead of in writing.
(2) A person who wants an extension of time must–
(a) apply when serving the application or representations for which it is needed; and
(b) explain the delay.

Costs out of central funds

Costs out of central funds

45.4.–(1) This rule applies where the court can order the payment of costs out of central funds. **B-755**
(2) In this rule, costs–
(a) include–
(i) on an appeal, costs incurred in the court that made the decision under appeal, and
(ii) at a retrial, costs incurred at the initial trial and on any appeal; but
(b) do not include costs met by legal aid.
(3) The court may make an order–
(a) on application by the person who incurred the costs; or
(b) on its own initiative.
(4) Where a person wants the court to make an order that person must apply as soon as practicable and–
(a) outline the type of costs and the amount claimed, if that person wants the court to direct an assessment; or

(b) specify the amount claimed, if that person wants the court to assess the amount itself.

(5) The general rule is that the court must make an order, but—

(a) the court may decline to make a defendant's costs order if, for example—

(i) the defendant is convicted of at least one offence, or

(ii) the defendant's conduct led the prosecutor reasonably to think the prosecution case stronger than it was; and

(b) the court may decline to make a prosecutor's costs order if, for example, the prosecution was started or continued unreasonably.

(6) If the court makes an order—

(a) the court may direct an assessment under, as applicable—

(i) Part III of the Costs in Criminal Cases (General) Regulations 1986, or

(ii) Part 3 of the Serious Crime Act 2007 (Appeals under Section 24) Order 2008;

(b) the court may assess the amount itself in a case in which either—

(i) the recipient agrees the amount, or

(ii) the court decides to allow a lesser sum than that which is reasonably sufficient to compensate the recipient for expenses properly incurred in the proceedings; and

(c) an order for the payment of a defendant's costs which includes an amount in respect of fees payable to a legal representative, or disbursements paid by a legal representative, must include a statement to that effect.

(7) If the court directs an assessment, the order must specify any restriction on the amount to be paid that the court considers appropriate.

(8) If the court assesses the amount itself, it must do so subject to any restriction on the amount to be paid that is imposed by regulations made by the Lord Chancellor.

Payment of costs by one party to another

Costs on conviction and sentence, etc.

B-756 **45.5.**—(1) This rule applies where the court can order a defendant to pay the prosecutor's costs if the defendant is—

(a) convicted or found guilty;

(b) dealt with in the Crown Court after committal for sentence there;

(c) dealt with for breach of a sentence; or

(d) in an extradition case—

(i) ordered to be extradited, under Part 1 of the Extradition Act 2003, or

(ii) sent for extradition to the Secretary of State, under Part 2 of that Act, or

(iii) unsuccessful on an appeal by the defendant to the High Court, or on an application by the defendant for permission to appeal from the High Court to the Supreme Court.

(2) The court may make an order—

(a) on application by the prosecutor; or

(b) on its own initiative.

(3) Where the prosecutor wants the court to make an order—

(a) the prosecutor must—

(i) apply as soon as practicable, and

(ii) specify the amount claimed; and

(b) the general rule is that the court must make an order if it is satisfied that the defendant can pay.

(4) A defendant who wants to oppose an order must make representations as soon as practicable.

(5) If the court makes an order, it must assess the amount itself.

Costs on appeal

B-757 **45.6.**—(1) This rule—

(a) applies where a magistrates' court, the Crown Court or the Court of Appeal can order a party to pay another person's costs on an appeal, or an application for permission to appeal; and

(b) authorises the Crown Court, in addition to its other powers, to order a party to pay another party's costs on an appeal to that court, except on an appeal under—

(i) section 108 of the Magistrates' Courts Act 1980, or

(ii) section 45 of the Mental Health Act 1983.

(2) In this rule, costs include–
(a) costs incurred in the court that made the decision under appeal; and
(b) costs met by legal aid.
(3) The court may make an order–
(a) on application by the person who incurred the costs; or
(b) on its own initiative.
(4) A person who wants the court to make an order must–
(a) apply as soon as practicable;
(b) notify each other party;
(c) specify–
(i) the amount claimed, and
(ii) against whom; and
(d) where an appellant abandons an appeal to the Crown Court by serving a notice of abandonment–
(i) apply in writing not more than 10 business days later, and
(ii) serve the application on the appellant and on the Crown Court officer.
(5) A party who wants to oppose an order must–
(a) make representations as soon as practicable; and
(b) where the application was under paragraph (4)(d), serve representations on the applicant, and on the Crown Court officer, not more than 5 business days after it was served.
(6) Where the application was under paragraph (4)(d), the Crown Court officer may–
(a) submit it to the Crown Court; or
(b) serve it on the magistrates' court officer, for submission to the magistrates' court.
(7) If the court makes an order, it may direct an assessment under rule 45.11, or assess the amount itself where–
(a) the appellant abandons an appeal to the Crown Court;
(b) the Crown Court decides an appeal, except an appeal under–
(i) section 108 of the Magistrates' Courts Act 1980, or
(ii) section 45 of the Mental Health Act 1983; or
(c) the Court of Appeal decides an appeal to which Part 40 applies (appeal to the Court of Appeal regarding reporting or public access restriction).
(8) If the court makes an order in any other case, it must assess the amount itself.

Costs on an application
45.7.–(1) This rule– **B-758**
(a) applies where the court can order a party to pay another person's costs in a case in which–
(i) the court decides an application for the production in evidence of a copy of a bank record,
(ii) a magistrates' court or the Crown Court decides an application to terminate a football banning order,
(iii) a magistrates' court or the Crown Court decides an application to terminate a disqualification for having custody of a dog,
(iv) the Crown Court allows an application to withdraw a witness summons, or
(v) the Crown Court decides an application relating to a deferred prosecution agreement under rule 11.5 (breach), rule 11.6 (variation) or rule 11.7 (lifting suspension of prosecution); and
(b) authorises the Crown Court, in addition to its other powers, to order a party to pay another party's costs on an application to that court under rule 11.5, 11.6 or 11.7.
(2) The court may make an order–
(a) on application by the person who incurred the costs; or
(b) on its own initiative.
(3) A person who wants the court to make an order must–
(a) apply as soon as practicable;
(b) notify each other party; and
(c) specify–
(i) the amount claimed, and
(ii) against whom.
(4) A party who wants to oppose an order must make representations as soon as practicable.

(5) If the court makes an order, it may direct an assessment under rule 45.11, or assess the amount itself.

Costs resulting from unnecessary or improper act, etc.

B-759 **45.8.**—(1) This rule applies where the court can order a party to pay another party's costs incurred as a result of an unnecessary or improper act or omission by or on behalf of the first party.

(2) In this rule, costs include costs met by legal aid.

(3) The court may make an order—

(a) on application by the party who incurred such costs; or

(b) on its own initiative.

(4) A party who wants the court to make an order must—

(a) apply in writing as soon as practicable after becoming aware of the grounds for doing so, and in any event no later than the end of the case;

(b) serve the application on—

(i) the court officer (or, in the Court of Appeal, the Registrar), and

(ii) each other party; and

(c) in that application specify—

(i) the party by whom costs should be paid,

(ii) the relevant act or omission,

(iii) the reasons why that act or omission meets the criteria for making an order,

(iv) the amount claimed, and

(v) those on whom the application has been served.

(5) Where the court considers making an order on its own initiative, it must—

(a) identify the party against whom it proposes making the order; and

(b) specify—

(i) the relevant act or omission,

(ii) the reasons why that act or omission meets the criteria for making an order, and

(iii) with the assistance of the party who incurred the costs, the amount involved.

(6) A party who wants to oppose an order must—

(a) make representations as soon as practicable; and

(b) in reply to an application, serve representations on the applicant and on the court officer (or Registrar) not more than 5 business days after it was served.

(7) If the court makes an order, it must assess the amount itself.

(8) To help assess the amount, the court may direct an enquiry by—

(a) the Lord Chancellor, where the assessment is by a magistrates' court or by the Crown Court; or

(b) the Registrar, where the assessment is by the Court of Appeal.

(9) In deciding whether to direct such an enquiry, the court must have regard to all the circumstances including—

(a) any agreement between the parties about the amount to be paid;

(b) the amount likely to be allowed;

(c) the delay and expense that may be incurred in the conduct of the enquiry; and

(d) the particular complexity of the assessment, or the difficulty or novelty of any aspect of the assessment.

(10) If the court directs such an enquiry—

(a) paragraphs (3) to (8) inclusive of rule 45.11 (assessment and re-assessment) apply as if that enquiry were an assessment under that rule (but rules 45.12 (appeal to a costs judge) and 45.13 (appeal to a High Court judge) do not apply);

(b) the authority that carries out the enquiry must serve its conclusions on the court officer as soon as reasonably practicable after following that procedure; and

(c) the court must then assess the amount to be paid.

Other costs orders

Costs against a legal representative

B-760 **45.9.**—(1) This rule applies where—

(a) a party has incurred costs—

(i) as a result of an improper, unreasonable or negligent act or omission by a legal or other representative or representative's employee, or

(ii) which it has become unreasonable for that party to have to pay because of such an act or omission occurring after those costs were incurred; and
(b) the court can–
(i) order the representative responsible to pay such costs, or
(ii) prohibit the payment of costs to that representative.
(2) In this rule, costs include costs met by legal aid.
(3) The court may make an order–
(a) on application by the person who incurred the costs; or
(b) on its own initiative.
(4) A party who wants the court to make an order must–
(a) apply in writing as soon as practicable after becoming aware of the grounds for doing so, and in any event no later than the end of the case;
(b) serve the application on–
(i) the court officer (or, in the Court of Appeal, the Registrar),
(ii) the representative responsible,
(iii) each other party, and
(iv) any other person directly affected; and
(c) in that application specify–
(i) the representative responsible,
(ii) the relevant act or omission,
(iii) the reasons why that act or omission meets the criteria for making an order,
(iv) the amount claimed, and
(v) those on whom the application has been served.
(5) Where the court considers making an order on its own initiative, it must–
(a) identify the representative against whom it proposes making that order; and
(b) specify–
(i) the relevant act or omission,
(ii) the reasons why that act or omission meets the criteria for making an order, and
(iii) with the assistance of the party who incurred the costs, the amount involved.
(6) A representative who wants to oppose an order must–
(a) [*identical to r.45.8(6)(a),B-759*];
(b) [*identical to r.45.8(6)(b), B-759*].
(7) If the court makes an order–
(a) the general rule is that it must do so without waiting until the end of the case, but it may postpone making the order; and
(b) it must assess the amount itself.
(8)-(10) [*Identical to r.45.8(8)-(10),B-759.*]
(11) Instead of making an order, the court may make adverse observations about the representative's conduct for use in an assessment where–
(a) a party's costs are–
(i) to be met by legal aid, or
(ii) to be paid out of central funds; or
(b) there is to be an assessment under rule 45.11.

Costs against a third party

45.10.–(1) This rule applies where– B-761
(a) there has been serious misconduct by a person who is not a party; and
(b) the court can order that person to pay a party's costs.
(2) In this rule, costs include costs met by legal aid.
(3) The court may make an order–
(a) on application by the person who incurred the costs; or
(b) on its own initiative.
(4) A party who wants the court to make an order must–
(a) apply in writing as soon as practicable after becoming aware of the grounds for doing so;
(b) serve the application on–
(i) the court officer (or, in the Court of Appeal, the Registrar),
(ii) the person responsible,
(iii) each other party, and

(iv) any other person directly affected; and
(c) in that application specify—
(i) the person responsible,
(ii) the relevant misconduct,
(iii) the reasons why the criteria for making an order are met,
(iv) the amount claimed, and
(v) those on whom the application has been served.
(5) Where the court considers making an order on its own initiative, it must—
(a) identify the person against whom it proposes making that order; and
(b) specify—
(i) the relevant misconduct,
(ii) the reasons why the criteria for making an order are met, and
(iii) with the assistance of the party who incurred the costs, the amount involved.
(6) A person who wants to oppose an order must—
(a) [*identical to r.45.8(6)(a),B-759*];
(b) [*identical to r.45.8(6)(b), B-759*].
(7) If the court makes an order—
(a) the general rule is that it must do so at the end of the case, but it may do so earlier; and
(b) it must assess the amount itself.
(8)-(10) [*Identical to r.45.8(8)-(10),B-759*].

Assessment of costs

Assessment and re-assessment

B-762 **45.11.**—(1) This rule applies where the court directs an assessment under—
(a) rule 33.48 (confiscation and related proceedings - restraint and receivership proceedings: rules that apply generally - assessment of costs);
(b) rule 45.6 (costs on appeal); or
(c) rule 45.7 (costs on an application).
(2) The assessment must be carried out by the relevant assessing authority, namely—
(a) the Lord Chancellor, where the direction was given by a magistrates' court or by the Crown Court; or
(b) the Registrar of Criminal Appeals, where the direction was given by the Court of Appeal.
(3) The party in whose favour the court made the costs order ("the applicant") must—
(a) apply for an assessment—
(i) in writing, in any form required by the assessing authority, and
(ii) not more than 3 months after the costs order; and
(b) serve the application on—
(i) the assessing authority, and
(ii) the party against whom the court made the costs order ("the respondent").
(4) The applicant must—
(a) summarise the work done;
(b) specify—
(i) each item of work done, giving the date, time taken and amount claimed,
(ii) any disbursements or expenses, including the fees of any advocate, and
(iii) any circumstances of which the applicant wants the assessing authority to take particular account; and
(c) supply—
(i) receipts or other evidence of the amount claimed, and
(ii) any other information or document for which the assessing authority asks, within such period as that authority may require.
(5) A respondent who wants to make representations about the amount claimed must—
(a) do so in writing; and
(b) serve the representations on the assessing authority, and on the applicant, not more than 15 business days after service of the application.
(6) The assessing authority must—
(a) if it seems likely to help with the assessment, obtain any other information or document;
(b) resolve in favour of the respondent any doubt about what should be allowed; and

(c) serve the assessment on the parties.
(7) Where either party wants the amount allowed re-assessed–
(a) that party must–
(i) apply to the assessing authority, in writing and in any form required by that authority,
(ii) serve the application on the assessing authority, and on the other party, not more than 15 business days after service of the assessment,
(iii) explain the objections to the assessment,
(iv) supply any additional supporting information or document, and
(v) ask for a hearing, if that party wants one;
(b) a party who wants to make representations about an application for re-assessment must–
(i) do so in writing,
(ii) serve the representations on the assessing authority, and on the other party, not more than 15 business days after service of the application, and
(iii) ask for a hearing, if that party wants one; and
(c) the assessing authority–
(i) must arrange a hearing, in public or in private, if either party asks for one,
(ii) subject to that, may re-assess the amount allowed with or without a hearing,
(iii) must re-assess the amount allowed on the initial assessment, taking into account the reasons for disagreement with that amount and any other representations,
(iv) may maintain, increase or decrease the amount allowed on the assessment,
(v) must serve the re-assessment on the parties, and
(vi) must serve reasons on the parties, if not more than 15 business days later either party asks for such reasons.
(8) A time limit under this rule may be extended even after it has expired–
(a) by the assessing authority, or
(b) by the Senior Costs Judge, if the assessing authority declines to do so.

Appeal to a costs judge
45.12.–(1) This rule applies where– B-763
(a) the assessing authority has re-assessed the amount allowed under rule 45.11; and
(b) either party wants to appeal against that amount.
(2) That party must–
(a) serve an appeal notice on–
(i) the Senior Costs Judge,
(ii) the other party, and
(iii) the assessing authority
not more than 15 business days after service of the written reasons for the re-assessment;
(b) explain the objections to the re-assessment;
(c) serve on the Senior Costs Judge with the appeal notice–
(i) the applications for assessment and re-assessment,
(ii) any other information or document considered by the assessing authority,
(iii) the assessing authority's written reasons for the re-assessment, and
(iv) any other information or document for which a costs judge asks, within such period as the judge may require; and
(d) ask for a hearing, if that party wants one.
(3) A party who wants to make representations about an appeal must–
(a) serve representations in writing on–
(i) the Senior Costs Judge, and
(ii) the applicant
not more than 15 business days after service of the appeal notice; and
(b) ask for a hearing, if that party wants one.
(4) Unless a costs judge otherwise directs, the parties may rely only on–
(a) the objections to the amount allowed on the initial assessment; and
(b) any other representations and material considered by the assessing authority.
(5) A costs judge–
(a) must arrange a hearing, in public or in private, if either party asks for one;
(b) subject to that, may determine an appeal with or without a hearing;
(c) may–

(i) consult the assessing authority,
(ii) consult the court which made the costs order, and
(iii) obtain any other information or document;
(d) must reconsider the amount allowed by the assessing authority, taking into account the objections to the re-assessment and any other representations;
(e) may maintain, increase or decrease the amount allowed on the re-assessment;
(f) may provide for the costs incurred by either party to the appeal; and
(g) must serve reasons for the decision on—
(i) the parties, and
(ii) the assessing authority.

(6) A costs judge may extend a time limit under this rule, even after it has expired.

Appeal to a High Court judge

B-764 **45.13.**—(1) This rule applies where—
(a) a costs judge has determined an appeal under rule 45.12; and
(b) either party wants to appeal against the amount allowed.

(2) A party who wants to appeal—
(a) may do so only if a costs judge certifies that a point of principle of general importance was involved in the decision on the review; and
(b) must apply in writing for such a certificate and serve the application on—
(i) the costs judge, and
(ii) the other party
not more than 15 business days after service of the decision on the review.

(3) That party must—
(a) appeal to a judge of the High Court attached to the Queen's Bench Division as if it were an appeal from the decision of a master under Part 52 of the Civil Procedure Rules 1998); and
(b) serve the appeal not more than 15 business days after service of the costs judge's certificate under paragraph (2).

(4) A High Court judge—
(a) may extend a time limit under this rule even after it has expired;
(b) has the same powers and duties as a costs judge under rule 45.12; and
(c) may hear the appeal with one or more assessors.

Application for an extension of time

B-765 **45.14.**—(1) A party who wants an extension of time under rule 45.11, 45.12 or 45.13 must—
(a) apply in writing;
(b) explain the delay; and
(c) attach the application, representations or appeal for which the extension of time is needed.

Criminal Procedure Rules 2020 (SI 2020/759), Pt 46

REPRESENTATIVES

Functions of representatives and their supporters

B-766 **46.1**—(1) Under these rules, anything that a party may or must do may be done—
(a) by a legal representative on that party's behalf;
(b) by a person with the corporation's written authority, where that corporation is a defendant; or
(c) with the help of a parent, guardian or other suitable supporting adult where that party is a defendant—
(i) who is under 18, or
(ii) whose understanding of what the case involves is limited
unless other legislation (including a rule) otherwise requires.

(2) A member, officer or employee of a prosecutor may, on the prosecutor's behalf—
(a) serve on the magistrates' court officer, or present to a magistrates' court, an application for summons or warrant under section 1 of the Magistrates' Courts Act 1980; or
(b) issue a written charge and requisition, or single justice procedure notice, under section 29 of the Criminal Justice Act 2003.

Notice of appointment, etc. of legal representative: general rules

B-767 **46.2.**—(1) This rule applies—

(a) in relation to–

(i) a party who does not have legal aid for the purposes of a case, and

(ii) a party to an extradition case in the High Court, whether that party has legal aid or not;

(b) where such a party–

(i) appoints a legal representative for the purposes of the case, or

(ii) dismisses such a representative, with or without appointing another; and

(c) where a legal representative for such a party withdraws from the case.

(2) Where paragraph (1)(b) applies, that party must give notice of the appointment or dismissal to–

(a) the court officer;

(b) each other party; and

(c) where applicable, the legal representative who has been dismissed,

as soon as practicable and in any event within 5 business days.

(3) Where paragraph (1)(c) applies, that legal representative must–

(a) as soon as practicable give notice to–

(i) the court officer,

(ii) the party whom he or she has represented, and

(iii) each other party; and

(b) where that legal representative has represented the defendant in an extradition case in the High Court, include with the notice–

(i) confirmation that the defendant has notice of when and where the appeal hearing will take place and of the need to attend, if the defendant is on bail,

(ii) details sufficient to locate the defendant, including details of the custodian and of the defendant's date of birth and custody reference, if the defendant is in custody, and

(iii) details of any arrangements likely to be required by the defendant to facilitate his or her participation in consequence of the representative's withdrawal, including arrangements for interpretation.

(4) Any such notice–

(a) may be given orally, but only if–

(i) it is given at a hearing, and

(ii) it specifies no restriction under paragraph (5)(b) (restricted scope of appointment); but

(b) otherwise, must be in writing.

(5) A notice of the appointment of a legal representative–

(a) must identify–

(i) the legal representative who has been appointed, with details of how to contact that representative, and

(ii) all those to whom the notice is given;

(b) may specify a restriction, or restrictions, on the purpose or duration of the appointment; and

(c) if it specifies any such restriction, may nonetheless provide that documents may continue to be served on the represented party at the representative's address until–

(i) further notice is given under this rule, or

(ii) that party obtains legal aid for the purposes of the case.

(6) A legal representative who is dismissed by a party or who withdraws from representing a party must, as soon as practicable, make available to that party such documents in the representative's possession as have been served on that party.

Application to change legal representative: legal aid

46.3.–(1) This rule applies in a magistrates' court, the Crown Court and the Court of Appeal– **B-768**

(a) in relation to a party who has legal aid for the purposes of a case; and

(b) where such a party wants to select a legal representative in place of the representative named in the legal aid representation order.

(2) Such a party must–

(a) apply in writing as soon as practicable after becoming aware of the grounds for doing so; and

(b) serve the application on–

(i) the court officer, and

(ii) the legal representative named in the legal aid representation order.

(3) The application must—

(a) explain what the case is about, including what offences are alleged, what stage it has reached and what is likely to be in issue at trial;

(b) explain how and why the applicant chose the legal representative named in the legal aid representation order;

(c) if an advocate other than that representative has been instructed for the applicant, explain whether the applicant wishes to replace that advocate;

(d) explain, giving relevant facts and dates—

(i) in what way, in the applicant's opinion, there has been a breakdown in the relationship between the applicant and the current representative such that neither the individual representing the applicant nor any colleague of his or hers any longer can provide effective representation, or

(ii) what other compelling reason, in the applicant's opinion, means that neither the individual representing the applicant nor any colleague of his or hers any longer can provide effective representation;

(e) give details of any previous application by the applicant to replace the legal representative named in the legal aid representation order;

(f) state whether the applicant—

(i) waives the legal professional privilege attaching to the applicant's communications with the current representative, to the extent required to allow that representative to respond to the matters set out in the application, or

(ii) declines to waive that privilege and acknowledges that the court may draw such inferences as it thinks fit in consequence;

(g) explain how and why the applicant has chosen the proposed new representative;

(h) include or attach a statement by the proposed new representative which—

(i) confirms that that representative is eligible and willing to conduct the case for the applicant,

(ii) confirms that that representative can and will meet the current timetable for the case, including any hearing date or dates that have been set, if the application succeeds, and

(iii) explains what, if any, dealings that representative has had with the applicant before the present case; and

(i) ask for a hearing, if the applicant wants one, and explain why it is needed.

(4) The legal representative named in the legal aid representation order must—

(a) respond in writing no more than 5 business days after service of the application; and

(b) serve the response on—

(i) the court officer,

(ii) the applicant, and

(iii) the proposed new representative.

(5) The response must—

(a) explain which, if any, of the matters set out in the application the current representative disputes;

(b) explain, as appropriate, giving relevant facts and dates—

(i) whether, and if so in what way, in the current representative's opinion, there has been a breakdown in the relationship with the applicant such that neither the individual representing the applicant nor any colleague of his or hers any longer can provide effective representation,

(ii) whether, in the current representative's opinion, there is some other compelling reason why neither the individual representing the applicant nor any colleague of his or hers any longer can provide effective representation, and if so what reason,

(iii) whether the current representative considers there to be a duty to withdraw from the case in accordance with professional rules of conduct, and if so the nature of that duty, and

(iv) whether the current representative no longer is able to represent the applicant through circumstances outside the representative's control, and if so the particular circumstances that render the representative unable to do so;

(c) explain what, if any, dealings the current representative had had with the applicant before the present case; and

(d) ask for a hearing, if the current representative wants one, and explain why it is needed.

(6) The court may determine the application–
(a) without a hearing, as a general rule; or
(b) at a hearing, which must be in private unless the court otherwise directs.
(7) Unless the court otherwise directs, any hearing must be in the absence of each other party and each other party's representative and advocate (if any).
(8) If the court allows the application, as soon as practicable–
(a) the current representative must make available to the new representative such documents in the current representative's possession as have been served on the applicant party; and
(b) the new representative must serve notice of appointment on each other party.
(9) Paragraph (10) applies where–
(a) the court refuses the application;
(b) in response to that decision–
(i) the applicant declines further representation by the current representative or asks for legal aid to be withdrawn, or
(ii) the current representative declines further to represent the applicant; and
(c) the court in consequence withdraws the applicant's legal aid.
(10) The court officer must serve notice of the withdrawal of legal aid on–
(a) the applicant; and
(b) the current representative.

Criminal Procedure Rules 2020 (SI 2020/759), Pt 47

INVESTIGATION ORDERS AND WARRANTS

Section 1: General rules

When this Part applies
47.1. This Part applies to the exercise of the powers listed in each of rules 47.4, 47.24, 47.35, 47.42, 47.46, 47.51, 47.54, 47.59, and 47.63. **★B-769**

[This rule is printed as amended, with effect from 8 February 2021, by SI 2021/40, r.27(a).]

Meaning of "court", "applicant" and "respondent"
47.2. In this Part– **B-770**
(a) a reference to the "court" includes a reference to any justice of the peace or judge who can exercise a power to which this Part applies;
(b) "applicant" means a person who, or an authority which, can apply for an order or warrant to which this Part applies; and
(c) "respondent" means any person–
(i) against whom such an order is sought or made, or
(ii) on whom an application for such an order is served.

Documents served on the court officer
47.3.–(1) Unless the court otherwise directs, the court officer may– **B-771**
(a) keep a written application; or
(b) arrange for the whole or any part to be kept by some other appropriate person, subject to any conditions that the court may impose.
(2) Where the court makes an order when the court office is closed, the applicant must, not more than 72 hours later, serve on the court officer–
(a) a copy of the order; and
(b) any written material that was submitted to the court.
(3) Where the court issues a warrant–
(a) the applicant must return it to the court officer as soon as practicable after it has been executed, and in any event not more than 3 months after it was issued (unless other legislation otherwise provides); and
(b) the court officer must–
(i) keep the warrant for 12 months after its return, and
(ii) during that period, make it available for inspection by the occupier of the premises to which it relates, if that occupier asks to inspect it.

SECTION 2: INVESTIGATION ORDERS

When this Section applies
47.4. This Section applies where– **B-772**

(a) a Circuit judge can make, vary or discharge an order for the production of, or for giving access to, material under paragraph 4 of Schedule 1 to the Police and Criminal Evidence Act 1984, other than material that consists of or includes journalistic material;
(b) for the purposes of a terrorist investigation, a Circuit judge can make, vary or discharge—
(i) an order for the production of, or for giving access to, material, or for a statement of its location, under paragraphs 5 and 10 of Schedule 5 to the Terrorism Act 2000 [ibid., §§ 25-50d, 25-50e],
(ii) an explanation order, under paragraphs 10 and 13 of Schedule 5 to the 2000 Act [ibid., §§ 25-50e, 25-50g], or
(iii) a customer information order, under paragraphs 1 and 4 of Schedule 6 to the 2000 Act;
(c) for the purposes of—
(i) a terrorist investigation, a Circuit judge can make, and the Crown Court can vary or discharge, an account monitoring order, under paragraphs 2 and 4 of Schedule 6A to the 2000 Act [ibid., §§ 25-110, 25-115], or
(ii) a terrorist financing investigation, a judge entitled to exercise the jurisdiction of the Crown Court can make, and the Crown Court can vary or discharge, a disclosure order, under paragraphs 9 and 14 of Schedule 5A to the 2000 Act [ibid., §§ 25-110, 25-115];
(d) for the purposes of an investigation to which Part 8 of the Proceeds of Crime Act 2002 or the Proceeds of Crime Act 2002 (External Investigations) Order 2014 applies, a Crown Court judge can make, and the Crown Court can vary or discharge—
(i) a production order, under sections 345 and 351 of the 2002 Act [ibid., §§ 15A-263, 15A-271] or under articles 6 and 12 of the 2014 Order,
(ii) an order to grant entry, under sections 347 [ibid., § 15A-267] and 351 of the 2002 Act or under articles 8 and 12 of the 2014 Order,
(iii) a disclosure order, under sections 357 and 362 of the 2002 Act [ibid., §§ 15A-280, 15A-287] or under articles 16 and 21 of the 2014 Order,
(iv) a customer information order, under sections 363 and 369 of the 2002 Act [ibid., §§ 15A-289, 15A-296] or under articles 22 and 28 of the 2014 Order, or
(v) an account monitoring order, under sections 370, 373 and 375 of the 2002 Act [ibid., §§ 15A-297, 15A-300, 15A-302] or under articles 29, 32 and 34 of the 2014 Order;
(e) in connection with an extradition request, a Circuit judge can make an order for the production of, or for giving access to, material under section 157 of the Extradition Act 2003.
(f) a magistrates' court can make a further information order under section 22B of the Terrorism Act 2000 in connection with—
(i) an investigation into whether a person is involved in the commission of an offence under any of sections 15 to 18 of the 2000 Act [§§ 25-21 to 25-24 in the main work],
(ii) determining whether such an investigation should be started, or
(iii) identifying terrorist property or its movement or use; and
(g) a magistrates' court can make a further information order under section 339ZH of the Proceeds of Crime Act 2002 [§26-49d in the main work] in connection with—
(i) an investigation into whether a person is engaged in money laundering,
(ii) determining whether such an investigation should be started, or
(iii) an investigation into money laundering by an authority in a country outside the United Kingdom.

Exercise of court's powers

★B-773 **47.5.**—(1) Subject to paragraphs (2), (3) and (4), the court may determine an application for an order, or to vary or discharge an order—
(a) at a hearing (which must be in private unless the court otherwise directs), or without a hearing; and
(b) in the absence of—
(i) the applicant,
(ii) any respondent,
(iii) any other person affected by the order.

(2) The court must not determine such an application in the applicant's absence if—
(a) the applicant asks for a hearing; or
(b) it appears to the court that—

(i) the proposed order may infringe legal privilege, within the meaning of section 10 of the Police and Criminal Evidence Act 1984 [ibid., § 15A-68], section 348 or 361 of the Proceeds of Crime Act 2002 [ibid., §§ 15A-268, 15A-286] or article 9 of the Proceeds of Crime Act 2002 (External Investigations) Order 2014,

(ii) the proposed order may require the production of excluded material, within the meaning of section 11 of the 1984 Act [ibid., § 15A-72], or

(iii) for any other reason the application is so complex or serious as to require the court to hear the applicant.

(3) The court must not determine such an application in the absence of any respondent or other person affected, unless—

(a) the absentee has had at least 2 business days in which to make representations; or

(b) the court is satisfied that—

(i) the applicant cannot identify or contact the absentee,

(ii) it would prejudice the investigation if the absentee were present,

(iii) it would prejudice the investigation to adjourn or postpone the application so as to allow the absentee to attend, or

(iv) the absentee has waived the opportunity to attend.

(4) The court must not determine such an application in the absence of any respondent who, if the order sought by the applicant were made, would be required to produce or give access to journalistic material, unless that respondent has waived the opportunity to attend.

(5) The court officer must arrange for the court to hear such an application no sooner than 2 business days after it was served, unless—

(a) the court directs that no hearing need be arranged; or

(b) the court gives other directions for the hearing.

(6) The court must not determine an application unless satisfied that sufficient time has been allowed for it.

(7) If the court so directs, the parties to an application may attend a hearing by live link or telephone.

(8) The court must not make, vary or discharge an order unless the applicant states, in writing or orally, that to the best of the applicant's knowledge and belief—

(a) the application discloses all the information that is material to what the court must decide; and

(b) the content of the application is true.

(9) Where the statement required by paragraph (8) is made orally—

(a) the statement must be on oath or affirmation, unless the court otherwise directs; and

(b) the court must arrange for a record of the making of the statement.

(10) The court may—

(a) shorten or extend (even after it has expired) a time limit under this Section;

(b) dispense with a requirement for service under this Section (even after service was required); and

(c) consider an application made orally instead of in writing.

(11) A person who wants an extension of time must—

(a) apply when serving the application for which it is needed; and

(b) explain the delay.

Rule 47.5 of the Criminal Procedure Rules 2020 (SI 2020/759) is temporarily amended by r.13(a) of the Criminal Procedure (Amendment No. 2) (Coronavirus) Rules 2020 (SI 2020/417) so as to remove "or telephone" in para.(7). This amendment ceases to have effect when ss.53 to 55 (and Schs 23 to 25) of the Coronavirus Act 2020 expire. This rule is also printed as amended, with effect from 8 February 2021, by SI 2021/40, r.27(b).

Application for order: general rules

47.6.—(1) This rule applies to each application for an order to which this Section applies. ★B-774

(2) The applicant must—

(a) apply in writing and serve the application on the court officer;

(b) demonstrate that the applicant is entitled to apply, for example as a constable or under legislation that applies to other officers;

(c) give the court an estimate of how long the court should allow—

(i) to read the application and prepare for any hearing, and

(ii) for any hearing of the application;
(d) attach a draft order in the terms proposed by the applicant;
(e) serve notice of the application on the respondent, if any, unless the court otherwise directs; and
(f) serve the application on any respondent to such extent, if any, as the court directs.

(3) A notice served on a respondent must—
(a) specify the material or information in respect of which the application is made; and
(b) identify—
(i) the power that the applicant invites the court to exercise, and
(ii) the conditions for the exercise of that power which the applicant asks the court to find are met.

(4) The applicant must serve any order made on a respondent.

[This rule is printed as amended, with effect from 8 February 2021, by SI 2021/40, r.27(c).]

Application containing information withheld from a respondent or other person

★B-775 **47.7.**—(1) This rule applies where an application includes information that the applicant thinks ought to be revealed only to the court.

(2) The application must—
(a) identify that information; and
(b) explain why that information ought not to be served on a respondent or other person.

(3) At a hearing of an application to which this rule applies—
(a) the general rule is that the court must consider, in the following sequence—
(i) representations first by the applicant and then by the respondent, if any, and any other person, in the presence of them all, and then
(ii) further representations by the applicant, in the others' absence; but
(b) the court may direct other arrangements for the hearing.

[This rule is printed as amended, with effect from 8 February 2021, by SI 2021/40, r.27(d).]

Application to vary or discharge an order

★B-776 **47.8.**—(1) This rule applies where one of the following wants the court to vary or discharge an order to which a rule in this Section refers—
(a) an applicant;
(b) a respondent; or
(c) a person affected by the order.

(2) That applicant, respondent or person affected must—
(a) apply in writing as soon as practicable after becoming aware of the grounds for doing so;
(b) serve the application on—
(i) the court officer, and
(ii) the respondent, applicant, or any person known to be affected, as applicable;
(c) explain why it is appropriate for the order to be varied or discharged;
(d) propose the terms of any variation; and
(e) ask for a hearing, if one is wanted, and explain why it is needed.

[This rule is printed as amended, with effect from 8 February 2021, by SI 2021/40, r.27(e).]

Application to punish for contempt of court

B-777 **47.9.**—(1) This rule applies where a person is accused of disobeying—
(a) a production order made under paragraph 4 of Schedule 1 to the Police and Criminal Evidence Act 1984;
(b) a production etc. order made under paragraph 5 of Schedule 5 to the Terrorism Act 2000;
(c) an explanation order made under paragraph 13 of that Schedule;
(d) an account monitoring order made under paragraph 2 of Schedule 6A to that Act;
(e) a production order made under section 345 of the Proceeds of Crime Act 2002 or article 6 of the Proceeds of Crime Act 2002 (External Investigations) Order 2014;
(f) an account monitoring order made under section 370 of the 2002 Act or article 29 of the 2014 Order; or
(g) a production order made under section 157 of the Extradition Act 2003.

(2) An applicant who wants the court to exercise its power to punish that person for contempt of court must comply with the rules in Part 48 (contempt of court).

Orders under the Police and Criminal Evidence Act 1984

Application for a production order under the Police and Criminal Evidence Act 1984

47.10.–(1) This rule applies where an applicant wants the court to make an order to which rule 47.4(a) refers. **B-778**

(2) As well as complying with rule 47.6 (application for order: general rules), the application must, in every case–

(a) specify the offence under investigation (and see paragraph (3)(a));
(b) describe the material sought;
(c) identify the respondent;
(d) specify the premises on which the material is believed to be, or explain why it is not reasonably practicable to do so;
(e) explain the grounds for believing that the material is on the premises specified, or (if applicable) on unspecified premises of the respondent;
(f) specify the set of access conditions on which the applicant relies (and see paragraphs (3) and (4)); and
(g) propose–
 (i) the terms of the order, and
 (ii) the period within which it should take effect.

(3) Where the applicant relies on paragraph 2 of Schedule 1 to the Police and Criminal Evidence Act 1984 ("the first set of access conditions": general power to gain access to special procedure material), the application must–

(a) specify the indictable offence under investigation;
(b) explain the grounds for believing that the offence has been committed;
(c) explain the grounds for believing that the material sought–
 (i) is likely to be of substantial value to the investigation (whether by itself, or together with other material),
 (ii) is likely to be admissible evidence at trial for the offence under investigation, and
 (iii) does not consist of or include items subject to legal privilege or excluded material;
(d) explain what other methods of obtaining the material–
 (i) have been tried without success, or
 (ii) have not been tried because they appeared bound to fail; and
(e) explain why it is in the public interest for the respondent to produce the material, having regard to–
 (i) the benefit likely to accrue to the investigation if the material is obtained, and
 (ii) the circumstances under which the respondent holds the material.

(4) Where the applicant relies on paragraph 3 of Schedule 1 to the Police and Criminal Evidence Act 1984 ("the second set of access conditions": use of search warrant power to gain access to excluded or special procedure material), the application must–

(a) state the legislation under which a search warrant could have been issued, had the material sought not been excluded or special procedure material (in this paragraph, described as "the main search power");
(b) include or attach the terms of the main search power;
(c) explain how the circumstances would have satisfied any criteria prescribed by the main search power for the issue of a search warrant; and
(d) explain why the issue of such a search warrant would have been appropriate.

Orders under the Terrorism Act 2000

Application for an order under the Terrorism Act 2000

47.11.–(1) This rule applies where an applicant wants the court to make one of the orders to which rule 47.4(b) and (c) refers. **★B-779**

(2) As well as complying with rule 47.6 (Application for order: general rules), the application must–

(a) specify the offence under investigation;
(b) explain how the investigation constitutes a terrorist investigation or terrorist financing investigation, as appropriate, within the meaning of the Terrorism Act 2000;
(c) identify any respondent; and
(d) give the information required by whichever of rules 47.12 to 47.16 applies.

[This rule is printed as amended, with effect from 8 February 2021, by SI 2021/40, r.27(f).]

Content of application for a production etc. order under the Terrorism Act 2000

B-780 **47.12.**—(1) As well as complying with rules 47.6 and 47.11, an applicant who wants the court to make an order for the production of, or for giving access to, material, or for a statement of its location, must—

(a) describe that material;

(b) explain why the applicant thinks the material is—

(i) in the respondent's possession, custody or power, or

(ii) expected to come into existence and then to be in the respondent's possession, custody or power within 28 days of the order;

(c) explain how the material constitutes or contains excluded material or special procedure material;

(d) confirm that none of the material is expected to be subject to legal privilege;

(e) explain why the material is likely to be of substantial value to the investigation;

(f) explain why it is in the public interest for the material to be produced, or for the applicant to be given access to it, having regard to—

(i) the benefit likely to accrue to the investigation if it is obtained, and

(ii) the circumstances in which the respondent has the material, or is expected to have it; and

(g) propose—

(i) the terms of the order, and

(ii) the period within which it should take effect.

(2) An applicant who wants the court to make an order to grant entry in aid of a production order must—

(a) specify the premises to which entry is sought;

(b) explain why the order is needed; and

(c) propose the terms of the order.

Content of application for a disclosure order or further information order under the Terrorism Act 2000

★B-781 **47.13.** (1) As well as complying with rules 47.6 and 47.11, an applicant who wants the court to make a disclosure order must—

(a) explain why the applicant thinks that—

(i) a person has committed an offence under any of sections 15 to 18 of the Terrorism Act 2000 [§§ 25-21 to 25-24 in the main work], or

(ii) property described in the application is terrorist property within the meaning of section 14 of the 2000 Act [§ 25-20 in the main work];

(b) describe in general terms the information that the applicant wants a person to provide;

(c) confirm that none of the information is—

(i) expected to be subject to legal privilege, or

(ii) excluded material;

(d) explain why the information is likely to be of substantial value to the investigation;

(e) explain why it is in the public interest for the information to be provided, having regard to the benefit likely to accrue to the investigation if it is obtained; and

(f) propose the terms of the order.

(2) As well as complying with rule 47.6, an applicant who wants the court to make a further information order must—

(a) identify the respondent from whom the information is sought and explain—

(i) whether the respondent is the person who made the disclosure to which the information relates or is otherwise carrying on a business in the regulated sector within the meaning of Part 1 of Schedule 3A to the 2000 Act, and

(ii) why the applicant thinks that the information is in the possession, or under the control, of the respondent;

(b) specify or describe the information that the applicant wants the respondent to provide;

(c) where the information sought relates to a disclosure of information by someone under section 21A of the 2000 Act (Failure to disclose: regulated sector) [§ 25-32 in the main work], explain—

(i) how the information sought relates to a matter arising from that disclosure,

(ii) how the information would assist in investigating whether a person is involved in the commission of an offence under any of sections 15 to 18 of that Act, or in determining whether an investigation of that kind should be started, or in identifying terrorist

property or its movement or use, and
(iii) why it is reasonable in all the circumstances for the information to be provided;
(d) where the information sought relates to a disclosure made under a requirement of the law of a country outside the United Kingdom which corresponds with Part III of the 2000 Act (Terrorist property), and an authority in that country which investigates offences corresponding with sections 15 to 18 of that Act has asked the National Crime Agency for information in connection with that disclosure, explain–
(i) how the information sought relates to a matter arising from that disclosure,
(ii) why the information is likely to be of substantial value to the authority that made the request in determining any matter in connection with the disclosure, and
(iii) why it is reasonable in all the circumstances for the information to be provided;
(e) confirm that none of the information is expected to be subject to legal privilege; and
(f) propose the terms of the order, including–
(i) how the respondent must provide the information required, and
(ii) the date by which the information must be provided.

(3) Rule 47.8 (Application to vary or discharge an order) does not apply to a further information order.

(4) Paragraph (5) applies where a party to an application for a further information order wants to appeal to the Crown Court from the decision of the magistrates' court.

(5) The appellant must–
(a) serve an appeal notice–
(i) on the Crown Court officer and on the other party,
(ii) not more than 15 business days after the magistrates' court's decision; and
(b) in the appeal notice, explain, as appropriate, why the Crown Court should (as the case may be) make, discharge or vary a further information order.

(6) Rule 34.11 (Constitution of the Crown Court) applies on such an appeal.

This rule is printed as amended, with effect from 8 February 2021, by SI 2021/40, r.27(g).]

Content of application for an explanation order under the Terrorism Act 2000

47.14. As well as complying with rules 47.6 and 47.11, an applicant who wants the court to make an explanation order must– **B-782**
(a) identify the material that the applicant wants the respondent to explain;
(b) confirm that the explanation is not expected to infringe legal privilege; and
(c) propose the terms of the order.

Content of application for a customer information order under the Terrorism Act 2000

47.15. As well as complying with rules 47.6 and 47.11, an applicant who wants the court to make a customer information order must– **B-783**
(a) explain why it is desirable for the purposes of the investigation to trace property said to be terrorist property within the meaning of the Terrorism Act 2000;
(b) explain why the order will enhance the effectiveness of the investigation; and
(c) propose the terms of the order.

Content of application for an account monitoring order under the Terrorism Act 2000

47.16. As well as complying with rules 47.6 and 47.11, an applicant who wants the court to make an account monitoring order must– **B-784**
(a) specify–
(i) the information sought,
(ii) the period during which the applicant wants the respondent to provide that information (to a maximum of 90 days), and
(iii) where, when and in what manner the applicant wants the respondent to provide that information;
(b) explain why it is desirable for the purposes of the investigation to trace property said to be terrorist property within the meaning of the Terrorism Act 2000;
(c) explain why the order will enhance the effectiveness of the investigation; and
(d) propose the terms of the order.

Orders under the Proceeds of Crime Act 2002

Application for an order under the Proceeds of Crime Act 2002

47.17. (1) This rule applies where an applicant wants the court to make one of the orders to **★B-785**

which rule 47.4(d) refers.

(2) As well as complying with rule 47.6 (application for order: general rules), the application must—

(a) identify—

(i) any respondent, and

(ii) the person or property the subject of the investigation;

(b) in the case of an investigation in the United Kingdom, explain why the applicant thinks that—

(i) the person under investigation has benefitted from criminal conduct, in the case of a confiscation investigation, or committed a money laundering offence, in the case of a money laundering investigation, or

(ii) the cash involved is property obtained through unlawful conduct, or is intended to be used in unlawful conduct, in the case of a detained cash investigation;

(c) in the case of an investigation outside the United Kingdom, explain why the applicant thinks that—

(i) there is an investigation by an overseas authority which relates to a criminal investigation or to criminal proceedings (including proceedings to remove the benefit of a person's criminal conduct following that person's conviction), and

(ii) in the case of a detained cash investigation, a detained property investigation or a frozen funds investigation, the cash or property involved, or the money held in the frozen account, was obtained through unlawful conduct or is intended to be used in unlawful conduct; and

(d) give the additional information required by whichever of rules 47.18 to 47.22 applies.

This rule is printed as amended, with effect from 8 February 2021, by SI 2021/40, r.27(h).]

Content of application for a production order under the Proceeds of Crime Act 2002

B-786 **47.18.** As well as complying with rules 47.6 and 47.17, an applicant who wants the court to make an order for the production of, or for giving access to, material, must—

(a) describe that material;

(b) explain why the applicant thinks the material is in the respondent's possession or control;

(c) confirm that none of the material is—

(i) expected to be subject to legal privilege, or

(ii) excluded material;

(d) explain why the material is likely to be of substantial value to the investigation;

(e) explain why it is in the public interest for the material to be produced, or for the applicant to be given access to it, having regard to—

(i) the benefit likely to accrue to the investigation if it is obtained, and

(ii) the circumstances in which the respondent has the material; and

(f) propose—

(i) the terms of the order, and

(ii) the period within which it should take effect, if 7 days from the date of the order would not be appropriate.

Content of application for an order to grant entry under the Proceeds of Crime Act 2002

B-787 **47.19.** An applicant who wants the court to make an order to grant entry in aid of a production order must—

(a) specify the premises to which entry is sought;

(b) explain why the order is needed; and

(c) propose the terms of the order.

Content of application for a disclosure order or further information order under the Proceeds of Crime Act 2002

★B-788 **47.20.** (1) As well as complying with rules 47.6 and 47.17, an applicant who wants the court to make a disclosure order must—

(a) describe in general terms the information that the applicant wants a person to provide;

(b) confirm that none of the information is—

(i) expected to be subject to legal privilege, or

(ii) excluded material;

(c) explain why the information is likely to be of substantial value to the investigation;

(d) explain why it is in the public interest for the information to be provided, having regard to the benefit likely to accrue to the investigation if it is obtained; and

(e) propose the terms of the order.

(2) As well as complying with rule 47.6, an applicant who wants the court to make a further information order must–

(a) identify the respondent from whom the information is sought and explain–
   (i) whether the respondent is the person who made the disclosure to which the information relates or is otherwise carrying on a business in the regulated sector within the meaning of Part 1 of Schedule 9 to the Proceeds of Crime Act 2002, and
   (ii) why the applicant thinks that the information is in the possession, or under the control, of the respondent;
(b) specify or describe the information that the applicant wants the respondent to provide;
(c) where the information sought relates to a disclosure of information under Part 7 of the Proceeds of Crime Act 2002 (Money laundering), explain–
   (i) how the information sought relates to a matter arising from that disclosure,
   (ii) how the information would assist in investigating whether a person is engaged in money laundering or in determining whether an investigation of that kind should be started, and
   (iii) why it is reasonable in all the circumstances for the information to be provided;
(d) where the information sought relates to a disclosure made under a requirement of the law of a country outside the United Kingdom which corresponds with Part 7 of the 2002 Act, and an authority in that country which investigates money laundering has asked the National Crime Agency for information in connection with that disclosure, explain–
   (i) how the information sought relates to a matter arising from that disclosure,
   (ii) why the information is likely to be of substantial value to the authority that made the request in determining any matter in connection with the disclosure, and
   (iii) why it is reasonable in all the circumstances for the information to be provided;
(e) confirm that none of the information is expected to be subject to legal privilege; and
(f) propose the terms of the order, including–
   (i) how the respondent must provide the information required, and
   (ii) the date by which the information must be provided.

(3) Rule 47.8 (Application to vary or discharge an order) does not apply to a further information order.

(4) Paragraph (5) applies where a party to an application for a further information order wants to appeal to the Crown Court from the decision of the magistrates' court.

(5) The appellant must–

(a) serve an appeal notice on the Crown Court officer and on the other party not more than 15 business days after the magistrates' court's decision; and
(b) in the appeal notice, explain, as appropriate, why the Crown Court should (as the case may be) make, discharge or vary a further information order.

(6) Rule 34.11 (Constitution of the Crown Court) applies on such an appeal.

This rule is printed as amended, with effect from 8 February 2021, by SI 2021/40, r.27(i).]

Content of application for a customer information order under the Proceeds of Crime Act 2002

47.21. As well as complying with rules 47.6 and 47.17, an applicant who wants the court to make a customer information order must– **B-789**

(a) explain why customer information about the person under investigation is likely to be of substantial value to that investigation;
(b) explain why it is in the public interest for the information to be provided, having regard to the benefit likely to accrue to the investigation if it is obtained; and
(c) propose the terms of the order.

Content of application for an account monitoring order under the Proceeds of Crime Act 2002

47.22. As well as complying with rules 47.6 and 47.17, an applicant who wants the court to make an account monitoring order for the provision of account information must– **B-790**

(a) specify–
   (i) the information sought,
   (ii) the period during which the applicant wants the respondent to provide that information (to a maximum of 90 days), and
   (iii) when and in what manner the applicant wants the respondent to provide that information;

(b) explain why the information is likely to be of substantial value to the investigation;
(c) explain why it is in the public interest for the information to be provided, having regard to the benefit likely to accrue to the investigation if it is obtained; and
(d) propose the terms of the order.

Application for a production order under the Extradition Act 2003

B-791 **47.23.**—(1) This rule applies where an applicant wants the court to make an order to which rule 47.4(e) refers.

(2) As well as complying with rule 47.6 (Application for order: general rules), the application must—

(a) identify the person whose extradition is sought;
(b) specify the extradition offence of which that person is accused;
(c) identify the respondent; and
(d) describe the special procedure or excluded material sought.

(3) In relation to the person whose extradition is sought, the application must explain the grounds for believing that—

(a) that person has committed the offence for which extradition is sought;
(b) that offence is an extradition offence; and
(c) that person is in the United Kingdom or is on the way to the United Kingdom.

(4) In relation to the material sought, the application must—

(a) specify the premises on which the material is believed to be;
(b) explain the grounds for believing that—
  (i) the material is on those premises,
  (ii) the material consists of or includes special procedure or excluded material, and
  (iii) the material would be likely to be admissible evidence at a trial in England and Wales for the offence for which extradition is sought;
(c) explain what other methods of obtaining the material—
  (i) have been tried without success, or
  (ii) have not been tried because they appeared bound to fail; and
(d) explain why it is in the public interest for the respondent to produce or give access to the material.

(5) The application must propose—

(a) the terms of the order, and
(b) the period within which it should take effect.

Section 3: Investigation warrants

When this Section applies

B-792 **47.24.** This Section applies where—

(a) a justice of the peace can issue a warrant under—
  (i) section 8 of the Police and Criminal Evidence Act 1984 [§ 15A-47 in the main work], or
  (ii) section 2 of the Criminal Justice Act 1987 [ibid., § 1-470];
(b) a Circuit judge can issue a warrant under—
  (i) paragraph 12 of Schedule 1 to the Police and Criminal Evidence Act 1984,
  (ii) paragraph 11 of Schedule 5 to the Terrorism Act 2000 [ibid., § 25-50f], or
  (iii) section 160 of the Extradition Act 2003;
(c) a Crown Court judge can issue a warrant under—
  (i) section 352 of the Proceeds of Crime Act 2002 [ibid., § 15A-272], or
  (ii) article 13 of the Proceeds of Crime Act 2002 (External Investigations) Order 2014; and
(d) a court to which these Rules apply can issue a warrant to search for and seize articles or persons under a power not listed in paragraphs (a), (b) or (c).

Exercise of court's powers

B-793 **47.25.** (1) The court must determine an application for a warrant—

(a) at a hearing, which must be in private unless the court otherwise directs;
(b) in the presence of the applicant; and
(c) in the absence of any person affected by the warrant, including any person in occupation or control of premises which the applicant wants to search.

(2) If the court so directs, the applicant may attend the hearing by live link or telephone.

(3) The court must not determine an application unless satisfied that sufficient time has been allowed for it.

(4) The court must not determine an application unless the applicant confirms, on oath or affirmation, that to the best of the applicant's knowledge and belief—

(a) the application discloses all the information that is material to what the court must decide, including any circumstances that might reasonably be considered capable of undermining any of the grounds of the application; and

(b) the content of the application is true.

(5) If the court requires the applicant to answer a question about an application—

(a) the applicant's answer must be on oath or affirmation;

(b) the court must arrange for a record of the gist of the question and reply; and

(c) if the applicant cannot answer to the court's satisfaction, the court may—

(i) specify the information the court requires, and

(ii) give directions for the presentation of any renewed application.

(6) Unless to do so would be inconsistent with other legislation, on an application the court may issue—

(a) a warrant in respect of specified premises;

(b) a warrant in respect of all premises occupied or controlled by a specified person;

(c) a warrant in respect of all premises occupied or controlled by a specified person which specifies some of those premises; or

(d) more than one warrant—

(i) each one in respect of premises specified in the warrant,

(ii) each one in respect of all premises occupied or controlled by a person specified in the warrant (whether or not such a warrant also specifies any of those premises), or

(iii) at least one in respect of specified premises and at least one in respect of all premises occupied or controlled by a specified person (whether or not such a warrant also specifies any of those premises).

Rule 47.25 of the Criminal Procedure Rules 2020 (SI 2020/759) is temporarily amended by r.13(b) of the Criminal Procedure (Amendment No. 2) (Coronavirus) Rules 2020 (SI 2020/417) so as to remove "or telephone" in para.(2). This amendment ceases to have effect when ss.53 to 55 (and Schs 23 to 25) of the Coronavirus Act 2020 expire.

Application for warrant: general rules

47.26.—(1) This rule applies to each application to which this Section applies. B-794

(2) The applicant must—

(a) apply in writing;

(b) serve the application on—

(i) the court officer, or

(ii) if the court office is closed, the court;

(c) demonstrate that the applicant is entitled to apply, for example as a constable or under legislation that applies to other officers;

(d) give the court an estimate of how long the court should allow—

(i) to read and prepare for the application, and

(ii) for the hearing of the application; and

(e) tell the court when the applicant expects any warrant issued to be executed.

(3) The application must disclose anything known or reported to the applicant that might reasonably be considered capable of undermining any of the grounds of the application.

(4) Where the application includes information that the applicant thinks should not be supplied under rule 5.7 (supply to a party of information or documents from records or case materials) to a person affected by a warrant, the applicant may—

(a) set out that information in a separate document, marked accordingly; and

(b) in that document, explain why the applicant thinks that that information ought not to be supplied to anyone other than the court.

(5) The application must include—

(a) a declaration by the applicant that to the best of the applicant's knowledge and belief—

(i) the application discloses all the information that is material to what the court must decide, including anything that might reasonably be considered capable of undermining any of the grounds of the application, and

(ii) the content of the application is true; and

(b) a declaration by an officer senior to the applicant that the senior officer has reviewed and authorised the application.

(6) The application must attach a draft warrant or warrants in the terms proposed by the applicant.

Information to be included in a warrant

B-795 **47.27.** (1) A warrant must identify—

(a) the person or description of persons by whom it may be executed;

(b) any person who may accompany a person executing the warrant;

(c) so far as practicable, the material, documents, articles or persons to be sought;

(d) the legislation under which it was issued;

(e) the name of the applicant;

(f) the court that issued it, unless that is otherwise recorded by the court officer;

(g) the court office for the court that issued it; and

(h) the date on which it was issued.

(2) A warrant must specify—

(a) either—

(i) the premises to be searched, where the application was for authority to search specified premises, or

(ii) the person in occupation or control of premises to be searched, where the application was for authority to search any premises occupied or controlled by that person; and

(b) the number of occasions on which specified premises may be searched, if more than one.

(3) A warrant must include, by signature, initial, or otherwise, an indication that it has been approved by the court that issued it.

(4) Where a warrant comprises more than a single page, each page must include such an indication.

(5) A copy of a warrant must include a prominent certificate that it is such a copy.

Application for warrant under section 8 of the Police and Criminal Evidence Act 1984

B-796 **47.28.** (1) This rule applies where an applicant wants a magistrates' court to issue a warrant or warrants under section 8 of the Police and Criminal Evidence Act 1984.

(2) As well as complying with rule 47.26, the application must—

(a) specify the offence under investigation (and see paragraph (3));

(b) so far as practicable, identify the material sought (and see paragraph (4));

(c) specify the premises to be searched (and see paragraphs (5) and (6));

(d) state whether the applicant wants the premises to be searched on more than one occasion (and see paragraph (7)); and

(e) state whether the applicant wants other persons to accompany the officers executing the warrant or warrants (and see paragraph (8)).

(3) In relation to the offence under investigation, the application must—

(a) state whether that offence is—

(i) an indictable offence, or

(ii) a relevant offence as defined in section 28D of the Immigration Act 1971; and

(b) explain the grounds for believing that the offence has been committed.

(4) In relation to the material sought, the application must explain the grounds for believing that that material—

(a) is likely to be of substantial value to the investigation (whether by itself, or together with other material);

(b) is likely to be admissible evidence at trial for the offence under investigation; and

(c) does not consist of or include items subject to legal privilege, excluded material or special procedure material.

(5) In relation to premises which the applicant wants to be searched and can specify, the application must—

(a) specify each set of premises;

(b) in respect of each set of premises, explain the grounds for believing that material sought is on those premises; and

(c) in respect of each set of premises, explain the grounds for believing that—

(i) it is not practicable to communicate with any person entitled to grant entry to the premises,

(ii) it is practicable to communicate with such a person but it is not practicable to communicate with any person entitled to grant access to the material sought,
(iii) entry to the premises will not be granted unless a warrant is produced, or
(iv) the purpose of a search may be frustrated or seriously prejudiced unless a constable arriving at the premises can secure immediate entry to them.

(6) In relation to premises which the applicant wants to be searched but at least some of which the applicant cannot specify, the application must–

(a) explain the grounds for believing that–
(i) because of the particulars of the offence under investigation it is necessary to search any premises occupied or controlled by a specified person, and
(ii) it is not reasonably practicable to specify all the premises which that person occupies or controls which might need to be searched;
(b) specify as many sets of premises as is reasonably practicable;
(c) in respect of each set of premises, whether specified or not, explain the grounds for believing that material sought is on those premises; and
(d) in respect of each specified set of premises, explain the grounds for believing that–
(i) it is not practicable to communicate with any person entitled to grant entry to the premises,
(ii) it is practicable to communicate with such a person but it is not practicable to communicate with any person entitled to grant access to the material sought,
(iii) entry to the premises will not be granted unless a warrant is produced, or
(iv) the purpose of a search may be frustrated or seriously prejudiced unless a constable arriving at the premises can secure immediate entry to them.

(7) In relation to any set of premises which the applicant wants to be searched on more than one occasion, the application must–

(a) explain why it is necessary to search on more than one occasion in order to achieve the purpose for which the applicant wants the court to issue the warrant; and
(b) specify any proposed maximum number of occasions.

(8) In relation to any set of premises which the applicant wants to be searched by the officers executing the warrant with other persons authorised by the court, the application must–

(a) identify those other persons, by function or description; and
(b) explain why those persons are required.

Application for warrant under section 2 of the Criminal Justice Act 1987

47.29. (1) This rule applies where an applicant wants a magistrates' court to issue a warrant or warrants under section 2 of the Criminal Justice Act 1987. **B-797**

(2) As well as complying with rule 47.26, the application must–

(a) describe the investigation being conducted by the Director of the Serious Fraud Office and include–
(i) an explanation of what is alleged and why, and
(ii) a chronology of relevant events;
(b) specify the document, documents or description of documents sought by the applicant (and see paragraphs (3) and (4)); and
(c) specify the premises which the applicant wants to be searched (and see paragraph (5)).

(3) In relation to each document or description of documents sought, the application must–

(a) explain the grounds for believing that each such document–
(i) relates to a matter relevant to the investigation, and
(ii) could not be withheld from disclosure or production on grounds of legal professional privilege; and
(b) explain the grounds for believing that–
(i) a person has failed to comply with a notice by the Director to produce the document or documents,
(ii) it is not practicable to serve such a notice, or
(iii) the service of such a notice might seriously impede the investigation.

(4) In relation to any document or description of documents which the applicant wants to be preserved but not seized under a warrant, the application must–

(a) specify the steps for which the applicant wants the court's authority in order to preserve and prevent interference with the document or documents; and
(b) explain why such steps are necessary.

(5) In respect of each set of premises which the applicant wants to be searched, the application must explain the grounds for believing that a document or description of documents sought by the applicant is on those premises.

(6) If the court so directs, the applicant must make available to the court material on which is based the information given under paragraph (2).

Application for warrant under paragraph 12 of Schedule 1 to the Police and Criminal Evidence Act 1984

B-798 **47.30.** (1) This rule applies where an applicant wants a Circuit judge to issue a warrant or warrants under paragraph 12 of Schedule 1 to the Police and Criminal Evidence Act 1984.

(2) As well as complying with rule 47.26, the application must—

(a) specify the offence under investigation (and see paragraph (3)(a));
(b) specify the set of access conditions on which the applicant relies (and see paragraphs (3) and (4));
(c) so far as practicable, identify the material sought;
(d) specify the premises to be searched (and see paragraphs (6) and (7)); and
(e) state whether the applicant wants other persons to accompany the officers executing the warrant or warrants (and see paragraph (8)).

(3) Where the applicant relies on paragraph 2 of Schedule 1 to the Police and Criminal Evidence Act 1984 ("the first set of access conditions": general power to gain access to special procedure material), the application must—

(a) specify the indictable offence under investigation;
(b) explain the grounds for believing that the offence has been committed;
(c) explain the grounds for believing that the material sought—
  (i) is likely to be of substantial value to the investigation (whether by itself, or together with other material),
  (ii) is likely to be admissible evidence at trial for the offence under investigation, and
  (iii) does not consist of or include items subject to legal privilege or excluded material;
(d) explain what other methods of obtaining the material—
  (i) have been tried without success, or
  (ii) have not been tried because they appeared bound to fail; and
(e) explain why it is in the public interest to obtain the material, having regard to—
  (i) the benefit likely to accrue to the investigation if the material is obtained, and
  (ii) the circumstances under which the material is held.

(4) Where the applicant relies on paragraph 3 of Schedule 1 to the Police and Criminal Evidence Act 1984 ("the second set of access conditions": use of search warrant power to gain access to excluded or special procedure material), the application must—

(a) state the legislation under which a search warrant could have been issued, had the material sought not been excluded or special procedure material (in this paragraph, described as "the main search power");
(b) include or attach the terms of the main search power;
(c) explain how the circumstances would have satisfied any criteria prescribed by the main search power for the issue of a search warrant; and
(d) explain why the issue of such a search warrant would have been appropriate.

(5) Where the applicant relies on the second set of access conditions and on an assertion that a production order made under paragraph 4 of Schedule 1 to the 1984 Act in respect of the material sought has not been complied with—

(a) the application must—
  (i) identify that order and describe its terms, and
  (ii) specify the date on which it was served; but
(b) the application need not comply with paragraphs (6) or (7).

(6) In relation to premises which the applicant wants to be searched and can specify, the application must (unless paragraph (5) applies)—

(a) specify each set of premises;
(b) in respect of each set of premises, explain the grounds for believing that material sought is on those premises; and
(c) in respect of each set of premises, explain the grounds for believing that—
  (i) it is not practicable to communicate with any person entitled to grant entry to the premises,
  (ii) it is practicable to communicate with such a person but it is not practicable to communicate with any person entitled to grant access to the material sought,

(iii) the material sought contains information which is subject to a restriction on disclosure or an obligation of secrecy contained in an enactment and is likely to be disclosed in breach of the restriction or obligation if a warrant is not issued, or
(iv) service of notice of an application for a production order under paragraph 4 of Schedule 1 to the 1984 Act may seriously prejudice the investigation.

(7) In relation to premises which the applicant wants to be searched but at least some of which the applicant cannot specify, the application must (unless paragraph (5) applies)–
(a) explain the grounds for believing that–
(i) because of the particulars of the offence under investigation it is necessary to search any premises occupied or controlled by a specified person, and
(ii) it is not reasonably practicable to specify all the premises which that person occupies or controls which might need to be searched;
(b) specify as many sets of premises as is reasonably practicable;
(c) in respect of each set of premises, whether specified or not, explain the grounds for believing that material sought is on those premises; and
(d) in respect of each specified set of premises, explain the grounds for believing that–
(i) it is not practicable to communicate with any person entitled to grant entry to the premises,
(ii) it is practicable to communicate with such a person but it is not practicable to communicate with any person entitled to grant access to the material sought,
(iii) the material sought contains information which is subject to a restriction on disclosure or an obligation of secrecy contained in an enactment and is likely to be disclosed in breach of the restriction or obligation if a warrant is not issued, or
(iv) service of notice of an application for a production order under paragraph 4 of Schedule 1 to the 1984 Act may seriously prejudice the investigation.

(8) In relation to any set of premises which the applicant wants to be searched by the officers executing the warrant with other persons authorised by the court, the application must–
(a) identify those other persons, by function or description; and
(b) explain why those persons are required.

Application for warrant under paragraph 11 of Schedule 5 to the Terrorism Act 2000

47.31.–(1) This rule applies where an applicant wants a Circuit judge to issue a warrant or warrants under paragraph 11 of Schedule 5 to the Terrorism Act 2000. **B-799**

(2) As well as complying with rule 47.26, the application must–
(a) specify the offence under investigation;
(b) explain how the investigation constitutes a terrorist investigation within the meaning of the Terrorism Act 2000;
(c) so far as practicable, identify the material sought (and see paragraph (4));
(d) specify the premises to be searched (and see paragraph (5)); and
(e) state whether the applicant wants other persons to accompany the officers executing the warrant or warrants (and see paragraph (6)).

(3) Where the applicant relies on an assertion that a production order made under paragraph 5 of Schedule 5 to the 2000 Act in respect of material on the premises has not been complied with–
(a) the application must–
(i) identify that order and describe its terms, and
(ii) specify the date on which it was served; but
(b) the application need not comply with paragraphs (4) or (5)(b).

(4) In relation to the material sought, unless paragraph (3) applies the application must explain the grounds for believing that–
(a) the material consists of or includes excluded material or special procedure material but does not include items subject to legal privilege;
(b) the material is likely to be of substantial value to a terrorist investigation (whether by itself, or together with other material); and
(c) it is not appropriate to make an order under paragraph 5 of Schedule 11 to the 2000 Act in relation to the material because–
(i) it is not practicable to communicate with any person entitled to produce the material,
(ii) it is not practicable to communicate with any person entitled to grant access to the material or entitled to grant entry to premises to which the application for the warrant relates, or

(iii) a terrorist investigation may be seriously prejudiced unless a constable can secure immediate access to the material.

(5) In relation to the premises which the applicant wants to be searched, the application must—

(a) specify—

(i) where paragraph (3) applies, the respondent and any premises to which the production order referred, or

(ii) in any other case, one or more sets of premises, or any premises occupied or controlled by a specified person (which may include one or more specified sets of premises);

(b) unless paragraph (3) applies, in relation to premises which the applicant wants to be searched but cannot specify, explain why—

(i) it is necessary to search any premises occupied or controlled by the specified person, and

(ii) it is not reasonably practicable to specify all the premises which that person occupies or controls which might need to be searched; and

(c) explain the grounds for believing that material sought is on those premises.

(6) In relation to any set of premises which the applicant wants to be searched by the officers executing the warrant with other persons authorised by the court, the application must—

(a) identify those other persons, by function or description; and

(b) explain why those persons are required.

Application for warrant under section 352 of the Proceeds of Crime Act 2002

B-800 **47.32.**—(1) This rule applies where an applicant wants a Crown Court judge to issue a warrant or warrants under—

(a) section 352 of the Proceeds of Crime Act 2002; or

(b) article 13 of the Proceeds of Crime Act 2002 (External Investigations) Order 2014 (S.I. 2014 No. 1893).

(2) As well as complying with rule 47.26, the application must—

(a) explain whether the investigation is a confiscation investigation, a money laundering investigation, a detained cash investigation, a detained property investigation, a frozen funds investigation or an external investigation;

(b) in the case of an investigation in the United Kingdom, explain why the applicant suspects that—

(i) the person under investigation has benefited from criminal conduct, in the case of a confiscation investigation, or committed a money laundering offence, in the case of a money laundering investigation, or

(ii) in the case of a detained cash investigation, a detained property investigation or a frozen funds investigation, the cash or property involved, or the money held in the frozen account, was obtained through unlawful conduct or is intended to be used in unlawful conduct;

(c) in the case of an investigation outside the United Kingdom, explain why the applicant believes that—

(i) there is an investigation by an overseas authority which relates to a criminal investigation or to criminal proceedings (including proceedings to remove the benefit of a person's criminal conduct following that person's conviction), and

(ii) the investigation is into whether property has been obtained as a result of or in connection with criminal conduct, or into the extent or whereabouts of such property;

(d) indicate what material is sought (and see paragraphs (4) and (5));

(e) specify the premises to be searched (and see paragraph (6)); and

(f) state whether the applicant wants other persons to accompany the officers executing the warrant or warrants (and see paragraph (7)).

(3) Where the applicant relies on an assertion that a production order made under sections 345 and 351 of the 2002 Act or under articles 6 and 12 of the 2014 Order has not been complied with—

(a) the application must—

(i) identify that order and describe its terms,

(ii) specify the date on which it was served, and

(iii) explain the grounds for believing that the material in respect of which the order was made is on the premises specified in the application for the warrant; but

(b) the application need not comply with paragraphs (4) or (5).

(4) Unless paragraph (3) applies, in relation to the material sought the application must—

(a) specify the material; or

(b) give a general description of the material and explain the grounds for believing that it relates to the person, cash, property or money under investigation and–
(i) in the case of a confiscation investigation, relates to the question whether that person has benefitted from criminal conduct, or to any question about the extent or whereabouts of that benefit,
(ii) in the case of a money laundering investigation, relates to the question whether that person has committed a money laundering offence,
(iii) in the case of a detained cash investigation, a detained property investigation or a frozen funds investigation into the derivation of cash, property or money, relates to the question whether that cash, property or money is recoverable property,
(iv) in the case of a detained cash investigation, a detained property investigation or a frozen funds investigation into the intended use of cash, property or money, relates to the question whether that cash, property or money is intended by any person to be used in unlawful conduct, or
(v) in the case of an investigation outside the United Kingdom, relates to that investigation.

(5) Unless paragraph (3) applies, in relation to the material sought the application must explain also the grounds for believing that–
(a) the material consists of or includes special procedure material but does not include excluded material or privileged material;
(b) the material is likely to be of substantial value to the investigation (whether by itself, or together with other material); and
(c) it is in the public interest for the material to be obtained, having regard to–
(i) other potential sources of information, and
(ii) the benefit likely to accrue to the investigation if the material is obtained.

(6) In relation to the premises which the applicant wants to be searched, unless paragraph (3) applies the application must–
(a) explain the grounds for believing that material sought is on those premises;
(b) if the application specifies the material sought, explain the grounds for believing that it is not appropriate to make a production order under sections 345 and 351 of the 2002 Act or under articles 6 and 12 of the 2014 Order because–
(i) it is not practicable to communicate with any person against whom the production order could be made,
(ii) it is not practicable to communicate with any person who would be required to comply with an order to grant entry to the premises, or
(iii) the investigation might be seriously prejudiced unless an appropriate person is able to secure immediate access to the material; and
(c) if the application gives a general description of the material sought, explain the grounds for believing that–
(i) it is not practicable to communicate with any person entitled to grant entry to the premises,
(ii) entry to the premises will not be granted unless a warrant is produced, or
(iii) the investigation might be seriously prejudiced unless an appropriate person arriving at the premises is able to secure immediate access to them;

(7) In relation to any set of premises which the applicant wants to be searched by those executing the warrant with other persons authorised by the court, the application must–
(a) identify those other persons, by function or description; and
(b) explain why those persons are required.

Application for warrant under section 160 of the Extradition Act 2003

47.33.–(1) This rule applies where an applicant wants a Circuit judge to issue a warrant or warrants under section 160 of the Extradition Act 2003. **B-801**

(2) As well as complying with rule 47.26, the application must–
(a) identify the person whose extradition is sought (and see paragraph (3));
(b) specify the extradition offence of which that person is accused;
(c) specify the material, or description of material, sought (and see paragraph (4)); and
(d) specify the premises to be searched (and see paragraph (5)).

(3) In relation to the person whose extradition is sought, the application must explain the grounds for believing that–
(a) that person has committed the offence for which extradition is sought;
(b) that offence is an extradition offence; and

(c) that person is in the United Kingdom or is on the way to the United Kingdom.

(4) In relation to the material sought, the application must explain the grounds for believing that—

(a) the material consists of or includes special procedure or excluded material; and

(b) the material would be likely to be admissible evidence at a trial in England and Wales for the offence for which extradition is sought.

(5) In relation to the premises which the applicant wants to search, the application must explain the grounds for believing that—

(a) material sought is on those premises; and

(b) one or more of the following conditions is satisfied, namely—

(i) it is not practicable to communicate with any person entitled to grant entry to the premises,

(ii) it is practicable to communicate with such a person but it is not practicable to communicate with any person entitled to grant access to the material sought, or

(iii) the material contains information which is subject to a restriction on disclosure or an obligation of secrecy contained in an enactment and is likely to be disclosed in breach of the restriction or obligation if a warrant is not issued.

(6) In relation to any set of premises which thc applicant wants to be searched by the officers executing the warrant with other persons authorised by the court, the application must—

(a) identify those other persons, by function or description; and

(b) explain why those persons are required.

Application for warrant under any other power

B-802 **47.34.**—(1) This rule applies—

(a) where an applicant wants a court to issue a warrant or warrants under a power (in this rule, "the relevant search power") to which rule 47.24(d) (other powers) refers; but

(b) subject to any inconsistent provision in legislation that applies to the relevant search power.

(2) As well as complying with rule 47.26, the application must—

(a) demonstrate the applicant's entitlement to apply;

(b) identify the relevant search power (and see paragraph (3));

(c) so far as practicable, identify the articles or persons sought (and see paragraph (4));

(d) specify the premises to be searched (and see paragraphs (5) and (6));

(e) state whether the applicant wants the premises to be searched on more than one occasion, if the relevant search power allows (and see paragraph (7)); and

(f) state whether the applicant wants other persons to accompany the officers executing the warrant or warrants, if the relevant search power allows (and see paragraph (8)).

(3) The application must—

(a) include or attach the terms of the relevant search power; and

(b) explain how the circumstances satisfy the criteria prescribed by that power for making the application.

(4) In relation to the articles or persons sought, the application must explain how they satisfy the criteria prescribed by the relevant search power about such articles or persons.

(5) In relation to premises which the applicant wants to be searched and can specify, the application must—

(a) specify each set of premises; and

(b) in respect of each, explain how the circumstances satisfy any criteria prescribed by the relevant search power—

(i) for asserting that the articles or persons sought are on those premises, and

(ii) for asserting that the court can exercise its power to authorise the search of those particular premises.

(6) In relation to premises which the applicant wants to be searched but at least some of which the applicant cannot specify, the application must—

(a) explain how the relevant search power allows the court to authorise such searching;

(b) specify the person who occupies or controls such premises;

(c) specify as many sets of such premises as is reasonably practicable;

(d) explain why—

(i) it is necessary to search more premises than those specified, and

(ii) it is not reasonably practicable to specify all the premises which the applicant wants to be searched;

(e) in respect of each set of premises, whether specified or not, explain how the circumstances satisfy any criteria prescribed by the relevant search power for asserting that the articles or persons sought are on those premises; and
(f) in respect of each specified set of premises, explain how the circumstances satisfy any criteria prescribed by the relevant search power for asserting that the court can exercise its power to authorise the search of those premises.

(7) In relation to any set of premises which the applicant wants to be searched on more than one occasion, the application must–
(a) explain how the relevant search power allows the court to authorise such searching;
(b) explain why the applicant wants the premises to be searched more than once; and
(c) specify any proposed maximum number of occasions.

(8) In relation to any set of premises which the applicant wants to be searched by the officers executing the warrant with other persons authorised by the court, the application must–
(a) identify those other persons, by function or description; and
(b) explain why those persons are required.

Section 4: Orders for the retention or return of property

When this Section applies

47.35.–(1) This Section applies where– B-803
(a) under section 1 of the Police (Property) Act 1897, a magistrates' court can–
(i) order the return to the owner of property which has come into the possession of the police or the National Crime Agency in connection with an investigation of a suspected offence, or
(ii) make such order with respect to such property as the court thinks just, where the owner cannot be ascertained; and
(b) a Crown Court judge can–
(i) order the return of seized property under section 59(4) of the Criminal Justice and Police Act 2001 [§ 15A-117 in the main work], or
(ii) order the examination, retention, separation or return of seized property under section 59(5) of the Act.

(2) In this Section, a reference to a person with "a relevant interest" in seized property means someone from whom the property was seized, or someone with a proprietary interest in the property, or someone who had custody or control of it immediately before it was seized.

Exercise of court's powers

47.36.–(1) The court may determine an application for an order– B-804
(a) at a hearing (which must be in private unless the court otherwise directs), or without a hearing; and
(b) in a party's absence, if that party–
(i) applied for the order, or
(ii) has had at least 10 business days in which to make representations.

(2) The court officer must arrange for the court to hear such an application no sooner than 10 business days after it was served, unless–
(a) the court directs that no hearing need be arranged; or
(b) the court gives other directions for the hearing.

(3) If the court so directs, the parties to an application may attend a hearing by live link or telephone.

(4) The court may–
(a) shorten or extend (even after it has expired) a time limit under this Section;
(b) dispense with a requirement for service under this Section (even after service was required); and
(c) consider an application made orally instead of in writing.

(5) A person who wants an extension of time must–
(a) apply when serving the application or representations for which it is needed; and
(b) explain the delay.

Rule 47.36 of the Criminal Procedure Rules 2020 (SI 2020/759) is temporarily amended by r.13(c) of the Criminal Procedure (Amendment No. 2) (Coronavirus) Rules 2020 (SI 2020/417) so as to remove "or telephone" in para.(3). This amendment ceases to have effect when ss.53 to 55 (and Schs 23 to 25) of the Coronavirus Act 2020 expire.

Application for an order under section 1 of the Police (Property) Act 1897

B-805 **47.37.**—(1) This rule applies where an applicant wants the court to make an order to which rule 47.35(1)(a) refers.

(2) The applicant must apply in writing and serve the application on—

(a) the court officer; and

(b) as appropriate—

(i) the officer who has the property,

(ii) any person who appears to be its owner.

(3) The application must—

(a) explain the applicant's interest in the property (either as a person who claims to be its owner or as an officer into whose possession the property has come);

(b) specify the direction that the applicant wants the court to make, and explain why; and

(c) include or attach a list of those on whom the applicant has served the application.

Application for an order under section 59 of the Criminal Justice and Police Act 2001

B-806 **47.38.**—(1) This rule applies where an applicant wants the court to make an order to which rule 47.35(1)(b) refers.

(2) The applicant must apply in writing and serve the application on—

(a) the court officer; and

(b) as appropriate—

(i) the person who for the time being has the seized property,

(ii) each person whom the applicant knows or believes to have a relevant interest in the property.

(3) In each case, the application must—

(a) explain the applicant's interest in the property (either as a person with a relevant interest, or as possessor of the property in consequence of its seizure, as appropriate);

(b) explain the circumstances of the seizure of the property and identify the power that was exercised to seize it (or which the person seizing it purported to exercise, as appropriate); and

(c) include or attach a list of those on whom the applicant has served the application.

(4) On an application for an order for the return of property under section 59(4) of the Criminal Justice and Police Act 2001, the application must explain why any one or more of these applies—

(a) there was no power to make the seizure;

(b) the property seized is, or contains, an item subject to legal privilege which is not an item that can be retained lawfully in the circumstances listed in section 54(2) of the Act [§ 15A-161 in the main work];

(c) the property seized is, or contains, excluded or special procedure material which is not material that can be retained lawfully in the circumstances listed in sections 55 and 56 of the Act; or

(d) the property seized is, or contains, something taken from premises under section 50 of the Act [[ibid., § 15A-106], or from a person under section 51 of the Act [ibid., § 15A-108], in the circumstances listed in those sections and which cannot lawfully be retained on the conditions listed in the Act.

(5) On an application for an order for the examination, retention, separation or return of property under section 59(5) of the 2001 Act, the application must—

(a) specify the direction that the applicant wants the court to make, and explain why;

(b) if applicable, specify each requirement of section 53(2) of the Act (examination and return of property [ibid., § 15A-111]) which is not being complied with; and

(c) if applicable, explain why the retention of the property by the person who now has it would be justified on the grounds that, even if it were returned, it would immediately become appropriate for that person to get it back under—

(i) a warrant for its seizure, or

(ii) a production order made under paragraph 4 of Schedule 1 to the Police and Criminal Evidence Act 1984, section 20BA of the Taxes Management Act 1970 or paragraph 5 of Schedule 5 to the Terrorism Act 2000.

Application containing information withheld from another party

B-807 **47.39.**—(1) This rule applies where—

(a) an applicant serves an application to which rule 47.37 (application for an order under section 1 of the Police (Property) Act 1897) or rule 47.38 (application for an order under section 59 of the Criminal Justice and Police Act 2001) applies; and

(b) the application includes information that the applicant thinks ought not be revealed to another party.

(2) The applicant must–

(a) omit that information from the part of the application that is served on that other party;

(b) mark the other part to show that, unless the court otherwise directs, it is only for the court; and

(c) in that other part, explain why the applicant has withheld that information from that other party.

(3) If the court so directs, any hearing of an application to which this rule applies may be, wholly or in part, in the absence of a party from whom information has been withheld.

(4) At any hearing of an application to which this rule applies–

(a) the general rule is that the court must consider, in the following sequence–

(i) representations first by the applicant and then by each other party, in all the parties' presence, and then

(ii) further representations by the applicant, in the absence of a party from whom information has been withheld; but

(b) the court may direct other arrangements for the hearing.

Representations in response

47.40.–(1) This rule applies where a person wants to make representations about an application under rule 47.37 or rule 47.38. **B-808**

(2) Such a person must–

(a) serve the representations on–

(i) the court officer, and

(ii) the applicant and any other party to the application;

(b) do so not more than 10 business days after service of the application; and

(c) ask for a hearing, if that person wants one.

(3) Representations in opposition to an application must explain why the grounds on which the applicant relies are not met.

(4) Where representations include information that the person making them thinks ought not be revealed to another party, that person must–

(a) omit that information from the representations served on that other party;

(b) mark the information to show that, unless the court otherwise directs, it is only for the court; and

(c) with that information include an explanation of why it has been withheld from that other party.

Application to punish for contempt of court

47.41.–(1) This rule applies where a person is accused of disobeying an order under section 59 of the Criminal Justice and Police Act 2001. **B-809**

(2) A person who wants the court to exercise its power to punish that person for contempt of court must comply with the rules in Part 48 (contempt of court).

SECTION 5: ORDERS FOR THE RETENTION OF FINGERPRINTS, ETC.

When this Section applies

47.42. This Section applies where– **B-810**

(a) a District Judge (Magistrates' Court) can make an order under–

(i) section 63F(7) or 63R(6) of the Police and Criminal Evidence Act 1984, or

(ii) paragraph 20B(5) or 20G(6) of Schedule 8 to the Terrorism Act 2000 [ibid., §§ 25-145b, 12-145g]; and

(b) the Crown Court can determine an appeal under–

(i) section 63F(10) of the Police and Criminal Evidence Act 1984, or

(ii) paragraph 20B(8) of Schedule 8 to the Terrorism Act 2000.

Exercise of court's powers

47.43.–(1) The court must determine an application under rule 47.44, and an appeal under rule 47.45– **B-811**

(a) at a hearing, which must be in private unless the court otherwise directs; and

(b) in the presence of the applicant or appellant.

(2) The court must not determine such an application or appeal unless any person served under those rules—

(a) is present; or

(b) has had an opportunity—

(i) to attend, or

(ii) to make representations.

Application to extend retention period

B-812 **47.44.**—(1) This rule applies where a magistrates' court can make an order extending the period for which there may be retained material consisting of—

(a) fingerprints taken from a person—

(i) under a power conferred by Part V of the Police and Criminal Evidence Act 1984,

(ii) with that person's consent, in connection with the investigation of an offence by the police, or

(iii) under a power conferred by Schedule 8 to the Terrorism Act 2000[ibid., §§ 25-134 et seq.] in relation to a person detained under section 41 of that Act [ibid., § 25-52];

(b) a DNA profile derived from a DNA sample so taken; or

(c) a sample so taken.

(2) A chief officer of police who wants the court to make such an order must—

(a) apply in writing—

(i) within the period of 3 months ending on the last day of the retention period, where the application relates to fingerprints or a DNA profile, or

(ii) before the expiry of the retention period, where the application relates to a sample;

(b) in the application—

(i) identify the material,

(ii) state when the retention period expires,

(iii) give details of any previous such application relating to the material, and

(iv) outline the circumstances in which the material was acquired;

(c) serve the application on the court officer, in every case; and

(d) serve the application on the person from whom the material was taken, where—

(i) the application relates to fingerprints or a DNA profile, or

(ii) the application is for the renewal of an order extending the retention period for a sample.

(3) An application to extend the retention period for fingerprints or a DNA profile must explain why that period should be extended.

(4) An application to extend the retention period for a sample must explain why, having regard to the nature and complexity of other material that is evidence in relation to the offence, the sample is likely to be needed in any proceedings for the offence for the purposes of—

(a) disclosure to, or use by, a defendant; or

(b) responding to any challenge by a defendant in respect of the admissibility of material that is evidence on which the prosecution proposes to rely.

(5) On an application to extend the retention period for fingerprints or a DNA profile, the applicant must serve notice of the court's decision on any respondent where—

(a) the court makes the order sought; and

(b) the respondent was absent when it was made.

Appeal

B-813 **47.45.**—(1) This rule applies where, under rule 47.44, a magistrates' court determines an application relating to fingerprints or a DNA profile and—

(a) the person from whom the material was taken wants to appeal to the Crown Court against an order extending the retention period; or

(b) a chief officer of police wants to appeal to the Crown Court against a refusal to make such an order.

(2) The appellant must—

(a) serve an appeal notice—

(i) on the Crown Court officer and on the other party, and

(ii) not more than 15 business days after the magistrates' court's decision, or, if applicable, service of notice under rule 47.44(5); and

(b) in the appeal notice, explain, as appropriate, why the retention period should, or should not, be extended.

(3) Rule 34.11 (constitution of the Crown Court) applies on such an appeal.

When this Section applies

47.46. This Section applies where– **B-814**

(a) a justice of the peace can make or discharge an investigation anonymity order, under sections 76 and 80(1) of the Coroners and Justice Act 2009 [§ 2-106, in the main work]; and

(b) a Crown Court judge can determine an appeal against –

(i) a refusal of such an order, under section 79 of the 2009 Act, or

(ii) a decision on an application to discharge such an order, under section 80(6) of the 2009 Act.

Exercise of court's powers

47.47.–(1) The court may determine an application for an investigation anonymity order, and any appeal against the refusal of such an order– **B-815**

(a) at a hearing (which must be in private unless the court otherwise directs); or

(b) without a hearing.

(2) The court must determine an application to discharge an investigation anonymity order, and any appeal against the decision on such an application–

(a) at a hearing (which must be in private unless the court otherwise directs); and

(b) in the presence of the person specified in the order, unless–

(i) that person applied for the discharge of the order,

(ii) that person has had an opportunity to make representations, or

(iii) the court is satisfied that it is not reasonably practicable to communicate with that person.

(3) The court may consider an application or an appeal made orally instead of in writing.

Application for an investigation anonymity order

47.48.–(1) This rule applies where an applicant wants a magistrates' court to make an investigation anonymity order. **B-816**

(2) The applicant must–

(a) apply in writing;

(b) serve the application on the court officer;

(c) identify the person to be specified in the order, unless–

(i) the applicant wants the court to determine the application at a hearing, or

(ii) the court otherwise directs;

(d) explain how the proposed order meets the conditions prescribed by section 78 of the Coroners and Justice Act 2009;

(e) say if the applicant intends to appeal should the court refuse the order;

(f) attach any material on which the applicant relies; and

(g) propose the terms of the order.

(3) At any hearing of the application, the applicant must–

(a) identify to the court the person to be specified in the order, unless–

(i) the applicant has done so already, or

(ii) the court otherwise directs; and

(b) unless the applicant has done so already, inform the court if the applicant intends to appeal should the court refuse the order.

Application to discharge an investigation anonymity order

47.49.–(1) This rule applies where one of the following wants a magistrates' court to discharge an investigation anonymity order– **B-817**

(a) an applicant; or

(b) the person specified in the order.

(2) That applicant or the specified person must–

(a) apply in writing as soon as practicable after becoming aware of the grounds for doing so;

(b) serve the application on–

(i) the court officer, and as applicable

(ii) the applicant for the order, and

(iii) the specified person;

(c) explain—

(i) what material circumstances have changed since the order was made, or since any previous application was made to discharge it, and

(ii) why it is appropriate for the order to be discharged; and

(d) attach—

(i) a copy of the order, and

(ii) any material on which the applicant relies.

(3) A party must inform the court if that party intends to appeal should the court discharge the order.

Appeal

B-818 **47.50.**—(1) This rule applies where one of the following ("the appellant") wants to appeal to the Crown Court—

(a) the applicant for an investigation anonymity order, where a magistrates' court has refused to make the order; or

(b) a party to an application to discharge such an order, where a magistrates' court has decided that application.

(2) The appellant must—

(a) serve on the Crown Court officer a copy of the application to the magistrates' court; and

(b) where the appeal concerns a discharge decision, notify each other party,

not more than 15 business days after the decision against which the appellant wants to appeal.

(3) The Crown Court must hear the appeal without justices of the peace.

Section 7: Investigation approval orders under the Regulation of Investigatory Powers Act 2000

When this Section applies

B-819 **47.51.**—(1) This Section applies where a justice of the peace can make an order approving—

(a) the grant or renewal of an authorisation, or the giving or renewal of a notice, under section 23A of the Regulation of Investigatory Powers Act 2000; and

(b) the grant or renewal of an authorisation under section 32A of the 2000 Act.

Exercise of court's powers

B-820 **47.52.**—(1) Rule 47.5 (investigation orders; exercise of court's powers) applies, subject to sections 23B(2) and 32B(2) of the Regulation of Investigatory Powers Act 2000.

(2) Where a magistrates' court refuses to approve the grant, giving or renewal of an authorisation or notice, the court must not exercise its power to quash that authorisation or notice unless the applicant has had at least 2 business days from the date of the refusal in which to make representations.

Application for approval for authorisation or notice

B-821 **47.53.**—(1) This rule applies where an applicant wants a magistrates' court to make an order approving—

(a) under sections 23A and 23B of the Regulation of Investigatory Powers Act 2000—

(i) an authorisation to obtain or disclose communications data, under section 22(3) of the 2000 Act, or

(ii) a notice that requires a postal or telecommunications operator if need be to obtain, and in any case to disclose, communications data, under section 22(4) of the 2000 Act; or

(b) under sections 32A and 32B of the Regulation of Investigatory Powers Act 2000, an authorisation for—

(i) the carrying out of directed surveillance, under section 28 of the 2000 Act, or

(ii) the conduct or use of a covert human intelligence source, under section 29 of the 2000 Act.

(2) The applicant must—

(a) apply in writing and serve the application on the court officer;

(b) attach the authorisation or notice which the applicant wants the court to approve;

(c) attach such other material (if any) on which the applicant relies to satisfy the court—

(i) as required by section 23A(3) and (4) of the 2000 Act, in relation to communications data,

(ii) as required by section 32A(3) and (4) of the 2000 Act, in relation to directed surveillance, or

(iii) as required by section 32A(5) and (6), and, if relevant, section 43(6A), of the 2000 Act, in relation to a covert human intelligence source; and

(d) propose the terms of the order.

SECTION 8: ORDERS FOR ACCESS TO DOCUMENTS, ETC. UNDER THE CRIMINAL APPEAL ACT 1995

When this Section applies

47.54. This section applies where the Crown Court can order a person to give the Criminal Cases Review Commission access to a document or other material under section 18A of the Criminal Appeal Act 1995. **B-822**

Exercise of court's powers

47.55.—(1) Subject to paragraphs (2), (3) and (4), the court may determine an application by the Criminal Cases Review Commission for an order— **B-823**

(a) at a hearing (which must be in private unless the court otherwise directs), or without a hearing; and

(b) in the absence of—

(i) the Commission,

(ii) the respondent, and

(iii) any other person affected by the order.

(2) The court must not determine such an application in the Commission's absence if—

(a) the Commission asks for a hearing; or

(b) it appears to the court that the application is so complex or serious as to require the court to hear the Commission.

(3) The court must not determine such an application in the absence of any respondent or other person affected, unless—

(a) the absentee has had at least 2 business days in which to make representations; or

(b) the court is satisfied that—

(i) the Commission cannot identify or contact the absentee,

(ii) it would prejudice the exercise of the Commission's functions to adjourn or postpone the application so as to allow the absentee to attend, or

(iii) the absentee has waived the opportunity to attend.

(4) The court must not determine such an application in the absence of any respondent who, if the order sought by the Commission were made, would be required to produce or give access to journalistic material, unless that respondent has waived the opportunity to attend.

(5) The court officer must arrange for the court to hear such an application no sooner than 2 business days after it was served, unless—

(a) the court directs that no hearing need be arranged; or

(b) the court gives other directions for the hearing.

(6) The court must not determine an application unless satisfied that sufficient time has been allowed for it.

(7) If the court so directs, the parties to an application may attend a hearing by live link or telephone.

(8) The court must not make an order unless an officer of the Commission states, in writing or orally, that to the best of that officer's knowledge and belief—

(a) the application discloses all the information that is material to what the court must decide; and

(b) the content of the application is true.

(9) Where the statement required by paragraph (8) is made orally—

(a) the statement must be on oath or affirmation, unless the court otherwise directs; and

(b) the court must arrange for a record of the making of the statement.

(10) The court may shorten or extend (even after it has expired) a time limit under this section.

Rule 47.55 of the Criminal Procedure Rules 2020 (SI 2020/759) (see the main work) is temporarily amended by r.13(d) of the Criminal Procedure (Amendment No. 2) (Coronavirus) Rules 2020 (SI 2020/417) so as to remove "or telephone" in para.(7). This amendment ceases to have effect when ss.53 to 55 (and Schs 23 to 25) of the Coronavirus Act 2020 expire.

Application for an order for access

47.56.—(1) Where the Criminal Cases Review Commission wants the court to make an order for access to a document or other material, the Commission must— **B-824**

(a) apply in writing and serve the application on the court officer;
(b) give the court an estimate of how long the court should allow—
(i) to read the application and prepare for any hearing, and
(ii) for any hearing of the application;
(c) attach a draft order in the terms proposed by the Commission; and
(d) serve the application and draft order on the respondent.

(2) The application must—
(a) identify the respondent;
(b) describe the document, or documents, or other material sought;
(c) explain the reasons for thinking that—
(i) what is sought is in the respondent's possession or control, and
(ii) access to what is sought may assist the Commission in the exercise of any of its functions; and
(d) explain the Commission's proposals for—
(i) the manner in which the respondent should give access, and
(ii) the period within which the order should take effect.

(3) The Commission must serve any order made on the respondent.

Application containing information withheld from a respondent or other person

B-825 **47.57.**—(1) This rule applies where—
(a) the Criminal Cases Review Commission serves an application under rule 47.56 (application for an order for access); and
(b) the application includes information that the Commission thinks ought not be revealed to a recipient.

(2) The Commission must—
(a) omit that information from the part of the application that is served on that recipient;
(b) mark the other part, to show that it is only for the court; and
(c) in that other part, explain why the Commission has withheld it from that recipient.

(3) A hearing of an application to which this rule applies may take place, wholly or in part, in the absence of that recipient and any other person.

(4) At a hearing of an application to which this rule applies—
(a) the general rule is that the court must consider, in the following sequence—
(i) representations first by the Commission and then by the other parties, in the presence of them all, and then
(ii) further representations by the Commission, in the others' absence; but
(b) the court may direct other arrangements for the hearing.

Application to punish for contempt of court

B-826 **47.58.**—(1) This rule applies where a person is accused of disobeying an order for access made under section 18A of the Criminal Appeal Act 1995.

(2) An applicant who wants the court to exercise its power to punish that person for contempt of court must comply with the rules in Part 48 (contempt of court).

[The next paragraph is B-830.]

Section 9: Orders for the Extension of a Moratorium Period under the Proceeds of Crime Act 2002

When this Section applies

★B-830 **47.59.**—(1) This Section applies where the Crown Court can extend a moratorium period under section 336A of the Proceeds of Crime Act 2002 .

(2) In this Section, "respondent" means, as well as a person within the meaning of rule 47.2(c), an "interested person" within the meaning of section 336D of the 2002 Act.

[This rule is printed as re-numbered, with effect from 8 February 2021, by SI 2021/40, r.27(l).]

Exercise of court's powers

★B-831 **47.60.**—(1) The court may determine an application to which rule 47.61 (application for extension of moratorium period) applies—
(a) at a hearing (which must be in private unless the court otherwise directs), or without a hearing; and

(b) in the absence of–
 (i) the applicant, and
 (ii) a respondent.

(2) The court must not determine such an application in the applicant's absence if the applicant asks for a hearing.

(3) The court must not determine such an application in the absence of a respondent unless–
(a) the absentee has had at least 2 business days in which to make representations; or
(b) the court is satisfied that–
 (i) the applicant cannot identify or contact the absentee,
 (ii) it would prejudice the investigation if the absentee were present,
 (iii) it would prejudice the investigation to adjourn or postpone the application so as to allow the absentee to attend, or
 (iv) the absentee has waived the opportunity to attend.

(4) The court officer must arrange for the court to hear such an application no sooner than 2 business days after notice of the application was served, unless–
(a) the court directs that no hearing need be arranged; or
(b) the court gives other directions for the hearing.

(5) If the court so directs, the parties to an application may attend a hearing by live link or telephone.

(6) The court must not extend a moratorium period unless the applicant states, in writing or orally, that to the best of the applicant's knowledge and belief–
(a) the application discloses all the information that is material to what the court must decide; and
(b) the content of the application is true.

(7) Where the statement required by paragraph (6) is made orally–
(a) the statement must be on oath or affirmation, unless the court otherwise directs; and
(b) the court must arrange for a record of the making of the statement.

(8) The court may–
(a) shorten or extend (even after it has expired) a time limit imposed by this rule;
(b) dispense with a requirement for service under this Section (even after service was required); and
(c) consider an application made orally instead of in writing.

Rule 47.60 of the Criminal Procedure Rules 2020 (SI 2020/759) is temporarily amended by r.13(f) of the Criminal Procedure (Amendment No. 2) (Coronavirus) Rules 2020 (SI 2020/417) so as to remove "or telephone" in para.(5). This amendment ceases to have effect when ss.53 to 55 (and Schs 23 to 25) of the Coronavirus Act 2020 expire. This rule is also printed as re-numbered and amended, with effect from 8 February 2021, by SI 2021/40, r.27(l) and (n).

Application for extension of moratorium period

47.61.–(1) This rule applies where an applicant wants the court to extend a moratorium period. **★B-832**

(2) The applicant must–
(a) apply in writing before the date on which the moratorium period otherwise would end;
(b) demonstrate that the applicant is entitled to apply as a senior officer within the meaning of section 336D of the Proceeds of Crime Act 2002;
(c) serve the application on the court officer;
(d) serve notice on each respondent that an application has been made; and
(e) serve the application on each respondent to such extent, if any, as the court directs.

(3) The application must specify–
(a) the disclosure in respect of which the application is made;
(b) the date on which the moratorium period began;
(c) the date and period of any previous extension of that period; and
(d) the date on which that period is due to end.

(4) The application must–
(a) describe the investigation being carried out in relation to that disclosure; and
(b) explain the grounds for believing that–
 (i) the investigation is being conducted diligently and expeditiously,
 (ii) further time is needed for conducting the investigation, and

(iii) it would be reasonable in all the circumstances for the moratorium period to be extended.

(5) A respondent who objects to the application must—

(a) serve notice of the objection on—

(i) the court officer, and

(ii) the applicant,

not more than 2 business days after service of notice of the application; and

(b) in that notice explain the grounds of the objection.

(6) The applicant must serve any order made on each respondent.

[This rule is printed as re-numbered, with effect from 8 February 2021, by SI 2021/40, r.27(l).]

Application containing information withheld from a respondent

★B-833 **47.62.**—(1) This rule applies where an application to extend a moratorium period includes an application to withhold information from a respondent.

(2) The applicant must—

(a) omit that information from any part of the application that is served on the respondent;

(b) mark the other part to show that, unless the court otherwise directs, it is only for the court; and

(c) in that other part, explain the grounds for believing that the disclosure of that information would have one or more of the following results—

(i) evidence of an offence would be interfered with or harmed,

(ii) the gathering of information about the possible commission of an offence would be interfered with,

(iii) a person would be interfered with or physically injured,

(iv) the recovery of property under this Act would be hindered, or

(v) national security would be put at risk.

(3) At any hearing of an application to which this rule applies—

(a) the court must first determine the application to withhold information, in the respondent's absence and that of any legal representative of the respondent; and

(b) if the court allows the application to withhold information, then in the following sequence—

(i) the court must consider representations first by the applicant and then by the respondent, in the presence of both, and

(ii) the court may consider further representations by the applicant in the respondent's absence and that of any legal representative of the respondent.

(4) If the court refuses an application to withhold information from the respondent, the applicant may withdraw the application to extend the moratorium period.

[This rule is printed as re-numbered, with effect from 8 February 2021, by SI 2021/40, r.27(l).]

Section 10: Orders for Access to Electronic Data under the Crime (Overseas Production Orders) Act 2019

When this Section applies

★B-834 **47.63.**—(1) This Section applies where the Crown Court can make an overseas production order under section 1 of the Crime (Overseas Production Orders) Act 2019.

(2) In this Section, a reference to a person affected by such an order includes a person by whom or on whose behalf there is stored any journalistic data specified or described in the application for that order.

[This rule is printed as re-numbered, with effect from 8 February 2021, by SI 2021/40, r.27(o).]

Exercise of court's powers

★B-835 **47.64.**—(1) Subject to paragraphs (2), (3) and (4), the court may determine an application under rule 47.65 for an overseas production order, or an application under rule 47.66 to vary or revoke an order—

(a) at a hearing (which must be in private unless the court otherwise directs), or without a hearing; and

(b) in the absence of—

(i) the applicant,

(ii) the respondent, and

(iii) any other person affected by the order.

(2) The court must not determine such an application in the applicant's absence if—

(a) the applicant asks for a hearing; or
(b) it appears to the court that–
(i) the proposed order may require the production of excepted electronic data, within the meaning of section 3 of the Crime (Overseas Production Orders) Act 2019, or
(ii) for any other reason the application is so complex or serious as to require the court to hear the applicant.

(3) The court must not determine such an application in the absence of any respondent or other person affected unless–
(a) the absentee has had at least 2 business days in which to make representations; or
(b) the court is satisfied that–
(i) the applicant cannot identify or contact the absentee,
(ii) it would prejudice the investigation if the absentee were present,
(iii) where journalistic data is sought, it would prejudice the investigation of another indictable offence or another terrorist investigation if the absentee were present,
(iv) it would prejudice the investigation to adjourn or postpone the application so as to allow the absentee to attend, or
(v) the absentee has waived the opportunity to attend.

(4) The court must not determine such an application in the absence of any respondent who, if the order sought by the applicant were made, would be required to produce or give access to journalistic data, unless that respondent has waived the opportunity to attend.

(5) The court officer must arrange for the court to hear such an application no sooner than 2 business days after notice of the application was served, unless–
(a) the court directs that no hearing need be arranged; or
(b) the court gives other directions for the hearing.

(6) The court must not determine an application unless satisfied that sufficient time has been allowed for it.

(7) If the court so directs, the parties to an application may attend a hearing by live link or telephone.

(8) The court must not make, vary or revoke an order unless the applicant states, in writing or orally, that to the best of the applicant's knowledge and belief–
(a) the application discloses all the information that is material to what the court must decide; and
(b) the content of the application is true.

(9) Where the statement required by paragraph (8) is made orally–
(a) the statement must be on oath or affirmation, unless the court otherwise directs; and
(b) the court must arrange for a record of the making of the statement.

(10) The court may–
(a) shorten or extend (even after it has expired) a time limit under this Section;
(b) dispense with a requirement for service under this Section (even after service was required); and
(c) consider an application made orally instead of in writing.

(11) A person who wants an extension of time must–
(a) apply when serving the application for which it is needed; and
(b) explain the delay.

Rule 47.64 of the Criminal Procedure Rules 2020 (SI 2020/759) is temporarily amended by r.13(g) of the Criminal Procedure (Amendment No. 2) (Coronavirus) Rules 2020 (SI 2020/417) so as to remove "or telephone" in para.(7). This amendment ceases to have effect when ss.53 to 55 (and Schs 23 to 25) of the Coronavirus Act 2020 expire. This rule is also printed as re-numbered and amended, with effect from 8 February 2021, by SI 2021/40, r.27(o) and (p).

Application for order

47.65.–(1) An applicant who wants the court to make an overseas production order must– ★B-836
(a) apply in writing and serve the application on the court officer;
(b) demonstrate that the applicant is entitled to apply;
(c) give the court an estimate of how long the court should allow–
(i) to read the application and prepare for any hearing, and
(ii) for any hearing of the application;
(d) attach a draft order in the terms proposed by the applicant;

(e) serve notice of the application on the respondent and on any other person affected by the order, unless the court otherwise directs; and
(f) serve the application on the respondent and on any such other person to such extent, if any, as the court directs.

(2) A notice served on the respondent and on any other person affected by the order must—
(a) specify or describe the electronic data in respect of which the application is made; and
(b) identify—
(i) the power that the applicant invites the court to exercise, and
(ii) the conditions for the exercise of that power which the applicant asks the court to find are met.

(3) The application must—
(a) specify the designated international co-operation arrangement by reference to which the application is made;
(b) identify the respondent;
(c) explain the grounds for believing that the respondent operates in, or is based in, a country or territory outside the United Kingdom which is a party to, or participates in, that designated international co-operation arrangement;
(d) specify or describe the electronic data in respect of which the order is sought;
(e) explain the grounds for believing that the electronic data sought does not consist of or include excepted electronic data;
(f) briefly describe the investigation for the purposes of which the electronic data is sought and explain—
(i) the grounds for believing that an indictable offence has been committed which is under investigation or in respect of which proceedings have begun, or
(ii) how the investigation constitutes a terrorist investigation within the meaning of the Terrorism Act 2000;
(g) explain the grounds for believing that the respondent has possession or control of all or part of the electronic data sought;
(h) explain the grounds for believing that the electronic data sought is likely to be of substantial value to the investigation, or to the proceedings (as the case may be), whether by itself or together with other material;
(i) where paragraph (3)(f)(i) applies, explain the grounds for believing that all or part of the electronic data sought is likely to be relevant evidence in respect of the offence concerned;
(j) explain the grounds for believing that it is in the public interest for the respondent to produce or give access to the electronic data sought, having regard to—
(i) the benefit likely to accrue to the investigation, or to the proceedings (as the case may be), if that data is obtained, and
(ii) the circumstances under which the respondent has possession or control of any of that data;
(k) specify—
(i) the person, or the description of person, to whom the applicant wants the court to order that electronic data must be produced or made accessible, and
(ii) the period by the end of which the applicant wants the court to order that that electronic data must be produced or made accessible (which must be a period of 7 days beginning with the day on which the order is served on the respondent, unless the court otherwise directs); and
(l) where the applicant wants the court to include a non-disclosure requirement in the order—
(i) explain why such a requirement would be appropriate, and
(ii) specify or describe when the applicant wants that requirement, if ordered, to expire.

(4) In the event that an overseas production order is made, the applicant must serve the order on the Secretary of State for service on the respondent.

(5) Where notice of the application was served on a respondent, in the event that the application is dismissed or abandoned the applicant must—
(a) promptly so notify that respondent; and
(b) where the application is dismissed, promptly inform that respondent if the court nonetheless orders that for a period that respondent must not—
(i) conceal, destroy, alter or dispose of any of the electronic data specified or described in the application, or
(ii) disclose the making of the application or its contents to any person.

[This rule is printed as re-numbered, with effect from 8 February 2021, by SI 2021/40, r.27(o).]

Application to vary or revoke an order

47.66.–(1) The orders to which this rule applies are– ★B-837

(a) an overseas production order;
(b) an order under section 8(4) of the Crime (Overseas Production Orders) Act 2019 maintaining an unexpired non-disclosure requirement;
(c) an order under section 13(3) of the 2019 Act maintaining a duty not to conceal, destroy, alter or dispose of electronic data, and not to disclose the making or content of an application for an overseas production order; and
(d) an order under section 13(4)(b) of the Act maintaining a duty not to conceal, destroy, alter or dispose of electronic data.

(2) This rule applies where one of the following wants the court to vary, to further vary or to revoke an order listed in paragraph (1)–

(a) the applicant for that order, or an equivalent appropriate officer;
(b) the respondent;
(c) another person affected by the order; or
(d) the Secretary of State.

(3) The applicant for the variation or revocation must–

(a) apply in writing as soon as practicable after becoming aware of the grounds for doing so;
(b) serve the application on–
  (i) the court officer, and
  (ii) as applicable, the applicant for the order, the respondent, any other person known to be affected and the Secretary of State; and
(c) ask for a hearing, if one is wanted, and explain why it is needed.

(4) Where the applicant wants the court to vary, or further vary, an overseas production order, the application must–

(a) specify or describe the electronic data in respect of which the varied order is sought (which may include electronic data not specified or described in the original order);
(b) satisfy or, as the case may be, continue to satisfy, the requirements of rule 47.65(3)(a) and (c) to (i) (which may be done by reference to the original application); and
(c) meet the requirements of rule 47.65(3)(j).

(5) Where the applicant wants the court to revoke an overseas production order, the application must–

(a) explain why revocation is appropriate;
(b) if the applicant wants the court, despite revocation, to maintain the requirement that for a period the respondent must not conceal, destroy, alter or dispose of any of the electronic data specified or described in the order–
  (i) explain why it would be appropriate to maintain that requirement, and
  (ii) specify or describe when the applicant wants that requirement, if maintained, to expire; and
(c) if the order includes an unexpired non-disclosure requirement that the applicant wants the court, despite revocation, to maintain–
  (i) explain why it would be appropriate to maintain that requirement, and
  (ii) specify or describe when the applicant wants that requirement, if maintained, to expire.

(6) Where the applicant wants the court to vary, to further vary or to revoke an order under section 8(4), section 13(3) or section 13(4)(b) of the 2019 Act the application must–

(a) explain–
  (i) what material circumstances have changed since the order was made, and
  (ii) why the order should be varied or revoked, as the case may be, as a result; and
(b) if applicable, specify the variation proposed.

[This rule is printed as re-numbered and amended, with effect from 8 February 2021, by SI 2021/40, r.27(o) and (r).]

Application containing information withheld from a respondent or other person

47.67.–(1) This rule applies where an application under rule 47.65 or 47.66 includes information that the applicant thinks ought to be revealed only to the court. ★B-838

(2) The application must–

(a) identify that information; and

(b) explain why that information ought not to be served on the respondent or another person.

(3) At a hearing of an application to which this rule applies—

(a) the general rule is that the court must consider, in the following sequence—

(i) representations first by the applicant and then by the respondent and any other person, in the presence of them all, and then

(ii) further representations by the applicant, in the others' absence; but

(b) the court may direct other arrangements for the hearing.

[This rule is printed as re-numbered and amended, with effect from 8 February 2021, by SI 2021/40, r.27(o) and (s).]

Application to punish for contempt of court

B-839 **47.68.**—(1) This rule applies where a person is accused of disobeying an order made by the court under the Crime (Overseas Production Orders) Act 2019.

(2) An applicant who wants the court to exercise its power to punish that person for contempt of court must comply with the rules in Part 48 (Contempt of court).

[This rule is printed as re-numbered, with effect from 8 February 2021, by SI 2021/40, r.27(o).]

CPD XI Other proceedings 47A: Investigation orders and warrants (substituted by Criminal Practice Directions 2015 (Amendment No. 8) [2019] EWCA Crim 495, Lord Burnett CJ)

B-840 **47A.1** Powers of entry, search and seizure, and powers to obtain banking and other confidential information, are among the most intrusive that investigators can exercise. Every application must be carefully scrutinised with close attention paid to what the relevant statutory provision requires of the applicant and to what it permits. CrimPR Part 47 must be followed, and the prescribed forms (retaining the Notes for Guidance section) must be used. These are designed to prompt applicants, and the courts, to deal with all of the relevant criteria.

47A.2 The issuing of a warrant or the making of such an order is never to be treated as a formality and it is therefore essential that the judge or magistrate considering the application is given, and must take, sufficient time for the purpose. The prescribed forms require the applicant to provide a time estimate, and listing officers and justices' legal advisers should take account of these.

47A.3 Applicants for orders and warrants owe the court duties of candour and truthfulness. On any application made without notice to the respondent, and so on all applications for search warrants, the duty of frank and complete disclosure is especially onerous. The applicant must draw the court's attention to any information that is unfavourable to the application. The existence of unfavourable information will not necessarily lead to the application being refused; it will be a matter for the court what weight to place on each piece of information. As Hughes LJ made clear in *Re Stanford International Limited* "In effect a prosecutor seeking an ex parte order must put on his defence hat and ask himself what, if he was representing the defendant or a third party with a relevant interest, he would be saying to the judge, and, having answered that question, that is what he must tell the judge". This is, as Aitkins LJ recognised, "a heavy burden but a vital safeguard. Full details must be given."

47A.4 Where an applicant supplements an application with additional oral or written information, on questioning by the court or otherwise, it is essential that the court keeps an adequate record. What is needed will depend upon the circumstances. The Rules require that a record of the 'gist' be retained. The purpose of such a record is to allow the sufficiency of the court's reasons for its decision subsequently to be assessed. The gravity of such decisions requires that their exercise should be susceptible to scrutiny and to explanation by reference to all of the information that was taken into account.

47A.5 The forms that accompany CrimPR Part 47 provide for the most frequently encountered applications. The included Notes for Guidance summarise for the applicant and the court the relevant criteria for making and considering an application. However, there are some hundreds of powers of entry, search and seizure, supplied by a corresponding number of legislative provisions. In any criminal matter, if there is no form designed for the particular warrant or order sought, the forms should still be used, as far as is practicable, and adapted as necessary. The applicant should pay particular attention to the specific legislative requirements for the granting of such an application to ensure that the court has all of the necessary information, and, if the court might be unfamiliar with the legislation, should provide a copy of the relevant provisions. Applicants must comply with the duties of candour and truthfulness, and include in their application the declarations required by the Rules and must make disclosure of any unfavourable information to the court.

Criminal Practice Direction XI (Other proceedings) 47B: Investigation orders and warrants in the Crown Court (inserted by Criminal Practice Directions 2015 (Amendment No. 8) [2019] EWCA Crim 495, Lord Burnett CJ)

47B.1 This section covers applications made under: **B-841**
(i) Schedule 1 Police and Criminal Evidence Act 1984 (PACE);
(ii) Section 2 Criminal Justice Act 1987;
(iii) Drug Trafficking Act 1994;
(iv) Part 8 of the Proceeds of Crime Act 2002;
(v) Section 5 Coroners and Justice Act 2009;
(vi) Terrorism Act 2000.

It does NOT cover applications under the Extradition Act 2003.

Crown Court centres

47B.2 Investigators must give careful consideration to which Crown Court centre is most appropriate to hear the application. In all cases, the application must explain the rationale for choosing the particular court centre. Relevant considerations will usually be: **B-842**

- where any subsequent proceedings are likely to be commenced;
- where a main suspect has some geographical connection; and/or
- where, in broad terms, the offending has taken place.

A court centre should not be chosen simply because it is most convenient or proximate to the investigators location. Any dispute over the proper venue for an application should be determined by the relevant Presiding Judges.

47B.3 Where the investigation is complex, lengthy and/or involves multiple suspects all applications should be made to one court centre. To ensure consistency, all subsequent applications arising out of the same or any connected investigation should be made to the same court centre and, where practicable, the same judge.

47B.4 Judges can refuse to determine applications and request they be resubmitted (if necessary to another court) where:

- the application is not in the proper form;
- there is an inaccurate reading time estimate; and/or
- there is insufficient justification for the application to be made at that court centre.

Dealing with applications without a hearing

47B.5 The court must not determine an application in the applicant's absence in the circumstances set out in CrimPR 47.5(2); or in the absence of any respondent in the circumstances set out in CrimPR 47.5(3) and (4). **B-843**

47B.6 When permitted by the rules, and where the application has been sufficiently completed and submitted on the correct form, there is a presumption that the application will be dealt with without a hearing. The judge is always entitled to require a hearing to clarify omissions or ambiguity on the application, or for any other reason.

47B.7 It will often not be appropriate for a court to deal with an application without a hearing in the following situations:

- where the investigation involved covert activity or the application is based on material gathered covertly;
- where the application is based on material which is especially sensitive and/or where it will be necessary to ensure the security at court of the material produced in support of the application;
- where the case may result in substantial local and/or national public interest;
- where the application is particularly lengthy, serious or complex.

47B.8 Applications should be sent electronically to the designated secure email address at the relevant court centre.

47B.9 A judge considering an application without a hearing will subject the application to the usual intense level of scrutiny ensuring that the relevant statutory requirements have been met. If the judge is not so satisfied then the judge will refuse the application, require further information to be served or adjourn it for a hearing in court, which can be carried out via live link or telephone, where permitted by the Rules. The Court will inform the applicant of the outcome and make the necessary arrangements for any additional hearings that may be required. There is no requirement for any order to be signed by the judge with a "wet ink" signature. The applicant will be notified electronically of any orders that are made.

47B.10 Applications considered without a hearing will be determined by a judge as soon as practicable. Approved orders will be returned electronically to the applicant and an electronic copy must be securely saved by the court. If there is a particular urgency with any application, that fact should be made clear to the court when it is served and the judge should expedite it where possible.

Listing

B-844 **47B.11** To assist the listing process, the applicant must supply a realistic estimate of the reading time required when the application is served. This estimate should be provided in the application and in the covering email to which it is attached. The covering email should also stipulate whether there have been any previous applications in the same or any connected investigation and provide the name of the judge who granted any previous Orders.

47B.12 Where the judge has decided that a hearing is required to determine or further consider the application, the expectation is that this hearing should usually take place by live link or telephone. 4 Where the judge directs a hearing at court, any additional material relied on by the applicant must be brought to court on the day of the hearing. Any additional material should not be retained by the court once the application has been determined, but must be taken away by the applicant at the end of the hearing.

47B.13 When listing such hearings consideration should be given to Division XIII Listing of these practice directions which states at A.1 that listing is a judicial responsibility and function. G.3(1) of that division envisages that such applications will be completed by 10.30am or start after 4.30pm so as not to interfere with trials. This general direction does not prevent a judge from considering applications outside of these times where other court business allows.

47B.14 However, as paragraph G.8 of Division XIII Listing makes clear, along with the relevant case law, that the search powers in PACE constitute "a serious inroad upon the liberty of the subject. The responsibility for ensuring that the procedure is not abused lies with circuit judges. It is of cardinal importance that circuit judges should be scrupulous in discharging that responsibility." 6 Accordingly, there must be adequate time allowed for the judge to read carefully the application and all the supporting evidence supplied with it. The judge will require sufficient time to enable a short judgment to be given, where necessary so that in the event of challenge in the Administrative Court there is an explanation of the reasons for the decision for that court to consider.

Darts recording

B-845 **47B.15** Hearings in court are required to be recorded whether on DARTS or some other secure method such as on a hand-held machine. Determination of the method of recording is a matter for the judge.

Criminal Procedure Rules 2020 (SI 2020/759), Pt 48

CONTEMPT OF COURT

General rules

When this Part applies

B-846 **48.1**—(1) This Part applies where the court can deal with a person for conduct—

(a) in contempt of court; or

(b) in contravention of the legislation to which rules 48.5 and 48.9 refer.

(2) In this Part, "respondent" means any such person.

Exercise of court's power to deal with contempt of court

B-847 **48.2**—(1) The court must determine at a hearing—

(a) an enquiry under rule 48.8; and

(b) an allegation under rule 48.9.

(2) The court must not proceed in the respondent's absence unless—

(a) the respondent's behaviour makes it impracticable to proceed otherwise; or

(b) the respondent has had at least 10 business days' notice of the hearing, or was present when it was arranged.

(3) If the court hears part of an enquiry or allegation in private, it must announce at a hearing in public—

(a) the respondent's name;

(b) in general terms, the nature of any conduct that the respondent admits, or the court finds proved; and

(c) any punishment imposed.

Notice of suspension of imprisonment by Court of Appeal or Crown Court

B-848 **48.3**—(1) This rule applies where—

(a) the Court of Appeal or the Crown Court suspends an order of imprisonment for contempt of court; and

(b) the respondent is absent when the court does so.

(2) The respondent must be served with notice of the terms of the court's order–

(a) by any applicant under rule 48.9; or

(b) by the court officer, in any other case.

Application to discharge an order for imprisonment

48.4–(1) This rule applies where the court can discharge an order for a respondent's imprisonment for contempt of court. **B-849**

(2) A respondent who wants the court to discharge such an order must–

(a) apply in writing, unless the court otherwise directs, and serve any written application on–

(i) the court officer, and

(ii) any applicant under rule 48.9 on whose application the respondent was imprisoned;

(b) in the application–

(i) explain why it is appropriate for the order for imprisonment to be discharged, and

(ii) give details of any appeal, and its outcome; and

(c) ask for a hearing, if the respondent wants one.

Contempt of court by obstruction, disruption, etc.

Initial procedure on obstruction, disruption, etc.

48.5–(1) This rule applies where the court observes, or someone reports to the court– **B-850**

(a) in the Court of Appeal or the Crown Court, obstructive, disruptive, insulting or intimidating conduct, in the courtroom or in its vicinity, or otherwise immediately affecting the proceedings;

(b) in the Crown Court, a contravention of–

(i) section 3 of the Criminal Procedure (Attendance of Witnesses) Act 1965 (disobeying a witness summons [§ 8-24, in the main work]);

(ii) section 20 of the Juries Act 1974 (disobeying a jury summons [ibid., § 28-41]);

(c) in a magistrates' court, a contravention of–

(i) section 97(4) of the Magistrates' Courts Act 1980 (refusing to give evidence), or

(ii) section 12 of the Contempt of Court Act 1981 (insulting or interrupting the court, etc. [ibid., § 28-81]);

(d) a contravention of section 9 of the Contempt of Court Act 1981 (without the court's permission, recording the proceedings, etc. [ibid., § 28-74]); or

(e) any other conduct with which the court can deal as, or as if it were, a criminal contempt of court, except failure to surrender to bail under section 6 of the Bail Act 1976 [ibid., § 3-31].

(2) Unless the respondent's behaviour makes it impracticable to do so, the court must–

(a) explain, in terms the respondent can understand (with help, if necessary)–

(i) the conduct that is in question,

(ii) that the court can impose imprisonment, or a fine, or both, for such conduct,

(iii) (where relevant) that the court has power to order the respondent's immediate temporary detention, if in the court's opinion that is required,

(iv) that the respondent may explain the conduct,

(v) that the respondent may apologise, if he or she so wishes, and that this may persuade the court to take no further action, and

(vi) that the respondent may take legal advice; and

(b) allow the respondent a reasonable opportunity to reflect, take advice, explain and, if he or she so wishes, apologise.

(3) The court may then–

(a) take no further action in respect of that conduct;

(b) enquire into the conduct there and then; or

(c) postpone that enquiry (if a magistrates' court, only until later the same day).

Review after temporary detention

48.6–(1) This rule applies in a case in which the court has ordered the respondent's immediate temporary detention for conduct to which rule 48.5 applies. **B-851**

(2) The court must review the case–

(a) if a magistrates' court, later the same day; or

(b) in the Court of Appeal or the Crown Court, no later than the next business day.

(3) On the review, the court must—
(a) unless the respondent is absent, repeat the explanations required by rule 48.5(2)(a); and
(b) allow the respondent a reasonable opportunity to reflect, take advice, explain and, if he or she so wishes, apologise.
(4) The court may then—
(a) take no further action in respect of the conduct;
(b) if a magistrates' court, enquire into the conduct there and then; or
(c) if the Court of Appeal or the Crown Court—
(i) enquire into the conduct there and then, or
(ii) postpone the enquiry, and order the respondent's release from such detention in the meantime.

Postponement of enquiry

B-852 **48.7**—(1) This rule applies where the Court of Appeal or the Crown Court postpones the enquiry.
(2) The court must arrange for the preparation of a written statement containing such particulars of the conduct in question as to make clear what the respondent appears to have done.
(3) The court officer must serve on the respondent—
(a) that written statement;
(b) notice of where and when the postponed enquiry will take place; and
(c) a notice that—
(i) reminds the respondent that the court can impose imprisonment, or a fine, or both, for contempt of court, and
(ii) warns the respondent that the court may pursue the postponed enquiry in the respondent's absence, if the respondent does not attend.

Procedure on enquiry

B-853 **48.8**—(1) At an enquiry, the court must—
(a) ensure that the respondent understands (with help, if necessary) what is alleged, if the enquiry has been postponed from a previous occasion;
(b) explain what the procedure at the enquiry will be; and
(c) ask whether the respondent admits the conduct in question.
(2) If the respondent admits the conduct, the court need not receive evidence.
(3) If the respondent does not admit the conduct, the court must consider—
(a) any statement served under rule 48.7;
(b) any other evidence of the conduct;
(c) any evidence introduced by the respondent; and
(d) any representations by the respondent about the conduct.
(4) If the respondent admits the conduct, or the court finds it proved, the court must—
(a) before imposing any punishment for contempt of court, give the respondent an opportunity to make representations relevant to punishment;
(b) explain, in terms the respondent can understand (with help, if necessary)—
(i) the reasons for its decision, including its findings of fact, and
(ii) the punishment it imposes, and its effect; and
(c) if a magistrates' court, arrange for the preparation of a written record of those findings.
(5) The court that conducts an enquiry—
(a) need not include the same member or members as the court that observed the conduct; but
(b) may do so, unless that would be unfair to the respondent.

Contempt of court by failure to comply with court order, etc.

Initial procedure on failure to comply with court order, etc.

B-854 **48.9**—(1) This rule applies where—
(a) a party, or other person directly affected, alleges—
(i) in the Crown Court, a failure to comply with an order to which applies rule 33.70 (compliance order, restraint order or ancillary order), rule 47.9 (certain investigation orders under the Police and Criminal Evidence Act 1984, the Terrorism Act 2000, the Proceeds of Crime Act 2002, the Proceeds of Crime Act 2002 (External Investigations) Order 2014 and the Extradition Act 2003), rule 47.41 (order for retention or return of property under section 59 of the Criminal Justice and Police Act 2001 [§ 15A-108

in the main work]) or rule 47.58 (order for access under section 18A of the Criminal Appeal Act 1995),

(ii) in the Court of Appeal or the Crown Court, any other conduct with which that court can deal as a civil contempt of court, or

(iii) in the Crown Court or a magistrates' court, unauthorised use of disclosed prosecution material under section 17 of the Criminal Procedure and Investigations Act 1996 [§ 12-88, in the main work]; or

(b) the court deals on its own initiative with conduct to which paragraph (1)(a) applies.

(2) Such a party or person must–

(a) apply in writing and serve the application on the court officer; and

(b) serve on the respondent–

(i) the application, and

(ii) notice of where and when the court will consider the allegation (not less than 10 business days after service).

(3) The application must–

(a) identify the respondent;

(b) explain that it is an application for the respondent to be dealt with for contempt of court;

(c) contain such particulars of the conduct in question as to make clear what is alleged against the respondent; and

(d) include a notice warning the respondent that the court–

(i) can impose imprisonment, or a fine, or both, for contempt of court, and

(ii) may deal with the application in the respondent's absence, if the respondent does not attend the hearing.

(4) A court which acts on its own initiative under paragraph (1)(b) must–

(a) arrange for the preparation of a written statement containing the same information as an application; and

(b) arrange for the service on the respondent of–

(i) that written statement, and

(ii) notice of where and when the court will consider the allegation (not less than 10 business days after service).

Procedure on hearing

48.10–(1) At the hearing of an allegation under rule 48.9, the court must– **B-855**

(a) ensure that the respondent understands (with help, if necessary) what is alleged;

(b) explain what the procedure at the hearing will be; and

(c) ask whether the respondent admits the conduct in question.

(2) If the respondent admits the conduct, the court need not receive evidence.

(3) If the respondent does not admit the conduct, the court must consider–

(a) the application or written statement served under rule 48.9;

(b) any other evidence of the conduct;

(c) any evidence introduced by the respondent; and

(d) any representations by the respondent about the conduct.

(4) If the respondent admits the conduct, or the court finds it proved, the court must–

(a) [*identical to r.48.8(4)(a), B-853*];

(b) [*identical to r.48.8(4)(b), B-853*]; and

(c) in a magistrates' court, arrange for the preparation of a written record of those findings.

Introduction of written witness statement or other hearsay

48.11–(1) Where rule 48.9 applies, an applicant or respondent who wants to introduce in evidence the written statement of a witness, or other hearsay, must– **B-856**

(a) serve a copy of the statement, or notice of other hearsay, on–

(i) the court officer, and

(ii) the other party; and

(b) serve the copy or notice–

(i) when serving the application under rule 48.9, in the case of an applicant, or

(ii) not more than 5 business days after service of that application or of the court's written statement, in the case of the respondent.

(2) Such service is notice of that party's intention to introduce in evidence that written witness statement, or other hearsay, unless that party otherwise indicates when serving it.

(3) A party entitled to receive such notice may waive that entitlement.

Content of written witness statement

B-857 **48.12**—(1) This rule applies to a written witness statement served under rule 48.11.

(2) Such a written witness statement must contain a declaration by the person making it that it is true to the best of that person's knowledge and belief.

Content of notice of other hearsay

B-858 **48.13**—(1) This rule applies to a notice of hearsay, other than a written witness statement, served under rule 48.11.

(2) Such a notice must—

(a) set out the evidence, or attach the document that contains it; and
(b) identify the person who made the statement that is hearsay.

Cross-examination of maker of written witness statement or other hearsay

B-859 **48.14**—(1) This rule applies where a party wants the court's permission to cross-examine a person who made a statement which another party wants to introduce as hearsay.

(2) The party who wants to cross-examine that person must—

(a) apply in writing, with reasons; and
(b) serve the application on—
  (i) the court officer, and
  (ii) the party who served the hearsay.

(3) A respondent who wants to cross-examine such a person must apply to do so not more than 5 business days after service of the hearsay by the applicant.

(4) An applicant who wants to cross-examine such a person must apply to do so not more than 3 business days after service of the hearsay by the respondent.

(5) The court—

(a) may decide an application under this rule without a hearing; but
(b) must not dismiss such an application unless the person making it has had an opportunity to make representations at a hearing.

Credibility and consistency of maker of written witness statement or other hearsay

B-860 **48.15**—(1) This rule applies where a party wants to challenge the credibility or consistency of a person who made a statement which another party wants to introduce as hearsay.

(2) The party who wants to challenge the credibility or consistency of that person must—

(a) serve notice of intention to do so on—
  (i) the court officer, and
  (ii) the party who served the hearsay; and
(b) in it, identify any statement or other material on which that party relies.

(3) A respondent who wants to challenge such a person's credibility or consistency must serve such a notice not more than 5 business days after service of the hearsay by the applicant.

(4) An applicant who wants to challenge such a person's credibility or consistency must serve such a notice not more than 3 business days after service of the hearsay by the respondent.

(5) The party who served the hearsay—

(a) may call that person to give oral evidence instead; and
(b) if so, must serve notice of intention to do so on—
  (i) the court officer, and
  (ii) the other party

  as soon as practicable after service of the notice under paragraph (2).

Magistrates' courts' powers to adjourn, etc.

B-861 **48.16**—(1) This rule applies where a magistrates' court deals with unauthorised disclosure of prosecution material under sections 17 and 18 of the Criminal Procedure and Investigations Act 1996 [§§ 12-88, 12-91 in the main work].

(2) The sections of the Magistrates' Courts Act 1980 listed in paragraph (3) apply as if in those sections—

(a) "complaint" and "summons" each referred to an application or written statement under rule 48.9;
(b) "complainant" meant an applicant; and
(c) "defendant" meant the respondent.

(3) Those sections are–
(a) section 51 (issue of summons on complaint);
(b) section 54 (adjournment);
(c) section 55 (non-appearance of defendant);
(d) section 97(1) (summons to witness);
(e) section 121(1) (constitution and place of sitting of court); and
(f) section 123 (defect in process).
(4) Section 127 of the 1980 Act (limitation of time) does not apply.

Court's power to vary requirements

48.17.–(1) The court may shorten or extend (even after it has expired) a time limit under rule 48.11, 48.14 or 48.15. **B-862**

(2) A person who wants an extension of time must–
(a) apply when serving the statement, notice or application for which it is needed; and
(b) explain the delay.

CPD XI Other proceedings 48A: Contempt in the face of the magistrates' court

General

48A.1 The procedure to be followed in cases of contempt of court is given in CrimPR Part 48. The magistrates' courts' power to deal with contempt in the face of the court is contained within section 12 of the Contempt of Court Act 1981. Magistrates' courts also have the power to punish a witness who refuses to be sworn or give evidence under section 97(4) of the Magistrates' Courts Act 1980. **B-863**

Contempt consisting of wilfully insulting anyone specified in section 12 or interrupting proceedings

48A.2 In the majority of cases, an apology and a promise as to future conduct should be sufficient for the court to order a person's release. However, there are likely to be certain cases where the nature and seriousness of the misconduct requires the court to consider using its powers, under section 12(2) of the Contempt of Court Act 1981, either to fine or to order the person's committal to custody. **B-864**

Imposing a penalty for contempt

48A.3 The court should allow the person a further opportunity to apologise for his or her contempt, and should follow the procedure at CrimPR 48.8(4). The court should consider whether it is appropriate to release the person or whether it must exercise its powers to fine the person or to commit the person to custody under section 12(2) of the 1981 Act. In deciding how to deal with the person, the court should have regard to the period for which he or she has been detained, whether the conduct was admitted and the seriousness of the contempt. Any period of committal to custody should be for the shortest period of time commensurate with the interests of preserving good order in the administration of justice. **B-865**

Criminal Procedure Rules 2020 (SI 2020/759), Pt 49

International Co-operation

Notice required to accompany process served outside the United Kingdom and translations

49.1.–(1) The notice which by virtue of section 3(4)(b) of the Crime (International Co-operation) Act 2003 (general requirements for service of process) must accompany any process served outside the United Kingdom must give the information specified in paragraphs (2) and (4) below. **B-866**

(2) The notice must–
(a) state that the person required by the process to appear as a party or attend as a witness can obtain information about his rights in connection therewith from the relevant authority; and
(b) give the particulars specified in paragraph (4) about that authority.
(3) The relevant authority where the process is served–
(a) at the request of the prosecuting authority, is that authority; or
(b) at the request of the defendant or the prosecutor in the case of a private prosecution, is the court by which the process is served.
(4) The particulars referred to in paragraph (2) are–
(a) the name and address of the relevant authority, together with its telephone and fax numbers and e-mail address; and

(b) the name of a person at the relevant authority who can provide the information referred to in paragraph (2)(a), together with his telephone and fax numbers and e-mail address.

(5) The justices' clerk or Crown Court officer must send, together with any process served outside the United Kingdom—

(a) any translation which is provided under section 3(3)(b) of the 2003 Act; and

(b) any translation of the information required to be given by this rule which is provided to him.

(6) In this rule, 'process' has the same meaning as in section 51(3) of the 2003 Act.

Proof of service outside the United Kingdom

B-867 **49.2.**—(1) A statement in a certificate given by or on behalf of the Secretary of State—

(a) that process has been served on any person under section 4(1) of the Crime (International Co-operation) Act 2003 (service of process otherwise than by post);

(b) of the manner in which service was effected; and

(c) of the date on which process was served;

shall be admissible as evidence of any facts so stated.

(2) In this rule, 'process' has the same meaning as in section 51(3) of the 2003 Act.

Supply of copy of notice of request for assistance abroad

B-868 **49.3.** Where a request for assistance under section 7 of the Crime (International Co-operation) Act 2003 is made by a justice of the peace or a judge exercising the jurisdiction of the Crown Court and is sent in accordance with section 8(1) of the 2003 Act, the justices' clerk or the Crown Court officer shall send a copy of the letter of request to the Secretary of State as soon as practicable after the request has been made.

Persons entitled to appear and take part in proceedings before a nominated court, and exclusion of the public

B-869 **49.4.** A court nominated under section 15(1) of the Crime (International Co-operation) Act 2003 (nominating a court to receive evidence) may—

(a) determine who may appear or take part in the proceedings under Schedule 1 to the 2003 Act before the court and whether a party to the proceedings is entitled to be legally represented; and

(b) direct that the public be excluded from those proceedings if it thinks it necessary to do so in the interests of justice.

Record of proceedings to receive evidence before a nominated court

B-870 **49.5.**—(1) Where a court is nominated under section 15(1) of the Crime (International Co-operation) Act 2003 the justices' clerk or Crown Court officer shall enter in an overseas record—

(a) details of the request in respect of which the notice under section 15(1) of the 2003 Act was given;

(b) the date on which, and place at which, the proceedings under Schedule 1 to the 2003 Act in respect of that request took place;

(c) the name of any witness who gave evidence at the proceedings in question;

(d) the name of any person who took part in the proceedings as a legal representative or an interpreter;

(e) whether a witness was required to give evidence on oath or (by virtue of section 5 of the Oaths Act 1978) after making a solemn affirmation; and

(f) whether the opportunity to cross-examine any witness was refused.

(2) When the court gives the evidence received by it under paragraph 6(1) of Schedule 1 to the 2003 Act to the court or authority that made the request or to the territorial authority for forwarding to the court or authority that made the request, the justices' clerk or Crown Court officer shall send to the court, authority or territorial authority (as the case may be) a copy of an extract of so much of the overseas record as relates to the proceedings in respect of that request.

Interpreter for the purposes of proceedings involving a television or telephone link

B-871 **49.6.**—(1) This rule applies where a court is nominated under section 30(3) (hearing witnesses in the UK through television links) or section 31(4) (hearing witnesses in the UK by telephone) of the Crime (International Co-operation) Act 2003.

(2) Where it appears to the justices' clerk or the Crown Court officer that the witness to be heard in the proceedings under Part 1 or 2 of Schedule 2 to the 2003 Act ('the relevant proceedings') is likely to give evidence in a language other than English, he shall make arrangements for an interpreter to be present at the proceedings to translate what is said into English.

(3) Where it appears to the justices' clerk or the Crown Court officer that the witness to be heard in the relevant proceedings is likely to give evidence in a language other than that in which the proceedings of the court referred to in section 30(1) or, as the case may be, 31(1) of the 2003 Act ('the external court') will be conducted, he shall make arrangements for an interpreter to be present at the relevant proceedings to translate what is said into the language in which the proceedings of the external court will be conducted.

(4) Where the evidence in the relevant proceedings is either given in a language other than English or is not translated into English by an interpreter, the court shall adjourn the proceedings until such time as an interpreter can be present to provide a translation into English.

(5) Where a court in Wales understands Welsh–

(a) paragraph (2) does not apply where it appears to the justices' clerk or Crown Court officer that the witness in question is likely to give evidence in Welsh;

(b) paragraph (4) does not apply where the evidence is given in Welsh; and

(c) any translation which is provided pursuant to paragraph (2) or (4) may be into Welsh instead of English.

Record of television link hearing before a nominated court

49.7.–(1) This rule applies where a court is nominated under section 30(3) of the Crime (International Co-operation) Act 2003. **B-872**

(2) The justices' clerk or Crown Court officer shall enter in an overseas record–

(a) details of the request in respect of which the notice under section 30(3) of the 2003 Act was given;

(b) the date on which, and place at which, the proceedings under Part 1 of Schedule 2 to that Act in respect of that request took place;

(c) the technical conditions, such as the type of equipment used, under which the proceedings took place;

(d) the name of the witness who gave evidence;

(e) the name of any person who took part in the proceedings as a legal representative or an interpreter; and

(f) the language in which the evidence was given.

(3) As soon as practicable after the proceedings under Part 1 of Schedule 2 to the 2003 Act took place, the justices' clerk or Crown Court officer shall send to the external authority that made the request a copy of an extract of so much of the overseas record as relates to the proceedings in respect of that request.

Record of telephone link hearing before a nominated court

49.8.–(1) This rule applies where a court is nominated under section 31(4) of the Crime (International Co-operation) Act 2003. **B-873**

(2) The justices' clerk or Crown Court officer shall enter in an overseas record–

(a) details of the request in respect of which the notice under section 31(4) of the 2003 Act was given;

(b) the date, time and place at which the proceedings under Part 2 of Schedule 2 to the 2003 Act took place;

(c) the name of the witness who gave evidence;

(d) the name of any interpreter who acted at the proceedings; and

(e) the language in which the evidence was given.

Overseas record

49.9.–(1) The overseas records of a magistrates' court shall be part of the register (within the meaning of section 150(1) of the Magistrates' Courts Act 1980). **B-874**

(2) The overseas records of any court shall not be open to inspection by any person except–

(a) as authorised by the Secretary of State; or

(b) with the leave of the court.

Overseas freezing orders

49.10.–(1) This rule applies where a court is nominated under section 21(1) of the Crime (International Co-operation) Act 2003 to give effect to an overseas freezing order. **B-875**

(2) Where the Secretary of State serves a copy of such an order on the court officer–

(a) the general rule is that the court must consider the order no later than the next business day; but

(b) exceptionally, the court may consider the order later than that, but not more than 5 business days after service.

(3) The court must not consider the order unless—

(a) it is satisfied that the chief officer of police for the area in which the evidence is situated has had notice of the order; and

(b) that chief officer of police has had an opportunity to make representations, at a hearing if that officer wants.

(4) The court may consider the order—

(a) without a hearing; or

(b) at a hearing, in public or in private.

Overseas forfeiture orders

B-876 **49.11.**—(1) This rule applies where—

(a) the Crown Court can—

(i) make a restraint order under article 5 of the Criminal Justice (International Co-operation) Act 1990 (Enforcement of Overseas Forfeiture Orders) Order 2005, or

(ii) give effect to an external forfeiture order under article 19 of that Order;

(b) the Director of Public Prosecutions or the Director of the Serious Fraud Office receives—

(i) a request for the restraint of property to which article 3 of the 2005 Order applies, or

(ii) a request to give effect to an external forfeiture order to which article 15 of the Order applies; and

(c) the Director wants the Crown Court to—

(i) make such a restraint order, or

(ii) give effect to such a forfeiture order.

(2) The Director must—

(a) apply in writing;

(b) serve the application on the court officer; and

(c) serve the application on the defendant and on any other person affected by the order, unless the court is satisfied that—

(i) the application is urgent, or

(ii) there are reasonable grounds for believing that to give notice of the application would cause the dissipation of the property which is the subject of the application.

(3) The application must—

(a) identify the property the subject of the application;

(b) identify the person who is or who may become the subject of such a forfeiture order;

(c) explain how the requirements of the 2005 Order are satisfied, as the case may be—

(i) for making a restraint order, or

(ii) for giving effect to a forfeiture order;

(d) where the application is to give effect to a forfeiture order, include an application to appoint the Director as the enforcement authority; and

(e) propose the terms of the Crown Court order.

(4) If the court allows the application, it must—

(a) where it decides to make a restraint order—

(i) specify the property the subject of the order,

(ii) specify the person or persons who are prohibited from dealing with that property,

(iii) specify any exception to that prohibition, and

(iv) include any ancillary order that the court believes is appropriate to ensure that the restraint order is effective; and

(b) where it decides to give effect to a forfeiture order, exercise its power to—

(i) direct the registration of the order as an order of the Crown Court,

(ii) give directions for notice of the order to be given to any person affected by it, and

(iii) appoint the applicant Director as the enforcement authority.

(5) Paragraph (6) applies where a person affected by an order, or the Director, wants the court to vary or discharge a restraint order or cancel the registration of a forfeiture order.

(6) Such a person must—

(a) apply in writing as soon as practicable after becoming aware of the grounds for doing so;

(b) serve the application on the court officer and, as applicable—

(i) the other party, and

(ii) any other person who will or may be affected;

(c) explain why it is appropriate, as the case may be—

(i) for the restraint order to be varied or discharged, or
(ii) for the registration of the forfeiture order to be cancelled;
(d) propose the terms of any variation; and
(e) ask for a hearing, if one is wanted, and explain why it is needed.
(7) The court may–
(a) consider an application
(i) at a hearing, which must be in private unless the court otherwise directs, or
(ii) without a hearing; and
(b) allow an application to be made orally.

[The next paragraph is B-883.]

Criminal Procedure Rules 2020 (SI 2020/759), Pt 50

EXTRADITION

Section 1: General rules

When this Part applies
50.1.–(1) This Part applies to extradition under Part 1 or Part 2 of the Extradition Act 2003. **B-883**
(2) Section 2 of this Part applies to proceedings in a magistrates' court, and in that Section–
(a) rules 50.3 to 50.7, 50.15 and 50.16 apply to extradition under Part 1 of the Act; and
(b) rules 50.3, 50.4 and 50.8 to 50.16 apply to extradition under Part 2 of the Act.
(3) Section 3 of this Part applies where–
(a) a party wants to appeal to the High Court against an order by the magistrates' court or by the Secretary of State; and
(b) a party to an appeal to the High Court wants to appeal further to the Supreme Court under–
(i) section 32 of the Act (appeal under Part 1 of the Act), or
(ii) section 114 of the Act (appeal under Part 2 of the Act).
(4) Section 4 of this Part applies to proceedings in a magistrates' court under–
(a) sections 54 and 55 of the Act (Request for consent to other offence being dealt with; Questions for decision at consent hearing); and
(b) sections 56 and 57 of the Act (Request for consent to further extradition to category 1 territory; Questions for decision at consent hearing).
(5) In this Part, and for the purposes of this Part in other rules–
(a) 'magistrates' court' means a District Judge (Magistrates' Courts) exercising the powers to which Section 2 of this Part applies;
(b) 'presenting officer' means an officer of the National Crime Agency, a police officer, a prosecutor and or other person representing an authority or territory seeking the extradition of a defendant;
(c) 'defendant' means a person arrested under Part 1 or Part 2 of the Extradition Act 2003.

Further objective in extradition proceedings
50.2. When exercising a power to which this Part applies, in furthering the overriding objective, in accordance with rule 1.3, the court must have regard to the importance of– **B-884**
(a) mutual confidence and recognition between judicial authorities in the United Kingdom and in requesting territories; and
(b) the conduct of extradition proceedings in accordance with international obligations, including obligations to deal swiftly with extradition requests.

Section 2: Extradition Proceedings in a Magistrates' Court

Exercise of magistrates' court powers
50.3.–(1) The general rule is that the magistrates' court must exercise its powers at a hearing in public, but– **★B-885**
(a) that is subject to any power the court has to–
(i) impose reporting restrictions,
(ii) withhold information from the public, or

(iii) order a hearing in private; and

(b) despite the general rule the court may, without a hearing—

(i) give any directions to which rule 50.4 applies (Case management in the magistrates' court and duty of court officer), or

(ii) determine an application which these Rules allow to be determined by a magistrates' court without a hearing in a case to which this Part does not apply.

(2) If the court so directs, a party may attend by live link any hearing except an extradition hearing under rule 50.6 or 50.13.

(3) Where the defendant is absent from a hearing—

(a) the general rule is that the court must proceed as if the defendant—

(i) were present, and

(ii) opposed extradition on any ground of which the court has been made aware;

(b) the general rule does not apply if the defendant is under 18;

(c) the general rule is subject to the court being satisfied that—

(i) the defendant had reasonable notice of where and when the hearing would take place,

(ii) the defendant has been made aware that the hearing might proceed in his or her absence, and

(iii) there is no good reason for the defendant's absence; and

(d) the general rule does not apply but the court may exercise its powers in the defendant's absence where—

(i) the court discharges the defendant,

(ii) the defendant is represented and the defendant's presence is impracticable by reason of his or her ill health or disorderly conduct, or

(iii) on an application under rule 50.32 (Application for consent to deal with another offence or for consent to further extradition), the defendant is represented or the defendant's presence is impracticable by reason of his or her detention in the territory to which he or she has been extradited.

(4) The court may exercise its power to adjourn—

(a) if either party asks, or on its own initiative; and

(b) in particular—

(i) to allow there to be obtained information that the court requires,

(ii) following a provisional arrest under Part 1 of the Extradition Act 2003, pending receipt of the warrant,

(iii) following a provisional arrest with a warrant under Part 2 of the Act, pending receipt of the extradition request,

(iv) following a provisional arrest without a warrant under Part 2 of the Act, pending receipt of evidence or information required by the court,

(v) if the court is informed that the defendant is serving a custodial sentence in the United Kingdom,

(vi) if it appears to the court that the defendant is not fit to be extradited, unless the court discharges the defendant for that reason,

(vii) where a court dealing with a warrant to which Part 1 of the Act applies is informed that another such warrant has been received in the United Kingdom,

(viii) where a court dealing with a warrant to which Part 1 of the Act applies is informed of a request for the temporary transfer of the defendant to the territory to which the defendant's extradition is sought, or a request for the defendant to speak to the authorities of that territory, or

(ix) during a hearing to which rule 50.32 applies (Application for consent to deal with another offence or for consent to further extradition).

(5) The court must exercise its power to adjourn if informed that the defendant has been charged with an offence in the United Kingdom.

(6) The general rule is that, before exercising a power to which this Part applies, the court must give each party an opportunity to make representations, unless that party is absent without good reason.

(7) The court may—

(a) shorten a time limit or extend it (even after it has expired), unless that is inconsistent with other legislation;

(b) direct that a notice or application be served on any person; and

(c) allow a notice or application to be in a different form to one set out in the Practice Direction, or to be presented orally.

(8) A party who wants an extension of time within which to serve a notice or make an application must–

(a) apply for that extension of time when serving that notice or making that application; and

(b) give the reasons for the application for an extension of time.

Rule 50.3 of the Criminal Procedure Rules 2020 (SI 2020/759) is temporarily amended by r.14(a) of the Criminal Procedure (Amendment No. 2) (Coronavirus) Rules 2020 (SI 2020/417) so that para.(2) is replaced with "(2) If the court so directs, a person must attend a hearing by live video link." This amendment ceases to have effect when ss.53 to 55 (and Schs 23 to 25) of the Coronavirus Act 2020 expire. This rule is also printed as amended, with effect from 8 February 2021, by SI 2021/40, r.29(b).

Case management in the magistrates' court and duty of court officer

50.4.–(1) The magistrates' court and the parties have the same duties and powers as under Part 3 (Case management), subject to– **B-886**

(a) rule 50.2 (Further objective in extradition proceedings); and

(b) paragraph (2) of this rule.

(2) Rule 3.6 (Application to vary a direction) does not apply to a decision to extradite or discharge.

(3) Where this rule applies, active case management by the court includes–

(a) if the court requires information from the authorities in the requesting territory–

(i) nominating a court officer, the designated authority which certified the arrest warrant where Part 1 of the Extradition Act 2003 Act applies, a party or other person to convey that request to those authorities, and

(ii) in a case in which the terms of that request need to be prepared in accordance with directions by the court, giving such directions accordingly; and

(b) giving such directions as are required where, under section 21B of the Extradition Act 2003 2, the parties agree–

(i) to the temporary transfer of the defendant to the requesting territory, or

(ii) that the defendant should speak with representatives of an authority in that territory.

(4) Where this rule applies, active assistance by the parties includes–

(a) applying for any direction needed as soon as reasonably practicable; and

(b) concisely explaining the reasons for any application for the court to direct–

(i) the preparation of a request to which paragraph (3)(a) applies, or

(ii) the making of arrangements to which paragraph (3)(b) applies.

(5) Where this rule applies, active assistance by the presenting officer includes–

(a) taking reasonable steps to ensure that the defendant will be able to understand (with help, if necessary)–

(i) what is alleged by the warrant, if Part 1 of the 2003 Act(1) applies, or

(ii) the content of the extradition request, if Part 2 of the Act applies; and

(b) providing in writing identification of the equivalent offence or offences under the law of England and Wales for the conduct being relied on if–

(i) this is raised for the defence as an issue and the court considers it necessary to identify the equivalent offence or offences in writing, or

(ii) the defendant is not represented.

(6) The court officer must–

(a) as soon as practicable, serve notice of the court's decision to extradite or discharge–

(i) on the defendant,

(ii) on the designated authority which certified the arrest warrant, where Part 1 of the 2003 Act applies, and

(iii) on the Secretary of State, where Part 2 of the Act applies; and

(b) give the court such assistance as it requires.

Extradition under Part 1 of the Extradition Act 2003

Preliminary hearing after arrest

50.5.–(1) This rule applies where the defendant is first brought before the court after– **B-887**

(a) arrest under a warrant to which Part 1 of the Extradition Act 2003 applies; or

(b) provisional arrest under Part 1 of the Act.

(2) The presenting officer must–

(a) serve on the court officer—
(i) the arrest warrant, and
(ii) a certificate, given by the authority designated by the Secretary of State, that the warrant was issued by an authority having the function of issuing such warrants in the territory to which the defendant's extradition is sought; or
(b) apply at once for an extension of time within which to serve that warrant and that certificate.

(3) An application under paragraph (2)(b) must—
(a) explain why the requirement to serve the warrant and certificate at once could not reasonably be complied with; and
(b) include—
(i) any written material in support of that explanation, and
(ii) representations about bail pending service of those documents.

(4) When the presenting officer serves the warrant and certificate, in the following sequence the court must—
(a) decide whether the defendant is the person in respect of whom the warrant was issued;
(b) explain, in terms the defendant can understand (with help, if necessary)—
(i) the allegation made in the warrant, and
(ii) that the defendant may consent to extradition, and how that may be done and with what effect;
(c) give directions for an extradition hearing to begin—
(i) no more than 21 days after the defendant's arrest, or
(ii) if either party so applies, at such a later date as the court decides is in the interests of justice;
(d) consider any ancillary application, including an application about bail pending the extradition hearing; and
(e) give such directions as are required for the preparation and conduct of the extradition hearing.

Extradition hearing

B-888 **50.6.**—(1) This rule applies at the extradition hearing directed under rule 50.5.

(2) In the following sequence, the court must decide—
(a) whether the offence specified in the warrant is an extradition offence;
(b) whether a bar to extradition applies, namely—
(i) the rule against double jeopardy,
(ii) absence of prosecution decision,
(iii) extraneous considerations,
(iv) the passage of time,
(v) the defendant's age,
(vi) speciality,
(vii) earlier extradition or transfer to the United Kingdom, or
(viii) forum;
(c) where the warrant alleges that the defendant is unlawfully at large after conviction, whether conviction was in the defendant's presence and if not—
(i) whether the defendant was absent deliberately, and
(ii) if the defendant was not absent deliberately, whether the defendant would be entitled to a retrial (or to a review of the conviction, amounting to a retrial);
(d) whether extradition would be—
(i) compatible with the defendant's human rights, and
(ii) proportionate;
(e) whether it would be unjust or oppressive to extradite the defendant because of his or her physical or mental condition;
(f) after deciding each of (a) to (e) above, before progressing to the next, whether to order the defendant's discharge; and
(g) whether to order the temporary transfer of the defendant to the territory to which the defendant's extradition is sought.

(3) If the court discharges the defendant, the court must consider any ancillary application, including an application about—
(a) reporting restrictions; or
(b) costs.

(4) If the court does not discharge the defendant, the court must–

(a) exercise its power to order the defendant's extradition;

(b) explain, in terms the defendant can understand (with help, if necessary), that the defendant may appeal to the High Court within the next 7 days; and

(c) consider any ancillary application, including an application about–

(i) bail pending extradition,

(ii) reporting restrictions, or

(iii) costs.

(5) If the court orders the defendant's extradition, the court must order its postponement where–

(a) the defendant has been charged with an offence in the United Kingdom; or

(b) the defendant has been sentenced to imprisonment or detention in the United Kingdom.

Discharge where warrant withdrawn

50.7.–(1) This rule applies where the authority that certified the warrant gives the court officer notice that the warrant has been withdrawn– **B-889**

(a) after the start of the hearing under rule 50.5; and

(b) before the court orders the defendant's extradition or discharge.

(2) The court must exercise its power to discharge the defendant.

Extradition under Part 2 of the Extradition Act 2003

Issue of arrest warrant

50.8.–(1) This rule applies where the Secretary of State serves on the court officer– **B-890**

(a) an extradition request to which Part 2 of the Extradition Act 2003 applies;

(b) a certificate given by the Secretary of State that the request was received in the way approved for the request; and

(c) a copy of any Order in Council which applies to the request.

(2) In the following sequence, the court must decide–

(a) whether the offence in respect of which extradition is requested is an extradition offence; and

(b) whether there is sufficient evidence, or (where the Secretary of State has so ordered, for this purpose) information, to justify the issue of a warrant of arrest.

(3) The court may issue an arrest warrant–

(a) without giving the parties an opportunity to make representations; and

(b) without a hearing, or at a hearing in public or in private.

Preliminary hearing after arrest

50.9.–(1) This rule applies where a defendant is first brought before the court after arrest under a warrant to which rule 50.8 applies. **B-891**

(2) In the following sequence, the court must–

(a) explain, in terms the defendant can understand (with help, if necessary)–

(i) the content of the extradition request, and

(ii) that the defendant may consent to extradition, and how that may be done and with what effect;

(b) give directions for an extradition hearing to begin–

(i) no more than 2 months later, or

(ii) if either party so applies, at such a later date as the court decides is in the interests of justice;

(c) consider any ancillary application, including an application about bail pending the extradition hearing; and

(d) give such directions as are required for the preparation and conduct of the extradition hearing.

Issue of provisional arrest warrant

50.10.–(1) This rule applies where a presenting officer wants a justice of the peace to issue a provisional arrest warrant under Part 2 of the Extradition Act 2003, pending receipt of an extradition request. **B-892**

(2) The presenting officer must–

(a) serve an application for a warrant on the court officer; and

(b) verify that application on oath or affirmation.

(3) In the following sequence, the justice must decide—
(a) whether the alleged offence is an extradition offence; and
(b) whether there is sufficient evidence, or (where the Secretary of State has so ordered, for this purpose) information, to justify the issue of a warrant of arrest.

Preliminary hearing after provisional arrest

★B-893 **50.11.**—(1) This rule applies where a defendant is first brought before the court after arrest—
(a) under a provisional arrest warrant to which rule 50.10 applies; or
(b) under section 74A of the Extradition Act 2003(1), without a warrant.
(2) Where paragraph (1)(b) applies the court must first—
(a) on the basis of such evidence or information as is produced to the court, decide whether a warrant to which rule 50.10 applies would be issued if the defendant were not already under arrest; and
(b) if no such warrant would be issued, order the defendant's discharge.
(3) Unless the court orders the defendant's discharge under paragraph (2), the court must—
(a) explain, in terms the defendant can understand (with help, if necessary)—
(i) the allegation in respect of which the defendant has been arrested, and
(ii) that the defendant may consent to extradition, and how that may be done and with what effect; and
(b) consider any ancillary application, including an application about bail pending receipt of the extradition request.

[This rule is printed as amended, with effect from 8 February 2021, by SI 2021/40, r.29(c).]

Arrangement of extradition hearing after provisional arrest

★B-894 **50.12.**—(1) This rule applies when the Secretary of State serves on the court officer—
(a) a request for extradition in respect of which a defendant has been arrested—
(i) under a provisional arrest warrant to which rule 50.10 applies, or
(ii) under section 74A of the Extradition Act 2003, without a warrant;
(b) a certificate given by the Secretary of State that the request was received in the way approved for the request; and
(c) a copy of any Order in Council which applies to the request.
(2) Unless a time limit for service of the request has expired, the court must—
(a) give directions for an extradition hearing to begin—
(i) no more than 2 months after service of the request, or
(ii) if either party so applies, at such a later date as the court decides is in the interests of justice;
(b) consider any ancillary application, including an application about bail pending the extradition hearing; and
(c) give such directions as are required for the preparation and conduct of the extradition hearing.

[This rule is printed as amended, with effect from 8 February 2021, by SI 2021/40, r.29(d).]

Extradition hearing

B-895 **50.13.**—(1) This rule applies at the extradition hearing directed under rule 50.9 or rule 50.12.
(2) In the following sequence, the court must decide—
(a) whether the documents served on the court officer by the Secretary of State include—
(i) those listed in rule 50.8(1) or rule 50.12(1), as the case may be,
(ii) particulars of the person whose extradition is requested,
(iii) particulars of the offence specified in the request, and
(iv) as the case may be, a warrant for the defendant's arrest, or a certificate of the defendant's conviction and (if applicable) sentence, issued in the requesting territory;
(b) whether the defendant is the person whose extradition is requested;
(c) whether the offence specified in the request is an extradition offence;
(d) whether the documents served on the court officer by the Secretary of State have been served also on the defendant;
(e) whether a bar to extradition applies, namely—
(i) the rule against double jeopardy,
(ii) extraneous considerations,

(iii) the passage of time,
(iv) hostage-taking considerations, or
(v) forum;

(f) where the request accuses the defendant of an offence, whether there is evidence which would be sufficient to make a case requiring an answer by the defendant if the extradition proceedings were a trial (unless the Secretary of State has otherwise ordered, for this purpose);

(g) where the request accuses the defendant of being unlawfully at large after conviction, whether the defendant was—
(i) convicted in his or her presence, or
(ii) absent deliberately;

(h) where the request accuses the defendant of being unlawfully at large after conviction, and the defendant was absent but not deliberately—
(i) whether the defendant would be entitled to a retrial (or to a review of the conviction amounting to a retrial), and
(ii) if so, whether there is evidence which would be sufficient to make a case requiring an answer by the defendant if the extradition proceedings were a trial (unless the Secretary of State has otherwise ordered, for this purpose);

(i) whether extradition would be compatible with the defendant's human rights;

(j) whether it would be unjust or oppressive to extradite the defendant because of his or her physical or mental condition; and

(k) after deciding each of (a) to (j) above, before progressing to the next, whether to order the defendant's discharge.

(3) If the court discharges the defendant, the court must consider any ancillary application, including an application about—
(a) reporting restrictions; or
(b) costs.

(4) If the court does not discharge the defendant, the court must—
(a) exercise its power to send the case to the Secretary of State to decide whether to extradite the defendant;
(b) explain, in terms the defendant can understand (with help, if necessary), that—
(i) the defendant may appeal to the High Court not more than 14 days after being informed of the Secretary of State's decision, and
(ii) any such appeal brought before the Secretary of State's decision has been made will not be heard until after that decision; and
(c) consider any ancillary application, including an application about—
(i) bail pending extradition,
(ii) reporting restrictions, or
(iii) costs.

(5) If the Secretary of State orders the defendant's extradition, the court must order its postponement where—
(a) the defendant has been charged with an offence in the United Kingdom; or
(b) the defendant has been sentenced to imprisonment or detention in the United Kingdom.

Discharge where extradition request withdrawn

50.14.—(1) This rule applies where the Secretary of State gives the court officer notice that the extradition request has been withdrawn— **B-896**
(a) after the start of the hearing under rule 50.9 or 50.11; and
(b) before the court—
(i) sends the case to the Secretary of State to decide whether to extradite the defendant, or
(ii) discharges the defendant.

(2) The court must exercise its power to discharge the defendant.

Evidence at Extradition Hearing

Introduction of additional evidence

50.15.—(1) Where a party wants to introduce evidence at an extradition hearing under the law that would apply if that hearing were a trial, the relevant Part of these Rules applies with such adaptations as the court directs. **B-897**

(2) If the court admits as evidence the written statement of a witness—
(a) each relevant part of the statement must be read or summarised aloud; or
(b) the court must read the statement and its gist must be summarised aloud.

(3) If a party introduces in evidence a fact admitted by another party, or the parties jointly admit a fact, a written record must be made of the admission.

Discharge after Failure to Comply with a Time Limit, etc.

Defendant's application to be discharged

★B-898 **50.16.**—(1) This rule applies where a defendant wants to be discharged—
(a) because of a failure—
(i) to give the defendant a copy of any warrant under which the defendant is arrested as soon as practicable after arrest,
(ii) to bring the defendant before the court as soon as practicable after arrest under a warrant,
(iii) to bring the defendant before the court no more than 48 hours after provisional arrest under Part 1 of the Extradition Act 2003,
(iv) to give the defendant a copy of any certificate enabling provisional arrest without a warrant under section 74A of the 2003 Act as soon as practicable after arrest, or
(v) to bring the defendant before the court as soon as practicable after arrest under that section;
(b) because of a defect in a certificate enabling arrest without a warrant under section 74A of the 2003 Act;
(c) because there were no reasonable grounds on which there could have been issued a certificate enabling arrest without a warrant under section 74A of the 2003 Act;
(d) following the expiry of a time limit for—
(i) service of a warrant to which Part 1 of the 2003 Act applies, after provisional arrest under that Part of the Act (48 hours, under section 6 of the Act, unless the court otherwise directs),
(ii) service of an extradition request to which Part 2 of the Act applies, after provisional arrest under that Part of the Act (45 days, under section 74 of the Act, unless the Secretary of State has otherwise ordered for this purpose),
(iii) receipt of an undertaking that the defendant will be returned to complete a sentence in the United Kingdom, where the court required such an undertaking (21 days, under section 37 of the Act),
(iv) making an extradition order, after the defendant has consented to extradition under Part 1 of the Act (10 days, under section 46 of the Act),
(v) extradition, where an extradition order has been made under Part 1 of the Act and any appeal by the defendant has failed (10 days, under sections 35, 36 and 47 of the Act, unless the court otherwise directs),
(vi) extradition, where an extradition order has been made under Part 2 of the Act and any appeal by the defendant has failed (28 days, under sections 117 and 118 of the Act),
(vii) the resumption of extradition proceedings, where those proceedings were adjourned pending disposal of another extradition claim which has concluded (21 days, under section 180 of the Act),
(viii) extradition, where extradition has been deferred pending the disposal of another extradition claim which has concluded (21 days, under section 181 of the Act), or
(ix) re-extradition, where the defendant has been returned to the United Kingdom to serve a sentence before serving a sentence overseas (as soon as practicable, under section 187 of the Act); or
(e) because an extradition hearing does not begin on the date arranged by the court.

(2) Unless the court otherwise directs—
(a) such a defendant must apply in writing and serve the application on—
(i) the magistrates' court officer,
(ii) the High Court officer, where paragraph (1)(d)(v) applies, and
(iii) the prosecutor;
(b) the application must explain the grounds on which it is made; and
(c) the court officer must arrange a hearing as soon as practicable, and in any event no later than the second business day after an application is served.

[This rule is printed as amended, with effect from 8 February 2021, by SI 2021/40, r.29(e).]

Section 3: Appeal to the High Court

Exercise of the High Court's powers

50.17.–(1) The general rule is that the High Court must exercise its powers at a hearing in public, but– **B-899**

(a) that is subject to any power the court has to–
   (i) impose reporting restrictions,
   (ii) withhold information from the public, or
   (iii) order a hearing in private;
(b) despite the general rule, the court may determine without a hearing–
   (i) an application for the court to consider out of time an application for permission to appeal to the High Court,
   (ii) an application for permission to appeal to the High Court (but a renewed such application must be determined at a hearing),
   (iii) an application for permission to appeal from the High Court to the Supreme Court,
   (iv) an application for permission to reopen a decision under rule 50.27 (Reopening the determination of an appeal), or
   (v) an application concerning bail; and
(c) despite the general rule the court may, without a hearing–
   (i) give case management directions,
   (ii) reject a notice or application and, if applicable, dismiss an application for permission to appeal, where rule 50.31 (Payment of High Court fees) applies and the party who served the notice or application fails to comply with that rule, or
   (iii) make a determination to which the parties have agreed in writing.

(2) If the High Court so directs, a party may attend a hearing by live link.

(3) The general rule is that where the High Court exercises its powers at a hearing it may do so only if the defendant attends, in person or by live link, but, despite the general rule, the court may exercise its powers in the defendant's absence if–

(a) the defendant waives the right to attend;
(b) subject to any appeal to the Supreme Court, the result of the court's order would be the discharge of the defendant; or
(c) the defendant is represented and–
   (i) the defendant is in custody, or
   (ii) the defendant's presence is impracticable by reason of his or her ill health or disorderly conduct.

(4) If the High Court gives permission to appeal to the High Court–

(a) unless the court otherwise directs, the decision indicates that the appellant has permission to appeal on every ground identified by the appeal notice;
(b) unless the court otherwise directs, the decision indicates that the court finds reasonably arguable each ground on which the appellant has permission to appeal; and
(c) the court must give such directions as are required for the preparation and conduct of the appeal, including a direction as to whether the appeal must be heard by a single judge of the High Court or by a divisional court.

(5) If the High Court decides without a hearing an application for permission to appeal from the High Court to the Supreme Court, the High Court must announce its decision at a hearing in public.

(6) The High Court may–

(a) shorten a time limit or extend it (even after it has expired), unless that is inconsistent with other legislation;
(b) allow or require a party to vary or supplement a notice that that party has served;
(c) direct that a notice or application be served on any person; and
(d) allow a notice or application to be in a different form to one set out in the Practice Direction, or to be presented orally.

(7) A party who wants an extension of time within which to serve a notice or make an application must–

(a) apply for that extension of time when serving that notice or making that application; and
(b) give the reasons for the application for an extension of time.

Rule 50.17 of the Criminal Procedure Rules 2020 (SI 2020/759) is temporarily amended by r.14(b) of the Criminal Procedure (Amendment No. 2) (Coronavirus) Rules 2020 (SI 2020/417) so that in para.(2) "party" is replaced with "person". This amendment ceases to have effect when ss.53 to 55 (and Schs 23 to 25) of the Coronavirus Act 2020 expire.

Case management in the High Court

B-900 **50.18.**—(1) The High Court and the parties have the same duties and powers as under Part 3 (Case management), subject to—

(a) rule 50.2 (Further objective in extradition proceedings); and
(b) paragraph (3) of this rule.

(2) A master of the High Court, a deputy master, or a court officer nominated for the purpose by the Lord Chief Justice—

(a) must fulfil the duty of active case management under rule 3.2, and in fulfilling that duty may exercise any of the powers of case management under—
(i) rule 3.5 (the court's general powers of case management),
(ii) rule 3.12(3) (requiring a certificate of readiness), and
(iii) rule 3.13 (requiring a party to identify intentions and anticipated requirements)
subject to the directions of a judge of the High Court; and
(b) must nominate a case progression officer under rule 3.4.

(3) Rule 3.6 (Application to vary a direction) does not apply to a decision to give or to refuse—

(a) permission to appeal; or
(b) permission to reopen a decision under rule 50.27 (Reopening the determination of an appeal).

Service of appeal notice

B-901 **50.19.**—(1) A party who wants to appeal to the High Court must serve an appeal notice on—

(a) in every case—
(i) the High Court officer,
(ii) the other party, and
(iii) the Director of Public Prosecutions, unless the Director already has the conduct of the proceedings;
(b) the designated authority which certified the arrest warrant, where Part 1 of the Extradition Act 2003 applies; and
(c) the Secretary of State, where the appeal is against—
(i) an order by the Secretary of State, or
(ii) an order by the magistrates' court sending a case to the Secretary of State.

(2) A defendant who wants to appeal must serve the appeal notice—

(a) not more than 7 days after the day on which the magistrates' court makes an order for the defendant's extradition, starting with that day, where that order is under Part 1 of the Extradition Act 2003; or
(b) not more than 14 days after the day on which the Secretary of State informs the defendant of the Secretary of State's decision, starting with that day, where under Part 2 of the Act—
(i) the magistrates' court sends the case to the Secretary of State for a decision whether to extradite the defendant, or
(ii) the Secretary of State orders the defendant's extradition.

(3) An authority or territory seeking the defendant's extradition which wants to appeal against an order for the defendant's discharge must serve the appeal notice—

(a) not more than 7 days after the day on which the magistrates' court makes that order, starting with that day, if the order is under Part 1 of the Extradition Act 2003;
(b) not more than 14 days after the day on which the magistrates' court makes that order, starting with that day, if the order is under Part 2 of the Act; or
(c) not more than 14 days after the day on which the Secretary of State informs the territory's representative of the Secretary of State's order, starting with that day, where the order is under Part 2 of the Act.

Form of appeal notice

B-902 **50.20.**—(1) An appeal notice constitutes—

(a) an application to the High Court for permission to appeal to that court; and
(b) an appeal to that court, if the court gives permission.

(2) An appeal notice must be in writing.

(3) In every case, the appeal notice must–
(a) specify–
(i) the date of the defendant's arrest under Part 1 or Part 2 of the Extradition Act 2003, and
(ii) the decision about which the appellant wants to appeal, including the date of that decision;
(b) identify each ground of appeal on which the appellant relies;
(c) summarise the relevant facts;
(d) identify any document or other material that the appellant thinks the court will need to decide the appeal; and
(e) include or attach a list of those on whom the appellant has served the appeal notice.

(4) If a defendant serves an appeal notice after the expiry of the time limit specified in rule 50.19 (Service of appeal notice)–
(a) the notice must–
(i) explain what the defendant did to ensure that it was served as soon as it could be, and
(ii) include or attach such evidence as the defendant relies upon to support that explanation; and
(b) where the appeal is on human rights grounds against an order for extradition made by the Secretary of State, the notice must explain why–
(i) the appeal is necessary to avoid real injustice, and
(ii) the circumstances are exceptional and make it appropriate to consider the appeal.

(5) Unless the High Court otherwise directs, the appellant may amend the appeal notice–
(a) by serving on those listed in rule 50.19(1) the appeal notice as so amended; and
(b) not more than 10 business days after service of the appeal notice.

(6) Where the appeal is against an order by the magistrates' court–
(a) if the grounds of appeal are that the magistrates' court ought to have decided differently a question of fact or law at the extradition hearing, the appeal notice must–
(i) identify that question,
(ii) explain what decision the magistrates' court should have made, and why, and
(iii) explain why the magistrates' court would have been required not to make the order under appeal, if that question had been decided differently; and
(b) if the grounds of appeal are that there is an issue which was not raised at the extradition hearing, or that evidence is available which was not available at the extradition hearing, the appeal notice must–
(i) identify that issue or evidence,
(ii) explain why it was not then raised or available,
(iii) explain why that issue or evidence would have resulted in the magistrates' court deciding a question differently at the extradition hearing, and
(iv) explain why, if the court had decided that question differently, the court would have been required not to make the order it made.

(7) Where the appeal is against an order by the Secretary of State–
(a) if the grounds of appeal are that the Secretary of State ought to have decided differently a question of fact or law, the appeal notice must–
(i) identify that question,
(ii) explain what decision the Secretary of State should have made, and why, and
(iii) explain why the Secretary of State would have been required not to make the order under appeal, if that question had been decided differently;
(b) if the grounds of appeal are that there is an issue which was not raised when the case was being considered by the Secretary of State, or that information is available which was not then available, the appeal notice must–
(i) identify that issue or information,
(ii) explain why it was not then raised or available,
(iii) explain why that issue or information would have resulted in the Secretary of State deciding a question differently, and
(iv) explain why, if the Secretary of State had decided that question differently, the order under appeal would not have been made.

Respondent's notice

50.21.–(1) A party on whom an appellant serves an appeal notice under rule 50.19 may serve a **B-903**

respondent's notice, and must do so if—
(a) that party wants to make representations to the High Court; or
(b) the court so directs.
(2) Such a party must serve any such notice on—
(a) the High Court officer;
(b) the appellant;
(c) the Director of Public Prosecutions, unless the Director already has the conduct of the proceedings; and
(d) any other person on whom the appellant served the appeal notice.
(3) Such a party must serve any such notice, as appropriate—
(a) not more than 10 business days after—
(i) service on that party of an amended appeal notice under rule 50.20(5) (Form of appeal notice), or
(ii) the expiry of the time for service of any such amended appeal notice
whichever of those events happens first; and
(b) not more than 5 business days after service on that party of—
(i) an appellant's notice renewing an application for permission to appeal, or
(ii) a direction to serve a respondent's notice.
(4) A respondent's notice must—
(a) give the date or dates on which the respondent was served with, as appropriate—
(i) the appeal notice,
(ii) the appellant's notice renewing the application for permission to appeal, or
(iii) the direction to serve a respondent's notice;
(b) identify each ground of opposition on which the respondent relies and the ground of appeal to which each such ground of opposition relates;
(c) summarise any relevant facts not already summarised in the appeal notice; and
(d) identify any document or other material that the respondent thinks the court will need to decide the appeal.

Renewing an application for permission to appeal, restoring excluded grounds, etc.

B-904 **50.22.**—(1) This rule—
(a) applies where the High Court—
(i) refuses permission to appeal to the High Court, or
(ii) gives permission to appeal to the High Court but not on every ground identified by the appeal notice; but
(b) does not apply where—
(i) a defendant applies out of time for permission to appeal to the High Court, and
(ii) the court for that reason refuses to consider that application.
(2) Unless the court refuses permission to appeal at a hearing, the appellant may renew the application for permission by serving notice on—
(a) the High Court officer;
(b) the respondent; and
(c) any other person on whom the appellant served the appeal notice,
not more than 5 business days after service of notice of the court's decision on the appellant.
(3) If the court refuses permission to appeal, the renewal notice must explain the grounds for the renewal.
(4) If the court gives permission to appeal but not on every ground identified by the appeal notice the decision indicates that—
(a) at the hearing of the appeal the court will not consider representations that address any ground thus excluded from argument; and
(b) an appellant who wants to rely on such an excluded ground needs the court's permission to do so.
(5) An appellant who wants to rely at the hearing of an appeal on a ground of appeal excluded from argument must—
(a) apply in writing, with reasons, and identify each such ground;
(b) serve the application on—
(i) the High Court officer, and
(ii) the respondent; and
(c) serve the application not more than 5 business days after—

(i) the giving of permission to appeal, or
(ii) the High Court officer serves notice of that decision on the applicant, if the applicant was not present in person or by live link when permission to appeal was given.

(6) Paragraph (7) applies where a party wants to abandon—
(a) a ground of appeal on which that party has permission to appeal; or
(b) a ground of opposition identified in a respondent's notice.

(7) Such a party must serve notice on—
(a) the High Court officer; and
(b) each other party,
before any hearing at which that ground will be considered by the court.

Appeal hearing

50.23.—(1) Unless the High Court otherwise directs, where the appeal to the High Court is under Part 1 of the Extradition Act 2003 the hearing of the appeal must begin no more than 40 days after the defendant's arrest. **B-905**

(2) Unless the High Court otherwise directs, where the appeal to the High Court is under Part 2 of the 2003 Act the hearing of the appeal must begin no more than 76 days after the later of—
(a) service of the appeal notice; or
(b) the day on which the Secretary of State informs the defendant of the Secretary of State's order, in a case in which—
(i) the appeal is by the defendant against an order by the magistrates' court sending the case to the Secretary of State, and
(ii) the appeal notice is served before the Secretary of State decides whether the defendant should be extradited.

(3) If the effect of the decision of the High Court on the appeal is that the defendant is to be extradited—
(a) the High Court must consider any ancillary application, including an application about—
(i) bail pending extradition,
(ii) reporting restrictions, or
(iii) costs; and
(b) the High Court is the appropriate court to order a postponement of the defendant's extradition where—
(i) the defendant has been charged with an offence in the United Kingdom, or
(ii) the defendant has been sentenced to imprisonment or detention in the United Kingdom.

(4) If the effect of the decision of the High Court on the appeal is that the defendant is discharged, the High Court must consider any ancillary application, including an application about—
(a) reporting restrictions; or
(b) costs.

Early termination of appeal: order by consent, etc.

50.24.—(1) This rule applies where— **B-906**
(a) an appellant has served an appeal notice under rule 50.19; and
(b) the High Court—
(i) has not determined the application for permission to appeal, or
(ii) where the court has given permission to appeal, has not determined the appeal.

(2) Where the warrant or extradition request with which the appeal is concerned is withdrawn—
(a) the party or person so informing the court must serve on the High Court officer—
(i) notice to that effect by the authority or territory requesting the defendant's extradition,
(ii) details of how much of the warrant or extradition request remains outstanding, if any, and of any other warrant or extradition request outstanding in respect of the defendant,
(iii) details of any bail condition to which the defendant is subject, if the defendant is on bail, and
(iv) details sufficient to locate the defendant, including details of the custodian and of the defendant's date of birth and custody reference, if the defendant is in custody; and
(b) paragraph (5) applies but only to the extent that the parties want the court to deal with an ancillary matter.

(3) Where a defendant with whose discharge the appeal is concerned consents to extradition, paragraph (5) applies but only to the extent that the parties want the court to—

(a) give directions for that consent to be given to the magistrates' court or to the Secretary of State, as the case may be; or
(b) deal with an ancillary matter.

(4) Paragraph (5) applies where the parties want the court to make a decision on which they are agreed—
(a) determining the application for permission to appeal or the appeal, as the case may be;
(b) specifying the date on which that application or appeal is to be treated as discontinued; and
(c) determining an ancillary matter, including costs, if applicable.

(5) The parties must serve on the High Court officer, in one or more documents—
(a) a draft order in the terms proposed;
(b) evidence of each party's agreement to those terms; and
(c) concise reasons for the request that the court make the proposed order.

Application for permission to appeal to the Supreme Court

B-907 **50.25.**—(1) This rule applies where a party to an appeal to the High Court wants to appeal to the Supreme Court.

(2) Such a party must—
(a) apply orally to the High Court for permission to appeal immediately after the court's decision; or
(b) apply in writing and serve the application on the High Court officer and every other party not more than 14 days after that decision.

(3) Such a party must—
(a) identify the point of law of general public importance that the appellant wants the High Court to certify is involved in the decision;
(b) serve on the High Court officer a statement of that point of law; and
(c) give reasons why—
(i) that point of law ought to be considered by the Supreme Court, and
(ii) the High Court ought to give permission to appeal.

(4) As well as complying with paragraph (3), a defendant's application for permission to appeal to the Supreme Court must include or attach any application for the following, with reasons—
(a) bail pending appeal; or
(b) permission to attend any hearing in the Supreme Court, if the appellant is in custody.

Determination of detention pending appeal to the Supreme Court against discharge

B-908 **50.26.** On an application for permission to appeal to the Supreme Court against a decision of the High Court which, but for that appeal, would have resulted in the defendant's discharge, the High Court must—
(a) decide whether to order the detention of the defendant; and
(b) determine any application for—
(i) bail pending appeal,
(ii) permission to attend any hearing in the Supreme Court, or
(iii) a representation order.

Reopening the determination of an appeal

B-909 **50.27.**—(1) This rule applies where a party wants the High Court to reopen a decision of that court which determines an appeal or an application for permission to appeal.

(2) Such a party must—
(a) apply in writing for permission to reopen that decision, as soon as practicable after becoming aware of the grounds for doing so; and
(b) serve the application on the High Court officer and every other party.

(3) The application must—
(a) specify the decision which the applicant wants the court to reopen; and
(b) give reasons why—
(i) it is necessary for the court to reopen that decision in order to avoid real injustice,
(ii) the circumstances are exceptional and make it appropriate to reopen the decision, and
(iii) there is no alternative effective remedy.

(4) The court must not give permission to reopen a decision unless each other party has had an opportunity to make representations.

Declaration of incompatibility with a Convention right

B-910 **50.28.**—(1) This rule applies where a party—

(a) wants the High Court to make a declaration of incompatibility with a Convention right under section 4 of the Human Rights Act 1998; or
(b) raises an issue that appears to the High Court may lead to the court making such a declaration.

(2) If the High Court so directs, the High Court officer must serve notice on–
(a) the relevant person named in the list published under section 17(1) of the Crown Proceedings Act 1947; or
(b) the Treasury Solicitor, if it is not clear who is the relevant person.

(3) That notice must include or attach details of–
(a) the legislation affected and the Convention right concerned;
(b) the parties to the appeal; and
(c) any other information or document that the High Court thinks relevant.

(4) A person who has a right under the 1998 Act to become a party to the appeal must–
(a) serve notice on–
(i) the High Court officer, and
(ii) the other parties,
if that person wants to exercise that right; and
(b) in that notice–
(i) indicate the conclusion that that person invites the High Court to reach on the question of incompatibility, and
(ii) identify each ground for that invitation, concisely outlining the arguments in support.

(5) The High Court must not make a declaration of incompatibility–
(a) less than 15 business days after the High Court officer serves notice under paragraph (2); and
(b) without giving any person who serves a notice under paragraph (4) an opportunity to make representations at a hearing.

Duties of court officers

50.29.–(1) The magistrates' court officer must– **B-911**
(a) keep any document or object exhibited in the proceedings in the magistrates' court, or arrange for it to be kept by some other appropriate person, until–
(i) 6 weeks after the conclusion of those proceedings, or
(ii) the conclusion of any proceedings in the High Court that begin within that 6 weeks;
(b) provide the High Court with any document, object or information for which the High Court officer asks, within such period as the High Court officer may require; and
(c) arrange for the magistrates' court to hear as soon as practicable any application to that court for bail pending appeal.

(2) A person who, under arrangements made by the magistrates' court officer, keeps a document or object exhibited in the proceedings in the magistrates' court must–
(a) keep that exhibit until–
(i) 6 weeks after the conclusion of those proceedings, or
(ii) the conclusion of any proceedings in the High Court that begin within that 6 weeks,
unless the magistrates' court or the High Court otherwise directs; and
(b) provide the High Court with any such document or object for which the High Court officer asks, within such period as the High Court officer may require.

(3) The High Court officer must–
(a) give as much notice as reasonably practicable of each hearing to–
(i) the parties,
(ii) the defendant's custodian, if any, and
(iii) any other person whom the High Court requires to be notified;
(b) serve a record of each order or direction of the High Court on–
(i) the parties,
(ii) any other person whom the High Court requires to be notified;
(c) if the High Court's decision determines an appeal or application for permission to appeal, serve a record of that decision on–
(i) the defendant's custodian, if any,
(ii) the magistrates' court officer, and
(iii) the designated authority which certified the arrest warrant, where Part 1 of the Extradition Act 2003 applies;

(d) where rule 50.24 applies (Early termination of appeal: order by consent, etc.), arrange for the High Court to consider the document or documents served under that rule; and
(e) treat the appeal as if it had been dismissed by the High Court where—
(i) the hearing of the appeal does not begin within the period required by rule 50.23 (Appeal hearing) or ordered by the High Court, or
(ii) on an appeal by a requesting territory under section 105 of the Extradition Act 2003, the High Court directs the magistrates' court to decide a question again and the magistrates' court comes to the same conclusion as it had done before.

Constitution of the High Court

B-912 **50.30.**—(1) A master of the High Court, a deputy master, or a court officer nominated for the purpose by the Lord Chief Justice, may exercise any power of the High Court to which the rules in this Section apply, except the power to—
(a) give or refuse permission to appeal;
(b) determine an appeal;
(c) reopen a decision which determines an appeal or an application for permission to appeal;
(d) grant or withhold bail; or
(e) impose or vary a condition of bail.

(2) Despite paragraph (1), such a master, deputy master or court officer may exercise one of the powers listed in paragraph (1)(a), (b), (d) or (e) if making a decision to which the parties have agreed in writing.

(3) A renewed application for permission to appeal to the High Court may be determined by—
(a) a single judge of the High Court other than the judge who first refused permission, or
(b) a divisional court.

(4) An appeal may be determined by—
(a) a single judge of the High Court; or
(b) a divisional court.

Payment of High Court fees

B-913 **50.31.**—(1) This rule applies where a party serves on the High Court officer a notice or application in respect of which a court fee is payable under legislation that requires the payment of such a fee.

(2) Such a party must pay the fee, or satisfy the conditions for any remission of the fee, when so serving the notice or application.

(3) If such a party fails to comply with paragraph (2), then unless the High Court otherwise directs—
(a) the High Court officer must serve on that party a notice requiring payment of the fee due, or satisfaction of the conditions for any remission of that fee, within a period specified in the notice;
(b) that party must comply with such a requirement; and
(c) until the expiry of the period specified in the notice, the High Court must not exercise its power—
(i) to reject the notice or application in respect of which the fee is payable, or
(ii) to dismiss an application for permission to appeal, in consequence of rejecting an appeal notice.

Section 4: Post-Extradition Proceedings

Application for consent to deal with another offence or for consent to further extradition

B-914 **50.32.**—(1) This rule applies where—
(a) a defendant has been extradited to a territory under Part 1 of the Extradition Act 2003; and
(b) the court officer receives from the authority designated by the Secretary of State a request for the court's consent to—
(i) the defendant being dealt with in that territory for an offence other than one in respect of which the extradition there took place, or
(ii) the defendant's further extradition from there to another such territory for an offence.

(2) The presenting officer must serve on the court officer—
(a) the request; and
(b) a certificate given by the designated authority that the request was made by a judicial authority with the function of making such requests in the territory to which the defendant was extradited.

(3) The court must–

(a) give directions for service by a party or other person on the defendant of notice that the request for consent has been received, unless satisfied that it would not be practicable for such notice to be served;

(b) give directions for a hearing to consider the request to begin–

(i) no more than 21 days after the request was received by the designated authority, or

(ii) at such a later date as the court decides is in the interests of justice; and

(c) give such directions as are required for the preparation and conduct of that hearing.

(4) At the hearing directed under paragraph (3), in the following sequence the court must decide–

(a) whether the consent requested is required, having regard to–

(i) any opportunity given for the defendant to leave the requesting territory after extradition which the defendant did not take within 45 days of arrival there,

(ii) if the defendant did not take such an opportunity, any requirements for consent imposed by the law of the requesting territory or by arrangements between that territory and the United Kingdom where the request is for consent to deal with the defendant in that territory for another offence, and

(iii) if the defendant did not take such an opportunity, any requirements for consent imposed by arrangements between the requesting territory and the United Kingdom where the request is for consent to extradite the defendant to another territory for an offence; and

(b) if such consent is required, then–

(i) whether the offence in respect of which consent is requested is an extradition offence, and

(ii) if it is, whether the court would order the defendant's extradition under sections 11 to 25 of the Extradition Act 2003 (bars to extradition and other considerations) were the defendant in the United Kingdom and the court was considering extradition for that offence.

(5) The court must give directions for notice of its decision to be conveyed to the authority which made the request.

(6) Rules 50.3 (Exercise of magistrates' court's powers) and 50.4 (Case management in the magistrates' court and duty of court officer) apply on an application under this rule.

CPD XI Other Proceedings 50A: Extradition: general matters and case management (as substituted by Criminal Practice Directions 2015 (Amendment No. 4) [2017] EWCA Crim 310, Lord Thomas CJ and amended by Criminal Practice Directions 2015 (Amendment No. 9) [2019] EWCA Crim 1603, Lord Burnett CJ)

General matters: expedition at all times

50A.1 Compliance with these directions is essential to ensure that extradition proceedings are dealt with expeditiously, both in accordance with the spirit of the Council Framework Decision of 13 June 2002 on the European Arrest Warrant and surrender procedures between Member States and the United Kingdom's other treaty obligations. It is of the utmost importance that orders which provide directions for the proper management and progress of cases are obeyed so that the parties can fulfil their duty to assist the court in furthering the overriding objective and in making efficient use of judicial resources. To that end: ★B-915

(i) the court may, and usually should, give case management directions, which may be based on a model, but adapted to the needs of the individual case, requiring the parties to supply case management information, consistently with the overriding objective of the Criminal Procedure Rules and compatibly with the parties' entitlement to legal professional and litigation privilege;

(ii) a defendant whose extradition is requested must expect to be required to identify what he or she intends to put in issue so that directions can be given to achieve a single, comprehensive and effective extradition hearing at the earliest possible date;

(iii) where the issues are such that further information from the requesting authority or state is needed then it is essential that the request is formulated clearly and in good time, in terms to which the parties can expect to contribute but which terms must be approved by the court, in order that those to whom the request is addressed will be able to understand what is sought, and why, and so can respond promptly;

(iv) where such a request or other document, including a formal notice to the defendant of a post-extradition consent request, requires transmission to an authority or other person in a requesting state or other place outside the UK, it is essential that clear and realistic directions for the transmission are given, identifying who is to be responsible and to what timetable, having regard to the capacity of the proposed courier. Once given, such directions must be promptly complied with and the court at once informed if difficulties are encountered.

(v) any skeleton argument must comply with the requirements of these Practice Directions and, if applicable, of the court. (Paragraphs XII D.17 to D.23 set out the general requirements for skeleton arguments. Paragraphs XI 50E.1 to 50E.7 set out some special requirements that apply in an extradition appeal to the High Court.)

General guidance under s. 2(7A) Extradition Act 2003 (as amended by the Anti-Social Behaviour, Crime and Policing Act 2014)

B-916 **50A.2** When proceeding under section 21A of the Act and considering under subsection (3)(a) of the Act the seriousness of the conduct alleged to constitute the extradition offence, the judge will determine the issue on the facts of each case as set out in the warrant, subject to the guidance in paragraph 50A.3 below.

50A.3 In any case where the conduct alleged to constitute the offence falls into one of the categories in the table at paragraph 50A.5 below, unless there are exceptional circumstances, the judge should generally determine that extradition would be disproportionate. It would follow under the terms of s. 21A(4)(b) of the Act that the judge must order the person's discharge.

50A.4 The exceptional circumstances referred to above in paragraph 50A.3 will include:

i. vulnerable victim;
ii. crime committed against someone because of their disability, gender-identity, race, religion or belief, or sexual orientation;
iii. significant premeditation;
iv. multiple counts;
v. extradition also sought for another offence;
vi. previous offending history.

50A.5 The table is as follows:

Category of offence	*Examples*
Minor theft - (not robbery/ burglary or theft from the person)	Where the theft is of a low monetary value and there is a low impact on the victim or indirect harm to others, for example: (a) Theft of an item of food from a supermarket; (b) Theft of a small amount of scrap metal from company premises; (c) Theft of a very small sum of money.
Minor financial offences (forgery, fraud and tax offences)	Where the sums involved are small and there is a low impact on the victim and / or low indirect harm to others, for example: (a) Failure to file a tax return or invoices on time; (b) Making a false statement in a tax return; (c) Dishonestly applying for a tax refund; (d) Obtaining a bank loan using a forged or falsified document; (e) Non-payment of child maintenance.
Minor road traffic, driving and related offences	Where no injury, loss or damage was incurred to any person or property, for example: (a) Driving whilst using a mobile phone; (b) Use of a bicycle whilst intoxicated.
Minor public order offences	Where there is no suggestion the person started the trouble and the offending behaviour was, for example:

Category of offence	*Examples*
	(a) Non-threatening verbal abuse of a law enforcement officer or government official; (b) Shouting or causing a disturbance, without threats; (c) Quarrelling in the street, without threats.
Minor criminal damage (other than by fire)	For example, breaking a window
Possession of controlled substance (other than one with a high capacity for harm such as heroin, cocaine, LSD or crystal meth)	Where it was possession of a very small quantity and intended for personal use

CPD XI Other proceedings 50B: Management of appeal to the High Court (as substituted by Criminal Practice Directions 2015 (Amendment No. 4) [2017] EWCA Crim 310, Lord Thomas CJ)

50B.1 Applications for permission to appeal to the High Court under the Extradition Act 2003 must be started in the Administrative Court of the Queen's Bench Division at the Royal Courts of Justice in London. **B-917**

50B.2 A Lord Justice of Appeal appointed by the Lord Chief Justice will have responsibility to assist the President of the Queen's Bench Division with overall supervision of extradition appeals.

Definitions

50B.3 Where appropriate "appeal" includes "application for permission to appeal". **B-918**

50B.4 "EAW" means European Arrest Warrant.

50B.5 A "nominated legal officer of the court" is a court officer assigned to the Administrative Court Office who is a barrister or solicitor and who has been nominated for the purpose by the Lord Chief Justice under CrimPR 50.18 and 50.30.

Forms

50B.6 The forms are to be used in the High Court, in accordance with CrimPR 50.19, 50.20, 50.21 and 50.22. **B-919**

50B.7 The forms may be amended or withdrawn from time to time, or new forms added, under the authority of the Lord Chief Justice: see *CrimPD I 5A.*

Management of the Appeal

50B.8 Where it is not possible for the High Court to begin to hear the appeal in accordance with time limits contained in CrimPR 50.23(1) and (2), the court may extend the time limit if it believes it to be in the interests of justice to do so and may do so even after the time limit has expired. **B-920**

50B.9 The power to extend those time limits may be exercised by a Lord Justice of Appeal, a Single Judge of the High Court, a Master of the Administrative Court or a nominated legal officer of the court.

50B.10 Case management directions setting down a timetable may be imposed upon the parties by a Lord Justice of Appeal, a Single Judge of the High Court, a Master of the Administrative Court or a nominated legal officer of the court. For the court's constitution and relevant powers and duties see section 4 of the Senior Courts Act 1981 and CrimPR 50.18 and 50.30.

Listing of Oral, Renewal and Substantive Hearings

50B.11 Arrangements for the fixing of dates for hearings will be made by a Listing Officer of the Administrative Court under the direction of the judge with overall responsibility for supervision of extradition appeals. **B-921**

50B.12 A Lord Justice of Appeal, a Single Judge of the High Court, a Master of the Administrative Court or a nominated legal officer of the court may give such directions to the Listing Officer as they deem necessary with regard to the fixing of dates, including as to whether cases in the same/related proceedings or raising the same or similar issues should be heard together or consecutively under the duty imposed by CrimPR 1.1 (2)(e). Parties must alert the nominated court officer for the need for such directions.

50B.13 Save in exceptional circumstances, regard will not be given to an advocate's existing commitments. This is in accordance with the spirit of the legislation that extradition matters should be dealt with expeditiously. Extradition matters are generally not so complex that an alternative advocate cannot be instructed.

50B.14 If a party disagrees with the time estimate given by the court, they must inform the Listing Office within 5 business days of the notification of the listing and they must provide a time estimate of their own.

Expedited appeals

B-922 **50B.15** The court may direct that the hearing of an appeal be expedited.

50B.16 The court will deal with requests for an expedited appeal without a hearing. Requests for expedition must be made in writing, either within the appeal notice, or by application notice, clearly marked with the Administrative Court reference number, which must be lodged with the Administrative Court Office or emailed to the appropriate email address: administrativecourtoffice.crimex@hmcts.x.gsi.gov.uk and notice must be given to the other parties.

50B.17 Any requests for an expedited appeal made to an out of hours judge must be accompanied by:

(i) a detailed chronology;
(ii) reasons why the application could not be made within court hours;
(iii) any orders or judgments made in the proceedings.

Amendment to Notices

B-923 **50B.18** Amendment to Notice of Appeal requiring permission:

(i) subject to CrimPR 50.20(5), an appeal notice may not be amended without the permission of the court: CrimPR 50.17(6)(b);
(ii) an application for permission to amend made before permission to appeal has been considered will be determined without a hearing;
(iii) an application for permission to amend after permission to appeal has been granted and any submissions in opposition will normally be dealt with at the hearing unless there is any risk that the hearing may have to be adjourned. If there is any risk that the application to amend may lead the other party to seek time to answer the proposed amendment, the application must be made as soon as practicable and well in advance of the hearing. A failure to make immediate applications for such an amendment is likely to result in refusal;
(iv) legal representatives or the appellant, if acting in person, must
   a. Inform the court at the time they make the application if the existing time estimate is affected by the proposed amendment; and
   b. Attempt to agree any revised time estimate no later than 5 business days after service of the application.
(v) where the appellant wishes to restore grounds of appeal excluded on the grant of permission to appeal, the procedure is governed by CrimPR 50.22.

50B.19 Amendment to Respondent's Notice:

(i) a respondent's notice may not be amended without the permission of the court: CrimPR 50.17(6)(b);
(ii) an application for permission to amend made before permission to appeal has been considered will be determined without a hearing;
(iii) an application for permission to amend after permission to appeal has been granted and any submissions in opposition will normally be dealt with at the hearing unless there is any risk that the hearing may have to be adjourned. If there is any risk that the application to amend may lead the other party to seek time to answer the proposed amendment, the application must be made as soon as practicable and well in advance of the hearing. A failure to make immediate applications for such an amendment is likely to result in refusal;
(iv) legal representatives or the appellant, if acting in person, must
   a. Inform the court at the time they make the application if the existing time estimate is affected by the proposed amendment; and
   b. Attempt to agree any revised time estimate no later than 5 business days after service of the application.

Use of Live-Links

B-924 **50B.20** When a party acting in person is in custody, the court office will request the institution to use live-link for attendance at any oral or renewal hearing or substantive appeal. The institution must give precedence to all such applications in the High Court over live-links to the lower courts, including the Crown Court.

Interpreters

B-925 **50B.21** It is the responsibility of the Listing Officer to ensure the attendance of an accredited interpreter when an unrepresented party in extradition proceedings is acting in person and does not understand or speak English.

50B.22 Where a party who does not understand or speak English is legally represented it is the responsibility of his/her solicitors to instruct an interpreter if required for any hearing in extradition proceedings.

Disposing of applications and appeals by way of consent

50B.23 CrimPR 50.24 governs the submission of Consent Orders and lists the essential requirements for such orders. Any Consent Order, the effect of which will be to allow extradition to proceed, must specify the date on which the appeal proceedings are to be treated as discontinued, for the purposes of section 36 or 118, as the case may be, of the Extradition Act 2003: whether that is to be the date on which the order is made or some later date. A Consent Order may be approved by a Lord Justice of Appeal, a Single Judge of the High Court or, under CrimPR 50.30(2), a nominated legal officer of the court. The order may, but need not, be pronounced in open court: CrimPR 50.17(1)(c)(iii). Once approved, the order will be sent to the parties and to any other person as required by CrimPR 50.29(3)(b), (c). **B-926**

50B.24 A Consent Order to allow an appeal brought under s.28 of the Extradition Act 2003 must provide:

(i) for the quashing of the decision of the District Judge in Westminster Magistrates' Court discharging the Requested Person;
(ii) for the matter to be remitted to the District Judge to hold fresh extradition proceedings;
(iii) for any ancillary matter, such as bail or costs.

50B.25 A Consent Order to allow an appeal brought under s.110 of the Extradition Act 2003 must provide:

(i) for the quashing of the decision of the Secretary of State for the Home Department not to order extradition;
(ii) for the matter to be remitted to the Secretary of State to make a fresh decision on whether or not to order extradition;
(iii) for any ancillary matter, such as bail or costs.

50B.26 Where:

(a) a Consent Order is intended to dispose of an application for permission to appeal which has not yet been considered by the court, the order must make clear by what means that will be achieved, bearing in mind that an application for permission which is refused without a hearing can be renewed under CrimPR 50.22(2). If the parties intend to exclude the possibility of renewal the order should declare either (i) that the time limit under rule 50.22(2) is reduced to nil, or (ii) permission to appeal is given and the appeal determined on the other terms of the order.
(b) one of the parties is a child or protected party, the documents served under CrimPR 50.24(5) must include an opinion from the advocate acting on behalf of the child or protected party and, in the case of a protected party, any relevant documents prepared for the Court of Protection.

Fees

50B.27 Applications to extend Representation Orders do not attract any fee. **B-927**

50B.28 Fees are payable for all other applications in accordance with the current Fees Order.

CPD XI Other proceedings 50C: Extradition: representation orders (as substituted by Criminal Practice Directions 2015 (Amendment No. 4) [2017] EWCA Crim 310, Lord Thomas CJ)

50C.1 Representation Orders may be granted by a Lord Justice of Appeal, a Single Judge of the High Court, a Master of the Administrative Court or a nominated legal officer of the court upon a properly completed CRM14 being lodged with the court. A Representation Order will cover junior advocate and solicitors for the preparation of the Notice of Appeal to determination of the appeal. **B-928**

50C.2 Applications to extend Representation Orders may be granted by a Lord Justice of Appeal, a Single Judge of the High Court, a Master of the Administrative Court or a nominated court officer who may direct a case management hearing before a Lord Justice of Appeal, a Single Judge, or a Master of the Administrative Court. Since these applications do not attract a fee, parties may lodge them with the court by attaching them to an email addressed to the nominated legal officer of the court.

50C.3 Applications to extend Representation Orders to cover the instruction of Queen's Counsel to appear either alone or with a junior advocate must be made in writing, either by letter or application notice, clearly marked with the Administrative Court reference number, which must be lodged with the Administrative Court Office or emailed to the appropriate email address: administrativecourtoffice.crimex@hmcts.x.gsi.gov.uk. The request must:

(i) identify the substantial novel or complex issues of law or fact in the case;

(ii) explain why these may only be adequately presented by a Queen's Counsel;
(iii) state whether a Queen's Counsel has been instructed on behalf of the respondent;
(iv) explain any delay in making the request;
(v) be supported by advice from junior advocate or Queen's Counsel.

B-929 **50C.4** Applications for prior authority to cover the cost of obtaining expert evidence must be made in writing, either by letter, clearly marked with the Administrative Court reference number, which must be sent or emailed to the Administrative Court Office. The request must:

(i) confirm that the evidence sought has not been considered in any previous appeals determined by the appellate courts;
(ii) explain why the evidence was not called at the extradition hearing in Westminster Magistrates' Court and what evidence can be produced to support that;
(iii) explain why the new evidence would have resulted in the District Judge deciding a question at the extradition hearing differently and whether, if so, the District Judge would have been required to make a different order as to discharge of the requested person;
(iv) explain why the evidence was not raised when the case was being considered by the Secretary of State for the Home Department or information was available that was not available at that time;
(v) explain why the new evidence would have resulted in the Secretary of State deciding a question differently, and if the question had been decided differently, the Secretary of State would not have ordered the person's extradition;
(vi) state when the need for the new evidence first became known;
(vii) explain any delay in making the request;
(viii) explain what relevant factual, as opposed to expert evidence, is being given by whom to create the factual basis for the expert's opinion;
(ix) explain why this particular area of expertise is relevant: for example why a child psychologist should be appointed as opposed to a social worker;
(x) state whether the requested person has capacity;
(xi) set out a full breakdown of all costs involved including any VAT or other tax payable, including alternative quotes or explaining why none are available;
(xii) provide a list of all previous extensions of the Representation Order and the approval of expenditure to date;
(xiii) provide a timetable for the production of the evidence and its anticipated effect on the time estimate and hearing date;
(xiv) set out the level of compliance to date with any directions order.

50C.5 Experts must have direct personal experience of and proven expertise in the issue on which a report is sought; it is only if they do have such experience and it is relevant, that they can give evidence of what they have observed.

50C.6 Where an order is granted to extend a Representation Order to obtain further evidence it will still be necessary for the party seeking to rely on the new evidence to satisfy the court hearing the application for permission or the substantive appeal that the evidence obtained should be admitted having regard to sections 27(4) and 29(4) of the Extradition Act 2003 and the judgment in *Szombathely City Court v Fenyvesi* [2009] EWHC 231 (Admin).

B-930 **50C.7** Applications to extend representation for the translation of documents must be made in writing, either by letter, clearly marked with the Administrative Court reference number, which must be sent to Administrative Court Office, The Royal Courts of Justice, Strand, London, WC2A 2LL or emailed to the appropriate email address: administrativecourtoffice.crimex@hmcts.x.gsi.gov.uk

The request should:

(i) explain the importance of the document for which a translation is being sought and the justification for obtaining it;
(ii) explain what it is believed to be contained in the document and the issues it will assist the court to address in hearing the appeal;
(iii) confirm that the evidence sought has not been considered in any previous appeals determined by the appellate courts;
(iv) confirm that the evidence sought was not called at the extradition hearing in the Westminster Magistrates' Court;
(v) explain why the evidence sought would have resulted in the District Judge deciding a question at the extradition hearing differently and whether, if so, the District Judge would have been required to make a different order as to discharge of the requested person;
(vi) confirm that the new evidence was not raised when the case was being considered by the Secretary of State for the Home Department;
(vii) explain why the new evidence sought would have resulted in the Secretary of State deciding a question differently, and if the question had been decided differently, the Secretary of State would not have ordered the person's extradition;

(viii) confirm when the need for the new evidence first became known;
(ix) explain any delay in making the request;
(x) explain fully the evidential basis for incurring the expenditure;
(xi) explain why the appellant cannot produce the evidence himself or herself in the form of a statement of truth;
(xii) set out a full breakdown of all costs involved including any VAT or other tax payable and the Legal Aid Agency contractual rates;
(xiii) provide a list of all previous extensions of the Representation Order and the expenditure to date.

50C.8 Where an order is made to extend representation to cover the cost of the translation of documents it will still be necessary for the party seeking to rely on the documents as evidence to satisfy the court that it should be admitted at the hearing of the appeal having regard to sections 27(4) and 29(4) of the Extradition Act 2003 and the judgment in *Szombathely City Court v Fenyvesi* [2009] EWHC 231 (Admin).

CPD XI Other proceedings 50D: Extradition: applications, etc (as substituted by Criminal Practice Directions 2015 (Amendment No. 4) [2017] EWCA Crim 310, Lord Thomas CJ and amended by Criminal Practice Directions 2015 (Amendment No. 5) [2017] EWCA Crim 1076, Lord Thomas CJ)

50D.1 Extension or abridgement of time: **B-931**
(i) any party who seeks extension or abridgment of time for the service of documents, evidence or skeleton arguments must apply to the High Court on the appropriate form and pay the appropriate fee;
(ii) applications for extension or abridgment of time may be determined by a Lord Justice of Appeal, a Single Judge of the High Court, a Master of the Administrative Court or a nominated legal officer of the court;
(iii) applications for extension of time must include a witness statement setting out the reasons for noncompliance with any previous order and the proposed timetable for compliance;
(iv) any application made to an out of hours judge must be accompanied with:
a. a detailed chronology;
b. reasons why the application could not be made within court hours;
c. any orders or judgments made in the proceedings.

Representatives

50D.2 CrimPR Part 46 applies. **B-932**

50D.3 Where under CrimPR 46.2(1)(c) a legal representative withdraws from the case then that representative should satisfy him or herself that the defendant is aware of the time and date of the appeal hearing and of the need to attend, by live link if the court has so directed. If the legal representative has any reason to doubt that the defendant is so aware then he or she should promptly notify the Administrative Court Office.

Application to adjourn

50D.4 Where a hearing date has been fixed, any application to vacate the hearing must be made **B-933**
on the appropriate form. A fee is required for the application if it is made within 14 days of the hearing date. The application must:
(i) explain the reasons why an application is being made to vacate the hearing;
(ii) detail the views of the other parties to the appeal;
(iii) include a draft order with the application notice.

50D.5 If the parties both seek an adjournment then the application must be submitted for consideration by a Lord Justice of Appeal, a Single Judge of the High Court or a Master of the Administrative Court. Exceptional circumstances must be shown if a date for the hearing has been fixed or the adjournment will result in material delay to the determination of the appeal.

50D.6 An application to adjourn following a compromise agreement must be supported by evidence justifying exceptional circumstances and why it is in compliance with the overriding objective.

Variation of directions

50D.7 Where parties are unable to comply with any order of the court they must apply promptly **B-934**
to vary directions before deadlines for compliance have expired and seek further directions. An application to vary directions attracts a fee and the application notice, to be submitted on the appropriate form, must:
(i) provide full and proper explanations for why the current and existing directions have not been complied with;

(ii) detail the views of the other parties to the appeal;

(iii) include a draft order setting out in full the timetable and directions as varied i.e. a superseding order which stands alone.

50D.8 A failure to make the application prior to the expiry of the date specified in the order will generally result in the refusal of the application unless good reasons are shown.

Application to certify a point of law of general public importance

B-935 **50D.9** Where an application is made under CrimPR 50.25(2)(b) the application must be made on the appropriate form accompanied by the relevant fee.

50D.10 Any response to the application must be made within 10 business days.

50D.11 Where an application to certify is granted but permission to appeal to the Supreme Court is refused, it shall be for those representing the Requested Person to apply for an extension of the Representation Order to cover proceedings in the Supreme Court, if so advised.

50D.12 The representation order may be extended by a Lord Justice of Appeal, a Single Judge of the High Court, a Master of the Administrative Court or a nominated legal officer of the court.

50D.13 The result of the application to certify a point of law of general public importance and permission to appeal to the Supreme Court may be notified in advance to the legal representatives but legal representatives must not communicate it to the Requested Person until 1 hour before the pronouncement is made in open court.

50D.14 There shall be no public announcement of the result until after it has been formally pronounced.

Application to reopen the determination of an appeal

B-936 **50D.15** An application under CrimPR 50.27 to reopen an appeal must be referred to the court that determined the appeal, but may if circumstances require be considered by a judge or judges other than those who determined the original appeal.

Application to extend required period for removal pursuant to section 36 of the Extradition Act 2003

B-937 **50D.16** Where an application is made for an extension of the required period within which to extradite a Requested Person it must be accompanied by:

(i) a witness statement explaining why it is not possible to remove the Requested Person within the required period and the proposed timetable for removal;

(ii) a draft order.

50D.17 The application to extend time may be made before or after the expiry of the required period for extradition, but the court will scrutinise with particular care an application made after its expiry.

50D.18 Where extensions of time are sought for the same reason in respect of a number of Requested Persons who are due to be extradited at the same time, a single application may be made to the court listing each of the Requested Persons for whom an extension is sought.

50D.19 The application may be determined by a Lord Justice of Appeal, a Single Judge of the High Court, a Master of the Administrative Court or a nominated legal officer of the court and a single order listing those persons may be granted.

Application for directions ancillary to a discharge pursuant to section 42 or 124 of the Extradition Act 2003

B-938 **50D.20** Where the High Court is informed that the warrant or extradition request has been withdrawn then unless ancillary matters are dealt with by Consent Order an application notice must be issued seeking any such directions. The notice of discharge of a Requested Person must be accompanied by:

(i) the notification by the requesting state that the EAW has been withdrawn together with a translation of the same;

(ii) a witness statement containing:

a. details of whether the withdrawn EAW is the only EAW outstanding in respect of the Requested Person;

b. details of other EAWs outstanding in respect of the Requested Person and the stage which the proceedings have reached;

c. whether only part of the EAW has been withdrawn;

d. details of any bail conditions;

e. details of any institution in which the Requested Person is being detained, the Requested Person's prison number and date of birth.

50D.21 The order for discharge may be made by a Lord Justice of Appeal, a Single Judge of the High Court, a Master of the Administrative Court or a nominated legal officer of the court.

50D.22 It is the responsibility of the High Court to serve the approved order on the appropriate institution and Westminster Magistrates' Court.

CPD XI Other proceedings 50E: Extradition: court papers (as substituted by Criminal Practice Directions 2015 (Amendment No. 4) [2017] EWCA Crim 310, Lord Thomas CJ)

Skeleton arguments

50E.1 The court on granting permission to appeal or directing an oral hearing for permission to appeal will give directions as to the filing of skeleton arguments. Strict compliance is required with all time limits. **B-939**

50E.2 A skeleton argument must:

(i) not normally exceed 25 pages (excluding front sheets and back sheets) and be concise;
(ii) be printed on A4 paper in not less than 12 point font and 1.5 line spacing;
(iii) define the issues in the appeal;
(iv) be set out in numbered paragraphs;
(v) be cross-referenced to any relevant document in the bundle;
(vi) be self-contained and not incorporate by reference material from previous skeleton arguments;
(vii) not include extensive quotations from documents or authorities.

50E.3 Where it is necessary to refer to an authority, the skeleton argument must:

(i) state the proposition of law the authority demonstrates; and
(ii) identify but not quote the parts of the authority that support the proposition.

50E.4 If more than one authority is cited in support of a given proposition, the skeleton argument must briefly state why.

50E.5 A chronology of relevant events will be necessary in most appeals.

50E.6 Where a skeleton argument has been prepared in respect of an application for permission to appeal, the same skeleton argument may be relied upon in the appeal upon notice being given to the court or a replacement skeleton may be lodged not less than 10 business days before the hearing of the appeal.

50E.7 At the hearing the court may refuse to hear argument on a point not included in a skeleton argument filed within the prescribed time.

Bundles

50E.8 The bundle for the hearing should be agreed by the parties save where the Requested Person is acting in person. In those circumstances the court expects the Requesting State to prepare the bundle. **B-940**

50E.9 The bundle must be paginated and indexed.

50E.10 Subject to any order made by the court, the following documents must be included in the appeal bundle:

(i) a copy of the appellant's notice;
(ii) a copy of any respondent's notice;
(iii) a copy of any appellant's or respondent's skeleton argument;
(iv) a copy of the order under appeal;
(v) a copy of any order made by the Court in the exercise of its case management powers;
(vi) any judgment of the Court made in a previous appeal involving the party or parties which is relevant to the present proceedings.
(vii) where the bundle of papers reaches more than 200 pages, the parties should agree a core appeal bundle which must contain (i)-(vi) above.

50E.11 The Bundle should only contain relevant documents and must not include duplicate documents.

50E.12 Bundles lodged with the court will not be returned to the parties but will be destroyed in the confidential waste system at the conclusion of the proceedings and without further notification.

CPD XI Other proceedings 50F: Extradition: consequences of non compliance with directions (as substituted by Criminal Practice Directions 2015 (Amendment No. 4) [2017] EWCA Crim 310, Lord Thomas CJ)

50F.1 Failure to comply with these directions will lead to applications for permission and appeals being dealt with on the material available to the court at the time when the decision is made. **B-941**

50F.2 Judges dealing with extradition appeals will seek full and proper explanations for any breaches of the rules and the provisions of this Practice Direction.

50F.3 If no good explanation can be given immediately by counsel or solicitors, the senior partner or the departmental head responsible is likely to be called to court to explain any failure to comply with a court order. Where counsel or solicitors fail to obey orders of the court and are unable to provide proper and sufficient reasons for their disobedience they may anticipate the matter being formally referred to the President of the Queen's Bench Division with a recommendation that the counsel or solicitors involved be reported to their professional bodies.

50F.4 The court may also refuse to admit any material or any evidence not filed in compliance with the order for directions or outside a time limit specified by the court.

50F.5 A failure to comply with the time limits or other requirements for skeleton arguments will have the consequences specified in 50E.7.

CPD XII General application A: Court dress

B-942 **A.1** In magistrates' courts, advocates appear without robes or wigs. In all other courts, Queen's Counsel wear a short wig and a silk (or stuff) gown over a court coat with bands, junior counsel wear a short wig and stuff gown with bands. Solicitors and other advocates authorised under the Courts and Legal Services Act 1990 wear a black solicitor's gown with bands; they may wear short wigs in circumstances where they would be worn by Queen's Counsel or junior counsel.

A.2 High Court Judges hearing criminal cases may wear the winter criminal robe year-round. However, scarlet summer robes may be worn.

CPD XII General application B: Modes of address and titles of judges and magistrates

Modes of Address

B-943 **B.1** The following judges, when sitting in court, should be addressed as 'My Lord' or 'My Lady', as the case may be, whatever their personal status:

(a) Judges of the Court of Appeal and of the High Court;
(b) any Circuit Judge sitting as a judge of the Court of Appeal (Criminal Division) or the High Court under section 9(1) of the Senior Courts Act 1981;
(c) any judge sitting at the Central Criminal Court;
(d) any Senior Circuit Judge who is an Honorary Recorder.

B.2 Subject to the paragraph above, Circuit Judges, qualifying judge advocates, Recorders and Deputy Circuit Judges should be addressed as 'Your Honour' when sitting in court.

District Judges (Magistrates' Courts) should be addressed as
"Sir [or Madam]" or "Judge" when sitting in Court.

Magistrates in court should be addressed through the Chairperson as "Sir [or Madam]" or collectively as "Your Worships".

Description

B-944 **B.3** In cause lists, forms and orders members of the judiciary should be described as follows:

(a) Circuit Judges, as 'His [or Her] Honour Judge A'. When the judge is sitting as a judge of the High Court under section 9(1) of the Senior Courts Act 1981, the words 'sitting as a judge of the High Court' should be added;
(b) Recorders, as 'Mr [or Mrs, Ms or Miss] Recorder B'. This style is appropriate irrespective of any honour or title which the recorder might possess, but if in any case it is desired to include an honour or title, the alternative description, 'Sir CD, Recorder' or 'The Lord D, Recorder' may be used;
(c) Deputy Circuit Judges, as 'His [or Her] Honour EF, sitting as a Deputy Circuit Judge'.
(d) qualifying judges advocates, as 'His [or Her] Honour GH, sitting as a qualifying judge advocate.'
(e) District Judges (Magistrates' Courts), as "District Judge (Magistrates' Courts) J"

CPD XII General application C: Availability of judgments given in the Court of Appeal and the High Court

B-945 **C.1** For cases in the High Court, reference should be made to Practice Direction 40E, the supplementary Practice Direction to the Civil Procedure Rules Part 40.

C.2 For cases in the Court of Appeal (Criminal Division), the following provisions apply.

Availability of reserved judgments before handing down, corrections and applications consequential on judgment

B-946 **C.3** Where judgment is to be reserved the Presiding Judge may, at the conclusion of the hearing, invite the views of the parties' legal representatives as to the arrangements to be made for the handing down of the judgment.

C.4 Unless the court directs otherwise, the following provisions apply where the Presiding Judge is satisfied that the judgment will attract no special degree of confidentiality or sensitivity.

C.5 The court will provide a copy of the draft judgment to the parties' legal representatives about three working days before handing down, or at such other time as the court may direct. Every page of every judgment which is made available in this way will be marked "Unapproved judgment: No permission is granted to copy or use in court." The draft is supplied in confidence and on the conditions that:

(a) neither the draft judgment nor its substance will be disclosed to any other person or used in the public domain; and

(b) no action will be taken (other than internally) in response to the draft judgment, before the judgment is handed down.

C.6 Unless the parties' legal representatives are told otherwise when the draft judgment is circulated, any proposed corrections to the draft judgment should be sent to the clerk of the judge who prepared the draft (or to the associate, if the judge has no clerk) with a copy to any other party's legal representatives, by 12 noon on the day before judgment is handed down.

C.7 If, having considered the draft judgment, the prosecution will be applying to the Court for a retrial or either party wishes to make any other application consequent on the judgment, the judge's clerk should be informed with a time estimate for the application by 12 noon on the day before judgment is handed down. This will enable the court to make appropriate listing arrangements and notify advocates to attend if the court so requires. There is no fee payable to advocates who attend the hand down hearing if not required to do so by the court. If either party is considering applying to the Court to certify a point for appeal to the Supreme Court, it would assist if the judge's clerk could be informed at the same time, although this is not obligatory as under section 34 of the Criminal Appeal Act 1968, the time limit for such applications is 28 days.

Communication to the parties including the defendant or the victim

C.8 The contents are not to be communicated to the parties, including to the defendant, respondent or the victim (defined as a person entitled to receive services under the Code of Practice for Victims of Crime) until two hours before the listed time for pronouncement of judgment. **B-947**

C.9 Judges may permit more information about the result of a case to be communicated on a confidential basis to the parties including to the defendant, respondent or the victim at an earlier stage if good reason is shown for making such a direction.

C.10 If, for any reason, the parties' legal representatives have special grounds for seeking a relaxation of the usual condition restricting disclosure to the parties, a request for relaxation of the condition may be made informally through the judge's clerk (or through the associate, if the judge has no clerk).

C.11 If the parties or their legal representatives are in any doubt about the persons to whom copies of the draft judgment may be distributed they should enquire of the judge or Presiding Judge.

C.12 Any breach of the obligations or restrictions in this section or failure to take reasonable steps to ensure compliance may be treated as contempt of court.

Restrictions on disclosure or reporting

C.13 Anyone who is supplied with a copy of the handed-down judgment, or who reads it in court, will be bound by any direction which the court may have given in a child case under section 39 of the Children and Young Persons Act 1933 or section 45 or 45A of the Youth Justice and Criminal Evidence Act 1999, or any other form of restriction on disclosure, or reporting, of information in the judgment. **B-948**

C.14 Copies of the approved judgment can be ordered from the official shorthand writers, on payment of the appropriate fee. Judgments identified as of legal or public interest will generally be made available on the website managed by BAILLI: *http://www.bailii.org/*

CPD XII General Application D: Citation of authority and provision of copies of judgments to the court and skeleton arguments (as amended by the Criminal Practice Directions 2015 (Amendment No. 6) [2018] EWCA Crim 516, Lord Burnett CJ and the Criminal Practice Directions 2015 (Amendment No. 9) [2019] EWCA Crim 1603, Lord Burnett CJ)

D.1 This Practice Direction applies to all criminal matters before the Court of Appeal (Criminal Division), the Crown Court and the magistrates' courts. In relation to those matters only, *Practice Direction (Citation of Authorities)* [2012] 1 W.L.R. 780 is hereby revoked. **B-949**

Citation of authority

D.2 In *Erskine; Williams* [2009] EWCA Crim 1425, [2010] 1 W.L.R. 183, (2009) 2 Cr. App. R. 29 the Lord Chief Justice stated: **B-950**

75. The essential starting point, relevant to any appeal against conviction or sentence, is that, adapting the well known aphorism of Viscount Falkland in 1641: if it is not *necessary* to refer to a previous decision of the court, it is *necessary* not to refer to it. Similarly, if it is not *necessary* to include a previous decision in the bundle of authorities, it is *necessary* to exclude it. That approach will be rigidly enforced.

76. It follows that when the advocate is considering what authority, if any, to cite for a proposition, only an authority which establishes the principle should be cited. Reference should not

be made to authorities which do no more than either (a) illustrate the principle or (b) restate it.

78. Advocates must expect to be required to justify the citation of each authority relied on or included in the bundle. The court is most unlikely to be prepared to look at an authority which does no more than illustrate or restate an established proposition.

80. ... In particular, in sentencing appeals, where a definitive Sentencing Guidelines Council guideline is available there will rarely be any advantage in citing an authority reached before the issue of the guideline, and authorities after its issue which do not refer to it will rarely be of assistance. In any event, where the authority does no more than uphold a sentence imposed at the Crown Court, the advocate must be ready to explain how it can assist the court to decide that a sentence is manifestly excessive or wrong in principle.

D.3 Advocates should only cite cases when it is necessary to do so; when the case identifies or represents a principle or the development of a principle. In sentencing appeals, other cases are rarely helpful, providing only an illustration, and this is especially true if there is a sentencing guideline. Unreported cases should only be cited in exceptional circumstances, and the advocate must expect to explain why such a case has been cited.

D.4 Advocates should not assume that because a case cited to the court is not referred to in the judgment the court has not considered it; it is more likely that the court was not assisted by it.

D.5 When an authority is to be cited, whether in written or oral submissions, the advocate should always provide the neutral citation followed by the law report reference.

D.6 The following practice should be followed:

i) Where a judgment is reported in the Official Law Reports (A.C., Q.B., Ch., Fam.) published by the Incorporated Council of Law Reporting for England and Wales or the Criminal Appeal Reports or the Criminal Appeal Reports (Sentencing) one of those two series of reports must be cited; either is equally acceptable. However, where a judgment is reported in the Criminal Appeal Reports or the Criminal Appeal Reports (Sentencing) that reference must be given in addition to any other reference. Other series of reports and official transcripts of judgment may only be used when a case is not reported, or not yet reported, in the Official Law Reports or the Criminal Appeal Reports or the Criminal Appeal Reports (Sentencing).

ii) If a judgment is not reported in the Official Law Reports, the Criminal Appeal Reports or the Criminal Appeal Reports (Sentencing), but it is reported in an authoritative series of reports which contains a headnote and is made by individuals holding a Senior Courts qualification (for the purposes of section 115 of the Courts and Legal Services Act 1990), that report should be cited.

iii) Where a judgment is not reported in any of the reports referred to above, but is reported in other reports, they may be cited.

iv) Where a judgment has not been reported, reference may be made to the official transcript if that is available, not the handed-down text of the judgment, as this may have been subject to late revision after the text was handed down. Official transcripts may be obtained from, for instance, BAILLI (*http://www.bailii.org/*).

D.7 In the majority of cases, it is expected that all references will be to the Official Law Reports and the Criminal Appeal Reports or the Criminal Appeal Reports (Sentencing); it will be rare for there to be a need to refer to any other reports. An unreported case should not be cited unless it contains a relevant statement of legal principle not found in reported authority, and it is expected that this will only occur in exceptional circumstances.

Provision of copies of judgments to the court

B-951 **D.8** The paragraphs below specify whether or not copies should be provided to the court. Authorities should not be included for propositions not in dispute. If more than one authority is to be provided, the copies should be presented in paginated and tagged bundles.

D.9 If required, copies of judgments should be provided either by way of a photocopy of the published report or by way of a copy of a reproduction of the judgment in electronic form that has been authorised by the publisher of the relevant series, but in any event-

i) the report must be presented to the court in an easily legible form (a 12-point font is preferred but a 10 or 11-point font is acceptable), and

ii) the advocate presenting the report must be satisfied that it has not been reproduced in a garbled form from the data source.

In any case of doubt the court will rely on the printed text of the report (unless the editor of the report has certified that an electronic version is more accurate because it corrects an error contained in an earlier printed text of the report).

D.10 If such a copy is unavailable, a printed transcript such as from BAILLI may be included.

Provision of copies to the Court of Appeal (Criminal Division)

B-952 **D.11** Advocates must provide to the Registrar of Criminal Appeals, with their appeal notice, respondent's notice or skeleton argument, a list of authorities upon which they wish to rely in their written or oral submissions. The list of authorities should contain the name of the applicant, appellant or respondent and the Criminal Appeal Office number where known. The list should include reference to the relevant paragraph numbers in each authority. An updated list can be provided if a new authority is issued, or in response to a respondent's notice or skeleton argument. From time to time, the Registrar may issue guidance as to the style or content of lists of authorities, including a suggested format; this guidance should be followed by all parties. The latest guidance is available from the Criminal Appeal Office.

D.12 If the case cited is reported in the Official Law Reports, the Criminal Appeal Reports or the Criminal Appeal Reports (Sentencing), the law report reference must be given after the neutral citation, and the relevant paragraphs listed, but copies should not be provided to the court.

D.13 If, exceptionally, reference is made to a case that is not reported in the Official Law Reports, the Criminal Appeal Reports or the Criminal Appeal Reports (Sentencing), three copies must be provided to the Registrar with the list of authorities and the relevant appeal notice or respondent's notice (or skeleton argument, if provided). The relevant passages of the authorities should be marked or sidelined.

Provision of copies to the Crown Court and the magistrates' courts

D.14 When the court is considering routine applications, it may be sufficient for the court to be referred to the applicable legislation or to one of the practitioner texts. However, it is the responsibility of the advocate to ensure that the court is provided with the material that it needs properly to consider any matter. **B-953**

D.15 If it would assist the court to consider any authority, the directions at paragraphs D.2 to D.7 above relating to citation will apply and a list of authorities should be provided.

D.16 Copies should be provided by the party seeking to rely upon the authority in accordance with CrimPR 24.13. This Rule is applicable in the magistrates' courts, and in relation to the provision of authorities, should also be followed in the Crown Court since courts often do not hold library stock (see CrimPR 25.17). Advocates should comply with paragraphs D.8 to D.10 relating to the provision of copies to the court.

Skeleton arguments

D.17 The court may give directions for the preparation of skeleton arguments. Such directions will provide for the time within which skeleton arguments must be served and for the issues which they must address. Such directions may provide for the number of pages, or the number of words, to which a skeleton argument is to be confined. Any such directions displace the following to the extent of any inconsistency. Subject to that, however, a skeleton argument must: **B-954**

i. not normally exceed 15 pages (excluding front sheets and back sheets) and be concise;
ii. be presented in A4 page size and portrait orientation, in not less than 12 point font and in 1.5 line spacing;
iii. define the issues;
iv. be set out in numbered paragraphs;
v. be cross-referenced to any relevant document in any bundle prepared for the court;
vi. be self-contained and not incorporate by reference material from previous skeleton arguments;
vii. not include extensive quotations from documents or authorities.

D.18 Where it is necessary to refer to an authority, the skeleton argument must:

i. state the proposition of law the authority demonstrates; and
ii. identify but not quote the parts of the authority that support the proposition.

D.19 If more than one authority is cited in support of a given proposition, the skeleton argument must briefly state why.

D.20 A chronology of relevant events will be necessary in most cases.

D.21 There are directions at paragraphs I 3C.3 and 3C.4 of these Practice Directions that apply to the service of skeleton arguments in support of, and in opposition to, an application to stay an indictment on the grounds of abuse of process; and directions at paragraphs IX 39F.1 to 39F.3 that apply to the service of skeleton arguments in the Court of Appeal. Where a skeleton argument has been prepared in respect of an application for permission to appeal, the same skeleton argument may be relied upon in the appeal upon notice being given to the court, or a replacement skeleton may be served to the timetable set out in those paragraphs. **★B-955**

D.22 At the hearing the court may refuse to hear argument on a point unless it is included in a skeleton argument which (i) is served within the required time, and (ii) complies with the requirements of these Practice Directions (as varied, if applicable, by direction of the court). Any application for a variation, or further variation, of those requirements must give reasons, and such an application must accompany any skeleton argument that does not comply.

D.23 In *James, Selby* [2016] EWCA Crim 1639; [2017] Crim. L.R. 228 the Court of Appeal observed (at paragraphs 52 to 54):

> "Legal documents of unnecessary and too often of excessive length offer very little assistance to the court. In *Tombstone Ltd v Raja* [2008] EWCA Civ 1441, [2009] 1 WLR 1143 Mummery LJ said:
>
> > "Practitioners ... are well advised to note the risk of the court's negative reaction to unnecessarily long written submissions. The skeleton argument procedure was introduced to assist the court, as well as the parties, by improving preparations for, and the efficiency of, adversarial oral hearings, which remain central to this court's public role... An unintended and unfortunate side effect of the growth in written advocacy... has been that too many practitioners, at increased cost to their clients and diminishing assistance to the court, burden their opponents and the court with written briefs."
>
> He might have penned those remarks had he been sitting in these two cases, and many more, in this Division. In *Standard Bank PLC v Via Mat International* [2013] EWCA Civ 490, [2013] 2 All E.R. (Comm) 1222 the excessive length of court documents prompted:
>
> > "It is important that both practitioners and their clients understand that skeleton arguments are not intended to serve as vehicles for extended advocacy and that in general a short, concise skeleton is both more helpful to the court and more likely to be persuasive than a longer document which seeks to develop every point which the advocate would wish to make in oral argument."
>
> No area of law is exempt from the requirement to produce careful and concise documents: *Tchenquiz v Director of the Serious Fraud Office* [2014] EWCA Civ 1333, [2015] 1 WLR 838, paragraph 10."

CPD XII General application E: Preparation of judgments: neutral vitation

B-956 **E.1** Since 11 January 2001 every judgment of the Court of Appeal, and of the Administrative Court, and since 14 January 2002 every judgment of the High Court, has been prepared and issued as approved with single spacing, paragraph numbering (in the margins) and no page numbers. In courts with more than one judge, the paragraph numbering continues sequentially through each judgment and does not start again at the beginning of each judgment. Indented paragraphs are not numbered. A unique reference number is given to each judgment. For judgments of the Court of Appeal, this number is given by the official shorthand writers, Merrill Legal Solutions (Tel: 020 7421 4000 ext.4036). For judgments of the High Court, it is provided by the Courts Recording and Transcription Unit at the Royal Courts of Justice. Such a number will also be furnished, on request to the Courts Recording and Transcription Unit, Royal Courts of Justice, Strand, London WC2A 2LL (Tel: 020 7947 7820), (e-mail: rcj.cratu@hmcts.gsi.gov.uk) for High Court judgments delivered outside London.

E.2 Each Court of Appeal judgment starts with the year, followed by EW (for England and Wales), then CA (for Court of Appeal), followed by Civ or Crim and finally the sequential number. For example, '*Smith v Jones* [2001] EWCA Civ 10'.

E.3 In the High Court, represented by HC, the number comes before the divisional abbreviation and, unlike Court of Appeal judgments, the latter is bracketed: (Ch), (Pat), (QB), (Admin), (Comm), (Admlty), (TCC) or (Fam), as appropriate. For example, '[2002] EWHC 123 (Fam)', or '[2002] EWHC 124 (QB)', or '[2002] EWHC 125 (Ch)'.

E.4 This 'neutral citation', as it is called, is the official number attributed to the judgment and must always be used at least once when the judgment is cited in a later judgment. Once the judgment is reported, this neutral citation appears in front of the familiar citation from the law reports series. Thus: '*Smith v Jones* [2001] EWCA Civ 10; [2001] QB 124; [2001] 2 All ER 364', etc.

E.5 Paragraph numbers are referred to in square brackets. When citing a paragraph from a High Court judgment, it is unnecessary to include the descriptive word in brackets: (Admin), (QB), or whatever. When citing a paragraph from a Court of Appeal judgment, however, 'Civ' or 'Crim' is included. If it is desired to cite more than one paragraph of a judgment, each numbered paragraph should be enclosed with a square bracket. Thus paragraph 59 in *Green v White* [2002] EWHC 124 (QB) would be cited: '*Green v White* [2002] EWHC 124 at [59]'; paragraphs 30 - 35 in Smith v Jones would be '*Smith v Jones* [2001] EWCA Civ 10 at [30] - [35]'; similarly, where a number of paragraphs are cited: '*Smith v Jones* [2001] EWCA Civ 10 at [30], [35] and [40 - 43]'.

E.6 If a judgment is cited more than once in a later judgment, it is helpful if only one abbreviation is used, e.g., '*Smith v Jones*' or 'Smith's case', but preferably not both (in the same judgment).

CPD XII General application F: Citation of Hansard

B-957 **F.1** Where any party intends to refer to the reports of Parliamentary proceedings as reported in the Official Reports of either House of Parliament ("Hansard") in support of any such argument as is permitted by the decisions in *Pepper v Hart* [1993] A.C. 593 and *Pickstone v Freemans PLC* [1989] A.C. 66, or otherwise, he must, unless the court otherwise directs, serve upon all other parties and the court copies of any such extract, together with a brief summary of the argument intended to be based upon such extract. No other report of Parliamentary proceedings may be cited.

F.2 Unless the court otherwise directs, service of the extract and summary of the argument shall be effected not less than 5 clear working days before the first day of the hearing, whether or not it has a fixed date. Advocates must keep themselves informed as to the state of the lists where no fixed date has been given. Service on the court shall be effected by sending three copies to the Registrar of Criminal Appeals, Royal Courts of Justice, Strand, London, WC2A 2LL or to the court manager of the relevant Crown Court centre, as appropriate. If any party fails to do so, the court may make such order (relating to costs or otherwise) as is, in all the circumstances, appropriate.

CPD XIII Listing A: Judicial responsibility for listing and key principles

Listing as a judicial responsibility and function

A.1 Listing is a judicial responsibility and function. The purpose is to ensure that all cases are brought to a hearing or trial in accordance with the interests of justice, that the resources available for criminal justice are deployed as effectively as possible, and that cases are heard by an appropriate judge or bench with the minimum of delay. **B-958**

A.2 The agreement reached between the Lord Chief Justice and the Secretary of State for Constitutional Affairs and Lord Chancellor set out in a statement to the House of Lords on 26 January 2004 ('the Concordat'), states that judges, working with HMCTS, are responsible for deciding on the assignment of cases to particular courts and the listing of those cases before particular judges. Therefore:

(a) The Presiding Judges of each circuit have the overall responsibility for listing at all courts, Crown and magistrates', on their circuit;

(b) Subject to the supervision of the Presiding Judges, the Resident Judge at each Crown Court has the general responsibility within his or her court centre for the allocation of criminal judicial work, to ensure the just and efficient despatch of the business of the court or group of courts. This includes overseeing the deployment of allocated judges at the court or group, including the distribution of work between all the judges allocated to that court. A Resident Judge must appoint a deputy or deputies to exercise his or her functions when he or she is absent from his or her court centre. See also paragraph A.5: Discharge of judicial responsibilities;

(c) The listing officer in the Crown Court is responsible for carrying out the day-to-day operation of listing practice under the direction of the Resident Judge. The listing officer at each Crown Court centre has one of the most important functions at that Crown Court and makes a vital contribution to the efficient running of that Crown Court and to the efficient operation of the administration of criminal justice;

(d) In the magistrates' courts, the Judicial Business Group, subject to the supervision of the Presiding Judges of the circuit, is responsible for determining the listing practice in that area. The day-to-day operation of that listing practice is the responsibility of the justices' clerk with the assistance of the listing officer.

Key principles of listing

A.3 When setting the listing practice, the Resident Judge or the Judicial Business Group should take into account principles a-j: **B-959**

(a) Ensure the timely trial of cases and resolution of other issues (such as confiscation) so that justice is not delayed. The following factors are relevant:

   i. In general, each case should be tried within as short a time of its arrival in the court as is consistent with the interests of justice, the needs of victims and witnesses, and with the proper and timely preparation by the prosecution and defence of their cases in accordance with the directions and timetable set;

   ii. Priority should be accorded to the trial of young defendants, and cases where there are vulnerable or young witnesses. In *Barker* [2010] EWCA Crim 4, the Lord Chief Justice highlighted "the importance to the trial and investigative process of keeping any delay in a case involving a child complainant to an irreducible minimum";

   iii. Custody time limits (CTLs) should be observed, see *CPD XIII Listing F*;

   iv. Every effort must be made to avoid delay in cases in which the defendant is on bail;

(b) Ensure that in the magistrates' court unless impracticable, non-custody anticipated guilty plea cases are listed 14 days after charge, and non-custody anticipated not guilty pleas are listed 28 days after charge;

(c) Provide, when possible, for certainty and/or as much advance notice as possible, of the trial date; and take all reasonable steps to ensure that the trial date remains fixed;
(d) Ensure that a judge or bench with any necessary authorisation and of appropriate experience is available to try each case and, wherever desirable and practicable, there is judicial continuity, including in relation to post-trial hearings;
(e) Strike an appropriate balance in the use of resources, by taking account of:
 i. The efficient deployment of the judiciary in the Crown Court and the magistrates' courts taking into account relevant sitting requirements for magistrates. See *CPD XIII Annex 1* for information to support judicial deployment in the magistrates' courts;
 ii. The proper use of the courtrooms available at the court;
 iii. The provision in long and/or complex cases for adequate reading time for the judiciary;
 iv. The facilities in the available courtrooms, including the security needs (such as a secure dock), size and equipment, such as video and live link facilities;
 v. The proper use of those who attend the Crown Court as jurors;
 vi. The availability of legal advisers in the magistrates' courts;
 vii. The need to return those sentenced to custody as soon as possible after the sentence is passed, and to facilitate the efficient operation of the prison escort contract;
(f) Provide where practicable:
 i. the defendant and the prosecution with the advocate of their choice where this does not result in any delay to the trial of the case; and,
 ii. for the efficient deployment of advocates, lawyers and associate prosecutors of the Crown Prosecution Service, and other prosecuting authorities, and of the resources available to the independent legal profession, for example by trying to group certain cases together;
(g) Meet the need for special security measures for category A and other highrisk defendants;
(h) Ensure that proper time (including judicial reading time) is afforded to hearings in which the court is exercising powers that impact on the rights of individuals, such as applications for investigative orders or warrants;
(i) Consider the significance of ancillary proceedings, such as confiscation hearings, and the need to deal with such hearings promptly and, where possible, for such hearings to be conducted by the trial judge;
(j) Provide for government initiatives or projects approved by the Lord Chief Justice.

A.4 Although the listing practice at each Crown Court centre and magistrates' court will take these principles into account, the listing practice adopted will vary from court to court depending particularly on the number of courtrooms and the facilities available, the location and the workload, its volume and type.

Discharge of judicial responsibilities

B-960 **A.5** The Resident Judge of each court is responsible for:
 i. ensuring that good practice is implemented throughout the court, such that all hearings commence on time;
 ii. ensuring that the causes of trials that do not proceed on the date originally fixed are examined to see if there is any systemic issue;
 iii. monitoring the general performance of the court and the listing practices;
 iv. monitoring the timeliness of cases and reporting any cases of serious concern to the Presiding Judge;
 v. maintaining and reviewing annually a list of Recorders, qualifying judge advocates and Deputy Circuit Judges authorised to hear appeals from the magistrates' courts unless such a list is maintained by the Presiding Judge.

A.6 The Judicial Business Group for each clerkship subject to the overall jurisdiction of the Presiding Judge is responsible for:
 i. monitoring the workload and anticipated changes which may impact on listing policies;
 ii. ensuring that any listing practice meets the needs of the system as a whole.

CPD XIII Listing B: Classification

B-961 **B.1** The classification structure outlined below is solely for the purposes of trial in the Crown Court. The structure has been devised to accommodate practical administrative functions and is not intended to reflect a hierarchy of the offences therein.

Offences are classified as follows:

Class 1: A:
 i. Murder;

ii. Attempted Murder;
iii. Manslaughter;
iv. Infanticide;
v. Child destruction (section 1(1) of the Infant Life (Preservation) Act 1929;
vi. Abortion (section 58 of the Offences Against the Person Act 1861);
vii. Assisting a suicide;
viii. Cases including section 5 of the Domestic Violence, Crime and Victims Act 2004, as amended (if a fatality has resulted);
ix. Soliciting, inciting, encouraging or assisting, attempting or conspiring to commit any of the above offences or assisting an offender having committed such an offence.

Class 1: B:
i. Genocide;
ii. Torture, hostage-taking and offences under the War Crimes Act 1991;
iii. Offences under ss.51 and 52 International Criminal Courts Act 2001;
iv. An offence under section 1 of the Geneva Conventions Act 1957;
v. Terrorism offences (where offence charged is indictable only and took place during an act of terrorism or for the purposes of terrorism as defined in s.1 of the Terrorism Act 2000);
vi. Piracy, under the Merchant Shipping and Maritime Security Act 1997;
vii. Treason;
viii. An offence under the Official Secrets Acts;
ix. Incitement to disaffection;
x. Soliciting, inciting, encouraging or assisting, attempting or conspiring to commit any of the above offences or assisting an offender having committed such an offence.#

Class 1: C:
i. Prison mutiny, under the Prison Security Act 1992;
ii. Riot in the course of serious civil disturbance;
iii. Serious gang related crime resulting in the possession or discharge of firearms, particularly including a campaign of firebombing or extortion, especially when accompanied by allegations of drug trafficking on a commercial scale;
iv. Complex sexual offence cases in which there are many complainants (often under age, in care or otherwise particularly vulnerable) and/or many defendants who are alleged to have systematically groomed and abused them, often over a long period of time;
v. Cases involving people trafficking for sexual, labour or other exploitation and cases of human servitude;
vi. Soliciting, inciting, encouraging or assisting, attempting or conspiring to commit any of the above offences or assisting an offender having committed such an offence.

Class 1: D:
i. Causing death by dangerous driving;
ii. Causing death by careless driving;
iii. Causing death by unlicensed, disqualified or uninsured driving;
iv. Any Health and Safety case resulting in a fatality or permanent serious disability;
v. Any other case resulting in a fatality or permanent serious disability;
vi. Soliciting, inciting, encouraging or assisting, attempting or conspiring to commit any of the above offences or assisting an offender having committed such an offence.

Class 2: A
i. Arson with intent to endanger life or reckless as to whether life was endangered;
ii. Cases in which explosives, firearms or imitation firearms are used or carried or possessed;
iii. Kidnapping or false imprisonment (without intention to commit a sexual offence but charged on the same indictment as a serious offence of violence such as under section 18 or section 20 of the Offences Against the Person Act 1861);
iv. Cases in which the defendant is a police officer, member of the legal profession or a high profile or public figure;
v. Cases in which the complainant or an important witness is a high profile or public figure;
vi. Riot otherwise than in the course of serious civil disturbance;
vii. Child cruelty;
viii. Cases including section 5 of the Domestic Violence, Crime and Victims Act 2004, as amended (if no fatality has resulted);
ix. Soliciting, inciting, encouraging or assisting, attempting or conspiring to commit any of the above offences or assisting an offender having committed such an offence.

Class 2: B
i. Any sexual offence, with the exception of those included in Class 1C;

ii. Kidnapping or false imprisonment (with intention to commit a sexual offence or charged on the same indictment as a sexual offence);
iii. Soliciting, inciting, encouraging or assisting, attempting or conspiring to commit any of the above offences or assisting an offender having committed such an offence.

Class 2: C
i. Serious, complex fraud;
ii. Serious and/or complex money laundering;
iii. Serious and/or complex bribery;
iv. Corruption;
v. Complex cases in which the defendant is a corporation (including cases for sentence as well as for trial);
vi. Any case in which the defendant is a corporation with a turnover in excess of £1bn (including cases for sentence as well as for trial);
vii. Soliciting, inciting, encouraging or assisting, attempting or conspiring to commit any of the above offences or assisting an offender having committed such an offence.

Class 3:All other offences not listed in the classes above.

Deferred Prosecution Agreements

B-962 **B.2** Cases coming before the court under section 45 and Schedule 17 of the Crime and Courts Act 2013 must be referred to the President of the Queen's Bench Division who will allocate the matter to a judge from a list of judges approved by the Lord Chief Justice. Only the allocated judge may thereafter hear any matter or make any decision in relation to that case.

Criminal Cases Review Commission

B-963 **B.3** Where the CCRC refers a case upon conviction from the magistrates' courts to the Crown Court, this shall be dealt with at a Crown Court centre designated by the Senior Presiding Judge.

CPD XIII Listing C: Referral of cases in the Crown Court to the resident judge and to the presiding judges (as amended by Criminal Practice Directions 2015 (Amendment No. 8) [2019] EWCA Crim 495, Lord Burnett CJ)

B-964 **C.1** This Practice Direction specifies:
(a) cases which must be referred to a Presiding Judge for release; and
(b) cases which must be referred to the Resident Judge before being assigned to a judge, Recorder or qualifying judge advocate to hear.

It is applicable to all Crown Courts, but its application may be modified by the Senior Presiding Judge or the Presiding Judges, with the approval of the Senior Presiding Judge, through the provision of further specific guidance to Resident Judges in relation to the allocation and management of the work at their court.

C.2 This Practice Direction does not prescribe the way in which the Resident Judge gives directions as to listing policy to the listing officer; its purpose is to ensure that there is appropriate judicial control over the listing of cases. However, the Resident Judge must arrange with the listing officers a satisfactory means of ensuring that all cases listed at their court are listed before judges, Recorders or qualifying judge advocates of suitable seniority and experience, subject to the requirements of this Practice Direction. The Resident Judge should ensure that listing officers are made aware of the contents and importance of this Practice Direction, and that listing officers develop satisfactory procedures for referral of cases to him or her.

C.3 In order to assist the Resident Judge and the listing officer, all cases sent to the Crown Court should where possible include a brief case summary prepared by the prosecution. The prosecutor should ensure that any factors that make the case complex, or would lead it to be referred to the Resident Judge or a Presiding Judge are highlighted. The defence may also send submissions to the court, again highlighting any areas of complexity or any other factors that might assist in the case being allocated to an appropriate judge.

Cases in the Crown Court to be referred to the Resident Judge

B-965 **C.4** All cases in Class 1A, 1B, 1C, 1D, 2A and 2C must be referred to the Resident Judge as must any case which appears to raise particularly complex, sensitive or serious issues.

C.5 Resident Judges should give guidance to the judges and staff of their respective courts as to which Class 2B cases should be referred to them following consultation with the Senior Presiding Judge. This will include any cases that may be referred to the Presiding Judge, see below. Class 2B cases to be referred to the Resident Judge are likely to be identified by the list officer, or by the judge at the first hearing in the Crown Court. Any appeal against conviction and/or sentence from a Youth Court involving a Class 2B case must be bought to the attention of the Resident Judge as soon as practicable. Where not provided with the appeal papers, the list officer must obtain a full summary of the prosecution case so as to allow an informed allocation decision to be made.

C.6 Once a case has been referred to the Resident Judge, the Resident Judge should refer the case to the Presiding Judge, following the guidance below, or allocate the case to an appropriate category of judge, and if possible to a named judge.

Cases in the Crown Court to be referred to a Presiding Judge

C.7 All cases in Class 1A, 1B and 1C must be referred by the Resident Judge to a Presiding Judge, as must a case in any class which is: **B-966**

i. An usually grave or complex case or one in which a novel and important point of law is to be raised;
ii. A case where it is alleged that the defendant caused more than one fatality;
iii. A non-fatal case of baby shaking where serious injury resulted;
iv. A case where the defendant is a police officer, or a member of the legal profession or a high profile figure;
v. A case which for any reason is likely to attract exceptional media attention;
vi. A case where a large organisation or corporation may, if convicted, be ordered to pay a very large fine;
vii. Any case likely to last more than three months.

C.8 Resident Judges are encouraged to refer any other case if they think it is appropriate to do so.

C.9 Presiding Judges and Resident Judges should agree a system for the referral of cases to the Presiding Judge, ideally by electronic means. The system agreed should include provision for the Resident Judge to provide the Presiding Judge with a brief summary of the case, a clear recommendation by the Resident Judge about the judges available to try the case and any other comments. A written record of the decision and brief reasons for it must be made and retained.

C.10 Once a case has been referred to the Presiding Judge, the Presiding Judge may retain the case for trial by a High Court Judge, or release the case back to the Resident Judge, either for trial by a named judge, or for trial by an identified category of judges, to be allocated by the Resident Judge.

CPD XIII Listing D: Authorisation of judges

D.1 Judges must be authorised by the Lord Chief Justice before they may hear certain types of case. **B-967**

D.2 Judges (other than High Court Judges) to hear Class 1A cases must be authorised to hear such cases. Any judge previously granted a 'Class 1' or 'murder' authorisation is authorised to hear Class 1A cases. Judges previously granted an 'attempted murder' (including soliciting, incitement or conspiracy thereof) authorisation can only deal with these cases within Class 1A.

D.3 Judges (other than High Court Judges) to hear sexual offences cases in Class 1C or any case within Class 2B must be authorised to hear such cases. Any judge previously granted a 'Class 2' or 'serious sex offences' authorisation is authorised to hear sexual offences cases in Class 1C or 2B. It is a condition of the authorisation that it does not take effect until the judge has attended the relevant Judicial College course; the Resident Judge should check in the case of newly authorised judges that they have attended the course. Judges who have been previously authorised to try such cases should make every effort to ensure their training is up-to-date and maintained by attending the Serious Sexual Offences Seminar at least once every three years. See *CPD XIII Annex 2* for guidance in dealing with sexual offences in the youth court.

D.4 Cases in the magistrates' courts involving the imposition of very large fines:

i. Where a defendant appears before a magistrates' court for an either way offence, to which CPD XIII Annex 3 applies the case must be dealt with by a DJ (MC) who has been authorised to deal with such cases by the Chief Magistrate.
ii. The authorised DJ (MC) must first consider whether such cases should be allocated to the Crown Court or, where the defendant pleads guilty, committed for sentence under s.3 Powers of Courts (Sentence) Act 2000, and must do so when the DJ (MC) considers the offence or combination of offences so serious that the Crown Court should deal with the defendant had they been convicted on indictment.
iii. If an authorised DJ (MC) decides not to commit such a case the reasons must be recorded in writing to be entered onto the court register.

CPD XIII Listing E: Allocation of business within the Crown Court (as amended by Criminal Practice Directions 2015 (Amendment No. 8) [2019] EWCA Crim 495, Lord Burnett CJ)

E.1 Cases in Class 1A may only be tried by: **B-968**

i. a High Court Judge, or

ii. a Circuit Judge, or Deputy High Court Judge, authorised to try such cases and provided that the Presiding Judge has released the case for trial by such a judge; or
iii. a Deputy Circuit Judge to whom the case has been specifically released by the Presiding Judge.

E.2 Cases in Class 1B may only be tried by:
i. a High Court Judge, or
ii. a Circuit Judge, or a Deputy High Court Judge, provided that the Presiding Judge has released the case for trial by such a judge; or
iii. a Deputy Circuit Judge to whom the case has been specifically released by the Presiding Judge.

E.3 Cases in Class 1C may only be tried by:
i. a High Court Judge, or
ii. a Circuit Judge, or a Deputy High Court Judge, or Deputy Circuit Judge, authorised to try such cases (if the case requires the judge to be authorised to hear sexual offences cases), provided that the Presiding Judge has released the case for trial by such a judge, or, if the case is a sexual offence, the Presiding Judge has assigned the case to that named judge.

See also *CPD XIII Listing C.*10

E.4 Cases in Class 1D and 2A may be tried by:
i. a High Court Judge, or
ii. a Circuit Judge, or Deputy High Court Judge, or Deputy Circuit Judge, or a Recorder or a qualifying judge advocate, provided that either the Presiding Judge has released the case or the Resident Judge has allocated the case for trial by such a judge; with the exception that Class 2A i) cases may not be tried by a Recorder or qualifying judge advocate.

E.5 Cases in Class 2B may be tried by:
i. a High Court Judge, or
ii. a Circuit Judge, or Deputy High Court Judge, or Deputy Circuit Judge, or a Recorder or a qualifying judge advocate, authorised to try such cases and provided that either the Presiding Judge has released the case or the Resident Judge has allocated the case for trial by such a judge.

E.6 Cases in Class 2C may be tried by:
i. a High Court Judge, or
ii. a Circuit Judge, or Deputy High Court Judge, or Deputy Circuit Judge, or a Recorder or a qualifying judge advocate, with suitable experience (for example, with company accounts or other financial information) and provided that either the Presiding Judge has released the case or the Resident Judge has allocated the case for trial by such a judge.

E.7 Cases in Classes 1D, 2A and 2C will usually be tried by a Circuit Judge.

E.8 Cases in Class 3 may be tried by a High Court Judge, or a Circuit Judge, a Deputy Circuit Judge, a Recorder or a qualifying judge advocate. A case in Class 3 shall not be listed for trial by a High Court Judge except with the consent of a Presiding Judge.

E.9 If a case has been allocated to a judge, Recorder or qualifying judge advocate, the preliminary hearing should be conducted by the allocated judge if practicable, and if not, if possible by a judge of at least equivalent standing. PCMHs should only be heard by Recorders or qualifying judge advocates with the approval of the Resident Judge.

E.10 For cases in Class 1A, 1B or 1C, or any case that has been referred to the Presiding Judge, the preliminary hearing and PCMH must be conducted by a High Court Judge; by a Circuit Judge; or by a judge authorised by the Presiding Judges to conduct such hearings. In the event of a guilty plea before such an authorised judge, the case will be adjourned for sentencing and will immediately be referred to the Presiding Judge who may retain the case for sentence by a High Court Judge, or release the case back to the Resident Judge, either for sentence by a named judge, or for sentence by an identified category of judges, to be allocated by the Resident Judge.

E.11 Appeals from decisions of magistrates' courts shall be heard by:
i. a Resident Judge, or
ii. a Circuit Judge, nominated by the Resident Judge, or
iii. a Recorder or qualifying judge advocate or a Deputy Circuit Judge listed by the Presiding Judge to hear such appeals; or, if there is no such list nominated by the Resident Judge to hear such appeals;
iv. and, no less than two and no more than four justices of the peace, none of whom took part in the decision under appeal;
v. where no Circuit Judge or Recorder or qualifying judge advocate satisfying the requirements above is available, by a Circuit Judge, Recorder, qualifying judge advocate or Deputy Circuit Judge selected by the Resident Judge to hear a specific case or cases listed on a specific day.

E.12 Appeals from the youth court in relation to sexual offences shall be heard by:

i. A Resident Judge or;
ii. a Circuit Judge nominated by the Resident Judge who is authorised under D.3 to hear sexual offences in Class 1C or Class 2B;
iii. and no less than two and no more than four justices of the peace, none of whom took part in the decision under appeal. The justices of the peace must have undertaken specific training to deal with youth matters.
iv. No appeal against conviction and/or sentence from a Youth Court involving a Class 1C or Class 2B offence shall be heard by a Recorder save with the express permission of the Presiding Judge of the Circuit.

E.13 Allocation or committal for sentence following breach (such as a matter in which a community order has been made, or a suspended sentence passed), should, where possible, be listed before the judge who originally dealt with the matter or, if not, before a judge of the same or higher level.

E.14 Applications for removal of a driving disqualification should be made to the location of the Crown Court where the order of disqualification was made. Where possible, the matter should be listed before the judge who originally dealt with the matter or, if not, before a judge of the same or higher level.

CPD XIII Listing F: Listing of trials, custody time limits and transfer of cases

Estimates of trial length

F.1 Under the regime set out in the Criminal Procedure Rules, the parties will be expected to provide an accurate estimate of the length of trial at the hearing where the case is to be managed based on a detailed estimate of the time to be taken with each witness to be called, and accurate information about the availability of witnesses. **B-969**

F.2 At the hearing the judge will ask the prosecution to clarify any custody time limit ('CTL') dates. The court clerk must ensure the CTL date is marked clearly on the court file or electronic file. When a case is subject to a CTL all efforts must be made at the first hearing to list the case within the CTL and the judge should seek to ensure this. Further guidance on listing CTL cases can be found below.

Cases that should usually have fixed trial dates

F.3 The cases where fixtures should be given will be set out in the listing practice applicable at the court, but should usually include the following: **B-970**

i. Cases in classes 1A, 1B, 1C, 2B and 2C;
ii. Cases involving vulnerable and intimidated witnesses (including domestic violence cases), whether or not special measures have been ordered by the court;
iii. Cases where the witnesses are under 18 or have to come from overseas;
iv. Cases estimated to last more than a certain time - the period chosen will depend on the size of the centre and the available judges;
v. Cases where a previous fixed hearing has not been effective;
vi. Re-trials; and,
vii. Cases involving expert witnesses.

Custody Time Limits

F.4 Every effort must be made to list cases for trial within the CTL limits set by Parliament. The guiding principles are: **B-971**

i. At the first hearing in the Crown Court, prosecution will inform the court when the CTL lapses.
ii. All efforts must be made to list the case within the CTL. The CTL may only be extended in accordance with s.22 Prosecution of Offences Act 1985 and the Prosecution of Offences (Custody Time Limits) Regulations 1987.
iii. If suitable, given priority and listed on a date not less than 2 weeks before the CTL expires, the case may be placed in a warned list.
iv. The CTL must be kept under continual review by the parties, HMCTS and the Resident Judge.
v. If the CTL is at risk of being exceeded, an additional hearing should take place and should be listed before the Resident Judge or trial judge or other judge nominated by the Resident Judge.
vi. An application to extend the CTL in any case listed outside the CTL must be considered by the court whether or not it was listed with the express consent of the defence.
vii. Any application to extend CTLs must be considered as a matter of urgency. The reasons for needing the extension must be ascertained and fully explained to the court.

viii. Where courtroom or judge availability is an issue, the court must itself list the case to consider the extension of any CTL. The Delivery Director of the circuit must provide a statement setting out in detail what has been done to try to accommodate the case within the CTL.

ix. Where courtroom or judge availability is not in issue, but all parties and the court agree that the case will not be ready for trial before the expiration of the CTL, a date may be fixed outside the CTL. This may be done without prejudice to any application to extend the CTLs or with the express consent of the defence; this must be noted on the papers.

F.5 As legal argument may delay the swearing in of a jury, it is desirable to extend the CTL to a date later than the first day of the trial.

Re-trials ordered by the Court of Appeal

B-972 **F.6** The Crown Court must comply with the directions of the Court of Appeal and cannot vary those directions without reference to the Court of Appeal.

F.7 In cases where a retrial is ordered by the Court of Appeal the CTL is 112 days starting from the date that the new indictment is preferred i.e. from the date that the indictment is delivered to the Crown Court. Court centres should check that CREST has calculated the dates correctly and that it has not used 182 days on cases that have previously been 'sent'.

Changes to the date of fixed cases

B-973 **F.8** Once a trial date or window is fixed, it should not be vacated or moved without good reason. Under the Criminal Procedure Rules, parties are expected to be ready by the trial date.

F.9 The listing officer may, in circumstances determined by the Resident Judge, agree to the movement of the trial to a date to which the defence and prosecution both consent, provided the timely hearing of the case is not delayed. The prosecution will be expected to have consulted the witnesses before agreeing to any change.

F.10 In all other circumstances, requests to adjourn or vacate fixtures or trial windows must be referred to the Resident Judge for his or her personal attention; the Resident Judge may delegate the decision to a named deputy.

Transferring cases to another court

B-974 **F.11** Transfer between courts on the same circuit must be agreed by the Resident Judges of each court, subject to guidance from the Presiding Judges of the circuit.

F.12 Transfer of trials between circuits must be agreed between the Presiding Judges and Delivery Directors of the respective circuits.

F.13 Transfers may be agreed either in specific cases or in accordance with general principles agreed between those cited above.

CPD XIII Listing G: Listing of hearings other than trials

B-975 **G.1** In addition to trials, the court's listing practice will have to provide court time for shorter matters, such as those listed below. These hearings are important, often either for setting the necessary case management framework for the proper and efficient preparation of cases for trial, or for determining matters that affect the rights of individuals. They must be afforded the appropriate level of resource that they require to be considered properly, and this may include judicial reading time as well as an appropriate length of hearing.

G.2 The applicant is responsible for notifying the court, and the other party if appropriate, and ensuring that the papers are served in good time, including a time estimate for judicial reading time and for the hearing. The applicant must endeavour to complete the application within the time estimate provided unless there are exceptional circumstances.

G.3 Hearings other than trials include the following:

i. Applications for search warrants and Production Orders, sufficient reading time must be provided, see G.8 below;

ii. Bail applications;

iii. Applications to vacate or adjourn hearings;

iv. Applications for dismissal of charges;

v. Preparation for trial hearings, plea and trial preparation hearings, and other pre-trial case management hearings

vi. Applications for disclosure of further unused material under section 8 of CPIA 1996;

vii. Case progression or case management hearings;

viii. Applications in respect of sentence indications not sought at the PTPH;

ix. Sentences;

x. Civil applications under the Anti-Social Behaviour, Crime and Policing Act 2014;

xi. Breach proceedings (and see paragraph G.12 beneath);
xii. Appeals from the magistrates' court: it is essential in all cases where witnesses are likely to be needed on the appeal to check availability before a date is fixed (and see paragraphs G.13 to G.15 beneath);
xiii. Appeals from the youth court: where the case involves a Class 2B offence then a directions hearing will be required before the re- hearing to consider special measures, ground rules and appropriate adjustments for the hearing of the trial.

G.4 Short hearings should not generally be listed before a judge such that they may delay the start or continuation of a trial at the Crown Court. It is envisaged that any such short hearing will be completed by 10.30am or start after 4.30pm.

G.5 Each Crown Court equipped with a video link with a prison must have in place arrangements for the conduct of PCMHs, other pre-trial hearings and sentencing hearings by video link.

Notifying sureties of hearing dates

G.6 Where a surety has entered into a recognizance in the magistrates' court in respect of a case allocated or sent to the Crown Court and where the bail order or recognizance refers to attendance at the first hearing in the Crown Court, the defendant should be reminded by the listing officer that the surety should attend the first hearing in the Crown Court in order to provide further recognizance. If attendance is not arranged, the defendant may be remanded in custody pending the recognisance being provided. **B-976**

G.7 The Court should also notify sureties of the dates of the hearing at the Crown Court at which the defendant is ordered to appear in as far in advance as possible: see the observations of Parker LJ in *Crown Court at Reading ex p. Bello* [1992] 3 All E.R. 353.

Applications for Production Orders and Search Warrants

G.8 The use of production orders and search warrants involve the use of intrusive state powers that affect the rights and liberties of individuals. It is the responsibility of the court to ensure that those powers are not abused. To do so, the court must be presented with a properly completed application, on the appropriate form, which includes a summary of the investigation to provide the context for the order, a clear explanation of how the statutory requirements are fulfilled, and full and frank disclosure of anything that might undermine the basis for the application. Further directions on the proper making and consideration of such applications will be provided by Practice Direction. However, the complexity of the application must be taken into account in listing it such that the judge is afforded appropriate reading time and the hearing is given sufficient time for the issues to be considered thoroughly, and a short judgment given. **B-977**

Confiscation and Related Hearings

G.9 Applications for restraint orders should be determined by the Resident Judge, or a judge nominated by the Resident Judge, at the Crown Court location at which they are lodged. **B-978**

G.10 In order to prevent possible dissipation of assets of significant value, applications under the Proceeds of Crime Act 2002 should be considered urgent when lists are being fixed. In order to prevent potential prejudice, applications for the variation and discharge of orders, for the appointment of receivers, and applications to punish alleged breaches of orders as a contempt of court should similarly be treated as urgent and listed expeditiously.

Confiscation Hearings

G.11 It is important that confiscation hearings take place in good time after the defendant is convicted or sentenced. **B-979**

Breach proceedings

G.12 As a general rule, proceedings to which CrimPR Part 32 applies (breach of community and other orders) should be brought in the court, and in case of the Crown Court at the Crown Court centre, at which the sentence was imposed, or in the magistrates' court at which the breach of a Crown Court order ordinarily would be dealt with. An exception to that general rule should be made, however, to reflect the application of CrimPR Part 1, the overriding objective, and the key listing principles at A above, where the defendant's home is significantly closer to another court with jurisdiction to determine the proceedings, in which case those proceedings should be brought in that court. If the court in which the breach proceedings are brought was not the sentencing court, or the magistrates' court for the Crown Court centre at which the sentence was passed, then the authority by which the proceedings are instituted must explain the reasons for choosing it. Any dispute over the proper venue for should be determined by the relevant Presiding Judges. **B-980**

Appeals from magistrates' courts

G.13 As a general rule, the hearing in the Crown Court of an appeal to which CrimPR Part 34 **B-981**

applies (appeal against conviction or sentence from a magistrates' court) should take place at the Crown Court centre to which that magistrates' court ordinarily sends cases for trial or commits for sentence. This general rule applies irrespective of the location of the magistrates' court at which the case first began, if that was not the court at which the defendant was convicted, or sentenced, or both, because the reasons that led to the case being dealt with at a different magistrates' court may apply equally to the hearing of the appeal.

G.14 There are two exceptions to that general rule, however, each of which reflects the application of CrimPR Part 1, the overriding objective, and the key listing principles at A above. First, if on an appeal against conviction witnesses are required to give evidence in person then the appeal should be heard at the Crown Court centre which is the most conveniently situated for the majority of those witnesses. This exception is likely to apply where the defendant's conviction and sentence have been imposed at a magistrates' court distant from the place at which the offence occurred, perhaps because the defendant had failed to attend a hearing at the court for that area and subsequently was arrested for breach of bail and convicted and sentenced at another court. The information required of the parties to the appeal by CrimPR 34.3 and by the associated appeal forms will be essential to determining the most appropriate venue for the appeal. Second, where the appeal is against sentence only, or if, exceptionally, on an appeal against conviction no witnesses are required to give evidence in person, then then the appeal should be heard at the Crown Court centre which is the closest to the defendant's home. This exception is likely to apply where the defendant has been convicted and sentenced at a magistrates' court for the area in which the offence occurred but at a distance from the defendant's usual or present residence. This exception must not, however, be allowed to operate to the disadvantage of any victim of the offence who is expected to attend the sentencing in the Crown Court.

G.15 Once an appeal is submitted to the Crown Court, arrangements for its hearing, at that or at another Crown Court centre if appropriate, must be made by Crown Court staff under the direction of the Resident judge or Resident judges concerned. Any dispute over the proper venue for the appeal should be determined by the relevant Presiding Judges.

CPD XIII Listing Annex 1: General principles for the deployment of the judiciary in the magistrates' court (as amended by Criminal Practice Directions 2015 (Amendment No. 6), unreported, 22 March 2018, Lord Burnett CJ)

B-982 This distils the full deployment guidance issued in November 2012. The relevant sections dealing specifically with the allocation of work within the magistrates' court have been incorporated into this practice direction. It does not seek to replace the guidance in its entirety.

Presumptions

B-983 **1** The presumptions which follow are intended to provide an acceptable and flexible framework establishing the deployment of the district judges (magistrates' courts) and magistrates. The system must be capable of adaptation to meet particular needs, whether of locality or caseload. In any event, the presumptions which follow are illustrative not exhaustive.

2 District judges (magistrates' courts) should generally (not invariably) be deployed in accordance with the following presumptions ("the presumptions"): (a) Cases involving complex points of law and evidence; (b) cases involving complex procedural issues; (c) long cases (included on grounds of practicality); (d) interlinked cases (given the need for consistency, together with their likely complexity and novelty); (e) cases for which armed police officers are required in court, such as high end firearms cases; (f) a share of the more routine business of the court, including case management and pre-trial reviews, (for a variety of reasons, including the need for district judges (magistrates' courts) to have competence in all areas of work and the desirability of an equitable division of work between magistrates and district judges (magistrates' courts), subject always to the interests of the administration of justice); (g) where appropriate, in supporting the training of magistrates; (h) occasionally, in mixed benches of district judges (magistrates' courts) and magistrates (with a particular view both to improving the case management skills of magistrates and to improving the culture of collegiality); (i) in the short-term tackling of particular local backlogs ("backlog busting"), sometimes in combination with magistrates from the local or (with the senior presiding judge's approval) adjoining benches.

3 In accordance with current arrangements certain classes of cases necessarily require district judges (magistrates' courts) and have therefore been excluded from the above presumptions; these are as follows: (a) extradition; (b) terrorism; (c) prison adjudications; (d) sex cases in the youth court as per Annex 2; (e) cases where the defendant is likely to be sentenced to a very large fine: see Annex 3; (f) the special jurisdiction of the Chief Magistrate.

4 In formulating the presumptions, the following considerations have been taken into account.

(a) The listing of cases is here, as elsewhere, a judicial function: see *CPD XIII Listing A*, para. 10. In the magistrates' courts the Judicial Business Group, subject to the supervision of the presiding judges of the circuit, is responsible for determining the day-to-day listing practice in that area. The day-to-day operation of that listing practice is the responsibility of the justices' clerk with the assistance of the listing officer.

(b) Equally, providing the training of magistrates is a responsibility of justices' clerks.

(c) It is best not to treat "high profile" cases as a separate category but to consider their listing in the light of the principles and presumptions. The circumstances surrounding high profile cases do not permit ready generalisation, save that they are likely to require especially sensitive handling. Listing decisions involving such cases will often benefit from good communication at a local level between the justices' clerk, the district judge (magistrates' courts) and the bench chairman.

(d) Account must be taken of the need to maintain the competences of all members of the judiciary sitting in the magistrates' court.

5 The Special Jurisdiction of the Senior District Judge (Chief Magistrate) concerns cases which fall into the following categories:

i. cases with a terrorism connection;
ii. cases involving war crimes and crimes against humanity;
iii. matters affecting state security;
iv. cases brought under the Official Secrets Act;
v. offences involving royalty or parliament;
vi. offences involving diplomats;
vii. corruption of public officials;
viii. police officers charged with serious offences;
ix. cases of unusual sensitivity.

6 Where cases fall within the category of the Special Jurisdiction they must be heard by:-

i. the Senior District Judge (or if not available);
ii. the Deputy Senior District Judge (or if not available);
iii. a District Judge approved by the Senior District Judge or his/her deputy for the particular case.

7 Where a doubt may exist as to whether or not a case falls within the Special Jurisdiction, reference should always be made to the Senior District Judge or to the Deputy Senior District Judge for clarification.

CPD XIII Listing Annex 2: Sexual offences in the Youth Court

Introduction

1 This annex sets out the procedure to be applied in the youth court in all cases involving allegations of sexual offences which are capable of being sent for trial at the Crown Court under the grave crime provisions. **B-984**

2 This applies to all cases involving such charges, irrespective of the gravity of the allegation, the age of the defendant and/or the antecedent history of the defendant. (So, for example, every allegation of sexual touching, under s.3 of the SOA 2003, is covered by this protocol.)

3 This does not alter the test (set out in the Sentencing Guidelines Council's definitive guideline, entitled "Overarching Principles–Sentencing Youths" [§§ S-15 et seq. in the Sentencing Guidelines Supplement.]) that the youth court must apply when determining whether a case is a "grave crime".

4 In the Crown Court, cases involving allegations of sexual offences frequently involve complex and sensitive issues and only those circuit judges and recorders who have been specifically authorised and who have attended the appropriate Judicial College course may try this type of work.

5 A number of district judges (magistrates' courts) have now undertaken training in dealing with these difficult cases and have been specifically authorised to hear cases involving serious sexual offences which fall short of requiring to be sent to the Crown Court ("an authorised district judge (magistrates' courts)"). As such, a procedure similar to that of the Crown Court will now apply to allegations of sexual offences in the youth court.

Procedure

6 The determination of venue in the youth court is governed by section 51 of the CDA 1998 [§ 1-24 in the main work], which provides that the youth must be tried summarily unless charged with such a grave crime that long-term detention is a realistic possibility (s.24(1) of the MCA 1980 [ibid., § 1-83]), or that one of the other exceptions to this presumption arises. **B-985**

7 Wherever possible such cases should be listed before an authorised district judge (magistrates' courts), to decide whether the case falls within the grave crime provisions and should therefore be sent for trial. If jurisdiction is retained and the allegation involves actual, or attempted, penetrative activity, the case must be tried by an authorised district judge (magistrates' courts). In all other cases, the authorised district judge (magistrates' courts) must consider whether the case is so serious and/or complex that it must be tried by an authorised district judge (magistrates' courts), or whether the case can be heard by any district judge (magistrates' courts) or any youth court bench.

8 If it is not practicable for an authorised district judge (magistrates' courts) to determine venue, any district judge (magistrates' courts) or any youth court bench may consider that issue. If jurisdiction is retained, appropriate directions may be given but the case papers, including a detailed case summary and a note of any representations made by the parties, must be sent to an authorized district judge (magistrates' courts) to consider. As soon as possible the authorised district judge (magistrates' courts) must decide whether the case must be tried by an authorised district judge (magistrates' courts) or whether the case is suitable to be heard by any district judge (magistrates' courts) or any youth court bench; however, if the case involves actual, or alleged, penetrative activity, the trial must be heard by an authorised district judge (magistrates' courts).

9 Once an authorised district judge (magistrates' courts) has decided that the case is one which must be tried by an authorised district judge (magistrates' courts), and in all cases involving actual or alleged penetrative activity, all further procedural hearings should, so far as practicable, be heard by an authorised district judge (magistrates' courts).

10 All cases which are remitted for sentence from the Crown Court to the youth court should be listed for sentence before an authorised district judge (magistrates' courts).

Arrangements for an authorised district judge (magistrates' courts) to be appointed

B-986 **11** Where a case is to be tried by an authorised district judge (magistrates' courts) but no such judge is available, the bench legal adviser should contact the Chief Magistrate's office for an authorised district judge (magistrates' courts) to be assigned.

CPD XIII Listing Annex 3: Cases involving very large fines in the magistrates' court (as amended by Criminal Practice Directions 2015 (Amendment No. 9) [2019] EWCA Crim 1603, Lord Burnett CJ)

B-987 **1** [*Applies following commencement of LASPOA 2012, s.85 (§ 1-120 in the main work).*]

2 An authorised district judge (magistrates' courts) must deal with any allocation decision, trial and sentencing hearing in the following types of cases which are triable either way: (a) cases involving death or significant, life changing injury or a high risk of death or significant, life-changing injury; (b) cases involving substantial environmental damage or polluting material of a dangerous nature; (c) cases where major adverse effect on human health or quality of life, animal health or flora has resulted; (d) cases where major costs through clean-up, site restoration or animal rehabilitation have been incurred; (e) cases where the defendant corporation has a turnover in excess of £10m but does not exceed £250m, and has acted in a deliberate, reckless or negligent manner; (f) cases where the defendant corporation has a turnover in excess of £250m; (g) cases where the court will be expected to analyse complex company accounts; (h) high profile cases or ones of an exceptionally sensitive nature.

3 The prosecution agency must notify the justices' clerk where practicable of any case of the type mentioned in paragraph 2 ..., no less than seven days before the first hearing to ensure that an authorised district judge (magistrates' courts) is available at the first hearing.

4 The justices' clerk shall contact the office of the Chief Magistrate to ensure that an authorised district judge (magistrates' courts) can be assigned to deal with such a case if there is not such a person available in the courthouse.

5 Where an authorised district judge (magistrates' courts) is not appointed at the first hearing the court shall adjourn the case. The court shall ask the accused for an indication of his plea, but shall not allocate the case nor, if the accused indicates a guilty plea, sentence him, commit him for sentence, ask for a pre-sentence report or give any indication as to likely sentence that will be imposed. The justices' clerk shall ensure an authorised district judge (magistrates' courts) is appointed for the following hearing.

6 When dealing with sentence, section 3 of the PCC(S)A 2000 [§ 5A-205 in the main work] can be invoked where, despite the magistrates' court having maximum fine powers available to it, the offence or combination of offences make it so serious that the Crown Court should deal with it as though the person had been convicted on indictment.

7 An authorised district judge (magistrates' courts) should consider allocating the case to the Crown Court or committing the accused for sentence.

CPD XIII Listing Annex 4: The management of terrorism cases

Application

B-988 **1** This annex applies to "terrorism cases". For the purposes of this annex a case is a "terrorism case" where:

(a) one of the offences charged against any of the defendants is indictable only and it is alleged by the prosecution that there is evidence that it took place during an act of terrorism or for the purposes of terrorism as defined in section 1 of the Terrorism Act 2000 [§ 25-13 in the main work]; this may include, but is not limited to:
  (i) murder;
  (ii) manslaughter;
  (iii) an offence under section 18 of the Offences against the Person Act 1861 (wounding with intent);
  (iv) an offence under section 23 or 24 of that Act (administering poison etc);
  (v) an offence under section 28 or 29 of that Act (explosives);
  (vi) an offence under section 2, 3 or 5 of the Explosive Substances Act 1883 (causing explosions);
  (vii) an offence under section 1 (2) of the Criminal Damage Act 1971 (endangering life by damaging property);
  (viii) an offence under section 1 of the Biological Weapons Act 1974 (biological weapons);
  (ix) an offence under section 2 of the Chemical Weapons Act 1996 (chemical weapons);
  (x) an offence under section 56 of the Terrorism Act 2000 (directing a terrorist organisation);
  (xi) an offence under section 59 of that Act (inciting terrorism overseas);
  (xii) offences under (v), (vii) and (viii) above given jurisdiction by virtue of section 62 of that Act (terrorist bombing overseas); and
  (xiii) an offence under section 5 of the Terrorism Act 2006 (preparation of terrorism acts);

(b) one of the offences charged is indictable only and includes an allegation by the prosecution of serious fraud that took place during an act of terrorism or for the purposes of terrorism as defined in section 1 of the Terrorism Act 2000 and the prosecutor gives a notice under section 51B of the CDA 1998 (notices in serious or complex fraud cases) [§ 1-26 in the main work]:

(c) one of the offences charged is indictable only, which includes an allegation that a defendant conspired, incited or attempted to commit an offence under sub-paragraphs (1)(a) or (b) above; or

(d) it is a case (which can be indictable only or triable either way) that a judge of the terrorism cases list (see paragraph 2(a) below) considers should be a terrorism case.

In deciding whether a case not covered by sub-paragraphs (1)(a), (b) or (c) above should be a terrorism case, the judge may hear representations from the CPS.

The terrorism cases list

2(a) All terrorism cases, wherever they originate in England and Wales, will be managed in a list known as the "terrorism cases list" by such judges of the High Court as are nominated by the President of the Queen's Bench Division. **B-989**

(b) Such cases will be tried, unless otherwise directed by the President of the Queen's Bench Division, by a judge of the High Court as nominated by the President of the Queen's Bench Division.

3 The judges managing the terrorism cases referred to in paragraph 2(a) will be supported by the London and South Eastern Regional Co-ordinator's Office (the "Regional Co-ordinator's Office"). An official of that office or an individual nominated by that office will act as the case progression officer for cases in that list for the purposes of rule 3.4 of the Criminal Procedure Rules.

Procedure after charge

4 Immediately after a person has been charged in a terrorism case, anywhere in England and Wales, a representative of the CPS will notify the person on the 24-hour rota for special jurisdiction matters at Westminster Magistrates' Court of the following information: **B-990**

(a) the full name of each defendant and the name of his solicitor of other legal representative, if known;

(b) the charges laid;

(c) the name and contact details of the crown prosecutor with responsibility for the case, if known; and

(d) confirmation that the case is a terrorism case.

5 The person on the 24-hour rota will then ensure that all terrorism cases wherever they are charged in England and Wales are listed before the Chief Magistrate or other District Judge designated under the Terrorism Act 2000. Unless the Chief Magistrate or other District Judge designated under the Terrorism Act 2000 directs otherwise, the first appearance of all defendants accused of terrorism offences will be listed at Westminster Magistrates' Court.

6 In order to comply with section 46 of the PACE Act 1984 [§ 3-164 in the main work], if a defendant in a terrorism case is charged at a police station within the local justice area in which Westminster Magistrates' Court is situated, the defendant must be brought before Westminster Magistrates' Court as soon as is practicable and in any event not later than the first sitting after he is charged with the offence. If a defendant in a terrorism case is charged in a police station outside the local justice area in which Westminster Magistrates' Court is situated, unless the Chief Magistrate or other designated judge directs otherwise, the defendant must be removed to that area as soon as is practicable. He must then be brought before [that court] as soon as is practicable after his arrival in the area and in any event not later than the first sitting of [that court] after his arrival in that area.

7 As soon as is practicable after charge a representative of the CPS will also provide the Regional Listing Co-ordinator's Office with the information listed in paragraph 4 above.

8 The Regional Co-ordinator's Office will then ensure that the Chief Magistrate and the Legal Aid Agency have the same information.

Cases to be sent to the Crown Court under section 51 of the Crime and Disorder Act 1998 [§ 1-24 in the main work]

B-991 **9** The court should ordinarily direct that the plea and trial preparation hearing should take place about 14 days after charge.

10 The sending magistrates' court should contact the Regional Listing Co-ordinator's Office who will be responsible for notifying the magistrates' court as to the relevant Crown Court to which to send the case.

11 In all terrorism cases, the magistrates' court case progression form for cases sent to the Crown Court under section 51 of the [1998 Act] should not be used. Instead of the automatic directions set out in that form, the magistrates' court shall make the following directions to facilitate the preliminary hearing at the Crown Court:

(a) three days prior to the preliminary hearing in the terrorism cases list, the prosecution must serve upon each defendant and the Regional Listing Co-ordinator:
- (i) a preliminary summary of the case;
- (ii) the names of those who are to represent the prosecution, if known;
- (iii) an estimate of the length of the trial;
- (iv) a suggested provisional timetable which should generally include:
  - the general nature of further enquiries being made by the prosecution,
  - the time needed for the completion of such enquiries,
  - the time required by the prosecution to review the case,
  - a timetable for the phased service of the evidence,
  - the time for the provision by the Attorney-General for his consent if necessary,
  - the time for service of the detailed defence case statement,
  - the date for the case management hearing, and
  - the estimated trial date;
- (v) a preliminary statement of the possible disclosure issues setting out the nature and scale of the problem, including the amount of unused material, the manner in which the prosecution seeks to deal with these matters and a suggested timetable for discharging their statutory duty; and
- (vi) any information relating to bail and custody time limits;

(b) one day prior to the preliminary hearing in the terrorist cases list, each defendant must serve in writing on the Regional Listing Co-ordinator and the prosecution:
- (i) the proposed representation;
- (ii) observations on the timetable; and
- (iii) an indication of plea and the general nature of the defence.

Cases to be sent to the Crown Court after the prosecutor gives notice under section 51D of the Crime and Disorder Act 1998 [§ 1-28 in the main work]

B-992 **12** If a terrorism case is to be sent to the Crown Court after the prosecutor gives a notice under section 51B of the CDA 1998 [§ 1-26 in the main work] the magistrates' court should proceed as in paragraphs 9–11 above.

13 When a terrorism case is so sent the case will go into the terrorism list and be managed by a judge as described in paragraph 2(a) above.

The preliminary hearing at the Crown Court

B-993 **14** At the plea and trial preparation hearing, the judge will determine whether the case is one to remain in the terrorism list and if so, give directions setting the provisional timetable.

15 The Legal Aid Agency must attend the hearing by an authorised officer to assist the court.

Use of video links

B-994 **16** Unless a judge otherwise directs, all Crown Court hearings prior to the trial will be conducted by video link for all defendants in custody.

Security

17 The police service and the prison service will provide the Regional Listing Co-ordinator's Office with an initial joint assessment of the security risks associated with any court appearance by the defendants within 14 days of charge. Any subsequent changes in circumstances or the assessment of risk which have the potential to impact upon the choice of trial venue will be notified to the Regional Listing Co-ordinator's Office immediately. **B-995**

CPD XIII Listing: Annex 5: Management of Cases from the Organised Crime Division of the Crown Prosecution Service

1 The Organised Crime Division (OCD) of the CPS is responsible for prosecution of cases from the National Crime Agency (NCA). Typically, these cases involve more than one defendant, are voluminous and raise complex and specialised issues of law. It is recognised that if not closely managed, such cases have the potential to cost vast amounts of public money and take longer than necessary. **B-996**

2 This annex applies to all cases handled by the OCD.

Designated court centres

3 Subject to the overriding discretion of the presiding judges of the circuit, OCD cases should normally be heard at Designated Court Centres (DCC). The process of designating court centres for this purpose has taken into account geographical factors and the size, security and facilities of those court centres. The designated court centres are: **B-997**

(a) Northern Circuit: Manchester, Liverpool and Preston;
(b) North Eastern Circuit: Leeds, Newcastle and Sheffield;
(c) Western Circuit: Bristol and Winchester;
(d) South Eastern Circuit (not including London): Reading, Luton, Chelmsford, Ipswich, Maidstone, Lewes and Hove;
(e) South Eastern Circuit (London only): Southwark, Blackfriars, Kingston, Woolwich, Croydon and the Central Criminal Court;
(f) Midland Circuit: Birmingham, Leicester and Nottingham;
(g) Wales Circuit: Cardiff, Swansea and Mold.

Selection of designated court centres

4 If arrests are made in different parts of the country and the OCD seeks to have all defendants tried by one Crown Court, the OCD will, at the earliest opportunity, write to the relevant court cluster manager with a recommendation as to the appropriate designated court centre, requesting that the decision be made by the relevant presiding judges. In the event that the designated court centre within one region is unable to accommodate a case, for example, as a result of a custody time limit expiry date, consideration may be given to transferring the case to a DCC in another region with the consent of the relevant presiding judges. **B-998**

5 There will be a single point of contact person at the OCD for each HMCTS region, to assist listing co-ordinators.

6 The single contact person for each HMCTS region will be the relevant cluster manager, with the exception of the South Eastern Circuit, where the appropriate person will be the Regional Listing Co-ordinator.

Designation of the trial judge

7 The trial judge will be assigned by the Presiding Judge at the earliest opportunity, and in accordance with *CPD XIII Listing E* [§ 2-22j in the main work]. Where the trial judge is unable to continue with the case, all further pre-trial hearings should be by a single judge until a replacement has been assigned. **B-999**

Procedure after charge

8 Within 24 hours of the laying of a charge, a representative of the OCD will notify the relevant cluster manager of the following information to enable an agreement to be reached between that cluster manager and the reviewing CPS lawyer before the first appearance as to the DCC to which the case should be sent: **B-1000**

(a) the full name of each defendant and the name of his legal representatives, if known;
(b) the charges laid; and
(c) the name and contact details of the crown prosecutor with responsibility for the case.

Exceptions

9 Where it is not possible to have a case dealt with at a DCC, the OCD should liaise closely with **B-1001**

the relevant cluster manager and the presiding judges to ensure that the cases are sent to the most appropriate court centre. This will, among other things, take into account the location of the likely source of the case, convenience of the witnesses, travelling distance for OCD staff and facilities at the court centres.

10 In the event that it is allocated to a non-designated court centre, the OCD should be permitted to make representations in writing to the presiding judges within 14 days as to why the venue is not suitable. The presiding judges will consider the reasons and, if necessary, hold a hearing. The CPS may renew their request at any stage where further reasons come to light that may affect the original decision on venue.

11 Nothing in this annex should be taken to remove the right of the defence to make representations as to the venue.

Criminal Costs Practice Direction (2015)

B-1002 For the *Criminal Costs Practice Direction (2015)*, see Appendix F.

APPENDIX C
The Duties of Advocates

I. CODE OF CONDUCT

Version 3.3 of the Bar Standards Board Handbook came into force on 24 May 2018. It contains (in Part 2) the Code of Conduct for the Bar of England and Wales. Part 1 of the handbook is an introduction. Parts 3 and 4 contain the scope of practice rules and the qualification rules. Part 5 comprises the enforcement regulations and Part 6 provides for the interpretation of terms used throughout the handbook. **C-1**

Within the code, there are "core duties", "outcomes", "rules" and "guidance". The significance of each is explained in the introductory section of the handbook. Thus the core duties (italicised words and expressions are defined in Part 6)–

> these underpin the entire regulatory framework and set the mandatory standards that all *BSB regulated persons* or *unregistered barristers* are required to meet. They also define the core elements of professional conduct. Disciplinary proceedings may be taken against a *BSB regulated person* or *unregistered barrister* if the *Bar Standards Board* believes there has been a breach by that person of the Core Duties set out in this *Handbook* and that such action would be in accordance with the *Enforcement Policy.*

The outcomes–

> these explain the reasons for the regulatory scheme and what it is designed to achieve. They are derived from the *regulatory objectives* as defined in the LSA and the risks which must be managed if those objectives are to be achieved. They are not themselves mandatory rules, but they are factors which *BSB regulated persons* or *unregistered barristers* should have in mind when considering how the Core Duties, Conduct Rules or Qualification Rules (as appropriate) should be applied in particular circumstances. The *Bar Standards Board* will take into account whether or not an Outcome has, or might have been, adversely affected when considering how to respond to alleged breaches of the Core Duties, Conduct Rules or Qualification Rules.

The conduct rules (i.e. those in the code of conduct)–

> "supplement the Core Duties and are mandatory. Disciplinary proceedings may be taken against a *BSB regulated person* or *unregistered barrister,* if the *Bar Standards Board* believes there has been a breach by that person of the Conduct Rules set out in Part 2 of this *Handbook* and that it would be in accordance with the *Enforcement policy* to take such action. However, the Conduct Rules are not intended to be exhaustive. In any situation where no specific Rule applies, reference should be made to the Core Duties. In situations where specific Rules do apply, it is still necessary to consider the Core Duties, since compliance with the Rules alone will not necessarily be sufficient to comply with the Core Duties."

The guidance is self-explanatory, its principal purpose being to assist in the interpretation of the core duties and rules.

The code of conduct itself is divided into four sections: A - Application, B - The Core Duties, C - The Conduct Rules, and D - Rules Applying to Particular Groups of Regulated Persons. The conduct rules are themselves divided into five sections, viz. C1 "You and the court", C2 "Behaving ethically", C3 "You and your client", C4 "You and your regulator" and C5 "You and your practice". So far as practice in court is concerned, the most important rules are contained in section C1. These, together with the core duties, are set in full, below. The handbook runs to a total of 274 pages and space precludes the inclusion of more detail. However it should be noted that C2 (behaving ethically) contains provisions relating to honesty, integrity and independence, referral fees, undertakings, discrimination and foreign work, and that C3 (you and your client) has rules relating to "best interests of each client, provision of a competent standard of work, and confidentiality", "not misleading clients and potential clients", "personal responsibility", "accepting instructions", "defining terms or basis on which instructions are accepted", "returning instructions", "requirement not to discriminate", "the 'cab-rank rule'" and the "quality assurance scheme for advocates rules". **C-2**

Core duties

C-3

CD1	You must observe your duty to the court in the administration of justice.
CD2	You must act in the best interests of each client.
CD3	You must act with honesty and integrity.
CD4	You must maintain your independence.
CD5	You must not behave in a way which is likely to diminish the trust and confidence which the public places in you or in the profession.
CD6	You must keep the affairs of each client confidential.
CD7	You must provide a competent standard of work and service to each client.
CD8	You must not discriminate unlawfully against any person.
CD9	You must be open and co-operative with your regulators.
CD10	You must take reasonable steps to manage your practice, or carry out your role within your practice, competently and in such a way as to achieve compliance with your legal and regulatory obligations.

Guidance to the core duties

C-4 gC1 The Core Duties are not presented in order of precedence, subject to the following:

.1 CD1 overrides any other core duty, if and to the extent the two are inconsistent. Rules C3.5 and C4 deal specifically with the relationship between CD1, CD2 and CD6 and you should refer to those rules and to the related Guidance;

.2 in certain other circumstances set out in this Code of Conduct one Core Duty overrides another. Specifically, Rule C16 provides that CD2 (as well as being subject to CD1) is subject to your obligations under CD3, CD4 and CD8.

gC2 Your obligation to take reasonable steps to manage your *practice*, or carry out your role within your *practice*, competently and in such a way as to achieve compliance with your legal and regulatory obligations (CD10) includes an obligation to take all reasonable steps to mitigate the effects of any breach of those legal and regulatory obligations once you become aware of the same.

The Conduct Rules

C.1 You and the court

Outcomes

C-5 oC1 The *court* is able to rely on information provided to it by those conducting litigation and by advocates who appear before it.

oC2 The proper administration of justice is served.

oC3 The interests of *clients* are protected to the extent compatible with outcomes oC1 and oC2 and the Core Duties.

oC4 Both those who appear before the *court* and *clients* understand clearly the extent of the duties owed to the *court* by advocates and those conducting litigation and the circumstances in which duties owed to *clients* will be overridden by the duty owed to the *court*.

oC5 *The public* has confidence in the administration of justice and in those who serve it.

Rules

C-6 rC3 You owe a duty to the *court* to act with independence in the interests of justice. This duty overrides any inconsistent obligations which you may have (other than obligations under the criminal law). It includes the following specific obligations which apply whether you are acting as an advocate or are otherwise involved in the conduct of litigation in whatever role (with the exception of Rule C3.1 below, which applies when acting as an advocate):

.1 you must not knowingly or recklessly mislead or attempt to mislead the *court*;

.2 you must not abuse your role as an advocate;

.3 you must take reasonable steps to avoid wasting the *court's* time;

.4 you must take reasonable steps to ensure that the *court* has before it all relevant decisions and legislative provisions;

.5 you must ensure that your ability to act independently is not compromised.

rC4 Your duty to act in the best interests of each *client* is subject to your duty to the *court*.

rC5 Your duty to the *court* does not require you to act in breach of your duty to keep the affairs of each *client* confidential.

Not misleading the court

rC6 Your duty not to mislead the *court* or to permit the *court* to be misled will include the following obligations: C-7

.1 you must not:

.a make submissions, representations or any other statement; or

.b ask questions which suggest facts to witnesses

which you know, or are instructed, are untrue or misleading.

.2 you must not call witnesses to give evidence or put affidavits or witness statements to the *court* which you know, or are *instructed,* are untrue or misleading, unless you make clear to the *court* the true position as known by or instructed to you.

Not abusing your role as an advocate

rC7 Where you are acting as an advocate, your duty not to abuse your role includes the following obligations: C-8

.1 you must not make statements or ask questions merely to insult, humiliate or annoy a witness or any other person;

.2 you must not make a serious allegation against a witness whom you have had an opportunity to cross-examine unless you have given that witness a chance to answer the allegation in cross-examination;

.3 you must not make a serious allegation against any person, or suggest that a person is guilty of a crime with which your *client* is charged unless:

.a you have reasonable grounds for the allegation; and

.b the allegation is relevant to your *client's* case or the credibility of a witness; and

.c where the allegation relates to a third party, you avoid naming them in open *court* unless this is reasonably necessary.

.4 you must not put forward to the *court* a personal opinion of the facts or the law unless you are invited or required to do so by the *court* or by law.

Guidance

Guidance on Rules rC3 - rC6 and relationship to CD1 and CD2

gC3 Rules rC3 – rC6 set out some specific aspects of your duty to the court (CD1). See CD1 and associated Guidance at gC1. C-9

gC4 As to your duty not to mislead the court:

.1 knowingly misleading the *court* includes being complicit in another person misleading the court;

.2 knowingly misleading the *court* also includes inadvertently misleading the court if you later realise that you have misled the *court,* and you fail to correct the position;

.3 recklessly means being indifferent to the truth, or not caring whether something is true or false; and

.4 the duty continues to apply for the duration of the case.

gC5 Your duty under Rule rC3.4 includes drawing to the attention of the court any decision or provision which may be adverse to the interests of your *client.* It is particularly important where you are appearing against a litigant who is not legally represented.

gC6 You are obliged by CD2 to promote and to protect your *client's* interests so far as that is consistent with the law and with your overriding duty to the *court* under CD1. Your duty to the *court* does not prevent you from putting forward your *client's* case simply because you do not believe that the facts are as your *client* states them to be (or as you, on your *client's* behalf, state them to be), as long as any positive case you put forward accords with your *instructions* and you do not mislead the *court.* Your role when acting as an advocate or conducting litigation is to present your *client's* case, and it is not for you to decide whether your *client's* case is to be believed.

gC7 For example, you are entitled and it may often be appropriate to draw to the witness's attention other evidence which appears to conflict with what the witness is saying and you are entitled to indicate that a *court* may find a particular piece of evidence difficult to accept. But if the witness maintains that the evidence is true, it should be recorded in the witness statement and you will not be misleading the *court* if you call the witness to confirm their witness statement. Equally, there may be circumstances where you call a hostile witness whose evidence you are instructed is untrue. You will not be in breach of Rule rC6 if you make the position clear to the court. See, further, the guidance at gC14.

gC8 As set out in Rule rC5, your duty to the *court* does not permit or require you to disclose confidential information which you have obtained in the course of your *instructions* and which your client has not authorised you to disclose to the *court.* However, Rule rC6 requires you not knowingly to mislead the *court.* There may be situations where you have obligations under both these rules.

gC9 Rule rC4 makes it clear that your duty to act in the best interests of your *client* is subject to your duty to the *court.* For example, if your *client* were to tell you that they have committed the crime with which they were charged, in order to be able to ensure compliance with Rule rC4 on the one hand and Rule rC3 and Rule rC6 on the other:

.1 you would not be entitled to disclose that information to the *court* without your *client's* consent; and

.2 you would not be misleading the *court* if, after your *client* had entered a plea of 'not guilty', you were to test in cross-examination the reliability of the evidence of the prosecution witnesses and then address the jury to the effect that the prosecution had not succeeded in making them sure of your *client's* guilt.

gC10 However, you would be misleading the *court* and would therefore be in breach of Rules rC5 and rC6 if you were to set up a positive case inconsistent with the confession, as for example by:

.1 suggesting to prosecution witnesses, calling your *client* or your witnesses to show; or submitting to the *jury*, that your *client did* not commit the crime; or

.2 suggesting that someone else had done so; or

.3 putting forward an alibi.

gC11 If there is a risk that the *court* will be misled unless you disclose confidential information which you have learned in the course of your *instructions*, you should ask the *client* for permission to disclose it to the *court.* If your *client* refuses to allow you to make the disclosure you must cease to act, and return your *instructions*: see Rules rC25 to rC27 below. In these circumstances you must not reveal the information to the *court.*

gC12 For example, if your *client* tells you that they have previous *convictions* of which the prosecution is not aware, you may not disclose this without their consent. However, in a case where mandatory sentences apply, the non-disclosure of the previous *convictions* will result in the *court* failing to pass the sentence that is required by law. In that situation, you must advise your *client* that if consent is refused to your revealing the information you will have to cease to act. In situations where mandatory sentences do not apply, and your *client* does not agree to disclose the previous *convictions*, you can continue to represent your *client* but in doing so must not say anything that misleads the *court.* This will constrain what you can say in mitigation. For example, you could not advance a positive case of previous good character knowing that there are undisclosed prior *convictions.* Moreover, if the *court* asks you a direct question you must not give an untruthful answer and therefore you would have to withdraw if, on your being asked such a question, your *client* still refuses to allow you to answer the question truthfully. You should explain this to your *client.*

gC13 Similarly, if you become aware that your *client* has a document which should be disclosed but has not been disclosed, you cannot continue to act unless your *client* agrees to the disclosure of the document. In these circumstances you must not reveal the existence or contents of the document to the *court.*

[The next paragraph is C-20.]

II. BAR COUNCIL GUIDANCE

Written standards of work

C-20 The Bar Council issued written standards for the conduct of professional work together with the eighth edition of the code of conduct. They did not form part of the code, but paragraph 701(d) obliged a barrister "to have regard to any relevant written standards." They can still be found on the website of the Bar Standards Board, but it does not appear that they are intended to have any continuing effect as there is a statement at the top of the page to the effect that, as from January 6, 2014, barristers should refer to the board's handbook (as to which, see above, C-1) for rules and guidance on their conduct as such.

[The next paragraph is C-46.]

Preparation of defence statements

C-46 As to guidance regarding the duties of counsel in relation to the preparation of defence statements, see § 12-122 in the main work.

III. MISCELLANEOUS AUTHORITIES ON DUTIES OF ADVOCATES

(1) Return of brief or instructions

Members of the criminal bar have a personal responsibility for compliance with provisions of the Code of Conduct relating to the return of instructions, of which their clerks should be aware. It is open to a court concerned with a problem caused by a late return of a brief to send a complaint to the Professional Conduct Committee of the Bar Council: *Sutton JJ., ex p. DPP*, 95 Cr. App. R. 180, DC, per Brooke J., at p. 186 (decided in relation to paragraphs 507 and 508 of the fifth edition of the Code of Conduct). **C-47**

The absence of what counsel would regard as sufficient time for preparation does not constitute an exception to the cab-rank rule requiring him to act for his client: see *Ulcay* (§ 4-67 in the main work).

(2) Duty not to accept certain instructions

Counsel should not appear for the prosecution in a case where the defendant is a person he has previously represented; para. 501(f) of the Code of Conduct for the Bar (6th ed.) referred to the risk that the barrister might have considential information or special knowledge disadvantageous to the defendant, his former client; it is contrary to the spirit of the code that a barrister should put himself in a position where such a risk might be perceived: *Dann* [1997] Crim. L.R. 46, CA. As to *Dann*, see further *Re T. and A. (Children) (Risk of Disclosure)* [2000] 1 F.L.R. 859, CA (Civ.Div.). **C-48**

(3) Duty in relation to the giving of advice and taking of instructions

Although not laid down in prescriptive form in the codes of conduct governing barristers and solicitors, solicitors and counsel should make a brief note of the advice given and the instructions received in conference on important issues as to the conduct of the defence (such as discussions relating to strategy, including as to whether the defendant should give evidence); such a note would be to the benefit of the client, in that it will serve to ensure that he has been given the appropriate advice; it would also serve to protect the advocate and his instructing solicitors from criticism based on assertions made after the event by a dissatisfied client: *Anderson, The Times*, 23 December 2010, CA. **C-48a**

(4) Duty of counsel to acquaint themselves with the terms of the indictment

See *Peckham*, 25 Cr. App. R. 125, CCA (prosecution), and *Olivo*, 28 Cr. App. R. 173, CCA (defence). **C-49**

(5) Duty concerning recent legislation

In *Isaacs, The Times*, 9 February 1990, the Court of Appeal said that when presenting cases at first instance or in appellate courts, counsel have a positive duty to inform the court of all relevant commencement dates of recent legislation. **C-50**

(6) Duty of counsel to inform themselves of the sentencing powers of the court

The Court of Appeal has repeatedly emphasised the duty of both counsel to inform themselves before the commencement of proceedings in the Crown Court of the sentencing powers of the court, including powers in relation to ancillary orders, such as costs, compensation, etc. The starting point is *Clarke (R.W.W.)*, 59 Cr. App. R. 298, CA. Lawton LJ concluded the judgment of the court with the following general observations and guidance. His Lordship's remarks are even more apposite today than when they were made: legislation in relation to sentence has become ever more complex. Sections 28 and 29 of the MCA 1952 were replaced by sections 37 and 38 respectively of the MCA 1980, which have themselves since been subject to extensive amendment. Section 37 was eventually repealed by the CDA 1998, and section 38 was repealed and replaced by section 3 of the PCC(S)A 2000. **C-51**

> "We adjudge that counsel as a matter of professional duty to the Court, and in the case of defending counsel to their client, should always before starting a criminal case satisfy themselves as to what the maximum sentence is. There can be no excuse for counsel not doing this and they should remember that the performance of this duty is particularly important in a case where a man has been committed to the Crown Court for sentencing pursuant to the provisions of sections 28 and 29 of the Magistrates' Courts Act 1952, and section 56 of the Criminal Justice Act 1967. Those statutory provisions are pregnant with dangers for court and for counsel and above all for accused persons...
>
> Secondly, those who administer the Crown Court should act as follows. Before the Crown Court came into existence..., it was the practice of many clerks of assize and many clerks of the peace to make a note on the documents put before the trial judge of the maximum sentence which could be passed and of the paragraphs in *Archbold's Criminal Pleading, Evidence and Practice* which dealt with the offence. In some Crown Courts this former practice has been followed. On the other hand it is clear from this case and from inquiries which we have made that it is not always followed. It should be; and it is particularly important that it should be when judges are asked to deal with cases committed for sentence under the statutory provisions to which I have already referred" (at pp. 301-302).

A reminder of the duty of counsel for both sides to ensure that sentences imposed, and orders made, are within the powers of the court, and to invite the court to vary a sentence if on subsequent consideration it appears to be unlawful, was given in *Komsta and Murphy*, 12 Cr. App. R.(S.) 63. Turner J. commented that it could not be too clearly understood that there was positive obligation on counsel, both for the prosecution and the defence, to ensure that no order was made that the court had no power to make. The PCC(S)A 2000, s. 155(1) (see § 5A-1229 in the main work) allowed the Crown Court to alter or vary any sentence or order, within the period of 28 [now 56] days of the making of the order. If it appeared to either counsel that the order was one which the court had no power to make, counsel should not hesitate to invite the court to exercise such powers.

See also *Richards, The Times,* 1 April 1993, CA, *Hartrey* [1993] Crim. L.R. 230, CA, *Johnstone (D.), The Times,* 18 June 1996, CA, *Bruley* [1996] Crim. L.R. 913, CA, *McDonnell* [1996] Crim. L.R. 914, CA, *Street,* 161 J.P. 28, CA, *Blight* [1999] Crim. L.R. 426, CA and, most recently, *Cain* [2006] EWCA Crim 3233; [2007] 2 Cr. App. R.(S.) 25. In *Blight,* it was said that counsel do not discharge their duty simply by having a copy of *Archbold* "to hand"; it is the duty of both counsel to be aware in advance of the powers of the court so that any error may be recited immediately; as to the defence counsel, it was said to be very difficult to see how mitigation can be done properly without having in the very front of the mind the powers within which the judge must exercise his duty. In *Cain,* it was said that defence advocates should ascertain and be prepared to assist the judge with any relevant legal restrictions on sentence, and the prosecution advocate should ensure that the sentencer does not, through inadvertence, impose an unlawful sentence; in particular, prosecution advocates should always be ready to assist the court by drawing attention to any statutory provisions that govern the court's sentencing powers and to any sentencing guidelines or guideline decisions of the Court of Appeal.

C-52 In *Reynolds* [2007] EWCA Crim 538; [2007] 2 Cr. App. R.(S.) 87, it was said that prosecuting and defence advocates must ensure that they are fully aware of the potential impact of the provisions of the dangerous offender provisions in Chapter 5 of Part 12 of the CJA 2003 (§§ 5A-572 et seq. in the main work), that they are able to assist the sentencer in that respect and are alert to any mistakes made in passing sentence so that any problem can be resolved before it is too late.

(7) Defendant absconding

C-53 See generally, §§ 3-222 et seq. in the main work, and *Shaw,* 70 Cr. App. R. 313, CA (§ 7-87 in the main work).

(8) Defendant not giving evidence

C-54 In *Bevan,* 98 Cr. App. R. 354, CA, it was held that where a defendant decides not to give evidence, it should be the invariable practice of counsel to record that decision and to cause the defendant to sign that record, indicating clearly first, that he has, of his own free will, decided not to give evidence and, secondly, that he has so decided bearing in mind the advice given to him by counsel. In the light of section 35 of the CJPOA 1994 (§ 4-377 in the main work), the advice of the Court of Appeal in *Bevan* is likely to become of greater importance than at the time of the decision. As to this, see also *Ebanks (Kurt) v The Queen* [2006] UKPC 16; [2006] 1 W.L.R. 1827 (§ 4-382 in the main work).

Bevan, above, was considered in *Good (Alfie)* [2016] EWCA Crim 1054. It was said that counsel's advice on the question whether to give evidence or not should include advice as to the likely direction to the jury on the issue and of the adverse inference that they might draw in light of that direction (pursuant to s.35 of the 1994 Act); and attention should also be drawn, where required, to the fact that, without evidence from the defendant, there will be no evidence to substantiate his case. Where a defendant decides not to give evidence, whether following advice or notwithstanding advice, the court said that it should be the invariable practice for counsel to make a record of the decision with a summary of the reasons; he should read this out to the defendant, who should then be asked to sign it; and that should be done before the time when the judge gives the warning about not giving evidence set out in section 35(2) of the 1994 Act; a photocopy of the endorsement should be made in chambers or in the office of an advocate as a record of the advice and the decision.

(9) Duties in relation to cross-examination

See §§ 8-216, 8-219 et seq. in the main work and, in relation to defence counsel's duty when cross-examining a co-defendant, see *Fenlon*, 71 Cr. App. R. 307, CA, and § 8-297 in the main work. **C-55**

(10) Duties in relation to the summing up

See §§ 4-433 et seq. in the main work. **C-56**

(11) Duties in relation to appeal

As to the duty to advise in relation to the possibility of an appeal against conviction or sentence, see §§ 7-165 et seq. in the main work. **C-57**

As to counsel's general duty in relation to the drafting of grounds of appeal, see § 7-168 in the main work. As to criticism of former counsel, see § 7-83 in the main work.

As to the duty of counsel for the prosecution, see § 7-201 in the main work.

The duty of a barrister to present his client's case before the Court of Appeal could not extend to advancing the client's assertion, unsubstantiated by any evidence, that the trial judge was corrupt or biased. A barrister's duty in such circumstances is either to decline to comply with the instructions or to withdraw from the case: *Thatcher v Douglas, The Times,* 8 January 1996, CA (Civ. Div.).

(12) Duties of prosecuting counsel

Apart from the matters mentioned above, see also (a) *The Role and Responsibilities of the Prosecution Advocate*, E-15 et seq.; (b) *Herbert*, 94 Cr. App. R. 230, CA (§ 4-173 in the main work) and *Richards and Stober*, 96 Cr. App. R. 258, CA (§ 19-103 in the main work), in relation to "plea-bargaining" and the acceptance of pleas, with particular reference to cases where there are two or more defendants; (c) §§ 4-342 et seq. in the main work, in relation to the opening of a case generally, and *Hobstaff*, 14 Cr. App. R.(S.) 605, CA, in relation to opening the facts on a plea of guilty; and (d) the Attorney-General's guidelines on the acceptance of pleas and the prosecutor's role in the sentencing exercise (Appendix A-276 et seq.). **C-58**

(13) Advocate as witness

In *Jacquith (or Jaquith) and Emode* [1989] Crim. L.R. 508 and 563, CA, junior counsel for one defendant has been called on his behalf to rebut a suggestion of recent invention made against him. The Court of Appeal said that the evidence on this point was admissible but it was very undesirable for counsel to give evidence on this point in court. In addition to the effect on the jury it caused embarrassment and difficulty to other members of the Bar who had to set about cross-examining a colleague. **C-59**

May L.J. said that the suggestion had been made that the court give some indication of its views concerning evidence given by counsel and also where a client alleged an attempt to pervert the court of justice by a co-defendant. their Lordships considered, however, that the right course would be to list points for consideration by the Bar Council and the Law Society. It was not sought to lay these maters down as ones of principle; their Lordships merely thought they deserved consideration.

1. No advocate should ever give evidence if that could possibly be avoided. 2. Where it was not possible for an advocate to avoid giving evidence, he should take no further part in the case. It necessarily followed that, if he was not being led, the trial must stop and a retrial be ordered. 3. There was a duty on counsel to anticipate circumstances in which he might be called upon to give evidence. Experienced counsel ought to be able to anticipate whether such a situation might arise. Where such a situation was anticipated, or envisaged even as a possibility, he should withdraw from the case. 4. Where it came to the notice of a legal adviser, through an accused person, that one of his co-defendants had attempted to pervert the court of justice, there was a duty on the legal adviser, usually the instructing solicitor, to take a detailed proof at once to provide a record and for further investigation. 5. Where the giving of evidence by an advocate caused real embarrassment or inhibition or difficulty regarding cross-examination by other advocates, the judge should exercise his discretion to discharge the jury and order a retrial.

(14) Co-habiting counsel

C-60 It is generally undesirable for husband and wife, or other partners living together, to appear as counsel on opposite sides in the same criminal matter since it might give rise to an apprehension that the proper conduct of the case had been in some way affected by that personal relationship: *Batt*, [1996] Crim. L.R. 910, CA. See also *Re L. (Minors) (Care Proceedings: Solicitors)* [2001] 1 W.L.R. 100, Fam D. (Wilson J).

APPENDIX E
Crown Prosecution Service

I. CODE FOR CROWN PROSECUTORS

A. INTRODUCTION

The Crown Prosecution Service is the principal public prosecuting authority for England and Wales and is headed by the Director of Public Prosecutions, who is to discharge his functions under the superintendence of the Attorney-General (Prosecution of Offences Act 1985, s.3(1)). The Attorney-General is accountable to Parliament for the Service. **E-1**

The Crown Prosecution Service is a national organisation consisting of 42 areas. Each area is headed by a Chief Crown Prosecutor and corresponds to a single police force area, with one for London. It was set up in 1986 to prosecute cases investigated by the police.

Although the Crown Prosecution Service works closely with the police, it is independent of them. The independence of crown prosecutors is of fundamental constitutional importance. Casework decisions taken with fairness, impartiality and integrity help deliver justice for victims, witnesses, defendants and the public.

The Crown Prosecution Service co-operates with the investigating and prosecuting agencies of other jurisdictions.

The Director of Public Prosecutions is responsible for issuing a Code for Crown Prosecutors under section 10 of the Prosecution of Offences Act 1985, giving guidance on the general principles to be applied when making decisions about prosecutions. This is the eighth edition of the code and replaces all earlier versions. It was issued on 26 October 2018.

B. THE CODE

Introduction

1.1. The Code for Crown Prosecutors (the Code) is issued by the Director of Public Prosecutions (DPP) under section 10 of the Prosecution of Offences Act 1985. This is the eighth edition of the Code and replaces all earlier versions. **E-2**

1.2. The DPP is the head of the Crown Prosecution Service (CPS), which is the principal public prosecution service for England and Wales. The DPP operates independently, under the superintendence of the Attorney General who is accountable to Parliament for the work of the CPS.

1.3. The Code gives guidance to prosecutors on the general principles to be applied when making decisions about prosecutions. The Code is issued primarily for prosecutors in the CPS but other prosecutors follow the Code, either through convention or because they are required to do so by law.

1.4. In this Code:

- "suspect" is used to describe a person who is under consideration as the subject of formal criminal proceedings;
- "defendant" is used to describe a person who has been charged or summonsed;
- "offender" is used to describe a person who has admitted guilt as to the commission of an offence, or who has been found guilty in a court of law.
- "victim" is used to describe a person against whom an offence has been committed, or the complainant in a case being considered or prosecuted by the CPS.

General Principles

2.1. The independence of the prosecutor is central to the criminal justice system of a democratic society. Prosecutors are independent from persons or agencies that are not part of the prosecution decision-making process. CPS prosecutors are also independent from the police and other investigators. Prosecutors must be free to carry out their professional duties without political interference and must not be affected by improper or undue pressure or influence from any source. **E-3**

2.2. It is not the function of the CPS to decide whether a person is guilty of a criminal offence, but to make assessments about whether it is appropriate to present charges for the criminal court to consider. The CPS assessment of any case is not in any sense a finding of, or implication of, any guilt or criminal conduct. A finding of guilt can only be made by a court.

2.3. Similarly, a decision not to bring criminal charges does not necessarily mean that an individual has not been a victim of crime. It is not the role of the CPS to make such determinations.

2.4. The decision to prosecute or to recommend an out-of-court disposal is a serious step that affects suspects, victims, witnesses and the public at large and must be undertaken with the utmost care.

2.5. It is the duty of prosecutors to make sure that the right person is prosecuted for the right offence and to bring offenders to justice wherever possible. Casework decisions taken fairly, impartially and with integrity help to secure justice for victims, witnesses, suspects, defendants and the public. Prosecutors must ensure that the law is properly applied, that relevant evidence is put before the court and that obligations of disclosure are complied with.

2.6. Although each case must be considered on its own facts and on its own merits, there are general principles that apply in every case.

2.7. When making decisions, prosecutors must be fair and objective. They must not let any personal views about the ethnic or national origin, gender, disability, age, religion or belief, sexual orientation or gender identity of the suspect, defendant, victim or any witness influence their decisions. Neither must they be motivated by political considerations. Prosecutors must always act in the interests of justice and not solely for the purpose of obtaining a conviction.

2.8. Prosecutors must be even-handed in their approach to every case, and have a duty to protect the rights of suspects and defendants, while providing the best possible service to victims.

2.9. The CPS is a public authority for the purposes of current, relevant equality legislation. Prosecutors are bound by the duties set out in this legislation.

2.10. Prosecutors must apply the principles of the European Convention on Human Rights, in accordance with the Human Rights Act 1998, at each stage of a case. They must comply with any guidelines issued by the Attorney General and with the policies and guidance of the CPS issued on behalf of the DPP, unless it is determined that there are exceptional circumstances. CPS guidance contains further evidential and public interest factors for specific offences and offenders and is available for the public to view on the CPS website. Prosecutors must also comply with the Criminal Procedure Rules and Criminal Practice Directions, and have regard to the Sentencing Council Guidelines and the obligations arising from international conventions.

2.11. The CPS prosecutes on behalf of some other Government departments. In such cases, prosecutors should have regard to any relevant enforcement policies of those departments.

2.12. Some offences may be prosecuted by either the CPS or by other prosecutors in England and Wales. When making decisions in these cases, CPS prosecutors may, where they think it appropriate, have regard to any relevant enforcement or prosecution policy or code of the other prosecutor.

2.13. Where the law differs in England and Wales prosecutors must apply the Code and have regard to any relevant policy, guidance or charging standard.

The Decision Whether to Prosecute

E-4 3.1. In more serious or complex cases, prosecutors decide whether a person should be charged with a criminal offence and, if so, what that offence should be. Prosecutors may also advise on or authorise out-of-court disposals as an alternative to prosecution. They make their decisions in accordance with this Code, the DPP's Guidance on Charging and any relevant legal guidance or policy. The police apply the same principles in deciding whether to start criminal proceedings against a person in those cases for which they are responsible.

3.2. The police and other investigators are responsible for conducting inquiries into any alleged crime and for deciding how to deploy their resources. This includes decisions to start or continue an investigation and on the scope of the investigation. Prosecutors should advise the police and other investigators about possible reasonable lines of inquiry, evidential requirements, pre-charge procedures, disclosure management and the overall investigation strategy. This can include decisions to refine or narrow the scope of the criminal conduct and the number of suspects under investigation. Such advice assists the police and other investigators to complete the investigation within a reasonable period of time and to build the most effective prosecution case.

3.3. Prosecutors cannot direct the police or other investigators. However, prosecutors must have regard to the impact of any failure to pursue an advised reasonable line of inquiry or to comply with a request for information, when deciding whether the application of the Full Code Test should be deferred or whether the test can be met at all.

3.4. Prosecutors should identify and, where possible, seek to rectify evidential weaknesses but, subject to the Threshold Test (see section 5), they should quickly stop cases which do not meet the evidential stage of the Full Code Test (see section 4) and which cannot be strengthened by further investigation, or where the public interest clearly does not require a prosecution (see section 4).

Although prosecutors primarily consider the evidence and information supplied by the police and other investigators, the suspect or those acting on their behalf may also submit evidence or information to the prosecutor, before or after charge, to help inform the prosecutor's decision. In appropriate cases, the prosecutor may invite the suspect or their representative to do so.

3.5. Prosecutors should not start or continue a prosecution where their view is that it is highly likely that a court will rule that a prosecution is an abuse of its process, and stay the proceedings.

3.6. Prosecutors review every case they receive from the police or other investigators. Review is a continuing process and prosecutors must take account of any change in circumstances that occurs as the case develops. This includes what becomes known of the defence case, any further reasonable lines of inquiry that should be pursued, and receipt of any unused material that may undermine the prosecution case or assist the defence case, to the extent that charges should be altered or discontinued or the prosecution should not proceed. If a case is to be stopped, care should be taken when choosing the method of termination, as this can affect the victim's position under the Victims' Right to Review scheme. Wherever possible, prosecutors should consult the investigator when considering changing the charges or stopping the case. Prosecutors and investigators work closely together, but the final responsibility for the decision whether or not a case should go ahead rests with the CPS.

3.7. Parliament has decided that a limited number of offences should only be taken to court with the agreement of the DPP. These are called consent cases. In such cases the DPP, or a prosecutor acting on their behalf, applies the Code in deciding whether to give consent to a prosecution.

3.8. There are also certain offences that can only be taken to court with the consent of the Attorney General. Prosecutors must follow current guidance when referring any such cases to the Attorney General. Some offences require the consent of a Secretary of State before a prosecution is started. Prosecutors must obtain such consent prior to charge and apply any relevant guidance in these cases. Additionally, the Attorney General will be kept informed of certain cases as part of their superintendence of the CPS and accountability to Parliament for its actions.

The Full Code Test

4.1. Prosecutors must only start or continue a prosecution when the case has passed both stages of the Full Code Test. The exception is when the Threshold Test may be applied (see section 5). **E-5**

4.2. The Full Code Test has two stages: (i) the evidential stage; followed by (ii) the public interest stage.

4.3. The Full Code Test should be applied:

a) when all outstanding reasonable lines of inquiry have been pursued; or
b) prior to the investigation being completed, if the prosecutor is satisfied that any further evidence or material is unlikely to affect the application of the Full Code Test, whether in favour of or against a prosecution.

4.4. In most cases prosecutors should only consider whether a prosecution is in the public interest after considering whether there is sufficient evidence to prosecute. However, there will be cases where it is clear, prior to reviewing all the evidence, that the public interest does not require a prosecution. In these instances, prosecutors may decide that the case should not proceed further.

4.5. Prosecutors should only take such a decision when they are satisfied that the broad extent of the criminality has been determined and that they are able to make a fully informed assessment of the public interest. If prosecutors do not have sufficient information to take such a decision, the investigation should continue and a decision taken later in accordance with the Full Code Test set out in this section.

The Evidential Stage

4.6. Prosecutors must be satisfied that there is sufficient evidence to provide a realistic prospect of conviction against each suspect on each charge.[1] They must consider what the defence case may be, and how it is likely to affect the prospects of conviction. A case which does not pass the evidential stage must not proceed, no matter how serious or sensitive it may be. **E-6**

4.7. The finding that there is a realistic prospect of conviction is based on the prosecutor's objective assessment of the evidence, including the impact of any defence and any other information that the suspect has put forward or on which they might rely. It means that an objective, impartial and reasonable jury or bench of magistrates or judge hearing a case alone, properly directed and acting in accordance with the law, is more likely than not to convict the defendant of the charge alleged. This is a different test from the one that the criminal courts themselves must apply. A court may only convict if it is sure that the defendant is guilty.

---

[1] For the purposes of the Code for Crown Prosecutors, "conviction" includes a finding that "the person did the act or made the omission" in circumstances where the person is likely to be found not guilty on the grounds of insanity.

4.8. When deciding whether there is sufficient evidence to prosecute, prosecutors should ask themselves the following:

Can the evidence be used in court? Prosecutors should consider whether there is any question over the admissibility of certain evidence. In doing so, prosecutors should assess:

- the likelihood of that evidence being held as inadmissible by the court; and
- the importance of that evidence in relation to the evidence as a whole.

Is the evidence reliable? Prosecutors should consider whether there are any reasons to question the reliability of the evidence, including its accuracy or integrity.

Is the evidence credible? Prosecutors should consider whether there are any reasons to doubt the credibility of the evidence.

Is there any other material that might affect the sufficiency of evidence? Prosecutors must consider at this stage and throughout the case whether there is any material that may affect the assessment of the sufficiency of evidence, including examined and unexamined material in the possession of the police, and material that may be obtained through further reasonable lines of inquiry.

The Public Interest Stage

E-7 4.9. In every case where there is sufficient evidence to justify a prosecution or to offer an out-of-court disposal, prosecutors must go on to consider whether a prosecution is required in the public interest.

4.10. It has never been the rule that a prosecution will automatically take place once the evidential stage is met. A prosecution will usually take place unless the prosecutor is satisfied that there are public interest factors tending against prosecution which outweigh those tending in favour. In some cases the prosecutor may be satisfied that the public interest can be properly served by offering the offender the opportunity to have the matter dealt with by an out-of-court disposal rather than bringing a prosecution.

4.11. When deciding the public interest, prosecutors should consider each of the questions set out below in paragraphs 4.14 a) to g) so as to identify and determine the relevant public interest factors tending for and against prosecution. These factors, together with any public interest factors set out in relevant guidance or policy issued by the DPP, should enable prosecutors to form an overall assessment of the public interest.

4.12. The explanatory text below each question in paragraphs 4.14 a) to g) provides guidance to prosecutors when addressing each particular question and determining whether it identifies public interest factors for or against prosecution. The questions identified are not exhaustive, and not all the questions may be relevant in every case. The weight to be attached to each of the questions, and the factors identified, will also vary according to the facts and merits of each case.

4.13. It is quite possible that one public interest factor alone may outweigh a number of other factors which tend in the opposite direction. Although there may be public interest factors tending against prosecution in a particular case, prosecutors should consider whether nonetheless a prosecution should go ahead and those factors put to the court for consideration when sentence is passed.

4.14. Prosecutors should consider each of the following questions:

a) **How serious is the offence committed?**
- The more serious the offence, the more likely it is that a prosecution is required.
- When assessing the seriousness of an offence, prosecutors should include in their consideration the suspect's culpability and the harm caused, by asking themselves the questions at b) and c).

b) **What is the level of culpability of the suspect?**
- The greater the suspect's level of culpability, the more likely it is that a prosecution is required.
- Culpability is likely to be determined by:
  i. the suspect's level of involvement;
  ii. the extent to which the offending was premeditated and/or planned;
  iii. the extent to which the suspect has benefitted from criminal conduct;
  iv. whether the suspect has previous criminal convictions and/or out-of-court disposals and any offending whilst on bail or whilst subject to a court order;
  v. whether the offending was or is likely to be continued, repeated or escalated;
  vi. the suspect's age and maturity (see paragraph d below).
- A suspect is likely to have a much lower level of culpability if the suspect has been compelled, coerced or exploited, particularly if they are the victim of a crime that is linked to their offending.
- Prosecutors should also have regard to whether the suspect is, or was at the time of the

offence, affected by any significant mental or physical ill health or disability, as in some circumstances this may mean that it is less likely that a prosecution is required. However, prosecutors will also need to consider how serious the offence was, whether the suspect is likely to re-offend and the need to safeguard the public or those providing care to such persons.

c) **What are the circumstances of and the harm caused to the victim?**
- The circumstances of the victim are highly relevant. The more vulnerable the victim's situation, or the greater the perceived vulnerability of the victim, the more likely it is that a prosecution is required.
- This includes where a position of trust or authority exists between the suspect and victim.
- A prosecution is also more likely if the offence has been committed against a victim who was at the time a person serving the public.
- It is more likely that prosecution is required if the offence was motivated by any form of prejudice against the victim's actual or presumed ethnic or national origin, gender, disability, age, religion or belief, sexual orientation or gender identity; or if the suspect targeted or exploited the victim, or demonstrated hostility towards the victim, based on any of those characteristics.
- Prosecutors also need to consider if a prosecution is likely to have an adverse effect on the victim's physical or mental health, always bearing in mind the seriousness of the offence, the availability of special measures and the possibility of a prosecution without the participation of the victim.
- Prosecutors should take into account the views expressed by the victim about the impact that the offence has had. In appropriate cases, this may also include the views of the victim's family.
- However, the CPS does not act for victims or their families in the same way as solicitors act for their clients, and prosecutors must form an overall view of the public interest.

d) **What was the suspect's age and maturity at the time of the offence?**
- The criminal justice system treats children and young people differently from adults and significant weight must be attached to the age of the suspect if they are a child or young person under 18.
- The best interests and welfare of the child or young person must be considered, including whether a prosecution is likely to have an adverse impact on their future prospects that is disproportionate to the seriousness of the offending.
- Prosecutors must have regard to the principal aim of the youth justice system, which is to prevent offending by children and young people. Prosecutors must also have regard to the obligations arising under the United Nations 1989 Convention on the Rights of the Child.
- Prosecutors should consider the suspect's maturity, as well as their chronological age, as young adults will continue to mature into their mid-twenties.
- As a starting point, the younger the suspect, the less likely it is that a prosecution is required.
- However, there may be circumstances which mean that, notwithstanding the fact that the suspect is under 18 or lacks maturity, a prosecution is in the public interest. These include where:
  - i. the offence committed is serious;
  - ii. the suspect's past record suggests that there are no suitable alternatives to prosecution; and
  - iii. the absence of an admission means that out-of-court disposals that might have addressed the offending behaviour are not available.

e) **What is the impact on the community?**
- The greater the impact of the offending on the community, the more likely it is that a prosecution is required.
- The prevalence of an offence in a community may cause particular harm to that community, increasing the seriousness of the offending.
- Community is not restricted to communities defined by location and may relate to a group of people who share certain characteristics, experiences or backgrounds, including an occupational group.
- Evidence of impact on a community may be obtained by way of a Community Impact Statement.

f) **Is prosecution a proportionate response?**
- In considering whether prosecution is proportionate to the likely outcome, the following may be relevant:

i. The cost to the CPS and the wider criminal justice system, especially where it could be regarded as excessive when weighed against any likely penalty. Prosecutors should not decide the public interest on the basis of this factor alone. It is essential that regard is also given to the public interest factors identified when considering the other questions in paragraphs 4.14 a) to g), but cost can be a relevant factor when making an overall assessment of the public interest.
ii. Cases should be prosecuted in accordance with principles of effective case management. For example, in a case involving multiple suspects, prosecution might be reserved for the main participants in order to avoid excessively long and complex proceedings.

g) **Do sources of information require protecting?**
- In cases where public interest immunity does not apply, special care should be taken when proceeding with a prosecution where details may need to be made public that could harm sources of information, ongoing investigations, international relations or national security. It is essential that such cases are kept under continuing review.

The Threshold Test

E-8 5.1. In limited circumstances, where the Full Code Test is not met, the Threshold Test may be applied to charge a suspect. The seriousness or circumstances of the case must justify the making of an immediate charging decision, and there must be substantial grounds to object to bail.

5.2. There must be a rigorous examination of the five conditions of the Threshold Test, to ensure that it is only applied when necessary and that cases are not charged prematurely. All five conditions must be met before the Threshold Test can be applied. Where any of the conditions are not met, there is no need to consider any of the other conditions, as the Threshold Test cannot be applied and the suspect cannot be charged.

First condition—There are reasonable grounds to suspect that the person to be charged has committed the offence

E-8a 5.3. Prosecutors must be satisfied, on an objective assessment of the evidence, that there are reasonable grounds to suspect that the person to be charged has committed the offence. The assessment must consider the impact of any defence or information that the suspect has put forward or on which they might rely.

5.4. In determining whether there are reasonable grounds to suspect, prosecutors must consider all of the material or information available, whether in evidential format or otherwise. Prosecutors must be satisfied that the material to be relied on at this stage is capable of being:
- put into an admissible format for presentation in court;
- reliable; and
- credible.

Second condition—Further evidence can be obtained to provide a realistic prospect of conviction

E-8b 5.5. Prosecutors must be satisfied that there are reasonable grounds to believe that the continuing investigation will provide further evidence, within a reasonable period of time, so that when all the evidence is considered together, including material which may point away from as well as towards a particular suspect, it is capable of establishing a realistic prospect of conviction in accordance with the Full Code Test.

5.6. The likely further evidence must be identifiable and not merely speculative.

5.7. In reaching this decision prosecutors must consider:
- the nature, extent and admissibility of any likely further evidence and the impact it will have on the case;
- the charges that all the evidence will support;
- the reasons why the evidence is not already available;
- the time required to obtain the further evidence, including whether it could be obtained within any available detention period; and
- whether the delay in applying the Full Code Test is reasonable in all the circumstances.

Third condition—The seriousness or the circumstances of the case justifies the making of an immediate charging decision

E-8c 5.8. The seriousness and the circumstances of the case should be assessed in relation to the alleged offending and should be linked to the level of risk created by granting bail.

Fourth condition—There are continuing substantial grounds to object to bail in accordance with the Bail Act 1976 and in all the circumstances of the case it is proper to do so

E-8d 5.9. This determination must be based on a proper risk assessment, which reveals that the suspect is not suitable to be bailed, even with substantial conditions. For example, a dangerous suspect who poses a serious risk of harm to a particular person or the public, or a suspect who poses a serious risk of absconding or interfering with witnesses. Prosecutors should not accept, without careful enquiry, any unjustified or unsupported assertions about risk if release on bail were to take place.

Fifth condition–It is in the public interest to charge the suspect

5.10. Prosecutors must apply the public interest stage of the Full Code Test based on the information available at that time. **E-8e**

Reviewing the Threshold Test

5.11. A decision to charge under the Threshold Test must be kept under review. The prosecutor should be proactive to secure from the police the identified outstanding evidence or other material in accordance with an agreed timetable. The evidence must be regularly assessed to ensure that the charge is still appropriate and that continued objection to bail is justified. The Full Code Test must be applied as soon as the anticipated further evidence or material is received and, in any event, in Crown Court cases, usually before the formal service of the prosecution case. **E-9**

Selection of Charges

6.1. Prosecutors should select charges which: **E-10**

- reflect the seriousness and extent of the offending;
- give the court adequate powers to sentence and impose appropriate post-conviction orders;
- allow a confiscation order to be made in appropriate cases, where a defendant has benefitted from criminal conduct; and
- enable the case to be presented in a clear and simple way.

6.2. This means that prosecutors may not always choose or continue with the most serious charge where there is a choice and the interests of justice are met by selecting the lesser charge.

6.3. Prosecutors should never proceed with more charges than are necessary just to encourage a defendant to plead guilty to a few. In the same way, they should never proceed with a more serious charge just to encourage a defendant to plead guilty to a less serious one.

6.4. Prosecutors should not change the charge simply because of the decision made by the court or the defendant about where the case will be heard.

6.5. Prosecutors must take account of any relevant change in circumstances as the case progresses after charge.

Out-of-Court Disposals

7.1. An out-of-court disposal may take the place of a prosecution if it is an appropriate response to the offender and/or the seriousness and consequences of the offending. **E-11**

7.2. Prosecutors must follow any relevant guidance when asked to advise on or authorise an out-of-court disposal, including any appropriate regulatory proceedings, a punitive or civil penalty, or other disposal. They should ensure that the appropriate evidential standard for the specific out-of-court disposal is met including, where required, a clear admission of guilt, and that the public interest would be properly served by such a disposal.

Court Venue

8.1. Prosecutors must have regard to the guidelines on sentencing and allocation when making submissions to the magistrates' court about where the defendant should be tried. **E-11a**

8.2. Speed must never be the only reason for asking for a case to stay in the magistrates' court. But prosecutors should consider the effect of any likely delay if a case is sent to the Crown Court, including the possible effect on any victim or witness.

8.3. Prosecutors should bear in mind that if confiscation proceedings are required, these may only take place in the Crown Court. Summary proceedings may be committed for that purpose, where appropriate.

Venue for Trial in Cases Involving Children and Young People

8.4. Prosecutors must bear in mind that children and young people (under 18s) should be tried in the youth court wherever possible. It is the court which is best designed to meet their specific needs. A trial of a child or young person in the Crown Court should be reserved for the most serious cases or where the interests of justice require a child or young person to be jointly tried with an adult. **E-12**

Accepting Guilty Pleas

E-12a 9.1. Defendants may want to plead guilty to some, but not all, of the charges. Alternatively, they may want to plead guilty to a different, possibly less serious, charge because they are admitting only part of the crime.

9.2. Prosecutors should only accept the defendant's plea if:

- the court is able to pass a sentence that matches the seriousness of the offending, particularly where there are aggravating features;
- it enables the court to make a confiscation order in appropriate cases, where a defendant has benefitted from criminal conduct; and
- it provides the court with adequate powers to impose other ancillary orders, bearing in mind that these can be made with some offences but not with others.

9.3. Particular care must be taken when considering pleas which would enable the defendant to avoid the imposition of a mandatory minimum sentence.

9.4. Prosecutors must never accept a guilty plea just because it is convenient.

9.5. In considering whether the pleas offered are acceptable, prosecutors should ensure that the interests and, where possible, the views of the victim, or in appropriate cases the views of the victim's family, are taken into account when deciding whether it is in the public interest to accept the plea. However, the decision rests with the prosecutor.

9.6. It must be made clear to the court on what basis any plea is advanced and accepted. In cases where a defendant pleads guilty to the charges but on the basis of facts that are different from the prosecution case, and where this may significantly affect sentence, the court should be invited to hear evidence to determine what happened, and then sentence on that basis.

9.7. Where a defendant has previously indicated that they will ask the court to take an offence into consideration when sentencing, but then declines to admit that offence at court, prosecutors will consider whether a prosecution is required for that offence. Prosecutors should explain to the defence advocate and the court that the prosecution of that offence may be subject to further review, in consultation with the police or other investigators wherever possible.

Reconsidering a Prosecution Decision

E-12b 10.1. People should be able to rely on decisions taken by the CPS. Normally, if the CPS tells a suspect or defendant that there will not be a prosecution, or that the prosecution has been stopped, the case will not start again. But occasionally there are cases where the CPS will overturn a decision not to prosecute or to deal with the case by way of an out-of-court disposal or when it will restart the prosecution, particularly if the case is serious.

10.2. These cases include:

- cases where a further review of the original decision shows that it was wrong and, in order to maintain confidence in the criminal justice system, a prosecution should be brought despite the earlier decision;
- cases which are stopped so that further anticipated evidence, which is likely to become available in the fairly near future, can be collected and prepared. In these cases, the prosecutor will tell the defendant that the prosecution may well start again;
- cases which are not prosecuted or are stopped because of a lack of evidence but where more significant evidence is discovered later; and
- cases involving a death in which a review following the findings of an inquest concludes that a prosecution should be brought, notwithstanding any earlier decision not to prosecute.

10.3. Victims may seek a review of certain CPS decisions not to start a prosecution or to stop a prosecution, under the Victims' Right to Review Scheme.

2018

C. AUTHORITIES

Charging of youths

E-12c Whereas the code for crown prosecutors requires consideration to be given to the interests of a child or young person when deciding whether it is in the public interest to prosecute (see now para. 4.12(d), E-7), there is no requirement that a crown prosecutor should obtain a risk assessment from the youth offending services or that he should contact the potential defendant's school: *R. (A.) v South Yorkshire Police and CPS*, 171 J.P. 465, DC.

In *D. and B. v Commr of Police for the Metropolis, CPS, Croydon JJ.* [2008] EWHC 442 (Admin); [2008] A.C.D. 47, DC, it was held that it was permissible for a crown prosecutor to decide that the combination of the seriousness of an offence and the public interest warranted prosecution, despite the fact that the particular circumstances of the offence would normally, in accordance with the guidance issued under section 65 of the CDA 1998, be such as to justify only a final warning.

Charging victims of human trafficking

What follows will have to be considered in the light of the defence provided by section 45 of the Modern Slavery Act 2015 (§ 19-464 in the main work). **E-12d**

Where it is possible that a defendant or potential defendant is a victim of human trafficking, a prosecutor should take cognisance of the CPS guidance on (i) the prosecution of defendants charged with immigration offences who might be victims of trafficking, and (ii) the prosecution of young offenders charged with offences who might be such victims; in particular, under (i), when deciding whether to prosecute, or to continue to prosecute, a "credible trafficked victim" for immigration offences, prosecutors should consider whether this would serve the public interest; and under (ii), a case should be discontinued on evidential grounds where there is clear evidence that a youth has a credible defence of duress, but, if the evidence is less certain, further details should be sought from the police and youth offender teams; the defence, on the other hand, should make inquiries wherever there is credible material showing that the defendant might have been a trafficked victim, especially if the client is young; as a signatory to the Council of Europe Convention on Action against Trafficking in Human Beings, the United Kingdom is required to identify and protect victims of trafficking, and, whereas the CPS guidance supports the purpose of the convention, a trial which had failed to have proper regard to it was not fair, either under the principles of the common law or under the principles enshrined in the ECHR: *O.* [2008] EWCA Crim 2835; *The Times,* 2 October 2008.

O. and the issues arising from it were further considered in *M. (L.), B. (M.) and G. (D.); Tabot; Tijani* [2010] EWCA Crim 2327; [2011] 1 Cr. App. R. 12. It was held that one way in which the duty under Article 26 of the Council of Europe Convention (to avoid the imposition of penalties on victims of human trafficking for their involvement in unlawful activities to the extent that they were compelled to become so involved) is met in England and Wales, is by means of the guidance given to prosecutors considering whether charges should be brought against those who are or may be victims of trafficking (the court pointed out that whilst the guidance is now set out in the context of immigration offences only, it should be taken to apply whatever the nature of the allegation). The effect of the CPS's guidance, according to the court, is to require of prosecutors a three-stage exercise, asking, first, whether there is reason to believe that the person has been trafficked, secondly, whether there is clear evidence of a common law defence (in which case, any proceedings will be discontinued on evidential grounds) and, thirdly, where there is no such evidence, but the offence may have been committed as a result of compulsion arising from the trafficking, whether the public interest requires a prosecution. It was said that Article 26 does not require a blanket immunity from prosecution for trafficked victims, and that there will normally be no reason not to prosecute a victim of trafficking if the offence appears to have been committed out-with any reasonable nexus of compulsion occasioned by the trafficking. The court said that material considerations for the prosecutor when deciding whether to pursue a prosecution will be the gravity of the offence, the degree of continuing compulsion and the alternatives reasonably available to the defendant. As to this case, see also § 17-105 in the main work.

Previously there was an expanded abuse of process jurisdiction in respects of victims of trafficking, see *N. (A.); Le* [2012] EWCA Crim 189; [2012] 1 Cr. App. R. 35 and *(C.); N. (H.V.); N. (T.H.); T. (H.D.) (Children's Commr for England and Equality and Human Rights Commission Intervening)* [2013] EWCA Crim 991; [2013] 2 Cr. App. R. 23. However, since the enactment of s.45 of the Modern Slavery Act 2015 (see § 19-464 in the main work), that expanded abuse of process jurisdiction no longer applies, and cases to which the 2015 Act applies should proceed on the basis that they will be stayed if, but only if, an abuse of process as conventionally defined is found: *DS* [2020] EWCA Crim 285. Under s.45 the responsibility for deciding the facts relevant to the status of the defendant as a victim of trafficking is unquestionably that of the jury, which they will have to consider on all properly admissible evidence. Additionally, in *DS* it was held that there is no basis for deriving a positive obligation not to prosecute victims of forced or compulsory labour from Art. 4 of the ECHR (see § 16-49 in the main work), and that there remains a need for prosecutors to consider carefully whether the s.45 defence is rebutted on the evidence.

The full code test/evidential stage

E-12e When applying the "realistic prospect of conviction" test, a prosecutor should adopt a "merits based" approach, imagining himself to be the fact finder and asking himself, whether, on balance, the evidence is sufficient to merit a conviction, taking into account what he knows about the defence case, rather than a predictive "bookmaker's" approach, based on past experience of similar cases; questions of how a jury are likely to see a case are not relevant at this stage but at a later stage, under the public interest test in paragraphs 5.6 to 5.13 of the code: *R. (F.B.) v DPP* [2009] EWHC 106 (Admin); [2009] 1 Cr. App. R. 38, DC. As to this case, see also §§ 1-420, 16-48 in the main work.

For a decision of the Grand Chamber of the European Court of Human Rights in relation to the evidential test, see *Armani Da Silva v U.K., The Times,* 26 April 2016, ECtHR (Grand Chamber) (§ 1-420 in the main work)

II. LEGAL GUIDANCE AND CHARGING STANDARDS

E-13 Apart from the code for crown prosecutors, the CPS has prepared legal guidance to prosecutors and caseworkers in relation to many criminal offences and procedural issues. It has never been suggested that such guidance has the force of law, or even parity of standing with the code. It is merely, in the words of the CPS website (where it is available to the public), "an aid to guide crown prosecutors and associate prosecutors in the use of their discretion in making decisions in cases", which "does not create any rights enforceable at law, in any legal proceedings", and is subject to the principles as set out in the code for crown prosecutors.

E-14 Incorporated within the guidance are various "charging standards" for various offences or groups of offences, such as offences against the person, driving offences, drug offences, public order offences and theft. They contain a mixture of propositions of law (as to the ingredients of the various offences, maximum penalties, available alternative verdicts, etc.) and guidance as to the various factors that should be taken into consideration in deciding which offence to charge. The standards emphasise that they:

(a) are not to be used in the determination of any pre-charge decision, such as the decision to arrest;
(b) do not override any guidance issued on the use of appropriate alternative forms of disposal short of charge, such as cautioning;
(c) do not override the principles set out in the code for crown prosecutors;
(d) do not override the need for consideration to be given in every case as to whether a charge or prosecution is in the public interest;
(e) do not override particular policy guidance involving hate crimes; and
(f) do not remove the need for each case to be considered on its individual merits or fetter the discretion of the police to charge and the CPS to prosecute the most appropriate offence depending on the particular facts of the case in question.

The following recitation of general charging principles is common to all the standards:

(a) the charge or charges preferred should accurately reflect the extent of the defendant's involvement and responsibility, thereby allowing the courts the discretion to sentence appropriately;
(b) the choice of charges should ensure the clear and simple presentation of the case, particularly where there is more than one defendant;
(c) it is wrong to encourage a defendant to plead guilty to a few charges by selecting more charges than are necessary;
(d) it is wrong to select a more serious charge which is not supported by the evidence in order to encourage a plea of guilty to a lesser allegation.

III. THE ROLE AND RESPONSIBILITIES OF THE PROSECUTION ADVOCATE

Foreword

E-15 The prosecution advocate plays an important public role and as such may be considered a cornerstone of an open and fair criminal justice system. The principles so well articulated by Farquharson L.J. and his committee as to the role of the prosecution advocate have served us well since they were published in 1986. However, the time has come for new guidance which, whilst building on the established principles, reflects the changes that have occurred in the criminal courts, at the Bar and within the Crown Prosecution Service over recent years.

I welcome and commend the new Guidelines which, whilst not legally binding unless expressly approved by the Court of Appeal, nonetheless provide important practical guidance for practitioners involved in the prosecution process.

Lord Woolf C.J.

Introduction

The work undertaken in 1986 by the committee chaired by Farquharson L.J. has, for over 15 years, provided valuable guidance as to role [*sic*] of the prosecution advocate and their relationship with the Crown Prosecution Service (CPS). **E-16**

However, the ever-evolving criminal justice system, changes at the Bar and developments in the CPS brought about by the implementation of Sir Iain Glidewell's Review, mean that the environment in which we all operate has radically changed since the original report was published.

Whilst the principles established by Farquharson L.J.'s committee have been enormously helpful and will continue to apply, the time has come for new guidance that reflects the changes and emphasises the new relationship that is developing between CPS Areas and the local Bar.

The new Guidelines have therefore been developed to take account of the changes and are the result of the Bar and CPS working in partnership and in consultation with the judiciary, Bar Council and Law Society.

We commend the Guidelines as providing valuable guidance and a framework within which the Bar and the CPS can work effectively together.

Lord Goldsmith Q.C., Attorney General
David Calvert-Smith Q.C., Director of Public Prosecutions

1. Pre-trial preparation

Farquharson

(a) *It is the duty of prosecution counsel to read the Instructions delivered to him expeditiously and to advise or confer with those instructing him on all aspects of the case well before its commencement.* **E-17**

1.1 The Crown Prosecution Service (CPS) will deliver instructions at a stage in the proceedings that allows sufficient time for the prosecution advocate adequately to consider, prepare and advise on the evidence before the court hearing or draft/agree the indictment. **E-18**

1.2 Where a CPS higher court advocate represents the prosecution at a Plea and Directions Hearing (PDH), the CPS will deliver instructions to the trial advocate no later than 10 working days after the date of the PDH.

1.3 The CPS will deliver instructions which:

i. address the issues in the case including any strategic decisions that have been or may need to be made;
ii. identify relevant case law;
iii. explain the basis and rationale of any decision made in relation to the disclosure of unused material;
iv. where practical, provide specific guidance or indicate parameters on acceptable plea(s); and
v. where a case is an appeal either to the Crown Court from the magistrates' court or is before the Court of Appeal, Divisional Court or House of Lords, address the issues raised in the notice of appeal, case stated, application for judicial review or petition.

Action on receipt of instructions

1.4 On receipt of instructions the prosecution advocate will consider the papers and advise the CPS, ordinarily in writing, or orally in cases of urgency where: **E-19**

i. the prosecution advocate forms a different view to that expressed by the CPS (or where applicable a previous prosecution advocate) on acceptability of plea;
ii. the indictment as preferred requires amendment;
iii. additional evidence is required;
iv. there is an evidential deficiency (which cannot be addressed by the obtaining of further evidence) and, applying the Code for Crown Prosecutors, there is no longer a realistic prospect of conviction; or the prosecution advocate believes that it is not in the public interest to continue the prosecution;
v. in order to expedite and simplify proceedings certain formal admissions should be made;

vi. the prosecution advocate, having reviewed previous disclosure decisions, disagrees with a decision that has been made; or is not satisfied that he or she is in possession of all relevant documentation; or considers that he or she has not been fully instructed regarding disclosure matters;

vii. a case conference is required (particularly where there is a sensitive issue, e.g. informant/ PII/ disclosure etc);

viii. the presentation of the case to the court requires special preparation of material for the jury or presentational aids.

E-20 1.5 The prosecution advocate will endeavour to respond within five working days of receiving instructions, or within such period as may be specified or agreed where the case is substantial or the issues complex.

1.6 Where the prosecution advocate is to advise on a specific aspect of the case other than 1.4 (i-viii), the advocate should contact the CPS and agree a realistic timescale within which advice is to be provided.

1.7 The prosecution advocate will inform the CPS without delay where the advocate is unlikely to be available to undertake the prosecution or advise within the relevant timescale.

1.8 When returning a brief, the advocate originally instructed must ensure that the case is in good order and should discuss outstanding issues or potential difficulties with the advocate receiving the brief. Where the newly instructed advocate disagrees with a decision or opinion reached by the original advocate, the CPS should be informed so that the matter can be discussed.

Case summaries

E-21 1.9 When a draft case summary is prepared by the CPS, the prosecution advocate will consider the summary and either agree the contents or advise the CPS of any proposed amendment.

1.10 In cases where the prosecution advocate is instructed to settle the case summary or schedules, the document(s) will be prepared and submitted to the CPS without delay.

Case management plan

E-22 1.11 On receipt of a case management plan the prosecution advocate, having considered the papers, will contact the Crown Prosecutor within seven days, or such period as may be specified or agreed where the case is substantial or the issues complex, to discuss and agree the plan. The plan will be maintained and regularly reviewed to reflect the progress of the case.

Keeping the prosecution advocate informed

E-23 1.12 The CPS will inform the prosecution advocate of developments in the case without delay and, where a decision is required which may materially affect the conduct and presentation of the case, will consult with the prosecution advocate prior to that decision.

1.3 Where the CPS is advised by the defence of a plea(s) of guilty or there are developments which suggest that offering no evidence on an indictment or count therein is an appropriate course, the matter should always be discussed with the prosecution advocate without delay unless to do so would be wholly impracticable.

Victims and witnesses

E-24 1.14 When a decision whether or not to prosecute is based on the public interest, the CPS will always consider the consequences of that decision for the victim and will take into account any views expressed by the victim or the victim's family.

1.15 The prosecution advocate will follow agreed procedures and guidance on the care and treatment of victims and witnesses, particularly those who may be vulnerable or have special needs.

Appeals

E-25 1.16 Where the prosecution advocate forms a different view to that expressed by the CPS on the conduct/approach to the appeal, the advocate should advise the CPS within FIVE working days of receiving instructions or such period as may be specified or agreed where the case is substantial or the issues complex.

PDH and other preliminary hearings

E-26 1.17 The principles and procedures applying to trials as set out in the following paragraphs will be equally applicable where the prosecution advocate is conducting a PDH or other preliminary hearing.

2. Withdrawal of instructions

Farquharson

E-27 (b) *A solicitor who has briefed counsel to prosecute may withdraw his instructions before the commencement of the trial up to the point when it becomes impracticable to do so, if he disagrees with the advice given by Counsel or for any other proper professional reason.*

2.1 The CPS will consult and take all reasonable steps to resolve any issue or disagreement and will only consider withdrawing instructions from a prosecution advocate as a last resort.

2.2 If the prosecution advocate disagrees with any part of his or her instructions the advocate should contact the responsible Crown Prosecutor to discuss the matter. Until the disagreement has been resolved the matter will remain confidential and must not be discussed by the prosecution advocate with any other party to the proceedings.

"Proper professional reason"

2.3 The prosecution advocate will keep the CPS informed of any personal concerns, reservations or ethical issues that the advocate considers have the potential to lead to possible conflict with his or her instructions. **E-28**

2.4 Where the CPS identifies the potential for professional embarrassment or has concerns about the prosecution advocate's ability or experience to present the case effectively to the court, the CPS reserves the right to withdraw instructions.

Timing

2.5 It is often difficult to define when, in the course of a prosecution it becomes impracticable to withdraw instructions as circumstances will vary according to the case. The nature of the case, its complexity, witness availability and the view of the court will often be factors that will influence the decision. **E-29**

2.6 In the majority of prosecutions it will not be practicable to withdraw instructions once the judge has called the case before the court as a preliminary step to the swearing of the jury.

2.7 If instructions are withdrawn, the prosecution advocate will be informed in writing and reasons will be given.

2.8 Instructions may only be withdrawn by or with the consent of the Chief Crown Prosecutor, Assistant Chief Crown Prosecutor, Head of a CPS Trials Unit or, in appropriate cases, Head of a CPS Criminal Justice Unit.

2.9 In relation to cases prosecuted by the CPS Casework Directorate, the decision may only be taken by the Director Casework or Head of Division.

3. Presentation and conduct

Farquharson

(c) *While he remains instructed it is for counsel to take all necessary decisions in the presentation and general conduct of the prosecution.* **E-30**

3.1 The statement at 3(c) applies when the prosecution advocate is conducting the trial, PDH or any other preliminary hearing, but is subject to the principles and procedures relating to matters of policy set out in section 4 below.

Disclosure of material

3.2 Until the conclusion of the trial the prosecution advocate and CPS have a continuing duty to keep under review decisions regarding disclosure. The prosecution advocate should in every case specifically consider whether he or she can satisfactorily discharge the duty of continuing review on the basis of the material supplied already, or whether it is necessary to inspect further material or to reconsider material already inspected. **E-31**

3.3 Disclosure of material must always follow the established law and procedure. Unless consultation is impracticable or cannot be achieved without a delay to the hearing, it is desirable that the CPS, and where appropriate the disclosure officer are consulted over disclosure decisions.

4. Policy decisions

Farquharson

(d) *Where matters of policy[2] fall to be decided after the point indicated in (b) above (including offering no* **E-32**

---

[2] "Policy" decisions should be understood as referring to non-evidential decisions on: the acceptance of pleas of guilty to lesser counts or groups of counts or available alternatives; offering no evidence on particular counts; consideration of a retrial; whether to lodge an appeal; certification of a point of law; and the withdrawal of the prosecution as a whole.

evidence on the indictment or on a particular count, or on the acceptance of pleas to lesser counts), it is the duty of Counsel to consult his Instructing Solicitor/Crown Prosecutor whose views at this stage are of crucial importance.

(e) *In the rare case where counsel and his instructing solicitor are unable to agree on a matter of policy, it is, subject to (g) below, for prosecution counsel to make the necessary decisions.*

Policy issues arising at trial

E-33 4.1 The prosecution advocate should alert the CPS at the first opportunity if a matter of policy is likely to arise.

4.2 The prosecution advocate must not give an indication or undertaking which binds the prosecution without first discussing the issue with the CPS.

CPS representation at Crown Court

E-34 4.3 Whenever possible, an experienced Crown Prosecutor will be available at the Crown Court to discuss and agree any issue involving the conduct or progress of the case.

4.4 When it is not possible to provide a Crown Prosecutor at court, an experienced caseworker will attend and facilitate communication between the prosecution advocate and the Crown Prosecutor having responsibility for the case.

4.5 In exceptional circumstances where it is not possible to contact a Crown Prosecutor, the prosecution advocate should ask the court to adjourn the hearing for a realistic period in order to consult with the CPS. Where an adjournment is refused, the prosecution advocate may make the decision but should record his or her reasons in writing.

Referral to senior CPS representative

E-35 4.6 Where an issue remains unresolved following consultation with a Crown Prosecutor; or where the case/issue under consideration is substantial, sensitive or complex; or the prosecution advocate disagrees with the advice of the Crown Prosecutor, the matter may be referred to the Chief Crown Prosecutor, the Director Casework or to a senior Crown Prosecutor with delegated authority to act on their behalf.

4.7 In order to ensure consultation takes place at the highest level appropriate to the circumstances and nature of the case, the court should be asked to adjourn if necessary. When an adjournment is sought, the facts leading to the application should be placed before the court only in so far as they are relevant to that application.

4.8 Where a Chief Crown Prosecutor has been directly involved in the decision making process and the issue remains unresolved, the matter may be referred to the Director of Public Prosecutions.

Farquharson

E-36 (f) *Where counsel has taken a decision on a matter of policy with which his Instructing Solicitor has not agreed, then it would be appropriate for the Attorney General to require Counsel to submit to him a written report of all the circumstances, including his reasons for disagreeing with those who instruct him.*

4.9 It will only be in exceptional circumstances that the Attorney General will require a written report. The prosecution advocate will first discuss the decision with the Chief Crown Prosecutor or the Director, Casework. Where, by agreement, the issue remains one that either party considers should be drawn to the attention of the Director of Public Prosecutions the prosecution advocate will, on request, provide a written report for submission to the Director of Public Prosecutions. If he considers it appropriate to do so, the Director of Public Prosecutions may refer the matter to the Attorney General.

4.10 Where there has been a disagreement on a matter of policy, provided that the CPS is satisfied that the prosecution advocate followed the principles set out in this document, the professional codes of conduct and was not *Wednesbury* unreasonable, the CPS will not apply sanctions in respect of any future work solely as a result of the decision in a particular case.

5. Change of advice

Farquharson

E-37 (g) *When counsel has had the opportunity to prepare his brief and to confer with those instructing him, but at the last moment before trial unexpectedly advises that the case should not proceed or that pleas to lesser offences should be accepted, and his Instructing Solicitor does not accept such advice, counsel should apply for an adjournment if instructed so to do.*

E-38 5.1 The CPS and the prosecution advocate should agree a period of adjournment that would allow a newly instructed advocate to prepare for trial. The period should be realistic and acknowledge that in such circumstances a case conference will usually be required.

5.2 The facts leading to the application for the adjournment should be placed before the court only in so far as they are relevant to that application.

6. Prosecution advocate's role in decision making at trial

Farquharson

(h) *Subject to the above, it is for prosecution counsel to decide whether to offer no evidence on a particular count or on the indictment as a whole and whether to accept pleas to a lesser count or counts.* **E-39**

6.1 The prosecution advocate may ask the defence advocate as to whether a plea will be forthcoming but at this initial stage should not suggest or indicate a plea that might be considered acceptable to the prosecution before a plea is offered.

6.2 Where the defence advocate subsequently offers details of a plea, the prosecution advocate may discuss the matter with a view to establishing an acceptable plea that reflects the defendant's criminality and provides the court with sufficient powers to sentence appropriately.

Responsibility of prosecution advocate to consult

6.3 Where the prosecution advocate forms the view that the appropriate course is to accept a plea before proceedings commence or continue, or to offer no evidence on the indictment or any part of it, the prosecution advocate should: **E-40**

i. whenever practicable, speak with the victim or victim's family attending court to explain the position;
ii. ensure that the interests of the victim or any views expressed by the victim or victim's family are taken into account as part of the decision making process; and
iii. keep the victim or victim's family attending court informed and explain decisions as they are made.

6.4 Where appropriate the prosecution advocate may seek an adjournment of the court hearing in order to facilitate discussion with the victim or victim's family.

6.5 The prosecution advocate should always comply with paragraph 6.3 and, where practicable, discuss the matter with the CPS before informing the defence advocate or the court that a plea is acceptable.

6.6 Where the defendant indicates an acceptable plea, unless the issue is simple, the defence should reduce the basis of the plea to writing. The prosecution advocate should show the CPS any written record relating to the plea and agree with the CPS the basis on which the case will be opened to the court.

6.7 It is the responsibility of the prosecution advocate to ensure that the defence advocate is aware of the basis on which the plea is accepted by the prosecution and the way in which the prosecution case will be opened to the court.

6.8 It will not be necessary for the prosecution advocate to consult the CPS where the plea or course of action accords with the written instructions received from the CPS, although paragraph 6.3 may still apply.

Prosecution advocate's role in sentencing

6.9 The prosecution advocate should always draw the court's attention to any matters, including aggravating or mitigating features, that might affect sentence. Additionally, the advocate should be in a position to assist the court, if requested, with any statutory provisions or sentencing guidelines and should always draw attention to potential sentencing errors. **E-41**

6.10 Where a discussion on plea and sentence takes place, the prosecution advocate must adhere to the Attorney General's Guidelines on the Acceptance of Pleas published on 7 December 2000.

7. Seeking judicial approval

Farquharson

(i) *If prosecution counsel invites the Judge to approve the course he is proposing to take, then he must abide by the judge's decision.* **E-42**

7.1 A discussion with the judge about the acceptability of a plea or conduct of the case should be held in the presence of the defendant unless exceptional circumstances apply.[3]

7.2 In exceptional circumstances, where the prosecution advocate considers it appropriate to communicate with the judge or seek the judge's view in chambers, the CPS should be consulted before such a step is taken.

7.3 Where discussions take place in chambers it is the responsibility of the prosecution advocate to remind the judge, if necessary, that an independent record must always be kept.

7.4 The prosecution advocate should also make a full note of such an event, recording all decisions and comments. This note should be made available to the CPS.

Farquharson

E-43 (j) *If prosecution counsel does not invite the judge's approval of his decision it is open to the judge to express his dissent with the course proposed and invite counsel to reconsider the matter with those instructing him, but having done so, the final decision remains with counsel.*

7.5 Where a judge expresses a view based on the evidence or public interest, the CPS will carry out a further review of the case.

7.6 The prosecution advocate will inform the CPS in a case where the judge has expressed a dissenting view and will agree the action to be taken. Where there is no CPS representative at court, the prosecution advocate will provide a note of the judge's comments.

7.7 The prosecution advocate will ensure that the judge is aware of all factors that have a bearing on the prosecution decision to adopt a particular course. Where there is a difference of opinion between the prosecution advocate and the CPS the judge will be informed as to the nature of the disagreement.

Farquharson

E-44 (k) *In an extreme case where the judge is of the opinion that the course proposed by counsel would lead to serious injustice, he may decline to proceed with the case until counsel has consulted with either the Director or the Attorney General as may be appropriate.*

7.8 As a preliminary step, the prosecution advocate will discuss the judge's observations with the Chief Crown Prosecutor in an attempt to resolve the issue. Where the issue remains unresolved the Director of Public Prosecutions will be consulted. In exceptional circumstances the Director of Public Prosecutions may consult the Attorney General.

E-45 **Note:** These Guidelines are subject to the Code of Conduct of the Bar of England and Wales (barrister advocates) and The Law Society's The Guide to the Professional Conduct of Solicitors (solicitor advocates). Whilst reference is made in the guidelines to the CPS and levels of authority within the Service, the guidelines may be adopted as best practice, with consequential amendments to levels of authority, by other prosecuting authorities.

These Guidelines may be amended at any time and copyright is waived.

These Guidelines are also available on the CPS Website: *www.cps.gov.uk.*

---

[3] For the purposes of these guidelines, "exceptional circumstances" would include the following:

(i) Where there is material or information which should not be made public, e.g. a police text, or for some other compelling reason such as a defendant or witness suffering, unknown to them, from a serious or terminal illness; or

(ii) There are sensitivities surrounding a prosecution decision or proposed action which need to be explained in chambers with a view to obtaining judicial approval. Such approval may be given in open court where it is necessary to explain a prosecution decision or action in order to maintain public confidence in the criminal justice system.

APPENDIX F
Practice Direction (Costs in Criminal Proceedings) 2015

I. COSTS IN CRIMINAL CASES (GENERAL) REGULATIONS 1986 (SI 1986/1335)

A. PRACTICE DIRECTION

On 29 September 2015, Lord Thomas CJ issued a new practice direction to replace the one issued by himself in October 2013 (*Practice Direction (Criminal Proceedings: Costs)* [2013] EWCA Crim 1632; [2013] 1 W.L.R. 3255), which had in turn replaced that issued by Lord Judge CJ in July 2010. The 2015 practice direction repeats the substance of the 2013 direction (as amended by *Practice Direction (Criminal Proceedings: Costs) (No. 2)* [2014] EWCA Crim 1570; [2014] 1 W.L.R. 3037), but has been revised to bring up to date references to the Criminal Procedure Rules and other legislation. It came into force on 5 October 2015. It was amended with effect from 4 April 2016, by *Practice Direction (Costs in Criminal Proceedings) 2015 (Amendment No. 1)* [2016] EWCA Crim 98, Lord Thomas CJ. The full text (as so amended) (apart from some paragraphs that do no more than restate the effect of legislation and Pt 9 (VAT)) is set out below, subject only to any necessary correction of references to legislation and case law. **F-1**

Practice Direction (Costs in Criminal Proceedings) (2015)

Part 1: General

1.1 Preamble (omitted) **F-2**

1.2 The Power to Award Costs

1.2.1 The powers enabling the court to award costs in criminal proceedings are primarily contained in Part II of the Prosecution of Offences Act 1985 ("the Act") (sections 16 to 19B), the Access to Justice Act 1999 and the Legal Aid, Sentencing and Punishment of Offenders Act 2012 (in relation to funded clients) and in regulations made under those Acts including the Costs in Criminal Cases (General) Regulations 1986, as amended ("the General Regulations"). References in this direction to sections and regulations by number alone are to the sections and regulations so numbered in the Act and the General Regulations unless otherwise stated. Schedule1 below sets out details of the relevant regulations.

1.2.2 Sections 16 and 16A of the Act make provision for the award of defence costs out of Central Funds (a defendant's costs order). Section 17 provides for an award of costs to a private prosecutor out of Central Funds. Section 18 gives power to order a convicted defendant or an unsuccessful appellant to pay costs to the prosecutor. Section 19(1) of the Act and Regulation 3 of the General Regulations provide for awards of costs between parties in respect of unnecessary or improper acts and omissions. Section 19A provides for the court to disallow or order a legal or other representative of a party to the proceedings to meet wasted costs. Regulations 3A to 3D of the General Regulations govern the making of wasted costs orders. Section 19B provides for the award of costs against third parties. Regulations 3E to 3I of the General Regulations apply to third party costs orders.

1.2.3 The Senior Courts also have the power under their inherent jurisdiction over officers of the court to order a solicitor personally to pay costs thrown away. The inherent jurisdiction of the court should be invoked only to avoid a clear injustice (*Symbol Park Lane Ltd v Steggles* [1985] 1 W.L.R. 668, CA (Civ. Div.)). Where the legislature has stepped in with particular legislation in a particular area (e.g. the wasted costs provisions) then, within that particular area, the existing inherent jurisdiction will be ousted or curtailed, at any rate in so far as the particular legislation is negative in character (*Shiloh Spinners Ltd v Harding* [1973] A.C. 691, HL; *Harrison v Tew* [1990] 2 A.C. 523, HL). Given the present provisions relating to costs, the exercise of the inherent jurisdiction will occur only in the rarest of circumstances.

1.2.4 Where the court orders a defendant to pay costs to the prosecutor; orders one party to pay costs to another party or a third party to pay costs; disallows or orders a legal or other representative to meet any wasted costs; or makes a defendant's costs order other than for the full amount; the order for costs must specify the sum to be paid or disallowed. Where the court is required to specify the amount of costs to be paid it cannot delegate the decision, but may require the assistance of the relevant assessing authority, in practice the National Taxing Team (for magistrates' courts and for the Crown Court) and the Registrar of Criminal Appeals (for the Court of Appeal): see CrimPR 45.8(8), 45.9(8) and 45.10(8). The rules provide also that a party who has incurred unnecessary or wasted costs should provide assistance to the court as to the amount involved, where the court considers making an order on its own initiative: CrimPR 45.8(5)(b)(iii), 45.9(5)(b)(iii) and 45.10(5)(b)(iii).

Extent of orders for costs from central funds

F-3 **1.3.1** Where a court orders that the costs of a defendant, appellant or private prosecutor should be paid from central funds, the order will be for such amount as the court considers sufficient reasonably to compensate the party for expenses incurred by him in the proceedings; unless the court considers that there are circumstances that make it inappropriate to allow the full amount in which event it will allow such lesser sum as it considers just and reasonable. This will include the costs incurred in the proceedings in the lower courts unless for good reason the court directs that such costs are not included in the order, but it cannot include expenses incurred which do not directly relate to the proceedings themselves, such as loss of earnings. Where the party in whose favour the costs order is made is legally aided, he will only recover his personal costs: see s.21(4A)(a) of the Act. Schedule 2 below sets out the extent of availability of costs from central funds and the relevant statutory authority.

1.3.2 If a defendant's costs order includes legal costs (sums paid for advocacy, litigation services or experts' fees) the order must include a statement to that effect.

Amount of costs to be paid

F-4 **1.4.1** If the court does not fix the amount of costs to be paid out of central funds, the costs will be determined in accordance with the General Regulations by the appropriate authority. The appropriate authority will calculate the amount payable in respect of legal costs at such rates and scales as are prescribed by the Lord Chancellor. Where the court makes a defendant's costs order, or an order in favour of a private prosecutor, but is of the opinion there are circumstances which make it inappropriate that the person in whose favour the order is made should recover the full amount of the costs, the court may assess the lesser amount that would in its opinion be just and reasonable, and specify that amount in the order. If the court is not in a position to specify the amount payable, the judge may make remarks which the appropriate authority will take into account as a relevant circumstance when determining the costs payable.

1.4.2 In respect of proceedings commenced on or after 1 October 2012 legal costs (sums paid for advocacy, litigation services or experts' fees) may only be included in a defendant's costs order to a defendant who is an individual and only in proceedings in a magistrates' court, appeals against conviction or sentence from a magistrates' court to the Crown Court, relevant Crown Court proceedings after 27 January 2014 (as to which see para 1.4.3 below) and appeals to the Court of Appeal (i) against a verdict of not guilty by reason of insanity (ii) against a finding under the Criminal Procedure (Insanity) Act 1964 that the appellant is under a disability or that he did the act or made the omission charged or (iii) under s.16A of the CAA 1968 (appeals against order made in cases of insanity or unfitness to plead).

1.4.3 After 27 January 2014 legal costs may be included in a defendant's costs order, provided that the defendant is an individual, in relevant proceedings in the Crown Court if the Director of Legal Aid Casework has made a determination of financial ineligibility in relation to that defendant. The relevant proceedings are those in which the accused has been sent by a magistrates' court to the Crown Court for trial, where a bill of indictment has been preferred (under s.2(2)(b) of the Administration of Justice (Miscellaneous Provisions) Act 1933 [§ 1-328]) or following an order for a retrial made by the Court of Appeal or the Supreme Court.

1.4.4 Where legal costs may be allowed, if the court fixes the amount to be paid to a defendant under s.16(6C) of the Act or under ss.62A(4) or 135A(4) of the Extradition Act 2003 it must calculate any amounts to be allowed in respect of legal costs in accordance with rates and scales prescribed by the Lord Chancellor.

1.4.5 Rules 45.2(6) and (7) of the Criminal Procedure Rules ("CrimPR") contain general rules about the amount of an award of costs that apply subject to any statutory limitation.

Criminal Procedure Rules

F-5 **1.5.1** Part 45 contains rules governing the procedure on the exercise of any of the powers to award costs listed in CrimPR 45.1. They include the powers contained in the Act and in the General Regulations. CrimPR Part 33 contains rules about the award of costs in restraint or receivership proceedings under the Proceeds of Crime Act 2002 (§§ 5B-232 and following)

1.5.2 The procedure for the assessment of costs under CrimPR 45.11 applies where the court makes an award between parties in one of the cases listed in r.45.11(1). The assessment of an award of costs out of central funds is governed by substantially similar procedures under (i) the General Regulations or (ii) the Serious Crime Act 2007 (Appeals under Section 24) Order 2008 (SI 2008/1863) [§§ 7-338 and following.].

PART 2: COSTS OUT OF CENTRAL FUNDS

In a magistrates' court

2.1.1 Where an information laid before a justice of the peace charging a person with an offence is not proceeded with or a magistrates' court dealing summarily with an offence dismisses the information the court may make a defendant's costs order. An order under s.16 of the Act may also be made in relation to breach of bind-over proceedings in a magistrates' court or the Crown Court: reg.14(4) of the General Regulations. Whether to make such an order is a matter in the discretion of the court in the light of the circumstances of each particular case. A defendant's costs order should normally be made unless there are positive reasons for not doing so, for example, where the defendant's own conduct has brought suspicion on himself and has misled the prosecution into thinking that the case against him was stronger than it was. Where the defendant has been acquitted on some counts but convicted on others the court may make an order that only part of the costs be paid: see paras 2.2.1 and 2.2.2 below. The court when declining to make a costs order should explain, in open court, that the reason for not making an order does not involve any suggestion that the defendant is guilty of any criminal conduct but the order is refused because of the positive reason that should be identified (*Hussain v U.K.* (2006) 43 E.H.R.R. 22). Where the court considers that it would be inappropriate that the defendant should recover all of the costs properly incurred, either the amount allowed must be specified in the order or the court may describe to the appropriate authority the reduction required. F-6

2.1.2 In respect of proceedings in a magistrates' court commenced on or after 1 October 2012 legal costs (sums paid for advocacy, litigation services or experts' fees) may only be allowed to a defendant who is an individual. Where legal costs may be allowed, if the court fixes the amount to be paid under s.16(6C) of the Act or under ss.62A(4) or 135A(4) of the Extradition Act 2003 it must calculate any amounts allowed in respect of legal costs in accordance with the rates and scales prescribed by the Lord Chancellor. If the court does not fix the amount of costs to be paid out of central funds, the costs will be determined by the appropriate authority in accordance with the General Regulations and any legal costs allowed will be calculated at the prescribed rates and scales.

In the Crown Court

2.2.1 Where a person is not tried for an offence for which he has been indicted, or in respect of which proceedings against him have been sent for trial or transferred for trial, or has been acquitted on any count in the indictment, the court may make a defendant's costs order in his favour. Whether to make such an order is a matter for the discretion of the court in the light of the circumstances of the particular case. A defendant's costs order should normally be made whether or not an order for costs between the parties is made, unless there are positive reasons for not doing so, for example, where the defendant's own conduct has brought suspicion on himself and has misled the prosecution into thinking that the case against him was stronger than it was. [Identical to penultimate sentence in para.2.1.1.] Where the court considers that it would be inappropriate that the defendant should recover all of the costs properly incurred, either the lesser amount must be specified in the order, or the court must describe to the appropriate authority the reduction required. F-7

2.2.2 Where a person is convicted of some count(s) in the indictment and acquitted on other(s) the court may exercise its discretion to make a defendant's costs order but may order that only a proportion of the costs incurred be paid. The court should make whatever order seems just having regard to the relative importance of the charges and the conduct of the parties generally. The proportion of costs allowed must be specified in the order.

2.2.3 The Crown Court may make a defendant's costs order in favour of a successful appellant: see s.16(3) of the Act.

2.2.4 In respect of proceedings in the Crown Court commenced on or after 1 October 2012 legal costs ... may only be allowed under a defendant's costs order to a defendant who is an individual and only (1) in respect of appeals against conviction or sentence from a magistrates' court; or (2) after 27 January 2014 in other relevant Crown Court proceedings provided that the Director of Legal Aid Casework has made a determination of financial ineligibility in relation to the defendant. The relevant proceedings are those in which the accused has been sent by a magistrates' court to the Crown Court for trial, where a bill of indictment has been preferred (under s.2(2)(b) of the Administration of Justice (Miscellaneous Provisions) Act 1933 [§ 1-328]) or following an order for a retrial made by the Court of Appeal or the Supreme Court. Where legal costs may be allowed, if the court fixes the amount to be paid under s.16(6C) of the Act it must calculate any amounts allowed in respect of legal costs in accordance with the rates and scales prescribed by the Lord Chancellor. [Identical to last sentence of para.2.1.2.]

In the High Court

2.3.1 The Divisional Court of the Queen's Bench Division may make a defendant's costs order on determining proceedings in a criminal cause or matter: see s.16(5)(a) of the Act. F-8

In the Court of Appeal (Criminal Division)

F-9 **2.4.1** A successful appellant under Part I of the Criminal Appeal Act 1968 may be awarded a defendant's costs order. Orders may also be made on an appeal against an order or ruling at a preparatory hearing (section 16(4A) of the 1985 Act), to cover the costs of representing an acquitted defendant in respect of whom there is an Attorney Generals' reference under section 36 of the Criminal Justice Act 1972 (see section 36(5) (5A) of the 1972 Act) and in the case of a person whose sentence is reviewed under section 36 of the Criminal Justice Act 1988 : see section 36 of, and paragraph 11 of Schedule 3 to, the 1988 Act.

2.4.2 On determining an application for leave to appeal to the Supreme Court under Part II of the Criminal Appeal Act 1968, whether by prosecutor or by defendant, the court may make a defendant's costs order

2.4.3 In considering whether to make such an order the court will have in mind the principles applied by the Crown Court in relation to acquitted defendants: see paras. 2.2.1 and 2.2.2 above.

2.4.4 In respect of appeals where the application for leave to appeal is made or notice of appeal given on or after 1 October 2012 legal costs ... may only be allowed under a defendant's costs order to a defendant who is an individual and only in appeals (i) against a verdict of not guilty by reason of insanity (ii) against a finding under the Criminal Procedure (Insanity) Act 1964 that the appellant is under a disability or that he did the act or made the omission charged or (iii) under s.16A of the CAA 1968 (appeal against order made in cases of insanity or unfitness to plead). If the court does not fix the amount of costs to be paid out of central funds, the costs will be determined in accordance with the General Regulations by the appropriate authority. The appropriate authority will calculate the amount payable in respect of legal costs at such rates and scales as are prescribed by the Lord Chancellor.

Costs of witness, interpreter or medical evidence

F-10 **2.5.1** The costs of attendance of a witness required by the accused, a private prosecutor or the court, or of an interpreter required because of the accused's lack of English or an intermediary under s.29 of the YJCEA 1999, or of an oral report by a medical practitioner are allowed out of central funds unless the court directs otherwise: see reg.16(1) of the General Regulations. In the case of a witness if, and only if, the court makes such a direction can the expense of the witness be claimed as a disbursement for the purposes of criminal legal aid. A witness includes any person properly attending to give evidence whether or not he gives evidence or is called, but it does not include a character witness unless the court has certified that the interests of justice require his attendance: see s.21(1) of the Act.

2.5.2 The Crown Court may order the payment out of central funds of such sums as appear to be sufficient reasonably to compensate any medical practitioner for the expenses, trouble or loss of time properly incurred in preparing and making a report on the mental condition of a person accused of murder: see s.34(5) of the Mental Health (Amendment) Act 1982 [§ 6-86].

Private prosecutor's costs from central funds

F-11 **2.6.1** There is no power to order the payment of costs out of central funds of any prosecutor who is a public authority, a person acting on behalf of a public authority, or acting as an official appointed by a public authority as defined in the Act. In the limited number of cases in which a prosecutor's costs may be awarded out of central funds, an application is to be made by the prosecution in each case. An order should be made save where there is good reason for not doing so, for example, where proceedings have been instituted or continued without good cause. This provision applies to proceedings in respect of an indictable offence or proceedings before the High Court in respect of a summary offence. Regulation 14(1) of the General Regulations extends it to certain committals for sentence from a magistrates' court.

2.6.2 Where the court is of the opinion that there are circumstances which make it inappropriate to award the full amount of costs out of central funds, the order must be for the payment of such lesser amount as is just and reasonable. Where the court considers it appropriate to do so, and the prosecutor agrees the amount, it must fix the amount. Otherwise it must make an order for such costs as are just and reasonable, describing in the order any reduction in the amount of costs required, and the costs will, be determined by the appropriate authority in accordance with the General Regulations.

2.6.3 For the purposes of an order under s.17 of the Act the costs of the prosecutor are taken to include the expense of compensating any witness for the expenses, travel and loss of time properly incurred in or incidental to his attendance.

2.6.4 If there has been misconduct a private prosecutor should not be awarded costs out of central funds (*Esher and Walton JJ, ex p. Victor Value & Co Ltd* (1967) 111 S.J. 473, DC).

2.6.5 Where the conduct of a private prosecution is taken over by the CPS the power of the court to order payment of prosecution costs out of central funds extends only to the period prior to the intervention of the CPS.

Procedure

2.7.1 CrimPR 45.4, and the general rules in the first section of CrimPR, Pt 45, apply to the exercise of the court's powers to award costs out of central funds. F-12

Part 3: Awards of Costs against Defendants

3.1 A Magistrates' Court or the Crown Court may make an order for costs against a person convicted of an offence before it or in dealing with it in respect of certain orders as to sentence specified in regulation 14(3) of the General Regulations. The Crown Court may make an order against an unsuccessful appellant and against a person committed by a Magistrates' Court in respect of the proceedings specified in regulation 14(1) (2). The court may make such order payable to the prosecutor as it considers just and reasonable: section 18(1) of the Act. F-13

3.2 In a Magistrates' Court where the defendant is ordered to pay a sum not exceeding £5 by way of fine, penalty, forfeiture or compensation the court must not make a costs order unless in the particular circumstances of the case it considers it right to do so: section 18(4) of the Act. Where the defendant is under 18 the amount of any costs awarded against him by a Magistrates' Court must not exceed the amount of any fine imposed on him: section 18(5).

3.3 The Court of Appeal (Criminal Division) may order an unsuccessful appellant to pay costs to such person as may be named in the order. Such costs may include the costs of any transcript obtained for the proceedings in the Court of Appeal: section 18(2),(6) of the Act.

3.4 An order should be made where the court is satisfied that the defendant or appellant has the means and the ability to pay. The order is not intended to be in the nature of a penalty which can only be satisfied on the defendant's release from prison. An order should not be made on the assumption that a third party might pay. Whilst the court should take into account any debt of the appellant or defendant, where the greater part of those debts relates to the offence itself, the court may still make an order for costs.

3.5 Where co-defendants are husband and wife, the couple's means should not be taken together. Where there are multiple defendants the court may make joint and several orders, but the costs ordered to be paid by an individual should be related to the costs in or about the prosecution of that individual. In a multi-handed case where some defendants have insufficient means to pay their share of the costs, it is not right for that share to be divided among the other defenders *[sic]*. F-14

3.6 The prosecution should serve upon the defence, at the earliest time, full details of its costs so as to give the defendant a proper opportunity to make representations upon them if appropriate. If a defendant wishes to dispute all or any of the prosecution's claim for costs, the defendant should, if possible, give proper notice to the prosecution of the objections proposed to be made or at least make it plain to the court precisely what those objections are. There is no provision for assessment of prosecution costs in a criminal case, such disputes have to be resolved by the court, which must specify the amount to be paid (see *Associated Octel Ltd* [§ 6-46]).

3.7 The principles to be applied in deciding on the amount of costs are those set out by the Court of Appeal in *Neville v Gardner Merchant* [§ 6-46]. The court when awarding prosecution costs may award costs in respect of time spent in bringing the offences to light, even if the necessary investigation was carried out, for example, by an environmental health official. Generally it will not be just or reasonable to order a defendant to pay costs of investigation which the prosecutor itself will not satisfy. In *Balshaw* [§ 6-46] the Court of Appeal considered the circumstances in which the CPS may be able to recover costs associated with the investigation incurred by the police, The Divisional Court has held that there is a requirement that any sum ordered to be paid by way of costs should not ordinarily be greatly at variance with any fine imposed. Where substantial research is required in order to counter possible defences, the court may also award costs in respect of that work if it considers it to be justified.

3.8 The High Court is not covered by s.18 of the Act but it has complete discretion over all costs between the parties in relation to proceedings before it (Senior Courts Act 1981, s.51).

3.9 An order under s.18 of the Act includes the cost of advice, assistance or representation provided under the criminal legal aid provisions: see s.21(4A)(b) of the Act.

3.10 CrimPR 45.5, 45.6 and the general rules in the first section of CrimPR, Pt 45, apply to the exercise of the court's powers to award costs against a defendant on conviction, sentence or appeal.

Part 4: Other Costs Orders

Costs incurred as a result of unnecessary or improper act or omission

4.1.1 A magistrates' court, the Crown Court and the Court of Appeal (Criminal Division) may order the payment of any costs incurred as a result of any unnecessary or improper act or omission by or on behalf of any party to the proceedings as distinct from his legal representative: s.19 of the Act and reg.3 of the General Regulations. The court may find it helpful to adopt a three stage F-15 approach. (a) Has there been an unnecessary or improper, act or omission? (b) As a result have any costs been incurred by another party? (c) If the answers to (a) and (b) are "yes", should the court exercise its discretion to order the party responsible to meet the whole or any part of the relevant costs, and if so what specific sum is involved? CrimPR 45.8 sets out the procedure. A form of application is set out in Sch.5 to this practice direction.

4.1.2 The court must hear the parties and may then order that all or part of the costs so incurred by one party shall be paid to him by the other party.

4.1.3 Before making such an order the court may take into account any other order as to costs and the order must specify the amount of the costs to be paid. The court is entitled to take such an order into account when making any other order as to costs in the proceedings: reg.3(2)-(4) of the General Regulations. The order can extend to legal aid costs incurred on behalf of any party: s.21(4A)(b) of the Act.

4.1.4 In a magistrates' court no order may be made which requires a convicted person under 17 to pay an amount by way of costs which exceeds the amount of any fine imposed upon him: reg.3(5) of the General Regulations.

4.1.5 Such an order is appropriate only where the failure is that of the defendant or of the prosecutor. Where the failure is that of a legal representative(s), paras 4.2 and 4.5 (below) may be more suitable.

4.1.6 Though the court cannot delegate its decision to the appropriate authority, it may require the assistance of that authority, in practice the National Taxing Team (for magistrates' courts and for the Crown Court) and the Registrar of Criminal Appeals (for the Court of Appeal): see CrimPR 45.8(8). The rule lists the circumstances of which the court must take account in deciding whether or not to seek such assistance. In most cases it will be neither necessary nor desirable to do so, bearing in mind the summary nature of the court's jurisdiction, the delay and expense that is otherwise liable to be incurred, and the rules that require claimants to specify in a written application the amount claimed and that require opponents to respond in writing, thus exposing the extent of any disagreement. However, in a few, exceptional, cases it may better meet the overriding objective to secure the assistance of an assessing authority than for the court to embark upon a complex assessment without such assistance. The rules provide also that a party who has incurred costs as a result of an unnecessary or improper act or omission by another party should provide assistance to the court as to the amount involved, where the court considers making an order on its own initiative: CrimPR 45.8(5)(b)(iii).

F-16 **4.2.1** Section 19A of the Act allows a magistrates' court, the Crown Court or the Court of Appeal (Criminal Division) to disallow or order the legal or other representative to meet the whole or any part of the wasted costs. The order can be made against any person exercising a right of audience or a right to conduct litigation (in the sense of acting for a party to the proceedings). "Wasted costs" are costs incurred by a party (which includes a legally aided party) as a result of any improper, unreasonable or negligent act or omission on the part of any representative or his employee, or which, in the light of any such act or omission occurring after they were incurred, the court considers it unreasonable to expect that party to pay: s.19A(3) of the Act; s.89(8) of the POCA 2002 [§ 5B-170]. CrimPR 45.9 sets out the procedure. A form of application is set out in Sch.5 to this practice direction.

4.2.2 The judge has a much greater and more direct responsibility for costs in criminal proceedings than in civil and should keep the question of costs in the forefront of his mind at every stage of the case and ought to be prepared to take the initiative himself without any prompting from the parties.

4.2.3 Regulation 3B of the General Regulations requires the court to specify the amount of the wasted costs and before making the order to allow the legal or other representative and any party to the proceedings to make representations. In making the order the court may take into account any other orders for costs and may take the wasted costs order into account when making any other order as to costs. The court should also give reasons for making the order and must notify any interested party (which includes the Legal Aid Agency and central funds determining authorities) of the order and the amount.

4.2.4 Judges contemplating making a wasted costs order should bear in mind the guidance given by the Court of Appeal in *In re A. Barrister (Wasted Costs Order) (No 1 of 1991)* [1993] Q.B. 293. The guidance, which is set out below, is to be considered together with all the statutory and other rules and recommendations set out by Parliament and in this practice direction.

(i) There is a clear need for any judge or court intending to exercise the wasted costs jurisdiction to formulate carefully and concisely the complaint and grounds upon which such an order may be sought. These measures are draconian and, as in contempt proceedings, the grounds must be clear and particular.

(ii) Where necessary a transcript of the relevant part of the proceedings under discussion should be available and in accordance with the rules a transcript of any wasted cost *[sic]* hearing must be made.

(iii) A defendant involved in a case where such proceedings are contemplated should be present if, after discussion with an advocate, it is thought that his interest may be affected and he should certainly be present and represented if the matter might affect the course of his trial. CrimPR 45.2(1) requires that the court must not make a costs order unless each party, and any other person affected, (a) is present, or (b) has had an opportunity to attend or to make representations.

(iv) A three stage test or approach is recommended when a wasted costs order is contemplated. (a) Has there been an improper, unreasonable or negligent act or omission? (b) As a result have any costs been incurred by a party? (c) If the answers to (a) and (b) are "yes", should the court exercise its discretion to disallow or order the representative to meet the whole or any part of the relevant costs, and if so what specific sum is involved?

(v) It is inappropriate to propose any settlement that the representative might forgo fees. The complaint should be formally stated by the judge and the representative invited to make his own comments. After any other party has been heard the judge should give his formal ruling. Discursive conversations may be unfair and should certainly not take place.

(vi) The judge must specify the sum to be allowed or ordered. Alternatively the relevant available procedure should be substituted should it be impossible to fix the sum: see para 4.2.7 below.

4.2.5 The Court of Appeal has given further guidance in *In re P. (A Barrister) (Wasted Costs Order)* [2001] EWCA Crim 1728; [2002] 1 Cr. App. R. 19 as follows: **F-17**

(i) the primary object is not to punish but to compensate, albeit as the order is sought against a non party, it can from that perspective be regarded as penal;

(ii) the jurisdiction is a summary jurisdiction to be exercised by the court which has "tried the case in the course of which the misconduct was committed";

(iii) fairness is assured if the lawyer alleged to be at fault has sufficient notice of the complaint made against him and a proper opportunity to respond to it;

(iv) because of the penal element a mere mistake is not sufficient to justify an order: there must be a more serious error;

(v) although the trial judge can decline to consider an application in respect of costs, for example on the ground that he or she is personally embarrassed by an appearance of bias, it will only be in exceptional circumstances that it will be appropriate to pass the matter to another judge, and the fact that, in the proper exercise of his judicial function, a judge has expressed views in relation to the conduct of a lawyer against whom an order is sought, does not of itself normally constitute bias or the appearance of bias so as to necessitate a transfer;

(vi) the normal civil standard of proof applies but if the allegation is one of serious misconduct or crime clear evidence will be required to meet that standard.

4.2.6 Though the court cannot delegate its decision to the appropriate authority, it may require the assistance of that authority, in practice the National Taxing Team (for magistrates' courts and for the Crown Court) and the Registrar of Criminal Appeals (for the Court of Appeal): see CrimPR 45.9(8). The rule lists the circumstances of which the court must take account in deciding whether or not to seek such assistance. In most cases it will be neither necessary nor desirable to do so, bearing in mind the summary nature of the court's jurisdiction, the delay and expense that is otherwise liable to be incurred, and the rules that require claimants to specify in a written application the amount claimed and that require opponents to respond in writing, thus exposing the extent of any disagreement. However, in a few, exceptional, cases it may better meet the overriding objective to secure the assistance of an assessing authority than for the court to embark upon a complex assessment without such assistance. The rules provide also that a party who has incurred costs as a result of an improper, unreasonable or negligent act or omission by a legal or other representative should provide assistance to the court as to the amount involved, where the court considers making an order on its own initiative: CrimPR 45.9(5)(b)(iii).

4.2.7 The court may postpone the making of a wasted costs order to the end of the case if it appears more appropriate to do so, for example, because the likely amount is not readily available, there is a possibility of conflict between the legal representatives as to the apportionment of blame, or the legal representative concerned is unable to make full representations because of a possible conflict with the duty to the client.

4.2.8 A wasted costs order should normally be made regardless of the fact that the client of the legal representative concerned is legally aided. However where the court is minded to disallow substantial legal aid costs, it may, instead of making a wasted costs order, make observations to the determining authority that work may have been unreasonably done: see para 4.3 below. This practice should only be adopted where the extent and amount of the costs wasted is not entirely clear.

Appeals against wasted costs orders

4.2.9 A party against whom a wasted costs order has been made may appeal against that order. In **F-18**

the case of an order made by a magistrates' court, appeal is to the Crown Court, and CrimPR, Pt 34 [§§ 2-117 and following] sets out the procedure. In the case of an order made at first instance by the Crown Court, the appeal is to the Court of Appeal and the procedure is set out in CrimPR, Pt 39 [§§ 7-380 and following]. In both cases the time limit for appeal is 21 days from the date of the order.

4.2.10 Having heard the submissions, the appeal court may affirm, vary or revoke the order as it thinks fit and must notify its decision to the appellant, any interested party and the court which made the order.

Disallowance of criminal legal aid costs

F-19 **4.3.1** Where it appears to any judge of the Crown Court or the Court of Appeal (Criminal Division), sitting in proceedings for which legal aid has been granted, that work may have been unreasonably done, e.g. if the represented person's case may have been conducted unreasonably so as to incur unjustifiable expense, or costs may have been wasted by failure to conduct the proceedings with reasonable competence or expedition, the judge may make observations to that effect for the attention of the appropriate authority. The judge or the court, as the case may be, should specify as precisely as possible the item, or items, which the determining officer should consider or investigate on the determination of the costs payable pursuant to the representation order. The precise terms of the observations must be entered in the court record.

4.3.2 Article [sic] 26 of the Criminal Legal Aid (Remuneration) Regulations 2013 [Appendix G-30] permits the appropriate officer to reduce any fee which would otherwise be payable by such proportion as the officer considers reasonable in the light of any adverse comments made by the court. The power to make adverse comments co-exists with the power to disallow fees when making a wasted costs order. Article [sic] 27 of the 2013 regulations [Appendix G-31] allows the determining officer to disallow the amount of the wasted costs order from the amount otherwise payable to the litigator or advocate and allows for deduction of a greater amount if appropriate.

4.3.3 Where the judge or the court has in mind making observations under para.4.3 the litigator or advocate whose fees or expenses might be affected must be informed of the precise terms thereof and of his right to make representations to the appropriate authority and be given a reasonable opportunity to show cause why the observations or direction should not be made.

4.3.4 Where such observations or directions are made the appropriate authority must afford an opportunity to the litigator or advocate whose fees might be affected to make representations in relation to them.

4.3.5 Whether or not observations under para.4.3.1 have been made the appropriate authority may consult the judge or the court on any matter touching the allowance or disallowance of fees and expenses, but if the observations then made are to the effect mentioned in para.4.3.1, the appropriate authority should afford an opportunity to the litigator or advocate concerned to make representations in relation to them.

Very High Cost Cases

F-20 **4.4.1** In proceedings which are classified as a very high cost case ("VHCC") as defined by reg.2 of the Criminal Legal Aid (Remuneration) Regulations 2013 [Appendix G-6], the judge or court should, at the earliest opportunity, ask the representative of the legally aided party whether they have notified the Lord Chancellor of the case in accordance with reg.12 of those regulations [Appendix G-16]. If they have not they should be warned that they may not be able to recover their costs.

Wasted costs orders in the High Court

F-21 **4.5.1** In the High Court (Divisional Court) where the court is considering whether to make an order under s.51(6) of the Senior Courts Act 1981 (a wasted costs order or disallowing wasted costs) it will do so in accordance with CPR, r.46.8 which contains similar provisions as to giving the legal representative a reasonable opportunity to attend a hearing to give reasons why the court should not make such an order.

Awards of costs against solicitors under the court's inherent jurisdiction

F-22 **4.6.1** In addition to the power under reg.3 of the General Regulations to order that costs improperly incurred be paid by a party to the proceedings and the power to make wasted costs orders under s.19A of the Act, the Senior Courts (which includes the Crown Court) may, in the exercise of its inherent jurisdiction over officers of the court, order a solicitor personally to pay costs thrown away by reason of a serious breach on the part of the solicitor of his duty to the court.

4.6.2 No such order may be made unless reasonable notice has been given to the solicitor of the matter alleged against him and he is given a reasonable opportunity of being heard in reply.

4.6.3 This power should be used only in exceptional circumstances not covered by the statutory powers: see para 1.2.3.

F-23 **4.7.1** The *[sic]* magistrates' court, the Crown Court and the Court of Appeal may make a third party costs order if there has been serious misconduct (whether or not constituting a contempt of court) by a third party and the court considers it appropriate, having regard to that misconduct, to make a third party costs order against him. A "third party costs order" is an order for the payment of costs incurred by a party to criminal proceedings by a person who is not a party to those proceedings ("the third party"): s.19B of the 1985 Act and regs 3E to 3I of the General Regulations. CrimPR, 45.10 sets out the procedure.

4.7.2 The court may make a third party costs order at any time during or after the criminal proceedings, but should only make such an order during the proceedings if it decides that there are good reasons to do so.

4.7.3 The court must notify the parties and the third party of those reasons and allow any of them to make representations.

4.7.4 A third party costs order may be made on the application of any party, or on the court's own initiative, but not in any other circumstances. Before making an order the court must allow the third party, and any other party, to make representations and may hear evidence.

4.7.5 When the court is making a third party costs order, it may take into account any other order as to costs in respect of the criminal proceedings, and may take the third party costs order into account when making any other order for costs in respect of those proceedings.

4.7.6 The order must specify the amount of costs to be paid, and the court must notify the third party and any interested party of the order and the amount ordered to be paid. [Next four sentences identical to first four sentences of para.4.1.6. save for reference to r.45.10(8) in lieu of reference to r.45.8(8).] The rules provide also that a party who has incurred costs as a result of serious misconduct by a third party should provide assistance to the court as to the amount involved, where the court considers making an order on its own initiative: CrimPR 45.10(5)(b)(iii).

4.7.7 If the court is considering making a third party costs order on its own initiative the appropriate officer should serve notice in writing on the third party and any other parties. Where a party applies for such an order the application must be in writing, and must contain the names and addresses of the applicant, the other parties and the third party against whom the order is sought, together with a summary of the facts upon which the applicant intends to rely, including in particular details of the alleged misconduct of the third party.

4.7.8 At the hearing of the application the court may proceed in the absence of the third party, and of any other party if satisfied that that party has been duly served with the notice by the appropriate officer, and with a copy of the application. The power to make a third party costs order extends to making such an order against a government department where there has been serious misconduct, including deliberate or negligent failure to attend to one's duties, or falling below a proper standard in that regard, but there is a higher threshold for liability than for a wasted costs order (*Ahmati* [2006] EWCA Crim 1826).

Appeals against third party costs orders

4.7.9 A third party against whom a third party costs order has been made may appeal against that order. In the case of an order made by a magistrates' court, appeal is to the Crown Court, and CrimPR, Pt 34 [§ 2-117 and following] sets out the procedure. In the case of an order made at first instance by the Crown Court, the appeal is to the Court of Appeal and the procedure is set out in CrimPR, Pt 39 [§§ 7-380 and following]. In both cases the time limit for appeal is 21 days from the date of the order. **F-24**

4.7.10 [Identical to para.4.2.10.]

Part 5: Assessment of Costs

Assessment of defence costs out of central funds

5.1.1 Where a legally aided defendant wishes to claim out of pocket expenses or costs for work which has not been done under the representation order, the assessment of those costs should be carried out at the same time as the assessment of his solicitor's costs under the representation order and the solicitors should ensure that the two claims are submitted together for assessment (*R. (Brewer) v Supreme Court Costs Office* [2006] EWHC 1955 (Admin); [2007] Costs L.R. 20, DC). **F-25**

Appeals to a costs judge

5.2.1 Under reg.9 of the General Regulations, or under CrimPR 45.11(7), a party dissatisfied with a costs assessment may apply to the relevant authority for a review of that assessment. Under reg.10 of the General Regulations, or under CrimPR 45.12, appeal against a decision on such a review lies to the senior costs judge of the Senior Courts Costs Office. Written notice of appeal must be given within 21 days of receipt of the reasons for the decision, or within such longer time as a costs judge may direct. **F-26**

5.2.2 The notice of appeal should be in the form set out in Sch.3 below (adapted where appropriate) setting out in separate numbered paragraphs each fee or item of costs or disbursement in respect of which the appeal is brought, showing the amount claimed for the item, the amount determined and the grounds of objection to the decision on the assessment or determination.

5.2.3 Advocates and litigators must provide detailed grounds of objection in respect of each item in accordance with reg.10(2) of the General Regulations, CrimPR 45.12(2)(b) and reg.29(5) of the Criminal Legal Aid (Remuneration) Regulations 2013 [Appendix G-33]. Reference to accompanying correspondence or documents is insufficient and will result in the appeal being dismissed.

5.2.4 The appeal must be accompanied by a cheque for the appropriate fee made payable to "H.M. Paymaster General". The notice must state whether the appellant wishes to appear or to be represented, or whether he will accept a decision given in his absence.

The following documents should be forwarded with the notice of appeal:

(a) a legible copy of the bill of costs (with any supporting submissions) showing the allowance made;
(b) a copy of the advocate's fee claim and any fee note, together with any note or memorandum by the advocate submitted to the determining authority;
(c) a copy of the original determination of costs and a copy of the redetermination;
(d) a copy of the appellant's representations made to the determining authority on seeking redetermination;
(e) the written reasons of the determining officer;
(f) a copy of the representation order and any authorities given under it.

Supporting papers

F-27 **5.3.1** Appellants who do not intend to appear at the hearing of their appeal should lodge all relevant supporting papers with the documents listed above. Appellants who do wish to attend the hearing of their appeal should not lodge their supporting papers until directed to do so by the Senior Courts Costs Office.

5.3.2 Appellants are reminded that it is their responsibility to procure the lodgment of the relevant papers, even if they are in the possession of the Crown Court or other persons. Appeals may be listed for dismissal if the relevant papers are not lodged when required.

5.3.3 Delays frequently arise in dealing with appeals by advocates because the relevant papers have been returned by the court to the litigator whose file may not be readily available or who may have destroyed the papers. These problems would be avoided if the advocate were, immediately on lodging with the court a request for redetermination, to ask instructing litigators to retain the relevant papers.

5.3.4 In complex or multi-handed appeals guidance should be sought from the Clerk of Appeals before lodging a large volume of papers to avoid duplication and unnecessary reading by the Costs Judge.

Time limits

F-28 **5.4.1** Appellants who are likely to be unable to lodge an appeal within the time limits should make an application prior to the expiry of the time limit seeking a reasonable extension with brief reasons for the request.

5.4.2 Appellants who have not been able to lodge an appeal within the time limits, and who have failed to make application before those time limits have expired, should make application to the costs judge for leave to appeal out of time in writing setting out in full the circumstances relied upon.

5.4.3 If the application is refused on the papers it may be renewed to a costs judge at an oral hearing. Such oral hearings should not be necessary if a full explanation is given in writing in the initial request for extension of time.

5.4.4 Appeals should not be delayed because certain relevant documents are not available. An accompanying note setting out the missing documents and an undertaking to lodge within a specified period, normally not exceeding 28 days, should be sent with the notice of appeal.

Appeals to the High Court

F-29 **5.5.1** An appellant desiring to appeal to a High Court judge from a decision of the costs judge should, within 21 days of the decision, request the costs judge to certify that a point of principle of general importance (specifying the same) is involved. The appeal can proceed only if such a certificate is granted. Such an appeal is instituted by appellant's notice under CPR, Pt 52 in the Queen's Bench Division within 21 days of the receipt of the costs judge's certificate. The times may be extended by a costs judge or a High Court judge as the case may be.

5.5.2 The appellant's notice must contain full particulars of the item or items, or the amount allowed in respect of which the appeal is brought. After issue of the notice the appellant must forthwith lodge with the clerk of appeals at the Senior Courts Costs Office all the documents used on the appeal to the costs judge.

5.5.3 The appellant's notice should be served in accordance with the provisions of CPR, Pt 6 and the practice direction thereto. It is no longer necessary to endorse an estimate of the length of hearing on the appellant's notice. The clerk of appeals will obtain from the judge a date for hearing and will notify the parties.

5.5.4 The appeal, which is final, will be heard by a judge of the Queen's Bench Division who will normally sit with two assessors, one of whom will be a costs judge and the other a practising litigator or advocate.

5.5.5 After the appeal has been heard and determined the clerk will obtain the documents together with a sealed copy of any order of the judge which may have been drawn up and will notify the court concerned of the result of the appeal.

Part 6: Contribution Orders and Recovery of Defence Costs Orders

Contribution orders in the Crown Court

6.1.1 In proceedings to which the Criminal Legal Aid (Contribution Orders) Regulations 2013 (SI 2013/483) [§6-218] apply, namely proceedings in the Crown Court, the represented defendant may be liable to make payments under an income contribution order. If the defendant is convicted or if the representation order is withdrawn, the defendant may be required to pay the whole or part of the cost of the representation under a capital contribution order. **F-30**

6.1.2 If the trial judge considers that there are exceptional reasons, a defendant who is acquitted may nevertheless be required to pay the whole or part of the costs of the representation in the Crown Court: reg.25(b).

6.1.3 Where a defendant is convicted of one or more, but not all, offences he may apply in writing to the trial judge (or a judge nominated for that purpose by the resident judge) for an order that he pay a proportion only of the costs of the representation in the Crown Court on the ground that it would be manifestly unreasonable that he pay the whole amount: reg.26. An application must be made within 21 days of the date on which the individual is dealt with. The judge may refuse the application or make an order specifying the proportion of costs which the defendant must pay.

Recovery of defence costs orders on appeals

6.2.1 Recovery of defence costs orders ("RDCOs") are created and regulated by the Criminal Legal Aid (Recovery of Defence Costs Orders) Regulations 2013 (SI 2013/511) [§6-193]. They may be made in proceedings in any court other than the magistrates' court or the Crown Court. **F-31**

6.2.2 Where an individual receives criminal legal aid in respect of proceedings, the court before which the proceedings are heard (other than a magistrates' court or the Crown Court) must make an order requiring him to pay some or all of the costs of any representation, except for the following:

- where the defendant has appeared in the magistrates' court and/or the Crown Court only;
- where the court has allowed the appeals of the defendant in respect of every conviction, unless the court considers it reasonable in all the circumstances to make an order; or
- where the defendant does not have capital exceeding £3,000 or equity in the main dwelling exceeding £100,000 or gross annual income exceeding £22,325; or
- where the defendant is in receipt of a qualifying benefit; or
- where the defendant is under the age of 18 on the date on which his application for legal aid was determined; or
- where it would not be reasonable to make an order on the basis of the information and evidence available; or
- where in the exceptional circumstances of the case an order would involve undue financial hardship: Criminal Legal Aid (Recovery of Defence Costs Orders) Regulations 2003, regs 6-11.

6.2.3 Where the court exercises its discretion on the basis of reasonableness or undue financial hardship it must give reasons for reaching that decision: reg.11.

6.2.4 Subject to the exceptions set out above, the court must make an RDCO and must give reasons for the terms of the order: reg.5.

6.2.5 The court (or the registrar of the Supreme Court or the Registrar of Criminal Appeals, as the case may be) must assess the financial resources of the defendant (including the resources of the defendant's partner unless the partner has a contrary interest) or refer the matter to the Director of Legal Aid Casework for assessment. When determining the amount, other than in exceptional circumstances, the court shall not take into account:

- the first £3,000 of available capital,
- the first £100,000 of equity in the main dwelling, or
- gross annual income of less than £22,235: reg.15.

These limits are prescribed and are subject to regular amendment.

6.2.6 The court may ask the defendant's litigator to provide an estimate of the total costs which **F-32**

are likely to be incurred under the representation order. It should be borne in mind that whilst the litigator may have little difficulty in producing an estimate of the costs incurred up until the point of request, this estimate may not be accurate. In a very high cost case which has been managed under contract, the litigator will be able to provide accurate figures of all costs incurred to date and to say what costs have been agreed as reasonable for the next stage of the case. Where an RDCO is made based on this estimate the defendant's litigator must inform the Lord Chancellor if it subsequently transpires that the costs incurred were lower than the amount ordered to be paid under an RDCO. In these circumstances, where the defendant has paid the amount ordered, the balance will be repaid to him: reg.19.

6.2.7 The defendant is obliged to provide such details or evidence of his means as is required by the court. At the end of the case where the court is considering whether to make an RDCO or what order to make, it may adjourn the making of the order and order that any further information which is required should be provided: reg.16. This power may be used where further information has come to light during the case about the defendant's means.

6.2.8 Where information required under the Regulations is not provided the court may nevertheless make an RDCO for the full cost of the representation incurred under the representation order or such proportion of the cost as the court considers reasonable: reg.17.

6.2.9 Where it appears to the court that the defendant has transferred any financial resources to another person, directly or indirectly deprived themselves of any resources, or converted any resources into resources which are to be disregarded under the regulations, the court must treat such financial resources as part of the defendant's financial resources or as not so converted. Where it appears to the court that another person has been substantially maintaining the defendant or the defendant's partner or that any of the financial resources of another person have been made available to the defendant or the defendant's partner, the court may assess the amount of the maintenance or the resources made available and treat such amounts as the resources of the defendant: reg.14.

Part 7: Costs in Restraint, Confiscation or Receivership Proceedings

The order for costs

F-33 **7.1.1** This part of the practice direction applies where the Crown Court is deciding whether to make an order for costs in relation to restraint proceedings or receivership proceedings brought under the POCA 2002. (Confiscation proceedings are treated for costs purposes as part of the criminal trial.) The court has discretion as to: whether costs are payable by one party to another; the amount of those costs; and, when they are to be paid. The general rule is that if the court decides to make an order about costs the unsuccessful party will be ordered to pay the costs of the successful party but the court may make a different order: CrimPR 33.47(3)

7.1.2 Attention is drawn to the fact that in receivership proceedings the rules provide that the Crown Court may make orders in respect of security to be given by a receiver to cover his liability for his acts and omissions as a receiver: CrimPR 33.60. The court may also make orders in relation to determining the remuneration of the receiver: CrimPR 33.61. (Paragraph 7.3 below deals with determination of the remuneration of a receiver.)

7.1.3 In deciding what if any order to make about costs the court is required to have regard to all the circumstances including the conduct of all the parties and whether a party has succeeded on part of an application, even if that party has not been wholly successful.

7.1.4 The rules set out the type of order which the court may make (the list is not exclusive):

(a) a proportion of another party's costs;
(b) a stated amount in respect of another party's costs;
(c) costs from or until a certain date only;
(d) costs incurred before proceedings have begun;
(e) costs relating to particular steps taken in the proceedings;
(f) costs relating only to a distinct part of the proceedings; and
(g) interest on costs from or until a certain date including a date before the making of an order.

7.1.5 The court is required, where it is practicable, to award a proportion (e.g. a percentage) of the costs, or costs between certain dates, rather than making an order relating only to a distinct part or issue in the proceedings. The latter type of order makes it extremely difficult for the costs to be assessed.

7.1.6 Where the court orders a party to pay costs it may, in addition, order an amount to be paid on account by one party to another before the costs are assessed. Where the court makes such an order, the order should state the amount to be paid and the date on or before which payment is to be made.

Assessment of costs

F-34 **7.2.1** Where the Crown Court makes an order for costs in restraint, or receivership, proceedings it may make an assessment of the costs itself there and then (a summary assessment), or order assessment of the costs under CrimPR 45.11: CrimPR 33.48(1). If the court neither makes an assessment of the costs nor orders assessment as specified above, the order for costs will be treated as an order for the amount of costs to be decided by assessment under r.45.11 unless the order otherwise provides.

7.2.2 Whenever the court awards costs to be assessed it should consider whether to exercise the power to order the paying party to pay such sum of money as it thinks just, on account of those costs.

7.2.3 In carrying out the assessment of costs the court or the assessing authority is required to allow only costs which are proportionate to the matters in issue, and to resolve any doubt which it may have, as to whether the costs were reasonably incurred or were reasonable and proportionate in amount, in favour of the paying party.

7.2.4 The court or assessing authority carrying out the assessment should have regard to all the circumstances in deciding whether costs were proportionately or reasonably incurred or proportionate and reasonable in amount. Effect must be given to any orders for costs which have already been made. The court or the assessing authority should also have regard to:

- (a) the conduct of all the parties, including in particular conduct before as well as during the proceedings;
- (b) the amount or value of any property involved;
- (c) the importance of the matter to all the parties;
- (d) the particular complexity of the matter or the difficulty or novelty of the questions raised;
- (e) the skill, effort, specialised knowledge and responsibility involved;
- (f) the time spent on the case; and
- (g) the place where and the circumstances in which work or any part of it was done.

7.2.5 In applying the test of proportionality regard should be had to the objective of dealing with cases justly. Dealing with a case justly includes, so far as practicable, dealing with it in ways which are proportionate to:

- (i) the amount of money involved;
- (ii) the importance of the case;
- (iii) the complexity of the issues; and
- (iv) the financial position of each party.

The relationship between the total of the costs incurred and the financial value of the claim may not be a reliable guide.

7.2.6 In any proceedings there will be costs which will inevitably be incurred and which are necessary for the successful conduct of the case. Litigators are not required to conduct litigation at rates which are uneconomic, thus in a modest claim the proportion of costs is likely to be higher than in a large claim and may even equal or possibly exceed the amount in dispute.

7.2.7 Where a hearing takes place, the time taken by the court in dealing with a particular issue may not be an accurate guide to the amount of time properly spent by the legal or other representatives in preparing for the trial of that issue.

7.2.8 The Criminal Procedure Rules do not apply to the assessment of costs in proceedings to the extent that s.26 of the LASPOA 2012 (costs in civil proceedings) applies and statutory instruments made under that Act make different provision.

Remuneration of a receiver

7.3.1 A receiver may only charge for his services if the Crown Court so directs and specifies the basis on which the receiver is to be remunerated: CrimPR 33.61(2). The Crown Court (unless it orders otherwise) is required to award such sum as is reasonable and proportionate in all the circumstances. In arriving at the figure for remuneration the court should take into account: **F-35**

- (a) the time properly given by the receiver and his staff to the receivership;
- (b) the complexity of the receivership;
- (c) any responsibility of an exceptional kind or degree which falls on the receiver in consequence of the receivership;
- (d) the effectiveness with which the receiver appears to be carrying out or to have carried out his duties; and
- (e) the value and nature of the subject matter of the receivership.

7.3.2 The Crown Court may instead of determining the receiver's remuneration itself refer it to be ascertained by the assessing authority of the Crown Court. In these circumstances CrimPR 45.11 to 45.13 (which deal with review by the assessing authority, further review by a costs judge and appeal to a High Court judge) have effect.

Procedure on appeal to the Court of Appeal

7.4 The costs of and incidental to all proceedings on an appeal to the criminal division of the Court of Appeal against orders made in restraint proceedings, or appeals against or relating to the making of receivership orders, are in the discretion of the court: POCA 2002, s.89(4) [§ 5B-170]. **F-36**

7.4.1 The court has full power to determine by whom and to what extent the costs are to be paid.

7.4.2 In any such proceedings the court may disallow or (as the case may be) order the legal or other representative concerned to meet the whole of any wasted costs or such part of them as may be determined in accordance with the Criminal Procedure Rules. (As to wasted costs orders, see Pt 4 above.)

7.4.3 These provisions have retrospective effect in relation to proceedings on appeals in respect of offences committed or alleged to have been committed on or after 24 March 2003: Courts Act 2003, s.94(3).

Part 8: Advice on Appeal to the Court of Appeal (Criminal Division)

F-37 **8.1** In all cases the procedure set out in "*A Guide to Proceedings in the Court of Appeal (Criminal Division)*" published by the Criminal Appeal Office with the approval of the Lord Chief Justice [Appendix J] should be followed.

8.2 This procedure requires that immediately following the conclusion of a case, legal representatives should see the defendant, and the advocate should express orally his final view as to the prospects of a successful appeal (whether against conviction or sentence or both). Litigators should not wait to be asked for advice by the defendant. In simple cases this will involve little or no expense. If the procedure is not followed and the work has not been done with due care, fees may be reduced accordingly. If there are no reasonable grounds of appeal, that should be confirmed in writing and a copy provided then or as soon as practicable thereafter, to the defendant by the litigator. Where the advocate's immediate and final view is that there are no reasonable grounds of appeal, no additional fee will normally be allowed. If there are reasonable grounds, grounds of appeal should be drafted, signed and sent to the instructing litigator as soon as possible. Litigators should immediately send a copy of the documents received from the advocate to the defendant. Provision for advice or assistance on appeal is included in the trial representation order issued by the Crown Court.

8.3 Notice and grounds (Form NG and the advocate's advice) should be lodged at the Crown Court (where the trial was conducted) within 28 days from the date of the conviction in the case of an application for leave to appeal against conviction and within 28 days from the date of sentence in the case of an application for leave to appeal against sentence. On a reference by the CCRC, Form NG and grounds should be served on the Registrar not more than 56 days after the Registrar has served notice that the CCRC has referred a conviction and not more than 28 days in the case of a sentence referral.

8.4 When (a) positive advice on appeal has been given; and (b) notice and grounds have been lodged with the Crown Court on the strength of that advice, the Registrar of Criminal Appeals is the authority for decisions about representation orders, in accordance with the principle that the court before which there are proceedings is the court with power to grant a right to representation. The Crown Court should not determine the fees in respect of the work in connection with the advice, notice and grounds unless the litigator confirms that the notice and grounds were not given on the litigator's or the advocate's advice. Where no notice of application is given, either because of unfavourable advice or despite favourable advice, the appropriate authority is the appropriate officer for the Crown Court.

8.5 If it appears that the defendant was never given advice, the Crown Court should direct the litigators' attention to this fact and if there is no satisfactory explanation as to why no advice was sent, the determining officer should bear this in mind when determining the litigator's costs and should draw the litigator's attention to the above mentioned guide.

8.6 Prior to the service of the notice and grounds of appeal, the Registrar of Criminal Appeals has no power to grant a representation order.

F-38 **8.7** The Crown Court can only amend a representation order in favour of fresh legal representatives if advice on appeal has not been given by trial legal representatives and it is necessary and reasonable for another legal representative to be instructed.

Part 9: VAT

F-38a [*Not set out in this work.*]

B. THE REGULATIONS

Costs in Criminal Cases (General) Regulations 1986 (SI 1986/1335)

Part I—

Preliminary (regs 1, 2)

Citation, commencement and interpretation

1.–(1) [*Citation and commencement.*] **F-39**

(2) In these Regulations, "the Act" means the Prosecution of Offences Act 1985 and expressions which are defined by regulations 4 and 15 have the meanings assigned to them by those regulations for the purposes of Parts III and V respectively of these Regulations.

2. [*Revocations.*]

PART II–

COSTS UNNECESSARILY OR IMPROPERLY INCURRED (REG.3)

Unnecessary or improper acts and omissions

3.–(1) Subject to the provisions of this regulation, where at any time during criminal proceedings– **F-40**

(a) a magistrates' court,

(b) the Crown Court, or

(c) the Court of Appeal is satisfied that costs have been incurred in respect of the proceedings by one of the parties as a result of an unnecessary or improper act or omission by, or on behalf of, another party to the proceedings, the court may, after hearing the parties, order that all or part of the costs so incurred by that party shall be paid to him by the other party.

(2) When making an order under paragraph (1), the court may take into account any other order as to costs which has been made in respect of the proceedings.

(3) An order made under paragraph (1) shall specify the amount of costs to be paid in pursuance of the order.

(4) Where an order under paragraph (1) has been made, the court may take that order into account when making any other order as to costs in respect of the proceedings.

(5) No order under paragraph (1) shall be made by a magistrates' court which requires a person under the age of seventeen who has been convicted of an offence to pay an amount by way of costs which exceeds the amount of any fine imposed on him.

[This regulation is printed as amended by the Costs in Criminal Cases (General) Regulations 2008 (SI 2008/2448).]

PART IIA–

WASTED COSTS ORDERS (REGS 3A–3D)

Application and definitions

3A. This Part of these Regulations applies to action taken by a court under section 19A of the Act and in this Part of these Regulations– **F-41**

"wasted costs order" means any action taken by a court under section 19A of the Act; and

"interested party" means the party benefiting from the wasted costs order and, where he was receiving services funded for him as part of the Criminal Defence Service, or provided for him under arrangements made for the purposes of Part 1 of the Legal Aid, Sentencing and Punishment of Offenders Act 2012, or an order for the payment of costs out of central funds was made in his favour, shall include the authority responsible for determining costs payable in respect of work done under the representation order, or under the determination for representation for the purposes of criminal proceedings, or out of central funds as the case may be.

[This regulation is printed as amended by the Costs in Criminal Cases (General) (Amendment) Regulations 2004 (SI 2004/2408); and the Legal Aid, Sentencing and Punishment of Offenders Act 2012 (Consequential, Transitional and Saving Provisions) Regulations 2013 (SI 2013/534).]

General

3B.–(1) A wasted costs order may provide for the whole or any part of the wasted costs to be disallowed or ordered to be paid and the court shall specify the amount of such costs. **F-42**

(3) When making a wasted costs order the court may take into account any other order as to costs in respect of the proceedings and may take the wasted costs order into account when making any other such order.

[This regulation is printed as amended by SI 2004/2408 (above); and the Costs in Criminal Cases (General) (Amendment) Regulations 2009 (SI 2009/2720).]

Appeals

3C.–(1) A legal or other representative against whom the wasted costs order is made may appeal– **F-43**

(a) in the case of an order made by a magistrates' court, to the Crown Court, and

(b) in the case of an order made at first instance by the Crown Court to the Court of Appeal.

(6) The appeal court may affirm, vary or revoke the order as it thinks fit.

[This regulation is printed as amended by SI 2004/2408, above; and SI 2009/2720 (above).]

F-44 **3D.** *Recovery of sums due under a wasted costs order (amended by SI 2013/534)*
Where the person required to make a payment in respect of sums due under a wasted costs order fails to do so, the payment may be recovered summarily as a sum adjudged to be paid as a civil debt by order of a magistrates' court by the party benefiting from the order, save that where he was receiving services funded for him as part of the Criminal Defence Service, or provided for him under arrangements made for the purposes of Pt 1 of the Legal Aid, Sentencing and Punishment of Offenders Act 2012, or an order for the payment of costs out of central funds was made in his favour, the power to recover shall be exercisable by the Lord Chancellor.

Part IIB—

Third party costs orders (regs 3E–3I)

Application and definitions

F-45 **3E.**—(1) This Part of these Regulations applies where there are, or have been criminal proceedings in a magistrates' court, the Crown Court or the Court of Appeal.

(2) In this Part of these Regulations—

"court" means the court in which the criminal proceedings are taking, or took, place;

"interested party" means the party benefiting from the third party costs order and, where he was receiving services funded for him as part of the Criminal Defence Service, or provided for him under arrangements made for the purposes of Part 1 of the Legal Aid, Sentencing and Punishment of Offenders Act 2012, or an order for the payment of costs out of central funds was made in his favour, shall include the authority responsible for determining costs payable in respect of work done under the representation order, or under the determination for representation for the purposes of criminal proceedings, or out of central funds as the case may be;

"party" means a party to the criminal proceedings;

"third party" means a person who is not a party;

"third party costs order" means an order as to the payment, by a third party, of costs incurred by a party in accordance with regulation 3F.

[This regulation is printed as amended by SI 2008/2448 and SI 2013/534]

General

F-46 **3F.**—(1) If—

(a) there has been serious misconduct (whether or not constituting a contempt of court) by a third party; and

(b) the court considers it appropriate, having regard to that misconduct, to make a third party costs order against him the court may order the third party to pay all or part of the costs incurred or wasted by any party as a result of the misconduct.

(6) A third party costs order shall specify the amount of costs to be paid in pursuance of the order.

(7) When a third party costs order has been made the court shall notify the third party and any interested party of the order and the amount ordered to be paid.

[This regulation is printed as amended by SI 2008/2448 and SI 2009/2720

Procedure for third party costs orders

F-47 **3G.** [*Revoked by SI 2009/2720.*]

Appeals

3H.—(1) A third party against whom a third party costs order is made may appeal—

(a) in the case of an order made by a magistrates' court, to the Crown Court; and

(b) in the case of an order made at first instance by the Crown Court, to the Court of Appeal.

(6) The appeal court may affirm, vary or revoke the order as it thinks fit.

[This regulation is printed as amended by SI 2009/2720]

Recovery of sums due under a third party costs order

3I. Where the person required to make a payment in respect of sums due under a third party costs order fails to do so, the payment may be recovered summarily as a sum adjudged to be paid as a civil debt by order of a magistrates' court by the party benefiting from the order, save that where he was receiving services funded for him as part of the Criminal Defence Service [, or provided for him under arrangements made for the purposes of Part 1 of the Legal Aid, Sentencing and Punishment of Offenders Act 2012,] 2 or an order for the payment of costs out of central funds was made in his favour, the power to recover shall be exercisable by the Lord Chancellor.] 1 **F-48**

[Inserted subject to the transitional provisions specified in SI 2004/2408 reg.2(3) by Costs in Criminal Cases (General)(Amendment) Regulations 2004/2408 reg.7 (October 18, 2004).]

PART III–

COSTS OUT OF CENTRAL FUNDS (REGS 4–13)

Application and definitions

4. This Part of these Regulations applies to costs payable out of central funds in pursuance of an order made under or by virtue of Part II of the Act and in this Part of these Regulations– **F-49**

"applicant" means the person in whose favour a costs order has been made;

"appropriate authority" has the meaning assigned to it by regulation 5;

"costs judge" means a taxing master of the Senior Courts;

"costs order" means an order made under or by virtue of Part II of the Act for the payment of costs out of central funds;

"determination of financial ineligibility", in relation to an individual and proceedings, means a determination under section 21 of the Legal Aid, Sentencing and Punishment of Offenders Act 2012 that the individual's financial resources are such that the individual is not eligible for representation under section 16 of that Act for the purposes of the proceedings;

"Director of Legal Aid casework" means the civil servant designated under section 4(1) of the Legal Aid, Sentencing and Punishment of Offenders Act 2012;

"disbursements" do not include any payment made out of central funds to a witness, interpreter, intermediary or medical practitioner in accordance with Part V of these Regulations;

"expenses" means out of pocket expenses, travelling expenses and subsistence allowance;

"presiding judge" means the judge who presided at the hearing in respect of which the costs are payable; and "relevant Crown Court proceedings" means any of the following–

(a) proceedings in the Crown Court in respect of an offence for which the accused has been sent by a magistrates' court to the Crown Court for trial;

(b) proceedings in the Crown Court relating to an offence in respect of which a bill of indictment has been preferred by virtue of section 2(2)(b) of the Administration of Justice (Miscellaneous Provisions) Act 1933;

(c) proceedings in the Crown Court following an order by the Court of Appeal or the Supreme Court for a retrial.

[This regulation is printed as amended by the Costs in Criminal Cases (General) Regulations 1999 (SI 1999/2096); the Constitutional Reform Act 2005, s.59(4); SI 2008/2448 and the Costs in Criminal Cases (General) (Amendment) (No. 2) Regulations 2013 (SI 2013/2830).]

Costs fixed by the court

4A. Where the court fixes an amount to be paid to the accused out of central funds in accordance with section 16(6C) of the Act or sections 62A(4) or 135A(4) of the Extradition Act 2003, it must, in relation to any amounts payable in respect of legal costs, calculate such amounts in accordance with the rates or scales or other provision made by the Lord Chancellor pursuant to regulation 7(7), whether or not that results in the fixing of an amount that the court considers reasonably sufficient or necessary to compensate the accused. **F-50**

[This regulation was inserted by the Costs in Criminal Cases (General) Regulations 2012 (SI 2012/1804).]

The appropriate authority

5.–(1) Costs shall be determined by the appropriate authority in accordance with these Regulations. **F-51**

(2) Subject to paragraph (3), the appropriate authority shall be–

(a) the registrar of criminal appeals in the case of proceedings in the Court of Appeal,

(b) the master of the Crown Office in the case of proceedings in a Divisional Court of the Queen's Bench Division,

(c) an officer appointed by the Lord Chancellor in the case of proceedings in the Crown Court or, subject to sub-paragraph (d), a magistrates' court,

(d) [a justices' legal adviser (a person nominated by the Lord Chancellor who is authorised to exercise functions under section 28(1) of the Courts Act 2003) in the case of proceedings in a magistrates' court [, where the costs consist solely of expenses claimed by the applicant

(3) The appropriate authority may appoint or authorise the appointment of determining officers to act on its behalf under these Regulations in accordance with directions given by it or on its behalf.

[This regulation is printed as amended by SI 2008/2448 and by reg.3 of the Courts and Tribunals (Judiciary and Functions of Staff) Act 2018 (Consequential, Transitional and Saving Provision) Regulations 2020 (SI 2020/100) so that in para.(2)(d), "the justices' clerk" is replaced with "a justices' legal adviser (a person nominated by the Lord Chancellor who is authorised to exercise functions under section 28(1) of the Courts Act 2003)"]

Claims for costs

F-52 **6.**—(1) Subject to regulation 12, no claim for costs shall be entertained unless it is submitted within three months of the date on which the costs order was made.

(2) Subject to paragraph (3), a claim for costs shall be submitted to the appropriate authority, in such form or manner as it may direct and shall be accompanied by receipts or other evidence of the applicant's payment of the costs claimed, and any receipts or other documents in support of any disbursements claimed.

(3) A claim shall—

(a) summarise the items of work done by a solicitor;

(b) state, where appropriate, the dates on which items of work were done, the time taken and the sums claimed,

(c) specify any disbursements claimed, including counsel's fees, the circumstances in which they were incurred and the amounts claimed in respect of them, and

(d) contain either full particulars, including the date and outcome, of any claim for payment in respect of services funded for the applicant as part of the Criminal Defence Service, or provided for him under arrangements made for the purposes of Part 1 of the Legal Aid, Sentencing and Punishment of Offenders Act 2012, or a certificate by the solicitor that he has not made, and will not make, any such claim.

(4) Where there are any special circumstances which should be drawn to the attention of the appropriate authority, the applicant shall specify them.

(5) The applicant shall supply such further particulars, information and documents as the appropriate authority may require.

[This regulation is printed as amended by SI 1999/2096; the Costs in Criminal Cases (General) (Amendment) Regulations 2001 (SI 2001/611); SI 2008/2448 and SI 2013/534]

The reference to a solicitor is to be taken as including a reference to:

(a) a body recognised by the Law Society under the Administration of Justice Act 1985, s.9 (Solicitors' Recognised Bodies Order 1991 (SI 1991/2684), arts 2 and 4, and Sch.1); and

(b) a licensed body, i.e. a body that holds a licence issued by the Law Society under Pt 5 of the Legal Services Act 2007 (Legal Services Act 2007 (Designation as a Licensing Authority) (No. 2) Order 2011 (SI 2011/2866), arts 1(3) and 8(1) and (2)(a), and Sch.2).

Determination of costs

F-53 **7.**—(1) The appropriate authority shall consider the claim and any further particulars, information or documents submitted by the applicant under regulation 6(5), and shall allow costs in respect of—

(a) such work as appears to it to have been actually and reasonably done; and

(b) such disbursements as appear to it to have been actually and reasonably incurred.

(2) In calculating costs under paragraph (1) the appropriate authority shall take into account all the relevant circumstances of the case including the nature, importance, complexity and difficulty of the work and the time involved.

(3) Any doubts which the appropriate authority may have as to whether the costs were reasonably incurred or were reasonable in amount shall be resolved against the applicant.

(4) The costs awarded shall not exceed the costs actually incurred.

(5) Subject to paragraph (6), the appropriate authority shall allow such legal costs as it considers reasonably sufficient to compensate the applicant for any expenses properly incurred by him in the proceedings.

(6) Where the subject of a costs order is an individual and–

(a) the order was made under section 16(1), (3) or (4)(a)(ii) or (iii) or (d) of the Act;

(b) the order was made under section 16 and includes legal costs that were incurred in proceedings in a court below which were–

(i) proceedings in a magistrates' court; or

(ii) proceedings on an appeal to the Crown Court under section 108 of the Magistrates' Courts Act 1980;

(c) the order includes an amount in respect of legal costs incurred in proceedings in a magistrates' court under the Extradition Act 2003, or

(d) the order was made under section 16(2) of the Act and–

(i) the legal costs were incurred in relevant Crown Court proceedings; and

(ii) the Director of Legal Aid Casework has made a determination of financial ineligibility in relation to the accused and those proceedings, the appropriate authority shall calculate amounts payable out of central funds in respect of legal costs to the individual in accordance with the rates or scales or other provision made by the Lord Chancellor pursuant to paragraph (7), whether or not that results in the fixing of an amount that the appropriate authority considers reasonably sufficient or necessary to compensate the individual.

(7) The Lord Chancellor shall, with the consent of the Treasury, determine provision (whether in the form of rates or scales or other provision) as to how amounts payable out of central funds in respect of legal costs shall be calculated.

[This regulation is printed as substituted by SI 2012/1804 and SI 2013/2830.]

Payment of costs

8.–(1) When the appropriate authority has determined the costs payable to an applicant in accordance with these Regulations, the appropriate authority shall notify the applicant of the costs payable and authorise payment accordingly. **F-54**

(2) Where the costs payable under paragraph (1) are varied as a result of a redetermination under regulation 9, an appeal to a costs judge under regulation 10, or an appeal to the High Court under regulation 11, then–

(a) where the costs are increased, the appropriate authority shall authorise payment of the increase;

(b) where the costs are decreased, the applicant shall repay the amount of such decrease; and

(c) where the payment of the costs of an appeal is ordered under regulation 10(14) or 11(8), the appropriate authority shall authorise such payment to the applicant.

[This regulation is printed as amended by SI 1999/2096; SI 2001/611; and SI 2008/2448]

Redetermination of costs by an appropriate authority

9.–(1) An applicant who is dissatisfied with the costs determined under these Regulations by an appropriate authority in respect of proceedings other than proceedings before a magistrates' court may apply to the appropriate authority to redetermine them. **F-55**

(2) Subject to regulation 12, the application shall be made, within 21 days of the receipt of notification of the costs payable under regulation 8(1), by giving notice in writing to the appropriate authority specifying the items in respect of which the application is made and the grounds of objection and shall be made in such form and manner as the appropriate authority may direct.

(3) The notice of application shall state whether the applicant wishes to appear or to be represented and, if the applicant so wishes, the appropriate authority shall notify the applicant of the time at which it is prepared to hear him or his representative.

(4) The notice of application shall be accompanied by any particulars, information and documents supplied under regulation 6 and the applicant shall supply such further particulars, information and documents as the appropriate authority may require.

(5) The appropriate authority shall redetermine the costs, whether by way of increase, decrease or at the level previously determined, in the light of the objections made by the applicant or on his behalf and shall notify the applicant of its decision.

(6) The applicant may request the appropriate authority to give reasons in writing for its decision and, if so requested, the appropriate authority shall comply with the request.

(7) Subject to regulation 12, any request under paragraph (6) shall be made within 21 days of receiving notification of the decision.

Appeals to a costs judge

F-56 **10.**—(1) Where the appropriate authority has given its reasons for its decision on a redetermination under regulation 9, an applicant who is dissatisfied with that decision may appeal to a costs judge.

(2) Subject to regulation 12, an appeal shall be instituted within 21 days of the receipt of the appropriate authority's reasons by giving notice in writing to the Senior Costs Judge specifying the items in respect of which the appeal is brought and the grounds of objection.

(3) The appellant shall send a copy of any notice given under paragraph (2) to the appropriate authority.

(4) The notice of appeal shall be accompanied by—

(a) a copy of the written notice given under regulation 9(2);

(b) any particulars, information and documents supplied to the appropriate authority under regulation 9, and

(c) the appropriate authority's reasons for its decision given under regulation 9(6).

(5) The notice of appeal shall state whether the appellant wishes to appear or to be represented or whether he will accept a decision given in his absence.

(6) The Senior Costs Judge may, and if so directed by the Lord Chancellor either generally or in a particular case shall, send to the Lord Chancellor a copy of the notice of appeal together with copies of such other documents as the Lord Chancellor may require.

(7) With a view to ensuring that the public interest is taken into account, the Lord Chancellor may arrange for written or oral representations to be made on his behalf and, if he intends to do so, he shall inform the Senior Costs Judge and the appellant.

(8) Any written representations made on behalf of the Lord Chancellor under paragraph (7) shall be sent to the Senior Costs Judge and to the appellant and, in the case of oral representations, the Senior Costs Judge and the appellant shall be informed of the grounds on which such representations will be made.

(9) The appellant shall be permitted a reasonable opportunity to make representations in reply.

(10) The costs judge shall inform the appellant (or his representative) and the Lord Chancellor, where representations have been or are to be made on his behalf, of the date of any hearing and, subject to the provisions of this regulation, may give directions as to the conduct of the appeal.

(11) The costs judge may consult the presiding judge, and the appropriate authority or the determining officer who redetermined the costs on its behalf as the case may be, and may require the appellant to provide any further information which he requires for the purpose of the appeal and, unless the costs judge otherwise directs, no further evidence shall be received on the hearing of the appeal and no ground of objection shall be valid which was not raised on the redetermination under regulation 9.

(12) The costs judge shall have the same powers as the appropriate authority under these Regulations and, in the exercise of such powers, may alter the redetermination of the appropriate authority in respect of any sum allowed, whether by increase or decrease, as he thinks fit.

(13) The costs judge shall communicate his decision and the reasons for it in writing to the appellant, the Lord Chancellor, and the appropriate authority or the determining officer who redetermined the costs on its behalf as the case may be.

(14) Save where he confirms or decreases the sums redetermined under regulation 9, the costs judge may allow the appellant a sum in respect of part or all of any reasonable costs (including any fee payable in respect of an appeal) incurred by him in connection with the appeal.

[This regulation is printed as amended by SI 1999/2096]

Appeals to the High Court

F-57 **11.**—(1) An applicant who is dissatisfied with the decision of a costs judge on an appeal under regulation 10 may apply to a costs judge to certify a point of principle of general importance.

(2) Subject to regulation 12, an application under paragraph (1) shall be made within 21 days of notification of a costs judge's decision under regulation 10(13).

(3) Where a cost judge certifies a point of principle of general importance, the applicant may appeal to the High Court against the decision of a costs judge on an appeal under regulation 10, and the Lord Chancellor shall be a respondent to the appeal.

(4) Subject to regulation 12, an appeal under paragraph (3) shall be instituted within 21 days of receiving a costs judge's certificate under paragraph (1).

(5) Where the Lord Chancellor is dissatisfied with the decision of a costs judge on an appeal under regulation 10 he may, if no appeal has been made by the applicant under paragraph (3), appeal to the High Court against that decision and the applicant shall be a respondent to the appeal.

(6) Subject to regulation 12, an appeal under paragraph (5) shall be instituted within 21 days of

receiving notification of the costs judge's decision under regulation 10(13).

(7) An appeal under paragraphs (3) and (5) shall be brought in the Queen's Bench Division, follow the procedure set out in Part 52 of the Civil Procedure Rules 1998 and shall be heard and determined by a single judge whose decision shall be final.

(8) The judge shall have the same powers as the appropriate authority and a costs judge under these Regulations and may reverse, affirm or amend the decision appealed against or make such other order as he thinks fit.

[This regulation is printed as amended by SI 1999/2096; and the Costs in Criminal Cases (General) (Amendment) Regulations 2005 (SI 2005/2622).]

Time limits

12.—(1) Subject to paragraph (2), the time limit within which there must be made or instituted— **F-58**

(a) a claim for costs by an applicant under regulation 6, an application for a redetermination under regulation 9, or a request for an appropriate authority to give reasons for its decision on a redetermination under regulation 9;

(b) an appeal to a Senior Costs Judge under regulation 10 or an application for a certificate under regulation 11; or

(c) an appeal to the High Court under regulation 11; may, for good reason, be extended by the appropriate authority, the Senior Costs Judge or the High Court, as the case may be.

(2) Where an applicant without good reason has failed (or, if an extension were not granted, would fail) to comply with a time limit, the appropriate authority, the Senior Costs Judge or the High Court, as the case may be, may, in exceptional circumstances, extend the time limit and shall consider whether it is reasonable in the circumstances to reduce the costs; provided that the costs shall not be reduced unless the representative has been allowed a reasonable opportunity to show cause orally or in writing why the costs should not be reduced.

(3) An applicant may appeal to the Senior Costs Judge against a decision made under this regulation by an appropriate authority in respect of proceedings other than proceedings before a magistrates' court and such an appeal shall be instituted within 21 days of the decision being given by giving notice in writing to the Senior Costs Judge specifying the grounds of appeal.

[This regulation is printed as amended by SI 1999/2096 and SI 2005/2622]

Supreme Court

13.—(1) In the case of proceedings in the Supreme Court, the costs payable to any person under section 16(5) or 17(1) of the Act shall be determined by such officer as may be prescribed by the Supreme Court. **F-59**

(2) Subject to paragraph (1), this Part of these regulations shall not apply to proceedings in the Supreme Court.

[This regulation is printed as amended by the Costs in Criminal Cases (General) (Amendment) Regulations 2009 (SI 2009/2720).]

PART IIIA—

FEES OF COURT APPOINTEES (REGS 13A-13C)

13A. Subject to the following provisions of this Part, Part III of these Regulations shall apply, with any necessary modifications, to the determination of the proper fee or costs of a court appointee. **F-60**

13B.—(1) For the purposes of this Part of the Regulations:—

(a) the reference to "solicitor" in regulation 6(3)(a) and any reference to "applicant" in Part III shall be construed as including a reference to a court appointee;

(b) any reference to "costs" in Part III shall be construed as including a reference to the proper fee or costs of a court appointee; and

(c) the words after paragraph (b) in regulation 7(1) shall be omitted.

13C. In this Part of the Regulations "court appointee" means:—

(a) a person appointed by the Crown Court under section 4A of the Criminal Procedure (Insanity) Act 1964 to put the case for the defence;

(b) a legal representative appointed by the court under section 38(4) of the Youth Justice and Criminal Evidence Act 1999 to cross-examine a witness in the interests of the accused.

[Part IIIA was inserted by the Costs in Criminal Cases (General) (Amendment) Regulations 1992 (SI 1992/323). Regulation 13C is printed as subsequently substituted by the Costs in Criminal Cases (General) (Amendment) Regulations 2000 (SI 2000/2094).]

PART IV—

MISCELLANEOUS APPLICATIONS OF THE ACT (REG.14)

Application of sections 16, 17 and 18 of the Act

F-61 **14.**—(1) Sections 17 and 18 of the Act shall apply to proceedings in the Crown Court in respect of a person committed by a magistrates' court to that Court—

(a) with a view to his being sentenced for an indictable offence in accordance with section [5 of the Powers of Criminal Courts (Sentencing) Act 2000]; or

(b) with a view to his being sentenced by the Crown Court under section 6(6) or 9(3) of the Bail Act 1976; or

(c) with a view to the making of a hospital order with an order restricting his discharge under Part III of the Mental Health Act 1983, as they apply where a person is convicted in proceedings before the Crown Court.

(2) Section 18 of the Act shall apply to proceedings in the Crown Court—

(a) in respect of a person committed by a magistrates' court as an incorrigible rogue under section 5 of the Vagrancy Act 1824 as if he were sent for trial before the Crown Court; and

(b) in respect of an appeal under section 14 of the Vagrancy Act 1824 as if the hearing of the appeal were a trial on indictment.

(3) Section 18 of the Act shall apply to proceedings in a magistrates' court or the Crown Court for dealing with an offender—

(a) under any of the following provisions of the Powers of Criminal Courts (Sentencing) Act 2000—

(i) section 13 (commission of further offence by person conditionally discharged);

(ii) section 119(1) or 123 (power of court on conviction of further offence to deal with suspended sentence and breach of requirement of suspended sentence supervision order);

(iii) paragraph 5 of Schedule 1 (power of court on referral back from panel);

(iv) Part II of Schedule 3 (breach of requirement of certain community orders);

(v) paragraphs 1 to 3 of Schedule 5 (breach etc of attendance centre order);

(vi) paragraphs 2 to 4 of Schedule 7 (breach of requirement of supervision order);

(vii) paragraphs 2 to 4 of Schedule 8 (breach of requirement of action plan order or reparation order); and

(b) under any of the following provisions of the Criminal Justice Act 2003—

(ai) section 256AC (breach of supervision requirements imposed under section 256AA);

(i) Part 2 of Schedule 8 (breach of requirement of community order);

(ii) Part 2 of Schedule 12 (breach of community requirement of suspended sentence order or conviction of further offence);

(iii) paragraphs 7 to 9 of Schedule 19A (breach, revocation or amendment of supervision default orders), as if the offender had been tried in those proceedings for the offence for which the order was made or the sentence passed.

(4) Section 16 of the Act shall apply to proceedings in a magistrates' court or the Crown Court in which it is alleged that an offender required to enter into a recognisance to keep the peace or be of good behaviour has failed to comply with a condition of that recognisance, as if that failure were an indictable offence.

[This regulation is printed as amended by the Costs in Criminal Cases (General) (Amendment) (No. 2) Regulations 1992 (SI 1992/2956); SI 2008/2448; the Costs in Criminal Cases (General) (Amendment) Regulations 2013 (SI 2013/2526); and the Costs in Criminal Cases (General) (Amendment) Regulations 2015 (SI 2015/12). The reference in square brackets in para.(1)(a) to s.5 of the PCC(S)A 2000 has been substituted by virtue of s.165(3) of, and Sch.11, para.1(4), to that Act.]

PART V—

ALLOWANCES TO WITNESSES (REGS 15-25)

Definitions

F-62 **15.** In this Part of these Regulations—

"expenses" include compensation to a witness for his trouble or loss of time and out of pocket expenses;

"proceedings in a criminal cause or matter" includes any case in which—

(a) an information charging the accused with an offence is laid before a justice of the peace for any area but not proceeded with; or

(b) the accused is sent for trial but not tried;

"professional witness" means a witness practising as a member of the legal or medical profession or as a dentist, veterinary surgeon or accountant who attends to give professional evidence as to matters of fact;

"private prosecutor" means any person in whose favour an order for the payment of costs out of central funds could be made under section 17 of the Act;

"the relevant amount" has the meaning assigned to it by regulation 17;

"witness" means any person properly attending to give evidence, whether or not he gives evidence or is called at the instance of one of the parties or of the court, but does not include–

(a) a person attending as a witness to character only unless the court has certified that the interests of justice required his attendance;

(b) a member of a police force attending court in his capacity as such;

(c) a full-time officer of an institution to which the Prison Act 1952 applies attending court in his capacity as such; or

(d) a prisoner in respect of any occasion on which he is conveyed to court in custody.

[This regulation is printed as amended by SI 2013/2526]

General

16.–(1) Where, in any proceedings in a criminal cause or matter in a magistrates' court, the Crown Court, a Divisional Court of the Queen's Bench Division, the Court of Appeal or the Supreme Court– **F-63**

(a) a witness attends at the instance of the accused, a private prosecutor or the court; or

(b) an interpreter is required because of the accused's lack of English; or

(ba) a witness called by the defendant is examined through an intermediary under section 29 of the Youth Justice and Criminal Evidence Act 1999; or

(bb) an intermediary is required to assist the defendant; or

(c) a medical practitioner makes a report otherwise than in writing, the expenses properly incurred by a witness referred to in sub-paragraph (a) or by that interpreter, intermediary or medical practitioner shall be allowed out of central funds in accordance with this Part of these Regulations, unless the court directs that the expenses are not to be allowed out of central funds.

(2) Subject to paragraph (3), any entitlement to an allowance under this Part of these Regulations shall be the same whether the witness, interpreter, intermediary or medical practitioner attends on the same day in one case or more than one case.

(3) Paragraph (2) shall not apply to allowances under regulation 25.

[This regulation is printed as amended by SI 2008/2448; SI 2009/2720 and SI 2013/2526]

Determination of rates or scales of allowances payable out of central funds

17. The Lord Chancellor shall, with the consent of the Treasury, determine the rates or scales of allowances payable out of central funds to witnesses, interpreters, intermediaries or medical practitioners and a reference in this Part of these Regulations to an allowance not exceeding the relevant amount means an amount calculated in accordance with the rates or scales so determined **F-64**

Witnesses other than professional or expert witnesses

18.–(1) A witness (other than a witness to whom regulation 19 or 20 applies) may be allowed– **F-65**

(a) a loss allowance not exceeding the relevant amount in respect of–

(i) any expenditure incurred (other than on travelling, lodging or subsistence) to which the witness would not otherwise be subject; or

(ii) any loss of earnings or of benefit under the enactments relating to National Insurance; and

(b) a subsistence allowance not exceeding the relevant amount.

(2) Any other person who in the opinion of the court necessarily attends for the purpose of any proceedings otherwise than to give evidence may be allowed the same allowances under paragraph (1) as if he attended as a witness other than a professional or expert witness.

(3) Paragraph (2) shall not apply to–

(a) a member of a police force attending court in his capacity as such;

(b) a full-time officer of an institution to which the Prison Act 1952 applies attending court in his capacity as such, or

(c) a prisoner in respect of any occasion on which he is conveyed to court in custody.

Professional witnesses

F-66 **19.** A professional witness may be allowed a professional witness allowance not exceeding the relevant amount

Expert witnesses etc.

20. (1) The court may make an allowance in respect of an expert witness for attending to give expert evidence and for work in connection with its preparation of such an amount as it may consider reasonable having regard to the nature and difficulty of the case and the work necessarily involved.

(2) Paragraph (1) shall apply, with the necessary modifications, to—

(a) an interpreter or intermediary, or

(b) a medical practitioner who makes a report otherwise than in writing for the purpose of section 11 of the Powers of Criminal Courts (Sentencing) Act 2000 as it applies to an expert witness.

Night allowances.

21. (1) A professional or expert witness who is necessarily absent from his place of residence overnight may be allowed a night allowance not exceeding the relevant amount.

(2) An interpreter, intermediary or medical practitioner who receives an allowance under regulation 20 may be allowed the same night allowance as if he attended as a professional or expert witness.

22. [*Seamen.*]

Prosecutors and defendants

F-67 **23.** A person in whose favour an order is made under section 16, 17 or 19(4) of the Act may be allowed the same subsistence allowance and travelling expenses as if he attended as a witness other than a professional or expert witness.

24. [*Travelling expenses.*]

Written medical reports

F-68 **25.**—(1) A medical practitioner who makes a written report to a court in pursuance of a request to which section 19(3B) of the Act applies may be allowed a medical report allowance not exceeding the relevant amount.

(2) A medical practitioner who makes a report to which paragraph (1) applies and incurs travelling expenses in connection with the preparation of that report may be allowed a travelling allowance not exceeding the relevant amount.

(3) Nothing in this regulation shall apply to a report by the medical officer of an institution to which the Prison Act 1952 applies.

[This regulation is printed as amended by SI 2009/2720]

Part VI—

Recovery of sums paid out of the legal aid fund or central funds (regs 26, 27)

Directions by the Lord Chancellor

F-69 **26.**—(1) The Lord Chancellor shall recover in accordance with directions given by him any sums paid out as part of the Criminal Defence Service, or by the Lord Chancellor under arrangements made for the purposes of Part 1 of the Legal Aid, Sentencing and Punishment of Offenders Act 2012 or central funds where a costs order has been made against a person in favour of—

(a) a person receiving services funded for him as part of the Criminal Defence Service, or by the Lord Chancellor under arrangements made for the purposes of Part 1 of the Legal Aid, Sentencing and Punishment of Offenders Act 2012, or

(b) a person in whose favour an order for the payment of costs out of central funds has been made.

(2) Directions given by the Lord Chancellor under this regulation may be given generally or in respect of a particular case and may require the payment of sums due under a costs order and stipulate the mode of payment and the person to whom payment is to be made.

(3) In this regulation and regulation 27 "costs order" shall include a wasted costs order as defined by regulation 3A, or a third party costs order as defined by regulation 3E, of these regulations.

[This regulation is printed as amended by the Costs in Criminal Cases (General) (Amendment) Regulations 1991 (SI 1991/789); SI 2004/2408; and SI 2013/534]

27. [*Recovery of sums due under a costs order.*]

C. ENFORCEMENT

Powers of Criminal Courts (Sentencing) Act 2000, ss.141, 142

Power of Crown Court to allow time for payment, or payment by instalments, of costs and compensation

141. Where the Crown Court makes any such order as is mentioned in Part I of Schedule 9 to the Administration of Justice Act 1970 (orders against accused for the payment of costs or compensation), the court may– **F-70**

(a) allow time for the payment of the sum due under the order;

(b) direct payment of that sum by instalments of such amounts and on such dates as the court may specify.

Power of Crown Court to order search of persons before it

142.–(1) [Power of Crown Court to order search of persons before it: see § 5A-416.] **F-71**

Administration of Justice Act 1970, s.41

41.–(1) In the cases specified in Part I of Schedule 9 to this Act (being cases where, in criminal proceedings, a court makes an order against the accused for the payment of costs, compensation, etc.) any sum required to be paid by such an order as is there mentioned shall be treated, for the purposes of collection and enforcement, as if it had been adjudged to be paid on a conviction by a magistrates' court, being– **F-72**

(a) where the order is made by a magistrates' court, that court; and

(b) in any other case, such magistrates' court as may be specified in the order.

(2) In the cases specified in Part II of the said Schedule (being cases where a court makes an order against the prosecutor in criminal proceedings, and certain cases where an order for costs arises out of an appeal to the Crown Court in proceedings which are not criminal) any sum required to be paid by such an order as is there mentioned shall be enforceable as if the order were for the payment of money recoverable summarily as a civil debt.

(3) Without prejudice to the foregoing subsections, but subject to subsection (4) below, in the cases specified in Schedule 9 to this Act any sum required to be paid by such an order as is there mentioned shall be enforceable by the High Court or the County Court (otherwise than by issue of a writ of fieri facias or other process against goods or by imprisonment or attachment of earnings) as if the sum were due in pursuance of a judgment or order of the High Court or county court as the case may be.

(4), (4A) [Repealed by High Court and County Courts Jurisdiction Order 1991 (SI 1991/724).]

(5) [*Transitional provisions.*]

(6) [Repealed by Magistrates' Courts Act 1980.]

(7) [Amends Courts-Martial (Appeals) Act 1968, s.32(2).]

(8) Subject to subsection (8A) below, where in the case specified in paragraph 10, 12B or 12C of Schedule 9 to this Act the Crown Court thinks that the period for which the person subject to the order is liable apart from this subsection to be committed to prison for default under the order is insufficient, it may specify a longer period for that purpose; and then, in the case of default–

(a) the specified period shall be substituted as the maximum for which the person may be imprisoned under section 76 of the Magistrates' Courts Act 1980; and

(b) paragraph 2 of Schedule 4 to that Act shall apply, with any necessary modifications, for the reduction of the specified period where, at the time of the person's imprisonment, he has made part payment under the order.

(8A) The Crown Court may not specify under subsection (8) above a period of imprisonment longer than that which it could order a person to undergo on imposing on him a fine equal in amount to the sum required to be paid by the order.

(9) Where a magistrates' court has power to commit a person to prison for default in paying a sum due under an order enforceable as mentioned in this section, the court shall not exercise the power unless it is satisfied that all other methods of enforcing payment have been tried or considered and either have proved unsuccessful or are likely to do so.

[This section is printed as amended by the CLA 1977, Sch.13; the MCA 1980, Schs 7 and 9; the County Courts Act 1984, Sch.2; the CJA 1988, s.106; the High Court and County Courts Jurisdiction Order 1991 (SI 1991/724); the Crime and Courts Act 2013, s.17(5), and Sch.9, para.52; and the Modern Slavery Act 2015, s.57(1), and Sch.5, para.11(1) and (2) (as amended by the Modern Slavery Act 2015 (Consequential Amendments) Regulations 2016 (SI 2016/244)).]

Administration of Justice Act 1970, Sch.9

SCHEDULE 9

PART I

Cases where Payment Enforceable as on Summary Conviction

Costs awarded by magistrates

F-73 1. Where a magistrates' court, on the summary trial of an information, makes an order as to costs to be paid by the accused to the prosecutor.

1A. Where a magistrates' court makes an order as to costs to be paid by the accused in exercise of any power in that behalf conferred by regulations made under section 19(1) of the Prosecution Offences Act 1985.

2. Where an appellant to the Crown Court against conviction or sentence by a magistrates' court abandons his appeal and the magistrates' court orders him to pay costs to the other party to the appeal.

Costs awarded by the Crown Court

F-74 3. Where a person appeals to the Crown Court against conviction or sentence by a magistrates' court, and the Crown Court makes an order as to costs to be paid by him.

4. Where a person is prosecuted or tried on indictment before the Crown Court and is convicted, and the court makes an order as to costs to be paid by him.

4A. Where the Crown Court makes an order as to costs to be paid by the accused in exercise of any power in that behalf conferred by regulations made under section 19(1) of the Prosecution of Offences Act 1985.

Costs awarded by the Court of Appeal (criminal division) or Supreme Court

F-75 6. Where the criminal division of the Court of Appeal makes an order as to costs to be paid by—

(a) an appellant;

(b) an applicant for leave to appeal to that court; or

(c) in the case of an application for leave to appeal to the Supreme Court, an applicant who was the appellant before the criminal division.

Miscellaneous orders for costs, compensation, etc.

F-76 9. Where a court makes an order by virtue of regulations made under section 19(5) of the Prosecution of Offences Act 1985 for the payment of costs by an offender.

9A. Where a court orders the payment of a charge in respect of relevant court costs under section 21A of the Prosecution of Offences Act 1985.

10. Where under section 130 of the Powers of Criminal Courts (Sentencing) Act 2000 a court orders the payment of compensation.

12. Where under section 137 of the Powers of Criminal Courts (Sentencing) Act 2000 a court orders any fine ... compensation or costs, or any sum awarded by way of satisfaction or compensation to be paid by the parent or guardian of a child or young person.

12A. Where under section 161A of the Criminal Justice Act 2003 a court orders the payment of a surcharge.

12B. Where under section 4 of the Prevention of Social Housing Fraud Act 2013 a court makes an unlawful profit order.

12C. Where under section 8 of the Modern Slavery Act 2015 a court makes a slavery and trafficking reparation order.

PART II

Cases where Costs Enforceable Summarily as Civil Debt

Costs awarded by magistrates

F-77 13. Where a magistrates' court makes an order as to costs to be paid by the prosecutor in exercise of any power in that behalf conferred by regulations made under section 19(1) of the Prosecution of Offences Act 1985.

14. Where an appellant to the Crown Court from a magistrates' court (otherwise than against conviction or sentence) abandons his appeal and the magistrates' court orders him to pay costs to the other party to the appeal.

Costs awarded by the Crown Court

16. Any order for the payment of costs made by the Crown Court, other than an order falling within Part I above, or an order for costs to be paid out of money provided by Parliament. **F-78**

Costs awarded by the Court of Appeal (criminal division)

16A. Where the criminal division of the Court of Appeal makes an order as to costs to be paid by the respondent or, in the case of an application for leave to appeal to the Supreme Court, an applicant who was the respondent before the criminal division, and does so in exercise of any power in that behalf conferred by regulations made under section 19(1) of the Prosecution of Offences Act 1985. **F-79**

[Schedule 9 is printed as amended by the Courts Act 1971, s.56(1) and (4), Sch.8, para.60, and Sch.11; the CJA 1972, Sch.6; the Costs in Criminal Cases Act 1973, Sch.1; the PCCA 1973, Sch.5; the CLA 1977, Sch.13; the Prosecution of Offences Act 1985, Schs 1 and 2; the PCC(S)A 2000, s.165(1), and Sch.9, para.43; the Domestic Violence, Crime and Victims Act 2004, s.14(3); the Constitutional Reform Act 2005, s.40(4), and Sch.9, para.22; the Prevention of Social Housing Fraud Act 2013, s.10, and Sch., paras 1 and 3; the CJCA 2015, s.54(2); and the Modern Slavery Act 2015, s.57(1), and Sch.5, para.11(1) and (3) (as amended by SI 2016/244.

Magistrates' Courts Act 1980, ss.75A, 76

75A. [*Costs of collecting sums adjudged to be paid by a conviction: see § 5A-421.*] **F-80**

Enforcement of sums adjudged to be paid

76.—(1) Subject to the following provisions of this Part of this Act, and to section 132 below ..., where default is made in paying a sum adjudged to be paid by a conviction or order of a magistrates' court, the court may issue a warrant of control for the purpose of recovering the sum or issue a warrant committing the defaulter to prison.

(2) A warrant of commitment may be issued as aforesaid either—

(a) where it appears on the return to a warrant of control that the money and goods of the defaulter are insufficient to pay the amount outstanding, as defined by paragraph 50(3) of Schedule 12 to the Tribunals, Courts and Enforcement Act 2007; or

(b) instead of a warrant of control.

(3) The period for which a person may be committed to prison under such a warrant as aforesaid shall not, subject to the provisions of any enactment passed after 31st December 1879, exceed the period applicable to the case under Schedule 4 to this Act.

[This section is printed as amended by the CJA 1982, s.78, and Sch.16; the Tribunals, Courts and Enforcement Act 2007, s.62(3), and Sch.13, para.46; and the Crime and Courts Act 2013, s.17(6), and Sch.10, para.49.]

Magistrates' Courts Act 1980, Sch.4

SCHEDULE 4

Maximum Periods of Imprisonment in Default of Payment

1. Subject to the following provisions of this Schedule, the periods set out in the second column of the following Table shall be the maximum periods applicable respectively to the amounts set out opposite thereto, being amounts due at the time the imprisonment or detention is imposed. **F-81**

An amount not exceeding £200	7 days
An amount exceeding £200 but not exceeding £500	14 days
An amount exceeding £500 but not exceeding £1,000	28 days
An amount exceeding £1,000 but not exceeding £2,500	45 days
An amount exceeding £2,500 but not exceeding £5,000	3 months
An amount exceeding £5,000 but not exceeding £10,000	6 months
An amount exceeding £10,000	12 months

2.—(1) Where the amount due at the time imprisonment or detention is imposed is so much of a sum adjudged to be paid by a summary conviction as remains due after part payment, then, subject to sub-paragraph (2) below, the maximum period applicable to the amount shall be the period applicable to the whole sum reduced by such number of days as bears to the total number of days therein the same proportion as the part paid bears to the whole sum.

(2) In calculating the reduction required under sub-paragraph (1) above, any fraction of a day shall be left out of account and the maximum period shall not be reduced to less than seven days.

[Paragraph 2(2) is printed as amended by the CJA 1991, Sch.11, para.28.]

APPENDIX G
Guidelines on Claims for Fees under a Crown Court Representation Order and in the Court of Appeal

A. SUMMARY OF SOURCE MATERIAL

Legislation

The Criminal Legal Aid (Remuneration) Regulations 2013 (SI 2013/435) (set out in full, G-6 and following) came into force on 1 April 2013. The substance of the 2013 regulations is almost identical to that of the Criminal Defence Service (Funding) Order 2007 (SI 2007/1174) as it read at the time it lapsed, and many, if not all, the authorities that related to the 2007 order at that time will simply carry across. Where they are referred to below in this appendix, references to provisions of the former legislation have simply been updated to refer to the corresponding provision of the 2013 regulations. **G-1**

A challenge to the 8.75 per cent reduction in litigators' fees effected by amendments to Schedules 2, 3 and 4 to SI 2013/435 (above) in the Criminal Legal Aid (Remuneration) (Amendment) Regulations 2014 (SI 2013/415) was rejected in *R. (London Criminal Courts Solicitors' Association) v Lord Chancellor* [2014] EWHC 3020 (Admin); [2015] 1 Costs L.R. 7, QBD (Burnett J).

On 3 August 2018, the Criminal Legal Aid (Remuneration) (Amendment) Regulations 2017 (SI 2017/1019) (see below), which reduced the maximum number of pages of prosecution evidence which could be counted in fixing graduated fees under the Litigator's Graduated Fees Scheme, were quashed on the basis that they were based on an unlawful consultation process: *R. (on the application of Law Society) v Lord Chancellor* [2018] EWHC 2094 (Admin), DC.

Recent amendments

SI 2013/435 was amended by the Criminal Legal Aid (Amendment) Regulations 2017 (SI 2017/1319) (with effect from 21 February 2018). The titles of the tables in paragraph 11(3) of Schedule 4 to SI 2013/435 (not set out in this Appendix) were amended to reflect the extension of legal aid to reviews of an individual's classification as a Category A prisoner, directions in relation to a prisoner's placement in a close supervision centre of a prison, directions in relation to a prisoner's placement in a separation centre within a prison, and all Parole Board hearings by SI 2017/1319. The amendments do not apply to a matter where a determination under section 15 of the 2012 Act (see § 6-186 in the main work) was made before 21 February 2018. **★G-1a**

SI 2013/435 was further amended by the Criminal Legal Aid (Remuneration) (Amendment) Regulations 2018 (SI 2018/220) (with effect from 1 April 2018). The 2018 Regulations amend the legal aid fees that are payable to advocates in criminal proceedings under the advocates' graduated fee scheme ("AGFS"), as set out in Schedule 1 to SI 2013/435. The 2018 Regulations make provision for advocates' fees to be determined according to a new banding structure for criminal offences. The 2018 Regulations amend regulations 2 (G-6), 21 (G-25a) and 28 (G-32) of SI 2013/435 as well as Sch. 1 (G-36 to G-71), Sch. 2, paras. 1 (G-73), 3 (G-75) and 29 (G-99), and Sch. 3, para.8 (G-107). The amendments have no effect in relation to proceedings in respect of which a determination under section 16 of the Legal Aid, Sentencing and Punishment of Offenders Act 2012 (see § 6-187 in the main work) is made before 1 April 2018.

Amendments to SI 2013/435 were then effected by the Criminal Legal Aid (Remuneration) (Amendment) (No. 2) Regulations 2018 (SI 2018/1323) so as to increase the fees payable for certain offences; to make fees for special preparation available for cases involving very unusual points of law, or novel factual issues; to make the fee payable where a guilty plea is entered at a plea and trial preparation hearing the fee payable for guilty pleas ordinarily, rather than the fixed fee for such a hearing; and to extend the 20% uplift to fees for each additional defendant that the advocate represents at a hearing to cases where a defendant enters a guilty plea at a plea and trial preparation hearing. The amendments made by SI 2018/1323 have no effect in relation to proceedings in respect of which a determination under s.16 of the Legal Aid, Sentencing and Punishment of Offenders Act 2012 (see § 6-187 in the main work) was made before 31 December 2018.

With effect from 1 May 2020, SI 2013/435 was further amended by the Criminal Legal Aid (Coronavirus, Remuneration) (Amendment) Regulations 2020 (SI 2020/472). For the effect of these further amendments see, below, Appendix G-25a.

The latest substantive amendments to SI 2013/435 are effected by the Criminal Legal Aid (Remuneration) (Amendment) Regulations 2020 (SI 2020/903). With effect from 17 September 2020, SI 2020/903 introduces new fees under the Advocates' Graduated Fee Scheme ("AGFS") and the Litigator's Graduated Fee Scheme for unused material; inserts into the AGFS new page limits for bands 2.1 to 17.1 for fees for special preparation; and amends the fees payable for guilty pleas and cracked trials to advocates to increase the fees payable in respect of all cracked trials and to remove the distinction between trials that crack in the first and second third and trials that crack in the last third. With effect from 19 October 2020, SI 2020/903 introduces a new fixed fee of £180.40 payable to a litigator in respect of a case sent for trial to the Crown Court. The amendments effected apply only to cases in which a determination under the LASPOA 2012, s.16 (§ 6-187 in the main work) was made on or after the date of amendment. Minor further amendments were, however, made by the Criminal Legal Aid (Remuneration) (Amendment) Regulations 2021 (SI 2021/80), with effect from 19 February 2021, to correct errors introduced by SI 2020/903 in relation to the fee to be paid for reviewing unused material.

The current regimes

G-2 Apart from a handful of historical cases which will be governed by the former provisions for ex post facto taxation (as to which see G-200 and following in the supplements to the 2010 edition of this work), advocates' fees in the Crown Court effectively fall into one of two regimes:

(i) *Graduated fees.* These were first introduced in 1997 for trials lasting up to 10 days, appeals and other minor Crown Court business: Legal Aid in Criminal and Care Proceedings (Costs) Regulations 1989 (SI 1989/343), Sch.3. The scheme was then extended to cover trials of up to 25 days and, as from 2005, of trials up to 40 days. As from 30 April 2007, it was intended that the scheme would cover all Crown Court work save for those cases contracted under the Very High Costs Case provisions: Criminal Defence Service (Funding) Order 2007 (SI 2007/1174), art.3(6A), and Sch.1, para.2(1). The 2007 scheme is sometimes referred to as the Revised Advocacy Graduated Fee Scheme (RAGFS). The details were contained in Schedule 1 to the 2007 order, which replaced Schedule 4 to the Criminal Defence Service (Funding) Order 2001 (SI 2001/855). The 2007 scheme (as amended) is now to be found in Schedule 1 to the Criminal Legal Aid (Remuneration) Regulations 2013 (SI 2013/435).

(ii) *Very High Cost Cases (VHCC).* This regime came into effect on 29 October 2001. All cases estimated to last more than 24 days are capable of being subject to a VHCC contract. As to the current VHCC regime, see G-199 to G-202.

Notes for guidance

(a) Graduated fees

G-3 The Ministry of Justice's Crown Court Fee Guidance "CCFG" (*https://www.gov.uk/government/publications/crown-court-fee-guidance*) is updated at regular intervals. However, while interesting and instructive, the guidance is not a source of law and, where there is any conflict between the guidance and the regulations, the regulations take precedence; the guidance is precisely that, not a source of law: *Metcalf* [2010] 4 Costs L.R. 646. Appendix J of the guidance document contains summaries of various costs judgments.

The Ministry of Justice also publishes calculators to assist in calculating LGFS and AGFS fees under the graduated fee scheme *https://www.gov.uk/government/publications/graduated-fee-calculators.*

(b) Very High Cost Cases

G-4 Very High Cost Cases are governed by the Very High Cost (Crime) Cases Arrangements 2013 (see G-199 to G-202). Additional guidance can be found at *https://www.gov.uk/guidance/high-cost-cases-crime.*

B. THE REMUNERATION REGULATIONS

Criminal Legal Aid (Remuneration) Regulations 2013 (SI 2013/435)

Citation and commencement

1. These Regulations may be cited as the Criminal Legal Aid (Remuneration) Regulations 2013 and shall come into force on 1st April 2013. **G-5**

Interpretation

2.–(1) In these Regulations– **G-6**

"the Act" means the Legal Aid, Sentencing and Punishment of Offenders Act 2012;

"advocate" means a barrister, a solicitor advocate or a solicitor who is exercising their automatic rights of audience in the Crown Court;

"AGFS Banding Document" means version 1.2 (December 2018) of the document called "Banding of Offences in the Advocates' Graduated Fee Scheme (AGFS)", published by the Ministry of Justice;

"appropriate officer" means–

(a) in the case of proceedings in the civil division of the Court of Appeal, the head of the civil appeals office;

(b) in the case of proceedings in the criminal division of the Court of Appeal, the registrar of criminal appeals;

(c) in the case of proceedings in the Crown Court, the Lord Chancellor;

(d) in respect of advice or assistance as to an appeal from the Crown Court to the Court of Appeal (except in the case of an appeal under section 9(11) of the Criminal Justice Act 1987 (preparatory hearings)) where, on the advice of any representative instructed, notice of appeal is given, or application for leave to appeal is made, whether or not such appeal is later abandoned, the registrar of criminal appeals;

(e) in respect of advice or assistance as to an appeal to the Courts-Martial Appeal Court, the registrar of criminal appeals;

(f) in respect of advice or assistance as to an appeal from the Court of Appeal to the Supreme Court, where the appeal is not lodged with the Supreme Court, the registrar of criminal appeals; and

(g) in any other case, the Lord Chancellor,

and, in any case, includes an officer designated by the person who is the appropriate officer by virtue of paragraphs (a) to (g) to act on his behalf for the purposes of these Regulations;

"assisted person" means an individual in whose favour a section 16 determination has been made;

"band" (in relation to a criminal offence) has the meaning given in paragraph 1(7) of Schedule 1;

"Class" (in relation to a criminal offence) has the meaning given in paragraph 1(7) of Schedule 2;

"fee earner" means a litigator, or person employed by a litigator, who undertakes work on a case;

"instructed advocate" means–

(a) where the section 16 determination provides for representation by a single advocate, the first barrister or solicitor advocate instructed in the case, who has primary responsibility for the case; or

(b) where the section 16 determination provides for representation by more than one advocate, each of–

(i) the leading instructed advocate; and

(ii) the led instructed advocate;

"leading instructed advocate" means the first leading barrister or solicitor advocate instructed in the case who has primary responsibility for those aspects of a case undertaken by a leading advocate;

"led instructed advocate" means the first led barrister or solicitor advocate instructed in the case who has primary responsibility for those aspects of the case undertaken by a led advocate;

"LGFS Table of Offences" means the table in Part 7 of Schedule 2;

"litigator" means the person referred to in the representation order as representing an assisted person, being a solicitor, firm of solicitors or other appropriately qualified person.

"main hearing" means—
- (a) in relation to a case which goes to trial, the trial;
- (b) in relation to a guilty plea (within the meaning of Schedule 1), the hearing at which pleas are taken or, where there is more than one such hearing, the last such hearing;
- (c) in relation to a cracked trial (within the meaning of Schedule 1), the hearing at which—
  - (i) the case becomes a cracked trial by meeting the conditions in the definition of a cracked trial, whether or not any pleas were taken at that hearing; or
  - (ii) a formal verdict of not guilty was entered as a result of the prosecution offering no evidence, whether or not the parties attended the hearing;
- (d) in relation to an appeal against conviction or sentence in the Crown Court, the hearing of the appeal;
- (e) in relation to proceedings arising out of a committal for sentence in the Crown Court, the sentencing hearing; and
- (f) in relation to proceedings arising out of an alleged breach of an order of the Crown Court, the hearing at which those proceedings are determined;

"related proceedings" means—
- (a) two or more sets of proceedings involving the same defendant which are prepared, heard or dealt with together; or
- (b) proceedings involving more than one defendant which arise out of the same incident, so that the defendants are charged, tried or disposed of together;

"relevant order" means whichever of the 2015 Duty Provider Crime Contract or the 2015 Own Client Crime Contract governs the provision of advice and assistance made available under sections 13 or 15 of the Act, for which remuneration is claimed;

"representation order" means a document which records a section 16 determination;

"representative" means a litigator or an advocate including, where appropriate, an instructed advocate or trial advocate;

"restriction order" has the meaning given in section 41 (power of higher courts to restrict discharge from hospital) of the Mental Health Act 1983;

"section 16 determination" means a determination made under section 16 of the Act that an individual qualities for representation for the purposes of criminal proceedings;

"senior solicitor" means a solicitor who, in the judgement of the appropriate officer, has the skill, knowledge and experience to deal with the most difficult and complex cases;

"solicitor advocate" means a solicitor who has obtained a higher courts advocacy qualification in accordance with regulations and rules of conduct of the Law Society;

"solicitor, legal executive or fee earner of equivalent experience" means a solicitor, Fellow of the Institute of Legal Executives or equivalent senior fee earner who, in the judgement of the appropriate officer, has good knowledge and experience of the conduct of criminal cases;

"trainee solicitor or fee earner of equivalent experience" means a trainee solicitor or other fee earner who is not a Fellow of the Institute of Legal Executives, who, in the judgement of the appropriate officer, carries out the routine work on a case;

"trial advocate" means, unless otherwise provided, an advocate instructed pursuant to a section 16 determination to represent the assisted person at the main hearing in any case;

"Very High Cost Case" means a case in which a section 16 determination has been made and which the Director classifies as a Very High Cost Case on the grounds that—
- (a) in relation to fees claimed by litigators—
  - (i) if the case were to proceed to trial, the trial would in the opinion of the Director be likely to last for more than 40 days and the Director considers that there are no exceptional circumstances which make it unsuitable to be dealt with under an individual case contract for Very High Cost Cases made by the Lord Chancellor under section 2(1) of the Act; or
  - (ii) if the case were to proceed to trial, the trial would in the opinion of the Director be likely to last no fewer than 25 and no more than 40 days and the Director considers that there are circumstances which make it suitable to be dealt with under an individual case contract for Very High Cost Cases made by the Lord Chancellor under section 2(1) of the Act;
- (b) in relation to fees claimed by advocates, if the case were to proceed to trial, the trial would in the opinion of the Director be likely to last for more than 60 days and the Director considers that there are no exceptional circumstances which make it unsuitable to be dealt with under an individual case contract for Very High Cost Cases made by the Lord Chancellor under section 2(1) of the Act;

"Very High Cost Case contract" means the 2013 VHCC contract between the Lord Chancellor and a representative for the provision of representation under section 16 of the Act (criminal legal aid).

(2) The fees and rates set out in the Schedules to these Regulations are exclusive of value added tax.

(3) A function of the Lord Chancellor or Director under these Regulations may be exercised by, or by an employee of, a person authorised for that purpose by the Lord Chancellor or Director respectively.

[This regulation is printed as amended (insertion of definition of "Very High Cost Case contract") by the Criminal Legal Aid (Remuneration) (Amendment) Regulations 2013 (SI 2013/2803), reg.3(1) and (3). The amendment applies in relation to fees for work undertaken on or after 2 December 2013: reg.4. It is also printed as further amended by the Criminal Legal Aid (Remuneration) (Amendment) Regulations 2015 (SI 2015/882), reg.2(1) and (2) (insertion of definitions of "main hearing" and "trial advocate", and inclusion of words "or trial advocate" at the end of the definition of "representative"). The amendments apply to criminal proceedings in the Crown Court in which a determination under the LASPOA 2012, s.16 (§ 6-187 in the main work) is made on or after 5 May 2015. It is further printed as amended by the Criminal Legal Aid (Remuneration) (Amendment) Regulations 2018 (SI 2018/220), regs. 2 and 3 (insertion of definitions of "AGFS Banding Document", "band", "Class", "LGFS Table of Offences", and "restriction order"). The amendments have no effect in relation to proceedings in respect of which a determination under s.16 of the LASPOA 2012 (see § 6-187 in the main work) is made before 1 April 2018.

It is most recently amended by the Criminal Legal Aid (Remuneration) (Amendment) (No. 2) Regulations 2018 (SI 2018/1323), reg.2, to update the definition of "AGFS Banding Document". For transitional provisions in relation to amendments made by SI 2018/1323, see G-1a.]

Scope

3.—(1) Regulations 5(2), 10 and 14(1) apply to proceedings in magistrates' courts and to proceedings in the Crown Court. **G-7**

(2) Regulation 8 and Schedule 4 apply to proceedings in magistrates' courts, to proceedings in the County Court, to proceedings in the Crown Court and to proceedings in the High Court.

(3) Regulations 16 and 31 and Schedule 5 apply to proceedings in magistrates' courts, to proceedings in the Crown Court and to proceedings in the Court of Appeal.

(4) Regulations 4, 5(1) and (3) to (8), 13, 14(2) to (9), 15, 17 to 24 and 28 to 30 and Schedules 1 and 2 apply to proceedings in the Crown Court only.

(5) Regulations 11 and 25 to 27, apply to proceedings in the Crown Court and to proceedings in the Court of Appeal.

(5A) Regulation 9 applies to proceedings in magistrates' courts, to proceedings in the Crown Court and to proceedings in the Court of Appeal.

(6) Regulation 6 and Schedule 3 apply to proceedings in the Court of Appeal only.

(7) Regulation 7 applies to proceedings in the Supreme Court only.

(8) With the exception of regulations 12 and 12A and paragraphs 13(8) and (9) of Schedule 2 and Schedule 6, these regulations do not apply to Very High Cost Cases.

(9) For the purpose of these regulations, any reference to the Court of Appeal includes as appropriate a reference to—

(a) the criminal division of the Court of Appeal;
(b) the civil division of the Court of Appeal;
(c) the Courts-Martial Appeal Court; and
(d) a Divisional Court of the High Court.

[This regulation is printed as amended (insertion of references to reg.12A and Sch.6) by the Criminal Legal Aid (Remuneration) (Amendment) Regulations 2013 (SI 2013/2803), reg.3(1) and (4). The amendment applies in relation to fees for work undertaken on or after 2 December 2013: above, reg.4. It is also printed as further amended by the Civil and Criminal Legal Aid (Remuneration) (Amendment) Regulations 2015 (SI 2015/325), reg.3(1) and (2); and the Criminal Legal Aid (Standard Crime Contract) (Amendment) Regulations 2017 (SI 2017/311).]

Claims for fees by advocates—Crown Court

4.—(1) Claims for fees by a trial advocate in proceedings in the Crown Court must be made and determined in accordance with the provisions of Schedule 1 to these Regulations. **G-8**

(2) A claim for fees under this regulation and Schedule 1 must be made by each trial advocate.

(3) Subject to regulation 31, a claim by a trial advocate for fees in respect of work done pursuant

to a section 16 determination must not be entertained unless the trial advocate submits it within three months of the conclusion of the proceedings to which it relates.

(4) A trial advocate must submit a claim for fees to the appropriate officer in such form and manner as the appropriate officer may direct.

(5) A trial advocate must supply such further information and documents as the appropriate officer may require.

(6) Where a confiscation hearing under Part 2 of the Proceeds of Crime Act 2002 (confiscation: England and Wales), section 2 of the Drug Trafficking Act 1994 (confiscation orders) or section 71 of the Criminal Justice Act 1988 (confiscation orders) is to be held more than 28 days after—

(a) the conclusion of the trial to which the section 16 determination relates; or

(b) the entering of a guilty plea,

a trial advocate may submit any claim for fees in respect of the trial or guilty plea as soon as the trial has concluded or the guilty plea has been entered.

(7) Where the section 16 determination provides for representation by—

(a) a single advocate other than a QC; or

(b) two or more advocates other than QC,

and a QC agrees to appear as the single advocate or as a leading junior, that QC must be treated for all the purposes of these Regulations as having been instructed in relation to that determination, and the remuneration of that QC must be determined as if the advocate were not a QC.

(8) In this regulation, where the main hearing is a trial, "trial advocate" means an advocate who—

(a) is instructed pursuant to a section 16 determination to represent the assisted person at the trial, and

(b) attends the first day of the trial.

[This regulation is printed as amended, with effect from 5 May 2015, by the Criminal Legal Aid (Remuneration) (Amendment) Regulations 2015 (SI 2015/882), reg.2(3)(a), (4)(a), (5)(a), (6)(a) and (7). For the transitional provision, see G-6.]

Claims for fees and disbursements by litigators–Crown Court

G-9 **5.**—(1) Claims for fees by litigators in proceedings in the Crown Court must be made and determined in accordance with the provisions of Schedule 2 to these Regulations.

(2) Claims for disbursements by litigators in proceedings in the Crown Court or in proceedings in a magistrates' court which are subsequently sent for trial to the Crown Court must be made and determined in accordance with the provisions of regulations 14 to 17.

(3) Subject to regulation 31, a claim by a litigator for fees in respect of work done pursuant to a section 16 determination must not be entertained unless the litigator submits it within three months of the conclusion of the proceedings to which it relates.

(4) Subject to paragraph (5), a claim by a litigator for fees in proceedings in the Crown Court must be submitted to the appropriate officer in such form and manner as the appropriate officer may direct and must be accompanied by the representation order and any receipts or other documents in support of any disbursement claimed.

(5) A claim under paragraph 20 or 26 of Schedule 2 to these Regulations must—

(a) summarise the items of work done by a fee earner in respect of which fees are claimed according to the classes specified in paragraph 26(2) of Schedule 2;

(b) state, where appropriate, the dates on which the items of work were done, the time taken, the sums claimed and whether the work was done for more than one assisted person;

(c) specify, where appropriate, the level of fee earner who undertook each of the items of work claimed; and

(d) give particulars of any work done in relation to more than one indictment or a retrial.

(6) Where the litigator claims that paragraph 29 of Schedule 2 applies in relation to an item of work, the litigator must give full particulars in support of the claim.

(7) The litigator must specify any special circumstances which the litigator considers should be drawn to the attention of the appropriate officer.

(8) The litigator must supply such further information and documents as the appropriate officer may require.

[This regulation is printed as amended by SI 2015/1678 (as to which, see G-1a).]

Proceedings in the Court of Appeal

G-10 **6.** Claims for fees by representatives in proceedings in the Court of Appeal must be made and determined in accordance with the provisions of Schedule 3 to these Regulations.

Proceedings in the Supreme Court

7.–(1) In proceedings in the Supreme Court, the fees payable to a representative in respect of advice and assistance or representation made available to an individual in accordance with sections 15 or 16 of the Act must be determined by such officer as may be prescribed by order of the Supreme Court. **G-11**

(2) Subject to paragraph (1), these Regulations do not apply to proceedings in the Supreme Court.

Claims for fees for certain categories of work to which the Standard Crime Contract applies

8.–(1) This regulation applies to– **G-12**

(a) advice and assistance provided pursuant to a determination made under section 13 or section 15 of the Act;

(b) representation in proceedings in a magistrates' court pursuant to a section 16 determination;

(c) representation pursuant to a section 16 determination in proceedings prescribed as criminal proceedings under section 14(h) of the Act; and

(d) representation in appeals by way of case stated to the High Court.

(2) Claims for fees in cases to which this regulation applies must–

(a) be made and determined in accordance with the 2017 Standard Crime Contract; and

(b) be paid in accordance with the rates set out in Schedule 4.

(3) In this regulation and in Schedule 4, "2017 Standard Crime Contract" means the contract so named between the Lord Chancellor and a person with whom the Lord Chancellor has made an arrangement under section 2(1) of the Act for the provision of advice, assistance and representation made available under sections 13, 15 and 16 of the Act.

[This regulation is printed as amended by the Criminal Legal Aid (Standard Crime Contract) (Amendment) Regulations 2017 (SI 2017/311).]

Payments from other sources

9. Where representation is provided in respect of any proceedings, the representative, whether acting pursuant to a section 16 determination or otherwise, must not receive or be a party to the making of any payment for work done in connection with those proceedings, except such payments as may be made– **G-13**

(a) by the Lord Chancellor; or

(b) in respect of any expenses or fees incurred in–

(i) preparing, obtaining or considering any report, opinion or further evidence, whether provided by an expert witness or otherwise; or

(ii) obtaining any transcripts or recordings,

where an application under regulation 13 for an authority to incur such fees or expenses has been refused by a committee appointed under arrangements made by the Lord Chancellor to deal with, amongst other things, appeals of, or review of, assessment of costs.

In connection with regulation 9, see *Banfield*, § 7-166.

Cases sent for trial to the Crown Court

10.– [Revoked.] **G-14**

[With effect from 19 October 2020, this regulation was omitted by SI 2020/903 (G-1a). The revocation applies only to criminal proceedings in which a determination under the LASPOA 2012, s.16 (§ 6-187 in the main work) was made on or after that date.]

Proceedings for contempt

11. Where representation is provided in proceedings referred to in section 14(g) of the Act (proceedings for contempt in the face of a court), the Lord Chancellor may only pay remuneration for services in accordance with Schedules 1, 2 and 3. **G-15**

Notification of Very High Cost Cases

12.–(1) A litigator who has conduct of a case which is, or is likely to be classified as, a Very High Cost Case, must notify the Lord Chancellor in writing as soon as practicable. **G-16**

(2) Where a litigator fails to comply with this regulation without good reason, and as a result there is a loss to public funds, the Lord Chancellor may refuse payment of the litigator's costs up to the extent of such loss.

(3) The Lord Chancellor must not refuse payment under paragraph (2) unless the litigator has been given a reasonable opportunity to show why the payment should not be refused.

Fees in Very High Cost Cases

12A. Where services consisting of representation made available under section 16 of the Act (criminal legal aid) are provided in a case which is the subject of a Very High Cost Case contract, fees for that case must be paid—

(a) in accordance with the terms of that contract; and

(b) at the rates set out for the appropriate category and level of representative set out in Schedule 6 to these Regulations.

[This regulation was inserted by the Criminal Legal Aid (Remuneration) (Amendment) Regulations 2013 (SI 2013/2803), reg.3(1) and (5). It applies in relation to fees for work undertaken on or after 2 December 2013: above, reg.4.]

Authorisation of expenditure

G-17 **13.**—(1) Where it appears to a litigator necessary for the proper conduct of proceedings in the Crown Court for costs to be incurred in relation to representation by taking any of the following steps—

(a) obtaining a written report or opinion of one or more experts;

(b) employing a person to provide a written report or opinion (otherwise than as an expert);

(c) obtaining any transcripts or recordings; or

(d) performing an act which is either unusual in its nature or involves unusually large expenditure,

the litigator may apply to the Lord Chancellor for prior authority to do so.

(2) Where the Lord Chancellor authorises the taking of any step referred to in paragraph (1), the Lord Chancellor shall also authorise the maximum to be paid in respect of that step.

(3) A representative assigned to an assisted person in any proceedings in the Crown Court may apply to the Lord Chancellor for prior authority for the incurring of travelling and accommodation expenses in order to attend at the main hearing in those proceedings.

[This regulation is printed as amended, with effect from 5 May 2015, by the Criminal Legal Aid (Remuneration) (Amendment) Regulations 2015 (SI 2015/882), reg.2(8). For the transitional provision, see G-6.]

The following authorities were decided under the corresponding provisions in earlier legal aid legislation: see, in particular, regulation 54 of the Legal Aid in Criminal and Care Proceedings (General) Regulations 1989 (SI 1989/344).

In *Silcott, Braithwaite and Raghip, The Times,* 9 December 1991, the Court of Appeal said that all members of the legal profession were under a duty not to involve the legal aid fund in unnecessary expenditure. If an expert consulted by the defence was hostile to the accused's case or his solicitor considered the opinion to be wrong or defective it was most unlikely that legal aid authority would be given on application by the solicitor to consult more than one expert and certainly no more than two. In the instant case, the opinions of two experts had been obtained on behalf of one defendant. They were adverse to the defendant. Neither expert was called, but both changed their views in the light of the opinion of a third expert, who had been consulted after the trial's conclusion. This demonstrated that a third opinion had been necessary in the interests of justice. "Expert shopping" was to be discouraged, but there were exceptional cases where the need for a further expert opinion could be demonstrated. In such cases counsel should be asked to advise on evidence in support of an extension of the legal aid certificate, if he thought it right to do so. The courts and those responsible for the legal aid fund must rely on proper professional standards being observed by all the lawyers concerned.

A judge has no power to authorise the incurring of costs under a legal aid order for an expert witness, although he may express his opinion as to the desirability of legal aid being so extended: *Donnelly* [1998] Crim. L.R. 131, CA.

G-18 **14.**—(1) A litigator may submit a claim to the appropriate officer for payment of a disbursement for which the litigator has incurred liability in proceedings in the Crown Court, or in proceedings in a magistrates' court which are subsequently sent for trial to the Crown Court, in accordance with the provisions of this regulation.

(2) A claim for payment under paragraph (1) may be made where—

(a) a litigator has obtained prior authority to incur expenditure of £100 or more under regulation 13; and

(b) the litigator has incurred such a liability.

(3) Without prejudice to regulation 17(4) and (5) a claim for payment under paragraph (1) must not exceed the maximum amount authorised under the prior authority.

(4) A claim for payment under paragraph (1) may be made at any time before the litigator submits a claim for fees under regulation 5.

(5) A claim for payment under paragraph (1) must be submitted to the appropriate officer in such form and manner as the appropriate officer may direct and must be accompanied by the authority to incur expenditure and any invoices or other documents in support of the claim.

(6) Subject to regulation 16, the appropriate officer must allow the disbursement subject to the limit in paragraph (3) if it appears to have been reasonably incurred in accordance with the prior authority.

(7) The appropriate officer must notify the litigator and, where the disbursement claimed includes the fees or charges of any person, may notify that person of the appropriate officer's decision.

(8) Where the appropriate officer allows the disbursement, the appropriate officer must notify the litigator and, where the disbursement includes the fees or charges of any person, may notify that person, of the amount payable, and must authorise payment to the litigator accordingly.

(9) Regulations 28 to 30 do not apply to a payment under this regulation.

[This regulation is printed as amended by SI 2015/1678 (G-1a).]

Interim disbursements and final determination of fees

15.—(1) On a final determination of fees, regulations 5(2) and 17 apply notwithstanding that a payment has been made under regulation 14. **G-19**

(2) Where the amount found to be due under regulation 17 in respect of a disbursement is less than the amount paid under regulation 14 ("the interim payment"), the appropriate officer must deduct the difference from the sum otherwise payable to the litigator on the determination of fees, and where the amount due under regulation 17 exceeds the interim payment, the appropriate officer must add the difference to the amount otherwise payable to the litigator.

Expert services

16.—(1) Subject to paragraph (2), the Lord Chancellor may provide for the payment of expert services only at the fixed fees or at rates not exceeding the rates set out in Schedule 5. **G-20**

(2) The appropriate officer may, in relation to a specific claim, increase the fixed fees or rates set out in Schedule 5 if that officer considers it reasonable to do so in exceptional circumstances.

(3) For the purposes of paragraph (2), exceptional circumstances are where the expert's evidence is key to the client's case and either—

(a) the complexity of the material is such that an expert with a high level of seniority is required; or

(b) the material is of such a specialised and unusual nature that only very few experts are available to provide the necessary evidence.

Determination of litigators' disbursements

17.—(1) Subject to paragraphs (2) to (5), the appropriate officer must allow such disbursements claimed under regulation 5(2) as appear to the appropriate officer to have been reasonably incurred. **G-21**

(2) If the disbursements claimed are abnormally large by reason of the distance of the court or the assisted person's residence or both from the litigator's place of business, the appropriate officer may limit reimbursement of the disbursements to what otherwise would, having regard to all the circumstances, be a reasonable amount.

(3) No question as to the propriety of any step or act in relation to which prior authority has been obtained under regulation 13 may be raised on any determination of disbursements, unless the litigator knew or ought reasonably to have known that the purpose for which the authority was given had failed or had become irrelevant or unnecessary before the disbursements were incurred.

(4) Where disbursements are reasonably incurred in accordance with and subject to the limit imposed by a prior authority given under regulation 13, no question may be raised on any determination of fees as to the amount of the payment to be allowed for the step or act in relation to which the authority was given.

(5) Where disbursements are incurred in taking any steps or doing any act for which authority may be given under regulation 13, without such authority having been given or in excess of any fee so authorised, payment in respect of those disbursements may nevertheless be allowed on a determination of disbursements payable under regulation 5.

(6) Paragraph (7) applies where the Lord Chancellor receives a request for funding of an expert service of a type not listed in Schedule 5.

(7) In considering the rate at which to fund the expert service the Lord Chancellor—

(a) must have regard to the rates set out in Schedule 5; and

(b) may require more than one quotation for provision of the service to be submitted to the Lord Chancellor.

Interim payment of litigators' fees

G-22 **17A.**—(1) A litigator may make a claim to the appropriate officer for an interim payment of the litigator's fees, in relation to proceedings in the Crown Court, in accordance with this regulation.

(2) Subject to paragraphs (3) to (6), a litigator may make a claim for an interim payment under this regulation in relation to one or more of the following stages in the proceedings—

(a) after the first hearing at which the assisted person enters a plea of not guilty;

(b) where representation is transferred to the litigator following the ordering of a retrial, after the date for the retrial has been set; and

(c) after commencement of a trial which is listed for 10 days or more.

(3) A litigator may not make a claim for an interim payment under paragraph (2)(a) or (b) in relation to a case committed or sent for trial to the Crown Court on the election of a defendant where the magistrates' court has determined the case to be suitable for summary trial.

(4) Subject to paragraphs (5) and (6), a litigator may make only one claim in relation to each of the stages in the proceedings set out in paragraph (2).

(5) A litigator may not make a claim for an interim payment under paragraph (2)(a) or (b) at the same time as, or after, that litigator has made a claim for an interim payment under paragraph (2)(c).

(6) A litigator may not make a claim for an interim payment under paragraph (2)(c) if the trial in question is a retrial and the litigator was the litigator for the first or a previous trial.

(7) A litigator may not make a claim for an interim payment at the same time as, or after, that litigator has made a claim under regulation 5.

(8) A litigator must make a claim for an interim payment to the appropriate officer in such form and manner as the appropriate officer may direct.

(9) A litigator must supply such information and documents as the appropriate officer may require to determine the claim for interim payment.

(10) Where a claim for an interim payment is made in accordance with this regulation, the appropriate officer must authorise payment.

(11) Where the claim is made under paragraph (2)(a) the amount of the interim payment is the sum of—

(a) the fee which, on a final determination of fees, would be paid to the litigator if paragraph 13 of Schedule 2 and the scenario "Before trial transfer (original litigator)" set out in the table following that paragraph applied; and

(b) any additional payments which, on a final determination of fees, would be paid to the litigator under paragraph 12 of Schedule 2.

(12) Where the claim is made under paragraph (2)(b), the amount of the interim payment is the sum of—

(a) the fee which, on a final determination of fees, would be paid to the litigator under paragraph 13 of Schedule 2 and the scenario "Transfer before cracked retrial (new litigator)" set out in the table following that paragraph; and

(b) any additional payments which, on a final determination of fees, would be paid to the litigator under paragraph 12 of Schedule 2.

(13) Where the claim is made under paragraph (2)(c), the amount of the interim payment is—

(a) the sum of—

(i) the fee determined in accordance with paragraph (14) on the basis that the trial length is one day; and

(ii) any additional payments which, on a final determination of fees, must be paid to the litigator under paragraph 12 of Schedule 2;

(b) less any amount paid to the litigator, in the proceedings in question, for a claim under paragraph (2)(a) or (b).

(14) The fee referred to in paragraph (13)(a)(i) is—

(a) where the number of pages of prosecution evidence is less than or equal to the PPE Cut-off specified in the table following paragraph 5(2) of Schedule 2, the basic fee specified in the table following paragraph 7(2) of that Schedule as appropriate to the offence with which the assisted person is charged and the number of pages of prosecution evidence served on the court;

(b) where the pages of prosecution evidence exceeds the PPE Cut-off specified in the table following paragraph 5(2) of Schedule 2, the final fee as calculated in accordance with paragraph 9(2) of that Schedule as appropriate to the offence with which the assisted person is charged and the number of pages of prosecution evidence served on the court.

(15) For purposes of paragraphs (11) to (14)—

(a) the number of defendants;

(b) the number of pages of prosecution evidence served on the court; and

(c) the offence with which the assisted person is charged are determined as at the date of the claim for the interim payment.

(16) Where a litigator has received a hardship payment under regulation 21, the amount of that hardship payment must be deducted from any interim payment payable to that litigator under this regulation.

(17) Where a litigator has already received one or more interim payments under this regulation, the amount to be deducted under paragraph (16) excludes any hardship payment already deducted from any earlier interim payment.

(18) Regulations 28 to 30 do not apply to a payment under this regulation.

(19) In this regulation, "cracked trial", "guilty plea" and "PPE cut-off" have the meaning given in Schedule 2.

(20) For the purpose of this regulation, the number of pages of prosecution evidence served on the court must be determined in accordance with paragraph 1(3) to (5) of Schedule 2.

[This regulation was inserted by the Criminal Legal Aid (Remuneration) (Amendment) (No. 2) Regulations 2014 (SI 2014/2422), reg.2(3), and Sched., with effect from 3 October 2014. The amendments made by those regulations apply to criminal proceedings in which a determination under the LASPOA 2012, s.16 (§ 6-187 in the main work) was made on or after 2 October 2014: reg.3. It is printed as further amended by SI 2015/1369 (G-1a); and SI 2015/1678 (G-1a).]

Interim payments in cases awaiting determination of fees

18.—(1) The appropriate officer must authorise an interim payment in respect of a claim for fees in proceedings in the Crown Court in accordance with this regulation. **G-23**

(2) Entitlement to a payment arises in respect of a claim for fees by a trial advocate, where—

(a) the graduated fee claimed in accordance with Schedule 1 is £4,000 or more (exclusive of value added tax); and

(b) the claim for fees is for less than the amount mentioned in sub-paragraph (a) but is related to any claim for fees falling under sub-paragraph (a).

(3) For the purposes of this regulation, the following claims for fees are related to each other—

(a) the claims of trial advocates acting in the same proceedings for a defendant; and

(b) the claims of any instructed advocate acting for any assisted person in related proceedings.

(4) Entitlement to a payment under paragraph (1) does not arise until three months have elapsed from the earlier of—

(a) the date on which the claim for fees is received by the appropriate officer for determination, except that where there are related claims for fees, the date on which the last claim is received by the appropriate officer; or

(b) three months after the conclusion of the last of any related proceedings.

(5) A trial advocate may submit a claim for an interim payment under this regulation where—

(a) no payment has been made under paragraph (1); and

(b) six months have elapsed from the conclusion of the proceedings against the assisted person.

(6) Subject to regulation 31, payment must not be made under this regulation unless the trial advocate has submitted a claim for fees in accordance with regulation 4(3).

(7) In this regulation, where the main hearing is a trial, "trial advocate" means an advocate who—

(a) is instructed pursuant to a section 16 determination to represent the assisted person at the trial, and

(b) attends the first day of the trial.

[This regulation is printed as amended, with effect from 5 May 2015, by the Criminal Legal Aid (Remuneration) (Amendment) Regulations 2015 (SI 2015/882), reg.2(3)(b), (4)(b), (5)(b) and (9). For the transitional provision, see G-6.]

Amount of interim payments in cases awaiting determination of fees

19.—(1) Where entitlement to an interim payment arises under regulation 18, the amount payable is 40% of the total claim for fees, less any sum already paid. **G-24**

(2) Regulations 28 to 30 do not apply to an interim payment under this regulation.

Staged payments in long Crown Court proceedings

20.—(1) An instructed advocate may submit a claim to the appropriate officer for a staged payment of the instructed advocate's fees in relation to proceedings in the Crown Court. **G-25**

(2) Where a claim is submitted in accordance with this regulation, a staged payment must be allowed where the appropriate officer is satisfied—

(a) that the claim relates to fees for a period of preparation of 100 hours or more, for which the instructed advocate will, subject to final determination of the fees payable, be entitled to be paid in accordance with Schedule 1; and

(b) that the period from sending for trial (or from the date of the section 16 determination, if later) to the conclusion of the Crown Court proceedings is likely to exceed 12 months, having regard, amongst other matters, to the number of defendants, the anticipated pleas and the weight and complexity of the case.

(3) In this regulation, "preparation" means—

(a) reading the papers in the case;

(b) contact with prosecutors;

(c) written or oral advice on plea;

(d) researching the law, preparation for examination of witnesses and preparation of oral submissions;

(e) viewing exhibits or undisclosed material at police stations;

(f) written advice on evidence;

(g) preparation of written submissions, notices or other documents for use at the trial;

(h) attendance at views at the scene of the alleged offence,

and is limited to preparation done before the trial, except in proceedings in which a preparatory hearing has been ordered under section 8 of the Criminal Justice Act 1987 (commencement of trial and arraignment), in which case it is limited to preparation done before the date on which the jury is sworn (or on which it became certain, by reason of pleas of guilty or otherwise, that the matter would not proceed to trial).

(4) The amount allowed for preparation falling within paragraph (3) must be determined by reference to the number of hours of preparation which it appears to the appropriate officer, without prejudice to the final determination of the fees payable, has been reasonably done, multiplied by the hourly rate for special preparation as set out in the table following paragraph 24 of Schedule 1, as appropriate to the category of advocate.

(5) A claim for staged payment of fees under this regulation must be made to the appropriate officer in such form and manner as the appropriate officer may direct, including such case plan as the appropriate officer may require for the purposes of paragraph (2)(a).

(6) An instructed advocate may claim further staged payments in accordance with this regulation in respect of further periods of preparation exceeding 100 hours which were not included in an earlier claim.

(7) Regulations 28 to 30 do not apply to a payment under this regulation.

[This regulation is printed as amended by SI 2015/1678 (G-1a).]

Hardship payments

G-25a **21.**—(1) Subject to paragraphs (5) and (6), the appropriate officer may allow a hardship payment to a representative in the circumstances set out in paragraph (2).

(2) Those circumstances are that the representative—

(a) represents the assisted person in proceedings in the Crown Court;

(b) applies for such payment, in such form and manner as the appropriate officer may direct, not less than one month after the representative was first instructed in those proceedings, or in related proceedings if the representative was instructed in those proceedings earlier than in the proceedings to which the application relates;

(c) is unlikely to receive final payment in respect of the proceedings, as determined under Schedule 1 or 2, within the three months following the application for the hardship payment; and

(d) satisfies the appropriate officer that, by reason of the circumstance in sub-paragraph (c), the representative is likely to suffer financial hardship.

(3) Every application for a hardship payment by an advocate must be accompanied by such information and documents as the appropriate officer may require as evidence of—

(a) the work done by the advocate in relation to the proceedings up to the date of the application; and

(b) the likelihood of financial hardship.

(4) Every application for a hardship payment by a litigator must be accompanied by such information and documents as the appropriate officer may require as evidence of—

(a) the Class of Offence with which the assisted person is charged, in accordance with the LFGS Table of Offences;

(b) the length of trial, where appropriate;

(c) the number of pages of prosecution evidence, determined in accordance with paragraph 1(2) of Schedule 2;
(d) the total number of defendants in the proceedings who are represented by the litigator, where appropriate;
(e) the likelihood of financial hardship.

(5) The amount of any hardship payment is at the discretion of the appropriate officer, but must not exceed such sum as would be reasonable remuneration for the work done by the representative in the proceedings up to the date of the application.

(6) A hardship payment must not be made if it appears to the appropriate officer that the sum which would be reasonable remuneration for the representative, or the sum required to relieve the representative's financial hardship, is less than £450 (excluding value added tax).

(7) Subject to paragraphs (9) and (10) where the appropriate officer allows a hardship payment under paragraph (1), the appropriate officer must authorise payment accordingly.

(8) Where the application for a hardship payment is made by an advocate other than a trial advocate, and the appropriate officer allows a hardship payment under paragraph (1)—

(a) payment must be made to the—
  (i) appropriate trial advocate who attends the first day of trial, where the trial has commenced;
  (ii) appropriate trial advocate, where a trial has not commenced, or
  (iii) appropriate instructed advocate, where there is no trial advocate, and;
(b) the appropriate officer must notify the advocate who made the application that payment has been made to the appropriate trial advocate or the appropriate instructed advocate.

(9) Where a litigator has received an interim payment under regulation 17A, the amount of that interim payment must be deducted from any hardship payment payable to that litigator under this regulation.

(10) Where a litigator has already received one or more hardship payments under this regulation, the amount deducted under paragraph (9) excludes any interim payment already deducted from any earlier hardship payment.

(11) In paragraph (8)—

"appropriate instructed advocate" means—
  (a) where the section 16 determination provides for representation by a single advocate, the instructed advocate, or
  (b) where the section 16 determination provides for representation by more than one advocate, the leading instructed advocate or the led instructed advocate, as appropriate, and

"appropriate trial advocate" means—
  (a) where the section 16 determination provides for representation by a single advocate, the trial advocate, or
  (b) where the section 16 determination provides for representation by more than one advocate, the leading trial advocate or the led trial advocate, as appropriate.

[This regulation is printed as amended by SI 2014/2422 (G-22). For the transitional provision, see G-22. It is printed as further amended, with effect from 5 May 2015, by the Criminal Legal Aid (Remuneration) (Amendment) Regulations 2015 (SI 2015/882), reg.2(3)(c) and (10) (for transitional provision, see G-6); by SI 2015/1369 (G-1a) ; and, with effect from 1 May 2020, by SI 2020/472 (so that in (2)(b), "six months" is replaced with "one month" and in (6) "£5,000" is replaced with "£450").]

Computation of final claim where an interim payment has been made

22.—(1) At the conclusion of a case in which one or more payments have been made to an instructed advocate, a trial advocate or a litigator under regulations 17A to 21, the trial advocate or litigator must submit a claim under regulation 4 or 5 for the determination of the overall remuneration, whether or not such a claim will result in any payment additional to those already made. **G-26**

(2) In the determination of the amount payable to a trial advocate or litigator under regulation 4 or 5—

(a) the appropriate officer must deduct the amount of any payment made under regulations 17A to 21 in respect of the same case from the amount that would otherwise be payable; and
(b) if the amount of the interim payment is greater than the amount that would otherwise be payable, the appropriate officer may recover the amount of the difference, either by way of repayment by the trial advocate or litigator or by way of deduction from any other amount that may be due to the trial advocate or litigator.

(3) In this regulation, where the main hearing is a trial, "trial advocate" means an advocate who—

(a) is instructed pursuant to a section 16 determination to represent the assisted person at the trial, and

(b) attends the first day of the trial.

[This regulation is printed as amended by SI 2014/2422 (G-22). For the transitional provision, see G-22. It is also printed as further amended, with effect from 5 May 2015, by the Criminal Legal Aid (Remuneration) (Amendment) Regulations 2015 (SI 2015/882), reg.2(3)(d), (6)(b) and (11). For the transitional provision, see G-6.]

Payment of fees to advocates–Crown Court

G-27 **23.**—(1) Having determined the fees payable to each trial advocate, in accordance with Schedule 1, the appropriate officer must notify each trial advocate of the fees payable and authorise payment accordingly.

(2) Where, as a result of any redetermination or appeal made or brought pursuant to regulations 28 to 30, the fees payable under paragraph (1) are altered—

(a) if they are increased, the appropriate officer must authorise payment of the increase; or

(b) if they are decreased, the trial advocate must repay the amount of such decrease.

(3) Where the payment of any fees of a trial advocate is ordered under regulation 29(12) or regulation 30(8), the appropriate officer must authorise payment.

(4) In this regulation, where the main hearing is a trial, "trial advocate" means an advocate who—

(a) is instructed pursuant to a section 16 determination to represent the assisted person at the trial, and

(b) attends the first day of the trial.

[This regulation is printed as amended, with effect from 5 May 2015, by the Criminal Legal Aid (Remuneration) (Amendment) Regulations 2015 (SI 2015/882), reg.2(3)(e), (5)(c), (6)(c) and (12). For the transitional provision, see G-6.]

Payment of fees to litigators–Crown Court

G-28 **24.**—(1) Having determined the fees payable to a litigator in accordance with Schedule 2, the appropriate officer must authorise payment accordingly.

(2) Where the appropriate officer determines that the fees payable under paragraph (1) are greater than or less than the amount claimed by the litigator under regulation 5(1), the appropriate officer must notify the litigator of the amount the appropriate officer has determined to be payable.

(3) Where, as a result of any redetermination or appeal made or brought pursuant to regulations 28 to 30, the fees payable under paragraph (1) are altered—

(a) if they are increased, the appropriate officer must authorise payment of the increase; or

(b) if they are decreased, the litigator must repay the amount of such decrease.

(4) Where the payment of any fees of the litigator is ordered under regulation 29(12) or regulation 30(8), the appropriate officer must authorise payment.

Recovery of overpayments

G-29 **25.**—(1) This regulation applies where a representative is entitled to be paid a certain sum ("the amount due") by virtue of the provisions of Schedule 1, 2 or 3 and, for whatever reason, the representative is paid an amount greater than that sum.

(2) Where this regulation applies, the appropriate officer may—

(a) require immediate repayment of the amount in excess of the amount due ("the excess amount"); or

(b) deduct the excess amount from any other sum which is or becomes payable to the representative by virtue of the provisions of Schedule 1, 2 or 3,

and where sub-paragraph (a) applies the representative must repay the excess amount to the appropriate officer.

(3) The appropriate officer may proceed under paragraph (2)(b) without first proceeding under paragraph (2)(a).

(4) Paragraph (2) applies notwithstanding that the representative to whom the excess amount was paid is exercising, or may exercise, a right under regulations 28 to 30.

(5) In this regulation, where the main hearing is a trial, "trial advocate" means, for the purposes of the meaning of "representative", the advocate who—

(a) is instructed pursuant to a section 16 determination to represent the assisted person at the trial, and

(b) attends the first day of the trial.

[This regulation is printed as amended, with effect from 5 May 2015, by the Criminal Legal Aid (Remuneration) (Amendment) Regulations 2015 (SI 2015/882), reg.2(13). For the transitional provision, see G-6.]

Adverse observations

26.—(1) Where in any proceedings to which Schedule 1, 2 or 3 applies, the court makes adverse observations concerning a representative's conduct of the proceedings, the appropriate officer may reduce any fee which would otherwise be payable in accordance with Schedule 1, 2 or 3 by such proportion as the appropriate officer considers reasonable. **G-30**

(2) Before reducing the fee payable to a representative in accordance with the provisions of paragraph (1), the appropriate officer must give the representative the opportunity to make representations about whether it is appropriate to reduce the fee and the extent to which the fee should be reduced.

Wasted costs orders

27.—(1) Subject to paragraph (2), where the court has disallowed the whole or any part of any wasted costs under section 19A of the Prosecution of Offences Act 1985 (costs against legal representatives etc), the appropriate officer, in determining fees in respect of work done by the representative against whom the wasted costs order was made, may deduct the amount in the wasted costs order from the amount otherwise payable in accordance with these Regulations. **G-31**

(2) Where the appropriate officer, in accordance with this regulation, is minded to disallow any amount of a claim for work done to which the wasted costs order relates, the appropriate officer must disallow that amount or the amount of the wasted costs order, whichever is the greater.

Redetermination of fees by appropriate officer

28.—(1) Where— **G-32**

(a) an advocate in proceedings in the Crown Court is dissatisfied with the decision not to allow any of the following fees, or with the number of hours allowed in the calculation of such a fee, namely—

(i) a special preparation fee under paragraph 17 of Schedule 1; or

(ii) a wasted preparation fee under paragraph 18 of Schedule 1; or

(b) a trial advocate in proceedings in the Crown Court is dissatisfied with—

(i) the decision not to allow an hourly fee in respect of attendance at conferences or views at the scene of the alleged offence under paragraph 19 of Schedule 1, or with the number of hours allowed in the calculation of such a fee;

(ii) the calculation by the appropriate officer of the fee payable to the trial advocate in accordance with Schedule 1; or

(iii) the decision of the appropriate officer under paragraph 3(3) of Schedule 1; or

(c) a litigator is dissatisfied with—

(i) the determination by the appropriate officer of the fee payable to the litigator in accordance with Schedule 2; or

(ii) the decision of the appropriate officer under paragraph 3(3) of Schedule 2,

the advocate, trial advocate or litigator, as the case may be, may apply to the appropriate officer to redetermine those fees, to review that decision or to reclassify the offence, as appropriate.

(2) An application under paragraph (1) may not challenge the quantum of any of the fees set out in Schedule 1 or Schedule 2.

(3) Subject to regulation 31, an application under paragraph (1), or paragraph 11(1) of Schedule 3, must be made—

(a) within 21 days of the receipt of the fees payable under regulation 23, regulation 24 or paragraph 10 of Schedule 3, as appropriate;

(b) by giving notice in writing to the appropriate officer, specifying the matters in respect of which the application is made and the grounds of objection; and

(c) in such form and manner as the appropriate officer may direct.

(4) The notice of application must be accompanied by the information and documents supplied under regulation 4, regulation 5 or Schedule 3, as appropriate.

(5) The notice of application must state whether the applicant wishes to appear or to be represented and, if the applicant so wishes, the appropriate officer must notify the applicant of the hearing date and time.

(6) The applicant must supply such further information and documents as the appropriate officer may require.

(7) The appropriate officer must, in the light of the objections made by the applicant or on behalf of the applicant—

(a) redetermine the fees, whether by way of confirmation, or increase or decrease in the amount previously determined;

(b) confirm—

(i) in the case of a redetermination requested by an advocate, the banding of the offence within band 17.1; or

(ii) in the case of a redetermination requested by a litigator, the classification of the offence within Class H; or

(c) re-band or reclassify the offence,

as the case may be, and must notify the applicant of his decision.

(8) Where the applicant so requests, the appropriate officer must give reasons in writing for the appropriate officer's decision.

(9) Subject to regulation 31, any request under paragraph (8) must be made within 21 days of receiving notification of the appropriate officer's decision under paragraph (7).

(10) In this regulation, where the main hearing is a trial, "trial advocate" means an advocate who—

(a) is instructed pursuant to a section 16 determination to represent the assisted person at the trial, and

(b) attends the first day of the trial.

[This regulation is printed as amended, with effect from 5 May 2015, by the Criminal Legal Aid (Remuneration) (Amendment) Regulations 2015 (SI 2015/882), reg.2(14) (for transitional provision, see G-6; by SI 2015/1369 (G-1a), with effect from 1 April 2016; and, with effect from 1 April 2018, by SI 2018/220 (G-1a) (for transitional provisions, see G-1a).]

Appeals to a costs judge

G-33 **29.**—(1) Where the appropriate officer has given his reasons for his decision under regulation 28(8), a representative who is dissatisfied with that decision may appeal to a costs judge.

(2) Subject to regulation 31, an appeal under paragraph (1) or paragraph 11(2) of Schedule 3 must be instituted within 21 days of the receipt of the appropriate officer's reasons, by giving notice in writing to the Senior Costs Judge.

(3) The appellant must send a copy of any notice of appeal given under paragraph (2) to the appropriate officer.

(4) The notice of appeal must be accompanied by—

(a) a copy of any written representations given under regulation 28(3);

(b) the appropriate officer's reasons for the appropriate officer's decision given under regulation 28(8); and

(c) the information and documents supplied to the appropriate officer under regulation 28.

(5) The notice of appeal must—

(a) be in such form as the Senior Costs Judge may direct;

(b) specify separately each item appealed against, showing (where appropriate) the amount claimed for the item, the amount determined and the grounds of the objection to the determination; and

(c) state whether the appellant wishes to appear or to be represented or whether the appellant will accept a decision given in the appellant's absence.

(6) The Senior Costs Judge may, and if so directed by the Lord Chancellor either generally or in a particular case must, send to the Lord Chancellor a copy of the notice of appeal together with copies of such other documents as the Lord Chancellor may require.

(7) With a view to ensuring that the public interest is taken into account, the Lord Chancellor may arrange for written or oral representations to be made on the Lord Chancellor's behalf and, if the Lord Chancellor intends to do so, the Lord Chancellor must inform the Senior Costs Judge and the appellant.

(8) Any written representations made on behalf of the Lord Chancellor under paragraph (7) must be sent to the Senior Costs Judge and the appellant and, in the case of oral representations, the Senior Costs Judge and the appellant must be informed of the grounds on which such representations will be made.

(9) The appellant must be permitted a reasonable opportunity to make representations in reply.

(10) The costs judge must inform the appellant (or the person representing him) and the Lord Chancellor, where representations have been or are to be made on the Lord Chancellor's behalf, of the date of any hearing and, subject to the provisions of this regulation, may give directions as to the conduct of the appeal.

(11) The costs judge may consult the trial judge or the appropriate officer and may require the

appellant to provide any further information which the costs judge requires for the purpose of the appeal and, unless the costs judge otherwise directs, no further evidence may be received on the hearing of the appeal and no ground of objection may be raised which was not raised under regulation 28.

(12) The costs judge has the same powers as the appropriate officer under these Regulations and, in the exercise of such powers, may alter the redetermination of the appropriate officer in respect of any sum allowed, whether by increasing or decreasing it, as the costs judge thinks fit.

(13) The costs judge must communicate his decision and the reasons for it in writing to the appellant, the Lord Chancellor and the appropriate officer.

(14) Where the costs judge increases the sums redetermined under regulation 28, the costs judge may allow the appellant a sum in respect of part or all of any reasonable costs incurred by the appellant in connection with the appeal (including any fee payable in respect of an appeal).

Appeals to the High Court

30.—(1) A representative who is dissatisfied with the decision of a costs judge on an appeal under regulation 29 may apply to a costs judge to certify a point of principle of general importance. **G-34**

(2) Subject to regulation 31, an application under paragraph (1) or paragraph 11(3) of Schedule 3 must be made within 21 days of receiving notification of a costs judge's decision under regulation 29(13).

(3) Where a costs judge certifies a point of principle of general importance the appellant may appeal to the High Court against the decision of a costs judge on an appeal under regulation 29, and the Lord Chancellor must be a respondent to such an appeal.

(4) Subject to regulation 31, an appeal under paragraph (3) must be instituted within 21 days of receiving notification of a costs judge's certificate under paragraph (1).

(5) Where the Lord Chancellor is dissatisfied with the decision of a costs judge on an appeal under regulation 29, the Lord Chancellor may, if no appeal has been made by an appellant under paragraph (3), appeal to the High Court against that decision, and the appellant must be a respondent to the appeal.

(6) Subject to regulation 31, an appeal under paragraph (5) must be instituted within 21 days of receiving notification of the costs judge's decision under regulation 29(13).

(7) An appeal under paragraph (3) or (5) must—

(a) be brought in the Queen's Bench Division;

(b) subject to paragraph (4), follow the procedure set out in Part 52 of the Civil Procedure Rules 1998; and

(c) be heard and determined by a single judge whose decision will be final.

(8) The judge has the same powers as the appropriate officer and a costs judge under these Regulations and may reverse, affirm or amend the decision appealed against or make such other order as the judge thinks fit.

Time limits

31.—(1) Subject to paragraph (2), the time limit within which any act is required or authorised to be done under these Regulations may, for good reason, be extended— **G-35**

(a) in the case of acts required or authorised to be done under regulations 29 or 30, by a costs judge or the High Court as the case may be; and

(b) in the case of acts required or authorised to be done by a representative under any other regulation, by the appropriate officer.

(2) Where a representative without good reason has failed (or, if an extension were not granted, would fail) to comply with a time limit, the appropriate officer, a costs judge or the High Court, as the case may be, may, in exceptional circumstances, extend the time limit and must consider whether it is reasonable in the circumstances to reduce the fees payable to the representative under regulations 4, 5 or 6, provided that the fees must not be reduced unless the representative has been allowed a reasonable opportunity to show cause orally or in writing why the fees should not be reduced.

(3) A representative may appeal to a costs judge against a decision made under this regulation by an appropriate officer and such an appeal must be instituted within 21 days of the decision being given by giving notice in writing to the Senior Costs Judge specifying the grounds of appeal.

(4) In this regulation, where the main hearing is a trial, "trial advocate" means, for the purposes of the meaning of "representative", the advocate who—

(a) is instructed pursuant to a section 16 determination to represent the assisted person at the trial, and

(b) attends the first day of the trial.

[This regulation is printed as amended, with effect from 5 May 2015, by the Criminal Legal Aid

(Remuneration) (Amendment) Regulations 2015 (SI 2015/882), reg.2(15). For the transitional provision, see G-6.]

Regulation 4

SCHEDULE 1

ADVOCATES' GRADUATED FEE SCHEME

PART 1

Definitions and Scope

Interpretation

G-36 1.—(1) In this Schedule—

"case" means proceedings in the Crown Court against any one assisted person—

(a) on one or more counts of a single indictment;

(b) arising out of a single notice of appeal against conviction or sentence, or a single committal for sentence, whether on one or more charges; or

(c) arising out of a single alleged breach of an order of the Crown Court,

and a case falling within paragraph (c) must be treated as a separate case from the proceedings in which the order was made;

"cracked trial" means a case on indictment in which—

(a) the assisted person enters a plea of not guilty to one or more counts at the first hearing at which he or she enters a plea and—

(i) the case does not proceed to trial (whether by reason of pleas of guilty or for other reasons) or the prosecution offers no evidence; and

(ii) either—

(aa) in respect of one or more counts to which the assisted person pleaded guilty, the assisted person did not so plead at the first hearing at which he or she entered a plea; or

(bb) in respect of one or more counts which did not proceed, the prosecution did not, before or at the first hearing at which the assisted person entered a plea, declare an intention of not proceeding with them; or

(b) the case is listed for trial without a hearing at which the assisted persons enters a plea;

"excluded hearing" means—

(a) the first hearing at which the assisted person enters a plea;

(b) any hearing which forms part of the main hearing, or

(c) any hearing for which a fee is payable under a provision of this Schedule other than paragraph 12(2);

"guilty plea" means a case on indictment which—

(a) is disposed of without a trial because the assisted person pleaded guilty to one or more counts; and

(b) is not a cracked trial;

"*Newton* hearing" means a hearing at which evidence is heard for the purpose of determining the sentence of a convicted person in accordance with the principles of *Newton* (1983) 77 Cr. App. R. 13;

"standard appearance" means an appearance by the trial advocate or substitute advocate in any of the following hearings unless it is an excluded hearing—

(b) a pre-trial review;

(bb) a case management hearing;

(c) the hearing of a case listed for plea which is adjourned for trial;

(d) any hearing (except a trial, the first hearing at which the assisted person enters a plea or a hearing referred to in paragraph 2(1)(b)) which is listed but cannot proceed because of the failure of the assisted person or a witness to attend, the unavailability of a pre-sentence report or other good reason;

(e) custody time limit applications;

(f) bail and other applications (except where any such applications take place in the course of a hearing referred to in paragraph 2(1)(b));

(g) the hearing of the case listed for mention only, including applications relating to the date of the trial (except where an application takes place in the course of a hearing referred to in paragraph 2(1)(b));

(i) a preliminary hearing; or

(j) a hearing, whether contested or not, relating to breach of bail, failure to surrender to bail or execution of a bench warrant,

provided that a fee is not payable elsewhere under this Schedule in respect of the hearing;

"substitute advocate" means an advocate who is not an instructed advocate or the trial advocate but who undertakes work on the case;

"unused material" means material disclosed pursuant to the prosecutors' obligations in Part 1 of the Criminal Procedure and Investigations Act 1996, but does not include—

(a) witness statements;

(b) documentary and pictorial exhibits;

(c) records of interviews with the assisted person; and

(d) records of interviews with other defendants.

(2) For the purposes of this Schedule, the number of pages of prosecution evidence served on the court must be determined in accordance with sub-paragraphs (3) to (5).

(3) The number of pages of prosecution evidence includes all—

(a) witness statements;

(b) documentary and pictorial exhibits;

(c) records of interviews with the assisted person; and

(d) records of interviews with other defendants,

which form part of the served prosecution documents or which are included in any notice of additional evidence.

(4) Subject to sub-paragraph (5), a document served by the prosecution in electronic form is included in the number of pages of prosecution evidence.

(5) A documentary or pictorial exhibit which—

(a) has been served by the prosecution in electronic form; and

(b) has never existed in paper form,

is not included within the number of pages of prosecution evidence unless the appropriate officer decides that it would be appropriate to include it in the pages of prosecution evidence taking into account the nature of the document and any other relevant circumstances.

(6) In proceedings on indictment in the Crown Court initiated otherwise than by sending for trial, the appropriate officer must determine the number of pages of prosecution evidence in accordance with sub-paragraphs (2) to (5) or as nearly in accordance with those sub-paragraphs as possible as the nature of the case permits.

(7) A reference in this Schedule to a "band" is to the band of the offence concerned set out in Table B in the AGFS Banding Document, as read in conjunction with Table A in that document.

(8) Where the band within which an offence described in Table B in the AGFS Banding Document falls depends on the facts of the case, the band within which the offence falls is to be determined by reference to Table A in that document.

[This paragraph is printed as amended by SI 2015/882, SI 2015/1678, SI 2018/220, and with effect from 17 September 2020, SI 2020/903. For the detail of each and the transitional provisions see G-1a.]

Application

2.—(1) Subject to sub-paragraphs (2) to (11), this Schedule applies to— G-37

(a) every case on indictment; and

(b) the following proceedings in the Crown Court—

(i) an appeal against conviction or sentence;

(ii) a sentencing hearing following a committal for sentence to the Crown Court; and

(iii) proceedings arising out of an alleged breach of an order of the Crown Court (whether or not this Schedule applies to the proceedings in which the order was made).

(2) Sub-paragraphs (3) and (4) apply where, following a trial, an order is made for a new trial and the same trial advocate appears at both trials where—

(a) the defendant is an assisted person at both trials; or

(b) the defendant is an assisted person at the new trial only; or

(c) the new trial is a cracked trial or guilty plea.

(3) Subject to sub-paragraph (4), in respect of a new trial, or if the trial advocate so elects, in respect of the first trial, the graduated fee payable to the trial advocate must be calculated in accordance with Part 2 or Part 3, as appropriate, except that the fee must be reduced by—

(a) 30%, where the new trial started within one month of the conclusion of the first trial;

(b) 20%, where the new trial did not start within one month of the conclusion of the first trial;

(c) 40%, where the new trial becomes a cracked trial or guilty plea within one month of the conclusion of the first trial; or

(d) 25% where the new trial becomes a cracked trial or guilty plea more than one month after the conclusion of the first trial.

(4) Where—

(a) in relation to the first trial, the case was sent for trial to the Crown Court on the election of a defendant where the magistrates' court had determined the case to be suitable for summary trial; and

(b) the new trial becomes a cracked trial or guilty plea,

the fee payable to the trial advocate must be

(i) the graduated fee calculated in accordance with Part 2, in respect of the first trial; and

(ii) the fixed fee set out in paragraph 10 in respect of the new trial.

(5) Sub-paragraphs (6) and (7) apply in the circumstances set out in sub-paragraph (2) but where a different trial advocate appears for the assisted person at each trial.

(6) Subject to sub-paragraph (7), in respect of each trial, the graduated fee payable to the trial advocate must be calculated in accordance with Part 2 or Part 3 as appropriate.

(7) Where—

(a) in relation to the first trial, the case was sent for trial to the Crown Court on the election of a defendant where the magistrates' court had determined the case to be suitable for summary trial; and

(b) the new trial becomes a cracked trial or guilty plea,

the fee payable to the trial advocate at the first trial must be the graduated fee, calculated in accordance with Part 2 and the fee payable to the trial advocate at the new trial must be the fixed fee set out in paragraph 10.

(8) Where following a case on indictment a *Newton* hearing takes place—

(a) for the purposes of this Schedule the case is to be treated as having gone to trial;

(b) the length of the trial is to be taken to be the combined length of the main hearing and the *Newton* hearing;

(c) the provisions of this Schedule relating to cracked trials and guilty pleas do not apply; and

(d) no fee is payable under paragraph 15 in respect of the *Newton* hearing.

(10) Where, at any time after proceedings are sent for trial to the Crown Court they are—

(a) discontinued by a notice served under section 23A of the Prosecution of Offences Act 1985 (discontinuance of proceedings after accused has been sent for trial), or

(b) dismissed pursuant to paragraph 2 of Schedule 3 to the Crime and Disorder Act 1998 (applications for dismissal),

the provisions of paragraph 22 apply.

(11) For the purposes of this Schedule, a case on indictment which discontinues at or before the first hearing at which the assisted person enters a plea otherwise than—

(a) by reason of a plea of guilty being entered; or

(b) in accordance with sub-paragraph (10),

must be treated as a guilty plea.

[Paragraph 2 is printed as amended by SI 2015/1678 (G-1a).]

Bands of offences

G-38 3.—(1) For the purposes of this Schedule—

(a) every indictable offence falls within the band of that offence set out in the AGFS Banding Document and, subject to sub-paragraph (2), indictable offences not specifically so listed are deemed to fall within band 17.1;

(b) conspiracy to commit an indictable offence contrary to section 1 of the Criminal Law Act 1977 (the offence of conspiracy), incitement to commit an indictable offence and attempts to commit an indictable offence contrary to section 1 of the Criminal Attempts Act 1981 (attempting to commit an offence) fall within the same band as the substantive offence to which they relate;

(c) where the AGFS Banding Document specifies that the band within which an offence falls depends on whether the value, amount or weight involved exceeds a stated limit, the value, amount or weight must be presumed not to exceed that limit unless the advocate making the claim under regulation 4 proves otherwise to the satisfaction of the appropriate officer;

(d) where more than one count of the indictment is for an offence in relation to which the band depends on the value, amount or weight involved, that value, amount or weight must be taken to the total value, amount or weight involved in all those offences, but where two or more counts relate to the same property, the value, amount or weight of that property must be taken into account once only;

(e) where an entry in the AGFS Banding Document specifies an offence as being contrary to a statutory provision, then subject to any express limitation in the entry that entry includes every offence contrary to that statutory provision whether or not the words of description in the entry are appropriate to cover all such offences;

(f) where in a case on indictment there is a hearing to determine the question of whether an assisted person is unfit to plead or unfit to stand trial, the trial advocate must elect whether that hearing falls within the same band as the indictable offence to which it relates or within band 5.3; and

(g) where in a case on indictment a restriction order is made, the offence is to be treated as if it falls within band 1.3, regardless of the band within which the offence would fall within the AGFS Banding Document but for this paragraph.

(2) Where an advocate in proceedings in the Crown Court is dissatisfied with the banding within band 17.1 of an indictable offence not listed in the AGFS Banding Document, the advocate may apply to the appropriate officer when lodging the claim for fees to re-band the offence.

(3) The appropriate officer must, in light of the objections made by the advocate–

(a) confirm the banding of the offence within band 17.1; or

(b) re-band the offence,

and must notify the advocate of the decision.

[This paragraph is printed as amended by SI 2018/220 (G-1a). The amendments have no effect in relation to proceedings in respect of which a determination under section 16 of the LASPOA 2012 (see § 6-187 in the main work) is made before 1 April 2018.]

Part 2
Graduated Fees for Trial

Calculation of graduated fees

4. The amount of the graduated fee for a single trial advocate representing one assisted person being tried on one indictment in the Crown Court in a trial lasting one to 40 days must be calculated in accordance with the following formula– **G-39**

GF = BF + (D x DAF)

where–

GF is the amount of the graduated fee;

BF is the basic fee specified as appropriate to the band of the offence for which the assisted person is tried and the category of trial advocate (see paragraph 5);

D is the number of days or parts of a day on which the advocate attends at court by which the trial exceeds 1 day;

DAF is the fee payable in respect of daily attendance at court for the number of days by which the trial exceeds 1 day, as appropriate to the band of the offence for which the assisted person is tried and the category of trial advocate (see paragraph 5A).

[This paragraph is printed as amended by SI 2018/220 (G-1a). The amendments have no effect in relation to proceedings in respect of which a determination under section 16 of the LASPOA 2012 (see § 6-187 in the main work) is made before 1 April 2018.]

Basic fees

5. For the purposes of paragraph 4, in relation to the offence concerned, the basic fee is the amount set out in the table following this paragraph which corresponds with the band within which that offence falls (as set out in column (1) of the table) and the category of the advocate concerned (as set out in columns (2) to (4) of the table). **G-40**

(1) Band of Offence	*(2) Junior Alone or Led Junior (£)*	*(3) Leading Junior (£)*	*(4) Queen's Counsel (£)*
1.1	8,585	12,880	17,170
1.2	4,295	6,445	8,590
1.3	2,575	3,865	5,150
1.4	2,145	3,220	4,290
2.1	8,585	12,880	17,170
2.2	2,575	3,865	5,150
3.1	3,535	5,305	7,070
3.2	2,020	3,030	4,040
3.3	1,200	1,800	2,400

(1) Band of Offence	*(2) Junior Alone or Led Junior (£)*	*(3) Leading Junior (£)*	*(4) Queen's Counsel (£)*
3.4	850	1,275	1,700
3.5	750	1,125	1,500
4.1	2,020	3,030	4,040
4.2	1,565	2,350	3,130
4.3	1,515	2,275	3,030
5.1	1,900	2,850	3,800
5.2	1,415	2,125	2,830
5.3	1,010	1,515	2,020
6.1	8,485	12,730	16,970
6.2	7,700	11,550	15,400
6.3	2,855	4,285	5,710
6.4	1,010	1,515	2,020
6.5	810	1,215	1,620
7.1	1,415	2,125	2,830
7.2	810	1,215	1,620
7.3	760	1,140	1,520
8.1	1,210	1,815	2,420
9.1	5,860	8,790	11,720
9.2	4,040	6,060	8,080
9.3	3,030	4,545	6,060
9.4	2,650	3,975	5,300
9.5	1,615	2,425	3,230
9.6	1,210	1,815	2,420
9.7	810	1,215	1,620
10.1	2,220	3,330	4,440
11.1	1,400	2,100	2,800
11.2	800	1,200	1,600
12.1	2,120	3,180	4,240
12.2	1,315	1,975	2,630
12.3	910	1,365	1,820
13.1	1,800	2,700	3,600
14.1	2,325	3,490	4,650
15.1	1,615	2,425	3,230
15.2	1,400	2,100	2,800
15.3	850	1,275	1,700
16.1	2,220	3,330	4,440
16.2	1,615	2,425	3,230
16.3	1,010	1,515	2,020
17.1	725	1,090	1,450

[This paragraph is printed as amended by SI 2018/220 (G-1a) and SI 2018/1323 (G-1a). For transitional provisions see G-1a.]

Daily attendance fees

G-41 5A. For the purposes of paragraph 4, in relation to the offence concerned, the daily attendance fee is the amount set out in the table following this paragraph which corresponds with the band within which that offence falls (as set out in column (1) of the table) and the category of the advocate concerned (as set out in columns (2) to (4) of the table).

(1) Band of Offence	*(2) Junior Alone or Led Junior (£)*	*(3) Leading Junior (£)*	*(4) Queen's Counsel (£)*
1.1	580	870	1,160
1.2	580	870	1,160
1.3	580	870	1,160
1.4	580	870	1,160
2.1	580	870	1,160
2.2	580	870	1,160
3.1	505	760	1,010
3.2	505	760	1,010
3.3	505	760	1,010
3.4	505	760	1,010
3.5	400	600	800
4.1	530	795	1,060
4.2	505	760	1,010
4.3	480	720	960
5.1	530	795	1,060
5.2	505	760	1,010
5.3	480	720	960
6.1	530	795	1,060
6.2	505	760	1,010
6.3	405	610	810
6.4	400	600	800
6.5	400	600	800
7.1	505	760	1,010
7.2	455	685	910
7.3	405	610	810
8.1	505	760	1,010
9.1	530	795	1,060
9.2	530	795	1,060
9.3	455	685	910
9.4	455	685	910
9.5	455	685	910
9.6	405	610	810
9.7	400	600	800
10.1	530	795	1,060
11.1	455	685	910
11.2	400	600	800
12.1	505	760	1,010
12.2	505	760	1,010
12.3	505	760	1,010
13.1	505	760	1,010
14.1	555	835	1,110
15.1	505	760	1,010
15.2	405	610	810
15.3	400	600	800
16.1	555	835	1,110
16.2	505	760	1,010
16.3	505	760	1,010
17.1	400	600	800

[This paragraph is printed as amended by SI 2018/220 (G-1a) and SI 2018/1323 (G-1a). For transitional provisions see G-1a.]

PART 3

Graduated Fees for Guilty Pleas and Cracked Trials

Scope of Part 3

G-42 6.—(1) Subject to sub-paragraph (2) and to paragraph 22, this Part does not apply to a case sent for trial to the Crown Court on the election of a defendant where the magistrates' court has determined the case to be suitable for a summary trial.

(2) This Part applies in all cases where the trial is a cracked trial because—

(a) the prosecution offer no evidence on all counts against the defendant and the judge directs that a not guilty verdict be entered; or

(b) after the election by the defendant mentioned in sub-paragraph (1)—

(i) there is a substantive change to a count on the indictment and the defendant pleads guilty; or

(ii) the defendant pleads guilty to one or more counts on the indictment and the prosecution offer no evidence on a remaining count, or otherwise do not proceed to trial on a remaining count.

[This paragraph was substituted by SI 2014/2422 (G-21a). For the transitional provision, see G-21a. It is printed as amended by SI 2015/1678 (G-1a); SI 2018/220 (G-1a) and, with effect from 31 December 2018, SI 2018/1323 (for the transitional provision, see G-1a).]

Calculation of fees in guilty pleas and cracked trials

G-43 7. The amount of the fee for a single trial advocate representing one assisted person where the case is—

(a) a guilty plea, is the fee specified in Table A following this paragraph;

(b) a cracked trial, is the fee specified in Table A1 following this paragraph,

as appropriate to the offence with which the assisted person is charged, and the category of the trial advocate.

[This paragraph is printed as substituted by SI 2020/903 (see G-1a), with effect from 17 September 2020. The substituted paragraph applies only to cases in which a determination under the LASPOA 2012, s.16 (§ 6-187 in the main work) was made on or after 17 September 2020.]

G-44 FEE FOR A GUILTY PLEA

G-44

(1) Band of offence	*(2) Junior Alone or Led Junior (£)*	*(3) Leading Junior (£)*	*(4) Queen's Counsel (£)*
1.1	4,295	6,440	8,585
1.2	2,150	3,220	4,295
1.3	1,290	1,930	2,575
1.4	1,075	1,610	2,145
2.1	4,295	6,440	8,585
2.2	1,290	1,930	2,575
3.1	1,770	2,650	3,535
3.2	1,010	1,515	2,020
3.3	600	900	1,200
3.4	425	640	850
3.5	375	565	750
4.1	1,010	1,515	2,020
4.2	785	1,175	1,565
4.3	760	1,135	1,515
5.1	950	1,425	1,900
5.2	710	1,060	1,415
5.3	505	760	1,010
6.1	4,245	6,365	8,485

(1) *Band of offence*	(2) *Junior Alone or Led Junior (£)*	(3) *Leading Junior (£)*	(4) *Queen's Counsel (£)*
6.2	3,850	5,775	7,700
6.3	1,430	2,140	2,855
6.4	505	760	1,010
6.5	405	610	810
7.1	710	1,060	1,415
7.2	405	610	810
7.3	380	570	760
8.1	605	910	1,210
9.1	2,930	4,395	5,860
9.2	2,020	3,030	4,040
9.3	1,515	2,275	3,030
9.4	1,325	1,990	2,650
9.5	810	1,210	1,615
9.6	605	910	1,210
9.7	405	610	810
10.1	1,110	1,665	2,220
11.1	700	1,050	1,400
11.2	400	600	800
12.1	1,060	1,590	2,120
12.2	660	985	1,315
12.3	455	685	910
13.1	900	1,350	1,800
14.1	1,165	1,745	2,325
15.1	810	1,210	1,615
15.2	700	1,050	1,400
15.3	425	640	850
16.1	1,110	1,665	2,220
16.2	810	1,210	1,615
16.3	505	760	1,010
17.1	365	545	725

Table A1: Fee for a Cracked Trial

G-44

(1) *Band of offence*	(2) *Junior Alone or Led Junior*	(3) *Leading Junior*	(4) *Queen's Counsel*
1.1	8,585	12,880	17,170
1.2	4,295	6,445	8,590
1.3	2,575	3,865	5,150
1.4	2,145	3,220	4,290
2.1	8,585	12,880	17,170
2.2	2,575	3,865	5,150
3.1	3,535	5,305	7,070
3.2	2,020	3,030	4,040
3.3	1,200	1,800	2,400
3.4	850	1,275	1,700
3.5	750	1,125	1,500
4.1	2,020	3,030	4,040
4.2	1,565	2,350	3,130
4.3	1,515	2,275	3,030

(1) Band of offence	*(2) Junior Alone or Led Junior*	*(3) Leading Junior*	*(4) Queen's Counsel*
5.1	1,900	2,850	3,800
5.2	1,415	2,125	2,830
5.3	1,010	1,515	2,020
6.1	8,485	12,730	16,970
6.2	7,700	11,550	15,400
6.3	2,855	4,285	5,710
6.4	1,010	1,515	2,020
6.5	810	1,215	1,620
7.1	1,415	2,125	2,830
7.2	810	1,215	1,620
7.3	760	1,140	1,520
8.1	1,210	1,815	2,420
9.1	5,860	8,790	11,720
9.2	4,040	6,060	8,080
9.3	3,030	4,545	6,060
9.4	2,650	3,975	5,300
9.5	1,615	2,425	3,230
9.6	1,210	1,815	2,420
9.7	810	1,215	1,620
10.1	2,220	3,330	4,440
11.1	1,400	2,100	2,800
11.2	800	1,200	1,600
12.1	2,120	3,180	4,240
12.2	1,315	1,975	2,630
12.3	910	1,365	1,820
13.1	1,800	2,700	3,600
14.1	2,325	3,490	4,650
15.1	1,615	2,425	3,230
15.2	1,400	2,100	2,800
15.3	850	1,275	1,700
16.1	2,220	3,330	4,440
16.2	1,615	2,425	3,230
16.3	1,010	1,515	2,020
17.1	725	1,090	1,450

[Paragraph 8 of SI 2013/435 and Table B that followed that paragraph were omitted by SI 2020/903 and new Table A1 inserted with effect from 17 September 2020. For transitional provision, see G-43.]

PART 4

Fixed Fee for Guilty Pleas and Cracked Trials

Scope of Part 4

G-45 9.—(1) Subject to sub-paragraph (2), this Part applies to a case sent for trial to the Crown Court on the election of a defendant where the magistrates' court has determined the case to be suitable for summary trial.

(2) This Part does not apply where the trial is a cracked trial because—

(a) the prosecution offer no evidence on all counts against the defendant and the judge directs that a not guilty verdict be entered; or

(b) after the election by the defendant mentioned in sub-paragraph (1)—

(i) there is a substantive change to a count on the indictment and the defendant pleads guilty; or

(ii) the defendant pleads guilty to one or more counts on the indictment and the prosecution offer no evidence on a remaining count, or otherwise do not proceed to trial on a remaining count.

[This paragraph was substituted by SI 2014/2422 (G-21a). For the transitional provision, see G-21a. It is printed as amended by SI 2015/1678 (G-1a); SI 2018/220 (G-1a); and, with effect from 31 December 2018, SI 2018/1323 (for the transitional provision, see G-1a).]

Fixed fee for guilty pleas or cracked trials

10. The fee payable to an advocate in relation to a guilty plea or cracked trial to which this Part applies is £365 per proceedings.

[This paragraph is printed as amended by SI 2018/1323 (G-1a): for the transitional provision, see G-1a.]

PART 5

Fixed Fees

General provisions

11.—(1) All work undertaken by an advocate in a case to which Part 4 applies is included within the fee set out in paragraph 10 except for attendance at a confiscation hearing to which paragraph 14 applies. **G-47**

(2) Except as provided under this Part, all work undertaken by an advocate in a case to which Part 3 applies is included within the basic fee specified in the table following paragraph 5, or the basic fee specified in the tables following paragraph 7, as appropriate to—

(a) the offence for which the assisted person is tried;
(b) the category of advocate; and
(c) whether the case is a cracked trial, guilty plea or trial.

[This paragraph is printed as amended by SI 2018/220 (G-1a) and, with effect from 17 September 2020, by SI 2020/903 (G-1a).]

Fees for standard appearance

12.—(2) The fee payable in respect of an appearance by the trial advocate or substitute advocate at a standard appearance is specified in the table following paragraph 24 as appropriate to the category of trial advocate or substitute advocate. **G-48**

(4) This paragraph does not apply to a standard appearance which is or forms part of the main hearing in a case or to a hearing for which a fee is payable elsewhere under this Schedule.

[This paragraph is printed as amended by SI 2015/1678 (G-1a) and, with effect from 1 April 2018, by SI 2018/220 (G-1a). The amendments effected by SI 2018/220 are of no effect in relation to proceedings in respect of which a determination under section 16 of the LASPOA 2012 (see § 6-187 in the main work) is made before 1 April 2018.]

Fees for abuse of process, disclosure, admissibility and withdrawal of plea hearings

13.—(1) This paragraph applies to— **G-49**

(a) the hearing of an application to stay the case on indictment or any count on the ground that the proceedings constitute an abuse of the process of the court;
(b) any hearing relating to the question of whether any material should be disclosed by the prosecution to the defence or the defence to the prosecution (whether or not any claim to public interest immunity is made);
(c) the hearing of an application under section 2(1) of the Criminal Procedure (Attendance of Witnesses) Act 1965 (issue of witness summons on application to Crown Court) for disclosure of material held by third parties;
(d) any hearing relating to the question of the admissibility as evidence of any material;
(da) a ground rules hearing ordered in a case in which a special measures direction provides for a recording to be admitted under section 28 (video recorded cross-examination or re-examination) of the Youth Justice and Criminal Evidence Act 1999, and for this purpose "special measures direction" has the meaning given in section 33(1) (interpretation etc. of Chapter I) of that Act; and
(e) the hearing of an application to withdraw a plea of guilty where the application is—
   (i) made by an advocate other than the advocate who appeared at the hearing at which the plea of guilty was entered; and
   (ii) unsuccessful.

(2) Where a hearing to which this paragraph applies is held on any day of the main hearing of a

case on indictment, no separate fee is payable in respect of attendance at the hearing, but the hearing is included in the length of the main hearing for the purpose of calculating the fees payable.

(3) Where a hearing to which this paragraph applies is held prior to the first or only day of the main hearing, it is not included in the length of the main hearing for the purpose of calculating the fees payable and the trial advocate or substitute advocate must be remunerated for attendance at such a hearing—

(a) in respect of any day where the hearing begins before and ends after the luncheon adjournment, at the daily rate set out in the table following paragraph 24 as appropriate to the category of trial advocate or substitute advocate; or

(b) in respect of any day where the hearing begins and ends before the luncheon adjournment, or begins after the luncheon adjournment, at the half-daily rate set out in the table following paragraph 24 as appropriate to the category of trial advocate or substitute advocate.

[This paragraph is printed as amended, with effect from 1 April 2018, by SI 2018/220 (G-1a). The amendments are of no effect in relation to proceedings in respect of which a determination under section 16 of the LASPOA 2012 (see § 6-187 in the main work) is made before 1 April 2018.]

Fees for confiscation hearings

G-50 14.—(1) This paragraph applies to—

(a) a hearing under Part 2 of the Proceeds of Crime Act 2002 (confiscation: England and Wales);

(b) a hearing under section 2 of the Drug Trafficking Act 1994 (confiscation orders); and

(c) a hearing under section 71 of the Criminal Justice Act 1988 (confiscation orders).

(2) A hearing to which this paragraph applies is not included in the length of the main hearing or of any sentencing hearing for the purpose of calculating the fees payable, and the trial advocate or substitute advocate must be remunerated in respect of such a hearing—

(a) where the number of pages of evidence is fewer than 51, for attendance—

(i) in respect of any day when the hearing begins before and ends after the luncheon adjournment, at the daily rate set out in the first section of the table following this sub-paragraph; or

(ii) in respect of any day when the hearing begins and ends before the luncheon adjournment, or begins after the luncheon adjournment, at the half-daily rate set out in the first section of that table,

as appropriate to the category of trial advocate or substitute advocate;

(b) where the number of pages of evidence is between 51 and 1000—

(i) at the rates for the relevant number of pages set out in the second section of the table following this sub-paragraph; and

(ii) where the hearing lasts for more than one day, for attendance on subsequent days or half-days at the daily rate or half-daily rate set out in the first section of that table,

as appropriate to the category of trial advocate or substitute advocate; or

(c) where the number of pages of evidence exceeds 1000—

(i) at the rates for 751 to 1000 pages set out in the second section of the table following this sub-paragraph;

(ii) with such fee as the appropriate officer considers reasonable for preparation in respect of the pages in excess of 1000, at the hourly rates for preparation set out in the third section of that table; and

(iii) where the hearing lasts for more than one day, for attendance on subsequent days or half-days at the daily rate or half-daily rate set out in the first section of that table,

as appropriate to the category of trial advocate or substitute advocate.

FEES FOR CONSFISCATION HEARINGS

	Fee for QC (£)	*Fee for Leading Junior (£)*	*Fee for Junior Alone (£)*	*Fee for Led Junior (£)*
1. Daily and half daily rates				
Half daily rate	263	197	131	131
Daily rate	502	349	240	240
2. Pages of evidence				
51-250	655	546	437	327
251-500	983	819	655	491

	Fee for QC (£)	*Fee for Leading Junior (£)*	*Fee for Junior Alone (£)*	*Fee for Led Junior (£)*
501-750	1,311	1,092	874	655
751-1000	1,965	1,638	1,311	983
3. Preparation				
Hourly rates	74.74	56.56	39.39	39.39

(3) In sub-paragraph (2) "evidence" means–

(a) the statement of information served under section 16 of the Proceeds of Crime Act 2002 and relied on by the prosecution for the purposes of a hearing under Part 2 of that Act, or a similar statement served and so relied on for the purposes of a hearing under section 2 of the Drug Trafficking Act 1994 or under section 71 of the Criminal Justice Act 1988 and, in each case, any attached annexes and exhibits;

(b) any other document which–

(i) is served as a statement or an exhibit for the purposes of the trial;

(ii) is specifically referred to in, but not served with, a statement mentioned in paragraph (a); and

(iii) the prosecution state that they intend to rely on in the hearing; and

(c) any written report of an expert obtained with the prior authority of the Lord Chancellor under regulation 13 or allowed by the appropriate officer under these Regulations, and any attached annexes and exhibits, other than documents contained in such annexes or exhibits which have also been served under paragraph (a) or (b) or which consist of financial records or similar data.

[This paragraph is printed as amended by SI 2018/1323 (G-1a): for the transitional provision, see G-1a.]

Fees for sentencing hearings

15.–(1) Subject to sub-paragraphs (2) to (4), the fee payable to an advocate for appearing at a sentencing hearing is the fixed sentencing hearing fee. **G-51**

(2) Where sentence has been deferred under section 1 (deferment of sentence) of the Powers of Criminal Courts (Sentencing) Act 2000, the fee payable to an advocate for appearing at a sentencing hearing is the fee for a deferred sentencing hearing for the category of the advocate concerned which is set out in the fixed fees table.

(3) Subject to sub-paragraph (4), where a hospital direction, a hospital order or a restriction order is in force in respect of an assisted person in a sentencing hearing, the fee payable to an advocate for appearing at the sentencing hearing is a fee (the "DAF equivalent fee") which is equal to the daily attendance fee under paragraph 5A which relates to the category of the advocate concerned and the band within which the offence for which the assisted person is to be sentenced falls.

(4) Where the sentencing hearing takes place on a day, or at a time, in respect of which an advocate receives, or is to receive, a banded fee–

(a) no fixed sentencing hearing fee is payable to the advocate for appearing at the sentencing hearing under sub-paragraph (1);

(b) no DAF equivalent fee is payable to the advocate for appearing at the sentencing hearing under sub-paragraph (3).

(5) In this paragraph–

"banded fee" means a basic fee under paragraph 5, a daily attendance fee under paragraph 5A or a basic fee (in respect of a guilty plea or a cracked trial) under paragraph 7;

"fixed fees table" means the table following paragraph 24;

"fixed sentencing hearing fee" means the fee for a sentencing hearing for the category of the advocate concerned which is set out in fixed fees table;

"hospital direction" has the meaning given in section 45A (power of higher courts to direct hospital admission) of the Mental Health Act 1983;

"hospital order" has the meaning given in section 37 (powers of courts to order hospital admission or guardianship) of the Mental Health Act 1983;

"sentencing hearing" means a sentencing hearing following a case on indictment to which this Schedule applies.

[This paragraph is printed as substituted by SI 2018/220 (G-1a) and, with effect from 17 September 2020, as subsequently amended by SI 2020/903 (G-1a).]

Fees for ineffective trials

16. The fee set out in the table following paragraph 24 as appropriate to the category of trial **G-52**

advocate is payable in respect of each day on which the case was listed for trial but did not proceed on the day for which it was listed, for whatever reason.

Fees for special preparation

G-53 17.—(1) This paragraph applies where, in any case on indictment in the Crown Court in respect of which a graduated fee is payable under Part 2 or Part 3—

(a) it has been necessary for an advocate to do work by way of preparation substantially in excess of the amount normally done for cases of the same type because the case involves a very unusual or novel point of law or factual issue; or

(b) the number of pages of prosecution evidence, as defined and determined in accordance with paragraph 1(2) to (5), exceeds—

(ai) in cases falling within bands 2.1 and 2.2 (terrorism offences), 750;

(bi) in cases falling within bands 3.1 to 3.5 (serious violence), 700;

(ci) in cases falling within bands 4.1. to 4.3 (sexual offences, children), 750;

(di) in cases falling within bands 5.1 to 5.3 (sexual offences, adult), 650;

(i) in cases falling within bands 6.1 to 6.5 (dishonesty offences, including proceeds of crime and money laundering), 30,000;

(ia) in cases falling within bands 7.1 to 7.3 (property damage offences), 550;

(ib) in cases falling within band 8.1 (offences against the public interest, unless standard), 600;

(ii) in cases falling within bands 9.1 to 9.7 (drugs offences), 15,000; or

(iia) in cases falling within band 10.1 (driving offences), 800;

(iib) in cases falling within bands 11.1 and 11.2 (burglary and robbery), 350;

(iic) in cases falling within bands 12.1 to 12.3 (firearms offences), 750;

(iid) in cases falling within band 13.1 (other offences against the person), 750;

(iie) in cases falling within band 14.1 (exploitation/human trafficking offences), 350;

(iif) in cases falling within bands 15.1 to 15.3 (public order offences), 150;

(iig) in cases falling within bands 16.1 to 16.3 (regulatory offences), 300;

(iih) in cases falling within band 17.1 (standard cases), 100;

(iii) in all other cases, 10,000, and the appropriate officer considers it reasonable to make a payment in excess of the graduated fee payable under this Schedule.

(2) Where this paragraph applies, a special preparation fee may be paid, in addition to the graduated fee payable under Part 2 or Part 3.

(3) The amount of the special preparation fee must be calculated—

(a) where sub-paragraph (1)(a) applies, from the number of hours preparation in excess of the amount the appropriate officer considers reasonable for cases of the same type;

(b) where sub-paragraph (1)(b) applies, from the number of hours which the appropriate officer considers reasonable to read the excess pages;

and in each case using the hourly fee rates set out in the table following paragraph 24 as appropriate to the category of trial advocate.

(4) Any claim for a special preparation fee under this paragraph must be made by a trial advocate, whether or not the trial advocate did the work claimed for.

(5) A trial advocate claiming a special preparation fee must supply such information and documents as may be required by the appropriate officer in support of the claim.

(6) In determining a claim under this paragraph, the appropriate officer must take into account all the relevant circumstances of the case, including, where special preparation work has been undertaken by more than one advocate, the benefit of such work to the trial advocate.

(7) In sub-paragraphs (4) and (5), where the main hearing is a trial, "trial advocate" means the advocate who—

(a) is instructed pursuant to a section 16 determination to represent the assisted person at the trial, and

(b) attends the first day of the trial.

[This paragraph is printed as amended by SI 2015/882, SI 2018/220 and SI 2018/1323 (G-1a): for transitional provisions, see G-1a.]

Fees for consideration of unused material

★G-53a 17A.—(1) This paragraph applies in respect of any case on indictment in the Crown Court, in respect of which a graduated fee is payable under Part 2 or Part 3, other than a guilty plea.

(2) In any case to which this paragraph applies, a fee ("the basic consideration fee") is payable to a

trial advocate in respect of the consideration of unused material which corresponds to the category of the advocate concerned specified in the table following this sub-paragraph, whether or not such consideration has actually occurred.

Category of advocate	*Fee (£)*
QC	112.11
Leading Junior	84.84
Junior alone or Led Junior	59.09

(3) This sub-paragraph applies where–

(a) a trial advocate has undertaken the consideration of unused material; and

(b) the advocate has spent in excess of three hours undertaking that consideration.

(4) In a case where sub-paragraph (3) applies–

(a) a fee ("the additional fee") is payable to the trial advocate in addition to the basic consideration fee; and

(b) the amount of the additional fee corresponds to the category of the advocate concerned specified in the table following paragraph 24.

(5) The additional fee is payable only where the appropriate officer considers it reasonable to make such a payment.

(6) A trial advocate claiming the additional fee must supply such information and documents as may be required by the appropriate officer in support of the claim.

(7) In determining whether it is reasonable to pay the additional fee, the appropriate officer must take into account–

(a) the reasonableness of the hours claimed in respect of the case taken as a whole; and

(b) the reasonableness of the hours claimed in respect of the consideration of the unused material.

[This paragraph is printed as inserted, with effect from 17 September 2020, by SI 2020/903 (G-1a). The insertion has effect only for cases in which a determination under the LASPOA 2012, s.16 (§ 6-187 in the main work) was made on or after 17 September 2020. It is also printed as subsequently amended, with effect from 19 February 2021, by SI 2021/80 (G-1a).]

Fees for wasted preparation

18.–(1) A wasted preparation fee may be claimed where a trial advocate in any case to which this paragraph applies is prevented from representing the assisted person in the main hearing by any of the following circumstances– **G-54**

(a) the trial advocate is instructed to appear in other proceedings at the same time as the main hearing in the case and has been unable to secure a change of date for either the main hearing or the other proceedings;

(b) the date fixed for the main hearing is changed by the court despite the trial advocate's objection;

(c) the trial advocate has withdrawn from the case with the leave of the court because of the trial advocate's professional code of conduct or to avoid embarrassment in the exercise of the trial advocate's profession;

(d) the trial advocate has been dismissed by the assisted person or the litigator; or

(e) the trial advocate is obliged to attend at any place by reason of a judicial office held by the trial advocate or other public duty.

(2) This paragraph applies to every case on indictment to which this Schedule applies provided that–

(a) the case goes to trial, and the trial lasts for five days or more; or

(b) the case is a cracked trial, and the number of pages of prosecution evidence exceeds 150.

(3) The amount of the wasted preparation fee must be calculated from the number of hours of preparation reasonably carried out by the trial advocate, using the hourly fee rates set out in the table following paragraph 24 as appropriate to the category of trial advocate, but no such fee is payable unless the number of hours of preparation is eight or more.

(4) Any claim for a wasted preparation fee under this paragraph must be made by a trial advocate, whether or not the trial advocate did the work claimed for.

(5) A trial advocate claiming a wasted preparation fee must supply such information and documents as may be required by the appropriate officer as proof of the circumstances in which the advocate was prevented from representing the assisted person and of the number of hours of preparation.

(6) In sub-paragraphs (4) and (5), where the main hearing is a trial, "trial advocate" means an advocate who—

(a) is instructed pursuant to a section 16 determination to represent the assisted person at the trial, and

(b) attends the first day of the trial.

[This paragraph is printed as amended, with effect from 5 May 2015, by the Criminal Legal Aid (Remuneration) (Amendment) Regulations 2015 (SI 2015/882), reg.2(4)(c), (6)(d) and (16)(c). For the transitional provision, see G-6.]

Fees for conferences and views

G-55 19.—(1) This paragraph applies to the following types of work—

(a) attendance by the trial advocate at pre-trial conferences with prospective or actual expert witnesses not held at court;

(b) attendance by the trial advocate at views at the scene of the alleged offence;

(c) attendance by the trial advocate at pre-trial conferences with the assisted person not held at court;

(d) reasonable travelling time by the trial advocate for the purpose of attending a view at the scene of the alleged offence; or

(e) reasonable travelling time by the trial advocate for the purpose of attending a pre-trial conference with the assisted person or prospective or actual expert witness, where the appropriate officer is satisfied that the assisted person or prospective or actual expert witness was unable or could not reasonably have been expected to attend a conference at the trial advocate's chambers or office.

(2) The fees payable in respect of attendance at the first three pre-trial conferences or views, as set out in sub-paragraph (1)(a) to (c), are included in the basic fee specified in the table following paragraph 5, or the basic fee specified in the tables following paragraph 7, as appropriate to the offence for which the assisted person is tried, the category of trial advocate and whether the case is a guilty plea, cracked trial or trial, provided that the trial advocate satisfies the appropriate officer that the work was reasonably necessary.

(3) The fee specified in the table following paragraph 24 as appropriate to the category of trial advocate is payable in the following circumstances, provided that the trial advocate satisfies the appropriate officer that the work was reasonably necessary—

(a) for trials lasting not less than 21 and not more than 25 days, and cracked trials where it was accepted by the court at the first hearing at which the assisted person entered a plea that the trial would last not less than 21 days and not more than 25 days, one further pre-trial conference or view not exceeding two hours;

(b) for trials lasting not less than 26 and not more than 35 days, and cracked trials where it was accepted by the court at the first hearing at which the assisted person entered a plea that the trial would last not less than 26 days and not more than 35 days, two further pre-trial conferences or views each not exceeding two hours; and

(c) for trials lasting not less than 36 days, and cracked trials where it was accepted by the court at the first hearing at which the assisted person entered a plea that the trial would last not less than 36 days and not more than 40 days, three further pre-trial conferences or views each not exceeding two hours.

(4) Travel expenses must be paid for all conferences and views set out in sub-paragraph (1)(a) to (c), provided that the trial advocate satisfies the appropriate officer that they were reasonably incurred.

(5) Travelling time must be paid for all conferences and views set out in sub-paragraph (1)(a) to (c), provided that the trial advocate satisfies the appropriate officer that it was reasonable.

[Paragraph 19 is printed as amended by SI 2015/1678, SI 2018/220 (G-1a) and, with effect from 17 September 2020, by SI 2020/903 (G-1a).]

Fees for further case management hearings and plea and trial preparation hearings

G-56 19A.—(1) The fee payable to a trial advocate for a further case management hearing or a plea and trial preparation hearing held at court is the fee which corresponds with a hearing of that description, and the category of the advocate concerned, which is set out in the table following paragraph 24.

(2) But if a guilty plea is entered at a plea and trial preparation hearing, the fee payable to the advocate for that hearing is the amount set out in Table A following paragraph 7 which corresponds with the band within which the offence falls and the category of the advocate concerned.

[This paragraph was inserted by SI 2018/220 (G-1a), and is printed as subsequently amended by SI 2018/1323 (G-1a) and SI 2020/903 (G-1a): for transitional provisions, see G-1a.]

Fees for appeals, committals for sentence and breach hearings

20.—(1) Subject to sub-paragraphs (4) to (7) and paragraph 26 the fee payable to a trial advocate in any of the hearings referred to in paragraph 2(1)(b) is the fixed fee specified in the table following paragraph 24. **G-57**

(2) Where a hearing referred to in paragraph 2(1)(b) is listed but cannot proceed because of the failure of the assisted person or a witness to attend, the unavailability of a pre-sentence report, or other good reason, the fee payable to the advocate is the fixed fee specified in the table following paragraph 24.

(3) Where—

(a) a bail application;

(b) a mention hearing; or

(c) any other application,

takes place in the course of a hearing referred to in paragraph 2(1)(b), the fee payable to the advocate is the fixed fee specified in the table following paragraph 24.

(4) Where it appears to the appropriate officer that the fixed fee allowed under sub-paragraph (1) would be inappropriate taking into account all of the relevant circumstances of the case the appropriate officer may instead allow fees of such amounts as appear to the appropriate officer to be reasonable remuneration for the relevant work in accordance with sub-paragraph (5).

(5) The appropriate officer may allow any of the following classes of fees to an advocate in respect of work allowed by the appropriate officer under this paragraph—

(a) a fee for preparation including, where appropriate, the first day of the hearing including, where they took place on that day—

(i) short conferences;

(ii) consultations;

(iii) applications and appearances (including bail applications);

(iv) views at the scene of the alleged offence; and

(v) any other preparation;

(b) a refresher fee for any day or part of a day for which a hearing continued, including, where they took place on that day—

(i) short conferences;

(ii) consultations;

(iii) applications and appearances (including bail applications);

(iv) views at the scene of the alleged offence; and

(v) any other preparation; and

(c) subsidiary fees for—

(i) attendance at conferences, consultations and views at the scene of the alleged offence not covered by paragraph (a) or (b);

(ii) written advice on evidence, plea, appeal, case stated or other written work; and

(iii) attendance at applications and appearances (including bail applications and adjournments for sentence) not covered by paragraph (a) or (b).

(6) Sub-paragraph (7) applies where the hearing—

(a) is an appeal from a magistrates' court;

(b) is heard in the Crown Court; and

(c) lasts for more than one day.

(7) Where this sub-paragraph applies, the fee payable to the advocate—

(a) for the first day of the hearing, is the basic fee for band 17.1, set out in the table following paragraph 5, for the category of the advocate concerned;

(b) for the second day, and any subsequent days, of the hearing, is the daily attendance fee for band 17.1, set out in the table following paragraph 5A, for the category of the advocate concerned.

[This paragraph is printed as amended, with effect from 1 April 2018, by SI 2018/220 (G-1a). The insertion has no effect in relation to proceedings in respect of which a determination under section 16 of the LASPOA 2012 (see § 6-187 in the main work) is made before 1 April 2018.]

Fees for contempt proceedings

21.—(1) Subject to sub-paragraph (2), remuneration for advocates in proceedings referred to in **G-58** section 14(g) of the Act in the Crown Court must be at the rates specified in the table following this sub-paragraph.

Category of advocate	*Payment rates (£ per day)*
QC	303
Leading junior	227
Led junior or junior acting alone	152

(2) Where an advocate and a litigator are instructed in proceedings referred to in section 14(g) of the Act, remuneration must be at the rates specified in the table following this sub-paragraph, as appropriate to the category of advocate.

Category of advocate	*Payment rates (£ per day)*
QC	177
Leading junior	126
Led junior or junior acting alone	101

[This paragraph is printed as amended by SI 2018/1323 (G-1a): for transitional provisions, see G-1a].

Discontinuance or dismissal of proceedings

G-59 22.—(1) This paragraph applies to proceedings which are sent for trial in the Crown Court.

(2) Where proceedings referred to in sub-paragraph (1) are discontinued by a notice served under section 23A of the Prosecution of Offences Act 1985 (discontinuance of proceedings after accused has been sent for trial) at any time before the prosecution serves its evidence in accordance with the Crime and Disorder Act 1998 (Service of Prosecution Evidence) Regulations 2005 the advocate must be paid 50% of the basic fee for a guilty plea, as specified in Table A following paragraph 7 as appropriate to the offence for which the assisted person is charged and the category of advocate.

(3) Where proceedings referred to in sub-paragraph (1) are discontinued by a notice served under section 23A of the Prosecution of Offences Act 1985 (discontinuance of proceedings after accused has been sent for trial) at any time after the prosecution serves its evidence in accordance with the Crime and Disorder Act 1998 (Service of Prosecution Evidence) Regulations 2005, the advocate must be paid a fee calculated in accordance with paragraph 7(a), as appropriate for representing an assisted person in a guilty plea.

(5) Where, at or before the first hearing at which the assisted person enters a plea—

(a) the prosecution offers no evidence and the assisted person is discharged; or

(b) the case is remitted to the magistrates' court in accordance with paragraph 10(3)(a), 13(2) or 15(3)(a) of Schedule 3 to the Crime and Disorder Act 1998,

the advocate instructed in the proceedings must be paid a fee calculated in accordance with paragraph 7(a), as appropriate for representing an assisted person in a guilty plea.

(6) Where an application for dismissal is made under paragraph 2 of Schedule 3 to the Crime and Disorder Act 1998, the advocate must be remunerated for attendance at the hearing of the application for dismissal—

(a) in respect of any day where the hearing begins before and ends after the luncheon adjournment, at the daily rate set out in the table following paragraph 24 as appropriate to the category of advocate; or

(b) in respect of any day where the hearing begins and ends before the luncheon adjournment, or begins after the luncheon adjournment, at the half-daily rate set out in that table as appropriate to the category of advocate,

provided that a fee is not payable elsewhere under this Schedule in respect of any day of the hearing.

(7) Where an application for dismissal is made under paragraph 2 of Schedule 3 to the Crime and Disorder Act 1998, and—

(a) the charge, or charges, are dismissed and the assisted person is discharged; or

(b) the case is remitted to the magistrates' court in accordance with paragraph 10(3)(a), 13(2) or 15(3)(a) of Schedule 3 to the Crime and Disorder Act 1998,

in respect of the first day of the hearing of the application to dismiss, the advocate instructed in the proceedings must be paid a fee calculated in accordance with paragraph 7(a), as appropriate for representing an assisted person in a guilty plea.

(8) Where an advocate represents more than one assisted person in proceedings referred to in sub-paragraph (1), the advocate must be paid a fixed fee of 20% of—

(a) the fee specified in sub-paragraph (2) where that sub-paragraph applies; or

(b) the basic fee specified in the tables following paragraph 7 where sub-paragraph (3), (4) or (5) applies, as appropriate for the circumstances set out in the relevant sub-paragraph,

in respect of each additional assisted person the advocate represents.

[This paragraph is printed as amended by SI 2015/1678 (G-1a), by SI 2018/220 (G-1a) and, with effect from 17 September 2020, by SI 2020/903 (G-1a).]

Noting brief fees

23. The fee payable to an advocate retained solely for the purpose of making a note of any hearing must be the daily fee set out in the table following paragraph 24. **G-60**

Fixed fees

24. The table following this paragraph sets out the fixed fees payable in relation to the category of work specified in the first column of the table. **G-61**

Category of work	*Paragraph providing for fee*	*Junior Alone or Led Junior (£)*	*Leading Junior (£)*	*Queen's Counsel (£)*
Standard Appearance	12(2)	91 per day	136 per day	182 per day
Abuse of process hearing	13(1)(a) and (3)	240 full day	349 full day	502 full day
		131 half day	197 half day	263 half day
Hearings relating to disclosure	13(1)(b), (c) and (3)	240 full day	349 full day	502 full day
		131 half day	197 half day	263 half day
Hearings relating to the admissibility of evidence	13(1)(d) and (3)	240 full day	349 full day	502 full day
		131 half day	197 half day	263 half day
Ground rules hearings	13(1)(da) and (3)	240 full day	349 full day	502 full day
		131 half day	197 half day	263 half day
Hearings on withdrawal of guilty plea	13(1)(e) and (3)	240 full day	349 full day	502 full day
		131 half day	197 half day	263 half day
Sentencing hearing	15	126 per day	192 per day	253 per day
Deferred sentencing hearing	15(2)	175 per day	240 per day	327 per day
Ineffective trial hearing	16	380 per day	380 per day	380 per day
Special preparation	17	39.39 per hour	56.56 per hour	74.74 per hour
Consideration of unused material in excess of three hours	17A(3)	39.39 per hour	56.56 per hour	74.74 per hour
Wasted preparation	18	39.39 per hour	56.56 per hour	74.74 per hour
Conferences and views	19	40.40 per hour	60.60 per hour	80.80 per hour
Further case management hearing	19A	101 per day	152 per day	202 per day
Plea and trial preparation hearing	19A	126 per day	192 per day	253 per day
Appeals to the Crown Court against sentence	20	250 per day	373 per day	498 per day
Appeals to the Crown Court against conviction	20	330 per day	496 per day	661 per day
Proceedings relating to the breach of an order of the Crown Court	20(1)	109 per day	153 per day	218 per day
Committal for sentence	20(1) and (2)	152 per day	227 per day	303 per day
Adjourned appeals, committals for sentence and breach hearings	20(2)	88 per day	131 per day	175 per day
Bail applications, mentions and other applications in appeal, committals for sentence and	20(3)	88 per day	131 per day	175 per day

Category of work	*Paragraph providing for fee*	*Junior Alone or Led Junior (£)*	*Leading Junior (£)*	*Queen's Counsel (£)*
breach hearings				
Second and subsequent days of an application to dismiss	22(6)	240 full day	349 full day	502 full day
		131 half day	197 half day	263 half day
Noting brief	23	109 per day	109 per day	109 per day
Hearing for mitigation of sentence	34	109 per day	175 per day	263 per day

[The table is printed as substituted by SI 2018/1323 (G-1a), and, with effect from 17 September 2020, by SI 2020/903 (G-1a): for transitional provisions, see G-1a.]

Warrant for arrest

G-62 24A.—(1) This paragraph applies where—

(a) the assisted person fails to attend a hearing;

(b) at that hearing the court issues a warrant for the arrest of the assisted person under section 7(1) (liability to arrest for absconding or breaking conditions of bail) of the Bail Act 1976 ("the warrant"); and

(c) the case does not proceed in the absence of the assisted person.

(2) Where in a case on indictment the warrant is not executed within three months of the date on which it was issued, the fee payable to the advocate is the fee for a guilty plea set out in Table A following paragraph 7 which corresponds with the band within which the offence concerned falls and the category of the advocate concerned.

(3) Where the warrant is issued during the course of proceedings referred to in paragraph 20, the fee payable to the advocate is the fee which corresponds with the category of work, and the category of the advocate concerned, which is set out in the table following paragraph 24.

(4) Sub-paragraph (5) applies where—

(a) a fee has been paid, or is payable, to the advocate in accordance with sub-paragraph (2);

(b) the warrant is executed within 15 months of the date on which it was issued;

(c) the case proceeds after the warrant has been executed; and

(d) the advocate submits a claim for fees for the determination of the advocate's overall remuneration in the case, in accordance with regulation 4.

(5) Where this sub-paragraph applies—

(a) the appropriate officer must deduct the amount paid or payable in accordance with sub-paragraph (2) from the amount payable to the advocate on the final determination of fees in the case; and

(b) if the fee paid or payable in accordance with sub-paragraph (2) is greater than the amount payable to the advocate on the final determination of fees in the case, the appropriate officer may recover the amount of the difference by way of repayment by the advocate.

[This paragraph was inserted by SI 2018/220 (G-1a) and is printed as further amended by SI 2020/903, with effect from 17 September 2020: for transitional provisions, see G-1a.]

PART 6
Miscellaneous

Identity of instructed advocate

G-63 25.—(1) Where an instructed advocate is appointed before the first hearing at which the assisted person enters a plea, the instructed advocate must notify the Court in writing as soon as the appointment is made and, where appropriate, must confirm whether the instructed advocate is the leading instructed advocate or the led instructed advocate.

(2) Where the section 16 determination provides for representation by a single advocate and no instructed advocate has been notified to the Court in accordance with sub-paragraph (1)—

(a) the barrister or solicitor advocate who attends the first hearing at which the assisted person enters a plea is deemed to be the instructed advocate; and

(b) the Court must make a written record of this fact.

(3) Where the section 16 determination provides for representation by a single advocate and no barrister or solicitor advocate attends the first hearing at which the assisted person enters a plea—

(a) the barrister or solicitor advocate who attends the next hearing in the case is deemed to be the instructed advocate; and

(b) the Court must make a written record of this fact.

(4) Where the section 16 determination provides for representation by more than one advocate, and no leading instructed advocate has been notified to the Court in accordance with sub-paragraph (1), the leading advocate who attends–

(a) the first hearing at which the assisted person enters a plea; or

(b) where no leading advocate attends the first hearing at which the assisted person enters a plea, the next hearing in the case attended by a leading advocate,

is deemed to be the leading instructed advocate, and the Court must make a written record of this fact.

(5) Where the section 16 determination provides for representation by more than one advocate, and no led instructed advocate has been notified to the Court in accordance with sub-paragraph (1), the led advocate who attends–

(a) the first hearing at which the assisted person enters a plea; or

(b) where no led advocate attends the first hearing at which the assisted person enters a plea, the next hearing in the case attended by a led advocate,

is deemed to be the led instructed advocate, and the Court must make a written record of this fact.

(6) Where a section 16 determination is amended after the first hearing at which the assisted person enters a plea to provide for representation by more than one advocate–

(a) the additional instructed advocate must notify the Court in writing of the additional instructed advocate's appointment within 7 days of the date on which the section 16 determination is amended; and

(b) each instructed advocate must notify the Court whether that instructed advocate is the leading instructed advocate or the led instructed advocate.

(7) Where no additional instructed advocate has been notified to the Court in accordance with sub-paragraph (6)(a), the advocate who attends the next hearing in the case is deemed to be an instructed advocate and the Court must record in writing whether that instructed advocate is the leading instructed advocate or the led instructed advocate, as appropriate to the circumstances of the case.

(8) Where–

(a) a case ceases to be a Very High Cost Case (in relation to fees claimed by advocates); and

(b) none of sub-paragraphs (1) to (7) applies,

the instructed advocate must notify the Court in writing of the instructed advocate's appointment within 7 days of the case ceasing to be a Very High Cost Case.

(9) The Court must attach–

(a) any notice received under sub-paragraph (1), (6) or (8); and

(b) any record made by it under sub-paragraph (2), (3), (4), (5) or (7),

to the representation order.

(10) An instructed advocate must remain as instructed advocate at all times, except where–

(a) a date for trial is fixed at or before the first hearing at which the assisted person enters a plea and the instructed advocate is unable to conduct the trial due to the instructed advocate's other pre-existing commitments;

(b) the instructed advocate is dismissed by the assisted person or the litigator; or

(c) the instructed advocate is required to withdraw because of his professional code of conduct.

(11) Where, in accordance with sub-paragraph (10), an instructed advocate withdraws, the instructed advocate must–

(a) immediately notify the court of the withdrawal–

(i) in writing; or

(ii) where the withdrawal takes place at a hearing, orally; and

(b) within 7 days of the date of the withdrawal, notify the court in writing of the identity of a replacement instructed advocate, who must fulfil all the functions of an instructed advocate in accordance with these Regulations.

(12) This paragraph does not apply to a claim for fees under paragraph 32, 33 or 34.

[Paragraph 25 is printed as amended by SI 2015/1678 (G-1a).]

Payment of fees to trial advocate

26.–(1) In accordance with regulation 23 the appropriate officer must notify each trial advocate of the total fees payable and authorise payment to the trial advocate accordingly. **G-64**

(2) Payment of the fees in accordance with sub-paragraph (1) must be made to each trial advocate.

(3) Where the section 16 determination provides for representation by a single advocate, the trial

advocate is responsible for arranging payment of fees to the instructed advocate and any substitute advocate who has undertaken work on the case.

(4) Where there are two trial advocates for an assisted person, payment must be made to each trial advocate individually, and—

(a) the leading trial advocate is responsible for arranging payment of fees to the instructed advocate and any substitute advocate who have undertaken work on the case of a type for which a leading advocate is responsible; and

(b) the led trial advocate is responsible for arranging payment of fees to the instructed advocate and any substitute advocate who have undertaken work on the case of a type for which a led advocate is responsible.

(4A) In this paragraph, where the main hearing is a trial, "trial advocate" means an advocate who—

(a) is instructed pursuant to a section 16 determination to represent the assisted person at the trial, and

(b) attends the first day of the trial.

(5) This paragraph does not apply to a claim for fees under paragraph 32, 33 or 34.

[This paragraph is printed as amended, with effect from 5 May 2015, by the Criminal Legal Aid (Remuneration) (Amendment) Regulations 2015 (SI 2015/882), reg.2(5)(d) and (16)(d). For the transitional provision, see G-6.]

Additional charges and additional cases

G-65 27.—(1) Where an assisted person is charged with more than one offence on one indictment, the fee payable to the trial advocate under this Schedule must be based on whichever of those offences the trial advocate selects.

(2) Where two or more cases to which this Schedule applies involving the same trial advocate are heard concurrently (whether involving the same or different assisted persons)—

(a) the trial advocate must select one case ("the principal case"), which must be treated for the purposes of remuneration in accordance with this Schedule;

(b) in respect of the main hearing in each of the other cases the trial advocate must be paid a fixed fee of 20% of—

(i) where the principal case is a case on indictment, the basic fee specified in the table following paragraph 5 or, where there is a guilty plea or a cracked trial, the basic fee specified in the tables following paragraph 7, which corresponds with the band within which the offence concerned falls and the category of the advocate concerned; or

(ii) the fixed fee for the principal case, where that is a case falling within paragraph 2(1)(b) or paragraph 10.

(3) Nothing in sub-paragraphs (4) to (6) permits a fixed fee under Part 5, other than one to which paragraph 14 applies, to be paid in a case to which Part 4 applies.

(4) Where a trial advocate or substitute advocate appears at a hearing specified in paragraph 12, 13, 14, 15, 16 or 19A, forming part of two or more cases involving different assisted persons, the trial advocate or substitute advocate must be paid—

(a) in respect of the first such case, the fixed fee for that hearing specified in the table following paragraph 24 or, where the hearing falls within paragraph 19A(2), the applicable fee specified in Table A following paragraph 7; and

(b) in respect of each of the other cases, 20% of that fee.

(5) Subject to sub-paragraphs (1) to (4), where a trial advocate or substitute advocate appears at a hearing forming part of two or more cases, the trial advocate or substitute advocate must be paid the fixed fee for that hearing specified in the table following paragraph 24 in respect of one such case, without any increase in respect of the other cases.

(6) Where a trial advocate selects—

(a) one offence, in preference to another offence, under sub-paragraph (1); or

(b) one case as the principal case, in preference to another case, under sub-paragraph (2),

that selection does not affect the trial advocate's right to claim any of the fees set out in the table following paragraph 24 to which the trial advocate would otherwise have been entitled.

[This paragraph is printed as amended by SI 2018/220 (G-1a), SI 2018/1323 (G-1a) and SI 2020/903 (G-1a): for transitional provisions, see G-1a.]

Multiple advocates

G-66 28. Where a section 16 determination provides for representation by three advocates in a case the provisions of this Schedule apply, and the fees payable to the led juniors in accordance with Part 2 or

Part 3 are payable to each led junior who is instructed in the case.

Non-local appearances

29. Where an advocate is instructed to appear in a court which is not within 40 kilometres of the advocate's office or chambers, the appropriate officer may allow an amount for travelling and other expenses incidental to that appearance, provided that the amount must not be greater than the amount, if any, which would be payable to a trial advocate from the nearest local Bar unless the advocate instructed to appear has obtained prior approval under regulation 13 for the incurring of such expenses or can justify the attendance having regard to all the relevant circumstances of the case. G-67

[This paragraph is printed as amended, with effect from 1 April 2018, by SI 2018/220 (G-1a). The insertion has no effect in relation to proceedings in respect of which a determination under section 16 of the LASPOA 2012 (see § 6-187 in the main work) is made before 1 April 2018.]

Assisted person unfit to plead or stand trial

31. Where in any case a hearing is held to determine the question of whether the assisted person is unfit to plead or to stand trial (a "fitness hearing")– G-68

(a) if a trial on indictment is held, or continues, at any time thereafter, the length of the fitness hearing is included in determining the length of the trial for the calculation of the graduated fee in accordance with Part 2 or Part 3;

(b) if a trial on indictment is not held, or does not continue, thereafter by reason of the assisted person being found unfit to plead or to stand trial, the trial advocate must be paid–

(i) a graduated fee calculated in accordance with paragraph 4 as appropriate to the combined length of–

(aa) the fitness hearing; and

(bb) any hearing under section 4A of the Criminal Procedure (Insanity) Act 1964 (finding that the accused did the act or made the omission charged against him); or

(ii) fee calculated in accordance with paragraph 7(b) as appropriate for representing an assisted person in a cracked trial,

whichever the trial advocate elects; and

(c) if at any time the assisted person pleads guilty to the indictable offence, the trial advocate must be paid either–

(i) a graduated fee calculated in accordance with paragraph 4 as appropriate to the length of the fitness hearing; or

(ii) fee calculated in accordance with paragraph 7(a) as appropriate for representing an assisted person in a guilty plea, whichever the trial advocate elects.

[This paragraph is printed as amended by SI 2020/903 (G-1a), with effect from 17 September 2020: for transitional provision see G-1a.]

Cross examination of witness

32.–(1) Where in any case on indictment an advocate is retained solely for the purpose of cross-examining a witness under section 38 of the Youth Justice and Criminal Evidence Act 1999 (defence representation for purposes of cross-examination), the advocate must be paid a graduated fee calculated in accordance with paragraph 4. G-69

(2) For the purposes of this paragraph the daily attendance fee is as set out in the table following paragraph 5A as appropriate to the number of days of attendance at court by the advocate.

[This paragraph is printed as amended, with effect from 1 April 2018, by SI 2018/220 (G-1a). The insertion has no effect in relation to proceedings in respect of which a determination under section 16 of the LASPOA 2012 (see § 6-187 in the main work) is made before 1 April 2018.]

Provision of written or oral advice

33.–(1) Where in any case on indictment an advocate is assigned pursuant to a section 16 determination solely for the purpose of providing written or oral advice, the advocate must be paid for the reasonable number of hours of preparation for that advice using the hourly fee rates for special preparation set out in the table following paragraph 24 as appropriate to the category of trial advocate. G-70

(2) An advocate claiming a fee for advice under this paragraph may apply to the appropriate officer to redetermine the fee under regulation 28 and the advocate must supply such information and documents as may be required by the appropriate officer as proof of the number of hours of preparation.

Mitigation of sentence

G-71 34.—(1) Where in any case on indictment an advocate is assigned pursuant to a section 16 determination to appear at a sentencing hearing solely for the purpose of applying to the court to mitigate the assisted person's sentence, the advocate must be paid in respect of that appearance the fee specified in the table following paragraph 24 together with a fee calculated from the reasonable number of hours of preparation for that appearance using the hourly fee rates for special preparation set out in the table following paragraph 24 as appropriate to the category of trial advocate.

(2) An advocate claiming an hourly preparation fee under this paragraph may apply to the appropriate officer to redetermine such hourly fee under regulation 28 and the advocate must supply such information and documents as may be required by the appropriate officer as proof of the number of hours of preparation.

Table of offences

G-72 The table of offences previously found in Pt 7 of Schedule 1 to the regulations is now found in Pt 7 of Schedule 2 (see G-101) by virtue of amendments effected by SI 2018/220 (G-1a).

Regulation 5

SCHEDULE 2

LITIGATORS' GRADUATED FEE SCHEME

PART 1

Definition and Scope

Interpretation

G-73 1.—(1) In this Schedule—

"case" means proceedings in the Crown Court against any one assisted person—

(a) on one or more counts of a single indictment;

(b) arising out of a single notice of appeal against conviction or sentence, or a single committal for sentence, whether on one or more charges; or

(c) arising out of a single alleged breach of an order of the Crown Court,

and a case falling within paragraph (c) must be treated as a separate case from the proceedings in which the order was made;

"cracked trial" means a case on indictment in which—

(a) the assisted person enters a plea of not guilty to one or more counts at the first hearing at which he or she enters a plea and

(i) the case does not proceed to trial (whether by reason of pleas of guilty or for other reasons) or the prosecution offers no evidence; and

(ii) either—

(aa) in respect of one or more counts to which the assisted person pleaded guilty, the assisted person did not so plead at the first hearing at which he or she entered a plea; or

(bb) in respect of one or more counts which did not proceed, the prosecution did not, before or at the first hearing at which the assisted person entered a plea, declare an intention of not proceeding with them; or

(b) the case is listed for trial without a hearing at which the assisted persons enters a plea;

"guilty plea" means a case on indictment which—

(a) is disposed of without a trial because the assisted person pleaded guilty to one or more counts; and

(b) is not a cracked trial;

"main hearing" means—

(a) in relation to a case which goes to trial, the trial;

(b) in relation to a guilty plea, the hearing at which pleas are taken or, where there is more than one such hearing, the last such hearing;

(c) in relation to a cracked trial, the hearing at which—

(i) the case becomes a cracked trial by meeting the conditions in the definition of a cracked trial, whether or not any pleas were taken at that hearing; or

(ii) a formal verdict of not guilty was entered as a result of the prosecution offering no evidence, whether or not the parties attended the hearing;

(d) in relation to an appeal against conviction or sentence in the Crown Court, the hearing of the appeal;

(e) in relation to proceedings arising out of a committal for sentence in the Crown Court, the sentencing hearing; and

(f) in relation to proceedings arising out of an alleged breach of an order of the Crown Court, the hearing at which those proceedings are determined;

"*Newton* hearing" means a hearing at which evidence is heard for the purpose of determining the sentence of a convicted person in accordance with the principles of *R. v. Newton* (1982) 77 Cr. App. R. 13;

"PPE Cut-off" means the number of pages of prosecution evidence for use in determining the fee payable to a litigator under this Schedule, as set out in the tables following paragraph 5(1) and (2);

"unused material" means material disclosed pursuant to the prosecutors' obligations in Part 1 of the Criminal Procedure and Investigations Act 1996, but does not include–

(a) witness statements;

(b) documentary and pictorial exhibits;

(c) records of interviews with the assisted person; and

(d) records of interviews with other defendants.

(2) For the purposes of this Schedule, the number of pages of prosecution evidence served on the court must be determined in accordance with sub-paragraphs (3) to (5).

(3) The number of pages of prosecution evidence includes all–

(a) witness statements;

(b) documentary and pictorial exhibits;

(c) records of interviews with the assisted person; and

(d) records of interviews with other defendants,

which form part of the served prosecution documents or which are included in any notice of additional evidence.

(4) Subject to sub-paragraph (5), a document served by the prosecution in electronic form is included in the number of pages of prosecution evidence.

(5) A documentary or pictorial exhibit which–

(a) has been served by the prosecution in electronic form; and

(b) has never existed in paper form,

is not included within the number of pages of prosecution evidence unless the appropriate officer decides that it would be appropriate to include it in the pages of prosecution evidence taking into account the nature of the document and any other relevant circumstances.

(6) In proceedings on indictment in the Crown Court initiated otherwise than by sending for trial, the appropriate officer must determine the number of pages of prosecution evidence in accordance with sub-paragraphs (2) to (5) or as nearly in accordance with those sub-paragraphs as possible as the nature of the case permits.

(7) A reference in this Schedule to a "Class" is to the Class for the offence concerned set out in the LGFS Table of Offences.

[This paragraph is printed as amended by SI 2015/1678 (G-1a); SI 2015/1369 (G-1a); SI 2018/220 (G-1a); and, with effect from 17 September 2020, by SI 2020/903 (G-1a). For the relevant transitional provisions, see G-1a.]

Application

2.–(1) Subject to sub-paragraphs (2) to (7), this Schedule applies to– G-74

(a) every case on indictment;

(b) the following proceedings in the Crown Court–

(i) an appeal against conviction or sentence from the magistrates' court;

(ii) a sentencing hearing following a committal for sentence to the Crown Court;

(iii) proceedings arising out of an alleged breach of an order of the Crown Court (whether or not this Schedule applies to the proceedings in which the order was made);

(c) a sentencing hearing following a case on indictment to which this Schedule applies, where sentence has been deferred under section 1 of the Powers of Criminal Courts (Sentencing) Act 2000 (deferment of sentence);

(d) any other post-sentence hearing.

(3) Where, at any time after proceedings are sent for trial to the Crown Court they are–

(a) discontinued by a notice served under section 23A of the Prosecution of Offences Act 1985 (discontinuance of proceedings after accused has been sent for trial); or

(b) dismissed pursuant to paragraph 2 of Schedule 3 to the Crime and Disorder Act 1998 (applications for dismissal),

the provisions of paragraphs 21 and 22 apply.

(4) Where, following a case on indictment, a *Newton* hearing takes place—

(a) for the purposes of this Schedule the case is to be treated as having gone to trial;

(b) the length of the trial is to be taken to be the combined length of the main hearing and the *Newton* hearing; and

(c) the provisions of this Schedule relating to cracked trials and guilty pleas will not apply.

(5) For the purposes of this Schedule, a case on indictment which discontinues at or before the first hearing at which the assisted person enters a plea otherwise than—

(a) by reason of a plea of guilty being entered; or

(b) in accordance with sub-paragraph (3),

must be treated as a guilty plea.

(6) For the purposes of this Schedule, where a trial that is not a Very High Cost Case (in relation to fees claimed by litigators) lasts over 200 days, it must be treated as if it had lasted 200 days.

(7) For the purposes of this Schedule, where the number of pages of prosecution evidence in a case which is not a Very High Cost Case (in relation to fees claimed by litigators) exceeds—

(a) the PPE Cut-off figure specified in the table following paragraph 5(2) as appropriate to the offence for which the assisted person is to be tried and the length of trial; and

(b) 10,000,

the case must be treated as though it had 6,000 pages of prosecution evidence.

[Paragraph 2 is printed so as to reflect the quashing of SI 2017/1019 (G-1a) in *R. (on the application of Law Society) v Lord Chancellor* (G-1).]

Class of offences

G-75 3.—(1) For the purposes of this Schedule—

(a) every indictable offence falls within the Class under which it is listed in the LGFS Table of Offences and, subject to sub-paragraph (2), indictable offences not specifically so listed are deemed to fall within Class H;

(b) conspiracy to commit an indictable offence contrary to section 1 of the Criminal Law Act 1977 (the offence of conspiracy), incitement to commit an indictable offence and attempts to commit an indictable offence contrary to section 1 of the Criminal Attempts Act 1981 (attempting to commit an offence) fall within the same Class as the substantive offence to which they relate;

(c) where the LGFS Table of Offences specifies that the Class within which an offence falls depends on whether the value involved exceeds a stated limit, the value must be presumed not to exceed that limit unless the litigator making the claim under regulation 5 proves otherwise to the satisfaction of the appropriate officer;

(d) where more than one count of the indictment is for an offence in relation to which the Class depends on the value involved, that value must be taken to be the total value involved in all those offences, but where two or more counts relate to the same property, the value of that property must be taken into account once only;

(e) where an entry in the LGFS Table of Offences specifies an offence as being contrary to a statutory provision, then subject to any express limitation in the entry that entry includes every offence contrary to that statutory provision whether or not the words of description in the entry are appropriate to cover all such offences;

(f) where in a case on indictment there is a hearing to determine the question of whether an assisted person is unfit to plead or unfit to stand trial, the litigator must elect whether that hearing falls within the same Class as the indictable offence to which it relates or within Class D;

(g) where in a case on indictment a restriction order is made, the offence falls within Class A, regardless of the Class under which the offence would be listed in the Table of Offences, but for this paragraph.

(2) Where a litigator in proceedings in the Crown Court is dissatisfied with the classification within Class H of an indictable offence not listed in the Table of Offences, the litigator may apply to the appropriate officer, when lodging the claim for fees, to reclassify the offence.

(3) The appropriate officer must, in light of the objections made by the litigator—

(a) confirm the classification of the offence within Class H; or

(b) reclassify the offence,

and must notify the litigator of the decision.

[This paragraph is printed as amended, with effect from 1 April 2018, by SI 2018/220 (G-1a). As to the transitional provision, see G-1a.]

Part 2
Graduated Fees for Guilty Pleas, Cracked Trials and Trials

Scope

4.—(1) Subject to sub-paragraph (2) and to paragraph 21, this Part does not apply to a guilty plea or cracked trial in a case sent for trial to the Crown Court on the election of a defendant where the magistrates' court has determined the case to be suitable for summary trial. G-76

(2) This Part applies in all cases where the trial is a cracked trial because the prosecution offer no evidence on all counts against a defendant and the judge directs that a not guilty verdict be entered.

[This paragraph was substituted by SI 2014/2422 (G-21a). For the transitional provision, see G-21a. It is printed as amended by SI 2015/1678 (G-1a).]

Pages of prosecution evidence

5.—(1) For the purposes of this Part, the PPE Cut-off figures in a cracked trial or guilty plea are specified in the table following this sub-paragraph, as appropriate to the offence with which the assisted person is charged. G-77

PPE Cut-off Figures in Cracked Trials and Guilty Pleas

	Class of offence										
Type of case	*A*	*B*	*C*	*D*	*E*	*F*	*G*	*H*	*I*	*J*	*K*
Cracked trial or guilty plea	80	70	40	80	40	50	50	40	40	80	120

(2) For the purposes of this Part, the PPE Cut-off figures in a trial are specified in the table following this sub-paragraph, as appropriate to the offence for which the assisted person is tried and the length of trial.

PPE Cut-off figures in trials

Trial length in days	*PPE Cut off A*	*PPE Cut off B*	*PPE Cut off C*	*PPE Cut off D*	*PPE Cut off E*	*PPE Cut off F*	*PPE Cut off G*	*PPE Cut off H*	*PPE Cut off I*	*PPE Cut off J*	*PPE Cut off K*
1	80	70	40	80	40	50	50	40	40	80	120
2	80	70	40	80	40	50	50	40	40	80	120
3	95	105	81	95	120	138	138	122	134	95	186
4	126	139	120	126	158	173	173	157	185	126	252
5	156	170	157	156	195	206	206	191	232	156	314
6	186	203	193	186	229	240	240	225	281	186	372
7	218	238	230	218	265	276	276	260	329	218	433
8	257	274	267	257	301	310	310	301	376	257	495
9	293	306	301	293	333	342	342	338	420	293	550
10	330	338	339	330	365	373	373	374	464	330	606
11	367	370	378	367	399	405	405	412	509	367	663
12	404	402	417	404	433	437	437	449	554	404	721
13	440	434	455	440	467	470	470	486	598	440	779
14	477	465	493	477	500	501	501	523	642	477	836
15	514	497	531	514	532	533	533	559	686	514	894
16	551	535	569	551	565	564	564	596	730	551	951
17	587	573	607	587	598	596	596	637	774	587	1,007
18	624	611	646	624	646	627	627	687	818	624	1,063
19	661	649	684	661	696	659	659	736	862	661	1,119
20	697	687	722	697	746	690	690	786	907	697	1,174
21	742	722	753	742	787	720	720	826	943	742	1,230
22	786	757	785	786	828	752	752	867	980	786	1,286
23	830	792	819	830	868	784	784	908	1,017	830	1,341
24	874	826	857	874	908	816	816	948	1,053	874	1,396
25	917	860	894	917	948	848	848	988	1,088	917	1,451
26	961	895	931	961	988	880	880	1,028	1,124	961	1,505
27	1,005	935	967	1,005	1,028	912	912	1,068	1,160	1,005	1,560
28	1,049	975	1,004	1,049	1,068	944	944	1,107	1,196	1,049	1,615

Trial length in days	*PPE Cut off A*	*PPE Cut off B*	*PPE Cut off C*	*PPE Cut off D*	*PPE Cut off E*	*PPE Cut off F*	*PPE Cut off G*	*PPE Cut off H*	*PPE Cut off I*	*PPE Cut off J*	*PPE Cut off K*
29	1,099	1,016	1,041	1,099	1,108	976	976	1,147	1,231	1,099	1,670
30	1,150	1,057	1,077	1,150	1,148	1,007	1,007	1,187	1,267	1,150	1,725
31	1,200	1,098	1,114	1,200	1,188	1,039	1,039	1,226	1,303	1,200	1,780
32	1,251	1,138	1,151	1,251	1,228	1,070	1,070	1,266	1,349	1,251	1,835
33	1,301	1,179	1,187	1,301	1,268	1,102	1,102	1,307	1,394	1,301	1,889
34	1,352	1,220	1,224	1,352	1,308	1,133	1,133	1,357	1,439	1,352	1,944
35	1,402	1,261	1,262	1,402	1,347	1,165	1,165	1,407	1,485	1,402	1,999
36	1,453	1,302	1,303	1,453	1,435	1,196	1,196	1,457	1,530	1,453	2,054
37	1,503	1,348	1,345	1,503	1,526	1,228	1,228	1,507	1,575	1,503	2,109
38	1,554	1,395	1,386	1,554	1,617	1,259	1,259	1,557	1,621	1,554	2,164
39	1,604	1,441	1,428	1,604	1,708	1,291	1,291	1,607	1,666	1,604	2,219
40	1,652	1,484	1,444	1,652	1,745	1,314	1,314	1,629	1,704	1,652	2,271
41	1,700	1,527	1,461	1,700	1,782	1,338	1,338	1,651	1,742	1,700	2,324
42	1,748	1,570	1,477	1,748	1,820	1,361	1,361	1,673	1,780	1,748	2,377
43	1,796	1,613	1,494	1,796	1,857	1,384	1,384	1,695	1,818	1,796	2,430
44	1,844	1,656	1,511	1,844	1,895	1,410	1,410	1,716	1,856	1,844	2,483
45	1,892	1,699	1,527	1,892	1,932	1,440	1,440	1,738	1,894	1,892	2,536
46	1,939	1,742	1,544	1,939	1,970	1,470	1,470	1,760	1,932	1,939	2,589
47	1,987	1,785	1,560	1,987	2,007	1,501	1,501	1,782	1,970	1,987	2,642
48	2,039	1,828	1,577	2,039	2,045	1,531	1,531	1,804	2,008	2,039	2,695
49	2,091	1,871	1,594	2,091	2,082	1,561	1,561	1,826	2,046	2,091	2,749
50	2,144	1,914	1,610	2,144	2,120	1,591	1,591	1,848	2,084	2,144	2,802
51	2,196	1,957	1,627	2,196	2,158	1,622	1,622	1,870	2,122	2,196	2,855
52	2,249	2,000	1,644	2,249	2,195	1,652	1,652	1,892	2,160	2,249	2,908
53	2,301	2,043	1,660	2,301	2,233	1,682	1,682	1,914	2,198	2,301	2,962
54	2,354	2,086	1,677	2,354	2,271	1,712	1,712	1,936	2,236	2,354	3,015
55	2,406	2,129	1,694	2,406	2,308	1,743	1,743	1,958	2,275	2,406	3,068
56	2,459	2,172	1,710	2,459	2,346	1,773	1,773	1,980	2,313	2,459	3,121
57	2,512	2,215	1,727	2,512	2,384	1,803	1,803	2,002	2,351	2,512	3,175
58	2,564	2,258	1,744	2,564	2,422	1,833	1,833	2,024	2,389	2,564	3,228

Trial length in days	*PPE Cut off A*	*PPE Cut off B*	*PPE Cut off C*	*PPE Cut off D*	*PPE Cut off E*	*PPE Cut off F*	*PPE Cut off G*	*PPE Cut off H*	*PPE Cut off I*	*PPE Cut off J*	*PPE Cut off K*
59	2,617	2,301	1,760	2,617	2,459	1,864	1,864	2,046	2,427	2,617	3,281
60	2,669	2,345	1,777	2,669	2,497	1,894	1,894	2,068	2,465	2,669	3,335
61	2,722	2,388	1,794	2,722	2,535	1,924	1,924	2,090	2,503	2,722	3,388
62	2,775	2,431	1,811	2,775	2,572	1,959	1,959	2,112	2,542	2,775	3,442
63	2,827	2,474	1,827	2,827	2,610	2,020	2,020	2,134	2,580	2,827	3,495
64	2,880	2,517	1,844	2,880	2,648	2,081	2,081	2,156	2,618	2,880	3,549
65	2,933	2,561	1,861	2,933	2,686	2,141	2,141	2,178	2,656	2,933	3,602
66	2,985	2,604	1,877	2,985	2,723	2,202	2,202	2,200	2,694	2,985	3,656
67	3,038	2,647	1,894	3,038	2,761	2,263	2,263	2,222	2,776	3,038	3,709
68	3,091	2,690	1,911	3,091	2,799	2,323	2,323	2,244	2,865	3,091	3,763
69	3,144	2,734	1,927	3,144	2,836	2,384	2,384	2,266	2,954	3,144	3,816
70	3,196	2,777	1,944	3,196	2,874	2,445	2,445	2,288	3,043	3,196	3,870
71	3,249	2,820	1,961	3,249	2,912	2,506	2,506	2,310	3,132	3,249	3,923
72	3,302	2,864	1,978	3,302	2,950	2,566	2,566	2,332	3,221	3,302	3,977
73	3,355	2,907	1,994	3,355	2,987	2,627	2,627	2,354	3,310	3,355	4,031
74	3,407	2,950	2,016	3,407	3,025	2,688	2,688	2,376	3,399	3,407	4,084
75	3,460	2,994	2,040	3,460	3,063	2,749	2,749	2,398	3,488	3,460	4,138
76	3,513	3,037	2,064	3,513	3,101	2,809	2,809	2,420	3,577	3,513	4,192
77	3,566	3,080	2,089	3,566	3,138	2,870	2,870	2,442	3,666	3,566	4,245
78	3,619	3,124	2,113	3,619	3,176	2,931	2,931	2,464	3,755	3,619	4,299
79	3,672	3,167	2,137	3,672	3,214	2,992	2,992	2,486	3,844	3,672	4,353
80	3,724	3,211	2,161	3,724	3,251	3,052	3,052	2,508	3,933	3,724	4,406
81	3,777	3,254	2,185	3,777	3,289	3,113	3,113	2,530	4,023	3,777	4,460
82	3,830	3,297	2,210	3,830	3,327	3,174	3,174	2,552	4,112	3,830	4,514
83	3,883	3,341	2,234	3,883	3,365	3,235	3,235	2,575	4,201	3,883	4,568
84	3,936	3,384	2,258	3,936	3,402	3,295	3,295	2,597	4,290	3,936	4,622
85	3,989	3,428	2,282	3,989	3,440	3,356	3,356	2,619	4,379	3,989	4,675
86	4,042	3,471	2,307	4,042	3,478	3,417	3,417	2,641	4,469	4,042	4,729
87	4,095	3,515	2,331	4,095	3,516	3,478	3,478	2,663	4,558	4,095	4,783
88	4,148	3,558	2,355	4,148	3,553	3,539	3,539	2,685	4,647	4,148	4,837

Trial length in days	*PPE Cut off A*	*PPE Cut off B*	*PPE Cut off C*	*PPE Cut off D*	*PPE Cut off E*	*PPE Cut off F*	*PPE Cut off G*	*PPE Cut off H*	*PPE Cut off I*	*PPE Cut off J*	*PPE Cut off K*
89	4,201	3,602	2,379	4,201	3,591	3,599	3,599	2,707	4,737	4,201	4,891
90	4,254	3,645	2,404	4,254	3,629	3,660	3,660	2,729	4,826	4,254	4,945
91	4,307	3,689	2,428	4,307	3,666	3,721	3,721	2,751	4,915	4,307	4,999
92	4,360	3,733	2,452	4,360	3,704	3,782	3,782	2,774	5,005	4,360	5,053
93	4,413	3,776	2,477	4,413	3,742	3,843	3,843	2,796	5,094	4,413	5,107
94	4,466	3,820	2,501	4,466	3,780	3,903	3,903	2,818	5,183	4,466	5,161
95	4,519	3,863	2,525	4,519	3,817	3,964	3,964	2,840	5,273	4,519	5,215
96	4,572	3,907	2,549	4,572	3,855	4,025	4,025	2,862	5,362	4,572	5,269
97	4,625	3,951	2,574	4,625	3,893	4,086	4,086	2,884	5,452	4,625	5,323
98	4,679	3,994	2,598	4,679	3,930	4,147	4,147	2,906	5,541	4,679	5,377
99	4,732	4,038	2,622	4,732	3,968	4,207	4,207	2,929	5,631	4,732	5,431
100	4,785	4,082	2,647	4,785	4,006	4,268	4,268	2,951	5,720	4,785	5,485
101	4,838	4,125	2,671	4,838	4,044	4,329	4,329	2,973	5,810	4,838	5,539
102	4,891	4,169	2,695	4,891	4,081	4,390	4,390	2,995	5,899	4,891	5,593
103	4,944	4,213	2,720	4,944	4,119	4,451	4,451	3,032	5,989	4,944	5,647
104	4,997	4,257	2,744	4,997	4,157	4,512	4,512	3,073	6,079	4,997	5,702
105	5,051	4,300	2,768	5,051	4,195	4,573	4,573	3,114	6,168	5,051	5,756
106	5,104	4,344	2,793	5,104	4,232	4,633	4,633	3,155	6,258	5,104	5,810
107	5,157	4,388	2,817	5,157	4,270	4,694	4,694	3,196	6,348	5,157	5,864
108	5,210	4,432	2,841	5,210	4,308	4,755	4,755	3,237	6,437	5,210	5,918
109	5,264	4,475	2,866	5,264	4,345	4,816	4,816	3,278	6,527	5,264	5,973
110	5,317	4,519	2,890	5,317	4,383	4,877	4,877	3,319	6,617	5,317	6,027
111	5,370	4,563	2,914	5,370	4,421	4,938	4,938	3,361	6,706	5,370	6,081
112	5,423	4,607	2,939	5,423	4,459	4,999	4,999	3,402	6,796	5,423	6,135
113	5,477	4,650	2,963	5,477	4,496	5,059	5,059	3,443	6,886	5,477	6,189
114	5,530	4,694	2,987	5,530	4,534	5,120	5,120	3,484	6,976	5,530	6,244
115	5,583	4,738	3,012	5,583	4,572	5,181	5,181	3,525	7,066	5,583	6,298
116	5,637	4,782	3,036	5,637	4,610	5,242	5,242	3,566	7,155	5,637	6,352
117	5,690	4,826	3,060	5,690	4,647	5,303	5,303	3,607	7,245	5,690	6,406
118	5,743	4,869	3,085	5,743	4,685	5,364	5,364	3,648	7,335	5,743	6,460

Trial length in days	*PPE Cut off A*	*PPE Cut off B*	*PPE Cut off C*	*PPE Cut off D*	*PPE Cut off E*	*PPE Cut off F*	*PPE Cut off G*	*PPE Cut off H*	*PPE Cut off I*	*PPE Cut off J*	*PPE Cut off K*
119	5,797	4,913	3,109	5,797	4,723	5,425	5,425	3,689	7,425	5,797	6,514
120	5,850	4,957	3,133	5,850	4,760	5,486	5,486	3,730	7,515	5,850	6,569
121	5,904	5,001	3,158	5,904	4,798	5,547	5,547	3,771	7,605	5,904	6,623
122	5,956	5,044	3,182	5,956	4,836	5,607	5,607	3,812	7,693	5,956	6,677
123	6,009	5,088	3,206	6,009	4,874	5,668	5,668	3,853	7,782	6,009	6,731
124	6,061	5,131	3,230	6,061	4,911	5,729	5,729	3,895	7,871	6,061	6,785
125	6,114	5,175	3,254	6,114	4,949	5,789	5,789	3,936	7,959	6,114	6,839
126	6,167	5,218	3,278	6,167	4,987	5,850	5,850	3,977	8,048	6,167	6,892
127	6,219	5,261	3,302	6,219	5,025	5,911	5,911	4,017	8,137	6,219	6,945
128	6,272	5,304	3,326	6,272	5,062	5,971	5,971	4,058	8,225	6,272	6,999
129	6,324	5,347	3,350	6,324	5,100	6,032	6,032	4,098	8,314	6,324	7,052
130	6,377	5,390	3,374	6,377	5,138	6,093	6,093	4,139	8,403	6,377	7,106
131	6,430	5,433	3,398	6,430	5,175	6,153	6,153	4,179	8,491	6,430	7,159
132	6,482	5,476	3,422	6,482	5,213	6,214	6,214	4,219	8,580	6,482	7,212
133	6,535	5,520	3,446	6,535	5,251	6,274	6,274	4,260	8,669	6,535	7,266
134	6,588	5,563	3,470	6,588	5,289	6,335	6,335	4,300	8,757	6,588	7,319
135	6,640	5,606	3,494	6,640	5,326	6,396	6,396	4,341	8,846	6,640	7,373
136	6,693	5,649	3,518	6,693	5,364	6,456	6,456	4,381	8,935	6,693	7,426
137	6,745	5,692	3,542	6,745	5,402	6,517	6,517	4,422	9,023	6,745	7,479
138	6,798	5,735	3,566	6,798	5,439	6,578	6,578	4,462	9,112	6,798	7,533
139	6,851	5,778	3,590	6,851	5,477	6,638	6,638	4,503	9,201	6,851	7,586
140	6,903	5,821	3,614	6,903	5,515	6,699	6,699	4,543	9,289	6,903	7,639
141	6,956	5,864	3,638	6,956	5,553	6,760	6,760	4,584	9,378	6,956	7,693
142	7,008	5,908	3,662	7,008	5,590	6,820	6,820	4,624	9,467	7,008	7,746
143	7,061	5,951	3,686	7,061	5,628	6,881	6,881	4,664	9,555	7,061	7,800
144	7,114	5,994	3,709	7,114	5,666	6,942	6,942	4,705	9,644	7,114	7,853
145	7,166	6,037	3,733	7,166	5,704	7,002	7,002	4,745	9,733	7,166	7,906
146	7,219	6,080	3,757	7,219	5,741	7,063	7,063	4,786	9,821	7,219	7,960
147	7,272	6,123	3,781	7,272	5,779	7,124	7,124	4,826	9,910	7,272	8,013
148	7,324	6,166	3,805	7,324	5,817	7,184	7,184	4,867	9,999	7,324	8,067

Trial length in days	*PPE Cut off A*	*PPE Cut off B*	*PPE Cut off C*	*PPE Cut off D*	*PPE Cut off E*	*PPE Cut off F*	*PPE Cut off G*	*PPE Cut off H*	*PPE Cut off I*	*PPE Cut off J*	*PPE Cut off K*
149	7,377	6,209	3,829	7,377	5,854	7,245	7,245	4,907	10,087	7,377	8,120
150	7,429	6,252	3,853	7,429	5,892	7,305	7,305	4,948	10,176	7,429	8,173
151	7,482	6,296	3,877	7,482	5,930	7,366	7,366	4,988	10,265	7,482	8,227
152	7,535	6,339	3,901	7,535	5,968	7,427	7,427	5,029	10,353	7,535	8,280
153	7,587	6,382	3,925	7,587	6,005	7,487	7,487	5,069	10,442	7,587	8,333
154	7,640	6,425	3,949	7,640	6,043	7,548	7,548	5,110	10,531	7,640	8,387
155	7,692	6,468	3,973	7,692	6,081	7,609	7,609	5,150	10,619	7,692	8,440
156	7,745	6,511	3,997	7,745	6,119	7,669	7,669	5,190	10,708	7,745	8,494
157	7,798	6,554	4,021	7,798	6,156	7,730	7,730	5,231	10,797	7,798	8,547
158	7,850	6,597	4,045	7,850	6,194	7,791	7,791	5,271	10,885	7,850	8,600
159	7,903	6,641	4,069	7,903	6,232	7,851	7,851	5,312	10,974	7,903	8,654
160	7,956	6,684	4,093	7,956	6,269	7,912	7,912	5,352	11,063	7,956	8,707
161	8,008	6,727	4,117	8,008	6,307	7,973	7,973	5,393	11,151	8,008	8,760
162	8,061	6,770	4,141	8,061	6,345	8,033	8,033	5,433	11,240	8,061	8,814
163	8,113	6,813	4,165	8,113	6,383	8,094	8,094	5,474	11,329	8,113	8,867
164	8,166	6,856	4,189	8,166	6,420	8,155	8,155	5,514	11,417	8,166	8,921
165	8,219	6,899	4,213	8,219	6,458	8,215	8,215	5,555	11,506	8,219	8,974
166	8,271	6,942	4,237	8,271	6,496	8,276	8,276	5,595	11,595	8,271	9,027
167	8,324	6,985	4,261	8,324	6,534	8,337	8,337	5,636	11,683	8,324	9,081
168	8,376	7,029	4,285	8,376	6,571	8,397	8,397	5,676	11,772	8,376	9,134
169	8,429	7,072	4,309	8,429	6,609	8,458	8,458	5,716	11,861	8,429	9,188
170	8,482	7,115	4,333	8,482	6,647	8,518	8,518	5,757	11,949	8,482	9,241
171	8,534	7,158	4,357	8,534	6,684	8,579	8,579	5,797	12,038	8,534	9,294
172	8,587	7,201	4,380	8,587	6,722	8,640	8,640	5,838	12,127	8,587	9,348
173	8,639	7,244	4,404	8,639	6,760	8,700	8,700	5,878	12,215	8,639	9,401
174	8,692	7,287	4,428	8,692	6,798	8,761	8,761	5,919	12,304	8,692	9,454
175	8,745	7,330	4,452	8,745	6,835	8,822	8,822	5,959	12,393	8,745	9,508
176	8,797	7,373	4,476	8,797	6,873	8,882	8,882	6,000	12,481	8,797	9,561
177	8,850	7,417	4,500	8,850	6,911	8,943	8,943	6,040	12,570	8,850	9,615
178	8,903	7,460	4,524	8,903	6,948	9,004	9,004	6,081	12,659	8,903	9,668

Trial length in days	*PPE Cut off A*	*PPE Cut off B*	*PPE Cut off C*	*PPE Cut off D*	*PPE Cut off E*	*PPE Cut off F*	*PPE Cut off G*	*PPE Cut off H*	*PPE Cut off I*	*PPE Cut off J*	*PPE Cut off K*
179	8,955	7,503	4,548	8,955	6,986	9,064	9,064	6,121	12,747	8,955	9,721
180	9,008	7,546	4,572	9,008	7,024	9,125	9,125	6,162	12,836	9,008	9,775
181	9,060	7,589	4,596	9,060	7,062	9,186	9,186	6,202	12,925	9,060	9,828
182	9,113	7,632	4,620	9,113	7,099	9,246	9,246	6,242	13,013	9,113	9,881
183	9,166	7,675	4,644	9,166	7,137	9,307	9,307	6,283	13,102	9,166	9,935
184	9,218	7,718	4,668	9,218	7,174	9,368	9,368	6,323	13,191	9,218	9,988
185	9,271	7,762	4,692	9,271	7,211	9,428	9,428	6,364	13,279	9,271	10,042
186	9,323	7,805	4,716	9,323	7,248	9,489	9,489	6,404	13,368	9,323	10,095
187	9,376	7,848	4,740	9,376	7,285	9,549	9,549	6,445	13,457	9,376	10,148
188	9,429	7,891	4,764	9,429	7,322	9,610	9,610	6,485	13,545	9,429	10,202
189	9,481	7,934	4,788	9,481	7,360	9,671	9,671	6,526	13,634	9,481	10,255
190	9,534	7,977	4,812	9,534	7,397	9,731	9,731	6,566	13,723	9,534	10,309
191	9,587	8,020	4,836	9,587	7,434	9,792	9,792	6,607	13,811	9,587	10,362
192	9,639	8,063	4,860	9,639	7,471	9,853	9,853	6,647	13,900	9,639	10,415
193	9,692	8,106	4,884	9,692	7,508	9,913	9,913	6,687	13,988	9,692	10,469
194	9,744	8,150	4,908	9,744	7,545	9,974	9,974	6,728	14,077	9,744	10,522
195	9,797	8,193	4,932	9,797	7,582	10,035	10,035	6,768	14,166	9,797	10,575
196	9,850	8,236	4,956	9,850	7,620	10,095	10,095	6,809	14,254	9,850	10,629
197	9,902	8,279	4,980	9,902	7,657	10,156	10,156	6,849	14,343	9,902	10,682
198	9,955	8,322	5,004	9,955	7,694	10,217	10,217	6,890	14,432	9,955	10,736
199	10,007	8,365	5,028	10,007	7,731	10,277	10,277	6,930	14,520	10,007	10,789
200	10,060	8,408	5,051	10,060	7,768	10,338	10,338	6,971	14,609	10,060	10,842

Cracked trial or guilty plea where the number of pages of prosecution evidence is less than or equal to the PPE Cut-off

6.—(1) Where in a cracked trial or guilty plea the number of pages of prosecution evidence is less than or equal to the PPE Cut-off specified in the table following paragraph 5(1) as appropriate to the Class of Offence with which the assisted person is charged, the total fee payable to the litigator is— **G-78**

(a) the basic fee, calculated in accordance with the table following sub-paragraph (2) of this paragraph;

(b) the defendant uplift, if any, calculated in accordance with the table following paragraph 12; and

(c) the adjustment for transfers and retrials, if any, calculated in accordance with paragraph 13.

(2) For the purposes of sub-paragraph (1), the basic fee appropriate to a cracked trial or a guilty plea is specified in the table following this sub-paragraph, in accordance with the type of case and Class of Offence with which the assisted person is charged.

BASIC FEES FOR CRACKED TRIALS AND GUILTY PLEAS (£)

	Class of Offence										
Type of case	*A*	*B*	*C*	*D*	*E*	*F*	*G*	*H*	*I*	*J*	*K*
Cracked trial	904.58	707.32	524.83	859.35	233.03	224.23	224.23	237.00	253.67	904.58	773.86
Guilty plea	680.39	556.11	442.91	646.36	184.70	195.81	195.81	190.97	174.60	680.39	640.84

[The table following para.6(2) is printed as substituted by SI 2016/313 (G-1a).

Trial where the number of pages of prosecution evidence is less than or equal to the PPE Cut-off

7.—(1) Where in a trial the number of pages of prosecution evidence is less than or equal to the PPE Cut-off specified in the table following paragraph 5(2) as appropriate to the offence for which the assisted person is tried and the length of trial, the total fee payable to the litigator is— **G-79**

(a) the basic fee, calculated in accordance with the table following sub-paragraph (2);

(b) the length of trial proxy, if any, calculated in accordance with the table following subparagraph (3);

(c) the defendant uplift, if any, calculated in accordance with the table following paragraph 12; and

(d) the adjustment for transfers and retrials, if any, calculated in accordance with paragraph 13.

(2) For the purposes of sub-paragraph (1), the basic fee appropriate to a trial is specified in the table following this sub-paragraph, in accordance with the offence for which the assisted person is tried.

	Class of Offence										
Type of case	A	B	C	D	E	F	G	H	I	J	K
Trial	1,467.58	1,097.66	739.59	1394.20	352.72	357.60	357.60	357.75	357.44	1,467.58	1,031.82

(3) For the purposes of sub-paragraph (1), the length of trial proxy is specified in the table following this sub-paragraph, in accordance with the offence for which the assisted person is tried and the length of trial.

Trial Length in Days	*Trial length proxy A*	*Trial length proxy B*	*Trial length proxy C*	*Trial length proxy D*	*Trial length proxy E*	*Trial length proxy F*	*Trial length proxy G*	*Trial length proxy H*	*Trial length proxy I*	*Trial length proxy J*	*Trial length proxy K*
1	0.00	0.00	0.00	0.00	0.00	0.00	0.00	0.00	0.00	0.00	0.00
2	0.00	0.00	0.00	0.00	0.00	0.00	0.00	0.00	0.00	0.00	0.00
3	252.54	452.88	432.51	239.92	716.58	644.94	644.94	703.69	862.39	252.54	574.13
4	769.79	879.65	843.33	731.30	1,033.65	898.77	898.77	1,009.83	1,320.93	769.79	1,140.63
5	1,261.16	1,285.08	1,233.61	1,198.10	1,334.86	1,139.90	1,139.90	1,300.64	1,756.54	1,261.16	1,678.81
6	1,761.17	1,695.98	1,621.20	1,673.12	1,617.11	1,386.43	1,386.43	1,589.05	2,200.59	1,761.17	2,181.04
7	2,253.87	2,102.22	2,011.03	2,141.18	1,915.45	1,632.83	1,632.83	1,879.51	2,637.65	2,253.87	2,713.26
8	2,746.56	2,508.44	2,400.87	2,609.24	2,213.79	1,875.25	1,875.25	2,169.97	3,074.70	2,746.56	3,245.48
9	3,210.92	2,874.04	2,751.71	3,050.38	2,482.29	2,093.45	2,093.45	2,431.38	3,473.43	3,210.92	3,724.49
10	3,675.29	3,239.65	3,102.56	3,491.52	2,750.81	2,311.64	2,311.64	2,692.79	3,872.17	3,675.29	4,203.48
11	4,143.10	3,605.74	3,462.93	3,935.94	3,031.66	2,536.06	2,536.06	2,961.38	4,279.02	4,143.10	4,703.99
12	4,607.74	3,971.38	3,823.47	4,377.35	3,312.59	2,760.47	2,760.47	3,229.64	4,686.22	4,607.74	5,204.80
13	5,072.39	4,337.02	4,175.80	4,818.77	3,593.15	2,983.98	2,983.98	3,492.07	5,086.28	5,072.39	5,705.63
14	5,537.03	4,702.67	4,528.13	5,260.19	3,865.07	3,203.34	3,203.34	3,754.51	5,486.32	5,537.03	6,206.43
15	6,001.68	5,068.31	4,880.46	5,701.59	4,136.15	3,422.69	3,422.69	4,016.95	5,886.37	6,001.68	6,707.21
16	6,466.32	5,433.96	5,232.79	6,143.00	4,407.26	3,642.05	3,642.05	4,279.39	6,286.42	6,466.32	7,207.20
17	6,930.96	5,799.60	5,585.12	6,584.42	4,678.35	3,861.41	3,861.41	4,541.82	6,686.47	6,930.96	7,693.86
18	7,395.60	6,165.24	5,937.45	7,025.83	4,949.45	4,080.76	4,080.76	4,804.26	7,086.52	7,395.60	8,180.52
19	7,860.25	6,530.88	6,289.77	7,467.24	5,220.54	4,300.12	4,300.12	5,066.69	7,486.57	7,860.25	8,667.17
20	8,324.89	6,896.53	6,642.11	7,908.66	5,491.63	4,519.48	4,519.48	5,329.13	7,886.63	8,324.89	9,153.84
21	8,798.40	7,234.27	6,931.61	8,358.47	5,715.66	4,698.94	4,698.94	5,544.96	8,215.37	8,798.40	9,640.50
22	9,271.81	7,571.99	7,221.19	8,808.22	5,939.70	4,878.48	4,878.48	5,760.90	8,544.12	9,271.81	10,127.16
23	9,737.21	7,909.69	7,510.79	9,250.36	6,157.06	5,058.02	5,058.02	5,976.83	8,872.90	9,737.21	10,613.82
24	10,202.62	8,239.72	7,800.39	9,692.49	6,374.43	5,237.57	5,237.57	6,192.76	9,198.07	10,202.62	11,100.48
25	10,668.04	8,569.74	8,088.48	10,134.63	6,591.80	5,417.10	5,417.10	6,405.21	9,519.15	10,668.04	11,587.14
26	11,133.44	8,899.77	8,371.53	10,576.78	6,809.17	5,596.65	5,596.65	6,615.99	9,840.24	11,133.44	12,073.81
27	11,598.84	9,229.80	8,654.60	11,018.90	7,026.53	5,776.19	5,776.19	6,826.76	10,161.33	11,598.84	12,560.46
28	12,064.25	9,559.83	8,937.65	11,461.05	7,243.91	5,955.73	5,955.73	7,037.54	10,482.41	12,064.25	13,047.13
29	12,529.67	9,889.86	9,220.70	11,903.18	7,461.27	6,133.18	6,133.18	7,248.30	10,803.51	12,529.67	13,533.78

Trial Length in Days	*Trial length proxy A*	*Trial length proxy B*	*Trial length proxy C*	*Trial length proxy D*	*Trial length proxy E*	*Trial length proxy F*	*Trial length proxy G*	*Trial length proxy H*	*Trial length proxy I*	*Trial length proxy J*	*Trial length proxy K*
30	12,995.07	10,219.88	9,503.75	12,345.31	7,678.63	6,309.59	6,309.59	7,459.07	11,124.59	12,995.07	14,020.44
31	13,460.48	10,549.91	9,786.81	12,787.46	7,896.01	6,486.01	6,486.01	7,669.85	11,445.67	13,460.48	14,507.11
32	13,925.88	10,879.95	10,069.87	13,229.59	8,113.38	6,662.43	6,662.43	7,880.61	11,766.76	13,925.88	14,993.76
33	14,391.30	11,209.97	10,352.92	13,671.73	8,330.74	6,838.84	6,838.84	8,091.39	12,087.84	14,391.30	15,480.43
34	14,856.70	11,540.00	10,635.97	14,113.87	8,548.11	7,015.26	7,015.26	8,302.16	12,408.93	14,856.70	15,967.09
35	15,322.11	11,870.03	10,919.03	14,556.01	8,765.48	7,191.68	7,191.68	8,512.93	12,730.02	15,322.11	16,453.75
36	15,787.52	12,200.05	11,202.09	14,998.14	8,982.84	7,368.10	7,368.10	8,723.70	13,051.10	15,787.52	16,940.41
37	16,252.93	12,530.09	11,485.14	15,440.28	9,200.22	7,544.51	7,544.51	8,934.48	13,372.19	16,252.93	17,427.07
38	16,718.33	12,860.11	11,768.20	15,882.42	9,417.58	7,720.93	7,720.93	9,145.25	13,693.28	16,718.33	17,913.73
39	17,183.74	13,190.13	12,051.25	16,324.55	9,634.94	7,897.35	7,897.35	9,356.02	14,014.36	17,183.74	18,400.40
40	17,622.38	13,492.13	12,163.57	16,741.26	9,722.09	8,027.76	8,027.76	9,447.16	14,282.00	17,622.38	18,865.89
41	18,063.40	13,796.43	12,277.13	17,160.24	9,811.54	8,158.44	8,158.44	9,539.40	14,551.22	18,063.40	19,334.83
42	18,504.54	14,100.82	12,390.73	17,579.32	9,901.04	8,289.12	8,289.12	9,631.68	14,820.51	18,504.54	19,803.93
43	18,945.79	14,405.31	12,504.33	17,998.51	9,990.58	8,419.82	8,419.82	9,723.97	15,089.84	18,945.79	20,273.20
44	19,387.15	14,709.89	12,617.96	18,417.79	10,080.16	8,550.52	8,550.52	9,816.28	15,359.23	19,387.15	20,742.61
45	19,828.61	15,014.56	12,731.61	18,837.18	10,169.77	8,681.22	8,681.22	9,908.63	15,628.69	19,828.61	21,212.18
46	20,270.18	15,319.32	12,845.28	19,256.68	10,259.43	8,811.94	8,811.94	10,000.97	15,898.19	20,270.18	21,681.91
47	20,711.85	15,624.18	12,958.98	19,676.26	10,349.13	8,942.66	8,942.66	10,093.35	16,167.76	20,711.85	22,151.80
48	21,153.65	15,929.14	13,072.69	20,095.97	10,438.87	9,073.39	9,073.39	10,185.75	16,437.38	21,153.65	22,621.84
49	21,595.54	16,234.19	13,186.44	20,515.76	10,528.64	9,204.12	9,204.12	10,278.16	16,707.05	21,595.54	23,092.04
50	22,037.53	16,539.33	13,300.19	20,935.66	10,618.45	9,334.88	9,334.88	10,370.61	16,976.79	22,037.53	23,562.39
51	22,479.65	16,844.56	13,413.98	21,355.67	10,708.32	9,465.63	9,465.63	10,463.06	17,246.59	22,479.65	24,032.91
52	22,921.86	17,149.88	13,527.78	21,775.77	10,798.21	9,596.40	9,596.40	10,555.54	17,516.43	22,921.86	24,503.58
53	23,364.19	17,455.30	13,641.60	22,195.99	10,888.15	9,727.16	9,727.16	10,648.04	17,786.33	23,364.19	24,974.41
54	23,806.62	17,760.82	13,755.44	22,616.29	10,978.13	9,857.94	9,857.94	10,740.56	18,056.29	23,806.62	25,445.40
55	24,249.16	18,066.42	13,869.31	23,036.69	11,068.14	9,988.72	9,988.72	10,833.10	18,326.31	24,249.16	25,916.54
56	24,691.80	18,372.13	13,983.20	23,457.22	11,158.20	10,119.52	10,119.52	10,925.66	18,596.39	24,691.80	26,387.85
57	25,134.56	18,677.92	14,097.11	23,877.83	11,248.29	10,250.32	10,250.32	11,018.24	18,866.52	25,134.56	26,859.31
58	25,577.42	18,983.81	14,211.04	24,298.55	11,338.39	10,381.13	10,381.13	11,110.84	19,136.71	25,577.42	27,330.92

Trial Length in Days	*Trial length proxy A*	*Trial length proxy B*	*Trial length proxy C*	*Trial length proxy D*	*Trial length proxy E*	*Trial length proxy F*	*Trial length proxy G*	*Trial length proxy H*	*Trial length proxy I*	*Trial length proxy J*	*Trial length proxy K*
59	26,020.39	19,289.79	14,325.00	24,719.38	11,428.49	10,511.95	10,511.95	11,203.47	19,406.96	26,020.39	27,802.70
60	26,463.47	19,595.86	14,438.97	25,140.29	11,518.59	10,642.77	10,642.77	11,296.10	19,677.26	26,463.47	28,274.63
61	26,906.66	19,902.03	14,552.97	25,561.32	11,608.70	10,773.60	10,773.60	11,388.77	19,947.62	26,906.66	28,746.72
62	27,349.94	20,208.30	14,666.99	25,982.45	11,698.80	10,904.44	10,904.44	11,481.46	20,218.04	27,349.94	29,218.96
63	27,793.35	20,514.64	14,781.02	26,403.69	11,788.90	11,035.28	11,035.28	11,574.16	20,488.52	27,793.35	29,691.37
64	28,236.86	20,821.10	14,895.09	26,825.02	11,879.00	11,166.14	11,166.14	11,666.89	20,759.04	28,236.86	30,163.93
65	28,680.48	21,127.63	15,009.17	27,246.45	11,969.10	11,297.01	11,297.01	11,759.62	21,029.63	28,680.48	30,636.65
66	29,124.20	21,434.28	15,123.28	27,667.99	12,059.20	11,427.88	11,427.88	11,852.39	21,300.28	29,124.20	31,109.52
67	29,568.03	21,741.01	15,237.40	28,089.63	12,149.30	11,558.76	11,558.76	11,945.17	21,570.97	29,568.03	31,582.55
68	30,011.97	22,047.83	15,351.55	28,511.37	12,239.40	11,689.65	11,689.65	12,037.98	21,841.73	30,011.97	32,055.74
69	30,456.02	22,354.74	15,465.72	28,933.21	12,329.50	11,820.54	11,820.54	12,130.81	22,112.55	30,456.02	32,529.08
70	30,900.17	22,661.76	15,579.91	29,355.16	12,419.60	11,951.45	11,951.45	12,223.66	22,383.42	30,900.17	33,002.60
71	31,344.44	22,968.86	15,694.12	29,777.22	12,509.70	12,082.36	12,082.36	12,316.53	22,654.35	31,344.44	33,476.26
72	31,788.81	23,276.06	15,808.35	30,199.37	12,599.80	12,213.28	12,213.28	12,409.42	22,925.33	31,788.81	33,950.08
73	32,233.28	23,583.35	15,922.61	30,621.63	12,689.90	12,344.21	12,344.21	12,502.32	23,196.37	32,233.28	34,424.05
74	32,677.87	23,890.74	16,036.89	31,043.98	12,780.00	12,475.14	12,475.14	12,595.26	23,467.47	32,677.87	34,898.19
75	33,122.56	24,198.21	16,151.19	31,466.43	12,870.10	12,606.09	12,606.09	12,688.21	23,738.63	33,122.56	35,372.48
76	33,567.36	24,505.78	16,265.50	31,889.00	12,960.20	12,737.03	12,737.03	12,781.18	24,009.84	33,567.36	35,846.92
77	34,012.28	24,813.45	16,379.85	32,311.66	13,050.30	12,867.99	12,867.99	12,874.16	24,281.10	34,012.28	36,321.53
78	34,457.29	25,121.21	16,494.21	32,734.43	13,140.40	12,998.95	12,998.95	12,967.17	24,552.43	34,457.29	36,796.30
79	34,902.42	25,429.06	16,608.60	33,157.30	13,230.50	13,129.94	13,129.94	13,060.21	24,823.82	34,902.42	37,271.22
80	35,347.65	25,737.00	16,723.00	33,580.26	13,320.60	13,260.92	13,260.92	13,153.27	25,095.26	35,347.65	37,746.29
81	35,792.99	26,045.04	16,837.42	34,003.35	13,410.70	13,391.90	13,391.90	13,246.34	25,366.75	35,792.99	38,221.52
82	36,238.43	26,353.17	16,951.88	34,426.52	13,500.80	13,522.90	13,522.90	13,339.43	25,638.30	36,238.43	38,696.92
83	36,683.99	26,661.40	17,066.35	34,849.80	13,590.90	13,653.90	13,653.90	13,432.55	25,909.92	36,683.99	39,172.47
84	37,129.65	26,969.72	17,180.83	35,273.17	13,681.01	13,784.93	13,784.93	13,525.68	26,181.58	37,129.65	39,648.18
85	37,575.42	27,278.13	17,295.35	35,696.65	13,771.11	13,915.94	13,915.94	13,618.83	26,453.30	37,575.42	40,124.04
86	38,021.30	27,586.64	17,409.90	36,120.24	13,861.21	14,046.97	14,046.97	13,712.01	26,725.09	38,021.30	40,600.06
87	38,467.29	27,895.23	17,524.45	36,543.93	13,951.31	14,178.01	14,178.01	13,805.21	26,996.93	38,467.29	41,076.24

Trial Length in Days	*Trial length proxy A*	*Trial length proxy B*	*Trial length proxy C*	*Trial length proxy D*	*Trial length proxy E*	*Trial length proxy F*	*Trial length proxy G*	*Trial length proxy H*	*Trial length proxy I*	*Trial length proxy J*	*Trial length proxy K*
88	38,913.39	28,203.93	17,639.03	36,967.72	14,041.41	14,309.06	14,309.06	13,898.42	27,268.82	38,913.39	41,552.58
89	39,359.59	28,512.71	17,753.63	37,391.61	14,131.51	14,440.10	14,440.10	13,991.66	27,540.77	39,359.59	42,029.07
90	39,805.90	28,821.60	17,868.25	37,815.60	14,221.61	14,571.17	14,571.17	14,084.91	27,812.78	39,805.90	42,505.73
91	40,252.32	29,130.57	17,982.89	38,239.70	14,311.71	14,702.24	14,702.24	14,178.20	28,084.84	40,252.32	42,982.53
92	40,698.83	29,439.63	18,097.56	38,663.90	14,401.81	14,833.32	14,833.32	14,271.49	28,356.97	40,698.83	43,459.49
93	41,145.47	29,748.80	18,212.24	39,088.20	14,491.91	14,964.40	14,964.40	14,364.81	28,629.15	41,145.47	43,936.62
94	41,592.21	30,058.05	18,326.95	39,512.60	14,582.01	15,095.49	15,095.49	14,458.15	28,901.38	41,592.21	44,413.90
95	42,039.06	30,367.40	18,441.68	39,937.10	14,672.11	15,226.59	15,226.59	14,551.52	29,173.67	42,039.06	44,891.33
96	42,486.02	30,676.84	18,556.44	40,361.72	14,762.22	15,357.69	15,357.69	14,644.89	29,446.03	42,486.02	45,368.93
97	42,933.08	30,986.38	18,671.21	40,786.43	14,852.32	15,488.81	15,488.81	14,738.25	29,718.43	42,933.08	45,846.68
98	43,380.25	31,296.01	18,786.00	41,211.24	14,942.42	15,619.94	15,619.94	14,831.63	29,990.89	43,380.25	46,324.60
99	43,827.53	31,605.73	18,900.82	41,636.15	15,032.52	15,751.07	15,751.07	14,925.00	30,263.42	43,827.53	46,802.66
100	44,274.91	31,915.55	19,015.65	42,061.17	15,122.62	15,882.21	15,882.21	15,018.37	30,535.98	44,274.91	47,280.88
101	44,722.41	32,225.46	19,130.51	42,486.29	15,212.72	16,013.36	16,013.36	15,111.74	30,808.63	44,722.41	47,759.26
102	45,170.01	32,535.45	19,245.39	42,911.51	15,302.82	16,144.51	16,144.51	15,205.11	31,081.31	45,170.01	48,237.80
103	45,617.73	32,845.55	19,360.30	43,336.84	15,392.92	16,275.67	16,275.67	15,298.48	31,354.06	45,617.73	48,716.50
104	46,065.54	33,155.74	19,475.21	43,762.27	15,483.02	16,406.84	16,406.84	15,391.85	31,626.86	46,065.54	49,195.35
105	46,513.46	33,466.03	19,590.12	44,187.79	15,573.12	16,538.02	16,538.02	15,485.22	31,899.72	46,513.46	49,674.36
106	46,961.50	33,776.40	19,705.04	44,613.42	15,663.22	16,669.21	16,669.21	15,578.59	32,172.64	46,961.50	50,153.43
107	47,409.64	34,086.84	19,819.95	45,039.15	15,753.32	16,800.40	16,800.40	15,671.96	32,445.62	47,409.64	50,632.48
108	47,857.89	34,397.27	19,934.87	45,465.00	15,843.43	16,931.60	16,931.60	15,765.33	32,718.65	47,857.89	51,111.54
109	48,306.24	34,707.71	20,049.78	45,890.93	15,933.53	17,062.82	17,062.82	15,858.70	32,991.74	48,306.24	51,590.60
110	48,754.70	35,018.15	20,164.69	46,316.97	16,023.63	17,194.03	17,194.03	15,952.07	33,264.88	48,754.70	52,069.66
111	49,203.28	35,328.59	20,279.60	46,743.12	16,113.73	17,325.26	17,325.26	16,045.44	33,538.08	49,203.28	52,548.71
112	49,651.95	35,639.02	20,394.51	47,169.36	16,203.83	17,456.49	17,456.49	16,138.81	33,811.34	49,651.95	53,027.77
113	50,100.74	35,949.45	20,509.43	47,595.72	16,293.93	17,587.73	17,587.73	16,232.18	34,084.66	50,100.74	53,506.84
114	50,549.63	36,259.89	20,624.34	48,022.16	16,384.03	17,718.99	17,718.99	16,325.55	34,358.03	50,549.63	53,985.89
115	50,998.64	36,570.33	20,739.25	48,448.70	16,474.13	17,850.24	17,850.24	16,418.92	34,631.46	50,998.64	54,464.95
116	51,447.75	36,880.77	20,854.17	48,875.36	16,564.23	17,981.51	17,981.51	16,512.29	34,904.94	51,447.75	54,944.01

Trial Length in Days	*Trial length proxy A*	*Trial length proxy B*	*Trial length proxy C*	*Trial length proxy D*	*Trial length proxy E*	*Trial length proxy F*	*Trial length proxy G*	*Trial length proxy H*	*Trial length proxy I*	*Trial length proxy J*	*Trial length proxy K*
117	51,896.97	37,191.20	20,969.08	49,302.12	16,654.33	18,112.78	18,112.78	16,605.66	35,178.49	51,896.97	55,423.07
118	52,346.29	37,501.64	21,083.99	49,728.98	16,744.43	18,244.06	18,244.06	16,699.03	35,452.09	52,346.29	55,902.12
119	52,795.73	37,812.07	21,198.91	50,155.94	16,834.53	18,375.35	18,375.35	16,792.40	35,725.74	52,795.73	56,381.19
120	53,245.27	38,122.51	21,313.82	50,583.00	16,924.63	18,506.65	18,506.65	16,885.77	35,999.46	53,245.27	56,860.25
121	53,694.91	38,432.95	21,428.73	51,010.17	17,014.73	18,637.95	18,637.95	16,979.14	36,273.23	53,694.91	57,339.30
122	54,137.91	38,743.38	21,543.64	51,431.02	17,104.83	18,768.69	18,768.69	17,072.51	36,543.17	54,137.91	57,818.36
123	54,580.90	39,053.82	21,658.55	51,851.87	17,194.93	18,899.43	18,899.43	17,165.88	36,813.11	54,580.90	58,297.42
124	55,023.91	39,360.61	21,771.79	52,272.71	17,285.03	19,030.16	19,030.16	17,259.25	37,083.05	55,023.91	58,775.55
125	55,466.90	39,666.39	21,884.98	52,693.55	17,375.13	19,160.90	19,160.90	17,352.62	37,353.00	55,466.90	59,247.42
126	55,909.89	39,972.16	21,998.17	53,114.41	17,465.23	19,291.63	19,291.63	17,445.93	37,622.93	55,909.89	59,719.29
127	56,352.90	40,277.95	22,111.36	53,535.25	17,555.33	19,422.37	19,422.37	17,537.91	37,892.88	56,352.90	60,191.17
128	56,795.89	40,583.73	22,224.55	53,956.10	17,645.43	19,553.11	19,553.11	17,629.88	38,162.82	56,795.89	60,663.04
129	57,238.88	40,889.51	22,337.74	54,376.94	17,735.53	19,683.85	19,683.85	17,721.85	38,432.76	57,238.88	61,134.92
130	57,681.88	41,195.29	22,450.92	54,797.79	17,825.63	19,814.58	19,814.58	17,813.82	38,702.70	57,681.88	61,606.79
131	58,124.87	41,501.07	22,564.12	55,218.63	17,915.74	19,945.32	19,945.32	17,905.79	38,972.65	58,124.87	62,078.65
132	58,567.87	41,806.85	22,677.30	55,639.48	18,005.84	20,076.06	20,076.06	17,997.76	39,242.58	58,567.87	62,550.53
133	59,010.87	42,112.63	22,790.49	56,060.32	18,095.94	20,206.79	20,206.79	18,089.73	39,512.53	59,010.87	63,022.41
134	59,453.86	42,418.40	22,903.68	56,481.17	18,186.04	20,337.53	20,337.53	18,181.70	39,782.47	59,453.86	63,494.28
135	59,896.86	42,724.19	23,016.87	56,902.01	18,276.14	20,468.27	20,468.27	18,273.66	40,052.42	59,896.86	63,966.15
136	60,339.86	43,029.97	23,130.07	57,322.86	18,366.24	20,599.01	20,599.01	18,365.63	40,322.36	60,339.86	64,438.02
137	60,782.85	43,335.75	23,243.25	57,743.70	18,456.34	20,729.74	20,729.74	18,457.60	40,592.30	60,782.85	64,909.90
138	61,225.85	43,641.53	23,356.44	58,164.56	18,546.44	20,860.48	20,860.48	18,549.57	40,862.24	61,225.85	65,381.77
139	61,668.84	43,947.30	23,469.63	58,585.40	18,636.54	20,991.22	20,991.22	18,641.54	41,132.19	61,668.84	65,853.64
140	62,111.84	44,253.09	23,582.82	59,006.25	18,726.64	21,121.95	21,121.95	18,733.52	41,402.13	62,111.84	66,325.52
141	62,554.83	44,558.86	23,696.01	59,427.09	18,816.74	21,252.69	21,252.69	18,825.48	41,672.07	62,554.83	66,797.38
142	62,997.82	44,864.65	23,809.20	59,847.94	18,906.84	21,383.43	21,383.43	18,917.46	41,942.01	62,997.82	67,269.26
143	63,440.83	45,170.43	23,922.38	60,268.79	18,996.95	21,514.17	21,514.17	19,009.43	42,211.96	63,440.83	67,741.13
144	63,883.82	45,476.21	24,035.58	60,689.64	19,087.05	21,644.90	21,644.90	19,101.39	42,481.89	63,883.82	68,213.00
145	64,326.82	45,781.99	24,148.77	61,110.47	19,177.15	21,775.64	21,775.64	19,193.36	42,751.84	64,326.82	68,684.88

Trial Length in Days	*Trial length proxy A*	*Trial length proxy B*	*Trial length proxy C*	*Trial length proxy D*	*Trial length proxy E*	*Trial length proxy F*	*Trial length proxy G*	*Trial length proxy H*	*Trial length proxy I*	*Trial length proxy J*	*Trial length proxy K*
146	64,769.82	46,087.77	24,261.95	61,531.33	19,267.25	21,906.38	21,906.38	19,285.32	43,021.78	64,769.82	69,156.75
147	65,212.81	46,393.55	24,375.15	61,952.17	19,357.35	22,037.11	22,037.11	19,377.30	43,291.72	65,212.81	69,628.62
148	65,655.81	46,699.32	24,488.33	62,373.03	19,447.45	22,167.85	22,167.85	19,469.27	43,561.66	65,655.81	70,100.49
149	66,098.81	47,005.10	24,601.52	62,793.86	19,537.55	22,298.59	22,298.59	19,561.24	43,831.61	66,098.81	70,572.37
150	66,541.80	47,310.89	24,714.71	63,214.71	19,627.65	22,429.33	22,429.33	19,653.21	44,101.54	66,541.80	71,044.25
151	66,984.79	47,616.67	24,827.90	63,635.56	19,717.75	22,560.06	22,560.06	19,745.18	44,371.49	66,984.79	71,516.11
152	67,427.79	47,922.44	24,941.09	64,056.41	19,807.85	22,690.80	22,690.80	19,837.15	44,641.43	67,427.79	71,987.98
153	67,870.78	48,228.23	25,054.28	64,477.25	19,897.95	22,821.54	22,821.54	19,929.12	44,911.37	67,870.78	72,459.86
154	68,313.78	48,534.00	25,167.46	64,898.10	19,988.05	22,952.27	22,952.27	20,021.09	45,181.32	68,313.78	72,931.73
155	68,756.78	48,839.79	25,280.66	65,318.94	20,078.16	23,083.01	23,083.01	20,113.05	45,451.26	68,756.78	73,403.61
156	69,199.78	49,145.56	25,393.84	65,739.79	20,168.26	23,213.74	23,213.74	20,205.02	45,721.20	69,199.78	73,875.48
157	69,642.77	49,451.34	25,507.03	66,160.63	20,258.36	23,344.49	23,344.49	20,297.00	45,991.14	69,642.77	74,347.34
158	70,085.77	49,757.13	25,620.22	66,581.48	20,348.46	23,475.22	23,475.22	20,388.96	46,261.09	70,085.77	74,819.22
159	70,528.77	50,062.91	25,733.41	67,002.33	20,438.56	23,605.96	23,605.96	20,480.93	46,531.02	70,528.77	75,291.10
160	70,971.76	50,368.69	25,846.61	67,423.17	20,528.66	23,736.70	23,736.70	20,572.91	46,800.97	70,971.76	75,762.97
161	71,414.76	50,674.46	25,959.79	67,844.02	20,618.76	23,867.43	23,867.43	20,664.87	47,070.91	71,414.76	76,234.84
162	71,857.75	50,980.24	26,072.98	68,264.86	20,708.86	23,998.17	23,998.17	20,756.85	47,340.85	71,857.75	76,706.71
163	72,300.74	51,286.02	26,186.17	68,685.72	20,798.96	24,128.91	24,128.91	20,848.82	47,610.79	72,300.74	77,178.59
164	72,743.74	51,591.80	26,299.36	69,106.56	20,889.06	24,259.64	24,259.64	20,940.78	47,880.74	72,743.74	77,650.46
165	73,186.74	51,897.59	26,412.55	69,527.40	20,979.16	24,390.38	24,390.38	21,032.75	48,150.67	73,186.74	78,122.33
166	73,629.73	52,203.37	26,525.74	69,948.25	21,069.26	24,521.12	24,521.12	21,124.72	48,420.62	73,629.73	78,594.21
167	74,072.73	52,509.14	26,638.92	70,369.10	21,159.36	24,651.85	24,651.85	21,216.69	48,690.56	74,072.73	79,066.07
168	74,515.73	52,814.93	26,752.12	70,789.95	21,249.46	24,782.59	24,782.59	21,308.66	48,960.50	74,515.73	79,537.95
169	74,958.72	53,120.70	26,865.30	71,210.79	21,339.56	24,913.33	24,913.33	21,400.63	49,230.44	74,958.72	80,009.83
170	75,401.72	53,426.48	26,978.49	71,631.63	21,429.66	25,044.06	25,044.06	21,492.60	49,500.39	75,401.72	80,481.69
171	75,844.72	53,732.26	27,091.68	72,052.49	21,519.76	25,174.81	25,174.81	21,584.57	49,770.33	75,844.72	80,953.57
172	76,287.71	54,038.04	27,204.87	72,473.33	21,609.86	25,305.54	25,305.54	21,676.54	50,040.28	76,287.71	81,425.44
173	76,730.70	54,343.83	27,318.06	72,894.18	21,699.96	25,436.28	25,436.28	21,768.51	50,310.22	76,730.70	81,897.32
174	77,173.70	54,649.60	27,431.25	73,315.02	21,790.06	25,567.02	25,567.02	21,860.48	50,580.16	77,173.70	82,369.19

Trial Length in Days	*Trial length proxy A*	*Trial length proxy B*	*Trial length proxy C*	*Trial length proxy D*	*Trial length proxy E*	*Trial length proxy F*	*Trial length proxy G*	*Trial length proxy H*	*Trial length proxy I*	*Trial length proxy J*	*Trial length proxy K*
175	77,616.70	54,955.38	27,544.44	73,735.87	21,880.16	25,697.75	25,697.75	21,952.44	50,850.10	77,616.70	82,841.06
176	78,059.69	55,261.16	27,657.63	74,156.71	21,970.26	25,828.49	25,828.49	22,044.41	51,120.05	78,059.69	83,312.94
177	78,502.69	55,566.94	27,770.82	74,577.56	22,060.36	25,959.23	25,959.23	22,136.39	51,389.98	78,502.69	83,784.80
178	78,945.69	55,872.72	27,884.00	74,998.40	22,150.47	26,089.96	26,089.96	22,228.35	51,659.93	78,945.69	84,256.68
179	79,388.68	56,178.50	27,997.20	75,419.25	22,240.57	26,220.70	26,220.70	22,320.32	51,929.87	79,388.68	84,728.55
180	79,831.68	56,484.28	28,110.38	75,840.09	22,330.67	26,351.44	26,351.44	22,412.30	52,199.81	79,831.68	85,200.42
181	80,274.68	56,790.07	28,223.58	76,260.94	22,420.77	26,482.17	26,482.17	22,504.26	52,469.75	80,274.68	85,672.30
182	80,717.67	57,095.84	28,336.77	76,681.78	22,510.87	26,612.91	26,612.91	22,596.24	52,739.70	80,717.67	86,144.17
183	81,160.67	57,401.62	28,449.95	77,102.64	22,599.68	26,743.65	26,743.65	22,688.21	53,009.63	81,160.67	86,616.04
184	81,603.66	57,707.40	28,563.15	77,523.48	22,688.43	26,874.38	26,874.38	22,780.17	53,279.58	81,603.66	87,087.91
185	82,046.65	58,013.18	28,676.33	77,944.32	22,777.18	27,005.13	27,005.13	22,872.14	53,549.52	82,046.65	87,559.79
186	82,489.66	58,318.96	28,789.52	78,365.17	22,865.93	27,135.86	27,135.86	22,964.11	53,819.46	82,489.66	88,031.67
187	82,932.65	58,624.74	28,902.71	78,786.02	22,954.68	27,266.60	27,266.60	23,056.08	54,089.40	82,932.65	88,503.53
188	83,375.65	58,930.52	29,015.90	79,206.87	23,043.43	27,397.34	27,397.34	23,148.05	54,359.35	83,375.65	88,975.40
189	83,818.64	59,236.30	29,129.09	79,627.71	23,132.18	27,528.06	27,528.06	23,240.02	54,629.29	83,818.64	89,447.28
190	84,261.64	59,542.08	29,242.28	80,048.55	23,220.93	27,658.81	27,658.81	23,331.99	54,899.23	84,261.64	89,919.15
191	84,704.64	59,847.86	29,355.46	80,469.41	23,309.68	27,789.55	27,789.55	23,423.96	55,169.18	84,704.64	90,391.03
192	85,147.63	60,153.64	29,468.66	80,890.25	23,398.43	27,920.28	27,920.28	23,515.94	55,439.11	85,147.63	90,862.90
193	85,590.63	60,459.41	29,581.84	81,311.10	23,487.18	28,051.02	28,051.02	23,607.90	55,709.06	85,590.63	91,334.76
194	86,033.62	60,765.20	29,695.03	81,731.94	23,575.92	28,181.76	28,181.76	23,699.87	55,979.00	86,033.62	91,806.64
195	86,476.61	61,070.98	29,808.22	82,152.79	23,664.67	28,312.49	28,312.49	23,791.84	56,248.94	86,476.61	92,278.52
196	86,919.61	61,376.76	29,921.41	82,573.64	23,753.42	28,443.23	28,443.23	23,883.80	56,518.88	86,919.61	92,750.39
197	87,362.61	61,682.54	30,034.60	82,994.48	23,842.17	28,573.96	28,573.96	23,975.78	56,788.83	87,362.61	93,222.26
198	87,805.60	61,988.32	30,147.79	83,415.33	23,930.92	28,704.70	28,704.70	24,067.75	57,058.76	87,805.60	93,694.13
199	88,248.61	62,294.10	30,260.97	83,836.17	24,019.67	28,835.45	28,835.45	24,159.72	57,328.71	88,248.61	94,166.01
200	88,691.60	62,599.87	30,374.17	84,257.02	24,108.42	28,966.17	28,966.17	24,251.69	57,598.65	88,691.60	94,637.88

[The tables following sub-paras 7(2) and (3) are printed as substituted by the SI 2016/313 (G-1a).]

Cracked trials and guilty pleas where the number of pages of prosecution evidence exceeds the PPE cut-off

8.—(1) Where in a cracked trial or guilty plea the number of pages of prosecution evidence exceeds the PPE Cut-off specified in the table following paragraph 5(1) as appropriate to the offence with which the assisted person is charged, the total fee payable to the litigator is— **G-80**

(a) the final fee, calculated in accordance with sub-paragraph (2) of this paragraph;

(b) the defendant uplift, if any, calculated in accordance with the table following paragraph 12; and

(c) the adjustment for transfers and retrials, if any, calculated in accordance with paragraph 13.

(2) For the purposes of sub-paragraph (1), the final fee payable to a litigator in a cracked trial or guilty plea is calculated in accordance with the following formula—

$F=I + (D \times i)$

Where—

- **F** is the amount of the final fee;
- **I** is the initial fee specified in the tables following this paragraph, as appropriate to the type of case, the offence with which the assisted person is charged and the number of pages of prosecution evidence;
- **D** is the difference between—
  - (i) the number of pages of prosecution evidence in the case; and
  - (ii) the lower number in the PPE range as specified in the tables following this paragraph, as appropriate to the type of case, the offence with which the assisted person is charged and the number of pages of prosecution evidence in the case;
- **i** is the incremental fee per page of prosecution evidence specified in the tables following this paragraph, as appropriate to the type of case, the offence with which the assisted person is charged and the number of pages of prosecution evidence in the case.

Table of Final Fees in Cracked Trials

Class of Offence	*PPE Range*	*Initial Fee (£)*	*Incremental fee per page of prosecution evidence (£)*
A and J	0-79	904.58	0
A and J	80-249	904.58	10.70
A and J	250-999	2,722.89	6.71
A and J	1000-2799	7,757.90	3.92
A and J	2800-4599	14,820.75	3.92
A and J	4600-6399	21,883.61	3.11
A and J	6400-8199	27,490.35	3.11
A and J	8200-9999	33,097.09	3.11
A and J	10,000	38,700.71	0
B	0-69	709.15	0
B	70-249	709.15	7.83
B	250-999	2,117.67	3.66
B	1000-2799	4,864.56	2.44
B	2800-4599	9,255.51	2.44
B	4600-6399	13,646.46	2.05
B	6400-8199	17,338.49	2.05
B	8200-9999	21,030.50	2.05
B	10,000	24,720.46	0
C	0-39	524.84	0
C	40-249	524.84	3.92
C	250-999	1,348.77	2.25
C	1000-2799	3,033.06	1.43
C	2800-4599	5,607.48	1.43
C	4600-6399	8,181.89	1.43

Class of Offence	*PPE Range*	*Initial Fee (£)*	*Incremental fee per page of prosecution evidence (£)*
C	6400-8199	10,756.31	1.43
C	8200-9999	13,330.74	1.43
C	10,000	15,903.73	0
D	0-79	859.35	0
D	80-249	859.35	10.14
D	250-999	2,582.50	6.11
D	1000-2799	7,163.76	3.61
D	2800-4599	13,655.74	3.61
D	4600-6399	20,147.71	2.96
D	6400-8199	25,474.79	2.96
D	8200-9999	30,801.87	2.96
D	10,000	36,125.98	0
E	0-39	233.03	0
E	40-249	233.03	4.60
E	250-999	1,199.43	1.46
E	1000-2799	2,291.54	0.61
E	2800-4599	3,390.26	0.61
E	4600-6399	4,488.97	0.61
E	6400-8199	5,587.69	0.61
E	8200-9999	6,686.41	0.61
E	10,000	7,784.51	0
F and G	0-49	224.22	0
F and G	50-249	224.22	4.42
F and G	250-999	1,107.53	1.79
F and G	1000-2799	2,450.39	0.70
F and G	2800-4599	3,704.67	0.70
F and G	4600-6399	4,958.94	0.70
F and G	6400-8199	6,213.21	0.70
F and G	8200-9999	7,467.49	0.70
F and G	10,000	8,721.06	0
H	0-39	237.00	0
H	40-249	237.00	4.26
H	250-999	1,131.61	1.56
H	1000-2799	2,298.20	0.70
H	2800-4599	3,550.79	0.70
H	4600-6399	4,803.37	0.70
H	6400-8199	6,055.96	0.70
H	8200-9999	7,308.55	0.70
H	10,000	8,560.44	0
I	0-39	253.68	0
I	40-249	253.68	5.92
I	250-999	1,496.80	2.31
I	1000-2799	3,231.91	0.90
I	2800-4599	4,847.36	0.90
I	4600-6399	6,462.79	0.90
I	6400-8199	8,078.23	0.90
I	8200-9999	9,693.67	0.90

Class of Offence	*PPE Range*	*Initial Fee (£)*	*Incremental fee per page of prosecution evidence (£)*
I	10,000	11,308.20	0
K	0-119	773.86	0
K	120-249	773.86	6.55
K	250-999	1,624.85	5.02
K	1000-2799	5,388.98	4.39
K	2800-4599	13,299.04	4.39
K	4600-6399	21,209.12	3.75
K	6400-8199	27,954.29	3.75
K	8200-9999	34,699.46	3.75
K	10,000	41,440.89	0

Table of Final Fees in Guilty Pleas

Class of Offence	*PPE Range*	*Initial Fee (£)*	*Incremental fee per page of prosecution evidence (£)*
A and J	0-79	680.39	0
A and J	80-399	680.39	5.62
A and J	400-999	2,478.29	2.96
A and J	1000-2799	4,256.09	1.89
A and J	2800-4599	7,666.89	1.89
A and J	4600-6399	11,077.68	1.12
A and J	6400-8199	13,090.60	1.12
A and J	8200-9999	15,103.53	1.12
A and J	10,000	17,115.33	0
B	0-69	556.11	0
B	70-399	556.11	4.52
B	400-999	2,046.59	2.28
B	1000-2799	3,411.75	1.45
B	2800-4599	6,025.92	1.45
B	4600-6399	8,640.11	1.06
B	6400-8199	10,555.35	1.06
B	8200-9999	12,470.60	1.06
B	10,000	14,384.78	0
C	0-39	442.91	0
C	40-399	442.91	2.66
C	400-999	1,401.88	1.46
C	1000-2799	2,276.27	0.79
C	2800-4599	3,699.93	0.79
C	4600-6399	5,123.61	0.79
C	6400-8199	6,547.28	0.79
C	8200-9999	7,970.95	0.79
C	10,000	9,393.82	0
D	0-79	646.36	0
D	80-399	646.36	5.23
D	400-999	2,320.66	2.75
D	1000-2799	3,968.37	1.71
D	2800-4599	7,046.20	1.71

Class of Offence	*PPE Range*	*Initial Fee (£)*	*Incremental fee per page of prosecution evidence (£)*
D	4600-6399	10,124.03	1.06
D	6400-8199	12,036.98	1.06
D	8200-9999	13,949.91	1.06
D	10,000	15,861.79	0
E	0-39	184.70	0
E	40-399	184.70	2.92
E	400-999	1,237.24	1.25
E	1000-2799	1,989.07	0.46
E	2800-4599	2,819.70	0.46
E	4600-6399	3,650.33	0.46
E	6400-8199	4,480.96	0.46
E	8200-9999	5,311.59	0.46
E	10,000	6,141.75	0
F and G	0-49	195.81	0
F and G	50-399	195.81	2.83
F and G	400-999	1,187.73	0.99
F and G	1000-2799	1,781.21	0.32
F and G	2800-4599	2,354.07	0.32
F and G	4600-6399	2,926.93	0.32
F and G	6400-8199	3,499.78	0.32
F and G	8200-9999	4,072.64	0.32
F and G	10,000	4,645.18	0
H	0-39	190.97	0
H	40-399	190.97	2.79
H	400-999	1,196.59	0.99
H	1000-2799	1,790.74	0.32
H	2800-4599	2,359.85	0.32
H	4600-6399	2,928.98	0.32
H	6400-8199	3,498.10	0.32
H	8200-9999	4,067.22	0.32
H	10,000	4,636.00	0
I	0-39	174.60	0
I	40-399	174.60	3.12
I	400-999	1,298.52	1.36
I	1000-2799	2,116.29	0.51
I	2800-4599	3,033.02	0.51
I	4600-6399	3,949.75	0.51
I	6400-8199	4,866.48	0.51
I	8200-9999	5,783.22	0.51
I	10,000	6,699.45	0
K	0-119	640.84	0
K	120-399	640.84	5.26
K	400-999	2,113.13	2.93
K	1000-2799	3,869.24	2.73
K	2800-4599	8,775.55	2.73
K	4600-6399	13,681.86	2.08
K	6400-8199	17,423.28	2.08

Class of Offence	PPE Range	Initial Fee (£)	Incremental fee per page of prosecution evidence (£)
K	8200-9999	21,164.71	2.08
K	10,000	24,904.04	0

[The above tables are printed as substituted by SI 2016/313 (G-1a) so as to reflect the quashing of SI 2017/1019 (G-1a) in *R. (on the application of Law Society) v Lord Chancellor* (G-1).]

Trials where the number of pages of prosecution evidence exceeds the PPE Cut-off

9.–(1) Where in a trial the number of pages of prosecution evidence exceeds the PPE Cut-off figure specified in the table following paragraph 5(2) as appropriate to the offence for which the assisted person is tried and the length of trial, the total fee payable to the litigator is– **G-81**

(a) the final fee, calculated in accordance with sub-paragraph (2) of this paragraph;

(b) the defendant uplift, if any, calculated in accordance with the table following paragraph 12; and

(c) the adjustment for transfers and retrials, if any, calculated in accordance with paragraph 13.

(2) For the purposes of sub-paragraph (1), the final fee is calculated in accordance with the following formula–

$F=I+(D \times i)$

Where–

- **F** is the amount of the final fee;
- **I** is the initial fee specified in the table following this paragraph as appropriate to the offence for which the assisted person is tried and the number of pages of prosecution evidence;
- **D** is the difference between–
  (i) the number of pages of prosecution evidence in the case; and
  (ii) the lower number in the PPE range as specified in the table following this paragraph, as appropriate to the offence for which the assisted person is tried and the number of pages of prosecution evidence in the case;
- **i** is the incremental fee per page of prosecution evidence specified in the table following this paragraph, as appropriate to the offence for which the assisted person is tried and the number of pages of prosecution evidence in the case.

TABLE OF FINAL FEES IN TRIALS

Class of Offence	PPE Range	Initial Fee (£)	Incremental fee per page (£)
A and J	0-79	1,467.58	0
A and J	80-209	1,467.58	16.58
A and J	210-699	3,622.54	12.66
A and J	700-1049	9,824.91	10.62
A and J	1050-1999	13,543.42	9.21
A and J	2000-3599	22,295.42	8.42
A and J	3600-5199	35,767.03	8.42
A and J	5200-6799	49,238.64	8.42
A and J	6800-8399	62,710.26	8.42
A and J	8400-9999	76,181.87	8.42
A and J	10,000	89,645.06	0
B	0-69	1,097.66	0
B	70-199	1,097.66	12.81
B	200-499	2,762.60	11.44
B	500-899	6,195.38	9.63
B	900-1299	10,048.21	8.09
B	1300-1999	13,285.03	7.09
B	2000-3299	18,249.51	7.09
B	3300-4999	27,469.24	7.09

Class of Offence	*PPE Range*	*Initial Fee (£)*	*Incremental fee per page (£)*
B	5000-5999	39,525.82	7.09
B	6000-7999	46,617.93	7.09
B	8000-8999	60,802.14	7.09
B	9000-9999	67,894.24	7.09
B	10,000	74,979.26	0
C	0-39	739.59	0
C	40-299	739.59	10.57
C	300-799	3,486.54	9.23
C	800-1249	8,101.74	7.73
C	1250-1999	11,578.09	6.83
C	2000-3199	16,700.93	4.72
C	3200-4559	22,368.79	4.72
C	4560-5919	28,792.38	4.72
C	5920-7279	35,215.96	4.72
C	7280-8639	41,639.54	4.72
C	8640-9999	48,063.12	4.72
C	10,000	54,482.00	0
D	0-79	1,394.20	0
D	80-209	1,394.20	15.75
D	210-699	3,441.41	12.03
D	700-1049	9,333.67	10.09
D	1050-1999	12,866.25	8.75
D	2000-3599	21,180.65	8.00
D	3600-5199	33,978.67	8.00
D	5200-6799	46,776.70	8.00
D	6800-8399	59,574.74	8.00
D	8400-9999	72,372.77	8.00
D	10,000	85,162.80	0
E	0-39	352.72	0
E	40-69	352.72	9.52
E	70-129	638.20	8.57
E	130-599	1,152.58	8.29
E	600-1349	5,049.74	5.44
E	1350-2999	9,131.96	2.39
E	3000-4749	13,072.77	2.39
E	4750-6499	17,252.41	2.39
E	6500-8249	21,432.04	2.39
E	8250-9999	25,611.69	2.39
E	10,000	29,788.93	0
F and G	0-49	357.60	0
F and G	50-229	357.60	7.31
F and G	230-699	1,673.21	6.96
F and G	700-1399	4,946.64	5.60
F and G	1400-1949	8,865.80	4.32
F and G	1950-3549	11,242.37	2.16
F and G	3550-5149	14,691.41	2.16
F and G	5150-6749	18,140.45	2.16
F and G	6750-8349	21,589.49	2.16

Class of Offence	*PPE Range*	*Initial Fee (£)*	*Incremental fee per page (£)*
F and G	8350-9999	25,038.53	2.16
F and G	10,000	28,593.21	0
H	0-39	357.75	0
H	40-249	357.75	8.60
H	250-619	2,162.92	7.15
H	620-1299	4,807.79	5.31
H	1300-2999	8,418.74	4.21
H	3000-4999	15,583.59	2.27
H	5000-5999	20,129.84	2.27
H	6000-6999	22,402.90	2.27
H	7000-7999	24,676.03	2.27
H	8000-8999	26,949.15	2.27
H	9000-9999	29,222.28	2.27
H	10,000	31,493.13	0
I	0-39	357.44	0
I	40-369	357.44	9.14
I	370-799	3,373.66	9.09
I	800-1299	7,282.43	8.99
I	1300-2699	11,779.02	7.08
I	2700-4199	21,697.63	3.04
I	4200-5359	26,264.52	3.04
I	5360-6519	29,796.25	3.04
I	6520-7679	33,327.97	3.04
I	7680-8839	36,859.71	3.04
I	8840-9999	40,391.43	3.04
I	10,000	43,920.11	0
J	0-79	1,467.58	0
J	80-209	1,467.58	16.58
J	210-699	3,622.54	12.66
J	700-1049	9,824.91	10.62
J	1050-1999	13,543.42	9.21
J	2000-3599	22,295.42	8.42
J	3600-5199	35,767.03	8.42
J	5200-6799	49,238.64	8.42
J	6800-8399	62,710.26	8.42
J	8400-9999	76,181.87	8.42
J	10,000	89,645.06	0
K	0-119	1,031.82	0
K	120-734	1,031.82	8.66
K	735-1289	6,356.06	8.72
K	1290-2399	11,193.67	8.87
K	2400-4499	21,042.53	8.84
K	4500-7999	39,605.74	8.84
K	8000-8399	70,544.40	8.84
K	8400-8799	74,080.24	8.84
K	8800-9199	77,616.08	8.84
K	9200-9599	81,151.94	8.84
K	9600-9999	84,687.78	8.84

Class of Offence	*PPE Range*	*Initial Fee (£)*	*Incremental fee per page (£)*
K	10,000	88,214.79	0

[The table in para.9 is printed as substituted by SI 2016/313 (G-1a), so as to reflect the quashing of SI 2017/1019 (G-1a) in *R. (on the application of Law Society) v Lord Chancellor* (G-1a).]

PART 3

Fixed Fee for Guilty Pleas and Cracked Trials

Scope of Part 3

G-82 10.—(1) Subject to sub-paragraph (2), this Part applies to a case sent for trial to the Crown Court on the election of a defendant where the magistrates' court has determined the case to be suitable for summary trial.

(2) This Part does not apply where the trial is a cracked trial because the prosecution offer no evidence on all counts against a defendant and the judge directs that a not guilty verdict be entered.

[This paragraph was substituted by SI 2014/2422 (G-22). For the transitional provision, see G-22. It is printed as amended by SI 2015/1678 (G-1a).]

Fixed fee for guilty pleas or cracked trials

11. The fee payable to a litigator in relation to a guilty plea or cracked trial to which this Part applies is £330.33 per proceedings.

[Paragraph 11 is printed as amended by SI 2016/303 (G-1a).]

PART 4

Defendant Uplifts, Retrials and Transfers

Defendant uplifts

G-83 12.—(1) The defendant uplift payable to a litigator is calculated in accordance with the table following this paragraph.

(2) Only one defendant uplift is payable in each case.

(3) In the table following this paragraph, the total fee means—

(a) in a cracked trial or guilty plea where the number of pages of prosecution evidence does not exceed the PPE Cut-off specified in the table following paragraph 5(1), the basic fee specified in the table following paragraph 6(2);

(b) in a trial where the number of pages of prosecution evidence does not exceed the PPE Cut-off specified in the table following paragraph 5(2), the basic fee specified in the table following paragraph 7(2) plus the length of trial proxy specified in the table following paragraph 7(3);

(c) in a cracked trial or guilty plea where the number of pages of prosecution evidence exceeds the PPE Cut-off specified in the table following paragraph 5(1), the final fee, as calculated in accordance with paragraph 8(2); and

(d) in a trial where the number of pages of prosecution evidence exceeds the PPE Cut-off specified in the table following paragraph 5(2), the final fee, as calculated in accordance with paragraph 9(2);

(e) where appropriate, the fee set out in paragraph 11.

(4) In a case where the representation of one defendant would attract a fixed fee under Part 3 and the representation of one or more of the other defendants would attract a graduated fee under Part 2, the total fee is the fee falling within whichever of paragraphs (a) to (d) of sub-paragraph (3) is appropriate.

DEFENDANT UPLIFTS

Total number of defendants represented by litigator	*Percentage uplift to total fee*
2–4	20%
5+	30%

Retrials and transfers

G-84 13.—(1) Where following a trial an order is made for a retrial and the same litigator acts for the assisted person at both trials the fee payable to that litigator is—

(a) in respect of the first trial, a fee calculated in accordance with the provisions of this Schedule; and

(b) in respect of the retrial, 25% of the fee, as appropriate to the circumstances of the retrial, in accordance with the provisions of this Schedule.

(2) Where—

(a) a case is transferred to a new litigator; or

(b) a retrial is ordered and a new litigator acts for the assisted person at the retrial,

the fee payable to the original litigator and the new litigator is a percentage of the total fee, calculated in accordance with the table following this paragraph, as appropriate to the circumstances and timing of the retrial, transfer or withdrawal of the section 16 determination.

(3) In sub-paragraph (2), "transfer" includes the making of a section 16 determination in favour of an individual who, immediately before the making of the section 16 determination—

(a) had represented themselves; or

(b) had been represented (otherwise than pursuant to a section 16 determination) by the litigator named in the order,

and for the purposes of that sub-paragraph the litigator is to be treated as a new litigator.

(4) For the purposes of sub-paragraph (2), a case is not transferred to a new litigator where—

(a) a firm of solicitors is named as litigator in the representation order and the solicitor or other appropriately qualified person with responsibility for the case moves to another firm;

(b) a firm of solicitors is named as litigator in the representation order and the firm changes (whether by merger or acquisition or in some other way), but so that the new firm remains closely related to the firm named in the order; or

(c) a solicitor or other appropriately qualified person is named as litigator in the representation order and responsibility for the case is transferred to another solicitor or appropriately qualified person in the same firm or a closely related firm.

(5) For the purposes of sub-paragraph (2), where a case which has been transferred to a new litigator is transferred again, that new litigator—

(a) must be treated as the original litigator, where the transfer takes place at any time before the trial or any retrial;

(b) must be treated as a new litigator, where the transfer takes place during the trial or any retrial; and

(c) must not receive any fee, where the transfer takes place after the trial or any retrial but before the sentencing hearing.

(6) Where a section 16 determination is withdrawn before the case ends, a litigator must receive a percentage of the total fee, in accordance with the table following this paragraph, as appropriate to the circumstances and timing of a transfer.

(7) In the table following this paragraph, the total fee means—

(a) in a cracked trial or guilty plea in a case to which Part 2 applies, where the number of pages of prosecution evidence is less than or equal to the PPE Cut-off specified in the table following paragraph 5(1), the basic fee as set out in the table following paragraph 6(2);

(b) in a trial where the number of pages of prosecution evidence is less than or equal to the PPE Cut-off specified in the table following paragraph 5(2), the basic fee specified in the table following paragraph 7(2) plus the length of trial proxy specified in the table following paragraph 7(3);

(c) in a cracked trial or guilty plea in a case to which Part 2 applies, where the number of pages of prosecution evidence exceeds the PPE Cut-off specified in the table following paragraph 5(1), the final fee as calculated in accordance with paragraph 8(2);

(d) in a trial where the number of pages of prosecution evidence exceeds the PPE Cut-off specified in the table following paragraph 5(2), the final fee, as calculated in accordance with paragraph 9(2);

(e) in a cracked trial or guilty plea in a case to which Part 3 applies, the fixed fee set out in paragraph 11.

(8) Where a case becomes a Very High Cost Case after a section 16 determination has been made and is transferred from the litigator named on the representation order to a new litigator—

(a) the original litigator must be remunerated in accordance with the individual Very High Cost Case contract entered into by that litigator; and

(b) the new litigator must be remunerated in accordance with the individual Very High Cost Case contract entered into by that litigator.

(9) Where a case becomes a Very High Cost Case after a section 16 determination has been made and the section 16 determination is withdrawn before the end of the case, the litigator must be

remunerated in accordance with the table following this paragraph as appropriate to the circumstances and timing of the withdrawal.

(10) Sub-paragraph (11) applies where—

(a) the case is a case to which Part 3 would apply if it resulted in a cracked trial or guilty plea; and

(b) at the time the case is transferred to a new litigator in accordance with sub-paragraph (2) it is not known whether the case would result in a cracked trial or guilty plea or whether it would proceed to trial.

(11) Where this sub-paragraph applies—

(a) for the purpose of a claim by the original litigator at the time of the transfer of the case, "total fee" in the table following this paragraph, means the fixed fee set out in paragraph 11;

(b) the original litigator may, if the case proceeds to trial, claim the difference between the payment received at the time of transfer of the case and the payment that would have been due at that time if that payment had been based on the case proceeding to trial.

(12) A litigator may not be treated both as an original litigator and as a new litigator in a case.

RETRIALS AND TRANSFERS

Scenario	*Percentage of the total fee*	*Case type used to determine total fee*	*Claim period*
Cracked trial before retrial, where there is no change of litigator	25%	Cracked trial	–
Retrial, where there is no change of litigator	25%	Trial	–
Up to and including plea and case management hearing transfer (original litigator)	25%	Cracked trial	–
Transfer at or before the first hearing at which the assisted person enters a plea – guilty plea (new litigator)	100%	Guilty plea	–
Transfer at or before the first hearing at which the assisted person enters a plea – cracked trial (new litigator)	100%	Cracked trial	–
Transfer at or before the first hearing at which the assisted person enters a plea – trial (new litigator)	100%	Trial	–
Before trial transfer (original litigator)	75%	Cracked trial	–
Before trial transfer – cracked trial (new litigator)	100%	Cracked trial	–
Before trial transfer – trial (new litigator)	100%	Trial	–
During trial transfer (original litigator)	100%	Trial	Claim up to and including the day before the transfer
During trial transfer (new litigator)	50%	Trial	Claim for the full trial length
Transfer after trial or guilty plea and before sentencing hearing (original litigator)	100%	Trial, cracked trial or guilty plea as appropriate	Claim for the full trial length, excluding the length of the sentencing hearing
Transfer after trial or guilty plea and before sentencing hearing (new litigator)	10%	Trial	Claim for one day, or for the length of the sentencing hearing if

Scenario	*Percentage of the total fee*	*Case type used to determine total fee*	*Claim period*
			longer than one day
Transfer before retrial (original litigator)	25%	Cracked trial	–
Transfer before cracked retrial (new litigator)	50%	Cracked trial	
Transfer before retrial (new litigator)	50%	Trial	Claim for the full retrial length
Transfer during retrial (original litigator)	25%	Trial	Claim up to and including the day before the transfer
Transfer during retrial (new litigator)	50%	Trial	Claim for the full retrial length
Transfer after retrial or cracked retrial and before sentencing hearing (original litigator)	25%	Trial or cracked trial as appropriate	Claim for the full retrial length, excluding the length of the sentencing hearing
Transfer after retrial or cracked retrial and before sentencing hearing (new litigator)	10%	Trial	Claim for one day, or for the length of the sentencing hearing if longer than one day

[Paragraph 13 is printed as amended by SI 2015/1678 (G-1a).]

PART 5
Fixed Fees

General provisions

14.–(1) All work undertaken by a litigator in a case to which Part 3 applies is included within the fee set out in paragraph 11 except for a defendant uplift as provided for in paragraph 22. **G-85**

(2) Except as provided under this Part, remuneration for all work undertaken by a litigator in a case to which Part 2 applies is included within the fee set out in Part 2 in this Schedule as appropriate to–

(a) the offence for which the assisted person is charged or tried;

(b) whether the case is a cracked trial, guilty plea or trial; and

(c) the number of pages of prosecution evidence.

Fees for appeals and committals for sentence hearings

15. The fee payable to a litigator instructed in– **G-86**

(a) an appeal against conviction from a magistrates' court;

(b) an appeal against sentence from a magistrates' court; or

(c) a sentencing hearing following a committal for sentence to the Crown Court,

is that set out in the table following paragraph 19.

Fees for hearing subsequent to sentence

16.–(1) The fee payable to a litigator instructed in relation to a hearing under an enactment listed in sub-paragraph (2) is that set out in the table following paragraph 19. **G-87**

(2) The enactments are–

(a) section 1CA of the Crime and Disorder Act 1998 (variation and discharge of orders under section 1C);

(b) section 155 of the Powers of Criminal Courts (Sentencing) Act 2000 (alteration of Crown Court sentence);

(c) section 74 of the Serious Organised Crime and Police Act 2005 (assistance by defendant: review of sentence).

Fees for contempt proceedings

17.–(1) This paragraph applies to proceedings referred to in section 14(g) of the Act in the Crown Court. **G-88**

(2) Where, in proceedings to which this paragraph applies, the contempt is alleged to have been committed by a person other than a defendant in a case to which this Schedule applies, remuneration for litigators must be at the rate set out in the table following paragraph 19.

(3) Where, in proceedings to which this paragraph applies, the contempt is alleged to have been committed by the defendant in a case to which this Schedule applies, all work undertaken by the litigator is included within—

(a) the fee payable under Part 2 of this Schedule, or

(b) in proceedings under paragraph 15 or paragraph 18, the fixed fee set out in the table following paragraph 19.

Fees for alleged breaches of a Crown Court order

G-89 18.—(1) This paragraph applies to proceedings in the Crown Court against one assisted person arising out of a single alleged breach of an order of the Crown Court.

(3) The fee payable to the litigator in respect of the proceedings to which this paragraph applies is that set out in the table following paragraph 19.

Fixed Fees

19. The table following this paragraph sets out the fixed fees payable in relation to the category of work specified in the first column of the table.

Types of proceedings	*Paragraph providing for fee*	*Fee payable – (£ per proceedings)*
Appeal against sentence from a magistrates' court	15	155.32
Appeal against conviction from a magistrates' court	15	349.47
Committal for sentence	15	232.98
Hearing subsequent to sentence	16	155.32
Contempt proceedings (where contempt is alleged to have been committed by a person other than the defendant)	17(2)	116.49
Alleged breach of a Crown Court order	18(2)	77.66

[The table in para.19 is printed as substituted by SI 2016/313 (G-1a).]

Fees for special preparation

G-90 20.—(1) This paragraph applies in any case on indictment in the Crown Court—

(a) where a documentary or pictorial exhibit is served by the prosecution in electronic form and—

(i) the exhibit has never existed in paper form; and

(ii) the appropriate officer does not consider it appropriate to include the exhibit in the pages of prosecution evidence; or

(b) in respect of which a fee is payable under Part 2 (other than paragraph 7), where the number of pages of prosecution evidence, as so defined, exceeds 6,000,

and the appropriate officer considers it reasonable to make a payment in excess of the fee payable under Part 2.

(2) Where this paragraph applies, a special preparation fee may be paid, in addition to the fee payable under Part 2.

(3) The amount of the special preparation fee must be calculated from the number of hours which the appropriate officer considers reasonable—

(a) where sub-paragraph (1)(a) applies, to view the prosecution evidence; and

(b) where sub-paragraph (1)(b) applies, to read the excess pages,

and in each case using the rates specified in the table following paragraph 27.

(4) A litigator claiming a special preparation fee must supply such information and documents as may be required by the appropriate officer in support of the claim.

(5) In determining a claim under this paragraph, the appropriate officer must take into account all the relevant circumstances of the case.

[Paragraph 20 is printed so as to reflect the quashing of SI 2017/1019 (G-1a) in *R. (on the application of Law Society) v Lord Chancellor* (G-1).]

Fees for consideration of unused material

20A.—(1) This paragraph applies in respect of any case on indictment in the Crown Court, in respect of which a graduated fee is payable under Part 2, other than a guilty plea. ★G-90a

(2) In any case to which this paragraph applies, a fee ("the basic consideration fee") is payable to a litigator in respect of the consideration of unused material whether or not such consideration has actually occurred.

(2A) The basic consideration fee in sub-paragraph (2) is £64.68

(3) This sub-paragraph applies where—

(a) a litigator has undertaken the consideration of unused material; and

(b) the litigator has spent in excess of three hours undertaking that consideration.

(4) In a case where sub-paragraph (3) applies—

(a) a fee ("the additional fee") is payable to the litigator in addition to the basic consideration fee; and

(b) the amount of the additional fee corresponds to the grade of fee earner concerned specified in the table following paragraph 27.

(5) The additional fee is payable only where the appropriate officer considers it reasonable to make such a payment.

(6) A litigator claiming the additional fee must supply such information and documents as may be required by the appropriate officer in support of the claim.

(7) In determining whether it is reasonable to pay the additional fee, the appropriate officer must take into account—

(a) the reasonableness of the hours claimed in respect of the case taken as a whole; and

(b) the reasonableness of the hours claimed in respect of the consideration of the unused material.

[This paragraph is printed as inserted, with effect from 17 September 2020, by SI 2020/903 (G-1a). The insertion has effect only for cases in which a determination under the LASPOA 2012, s.16 (§ 6-187 in the main work) was made on or after 17 September 2020. It is also printed as subsequently amended, with effect from 19 February 2021, by SI 2021/80 (G-1a).]

Discontinuance or dismissal of proceedings

21.—(1) This paragraph applies to proceedings which are sent for trial to the Crown Court. G-91

(2) Where proceedings to which this paragraph applies are discontinued by a notice served under section 23A of the Prosecution of Offences Act 1985 (discontinuance of proceedings after accused has been sent for trial) at any time before the prosecution serves its evidence in accordance with the Crime and Disorder Act 1998 (Service of Prosecution Evidence) Regulations 2005 the litigator must be paid 50% of the basic fee for a guilty plea, as specified in the table following paragraph 6, as appropriate to the offence for which the assisted person is charged.

(3) Where proceedings to which this paragraph applies are discontinued by a notice served under section 23A of the Prosecution of Offences Act 1985 (discontinuance of proceedings after accused has been sent for trial) at any time after the prosecution serves its evidence in accordance with the Crime and Disorder Act 1998 (Service of Prosecution Evidence) Regulations 2005, the litigator must be paid a fee calculated in accordance with paragraph 6, or, where appropriate, paragraph 8, as appropriate for representing an assisted person in a guilty plea.

(4) Where an application for dismissal is made under paragraph 2 of Schedule 3 to the Crime and Disorder Act 1998, section 6 of the Criminal Justice Act 1987 or paragraph 5 of Schedule 6 to the Criminal Justice Act 1991, and—

(a) the charge, or charges are dismissed and the assisted person is discharged; or

(b) the case is remitted to the magistrates' court in accordance with paragraph 10(3)(a), 13(2) or 15(3)(a) of Schedule 3 to the Crime and Disorder Act 1998,

the litigator instructed in the proceedings must be paid a fee calculated in accordance with paragraph 6, or where appropriate, paragraph 8, as appropriate for representing an assisted person in a guilty plea.

(6) Where, at or before the first hearing at which the assisted person enters a plea—

(a) the prosecution offers no evidence and the assisted person is discharged; or

(b) the case is remitted to the magistrates' court in accordance with paragraph 10(3)(a), 13(2) or 15(3)(a) of Schedule 3 to the Crime and Disorder Act 1998,

the litigator must be paid a fee calculated in accordance with paragraph 6 or where appropriate paragraph 8, as appropriate for representing an assisted person in a guilty plea.

[Paragraph 21 is printed as amended by SI 2015/1678 (G-1a).]

Defendant uplifts

G-92 22.—(1) Where a litigator represents more than one assisted person in proceedings referred to in paragraph 21(2), (3), (4) or (5), a defendant uplift is payable.

(2) The defendant uplift must be calculated in accordance with the table following this paragraph.

(3) In the table following this paragraph, the total fee means—

(a) the fee specified in sub-paragraph (2) of paragraph 21 where that sub-paragraph applies;

(b) the basic fee (B) specified in the table following paragraph 6, or, where appropriate, the initial fee specified in paragraph 8, where paragraph 21(3), (4) or (5) applies, as appropriate for the circumstances set out in that sub-paragraph; or

(c) where appropriate the fee set out in paragraph 11.

(4) In a case where the representation of one defendant would attract a fixed fee under Part 3 and the representation of one or more of the other defendants would attract a graduated fee under Part 2, the total fee in the table following this paragraph means the fee falling within sub-paragraph (3)(b).

Defendant Uplifts

Total number of defendants represented by litigator	*Percentage uplift to total fee*
2–4	20%
5+	30%

Warrant for arrest

G-93 23.—(1) This paragraph applies where—

(a) the assisted person fails to attend a hearing;

(b) at that hearing the court issues a warrant for the arrest of the assisted person, pursuant to section 7(1) of the Bail Act 1976 ("the warrant"); and

(c) the case does not proceed in the absence of the assisted person.

(2) Where in a case on indictment the warrant is not executed within three months of the date on which it was issued, the fee payable to the litigator is—

(a) where the warrant is issued at or before the first hearing at which the assisted person enters a plea, the fee payable for a guilty plea in accordance with paragraph 6 or where appropriate paragraph 8;

(b) where the warrant is issued after the first hearing at which the assisted person enters a plea but before the trial, the fee payable for a cracked trial in accordance with paragraph 6 or where appropriate paragraph 8, as appropriate to the Class of Offence with which the assisted person is charged; and

(c) where the warrant is issued during the trial, and the trial is aborted as a result, the fee payable for a trial as if the trial had ended on the day the warrant was issued.

(3) Where the warrant is issued during the course of proceedings referred to in paragraph 15 or 18 the fee payable to the litigator is the fee set out in the table following paragraph 19, as appropriate to the type of proceedings.

(4) Sub-paragraph (5) applies where—

(a) a fee has been paid, or is payable, to the litigator in accordance with sub-paragraph (2);

(b) the warrant is executed within 15 months of the date on which it was issued;

(c) the case proceeds after the warrant has been executed; and

(d) the litigator submits a claim for fees for the determination of the litigator's overall remuneration in the case, in accordance with regulation 5.

(5) Where this sub-paragraph applies—

(a) the appropriate officer must deduct the amount paid or payable in accordance with sub-paragraph (2) from the amount payable to the litigator on the final determination of fees in the case; and

(b) if the fee paid or payable in accordance with sub-paragraph (2) is greater than the amount payable to the litigator on the final determination of fees in the case, the appropriate officer may recover the amount of the difference by way of repayment by the litigator.

[Paragraph 23 is printed as amended by SI 2015/1678 (G-1a).]

Part 6

Miscellaneous

Additional charges

G-94 24.—(1) Where an assisted person is charged with more than one offence on one indictment, the fee payable to the litigator under this Schedule must be based on whichever of those offences the litigator selects.

(2) Where a litigator selects one offence, in preference to another offence, under sub-paragraph (1) that selection does not affect the litigator's right to claim any of the fees provided for in Part 5 of this Schedule to which the litigator would otherwise have been entitled.

Assisted person unfit to plead or stand trial

25. Where in any case a hearing is held to determine the question of whether the assisted person is unfit to plead or to stand trial (a "fitness hearing")— G-95

(a) if a trial on indictment is held, or continues, at any time thereafter, the length of the fitness hearing is included in determining the length of the trial for the calculation of the fee in accordance with Part 2;

(b) if a trial on indictment is not held, or does not continue, thereafter by reason of the assisted person being found unfit to plead or to stand trial, the litigator must be paid—

(i) a fee calculated in accordance with paragraph 7 or where appropriate paragraph 9, as appropriate to the combined length of—

(aa) the fitness hearing; and

(bb) any hearing under section 4A of the Criminal Procedure (Insanity) Act 1964 (finding that the accused did the act or made the omission charged against him); or

(ii) a fee calculated in accordance with paragraph 6, or where appropriate paragraph 8, as appropriate, for representing an assisted person in a cracked trial,

whichever the litigator elects; and

(c) if at any time the assisted person pleads guilty to the indictable offence, the litigator must be paid either—

(i) a fee calculated in accordance with paragraph 7 or, where appropriate, paragraph 9, as appropriate to the length of the fitness hearing; or

(ii) a fee calculated in accordance with paragraph 6 or, where appropriate, paragraph 8, as appropriate for representing an assisted person in a guilty plea,

whichever the litigator elects.

Fees for confiscation proceedings

26.—(1) This paragraph applies to— G-96

(a) proceedings under Part 2 of the Proceeds of Crime Act 2002 (confiscation: England and Wales);

(b) proceedings under section 2 of the Drug Trafficking Act 1994 (confiscation orders); and

(c) proceedings under section 71 of the Criminal Justice Act 1988 (confiscation orders).

(2) Where this paragraph applies, the appropriate officer may allow work done in the following classes by a litigator—

(a) preparation, including taking instructions, interviewing witnesses, ascertaining the prosecution case, preparing and perusing documents, dealing with letters and telephone calls, instructing an advocate and expert witnesses, conferences, consultations and work done in connection with advice on appeal;

(b) attending at court where an advocate is instructed, including conferences with the advocate at court;

(c) travelling and waiting; and

(d) writing routine letters and dealing with routine telephone calls.

(3) The appropriate officer must consider the claim, any further particulars, information or documents submitted by the litigator under regulation 5 and any other relevant information and must allow such work as appears to him to have been reasonably done in the proceedings.

(4) Subject to sub-paragraph (3), the appropriate officer must allow fees under this paragraph in accordance with paragraph 27.

(5) The appropriate officer must allow fees in accordance with paragraphs 27 to 29 as appropriate to such of the following grades of fee earner as the appropriate officer considers reasonable—

(a) senior solicitor;

(b) solicitor, legal executive or fee earner of equivalent experience; or

(c) trainee or fee earner of equivalent experience.

Prescribed fee rates

27. Subject to paragraphs 28 and 29, for proceedings in the Crown Court to which paragraph 26 applies the appropriate officer must allow fees for work under paragraph 26(2) at the following G-97

prescribed rates—

Class of work	*Grade of fee earner*	*Rate*	*Variations*
Preparation	Senior solicitor	£48.36 per hour	£50.87 per hour for a fee hour earner whose office is situated within the City of London or a London borough
	Solicitor, legal executive or fee earner of equivalent experience	£41.06 per hour	£43.12 per hour for a fee earner whose office is situated within the City of London or a London borough
	Trainee or fee earner of equivalent experience	£27.15 per hour	£31.03 per hour for a fee earner whose office is situated within the City of London or a London borough
Consideration of unused material in excess of 3 hours	Senior solicitor	£48.36 per hour	£50.87 per hour for a fee earner whose office is situated within the City of London or a London Borough
	Solicitor, legal executive or fee earner of equivalent experience	£41.06 per hour	£43.12 per hour for a fee earner whose office is situated within the City of London or a London Borough
	Trainee or fee earner of equivalent experience	£27.15 per hour	£31.03 per hour for a fee earner whose office is situated within the City of London or a London Borough.
Attendance at court where more than one representative instructed	Senior solicitor	£38.55 per hour	
	Solicitor, legal executive or fee earner of equivalent experience	£31.03 per hour	
	Trainee or fee earner of equivalent experience	£18.71 per hour	
Travelling and waiting	Senior solicitor	£22.58 per hour	
	Solicitor, legal executive or fee earner of equivalent experience	£22.58 per hour	
	Trainee or fee earner of equivalent experience	£11.41 per hour	
Writing routine letters and dealing with routine telephone calls		£3.15 per item	£3.29 per item for a fee earner whose office is situated within the City of London or a London borough.

[The table in para.27 is printed as substituted by SI 2016/313 (G-1a) and, with effect from 17 September 2020, as amended by SI 2020/903 (G-1a): for the relevant transitional provisions, see G-1a.]

Allowing fees at less than the prescribed rates

28. In respect of any item of work, the appropriate officer may allow fees at less than the relevant prescribed rate specified in paragraph 27 where it appears to the appropriate officer reasonable to do so having regard to the competence and despatch with which the work was done. G-98

Allowing fees at more than the prescribed rates

29.—(1) Upon a determination the appropriate officer may, subject to the provisions of this paragraph, allow fees at more than the relevant prescribed rate specified in paragraph 27 for preparation, attendance at court where more than one representative is instructed, routine letters written and routine telephone calls, in respect of offences in Class A, B, C, D, G, I, J or K in the LGFS Table of Offences. G-99

(2) The appropriate officer may allow fees at more than the prescribed rate where it appears to the appropriate officer, taking into account all the relevant circumstances of the case, that—

(a) the work was done with exceptional competence, skill or expertise;

(b) the work was done with exceptional despatch; or

(c) the case involved exceptional complexity or other exceptional circumstances.

(3) Paragraph 3 of Schedule 1 applies to litigators in respect of proceedings in the Crown Court as it applies to advocates.

(4) Where the appropriate officer considers that any item or class of work should be allowed at more than the prescribed rate, the appropriate officer must apply to that item or class of work a percentage enhancement in accordance with the following provisions of this paragraph.

(5) In determining the percentage by which fees should be enhanced above the prescribed rate the appropriate officer must have regard to—

(a) the degree of responsibility accepted by the fee earner;

(b) the care, speed and economy with which the case was prepared; and

(c) the novelty, weight and complexity of the case.

(6) The percentage above the relevant prescribed rate by which fees for work may be enhanced must not exceed 100%.

(7) The appropriate officer may have regard to the generality of proceedings to which these Regulations apply in determining what is exceptional within the meaning of this paragraph.

[This paragraph is printed as amended, with effect from 1 April 2018, by SI 2018/220 (G-1a). As to the transitional provision, see G-1a.]

In *Farrell and Selby* [2007] 3 Costs L.R. 495, it was held in relation to the provisions of paragraph 4 of Part 1 of Schedule 2 to the Criminal Defence Service (Funding) Order 2001 (SI 2001/855) for paying enhanced rates to solicitors, (i) it was open to a determining officer to apply different rates of enhancement to different items of work; since a determining officer was required, in deciding on the rate of enhancement, to have regard, inter alia, to the "degree of responsibility accepted by the solicitor and his staff", it was permissible for a determining officer to apply a lesser rate of enhancement to work of a routine nature done by Grade B fee earners than that applied to the senior fee earners to whom they reported; (ii) when enhancement was appropriate, a determining officer should first assess what enhanced rate would have been applied if legal aid had been granted prior to 1 October 1994 (the date of commencement of the revised rules as to enhancement introduced by the Legal Aid in Criminal and Care Proceedings (Costs) (Amendment) (No. 3) Regulations 1994 (SI 1994/2218)), viz. the hourly broad average direct cost rate plus an appropriate uplift for care and conduct, and then he should adjust the resulting figure upwards to allow for subsequent inflation; he should then decide on a rate of enhancement such as would match this figure; where, however, the figure exceeded the maximum enhanced rate under the 2001 order, then the determining officer should apply the maximum enhanced rate. Since the provisions under consideration corresponded to those of paragraph 6 of Schedule 2 to the Criminal Defence Service (Funding) Order 2007 (SI 2007/1174) (prior to amendment), it could safely be taken that this decision carried across to that order (prior to amendment) with the effect—as in this case—that, wherever enhanced rates are appropriate, the rate of enhancement is always going to be 100 per cent because the 1994 hourly direct cost plus uplift for care and attention, plus uplift for inflation is always going to exceed twice the current hourly rates, which have remained unchanged for many years. This was confirmed in *Bowles* [2007] 3 Costs L.R. 514. Whilst the provision for payment at enhanced rates under the 2013 regulations relates only to fees payable under paragraph 26, the provisions of paragraph 29 correspond to paragraph 6 of the unamended Schedule 2, and it would appear that the decision in *Farrell and Selby* will carry across to this paragraph in the same way that it carried across to paragraph 6. G-100

Table of offences

G-101 At the end of Schedule 2 to the regulations (in Pt 7), there is a table of offences. For the effect thereof, see G-119, G-168 and following. Until the amendments effected by SI 2018/220 (G-1a) on 1 April 2018, this table was in Pt 7 of Schedule 1.

Regulation 6

SCHEDULE 3

PROCEEDINGS IN THE COURT OF APPEAL

General provisions

G-102 1.—(1) The provisions of this Schedule apply to proceedings in the Court of Appeal.

(2) In determining fees the appropriate officer must, subject to the provisions of this Schedule—

(a) take into account all the relevant circumstances of the case including the nature, importance, complexity or difficulty of the work and the time involved; and

(b) allow a reasonable amount in respect of all work actually and reasonably done.

Claims for fees and disbursements by litigators

2.—(1) Subject to regulation 31, no claim by a litigator for fees and disbursements in respect of work done in proceedings in the Court of Appeal pursuant to a section 16 determination must be entertained unless the litigator submits it within three months of the conclusion of the proceedings to which it relates.

(2) Subject to sub-paragraph (3), a claim for fees in proceedings in the Court of Appeal must be submitted to the appropriate officer in such form and manner as the appropriate officer may direct and must be accompanied by the representation order and any receipts or other documents in support of any disbursement claimed.

(3) A claim must—

(a) summarise the items of work done by a fee earner in respect of which fees are claimed according to the classes specified in paragraph 3(1);

(b) state, where appropriate, the dates on which the items of work were done, the time taken, the sums claimed and whether the work was done for more than one assisted person;

(c) specify, where appropriate, the level of fee earner who undertook each of the items of work claimed;

(d) give particulars of any work done in relation to more than one indictment or a retrial; and

(e) specify any disbursements claimed, the circumstances in which they were incurred and the amounts claimed in respect of them.

(4) Where the litigator claims that paragraph 8(1) applies in relation to an item of work, the litigator must give full particulars in support of the claim.

(5) The litigator must specify any special circumstances which the litigator considers should be drawn to the attention of the appropriate officer.

(6) The litigator must supply such further information and documents as the appropriate officer may require.

(7) Where a retrospective section 16 determination has been made under regulations made under section 19 of the Act in respect of any proceedings where an appellant has been successful on appeal and granted a defendant's costs order under section 16(4) of the Prosecution of Offences Act 1985 (defence costs), the litigator must certify that no claim for fees incurred before the retrospective section 16 determination was made has been or will be made from central funds in relation to that work.

Determination of litigators' fees

G-103 3.—(1) The appropriate officer may allow work done in the following classes by fee earners—

(a) preparation, including taking instructions, interviewing witnesses, ascertaining the prosecution case, advising on plea and mode of trial, preparing and perusing documents, dealing with letters and telephone calls which are not routine, preparing for advocacy, instructing an advocate and expert witnesses, conferences, consultations, views and work done in connection with advice on appeal;

(b) advocacy, including applications for bail and other applications to the court;

(c) attending at court where an advocate is assigned, including conferences with the advocate at court;

(d) travelling and waiting; and

(e) writing routine letters and dealing with routine telephone calls.

(2) The appropriate officer must consider the claim, any further information or documents

submitted by the fee earner under paragraph 2 and any other relevant information and must allow—

(a) such work as appears to the appropriate officer to have been reasonably done pursuant to the section 16 determination (including any representation or advice which is deemed to be work done pursuant to that determination) by a fee earner, classifying such work according to the classes specified in sub-paragraph (1) as the appropriate officer considers appropriate; and

(b) such time in each class of work allowed by him (other than routine letters written and routine telephone calls) as the appropriate officer considers reasonable.

(3) The fees allowed in accordance with this Schedule are those appropriate to such of the following grades of litigator as the appropriate officer considers reasonable—

(a) senior solicitor;

(b) solicitor, legal executive or fee earner of equivalent experience; or

(c) trainee or fee earner of equivalent experience.

Determination of litigators' disbursements

4. The appropriate officer must allow such disbursements claimed under paragraph 2 as appear to the appropriate officer to have been reasonably incurred, provided that— **G-104**

(a) if they are abnormally large by reason of the distance of the court or the assisted person's residence or both from the litigator's place of business, the appropriate officer may limit reimbursement of the disbursements to what otherwise would, having regard to all the circumstances, be a reasonable amount; and

(b) the cost of a transcript, or any part thereof, of the proceedings in the court from which the appeal lies obtained otherwise than through the registrar must not be allowed except where the appropriate officer considers that it is reasonable in all the circumstances for such disbursement to be allowed.

Claims for fees by advocates

5.—(1) Subject to regulation 31, a claim by an advocate for fees for work done in proceedings in the Court of Appeal pursuant to a section 16 determination must not be entertained unless the advocate submits it within three months of the conclusion of the proceedings to which the section 16 determination relates.

(2) Where the advocate claims that paragraph 9(4) applies in relation to an item of work the advocate must give full particulars in support of his claim.

(3) Subject to sub-paragraph (4), a claim for fees by an advocate in proceedings in the Court of Appeal must be submitted to the appropriate officer in such form and manner as the appropriate officer may direct.

(4) A claim must—

(a) summarise the items of work done by an advocate in respect of which fees are claimed according to the classes specified in paragraph 6(2);

(b) state, where appropriate, the dates on which the items of work were done, the time taken, the sums claimed and whether the work was done for more than one assisted person; and

(c) give particulars of any work done in relation to more than one indictment or a retrial.

(5) The advocate must specify any special circumstances which the advocate considers should be drawn to the attention of the appropriate officer.

(6) The advocate must supply such further information and documents as the appropriate officer may require.

Determination of advocate's fees

6.—(1) The appropriate officer must consider the claim, any further particulars and information submitted by an advocate under paragraph 5 and any other relevant information and must allow such work as appears to the appropriate officer to have been reasonably done. **G-105**

(2) The appropriate officer may allow any of the following classes of fee to an advocate in respect of work allowed by him under this paragraph—

(a) a basic fee for preparation including preparation for a pre-trial review and, where appropriate, the first day's hearing including, where they took place on that day, short conferences, consultations, applications and appearances (including bail applications), views and any other preparation;

(b) a refresher fee for any day or part of a day during which a hearing continued, including, where they took place on that day, short conferences, consultations, applications and appearances (including bail applications), views at the scene of the alleged offence and any other preparation;

(c) subsidiary fees for—
(i) attendance at conferences, consultations and views at the scene of the alleged offence not covered by paragraph (a) or (b);
(ii) written advice on evidence, plea or appeal or other written work; and
(iii) attendance at pre-trial reviews, applications and appearances (including bail applications and adjournments for sentence) not covered by paragraph (a) or (b).

(3) Where a section 16 determination provides for representation by—
(a) a single advocate other than a QC; or
(b) two advocates other than QC,

and a QC agrees to appear as the single advocate or as a leading junior, that QC must be treated for all the purposes of this Schedule as having been instructed pursuant to that section 16 determination, and the remuneration of the QC must be determined as if the advocate were not a QC.

In connection with this paragraph, see *Bromige*, G-179.

Litigators' fees for proceedings in the Court of Appeal

G-106 7.—(1) For proceedings in the Court of Appeal the appropriate officer must allow fees for work by litigators at the following prescribed rates

Class of work	*Grade of fee earner*	*Rate*	*Variations*
Preparation	Senior solicitor	£48.36 per hour	£50.87 per hour for a litigator whose office is situated within the City of London or a London borough
	Solicitor, legal executive or fee earner of equivalent experience	£41.06 per hour	£43.12 per hour for a litigator whose office is situated within the City of London or a London borough
	Trainee or fee earner of equivalent experience	£27.15 per hour	£31.03 per hour for a litigator whose office is situated within the City of London or a London borough
Advocacy	Senior solicitor	£58.40 per hour	
	Solicitor	£51.10 per hour	
Attendance at court where more than one representative assigned	Senior solicitor	£38.55 per hour	
	Solicitor, legal executive or fee earner of equivalent experience	£31.03 per hour	
	Trainee or fee earner of equivalent experience	£18.71 per hour	
Travelling and waiting	Senior solicitor	£22.58 per hour	
	Solicitor, legal executive or fee earner of equivalent experience	£22.58 per hour	
	Trainee or fee earner of equivalent experience	£11.41 per hour	
Routine letters written and routine telephone calls		£3.15 per item	£3.29 per item for a litigator whose office is situated within the City of London or a London borough.

(2) In respect of any item of work, the appropriate officer may allow fees at less than the relevant prescribed rate specified in the table following sub-paragraph (1) where it appears to the appropriate officer reasonable to do so having regard to the competence and despatch with which the work was done.

[The table in para.7 is printed as substituted by SI 2016/313 (G-1a).]

Allowance of litigators' fees at more than the prescribed rate

8.—(1) Upon a determination of fees the appropriate officer may, subject to the provisions of this paragraph, allow fees at more than the relevant prescribed rate specified in paragraph 7 for preparation, advocacy, attendance at court where more than one representative is assigned, routine letters written and routine telephone calls, in respect of offences in Class A, B, C, D, G, I, J or K in the LGFS Table of Offences. **G-107**

(2) The appropriate officer may allow fees at more than the prescribed rate where it appears to the appropriate officer, taking into account all the relevant circumstances of the case, that—

(a) the work was done with exceptional competence, skill or expertise;

(b) the work was done with exceptional despatch; or

(c) the case involved exceptional complexity or other exceptional circumstances.

(3) Paragraph 3 of Schedule 1 applies to litigators in respect of proceedings in the Court of Appeal as it applies to advocates.

(4) Where the appropriate officer considers that any item or class of work should be allowed at more than the prescribed rate, the appropriate officer must apply to that item or class of work a percentage enhancement in accordance with the following provisions of this paragraph.

(5) In determining the percentage by which fees should be enhanced above the prescribed rate the appropriate officer may have regard to—

(a) the degree of responsibility accepted by the fee earner;

(b) the care, speed and economy with which the case was prepared; and

(c) the novelty, weight and complexity of the case.

(6) The percentage above the relevant prescribed rate by which fees for work may be enhanced must not exceed 100%.

(7) The appropriate officer may have regard to the generality of proceedings to which these Regulations apply in determining what is exceptional within the meaning of this paragraph.

[This paragraph is printed as amended, with effect from 1 April 2018, by SI 2018/220 (G-1a). As to the transitional provision, see G-1a.]

Advocates' fees for proceedings in the Court of Appeal

9.—(1) Subject to sub-paragraph 9(4), for proceedings in the Court of Appeal the appropriate officer must allow fees for work by advocates at the following prescribed rates— **G-108**

JUNIOR COUNSEL

Type of proceedings	*Basic fee*	*Full day refresher*	*Subsidiary fees*		
			Attendance at consultation, conferences and views	*Written work*	*Attendance at pretrial reviews, applications and other appearances*
All appeals	Maximum amount: £545.00 per case	Maximum amount: £178.75 per day	£33.50 per hour, minimum amount: £16.75	Maximum amount: £58.25 per item	Maximum amount: £110 per appearance

QC

Type of proceedings	*Basic fee*	*Full day refresher*	*Subsidiary fees*		
			Attendance at consultation, conferences and views	*Written work*	*Attendance at pretrial reviews, applications and other appearances*
All appeals	Maximum amount: £5,400.00 per case	Maximum amount: £330.50 per day	£62.50 per hour, minimum amount: £32.00	Maximum amount: £119.50 per item	Maximum amount: £257.50 per appearance

(2) Where an hourly rate is specified in the table following sub-paragraph (1), the appropriate officer must determine any fee for such work in accordance with that hourly rate, provided that the fee determined must not be less than the minimum amount specified.

(3) Where a refresher fee is claimed in respect of less than a full day, the appropriate officer must allow such fee as appears to the appropriate officer reasonable having regard to the fee which would be allowable for a full day.

(4) Where it appears to the appropriate officer, taking into account all the relevant circumstances of the case, that owing to the exceptional circumstances of the case the amount payable by way of fees in accordance with the table following sub-paragraph (1) would not provide reasonable remuneration for some or all of the work the appropriate officer has allowed, the appropriate officer may allow such amounts as appear to the appropriate officer to be reasonable remuneration for the relevant work.

Payment of fees

G-109 10.—(1) Having determined the fees payable to a representative in accordance with the terms of this Schedule, the appropriate officer must notify the representative of the fees payable and authorise payment accordingly.

(2) Where, as a result of any redetermination or appeal made or brought pursuant to paragraph 11, the fees payable under paragraph (1) are altered—

(a) if they are increased, the appropriate officer must authorise payment of the increase; and

(b) if they are decreased, the representative must repay the amount of such decrease.

(3) Where the payment of any fees of the representative is ordered under regulation 29(12) or regulation 30(8), the appropriate officer must authorise payment.

Redeterminations and appeals

G-110 11.—(1) Where a representative is dissatisfied with—

(a) the fees determined in accordance with the provisions of this Schedule; or

(b) the decision of the appropriate officer under paragraph 3(3) of Schedule 1,

he may apply to the appropriate officer to redetermine those fees or reclassify the offence, in accordance with the provisions of regulation 28(3) to (9).

(2) Where—

(a) a representative has made an application to the appropriate officer under sub-paragraph (1); and

(b) the appropriate officer has given his reasons for a decision under regulation 28(7),

a representative who is dissatisfied with that decision may appeal to a costs judge, in accordance with the provisions of regulation 29(2) to (14).

(3) A representative who is dissatisfied with the decision of a costs judge on an appeal under subparagraph (2) may apply to a costs judge to certify a point of principle of general importance, and the provisions of regulation 30(2) to (8) apply.

Regulation 8

SCHEDULE 4

RATES PAYABLE FOR THE CLAIMS SPECIFIED IN REGULATION 8

G-111 [*Sets out the rates payable for proceedings in a magistrates' court and certain other work to which the 2015 Duty Provider Contract or the 2015 Own Client Contract applies. It has been amended by the Criminal Legal Aid (Remuneration) (Amendment) Regulations 2013 (SI 2013/2803), the Criminal Legal Aid (Remuneration) (Amendment) Regulations 2014 (SI 2014/415), the Civil and Criminal Legal Aid (Remuneration) Regulations 2015 (SI 2015/325), the Criminal Legal Aid (Remuneration etc.) (Amendment) Regulations 2015 (SI 2015/1369), the Criminal Legal Aid (Remuneration) (Amendment) Regulations 2016 (SI 2016/313), the Criminal Legal Aid (Standard Crime Contract) (Amendment) Regulations 2017 (SI 2017/311), the Criminal Legal Aid (Amendment) Regulations 2017 (SI 2017/1319) and the Criminal Legal Aid (Remuneration) (Amendment) Regulations 2020 (SI 2020/903).*]

Regulation 16

SCHEDULE 5

EXPERTS' FEES AND RATES

Expert	*Non-London - hourly rate unless stated to be a fixed fee*	*London - hourly rate unless stated to be a fixed fee*
A&E consultant	£100.80	£108
Accident reconstruction	£72	£54.40
Accountant	£64	£64
Accountant (general staff)	£40	£40
Accountant (manager)	£86.40	£86.40
Accountant (partner)	£115.20	£115.20
Anaesthetist	£108	£72
Architect	£79.20	£72
Back calculations	£144 fixed fee	£151.20 fixed fee
Benefit expert	£72	£72
Cardiologist	£115.20	£72
Cell telephone site analysis	£72	£72
Child psychiatrist	£108	£72
Child psychologist	£100.80	£72
Computer expert	£72	£72
Consultant engineer	£72	£54.40
Dentist	£93.60	£72
Dermatologist	£86.40	£72
Disability consultant	£54.40	£54.40
DNA (testing of sample)	£252 per test	£252 per test
DNA (preparation of report)	£72	£72
Doctor (GP)	£79.20	£72
Drug expert	£72	£72
Employment consultant	£54.40	£54.40
Enquiry agent	£25.60	£18.40
ENT surgeon	£100.80	£72
Facial mapping	£108	£72
Fingerprint expert	£72	£37.60
Fire investigation	£72	£54.40
Firearm expert	£72	£72
Forensic scientist	£90.40	£72
General surgeon	£108	£72
Geneticist	£86.40	£72
GP (records report)	£50.40 fixed fee	£72 fixed fee
Gynaecologist	£108	£72
Haematologist	£97.60	£72

Expert	*Non-London - hourly rate unless stated to be a fixed fee*	*London - hourly rate unless stated to be a fixed fee*
Handwriting expert	£72	£72
Interpreter	£28	£25
Lip reader/Signer	£57.60	£32.80
Mediator	£100.80	£100.80
Medical consultant	£108	£72
Medical microbiologist	£108	£72
Medical report	£79.20	£72
Meteorologist	£100.80	£144 fixed fee
Midwife	£72	£72
Neonatologist	£108	£72
Neurologist	£122.40	£72
Neuropsychiatrist	£126.40	£72
Neuroradiologist	£136.80	£72
Neurosurgeon	£136.80	£72
Nursing expert	£64.80	£64.80
Obstetrician	£108	£72
Occupational therapist	£54.40	£54.40
Oncologist	£112	£72
Orthopaedic surgeon	£115.20	£72
Paediatrician	£108	£72
Pathologist	£122.40	£432 fixed fee
Pharmacologist	£97.60	£72
Photographer	£25.60	£18.40
Physiotherapist	£64.80	£64.80
Plastic surgeon	£108	£72
Process server	£25.60	£18.40
Psychiatrist	£108	£72
Psychologist	£93.60	£72
Radiologist	£108	£72
Rheumatologist	£108	£72
Risk assessment expert	£50.40	£50.40
Speech therapist	£79.20	£72
Surgeon	£108	£72
Surveyor	£40	£40
Telecoms expert	£72	£72
Toxicologist	£108	£72
Urologist	£108	£72
Vet	£72	£72
Voice recognition	£93.60	£72

[Schedule 5 is printed as substituted by the Criminal Legal Aid (Remuneration) (Amendment) Regulations 2013 (SI 2013/2803), reg.3(1) and (7), and Sch.1.]

SCHEDULE 6

Fees in Very High Cost Cases

Part 1

Interpretation and Application

Interpretation

G-112 1.—(1) In this Schedule—

(a) a reference to a level is a reference to that level as defined in the Very High Cost Case contract;

(b) a reference to a category is a reference to that category as defined in that contract;

(c) the standard rates apply to work as described in the Very High Cost Case contract Guide; and

(d) the preliminary hearing, half day and full day rates apply as described in the Very High Cost Case contract Guide.

(2) In this Part–

(a) "Task List" has the meaning given in the Very High Cost Case contract;

(b) "parties" means the representative who has signed the Very High Cost Case contract and the Lord Chancellor.

(3) In Table 2, a junior may be either a barrister or a solicitor-advocate.

Application

2.–(1) This paragraph makes provision in relation to the application of this Schedule to work done in a case which is the subject of a Very High Cost Case contract signed by the parties before 2nd December 2013. **G-113**

(2) Part 2 of this Schedule applies to work done pursuant to any Task List agreed between the parties before 2nd December 2013.

(3) Subject to sub-paragraph (4), Part 3 of this Schedule applies to work done pursuant to any Task List agreed between the parties on or after 2nd December 2013.

(4) Part 2 of this Schedule applies to work done in a case in which–

(a) the court has set a trial date before 2nd December 2013; and

(b) that trial date is on or before 31st March 2014.

(5) For the purpose of sub-paragraph (4), any adjournment or postponement of a trial which takes place after the trial date is set must be disregarded.

3. Part 3 of this Schedule applies to work done in a case which is the subject of a Very High Cost Case contract signed by the parties on or after 2nd December 2013.

PART 2

TABLE 1: PREPARATION (HOURLY RATES)

G-114

	Category 1 (£)	*Category 2 (£)*	*Category 3 (£)*	*Category 4 (£)*	*Standard Rates (£)*
Litigator					
Level A	145.00	113.00	91.00	91.00	55.75
Level B	127.00	100.00	79.00	79.00	47.25
Level C	84.00	65.00	51.00	51.00	34.00
Pupil/junior	45.00	36.00	30.00	30.00	
Barrister					
QC	145.00	113.00	91.00	91.00	
Leading junior	127.00	100.00	79.00	79.00	
Led junior	91.00	73.00	61.00	61.00	
Junior alone	100.00	82.00	70.00	70.00	
2nd Led junior	63.00	50.00	43.00	43.00	
Solicitor Advocate					
Leading level A	145.00	113.00	91.00	91.00	
Led level A	127.00	100.00	79.00	79.00	
Leading level B	127.00	100.00	79.00	79.00	
Led level B	104.00	86.00	66.00	66.00	
Level A alone	131.00	109.00	88.00	88.00	
Level B alone	113.00	95.00	75.00	75.00	
Second advocate	63.00	50.00	43.00	43.00	

TABLE 2: ADVOCACY RATES

G-115

	Preliminary hearing (£)	*Half day (£)*	*Full day (£)*
QC	113.00	238.00	476.00
Leading junior	86.00	195.00	390.00
Led junior	58.00	126.00	252.00
Junior alone	67.00	143.00	285.00
2nd Led junior	34.00	64.00	128.00
Noting junior	29.00	55.00	109.00

[The next paragraph is G-117.]

TABLE 3: ATTENDANCE AT COURT WITH ADVOCATE (HOURLY RATES FOR LITIGATORS)

G-117

	£
Level A	42.25
Level B	34.00
Level C	20.50

TABLE 4: TRAVELLING, WAITING AND MILEAGE

G-118

	£
Travelling (hourly rates)	25.00 (up to a maximum of 4 hours in one day)
Waiting (hourly rates)	25.00
Mileage	00.45 per mile

PART 3

TABLE 1: PREPARATION (HOURLY RATES)

G-119

	Category 1 (£)	*Category 2 (£)*	*Category 3 (£)*	*Category 4 (£)*	*Standard Rates (£)*
Litigator					
Level A	101.50	79.10	63.70	63.70	39.03
Level B	88.90	70.00	55.30	55.30	33.08
Level C	58.80	45.50	35.70	35.70	24.50
Pupil/junior	31.50	25.20	21.00	21.00	
Barrister					
QC	101.50	79.10	63.70	63.70	
Leading junior	88.90	70.00	55.30	55.30	
Led junior	63.70	51.10	42.70	42.70	
Junior alone	70.00	57.40	49.00	49.00	
2nd Led junior	44.10	35.00	30.10	30.10	
Solicitor Advocate					
Leading level A	101.50	79.10	63.70	63.70	
Led level A	88.90	70.00	55.30	55.30	
Leading level B	88.90	70.00	55.30	55.30	
Led level B	72.80	60.20	46.20	46.20	
Level A alone	91.70	76.30	61.60	61.60	
Level B alone	79.10	66.50	52.50	52.50	
Second advocate	44.10	35.00	30.10	30.10	

TABLE 2: ADVOCACY RATES

	Preliminary hearing (£)	*Half day (£)*	*Full day (£)*
QC	79.10	166.60	333.20
Leading junior	60.20	136.50	273.00
Led junior	40.60	88.20	176.40
Junior alone	46.90	100.10	199.50
2nd Led junior	23.80	44.80	89.60
Noting junior	20.30	38.50	76.30

G-120

TABLE 3: ATTENDANCE AT COURT WITH ADVOCATE (HOURLY RATES FOR LITIGATORS)

	£
Level A	29.58
Level B	23.80
Level C	14.35

G-121

TABLE 4: TRAVELLING, WAITING AND MILEAGE

	£
Travelling (hourly rates)	25.00 (up to a maximum of 4 hours in one day)
Waiting (hourly rates)	25.00
Mileage	00.45 per mile

G-122

[Schedule 6 was inserted by the Criminal Legal Aid (Remuneration) (Amendment) Regulations 2013 (SI 2013/2803), reg.3(1) and (8), and Sch.2. It applies in relation to fees for work undertaken on or after 2 December 2013: reg.4.]

C. REPRESENTATION ORDERS

Representatives are entitled to claim and be remunerated only for work done in respect of Crown Court proceedings in accordance with the provisions of the schedules to the remuneration regulations: SI 2013/435, regs 4, 5 and 9. G-123

Existence of a valid representation order

Payment can only be made for work done under a representation order. There is no power under the legislation to make a payment in respect of work actually and reasonably undertaken by counsel in the genuine but mistaken belief that the appropriate order was in existence. G-124

Solicitors are obliged to enclose a copy of the representation order with counsel's instructions, and to inform counsel of any subsequent amendments: *General Criminal Contract: Contract Specification*, Part B, para.5.4. It is, however, incumbent upon counsel to check whether the appropriate order exists. If it is not with his instructions, then it is his duty, if he seeks to look to the legal aid fund thereafter for remuneration, to see that the appropriate authority is obtained and supplied to him: *Hunt v East Dorset Health Authority* [1992] 1 W.L.R. 785 at 788 (Hobhouse J); and *Welsby* [1998] 1 Cr. App. R. 197, Crown Court (Ebsworth J) (counsel has a professional duty to ensure that he is covered by appropriate certificate).

Determining the effective date of a representation order

The effective date of a representation order for the purposes of determining which regulations apply is the date upon which representation was first granted to counsel's instructing solicitors and not the date of the later representation order under which they instructed counsel: *Hadley* [2005] 3 Costs L.R. 548. G-125

Orders made ultra vires

Representation orders assigning solicitors or counsel which are made ultra vires are invalid, G-126 and work done under such an order cannot be remunerated. However, where it is possible to construe an order as *intra vires,* that construction should be adopted: *O'Brien and Oliffe* [1985] 81 Cr. App. R. 25 at 30 (Hobhouse J). There is no power to backdate a representation order: *Welsby,* above; *Conroy* [2004] Costs L.R. 182.

Representation by an advocate

G-127 As to when a representation order may include representation by one or more advocates or by a Queen's Counsel, see regulations 16 to 20 of the Criminal Legal Aid (Determinations by a Court and Choice of Representative) Regulations 2013 (SI 2013/614) (§§ 6-270 to 6-275).

See also *Newport* (G-164 where two juniors appeared for the defendant). Queen's Counsel must be remunerated at the appropriate rate for junior counsel where he agrees to act as a sole advocate or as a leading junior: SI 2013/435, reg.4(7).

Orders for Queen's Counsel acting alone

G-127a Where prior authority has been obtained to instruct a Queen's Counsel alone, the propriety of the order may not be challenged on the determination of Queen's Counsel's fees unless the solicitor knew or ought reasonably to have known that the purpose for which the authority had been given had failed or become irrelevant or unnecessary before the fees were incurred: SI 2013/435, reg.17(3).

Work done under the order

G-128 The work claimed for must have been done under the order. Work done before the date of commencement of the representation order cannot be claimed or allowed: *Clarke* [1997] Costs L.R. (Core Vol.) 496. An order cannot be backdated in respect of proceedings in the Crown Court: *North Staffordshire JJ, ex p. O'Hara* [1994] C.O.D. 248, DC; *Welsby* [1998] 1 Cr. App. R. 197, Crown Court (Ebsworth J).

"Topping up"

G-129 An assisted person's solicitor or advocate is prohibited from receiving or being party to the making of any payment for work done in connection with the proceedings in respect of which the representation order was made other than payments by the Lord Chancellor or in respect of various specified disbursements: SI 2013/435, reg.9. These provisions are designed to prevent "topping" up of fees, rather than to prevent counsel from receiving payment for private fees incurred before the representation order was granted or *ex gratia* payments from solicitors who wrongly instructed counsel in the mistaken belief that he was covered by a representation order. However, once a representation order has been granted, the prohibition applies to all solicitors and advocates and not merely those persons acting under the representation order: *Grant* [2006] Costs L.R. 173.

D. REASONABLE REMUNERATION

G-130 The basic principle of remuneration under the former ex post facto regime was that counsel should receive reasonable remuneration for work actually and reasonably undertaken by him. Assessment of the work undertaken and the remuneration claimed was made in each case after the event by experienced officers appointed by the Lord Chancellor's department and subject to the appellate and expert supervision of costs judges and the High Court.

G-131 Graduated fees are calculated by reference to pre-determined fixed fees. Although allowances are made for different classes of case and for the length and size of each case, the scheme necessarily embraces a "swings and roundabouts" principle. Save in exceptional cases, graduated fees draw no distinction between straightforward and complex cases of the same length, class and size.

When they were introduced in 1997, it was intended that they would be cost neutral. The extension of fees to cover 25 to 40 day cases represented a diminution in fees for defence work, balanced by an increase in the fees of prosecution counsel who are now subject to a similar scheme. The further extension of the scheme in 2007 to all trials on indictment save for those covered by VHCC contracts was a far remove from its original ambit, and may give rise to some serious underfunding of cases or aspects of cases. It remains to be seen whether the recent changes to the AGFS scheme (including the removal, for most cases, for payments for PPE), address or exacerbate this problem.

Very High Cost Cases are remunerated by an hourly preparation fee and refreshers which fall within prescribed bands. The categorisation of the class of case, rates of remuneration, refreshers and the number of hours of preparation allowed to counsel must be agreed before the work is undertaken.

E. INTERIM FEES AND OTHER PRE-ASSESSMENT PAYMENTS

(1) Staged payments for preparation in long cases

Where the period from sending to the Crown Court to the conclusion of the proceedings is likely to exceed 12 months, a legal representative may apply for staged payments (i.e. interim fees for the preparation of a case) in respect of each period of preparation of 100 hours or more undertaken before trial or, in serious fraud cases, before the empanelling of a jury. Preparation in this context is widely defined and includes, inter alia, conferences with the defendant, written advice on evidence or plea, legal research and preparation for oral or written submissions: SI 2013/435, reg.20. G-132

(2) Interim payment of expenses

A litigator may make a claim for an interim payment of disbursements in accordance with the provisions of regulation 14 of SI 2013/435. G-133

(3) Interim payment pending determination

Entitlement

In certain circumstances, an advocate may claim an interim payment of 40 per cent of the total claim less any sum already paid: SI 2013/435, reg.19(1). Such payments may only be made where, (a) the basic fee claimed by counsel, or the total costs claimed by a solicitor in a related claim, or the basic fee claimed by counsel in a related claim, exceeds £4,000 (exclusive of VAT); and (b) three months have elapsed from either the date on which the bill is ready to tax or, if earlier, three months after the conclusion of the last of any related proceedings. A bill is deemed to be ready to tax on the date of receipt of the last bill in a related claim. Related claims are claims for costs of solicitors and counsel in the same proceedings acting for the same defendant or acting in related proceedings. Related proceedings are those involving the same defendant which are prepared, heard, or dealt with together, or proceedings involving more than one defendant arising out of the same incident so that the defendants are charged, tried, or disposed of together: SI 2013/435, reg.18. G-134

There is no right of re-determination or appeal against the interim award: SI 2013/435, reg.19(2).

Claims

An advocate may submit a claim for interim payment where, (a) he is entitled to such payment; (b) no payment has been made; (c) six months have elapsed since the conclusion of the proceedings against the defendant he represented; and (d) counsel has submitted a proper claim under regulation 4(3) (three-month time limit for the submission of claims): SI 2013/435, reg.18(2)-(6). G-135

(4) Hardship payments

A discretionary hardship payment may be made on proof of the likelihood of financial hardship. The proof required is left to the discretion of taxing officers. Counsel are advised to contact their circuit representative, before submitting a claim, to determine the form of proof likely to be acceptable. The sum paid cannot exceed the amount which is likely to be eventually paid, but payment will not be made for sums less than £5,000. Claims may only be made: (a) at least six months after the legal representative was first instructed, and (b) where final payment is unlikely to be made within the next three months by reason of which the applicant is likely to suffer financial hardship: SI 2013/435, reg.21. G-136

(5) Obligations to submit claims

Any person who has received a staged, interim or hardship payment must submit a claim under G-137 the appropriate regulation for final determination of his overall remuneration: SI 2013/435, reg.22(1). Any such payment will be set off against the overall remuneration on final determination and excess payments can be recovered: reg.22(2).

F. GRADUATED FEES

(1) Introduction

G-138 As to the introduction of the scheme for graduated fees, see G-2.

The scheme determines the taxation and payment of fees for advocacy and preparation in something of a mechanistic or formulaic way: *Meeke and Taylor v Secretary of State for Constitutional Affairs* [2006] Costs L.R. 1. It is a comprehensive scheme which must be applied by examining the particular wording of the legislation: *Kemp*, summarised in Appendix J of the CCFG guidance document (see G-3). There is no "equity" in the regulations; they have to be construed and given effect however hard the result might be: *Riddell*, summarised in Appendix J of the CCFG guidance document (see G-3), even where payment is morally due: see *Dhaliwal* [2004] 4 Costs L.R. 689. Conversely, as was pointed out in *Chubb* [2002] 2 Costs L.R. 333:

> "As has often been said, when the graduated fee system was introduced, it was on a principle which was expressed as being 'swings and roundabouts'. It is perfectly reasonable where the system operates against the Lord Chancellor's Department, that an appeal should be launched. There are many occasions, in my experience, when the graduated fee system has operated very much to the disadvantage of members of the bar and there is no reason why the bar should not take advantage when it operates in their favour."

References within this section to paragraphs are references to paragraphs in Schedule 1 to SI 2013/435 (unless otherwise stated).

(2) Cases on indictment

Scheduled offences

G-139 A "case" includes proceedings in the Crown Court against any one assisted person on one or more counts of a single indictment: SI 2013/435, Sch.1, para.1(1). Where counts or defendants are severed and dealt with separately, then each separate indictment is a separate case. Conversely, indictments which are joined should be treated as one case: CCFG 2.1.3 *Chubb* [2002] 2 Costs L.R. 333. A "case" should not be confused with a trial; there may be two trials in one case: *Bond* [2005] 3 Costs L.R. 532.

All cases on indictment now fall within the scheme unless specifically excluded: SI 2013/435, Sch.1, para.2. As to pre-indictment hearings, see G-145.

In *Hussain* [2011] 4 Costs L.R. 689, after one defendant was committed for trial and a plea and case management hearing was conducted in relation to a single-count indictment, a second defendant was committed for trial, as a result of which a second indictment was preferred which included the allegation against the first defendant in the single-count indictment, and the defendants were in due course tried on the second indictment. It was held that: (i) whereas paragraph 1(1) of Schedule 2 to SI 2013/435 (G-73) provides that "'case' means proceedings in the Crown Court against any one assisted person—(a) on one or more counts of a single indictment ...", there were two "cases"; (ii) in respect of the second indictment, the solicitors were entitled to a graduated fee for trial, together with the appropriate uplift for representing more than one defendant; and (iii) in respect of the first indictment, they were entitled to a graduated fee for a cracked trial. The costs judge observed that whilst it might be thought that the solicitors had obtained something of a windfall for, in layman's terms, this was really only one case, the regulations must be applied mechanistically.

Introduction of new AFGS Scheme

G-140 The Criminal Legal Aid (Remuneration) (Amendment) Regulations 2018 (SI 2018/220), with effect from 1 April 2018, amended the legal aid fees that are payable to advocates in criminal proceedings under the advocates' graduated fee scheme ("AGFS"), as set out in Schedule 1 to SI 2013/435. The 2018 Regulations make provision for advocates' fees to be determined according to a new banding structure for criminal offences set out in version 1.1 (February 2018) of the document called "Banding of Offences in the Advocates' Graduated Fee Scheme (AGFS)", published by the Ministry of Justice (available at *https://www.gov.uk/government/publications/banding-of-offences-in-the-advocates-graduated-fee-scheme*). This new banding structure replaces the table of offences previously set out in Schedule 1 to SI 2013/435 for the purposes of advocate's fees. This table has been moved by the 2018 Regulations into Schedule 2 to SI 2013/435, however, and continues to be relevant in relation to the operation of the litigator's graduated fee scheme ("LGFS"). These amendments have no effect in relation to proceedings in respect of which a determination under section 16 of the LASPOA 2012 (see § 6-187 in the main work) is made before 1 April 2018.

AFGS Bands

The new AFGS scheme uses a new banding structure for offences, replacing the classes used by the table of offences previously found in Schedule 1 to SI 2013/435, and now found in Schedule 2 to SI 2013/435. Offences are set out by a top-tier category, with lower-tier banding differentiating specific types of cases. The top-tier categories are set out below for convenience. For the full list of offences and bands, see version 1.2 (December 2018) of the document called "Banding of Offences in the Advocates' Graduated Fee Scheme (AGFS)", published by the Ministry of Justice (available at *https://www.gov.uk/government/publications/banding-of-offences-in-the-advocates-graduated-fee-scheme*). G-141

Cases which do not appear in the table of offences are deemed to fall within Band 17.1: SI 2013/435, Sch.2, para.3(1)(a). An advocate who is dissatisfied with that deemed classification may apply to the appropriate officer to re-band the offence: SI 2013/435, Sch.2, para.3(2).

Category 1	Murder/Manslaughter
Category 2	Terrorism
Category 3	Serious Violence
Category 4	Sexual Offences (children) - defendant or victim a child at the time of offence
Category 5	Sexual Offences (adult)
Category 6	Dishonesty (to include Proceeds of Crime and Money Laundering)
Category 7	Property Damage Offences
Category 8	Offences Against the Public Interest
Category 9	Drugs Offences
Category 10	Driving Offences
Category 11	Burglary & Robbery
Category 12	Firearms Offences
Category 13	Other Offences Against the Person
Category 14	Exploitation / Human Trafficking Offences
Category 15	Public Order Offences
Category 16	Regulatory Offences
Category 17	Standard Cases

Where counts of differing classes appear in the same indictment, the fee is based upon the class selected by the advocate: SI 2013/435, Sch.1, para.27(1). Where an indictment is drafted in such a way that the offence charged could fall into either of two different classes in the table of offences, the advocate may choose the class to which the case is to be assigned for the purpose of calculating the fees payable: *Lord Chancellor v Ahmed* [2014] Costs L.R. 21, QBD (Andrews J). G-141a

Conspiracy, incitement or attempt to commit an offence fall within the same band as the substantive offence: SI 2013/435, Sch.1, para.3(1)(b). Where the appropriate class depends upon a value, the lower value is presumed unless the claimant "proves otherwise to the satisfaction of the appropriate authority": SI 2013/435, Sch.1, para.3(1)(c). This may be done by extracts from the indictment or witness statements. Values relating to offences taken into consideration should be excluded from the computation: *Knight* (2003), summarised in Appendix J of the CCFG guid- G-142 ance document (see G-3). The proof required is proof on a balance of probabilities, and the appropriate officer must take a common sense approach in deciding whether the burden has been discharged: *Garness* [2014] Costs L.R. 201.

In *O'Donnell and Fawley* [2012] 2 Costs L.R. 431, it was held that the scheme is mechanistic and that there is no discretion for the court to say that, because the defendants may have been shown to have committed offences in a different class, which would attract a higher fee, it is permissible to reclassify the offence actually charged accordingly.

The calculation of values

G-143 The property values of each count falling within the same class may be aggregated, provided the same property is not counted twice: SI 2013/435, Sch.1, para.3(1)(d). However, offences taken into consideration are excluded from the calculation, even where it is agreed that the counts on the indictment are to be treated merely as sample counts: (*Knight* (2003) summarised in Appendix J of the CCFG guidance document (see G-3).

In *Wei* [2010] 5 Costs L.R. 846, it was held that "value", for the purposes of paragraph 3 of Schedule 2 to SI 2013/435 and the table of offences in Part 7 of Schedule 1 must, in the context of an offence of dishonesty, such as possession of articles for use in fraud, mean the value of the dishonest enterprise, and not the value of the particular articles. The court said that the obvious intention was to provide greater remuneration for more complex and lengthy cases within the confines of the formulaic graduated fee system.

It is submitted that the same reasoning applies to the new AFGS Banding Document, and continues to apply to the table of offences now found in Part 7 of Schedule 2.

Table of offences: LGFS

G-144 The table of offences in Schedule 2 to SI 2013/435 contains offences listed by statute with a description set out only for convenience. The statutory reference includes every offence contrary to that reference, whether or not the description of the offence is apt to describe the offence actually charged: SI 2013/435, Sch.2, para.3(1)(e). Cases which do not appear in the table of offences are deemed to fall within Class H: SI 2013/435, Sch.2, para.3(1)(a). A litigator who is dissatisfied with that deemed classification may apply to the appropriate officer to reclassify the offence: SI 2013/435, Sch.2, para.3(2).

The offences are divided into the following classes:

Class A	Homicide and related grave offences
Class B	Offences involving serious violence or damage and serious drug offences
Class C	Lesser offences involving violence or damage, and less serious drug offences
Class D	Sexual offences and offences against children
Class E	Burglary and going equipped
Class F	Other offences of dishonesty including those where the value does not exceed £30,000
Class G	Other more serious offences of dishonesty including those where the value exceeds £30,000 but does not exceed £100,000
Class H	Miscellaneous lesser offences
Class I	Offences against public justice and similar offences
Class J	Serious sexual offences
Class K	The most serious offences of dishonesty and other offences where the value exceeds £100,000

Where counts of differing classes appear in the same indictment, the fee is based upon the class selected by the litigator: SI 2013/435, Sch.2, para.24(1).

The offences are summarised and listed alphabetically by statute: G-186 to G-198.

Preliminary hearings

G-145 In *Lord Chancellor v Shapiro* [2010] Costs L.R. 769, QBD (Sweeney J), it was held that for a first hearing in the Crown Court of a case sent for trial under section 51 of the CDA 1998 (§ 1-24 in the main work) to fall within the graduated fee scheme there must be an indictment in existence at the time. It was said that since the order makes no specific provision for such hearings, it follows that they fall to be remunerated as part of the basic fee if there is an indictment in existence at the time, and, if there is not, there is no provision for payment; in particular, the order making no provision for ex post facto taxation (except in strictly limited circumstances), there is no power to make a payment on an ex post facto basis. For criticism of this decision, see the commentary in CLW/10/38/8.

Pleas and directions hearings and pre-trial reviews

Pleas and directions hearings are not defined under the regulations. Accordingly if a matter is listed as a pleas and directions hearing, it will be so treated. There is nothing to prevent a pleas and directions hearing from being adjourned, or there being more than one or even a series of such hearings. However, the listing of the case is not necessarily determinative. For example, although a case may be listed as a pleas and directions hearing, if a defendant pleads at that hearing and is sentenced, it cannot be said that a pleas and directions hearing has taken place: *Johnson* [2006] 5 Costs L.R. 852. **G-146**

Fees for oral hearings which fall within the definition of a standard appearance are deemed to be included in the basic fee: see G-129. Case management hearings which are not standard appearances are remunerated according to the fees set out in the table following paragraph 24: SI 2013/435, Sch.1, para.12(2). As to standard appearances, see G-150.

The start of the main hearing

In *Lord Chancellor v Ian Henery Solicitors Ltd* [2012] Costs L.R. 205, QBD (Spencer J), it was held that when considering the question whether, and if so on what date, a case has proceeded to trial, the following principles apply: **G-147**

(i) whether or not a jury have been sworn is not conclusive;
(ii) there can be no doubt that a trial will have begun if the jury have been sworn, the case has been opened, and evidence has been called;
(iii) a trial will also have begun if the jury have been sworn and the case has been opened to any extent, even if only for a few minutes (*Meeke and Taylor v Secretary of State for Constitutional Affairs* [2006] Costs L.R. 1, QBD (David Clarke J));
(iv) a trial will not have begun, even if the jury have been sworn (and whether or not the defendant has been put in the charge of the jury), if there has been no trial in a meaningful sense, e.g. because, before the case can be opened, the defendant pleads guilty (*Brook* [2004] Costs L.R. 178, *Baker and Fowler* [2004] 4 Costs L.R. 693, and *Sanghera* [2008] 5 Costs L.R. 823);
(v) a trial will have begun, even if there has been no empanelment of a jury, if submissions have begun in a continuous process resulting in the empanelling of a jury, the opening of the case, and the leading of evidence (considering *Wembo* [2011] 5 Costs L.R. 926, *Bullingham* [2011] 6 Costs L.R. 1078, and an unreported decision of Mitting J in December 2005, in the case of *Smith*);
(vi) if, in accordance with modern practice in long cases, a jury have been selected but not sworn, then provided the court is dealing with substantial matters of case management it may well be that the trial has begun in a meaningful sense; and
(vii) where there is likely to be any difficulty in deciding whether a trial has begun, and if so when it began, the judge should be prepared, upon request, to indicate his view on the matter for the benefit of the parties and the determining officer, in the light of these principles.

In *Budai* [2011] 6 Costs L.R. 1073, the costs judge acknowledged the principle in (v), above, but held that this did not cover a case where, on the day listed for trial, all that was done was that interpreters were sworn, a potential panel of 18 jurors was selected (prior to their being sent away until the following day to assess their availability for a lengthy trial) and there was a direction made regarding the amendment of the indictment. On the other side of the line are *Wembo*, above (where, immediately prior to a jury being empanelled, counsel had attended two days of hearings that related to a witness anonymity order, those days had formed part of the trial for the purposes of calculating the graduated fee); and *Bullingham*, above (where a jury had not been empanelled, but the judge directed that there should be a voir dire to determine the admissibility of evidence which the prosecution wanted to open to the jury, and there was such a voir dire at which evidence was called, the trial started with the giving of that direction even though the effect of the ruling on the voir dire was that the prosecution decided to accept pleas to lesser offences in consequence of which the defendant pleaded guilty and there was no requirement for a jury). The reasoning in *Bullingham* was expressly approved in *Lord Chancellor v Ian Henery Solicitors Ltd*, above, but it is submitted that the result is difficult to justify, not least for its failure to give effect to the obvious purpose of paragraph 13 of Schedule 1 (§ G-49), which the costs judge did not even refer to. Sub-paragraph (1)(d) expressly contemplates that a hearing as to the admissibility of evidence may take place before the main hearing of a case (trial or cracked trial), and if it does, it is to be remunerated in accordance with that paragraph. The decision of the costs judge effectively emasculates this by converting the admissibility hearing into the main hearing. See also the commentary in CLW/12/01/14.

The start of a preparatory hearing is the commencement of the trial for the purposes of the regulations: *Jones*; summarised in Appendix J of the CCFG.

Calculating the length of the main hearing

G-148 Length of the main hearing means the number of days of the main hearing together with the number of days of any *Newton* hearing in relation to the assisted person whose trial is under consideration: SI 2013/435, reg.2(1), and Sch.1, para.2(8). Thus, where counsel successfully submits that there is no case to answer, the main hearing ceases, despite the fact that the trial may continue against the co-defendants: *Secretary of State for Constitutional Affairs v Stork* [2005] EWHC 1763 (QB); *The Times*, 7 October 2005, QBD (Gray J). This can lead to harsh anomalies, as where a defendant pleads guilty shortly after a jury have been sworn during an estimated three-week trial; despite preparation for a three-week trial, counsel will be remunerated as for a one day trial: *Meeke and Taylor v Secretary of State for Constitutional Affairs*, above. Non-sitting days cannot be included: *Nassir*, summarised in Appendix J of the CCFG guidance document (see G-3). Applications relating to abuse of process, disclosure and witness summonses are to be treated as part of the main hearing where they are heard during the main hearing: SI 2013/435, Sch.1, para.13(2). The length of a fitness hearing which precedes a trial on indictment must also be included in determining the length of the trial: SI 2013/435, Sch.1, para.31(a). Confiscation proceedings are excluded from the computation: SI 2013/435, Sch.1, para.14(2).

Where, during the currency of a trial, there had been a day when one juror could not attend, but the judge had directed all counsel to attend in order that agreement should be reached as to how to reduce one section of the evidence, counsel was not entitled to count that day as a day of the trial; although the judge had indicated he would be available in case there was some issue on which agreement could not be reached, it had not been necessary to involve the judge and the case had not been called on in court; counsel was, however, entitled to a non-effective hearing fee for that day (under Sch.1, para.16 (G-52)); the case was listed for that day, counsel had been obliged to attend, but in fact the trial did not proceed on that day: *Budai*, above.

Fees for contested trials

G-149 The calculation of any graduated fee involves arcane formulae: SI 2013/435, Sch.1, para.4. To calculate the correct fee, the appropriate figures should be substituted from the tables of fees: SI 2013/435, Sch.1, paras. 5 and 5A.

Standard appearances

G-150 Standard appearances are defined in SI 2013/435 as appearances which do not form part of the main hearing, and constitute (i) pre-trial reviews; (ii) the hearing of a case listed for plea which is adjourned for trial; (iii) custody time limit, bail and other applications; (iv) mentions, including applications relating to the date of trial; (v) a hearing, whether contested or not, relating to breach of bail, failure to surrender to bail or execution of a bench warrant; and (vi) any hearing (except a trial, the first hearing at which the assisted person enters a plea, appeal against conviction or sentence, sentencing hearing following a committal for sentence to the Crown Court, or proceedings arising out of an alleged breach of an order of the Crown Court) which is listed but cannot proceed because of the failure of the assisted person or a witness to attend, the unavailability of a pre-sentence report or other good reason: Sch.1, para.1(1). Prior to amendment by SI 2018/220 (G-1a) standard appearances also included (i) plea and case management hearings; (ii) pre-trial preparation hearings; and (iii) a sentencing hearing other than one following a committal for sentence to the Crown Court, or one where sentence has been deferred under the PCC(S)A 2000, s.1, or one where the advocate has been instructed solely for the purposes of entering a plea in mitigation under paragraph 34 of Schedule 1. The fee payable in respect of a standard appearance is set out in the table in paragraph 24: Sch.1, para.12(2).

Trial of Bail Act offences

The trial of any Bail Act 1976 offence in the Crown Court entitles counsel who attends to apply for a new "trial" fee for the contested trial or plea: *Shaw* [2005] 2 Costs L.R. 326; *Despres* [2005] 4 Costs L.R. 750. **G-151**

Sendings to the Crown Court

Where cases are sent to the Crown Court under the CDA 1998, s.51, and are discontinued before the prosecution serve their evidence, the advocate is entitled to 50 per cent of the fee calculated on the basis of a guilty plea: SI 2013/435, Sch.1, para.22(2), together with an additional 20 per cent of that fee for each additional person represented: para.22(8)(a). Once the prosecution have served their evidence, discontinuance, the offering of no evidence at a pleas and case management hearing, or the remitting of the case to the magistrates' court at such hearing because the indictment contains no indictable offence, is treated for the purposes of calculating the relevant fee as if each was a guilty plea, para.22(3) and (5). An advocate representing more than one person in the latter circumstances is entitled to 20 per cent of the appropriate basic fee for each additional person he represents: para.22(8)(b). **G-152**

Dismissal hearings

Where a successful application for dismissal is made under the CDA 1998, Sch.3, para.2, with the result that the case is dismissed or remitted back to the magistrates' court, the fee is calculated as if the matter had been disposed of by a guilty plea, together with an attendance fee based upon the total number of days and half days occupied by the hearing: SI 2013/435, Sch.1, para.22(6) and (7). A full day's hearing is any court day which begins before and ends after the luncheon adjournment: para.22(6)(a). An advocate representing more than one person in such circumstances is entitled to 20 per cent of the appropriate basic fee for each additional person he represents: para.22(8)(b). **G-153**

Transfers

A case will be "transferred" to a new litigator for the purposes of paragraph 13(2)(a) of Schedule 2 to the Criminal Legal Aid (Remuneration) Regulations 2013 (SI 2013/435) (G-84) where the representation order has been amended to substitute the new litigator and the new litigator has agreed to accept the instructions and has carried out a conflicts check; an amended representation order will not be effective to transfer a case to a new litigator who has not carried out a conflicts check because it is incumbent upon any firm of solicitors to carry out such a check before accepting instructions and, therefore, in such circumstances, it cannot be said that the new litigator has been "instructed" until that duty has been discharged: *Tuckers Solicitors v Lord Chancellor* [2014] Costs L.R. 29, QBD (Andrews J) (considering a corresponding provision in the Criminal Defence Service (Funding) Order 2007 (SI 2007/1174), and observing that, in practice, it would be desirable if, when the Crown Court sends information to the putative new litigator, it were to include the indictment, witness list and, if available, the case summary, rather than leaving it to the former solicitors to do so). **G-154**

In *Rayan* [2010] 6 Costs L.R. 969, it was held that, for the purposes of paragraph 13(2) of Schedule 2 to SI 2013/435 (G-84), which provides that where a case is transferred from one litigator to another, the original litigator is entitled to 25 per cent of the cracked trial fee where the transfer took place "up to and including plea and case management hearing" or a fee of 75 per cent of the cracked trial fee for a "before trial transfer", the reference to a "plea and case management hearing" must be taken to be a reference to an effective such hearing. An effective hearing, it was held, requires there to have been a plea, and for case management directions of sufficient substance to have been made such that the hearing could be described as a plea and case management hearing.

Retrials

G-155 A standard graduated fee is paid for retrials, where the same advocate appears, subject to the following discounts based upon the time elapsed from the conclusion of the first trial to the start of the retrial: SI 2013/435, Schedule 1, para.2(3):

30 per cent	retrial starts within one month
20 per cent	retrial starts after one month
40 per cent	retrial is cracked or becomes a guilty plea within one month
25 per cent	retrial is cracked or becomes a guilty plea after one month.

No discounts are applied where the advocate who conducts the retrial is not the advocate who conducted the original trial: ., Schedule 1, para.2(5) and (6)

In *Connors* [2014] Costs L.R. 942 it was held that under the graduated fee scheme for advocates as set out in Schedule 1 to the Criminal Defence Service (Funding) Order 2007 (SI 2007/1174), where there is a trial followed by a retrial with the same advocate acting in both trials, the advocate does not have to wait until the conclusion of the second trial to claim payment for the first trial. Furthermore, an advocate need not wait until the conclusion of the second trial before electing to have the reduced fee applied to the first trial under paragraph 2(4) of Schedule 1 to the 2007 order (now under Sch.1, para.2(2) and (3), to SI 2013/435 (G-37)). If it turned out that there should have been a greater reduction than the one actually applied, the Legal Aid Agency could recoup any excess payment via article 26 of the 2007 order (now via reg.25 of SI 2013/435 (G-29)).

Where the case was sent to the Crown Court on the election of the defendant where the magistrates' court had determined the case to be suitable for summary trial, and the new trial becomes a cracked trial or guilty plea, the advocate will receive a graduated fee for the first trial and a fixed fee for the second trial: SI 2013/435, Sch.1, para.2(4). This also applies where the trial advocate is different at the second trial: SI 2013/435, Sch.1, para.2(5) and (7).

G-156 Where a defence advocate was initially retained privately but, the jury at the first trial having been unable to agree on a verdict, was then instructed for the retrial under a representation order, the defendant having run out of money, and where the defendant was acquitted at the retrial with a defendant's costs order being made in his favour, no payment could be made under the defendant's costs order out of central funds in respect of work done in preparation for the retrial between the date of the first trial and the grant of the representation order; the graduated fee payable for a retrial under the Criminal Defence Service (Funding) Order 2001 (SI 2001/855) was intended to allow for all preparation carried out for that retrial; to have authorised the payment would have resulted in a double payment out of public funds effectively in respect of the same work: *Long* [2009] Costs L.R. 151. The result would be the same under SI 2013/435.

In *Lord Chancellor v Purnell and McCarthy* [2010] Costs L.R. 81, QBD (Sir Christopher Holland), where a full trial had been conducted in which the jury had acquitted the defendant on the main charge of murder, but had been unable to agree on an alternative charge of manslaughter and on another count of violent disorder, where a date for a retrial had been fixed, where the prosecution eventually decided to offer no evidence, and where it was clear that counsel had not, meanwhile, been standing by awaiting a decision by the prosecution whether to proceed (it was not the case that the matter had been adjourned after trial to allow the prosecution time to decide whether they intended to proceed further) but, on the contrary, had begun preparing for the retrial, it was held that counsel were entitled to a graduated fee for a "cracked trial". They had every reason to expect and prepare for a retrial, as the case was serious and had so far featured a finding by at least three jurors that manslaughter had been proved against the defendant to the criminal standard. Under the 2001 order, there was no provision for any percentage reduction of the fee in such cases. This, however, has since been remedied: see now SI 2013/435, Sch.1, para.2(2) and (3) (G-37).

In *Seivwright* [2011] 2 Costs L.R. 327, it was held that paragraph 13(1) of Schedule 2 to SI 2013/435 (G-83) applies only where the retrial follows a trial and an order has been made for a retrial following appeal or where a jury have failed to reach a verdict, and that "retrial" for this purpose means a new trial which is not part of the same procedural and temporal matrix as the first trial. It was said that whilst this conclusion might be thought to conflict with the Litigator Graduated Fee Scheme Guidance published by the Legal Services Commission, that was merely guidance and not a source of law that was binding. On the facts, it was held that where the trial had commenced on a Monday, the jury had been discharged on the Thursday, the matter was listed for mention on the Friday when it was agreed that a new jury would be empanelled on the following Monday, and where they were so empanelled, there was but one trial.

In *Nettleton* [2014] Costs L.R. 387, it was held that where the question arises whether "an order [was] made for a retrial", this is not to be confined to cases where one jury are discharged following a disagreement and an order for a new trial is made before a different jury, but it does not extend to every interruption to the trial process, even if it involves the discharge of one jury and the empanelment of a fresh jury. The question is whether the new proceeding was part of the same procedural and temporal matrix as the prior proceeding (see *Seivwright*, above). If there is a continuous process, even a long gap will not necessarily render the second proceeding a "retrial", and the fact that additional evidence has been served by the prosecution, including from one or more new witnesses, will not per se render the new proceeding a retrial. In this case, it was held that it was clear that there had been a trial and a retrial where the jury at the original hearing had been discharged following the arrest of the judge, and there had then been a four-month gap before the second proceeding began with a new judge, new jury and, in the case of some defendants, new counsel.

Guilty pleas

SI 2013/435 defines a guilty plea as a case on indictment which is disposed of without trial because of the guilty plea, and is not a cracked trial: Sch.1, para.1(1). Cases which result in a *Newton* hearing are excluded: Sch.1, para.2(8)(c); and see G-170. **G-157**

The graduated fee for guilty pleas is as set out in the table of fees SI 2013/435, Sch.1, paras 7 and 8.

Graduated fees for guilty pleas under Part 3 of Schedule 1 to SI 2013/435 no longer apply to cases committed to the Crown Court on the election of the defendant where the magistrates' court determined that the case was suitable for summary trial: SI 2013/435, Sch.1, para.6 and is subject to a fixed fee as set out in Sched.1, paras 9 and 10.

In *Agbobu* [2009] 2 Costs L.R. 374, it was held that even though a case may not be a "guilty plea" within the definition in paragraph 1(1) of Schedule 2 to SI 2013/435 (G-73), paragraph 21(4) of Part 3 of that schedule (G-91) nevertheless provides that "where an application for dismissal is made ... and–(a) the charge, or charges are dismissed and the assisted person is discharged; ... the litigator instructed in the proceedings must be paid a fee calculated in accordance with paragraph 6, or where appropriate, paragraph 8, as appropriate for representing an assisted person in a guilty plea". Accordingly, the fee payable for a litigator representing a defendant against whom charges were dismissed was that payable for a guilty plea and not a cracked trial.

Cracked trials

A cracked trial is a case on indictment in which (a) the assisted person enters a plea of not guilty to one or more counts at the first hearing at which he or she enters a plea and (i) the case does not proceed to trial (whether by reason of pleas of guilty or for other reasons) or the prosecution offer no evidence; and (ii) either (aa) in respect of one or more counts to which the assisted person pleaded guilty, he did not so plead at the first hearing at which he entered a plea; or (bb) in respect of one or more counts which did not proceed, the prosecution did not, before or at the first hearing at which the assisted person entered a plea, declare an intention of not proceeding with them; or (b) the case is listed for trial without hearing at which the assisted persons enters a plea: SI 2013/435, Sch.1, para.1(1) (the definition is defective in that in (b) there is no reference to the case not proceeding to trial (read literally it would cover cases that go to trial where no plea and case management hearing took place)). The rationale for the cracked trial fee is that it provides some element of compensation for the loss of refreshers and trial length increments which otherwise would have been payable: *Frampton* [2005] 3 Costs L.R. 527. Graduated fees for guilty pleas under Part 3 of Schedule 1 to SI 2013/435 no longer apply to cases committed to the Crown Court on the election of the defendant where the magistrates' court determined that the case was suitable for summary trial: SI 2013/435, Sch.1, para.6. **G-158**

The essence of a cracked trial is that after the conclusion of a pleas and directions hearing there are still counts on which the prosecution and defence do not agree so that a trial remains a real possibility: 3.1.23 CCFG guidance document (see G-3) A case listed for a plea and directions hearing is ultimately defined by what actually happens at that hearing. If a defendant pleads guilty at what is listed as a plea and directions hearing, the plea obviates the need for such a hearing. Accordingly, an advocate is entitled to a fee for a cracked trial: *Johnson* [2006] 5 Costs L.R. 852 (note that this flies in the face of the definition of a "cracked trial": see (a), above). Where an indictment containing two counts was listed for trial following a plea and directions hearing, but the defendant pleaded guilty to one count, which was acceptable to the prosecution, whereupon the case was put back for sentence, and where, at the adjourned hearing, a formal not guilty verdict was entered on the other count and where the defendant was represented by different counsel on the two occasions, it was counsel who represented him on the first occasion who was entitled to the "cracked trial" fee as what happened on that occasion came within the definition of a "cracked trial" (viz. case was one in which a plea and directions hearing took place, the case did not proceed to trial, but the guilty plea was not entered at that hearing): *Johnson (Craig)* [2007] 2 Costs L.R. 316. Once a meaningful trial has started, a change of plea cannot convert the trial into a cracked trial: *Maynard*; *Karra* (Both in Appendix J of the CCFG and *Meeke and Taylor v Secretary of State for Constitutional Affairs* [2006] Costs L.R. 1, QBD (David Clarke J). Where a jury were discharged on the second day of a trial on a three count indictment, and on the following working day the prosecution added a new lesser count, and, before a new jury were sworn, the defendant offered sufficient pleas to the indictment, counsel was entitled to a fee for the first (abortive) trial, and a cracked trial fee for the later hearing at which pleas were tendered: *Frampton*, above.

Cracked trial fees do not apply where a person pleads not guilty at a pleas and directions hearing, but later the same day changes his plea; a guilty plea fee is appropriate: *Baxter*, (See Appendix J of the CCFG; G-3).

The fee for a cracked trial is calculated by reference to when the case cracked, i.e. in the first, second or third part of a period calculated from the date when the court first fixed the date of trial or first ordered that the case should be placed into a warned list, to the date of that first fixture or the date of the start of that warned list. The fact that the fixture might later be broken, or the case moved to another warned list is immaterial and does not affect the calculation. Where the number of days in the period cannot be equally divided by three, the remainder is simply added to the last third of the period: SI 2013/435, Sch.1, paras 7 and 8. The fee is payable to the advocate who appeared at the hearing where pleas were entered or the last such hearing if there was more than one: *Faulkner*, [2003] 1 Costs L.R. 148.

In *Carty* [2009] 3 Costs L.R. 500, it was held that where the prosecution of one of several defendants was stayed, the case fell within the definition of a "cracked trial". The fact that the defendant's advocate had not been present on the occasion of the stay (which had been ordered at a hearing when the principal defendant, being before the court on a separate indictment, had then entered acceptable pleas to the indictment in question) did not preclude payment. Moreover, since 1996, there had been an administrative practice which permitted the prosecution to offer no evidence and an acquittal to be pronounced in open court without the legal representatives being present, and paragraph 2.1.31 of the CCFG (G-3) permitted a cracked trial fee to be paid in such circumstances. For this purpose, there was no reason to differentiate between a cracked trial arising from the prosecution offering no evidence and one arising from a stay.

In *Harris* [2009] 3 Costs L.R. 507, where the defendant had pleaded guilty at a pleas and directions hearing to various offences, but where his "benefit" for the purpose of confiscation proceedings under the CJA 1988 had not yet been agreed, and where sentence and those proceedings had therefore been adjourned, the matter was held not to fall within the definition of a "cracked trial" in paragraph 9(3) of Schedule 4 to the Criminal Defence Service (Funding) Order 2001 (SI 2001/855) (which corresponds to the current definition), and the hearing at which the confiscation order was eventually made was said not to fall within the definition of a *Newton* hearing (*Newton* (1983) 77 Cr App R. 13, CA) under paragraph 1(1) (corresponding to the definition in para.1(1) of Sch.1 to SI 2013/435) for the purposes of paragraph 2(6) (see now para.2(6) of Sch.1 to SI 2013/435, G-37). The prosecution had accepted the basis of the defendant's guilty plea, but in the knowledge that it would take further time, and in all likelihood another hearing, to work out the defendant's benefit. The matter, therefore, fell within the definition of "guilty plea" under paragraph 9(5).

As to the distinction between a "trial" and a "cracked trial", see also G-147.

Calculating the pages of prosecution evidence

Due to amendments effected by SI 2018/220 (G-1a) the number of pages of evidence is now far less relevant for the payment of fees in relation to cases where legal aid is provided after 1 April 2018. Their relevance is limited to fees for special preparation under para.17(1)(b). This section has been preserved, however, for reference in cases where representation orders were issued prior to that date. Prosecution evidence includes all witness statements, documentary and pictorial exhibits and records of interview with any defendant served on the defence pursuant to the Crime and Disorder Act 1998 (Service of Prosecution Evidence) Regulations 2005 (SI 2005/902) (§§ 1-51, 1-52 in the main work), or included in any notice of additional evidence, and now includes documents served in electronic form, except for a documentary or pictorial exhibit which has never existed in paper form, unless the appropriate officer decides that it would be appropriate to include it in the page count taking into account the nature of the document and any other relevant circumstances: SI 2013/435, Sch.1, para.1(2) to (5), and Sch.2, para.1(2) to (5). The first 50 pages must be excluded for the purposes of the calculation: SI 2013/435, Sch.1, para.4. Additional documents cannot be included in the computation unless accompanied by a written notice of additional evidence: *Sturdy*, summarised in Appendix J of the CCFG; *Gkampos* [2011] Costs L.R. 142 (pages of antecedent materials relating to the defendant); and *Ward* [2012] 3 Costs L.R. 605; but see *Qu* [2012] 3 Costs L.R. 599 (evidence served by prosecution during trial and on which they intended to rely to be included in page count, though not accompanied by formal notice of additional evidence (see CLW/12/26/12 for the suggestion that the costs judge arrived at the correct result, but not necessarily for the right reasons)). Where one or more notices of additional evidence have been served, a page count should include the contents of all such notices, unless all sides are agreed that service of a particular notice was an administrative error; and it is irrelevant when a notice was served, or whether it was requested by the defence or prosecution: *Taylor* [2005] 4 Costs L.R. 712 (notice served on day jury retired). A prosecution notice of intention to adduce bad character evidence does not fall within the term "any notice of additional evidence": *McCall* [2011] 5 Costs L.R. 914 (but for a critique of the reasoning, see CLW/11/40/5). Where the Crown have exhibited and served tapes of interview, and defence counsel considers that a transcript of the interview is necessary, the pages of transcript should be included in the computation: *Brazier*, summarised in Appendix J of the CCFG. Taxing officers have been directed to include the fullest transcript produced, together with the version in the transfer bundle (if shorter), and also to include any video evidence transcripts requested by the judge:, CCFG. Appendix D.3. Taxing officers have been directed to exclude title and separator pages: CCFG. Appendix D.4; and any additional edited versions of transcripts placed before a jury: CCFG. Appendix D.4. And nor should pages comprising admissions and a jury bundle consisting of, inter alia, an index and details of the defendants: *Wei* [2010] 5 Costs L.R. 846. No allowance is made for small or large typefaces or for line spacing. Unused material is also excluded. G-159

Whereas paragraph 1(3) of Schedule 2 to SI 2013/435 (G-73) lists the documents that may be included when calculating the "pages of prosecution evidence" for the purposes of determining a litigator's fee under the graduated fee scheme, the list is to be taken to be exhaustive, notwithstanding that it does not include documents which will have to be read in most cases or even referred to in court (such as the indictment, custody records, correspondence, crime reports, and unused material): *Tucker* [2009] 5 Costs L.R. 850.

In *Jalibaghodelehzi* [2014] 4 Costs L.R. 781, it was held that when deciding whether a documentary or pictorial exhibit fell within paragraph 1(2C) of Schedule 1 to the Criminal Defence Service (Funding) Order 2007 (SI 2007/1174) (see now the corresponding provision in paragraph 1(5) of Schedules 1 and 2 to SI 2013/435 (G-36, G-73)), such exhibits should be included if they required a similar degree of consideration to evidence served on paper. Thus, if thousands of pages of raw telephone data were served and the task of the defence lawyers was simply to see whether their client's mobile phone number appeared anywhere (a task more easily done by electronic search), it would be difficult to conclude that the pages should be treated as part of the page count. However, if the evidence served electronically was an important part of the prosecution case, it would be difficult to conclude that the pages should not be included in the page count.

A submission that *Jalibaghodelehzi* (above) was wrongly decided was rejected in *Napper* [2014]

Costs L.R. 947. In that case it was held that any documentary or pictorial exhibit served electronically is to be included in the page count where it previously existed in paper form. Where it had not previously existed in paper form, or it was impossible to determine whether it had previously existed in paper form, then determining officers are required to consider the nature of the documents and all the relevant circumstances, including the significance of the documents in the case as a whole. The court said that the task of a determining officer under paragraph 1(2C) of Schedule 1 to the 2007 order (above) was not merely to make a determination as to whether such evidence would in practice have been served in paper form prior to the amendments made by the Criminal Defence Service (Funding) (Amendment) Order 2012 (SI 2012/750). However, where the litigator and the advocate are one and the same person, this is a circumstance to be taken into account. It was stated that in such a case, if it is appropriate to include exhibits falling within paragraph (2C) in the page count for the purposes of calculating the litigator's fee, it will not be appropriate to include them again when calculating the fee payable under Schedule 1.

Jalibaghodelehzi and *Napper* (above) were approved and followed in *Dodd* [2014] Costs L.R. 1131; and the factual narrative revealed in *Sana* [2014] Costs L.R. 1143, suggests that, in that case at least, the Legal Aid Agency had accepted and applied the approach in *Jalibaghodelehzi* and *Napper*. In *Furniss* [2015] Costs L.R. 151, Crown Court at Nottingham, Haddon-Cave J (i) approved *Jalibaghodelehzi*, (ii) said that cell site, telephone, and similar material served by the prosecution in digital form must be included as pages of prosecution evidence for graduated fee purposes, irrespective of how important or central it is to the prosecution case (thus going further than the costs judges in *Jalibaghodelehzi*, *Napper* and *Dodd*), and (iii) opined that the page-count limit of 10,000 pages in the graduated fee scheme for advocates constituted an artificial cap on their remuneration irrespective of the work actually done, and that, whilst it was possible to divine a pragmatic reason for a rough-and-ready cap where the actual page count was not significantly above the maximum (say 20–30 per cent), where it vastly exceeded 10,000 pages, such a restriction was manifestly disproportionate and could not rationally have been intended to apply. However, it appears that no argument to the contrary was advanced (and certainly none on behalf of the Lord Chancellor), and it is submitted that his Lordship's remarks (which included gratuitous suggestions as to the computation of the page count in confiscation proceedings and as to costs against the Legal Aid Agency on an indemnity basis if advocates have to bring further appeals on these points to costs judges), made in the context of a Crown Court trial and wholly outside the legislative framework for the determination of legal aid fees, are of doubtful authoritative status (as to which, see the commentary in CLW/15/05/8).

It was held in *Thompson* [2015] 1 Costs L.R. 173 that *Furniss* (above) is binding on costs judges. However, it was further held that *Furniss* was only concerned with cases in which the representation order was granted before 1 April 2012 (the date on which the amendments to the Criminal Defence Service (Funding) Order 2007 (SI 2007/1174) effected by the Criminal Defence Service (Funding) (Amendment) Order 2012 (SI 2012/750), came into force), and that where a representation order was granted before that date (as in the instant case), costs judges had no discretion to include the material referred to in *Furniss* in the page count. In the instant appeal, the Lord Chancellor did not appear but made a written submission in which he pointed out that, on any view, *Furniss* did not apply to the case, and more generally, he took issue with the status of *Furniss*.

In *Manning*, unreported, 3 April 2015, Crown Court at Manchester (HH Judge Mansell QC), the judge found that *Furniss* was not only not binding on the Crown Court, but that the reasoning was flawed for the reasons given in the commentary in CLW/15/05/8. The judge further found that it is no part of the function of a trial judge to dictate to the prosecution how to serve their evidence or to direct them to make agreements with the defence so as to affect the calculation of defence graduated fees (or to dictate to the determining officer how fees are to be calculated under the Criminal Legal Aid (Remuneration) Regulations 2013 (SI 2013/435) (G-5 and following) in any given case).

In *Jagelo*, unreported, 6 January 2016, Costs Judge Rowley held that *Furniss* is not binding on costs judges, and that the provision for the graduated fee payable for a given case to be supplemented by a payment under the special preparation arrangements where the number of pages exceeded 10,000 was compatible with the right of a defendant, under Article 6(3)(c) of the ECHR (§ 16-72 in the main work), to receive representation that was adequately remunerated, such that there was no need to read down paragraph 2(7) of Schedule 2 (G-74) to remove or restrict the cap; the special preparation process is neither arbitrary nor irrational in principle.

The most authoritative pronouncement on this topic must now be taken to be the judgment of Holroyde J in *Lord Chancellor v S.V.S. Solicitors* [2017] EWHC 1045 (QB); [2017] 4 W.L.R. 87. His Lordship held (having considered considering *Furniss*, above, and *Lord Chancellor v Edward Hayes LLP* [2017] EWHC 138 (QB); [2017] Costs L.R. 147 (Nicola Davies J)), that, when calculating the number of pages of prosecution evidence in a case falling within the graduated fee scheme– **G-160**

(a) the starting point is that only served evidence and exhibits can be counted; material that is only disclosed as unused material cannot be counted;
(b) in this context, references to "served" evidence and exhibits must mean "served as part of the evidence and exhibits in the case"; evidence may be served even though the prosecution do not specifically rely on every part of it;
(c) where evidence and exhibits are formally served as part of the material on the basis of which a defendant is sent for trial, or under a subsequent notice of additional evidence, and are recorded as such in the relevant notices, there is no difficulty; however, paragraph 1(3) (of Sch.2) only says that the number of pages of prosecution evidence "includes" such material; it does not say that the number of pages "comprises only" such material; "service" may therefore be informal (though formal service is to be preferred); it would be in nobody's interests to penalise informality if, in sensibly and cooperatively progressing a trial, the advocates dispensed with the need for service of a notice of additional evidence; service on the court is not a necessary precondition of evidence counting as part of the pages of prosecution evidence;
(d) where the prosecution seek to rely on only part of the data recovered from a particular source, and therefore serve an exhibit that contains only some of the data, issues may arise as to whether all of the data should be exhibited; the resolution of such issues will depend on the circumstances of the particular case, and on whether the data that has been exhibited can only fairly be considered in the light of the totality of the data; if, exceptionally, the parties are unable to agree as to what should be served, the trial judge can be asked whether he is prepared to make a ruling in the exercise of his case management powers, and if he is, will have to consider all the circumstances of the case before deciding whether the prosecution should be directed either to exhibit the underlying material or to present their case without the extracted material on which they seek to rely;
(e) if (regrettably) the status of particular material has not been clearly resolved between the parties, or (exceptionally) by a ruling of the trial judge, then the determining officer (or, on appeal, the costs judge) will have to determine it in the light of all the information that is available (and would be entitled to regard the failure of the parties to reach any agreement, or to seek a ruling from the trial judge, as a powerful indication that the prosecution's initial view as to the status of the material was correct); if he is unable to conclude that material was in fact served, then it must be treated as unused material, even if it was important to the defence;
(f) if an exhibit is served in electronic form and in circumstances that come within paragraph 1(5), a determining officer or costs judge has discretion as to whether it is appropriate to include it in the pages of prosecution evidence; that is an important and valuable control mechanism that ensures that public funds are not expended inappropriately;
(g) if an exhibit is served in electronic form but the determining officer or costs judge considers it inappropriate to include it in the page count, a claim for special preparation may be made by the solicitors in the circumstances set out in paragraph 20 of Schedule 2 (G-76); and
(h) if material that has been disclosed as unused material has not in fact been served (even informally) as evidence or exhibits, and the determining officer has not concluded that it should have been served, then it cannot be included in the number of pages of prosecution evidence; in such circumstances, the discretion under paragraph 1(5) does not apply.

The decisions of the costs judges in *O'Cuneff* [2010] 3 Costs L.R. 476, *Burbidge* [2010] 4 Costs L.R. 639, and *Ibefune*, unreported, 24 June 2010, evidence a conflict as between them and the Legal Services Commission as to the weight to be given to the number of pages of prosecution evidence agreed between the parties and the Crown Court at the end of the case. The commission's stance of not accepting this figure without additional objective evidence has now, however, been fully vindicated by *Criminal Practice Direction I (General matters) 3B* (Appendix B-19). This inserts new requirements relating to the pagination and indexing of served evidence (as to which, **G-161** see § 4-344 in the main work). It was plainly no coincidence that, in doing so, the practice direction adopted the (then) definition of "pages of prosecution evidence" contained in the Criminal Defence Service (Funding) Order 2007 (SI 2007/1174). Compliance with the requirements of the new provisions by the prosecution will supply the commission (and costs judges) with an objective measure of the number of pages of prosecution evidence.

In *Greenwood* [2010] 2 Costs L.R. 268, it was held that whereas paragraph 13(2) of Schedule 2 to SI 2013/435 (G-84) provides that "where ...a case is transferred to a new litigator ... the fee payable to the original litigator and the new litigator is a percentage of the total fee, calculated in accordance with the table following this paragraph, as appropriate to the circumstances and timing of the ... transfer", and whereas the table provides that where a case is transferred prior to the plea and case management hearing the original litigator should receive 25 per cent of a cracked trial fee, in calculating that fee, the number of pages of prosecution evidence should be taken to be the number of such pages served on the court as at the date of transfer.

Images and photographs

G-162 See now paragraphs 1(2) to (5) of Schedules 1 and 2 to SI 2013/435. For authorities on the former provision, which will still apply where the representation order was granted before 1 April 2012, see *Rigelsford* [2006] 3 Costs L.R. 518, and *Austin* [2006] 5 Costs L.R. 857.

Fees for leading and junior counsel

G-163 Under SI 2013/435, fees payable to Queen's Counsel, leading juniors and led juniors are not directly related, and are calculated from the relevant tables: see, for example, the tables following paragraphs 5 and 8 of Schedule 1. Where two or more led juniors are instructed in the same case, each is paid as if they were the sole junior: Sch.1, para.28.

G-164 In *Newport* [2009] 6 Costs L.R. 983, where two juniors appeared for the defendant when the representation order authorised instruction of junior counsel and Queen's Counsel, it was held that whilst a strict approach would lead to the conclusion that the leading junior was entitled to no payment, such an outcome would be unjust. Justice demanded that some payment should be made, especially given that the representation order had contemplated payment of two counsel. However, it was said that payment should be at the rate applicable to a leading junior. As to this case, see also G-224.

Advocates instructed for limited purposes

G-165 Advocates retained for a limited purpose are remunerated according to the specific provisions of SI 2013/435. The limited purposes are:

(a) the cross-examination of witnesses under the YJCEA 1999, s.38, which is remunerated as if for trial, save that the daily attendance fee is calculated by reference to the number of days the advocate actually attended court, instead of the number of days of the trial itself: SI 2013/435, Sch.1, para.32;
(b) the provision of written or oral advice: see G-179;
(c) mitigation of sentence on indictment, which is remunerated as for a sentencing hearing together with a fee based on the fixed hourly special preparation rate according to the "reasonable number of hours" taken: SI 2013/435, Sch.1, para.34(1); and an advocate who is discontented with the fee paid may seek a redetermination: para.34(2).

Instructed and substitute advocates

G-166 An instructed advocate is the first advocate instructed in the case who has primary responsibility for the case, or, where a representation order provides for more than one advocate, it means both the first advocate instructed who has primary responsibility for those aspects of a case undertaken by a leading advocate and the first advocate instructed who has primary responsibility for those aspects of a case undertaken by a led advocate: SI 2013/435, reg.2(1).

An instructed advocated remains an instructed advocate at all times, although provision is made for the instructed advocate to be changed, where, for example, he is unable to conduct the trial because of a clash of commitments, is dismissed by the client, or professionally embarrassed: see Sch.1, para.25(10). If the instructed advocate cannot attend a preliminary hearing, and sends a substitute advocate, he nevertheless remains responsible both for the conduct of the case and the ultimate payment of the substitute advocate.

Instructed advocates appointed before the pleas and directions hearing must in writing inform the court of their appointment as soon as they are appointed, otherwise the advocate who attends the pleas and directions hearing will be deemed to be the instructed advocate. If no advocate attends the plea and directions hearing, the advocate who attends the next hearing will be deemed to be and will be recorded by the court as the instructed advocate: see Sch.1, para.25(1)-(6). Where the representation order is amended after a plea and case management hearing to include a second advocate, each advocate must notify the court in writing whether they are the led or leading advocate. Where no additional instructed advocate is notified to the court in writing within seven days of the plea and case management hearing, the advocate to appear at the next hearing is deemed to be the instructed advocate and the court will record in writing whether he is the leading instructed advocate or the led instructed advocate, as appropriate to the circumstances of the case., para.25(7).

Sentencing hearings in cases on indictment

Any person appearing at a sentencing hearing in a case on indictment is entitled to a fixed fee: SI 2013/435, Sch.1, para.15. **G-167**

A contested application for an anti-social behaviour order at a sentencing hearing does not attract a separate or additional fee: *Brinkworth* [2006] 3 Costs L.R. 512.

Under SI 2013/435, an advocate instructed solely for the purpose of mitigation shall be paid the fee payable under paragraph 15 together with a fee calculated by reference to the reasonable number of hours of preparation for that appearance multiplied by the hourly rate set out in the table following paragraph 24 which is appropriate to the category of trial advocate: Sch.1, para.34(1). The advocate may apply for redetermination of such fee and shall supply such information and documents as may be required by the appropriate officer as proof of the number of hours of preparation: Sch.1, para.34(2).

Fitness hearings

A fitness hearing is a hearing to determine whether a defendant is fit to plead or stand trial: SI 2013/435, Sch.1, para.31. If there is a trial on indictment at any time thereafter, the length of the fitness hearing shall be included in determining the length of the trial: para.31(a). Where a person pleads guilty at any time after a fitness hearing is held, the advocate may elect to be paid either as if the fitness hearing was a trial or for the guilty plea: Sch.1, para.31(c). Where a person is found to be unfit, the trial advocate may elect to treat the fitness hearing either as a trial or as a cracked trial: Sch.1, para.31(b). **G-168**

Cross-examination of vulnerable witnesses

Where an advocate is retained solely for the purpose of cross-examining a vulnerable witness under section 38 of the YJCEA 1999, the graduated fee shall be assessed as though the matter was a trial, with the length of trial uplift and refresher calculated by reference to the number of days the advocate attended court: SI 2013/435, Sch.1, para.32. **G-169**

Newton hearings

Where a *Newton* hearing takes place following a trial on indictment the provisions relating to cracked trials, guilty pleas and sentencing hearings do not apply. The hearing is remunerated as for a contested trial. For the purposes of computation, the length of the *Newton* hearing is added to the main hearing: SI 2013/435, Sch.1, para.2(8). Thus the main hearing starts on the day the plea is entered, even if this occurred during a pleas and directions hearing: *Gemeskel.* summarised in Appendix J of the CCFG. The advocate who attended the main hearing should claim the whole fee and remunerate the other advocate (if any) who attended the *Newton* hearing: CCFG: section 2.2.4 **G-170**

Where a *Newton* hearing does not take place because the basis of plea was subsequently agreed, the case reverts to a guilty plea or cracked trial as appropriate: Appendix J, CCFG. If the hearing is aborted, the usual rules apply: see G-181, and *Ayres* [2002] 2 Costs L.R. 330.

In *Newton*, the Court of Appeal clearly envisaged circumstances in which a sentencing judge could reach a conclusion without hearing evidence. However, the regulations define a *Newton* hearing as one at which evidence is heard for the purpose of determining the sentence of a convicted person in accordance with the *Newton* principles. Accordingly, a *Newton* hearing at which no evidence is called can only be remunerated by a standard appearance fee as it is not a *Newton* hearing for the purposes of the regulations: *Hunter-Brown summarised in Appendix J of the CCFG guidance document (see G-3)* Appendix J, CCFG

Evidence given by a defendant, who had already pleaded guilty, in the trial of a co-defendant (with cross-examination on his basis of plea), and which was referred to by the judge when giving reasons for rejecting his basis of plea when he later passed sentence, was not a *Newton* hearing within sub-paragraph 1(1) of Schedule 2 to SI 2013/435 (G-36); the evidence had not been given for the purpose of determining sentence as required by that provision: *Hunt* [2016] 2 Costs L.R. 429.

Where a *Newton* hearing is held on a committal for sentence, the only fee payable under Schedule 1 to SI 2013/435 is the fixed fee payable for a committal for sentence: *Holden* [2010] 5 Costs L.R. 851.

Adverse judicial comment and reduction of graduated or fixed fees

G-171 Where a trial judge makes adverse observations concerning an advocate's conduct of a graduated or fixed fee case, the appropriate authority may reduce the fee by such proportion as it "considers reasonable", having first given the advocate the opportunity to make representations about the extent of the reduction: SI 2013/435, reg.26. See also G-30.

(3) Additional fees

Confiscation proceedings

G-172 Hearings under section 2 of the DTA 1994, section 71 of the CJA 1988 or Part 2 of the PCA 2002 are excluded from the length computation of the main hearing and are remunerated separately as work for which a daily or half-daily fee is payable: SI 2013/435, Sch.1, para.14(1) and (2). Entitlement to the daily fee arises where the hearing begins before but ends after the luncheon adjournment; a half-daily fee is paid where the hearing ends before or begins after the luncheon adjournment: SI 2013/435, Sch.1, para.14(2). The appropriate rates are set out in the table following paragraph 14(2).

Abuse of process, disclosure and witness summonses' etc.

G-173 Applications relating to abuse of process, disclosure or witness summonses heard before the main hearing are paid at the daily rates set out in the table following paragraph 24: SI 2013/435, Sch.1, para.13(2). As to remuneration for such applications where they take place as part of the main hearing, see G-148. A hearing merely relating to the failure of the prosecution to comply with an earlier disclosure order attracts only a standard appearance fee: CCFG, Paragraph 2.13.4

In respect of representation orders granted on or after 30 April 2007, these provisions were extended to include applications relating to the admissibility of evidence, and an unsuccessful application to withdraw a guilty plea made by an advocate other than the advocate who appeared at the hearing where the plea was tendered: see now SI 2013/435, Sch.1, para.13(1)(d) and (e).

Conferences and views

G-174 The first three pre-trial conferences or views are not separately remunerated; the fees are deemed to be included in the basic fee: Sch.1, para.19(2). Thereafter, the permitted number of further conferences or views (each not exceeding two hours) is as follows:

1 conference	trials of more than 20 but less than 26 days
2 conferences	trials of more than 25 days but less than 36 days
3 conferences	trials of more than 35 days

The number of further conferences allowed in respect of cracked trials is similar, save that the anticipated length of trial is that accepted by the court at the plea and case management hearing (save that, on a literal reading of the legislation, three conferences will only be paid for where it was accepted that the trial would last not more than 40 days): Sch.1, para.19(3).

G-175 Conferences include conferences with expert witnesses: SI 2013/435, Sch.1, para.19(1)(a). Travel expenses and the time taken in travelling, including time taken to travel to a conference with a defendant who could not reasonably be expected to attend counsel's chambers, are remunerated at the specified hourly rate: Sch.1, para.19(5). Where such fees are allowed, reasonable travelling expenses may also be claimed: para.19(4). The local bar rule has no application to such fees: *Carlyle* [2002] 1 Costs L.R. 192.

Special preparation

Special preparation is now only available in respect of novel points of law, not very unusual points of law or very unusual or novel factual issues, where the representation order was issued after 1 April 2018: SI 2018/220. This section has been preserved in full for cases dealing with orders prior to that date. Special preparation is preparation substantially in excess of the amount normally done for cases of the type in question and undertaken because the case involves "a very unusual or novel point of law or factual issue": SI 2013/435, Sch.1, para.17(1)(a). "Very" qualifies both "unusual" and "novel" and the phrase "very unusual or novel" qualifies both the expressions "point of law" and "factual issue": *Meeke and Taylor v Secretary of State for Constitutional Affairs* [2006] Costs L.R. 1, QBD (David Clarke J). Remuneration is calculated at an hourly rate for "the number of hours preparation in excess of the amount the appropriate officer considers reasonable for cases of the same type": SI 2013/435, Sch.1, para.17(3)(a); and with no enhancement under paragraph 29 of Schedule 2: *Lord Chancellor v McLarty & Co. Solicitors* [2012] Costs L.R. 190, QBD (Burnett J). G-176

What falls to be compensated is the extra work caused by the unusual or novel point by comparison with the sort of case involved without the unusual or novel point; as the term is used in relation to the quantification of fees, "type" in this context should be defined as an indication of weight; but the exercise does not include any consideration of the reasonableness of the time claimed; thus, once the determining officer has resolved that the case qualifies for a special preparation fee, he must assess the number of hours worked in excess of the norm and compensate for those hours at the prescribed hourly rate: *Goodwin* [2008] 3 Costs L.R. 497.

Goodwin, above, was considered in *Kholi* [2010] 6 Costs L.R. 982, in which it was held that under paragraph 52(i) of the Guidance Manual for the CPS Graduated Fee Scheme (which is in materially identical terms to para.17(1)(a) of Sch.1 to SI 2013/435 (G-53)), it is only those hours of work attributable to the unusual or novel point of law or factual issue which was involved, which fall to be remunerated as special preparation; it is not the case that all time spent by the advocate in preparation over and above the norm for the type of case should be so remunerated.

The concept of "normal preparation" done for a case of the same type is wholly artificial. Other than in routine cases of burglary and theft, in virtually all other crimes in the criminal calendar, the circumstances vary infinitely: *Briers* [2005] Costs L.R. 146. The test is "What is the normal preparation for this offence?" not "What is the normal preparation for a case exhibiting these particular facts": *Briers*, above; *Ward-Allen* [2005] 4 Costs L.R. 745.

It is for counsel to differentiate between what he considers to be the normal preparation for a case of that type and the actual preparation that he has carried out: *Briers*, above; *Marandola* [2006] 1 Costs L.R. 184.

Very unusual or novel points of law have an obvious meaning, namely a point of law which either has never been raised or decided (novel) or which is outwith the usual professional experience (very unusual): *Ward-Allen*, above. Some further assistance can be found in *Perry v Lord Chancellor*, *The Times*, 26 May 1994, although it should be noted that that case was not concerned with these regulations.

Very unusual or novel factual issues have a similar meaning, namely a factual issue which either has never been raised or which is outwith the usual professional experience: *Ward-Allen*, above. Such issues might cover extremely rare medical conditions, such as Munchausen's Syndrome by Proxy or "pubic symphysitis dysfunction", the exceptional, if not unique, nature of which was held in *Bishop* [2008] 5 Costs L.R. 808, to justify a special preparation fee where it had contributed to prosecution material of over 600 pages (not served as part of the page count); novel issues might, for example have included DNA fingerprinting when it was introduced, but it would not qualify now. A case involving "shaken baby syndrome" does not necessarily attract a special preparation fee, unless there are additional medical complications: *Khair* [2005] 3 Costs L.R. 542. A special preparation fee was allowed in *Thompson* [2006] 4 Costs L.R. 668 where the defendant was accused of murdering her husband 10 years earlier. Counsel had to consider not only pathology and toxicology reports, but also a psychiatric profile on the husband prepared by a psychiatrist who had never met him, and issues arising in diabetology and physiology. Transcripts of the original coroner's inquest and the defendant's previous trials for theft and attempted murder of another husband were also served.

The novelty of the bad character provisions of the CJA 2003 did not provide grounds for claiming a special preparation fee; the criminal law is constantly changing: *Christie* [2010] 4 Costs L.R. 634.

A special preparation fee would be reasonable where counsel had to check a sample of over 33,000 original photographs of which the prosecution had only copied a representative fraction for use at trial: *Rigelsford* [2006] 3 Costs L.R. 518; and see G-162. But the mere fact that preparation properly undertaken for a complex three-week rape trial was "wasted" because the defendant decided to plead guilty during the prosecution opening did not justify a special preparation fee: *Meeke and Taylor v Secretary of State for Constitutional Affairs*, above.

A large quantity of unused material does not of itself give rise to a novel or unusual factual issue even where it is accepted that detailed examination of the material was necessary: *Lawrence* [2007] Costs L.R. 138; and even where the trial judge has extended a representation order to allow two juniors to peruse such material: *Dhaliwal* [2004] Costs L.R. 689. Such work is not remunerated under the graduated fee scheme or indeed at all. Nor does the mere failure of the scheme to accommodate unused material amount to a breach of the principle of equality of arms: *Marandola*, above.

An advocate can also claim a special preparation fee where the prosecution evidence exceeds 10,000 pages and the appropriate officer considers that it is reasonable to make a payment in excess of the graduated fee which would otherwise be payable; the fee is calculated by reference to the number of hours which the appropriate officer considers reasonable to read the excess pages, using the current hourly fee rate: SI 2013/435, Sch.1, para.17(1)(b), (2) and (3)(b); and Sch.2, para.20(1)(b). As to this particular provision, see *Furniss* and *Jagelo*, G-159.

An advocate making a claim for special preparation should provide the Legal Aid Agency with dates, times and descriptions of the work completed, and the page count of any material considered, and any documents produced as a result of the special preparation should be annexed to the claim form, and the claim should relate each item of special preparation to the very unusual or novel point of law or fact that gave rise to the need for special preparation in the first place: *French* [2014] 4 Costs L.R. 786.

An advocate's failure to keep a contemporaneous work log may result in rejection of a claim for a special preparation fee: *Dunne* [2013] Costs L.R. 1031 (considering the corresponding provision in the Criminal Defence Service (Funding) Order 2007 (SI 2007/1174).

Evidence served electronically: LGFS and cases prior to 1 April 2018

G-177 A special preparation fee may also be claimed where a documentary or pictorial exhibit, which has never existed in paper form, is served by the prosecution in electronic form, and the appropriate officer does not consider it appropriate to include it in the pages of prosecution evidence; and such fee may be paid if the appropriate officer considers it reasonable to make a payment in excess of the fee otherwise payable under the graduated fee scheme, with the amount of the payment depending on the number of hours which the appropriate officer considers reasonable to view the exhibit: see Sch.1, para.17(1)(c) and (2), and Sch.2, para.20(1)(a) and (2). However, by virtue of the amendments effected by SI 2018/220 (G-1a), special preparation fees are no longer available for electronically served evidence in relation to advocates fees payable under a representation order issued on or after 1 April 2018. The drafting of these provisions in the two schedules is slightly different, but it is submitted that the intent is the same. As to the drafting, this - taken at face value - gives the appropriate officer a discretion whether to make a payment even where he considers it reasonable to do so. It is submitted, however, that the legislation is unlikely to be so construed: if the appropriate officer considers it reasonable to make a payment, then it is likely to be held that he should do so. The revised wording of these provisions (introduced by the Criminal Defence Service (Funding) (Amendment) Order 2001 (SI 2012/750)) was doubtless intended to avoid the difficulties caused by the former wording and which gave rise to a series of decisions, such as *Rigelsford* [2006] 3 Costs L.R. 518, *Austin* [2006] 5 Costs L.R. 857, *Lord Chancellor v Michael J. Reed Ltd* [2009] EWHC 2981 (QB); [2010] Costs 1 L.R. 72, QBD (Penry-Davey J), *Lord Chancellor v McLarty & Co. Solicitors* [2011] EWHC 3182 (QB); [2012] 1 Costs L.R. 190 (Burnett J), and *Jones* [2010] 3 Costs L.R. 469. For details of these authorities, which will still have application to cases in which a representation order was granted before 1 April 2012, see previous supplements.

Lord Chancellor v Michael J. Reed Ltd (above) was followed in *Osoteko* [2014] 1 Costs L.R. 190, but the costs judge certified a point of principle of general importance, viz. whether that case had created too narrow a definition of pages of prosecution evidence. The appeal to the High Court (see *Maclaverty Cooper Atkins v Lord Chancellor* [2014] EWHC 1387 (QB); [2014] 4 Costs L.R. 629 (Akenhead J)) was dismissed, the court approving and following *Lord Chancellor v Michael J. Reed Ltd.*

Listening to or viewing tapes

There is now no provision for any separate payment for listening to or viewing tapes. These are now treated as being rolled up within the whole of the graduated fee. **G-178**

Provision of written or oral advice

Any advocate instructed solely to provide written or oral advice shall be paid a fee calculated from the reasonable number of hours of preparation for that advice using the appropriate hourly rate in the table following paragraph 24 of Schedule 1 to SI 2013/435: see Sch.1, para.33(1). The advocate may apply for re-determination of such fee under regulation 28, and he shall supply such information and documents as may be required by the appropriate officer as proof of the number of hours of preparation: Sch.1, para.33(2). **G-179**

As to whether a solicitor may properly instruct counsel other than counsel who appeared at trial to advise on the question of appeal where trial counsel has advised in the negative, see *Umezie*, § 7-165 in the main work.

Umezie was considered in *Bromige* [2011] Costs L.R. 145, in which it was held that where solicitors, on receipt of trial counsel's negative advice as to the prospects of a successful appeal against sentence, instructed fresh counsel to advise on the question, trial counsel's negative advice (whether written or oral) did not terminate the representation order; paragraph A1-2 of the Guide to Commencing Proceedings in the Court of Appeal (Criminal Division) (Appendix J-4) did not preclude payment of a fee for subsequent advice given by fresh counsel in relation to the appeal, because that paragraph was only concerned with the amendment of representation orders, and no amendment to the representation order granted by the magistrates' court was necessary to instruct fresh counsel to advise; however, fresh counsel's claim for a fee for his advice could only fall within paragraph 6 of Schedule 3 to SI 2013/435 (G-105), which provides, that upon the determination of an advocate's fees in proceedings in the Court of Appeal, "the appropriate officer must consider the claim ... and must allow such work as appears to him to have been reasonably done"; as a general principle it will not be reasonable to obtain advice on a point that has already been the subject of advice, with the obvious exceptions to this principle being if the initial advice is incompetent or ambiguous, or if there is a change in circumstances or if new evidence has come to light; the reason given in this case for seeking further advice, viz. that the solicitors were not convinced as to the correctness of the negative oral advice from trial counsel, was not sufficient; therefore the work done by fresh counsel was not reasonably done for the purposes of paragraph 6 because no good reason had been shown for instructing him to give advice on a point that had already been the subject of advice. For the submission that the costs judge's reliance on paragraph 6 of Schedule 3 is unsustainable, see CLW/11/08/45.

(4) Acting for more than one defendant, or in more than one "case"

The definition of "case" in paragraph 1(1) of Schedule 2 (G-73) could not possibly lead to the conclusion that if a litigator represents more than one defendant charged and tried on the same indictment that litigator is then entitled to be paid on the basis that there are as many cases as there are defendants: *Lord Chancellor v Eddowes Perry and Osbourne Ltd* [2011] Costs L.R. 498, QBD (Spencer J). As to this case, see also G-226. **G-180**

An uplift of one-fifth for each additional defendant represented may only be claimed where the regulations so provide: SI 2013/435, Sch.1, para.27(2). Where an advocate acts for more than one defendant, the advocate must select the case on which remuneration is to be based (the principal case). Claims for such uplifts may be made for pleas and directions hearings, some aborted hearings, main hearings, appeals against conviction, committals for sentence, proceedings for a breach of a Crown Court order, disclosure, abuse and witness summons hearings, and confiscation proceedings: SI 2013/435, Sch.1, para.27(4). But no uplifts for these hearings, with the exception of confiscation proceedings, are payable in cases that were committed to the Crown Court on the election of the defendant, where the magistrates' court had determined that the case was suitable for summary trial: para.27(3). In respect of a trial, the uplift is limited to one-fifth of the basic fee and not the basic fee enhanced by reference to the prosecution evidence, witnesses and length of trial uplift: para.27(2)(b), i.e. where the main hearing in each case was heard concurrently: *Fletcher*, CCFG paragraph 2.27.2.

The above provisions also apply where the advocate conducts two or more cases concurrently: SI 2013/435, Sch.1, para.27(2). Proceedings arising out of a single notice of appeal against conviction or sentence, or single committal for sentence, constitute a separate "case": para.1(1) of Schedule 1 to SI 2013/435. As a case means proceedings on one or more counts of a single indictment, it is submitted that two trials arising from a severed indictment give rise to two separate graduated fees, as the trials are not heard concurrently.

In *Fury* [2011] 5 Costs L.R. 919, it was said that if a hearing deals with one case then another, independently of each other, it will be hearing them consecutively; hearings will be concurrent only if they are combined or conjoined or somehow interlinked; this will be so where the main hearings of a number of cases against the same defendant are listed together and the defendant either pleads guilty or is to be sentenced in all of the cases; the cases will impact on each other either as to the directions that are given for sentencing or as to the sentences that are imposed; they will not be considered independently of each other. For criticism of the actual decision in this case (cases were not heard concurrently where, as part of an agreed package, defendant pleaded guilty to one indictment and prosecution offered no evidence on the other, all counts having originally been in the same indictment), see CLW/11/40/3.

In *Sturmer and Lewis* [2009] 2 Costs L.R. 364, it was said that the combined effect of paragraph 15 and the table in paragraph 19 of Schedule 2 to SI 2013/435 (G-86, G-89) is that where a litigator is "instructed in ... a sentencing hearing following a committal for sentence to the Crown Court", the "fee payable ... is that set out in the table" (para.15), i.e. "£210.64" per proceedings (the table). "Proceedings" can involve more than one defendant and, if there is only one "proceedings", only one fee will be payable, however many defendants are represented by the litigator.

(5) Abortive hearings

G-181 The payment of fixed fees for abortive hearings is limited to ineffective trials: see Sch.1, para.16. As to this, see *Budai*, G-148.

(6) Wasted preparation

G-182 Wasted preparation occurs where an advocate does not represent his client because of (a) a clash of listings and the advocate has been unable to secure a change of date for either hearing; or (b) a fixture for a main hearing is altered by the court despite the advocate's objection; or (c) the advocate withdraws with leave of the court because of professional embarrassment; or (d) the advocate is dismissed by the client; or (e) the advocate is obliged to undertake judicial or other public duties: SI 2013/435, Sch.1, para.18(1). The hourly fee may be claimed only where eight or more hours of preparation have been undertaken, and (a) the trial lasted for five days or more, or (b) in the case of a cracked trial, there are more than 150 pages of prosecution evidence: SI 2013/435, Sch.1, para.18(2). The wasted preparation fee is calculated by reference to the number of hours of preparation reasonably carried out by the advocate, who must supply such information and documents in support of the claim as may be required: SI 2013/435, Sch.1, para.18(3) and (5).

The requirements of paragraph 18(1) were satisfied where, following the vacation of the trial date by the trial judge and his proposal of a new date, counsel had written objecting to the new date (on the grounds that he had booked and paid for a holiday abroad that started within 10 days of the new date), but where, despite that objection, the trial had gone ahead on the proposed date, with the result that counsel had had to return the brief: *Ghaffar* [2009] Costs L.R. 980. The fact that counsel's objection was to the new date, and not to the vacation of the original fixture, was not a valid ground for refusing a wasted preparation fee in respect of the substantial preparation done by counsel prior to the vacation of the original fixture. Changing a fixture is a process and an objection to part of that process is therefore an objection to the change. There was nothing in paragraph 18(1)(b) that restricted it to counsel's professional commitments.

(7) Appeals, pleas before venue, committals and other fees

Graduated fixed fees are also payable in respect of committals for sentence (which include plea before venue cases), appeals from magistrates' courts and breach of Crown Court orders: SI 2013/435, Sch.1, para.20; noting briefs, para.23; bail and other applications, and mentions when not forming part of a main hearing or other hearing for which a fixed fee is provided: para.20(3). The appropriate rate is that listed in the table following paragraph 24. After the Crown Court is seized of a case, any bail applications, or executions of bench warrants made in a magistrates' court are remunerated as if made in the Crown Court: *Bailey*, CCFG Appendix J. As to trials of Bail Act 1976 offences, see G-151. **G-183**

(8) Contempt proceedings

Remuneration for proceedings for contempt in the face of the court is fixed at discrete daily rates: SI 2013/435, reg.11, and Sch.1, para.21. The fees are fixed and there is no discretion to allow ex post facto payment, however regrettable and unfair the result may be: *Russell* [2006] 5 Costs L.R. 841. Such payments do not fall within the graduated fee scheme and, therefore, such hearings do not form part of the main hearing or the sentencing hearing. **G-184**

(9) Travel expenses

Travel and hotel expenses may be claimed subject to the usual 40 kilometre local bar rule: SI 2013/435, Sch.1, para.29 (see generally G-209). Expenses should not be paid in respect of conferences for which advocates are not entitled to be remunerated, unless the conference was abortive due to circumstances beyond the advocate's control: *Pickett*, [2004] 3 Costs L.R. 529. **G-185**

(10) Table of offences: LGFS

The effect of the table of offences at the end of Schedule 2 to SI 2013/435 (as amended by the Protection of Freedoms Act 2012 (Consequential Amendments) Order 2013 (SI 2013/862) and moved by SI 2018/220 (G-1a)) is set out in the following paragraphs. Offences are divided into those below £30,000, those where the value is £30,000 or more, but less than £100,000, and those where the value involved is £100,000 or more. As to the method of calculation for the purposes of determining value, see G-144. As to conspiracy, incitement and attempt, see G-143. It should be noted that there are various errors in the table: for example, it refers to section 39 (rather than section 139) of the CJA 1988 (this has been corrected below) and it refers to various measures that have been repealed and replaced, including the Post Office Act 1953, the Merchant Shipping Act 1970 and the Air Navigation Order 2005 (SI 2005/1970)). **G-186**

An "armed robbery" (see the Theft Act 1968 entries) arises where the offender was armed with a firearm or imitation firearm, or was thought by the victim to have been so armed, or was armed with an offensive weapon: *Stables* [2000] 1 WLUK 69.

Where a judge proposes to try an offence under the Bail Act 1976, s.6, in respect of a defendant who is first brought up before him for non-attendance, then there is a trial or guilty plea under the graduated fee scheme: *Shaw* [2005] 2 Costs L.R. 326.

As several statutes are listed under more than one class, the following is a list of the statutes and orders featured in the table, with the classes in which they appear— **G-187**

Air Navigation Order 2005 (SI 2005/1970)	H
Aviation Security Act 1982	B
Bail Act 1976	H
Bribery Act 2010	I
Child Abduction Act 1984	C
Children and Young Persons Act 1933	B, J

Cremation Act 1902	I
Crime and Disorder Act 1998	B, C, H
Criminal Damage Act 1971	B, C
Criminal Justice Act 1961	C
Criminal Justice Act 1967	I
Criminal Justice Act 1988	H
Criminal Justice Act 1991	B
Criminal Justice (International Co-operation) Act 1990	B
Criminal Justice (Terrorism and Conspiracy) Act 1998	I
Criminal Justice and Public Order Act 1994	I
Criminal Law Act 1967	I
Criminal Law Act 1977	C
Customs and Excise Management Act 1979	B, C, F, G, H, K
Dangerous Dogs Act 1991	C
Disorderly Houses Act 1751	H
Domestic Violence, Crime and Victims Act 2004	B
Drug Trafficking Act 1994	B, I
Drug Trafficking Offences Act 1986	C
European Communities Act 1972	I
Explosive Substances Act 1883	A, B
Firearms Act 1968	B, C
Firearms (Amendment) Act 1988	C
Forgery Act 1861	F, I
Forgery and Counterfeiting Act 1981	F, G, K
Fraud Act 2006	F, G, K
Hallmarking Act 1973	F, G, K
Identity Cards Act 2006	F
Immigration Act 1971	C
Indecency with Children Act 1960	J
Indecent Displays (Control) Act 1981	H
Infant Life (Preservation) Act 1929	A
Infanticide Act 1938	A
Insolvency Act 1986	G
Magistrates' Courts Act 1980	I
Malicious Damage Act 1861	H
Mental Health Act 1959	J
Mental Health Act 1983	D
Merchant Shipping Act 1970	H
Misuse of Drugs Act 1971	B, C, H
Nuclear Material (Offences) Act 1983	B
Obscene Publications Act 1959	H
Offences against the Person Act 1861	A, B, C, H
Perjury Act 1911	I
Post Office Act 1953	H
Prevention of Corruption Act 1906	I
Prevention of Crime Act 1953	H
Prison Act 1952	C
Prison Security Act 1992	B

Proceeds of Crime Act 2002	B
Prohibition of Female Circumcision Act 1985	C
Protection from Eviction Act 1977	H
Protection from Harassment Act 1997	H
Protection of Children Act 1978	J
Public Bodies Corrupt Practices Act 1889	I
Public Order Act 1986	B, C, H
Public Passenger Vehicles Act 1981	H
Road Traffic Act 1960	H
Road Traffic Act 1988	B, H
Road Traffic Regulation Act 1984	H
Sexual Offences Act 1956	D, H, J
Sexual Offences Act 1967	D, H
Sexual Offences Act 2003	D, J
Sexual Offences (Amendment) Act 2000	D
Stamp Duties Management Act 1891	F, G, K
Submarine Telegraph Act 1885	C
Suicide Act 1961	B
Taking of Hostages Act 1982	B
Terrorism Act 2000	B, C
Theatres Act 1968	H
Theft Act 1968	B, C, E, F, G, H, K
Theft Act 1978	F, G, H, K
Trade Descriptions Act 1968	H, I
Treason Act 1842	C
Value Added Tax Act 1994	F, G, K
Vehicle Excise and Registration Act 1994	H

Class A: homicide and related grave offences

(i) Common law offences
Murder and manslaughter **G-188**

(ii) Offences created by primary or secondary legislation
Those contrary to the following provisions:
Explosive Substances Act 1883, ss.2 and 3;
Infant Life (Preservation) Act 1929, s.1(1);
Infanticide Act 1938, s.1(1);
Offences against the Person Act 1861, s.4.

Class B: offences involving serious violence or damage, and serious drugs offences

(i) Common law offences
Kidnapping and false imprisonment **G-189**

(ii) Offences created by primary or secondary legislation
Those contrary to the following provisions:
Aviation Security Act 1982, s.2(1)(b);
Crime and Disorder Act 1998, s.30(1);
Children and Young Persons Act 1933, s.1;
Criminal Damage Act 1971, s.1(2) and (where the value exceeds £30,000) s.1(3);
Criminal Justice Act 1991, s.90;
Criminal Justice (International Co-operation) Act 1990, ss.12 and 18;
Customs and Excise Management Act 1979, s.50 (Class A or B drugs), s.85, s.170(2)(b) or (c) (in relation to Class A or B drugs);

Domestic Violence, Crime and Victims Act 2004, s.5;
Drug Trafficking Act 1994, ss.49, 50, 51, 52 and 53;
Explosive Substances Act 1883, s.4(1);
Firearms Act 1968, ss.5, 16, 17 and 18;
Misuse of Drugs Act 1971, s.4 (Class A or B drug), s.5(3) (Class A or B drug), ss.6, 8, 9, 12 and 13;
Nuclear Material (Offences) Act 1983, s.2;
Offences against the Person Act 1861, ss.16, 17, 18, 21, 22, 23, 28, 29, 30, 32, 33, 34 and 58;
Prison Security Act 1992, s.1;
Proceeds of Crime Act 2002, ss.327, 328, 329, 330, 331, 332, 333, 339(1A);
Public Order Act 1986, ss.1, 2 and 38;
Road Traffic Act 1988, ss.1, 3A and 22A;
Suicide Act 1961, s.2;
Taking of Hostages Act 1982, s.1;
Terrorism Act 2000, ss.11, 12, 13, 15, 16, 17, 18, 39, 54, 56, 57, 58 and 59;
Theft Act 1968, s.8(1) (if "armed"), s.8(2) (if "with weapon"), s.10, s.12A (if resulting in death) and 21.

Class C: lesser offences involving violence or damage, and less serious drugs offences

(i) Common law offences

G-190 Permitting an escape, rescue, breach of prison and escaping from lawful custody without force

(ii) Offences created by primary or secondary legislation

Those contrary to the following provisions:
Child Abduction Act 1984, ss.1 and 2;
Crime and Disorder Act 1998, ss.29(1) and 30(1);
Criminal Damage Act 1971, s.1(1) and, where the offence does not also fall within section 1(2) and where the value of the damage is less than £30,000, s.1(3), s.2 and s.3;
Criminal Justice Act 1961, s.22;
Criminal Law Act 1977, s.51;
Customs and Excise Management Act 1979, s.50 (in relation to Class C drugs), s.68A(1) and (2), s.86, s.170(2)(b), (c) (in relation to Class C drugs);
Dangerous Dogs Act 1991, s.3;
Drug Trafficking Offences Act 1986, ss.26B and 26C;
Firearms Act 1968, ss.1, 2, 3, 4, 19, 20, 21(4), 21(5) and 42;
Firearms (Amendment) Act 1988, s.6(1);
Immigration Act 1971, s.25;
Misuse of Drugs Act 1971, s.4 (Class C drug), s.5(2) (Class A drug), s.5(3) (Class C drug);
Offences against the Person Act 1861, ss.20, 24, 26, 27, 31, 37, 47, 59, 60 and 64;
Prison Act 1952, s.39;
Prohibition of Female Circumcision Act 1985, s.1;
Public Order Act 1986, ss.18 to 23;
Submarine Telegraph Act 1885, s.3;
Terrorism Act 2000, s.19;
Theft Act 1968, s.8(1) (other than when "armed");
Treason Act 1842, s.2.

Class D: sexual offences and offences against children

Offences created by primary or secondary legislation

G-191 Those contrary to the following provisions:
Criminal Law Act 1977, s.54;
Mental Health Act 1983, s.127;
Sexual Offences Act 1956, s.4, s.9, s.10 (other than by man with girl under 13), s.11, s.13 (between male aged 21 or over and male under 16), ss.14, 15, 19, 21, 23, 27, 29, 30 and 31;
Sexual Offences Act 1967, s.5;
Sexual Offences Act 2003, s.3, s.4 (without penetration), ss.11 to 13, 15 to 19, 32, 33, 36, 37, 40, 41, 52, 53, 61 to 67, 69 and 70;

Sexual Offences (Amendment) Act 2000, s.3.

Class E: burglary, etc.

Offences created by primary or secondary legislation

Those contrary to the following provisions: G-192

Theft Act 1968, ss.9 and 25

Classes F, G and K: other offences of dishonesty (offences always in Class F)

Offences created by primary or secondary legislation

Those contrary to the following provisions: G-193

Forgery Act 1861, ss.36, 37;

Identity Cards Act 2006, s.25(1), (3) and (5).

Classes F, G and K: other offences of dishonesty (offences always in Class G)

Offences created by primary or secondary legislation

Those contrary to the following provisions: G-194

Customs and Excise Management Act 1979, s.50 (counterfeit notes or coins), s.170(2)(b) or (c) (counterfeit notes or coins);

Forgery and Counterfeiting Act 1981, ss.14 to 17;

Insolvency Act 1986, s.360.

Classes F, G and K: other offences of dishonesty (offences in Class G if value exceeds £30,000, in Class K if value exceeds £100,000 and otherwise in Class F)

Offences created by primary or secondary legislation

Those contrary to the following provisions: G-195

Customs and Excise Management Act 1979, s.50 (to the extent not specified elsewhere), s.168, s.170(1)(b), s.170(2)(b), (c) (to the extent not specified elsewhere);

Forgery and Counterfeiting Act 1981, ss.1 to 5;

Fraud Act 2006, ss.2, 3, 4, 6, 7, 9 and 11;

Hallmarking Act 1973, s.6;

Stamp Duties Management Act 1891, s.13;

Theft Act 1968, ss.1, 11, 13, 15, 16, 17 and 22;

Theft Act 1978, ss.1 and 2;

Value Added Tax Act 1994, s.72(1)-(8).

Class H: miscellaneous other offences

(i) Common law offences

Keeping a disorderly house, outraging public decency G-196

(ii) Offences created by primary or secondary legislation

Those contrary to the following provisions:

Air Navigation Order 2005 (SI 2005/1970), art.75;

Bail Act 1976, s.9(1);

Crime and Disorder Act 1998, ss.1(10), 2(8), 31(1) and 32(1);

Criminal Justice Act 1988, s.139;

Customs and Excise Management Act 1979, ss.13 and 16;

Disorderly Houses Act 1751, s.8;

Indecent Displays (Control) Act 1981, s.1;

Malicious Damage Act 1861, s.36;

Merchant Shipping Act 1970, s.27;

Misuse of Drugs Act 1971, s.5(2) (Class B or C drug); s.11;

Obscene Publications Act 1959, ss.1 and 2;

Offences against the Person Act 1861, ss.35 and 38;

Post Office Act 1953, s.11;

Prevention of Crime Act 1953, s.1;

Protection from Eviction Act 1977, s.1;
Protection from Harassment Act 1997, ss.3(6), 4(1) and 5(5);
Public Order Act 1986, s.3;
Public Passenger Vehicles Act 1981, s.65;
Road Traffic Act 1960, s.233;
Road Traffic Act 1988, ss.2 and 173;
Road Traffic Regulation Act 1984, s.115;
Sexual Offences Act 1956, ss.2, 3, 12, 13 (other than where one participant over 21 and the other under 16), 22, 24 and 32;
Sexual Offences Act 1967, s.4;
Theatres Act 1968, s.2;
Theft Act 1968, s.12A (but not where death results);
Theft Act 1978, s.3;
Trade Descriptions Act 1968, ss.1, 8, 9, 12, 13 and 14;
Vehicle Excise and Registration Act 1994, s.44.

Class I: offences against public justice and similar offences

(i) Common law offences

G-197 Embracery, fabrication of evidence with intent to mislead tribunal, perverting the course of justice and personation of jurors

(ii) Offences created by primary or secondary legislation

Those contrary to the following provisions:
Bribery Act 2010, ss.1, 2 and 6;
Cremation Act 1902, s.8(2);
Criminal Justice Act 1967, s.89;
Criminal Justice (Terrorism and Conspiracy) Act 1998, s.5;
Criminal Justice and Public Order Act 1994, ss.51(1) and (2), 75(1) and (2);
Criminal Law Act 1967, ss.4(1) and 5;
Drug Trafficking Act 1994, s.58(1);
European Communities Act 1972, s.11;
Forgery Act 1861, s.34;
Magistrates' Courts Act 1980, s.106;
Perjury Act 1911, ss.1 to 7(2);
Prevention of Corruption Act 1906, s.1;
Public Bodies Corrupt Practices Act 1889, s.1;
Trade Descriptions Act 1968, s.29(2).

Class J: serious sexual offences

Offences created by primary or secondary legislation

G-198 Those contrary to the following provisions:
Children and Young Persons Act 1933, ss.25, 26;
Indecency with Children Act 1960, s.1(1);
Protection of Children Act 1978, s.1;
Sexual Offences Act 1956, ss.1(1), 5, 6, 7, 10, 12 (of person under 16), 16, 17, 20, 25, 26 and 28;
Sexual Offences Act 2003, ss.1, 2, 4 (activity involving penetration), 5 to 10, 14, 25, 26, 30, 31, 34, 35, 38, 39, 47 to 50 and 57 to 59A.

G. VERY HIGH COST CASES

Definition

G-199 For the definition of a "Very High Cost Case", see regulation 2 of SI 2013/435 (G-6). Regulation 3(8) (G-7) provides that the regulations (with the exception of reg.12 and para.13(8) and (9) of Schedule 2) do not apply to Very High Costs Cases.

Background

G-200 Unlike the former scheme for the ex post facto taxation of fees (as to which, see Appendix G in the supplements to the 2010 edition of this work) and the graduated fee scheme, the Very High Cost Case ("VHCC") regime is not concerned with fee assessment after the completion of a case. VHCCs operate under a contract-based system where litigators' and advocates' tasks and the time allotted for each task are agreed or determined before the work is undertaken. They are managed by the Complex Crime Unit of the Legal Aid Agency (an executive agency of the Ministry of Justice). More guidance can be found at *https://www.gov.uk/guidance/high-cost-cases-crime*

Notification and classification

Litigators (referred to by the Legal Aid Agency as "organisations") are required to notify the Legal Aid Agency of any case which is, or is likely to be, a VHCC: SI 2013/435, reg.12. Notification is effected by submitting a VHCC Notification Request Form 2013, which is available on the agency's website. If a case qualifies, or if an organisation is in any doubt about this, the organisation should make the notification within five business days of the earliest hearing at which the court sets a trial estimate, or the organisation identifying that the case will be or is likely to be a VHCC, or the organisation receiving a VHCC notification request form 2013 from the agency. If the notification requirements are not met, and the agency is likely to or will suffer financial loss as a result, it may, in discharging its functions under the LASPOA 2012: (a) impose any sanction on the organisation in accordance with any other legal aid agreement or contract; (b) exclude the organisation from undertaking VHCC work or Individual Case Contract work on the case that it failed to notify; (c) where it persistently breaches this duty, exclude the organisation from undertaking future VHCC work or Individual Case Contract Work or reduce or refuse any payment to the organisation in relation to the case. **G-201**

Part A of the current (2013) arrangements sets out the obligations and processes for notification and classification for all cases which may be classified as VHCCs on or after 1 April 2013. Part B applies to cases which fall to be classified on or after that date and where the trial would in the opinion of the Director of Legal Aid Casework be likely to last for more than 60 days (para.1.4). Part C applies to cases which fall to be classified on or after that date where the case satisfies the definition of a Very High Cost Case (in reg.2(1) of SI 2013/435 (G-6)) and the trial would in the opinion of the agency be likely to last for less than 61 days. Paragraph 5.4 of the arrangements states that where it is the opinion of the agency that a case will last no fewer than 25 days and no more than 40 days, it will only be classified as a Very High Cost Case if it is prosecuted by the Serious Fraud Office or it is a terrorism case.

Where a case satisfies the definition of a VHCC for organisations, the agency will issue a VHCC decision letter. If the case is one which in the director's opinion will last more than 60 days, the agency will issue a 2013 VHCC Contract (for organisations). In other cases, the agency will issue a 2013 Individual Case Contract (for organisations).

Where the case satisfies the definition of a VHCC for advocates, and a self-employed advocate has been instructed, the agency will issue a VHCC decision letter and a 2013 VHCC contract (for self-employed advocates) to the self-employed advocate. Exceptional circumstances apart, organisations and advocates must meet the eligibility criteria set out in the arrangements before they can undertake work on a Very High Cost Case.

For information as to the working of earlier arrangements, see the second supplement to the 2013 edition of this work.

Paragraph 13(9) of Schedule 2 is not to be construed literally; where, therefore, a very high cost case panel firm was instructed under the representation order prior to the case being classified as a very high cost case, where it continued to act after such classification and where, after the defendant had pleaded guilty and been put back for sentence, the representation order was withdrawn (apparently on the application of the solicitors) by order of the court, solicitors and counsel fell to be remunerated under the very high cost cases regime, not the graduated fee regime; paragraph 13(9) had no application to this situation; rather, it was intended to deal with the remuneration of a non-panel firm where a case is reclassified as a very high cost case whereupon the representation order is withdrawn (rather than being transferred to another litigator, in which case para.13(8) is engaged): *Lord Chancellor v Alexander Johnson & Co. Solicitors and McCarthy* [2011] 6 Costs L.R. 987, QBD (Davis J).

Remuneration

Once a case is classified as a VHCC, the Legal Aid Agency will assign it to one of four categories **G-202** against the criteria contained in clause 4.21 of the VHCC Specification (see also §§ 4.12 and following in the VHCC Guidance, *https://www.gov.uk/government/publications/high-cost-case-arrangements-and-contract-documents*). For this purpose, the contracted organisation is required to submit a completed VHCC category assessment sheet within 15 business days of the decision letter: Arrangements, para.8.2(c). The category to which the case is assigned determines the hourly rate payable for preparatory work undertaken by litigators. Advocacy rates are non-category specific.

Self-employed advocates are remunerated directly by the Legal Aid Agency: clause 5.21 of the VHCC Specification (for organisations). Where the VHCC has been classified both as a VHCC for organisations and for advocates, self-employed advocates must claim under their VHCC contract. Where the case is a VHCC for organisations but has not been classified as a VHCC for advocates, any self-employed advocate must claim under the advocates' graduated fee scheme. Employed advocates must claim payment through their organisation, whether under the graduated fee scheme (where the VHCC has not been classified as a VHCC for advocates) or under the VHCC scheme (where the VHCC is a VHCC in relation to both organisations and advocates).

As to rates of payments, these are now determined by regulation 12A of, and Schedule 6 (G-16, G-112 to G-122 and following) to the Criminal Legal Aid (Remuneration) Regulations 2013 (SI 2013/435) for cases subject to the 2013 VHCC contract, and by the provisions of the Criminal Defence Service (Very High Cost Cases) (Funding) Order 2013 (SI 2013/2804) for work undertaken on or after 2 December 2013 (unless the trial date was set before that date and is before April 2014), in a "pre-commencement case" (as to which, see the Legal Aid, Sentencing and Punishment of Offenders Act 2012 (Consequential, Transitional and Saving Provisions) Regulations 2013 (SI 2013/534), reg.2) that was the subject of a contract made between the Legal Services Commission and members of the (now abolished) Very High Cost Case (Crime) Panel (art.3 and Sch.1) or was the subject of a 2010 VHCC contract (art.4 and Sch.2). SI 2013/2804 also amended paragraph 25 (Very High Cost Cases) of Schedule 2 (litigators' graduated fee scheme) to the Criminal Defence Service (Funding) Order 2007 (SI 2007/1174) (which was revoked by the Criminal Defence Service (Funding) (Amendment) Order 2011 (SI 2011/2065) in relation to proceedings in which a representation order was granted on or after 3 October 2011) to provide for reduced fees for work done on or after 2 December 2013 (unless the trial date was set before that date and is before April 2014), in a Very High Costs Case where a litigator instructed an advocate who was not a member of the Very High Cost Case (Crime) Panel.

In practice, advocates in Very High Cost Cases are not remunerated in accordance with the hourly rates set out in Sch.6 to SI 2013/4355, but are instead remunerated under the Interim Fixed Fee Offer ("IFFO") scheme. This scheme involves the Legal Aid Agency agreeing with the advocate(s), at as early a stage of the proceedings as possible, a fixed fee, payable in three instalments, to cover all the work to be carried out in the case by the advocate(s). Advocates negotiate fees directly with the Legal Aid Agency. A final offer under the IFFO scheme is subject to judicial review: *R. (Ames) v Lord Chancellor* [2018] EWHC 2250 (Admin); [2018] A.C.D. 115, DC.

H. PREPARATION AND SUBMISSION OF CLAIMS

(1) The preparation of claims

G-203 There is no mandatory graduated fee form. The use of computer-generated forms is permitted and this allows only the relevant data to be submitted. As to graduated fees generally, see G-138 to G-170.

(2) Time limits for the submission of claims

G-204 No claim by an advocate for fees for work done shall be entertained unless submitted within three months of the conclusion of the proceedings to which it relates: SI 2013/435, reg.4(3). However, where a confiscation hearing under section 2 of the DTA 1994, section 71 of the CJA 1988 or Part 2 of the PCA 2002 is held more than 28 days after a person has been found or pleaded guilty, a graduated fee claim can be submitted despite the fact that the proceedings have not yet been completed: reg.4(6). The time limit may be extended for "good reason": reg.31(1); for example, where the claim is particularly complicated and difficult to prepare, where a co-defendant's case is awaiting disposal, or because there is a genuine misunderstanding about the submission of a claim. Extensions should be sought before the time limit expires.

Where there are no good reasons, the time may be extended in "exceptional circumstances", in which case the appropriate authority shall consider whether it is reasonable to reduce the fee: SI 2013/435, reg.31(2). An advocate should be given a reasonable opportunity to show cause why his costs should not be reduced (above). Any reduction may be challenged by appeal to the taxing master: G-222. As to what may constitute "good reason" or "exceptional circumstances", see G-222. G-205

Notwithstanding that a representation order may be expressed to cover proceedings in the Crown Court "and in the event of [the defendant] being convicted or sentenced ..., advice and assistance in regard to the making of an appeal", the legislation is clear as to the need for a claim in relation to work done in the Crown Court to be submitted within three months of the conclusion of the proceedings in that court, rather than within three months of the date on which an application for leave to appeal to the Court of Appeal was refused: *White* [2008] 3 Costs L.R. 479.

In *Dumbaya* [2012] 5 Costs L.R. 976, the costs judge took a different view and held that since "representation" for the purposes of Part I of the Access to Justice Act 1999, "includes ... subject to any time limits which may be prescribed, advice and assistance as to any appeal" (the 1999 Act, s.26), proceedings should not be regarded as "concluded" until any such advice or assistance has been given. For corresponding provision in the LASPOA 2012, see section 42(1).

The Legal Services Commission disagreed with the judge in *Dumbaya*. Its November 2012 guidance provides that (i) the "conclusion of the proceedings" for litigators is the date on which the defendant was acquitted or sentenced; where confiscation proceedings follow sentence, these will be treated as separate proceedings; (ii) the "conclusion of the proceedings" for advocates is the date on which the defendant was acquitted or sentenced or on which confiscation proceedings are concluded; (iii) the commission is currently seeking clarification (in light of conflicting authorities) on whether the time taken, following conviction, to obtain and provide advice on appeal can be taken into account when determining when proceedings conclude, but, pending clarification, proposes to use the date of sentence or acquittal as the conclusion of proceedings; advocates or litigators who risk not meeting the three-month time limit as a result of obtaining or providing advice on appeal should contact the commission for an extension; (iv) bereavement, serious illness, burglary, and flooding in an office, are examples of what are likely to constitute "good reason", but delay in obtaining evidence (including prosecution page counts) and administrative errors will not; (v) those who believe that they are unlikely to meet the time limit should email requesting an extension as soon as possible with grounds; advocates, if appropriate, should provide the name of any firm that is refusing to provide relevant documents; (vi) while the disallowance of the entirety of a claim might constitute a disproportionate sanction and, accordingly, an "exceptional" circumstance, as might the length of the delay and the amount of money involved, a rigid framework for imposing financial penalties is not suitable, and claims must instead be assessed on a case-by-case basis; (vii) accordingly, litigators and advocates who submit claims out of time without "good reason" should provide an explanation as to the impact on them of a total disallowance or reduction of fees for the specific case; although the amount of detail need not be equivalent to that provided when asking for payments to be expedited on hardship grounds, it must be sufficient to enable the determining officer to understand the impact of any decision to disallow or reduce fees.

It is submitted that the commission's stance that proceedings conclude upon acquittal or sentence is to be preferred to the approach of the costs judge in *Dumbaya*, above. As there is no provision under the 2007 order for payment for advice or assistance on appeal, there seems little point in delaying the date on which the proceedings may be said to have concluded. Any other view also introduces uncertainty.

(3) Submitting an amended claim

Where a genuine error is made in submitting a graduated fee claim, counsel should not be precluded for all time from submitting an amended claim where the refusal to permit him to do so could result in his being deprived of fees to which he would have been entitled had the claim been advanced correctly in the first place: *Hann* [2009] 5 Costs L.R. 833. Where, therefore, counsel, as a result of a genuine error, had submitted a claim for a cracked trial where the case was disposed of as a guilty plea (albeit there had been a long delay between plea and sentence, throughout which it had been on the cards that a *Newton* hearing would eventually be required), it G-206 was held that counsel (who had been paid the appropriate graduated fee for a guilty plea) should be granted an extension of time in which to submit an amended claim for a guilty plea plus a special preparation fee (under what is now SI 2013/435, Sch.1 para.17). See also *Lafayette* [2010] 4 Costs L.R. 650 (there is no good reason why a lawyer who has submitted a claim should not be permitted to amend it before it has been determined).

I. DISBURSEMENTS AND EXPENSES

(1) Disbursements

G-207 A barrister is not entitled to claim for disbursements or expenses other than those permitted under SI 2013/435.

For an example of the Legal Services Commission successfully questioning, pursuant to regulation 17 of SI 2013/435 (G-21), the propriety of incurring costs where the defence had sought, and obtained, prior authority to incur those costs, see *Ward* [2012] 3 Costs L.R. 605. The costs related to the printing of a large quantity of documentation that had been contained on two computer discs and a memory stick. The solicitors had obtained authority on the ground that the files were inaccessible electronically, or that the software would corrupt their own network or that specialist software was needed to download and read the material. However, this only applied to the documents on the memory stick, and when the decision was taken not to print off the material on the memory stick, the solicitors "knew or ought reasonably to have known that the purpose for which authority had been given had failed or had become irrelevant or unnecessary before the disbursements were incurred." It had not been reasonable to incur the considerable costs when the prosecution did not intend to print the material off, and when there was no real difficulty in accessing it electronically. However, it was held that the purchase of a hard drive used by a computer expert instructed to analyse computers that had been seized was reasonable; it was inevitable that the contents would have to be copied on to a new drive, rather than a previously used drive, to avoid contamination, and such a purchase would not be part of the expert's overheads because once the drive was used, it could not be re-used for the same purpose.

(2) Travelling and accommodation expenses

Entitlement under the regulations

G-208 Travel and other expenses incidental to appearance at court may be claimed provided the court is not within 40 kilometres of the advocate's office or chambers. Unless prior approval for the expenditure has been obtained under the regulations, or unless the advocate can justify his attendance having regard to all the relevant circumstances of the case, the amount payable shall not be greater than that, if any, payable to a trial advocate from the nearest local Bar or the nearest advocate's office (whichever is the nearer): SI 2013/435, Sch.1, para.29. As to interim payment of travel and accommodation expenses, see G-133.

Local bars

G-209 In *Comer* [2009] 6 Costs L.R. 972, it was said that in paragraph 29 of Schedule 1 to SI 2013/435 (G-67), the juxtaposition of the phrase "local Bar" with the phrase "advocate's office" suggests that a fairly modest number of practitioners can constitute a local bar. The existence of a bar mess is not a prerequisite, and whether the barristers based in an area constitute a local bar will be a question of feel. In this case, the view of the resident judge that "there is a healthy local bar" was considered to be the best evidence of such a bar. As to this case, see also G-211.

An advocate may be able to justify his attendance in a distant court which is usually serviced by a local bar where:

(a) the instruction of local counsel might lead to suspicion of prejudice, lack of independence or lack of objectivity (e.g. cases of local notoriety involving public figures or officials);
(b) there are insufficient local counsel whom instructing solicitors consider are sufficiently experienced to undertake the case in question so as to give the client a reasonable choice;
(c) the services of an advocate who has specialised experience and knowledge of the type of case of an unusual or technical nature are required;
(d) the advocate has previously been instructed in related matters which would assist him in the presentation or preparation of the case in question: *Conboy* (1990) Costs L.R. 493.

It is submitted that a further justification arises where an advocate is forced to follow a particular judge on circuit who is seized of his case and it was not reasonable to instruct another local advocate for that particular hearing. Where an advocate is instructed from outside a local bar for any of the above reasons it is advisable that he obtains a letter from his instructing solicitor explaining why he was instructed, and for his clerk to obtain prior approval for incurring such expenses from the court. This applies also to Queen's Counsel practising off-circuit: G-210.

Queen's Counsel and local bars

Queen's Counsel should not be regarded as being "local" to any particular bar, even though his chambers are in one particular place. Where Queen's Counsel practises on circuit, he should as a general rule receive an amount in respect of travelling and hotel expenses actually and reasonably incurred and necessarily and exclusively attributable to his attendance at a court on the circuit on which he practises: *Thomas; Davidson; Hutton* [1997] Costs L.R. (Core Vol.) 469. Where Queen's Counsel practises outside his circuit, the "local bar" rules apply: G-209. **G-210**

Expenses reasonably incurred

The reasonableness of an advocate's claim for travel and hotel expenses should be judged not by reference to the expenses incurred by other advocates in the same case, but in relation to the demands upon the advocate in putting forward his lay client's case and his own particular circumstances in relation to the conduct of the trial: *Plews* (1984) Costs L.R. 466; G-213. **G-210a**

The regulations refer to expenditure "reasonably incurred", whereas earlier regulations referred to expenses "actually and reasonably incurred". In *Conboy* (1990) Costs L.R. 493, the taxing master observed that the current wording is wider. It is submitted that the alteration acknowledges an advocate's entitlement to recover a reasonable amount in respect of expenses necessarily and exclusively attributable to attendance at court. Thus, where the expense incurred was reasonable, an advocate should recover in full. Where the travel undertaken or accommodation used was reasonable but the cost incurred was excessive, an advocate may only claim for and recover a reasonable amount being a sum no greater than that which he would have incurred had his expenses been reasonable.

Travel to court

Actual expenses incurred in travelling from an advocate's home to court will only be allowed if his home is nearer to court than his chambers, otherwise his journey is deemed to start from chambers: *Slessor* (1984) Costs L.R. 438. And, in such a case, he will only be entitled to travelling expenses actually incurred, i.e. from home to court: *Comer* [2009] 6 Costs L.R. 972 (as to which, see also G-209). **G-211**

(i) Public transport expenses

Where expenses are recoverable, travel costs are generally limited to the cost of public transport actually incurred, together with the expense incurred in getting from the starting point to the railhead or coach station and the expense incurred from getting from the terminal to the court: *Slessor*, above. **G-212**

(ii) Car expenses

Where an advocate chooses to journey by car, the expenses allowed will not exceed the equivalent cost of public transport: *Slessor*, above; *Conboy*, above. The expenses of travel by car will be allowed where public transport is not available or is not reasonably convenient. What is "not reasonably convenient" is a matter for the discretion of the taxing officer. What may be convenient in one case may not be convenient in another. The time spent in getting from the starting point to the railhead, and from the terminus to court is always relevant: if it is considerable, the use of a car may be justified. Taxing officers have been urged to adopt a flexible and broad approach to the problem: *Slessor*, above. Where the case papers are heavy and bulky, an advocate may be justified in using a car (an example given by the taxing officer in argument in *Conboy*, above). In *Plews* (1984) Costs L.R. 466, counsel would have had to catch a 7.15 a.m. train from London to allow him to arrive at court in sufficient time to robe, see his client and solicitor, and to hold any pre-hearing discussions. It was therefore reasonable for counsel, bearing in mind that he had to travel from his home to the station and was faced with a full day in court, to travel by car. **G-213**

(iii) Expenses for reasonable travel by car

G-214 In *Plews*, above, counsel's claim, based on a mileage rate less than that prescribed for medical practitioners in regulations then current, was considered reasonable, the taxing master observing that a claim based upon the equivalent rate would have been allowed. The usual means of estimating the expenses of travel by car is the standard mileage rate which is calculated by reference to the average cost of running a motor car, including such matters as depreciation, insurance, maintenance, etc., which are referable to the running of a car of the relevant engine capacity. Although the rate is not a precise measure of the actual cost of a particular form of transport, it is intended to provide a mechanism for reimbursing expenses incurred when travelling by car: *Conboy*, above. Where it is reasonable to incur the expense of travelling by car it must also be reasonable to incur necessary and consequential costs of car parking (if any).

The Legal Services Commission announced an increase in its rates for civil solicitors from 36p per mile to 45p per mile as from 2 April 2001. It is submitted that it is reasonable that similar rates should apply to criminal advocates.

Accommodation expenses

G-215 Hotel or accommodation expenses cannot be divorced from travelling expenses. They should be paid instead of travelling expenses where an advocate reasonably chooses, or by reason of distance is obliged, to stay near a court distant from his chambers rather than travel daily. Where an advocate claims expenses for overnight accommodation and the cost equals or is less than that of the daily travel for which he would be entitled to be reimbursed, such expenses should be allowed. Where the hotel expenses are more than the cost of daily travel, they should be allowed if, having regard to the demands of the case on an advocate, including the need for conferences after court and overnight preparation, the advocate could not have returned home at a reasonable hour: *Plews*, above.

Conference travel expenses and travel time

G-216 Travel expenses reasonably incurred and necessarily and exclusively attributable to attending a conference should be reimbursed where an advocate attends a conference in prison where the authorities will only produce the client at the place of detention; the same principle applies when the client is a patient in a psychiatric hospital: *Hindle* [1997] Costs L.R. (Core Vol.) 486 .

J. PROCEEDINGS IN THE COURT OF APPEAL

General principles

G-217 Payment for proceedings in the Court of Appeal is governed by Schedule 3 to SI 2013/435 (G-102 to G-110), which provides for ex post facto taxation, the overriding principles being that the appropriate officer should, in determining fees, allow a "reasonable amount" in respect of all work "actually and reasonably done".

Advice on appeal

G-218 As to this, see, in particular, *Umezie*, § 7-165 in the main work, and *Bromige*, G-179.

Solicitor advocates

G-219 In *Mansell* [2011] 3 Costs L.R. 531, it was held that: (i) under SI 2013/435, the fees of a solicitor advocate in the Court of Appeal fall to be determined under Schedule 3 as if he were an advocate, and not a litigator; (ii) a solicitor advocate is an "advocate" for all proceedings covered by SI 2013/435, including in the Court of Appeal (see the definition of "advocate" in reg.2, G-6); and (iii) that paragraph 3 of Schedule 3 (determination of litigators' fees (G-83)), which permits payment of advocacy by litigators, does not mean that all advocacy by solicitors is payable under that paragraph.

K. DETERMINATIONS AND APPEALS

(1) The taxing authorities

G-220 Graduated fee claims are determined by Crown Court taxing officers and should usually be paid within 10 working days of receipt of the claim.

Applications for re-determination are addressed to the chief clerk of the Crown Court or the regional taxation director as appropriate. The re-determination does not have to be carried out by the original officer, although this is usually the case. Where difficult points of principle arise or large sums are in dispute the matter is referred to the regional taxing director or his assistant. Appeals from re-determinations are heard by costs judges appointed by the Lord Chancellor.

(2) Guide to the process of determination and appeal

A brief outline of the various stages of the determination of an advocate's fees is set out below. **G-221**
The regulations referred to are those of SI 2013/435 (§§ G-5 to G-123). The table below is merely intended as a guide to the relevant procedures.

As to the circumstances in which an advocate or a litigator may apply to the appropriate officer for a redetermination of his fees, for a review of specified decisions or for an offence to be reclassified, see regulation 28 of SI 2013/435 (G-32).

The references in the last column in the tables below are references to regulations of SI 2013/435.

Stage	*Description*	*reg.*
Submission of Claim		4
Time limit	Within 3 months of conclusion of proceedings (see G-196)	4(3)
Particulars submitted in all cases	In the form and manner directed by the appropriate officer	4(3)
Interim payments (40% of total claim less any sum paid)		19
Definition	Payable where:	18
	(a) the basic fee claimed by any counsel in any related proceedings exceeds £4,000, and	18(2)
	(b) 3 months have elapsed from the date of the conclusion of related proceedings or the date on which the bill is ready to tax, whichever is earlier.	18(4)
Related proceedings	Proceedings involving the same defendant heard or dealt with together or proceedings involving more than one defendant arising out of the same incident so that defendants are charged, tried or disposed of together.	18(3)
When the bill is ready to tax	Date of receipt of last bill in related proceedings.	18(4)
Entitlement	Where counsel is entitled to an interim payment but no interim payment has been made and counsel has submitted his claim.	18(4), (5)
Time limit	6 months after the conclusion of proceedings against the defendant represented.	18(5)
Determination and notification of costs; authorisation of payment		
	Costs determined in accordance with Schedule 1.	23(1)
	Counsel notified of costs payable and payment authorised.	23(1)
Re-calculation of graduated fee or re-determination of decision to allow special or wasted preparation fee, or classification of offence		
Time limit	Within 21 days of receipt or notification of costs payable.	28(3)
Particulars to be submitted	(a) Written notice specifying matters in respect of which application is made,	28(3), (5)

Stage	*Description*	*reg.*
	grounds of objection and whether counsel wishes to appear or to be represented.	
	(b) Documents and information supplied with submission of claim.	28(4)
	(c) Further information, particulars and documents as required by the appropriate officer.	28(6)
Re-determination of decision not to allow conference fee (time limit and particulars as above)		28(1)(b)
Re-determination by the appropriate officer		28(7)
Application for written reasons		28(8)
Time limit	21 days of notification of the decision	28(8), (9)
Appeal to costs judge		29(1)
Time limit	21 days of receipt of written reasons.	29(2)
Particulars to be submitted to costs judge and appropriate officer	(a) Copy of written representations on application for re-determination. (b) Appropriate officer's written reasons. (c) All documents supplied hereto.	29(4)
Form of notice of appeal	(a) As directed by the costs judge. (b) Specifying separately each item appealed against, showing amount claimed and determined for each item and the ground of objection. (c) Stating whether appellant wishes to appear or to be represented.	29(5)
Lord Chancellor's written representations	Where the Lord Chancellor makes written representations, counsel shall have a reasonable opportunity to make representations in reply.	29(9)
Notification of hearing	The costs judge shall inform counsel of hearing date and give directions as to conduct of appeal.	29(10)
No further evidence	Unless costs judge otherwise directs no other evidence shall be raised at the hearing nor objection taken which was not raised at redetermination.	29(11)
Notification of costs judge's decision		29(13)
Costs	Costs may be awarded where the appeal is allowed.	29(14)
Appeals to the High Court		30
Right of appeal	Right of appeal to single QBD judge from costs judge's decision on a point of principle of public importance.	30(7)
Application for costs judge's certificate	Counsel may apply to the costs judge to certify a point of principle of general importance.	30(1)
Time limit for application	Within 21 days of notification of costs judge's decision.	30(2)
Time limit for appeal	Within 21 days from receipt of costs judge's certificate.	
Appeal by Lord Chancellor	Within 21 days of notification of costs judge's decision, the Lord Chancellor may appeal the decision if counsel does not do so.	30(5)

(3) The enforcement and extension of time limits

Time limits may be extended for good reason by the appropriate authority, i.e. the appropriate officer, costs judge, or the High Court: SI 2013/435, reg.31(1). Where for no good reason the time limit is not adhered to, the appropriate authority may in exceptional circumstances extend the time limit and shall consider whether it is reasonable in the circumstances to reduce the costs, subject to granting the advocate a reasonable opportunity to state either orally or in writing why the costs should not be reduced: reg.31(2). A decision not to extend time, or to reduce costs for claims out of time may be appealed by notice in writing to the senior costs judge specifying the grounds of appeal. The appeal must be instituted within 21 days of the decision being given: reg.31(3); and see G-198. For the latest guidance from the Legal Services Commission on the submission of late claims and what may or may not be treated as "good reason" or "exceptional circumstances", see G-205. G-222

It was held in *Mahmood* [2008] 2 Costs L.R. 326, that where a 10 per cent penalty was imposed following a delay of over two months in submitting a claim for costs, but where the representative had only received a notice, prior to the case being tried, stating that all late claims would be the subject of a penalty unless there was a good reason, this did not constitute notice to show cause why the claim should not be reduced. The determining officer had clearly not considered the circumstances of the particular case on its own merits.

In *Roberts* [2008] 2 Costs L.R. 323, the oversight of two fee earners, the holiday of one of those fee-earners (even if well-deserved), and a subsequent systematic firm-wide failure did not constitute "good reason" or "exceptional circumstances" so as to justify an extension of time, following a delay of 17 months in submitting a claim for costs. Nor did previous good character constitute "exceptional circumstances", although it was said that it might amount to mitigating circumstances when considering the extent of any reduction in costs (were an extension to be granted). This was the case despite a general softening in the attitude to the delay.

A misunderstanding of the legislation cannot amount to "good reason", but could amount to "exceptional circumstances" where the evidence was that other bills that had been submitted late for like reason in the past had been accepted: *White* [2008] 3 Costs L.R. 479. But a simple failure to follow up a case could rarely constitute "good reason" or "exceptional circumstances", and it made no difference that the firm in question had generally had a good record for submitting claims in time: *Johnson* [2008] 6 Costs L.R. 983.

Neither "mere oversight" on the part of leading counsel nor a mistaken belief on the part of junior counsel that leading counsel's clerk was dealing with their fees could amount to "good reason" for not submitting their claims on time; but disallowance of fees *in toto* may be so disproportionate as to amount to "exceptional circumstances": see *Lafayette* [2010] 4 Costs L.R. 650.

In *Griffin* [2008] 3 Costs L.R. 483, leading counsel had been under the mistaken impression that his junior was going to prepare a taxation note to be agreed between them before submission. However, in the event, his junior submitted his own claim independently and sent a copy of his taxation note to his leader, such note making it plain that he had submitted a claim and asserting, mistakenly, that leading counsel had already submitted his own claim. It was held that as this was already seven months out of time, and leading counsel only submitted his own claim after a further two years, neither the misunderstanding as between leader and junior, nor extreme pressure of work plus some personal pressure over the two years that followed discovery of the fact that his junior had submitted his own claim, could amount to "good reason" for the failure to submit the claim within the three-month time limit; nor could they amount to "exceptional circumstances" so as to justify an extension of time despite the absence of good reason. There had been no obligation on the determining officer to remind counsel that his claim was late and the absence, at the time, of published criteria to be applied to the submission of late claims, did not avail counsel. What was critical to the outcome was the fact that two years before his eventual submission of his claim, he had been alerted by his junior's note to the fact that he would need to submit his own claim and he had failed then to take any steps to address the situation.

In *Islami* [2009] 6 Costs L.R. 988, following a ruling that total disallowance of a claim by solicitors for £58,060.13 (including disbursements and travelling expenses) due to delay (of three years and nine months) would be so disproportionate (because of the substantial effect that this would have on the firm's profits) as to amount to "exceptional circumstances" and that the claim should G-223 be re-submitted, albeit that a five per cent penalty should be applied to the sum ultimately allowed, it was held that the fact that an administrative officer at the firm had then not complied with her instructions to submit the relevant documents for taxation, and the fact that this was only discovered during her ensuing extensive sick leave, did not amount to a "good reason" for a further delay of nine months in re-submitting the claim. In these circumstances, total disallowance of the claim, and the ensuing effect on the firm's profits, was no longer a disproportionate penalty sufficient to constitute "exceptional circumstances". Had the sum been needed with the urgency suggested at the original hearing, the firm would have ensured that the claim was re-submitted immediately and carefully tracked. Instead, the administrative problems identified at the original hearing had clearly not been resolved. However, it was said that this conclusion should be applied only to the profit costs and that the claim, so far as it related to disbursements (which had long since been paid out by the firm), should still be determined (without penalty), provided that the necessary papers were lodged within 14 days.

A reduction of an out-of-time claim to zero is not automatically to be regarded as so disproportionate as to give rise to "exceptional circumstances", but the shortness of the delay, the amount of money involved and the impact on the advocate or litigator involved are capable of constituting exceptional circumstances; each case must, however, turn on its own facts; there can be no hard and fast rules or pre-set scales: *Grigoropolou* [2012] 5 Costs L.R. 982.

G-224 In *Newport* [2009] 6 Costs L.R. 983, it was said that, although it has often been stated that barristers must have suitable systems in place to ensure that claims for fees and requests for redeterminations are made within the relevant time limits, and although the delay in this particular case was significant (over three years after the determining officer had refused payment), "exceptional circumstances" for extending the time to apply for a redetermination had been made out where counsel had trusted his senior clerk to ensure that the claim and any appeal procedure was appropriately and punctually concluded, but where he had been deliberately misled by the clerk, who failed, despite counsel's regular enquiries, to inform counsel that his claim had been refused *in toto*. This was found to be a rare and regrettable situation and not akin to an argument that "pressures of work" constituted exceptional circumstances (which would not be successful).

(4) Re-determinations and appeals

Graduated fees

G-225 An advocate may only seek re-determination or appeal in respect of graduated fees where, (a) the issue is either whether the graduated fee scheme applied to the relevant proceedings, or (b) complaint is made as to the calculation of the remuneration payable, or (c) where the advocate is dissatisfied with a refusal to allow a special preparation fee or the number of hours allowed in the calculation of such fee; or (d) where the advocate is dissatisfied with the classification of an offence which does not appear in the Table of offences: SI 2013/435, reg.28(3). Under SI 2013/435 a re-determination may also be sought in respect of a decision not to allow an hourly fee in respect of attendance at conferences or views at the scene of the alleged offence, or of the number of hours allowed in the calculation of such a fee: see reg.28(1)(b)(i).

Re-determination

G-226 On an application for re-determination an advocate shall specify the grounds of his objection to all or any part of the determination (SI 2013/435, reg.28(3)(b)) and may appear in person or through another to make representations: SI 2013/435, reg.28(5). An advocate is not obliged to provide fresh information or material to assist the determining officer in the redetermination. If no additional information is provided, the determining officer has a duty to redetermine on the basis of the information already supplied: *O'Brien* [2003] 4 Costs L.R. 625. Many appeals which might otherwise have succeeded have failed because the representations made to the appropriate officer have been perfunctory and inexplicit: *Davies* [1997] Costs L.R. (Core Vol.) 472.

As from 1 January 1994, the General Council of the Bar has agreed that all requests for fees to be re-determined or for written reasons to be provided should be signed by counsel personally.

Re-determination should, where possible, be carried out by the officer who determined costs. Where cases are cited in support of the re-determination, sufficient references must be given to allow an advocate to identify and look them up: *Pelepenko*, summarised in Appendix J of the CCFG guidance document (see G-3).

Where the Legal Aid Agency makes a decision to recover an overpayment of fees pursuant to regulation 25 of SI 2013/435 (G-29) and the litigator requests a review, a subsequent confirmation by the commission of its decision to recoup constitutes a redetermination within the meaning of regulation 28 (G-32), so as to allow the litigator to appeal to a costs judge pursuant to regulation 29(1) (G-33): *Lord Chancellor v Eddowes Perry and Osbourne Ltd* [2011] Costs L.R. 498, QBD (Spencer J) (disapproving *Charlery; Small* [2011] 2 Costs L.R. 331). As to this case, see also G-180.

Further evidence on appeal and supplemental written reasons

On appeal before a costs judge no further evidence shall be received and no ground of objection shall be valid which was not raised on the application for re-determination unless the costs judge otherwise directs: SI 2013/435, reg.29(11). These provisions are strictly applied. A costs judge will rarely accede to a request to adduce further evidence or allow a fresh objection to be raised. Where written reasons do not address a point raised in the claim, counsel cannot pursue the matter in the appeal. The proper method of dealing with such an omission is to seek supplemental written reasons from the appropriate officer. **G-227**

Appeals

The right of appeal to a costs judge is effectively limited in that no appeal lies against a determination unless the advocate has applied for a re-determination and, thereafter, for written reasons under SI 2013/435, reg.29(1). **G-228**

An advocate wishing to appeal must have regard to, and be familiar with, the provisions of Part 5 of the *Criminal Costs Practice Directions* (2015) (§§ 6-153 to 6-157).

Representation, costs and expenses of appeal

For the purposes of an appeal to a costs judge, an advocate is treated as the appellant and can elect to be represented at the hearing. A successful appellant may be awarded a sum in respect of part or all of any reasonable costs incurred in connection with the appeal: SI 2013/435, reg.29(14); and see *Boswell; Halliwell* [1987] 1 W.L.R. 705 (Leggatt J). **G-229**

A barrister without the intervention of a solicitor may accept a brief or instructions, with or without fee, directly from, and represent, another barrister on that other barrister's appeal as to his fees before a costs judge. A professional fee payable by one barrister to another for conducting the former's appeal is capable of constituting part of the costs incurred by the appellant counsel: *Boswell; Halliwell*, above. In assessing such costs the costs judge is entitled to take account of time and skill expended by the appellant or his counsel in the drawing of grounds and preparation of the appeal, and the conduct of the hearing, and travel and subsidence costs. Costs incurred in instructing other counsel are clearly reasonable where there is some technical question on the applicability of some part of the regulations or other issue which legitimately deserves the attention of specialist costs counsel. Costs are not reasonably incurred if trial counsel is available, could easily have represented himself and the only real issue is the weight of the case or the value of a particular item of work undertaken: *Jackson v Lord Chancellor* [2003] EWHC 626 (QB); [2003] 3 Costs L.R. 395; and *Martin* [2007] Costs L.R. 128. A successful appellant will ordinarily be entitled to the return of the fee payable in respect of the appeal.

Appeals to the single judge

As to appeals from a costs judge to the High Court, see SI 2013/435, reg.30. The ambit of an appeal is strictly limited to the point of principle certified by the costs judge as being of general importance (such certificate being a pre-condition to an appeal): *Patten v Lord Chancellor*, 151 N.L.J. 851, QBD (Leveson J), not following *Harold v Lord Chancellor* [1999] Costs L.R. 14. Although *Patten* was concerned with the interpretation of regulation 16 of the Legal Aid in Criminal and Care Proceedings (Costs) Regulations 1989 (SI 1989/343), regulation 29 of SI 2013/435 is worded in almost identical terms. A refusal of a costs judge to certify that the matter raises a point of principle of general importance is not susceptible to judicial review: *Supreme Court Taxing Office, exp. John Singh & Co* [1997] 1 Costs L.R. 49, CA (Civ. Div). As to the limited scope for a challenge, by way of judicial review, to the substantive decision of a costs judge where a certificate has been refused, see § 6-80 in the main work. **G-230**

(5) Recovery of overpayment

Where an advocate receives a sum in excess of his entitlement, the taxing authority may either **G-231** require immediate repayment of that excess, or deduct the excess from any other sum payable to the advocate under the regulations: SI 2013/435, reg.25. These provisions apply notwithstanding the fact that a re-determination or appeal has been or may be requested: SI 2013/435, reg.25(4).

(6) Appeals under VHCCs

G-232 Under the arrangements that came into force on 1 April 2013 (G-200 to G-202 and following), both the VHCC Specification for organisations and that for advocates provide for a right of appeal to the VHCC Appeals Panel. The details are set out in paragraph 6 of the specifications, with paragraph 6.4 listing the issues in relation to which there is a right of appeal (e.g. the category to which a case has been assigned) and paragraph 6.5 listing those issues in relation to which there is no right of appeal. The appeal process, including time limits, is provided for by paragraphs 6.6 to 6.30. The appeal will normally be determined by a single adjudicator but may be referred to an appeals committee. The decision of the adjudicator or committee is final (para.6.28), but is binding only in relation to the particular appeal (para.6.29). Anonymised versions of decisions will be published on the Legal Aid Agency's website (para.6.30). There are not, however, currently any published cases on *https://www.gov.uk/government/publications/high-cost-case-arrangements-and-contract-documents* or *https://www.gov.uk/guidance/high-cost-cases-crime*

APPENDIX H
Sexual Offences (Historical Offences Not Included in the Main Work)

A. INTRODUCTION

The history of the sexual offences legislation since 1956 is set out in detail at §§ 20-288 to 20-298 in the main work. In addition, some of the most commonly indicted pre-1956 offences are set out from §§ 20-309 and following in the main work. The remaining statutory provisions contained in this appendix were repealed with effect from 1 May 2004, by the SOA 2003, but, as stated in the main work, they have continuing effect in relation to conduct occurring prior to that date. It should be borne in mind that this appendix states the law as at 30 April 2004, and that, therefore, there may yet be prosecutions for offences committed prior to even earlier material changes in the law: see, in particular, the amendments effected by the SOA 1985 and the CJPOA 1994 (summarised at §§ 20-290, 20-291 in the main work). **H-1**

B. SEXUAL OFFENCES ACT 1956

(1) Administering drugs to obtain or facilitate intercourse

(a) Statute

Sexual Offences Act 1956, s.4

4.—(1) It is an offence for a person to apply or administer to, or cause to be taken by, a woman any drug, matter or thing with intent to stupefy or overpower her so as thereby to enable any man to have unlawful sexual intercourse with her. **H-2**

(2) [*Repealed by Criminal Justice and Public Order Act 1994, s.33(1).*]

As to the meaning of "sexual intercourse", see § 20-300 in the main work; as to the use of the words "man" and "woman", see § 20-303 in the main work, H-87.

For anonymity provisions, see §§ 20-7 and following in the main work.

(b) Allocation and class of offence

This offence is triable only on indictment: SOA 1956, s.37(2), and Sch.2, para.9. As to the classification of offences, see § 2-22c in the main work. **H-3**

(c) Alternative verdicts

As to the possibility of a conviction of this offence on a charge of rape, see § 20-315 in the main work. **H-4**

(d) Sentence

Imprisonment not exceeding two years: SOA 1956, s.37(3), and Sch.2, para.9. **H-5**

(e) Elements

"Unlawful" sexual intercourse means illicit sexual intercourse, i.e. outside the bond of marriage: *Chapman* [1959] 1 Q.B. 100; (1958) 42 Cr. App. R. 257, CCA (considering s.19 of the 1956 Act, H-38). **H-6**

The essence of the offence is the administering of the drug. If there has been only one administration, there can be only one offence, even though the intention of the administration was to enable more than one man to have intercourse with the woman: *Shillingford and Vanderwall* (1968) 52 Cr. App. R. 188, CA.

(2) Sexual intercourse with a girl under 16

(a) Statute

H-6a Prosecution for this offence are now time-barred. This section is reproduced to show the historical position.

Sexual Offences Act 1956, s.6

H-7 **6.**—(1) It is an offence, subject to the exceptions mentioned in this section, for a man to have unlawful sexual intercourse with a girl ... under the age of sixteen.

(2) Where a marriage is invalid under section two of the Marriage Act 1949, or section one of the Age of Marriage Act 1929 (the wife being a girl under the age of sixteen), the invalidity does not make the husband guilty of an offence under this section because he has sexual intercourse with her, if he believes her to be his wife, and has reasonable cause for the belief.

(3) A man is not guilty of an offence under this section because he has unlawful sexual intercourse with a girl under the age of sixteen, if he is under the age of twenty-four and has not previously been charged with a like offence, and he believes her to be of the age of sixteen or over and has reasonable cause for the belief.

In this subsection "a like offence" means an offence under this section or an attempt to commit one, or an offence under paragraph (1) of section five of the Criminal Law Amendment Act 1885 (the provision replaced for England and Wales by this section).

[This section is printed as repealed in part by the CLA 1967, s.10(1), and Sch.2, para.14.]

As to the meaning of "sexual intercourse", see § 20-300 in the main work; as to the use of the words "man" and "girl", see § 20-303 in the main work, H-87.

As to the proof of exceptions, see the SOA 1956, s.47, § 20-306 in the main work.

For anonymity provisions, see §§ 20-7 and following in the main work.

Marriage Act 1949, s.2

Marriages of persons under sixteen

H-8 **2.** A marriage solemnized between persons either of whom is under the age of sixteen shall be void.

(b) Indictment

Statement of Offence

Sexual intercourse with a girl under 16, contrary to section 6(1) of the Sexual Offences Act 1956.

Particulars of Offence

A B, on the ___ day of ___, 20_, had sexual intercourse with J N, a girl under the age of 16 years.

(c) Allocation and classification of offences

H-9 This offence and an attempt to commit it are triable either way: MCA 1980, s.17(1), and Sch.1 (§ 1-125 in the main work). As to the classification of offences, see § 2-22c in the main work.

(d) Alternative verdicts

H-10 Indecent assault, contrary to section 14(1) of the 1956 Act (§ 20-361 in the main work): *McCormack* [1969] 2 Q.B. 442; (1969) 53 Cr. App. R. 514, CA. As to alternative verdicts generally, see §§ 4-516 and following in the main work.

(3) Intercourse with defectives

(a) Statute

Sexual Offences Act 1956, ss.7, 9

Intercourse with defective

H-11 **7.**—(1) It is an offence, subject to the exception mentioned in this section, for a man to have unlawful sexual intercourse with a woman who is a defective.

(2) A man is not guilty of an offence under this section because he has unlawful sexual intercourse with a woman if he does not know and has no reason to suspect her to be a defective.

[This section is printed as substituted by the MHA 1959, s.127(1)(a).]

Procurement of defective

9.—(1) It is an offence, subject to the exception mentioned in this section, for a person to procure a woman who is a defective to have unlawful sexual intercourse in any part of the world. **H-12**

(2) A person is not guilty of an offence under this section because he procures a defective to have unlawful sexual intercourse, if he does not know and has no reason to suspect her to be a defective.

As to the meaning of "sexual intercourse", see § 20-300 in the main work; as to the use of the words "man" and "woman", see § 20-303 in the main work, H-87; as to the meaning of "defective", see H-15

For anonymity provisions, see §§ 20-7 and following in the main work.

As to the burden of proof in relation to the exception in subsection (2) of both sections, see section 47 of the Act, § 20-306 in the main work.

(b) Allocation and classification of offences

Offences against sections 7 and 9, and attempts to commit them, are triable only on indictment: SOA 1956, s.37(2), and Sch.2, paras 11(a), (b), and 13(a), (b). As to the classification of offences, see § 2-22c in the main work. **H-13**

For further guidance on sentencing in historic sexual cases see § 20-385 in the main work.

(c) Sentence

Offences against sections 7 and 9, and attempts to commit them: imprisonment not exceeding two years– SOA 1956, s.37(3), and Sch.2, paras 11(a), (b), and 13(a), (b). For an illustrative example, see *Adcock* [2000] 1 Cr. App. R.(S.) 563, CA. **H-14**

(d) Elements

"Defective"

Sexual Offences Act 1956, s.45

Meaning of defective

45. In this Act "defective" means a person suffering from a state of arrested or incomplete development of mind which includes severe impairment of intelligence and social functioning. **H-15**

[This section is printed as substituted by the MHA 1959, s.127(1); and as amended by the Mental Health (Amendment) Act 1982, Sch.3.]

The words "severe impairment of intelligence and social functioning" are ordinary English words and not words of art; they were inserted in the definition to protect women, if defectives, from exploitation. Severe impairment is to be measured against the standards of normal persons: *Hall (J.H.)* (1988) 86 Cr. App. R. 159, CA. The trial judge's direction that it was for them to decide on all the evidence whether the victim was severely impaired within the ordinary meaning of those words was correct.

"Unlawful" sexual intercourse

See *Chapman*, H-6. **H-16**

"Procure"

See H-58. **H-17**

(4) Incest by a man

(a) Statute

Sexual Offences Act 1956, s.10

10.—(1) It is an offence for a man to have sexual intercourse with a woman whom he knows to be his grand-daughter, daughter, sister or mother. **H-18**

(2) In the foregoing subsection "sister" includes half-sister and for the purposes of that subsection any expression importing a relationship between two people shall be taken to apply notwithstanding that the relationship is not traced through lawful wedlock.

As to the meaning of "sexual intercourse", see § 20-300 in the main work; as to the use of the words "man" and "woman", see § 20-303 in the main work, H-87.

For anonymity provisions, see §§ 20-7 and following in the main work.

(b) Indictment

Statement of Offence

Incest, contrary to section 10(1) of the Sexual Offences Act 1956.

Particulars of Offence

A B, being a male person, on the ___ day of ___, 20_, had sexual intercourse with J N, whom he knew to be his daughter [if under the age of 13, add her age].

Where a brother and sister were charged in separate counts of the same indictment with committing incest and were tried separately, with the result that the brother was convicted and the sister acquitted, it was held that the acquittal of the sister did not make the conviction of the brother bad: *Gordon* (1927) 19 Cr. App. R. 20, CCA. As to inconsistent verdicts generally, see §§ 7-70 and following in the main work.

(c) Allocation and classification of offences

H-19 This offence, and an attempt to commit it, are triable only on indictment: SOA 1956, s.37(2), and Sch.2, para.14(a), (b). As to the classification of offences, see § 2-22c in the main work.

(d) Alternative verdicts

H-20 On a charge of the full offence, unlawful sexual intercourse with a girl under 13 (s.5) (the alternative for a girl under 16 (s.6) is time-barred and not available): SOA 1956, s.37(4), and Sch.2, para.14(a).

(e) Restriction on prosecution

H-21 A prosecution for this offence, or an attempt to commit it, may not be commenced except by or with the consent of the DPP: SOA 1956, s.37(2), and Sch.2, para.14(a), (b).

(f) Sentence

Maximum

H-22 The full offence and an attempt to commit it: if with a girl under 13, and so charged in the indictment, life imprisonment, otherwise imprisonment not exceeding seven years—SOA 1956, s.37(3), and Sch.2, para.14(a), (b).

For further guidance on sentencing in historic sexual cases see § 20-385 in the main work.

(g) Effect of adoption

H-23 The prohibition contained in section 10(1) applies notwithstanding the adoption of one of the parties: Adoption and Children Act 2002, s.74(1)(b) (whilst this provision was amended to substitute a reference to sections 64 and 65 of the SOA 2003 for the references to sections 10 and 11 of the 1956 Act, its previous operation will be saved by virtue of section 16 of the Interpretation Act 1978).

(h) Elements

H-24 If a man makes a genuine mistake as to the identity of the person with whom he has intercourse, he will not commit the offence: *Baillie-Smith* (1977) 64 Cr. App. R. 76, CA (intercourse with daughter, thinking her to be his wife).

As to the abolition of the common law presumption that a boy under 14 is incapable of sexual intercourse, see 20-385.

(i) Evidence

The relationship between the parties may be proved by oral evidence or by certificates of marriage and birth, coupled with identification. An admission by the defendant that the person with whom the offence had been committed was his daughter may be sufficient evidence of the relationship: *Jones (Evan)* (1934) 24 Cr. App. R. 55, CCA. **H-25**

Evidence tending to show pre-existent sexual passion between the parties is admissible: *Ball* [1911] A.C. 47, HL.

The defendant was charged with incest with S, who was alleged to be his daughter. His defence was that he had no knowledge that S was his daughter. He desired to give evidence:

(a) that he had been told by his first wife (the mother of S) that S had been begotten by another man and that he believed that statement to be true;
(b) that he had told his second wife that he was not the father of S;
(c) explaining statements which he had made on certain occasions acknowledging S to be his daughter.

It was held (on appeal) that this evidence was relevant to the issue whether the defendant knew that S was his daughter and that he was entitled to give any evidence relevant to that issue, including evidence of an admission by his first wife: *Carmichael* [1940] 1 K.B. 630; (1940) 27 Cr. App. R. 183, CCA.

(5) Incitement to incest of girls under 16

See the CLA 1977, s.54, H-107. **H-26**

(6) Incest by a woman

(a) Statute

Sexual Offences Act 1956, s.11

11.—(1) It is an offence for a woman of the age of sixteen or over to permit a man whom she knows to be her grandfather, father, brother or son to have sexual intercourse with her by her consent. **H-27**

(2) In the foregoing subsection "brother" includes half-brother, and for the purposes of that subsection any expression importing a relationship between two people shall be taken to apply notwithstanding that the relationship is not traced through lawful wedlock.

As to the meaning of "sexual intercourse", see § 20-300 in the main work; as to the use of the words "woman" and "man", see § 20-303 in the main work, H-87.

For anonymity provisions, see §§ 20-7 and following in the main work.

(b) Indictment

Statement of Offence

Incest, contrary to section 11(1) of the Sexual Offences Act 1956.

Particulars of Offence

A B, being a female person of the age of 18, on the ___ day of ___, 20_, with her consent permitted J N, whom she knew to be her father, to have sexual intercourse with her.

(c) Allocation and classification of offences

This offence, and an attempt to commit it, are triable only on indictment: SOA 1956, s.37(2), and Sch.2, para.15(a), (b). As to the classification of offences, see § 2-22c in the main work. **H-28**

(d) Restriction on prosecution

H-29 A prosecution for this offence or an attempt to commit it may not be commenced except by or with the consent of the DPP: SOA 1956, s.37(2), and Sch.2, para.15(a), (b).

(e) Sentence

H-30 The full offence: imprisonment not exceeding seven years—SOA 1956, s.37(3), and Sch.2, para.15(a).

Attempt: imprisonment not exceeding two years—para.15(b).

For further guidance on sentencing in historic sexual cases, see § 20-385 in the main work.

(f) Effect of adoption

H-31 The prohibition contained in section 11(1) applies notwithstanding the adoption of one of the parties: Adoption and Children Act 2002, s.74(1)(b).

(g) Elements

H-32 The common law presumption as to incapacity in relation to boys under 14 years of age (§ 20-301 in the main work) had no application where a woman was charged with committing incest with such a boy: *Pickford* [1995] 1 Cr. App. R. 420, CA.

(7) Gross indecency

H-32a No proceedings for an offence under this section may be commenced after the expiration of 12 months from the date on which the offence was committed: SOA 1956, s7(1) and (2)(a). Prosecution for this offence is now time-barred.

(a) Statute

Sexual Offences Act 1956, s.13

H-33 **13.** It is an offence for a man to commit an act of gross indecency with another man otherwise than in the circumstances described below, whether in public or private, or to be a party to the commission by a man of an act of gross indecency with another man, or to procure the commission by a man of an act of gross indecency with another man.

The circumstances referred to above are that the man is under the age of sixteen and the other man has attained that age.

[This section is printed as amended by the Sexual Offences (Amendment) Act 2000, s.2(2)(a) and (b).]

No proceedings for an offence under this section may be commenced after the expiration of 12 months from the date on which the offence was committed: SOA1956, s.7(1) and (2)(a) and therefore is now time-barred.

(8) Abduction of woman by force or for the sake of her property

(a) Statute

Sexual Offences Act 1956, s.17

H-34 **17.**—(1) It is an offence for a person to take away or detain a woman against her will with the intention that she shall marry or have unlawful sexual intercourse with that or any other person, if she is so taken away or detained either by force or for the sake of her property or expectations of property.

(2) In the foregoing subsection, the reference to a woman's expectations of property relates only to property of a person to whom she is next of kin or one of the next of kin, and "property" includes any interest in property.

[This section is printed as effectively amended by the CLA 1967, s.12(5)(a).]

As to the meaning of "sexual intercourse", see § 20-300 in the main work; as to the use of the word "woman", see § 20-303 in the main work.

(b) Indictment

Statement of Offence

Abduction, contrary to section 17(1) of the Sexual Offences Act 1956.

Particulars of Offence

A B, on the___ day of___, 20_, took away [or detained] J N against her will and by force [or for the sake of her property or expectations of property] with the intention that she should have unlawful sexual intercourse with him the said A B or with another [or with the intention that she should marry him the said A B or another].

(c) Allocation and class of offence

This offence is triable on indictment only: SOA 1956, s.37(2), and Sch.2, para.4. As to the classification of offences, see § 2-22c in the main work. **H-35**

(d) Sentence

Imprisonment not exceeding 14 years: SOA 1956, s.37(3), and Sch.2, para.4. **H-36**

(e) Elements

As to the meaning of "unlawful" sexual intercourse, see H-6. **H-37**

If the woman is taken away with her own consent, but afterwards refuses to continue further with the offender, and is forcibly detained by him, this is within the statute: see 1 Hawk. c.41 (*Forcible Marriage*), s.7.

(9) Abduction of unmarried girl under 18 from parent or guardian

(a) Statute

Sexual Offences Act 1956, s.19

19.—(1) It is an offence, subject to the exception mentioned in this section, for a person to take an unmarried girl under the age of eighteen out of the possession of her parent or guardian against his will, if she is taken with the intention that she shall have unlawful sexual intercourse with men or with a particular man. **H-38**

(2) A person is not guilty of an offence under this section because he takes such a girl out of the possession of her parent or guardian as mentioned above, if he believes her to be of the age of eighteen or over and has reasonable cause for the belief.

(3) In this section "guardian" means any person having the parental responsibility for or care of the girl.

[This section is printed as amended by the Children Act 1989, s.108(4), and Sch.12, para.11.]

As to the meaning of "sexual intercourse", see § 20-300 in the main work; as to the use of the words "girl" and "man", see § 20-303 in the main work, H-87; as to the meaning of "parental responsibility", see § 20-304 in the main work.

For the burden of proof of exceptions, see section 47 of the 1956 Act, § 20-304 in the main work.

(b) Indictment

Statement of Offence

Abduction of girl, contrary to section 19(1) of the Sexual Offences Act 1956.

Particulars of Offence

A B, on the ___ day of ___, 20_, unlawfully took or caused to be taken J N, an unmarried girl under the age of 18, out of the possession and against the will of her father [or mother or of C D then having parental responsibility for or care of her] with an intent unlawfully to have sexual intercourse with her [or that she should have unlawful sexual intercourse with E F or generally].

(c) Allocation and class of offence

H-39 This offence is triable on indictment only: SOA 1956, s.37(2), and Sch.2, para.20. As to the classification of offences, see § 2-22c in the main work.

(d) Sentence

H-40 Imprisonment not exceeding two years: SOA 1956, s.37(3), and Sch.2, para.20.

(e) Elements

H-41 As to the meaning of "unlawful" sexual intercourse, see H-6.

Upon an indictment under this section for taking a girl out of the possession of her father, it was proved that at the time of the commission of the alleged offence she was employed by another person as barmaid at a distance from her father's home. It was held that she was under the lawful charge of her employer and not in the possession of her father, and that therefore the defendant could not be convicted of the offence with which he was charged: *Henkers* (1886) 16 Cox 257. The age of the girl must be proved by the prosecution, as H-49. The presumption of the CYPA 1933, s.99, does not apply to this offence: see the proviso to Schedule 1 to the 1933 Act (as to which see H-49).

(10) Abduction of unmarried girl under 16 from parent or guardian

(a) Statute

Sexual Offences Act 1956, s.20

H-42 **20.**—(1) It is an offence for a person acting without lawful authority or excuse to take an unmarried girl under the age of sixteen out of the possession of her parent or guardian against his will.

(2) In the foregoing subsection "guardian" means any person having parental responsibility for or care of the girl.

[This section is printed as amended by the Children Act 1989, s.108(4), and Sch.12, para.12.]

As to the use of the word "girl", see § 20-303 in the main work; as to the meaning of "parental responsibility", see § 20-304 in the main work.

See now section 2 of the Child Abduction Act 1984 (§ 19-397 in the main work) which covers much the same ground and is not limited to the abduction of girls.

(b) Indictment

Statement of Offence

Abduction of a girl, contrary to section 20(1) of the Sexual Offences Act 1956.

Particulars of Offence

A B, on the ___ day of ___, 20_, unlawfully took or caused to be taken J N, an unmarried girl aged 14, out of the possession and against the will of her father [or mother or of E F then having parental responsibility for or care of her].

(c) Allocation and class of offence

H-43 This offence is triable on indictment only: SOA 1956, s.37(2), and Sch.2, para.21. As to the classification of offences, see § 2-22c in the main work.

(d) Sentence

H-44 Imprisonment not exceeding two years: SOA 1956, s.37(3), and Sch.2, para.21.

(e) Elements

That the girl was in the possession of her father, etc

This is a question for the jury: *Mace*, 50 J.P. 776. A girl will still be in the possession of her parent/guardian even while she is away from home if she intends to return; and if, when so out of the house, the defendant induces her to run away with him, he is guilty: *Mycock* (1871) 12 Cox 28. See also *Baillie* (1859) 8 Cox 238; *Green* (1862) 3 F. & F. 274; and *Miller* (1876) 13 Cox 179. **H-45**

The taking

The taking need not be by force, either actual or constructive, and it is immaterial whether the girl consents or not: *Manktelow* (1853) 6 Cox 143, and see *Kipps* (1850) 4 Cox 167; *Booth* (1872) 12 Cox 231; and *Robins* (1844) 1 C. & K. 456 (where the girl positively encouraged the defendant). **H-46**

The words "taking out of the possession and against the will" of the parent mean some conduct amounting to a substantial interference with the possessory relationship of parent and child: *Jones (J.W.)* [1973] Crim. L.R. 621 (Swanwick J)–attempt to take girls (aged 10) for a walk with a view to indecently assaulting them held not to constitute an attempt to commit the offence. (Cf. *Leather* (1994) 98 Cr. App. R. 179, CA, decided on the Child Abduction Act 1984 (§ 19-398 in the main work).)

It is no defence that the defendant acted in concert with the girl and had no intention of keeping her away from her home permanently: *Timmins* (1860) 8 Cox 401; *Frazer and Norman*, 67 E.R. 306, at 446. See also *Baillie*, above at 238.

Instead of a taking, it can be shown that a girl left her parent or guardian, in consequence of some persuasion, inducement or blandishment held out to her by the defendant: *Henkers* (1886) 16 Cox 257, following *Olifier* (1866) 10 Cox 402.

Where a man induces a girl, by promise of what he will do for her, to leave her father's house and live with him, he may be convicted, although he is not actually present or assisting her at the time when she leaves her father's roof: *Robb* (1864) 4 F. & F. 59. If the girl leaves her father, without any persuasion, inducement or blandishment held out to her by the defendant, so that she has got fairly away from home, and then goes to him, although it may be his moral duty to return her to her father's custody, yet his not doing so is no infringement of this statute, for the statute does not say he shall restore, but only that he shall not take her away: *Olifier*, above, and this is so even though it be proved that before she so left he had taken her about to places of amusement and had intercourse with her: *Kauffman*, 68 J.P. 189. If the suggestion to go away with the defendant comes from the girl only, and he takes merely the passive part of yielding to her suggestion, he is entitled to an acquittal: *Jarvis* (1903) 20 Cox 249. It is submitted that the ruling to the contrary in *Biswell* (1847) 2 Cox 279 is not law. For a discussion of the authorities, see *Mackney* (1903) 29 Vict.L.R. 22, where the English cases are considered. **H-47**

Against the will, etc

If the defendant induced the parents, by false and fraudulent representations, to allow him to take the child away, this is an abduction: *Hopkins* (1842) C. & Mar. 254. **H-48**

Where the girl's mother had encouraged her in a lax course of life, by permitting her to go out alone at night and dance at public-houses, from one of which she went away with the defendant, Cockburn C.J. ruled that she could not be said to be taken away against her mother's will: *Primelt* (1858) 1 F. & F. 50.

To prove this element of the offence, it has been said that the parent or guardian must be called: *Nash, The Times,* 2 July 1903. Sed quaere.

Under 16, etc

Prove that she was under the age of 16 years and unmarried. As to the power of a court to presume her age from her appearance, see the CYPA 1933, s.99(2) and Sch.1 (§ 19-408 in the main work (prior to its repeal by the SOA 2003, the proviso to Sch.1 stipulated that s.99(2) did apply to offences under s.20)). It is no defence that the defendant did not know her to be under 16, or might suppose from her appearance that she was older: *Olifier*, above; *Mycock*, above; *Booth*, above; or even that the defendant bona fide believed and had reasonable grounds for believing that she was over 16: *Prince* (1875) L.R. 2 C.C.R. 154. Doubts about Prince were expressed by the **H-49**

House of Lords in *B. (a Minor) v DPP* [2000] 2 A.C. 428 and *K.* [2001] UKHL 41; [2002] 1 A.C. 462, but its correctness did not fall to be decided upon. Those expressions of doubt are likely to found a challenge to Prince, but it is submitted that the express provision of a defence based on mistake as to age in relation to the offence contrary to section 19 (H-38) makes it abundantly clear that Parliament intended that there should be no corresponding defence in relation to the abduction of a girl under 16.

Mens rea

H-50 The act of abduction is positively prohibited, and therefore the absence of a corrupt motive is no answer to the charge: see *Booth*, above.

If the defendant, at the time he took the girl away, did not know, and had no reason to know, that she was subject to the parental responsibility and care of her father, mother or some other person, he is not guilty of this offence: *Hibbert* (1869) L.R. 1 C.C.R. 184.

Without lawful authority or excuse

H-51 The defendant must show that he had either lawful authority or a lawful excuse; motive is irrelevant: *Tegerdine* (1982) 75 Cr. App. R. 298, CA (statutory history reviewed). It is submitted that the burden on the defendant is merely an evidential one, which is discharged if there is sufficient evidence to raise an issue on the matter: cf. the specific provision in section 47 in relation to "exceptions" under the Act.

(11) Abduction of defective from parent or guardian

(a) Statute

Sexual Offences Act 1956, s.21

H-52 **21.**—(1) It is an offence, subject to the exception mentioned in this section, for a person to take a woman who is a defective out of the possession of her parent or guardian against his will, if she is so taken with the intention that she shall have unlawful sexual intercourse with men or with a particular man.

(2) A person is not guilty of an offence under this section because he takes such a woman out of the possession of her parent or guardian as mentioned above, if he does not know and has no reason to suspect her to be a defective.

(3) In this section "guardian" means any person having parental responsibility for or care of the woman.

[This section is printed as amended by the Children Act 1989, s.108(4), and Sch.12, para.13.]

As to the meaning of "sexual intercourse", see § 20-300 in the main work; as to the meaning of "unlawful" sexual intercourse, see H-6; as to the use of the words "man" and "woman", see § 20-303 in the main work, H-87; as to the meaning of "defective", see H-15; as to the meaning of "parental responsibility", see § 20-304 in the main work.

For the burden of proof of exceptions, see section 47 of the 1956 Act, § 20-306 in the main work.

(b) Allocation and class of offence

H-53 This offence is triable on indictment only: SOA 1956, s.37(2), and Sch.2, para.22. As to the classification of offences, see § 2-22c in the main work.

(c) Sentence

H-54 Imprisonment not exceeding two years: SOA 1956, s.37(3), and Sch.2, para.22.

(12) Causing prostitution of women

(a) Statute

Sexual Offences Act 1956, s.22

H-55 **22.**—(1) It is an offence for a person—

(a) to procure a woman to become, in any part of the world, a common prostitute; or
(b) to procure a woman to leave the United Kingdom, intending her to become an inmate of or frequent a brothel elsewhere; or
(c) to procure a woman to leave her usual place of abode in the United Kingdom, intending her to become an inmate of or frequent a brothel in any part of the world for the purposes of prostitution.

(2) [*Repealed by* Criminal Justice and Public Order Act 1994, s.33(1).]

As to the use of the word "woman", see § 20-303 in the main work.

(b) Indictment

Statement of Offence

Procuring a woman to become a common prostitute, contrary to section 22(1)(a) of the Sexual Offences Act 1956.

Particulars of Offence

A B, on or about the ___ day of ___, 20_, at _____ procured C D, a woman, to become a common prostitute.

(c) Allocation and classification of offences

This offence, and an attempt to commit it, are triable on indictment only: SOA 1956, s.37(2), and Sch.2, para.23(a), (b). As to the classification of offences, see § 2-22c in the main work. **H-56**

(d) Sentence

The full offence, and an attempt to commit it: imprisonment not exceeding two years: SOA 1956, s.37(3), and Sch.2, para.23(a), (b). **H-57**

(e) Elements

"Procure"

As to the meaning of the word "procure" in general, see §§ 18-22, 18-23 in the main work, and see *Att.-Gen.'s Reference (No. 1 of 1975)* [1975] Q.B. 773; (1975) 61 Cr. App. R. 118, CA; *Re Royal Victoria Pavilion, Ramsgate* [1961] Ch. 581, Ch D, and *Blakely v DPP* [1991] R.T.R. 405, DC. In the first of these authorities, Lord Widgery CJ said that to procure, "means to produce by endeavour. You procure a thing by setting out to see that it happens and taking the appropriate steps to produce that happening" (at pp.779, 121). In *Re Royal Victoria Pavilion, Ramsgate,* Pennycuick J (at p.587) defined "to procure" as "to obtain by care and effort" or "to see to it". **H-58**

In *Broadfoot* (1977) 64 Cr. App. R. 71, CA, the court described *Att.-Gen's Reference (No. 1 of 1975),* above, as a useful guide. Whilst saying that the interpretation of the word was a matter of common sense for the jury to determine in the light of the particular facts, the court appears to have approved (see p.74) the suggestion of Shaw LJ, during argument, that it could be regarded as bringing about a course of conduct which the woman in question would not have embarked upon of her own volition. *Christian* (1913) 23 Cox 541, was distinguished. It was there held that procuration could be negatived by evidence showing the girl was not really procured, because she needed no procuring, and acted of her own free will.

If a woman is already a common prostitute she cannot become one and accordingly cannot be procured to become one. It follows that if there is evidence of procuration but "the woman" is a police officer it is a good defence to a charge of attempting to procure a woman to become a prostitute contrary to section 1(1) of the Criminal Attempts Act 1981, that the defendant thought that "the woman" he was attempting to procure was already a prostitute. If he believed (or might have believed) that, it could not be said that he was trying to procure her to become that which he believed she already was. Section 1(3) of the 1981 Act (§ 33-128 in the main work) is concerned with the converse case where the woman is a common prostitute but the defendant believes she is not. In such circumstances, he may be convicted of an attempt even though the commission of the offence is impossible: *Brown (R.A.)* (1985) 80 Cr. App. R. 36, CA.

As to "attempting to do the impossible", see also § 33-137 in the main work.

"Common prostitute"

H-59 This includes a woman who offiers her body commonly for acts of lewdness for payment although there is no act or offer of an act of ordinary sexual intercourse: *De Munck* [1918] 1 K.B. 635; (1919) 13 Cr. App. R. 113, CCA. The word "common" in the term "common prostitute" is not mere surplusage—a common prostitute is any woman who offers herself commonly for lewdness for reward. Whether or not the performance by a woman of a single act of lewdness with a man on one occasion for reward constitutes the woman a prostitute, it plainly does not make her a woman who offers herself commonly for lewdness. That must be someone who is prepared for reward to engage in acts of lewdness with all and sundry or with anyone who may hire her for that purpose: *Morris-Lowe* (1985) 80 Cr. App. R. 114, CA, applying *De Munck*, above.

It is not necessary that she should have submitted to acts of lewdness in a passive way. Active acts of indecency by the woman herself, e.g. masturbation by her of clients when acting as a masseuse will fall within the section: *Webb* [1964] 1 Q.B. 357; (1963) 47 Cr. App. R. 265, CCA.

In *McFarlane* [1994] Q.B. 419; (1994) 99 Cr. App. R. 8, CA, it was held in relation to a prosecution under section 30 of the 1956 Act that the essence of prostitution is the making of an offer of sexual services for reward, and that it is immaterial that the person making the offer does not intend to perform them and does not do so. It is obviously desirable that "prostitution" is given the same meaning wherever it appears in a statute; accordingly, this decision is likely to be applied to section 22. For a criticism of this decision, see the 1996 edition of this work.

(13) Procuration of girl under 21

(a) Statute

Sexual Offences Act 1956, s.23

H-60 **23.**—(1) It is an offence for a person to procure a girl under the age of twenty-one to have unlawful sexual intercourse in any part of the world with a third person.

(2) [*Repealed by* Criminal Justice and Public Order Act 1994, s.33(1).]

As to the meaning of "sexual intercourse", see § 20-300 in the main work; as to the use of the word "girl", see § 20-303 in the main work.

(b) Allocation and classification of offences

H-61 This offence, and an attempt to commit it, are triable on indictment only: SOA 1956, s.37(2), and Sch.2, para.24(a), (b). As to the classification of offences, see § 2-22c in the main work.

(c) Sentence

H-62 The full offence, and an attempt to commit it: imprisonment not exceeding two years; SOA 1956, s.37(3), and Sch.2, para.24(a), (b).

(d) Elements

H-63 As to the meaning of "procure", see H-58. As to the meaning of "unlawful" sexual intercourse, see H-6.

Before the defendant can be found guilty of an offence contrary to this section, it is necessary to prove that unlawful sexual intercourse did take place; if intercourse is not proved to have taken place but procurement with the intention that it should take place is proved, there may be a conviction of an attempt to commit the full offence: *Johnson* [1964] 2 Q.B. 404; (1964) 48 Cr. App. R. 25, CCA. As to the difference between an attempt and an intention, see *Landow* (1913) 8 Cr. App. R. 218, CCA. As to conspiracy with the procurer, see *Mackenzie and Higginson* (1911) 6 Cr. App. R. 64, CCA.

(14) Detention of a woman in brothel or other premises

(a) Statute

Sexual Offences Act 1956, s.24

24.—(1) It is an offence for a person to detain a woman against her will on any premises with the intention that she shall have unlawful sexual intercourse with men or with a particular man, or to detain a woman against her will in a brothel. **H-64**

(2) Where a woman is on any premises for the purpose of having unlawful sexual intercourse or is in a brothel, a person shall be deemed for the purpose of the foregoing subsection to detain her there if, with the intention of compelling or inducing her to remain there, he either withholds from her her clothes or any other property belonging to her or threatens her with legal proceedings in the event of her taking away clothes provided for her by him or on his directions.

(3) A woman shall not be liable to any legal proceedings, whether civil or criminal, for taking away or being found in possession of any clothes she needed to enable her to leave premises on which she was for the purpose of having unlawful sexual intercourse or to leave a brothel.

As to the meaning of "sexual intercourse", see § 20-300 in the main work; as to the use of the words "man" and "woman", see § 20-303 in the main work, H-87.

(b) Indictment

Statement of Offence

Detaining a woman against her will for unlawful sexual intercourse [or in a brothel], contrary to section 24(1) of the Sexual Offences Act 1956.

Particulars of Offence

A B, on or about the ___ day of ___, 20_, detained C D, a woman, against her will at ___ intending her to have unlawful sexual intercourse with men [or with E F, a man] [or detained C D, a woman, against her will at ___, a brothel].

(c) Allocation and class of offence

This offence is triable on indictment only: SOA 1956, s.37(2), and Sch.2, para.25. As to the classification of offences, see § 2-22c in the main work. **H-65**

(d) Sentence

Imprisonment not exceeding two years: SOA 1956, s.37(3), and Sch.2, para.25. **H-66**

(e) Elements

Unlawful sexual intercourse

See H-6. **H-67**

"Brothel"

See §§ 20-222 and following in the main work. **H-68**

(f) Evidence

See §§ 20-222, 20-223 in the main work. **H-69**

(15) Allowing premises to be used for intercourse

(a) Statute

Sexual Offences Act 1956, ss.25, 26, 27

Permitting girl under thirteen to use premises for intercourse

25. It is an offence for a person who is the owner or occupier of any premises, or who has, or acts **H-70**

or assists in, the management or control of any premises, to induce or knowingly suffer a girl under the age of thirteen to resort to or be on those premises for the purpose of having unlawful sexual intercourse with men or with a particular man.

[This section is printed as effectively amended by the CLA 1967, s.12(5)(a).]

Permitting girl between thirteen and sixteen to use premises for intercourse

H-71 **26.** It is an offence for a person who is the owner or occupier of any premises, or who has, or acts or assists in, the management or control of any premises, to induce or knowingly suffer a girl ... under the age of sixteen, to resort to or be on those premises for the purpose of having unlawful sexual intercourse with men or with a particular man.

[The words omitted were repealed by the CLA 1967, s.10(1), and Sch.2, para.14. This repeal renders the marginal note misleading.]

Permitting defective to use premises for intercourse

H-72 **27.**—(1) It is an offence, subject to the exception mentioned in this section, for a person who is the owner or occupier of any premises, or who has, or acts or assists in, the management or control of any premises, to induce or knowingly suffer a woman who is a defective to resort to or be on those premises for the purpose of having unlawful sexual intercourse with men or with a particular man.

(2) A person is not guilty of an offence under this section because he induces or knowingly suffers a defective to resort to or be on any premises for the purpose mentioned, if he does not know and has no reason to suspect her to be a defective.

As to the meaning of "sexual intercourse", see § 20-300 in the main work; as to the use of the words "man", "woman" and "girl", see § 20-303 in the main work, H-87; as to the meaning of "defective", see H-15.

For the burden of proof of exceptions, see section 47 of the 1956 Act, § 20-306 in the main work.

(b) Allocation and classification of offences

H-73 Section 25—this offence is triable only on indictment: SOA 1956, s.37(2), and Sch.2, para.6.

Section 26—this offence is triable either way: MCA 1980, s.17(1), and Sch.1 (§ 1-125 in the main work).

Section 27—this offence is triable only on indictment: SOA 1956, s.37(2), and Sch.2, para.27.

As to the classification of offences, see § 2-22c in the main work.

(c) Sentence

H-74 Section 25—life imprisonment: SOA 1956, s.37(3), and Sch.2, para.6.

Section 26—imprisonment not exceeding two years: SOA 1956, s.37(3), and Sch.2, para.26. The penalty on summary conviction is provided for by the MCA 1980, s.32 (§ 1-119 in the main work).

Section 27—imprisonment not exceeding two years: SOA 1956, s.37(3), and Sch.2, para.27.

(d) Elements

"Management", "assists in the management"

H-75 See the following cases, decided in relation to section 33 of the 1956 Act ("assisting in the management of a brothel"): *Abbott v Smith* [1965] 2 Q.B. 662, DC (meaning of "management"); *Gorman v Standen Palace-Clark v Standen* [1964] 1 Q.B. 294; (1964) 48 Cr. App. R. 30, DC; *Jones and Wood v DPP* (1993) 96 Cr. App. R. 130, DC; and *Elliott v DPP*; *Dublides v DPP*, *The Times*, 19 January 1989, DC ("assisting in the management"). In the last of these cases, the court appears to have accepted a distinction between assisting in the management of premises and assisting the management of premises.

"Unlawful" sexual intercourse

H-76 See H-6.

"Knowingly suffer"

H-77 In *Webster* (1885) 16 Q.B.D. 134, it was held that the words "knowingly suffer" mean that the defendant knew of the girl's purpose in being on the premises and did not prevent the unlawful sexual intercourse from occurring when it was in his power to do so. The girl was the defendant's daughter, and the premises were her home, where she resided with the defendant. But see *Merthyr Tydfil JJ.* (1894) 10 T.L.R. 375, where a mother was held not within the section, who for the purposes of obtaining conclusive evidence against a man who had seduced her daughter, permitted him to come to her house to repeat his unlawful intercourse.

(16) Causing or encouraging prostitution, etc.

(a) Statute

Sexual Offences Act 1956, ss.28, 29

Causing or encouraging prostitution of, intercourse with, or indecent assault on, girl under sixteen

28.—(1) It is an offence for a person to cause or encourage the prostitution of, or the commission of unlawful sexual intercourse with, or of an indecent assault on, a girl under the age of sixteen for whom he is responsible. **H-78**

(2) Where a girl has become a prostitute, or has had unlawful sexual intercourse, or has been indecently assaulted, a person shall be deemed for the purposes of this section to have caused or encouraged it, if he knowingly allowed her to consort with, or to enter or continue in the employment of, any prostitute or person of known immoral character.

(3) The persons who are to be treated for the purposes of this section as responsible for a girl are (subject to subsection (4) of this section)—

(a) her parents;

(b) any person who is not a parent of hers but who has parental responsibility for her; and

(c) any person who has care of her.

(4) An individual falling within subsection (3)(a) or (b) of this section is not to be treated as responsible for a girl if—

(a) a residence order under the Children Act 1989 is in force with respect to her and he is not named in the order as the person with whom she is to live; or

(aa) a special guardianship order under that Act is in force with respect to her and he is not her special guardian; or

(b) a care order under that Act is in force with respect to her.

(5) If, on a charge of an offence against a girl under this section, the girl appears to the court to have been under the age of sixteen at the time of the offence charged, she shall be presumed for the purposes of this section to have been so, unless the contrary is proved.

[This section is printed as amended by the Children Act 1989, s.108(4), and Sch.12, para.14; and the Adoption and Children Act 2002, s.139(1), and Sch.3, para.8.]

Causing or encouraging prostitution of defective

29.—(1) It is an offence, subject to the exception mentioned in this section, for a person to cause or encourage the prostitution in any part of the world of a woman who is a defective. **H-79**

(2) A person is not guilty of an offence under this section because he causes or encourages the prostitution of such a woman, if he does not know and has no reason to suspect her to be a defective.

As to the meaning of "sexual intercourse", see § 20-300 in the main work; as to the use of the words "woman" and "girl", see § 20-303 in the main work, H-87; as to the meaning of "parental responsibility", see § 20-304 in the main work; as to the meaning of "defective", see H-15.

For the burden of proof of exceptions, see section 47 of the 1956 Act, § 20-306 in the main work.

(b) Allocation and classification of offences

These offences are triable only on indictment: SOA 1956, s.37(2), and Sch.2, paras 28 and 29. As to the classification of offences, see § 2-22c in the main work. **H-80**

(c) Sentence

Sections 28 and 29—imprisonment not exceeding two years: SOA 1956, s.37(3), and Sch.2, paras 28 and 29. **H-81**

(d) Elements

H-82 As to what constitutes "causing" or "encouraging", see *Ralphs* (1914) 9 Cr. App. R. 86, CCA; *Chainey* [1914] 1 K.B. 137; (1914) 9 Cr. App. R. 175, CCA.

In *Drury* (1974) 60 Cr. App. R. 195, CA, it was held that there was evidence on which it could be held that a girl (aged 14) was in the care of the defendant where, at the time of the assault by a friend of the defendant, she was babysitting for him. The case was decided on the original wording of section 28(3)(c), viz. "any other person who has the custody, charge or care of her". The 1989 amendment (above) would not appear to affect this point. As to encouragement, the court said that there must be encouragement in fact and an intention to encourage.

A doctor who in the exercise of his clinical judgment gives contraceptive advice and treatment to a girl under 16 without her parents' consent does not commit an offence under section 6 or 28 of the 1956 Act, because the bona fide exercise by the doctor of his clinical judgment negates the mens rea which is an essential ingredient of those offences: *Gillick v West Norfolk and Wisbech Area Health Authority* [1986] A.C. 112, HL.

As to the meaning of "unlawful" sexual intercourse, see H-6. This offence cannot be prosecuted in relation to unlawful sexual intercourse as that offence is now time-barred see § 20-315 in the main work.

(17) Man living on earnings of prostitution

(a) Statute

Sexual Offences Act 1956, s.30

H-83 **30.**—(1) It is an offence for a man knowingly to live wholly or in part on the earnings of prostitution.

(2) For the purposes of this section a man who lives with or is habitually in the company of a prostitute, or who exercises control, direction or influence over a prostitute's movements in a way which shows he is aiding, abetting or compelling her prostitution with others, shall be presumed to be knowingly living on the earnings of prostitution, unless he proves the contrary.

As to the use of the word "man", see § 20-303 in the main work, H-87.

(b) Indictment

Statement of Offence

Living on prostitution, contrary to section 30(1) of the Sexual Offences Act 1956.

Particulars of Offence

A B, being a man, on the ___ day of ___, 20_, and on other days between that date and the ___ day of ___, 20_, knowingly lived wholly or in part on the earnings of the prostitution of J N.

In an indictment for this offence a person may be charged with having committed the offence on one specified day only: *Hill* (1914) 10 Cr. App. R. 56, CCA. Evidence is admissible to show what the defendant's relations with the woman in question had been either before or after the day specified in the indictment: above.

As to the application of the alibi notice provisions to this offence, see *Hassan* (1970) 54 Cr. App. R. 56, CA (§ 12-66 in the main work).

(c) Allocation and class of offence

H-84 This offence is triable either way: SOA 1956, s.37(2), and Sch.2, para.30. As to the classification of offences, see § 2-22c in the main work.

(d) Sentence

Maximum

H-85 On conviction on indictment, imprisonment not exceeding seven years; on summary conviction, six months, or a fine not exceeding £5,000: SOA 1956, s.37(3), and Sch.2, para.30 (as amended by the Street Offences Act 1959, s.4), and the MCA 1980, ss.32, 34(3)(a).

Guidelines

A sentence exceeding two years should be reserved for cases where there is some evidence of physical or mental coercion of the prostitutes involved, or of corruption. The existence of such coercion or corruption is the crucial sentencing factor: *Farrugia* (1979) 69 Cr. App. R. 108, CA. See also *Thomas* (1983) 5 Cr. App. R.(S.) 138, CA; *El-Gazzar* (1986) 8 Cr. App. R.(S.) 182, CA; *Malik* [1998] 1 Cr. App. R.(S.) 115, CA; and CSP B5-1. **H-86**

(e) Elements

"Man"

In *Tan* [1983] Q.B. 1053; (1983) 76 Cr. App. R. 300, CA, it was held that a person who was born a man and who remained biologically a man was a man for all purposes although he had undergone hormone treatment and surgical treatment consisting of sex-change operations and had become philosophically or psychologically female (applying *Corbett v Corbett* [1971] P. 83). **H-87**

Prostitution

As to what constitutes "prostitution", see § 20-177 in the main work, H-59. As to proving that at the material time the woman was a prostitute, see § 20-224 in the main work, and *Wilson (D.T.)* (1984) 78 Cr. App. R. 247, CA, in which *Woodhouse v Hall* (1981) 72 Cr. App. R. 39, DC, was applied in the context of a prosecution under section 30. **H-88**

Knowingly living on earnings of prostitution

There are three distinct foundations upon which the prosecution can rely in order to raise a presumption that an offence has been committed under section 30(2) (H-83): **H-89**

(a) proof that the accused was at the material time living with the prostitute;
(b) proof that he was habitually at the material time in her company;
(c) proof that he exercised control, direction or influence over her movements in a way which showed him to be aiding or abetting her prostitution.

Once evidence giving rise to the presumption has been led, it then has two facets: (a) it is presumed that he is living on immoral earnings; and (b) it is presumed that he is doing so knowingly: *Clarke* (1976) 63 Cr. App. R. 16, CA. It is not necessary to prove that he was living with or habitually in the company of such a prostitute in a way which showed that he was aiding, abetting or compelling her prostitution with others: above. See also *Lawrence*, H-206.

In *Stewart* (1986) 83 Cr. App. R. 327, CA, the court was referred to *Silver* (1956) 40 Cr. App. R. 32, CCC (Judge Maude); *Thomas* (1957) 41 Cr. App. R. 121, CCA; *Shaw v DPP* [1962] A.C. 220, HL; *Calderhead and Bidney* (1979) 68 Cr. App. R. 37, CA; and *Wilson (D.T.)*, above. Mustill LJ said, in giving the court's judgment: **H-90**

> "What we collect from them is as follows: according to the literal meaning of the section any person who supplies goods or services to a prostitute is in one sense living off the earnings of prostitution: for in part he earns his livelihood from payments which the woman would not be able to make but for her trade. This cannot be the right view. There has to be a closer connection between the receipt of money and the trade before the recipient commits an offence. We doubt whether it is possible to devise a definition of the type and closeness of the necessary connection which will deal with all the circumstances which may arise; and, indeed, it is dangerous to treat words or phrases from judgments delivered in relation to one set of facts, as if they provided a statutory gloss which can be reliably applied to facts of a quite different nature ... .
>
> Subject to this reservation, we believe that an approach which will often be useful is to identify for the jury the flavour of the words 'living off', and then to express this general concept in the shape of guidance more directly referable to the case in hand. In our judgment, the word 'parasite' (to be found in the speech of Lord Reid in *Shaw v DPP* ...), or some expanded equivalent, provides a useful starting point for this exercise, and does express a concept which accounts for all the reported cases except for *Silver*.
>
> Adopting this general approach, and dealing specifically with a defendant who supplies goods or services to a prostitute, a good working test, sufficient to deal with many cases, is whether the fact

of supply means that the supplier and the prostitute were engaged in the business of prostitution together: and 'the fact of supply' will include the scale of supply, the price charged and the nature of the goods or services. It will be impossible to say in advance that certain categories of supplies must necessarily fall outside the section, any more than that other categories must be within it, but the idea of participation in the prostitute's business will enable the jury to distinguish readily between (say) the supplier of groceries on the one hand and the publisher of prostitutes' advertisements on the other. There will remain a residue of more difficult cases, and these include the situation where premises are let at a market rent with knowledge of the purpose to which they are to be put. We see no room here for any rule of thumb distinction between premises which are or are not let at abnormally high rates. Certainly, the jury will find it easier to infer in the former case that the lessor participates in the woman's earnings. ... We can, however, see no logic in the suggestion that the lessor cannot be convicted unless the rent is exorbitant and indeed the judgment of Ashworth J in *Shaw v DPP* (at p.230) and the speech of Lord Simonds in the same case (at p.265 ... see the words 'whatever the rent') are authority for the view that the presence or absence of this factor is not conclusive. Nor in our opinion is the question whether the premises are occupied or capable of occupation as residential premises to be taken as the touchstone.

Instead, the judge must bear in mind when framing his direction the distinction between the offence under section 30(1), and the offences under sections 34, 35 and 36, and must not allow the jury to believe that knowledge of use to which the premises are put will be sufficient in itself to found a conviction. He must draw the attention of the jury to whatever factors are material to the individual case. These will often include, but not be limited to, the nature and location of the premises, the involvement of the lessor in adapting, furnishing or outfitting the premises for prostitution, the duration of the letting, the hours during which the premises are occupied, the rent at which they are let, the method of payment of rent, the fact that the prostitute does or does not live as well as work at the premises, the presence or absence of a personal relationship between the lessor and the lessee, the steps taken by the lessor to remove the prostitutes from his premises, and the steps taken by the lessor to disguise his relationship with the premises and the persons working there. Having presented the facts to the jury, the judge will invite them to consider whether they are sure that the lessor was involved together with the prostitute in the business of prostitution" (at pp.332–333).

H-91 Mustill LJ then said that in the opinion of the court, the judge's direction, that where a letting was referable to prostitution and nothing else it was immaterial whether the letting was at a higher than normal rent, was correct, and to the extent that *Silver*, above, is a decision to the contrary, it should not be followed.

It is essential that a jury should receive a clear and careful direction with regard to this offence and the burden of proof in relation to it. In particular, where the prosecution rely on subsection (2), the jury's attention should be directed to the various alternatives contained in the subsection, and to any evidence relating to any of those alternatives: *Lawrence* (1963) 47 Cr. App. R. 72, CCA.

In *Howard* (1992) 94 Cr. App. R. 89, CA, Lord Lane CJ said that what is required is a simple direction based primarily on what was said in *Shaw v DPP*, above, and *Stewart*, above, adjusted to the facts of the particular case.

(f) Evidence

H-92 That the defendant knowingly lived wholly or in part on the earnings of prostitution is usually proved by evidence that the prostitute paid the rent of rooms where both were living together, or paid for his food, or supplied him with money, or paid for drink consumed by him in public-houses, or the like. Whether conversation and association with a prostitute amounts to proof that the defendant was habitually in her company is a question of fact for the jury: *Ptohopoulos* (1968) 52 Cr. App. R. 47, CA.

There need not be proof that the prostitute handed money to the defendant if the evidence establishes that what the defendant received was earned by the prostitute (see *Calvert v Mayes* [1954] 1 Q.B. 242, approved in *Shaw*). Nor, as was held in *Ansell* [1975] Q.B. 215; (1974) 60 Cr. App. R. 45, CA, if the money comes from the men with whom the prostitutes are dealing and not from the prostitutes themselves, does that fact in law prevent the money being the earnings of prostitution: see, for example, *Farrugia* (1979) 69 Cr. App. R. 108, CA.

(18) Woman exercising control over prostitute

(a) Statute

Sexual Offences Act 1956, s.31

31. It is an offence for a woman for purposes of gain to exercise control, direction or influence over a prostitute's movements in a way which shows she is aiding, abetting or compelling her prostitution. H-93

As to the use of the word "woman", see § 20-303 in the main work. As to the meaning of "prostitution", see § 20-177 in the main work, H-59.

(b) Allocation and class of offence

This offence is triable either way: SOA 1956, s.37(2), and Sch.2, para.31. As to the classification of offences, see § 2-22c in the main work. H-94

(c) Sentence

On conviction on indictment, imprisonment not exceeding seven years; on summary conviction, six months, or a fine not exceeding £5,000: SOA 1956, s.37(3), and Sch.2, para.31 (as amended by the Street Offences Act 1959, s.4), and the MCA 1980, ss.32, 34(3)(a). H-95

(19) Solicitation for immoral purposes

(a) Statute

Sexual Offences Act 1956, s.32

32. It is an offence for a man persistently to solicit or importune in a public place for immoral purposes. H-96

As to the use of the word "man", see § 20-303 in the main work, H-87.

(b) Mode of trial

This offence is triable either way: SOA 1956, s.37(2), and Sch.2, para.32. H-97

(c) Sentence

On conviction on indictment, imprisonment not exceeding two years; on summary conviction, six months, or a fine not exceeding £5,000: SOA 1956, s.37(3), and Sch.2, para.32, and the MCA 1980, ss.32, 34(3)(a). H-98

(d) Elements

"persistently"

Two separate acts of importuning within the period named in the information or indictment are sufficient to render the importuning persistent: *Dale v Smith* [1967] 1 W.L.R. 700, DC (justices entitled to treat the use of the word "Hello" by the defendant to a youth in a public lavatory as an act of importuning, in view of the fact that the same word had been used by the defendant to another youth on the previous evening and had been followed by an undoubted act of importuning, viz. an invitation to look at indecent photographs). H-99

"solicit"

In *Behrendt v Burridge* (1976) 63 Cr. App. R. 202, DC, the defendant was observed for about 50 minutes sitting on a high stool in the bay window of a house. She sat silent and motionless, H-100 dressed in a low cut top and mini-skirt. The bay window was illuminated by a red light. She was charged with soliciting for the purpose of prostitution, contrary to section 1 of the Street Offences Act 1959. The Divisional Court said that the fact that her behaviour could be described as an explicit form of advertising was not decisive in her favour: advertising and soliciting are not mutually exclusive. It was clear that she was soliciting in the sense of tempting or allowing prospective customers to come in for the purposes of prostitution.

See also *Horton v Mead* [1913] 1 K.B. 154, DC, and *Burge v DPP* [1962] 1 W.L.R. 265, DC.

"importune"

H-101 See *Dale v Smith*, H-99.

"public place"

H-102 No definition appears in the 1956 Act, but it is a frequently used expression in legislation: see, for example, the Public Order Act 1936, s.9 (§ 25-329 in the main work), the Prevention of Crime Act 1953, s.1(4) (§ 5A-689 in the main work) and the Firearms Act 1968, s.57(4) (§ 24-120 in the main work).

"for immoral purposes"

H-103 An immoral purpose within section 32 has to be some kind of sexual activity: *Crook v Edmondson* [1966] 2 Q.B. 81, DC; *Kirkup* (1993) 96 Cr. App. R. 352, CA.

Section 32 applies both to heterosexual and homosexual behaviour: *Goddard* (1991) 92 Cr. App. R. 185, CA.

Although section 1 of the SOA 1967 (§ 20-350 in the main work) prevents homosexual practices in private between consenting parties who have attained the age of 16 from being a criminal offence, the 1967 Act did not change the law to the extent of preventing approaches for such purposes from being the offence of persistently importuning for "immoral purposes": *Ford* (1978) 66 Cr. App. R. 46, CA. The judge correctly ruled that the conduct complained of could amount to an offence and correctly left the jury to decide whether the conduct was or was not immoral.

Similarly, in *Goddard*, above, the unchallenged evidence of two young women was that they had had explicit sexual invitations made to them by G. It was held: (a) that it did not matter that the proposed sexual activity may be within the law; and (b) that it was a matter for the jury to decide, whether the invitations were for sexually immoral purposes, considering the circumstances in which the overtures were made and the nature of the overtures. This decision effectively overruled that part of the majority decision in *Crook v Edmondson*, above, which had held that "immoral purposes" was to be confined to purposes declared to be offences under other provisions of the 1956 Act.

The correct procedure is for the trial judge to rule whether the acts complained of could amount to an offence and, provided they are so capable, to leave it to the jury to decide whether the conduct, in fact, involved an immoral purpose, applying contemporary standards of morality: *Goddard*, above.

C. SEXUAL OFFENCES ACT 1967

(1) Procuring others to commit homosexual acts

Sexual Offences Act 1967, s.4

H-104 **4.**—(1) A man who procures another man to commit with a third man an act of buggery which by reason of section 1 of this Act is not an offence shall be liable on conviction on indictment to imprisonment for a term not exceeding two years.

(2) [*Repealed by* Criminal Law Act 1977, Sch.13.]

(3) It shall not be an offence under section 13 of the Act of 1956 for a man to procure the commission by another man of an act of gross indecency with the first-mentioned man which by reason of section 1 of this Act is not an offence under the said section 13.

The offence under subsection (1) is triable either way: MCA 1980, s.17(1), and Sch.1 (§ 1-119 in the main work).

As to the use of the word "man", see § 20-303 in the main work, H-87.

As to the offence of buggery, see §§ 20-348 and following in the main work.
For section 13 of the 1956 Act, see H-33.
As to "procures", see H-58.

(2) Living on earnings of male prostitution

Sexual Offences Act 1967, s.5

5.–(1) A man or woman who knowingly lives wholly or in part on the earnings of prostitution of another man shall be liable– **H-105**

(a) on summary conviction to imprisonment for a term not exceeding six months, or

(b) on conviction on indictment to imprisonment for a term not exceeding seven years.

(2) [*Repealed by* Criminal Law Act 1977, Sch.13.]

(3) Anyone may arrest without a warrant a person found committing an offence under this section.

As to the use of the words "man" and "woman", see § 20-303 in the main work and–in relation to "man"–see *Tan* [1983] Q.B. 1053; (1983) 76 Cr. App. R. 300, CA, H-87. **H-106**

As to the classification of offences, see § 2-22c in the main work.

Subsection (3) has ceased to have effect by virtue of the PACE Act 1984, s.26(1) (§ 15-188 in the main work).

D. CRIMINAL LAW ACT 1977

Criminal Law Act 1977, s.54

Incitement of girls under 16

54.–(1) It is an offence for a man to incite to have sexual intercourse with him a girl under the age of sixteen whom he knows to be his grand-daughter, daughter or sister. **H-107**

(2) In the preceding subsection "man" includes boy, "sister" includes half-sister, and for the purposes of that subsection any expression importing a relationship between two people shall be taken to apply notwithstanding that the relationship is not traced through lawful wedlock.

(3) The following provisions of section 1 of the Indecency with Children Act 1960, namely–

...

subsection (3) (references in Children and Young Persons Act 1933 to the offences mentioned in Schedule 1 to that Act to include offences under that section);

subsection (4) (offences under that section to be deemed offences against the person for the purpose of section 3 of the Visiting Forces Act 1952),

shall apply in relation to offences under this section.

(4) A person guilty of an offence under this section shall be liable–

(a) on summary conviction, to imprisonment for a term not exceeding six months or to a fine not exceeding the prescribed sum or both;

(b) on conviction on indictment to imprisonment for a term not exceeding two years.

[This section is printed as effectively amended by the MCA 1980, s.32(2) (substitution of reference to "the prescribed sum"); and as repealed in part by the PACE Act 1984, Sch.7.]

As to Schedule 1 to the CYPA 1933, see § 19-408 in the main work. **H-108**

As to "the prescribed sum", see the MCA 1980, s.32(2) and (9) (§ 1-119 in the main work).

For anonymity provisions, see §§ 20-7 and following in the main work.

Section 54 filled a lacuna in the law, identified in *Whitehouse* [1977] Q.B. 868; (1977) 65 Cr. App. R. 33, CA.

As to incitement at common law, see § 33-74 in the main work.

E. SEXUAL OFFENCES (AMENDMENT) ACT 2000

(1) Statute

Sexual Offences (Amendment) Act 2000, ss.3, 4

Abuse of position of trust

3.–(1) Subject to subsections (2) and (3) below, it shall be an offence for a person aged 18 or over– **H-109**

(a) to have sexual intercourse (whether vaginal or anal) with a person under that age; or
(b) to engage in any other sexual activity with or directed towards such a person,

if (in either case) he is in a position of trust in relation to that person.

(2) Where a person ("A") is charged with an offence under this section of having sexual intercourse with, or engaging in any other sexual activity with or directed towards, another person ("B"), it shall be a defence for A to prove that, at the time of the intercourse or activity—

(a) he did not know, and could not reasonably have been expected to know, that B was under 18;
(b) he did not know, and could not reasonably have been expected to know, that B was a person in relation to whom he was in a position of trust; or
(c) he was lawfully married to B.

(3) It shall not be an offence under this section for a person ("A") to have sexual intercourse with, or engage in any other sexual activity with or directed towards, another person ("B") if immediately before the commencement of this Act—

(a) A was in a position of trust in relation to B; and
(b) a sexual relationship existed between them.

(4) A person guilty of an offence under this section shall be liable—

(a) on summary conviction, to imprisonment for a term not exceeding six months, or to a fine not exceeding the statutory maximum, or to both;
(b) on conviction on indictment, to imprisonment for a term not exceeding five years, or to a fine, or to both.

(5) In this section, "sexual activity"—

(a) does not include any activity which a reasonable person would regard as sexual only with knowledge of the intentions, motives or feelings of the parties; but
(b) subject to that, means any activity which such a person would regard as sexual in all the circumstances.

As to "the commencement of this Act", see the Sexual Offences (Amendment) Act 2000 (Commencement No. 1) Order 2000 (SI 2000/3303), which brought the Act into force on 8 January 2001.

Meaning of "position of trust"

H-110 **4.**—(1) For the purposes of section 3 above, a person aged 18 or over ("A") is in a position of trust in relation to a person under that age ("B") if any of the four conditions set out below, or any condition specified in an order made by the Secretary of State by statutory instrument, is fulfilled.

(2) The first condition is that A looks after persons under 18 who are detained in an institution by virtue of an order of a court or under an enactment, and B is so detained in that institution.

(3) The second condition is that A looks after persons under 18 who are resident in a home or other place in which—

(a) accommodation and maintenance are provided by an authority under section 23(2) of the Children Act 1989 or Article 27(2) of the Children (Northern Ireland) Order 1995;
(b) accommodation is provided by a voluntary organisation under section 59(1) of that Act or Article 75(1) of that Order; or
(c) accommodation is provided by an authority under section 26(1) of the Children (Scotland) Act 1995,

and B is resident, and is so provided with accommodation and maintenance or accommodation, in that place.

(4) The third condition is that A looks after persons under 18 who are accommodated and cared for in an institution which is—

(a) a hospital;
(b) a residential care home, nursing home, mental nursing home or private hospital;
(c) a community home, voluntary home, children's home or residential establishment; or
(d) a home provided under section 82(5) of the Children Act 1989,

and B is accommodated and cared for in that institution.

(5) The fourth condition is that A looks after persons under 18 who are receiving full-time education at an educational institution, and B is receiving such education at that institution.

(6) No order shall be made under subsection (1) above unless a draft of the order has been laid before and approved by a resolution of each House of Parliament.

(7) A person looks after persons under 18 for the purposes of this section if he is regularly involved in caring for, training, supervising or being in sole charge of such persons.

(8) For the purposes of this section a person receives full-time education at an educational institution if–

(a) he is registered or otherwise enrolled as a full-time pupil or student at the institution; or
(b) he receives education at the institution under arrangements with another educational institution at which he is so registered or otherwise enrolled.

(9) In this section, except where the context otherwise requires–

"authority" means–

(a) in relation to Great Britain, a local authority; and
(b) [*Northern Ireland*];

"children's home" has–

(a) in relation to England and Wales, the meaning which would be given by subsection (3) of section 63 of the Children Act 1989 if the reference in paragraph (a) of that subsection to more than three children were a reference to one or more children; and
(b) [*Northern Ireland*];

"community home" has the meaning given by section 53(1) of the Children Act 1989;

"hospital" has–

(a) in relation to England and Wales, the meaning given by section 128(1) of the National Health Service Act 1977;
(b) [*Scotland*]; and
(c) [*Northern Ireland*];

"mental nursing home" has, in relation to England and Wales, the meaning given by section 22(1) of the Registered Homes Act 1984

"nursing home"–

(a) in relation to England and Wales, has the meaning given by section 21(1) of the Registered Homes Act 1984;
(b) [*Scotland*];
(c) [*Northern Ireland*];

"private hospital" has–

(a) [*Scotland*]; and
(b) [*Northern Ireland*];

"residential care home"–

(a) in relation to England and Wales, has the meaning given by section 1(2) of the Registered Homes Act 1984;
(b) [*Scotland*]; and
(c) [*Northern Ireland*];

"residential establishment" has the meaning given by section 93(1) of the Children (Scotland) Act 1995 as the meaning of that expression in Scotland;

"voluntary home" has–

(a) in relation to England and Wales, the meaning given by section 60(3) of the Children Act 1989; and
(b) [*Northern Ireland*].

(2) Indictment

Statement of Offence

Abuse of a position of trust, contrary to section 3(1)(a) of the Sexual Offences (Amendment) Act 2000.

Particulars of Offence

A B, on the ___ day of ___, 20_, being a person of the age of at least 18 years, had sexual intercourse with J N, being a person under the age of 18 years, and being at the time in a position of trust in relation to J N, in that at the time he looked after persons under the age of 18 years who were receiving full-time education at _____ school, and J N was at the time in receipt of such education at the aforesaid school.

(3) Allocation and class of offence

This offence is triable either way: s.3(4), above. As to the classification of offences, see § 2-22c in the main work. **H-111**

(4) Sentence

See s.3(4), above. **H-112**

The setting out of the various positions of trust in section 4(2) to (5) is not to be taken as indicative of descending seriousness: *Hubbard* [2002] EWCA Crim 494; [2002] 2 Cr. App. R.(S.) 101.

APPENDIX J
A Guide to Commencing Proceedings in the Court of Appeal (Criminal Division)

Appendix J

A. Applications for Leave to Appeal Conviction, Sentence and Confiscation orders

A1. Advice and Assistance

J-1 A1-1. Provision for advice and assistance on appeal is included in the trial representation order issued by the Crown Court. Solicitors should not wait to be asked for advice by the defendant. Immediately following the conclusion of the case, the legal representatives should see the defendant and advocates should express orally a view as to the prospects of a successful appeal (whether against conviction or sentence or both). If there are reasonable grounds, grounds of appeal should be drafted, signed and sent to instructing solicitors as soon as possible, bearing in mind the time limits that apply to lodging an appeal (see *section A6. Time Limits*). Solicitors should immediately send a copy of the documents received from the advocate to the defendant.

A1-2. Prior to the lodging of the notice and grounds of appeal by service of Form NG, the Registrar has no power to grant a representation order. The Crown Court can only amend a representation order in favour of fresh legal representatives if advice on appeal has not been given by trial representatives and it is necessary and reasonable for another legal representative to be instructed. Where advice on appeal has been given by trial legal representatives, application for funding prior to the lodging of the notice and grounds of appeal may only be made to the Legal Aid Authority (LAA).

A1-3. Once the Form NG has been lodged, the Registrar is the relevant authority for decisions about whether an individual qualifies for representation for the purposes of criminal proceedings before the Court of Appeal Criminal Division (ss.16(1) & 19(1) Legal Aid, Sentencing and Punishment of Offenders Act 2012 and Reg.8 Criminal Legal Aid (Determinations by a Court and Choice of Representative) Regulations 2013).

A1-4. Where, in order to settle grounds of appeal, work of an exceptional nature is contemplated or where the expense will be great, legal representatives should not contact the LAA for funding but should submit a Form NG with provisional grounds of appeal and with a note to the Registrar requesting a representation order to cover the specific work considered necessary to enable final grounds of appeal to be settled. The Registrar will then consider whether it is appropriate to grant funding for this purpose.

A2. Lodging Form NG and grounds of appeal

J-2 A2-1. In respect of applications lodged **before 1 October 2018**, where the advocate has advised an appeal and the defendant's instructions have been obtained, the solicitor should lodge Form NG and signed grounds of appeal at the **Crown Court** where the defendant appeared accompanied by such other forms as may be appropriate.

A2-2. Following a change in procedure, which comes into force on the **1 October 2018**, Form NG, signed grounds of appeal and any such accompanying forms must be **lodged directly on the Registrar of Criminal Appeals** (CrimPR 39.2). A separate Form NG should be completed for each substantive application which is being made. Each application (conviction, sentence and confiscation order) has its own Form NG and must be drafted and lodged as a stand-alone application (*CPD IX Appeal 39C*).

A2-3. Electronic service at criminalappealoffice.applications@hmcts.x.gsi.gov.uk is encouraged, with large attachments being sent in clearly marked separate emails. Service will be accepted by post at the Criminal Appeal Office, Royal Courts of Justice, Strand, London, WC2A 2LL. Representatives must not lodge Form NG and grounds of appeal on to the Digital Case System (DCS), as this will not alert the Criminal Appeal Office ("CAO") and service will not be effected. However, should the grounds of appeal rely upon trial documents that are already uploaded to the DCS, advocates are encouraged to identify the location of the document on the DCS in their grounds of appeal, which can then be obtained by the CAO. If Form NG and grounds of appeal are lodged with the Crown

Court on or after the 1 October 2018, service will not be effected and the Crown Court will send the documents back to the representatives.

A2-4. Direct Lodgment on the Registrar of Criminal Appeals applies to all applications to appeal conviction, sentence and confiscation falling within Part 39 of the CrimPR (*see Section D. Other Appeals for specific information on where to lodge applications in relation to other types of appeal*).

A2.5. It should be noted that Form NG and grounds of appeal are required to be served within the relevant time limit in all cases whether or not leave to appeal is required (e.g. where a trial Judge's certificate has been granted). However, on a reference by the Criminal Cases Review Commission (CCRC), if no Form NG and grounds are served within the required period, then the reference shall be treated as the appeal notice (CrimPR 39.5 (2)).

A3. Form NG and grounds of appeal

A3-1. Grounds must be settled with sufficient particularity to enable the Registrar, and subsequently the Court, to identify clearly the matters relied upon. A mere formula such as "the conviction is unsafe" or "the sentence is in all the circumstances too severe" will be deemed ineffective. **J-3**

A3-2. CrimPR 39.3 (1) sets out the information that *must* be contained in the appeal notice. The notice must:

(a) Specify:
  (i) the conviction, verdict or finding,
  (ii) the sentence, or
  (iii) the order, or the failure to make an order
  about which the appellant wants to appeal;
(b) identify each ground of appeal on which the appellant relies (and see paragraph (2));
(c) identify the transcript that the appellant thinks the Court will need, if the appellant wants to appeal against a conviction (*see section A7. Transcripts and notes of evidence*);
(d) identify the relevant sentencing powers of the Crown Court, if sentence is in issue;
(e) include or attach any application for the following, with reasons-
  (i) permission to appeal, if the appellant needs the court's permission,
  (ii) an extension of time within which to serve the appeal notice,
  (iii) bail pending appeal,
  (iv) a direction to attend in person a hearing that the appellant could attend by live link, if the appellant is in custody,
  (v) the introduction of evidence, including hearsay evidence and evidence of bad character
  (vi) an order requiring a witness to attend court,
  (vii) a direction for special measures for a witness,
  (viii) a direction for special measures for the giving of evidence by the appellant;
(f) identify any other document or thing that the appellant thinks the Court will need to decide the appeal.

A3-3. The grounds of appeal should set out the relevant facts and nature of the proceedings *concisely* in one all-encompassing document, not separate grounds of appeal and advice (*CPD IX Appeal 39C*). Pursuant to CrimPR 39.3(2) the grounds must:

(a) include in no more than the first two pages a summary of the grounds that makes what then follows easy to understand;
(b) in each ground of appeal identify the event or decision to which that ground relates;
(c) in each ground of appeal summarise the facts relevant to that ground, but only to the extent necessary to make clear what is in issue;
(d) concisely outline each argument in relation to each ground;
(e) number each ground consecutively if there is more than one;
(f) identify any relevant authority and
  i) state the proposition of law that the authority demonstrates, and
  ii) identify the parts of the authority that support that proposition; and
(g) where the Criminal Cases Review Commission refers a case to the court, explain how each ground of appeal relates (if it does) to the reasons for the reference.

A3-4. The intended readership of this document is the Court and not the lay or professional client. Its purpose is to enable the single Judge to grasp quickly the facts and issues in the case. In appropriate cases, draft grounds of appeal may be perfected before submission to the single Judge. A **separate** list of authorities must be provided which should contain the appellant's name and refer to the relevant paragraph numbers in each authority (CPD XII General Application D1) (*see section A8-5*).

A3-5. Failure to comply with the requirements in CrimPR 39 and the CPD referred to above, will result in a direction from the Registrar that the defects be remedied prior to the case being allocated to a single Judge. Failure to do so may be brought to the attention of the single Judge and/or full Court and legal representatives may be personally required to explain the reasons for non-compliance.

A3-6. Advocates should not settle or sign grounds unless they consider that they are properly arguable. An advocate should not settle grounds they cannot support because they are "instructed" to do so by a defendant.

A4. Applications by fresh legal representatives

J-4 A4-1. In all cases where fresh solicitors or fresh advocates are instructed, who did not act for the appellant at trial, it is necessary for the fresh solicitors or advocate to approach the solicitors and/or advocate who previously acted to ensure that the facts upon which the grounds of appeal are premised are correct, unless there are exceptional circumstances and good and compelling reasons not to do so. Such exceptional circumstances would likely be very rare (*McCook* [2014] EWCA Crim 734; [2016] 2 Cr. App. R.30). Where necessary, further steps should be taken to obtain objective and independent evidence to establish the factual basis for the appeal (*Lee* [2014] EWCA Crim 2928). The duty to make proper and diligent enquiries of previous representatives is not restricted to cases where criticism is being made of the trial representatives. It extends to all cases where there are fresh representatives acting (*McGill & others* [2017] EWCA Crim 1228).

A4-2. In cases where fresh representatives seek to adduce fresh evidence that was not adduced at trial, not only will the fresh representatives be required to comply with their duties pursuant to McCook; but the Registrar will usually also instigate the "waiver of privilege" procedure or require written reasons as to why the procedure should not be instigated (*Singh* [2017] EWCA Crim 466).

A4-3. Where a ground of appeal by fresh representatives criticises trial advocates and/or trial solicitors and in any other circumstance the Registrar considers necessary as set out above, the Registrar will instigate the waiver of privilege procedure. The appellant will be asked to waive privilege in respect of instructions to and advice at trial from legal representatives. If the appellant does waive privilege, the grounds of appeal are sent to the appropriate trial representative(s) and they are invited to respond. Any response will be sent to the appellant and his fresh legal representatives for comment. All of these documents will be sent to the single Judge when considering the application for leave. If the criticism is implicit, the Registrar may still instigate the procedure or he will refer the decision whether to instigate the procedure to a single Judge (*JH* [2014] EWCA Crim 2618). The single Judge may draw inferences from any failure to participate in the process. Waiver of privilege is a procedure that should be instigated by the Registrar and not by fresh legal representatives. However, if it is clear that the procedure will need to be instigated, the fresh representatives should lodge a signed waiver of privilege with the grounds of appeal (and any fresh evidence) but go no further.

A5. Specific grounds of appeal

Applications to call fresh evidence

J-5 A5-1.1 Where grounds of appeal rely upon fresh evidence that was not adduced at trial, an application pursuant to s. 23 Criminal Appeals Act 1968 must be made. If the fresh evidence is provided by a witness, representatives should obtain a statement from the witness in the form prescribed by s9 of the Criminal Justice Act 1967. If the fresh evidence is documentary or real evidence, the representatives should obtain statements from all those involved formally exhibiting the evidence. A Form W should be lodged in respect of each witness dealing with the fresh evidence. The Form W should indicate whether there is an application for a witness order. The Registrar or single Judge may direct the issue of a witness order but only the Court hearing the appeal may give leave for a witness to be called and then formally receive the evidence under s23 of the Criminal Appeal Act 1968.

A5-1.2 A supporting witness statement (in s9 form), or an affidavit from the appellant's solicitor must accompany the fresh evidence and Form W(s), setting out why the evidence was not available at trial and how it has come to light (*Gogana The Times* 12/07/1999). This will implicitly require fresh representatives to comply with McCook (*see section A4. Applications by fresh legal representatives*).

Insufficient weight given to assistance to prosecution authorities

J-6 Where a ground of appeal against sentence is that the Judge has given insufficient weight to the assistance given to the prosecution authorities, the "text" which had been prepared for the sentencing Judge is obtained by the Registrar. Grounds of appeal should be drafted in an anodyne form with a note to the Registrar alerting him to the existence of a "text". The CAO will obtain the "text" and the single Judge will have seen it when considering leave as will the full Court before the appeal hearing and it need not be alluded to in open Court.

Applications based on a change in law

A5-3.1 If an application to appeal which is based on a change in law is lodged within time, (see *A6. Time Limits*) the test to be applied by the Court of Appeal is whether the conviction is unsafe (*Johnson & Ors* [2016] EWCA Crim 1613). J-7

A5-3.2 If an application which is based on a change in law is lodged outside the time limits, exceptional leave will be required. Exceptional leave will only be granted if the applicant would otherwise suffer "substantial injustice" due to the change in law. Grounds of appeal should therefore set out why the substantial injustice test is met (*Johnson & Ors* [2016] EWCA Crim 1613). For examples of how the Court of Appeal has applied these principles see: *Uthayakumar* [2014] EWCA Crim 123 and *Ordu* [2017] EWCA Crim 4.

A6. Time Limits

A6-1. Notice and grounds should be lodged within 28 days from the date of conviction, sentence, verdict, finding or decision that is being appealed (s. 18 Criminal Appeal Act 1968 and CrimPR 39.2(1)). On a reference by the CCRC, Form NG and grounds should be served on the Registrar not more than 28 days after the Registrar has served notice that the CCRC has referred a conviction or sentence (CrimPR 39.2 (2)). J-8

A6-2. Where sentences were passed on different dates there may be two appeals against sentence. For example, there may be an appeal against a custodial term and an appeal against a confiscation order (*Neal* [1992] 2 Cr. App. R.(S) 352).

A6-3. An application for an extension of the 28 day period in which to give notice of an application must always be supported by details of the delay and the reasons for it (*Wilson* [2016] EWCA Crim 65). Often a chronology will assist. It is not enough merely to tick the relevant box on the Form NG.

A6-4. For out of time applications based on a change in law see A5-3. above.

A6-5. Applications for an extension of time should be submitted when the application for leave to appeal against either conviction or sentence is made and not in advance. Notwithstanding the terms of s18 (3) Criminal Appeal Act 1968, it has long been the practice of the Registrar to require the extension of time application to be made at the time of service of the notice and grounds of appeal. This practice is now reflected in CrimPR 36.4 and 39.3(2)(h)(ii).

A7. Transcripts and notes of evidence

A7-1. In publicly funded conviction cases, transcripts of the summing up and proceedings up to and including verdict are obtained as a matter of course. There is an obligation under CrimPR 39.3(2)(c) for advocates to identify any further transcript which they consider the Court will need and to provide a note of dates and times to enable an order to be placed with the transcription company. This is particularly important where there have been early directions and/or a split summing-up. Whether or not any further transcript is required is a matter for the judgment of the Registrar or his staff. Transcripts of evidence are not usually ordered; it may be appropriate for the advocate to provide an agreed note of evidence. J-9

A7-2. In sentence cases, transcripts of the prosecution opening of facts on a guilty plea and the Judge's observations on passing sentence are usually obtained. The Registrar will also obtain the relevant transcript in an application for leave to appeal against a confiscation order, an interlocutory appeal from a preparatory hearing or any other appeal providing the application has not been made by the prosecution.

A7-3. A transcript should only be requested if it is essential for the proper conduct of the appeal in light of the grounds. If the Registrar and the advocate are unable to agree the extent of the transcript to be obtained, the Registrar may refer that matter to a Judge.

A7-4. In certain circumstances the costs of unnecessary transcripts may be ordered to be paid by the appellant. Where a transcript is obtained otherwise than through the Registrar, the cost may be disallowed on taxation of public funding.

A7-5. If an appellant is paying privately for his legal representation, an order for transcripts should be placed directly with the transcription company and a copy provided to the Registrar upon receipt. If the Registrar has already obtained transcripts in a private case, the appellant's legal representatives will be required to pay the cost of the transcripts before they are released to them.

A8. Perfection of grounds of appeal

A8-1. The purpose of perfection is (a) to save valuable judicial time by enabling the Court to identify at once the relevant parts of the transcript and (b) to give the advocate the opportunity to J-10 reconsider the original grounds in the light of the transcript. Perfected grounds should consist of a fresh document which supersedes the original grounds of appeal and contains inter alia references by page number and letter (or paragraph number) to all relevant passages in the transcript.

A8-2. In conviction or confiscation appeals, the Registrar will almost certainly invite the advocate to perfect grounds to assist the single Judge or full Court. As a general rule, the advocate will not be invited to perfect the grounds of appeal in a sentence case. Where an advocate indicates a wish to perfect grounds of appeal against sentence, the Registrar will consider the request and will only invite perfection where he considers it necessary for the assistance of the single Judge or full Court.

A8-3. If perfection is appropriate, the advocate will be sent a copy of the transcript and asked to perfect the grounds, usually within 14 days. In the absence of any response from the advocate, the existing notice and grounds of appeal will be placed before the single Judge or the Court without further notice. If an advocate does not wish to perfect the grounds, a note to that effect will ensure that the case is not unnecessarily delayed.

A8-4. If, having considered the transcript, the advocate is of the opinion that there are no valid grounds, the reasons should be set out in a further advice and sent to his instructing solicitors. The Registrar should be informed that this has been done, but the advocate should not send the Registrar a copy of that advice. Solicitors should send a copy to the appellant and obtain instructions, at the same time explaining that if the appellant persists with his application the Court may consider whether to make a loss of time order.

A8-5. Advocates should identify any relevant authorities (CrimPR 39.3(2)(g)) and submit a separate list of authorities with the perfected grounds of appeal and include copies of any unreported authorities.

A9. Respondent's Notice

J-11 A9-1. The Criminal Procedure Rules provide for the service of a Respondent's Notice. Pursuant to CrimPR 39.6(1) the Registrar may serve the appeal notice on any party directly affected by the appeal (usually the prosecution) and must do so in a CCRC case. That party may then serve a Respondent's Notice if it wishes to make representations and must do so if the Registrar so directs (CrimPR 39.6(2)(b)). If directed, the Respondent's Notice should be served within 14 days (CrimPR 39.6(4)(a)). However, unless the case is urgent (in which case the Registrar may impose a deadline shorter than 14 days), 21 days is normally allowed for service. The Respondent's Notice should be served on the Registrar and any other party on whom the Registrar served the appeal notice.

A9-2. The Respondent's Notice must be in the specified Form RN and should set out the grounds of opposition (CrimPR 39.6(5)) including the information set out in CrimPR 39.6(6).

A9-3. In practice, this procedure primarily applies prior to consideration of leave by the single Judge. However, a Respondent's Notice may be sought at any time in the proceedings including at the direction of the single Judge. The Attorney General and the Registrar, following consultation with representatives from the Crown Prosecution Service (CPS) and the Revenue and Customs Prosecution Office (RCPO), have agreed guidance on types of cases and/or issues where the Registrar should consider whether to serve an appeal notice and direct or invite a party to serve a Respondent's Notice before the consideration of leave by the single Judge.

Examples of when the Registrar might direct a Respondent's Notice include:

(i) where the grounds concern matters which were the subject of public interest immunity (PII);
(ii) allegations of jury irregularity;
(iii) criticisms of the prosecution or the conduct of the Judge;
(iv) complex frauds;
(v) inconsistent verdicts;
(vi) fresh evidence;
(vii) where the grounds claim that the wrong statute, rule or regulation was applied.

The CPS will always be invited to lodge a Respondent's Notice in the following cases:

(i) all *conviction and sentence* applications involving a fatality;
(ii) all *conviction applications* involving rape, attempted rape or a serious sexual offence;
(iii) all *conviction applications* where a CPS Complex Casework Unit dealt with the case;
(iv) all *conviction applications* where the offence was perverting the course of justice, misconduct in public office and any conspiracy.

A9-4. In conviction cases where leave to appeal has been granted or where the application for leave has been referred to the full Court, the Crown is briefed to attend the hearing and required to submit a Respondent's Notice/skeleton argument. In relation to sentence cases where leave has been granted, referred or an appellant is represented on a renewed application, the sentence protocol set out in *CPD IX Appeal 39A Appeals against conviction and sentence - the provision of notice to the prosecution*, will apply. In those cases, a Respondent's Notice/skeleton argument will have to be served when the

Crown indicates a wish to attend a hearing or when the Registrar directs the Crown to attend. There is no need to serve a skeleton argument in addition to a Respondent's Notice.

A10. Referral by the Registrar

A10-1. Where leave to appeal is required, the Registrar, having obtained the necessary documents, will usually refer the application(s) to a single Judge for a decision (on the papers) under s. 31 Criminal Appeal Act 1968. The Registrar does have the power to refer an application for leave directly to the full Court, in which case he will usually grant the advocate a representation order for the hearing. Where an application is referred because an unlawful sentence has been passed or other procedural error identified, a representation order will ordinarily be granted unless the error is such that the Court could correct it on the papers, but advocates should be aware that the Court may make observations for the attention of the determining officer that a full fee should not be allowed on taxation. A representation order will not be granted where the presence of an advocate is not required, such as where there has been a technical error that the Court can correct without the need for oral argument. An applicant would not have the right to attend the hearing because the appeal is on a point of law only (s.22 Criminal Appeal Act 1968; *Hyde and others* [2016] EWCA Crim 1031; [2016] 1 WLR 4020). **J-12**

A10-2. Leave to appeal is required in all cases except:

- Where the trial or sentencing Judge has certified that the case is fit for appeal;
- Where the appeal has been referred by the Criminal Cases Review Commission (CCRC);
- Where the appeal is under s13 Administration of Justice Act 1960 (contempt proceedings);
- Where there is no provision for the grant of leave by a Single Judge; for example an appeal against an order for trial without jury (*see Section D Other Appeals*).

A10-3. Where leave to appeal is not required, the Registrar will usually grant a representation order for the hearing of the appeal.

A11. Oral applications for leave to appeal

All applications for leave (together with any ancillary applications such as for bail, extension of time, or a representation order) are normally considered by a single Judge on the papers, unless it can be demonstrated that there are exceptional reasons why an oral hearing is required. An advocate or solicitors may request an oral hearing, but that request must be supported by written reasons stating why the case is exceptional and any reasons why that hearing should be expedited (expedition will be a matter for the Registrar). That application should be copied to the prosecution. The single Judge determining the substantive application will then decide whether an oral hearing should be arranged. An advocate may make an application for a representation order at the hearing itself. Oral applications for leave and bail are usually heard in Court but in chambers at 9.30am before the normal Court sittings. Advocates appear unrobed. If the advocate considers that an application may take longer than 20 minutes, the Registrar must be notified. If the single Judge declines to hear the application at an oral hearing, the application will then be considered on the papers by that Judge. **J-13**

A12. Powers of the single Judge

The single Judge may grant the application for leave, refuse it or refer it to the full Court. In conviction cases and in sentence cases where appropriate, the single Judge may grant limited leave i.e. leave to argue some grounds but not others. Advocates must notify the Registrar within 14 days whether the grounds upon which leave has been refused are to be renewed before the full Court. If a representation order is granted, in a limited leave case, public funding will only cover grounds of appeal which the single Judge or the full Court say are arguable (*Cox & Thomas* [1999] 2 Cr App Rep 6 and *Hyde and others* [2016] EWCA Crim 1031; [2016] 1 WLR 4020). The single Judge may also grant, refuse or refer any ancillary application. **J-14**

A13. Bail pending appeal (CrimPR 39.8)

A13-1. Bail may be granted (a) by a single Judge or the full Court or (b) by a trial or sentencing Judge who has certified the case fit for appeal. In the latter case, bail can only be granted within 28 days of the conviction or sentence which is the subject of the appeal and may not be granted if an application for bail has already been made to the Court of Appeal (CPD III Custody and bail 14H.5). **J-15**

A13-2. An application to the Court of Appeal for bail pending appeal must be supported by a completed Form B which must be served on the Registrar and the prosecution. The Court must not decide such an application without giving the prosecution the opportunity to make representations.

A13-3. An application for bail will not be considered by a single Judge or the Court until notice of application for leave to appeal conviction or sentence or notice of appeal has first been given. In practice, Judges will also require the relevant transcripts to be available so they may consider the merits of the substantive application at the same time as the bail application.

A13-4. Where bail is granted pending appeal, the Court may attach any condition that must be met before the party is released, and may direct how such a condition must be met. The Registrar must serve a certificate recording any such condition on the party, the party's custodian and any other person directly affected by the condition (CrimPR 39.9). A condition of residence is always attached.

A14. Funding for grant of leave or reference to full Court

J-16 A14-1. Where the single Judge grants leave or refers an application to the Court, it is usual to grant a representation order for the preparation and presentation of the appeal. This is usually limited to the services of an advocate only. The advocate who settled grounds of appeal will usually be the assigned advocate. If the applicant is a litigant in person, an advocate may be assigned by the Registrar. In such cases the Registrar will provide a brief but does not act as an appellant's solicitor. The Registrar may assign one advocate to represent more than one appellant if appropriate. If it is considered that a representation order for two advocates and/or solicitors is required, the advocate should notify the Registrar and provide written justification in accordance with Criminal Legal Aid (Determinations by a Court and Choice of Representative) Regulations 2013 (S.I. 2013/614).

A14-2. If solicitors are assigned, it should be noted that by virtue of Regulation 12 of the Criminal Legal Aid (Determinations by a Court and Choice of Representative) Regulations 2013, SI 2013/614, a representation order can only be issued to a solicitor if they hold a Standard Crime Contract with the LAA. A solicitor not holding such a franchise may apply to the LAA for an individual case contract (ICC) by virtue of which the solicitor is employed on behalf of the LAA to represent an appellant in a given case.

A14-3. In some circumstances, the Registrar may refer an application to the full Court. This may be because there is a novel point of law, there is fresh evidence to be considered pursuant to s.23 of the Criminal Appeal Act 1968 or because in a sentence case, the sentence passed is very short. A representation order for an advocate is usually granted. The advocate for the prosecution usually attends a Registrar's referral.

A15. Refusal by the Single Judge

J-17 A15-1. Where the single Judge refuses leave to appeal, the Registrar sends a notification of the refusal, including any observations which the Judge may have made, to the appellant, who is informed that he may require the application to be considered by the Court by serving a renewal notice (Form SJ-Renewal) upon the Registrar within 14 days from the date on which the notice of refusal was served on him.

A15-2. A refused application which is not renewed within 14 days lapses. An appellant may apply for an extension of time in which to renew his application for leave (CrimPR 36.3 - 36.5 and s.31 Criminal Appeal Act 1968). The Registrar will normally refer such an application to the Court to be considered at the same time as the renewed application for leave to appeal. An application for an extension of time in which to renew must be supported by cogent reasons.

A15-3. If it is intended that an advocate should represent the appellant at the hearing of the renewed application for leave to appeal, whether privately instructed or on a pro bono basis, such intention must be communicated to the CAO in writing as soon as that decision has been made. Whilst a representation order is not granted by the Registrar in respect of a renewed application for leave, the advocate may apply at the hearing to the Court for a representation order to cover that appearance and any further work done in preparation of the renewal retrospectively. In practice, this is only granted where the application for leave is successful.

A16. Directions for loss of time

J-17a A16-1. S.29 Criminal Appeal Act 1968 empowers the Court to direct that time spent in custody as an appellant shall not count as part of the term of any sentence to which the appellant is for the time being subject. The Court will do so where it considers that an application is wholly without merit. Such an order may not be made where leave to appeal or a trial Judge's certificate has been granted, on a reference by the CCRC or where an appeal has been abandoned. An appeal is not built into the trial process but must be justified on properly arguable grounds (*Fortean* [2009] EWCA Crim 437; [2009] Crim LR 798).

A16-2. The only means the Court has of discouraging unmeritorious applications which waste precious time and resources is by using the powers in the Criminal Appeal Act 1968 and the Prosecution of Offences Act 1985. In every case where the Court is presented with an unmeritorious application, consideration should be given to exercising these powers.

A16-3. The mere fact that an advocate has advised that there are grounds of appeal will not be a sufficient answer to the question as to whether or not an application has indeed been brought which was wholly without merit (*Gray and Others* [2014] EWCA Crim 2372; [2015] 1 Cr App Rep (S) 197).

A16-4. The Form SJ, on which the single Judge records his decisions, and the reverse of which is used by appellants to indicate their wish to renew, includes:

- a box for the single Judge to initial in order to indicate that that the full Court should consider loss of time or a costs order if the application is renewed; and
- a box for the applicant to give reasons why such an order should not be made, whether or not an indication has been given by a single Judge.

A16-5. Where the single Judge has not indicated that the full Court should consider making a loss of time order because the applicant is not in custody, the single Judge also has the option of considering whether to make any directions in respect of costs, which could include the prosecution costs (usually in providing a Respondent's Notice). The Practice Direction in relation to costs should be followed.

A17. Abandonment

A17-1. An appeal or application may be abandoned at any time before the hearing without leave by completing and lodging Form A. An oral instruction or letter indicating a wish to abandon is insufficient. **J-18**

A17-2. At the hearing, an application or appeal can only be abandoned with the permission of the Court (CrimPR 36.13(2)(b)). An appeal or application which is abandoned is treated as being a final determination of the full Court (CrimPR 36.13(4)(c)).

A17-3. A notice of abandonment cannot be withdrawn nor can it be conditional. A person who wants to reinstate an application or appeal after abandonment must apply in writing to the Registrar with reasons (CrimPR 36.13(5)). The Court has power to allow reinstatement only where the purported abandonment can be treated as a nullity and the applicant must provide the Court with the relevant information to determine the application (*Medway* (1976) 62 Cr. App. R. 85 and *Zabotka* [2016] EWCA Crim 1771).

A17-4. An application to treat the abandonment as a nullity is heard by the full Court. If the Court does agree to treat the abandonment as a nullity, the status of the application is restored as if there had been no interruption.

A18. Case Management Duties

A18-1. CrimPR 36.2 gives the Court and parties the same powers and duties of case management as in Part 3 of the Rules. In accordance with those duties, for each application received, the Registrar nominates a case progression officer, (the 'responsible officer'). There is also a duty on the parties to actively assist the Court to progress cases. Close contact between the advocate and solicitors and the responsible officer is encouraged in order to facilitate the efficient preparation and listing of appeals, especially in complex cases and those involving witnesses. **J-19**

A18-2. Powers under the Criminal Appeal Act 1968 exercisable by the single Judge and the Registrar are contained in s.31 Criminal Appeal Act 1968 (as amended by s.87 Courts Act 2003, s.331 & Sched.32 Criminal Justice Act 2003 and Sched.8 Criminal Justice and Immigration Act 2008). These powers include the power to make procedural directions for the efficient and effective preparation of an application or appeal and the power to make an order under s.23(1)(a) Criminal Appeal Act 1968 for the production of evidence etc. necessary for the determination of the case.

A18-3. Where the Registrar refuses an application by an appellant to exercise any of the Registrar's case management powers under s.31 Criminal Appeal Act 1968 in the appellant's favour, the appellant is entitled to have the application determined by a single Judge (s. 31A (4) of the Act). There is no provision for any appeal against a procedural direction given by a single Judge and thus such decisions are final.

B. Interlocutory Appeals against rulings in Preparatory Hearings

Appeal against a ruling pursuant to s.9 of the Criminal Justice Act 1987 or a decision pursuant to s.35 of the Criminal Procedure and Investigations Act 1996 (Part 37 CrimPR)

B1. Where a Judge has ordered a preparatory hearing, they may make a ruling as to the admissibility of evidence and any other question of law relating to the case (s.9(3)(b) & (c) CJA 1987 and s.31(3)(a) &(b) CPIA 1996). Given the co-extensive powers of case management outside the preparatory hearing regime, Courts should now be very cautious about directing a preparatory hearing (barring terrorist cases) (*L & L* [2018] EWCA Crim 69; *BM* [2018] EWCA Crim 560). **J-20**

B2. Pursuant to s.9(11) CJA 1987 and s.35(1) CPIA 1996 the defence or the prosecution may appeal to the CACD (and ultimately to the Supreme Court) against such a ruling, but only with the leave of the trial Judge, single Judge or the full Court. As to the scope of a Judge's powers in relation to a preparatory hearing and thus the extent of appeal rights, see the decision of the House of Lords in *H* [2007] UKHL 7 on appeal from [2006] EWCA Crim 1975; *VGA* [2010] EWCA Crim 2742.

B3. If the trial date is imminent and the application is urgent, the Registrar should be notified so that he may consider referring the application directly to the full Court.

B4. If an application for leave to appeal is made to the trial Judge, it should be made orally immediately after the ruling, or within two business days by serving a notice of an application on the appropriate officer of the Crown Court and all parties directly affected (CrimPR 37.4). Whether leave is granted by the trial Judge or not or no such application is made to the trial Judge, notice of an appeal or application for leave to appeal **(Form NG (Prep))** is to be served on the Registrar, the Crown Court and the parties within five business days of the ruling or the trial Judge's decision whether to grant leave (CrimPR 37.2).

B5. The notice and grounds of appeal having been served on the other parties, grounds of opposition should be served in a Respondent's Notice **(Form RN (Prep))** within five business days of service of the appeal notice (CrimPR 37.5).

B6. Defence representatives are usually covered by the Crown Court representation order if one is in force (Paragraph 2(2), Schedule 3, Access to Justice Act 1999).

B7. If the relevant time limits are not complied with, the Court has power to grant an extension of time. Where a single Judge refuses leave to appeal or an extension of time within which to serve a notice, the application may be renewed for determination by the full Court by serving the notice of renewal, appropriately completed, upon the Registrar within five business days of the refusal being served (CrimPR 37.7).

C. Appeals by a prosecutor against a "terminating" ruling

S.58 Criminal Justice Act 2003 (Part 38 CrimPR)

J-21 C1. S.58 Criminal Justice Act 2003 provides the prosecution with a right of appeal in relation to a "terminating" ruling: a ruling where the prosecution agree to the defendant's acquittal if the appeal is not successful (*Y* [2008] EWCA Crim 10). This is wide enough to encompass a case-management decision (*C* [2007] EWCA Crim 2532).

C2. There is no right of appeal in respect of a ruling that the jury be discharged or a ruling in respect of which there is a right of appeal to the Court of Appeal by virtue of another enactment (s.57(2) CJA 2003). The prosecution should therefore consider whether there is a right of appeal under s.9 CJA 1987 or s.35 CPIA 1996.

C3. The prosecution must inform the Court that it intends to appeal or request an adjournment to consider whether to appeal (s.58(4) CJA 2003), which will be until the next business day (CrimPR 38.2(2)). The Judge has discretion to adjourn for longer if there is a real reason for doing so (*H* [2008] EWCA Crim 483). The prosecution can ask the trial Judge to grant leave to appeal immediately after the ruling or after the granted adjournment to consider the same (CrimPR 38.5). Leave should be granted only where the Judge considers there is a real prospect of success and not to speed up the hearing of the appeal (*JG* [2006] EWCA Crim 3276). If the prosecution do not ask the trial judge for leave to appeal, the notice and application to appeal **(Form NG (Pros))** must be served on the Crown Court, Registrar and every defendant affected by the ruling the next business day if the trial Judge expedites the appeal or five business days after telling the Judge of the intent to appeal if the Judge does not expedite the same (CrimPR 38.3). The prosecution must give the undertaking (as to the defendant's acquittal if the appeal is abandoned or leave to appeal is not obtained) at the time when it informs the Court of its intention to appeal. The failure to give it then is fatal to an application to the Court of Appeal for leave (ss.58(8) CJA 2003) (*LSA* [2008] EWCA Crim 1034; *NT* [2010] EWCA Crim 711; *B* [2014] EWCA Crim 2078).

C4. Whether or not leave is granted, the trial Judge must decide if the appeal is to be expedited and if so, adjourn the case. If he decides that the appeal should not be expedited then he can adjourn the case or discharge the jury (s.59 CJA 2003).

C5. The notice and grounds of appeal having been served on the other parties, grounds of opposition should be served in a Respondent's Notice **(Form RN (Prep))**. The Respondent's Notice must be served the next business day if the trial judge expedites the appeal or within five business days of service of the appeal notice if the appeal is not expedited (CrimPR 37.5).

C.6. Defence representatives are usually covered by the Crown Court representation order if one is in force (such proceedings being considered incidental within Paragraph 5(3) of Schedule 3 to the Legal Aid, Sentencing and Punishment of Offenders Act 2012).

C7. Expedition does not impose time limits on the Registrar or Court of Appeal. However, if leave has not been granted by the trial Judge, the application may be referred to the full Court by the Registrar to ensure that the matter is dealt with quickly.

C8. The Registrar endeavours to list prosecution appeals where a jury has not been discharged as quickly as possible. He is unlikely to be able to list an appeal in less than a week from the ruling because it is necessary for the prosecution to obtain transcripts, papers to be copied and the Judges to read their papers. It is of great assistance if it is anticipated that there is to be an appeal against a ruling where the jury has not been discharged that a phone call is made to the Registrar or CAO General Office (020 7947 6011) notifying the office even before the appeal notice is sent, so that preliminary views can be taken as to the constitution which may be able to hear the appeal. The listing of an urgent appeal invariably means that other cases have to be removed from the list.

D. Other Appeals

D1. Prosecution appeal against the making of a confiscation order or where the Court declines to make one (save on reconsideration of benefit)

- S.31(1) & (2) Proceeds of Crime Act 2002 **J-22**
- Part 42 CrimPR
- Proceedings are commenced by serving a **Form PoCA 1** on the defendant and the Crown Court within 28 days of the decision appealed against (Article 3(2)(a) Proceeds of Crime Act (Appeals under Part 2) Order 2003)
- A Respondent's Notice **Form PoCA 2** is to be served on the Registrar of Criminal Appeals and the appellant not later than 14 days after receiving **Form PoCA 1**
- An undischarged Crown Court representation order will cover advice and assistance on the merits of opposing the appeal and drafting the Respondent's Notice, otherwise an application for a representation order can be made to the Registrar. In any event where an application for a representation order is made on Form **PoCA 2**, the Registrar will consider a representation order for the hearing
- Leave to appeal can be granted by a single Judge or the full Court

D2. Prosecution and third party appeal against a determination, under S.10A Proceeds of Crime Act 2002, of the extent of the defendant's interest in property

- S.31(4) & (5) Proceeds of Crime Act 2002 **J-23**
- Part 42 CrimPR
- Proceedings are commenced by serving a **Form PoCa 1** on the defendant and the Crown Court within 28 days of the decision appealed against
- A Respondent's Notice **Form PoCA 2** is to be served on the Registrar of Criminal Appeals and the appellant not later than 14 days after receiving **Form PoCA 1**
- An undischarged Crown Court representation order will cover advice and assistance on the merits of opposing the appeal and drafting the Respondent's Notice, otherwise an application for a representation order can be made to the Registrar. In any event where an application for a representation order is made on **Form PoCA 2**, the Registrar will consider a representation order for the hearing
- Leave to appeal can be granted by a single Judge or the full Court

D3. Appeal in relation to a restraint order

- S.43 Proceeds of Crime Act 2002 **J-24**
- Part 42 CrimPR
- The prosecution or an accredited financial investigator can appeal a refusal to make a restraint order. A person who applied for an order or who is affected by the order can apply to the Crown Court to vary or discharge the order and then appeal that decision to the Court of Appeal
- Proceedings are commenced by serving a **Form PoCA 3** on the Crown Court within 28 days of the decision being appealed. **Form PoCA 3** must then be served on any respondent, any person who holds realisable property to which the appeal relates, or is affected by the appeal, not later than seven days after the form is lodged at the Crown Court. The documents which are to be served with **Form PoCA3** are set out in CrimPR 42.15
- A Respondent's Notice **Form PoCA 4** is to be served on the Registrar of Criminal Appeals not later than 14 days after the respondent is notified that the appellant has leave to appeal or notified that the application for leave and the appeal are to be heard together. **Form PoCA 4**

is then to be served on the appellant and any other respondent as soon as is practicable and not later than seven days after it was served on the Registrar
- Criminal Defence Service Regulations do not apply to these proceedings and thus no representation orders will be granted by the Registrar or the Court
- Leave to appeal can be granted by a single Judge or full Court
- An application for a restraint order can be made as soon as a criminal investigation has begun. The proposed defendant may not have been charged (s.40 Proceeds of Crime Act 2002)

D4. Appeal in relation to a receivership order

J-25
- S.65 Proceeds of Crime Act 2002
- Part 42 CrimPR
- The appointment, non-appointment or powers of a receiver can be appealed, as can an order giving a direction to a receiver and the variation or discharge of a receivership order. An appeal can be brought by the person who applied for the order, a person who is affected by the order or the receiver
- Proceedings are commenced by serving a **Form PoCA 3** on the Crown Court within 28 days of the decision being appealed
- **Form PoCA 3** must then be served on any respondent and any person who holds realisable property to which the appeal relates, or is affected by the appeal, not later than seven days after the form is lodged at the Crown Court
- A Respondent's Notice **Form PoCA 4** to be served on the Registrar of Criminal Appeals not later than 14 days after the respondent is notified that the appellant has leave to appeal or is notified that the application for leave and the appeal are to be heard together. **Form PoCA 4** is then to be served on the appellant and any other respondent as soon as is practicable and not later than seven days after it was served on the Registrar
- Criminal Defence Service Regulations do not apply to these proceedings and thus no representation orders will be granted by the Registrar or the Court
- Leave to appeal can be granted by a single Judge or full Court

D5. Appeal against an order of the Crown Court in the exercise of its jurisdiction to punish for contempt - usually a finding of contempt or sentence for contempt

J-26
- S.13 Administration of Justice Act 1960
- Part 39 CrimPR
- Anyone dealt with by the Crown Court for contempt may appeal
- Proceedings are commenced by lodging a **Form NG** at the Crown Court (if the notice and grounds are lodged before 1 October 2018) or directly on the Registrar of Criminal Appeals (if the notice and grounds are lodged on or after 1 October 2018) not more than 28 days after the order to be appealed (*see section A2. Lodging Form NG and grounds of appeal*)
- The Registrar may direct a Respondent's Notice **Form RN** or the prosecution may serve one if they wish to make representations to the Court
- An undischarged Crown Court representation order will cover advice and assistance on appeal. The Registrar will consider a representation order for the hearing (s.19 Legal Aid, Sentencing and Punishment of Offenders Act 2012; Reg.8 Criminal Legal Aid (Determinations by Court and Choice of Representative) Regulations 2013 [SI 2013/614])
- No leave to appeal is required. The appeal is as of right (s. 13 Administration of Justice Act 1960)
- Appeals occur most frequently when an appellant wishes to appeal a sentence for failing to appear at the Crown Court as the failing to appear is dealt with as if it were contempt

D6. Appeal against a minimum term set or reviewed by a High Court Judge

J-27
- Para. 14 of Schedule 22 Criminal Justice Act 2003
- Part 39 CrimPR
- A defendant with a mandatory life sentence imposed before 18 December 2003 who has had his minimum term set or reviewed by a High Court Judge can appeal
- Proceedings are commenced by service of **Form NG (MT)** on the Registrar not more than 28 days after the decision
- The Registrar may direct a Respondent's Notice **Form RN** or the prosecution may serve one if they wish to make representations to the Court

- An application for a representation order can be made to the Registrar (s.19 Legal Aid, Sentencing and Punishment of Offenders Act 2012; Reg.8 Criminal Legal Aid (Determinations by Court and Choice of Representative) Regulations 2013 [SI 2013/614])
- Leave to appeal is required and can be granted by the full Court or a single Judge (Part 2 Para.8 Criminal Justice Act 2003 (Mandatory Life Sentences: Appeals in Transitional Cases Order 2003) [S.I. 2005/2798])

D7. Attorney General's reference of an unduly lenient sentence

- S.36 Criminal Justice Act 1988 J-28
- Part 41 CrimPR
- The Attorney General can refer sentences only in relation to specific offences or sentences (ss.35 & 36 Criminal Justice Act 1988 and Criminal Justice Act 1988 (Reviews of Sentencing) Order 2006)
- Although CrimPR 41.3(1) implies there is a specific form to commence proceedings, in practice a standard letter with supporting documents is sent to the Registrar of Criminal Appeals by the Attorney General's Office no more than 28 days after sentence
- If the defendant wishes to make representations to the Court he must serve a Respondent's Notice within 14 days of the Registrar serving the application upon him. Again, there is no specific form available
- Representation orders are granted by the Registrar to respond to an Attorney General's reference
- The leave of the Court of Appeal is required

D8. Attorney General's reference of a point of law on an acquittal

- S.36 Criminal Justice Act 1972 J-29
- Part 41 Crim PR
- The Attorney General can refer a point of law to the Court of Appeal for their opinion on the acquittal on indictment of the defendant
- Although CrimPR 41.3(1) implies there is a specific form to commence proceedings, there is no such form and CrimPR 70.3 sets out what should be included in the reference. All references which identify the defendant should be excluded
- There is no time limit
- If the defendant wishes to make representations to the Court he must serve a Respondent's Notice within 28 days of the Registrar serving the application upon him. Again there is no specific form available
- Representation orders are granted by the Registrar to respond to an Attorney General's reference
- Leave is not required

D9. Appeal against a finding of unfitness to plead or a finding that the accused did the act or made the omission charged

- S.15 Criminal Appeal Act 1968 J-30
- Part 39 CrimPR
- The accused can appeal (by the person appointed to represent the accused) against a finding of unfitness to plead (but not fitness to plead) and that he did the act or made the omission charged. The appeal does not lie until both findings have been made
- Proceedings are commenced by the service of **Form NG** on the Crown Court (if the application is lodged prior to the 1 October 2018) or directly on the Registrar of Criminal Appeals (if the application is lodged on or after the 1 October 2018) not more than 28 days after the finding made which the accused wishes to appeal (*see section A2. Lodging of Form NG and grounds of appeal*)
- The prosecution should serve a Respondent's Notice **Form RN** if directed by the Registrar or if they wish to make representations to the court
- The costs of the person appointed to put the case on appeal are paid from central funds, but the mechanism will depend on the outcome of the appeal proceedings, thus the issue should be considered only at the conclusion of proceedings. Where an appeal is allowed, the Court may make a defendant's costs order under s16(4)(a)(iii) of the Prosecution of Offences Act 1985, which will include legal costs (s16A(3)(c)). Where leave to appeal is not granted or the appeal is not successful, the costs of the person appointed to put the case on appeal are

covered by Part IIIA of the regulations made under s19(3)(d) of the 1985 Act (*Antoine* [1999] 2 Cr. App.R.225)
- Leave to appeal may be granted by the Crown Court Judge, a single Judge or the full Court

D10. Appeal against a verdict of not guilty by reason of insanity

J-31
- S.12 Criminal Appeal Act 1968
- Part 39 CrimPR
- The defendant can appeal a verdict of not guilty by reason of insanity
- Proceedings are commenced by the service of **Form NG** on the Crown Court (if the application is lodged prior to the 1 October 2018) or directly on the Registrar of Criminal Appeals (if the application is lodged on or after 1 October 2018) not more than 28 days after the verdict (*see section A2. Lodging of Form NG and grounds of appeal*)
- The prosecution should serve a Respondent's Notice **Form RN** if directed by the Registrar or if they wish to make representations to the court
- S.16(4) Prosecution of Offences Act 1985 provides that where the Court of Appeal **allows an appeal** then the court may make a defendant's costs order. If the appeal is not allowed costs from central funds should be available on the same basis as was allowed in *Antoine* (above) in the absence of any statutory provision
- Leave to appeal may be granted by the Crown Court Judge, a single Judge or the full Court

D11. Appeal against the order following a verdict of not guilty by reason of insanity or a finding of unfitness to plead

J-32
- S.16A Criminal Appeal Act 1968
- Part 39 CrimPR
- An accused who, as a result of a verdict of not guilty by reason of insanity or a finding of fitness to plead has a hospital order, interim hospital order or supervision order made against him may appeal against the order
- Proceedings are commenced by the service of **Form NG** on the Crown Court (if the application is lodged prior to the 1 October 2018) or directly on the Registrar of Criminal Appeals (if the application is lodged on or after 1 October 2018) not more than 28 days after the verdict (*see section A". Lodging Form NG and grounds of appeal*)
- The prosecution should serve a Respondent's Notice **Form RN** if directed by the Registrar or if they wish to make representations to the court
- S.16(4) Prosecution of Offences Act 1985 provides that where the Court of Appeal **allows an appeal** then the court may make a defendant's costs order. If the appeal is not allowed costs from central funds should be available on the same basis as was allowed in *Antoine* (above) in the absence of any statutory provision
- Leave to appeal may be granted by the Crown Court Judge, a single Judge or the full Court

D12. Appeal against review of sentence

J-33
- S.74(8) Serious Organised Crime and Police Act 2005
- Part 39 Crim PR
- A defendant or specified prosecutor may appeal
- Proceedings are commenced by serving a **Form NG (RD)** on the Crown Court (if the application is lodged prior to 1 October 2018) or directly on the Registrar of Criminal Appeals (if the application is lodged on or after 1 October 2018) not more than 28 days after the review (*see section A2. Lodging Form NG and grounds of appeal*)
- A Respondent's Notice **Form RN** should be served if directed by the Registrar or if the respondent wishes to make representations to the Court
- An application for a representation order can be made to the Registrar (Legal Aid, Sentencing and Punishment of Offenders Act 2012 s.19; Reg .9 Criminal Legal Aid (General) Regulations 2013)
- Leave to appeal can be granted by the single Judge or full Court (Serious Organised Crime and Police Act 2005 (Appeals under s.74) Order 2006/21)

D13. Appeal against an order for trial by jury of sample counts

J-34
- S.18 Domestic Violence, Crime and Victims Act 2004
- Part 37 Crim PR

- The defendant and the prosecution can appeal the determination of an application to make the order
- An application for the jury to try some counts as sample counts and the Judge to try the remainder if the jury convict, must be determined at a preparatory hearing and s.18 confers rights of interlocutory appeal. A **Form NG (Prep)** must be served on the Crown Court, the Registrar and any party directly affected not more than five business days after the order or the Crown Court Judge granting or refusing leave (*For applications to the Crown Court Judge see Part B above*)
- A Respondent's Notice **Form RN (Prep)** should be served if the Court directs or the prosecution (or any party affected) wants to make representations to the Court
- Defence representatives are usually covered by the Crown Court representation order if one is in force, the proceedings being considered incidental within Paragraph 5(3) of Schedule 3 to Legal Aid, Sentencing and Punishment of Offenders Act 2012
- The Crown Court Judge, single Judge or full Court can grant leave

D14. Appeal against an order relating to a trial to be conducted without a jury where there is a danger of jury tampering

- S.45(5) and (9) Criminal Justice Act 2003 amending s.9(11) Criminal Justice Act 1987 and s.35(1) Criminal Procedure and Investigations Act 1994 **J-35**
- Part 37 CrimPR
- The prosecution can appeal the refusal to make an order; the defence can appeal the making of an order
- A **Form NG (Prep)** must be served on the Crown Court, the Registrar and any party directly affected not more than five business days after the order or the Crown Court Judge granting or refusing leave (*For applications to the Crown Court Judge see Part B above*)
- A Respondent's Notice **Form RN (Prep)** should be served if the Court directs or the Crown (or any party affected) wants to make representations to the Court
- Defence representatives are usually covered by the Crown Court representation order if one is in force, the proceedings being considered incidental within Paragraph 5(3) of Schedule 3 to Legal Aid, Sentencing and Punishment of Offenders Act 2012
- The Crown Court Judge, single Judge or full Court can grant leave

D15. Appeal against an order that a trial should continue without a jury or a new trial take place without a jury after jury tampering

- S.47 Criminal Justice Act 2003 **J-36**
- Part 37 CrimPR (relating to appeals against an order made in a preparatory hearing notwithstanding there will have been no preparatory hearing)
- Both the prosecution and defence can appeal a decision that the trial should continue without a jury or a new trial should take place without a jury
- **A Form NG (Prep)** must be served on the Crown Court, the Registrar and any party directly affected not more than five business days after the order or the Crown Court Judge granting or refusing leave (*For applications to the Crown Court Judge see Part B above*)
- A Respondent's Notice **Form RN (Prep)** should be served if the Court directs or the Crown (or any party affected) wants to make representations to the Court
- Defence representatives are usually covered by the Crown Court representation order if one is in force, the proceedings being considered incidental within Paragraph 5(3) of Schedule 3 to Legal Aid, Sentencing and Punishment of Offenders Act 2012
- The Crown Court Judge, single Judge or full Court can grant leave

D16. Appeal against orders restricting or preventing reports or restricting public access

- S.159 Criminal Justice Act 1988 **J-37**
- Part 40 CrimPR
- A person aggrieved may appeal
- Applications against orders restricting reporting shall be made within 10 business days after the date on which the order was made by lodging **Form NG (159)** on the Registrar, the Crown Court, the prosecutor and defendant and any other affected person. Applications against orders to restrict public access must be made the next business day after the order was made. If advance notice of an order restricting public access is given, then advance notice of an intention to appeal may be made not more than five business days after the advance notice is displayed

- A person on whom an appeal notice is served should serve a Respondent's Notice **Form RN (159)** if he wishes to make representations to the Court or the Court so directs within three business days
- The Court may make such order as to costs as it thinks fit (s.159(5)(c) Criminal Justice Act 1988), but not out of central funds (*Holden and others v CPS No.2* [1994] 1 AC 22)
- A single Judge or the full Court can grant leave (s.31(2B) Criminal Appeal Act 1968)
- Applications for leave to appeal and appeals in relation to reporting restrictions *may* be heard in private (CrimPR 36.6(1)). Applications for leave to appeal and appeals relating to restricting public access may be decided without a hearing but the decision must be announced at a hearing in public (Crim PR 36.6(3)). In either case, if the hearing relates to public interest immunity, it must be in private unless the Court otherwise directs (Crim PR 36.6(2))

D17. Appeal against a wasted costs order

J-38
- Regulation 3C Costs in Criminal Cases (General) Regulations 1986
- A legal or other representative against whom a wasted costs order has been made in the Crown Court
- There is no specific form. Notice of appeal should be served on any interested party within 21 days of the order being made.
- Any interested party can make representations orally or in writing
- Leave to appeal is not required (s. 19 A Prosecution of Offences Act 1985)

D18. Appeal relating to Serious Crime Prevention Orders

J-39
- S.24 Serious Crime Act 2007
- Part 39 CrimPR
- A person subject to the order, an applicant authority or anyone given the opportunity to make representations at the Crown Court about the making, variation or non-variation of an order
- Proceedings are commenced by the service of **Form NG (SCPO)** on the Crown Court (if the application is lodged prior to 1 October 2018) or directly on the Registrar of Criminal Appeals (if the application is lodged on or after 1 October 2018) not more than 28 days after the order (*see section A2. Lodging Form NG and grounds of appeal*)
- A Respondent's Notice **Form RN** should be served if directed by the Registrar or if the respondent wishes to make representations to the Court. Proceedings before the Crown Court or the Court of Appeal relating to serious crime prevention orders and arising by virtue of ss.19, 20, 21 or 24 of the Serious Crime Act 2007 are criminal proceedings for the purposes of Legal Aid, Sentencing and Punishment of Offenders Act 2012 s.19; Reg.9(s) Criminal Legal Aid (General) Regulations 2013. Accordingly, the Registrar may grant a representation order to a person subject to the order. A person who made representations at the Crown Court can apply to the LAA for a representation order. The Court has discretion to order costs as it thinks fit (Part 3 Orders as to costs Serious Crime Act 2007 (Appeals under s.24) Order 2008/1863)
- Leave can be granted by the Crown Court Judge, full Court or single Judge (Art.9 Serious Crime Act 2007 (Appeals under s.24) Order 2008/1863)

D19. Appeal against the failure to make a football banning order

J-40
- S.14A(5A) Football Spectators Act 1989
- Part 39 CrimPR
- The CACD has no power to deal with these. An appeal lies to the Civil Division (*Boggild* [2011] EWCA Crim 1928)

E. Application for a Retrial for a Serious Offence

E1. Application by a prosecutor to quash an acquittal and seek a retrial of a qualifying offence (S.76(1) Criminal Justice Act 2003 and Part 27 CrimPR)

J-41 E1-1. There must be new and compelling evidence and it must be in the interests of justice for the acquitted person to be re-tried (ss.78 and 79 Criminal Justice Act 2003 and *Dunlop* [2006] EWCA Crim 1354; *Sanjuliano* [2007] EWCA Crim 3130). Evidence was "new" if it had not been adduced at trial and for the purposes of s.78(2) evidence was "adduced" if it had been put forward in evidence (*Henry* [2014] EWCA Crim. 1816; [2015] 2 Cr. App. R. 1).

E1-2. Proceedings can begin in one of two ways:

(1) By serving notice of the application under s.76 on the Registrar of Criminal Appeals and

the acquitted person within two days of the decision having been made (s.80 Criminal Justice Act 2003). This notice charges the acquitted person with the offence. It requires the personal written consent of the Director of Public Prosecutions (DPP) (s.76(3)).

If the acquitted person is not in custody the prosecution can ask the Crown Court to issue:

i) A summons for the acquitted person to appear before the Court of Appeal for the hearing of the application

ii) A warrant for his arrest (s.89(3))

Once arrested on the warrant the acquitted person must be brought before the Crown Court within 48 hours (s.89(6)).

(2) An acquitted person may be charged with the offence *before* an application under s76 has been made. This may be after an arrest in an investigation authorised by the DPP (s 85(2)) or where no authorisation has been given, after arrest under a warrant issued by a justice of the peace (s87(1) Criminal Justice Act 2003). Having been charged, the acquitted person must be brought before the Crown Court to consider bail within 24 hours (s.88(2) Criminal Justice Act 2003). He can then be remanded in custody or on bail for 42 days whilst an application under s.76 is prepared (s.88(6)) unless extended by s.88(8) Criminal Justice Act 2003). Once a notice of application under s.76 has been made, stating that the acquitted person has previously been charged with the offence, the acquitted person must be brought before the Crown Court to consider bail within 48 hours of the notice being given to the Registrar, if the acquitted person is already in custody under s.88 (above) (s.89(2)).

E1-3. Thus in either case, bail is dealt with largely by the Crown Court. The Court of Appeal only considers bail on the adjournment of the hearing of the application under s.76 (s.90 (1) Criminal Justice Act 2003).

E1-4. The notice **(Form NG (ACQ))** should where practicable be accompanied by the witness statements which are relied on as the new and compelling evidence, the original witness statements, unused statements, indictment, paper exhibits from the original trial, any relevant transcripts from the original trial and any other documents relied on (CrimPR 27.2(2)).

E1-5. An acquitted person who wants to oppose a s.76 application must serve a response **(Form RN (ACQ))** not more than 28 days after receiving the notice (CrimPR 27.3(2)).

E2. Application by a prosecutor for a determination whether a foreign acquittal is a bar to a trial and if so, an order that it not be a bar (S.76(2) Criminal Justice Act 2003 and Part 27 CrimPR)

E2-1. The prosecution can apply, with the personal written consent of the DPP (s.76(3) Criminal Justice Act 2003) for a determination whether an acquittal outside the UK is a bar to the acquitted person being tried in England and Wales and if it is found to be so, an order that the acquittal not be a bar. Proceedings can begin in the same way as for an application under s.76(1). **J-42**

E3. Application for restrictions on publication relating to an application under s.76 (S.82 Criminal Justice Act 2003 and Part 27 CrimPR)

E3-1. An application can be made by the DPP for reporting restrictions. This can be made after a notice of an application for a re-trial has been made and may also be made by the Court of its own motion (s.82(5) Criminal Justice Act 2003). An application can also be made by the DPP for reporting restrictions **before** a notice of an application for a retrial if an investigation has been commenced (s.82(6) Criminal Justice Act 2003). The application for reporting restrictions must be served on the Registrar **(Form REP (ACQ))** and (usually) the acquitted person (CrimPR 27.8(1)). **J-43**

E3-2. A party who wants to vary or revoke an order for restrictions on publication under s.82(7) may apply to the Court of Appeal in writing at any time after the order was made (CrimPR 27.9(1)).

E4. Representation orders

E4-1. The Registrar will grant a representation order to the acquitted person for solicitors and counsel to respond to any of the above applications. **J-44**

APPENDIX N
Protocols

A. CONTROL AND MANAGEMENT OF HEAVY FRAUD AND OTHER COMPLEX CRIMINAL CASES

A protocol issued by the Lord Chief Justice of England and Wales N-1

22 March 2005

Other issues

Defence representation and defence costs
Assistance to the Judge
Jury Management
Maxwell hours
Livenote

Other issues

Defence representation and defence costs
Assistance to the Judge

Introduction

N-2 There is a broad consensus that the length of fraud and trials of other complex crimes must be controlled within proper bounds in order:

(i) To enable the jury to retain and assess the evidence which they have heard. If the trial is so long that the jury cannot do this, then the trial is not fair either to the prosecution or the defence.

(ii) To make proper use of limited public resources: see *Jisl* [2004] EWCA Crim. 696 at [113]-[121].

There is also a consensus that no trial should be permitted to exceed a given period, save in exceptional circumstances; some favour 3 months, others an outer limit of 6 months. Whatever view is taken, it is essential that the current length of trials is brought back to an acceptable and proper duration.

This Protocol supplements the Criminal Procedure Rules and summarises good practice which experience has shown may assist in bringing about some reduction in the length of trials of fraud and other crimes that result in complex trials. Flexibility of application of this Protocol according to the needs of each case is essential; it is designed to inform but not to proscribe.

This Protocol is primarily directed towards cases which are likely to last eight weeks or longer. It should also be followed, however, in all cases estimated to last more than four weeks. This Protocol applies to trials by jury, but many of the principles will be applicable if trials without a jury are permitted under s.43 of the Criminal Justice Act 2003.

The best handling technique for a long case is continuous management by an experienced Judge nominated for the purpose.

It is intended that this Protocol be kept up to date; any further practices or techniques found to be successful in the management of complex cases should be notified to the office of the Lord Chief Justice.

1. The investigation

(i) The role of the prosecuting authority and the judge

N-3 (a) Unlike other European countries, a judge in England and Wales does not directly control the investigation process; that is the responsibility of the Investigating Authority, and in turn the Prosecuting Authority and the prosecution advocate. Experience has shown that a prosecution lawyer (who must be of sufficient experience and who will be a member of the team at trial) and the prosecution advocate, if different, should be involved in the investigation as soon as it appears that a heavy fraud trial or other complex criminal trial is likely to ensue. The costs that this early preparation will incur will be saved many times over in the long run.

(b) The judge can and should exert a substantial and beneficial influence by making it clear that, generally speaking, trials should be kept within manageable limits. In most cases 3 months should be the target outer limit, but there will be cases where a duration of 6 months, or in exceptional circumstances, even longer may be inevitable.

(ii) Interviews

N-4 (a) At present many interviews are too long and too unstructured. This has a knock-on effect on the length of trials. Interviews should provide an opportunity for suspects to respond to the allegations against them. They should not be an occasion to discuss every document in the case. It should become clear from judicial rulings that interviews of this kind are a waste of resources.

(b) The suspect must be given sufficient information before or at the interview to enable them to meet the questions fairly and answer them honestly; the information is not provided to give him the opportunity to manufacture a false story which fits undisputable facts.
(c) It is often helpful if the principal documents are provided either in advance of the interview or shown as the interview progresses; asking detailed questions about events a considerable period in the past without reference to the documents is often not very helpful.

(iii) The prosecution and defence teams

(a) **The Prosecution Team**

While instructed it is for the lead advocate for the prosecution to take all necessary decisions in the presentation and general conduct of the prosecution case. The prosecution lead advocate will be treated by the court as having that responsibility. **N-5**

However, in relation to policy decisions the lead advocate for the prosecution must not give an indication or undertaking which binds the prosecution without first discussing the issue with Director of the Prosecuting authority or other senior officer.

"Policy" decisions should be understood as referring to non-evidential decisions on: the acceptance of pleas of guilty to lesser counts or groups of counts or available alternatives: offering no evidence on particular counts; consideration of a re-trial; whether to lodge an appeal; certification of a point of law; and the withdrawal of the prosecution as a whole (for further information see the "Farquharson Guidelines" on the role and responsibilities of the prosecution advocate).

(b) **The Defence Team**

In each case, the lead advocate for the defence will be treated by the court as having responsibility to the court for the presentation and general conduct of the defence case.

(c) In each case, a case progression officer must be assigned by the court, prosecution and defence from the time of the first hearing when directions are given (as referred to in paragraph 3(iii)) until the conclusion of the trial.
(d) In each case where there are multiple defendants, the LSC will need to consider carefully the extent and level of representation necessary.

(iv) Initial consideration of the length of a case

If the prosecutor in charge of the case from the Prosecuting Authority or the lead advocate for the prosecution consider that the case as formulated is likely to last more than 8 weeks, the case should be referred in accordance with arrangements made by the Prosecuting Authority to a more senior prosecutor. The senior prosecutor will consider whether it is desirable for the case to be prosecuted in that way or whether some steps might be taken to reduce its likely length, whilst at the same time ensuring that the public interest is served. **N-6**

Any case likely to last 6 months or more must be referred to the Director of the Prosecuting Authority so that similar considerations can take place.

(v) Notification of cases likely to last more than 8 weeks

Special arrangements will be put in place for the early notification by the CPS and other Prosecuting Authorities, to the LSC and to a single designated officer of the Court in each Region (Circuit) of any case which the CPS or other Prosecuting Authority consider likely to last over 8 weeks. **N-7**

(vi) Venue

The court will allocate such cases and other complex cases likely to last 4 weeks or more to a specific venue suitable for the trial in question, taking into account the convenience to witnesses, the parties, the availability of time at that location, and all other relevant considerations. **N-8**

2. Designation of the trial judge

The assignment of a judge

(a) In any complex case which is expected to last more than four weeks, the trial judge will be assigned under the direction of the Presiding Judges at the earliest possible moment. **N-9**
(b) Thereafter the assigned judge should manage that case "from cradle to grave"; it is essential that the same judge manages the case from the time of his assignment and that arrangements are made for him to be able to do so. It is recognised that in certain court centres

with a large turnover of heavy cases (*e.g.* Southwark) this objective is more difficult to achieve. But in those court centres there are teams of specialist judges, who are more readily able to handle cases which the assigned judge cannot continue with because of unexpected events; even at such courts, there must be no exception to the principle that one judge must handle all the pre-trial hearings until the case is assigned to another judge.

3. Case management

(i) Objectives

N-10 (a) The number, length and organisation of case management hearings will, of course, depend critically on the circumstances and complexity of the individual case. However, thorough, well-prepared and extended case management hearings will save court time and costs overall.

(b) Effective case management of heavy fraud and other complex criminal cases requires the judge to have a much more detailed grasp of the case than may be necessary for many other Plea and Case Management Hearings (PCMHs). Though it is for the judge in each case to decide how much pre-reading time he needs so that the judge is on top of the case, it is not always a sensible use of judicial time to allocate a series of reading days, during which the judge sits alone in his room, working through numerous boxes of ring binders.

See paragraph 3(iv)(e) below

(ii) Fixing the trial date

N-11 Although it is important that the trial date should be fixed as early as possible, this may not always be the right course. There are two principal alternatives:

(a) The trial date should be fixed at the first opportunity—*i.e.* at the first (and usually short) directions hearing referred to in The first hearing for the giving of initial directions. From then on everyone must work to that date. All orders and pre-trial steps should be timetabled to fit in with that date. All advocates and the judge should take note of this date, in the expectation that the trial will proceed on the date determined.

(b) The trial date should not be fixed until the issues have been explored at a full case management hearing (referred to in The first Case Management Hearing), after the advocates on both sides have done some serious work on the case. Only then can the length of the trial be estimated.

Which is apposite must depend on the circumstances of each case, but the earlier it is possible to fix a trial date, by reference to a proper estimate and a timetable set by reference to the trial date, the better.

It is generally to be expected that once a trial is fixed on the basis of the estimate provided, that it will not be **increased** if, and only if, the party seeking to extend the time justifies why the original estimate is no longer appropriate.

(iii) The first hearing for the giving of initial directions

N-12 At the first opportunity the assigned judge should hold a short hearing to give initial directions. The directions on this occasion might well include:

(a) That there should be a full case management hearing on, or commencing on, a specified future date by which time the parties will be properly prepared for a meaningful hearing and the defence will have full instructions.

(b) That the prosecution should provide an outline written statement of the prosecution case at least one week in advance of that case management hearing, outlining in simple terms:

(i) the key facts on which it relies;

(ii) the key evidence by which the prosecution seeks to prove the facts.

The statement must be sufficient to permit the judge to understand the case and for the defence to appreciate the basic elements of its case against each defendant. The prosecution may be invited to highlight the key points of the case orally at the case management hearing by way of a short mini-opening. The outline statement should not be considered binding, but it will serve the essential purpose in telling the judge, and everyone else, what the case is really about and identifying the key issues.

(c) That a core reading list and core bundle for the case management hearing should be delivered at least one week in advance.

(d) Preliminary directions about disclosure: see paragraph 4.

(iv) The first case management hearing

N-13 (a) At the first case management hearing:

(1) the prosecution advocate should be given the opportunity to highlight any points from the prosecution outline statement of case (which will have been delivered at least a week in advance;

(2) each defence advocate should be asked to outline the defence.

If the defence advocate is not in a position to say what is in issue and what is not in issue, then the case management hearing can be adjourned for a short and limited time and to a fixed date to enable the advocate to take instructions; such an adjournment should only be necessary in exceptional circumstances, as the defence advocate should be properly instructed by the time of the first case management hearing and in any event is under an obligation to take sufficient instructions to fulfil the obligations contained in sections 33–39 of Criminal Justice Act 2003.

(b) There should then be a real dialogue between the judge and all advocates for the purpose of identifying:

(i) the focus of the prosecution case;
(ii) the common ground;
(iii) the real issues in the case. (Rule 3.2 of the Criminal Procedure Rules.)

(c) The judge will try to generate a spirit of co-operation between the court and the advocates on all sides. The expeditious conduct of the trial and a focussing on the real issues must be in the interests of **all** parties. It cannot be in the interests of any defendant for his good points to become lost in a welter of uncontroversial or irrelevant evidence.

(d) In many fraud cases the primary facts are not seriously disputed. The real issue is what each defendant knew and whether that defendant was dishonest. Once the judge has identified what is in dispute and what is not in dispute, the judge can then discuss with the advocate how the trial should be structured, what can be dealt with by admissions or agreed facts, what uncontroversial matters should be proved by concise oral evidence, what timetabling can be required under Rule 3.10 Criminal Procedure Rules, and other directions.

(e) In particularly heavy fraud or complex cases the judge may possibly consider it necessary to allocate a whole week for a case management hearing. If that week is used wisely, many further weeks of trial time can be saved. In the gaps which will inevitably arise during that week (for example while the advocates are exploring matters raised by the judge) the judge can do a substantial amount of informed reading. The case has come "alive" at this stage. Indeed, in a really heavy fraud case, if the judge fixes one or more case management hearings on this scale, there will be need for fewer formal reading days. Moreover a huge amount can be achieved in the pre-trial stage, if all trial advocates are gathered in the same place, focussing on the case **at the same time**, for several days consecutively.

(f) Requiring the defence to serve proper case statements may enable the court to identify

(i) what is common ground and
(ii) the real issues.

It is therefore important that proper defence case statements be provided as required by the Criminal Procedure Rules; judges will use the powers contained in ss.28–34 of the Criminal Proceedings and Evidence Act 1996 [*sic*] (and the corresponding provisions of the CJA 1987, ss.33 and following of the Criminal Justice Act 2003) and the Criminal Procedure Rules to ensure that realistic defence case statements are provided.

(g) Likewise this objective may be achieved by requiring the prosecution to serve draft admissions by a specified date and by requiring the defence to respond within a specified number of weeks.

(v) Further case management hearings

(a) The date of the next case management hearing should be fixed at the conclusion of the hearing so that there is no delay in having to fix the date through listing offices, clerks and others. **N-14**

(b) If one is looking at a trial which threatens to run for months, pre-trial case management on an intensive scale is essential.

(vi) Consideration of the length of the trial

(a) Case management on the above lines, the procedure set out in paragraph 1(iv), may still be insufficient to reduce the trial to a manageable length; generally a trial of 3 months should be the target, but there will be cases where a duration of 6 months or, in exceptional circumstances, even longer may be inevitable. **N-15**

(b) If the trial is not estimated to be within a manageable length, it will be necessary for the judge to consider what steps should be taken to reduce the length of the trial, whilst still ensuring that the prosecution has the opportunity of placing the full criminality before the court.

(c) To assist the judge in this task,
  (i) the lead advocate for the prosecution should be asked to explain why the prosecution have rejected a shorter way of proceeding; they may also be asked to divide the case into sections of evidence and explain the scope of each section and the need for each section;
  (ii) the lead advocates for the prosecution and for the defence should be prepared to put forward in writing, if requested, ways in which a case estimated to last more than three months can be shortened, including possible severance of counts or defendants, exclusions of sections of the case or of evidence or areas of the case where admissions can be made.

(d) One course the judge may consider is pruning the indictment by omitting certain charges and/or by omitting certain defendants. The judge must not usurp the function of the prosecution in this regard, and he must bear in mind that he will, at the outset, know less about the case than the advocates. The aim is achieve [*sic*] fairness to all parties

(e) Nevertheless, the judge does have two methods of pruning available for use in appropriate circumstances:
  (i) persuading the prosecution that it is not worthwhile pursuing certain charges and/or certain defendants;
  (ii) severing the indictment. Severance for reasons of case management alone is perfectly proper, although judges should have regard to any representations made by the prosecution that severance would weaken their case. Indeed the judge's hand will be strengthened in this regard by rule 1.1(2)(g) of the Criminal Procedure Rules. However, before using what may be seen as a blunt instrument, the judge should insist on seeing full defence statements of all affected defendants. Severance may be unfair to the prosecution if, for example, there is a cut-throat defence in prospect. For example, the defence of the principal defendant may be that the defendant relied on the advice of his accountant or solicitor that what was happening was acceptable. The defence of the professional may be that he gave no such advice. Against that background, it might be unfair to the prosecution to order separate trials of the two defendants.

(vii) The exercise of the powers

N-16 (a) The Criminal Procedure Rules require the court to take a more active part in case management. These are salutary provisions which should bring to an end interminable criminal trials of the kind which the Court of Appeal criticised in *Jisl* [2004] EWCA 696 at [113]-[121].

(b) Nevertheless these salutary provisions do not have to be used on every occasion. Where the advocates have done their job properly, by narrowing the issues, pruning the evidence and so forth, it may be quite inappropriate for the judge to "weigh in" and start cutting out more evidence or more charges of his own volition. It behoves the judge to make a careful assessment of the degree of judicial intervention which is warranted in each case.

(c) The note of caution in the previous paragraph is supported by certain experience which has been gained of the Civil Procedure Rules (on which the Criminal Procedure Rules are based). The CPR contain valuable and efficacious provisions for case management by the judge on his own initiative which have led to huge savings of court time and costs. Surveys by the Law Society have shown that the CPR have been generally welcomed by court users and the profession, but there have been reported to have been isolated instances in which the parties to civil litigation have faithfully complied with both the letter and the spirit of the CPR, and have then been aggrieved by what was perceived to be unnecessary intermeddling by the court.

(viii) Expert evidence

N-17 (a) Early identification of the subject matter of expert evidence to be adduced by the prosecution and the defence should be made as early as possible, preferably at the directions hearing.

(b) Following the exchange of expert evidence, any areas of disagreement should be identified and a direction should generally be made requiring the experts to meet and prepare, after discussion, a joint statement identifying points of agreement and contention and areas where the prosecution is put to proof on matters of which a positive case to the contrary is not advanced by the defence. After the statement has been prepared it should be served on the court, the prosecution and the defence. In some cases, it might be appropriate to provide that to the jury.

(ix) Surveillance evidence

(a) Where a prosecution is based upon many months' observation or surveillance evidence and it appears that it is capable of effective presentation based on a shorter period, the advocate should be required to justify the evidence of such observations before it is permitted to be adduced, either substantially or in its entirety. **N-18**
(b) Schedules should be provided to cover as much of the evidence as possible and admissions sought.

4. Disclosure

[*Replaced by the 2013 judicial protocol on disclosure: see* post, *N-52* et seq.] **N-19**

5. Abuse of process

(i) Applications to stay or dismiss for abuse of process have become a normal feature of heavy and complex cases. Such applications may be based upon delay and the health of defendants. **N-20**
(ii) Applications in relation to absent special circumstances [*sic*] tend to be unsuccessful and not to be pursued on appeal. For this reason there is comparatively little Court of Appeal guidance: but see: *Harris and Howells* [2003] EWCA Crim. 486. It should be noted that abuse of process is not there to discipline the prosecution or the police.
(iii) The arguments on both sides must be reduced to writing. Oral evidence is seldom relevant.
(iv) The judge should direct full written submissions (rather than "skeleton arguments") on any abuse application in accordance with a timetable set by him; these should identify any element of prejudice the defendant is alleged to have suffered.
(v) The judge should normally aim to conclude the hearing within an absolute maximum limit of one day, if necessary in accordance with a timetable. The parties should therefore prepare their papers on this basis and not expect the judge to allow the oral hearing to be anything more than an occasion to highlight concisely their arguments and answer any questions the court may have of them; applications will not be allowed drag on.

6. The trial

(i) The particular hazard of heavy fraud trials

A heavy fraud or other complex trial has the potential to lose direction and focus. This is a disaster for three reasons: **N-21**
(a) the jury will lose track of the evidence, thereby prejudicing both prosecution and defence;
(b) the burden on the defendants, the judge and indeed all involved will become intolerable;
(c) scarce public resources are wasted. Other prosecutions are delayed or—worse—may never happen. Fraud which is detected but not prosecuted (for resource reasons) undermines confidence.

(ii) Judicial mastery of the case

(a) It is necessary for the judge to exercise firm control over the conduct of the trial at all stages. **N-22**
(b) In order to do this the judge must read the witness statements and the documents, so that the judge can discuss case management issues with the advocates on—almost—an equal footing.
(c) To this end, the judge should not set aside weeks or even days for pre-reading (see paragraph 3(i)(b)). Hopefully the judge will have gained a good grasp of the evidence during the case management hearings. Nevertheless, realistic reading time must be provided for the judge in advance of trial.
(d) The role of the judge in a heavy fraud or other complex criminal trial is different from his/her role in a "conventional" criminal trial. So far as possible, the judge should be freed

from other duties and burdens, so that he/she can give the high degree of commitment which a heavy fraud trial requires. This will pay dividends in terms of saving weeks or months of court time.

(iii) The order of the evidence

N-23 (a) By the outset of the trial at the latest (and in most cases very much earlier) the judge must be provided with a schedule, showing the sequence of prosecution (and in an appropriate case defence) witnesses and the dates upon which they are expected to be called. This can only be prepared by discussion between prosecution and defence which the judge should expect, and say he/she expects, to take place: See: Criminal Procedure Rule 3.10. The schedule should, in so far as it relates to prosecution witnesses, be developed in consultation with the witnesses, via the witness care units, and with consideration given to their personal needs. Copies of the schedule should be provided for the Witness Service.

(b) The schedule should be kept under review by the trial judge and by the parties. If a case is running behind or ahead of schedule, each witness affected must be advised by the party who is calling that witness at the earliest opportunity.

(c) If an excessive amount of time is allowed for any witness, the judge can ask why. The judge may probe with the advocates whether the time envisaged for the evidence-in-chief or cross-examination (as the case may be) of a particular witness is really necessary.

(iv) Case management sessions

N-24 (a) The order of the evidence may have legitimately to be departed from. It will, however, be a useful for tool for monitoring the progress of the case. There should be periodic case management sessions, during which the judge engages the advocates upon a stock-taking exercise: asking, amongst other questions, "where are we going?" and "what is the relevance of the next three witnesses?". This will be a valuable means of keeping the case on track. Rule 3.10 of the Criminal Procedure Rules will again assist the judge.

(b) The judge may wish to consider issuing the occasional use of "case management notes" to the advocates, in order to set out the judge's tentative views on where the trial may be going off track, which areas of future evidence are relevant and which may have become irrelevant (*e.g.* because of concessions, admissions in cross-examination and so forth). Such notes from the judge plus written responses from the advocates can, cautiously used, provide a valuable focus for debate during the periodic case management reviews held during the course of the trial.

(v) Controlling prolix cross-examination

N-25 (a) Setting **rigid** time limits in advance for cross-examination is rarely appropriate—as experience has shown in civil cases; but a timetable is essential so that the judge can exercise control and so that there is a clear target to aim at for the completion of the evidence of each witness. Moreover the judge can and should indicate when cross-examination is irrelevant, unnecessary or time wasting. The judge may limit the time for further cross-examination of a particular witness.

(vi) Electronic presentation of evidence

N-26 (a) Electronic presentation of evidence (EPE) has the potential to save huge amounts of time in fraud and other complex criminal trials and should be used more widely.

(b) HMCS is providing facilities for the easier use of EPE with a standard audio visual facility. Effectively managed, the savings in court time achieved by EPE more than justify the cost.

(c) There should still be a core bundle of those documents to which frequent reference will be made during the trial. The jury may wish to mark that bundle or to refer back to particular pages as the evidence progresses. EPE can be used for presenting all documents not contained in the core bundle.

(d) Greater use of other modern forms of graphical presentations should be made wherever possible.

(vii) Use of interviews

N-27 The judge should consider extensive editing of self serving interviews, even when the defence want the jury to hear them in their entirety; such interviews are not evidence of the truth of their contents but merely of the defendant's reaction to the allegation.

(viii) Jury management

(a) The jury should be informed as early as possible in the case as to what the issues are in a manner directed by the Judge. **N-28**
(b) The jury must be regularly updated as to the trial timetable and the progress of the trial, subject to warnings as to the predictability of the trial process.
(c) Legal argument should be heard at times that causes the least inconvenience to jurors.
(d) It is useful to consider with the advocates whether written directions should be given to the jury and, if so, in what form.

(ix) Maxwell hours

(a) Maxwell hours should only be permitted after careful consideration and consultation with the Presiding Judge. **N-29**
(b) Considerations in favour include:
  (i) legal argument can be accommodated without disturbing the jury;
  (ii) there is a better chance of a representative jury;
  (iii) time is made available to the judge, advocates and experts to do useful work in the afternoons
(c) Considerations against include:
  (i) the lengthening of trials and the consequent waste of court time;
  (ii) the desirability of making full use of the jury once they have arrived at court;
  (iii) shorter trials tend to diminish the need for special provisions *e.g.* there are fewer difficulties in empanelling more representative juries;
  (iv) they are unavailable if any defendant is in custody.
(d) It may often be the case that a maximum of one day of Maxwell hours a week is sufficient; if so, it should be timetabled in advance to enable all submissions by advocates, supported by skeleton arguments served in advance, to be dealt with in the period after 1:30 pm on that day.

(x) Livenote

If Livenote is used, it is important that all users continue to take a note of the evidence, otherwise considerable time is wasted in detailed reading of the entire daily transcript. **N-30**

7. Other issues

(i) Defence representation and defence costs

(a) Applications for change in representation in complex trials need special consideration; the ruling of HH Judge Wakerley QC (as he then was) in *Asghar Ali* has been circulated by the JSB. **N-31**
(b) Problems have arisen when the Legal Services Commission have declined to allow advocates or solicitors to do certain work; on occasions the matter has been raised with the judge managing or trying the case.
(c) The Legal Services Commission has provided guidance to judges on how they can obtain information from the LSC as to the reasons for their decisions; further information in relation to this can be obtained from *Nigel Field, Head of the Complex Crime Unit, Legal Services Commission, 29-37 Red Lion Street, London, WC1R 4PP.*

(ii) Assistance to the judge

Experience has shown that in some very heavy cases, the judge's burden can be substantially offset with the provision of a judicial assistant or other support and assistance. **N-32**

[The next paragraph is N-52.]

B. DISCLOSURE OF UNUSED MATERIAL IN CRIMINAL CASES

Foreword

[*Identical to the foreword to the Attorney-General's guidelines*: ante, *§ A-242a*.] **N-52**

Introduction

N-53 This protocol is prescribed for use by CPD IV Disclosure 22A: Disclosure of Unused Material. It is applicable in all the criminal courts of England and Wales, including the Crown Court, the Court Martial[1] and the magistrates' courts. It replaces the previous judicial document 'Disclosure: a Protocol for the Control and Management of Unused Material in the Crown Court'[2] and it also replaces section 4 'Disclosure' of the Lord Chief Justice's Protocol on the Control and Management of Heavy Fraud and Other Complex Criminal Cases, dated 22 March 2005.[3]

This protocol is intended to provide a central source of guidance for the judiciary, although that produced by the Attorney General also requires attention.

In summary, this judicial protocol sets out the principles to be applied to, and the importance of, disclosure; the expectations of the court and its role in disclosure, in particular in relation to case management; and the consequences if there is a failure by the prosecution or defence to comply with their obligations.

Readers should note that a review of disclosure in the magistrates' courts is currently being undertaken by H.H.J. Kinch Q.C. and the Chief Magistrate, on behalf of Lord Justice Gross, the Senior Presiding Judge. Amendments may therefore be made following the recommendations of that review, and in accordance with other forthcoming changes to the criminal justice system.

The importance of disclosure for fair trials

N-54 1. Disclosure remains one of the most important - as well as one of the most misunderstood and abused - of the procedures relating to criminal trials. Lord Justice Gross' review has reemphasised the need for all those involved to understand the statutory requirements and to undertake their roles with rigour, in a timely manner.

2. The House of Lords stated in *H.* [2004] UKHL 3; [2004] 2 A.C. 134; [2004] 2 Cr. App. R. 10:

> "Fairness ordinarily requires that any material held by the prosecution which weakens its case or strengthens that of the defendant, if not relied on as part of its formal case against the defendant, should be disclosed to the defence. Bitter experience has shown that miscarriages of justice may occur where such material is withheld from disclosure. The golden rule is that full disclosure of such material should be made" ([2004] 2 A.C. 134, at 147).

The Criminal Cases Review Commission has recently noted that failure to disclose material to the defence to which they were entitled remains the biggest single cause of miscarriages of justice.

3. However, it is also essential that the trial process is not overburdened or diverted by erroneous and inappropriate disclosure of unused prosecution material or by misconceived applications. Although the drafters of the Criminal Procedure and Investigations Act 1996 ('CPIA 1996') cannot have anticipated the vast increase in the amount of electronic material that has been generated in recent years, nevertheless the principles of that Act still hold true. Applications by the parties or decisions by judges based on misconceptions of the law or a general laxity of approach (however well-intentioned) which result in an improper application of the disclosure regime have, time and again, proved unnecessarily costly and have obstructed justice. As Lord Justice Gross noted, the burden of disclosure must not be allowed to render the prosecution of cases impracticable.

4. The overarching principle is that unused prosecution material will fall to be disclosed if, and only if, it satisfies the test for disclosure applicable to the proceedings in question, subject to any overriding public interest considerations. The test for disclosure will depend on the date the criminal investigation in question commenced, as this will determine whether the common law disclosure regime applies, or either of the two disclosure regimes under the CPIA 1996.

5. The test for disclosure under section 3 of the CPIA 1996 as amended will be applicable in nearly every case and all those involved in the process will need to be familiar with it. Material fulfils the test if - but only if - it "might reasonably be considered capable of undermining the case for the prosecution ... or of assisting the case for the accused."

6. The disclosure process must be led by the prosecution so as to trigger comprehensive defence engagement, supported by robust judicial case management. Active participation by the court in the

---

[1] The timetables given here may vary in the Court Martial and reference should be made to the Criminal Procedure and Investigations Act 1996 (Application to the Armed Forces) Order 2009 and to any practice note issued by the Judge Advocate General.

[2] The previous judicial protocol was endorsed by the Court of Appeal in *K* [2006] EWCA Crim. 724; [2006] 2 All ER 552 (Note).

[3] This protocol also replaces the Protocol for the Provision of Advance Information, Prosecution Evidence and Disclosure of Unused Material in the Magistrates' Courts, dated 12 May 2006, which was adopted as part of the Stop Delaying Justice initiative.

disclosure process is a critical means of ensuring that delays and adjournments are avoided, given failures by the parties to comply with their obligations may disrupt and (in some cases) frustrate the course of justice.

Disclosure of unused material in criminal cases

7. The court should keep the timetable for prosecution and defence disclosure under review from the first hearing. Judges should as a matter of course ask the parties to identify the issues in the case, and invite the parties to indicate whether further disclosure is sought, and on what topics. For example, it is not enough for the judge to rely on the content of the PCMH form. Proper completion of the disclosure process is a vital part of case preparation, and it may well affect the progress of the case. The court will expect disclosure to have been considered from the outset; the prosecution and defence advocates need to be aware of any potential problems and substantive difficulties should be explained to the judge; and the parties should propose a sensible timetable. Realism is preferable to optimistic but unachievable deadlines which may dislocate the court schedule and imperil the date of trial. It follows that judges should not impose deadlines for service of the case papers or disclosure until they are confident that the prosecution advocate has taken instructions from the individuals who are best placed to evaluate the work to be undertaken. **N-55**

8. The advocates - both prosecution and defence - must be kept fully informed throughout the course of the proceedings as to any difficulties which may prevent them from complying with their disclosure obligations. When problems arise or come to light after directions have been given, the advocates should notify the court and the other party (or parties) immediately rather than waiting until the date set by the court for the service of the material is imminent or has passed, and they must provide the court with a suggested timetable in order to resolve the problem. The progress of the disclosure process should be reviewed at every hearing. There remains no basis in practice or law for counsel to counsel disclosure.

9. If there is a preliminary hearing the judge should seize the opportunity to impose an early timetable for disclosure and to identify any likely problems including as regards third party material and material that will require an application to the Family Court. In an appropriate case the court should consider holding a joint criminal/care directions hearing. See "Material held by Third Parties", from paragraph 44 below.

10. For the PCMH to be effective, the defence must have a proper opportunity to review the case papers and consider initial disclosure, with a view to preparing a properly completed defence statement which will inform the judge's conduct of the PCMH, and inform the prosecution of the matters required by sections 5, 6A and 6C of the CPIA. As the Court of Appeal noted in *Newell* [2012] EWCA Crim. 650; [2012] 2 Cr. App. R. 10, "a typed defence statement must be provided before the PCMH. If there is no defence statement by the time of the PCMH, then a judge will usually require the trial advocate to see that such a statement is provided and not proceed with the PCMH until that is done. In the ordinary case the trial advocate will be required to do that at the court and the PCMH resumed later in the day to avoid delay". There may be some instances when there will be a well-founded defence application to extend the 28-day time limit for serving a proper defence statement. In a proper case (but never routinely), it may be appropriate to put the PCMH back by a week or more, to enable an appropriate defence statement to be filed.

11. The defence statement can be admitted into evidence under section 6E(4) of the CPIA 1996. However, information included on the PCMH form (which is primarily an administrative form) will not usually be admitted in evidence when the defence advocate has complied with the letter and the spirit of the Criminal Procedure Rules.[4] Introducing the PCMH form (or part of it) during the trial is likely to be an exceptional event. The status of the trial preparation form in the magistrates' court is somewhat different, as discussed below.

12. The court should not extend time lightly or as a matter of course. If an extension is sought, it ought to be accompanied by an appropriate explanation. For instance, it is not sufficient for the prosecutor merely to say that the investigator has delivered the papers late: the underlying reasons are to be provided to the court. The same applies if the defence statement is delayed. Whichever party is at fault, realistic proposals for service are to be set out.

13. Judges should not allow the prosecution to avoid their statutory responsibility for reviewing the unused material by the expedient of permitting the defence to have access to (or providing the defence with copies of) the material listed in the schedules of non-sensitive unused prosecution material irrespective of whether it satisfies, wholly or in part, the relevant test for disclosure. Additionally, it is for the prosecutor to decide on the manner of disclosure, and it does not have to mirror the form in which the information was originally recorded. Rose L.J. gave guidance on case management

[4] *Newell* [2012] EWCA Crim. 650; [2012] 2 Cr. App. R. 10.

issues in this context in *CPS (Interlocutory Application under sections 35/36 CPIA)* [2005] EWCA Crim. 2342. Allowing the defence to inspect items that fulfil the disclosure test is also a valid means of providing disclosure.

14. The larger and more complex the case, the more important it is for the prosecution to adhere to the overarching principle and ensure that sufficient prosecution attention and resources are allocated to the task. Handing the defendant the "keys to the warehouse" has been the cause of many gross abuses in the past, resulting in considerable expenditure by the defence without any material benefit to the course of justice. The circumstances relating to large and complex cases are outlined below.

15. The court will require the defence to engage and assist in the early identification of the real issues in the case and, particularly in the larger and more complex cases, to contribute to the search terms to be used for, and the parameters of, the review of any electronically held material (which can be very considerable). Any defence criticisms of the prosecution approach to disclosure should be timely and reasoned; there is no place for disclosure "ambushes" or for late or uninformative defence statements. Admissions should be used so far as possible to narrow the real issues in dispute.

16. A constructive approach to disclosure is a necessary part of professional best practice, for the defence and prosecution. This does not undermine the defendant's legitimate interests, it accords with his or her obligations under the rules and it ensures that all the relevant material is provided. Delays and failures by the prosecution and the defence are equally damaging to a timely, fair and efficient trial, and judges should be vigilant in preventing and addressing abuses. Accordingly, whenever there are potential failings by either the defence or the prosecution, judges, in exercising appropriate oversight of disclosure, should carefully investigate the suggested default and give timely directions.

17. In the Crown Court, the defence statement is to be served within 28 days of the date when the prosecution complies with its duty of initial disclosure (or purports to do so) and whenever section 5(5) of the CPIA applies to the proceedings, and the defence statement must comply with section 6A of the CPIA. Service of the defence statement is a most important stage in the disclosure process, and timely service is necessary to facilitate proper consideration of the disclosure issues well in advance of the trial date. Judges expect a defence statement to contain a clear and detailed exposition of the issues of fact and law. Defence statements that merely rehearse the suggestion that the defendant is innocent do not comply with the requirements of the CPIA.

18. The prosecutor should consider the defence statement carefully and promptly provide a copy to the disclosure officer, to assist the prosecution in its continuing disclosure obligations. The court expects the Crown to identify any suggested deficiencies in the defence statement, and to draw these to the attention of the defence and the court; in particular in large and complex cases, it will assist the court if this is in writing. Although the prosecution's ability to request, and the court's jurisdiction to give, an adverse inference direction under section 11 of CPIA is not contingent on the prosecution having earlier identified any suggested deficiencies, nevertheless the prosecutor must provide a timely written explanation of its position.

19. Judges should examine the defence statement with care to ensure that it complies with the formalities required by the CPIA. As stated in *H.* (*supra*) (para. 35):

> "If material does not weaken the prosecution case or strengthen that of the defendant, there is no requirement to disclose it. For this purpose the parties' respective cases should not be restrictively analysed. But they must be carefully analysed, to ascertain the specific facts the prosecution seek to establish and the specific grounds on which the charges are resisted. The trial process is not well served if the defence are permitted to make general and unspecified allegations and then seek far-reaching disclosure in the hope that material may turn up to make them good. Neutral material or material damaging to the defendant need not be disclosed and should not be brought to the attention of the court."

20. If no defence statement - or an inadequate defence statement - is served within the relevant time limits, the judge should investigate the position. At every PCMH where there is no defence statement, including those where an extension has been given, or the time for filing has not yet expired, the defence should be warned in appropriate terms that pursuant to section 6E(2) of the CPIA an adverse inference may be drawn during the trial, and this result is likely if there is no justification for the deficiency. The fact that a warning has been given should be noted.

21. An adverse inference may be drawn under section 11 of the CPIA if the accused fails to discharge his or her disclosure obligations. Whenever the amended CPIA regime applies, the prosecution may comment on any failure in defence disclosure (except where the failure relates to a point of law) without leave of the court, but counsel should use a measure of judgment as to whether

it is wise to embark on cross-examination about such a failure.[5] If the accused is cross-examined about discrepancies between his evidence and his defence statement, or if adverse comment is made, the judge must give appropriate guidance to the jury.[6]

22. In order to secure a fair trial, it is vital that the prosecution is mindful of its continuing duty of disclosure. Once the defence statement has been received, the Crown must review disclosure in the light of the issues identified in the defence statement. In cases of complexity, the following steps are then likely to be necessary:

i. service by the prosecution of any further material due to the defence following receipt of the defence statement;
ii. any defence request to the prosecution for service of additional specific items; as discussed below, these requests must be justified by reference to the defence statement and they should be submitted on the section 8 form;
iii. prosecution response to the defence request;
iv. if the defence considers that disclosable items are still outstanding, a section 8 application should be made using the appropriate form.

23. It follows that all requests by the defence to the prosecution for disclosure should be made on the section 8 application form, even if no hearing is sought in the first instance. Discussion and co-operation between the parties outside of court is encouraged in order to ensure that the court is only asked to issue a ruling when strictly necessary. However, use of the section 8 form will ensure that focussed requests are clearly set out in one place.

24. The judge should set a date as part of the timetabling exercise by which any application under section 8 is to be made, if this appears to be a likely eventuality.

25. The court will require the section 8 application to be served on the prosecution well in advance of the hearing - indeed, prior to requesting the hearing - to enable the Crown to identify and serve any items that meet the test for disclosure.

26. Service of a defence statement is an essential precondition for an application under section 8, and applications should not be heard or directions for disclosure issued in the absence of a properly completed statement (see Part 22 of the Criminal Procedure Rules). In particular, blanket orders in this context are inconsistent with the statutory framework for disclosure laid down by the CPIA and the decision of the House of Lords in *H.* (*supra*). It follows that defence requests for disclosure of particular pieces of unused prosecution material which are not referable to any issue in the case identified in the defence statement should be rejected.

27. Judges must ensure that defendants are not prejudiced on account of the failures of their lawyers, and, when necessary, the professions should be reminded that if justice is to be done, and if disclosure is to be dealt with fairly in accordance with the law, a full and careful defence statement and a reasoned approach to section 8 applications are essential. In exploring the adequacy of the defence statement, a judge should always ask what the issues are and upon what matters of fact the defendant intends to rely[7] and on what matters of fact the defendant takes issue.

Listing

28. Sufficient time is necessary for the judge properly to undertake the PCMH, and this is a paramount consideration when listing cases. Unless the court is able to sit early, judges who are part heard on trials are probably not best placed to conduct PCMHs. **N-56**

29. Cases that raise particularly difficult issues of disclosure should be referred to the resident judge for directions (unless a trial judge has been allocated) and, for trials of real complexity, the trial judge should be identified at an early stage, prior to the PCMH if possible. Listing officers, working in consultation with the resident judge and, if allocated, the trial judge, should ensure that sufficient time is allowed for judges to prepare and deal with prosecution and defence applications relating to disclosure, particularly in the more complex cases.

Magistrates' courts (including the youth court)

30. The principles relating to disclosure apply equally in the magistrates' courts. It follows that whilst disclosure of unused material in compliance with the statutory test is undoubtedly essential in order to achieve justice, it is critical that summary trials are not delayed or made over-complicated by misconceived applications for, or inappropriate disclosure of, prosecution material. **N-57**

31. Magistrates will rely on their legal advisers for guidance, and the latter should draw the attention of the parties and the court to the statutory provisions and the applicable case law. Cases raising

---

[5] *Essa* [2009] EWCA Crim. 43, para. 22.
[6] *Hanyes* [2011] EWCA Crim. 3281.
[7] *Rochford* [2010] EWCA Crim. 1928; [2011] 1 Cr. App. R. 11.

disclosure issues of particular complexity should be referred to a District Judge (Magistrates' Courts), if available.

32. Although service of a defence statement is voluntary for summary trials (s.6 CPIA), the defendant cannot make an application for specific disclosure under section 8 CPIA, and the court cannot make any orders in this regard, unless a proper defence statement has been provided. It follows that although providing a defence statement is not mandatory, it remains a critical stage in the disclosure process. If disclosure issues are to be raised by the defence, a defence statement must be served well in advance of the trial date. Any section 8 application must be made in strict compliance with the rules.

33. The case-management forms used in the magistrates' courts fulfil some of the functions of a defence statement, and the prosecution must take into account the information provided as to the defence case when conducting its on-going review of unused material. As the Court of Appeal noted in *Newell* (*supra*), admissions can be made in the trial preparation form and the defence is able to identify the matters that are not in issue. Admissions made in these circumstances may be admissible during the trial. However, other information on the form that does not come within the section relating to admissions should be treated in the same way as the contents of a PCMH form in the Crown Court and it should not generally be introduced as part of the evidence at trial. However, the contents of the trial preparation form do not replace the need to serve a defence statement if the defendant seeks to apply for disclosure under section 8 CPIA.

34. The standard directions require that any defence statement is to be served within 14 days of the date upon which the prosecution has complied with, or purported to comply with, the duty to provide initial disclosure. There may be some instances when there will be a wellfounded defence application to extend the 14-day time limit for serving the defence statement. These applications must be made in accordance with the Criminal Procedure Rules, in writing and before the time limit expires.

35. Although CCTV footage frequently causes difficulties, it is to be treated as any other category of unused material and it should only be disclosed if the material meets the appropriate test for disclosure under the CPIA. The defence should either be provided with copies of the sections of the CCTV or afforded an opportunity to view them. If the prosecution refuses to disclose CCTV material that the defence considers to be discloseable, the courts should not make standard or general directions requiring the prosecutor to disclose material of this kind in the absence of an application under section 8. When potentially relevant CCTV footage is not in the possession of the police, the guidance in relation to third party material will apply, although the police remain under a duty to pursue all reasonable lines of inquiry, including those leading away from a suspect, whether or not defence requests are made.

36. The previous convictions of witnesses and any disciplinary findings against officers in the case are frequently discloseable and care should be taken to disclose them as appropriate. Documents such as crime reports or records of emergency calls should not be provided on a routine basis, for instance as part of a bundle of disclosed documents, irrespective of whether the material satisfies the appropriate test for disclosure. Defence advocates should not request this material in standard or routine correspondence, and instead focussed consideration should be given to the circumstances of the particular case. Unjustified requests for disclosure of material of this kind are routinely made, frequently leading to unnecessary delays and adjournments. The prosecution should always consider whether the request is properly made out.

37. The supervisory role of the courts is critical in this context, and magistrates must guard against granting unnecessary adjournments and issuing unjustified directions.

Large and complex cases in the Crown Court

N-58 38. Disclosure is a particular problem with the larger and more complex cases, which require a scrupulous approach by the parties and robust case management by the judiciary. If possible, the trial judge should be identified at the outset.

39. The legal representatives need to fulfil their duties in this context with care and efficiency; they should co-operate with the other party (or parties) and the court; and the judge and the other party (or parties) are to be informed of any difficulties, as soon as they arise. The court should be provided with an up-to-date timetable for disclosure whenever there are material changes in this regard. A disclosure-management document, or similar, prepared by the prosecution will be of particular assistance to the court in large and complex cases.

40. Judges should be prepared to give early guidance as to the prosecution's approach to disclosure, thereby ensuring early engagement by the defence.

41. Cases of this nature frequently include large volumes of digitally stored material. The Attorney General's 2011 guidance (now included as an annex to the Attorney General's Guidelines on Disclosure 2013) is of particular relevance and assistance in this context.

42. Applications for witness anonymity orders require particular attention; as the Court of Appeal noted in *Mayers* [2008] EWCA Crim. 2989; [2009] 1 Cr. App. R. 30, in making such an application, the prosecution's obligations of disclosure "go much further than the ordinary duties of disclosure".

43. If the judge considers that there are reasonable grounds to doubt the good faith of the investigation, he or she will be concerned to see that there has been independent and effective appraisal of the documents contained in the disclosure schedule and that its contents are adequate. In appropriate cases where this issue has arisen and there are grounds which show there is a real issue, consideration should be given to receiving evidence on oath from the senior investigating officer at an early case management hearing.

Material held by third parties

44. Where material is held by a third party such as a local authority, a social services department, hospital or business, the investigators and the prosecution may need to make enquiries of the third party, with a view to inspecting the material and assessing whether the relevant test for disclosure is met and determining whether any or all of the material should be retained, recorded and, in due course, disclosed to the accused. If access by the prosecution is granted, the investigators and the prosecution will need to establish whether the custodian of the material intends to raise PII issues, as a result of which the material may have to be placed before the court for a decision. This does not obviate the need for the defence to conduct its own enquiries as appropriate. Speculative enquiries without any proper basis in relation to third party material - whether by the prosecution or the defence - are to be discouraged, and, in appropriate cases, the court will consider making an order for costs where an application is clearly unmeritorious and misconceived. **N-59**

45. The 2013 Protocol and Good Practice Model on Disclosure of Information in Cases of Alleged Child Abuse and Linked Criminal and Care Directions Hearings has recently been published. It provides a framework and timetable for the police and CPS to obtain discloseable material from local authorities, and for applications to be made to the Family Court. It is applicable to all cases of alleged child abuse where the child is aged 17 years or under. It is not binding on local authorities, but it does represent best practice and therefore should be consulted in all such cases. Delays in obtaining this type of material have led to unacceptable delays to trials involving particularly vulnerable witnesses and every effort must be made to ensure that all discloseable material is identified at an early stage so that any necessary applications can be made and the defence receive material to which they are entitled in good time.

46. There is no specific procedure for disclosure of material held by third parties in criminal proceedings, although the procedure established under section 2 of the Criminal Procedure (Attendance of Witnesses) Act 1965 or section 97 of the Magistrates' Courts Act 1980 is often used for this purpose. Where the third party in question declines to allow inspection of the material, or requires the prosecution to obtain an order before providing copies, the prosecutor will need to consider whether it is appropriate to obtain a witness summons under either section 2 of the Criminal Procedure (Attendance of Witnesses) Act 1965 or section 97 of the Magistrates' Courts Act 1980. Part 28 of the Criminal Procedure Rules and paragraphs 3.5 and 3.6 of the Code of Practice under the CPIA 1996 should be followed.

47. Applications for third party disclosure must identify the documents that are sought and provide full details of why they are discloseable. This is particularly relevant when access is sought to the medical records of those who allege they are victims of crime. It should be appreciated that a duty to assert confidentiality may arise when a third party receives a request for disclosure, or the right to privacy may be claimed under Article 8 of the ECHR (see in particular Crim. P.R., Pt 28.6). Victims do not waive the confidentiality of their medical records, or their right to privacy under Article 8 of the ECHR, by making a complaint against the accused. The court, as a public authority, must ensure that any interference with the right to privacy under Article 8 is in accordance with the law, and is necessary in pursuit of a legitimate public interest. General and unspecified requests to trawl through such records should be refused. Confidentiality rests with the subject of the material, not with the authority holding it. The subject is entitled to service of the application and has the right to make representations: Criminal Procedure Rule 22.3 and *R. (B.) v Stafford Combined Court* [2006] EWHC 1645 (Admin.); [2006] 2 Cr. App. R. 34. The 2013 Protocol and Good Practice Model at paragraph 13 should be followed. It is likely that the judge will need to issue directions when issues of this kind are raised (*e.g.* whether enquiries with the third party are likely to be appropriate; who is to make the request; what material is to be sought, and from whom; and a timetable should be set).

48. The judge should consider whether to take any steps if a third party fails, or refuses, to comply with a request for disclosure, including suggesting that either of the parties pursue the request and, if necessary, make an application for a witness summons. In these circumstances, the

court will need to set an appropriate timetable for compliance with Part 28 of the rules. Any failure to comply with the timetable must immediately be referred back to the court for further directions, although a hearing will not always be necessary. Generally, it may be appropriate for the defence to pursue requests of this kind when the prosecution, for good reason, decline to do so and the court will need to ensure that this procedure does not delay the trial.

49. There are very limited circumstances in which information relating to Family Court proceedings (*e.g.* where there have been care proceedings in relation to a child who has complained to the police of mistreatment) may be communicated without a court order: see the Family Procedure Rules 12.73. Reference should be made to the 2013 Protocol and Good Practice Model. In most circumstances, a court order will be required and paragraph 11 of the Protocol which sets out how an application should be made should be followed.

Other government departments

N-60 50. Material held by other government departments or other Crown agencies will not be prosecution material for the purposes of section 3(2) or section 8(4) of the CPIA if it has not been inspected, recorded and retained during the course of the relevant criminal investigation. The *CPIA Code of Practice and the Attorney General's Guidelines on Disclosure*, however, impose a duty upon the investigators and the prosecution to pursue all reasonable lines of inquiry and that may involve seeking disclosure from the relevant body.

International matters

N-61 51. The obligations of the Crown in relation to relevant third-party material held overseas are as set out in *Flook* [2009] EWCA Crim. 682; [2010] 1 Cr. App. R. 30: the Crown must pursue reasonable lines of enquiry and if it appears there is relevant material, all reasonable steps must be taken to obtain it, whether formally or otherwise. To a great extent, the success of these enquiries will depend on the laws of the country where the material is held and the facts of the individual case. It needs to be recognised that when the material is held in a country outside of the European Union, the power of the Crown and the courts of England and Wales to obtain third-party material may well be limited. If informal requests are unsuccessful, the avenues are limited to the Crime (International Co-operation) Act 2003 and any applicable international conventions. It cannot, in any sense, be guaranteed that a request to a foreign government, court or body will produce the material sought. Additionally, some foreign authorities may be prepared to show the material in question to the investigating officers, whilst refusing to allow the material to be copied or otherwise made available.

52. As the Court of Appeal observed in *Khyam* [2008] EWCA Crim. 1612; [2009] 1 Cr. App. R.(S.) 77:

> "The prosecuting authorities in this jurisdiction simply cannot compel authorities in a foreign country to acknowledge, let alone comply with, our disclosure principles" (at [37]).

The obligation is therefore to take reasonable steps. Whether the Crown has complied with that obligation is for the courts to judge in each case.

53. It is, therefore, important that the prosecution sets out the position clearly in writing, including any inability to inspect or retrieve any material that potentially ought to be disclosed, along with the steps that have been taken.

Applications for non-disclosure in the public interest

N-62 54. Applications in this context, whenever possible, should be considered by the trial judge. The House of Lords in *H.* (*supra*) has provided useful guidance as to the proper approach to be applied (para. [36]):

> "When any issue of derogation from the golden rule of full disclosure comes before it, the court must address a series of questions:
>
> (1) What is the material which the prosecution seek to withhold? This must be considered by the court in detail.
>
> (2) Is the material such as may weaken the prosecution case or strengthen that of the defence? If No, disclosure should not be ordered. If Yes, full disclosure should (subject to (3), (4) and (5) below) be ordered.
>
> (3) Is there a real risk of serious prejudice to an important public interest (and, if so, what) if full disclosure of the material is ordered? If No, full disclosure should be ordered.
>
> (4) If the answer to (2) and (3) is Yes, can the defendant's interest be protected without disclosure or disclosure be ordered to an extent or in a way which will give adequate

protection to the public interest in question and also afford adequate protection to the interests of the defence?

This question requires the court to consider, with specific reference to the material which the prosecution seek to withhold and the facts of the case and the defence as disclosed, whether the prosecution should formally admit what the defence seek to establish or whether disclosure short of full disclosure may be ordered. This may be done in appropriate cases by the preparation of summaries or extracts of evidence, or the provision of documents in an edited or anonymised form, provided the documents supplied are in each instance approved by the judge. In appropriate cases the appointment of special counsel may be a necessary step to ensure that the contentions of the prosecution are tested and the interests of the defendant protected (see para. [22] above). In cases of exceptional difficulty the court may require the appointment of special counsel to ensure a correct answer to questions (2) and (3) as well as (4).

(5) Do the measures proposed in answer to (4) represent the minimum derogation necessary to protect the public interest in question? If No, the court should order such greater disclosure as will represent the minimum derogation from the golden rule of full disclosure.

(6) If limited disclosure is ordered pursuant to (4) or (5), may the effect be to render the trial process, viewed as a whole, unfair to the defendant? If Yes, then fuller disclosure should be ordered even if this leads or may lead the prosecution to discontinue the proceedings so as to avoid having to make disclosure.

(7) If the answer to (6) when first given is No, does that remain the correct answer as the trial unfolds, evidence is adduced and the defence advanced?

It is important that the answer to (6) should not be treated as a final, once-and-for-all, answer but as a provisional answer which the court must keep under review."

55. In this context, the following matters are to be emphasised:

a. the procedure for making applications to the court is set out in the Criminal Procedure Rules, Pt 22;

b. when the PII application is a Type 1 or Type 2 application, proper notice to the defence is necessary to enable the accused to make focused submissions to the court and the notice should be as specific as the nature of the material allows; it is appreciated that in some cases only the generic nature of the material can be identified; in some wholly exceptional cases (Type 3 cases) it may be justified to give no notice at all; the judge should always ask the prosecution to justify the form of notice (or the decision to give no notice at all);

c. the prosecution should be alert to the possibility of disclosing a statement in a redacted form by, for example, simply removing personal details; this may obviate the need for a PII application, unless the redacted material satisfies the test for disclosure;

d. except when the material is very short (for instance only a few sheets), or for reasons of sensitivity, the prosecution should supply securely sealed copies to the judge in advance, together with a short statement explaining the relevance of each document, how it satisfies the disclosure test and why it is suggested that disclosure would result in a real risk of serious prejudice to an important public interest; in undertaking this task, the use of merely formulaic expressions is to be discouraged; in any case of complexity a schedule of the material should be provided, identifying the particular objection to disclosure in relation to each item, and leaving a space for the judge's decision;

e. the application, even if held in private or in secret, should be recorded; the judge should give some short statement of reasons; this is often best done document by document as the hearing proceeds;

f. the recording, copies of the judge's orders (and any copies of the material retained by the court) should be clearly identified, securely sealed and kept in the court building in a safe or locked cabinet consistent with its security classification, and there should be a proper register of the contents; arrangements should be made for the return of the material to the prosecution once the case is concluded and the time for an appeal has elapsed.

Conclusion

56. Historically, disclosure was viewed essentially as being a matter to be resolved between the parties, and the court only became engaged if a particular issue or complaint was raised. That perception is now wholly out of date. The regime established under the Criminal Justice Act 2003 and the Criminal Procedure Rules gives judges the power - indeed, it imposes a duty on the judiciary - actively to manage disclosure in every case. The efficient, effective and timely resolution of these issues is a critical element in meeting the overriding objective of the Criminal Procedure Rules of dealing with cases justly. **N-63**

Calendars and Notable Dates

2017

JANUARY

M	T	W	Th	F	Sa	Su
						1
2	3	4	5	6	7	8
9	10	11	12	13	14	15
16	17	18	19	20	21	22
23	24	25	26	27	28	29
30	31					

FEBRUARY

M	T	W	Th	F	Sa	Su
		1	2	3	4	5
6	7	8	9	10	11	12
13	14	15	16	17	18	19
20	21	22	23	24	25	26
27	28					

MARCH

M	T	W	Th	F	Sa	Su
		1	2	3	4	5
6	7	8	9	10	11	12
13	14	15	16	17	18	19
20	21	22	23	24	25	26
27	28	29	30	31		

APRIL

M	T	W	Th	F	Sa	Su
					1	2
3	4	5	6	7	8	9
10	11	12	13	14	15	16
17	18	19	20	21	22	23
24	25	26	27	28	29	30

MAY

M	T	W	Th	F	Sa	Su
1	2	3	4	5	6	7
8	9	10	11	12	13	14
15	16	17	18	19	20	21
22	23	24	25	26	27	28
29	30	31				

JUNE

M	T	W	Th	F	Sa	Su
			1	2	3	4
5	6	7	8	9	10	11
12	13	14	15	16	17	18
19	20	21	22	23	24	25
26	27	28	29	30		

JULY

M	T	W	Th	F	Sa	Su
					1	2
3	4	5	6	7	8	9
10	11	12	13	14	15	16
17	18	19	20	21	22	23
24	25	26	27	28	29	30
31						

AUGUST

M	T	W	Th	F	Sa	Su
	1	2	3	4	5	6
7	8	9	10	11	12	13
14	15	16	17	18	19	20
21	22	23	24	25	26	27
28	29	30	31			

SEPTEMBER

M	T	W	Th	F	Sa	Su
				1	2	3
4	5	6	7	8	9	10
11	12	13	14	15	16	17
18	19	20	21	22	23	24
25	26	27	28	29	30	

OCTOBER

M	T	W	Th	F	Sa	Su
						1
2	3	4	5	6	7	8
9	10	11	12	13	14	15
16	17	18	19	20	21	22
23	24	25	26	27	28	29
30	31					

NOVEMBER

M	T	W	Th	F	Sa	Su
		1	2	3	4	5
6	7	8	9	10	11	12
13	14	15	16	17	18	19
20	21	22	23	24	25	26
27	28	29	30			

DECEMBER

M	T	W	Th	F	Sa	Su
				1	2	3
4	5	6	7	8	9	10
11	12	13	14	15	16	17
18	19	20	21	22	23	24
25	26	27	28	29	30	31

2018

JANUARY

M	T	W	Th	F	Sa	Su
1	2	3	4	5	6	7
8	9	10	11	12	13	14
15	16	17	18	19	20	21
22	23	24	25	26	27	28
29	30	31				

FEBRUARY

M	T	W	Th	F	Sa	Su
			1	2	3	4
5	6	7	8	9	10	11
12	13	14	15	16	17	18
19	20	21	22	23	24	25
26	27	28				

MARCH

M	T	W	Th	F	Sa	Su
			1	2	3	4
5	6	7	8	9	10	11
12	13	14	15	16	17	18
19	20	21	22	23	24	25
26	27	28	29	30	31	

APRIL

M	T	W	Th	F	Sa	Su
						1
2	3	4	5	6	7	8
9	10	11	12	13	14	15
16	17	18	19	20	21	22
23	24	25	26	27	28	29
30						

MAY

M	T	W	Th	F	Sa	Su
	1	2	3	4	5	6
7	8	9	10	11	12	13
14	15	16	17	18	19	20
21	22	23	24	25	26	27
28	29	30	31			

JUNE

M	T	W	Th	F	Sa	Su
				1	2	3
4	5	6	7	8	9	10
11	12	13	14	15	16	17
18	19	20	21	22	23	24
25	26	27	28	29	30	

JULY

M	T	W	Th	F	Sa	Su
						1
2	3	4	5	6	7	8
9	10	11	12	13	14	15
16	17	18	19	20	21	22
23	24	25	26	27	28	29
30	31					

AUGUST

M	T	W	Th	F	Sa	Su
		1	2	3	4	5
6	7	8	9	10	11	12
13	14	15	16	17	18	19
20	21	22	23	24	25	26
27	28	29	30	31		

SEPTEMBER

M	T	W	Th	F	Sa	Su
					1	2
3	4	5	6	7	8	9
10	11	12	13	14	15	16
17	18	19	20	21	22	23
24	25	26	27	28	29	30

OCTOBER

M	T	W	Th	F	Sa	Su
1	2	3	4	5	6	7
8	9	10	11	12	13	14
15	16	17	18	19	20	21
22	23	24	25	26	27	28
29	30	31				

NOVEMBER

M	T	W	Th	F	Sa	Su
			1	2	3	4
5	6	7	8	9	10	11
12	13	14	15	16	17	18
19	20	21	22	23	24	25
26	27	28	29	30		

DECEMBER

M	T	W	Th	F	Sa	Su
					1	2
3	4	5	6	7	8	9
10	11	12	13	14	15	16
17	18	19	20	21	22	23
24	25	26	27	28	29	30
31						

2019

JANUARY

M	T	W	Th	F	Sa	Su
	1	2	3	4	5	6
7	8	9	10	11	12	13
14	15	16	17	18	19	20
21	22	23	24	25	26	27
28	29	30	31			

FEBRUARY

M	T	W	Th	F	Sa	Su
				1	2	3
4	5	6	7	8	9	10
11	12	13	14	15	16	17
18	19	20	21	22	23	24
25	26	27	28			

MARCH

M	T	W	Th	F	Sa	Su
				1	2	3
4	5	6	7	8	9	10
11	12	13	14	15	16	17
18	19	20	21	22	23	24
25	26	27	28	29	30	31

APRIL

M	T	W	Th	F	Sa	Su
1	2	3	4	5	6	7
8	9	10	11	12	13	14
15	16	17	18	19	20	21
22	23	24	25	26	27	28
29	30					

MAY

M	T	W	Th	F	Sa	Su
		1	2	3	4	5
6	7	8	9	10	11	12
13	14	15	16	17	18	19
20	21	22	23	24	25	26
27	28	29	30	31		

JUNE

M	T	W	Th	F	Sa	Su
					1	2
3	4	5	6	7	8	9
10	11	12	13	14	15	16
17	18	19	20	21	22	23
24	25	26	27	28	29	30

JULY

M	T	W	Th	F	Sa	Su
1	2	3	4	5	6	7
8	9	10	11	12	13	14
15	16	17	18	19	20	21
22	23	24	25	26	27	28
29	30	31				

AUGUST

M	T	W	Th	F	Sa	Su
			1	2	3	4
5	6	7	8	9	10	11
12	13	14	15	16	17	18
19	20	21	22	23	24	25
26	27	28	29	30	31	

SEPTEMBER

M	T	W	Th	F	Sa	Su
						1
2	3	4	5	6	7	8
9	10	11	12	13	14	15
16	17	18	19	20	21	22
23	24	25	26	27	28	29
30						

OCTOBER

M	T	W	Th	F	Sa	Su
	1	2	3	4	5	6
7	8	9	10	11	12	13
14	15	16	17	18	19	20
21	22	23	24	25	26	27
28	29	30	31			

NOVEMBER

M	T	W	Th	F	Sa	Su
				1	2	3
4	5	6	7	8	9	10
11	12	13	14	15	16	17
18	19	20	21	22	23	24
25	26	27	28	29	30	

DECEMBER

M	T	W	Th	F	Sa	Su
						1
2	3	4	5	6	7	8
9	10	11	12	13	14	15
16	17	18	19	20	21	22
23	24	25	26	27	28	29
30	31					

2020

JANUARY

M	T	W	Th	F	Sa	Su
		1	2	3	4	5
6	7	8	9	10	11	12
13	14	15	16	17	18	19
20	21	22	23	24	25	26
27	28	29	30	31		

FEBRUARY

M	T	W	Th	F	Sa	Su
					1	2
3	4	5	6	7	8	9
10	11	12	13	14	15	16
17	18	19	20	21	22	23
24	25	26	27	28	29	

MARCH

M	T	W	Th	F	Sa	Su
						1
2	3	4	5	6	7	8
9	10	11	12	13	14	15
16	17	18	19	20	21	22
23	24	25	26	27	28	29
30	31					

APRIL

M	T	W	Th	F	Sa	Su
		1	2	3	4	5
6	7	8	9	10	11	12
13	14	15	16	17	18	19
20	21	22	23	24	25	26
27	28	29	30			

MAY

M	T	W	Th	F	Sa	Su
				1	2	3
4	5	6	7	8	9	10
11	12	13	14	15	16	17
18	19	20	21	22	23	24
25	26	27	28	29	30	31

JUNE

M	T	W	Th	F	Sa	Su
1	2	3	4	5	6	7
8	9	10	11	12	13	14
15	16	17	18	19	20	21
22	23	24	25	26	27	28
29	30					

JULY

M	T	W	Th	F	Sa	Su
		1	2	3	4	5
6	7	8	9	10	11	12
13	14	15	16	17	18	19
20	21	22	23	24	25	26
27	28	29	30	31		

AUGUST

M	T	W	Th	F	Sa	Su
					1	2
3	4	5	6	7	8	9
10	11	12	13	14	15	16
17	18	19	20	21	22	23
24	25	26	27	28	29	30
31						

SEPTEMBER

M	T	W	Th	F	Sa	Su
	1	2	3	4	5	6
7	8	9	10	11	12	13
14	15	16	17	18	19	20
21	22	23	24	25	26	27
28	29	30				

OCTOBER

M	T	W	Th	F	Sa	Su
			1	2	3	4
5	6	7	8	9	10	11
12	13	14	15	16	17	18
19	20	21	22	23	24	25
26	27	28	29	30	31	

NOVEMBER

M	T	W	Th	F	Sa	Su
						1
2	3	4	5	6	7	8
9	10	11	12	13	14	15
16	17	18	19	20	21	22
23	24	25	26	27	28	29
30						

DECEMBER

M	T	W	Th	F	Sa	Su
	1	2	3	4	5	6
7	8	9	10	11	12	13
14	15	16	17	18	19	20
21	22	23	24	25	26	27
28	29	30	31			

2021

JANUARY

M	T	W	Th	F	Sa	Su
				1	2	3
4	5	6	7	8	9	10
11	12	13	14	15	16	17
18	19	20	21	22	23	24
25	26	27	28	29	30	31

FEBRUARY

M	T	W	Th	F	Sa	Su
1	2	3	4	5	6	7
8	9	10	11	12	13	14
15	16	17	18	19	20	21
22	23	24	25	26	27	28

MARCH

M	T	W	Th	F	Sa	Su
1	2	3	4	5	6	7
8	9	10	11	12	13	14
15	16	17	18	19	20	21
22	23	24	25	26	27	28
29	30	31				

APRIL

M	T	W	Th	F	Sa	Su
			1	2	3	4
5	6	7	8	9	10	11
12	13	14	15	16	17	18
19	20	21	22	23	24	25
26	27	28	29	30		

MAY

M	T	W	Th	F	Sa	Su
					1	2
3	4	5	6	7	8	9
10	11	12	13	14	15	16
17	18	19	20	21	22	23
24	25	26	27	28	29	30
31						

JUNE

M	T	W	Th	F	Sa	Su
	1	2	3	4	5	6
7	8	9	10	11	12	13
14	15	16	17	18	19	20
21	22	23	24	25	26	27
28	29	30				

JULY

M	T	W	Th	F	Sa	Su
			1	2	3	4
5	6	7	8	9	10	11
12	13	14	15	16	17	18
19	20	21	22	23	24	25
26	27	28	29	30	31	

AUGUST

M	T	W	Th	F	Sa	Su
						1
2	3	4	5	6	7	8
9	10	11	12	13	14	15
16	17	18	19	20	21	22
23	24	25	26	27	28	29
30	31					

SEPTEMBER

M	T	W	Th	F	Sa	Su
		1	2	3	4	5
6	7	8	9	10	11	12
13	14	15	16	17	18	19
20	21	22	23	24	25	26
27	28	29	30			

OCTOBER

M	T	W	Th	F	Sa	Su
				1	2	3
4	5	6	7	8	9	10
11	12	13	14	15	16	17
18	19	20	21	22	23	24
25	26	27	28	29	30	31

NOVEMBER

M	T	W	Th	F	Sa	Su
1	2	3	4	5	6	7
8	9	10	11	12	13	14
15	16	17	18	19	20	21
22	23	24	25	26	27	28
29	30					

DECEMBER

M	T	W	Th	F	Sa	Su
		1	2	3	4	5
6	7	8	9	10	11	12
13	14	15	16	17	18	19
20	21	22	23	24	25	26
27	28	29	30	31		

2022

JANUARY

M	T	W	Th	F	Sa	Su
					1	2
3	4	5	6	7	8	9
10	11	12	13	14	15	16
17	18	19	20	21	22	23
24	25	26	27	28	29	30
31						

FEBRUARY

M	T	W	Th	F	Sa	Su
	1	2	3	4	5	6
7	8	9	10	11	12	13
14	15	16	17	18	19	20
21	22	23	24	25	26	27
28						

MARCH

M	T	W	Th	F	Sa	Su
	1	2	3	4	5	6
7	8	9	10	11	12	13
14	15	16	17	18	19	20
21	22	23	24	25	26	27
28	29	30	31			

APRIL

M	T	W	Th	F	Sa	Su
				1	2	3
4	5	6	7	8	9	10
11	12	13	14	15	16	17
18	19	20	21	22	23	24
25	26	27	28	29	30	

MAY

M	T	W	Th	F	Sa	Su
						1
2	3	4	5	6	7	8
9	10	11	12	13	14	15
16	17	18	19	20	21	22
23	24	25	26	27	28	29
30	31					

JUNE

M	T	W	Th	F	Sa	Su
		1	2	3	4	5
6	7	8	9	10	11	12
13	14	15	16	17	18	19
20	21	22	23	24	25	26
27	28	29	30			

JULY

M	T	W	Th	F	Sa	Su
				1	2	3
4	5	6	7	8	9	10
11	12	13	14	15	16	17
18	19	20	21	22	23	24
25	26	27	28	29	30	31

AUGUST

M	T	W	Th	F	Sa	Su
1	2	3	4	5	6	7
8	9	10	11	12	13	14
15	16	17	18	19	20	21
22	23	24	25	26	27	28
29	30	31				

SEPTEMBER

M	T	W	Th	F	Sa	Su
			1	2	3	4
5	6	7	8	9	10	11
12	13	14	15	16	17	18
19	20	21	22	23	24	25
26	27	28	29	30		

OCTOBER

M	T	W	Th	F	Sa	Su
					1	2
3	4	5	6	7	8	9
10	11	12	13	14	15	16
17	18	19	20	21	22	23
24	25	26	27	28	29	30
31						

NOVEMBER

M	T	W	Th	F	Sa	Su
	1	2	3	4	5	6
7	8	9	10	11	12	13
14	15	16	17	18	19	20
21	22	23	24	25	26	27
28	29	30				

DECEMBER

M	T	W	Th	F	Sa	Su
			1	2	3	4
5	6	7	8	9	10	11
12	13	14	15	16	17	18
19	20	21	22	23	24	25
26	27	28	29	30	31	

2023

JANUARY

M	T	W	Th	F	Sa	Su
						1
2	3	4	5	6	7	8
9	10	11	12	13	14	15
16	17	18	19	20	21	22
23	24	25	26	27	28	29
30	31					

FEBRUARY

M	T	W	Th	F	Sa	Su
		1	2	3	4	5
6	7	8	9	10	11	12
13	14	15	16	17	18	19
20	21	22	23	24	25	26
27	28					

MARCH

M	T	W	Th	F	Sa	Su
		1	2	3	4	5
6	7	8	9	10	11	12
13	14	15	16	17	18	19
20	21	22	23	24	25	26
27	28	29	30	31		

APRIL

M	T	W	Th	F	Sa	Su
					1	2
3	4	5	6	7	8	9
10	11	12	13	14	15	16
17	18	19	20	21	22	23
24	25	26	27	28	29	30

MAY

M	T	W	Th	F	Sa	Su
1	2	3	4	5	6	7
8	9	10	11	12	13	14
15	16	17	18	19	20	21
22	23	24	25	26	27	28
29	30	31				

JUNE

M	T	W	Th	F	Sa	Su
			1	2	3	4
5	6	7	8	9	10	11
12	13	14	15	16	17	18
19	20	21	22	23	24	25
26	27	28	29	30		

JULY

M	T	W	Th	F	Sa	Su
					1	2
3	4	5	6	7	8	9
10	11	12	13	14	15	16
17	18	19	20	21	22	23
24	25	26	27	28	29	30
31						

AUGUST

M	T	W	Th	F	Sa	Su
	1	2	3	4	5	6
7	8	9	10	11	12	13
14	15	16	17	18	19	20
21	22	23	24	25	26	27
28	29	30	31			

SEPTEMBER

M	T	W	Th	F	Sa	Su
				1	2	3
4	5	6	7	8	9	10
11	12	13	14	15	16	17
18	19	20	21	22	23	24
25	26	27	28	29	30	

OCTOBER

M	T	W	Th	F	Sa	Su
						1
2	3	4	5	6	7	8
9	10	11	12	13	14	15
16	17	18	19	20	21	22
23	24	25	26	27	28	29
30	31					

NOVEMBER

M	T	W	Th	F	Sa	Su
		1	2	3	4	5
6	7	8	9	10	11	12
13	14	15	16	17	18	19
20	21	22	23	24	25	26
27	28	29	30			

DECEMBER

M	T	W	Th	F	Sa	Su
				1	2	3
4	5	6	7	8	9	10
11	12	13	14	15	16	17
18	19	20	21	22	23	24
25	26	27	28	29	30	31

2024

JANUARY

M	T	W	Th	F	Sa	Su
1	2	3	4	5	6	7
8	9	10	11	12	13	14
15	16	17	18	19	20	21
22	23	24	25	26	27	28
29	30	31				

FEBRUARY

M	T	W	Th	F	Sa	Su
			1	2	3	4
5	6	7	8	9	10	11
12	13	14	15	16	17	18
19	20	21	22	23	24	25
26	27	28	29			

MARCH

M	T	W	Th	F	Sa	Su
				1	2	3
4	5	6	7	8	9	10
11	12	13	14	15	16	17
18	19	20	21	22	23	24
25	26	27	28	29	30	31

APRIL

M	T	W	Th	F	Sa	Su
1	2	3	4	5	6	7
8	9	10	11	12	13	14
15	16	17	18	19	20	21
22	23	24	25	26	27	28
29	30					

MAY

M	T	W	Th	F	Sa	Su
		1	2	3	4	5
6	7	8	9	10	11	12
13	14	15	16	17	18	19
20	21	22	23	24	25	26
27	28	29	30	31		

JUNE

M	T	W	Th	F	Sa	Su
					1	2
3	4	5	6	7	8	9
10	11	12	13	14	15	16
17	18	19	20	21	22	23
24	25	26	27	28	29	30

JULY

M	T	W	Th	F	Sa	Su
1	2	3	4	5	6	7
8	9	10	11	12	13	14
15	16	17	18	19	20	21
22	23	24	25	26	27	28
29	30	31				

AUGUST

M	T	W	Th	F	Sa	Su
			1	2	3	4
5	6	7	8	9	10	11
12	13	14	15	16	17	18
19	20	21	22	23	24	25
26	27	28	29	30	31	

SEPTEMBER

M	T	W	Th	F	Sa	Su
						1
2	3	4	5	6	7	8
9	10	11	12	13	14	15
16	17	18	19	20	21	22
23	24	25	26	27	28	29
30						

OCTOBER

M	T	W	Th	F	Sa	Su
	1	2	3	4	5	6
7	8	9	10	11	12	13
14	15	16	17	18	19	20
21	22	23	24	25	26	27
28	29	30	31			

NOVEMBER

M	T	W	Th	F	Sa	Su
				1	2	3
4	5	6	7	8	9	10
11	12	13	14	15	16	17
18	19	20	21	22	23	24
25	26	27	28	29	30	

DECEMBER

M	T	W	Th	F	Sa	Su
						1
2	3	4	5	6	7	8
9	10	11	12	13	14	15
16	17	18	19	20	21	22
23	24	25	26	27	28	29
30	31					

HOLIDAYS AND NOTABLE DATES

Holiday, etc.	*2017*	*2018*	*2019*	*2020*	*2021*	*2022*	*2023*	*2024*
New Year's Day	Jan. 1	Jan. 1	Jan. 1	Jan. 1	Jan. 1	Jan. 1	Jan. 1	Jan. 1
New Year Holiday (England)	–	–	–	–	–	–	–	–
New Year Holiday (Scotland)	Jan. 2	Jan. 2	Jan. 2	Jan. 2	Jan. 2	Jan. 2	Jan. 2	Jan. 2
St David's Day (Wales)	Mar. 1	Mar. 1	Mar. 1	Mar. 1	Mar. 1	Mar. 1	Mar. 1	Mar. 1
St Patrick's Day (Ireland)	Mar. 17	Mar. 17	Mar. 17	Mar. 17	Mar. 17	Mar. 17	Mar. 17	Mar. 17
Good Friday	Apr. 14	Mar. 30	Apr. 19	Apr. 10	Apr. 2	Apr. 15	Apr. 7	Mar. 29
Easter Monday	Apr. 17	Apr. 2	Apr. 22	Apr. 13	Apr. 5	Apr. 18	Apr. 10	Apr. 1
St George's Day (England)	Apr. 23	Apr. 23	Apr. 23	Apr. 23	Apr. 23	Apr. 23	Apr. 23	Apr. 23
May Day Holiday	May 1	May 7	May 6	May 8	May 3	May 2	May 1	May 6
Spring Bank Holiday	May 29	May 28	May 27	May 25	May 31	May 30	May 29	May 27
August Bank Holiday	Aug. 28	Aug. 27	Aug. 26	Aug. 31	Aug. 30	Aug. 29	Aug. 28	Aug. 26
St Andrew's Day (Scotland)	Nov. 30	Nov. 30	Nov. 30	Nov. 30	Nov. 30	Nov. 30	Nov. 30	Nov. 30
Christmas Day	Dec. 25	Dec. 25	Dec. 25	Dec. 25	Dec. 25	Dec. 25	Dec. 25	Dec .25
Boxing Day	Dec. 26	Dec. 26	Dec. 26	Dec. 26	Dec. 26	Dec. 26	Dec. 26	Dec. 26

INDEX

LEGAL TAXONOMY

FROM SWEET & MAXWELL

This index has been prepared using Sweet & Maxwell's Legal Taxonomy. Main index entries conform to keywords provided by the Legal Taxonomy except where references to specific documents or non-standard terms (denoted by quotation marks) have been included. These keywords provide a means of identifying similar concepts in other Sweet & Maxwell publications and online services to which keywords from the Legal Taxonomy have been applied. Readers may find some minor differences between terms used in the text and those which appear in the index. Suggestions to *sweetandmaxwell.taxonomy@tr.com.*

All references are to paragraph numbers.